Pageant of Europe

Sources and Selections
from the Renaissance to the Present Day

RAYMOND PHINEAS STEARNS

DEPARTMENT OF HISTORY IN
THE UNIVERSITY OF ILLINOIS

New York   HARCOURT, BRACE AND COMPANY   *1947*

To my beloved wife

ELIZABETH SCOTT STEARNS

1905-1946

PREFACE

THIS BOOK is designed primarily for college survey courses in modern European history. It is prepared in the time-tested belief that college students profit from judicious exposure to the raw materials out of which, directly or indirectly, the compressed treatments of textbooks are constructed. It is intended to supplement and to illustrate textbook and other reading materials, not to supplant them. Moreover, it is prepared with the needs of undergraduate students constantly in view. Advanced students may find it a convenient collection of materials, but the volume is planned for the younger student, not for the research scholar.

In order to assist students in the use of this book, the selections and documents are arranged topically and presented with explanatory and interpretative settings. The topics around which the selections are grouped have been chosen to parallel and supplement those treated in the European History textbooks most widely used in American colleges and universities. To make the materials as vital as possible to students, and to increase their value as illustrations of the textbook narrative, each selection is presented, in so far as possible, as a specific example of a particular individual, idea, or historical trend. Further, the date of the selection is cited, in so far as an accurate date can be assigned. Whenever possible the date cited is that of the actual writing of the selection; when that date cannot be ascertained, the date used is that of the actual publication of the work from which the selection is taken. The scope of the sources and documents is purposefully wide to assist students in attaining a meaningful interrelation of political, economic, and cultural events.

At base, of course, the selection of topics and of specific materials is personal and somewhat arbitrary, the result of much winnowing. I cannot reasonably expect every informed reader's judgment to coincide with my own, and I am aware of many omissions—some made because of the lack of suitable material, more because of space considerations. I have consciously excluded most American items, on the ground that adequate collections are widely available in the American field. In deciding upon specific selections, I have given constant attention to readability for students' use, illustrative value, relative importance for the topics under treatment, and reliability as historical material. The length of selections is, of course, a necessary consideration throughout. I have not hesitated to condense and to make extracts of the sources employed, but I have tried to avoid the inclusion of too many brief excerpts which often confuse students by their multiplicity and fail to give the literary or intellectual flavor of the original material. The source of each selection is noted; all omissions from the originals are indicated in the usual fashion; and all materials in square brackets are my own insertions. However, in borrowing the works of our ancestors from a variety of fields, from several languages, and from widely separated periods of time, I have

v

not attempted to reduce them uniformly to present-day standards of orthography, punctuation, and paragraphing. I have endeavored to preserve the original meaning throughout.

I am deeply indebted to many persons for their helpfulness in the preparation of this volume. I wish particularly to thank Professor Ferdinand Schevill for a critical reading of the early portions of the text and for a detailed review with me, in the light of his long teaching career and wide scholarly achievement, of the entire plan of the book. And while this volume has not been designed to accompany any one textbook alone, it is nevertheless well adapted to the new and revised edition of Professor Schevill's *History of Europe from the Reformation to the Present Day.*

Among others to whom I feel an especial debt of gratitude, I wish to acknowledge the assistance of Professor Franklin D. Scott, of Northwestern University, who has given generously of his wide knowledge, since this book was begun. I desire to thank my colleagues at the University of Illinois for their helpful suggestions, particularly Professors Theodore Calvin Pease, Frederick C. Dietz, Raymond C. Werner, Mary Lucille Shay, John Black Sirich and Dr. Josephine Bunch. Mrs. Reva S. Ludwig, besides a careful reading of most of the manuscript, has typed the greater portion of it. And lastly, though words cannot characterize a cherished partnership of twenty years, I wish to express affectionate appreciation to my late wife, Elizabeth Scott Stearns, whose wise counsel and untiring helpfulness were terminated by death just short of the completion of this book.

R. P. S.

Urbana, Illinois
July 1, 1947

THE PLAN OF THE BOOK

vii

TABLE OF CONTENTS

PART TWO

The Era of Enlightened Despotism (c. 1648-1815)

PART THREE

The Triumph of the Bourgeoisie, 1815-1914

PART FOUR

The Twentieth Century: Wars and Rumors of Wars, 1914-1945

"new spirit" appears to have been a blend of two factors, increasing secularism and intensified individualism. By secularism is meant a concern with the worldly affairs of this life and a corresponding lack of concern for the otherworldliness of the hereafter. Closely related to this secularism was the development of intensified individualism, which signified a new self-assertiveness of individual personalities. Accordingly, many writers have described the Renaissance as an era wherein man "rediscovered the world and rediscovered himself."

But the rediscovery of the world embraced within itself two important phases of the Renaissance. On the one hand, it constituted a vast shift in emphasis in the aims and purposes of man. The Middle Ages had tended to place almost exclusive emphasis upon the world as a place in which to prepare for a life beyond; consequently, the noblest study was theology, soul-saving was man's most important task, all human exertion was devoted to contemplation of the joys of the hereafter, this world was but a dark, uninteresting anteroom to Heaven. This medieval outlook is excellently portrayed by John Addington Symonds as follows: [1]

> During the Middle Ages man had lived enveloped in a cowl. He had not seen the beauty of the world, or had seen it only to cross himself and turn aside, to tell his beads and pray. Like St. Bernard [1090-1153] travelling along the shores of Lake Leman [Geneva], and noticing neither the azure of the waters, nor the luxuriance of the vines, nor the radiance of the mountains with their robe of sun and snow, but bending a thought-burdened forehead over the neck of his mule; even like this monk, humanity had passed, a careful pilgrim, intent on the terrors of sin, death, and judgment, along the highways of the world, and had scarcely known that they were sightworthy, or that life is a blessing. Beauty is a snare, pleasure a sin, the world a fleeting show, man fallen and lost, death the only certainty; ignorance is acceptable to God as a proof of faith and submission; abstinence and mortification are the only safe rules of life: these were the fixed ideas of the ascetic medieval Church.

The Renaissance did not eradicate these ideas completely by any means; but worldliness gradually took precedence over otherworldliness in the minds of most men. Like the Ancients, men found frank delight in living, felt joy in sensuous beauty, trusted nature and natural human impulses. In vivid contrast to St. Bernard consider Petrarch, the "first modern man," who, in 1335, made the difficult ascent of Mount Ventaux in France for the pure delight of the experience. Petrarch loved the fields and flowers, the hills and waterfalls, the birds and animals, the blue skies and rolling clouds. He felt a wholesome ecstasy in the beauties of this world and exalted heavenly things by stressing things terrestrial. Unlike St. Bernard, who loved God in spite of this world, Petrarch loved God the more because of this world. In worldly things he saw no barriers along the way to heaven. In this attitude, he profoundly modified the medieval viewpoint and closely approximated the outlook of modern times.

[1] *A Short History of the Renaissance in Italy Taken from the Work of John Addington Symonds* by Lieut.-Colonel Alfred Pearson, New York, n. d., 5. Reprinted by permission of Henry Holt and Company.

It was the rediscovered joy in the things of this world which caused men and women of the Renaissance to turn to ancient Latin and Greek writings, to imitate ancient classical styles in literature, language, and art. Finding ancient works compatible with the "new spirit," men of the Renaissance ignored their paganism, gained inspiration from them, and sought so diligently after them that an entire revival of ancient literature and art took place. As a result physics again took precedence over metaphysics, science replaced theology as man's chief concern, a full life in this world, even one devoted primarily to material pursuits, was no longer considered inimical to admission to the life hereafter. In fact, the practice of these material pursuits led to the second Renaissance phase in the rediscovery of the world. In the interests of expanding commerce and personal gain, new routes to the Indies were sought, and in the competition for trade supremacy the coast of Africa was explored, the New World was discovered, geographical knowledge was mightily expanded, and the civilization of Renaissance Europe was planted overseas. Thus, "the rediscovery of the world" embraced both a new materialism and a real expansion of geographical knowledge.

Interrelated with the rediscovery of the world was the "rediscovery of man," but it was even more complex in its historical manifestations. Fundamentally, as stated above, it was a new self-assertiveness, an intensified individualism. But because individualism is individualistic, this phase of the "new spirit" of the Renaissance permeated the whole life of man. It was manifested in the emancipation of the human mind from the authoritarian shackles of the Church, the State, the Schoolmen, and the Ancients. It was demonstrated by such Renaissance events as the Italian painters' discard of austere, impersonal medieval art forms in favor of natural, living models, by the humanists' rejection of scholasticism in literature and philosophy, by the rising national monarchs' unconcern for the medieval ideal of political unity in the whole Christian world, by Copernicus's assertion of the heliocentric theory of the universe against the institutionalized wisdom of the church, by Columbus's rejection of the geographical limits set by Ptolemy and Strabo, and by Luther's assertion against churchly authority of the right of private judgment in religious affairs. Man not only found new joys in this earthly existence but also he came to have a greater faith in his own powers as an individual. One of the ideals of the Renaissance was the development of many-sided giants, men versatile enough to master all phases of human endeavor. One of the earliest of these Renaissance geniuses was the Italian Vittorino da Feltre (1378-1446), an educational reformer who endeavored to develop the entire nature of his students, intellectually, morally, and physically. Many other men exemplified this Renaissance versatility, such as Fillippo Brunelleschi (1379-1446), Florentine sculptor, architect, goldsmith, clockmaker, mathematician, and theologian; Michelangelo (1475-1564), painter, sculptor, architect, engineer, physician, and poet; Leonardo da Vinci (1452-1519), painter, sculptor, mathematician, musician, anatomist, engineer, inventor, and amazing athlete; Lorenzo de' Medici (1449-1492), statesman, banker, philosopher, poet, patron of arts and letters; and Leo Battista Alberti (?1404-1472), astonishingly skilled in law, music, physics, mathematics, and painting, one who gave expression to man's new faith in man when he wrote "Men can do all things if they will." With such self-esteem, manifold accomplishments, and worldly aims, it is small wonder that men of the Renaissance became vain, self-seeking, ambitious, restless, endowed with a limitless curiosity about things of this world, impatient and critical of established authorities, experimental in nature —in short, highly individualistic and self-assertive in all phases of human activity. Herein lies the essence of the "new spirit" of Renaissance society.

Naturally, manifestations of the Renaissance era were not identical in all parts of Europe. They varied in nature as traditions, language, customs, geography, and other circumstances varied from community to community. Renaissance Rome varied from Renaissance Florence, Renaissance Italy demonstrated important differences from Renaissance Germany; and in some whole areas, such as Russia and the Ottoman Empire, developments peculiar to the Renaissance in the rest of Europe hardly took root at all and then only tardily and in a very limited degree. Moreover, no one can state exactly *where* or exactly *when* the Renaissance began. But everyone agrees that the significant developments are noticeable first in Italy.

It is possible, of course, that this is because of some peculiar genius of the Italian people. But it appears more likely to have been the result of the geographical position and cultural heritage of the Italian city-states. Situated midway between the Near East and western Europe, with sea lanes to eastern Mediterranean ports and good overland routes to Asia, merchants and princes of Venice, Florence, Milan, and other Italian cities were enabled to take an early lead in the expanding commerce between Europe and the Orient in the late Middle Ages. This trade stimulated the growth of Italian cities, led to vital readjustments in the Italian social and economic system, gave rise to concentrations of wealth and capital, the growth of new industries, and the emergence of a financially strong middle class in the Italian city-states. At the same time, Italy was the only *Christian* area with the traditions and extensive tangible architectural and literary remains of ancient society, from which men of the early Renaissance drew much of their intellectual and artistic stimulation. Moreover, in Italy was the traditional head of the western church; the Papacy, long in exile at Avignon (1305-77), had only recently returned to Rome (1377). Once returned, free from the shackles of foreign domination, the Papacy soon gained the leadership of vigorous Italian popes who were anxious to build up a powerful temporal state at Rome and to make Rome worthy of its recovered prestige. Thus Italy first combined the economic, intellectual, and social ingredients for the outburst of Renaissance culture: wealth, ancient remains, and prestige-seeking merchant-princes, popes, and middle-class men who were to become immortal as patrons of literature, art, science, and education. Without this financial patronage, few of the Renaissance achievements in literature, art, and science would have been possible; and it is only as commercial centers and wealth move into western Europe that these phases of Renaissance culture become significant there. The greatest cultural achievements of man appear always to occur in the wake of an era of unusual material prosperity, and the Renaissance is no exception. Such an era provides a "leisure class," creates *men* and *communities* of wealth which serve as patrons of art, literature, and learning. It is to the immortal credit of Italian merchants, princes, popes, and city-states of the Renaissance period that their prosperity was not wholly dissipated in wars and riotous living, that much of it was employed to finance the achievements of Renaissance masters. And if the Italian people as a whole demonstrated any peculiar genius in this period, it was their capacity to accept enthusiastically the new literature, the new art, and the new learning. The "new spirit" of the Renaissance seemed to permeate all Italian society so that even the humblest city dweller became something of a critic and connoisseur of poetry, books, paintings, architecture, and sculpture.

Consequently, in any consideration of the Renaissance era our attention is first directed to Italian achievements, then to the spread of Renaissance culture until it permeated most of Europe. The following selections, without pretending to be more than "samples" of a vast literature, are presented as illustrative of the Renaissance era in European history.

2   THE REINTERPRETATION OF CLASSICAL SURVIVALS: ITALIAN LITERATURE

1. Humanism: History and Definition

The term "humanism" is widely employed to denote a new literary, intellectual, and spiritual emphasis which arose during the Renaissance and still exerts a powerful influence in the Western world. A recent explanation of its origin and meaning follows.

From SCHEVILL, *History of Florence* (1936) [1]

The early Middle Ages, the true age of faith, had a markedly transcendental character, for they inculcated the vanity of the brief and imperfect Here and exalted the eternity of the Hereafter as alone worthy of the regard of a true Christian. Even though the later Middle Ages made a concession to our mortal state by authorizing the pursuit of mundane knowledge through the exercise of reason, the transcendental emphasis was not greatly

[1] Ferdinand Schevill, *History of Florence from the Founding of the City through the Renaissance,* Harcourt, Brace, 1936, 314, 316-18. Reprinted by permission of Ferdinand Schevill.

modified. While the thirteenth-century intellectuals, overwhelmingly members of the clergy confined within the barriers of their class, wrestled with the difficult abstractions of philosophy, the great body of the laity, composed of merchants, lawyers, physicians, and artisans, continued to occupy themselves with the pressing practical problems of living. They struggled to rise in the world by the successful exercise of their craft or profession; they traveled and became acquainted with other peoples, other countries, other customs; and, as citizens of an expanding town, they tried to contribute to its expansion and to win the right to participate in the conduct of its affairs. For these men constituting the urban laity, the transcendental message of the clergy imperceptibly began to lose its lure. Passionately concerned with the earth and with their human kind, they gradually, so gradually that it long escaped their own notice, set up for themselves a new scale of values. Inevitably the heaven of the teachers and preachers faded from view in measure as the urban laymen became increasingly absorbed with the engrossing concerns of everyday life. In brief, there took place a switch of attention, a mental re-orientation, which in the course of time received the name of humanism. Humanism is derived from the Latin *humanitas* (and ultimately from *homo,* that is, man), and its becoming a banner and a watch cry signified that the intellectual revolution produced by the urban movement had reached the stage when the Hereafter with its remote, presumptive glories would be gradually dethroned to be replaced by the Here with its pungent, ever-present, life-giving realities.

It was in the fourteenth century that humanism came clearly into view under its first great champion, Petrarch. But since it was, as we have been insisting, a consequence of the earth-directed communal movement, it had been in obscure gestation for several generations before; in the person of Petrarch, it presented itself to the eyes of men. . . .

It was by casting aside the medieval glasses and facing the world with so direct a gaze that . . . Petrarch was able to render both the language and literature of Rome a revolutionary service. A circumstance absolutely determinative of his outlook was that, although educated under the scholastic curriculum, he reacted violently against its dialectical exercises and the domination of the crabbed, abused Latin to which the needs of dialectics had reduced the once proud speech of the former rulers of the world. He wanted the original beauty of the language to be restored and the ancient authors to be studied for their value as literature. Not content to preach, he set an example by teaching himself to write Latin in at least an approach to the older manner and by probing the Latin authors to their stylistic core. An outstanding feature of the literature of Rome was that it represented an urban civilization which, having freed it-

self from religious tutelage, faced the world relying on no other support than our five frail senses and our imperfect reason. In the fourteenth century, a new urban civilization was arising, and to it, still groping in the dark, the older civilization, as disclosed by its literary remains, became a light and an inspiration. In short the time was ripe and Petrarch's message found an extraordinary response throughout the length and breadth of Italy. In measure as ever larger bodies of men discarded the old scholastic in favor of the new classical learning, there arose a demand for copies of the Latin writings, which Petrarch was extolling as the fountainhead of wisdom. While the existing works were rapidly multiplied by copyists, a feverish search began for missing works which ancient or recent neglect had permitted to drop from sight. In case the preserved or rediscovered texts of a given work showed different readings these had to be carefully compared in the hope of restoring as far as possible the exact words and turns of phrase the classical master had used. Such labor called for scholarly diligence and critical acumen and laid the foundations of classical philology, an entirely new field of study. Finally, in measure as the enthusiasm elicited by the reglimpsed world of antiquity continued to grow, the Latin literary monuments figured more and more prominently in the education of the young, thereby preparing the way for a revised curriculum which should no longer be dominated by the logical exercises and philosophic teachings of the schoolman.

From its practitioners beginning with Petrarch himself the new literary interests received the name of *studia humaniora,* for which the approximate English equivalent is humanism. Later generations, however, adopted a different emphasis and brought other terms into vogue, such as the revival of learning (or antiquity) and the Renaissance. As they still figure with humanism in all discussions of the period, we have three vaguely synonymous terms which have been subjected to a distressingly loose usage by many generations of writers. Under the circumstances every new writer should feel obliged to make clear the meaning he proposes to attach to each expression. To begin with humanism, after what has just gone before there should not be any doubt as to how it is here employed. We hold it to be a movement of the human mind which began when, following the rise of the towns, the urban intelligentsia slowly turned away from the transcendental values imposed by religion to the more immediately perceptible values of nature and of man. Inaugurated timidly in the twelfth and thirteenth centuries, humanism first arrived at consciousness of itself in the fourteenth century and, holding the scene ever since, has, apart from an occasional setback, steadily widened its empire. For reasons heretofore set forth it happened that, beginning with Petrarch, the mounting secular interests were deflected toward classical literature and led to an eager revival of antiquity. Consequently, since humanism did not become an active force till Petrarch's time, there has been a tendency to equate it with the revival of learning. But that is an ill-advised procedure, as the part can never be equal to the whole. In other words, the revival of learning was the particular turn taken under Petrarch's direction by the great secularizing movement which had set in with the communal revolution and which in one form or another has gone on uninterruptedly to our own day. It is therefore the writer's contention that humanism is a force which has been a factor in the civilization of the occident ever since the communal revolution, while the revival of learning is no more than the first

conscious phase of humanism dating from the fourteenth century and owing its special character to an inspired leader. It helps to maintain the distinction between the two terms to think of the revival of learning as a literary movement of limited duration and of humanism as a far more inclusive and continuous social and intellectual phenomenon. Accepting this relation to each other of humanism and the revival of learning (or antiquity), we should not find it difficult to differentiate them both from a term of much later origin, the Renaissance . . . applying . . . to the particular period or phase of western civilization which . . . marks the close of the Middle Ages and continues for some two or three hundred years . . . an European epoch with an indeterminate beginning and end.

2. Francesco Petrarch (1304-1374): "The First Modern Scholar"

PETRARCH ON HUMANISM AND RELIGION

Humanism did not develop without opposition; its opponents consisted of two groups of men. One group was composed primarily of churchmen who objected to humanistic learning because, as they insisted, it was a reversion to pagan ideals, a substitution of ancient mythology for the proper teachings of the Scriptures and of Christian saints and, on both counts, an intolerable anti-Christian influence. The other group, chiefly university professors, objected to humanism not only because it was anti-Christian but also because it upset the curricula and threatened to undermine the positions of whole university faculties. Against both these groups Francesco Petrarch found it necessary to defend the new learning.

Of Petrarch himself be it said that he is generally recognized as the earliest important humanist. He knew little Greek, but he became a self-taught master of Latin prose and verse in enthusiastic imitation of Roman writers, and his works mark clearly both his passion for ancient literature and his worldly, or secular, outlook. He loved the outdoors and he loved his Laura and, while Laura became another's wife, Petrarch never ceased to sing in her praise. But he was no lovesick romantic. He foresaw the values of humanism with remarkable clarity, and he met the opponents of the new learning with vigorous rebuttals. In a letter to his friend and pupil, Boccaccio, Petrarch supported humanism against the charge of being anti-Christian. An old man had written to Boccaccio and had claimed to have had a vision wherein Christ had appeared with messages for Boccaccio, Petrarch, and others urging them, upon pain of death, to renounce humanistic learning. Petrarch questioned the old man's veracity and scoffed at the prophecies. He counseled Boccaccio, who had been much shaken by the old man's words, as follows.

From PETRARCH, Letter to Boccaccio (1362) [1]

Neither exhortations to virtue nor the argument of approaching death should divert us from literature; for in a good mind it excites the love of virtue, and dissipates, or at least diminishes, the fear of death. To desert our studies shows want of self-confidence rather than wisdom, for letters do not hinder but aid the properly

[1] This and the next selection are quoted from James Harvey Robinson and Henry Winchester Rolfe, *Petrarch, the First Modern Scholar and Man of Letters,* 2nd ed. rev., 1914, 391-96. Courtesy G. P. Putnam's Sons.

constituted mind which possesses them; they facilitate our life, they do not retard it. . . . If it were otherwise, surely the zeal of certain persons who persevered to the end could not have roused such admiration. Cato, I never forget, acquainted himself with Latin literature as he was growing old, and Greek when he had really become an old man. Varro, who reached his hundredth year still reading and writing, parted from life sooner than from his love of study. Livius Drusus, although weakened by age and afflicted with blindness, did not give up his interpretation of the civil law, which he carried on to the great advantage of the state. . . .

Besides these and innumerable others like them, have not all those of our own religion whom we should wish most to imitate devoted their whole lives to literature, and grown old and died in the same pursuit? Some, indeed, were overtaken by death while still at work reading or writing. To none of them, so far as I know, did it prove a disadvantage to be noted for secular learning. . . .

While I know that many have become famous for piety without learning, at the same time I know of no one who has been prevented by literature from following the path of holiness. The apostle Paul was, to be sure, accused of having his head turned by study, but the world has long ago passed its verdict upon this accusation. If I may be allowed to speak for myself, it seems to me that, although the path to virtue by the way of ignorance may be plain, it fosters sloth. The goal of all good people is the same, but the ways of reaching it are many and various. Some advance slowly, others with more spirit; some obscurely, others again conspicuously. One takes a lower, another a higher path. Although all alike are on the road to happiness, certainly the more elevated path is the more glorious. Hence ignorance, however devout, is by no means to be put on a plane with the enlightened devoutness of one familiar with literature. Nor can you pick me out from the whole array of unlettered saints, an example so holy that I cannot match it with a still holier one from the other group.

PETRARCH'S OPPOSITION TO SCHOLASTICISM

Most of the university professors who denounced humanism were "scholastics," that is, adherents of the system of learning known as "scholasticism." Scholastics held that the furtherance of man's salvation was the supreme purpose of knowledge and that the foremost task of the scholar was to demonstrate the complete accord of philosophy with Christian dogma. Their chief distinguishing mark had become their method, which was rigidly formal according to the rules of logic and modes of reasoning set forth by Aristotle and other dialectics. Humanists as a whole, and Petrarch in particular, had small regard for scholastic learning. When Petrarch's friend Tomasso da Messina wrote of "a certain old logician" who loudly threatened to make war "upon our studies," Petrarch warned Tomasso that "if you are seeking virtue or truth, avoid persons of that stripe altogether," and continued in the following vein.

From PETRARCH, Letter to Tomasso (*c.* 1326) [1]

There is one thing which I myself long ago observed, and of which you now warn me anew. These logicians seek to cover their teachings with the splendour of Aristotle's name; they claim that Aristotle was wont to argue in the same way. They would have some excuse, I readily confess, if they followed in the steps of illustrious leaders, for even Cicero says

[1] *Ibid.,* 219-23.

that it would give him pleasure to err with Plato, if err he must. But they all deceive themselves. Aristotle was a man of the most exalted genius, who not only discussed but wrote upon themes of the very highest importance. How can we otherwise explain so vast an array of works, involving such prolonged labour, and prepared with supreme care amid such serious preoccupations—especially those connected with the guardianship of his fortunate pupil—and within the compass, too, of a life by no means long?— for he died at about sixty-three, the age which all writers deem so unlucky. Now why should these fellows diverge so widely from the path of their leader? . . . Who does not laugh at their trivial conclusions, with which, although educated men, they weary both themselves and others? They waste their whole lives in such contentions. Not only are they good for nothing else, but their perverted activity renders them actually harmful. Disputations such as they delight in are made a subject of mirth by Cicero and Seneca, in several passages. We find an example in the case of Diogenes, whom a contentious logician addressed as follows: "What I am, you are not." Upon Diogenes conceding this, the logician added, "But I am a man." As this was not denied, the poor quibbler propounded the conclusion, "Therefore you are not a man." "The last statement is not true," Diogenes remarked, "but if you wish it to be true, begin with me in your major premise." Similar absurdities are common enough with them. What they hope to gain from their efforts, whether fame or amusement, or some light upon the way to live righteously and happily, they may know; to me, I confess, it is the greatest of mysteries. . . .

On hearing such things as these, those of whom we are speaking grow furious—

indeed the chatter of this disputatious man usually verges closely on anger. "So you set yourself up to condemn logic," they cry. Far from it. . . . I know that it is one of the liberal studies, a ladder for those who are striving upwards, and by no means a useless protection to those who are forcing their way through the thorny thickets of philosophy. It stimulates the intellect, points out the way of truth, shows us how to avoid fallacies, and finally, if it accomplishes nothing else, makes us ready and quickwitted.

All this I readily admit, but because a road is proper for us to traverse, it does not immediately follow that we should linger on it forever. No traveller, unless he be mad, will forget his destination on account of the pleasures of the way; his characteristic virtue lies, on the contrary, in reaching his goal as soon as possible, never halting on the road. And who of us is not a traveller? . . . Dialectics may form a portion of our road, but certainly not its end: it belongs to the morning of life, not to its evening. We may have done once with perfect propriety what it would be shameful to continue. If as mature men we cannot leave the schools of logic because we have found pleasure in them as boys, why should we blush to . . . be rocked again in the cradle of our childhood? . . .

Use my arguments with the disciples of your ancient logician. Do not deter them from the study of logic; urge them rather to hasten through it to better things. Tell the old fellow himself that it is not the liberal arts which I condemn, but only hoary-headed children. Even as nothing is more disgraceful, as Seneca says, than an old man just beginning his alphabet, so there is no spectacle more unseemly than a person of mature years devoting himself to dialectics. But if your friend begins to vomit forth syllogisms, I advise you to take flight, bidding him argue with Enceladus. Farewell.

PETRARCH THE POET

Petrarch was a humanist poet of renown. Translations of three of his poems follow as illustrations of his art. The first is in praise of poetry, the second is an example of his love poems to Laura, and the third depicts his exquisite appreciation of nature—all three poems very earthly, wholly secular, and conforming closely to ancient patterns.

From PETRARCH, *The Sonnets* (c. 1535) [1]

TO A FRIEND, ENCOURAGING HIM TO PURSUE POETRY

Torn is each virtue from its earthly throne
By sloth, intemperance, and voluptuous
    ease;
E'en nature deviates from her wonted
    ways,
Too much the slave of vicious custom
    grown.
Far hence is every light celestial gone,
That guides mankind through life's per-
    plexing maze;
And those, whom Helicon's sweet waters
    please,
From mocking crowds receive contempt
    alone.
Who now would laurel, myrtle-wreaths
    obtain?
Let want, let shame, Philosophy attend!
Cries the base world, intent on sordid
    gain.
What though thy favourite path be trod
    by few;
Let it but urge thee more, dear gentle
    friend,
Thy great design of glory to pursue.

[1] *The Sonnets, Triumphs, and Other Poems of Petrarch,* translated by various hands, London, 1859 (Bohn's Illustrated Library), 6-7, 88-89, 172-73.

HE PAINTS THE BEAUTIES OF LAURA, PROTESTING
HIS UNALTERABLE LOVE

Loose to the breeze her golden tresses
flow'd
Wildly in thousand mazy ringlets blown,
And from her eyes unconquer'd glances
shone,
Those glances now so sparingly bestow'd.
And true or false, meseem'd some signs
she show'd
As o'er her cheek soft pity's hue was
thrown;
I, whose whole breast with love's soft
food was sown,
What wonder if at once my bosom
glow'd?
Graceful she moved, with more than mor-
tal mien,
In form an angel: and her accents won
Upon the ear with more than human
sound.
A spirit heavenly pure, a living sun,
Was what I saw; and if no more 'twere
seen,
T' unbend the bow will never heal the
wound.

THE VISION OF THE FAWN

Beneath a laurel, two fair streams be-
tween,
At early sunrise of the opening year,
A milk-white fawn upon the meadow
green,
Of gold its either horn, I saw appear;
So mild, yet so majestic, was its mien,
I left, to follow, all my labours here,
As miners after treasure, in the keen
Desire of new, forget the old to fear.
"Let none impede"—so, round its fair
neck, run
The words in diamond and topaz writ—
"My lord to give me liberty sees fit."
And now the sun his noontide height had
won
When I, with weary though unsated view,
Fell in the stream—and so my vision flew.

3. Boccaccio and Renaissance Society

Giovanni Boccaccio (1313-1375), friend, pupil, and fellow humanist of Petrarch, made some progress in the study of Greek. Like Petrarch, he ransacked Italy for ancient manuscripts and became very proud of his Latin style in imitation of the ancients. Ironically, however, he is most famous for a series of lively tales written in the vernacular (Tuscan) tongue and called *The Decameron,* a work of which Boccaccio himself was somewhat ashamed. Subsequent generations, however, view *The Decameron* as an excellent example of the coarse language and crude morality of Renaissance Italian society. The tales are almost purely pagan in tone, with little evidence of Christian sentiments or teachings. Sensual, worldly, and often indelicate in modern eyes, *The Decameron* is a distinctively Renaissance piece of literature. That it was written in a fine Italian prose style contributed much to the growth of an Italian vernacular literature. Composed between 1350 and 1354, it opens with an excellent description of the Black Death in Florence in 1348.

From BOCCACCIO, *The Decameron* (c. 1350) [1]

In the year then of our Lord 1348, there happened at Florence, the finest city in all Italy, a most terrible plague; which, whether owing to the influence of the planets, or that it was sent from God as a just punishment for our sins, had broken out some years before in the Levant; and after passing from place to place, and making incredible havoc all the way, had now reached the west; where, spite of all the means that art and human foresight

[1] *The Decameron; or, Ten Days' Entertainment of Boccaccio,* Albert & Charles Boni, 1926, xix-xx, xxiv-xxvii.

could suggest, as keeping the city clear from filth, and excluding all suspected persons; notwithstanding frequent consultations what else was to be done; nor omitting prayers to God in frequent processions: in the spring of the foregoing year, it began to show itself in a sad and wonderful manner; and, different from what it had been in the east, where bleeding from the nose is the fatal prognostic, here there appeared certain tumours in the groin, or under the armpits, some as big as a small apple, others as an egg; and afterwards purple spots in most parts of the body: in some cases large and but few in number, in others less and more numerous, both sorts the usual messengers of death. To the cure of this malady, neither medical knowledge nor the power of drugs was of any effect; whether because the disease was in its own nature mortal, or that the physicians (the number of whom, taking quacks and women pretenders into account, was grown very great) could form no just idea of the cause, nor consequently ground a true method of cure; whichever was the reason, few or none escaped; but they generally died the third day from the first appearance of the symptoms, without a fever or other bad circumstance attending. And the disease, by being communicated from the sick to the well, seemed daily to get ahead, and to rage the more, as fire will do by laying on fresh combustibles. . . .

But I am weary of recounting our late miseries; therefore, passing by everything that I can well omit, I shall only observe, that the city being left almost without inhabitants, it happened one Tuesday in the evening as I was informed by persons of good credit, that seven ladies all in deep mourning, as most proper for that time, had been attending Divine service (being the whole congregation), in new St. Mary's Church: who, as united by the ties either of friendship or relation, and of suitable years; viz., the youngest not less than eighteen, nor the eldest exceeding twenty-eight; so were they all discreet, nobly descended, and perfectly accomplished, both in person and behaviour. I do not mention their names, lest they should be displeased with some things said to have passed in conversation, there being a greater restraint on those diversions now. . . . And that I may relate therefore all that occurred without confusion, I shall affix names to every one bearing some resemblance to the quality of the person. The eldest then I call Pampinea, the next to her Flammetta, the third Philomena, the fourth Emilia, the fifth Lauretta, the sixth Neiphile, the youngest Eliza: who being got together by chance rather than any appointment, into a corner of the church, and there seated in a ring; and leaving off their devotions, and falling into some discourse together concerning the nature of the times; in a little while Pampinea thus began:

"My dear girls, you have often heard, as well as I, that no one is injured, where we only make an honest use of our own reason: now reason tells us that we are to preserve our lives by all possible means: and, in some cases, at the expense of the lives of others. And if the laws which regard the good of the community allow this, may not we much rather (and all that mean honestly as we do), without giving offence to any, use the means now in our power for our own preservation? . . . We stay here for no other purpose, that I can see, but to observe what numbers come to be buried, or to listen if the monks, who are now reduced to a very few, sing their services at the proper times, or else to show by our habits the greatness of our distress. And if we go from hence, we are saluted with numbers of the dead and sick carried along the streets; or with persons who had been outlawed for their villainies, now facing it out publicly, in defiance of the laws. Or we see the scum of the city enriched with the public calamity, and insulting us with reproachful ballads. Nor is anything talked of but that such an one is dead or dying; and, were any left to mourn, we should hear nothing but lamentations. . . .

"Therefore the case is the same, whether we stay here, depart hence, or go home; especially as there are few who are able to go, and have a place to go to, left but ourselves. And those few, I am told, fall into all sorts of debauchery; and even the religious and ladies shut up in monasteries, supposing themselves entitled to equal liberties with others, are as bad as the worst. . . . Wherefore, lest through our own wilfulness or neglect, this calamity, which might have been prevented, should befall us, I should think it best (and I hope you will join with me) for us to quit the town, and avoiding, as we would death itself, the bad example of others, to choose some place of retirement, of which every one of us has more than one, where we may make ourselves innocently merry, without offering the least violence to the dictates of reason and our own consciences. There will our ears be entertained with the warbling of the birds, and our eyes with the verdure of the hills and valleys; with the waving of corn-fields like the sea itself; with trees of a thousand different kinds, and a more open and serene sky which, however overcast, yet affords a far more agreeable prospect than these desolate walls. The air also is pleasanter, and there is greater plenty of everything, attended with fewer inconveniences: for, though people die there as well as here, yet we shall have fewer such objects before us, as the inhabitants are less in number; and on the other part, if I judge right, we desert nobody, but are rather ourselves forsaken. For all our friends, either by death, or endeavouring to avoid it, have left us, as if we in no way belonged to them. As no blame then can ensue by following this advice, and perhaps sickness and death by not doing so, I would have us take our maids, and everything we may be supposed to want, and to remove every day to a different place, taking all the diversions in the meantime which the seasons will permit; and there continue, unless death should interpose, till we see what end Providence designs for these things."

[And so the ladies, in company with some gentlemen bent upon the same purpose, took refuge in a villa outside Florence, where they amused themselves by telling tales—the tales which make up the remainder of *The Decameron*.]

4. Benvenuto Cellini in Rome

Probably the most human document of Renaissance Italy is *The Life of Benvenuto Cellini Written by Himself*. Cellini (1500-1571) was born in Florence, the son of a servant of the House of Medici. His father wanted him to become a musician, but he preferred the goldsmith's art, went to Rome, became a worshiper of Michelangelo, executed several works for Pope Clement VII, and became Stamp Master (of dies for the papal mint). Failing to get on well with Pope Paul III, who succeeded Clement in 1534, Cellini tried to attach himself to the court of Francis I of France. Unjustly imprisoned in Rome on the charge of having stolen papal jewels several years before, during the Sack of Rome (1527), Cellini was badly treated, but finally escaped and began work for Francis I in 1540. After a few years he tired of the French scene, returned to Florence, and worked for Cosimo de' Medici for the rest of his life. He became famous as an artist, but his rollicking, boastful autobiography has made him more famous still. Below is a selection from Cellini's *Life* describing his first visit to Rome as a youth still in his teens.

From *The Life of Cellini* (c. 1562) [1]

At Siena I waited for the mail to Rome, which I afterwards joined; and when we passed the Paglia, we met a courier carrying news of the new Pope, Clement VII [1523-1534]. Upon my arrival in Rome, I went to work in the shop of the master-goldsmith Santi. He was dead; but a son of his carried on the business. He did not work himself, but entrusted all his commissions to a young man named Lucagnolo from Iesi, a country fellow, who while yet a child had come into Santi's service. This man was short but well proportioned, and was a more skilful craftsman than any one whom I had met with up to that time; remarkable for facility and excellent in design. He executed large plate only; that is to say, vases of the utmost beauty, basins, and such pieces. Having put myself to work there, I began to make some candelabra for the Bishop of Salamanca, a Spaniard. They were richly chased, so far as that sort of work admits. A pupil of Raffaello da Urbino called Gian Francesco, and commonly known as Il Fattore, was a painter of great ability; and being on terms of friendship with the Bishop, he introduced me to his favour, so that I obtained many commissions from that prelate, and earned considerable sums of money.

During that time I went to draw, sometimes in Michel Agnolo's chapel, and sometimes in the house of Agostino Chigi of Siena, which contained many incomparable paintings by the hand of

[1] *The Life of Benvenuto Cellini Written by Himself*, ed. and trans. by John Addington Symonds, 1906, Bk. I, 113-20. Reprinted by permission of Coward-McCann, Inc.

that great master Raffaello. This I did on feast-days, because the house was then inhabited by Messer Gismondo, Agostino's brother. They plumed themselves exceedingly when they saw young men of my sort coming to study in their palaces. Gismondo's wife, noticing my frequent presence in that house—she was a lady as courteous as could be, and of surpassing beauty—came up to me one day, looked at my drawings, and asked me if I was a sculptor or a painter; to whom I said I was a goldsmith. She remarked that I drew too well for a goldsmith; and having made one of her waiting-maids bring a lily of the finest diamonds set in gold, she showed it to me, and bade me value it. I valued it at 800 crowns. Then she said that I had very nearly hit the mark, and asked me whether I felt capable of setting the stones really well. I said that I should much like to do so, and began before her eyes to make a little sketch for it, working all the better because of the pleasure I took in conversing with so lovely and agreeable a gentlewoman. When the sketch was finished, another Roman lady of great beauty joined us; she had been above, and now descending to the ground-floor, asked Madonna Porzia what she was doing there. She answered with a smile: "I am amusing myself by watching this worthy young man at his drawing; he is as good as he is handsome." I had by this time acquired a trifle of assurance, mixed, however, with some honest bashfulness; so I blushed and said: "Such as I am, lady, I shall ever be most ready to serve you." The gentlewoman, also slightly blushing, said: "You know well that I want you to serve me"; and reaching me the lily, told me to take it away; and gave me besides twenty golden crowns which she had in her bag, and added: "Set me the jewel after the fashion you have sketched, and keep for me the old gold in which it is now set."

. . . I set myself to making a little model of wax, in order to show how the jewel would look when it was completed. This I took to Madonna Porzia, whom I found with the same Roman lady. Both of them were highly satisfied with my work, and treated me so kindly that, being somewhat emboldened, I promised the jewel should be twice as good as the model. Accordingly I set hand to it, and in twelve days I finished it in the form of a fleur-de-lys, as I have said above, ornamenting it with little masks, children, and animals, exquisitely enamelled, whereby the diamonds which formed the lily were more than doubled in effect.

While I was working at this piece, Lucagnolo, of whose ability I have before spoken, showed considerable discontent, telling me over and over again that I might acquire far more profit and honour by helping him to execute large plate, as I had done at first. I made him answer that, whenever I chose, I should always be capable of working at great silver pieces; but that things like that on which I was now engaged were not commissioned every day; and beside their bringing no less honour than large silver plate, there was also more profit to be made by them. He laughed me in the face, and said: "Wait and see, Benvenuto; for by the time that you have finished that work of yours, I will make haste to have finished this vase, which I took in hand when you did the jewel; and then experience shall teach you what profit I shall get from my vase, and what you will get from your ornament." I answered that I was very glad indeed to enter into such a competition with so good a craftsman as he was, because the end would show which of us was mistaken. Accordingly both the one and the other of us, with a scornful smile upon our lips, bent our heads in grim earnest to the work, which both were now desirous of accomplishing; so that

after about ten days, each had finished his undertaking with great delicacy and artistic skill.

Lucagnolo's was a huge silver piece, used at the table of Pope Clement, into which he flung away bits of bone and the rind of divers fruits, while eating; an object of ostentation rather than necessity. The vase was adorned with two fine handles, together with many masks, both small and great, and masses of lovely foliage, in as exquisite a style of elegance as could be imagined; on seeing which I said it was the most beautiful vase that ever I set eyes on. Thinking he had convinced me, Lucagnolo replied: "Your work seems to me no less beautiful, but we shall soon perceive the difference between the two." So he took his vase and carried it to the Pope, who was very well pleased with it, and ordered at once that he should be paid at the ordinary rate of such large plate. Meanwhile I carried mine to Madonna Porzia, who looked at it with astonishment, and told me I had far surpassed my promise. . . .

On the day following, Madonna Porzia sent a major-domo of hers to my shop, who called me out, and putting into my hands a paper packet full of money from his lady . . . hinted that the money sent me was not the entire payment merited by my industry, and other messages were added worthy of so courteous a lady. Lucagnolo, who was burning to compare his packet with mine, burst into the shop; then in the presence of twelve journeyman and some neighbours, eager to behold the result of this competition, he seized his packet, scornfully exclaiming "Ou! ou!" three or four times, while he poured his money on the counter with a great noise. They were twenty-five crowns in giulios; and he fancied that mine would be four or five crowns *di moneta*. I for my part, stunned and stifled by his cries, and by the looks and smiles of the bystanders, first peeped into my packet; then, after seeing that it contained nothing but gold, I retired to one end of the counter, and, keeping my eyes lowered and making no noise at all, I lifted it with both hands suddenly above my head, and emptied it like a mill hopper. My coin was twice as much as his; which caused the onlookers, who had fixed their eyes on me with some derision, to turn round suddenly to him and say: "Lucagnolo, Benvenuto's pieces, being all of gold and twice as many as yours, make a far finer effect." I thought for certain that, what with jealousy and what with shame, Lucagnolo would have fallen dead upon the spot; and though he took the third part of my gain, since I was a journeyman (for such is the custom of the trade, two-thirds fall to the workman and one-third to the masters of the shop), yet inconsiderate envy had more power in him than avarice: it ought indeed to have worked quite the other way, he being a peasant's son from Iesi. He cursed his art and those who taught it him, vowing that thenceforth he would never work at large plate, but give his whole attention to those whoreson gewgaws, since they were so well paid.

5. Nicolas V and the Founding of the Vatican Library

New values seen in ancient writings led Renaissance scholars and patrons to a systematic search for forgotten works of classical authors—a quest for manuscripts both in the West and in Greece and Byzantium. Some scholars, such as Poggio Bracciolini (1380-1459), gained great distinction for the number of "lost" works they brought to light. The collection of these materials led to a lively business in book and manuscript selling and to the foundation of great classical libraries, some of which exist today, such as the Medici Library in Florence and the Papal Library in Rome. Vespasiano da Bisticci (1421-1498), a Florentine bookseller, wrote an account of the collections of Pope Nicolas V (1447-1455), the founder of the great Vatican Library. Part of this description is given below as illustrative of a collecting mania which permeated Renaissance Italy and, to some degree, all Europe.

From BISTICCI, *Life of Nicholas V* (c. 1455) [1]

A great quantity of money came . . . to the Apostolic See, and with this the pope commenced building in many places, and sent for Greek and Latin books, wherever he was able to find them, without regard to price. He gathered together a large band of writers, the best that he could find, and kept them in constant employment. He also summoned a number of learned men, both for the purpose of composing new works, and of translating such works as were not already tranlated, giving them most abundant provision for their needs meanwhile; and when the works were translated and brought to him, he gave them large sums of money, in order that they should do more willingly that which they undertook to do. He made great provision for the needs of learned men. He gathered together great numbers of books upon every subject, both Greek and Latin, to the number of 5000 volumes. So at his death it was found by inventory that never since the time of Ptolemy had half the number of books of every kind been brought together. All books he caused to be copied, without regard to what it cost him, and there were

1 Vespasiano da Bisticci, *Life of Nicholas V* as translated and quoted in Merrick Whitcomb, *A Literary Source-Book of the Renaissance,* 2nd ed., 1903, 74-76. Reprinted by permission of the University of Pennsylvania Press.

few places where his Holiness had not copiers at work. When he could not find a book, nor secure it in any way, he had it copied. After he had assembled at Rome, as I said above, many learned men at large salaries, he wrote to Florence to Messer Giannozzo Manetti, that he should come to Rome to translate and compose for him. And when Manetti left Florence and came to Rome, the pope, as was his custom, received him with honor, and assigned to him, in addition to his income as secretary, six hundred ducats, urging him to attempt the translation of the books of the Bible and of Aristotle, and to complete the book already commenced by him, *Contra Judeos et gentes;* a wonderful work, if it had been completed, but he carried it only to the tenth book. Moreover, he translated the New Testament, and the Psalter *De hebraica Veritate,* with five apologetical books in defense of this Psalter; showing that in the Holy Scriptures there is not one syllable that does not contain the greatest of mysteries.

It was pope Nicholas' intention to found a library in St. Peter's, for the general use of the whole Roman curia, which would have been an admirable thing indeed, if he had been able to carry it out, but death prevented his bringing it to completion. He illumined the Holy Scriptures with innumerable books, which he caused to be translated; and in the same way with the humanities, including certain works upon grammar, of use in learning Latin. The *Orthography* of Messer Giovanni Tortelle, who was of his Holiness' household and worked upon the library, a worthy book and useful to grammarians; the *Iliad* of Homer; Strabo's *De situ orbis* he caused to be translated by Guerrino, and gave him 500 florins for each part, that is to say, Asia, Africa and Europe; that was in all 1500 florins. Herodotus and Thucydides he had translated by Lorenzo

Valla, and rewarded him liberally for his trouble; Xenophon and Diodorus by Messer Poggio; Polybius by Nicolo Perotto, whom, when he handed it to him, he gave 500 brand new papal ducats in a purse, and said to him, that it was not what he deserved, but that in time he would take care to satisfy him. The work of Philo the Jew, a book of the greatest worth, of which the Latin tongue had as yet no knowledge; Theophrastus *De Plantis,* a most able work; *Problemata Aristoteles;* these two were translated by Theodorus the Greek, a man of great learning and eloquence. The Republic of Plato and his Laws, the *Posteriora,* the Ethics and Physics, *Magna Moralia,* and Metaphysics, the Greater Rhetoric, George of Trebisond. *De Animalibus* of Aristotle, by Theodorus, a most excellent work. Sacred works, the works of Dionysius the Areopagite, an admirable book, translated by Brother Ambrogio. There were before this other translations utterly barbarous. I was told by pope Nicholas that this translation was so good, that one got a better idea from the simple text than from the other texts accompanied with elaborate comments. The wonderful book, *De praeparatione evangelica,* of Eusebius Pamphili, a work of great erudition. Many works of St. Basil, of St. Gregory of Nazianzus; Chrysostom on St. Matthew, about eighty homilies, which had been lost for 500 years or more; for twenty-five homilies were translated by Orosius more than 500 years ago, and the work was much sought for by ancients and moderns; for it is written, that St. Thomas Aquinas, on his way to Paris, when, as he was approaching, the city was pointed out to him, said: "I would rather at this moment have St. John Chrysostom on St. Matthew than Paris." Such a reputation it had! This was translated by George of Trebisond. Cyril on

Genesis, and on St. John, excellent works. Many other works translated and composed at the desire of his Holiness, of which I have no knowledge. I have mentioned only those of which I have knowledge.

6. *The Renaissance and Italian Nationalism*

One of the characteristics of the Renaissance era was the rise of that powerful mass emotion known today as nationalism. Accompanying the rise of unified monarchies was the growth of the new spirit of nationalism. Feudal peoples had subscribed, in theory at least, to internationalism. The Holy Roman Empire symbolized political and temporal unity in Christendom; the Roman Catholic Church claimed spiritual and ecclesiastical unity; and the use of the Latin tongue gave linguistic and cultural unity. During the Renaissance, however, this ideal of unity was destroyed. Nationalism slowly pushed aside internationalism. National monarchs rivaled the Holy Roman Emperor; the church was nationalized to a considerable degree and its pretended unity was destroyed by the Protestant Revolt; the vernacular tongues displaced Latin and gradually gave rise to national literatures and nationalized cultures.

This nationalization of Europe was produced by a conjunction of events. Ambitious kings encouraged it for obvious political purposes. Their administration of royal authority demanded it; their financial needs required it; and their wars with one another nourished it. But in addition to these political

forces, Renaissance writers fostered nationalism by their frequent use of the vernacular tongue in preference to Latin. Chaucer in England, Cervantes in Spain, Rabelais in France—these and others are well known for their roles in the creation of vernacular writings for their respective nations.

DANTE'S NATIONALISM: HIS DEFENSE OF HIS NATIVE TONGUE

One of the first Italians to employ the "vulgar" tongue wrote a defense of his use of Italian. This man was the Florentine poet Dante Alighieri (1265-1321). As the quotation below will show, Dante was largely impelled to write in his native Italian out of nationalistic fervor. His *Convivio* (*The Banquet*) was written in Italian, as he says, for three reasons: First, because the vulgar tongue is flexible and admits change whereas Latin is fixed; second, because he was writing for the common people who rarely knew Latin; and third, because of national sentiment, as Dante himself explains.

From DANTE, *Convivio* (c. 1304) [1]

I say that the plan of my whole apology requires me to show how I was moved to this course through natural affection for my own native speech; and this is the third and last reason that impelled me to it. I say that natural affection chiefly moves a lover to three things, firstly, to magnify the object loved; secondly, to be jealous for it; thirdly, to defend it, as every one may see constantly happen. These three things made me choose this, namely, our vulgar tongue which natu-

[1] From *Dante's Convivio*, trans. by William Walrond Jackson, 1909, 55-65. By permission of The Clarendon Press, Oxford.

rally as well as for incidental reasons, I love and have loved.

I was moved in the first place by the wish to magnify it. . . .

I was moved in the second place by jealousy for it. . . .

Furthermore, I was moved by the wish to defend it against its numerous accusers who disparage it, and praise the other popular languages. . . .

To the perpetual shame and disgrace of these wicked men of Italy, who praise the vulgar tongue of other nations and disparage their own, I say that they are impelled to do this by five detestable causes. The first is blindness of discernment; the second, knavish excusing of themselves; the third, greed of vainglory; the fourth, an objection prompted by envy; the fifth and last, cowardice of mind, that is pusillanimity. . . .

But nevertheless I ought to show that I feel not only love but most perfect love for my native tongue, and furthermore I ought to censure her adversaries. In proving this to any one who will rightly understand, I shall say first how I became her friend and then how this friendship was confirmed. . . .

This vulgar tongue of mine brought together my two parents, for they conversed in it, even as the fire disposes the iron for the use of the smith who makes the knife. Wherefore it is plain that my native tongue had a share in begetting me, and thus is, in a sense, the cause of my being. Moreover, this my native speech ushered me into the path of knowledge which is our final perfection, in so far as I began Latin with her aid, and with her aid I learned it, Latin which afterwards opened me the way to go onwards: and thus it is obvious to all and is by me acknowledged that she has been to me the greatest of benefactors.

MACHIAVELLI AND ITALIAN NATIONALISM

Probably the greatest Renaissance writer to foster nationalism was Niccolo Machiavelli (1469-1527). Machiavelli was the son of a Florentine lawyer of good family but meager fortune. In 1498 he was appointed secretary to the Council of Ten for Peace and Liberty; that is, a secretary in the Foreign Office of the Florentine Republic. It was a subordinate post, but in this capacity Machiavelli was employed in diplomatic missions to other Italian states and he found a rare opportunity to study the minds and motives of men. Likewise, in this capacity Machiavelli came to abhor the mutual jealousies and greed which kept Italy divided into petty city-states helpless against and constantly the prey of the cunning diplomacy and superior force of its neighbors, especially the Empire, France, and Spain. Thus, as an Italian patriot—and, incidentally, as a bid for employment by the Medici, who controlled Florence and the Papacy—Machiavelli wrote (1513) Il Principe, "The Prince."

The Prince, politely and significantly dedicated to "The Magnificent Lorenzo di Piero de' Medici," is a collection of rules, justified by history and hardheaded experience, by which a prince might unite Italy, free it from foreign intervention, and regenerate and mold its people into a national state. Machiavelli intended his rules to be practical. As contemporary Italian politics were in a very low ethical and moral state, Machiavelli's recommendations, in a realistic fashion, were little concerned with moral and ethical values. He recognized that "to slaughter fellow-citizens, to betray friends, to be devoid of honour, pity, religion, cannot be counted as merits, for these are means that may lead to power, but confer no glory." But, as it appeared to Machiavelli, power was the most immediate need of a liberating prince; glory might be cultivated later. And so *The Prince* is represented as one who is entirely free from emotional disturbances, ready to take every advantage of existing circumstances, strong enough to sin boldly if his country's welfare depends upon it, shrewd in comprehending human nature in whatever form he finds it, ready to combat evil with evil, toy with the passions of men, use men as his purposes require. Moreover, he must be thorough, self-reliant, never hesitant. He must abolish mercenaries and create a national army of his own subjects. In short, if such a man could be found who was dead to every sentiment but love of country, more willing to save his fatherland than his own soul, careless of justice and injustice alike, of mercy or cruelty, of honor or disgrace, such a man might free Italy from the foreign yoke and create of the discordant Italian cities a national state. With such sentiments, it is easy to understand how the term "Machiavellian" has come to designate low cunning and unmoral action in nearly every modern language.

Machiavelli's book treats of princes who would encroach upon their neighbors in order to enlarge their dominions, "Of new Princedoms acquired by the aid of others and by good fortune," "Of those who by Crime come to be Princes," "Of the civil Princedom," "Of the duty of a Prince in respect of military affairs," "How Princes should keep faith," and so on until the last chapter is "An Exhortation to liberate Italy from the Barbarians." Illustrative selections follow.

From MACHIAVELLI, *The Prince* (1513) [1]

OF CRUELTY AND CLEMENCY, AND WHETHER IT IS BETTER TO BE LOVED OR FEARED

And here comes in the question whether it is better to be loved rather than feared, or feared rather than loved. It might be answered that we should wish to be both; but since love and fear can hardly exist together, if we must choose between them, it is far safer to be feared than loved. For of men it may generally be affirmed that they are thankless, fickle, false, studious to avoid danger, greedy of gain, devoted to you while you confer benefits upon them, and ready, as I said before, while the need is remote, to shed their blood, and sacrifice their property, their lives, and their children for you; but when it comes near they turn against you. The Prince, therefore, who without otherwise securing himself builds wholly on their professions is undone. For the friendships we buy with a price, and do not gain by greatness and nobility of character, though fairly earned are not made good, but fail us when we need them most.

Moreover, men are less careful how they offend him who makes himself loved than him who makes himself feared. For love is held by the tie of obligation, which, because men are a sorry breed, is broken on every prompting of self-interest; but fear is bound by the apprehension of punishment which never loosens its grasp.

Nevertheless a Prince should inspire fear in suchwise that if he do not win love he may escape hate. For a man may very well be feared and yet not hated, as will always be the case so long as he does not intermeddle with the property or with the women of his citizens and subjects.

[1] The following quotations are from *The Prince*, trans. by Ninian Hill Thomson, 3d ed., rev., Oxford, 1913, 120-21, 125-30, 190-198. By permission of the Clarendon Press, Oxford.

And if constrained to put any one to death, he should do so only when there is manifest cause or reasonable justification. But, above all, he must abstain from the property of others. For men will sooner forget the death of their father than the loss of their patrimony.

HOW PRINCES SHOULD KEEP FAITH

Every one recognizes how praiseworthy it is in a Prince to keep faith, and to act uprightly and not craftily. Nevertheless . . . Princes who have set little store by their word . . . have accomplished great things, and in the end had the better of those who trusted to honest dealing.

Be it known, then, that there are two ways of contending, one in accordance with the laws, the other by force; the first of which is proper to men, the second to beasts. But since the first method is often ineffectual, it becomes necessary to resort to the second. A Prince should, therefore, understand how to use well both the man and the beast. . . .

But since a Prince should know how to use the beast's nature wisely, he ought of beasts to choose both the lion and the fox; for the lion cannot guard himself from the toils, nor the fox from wolves. He must therefore be a fox to discern toils, and a lion to drive off wolves.

To rely wholly on the lion is unwise; and for this reason a prudent Prince neither can nor ought to keep his word when to keep it is hurtful to him and the causes which led him to pledge it are removed. If all men were good, this would not be good advice, but since they are dishonest and do not keep faith with you, you, in return, need not keep faith with them; and no Prince was ever at a loss for plausible reasons to cloak a breach of faith. . . .

Thus, it is well to seem merciful, faithful, humane, religious, and upright, and also to be so; but the mind should remain so balanced that were it needful not to be so, you should be able and know how to change to the contrary. . . . A Prince should therefore be very careful that nothing ever escapes his lips which is not replete with the five qualities above named, so that to see and hear him, one would think him the embodiment of mercy, good faith, integrity, kindliness, and religion. And there is no virtue which it is more necessary for him to seem to possess than this last; because men in general judge rather by the eye than by the hand, for all can see but few can touch. . . .

Moreover, in the actions of all men, and most of all of Princes, where there is no tribunal to which we can appeal, we look to results. Wherefore if a Prince succeeds in establishing and maintaining his authority, the means will always be judged honourable and be approved by every one.

AN EXHORTATION TO LIBERATE ITALY FROM THE BARBARIANS

Turning over in my mind all the matters which have above been considered, and debating with myself whether in Italy at the present hour the times are such as might serve to win honour for a new Prince, and whether fit opportunity now offers for a prudent and valiant leader to bring about changes glorious for himself and advantageous for the whole Italian people, it seems to me that so many conditions combine to further such an enterprise, that I know of no time so favourable to it as now. . . .

We see how she [Italy] prays God to send some one to rescue her from these barbarous cruelties and oppressions. We see, too, how ready and eager she is to follow any standard were there only some one to raise it. But at present we see no one except in your illustrious House (pre-eminent by its virtues and good fortune, and favoured by God and by the Church whose headship it now holds), who could assume the part of a deliverer. . . .

If, then, your illustrious House should seek to follow the example of those great men who have delivered their country in past ages, it is before all things necessary, as the true foundation of every such attempt, to be provided with national troops, since you can have no braver, truer, or more faithful soldiers; and although every single man of them be good, collectively they will be better, seeing themselves commanded by their own Prince, and honoured and maintained by him. That you may be able, therefore, to defend yourself against the foreigner with Italian valour, the first step is to provide yourself with an army such as this. . . .

This opportunity, then, for Italy at last

to look on her deliverer, ought not to be allowed to pass away. . . . What gates would be closed against him? What people would refuse him obedience? What jealousy would stand in his way? What Italian but would yield him homage? This barbarian tyranny stinks in all nostrils.

Let your illustrious House therefore take upon itself this charge with all the courage and all the hopes with which a just cause is undertaken, so that under your standard this our country may be ennobled, and under your auspices be fulfilled the words of Petrarch:

"Brief will be the strife
When valour arms against barbaric rage;
For the bold spirit of a bygone age
Still warms Italian hearts with life."

---

3 THE LITERARY RENAISSANCE IN TRANS-ALPINE EUROPE

1. The Renaissance in the Germanies

The new developments of the Renaissance era in Italy spread rapidly to other parts of Europe. The means for their dissemination were varied in nature. Italian scholars and artists, in their restless search for knowledge, traveled widely and, to some degree, carried the "new spirit" with them. Italian academies and universities gained such transcendent renown that students from transalpine Europe flocked to them, became imbued with the "new learning," and carried it back to their own lands. Italian financiers extended their opera-

tions and their patronage into German, Flemish, French, English, and Spanish cities, local competitors arose, and, as the centers of trade shifted westward, an urban movement and a material prosperity occurred in western Europe as it had occurred earlier in Italy with similar social results and a like stimulus to art and letters. European monarchs, exasperated by the double-dealing diplomacy of popes and other Italian princes, were led to invade Italy, and their armies returned home not only with the spoils of victory but also with a real desire to imitate and to emulate the culture of the vanquished. And lastly, the invention and use of printing, itself a

Renaissance achievement, exerted a tremendous influence in stimulating and spreading the "new learning" and humanistic literature.

As the new intellectual attitudes which had evolved in Italy during the Renaissance era were carried into transalpine Europe they underwent subtle changes. These changes were most evident in the Germanies (the Holy Roman Empire). One scholar has described them in the following selection.

From CREIGHTON, *History of the Papacy* (1894) [1]

Germany was the first country which distinctly admitted the influence of Italy; but it did not, in so doing, absorb the Italian spirit. The new learning won its way gradually through students, teacher, and universities; it was not carried home to the minds of the people by a great outburst of art and architecture, by the pomp and pageantry of princely and municipal life, such as dazzled the eyes of the Italians. It came from above, and won its way by conflict with old institutions and old modes of thought. The result was that it wore from the beginning the appearance of a reforming and progressive system, which proposed new modes of teaching and criticised existing methods. Moreover, in Germany there had been a quiet but steady current of conservative reform in ecclesiastical matters, which had created an amount of seriousness not to be found in Italy, and was too powerful to be neglected by the leaders of a new movement. There had been a continuous attempt to deal by personal perseverance with the acknowledged evils of the times; there had been a succession of men who in their own ways laboured to heighten

[1] Mandell Creighton, *A History of the Papacy during the Period of the Reformation*, 5 vols., 1882-1894, V, 3-4. By permission of Longmans, Green and Company.

the religious, moral, and social life of the people. The new learning had to take account of these men, and at first wore the aspect of an aid to their endeavours. If it came as an impulse, it was valued as suggesting a method. What in Italy was frivolous and superficial was esteemed in Germany for its practical utility. Culture did not remain as an individual possession; it must render its meed of service to social improvement.

Thus there was a breach between the Italian and German point of view, a breach which neither country clearly recognised but which prevented them from understanding one another when the crisis came. The Germans had drifted farther than they knew from the sentiment of the traditions of the past, and showed themselves singularly open to the pleadings of homely common-sense. The Italians, as soon as they were challenged, abandoned their intellectual indifference and took refuge in the sentiment of the past. The conscientious endeavours of the Germans to amend the old system rendered them, as a matter of fact, more ready to revolt from it than did the contemptuous disregard of the Italians, which rested on moral indifference rather than on intellectual disapproval.

2. Humanism in Transalpine Europe: Examples from the Works of Erasmus

ERASMUS ON THE NEW AGE OF LEARNING

Though he was by no means the first transalpine humanist, Desiderius Erasmus (1466-1536) is universally recognized as one of the greatest. A native of Rotterdam, he traveled, studied, and taught in the Germanies, France, Switzerland, and England. Wherever he went, he made friends with the best scholars of his day, and he kept up a voluminous correspondence with them all. "For my part," he once wrote, "my whole soul is bent on acquiring the most perfect learning, and hence I have a supreme disregard for learning of a trivial kind." Repeatedly he prophesied the near approach of a new age of learning and culture, as in the following letter to a fellow humanist.

From ERASMUS, Letter to Capito (1517) [1]

But at the present moment I could almost wish to be young again, for no other reason but this, that I anticipate the near approach of a golden age; so clearly do we see the minds of princes, as if changed by inspiration, devoting all their energies to the pursuit of peace. The chief movers in this matter are Pope Leo, and Francis, king of France. . . .

There is nothing this king does not do or does not suffer, in his desire to avert war and consolidate peace; submitting, of his own accord, to conditions which might be deemed unfair, if he preferred to have regard to his own greatness and dignity, rather than to the general advantage of the world; and exhibiting in this, as in every thing else, a magnanimous and truly royal character. Therefore, when I see that the highest sovereigns of Europe, Francis of France, Charles the King Catholic, Henry of England and the Emperor Maximilian, have set all their warlike preparations aside, and established peace upon solid, and, as I trust, adaman-

tine foundations, I am led to a confident hope, that not only morality and Christian piety, but also a genuine and purer literature may come to renewed life or greater splendour; especially as this object is pursued with equal zeal in various regions of the world—at Rome by Pope Leo, in Spain by the Cardinal of Toledo, in England by Henry, eighth of the name, himself not unskilled in Letters, and among ourselves by our young King Charles. In France King Francis, who seems as it were born for this object, invites and entices from all countries men that excel in merit or in learning. Among the Germans the same object is pursued by many of their excellent Princes and Bishops, and especially by Maximilian Caesar, whose old age, weary of so many wars, has determined to seek rest in the employments of peace, a resolution more becoming to his own years, while it is fortunate for the Christian world. To the piety of these princes it is due, that we see everywhere, as if upon a given signal, men of genius are arising and conspiring together to restore the best literature. . . .

Polite letters, which were almost extinct, are now cultivated and embraced by Scots, by Danes and by Irishmen. Medicine has a host of champions; at Rome Nicolas of Leonice; at Venice Ambrosius Leo of Nola, in France William Cop, and John Ruelle, and in England Thomas Linacre. The Imperial Law is restored at Paris by William Budè, in Germany by Udalric Zasy; and Mathematics at Basel by Henry of Glaris. In the Theological sphere there was no little to be done, because this science has been hitherto mainly professed by those who are most pertinacious in their abhorrence of the better literature, and are the more successful in defending their own ignorance as they do it under pretext of piety, the

[1] This and the next selection are from *The Epistles of Erasmus from His Earliest Letters to His Fifty-first Year, Arranged in Order of Time,* ed. by Francis Morgan Nichols, 3 vols., 1904. Erasmus to Guolfangus Fabritius Capito, Antwerp, 1516-17, II, 506-08. By permission of Longmans, Green and Company.

unlearned vulgar being induced to believe, that violence is offered to Religion, if any one begins to assault upon their barbarism. For in the presence of an ignorant mob they are always ready to scream and excite their followers to stone-throwing, if they see any risk of not being thought omniscient. But even here I am confident of success, if the knowledge of the three languages continues to be received in schools, as it has now begun. For the most learned and least churlish men of the profession do in some measure assist and favour the new system; and in this matter we are especially indebted to the vigourous exertions of James Lefèvre of Etaples, whom you resemble not only in name, but in a number of accomplishments.

The humblest part of the work has naturally fallen to my lot. Whether my contribution has been worth anything, I cannot say; at any rate those who object to the world regaining its senses, are as angry with me, as if my small industry had had some influence; although the work was not undertaken by me with any confidence that I could myself teach anything magnificent, but I wanted to construct a road for other persons of higher aims, so that they might be less impeded by pools and stumbling-blocks in carrying home those fair and glorious treasures.

ERASMUS CONDEMNS SCHOLASTIC DIVINES

Like Petrarch [see page 12], Erasmus had no use for scholasticism. As a student at Paris he became especially embittered toward the dialectical formalities of such scholastic theologians as Duns Scotus. The following letter to Thomas Grey set forth his opinion of scholastic divines in emphatic but humorous terms.

From ERASMUS, Letter to Thomas Grey (1497) [1]

There was once a man called Epimenides, the same who wrote that all Cretans are liars, being himself a Cretan and yet for the moment telling no lie. He lived to a great age, but this was not enough, for long after his death his skin was found with marks of letters on it. Some declare that it is preserved in these days at Paris in the Sorbonne, that sacrosanct temple of Scotistic theology. . . . For indeed they are said to go to it for oracles, whenever they are at a loss for syllogisms, and no one is allowed to set eyes on it, unless he has borne the title of M.N. [Magister Noster or "Professor"] for full fifteen years. If any other person ventures to direct his profane glances towards it, he straightway becomes as blind as a mole. . . . Epimenides also published theological books, for he was most distinguished in the profession of theology; but prophet and poet have been held to be the same. In these works he put together such knotty syllogisms as not even he was able to untie, and compounded mysteries which he could never have understood himself, if he had not been a prophet.

He is said once upon a time to have gone out of his city to take a walk, being out of humour with everything at home. After a while he betook himself to a cavern which had a deep recess. This he may have done either because he suffered from the heat, or because he had lost his way (for Divines do this sometimes) and was afraid of being exposed by night to the wild beasts in the open country, or, as is most likely, merely to seek a suitable place for meditation. While he was biting his nails there, and making many discoveries about *instances* and *quiddities* and *formalities*, he was overcome with sleep. I know you will not believe me, if

[1] Paris, 1497, *ibid.*, I, 142-44.

I tell you that he did not wake till the evening of the next day, though even drunkards sleep longer than that. But this theological slumber was prolonged, as is constantly affirmed by authors, for forty-seven years, and they say that there is some mysterious meaning in his sleep ending at that time, neither sooner nor later. For my part I think Epimenides was uncommonly fortunate in coming to himself even so late as he did. Most divines of our time never wake at all; and when they sleep on mandragora, they think themselves most awake. But to return to the waking of Epimenides. After he had risen and rubbed his eyes, being not quite sure whether he was awake or asleep, he walked out of the cave, and when he saw the whole appearance of the country altered, while the very entrance of the cavern was changed by the moss and briars that had grown over it, the man began to doubt his own identity. He goes into the city, where he finds everything new. He addresses each person he meets: "Ho there! do not you recognize Epimenides?" The other thinks he is mocked, and bids him go to the devil or look out for a stranger. In this ridiculous way he walked about for several months, until he fell in with some old boon companions, by whom he was recognized.

But look now, my Thomas, what do you suppose Epimenides dreamed of, all those years? What else but those subtlest of subtleties of which the Scotists now make boast? For I am ready to swear that Epimenides came to life again in Scotus. What if you saw Erasmus sit gaping among those blessed Scotists, while Gryllard is lecturing from his lofty chair? If you observed his contracted brow, his staring eyes, his anxious face, you would say he was another man. They assert that the mysteries of this science cannot be comprehended by one who has any commerce at all with the Muses or with the Graces. If you have touched good letters, you must unlearn what you have learnt; if you have drunk of Helicon, you must get rid of the draught. I do my best to speak nothing in true Latin, nothing elegant or witty, and I seem to make some progress. There is hope that they will acknowledge Erasmus some time or other. But what, you will say, is the upshot of all this? It is that you are not henceforth to expect anything from Erasmus that would savour of his ancient studies or character. Remembering amongst whom I live, with whom I daily sit, you must look out for another comrade.

Sweet Grey, do not mistake me. I would not have you construe this as directed against Theology itself, which, as you know, I have always regarded with special reverence. I have only amused myself in making game of some pseudo-theologians of our time, whose brains are rotten, their language barbarous, their intellects dull, their learning a bed of thorns, their manners rough, their life hypocritical, their talk full of venom, and their hearts as black as ink. Farewell.

ERASMUS SATIRIZES RENAISSANCE SOCIETY

The work for which Erasmus gained contemporary renown and enduring fame was his *Praise of Folly* (1511). Dedicated to his great English friend, Sir Thomas More, Erasmus claimed to have written the book while traveling from Italy to England. Thinking about More, he said, he decided to write on folly and explained it by a bilingual pun: "How! what maggot (say you) put this in your head? Why, the first hint, Sir, was your own surname of More, which [in Greek, Μωρία] comes as near the literal sound of the word, as you yourself are distant from the signification of it." Moreover, said Erasmus, as Homer had written about a war between frogs and mice, Virgil about a gnat, and Ovid about a nut, he felt justified in selecting such a silly subject as folly. Actually, the book was a superb satire upon the abuses, hypocrisies, and follies of his age—in church, state, education, and society at large. "I have praised Folly," he said, "in such a manner as not to have deserved the name of fool for my pains."

From ERASMUS, *Praise of Folly* (1511) [1]

And indeed the whole proceedings of the world are nothing but one continued scene of Folly, all the actors being equally fools and madmen. . . . It is Folly that, in a several dress, governs cities, appoints magistrates, and supports judicatures; and in short, makes the whole course of man's life a mere children's play, and worse than push-pin diversion. The inventions of all arts and sciences are likewise owing to the same cause; for what sedentary, thoughtful men would have beat their brains in the search of new and unheard-of-mysteries, if not egged on by the bubbling hopes of credit and reputation? They think a little glittering flash of vainglory is a sufficient reward for all their sweat, and toil, and tedious drudgery, while they that are supposedly more foolish, reap advantage of the others' labours.

And now since I have made good my title to valour and industry, what if I challenge an equal share of wisdom? How! this (you will say) is absurd and contradictory; the east and west may as soon shake hands as Folly and Wisdom be reconciled. Well, but have a little patience and I will warrant you I will make out my claim. First then, if wisdom (as

[1] *Erasmus in Praise of Folly, with Portrait, Life of Erasmus, and His Epistle Addressed to Sir Thomas More,* Reaves & Turner, London, 1870, 44, 48-51, 81-87.

must be confessed) is no more than a readiness of doing good, and an expedite method of becoming serviceable to the world, to whom does this virtue more properly belong? To the wise man, who partly out of modesty, partly out of cowardice, can proceed resolutely in no attempt; or to the fool, that goes hand over head, leaps before he looks, and so ventures through the most hazardous undertaking without any sense or prospect of danger? In the undertaking any enterprise the wise man shall run to consult with his books, and daze himself with poring upon musty authors, while the dispatchful fool shall rush bluntly on, and have done the business, while the other is thinking of it. For the two greatest lets and impediments to the issue of any performance are modesty, which casts a mist before men's eyes; and fear, which makes them shrink back, and recede from any proposal: both these are banished and cashiered by Folly, and in their stead such a habit of fool hardiness introduced, as mightily contributes to the success of all enterprizes.

Farther, if you will have wisdom taken in the other sense, of being a right judgment of things, you shall see how short wise men fall of it in this acceptation.

First, then, it is certain that all things, like so many Janus's, carry a double face, or rather bear a false aspect, most things being really in themselves far different from what they are in appearance to others: so as that which at first blush proves alive, is in truth dead; and that again which appears as dead, at a nearer review seems to be alive: beautiful seems ugly, wealthy poor, scandalous is thought creditable, prosperous passes for unlucky, friendly for what is most opposite, and innocent for what is hurtful and pernicious. In short, if we change the tables, all things are found placed in a quite different posture from what just before they appeared to stand in.

If this seem too darkly and unintelligibly expressed I will explain it by the familiar instance of some great king or prince, whom every one shall suppose to swim in a luxury of wealth, and to be a powerful lord and master, when, alas, on the one hand he has poverty of spirit enough to make him a mere beggar, and on the other side he is worse than a galley-slave to his own lusts and passions. . . .

The next to be placed among the regiment of fools are such as make a trade of telling or inquiring after incredible stories of miracles and prodigies: never doubting that a lie will choke them, they will muster up a thousand several strange relations of spirits, ghosts, apparitions, raising of the devil, and such like bugbears of superstition, which the farther they are from being probably true, the more greedily they are swallowed, and the more devoutly believed. And these absurdities do not only bring an empty pleasure, and cheap divertisement, but they are a good trade, and procure a comfortable income to such priests and friars as by this craft get their gain. To these again are nearly related such others as attribute strange virtues to the shrines and images of saints and martyrs. . . .

What shall I say of such as cry up and maintain the cheat of pardons and indulgences? that by these compute the time of each soul's residence in purgatory, and assign them a longer or shorter continuance, according as they purchase more or fewer of these paltry pardons, saleable exemptions? or what can be said bad enough of others, as pretend that by the force of such magical charms, or by the fumbling over their beads in the rehearsal of such and such petitions, (which some religious impostors invented, either for diversion, or what is more likely for advantage,) they shall procure riches, honour, pleasure,

health, long life, a lusty old age, nay, after death a sitting at the right hand of our Saviour in his kingdom; though as to this last part of their happiness, they care not how long it be deferred, having scarce any appetite toward a tasting the joys of heaven, till they are surfeited, glutted with, and can no longer relish their enjoyments on earth. By this easy way of purchasing pardon, any notorious highwayman, any plundering soldier, or any bribe-taking judge, shall disburse some part of their unjust gains, and so think all their grossest impieties sufficiently atoned for; so many perjuries, lusts, drunkenness, quarrels, bloodsheds, cheats, treacheries, and all sorts of debaucheries, shall all be, as it were, struck a bargain for, and such a contract made, as if they had paid off all arrears, and might now begin upon a new score. . . .

Several of these fooleries, which are so gross and absurd, as I myself am even ashamed to own, are practised and admired, not only by the vulgar, but by such proficients in religion as one might well expect should have more wit.

From the same principles of folly proceeds the custom of each country's challenging their particular guardian-saint; nay, each saint has his distinct office allotted to him, and is accordingly addressed to upon the respective occasions: as one for the toothache, a second to grant an easy delivery in child-birth, a third to help persons to lost goods, another to protect seamen in a long voyage, another to guard the farmer's cows and sheep, and so on; for to rehearse all instances would be extremely tedious.

There are some more catholic saints petitioned to upon all occasions, as more especially the Virgin Mary, whose blind devotees think it manners now to place the mother before the son.

And of all the prayers and intercessions that are made to these respective saints the substance of them is no more than downright Folly. Among all the trophies that for tokens of gratitude are hung upon the walls and ceilings of churches, you shall find no relics presented as a memorandum of any that were ever of Folly, or had been made one dram the wiser. One perhaps after shipwreck got safe to shore; another recovered when he had been run through by an enemy; one, when all his fellow soldiers were killed upon the spot, as cunningly perhaps as cowardly, made his escape from the field; another, while he was hanging, the rope broke, and so he saved his neck, and renewed his licence for practising his old trade of thieving; another broke jail, and got loose; a patient, against his physician's will, recovered of a dangerous fever; another drank poison, which putting him into a violent looseness, did his body more good than hurt, to the great grief of his wife, who hoped upon this occasion to have become a joyful widow; another had his waggon overturned, and yet none of his horses lamed; another had caught a grievous fall, and yet recovered from the bruise; another had been tampering with his neighbour's wife, and escaped very narrowly from being caught by the enraged cuckold in the very act. After all these acknowledgments of escapes from such singular dangers, there is none (as I have before intimated) that return thanks for being freed from Folly; Folly being so sweet and luscious, that it is rather sued for as a happiness, than deprecated as a punishment. But why should I launch out into so wide a sea of superstitions?

"Had I as many tongues as Argus eyes,
  Briareus hands, they all would not suffice
Folly in all her shapes t'epitomize."

Almost all Christians being wretchedly enslaved to blindness and ignorance, which the priests are so far from preventing or removing, that they blacken the darkness, and promote the delusion; wisely foreseeing that the people (like cows, which never give down their milk so well as when they are gently stroked,) would part with less if they knew more, their bounty proceeding only from a mistake of charity. Now if any grave wise man should stand up, and unseasonably speak the truth, telling every one that a pious life is the only way of securing a happy death; that the best title to a pardon of our sins is purchased by a hearty abhorrence of our guilt, and sincere resolutions of amendment; that the best devotion which can be paid to any saints is to imitate them in their exemplary life: if he should proceed thus to inform them of their several mistakes, there would be quite another estimate put upon tears, watchings, masses, fastings, and other severities, which before were so much prized, as persons will now be vexed to lose that satisfaction they formerly found in them.

ERASMUS DEFENDS HIS TRANSLATION OF THE NEW TESTAMENT

Erasmus' work as a humanist scholar and as a critic of the church culminated in the publication (1516) of the Greek text of the New Testament accompanied by a Latin translation which exposed many errors of the Vulgate. Having studied Greek for years, Erasmus long since had concluded "that Latin erudition, however ample, is crippled and imperfect without Greek. We have in Latin at best some small streams and turbid pools, while they [the Greeks] have the clearest springs and rivers flowing with gold. I see it is mere madness to touch with the little finger that principal part of theology which treats of the divine mysteries, without being furnished with the apparatus of Greek."[1] It was with the scholarly intention of correcting errors in existing translations of the Scriptures that Erasmus prepared his New Testament. But, because his translation differed from existing texts, many churchmen criticized his work, challenged his authority to do it, and charged him with unchurchly motives for his pains. Erasmus' reply to his critics is given below. It is part of a letter he wrote to an English friend.

From ERASMUS, Letter to Henry Bullock (1516) [2]

I am truly glad to hear, that the New Testament, as restored by our industry, is approved at Cambridge by the best people; although I have been told by some credible persons, that one of the most theological of your colleges, composed of pure Areopagites [members of a Greek court which tried only capital crimes (such as translating the New Testament!)], has passed a serious resolution, that no one shall either by horse, or boat, or cart or porter, bring that volume within the precincts of the college. I beseech you, most learned Bullock, ought one to laugh or weep over such proceedings? . . .

They say it is wrong to attempt such a work unless by the authority of a General Council. . . . But I should like to have an answer from them to this question. Was that very version, of which they are so fond [The Vulgate], undertaken by the translator [St. Jerome, at the end of the fourth century] under the authority of a General Council, or was it first published, and afterwards approved by the judgment of the Fathers? I believe it was written first, and approved afterwards;

and the same may take place with respect to my edition, though that is a thing I neither solicit nor expect. But I have conceded too much; it is more probable that the received version crept into use, and only gained strength by the progress of time. For if it had been approved and promulgated by the public judgment of a Council, it would have been in universal use. As it is, one text is cited by Ambrose, another by Augustine, another by Hilary and another by Jerome. Indeed the copies now in use do not agree. So that, if they think the Christian religion is upset if there is any variation in any part of the book, we were already subject to that risk, though we may have been sleeping through it. . . . Finally, why are we more alarmed at a various reading in the Sacred Books, than we are at a various interpretation? Surely there is equal danger in both cases. And we constantly find that the explanations given are not only different but conflicting.

Again, let them clear up, if they can, this dilemma. Do they allow any change to be made in the sacred text, or whether a change is rightly made or not? If none, what will they do with those passages where the existence of an error is too manifest to be concealed? Will they desire to follow the example of the priest, who having been used to say *mumpsimus* for twenty years, refused to change his practice, when told that he ought to read *sumpsimus*? . . .

But it will be said, that what is expedient in human science is a serious danger, if applied to the sacred books in all parts and by any one who pleases. Now in the first place I do not change all parts, for there is only a question about a few passages, the main substance remaining unaltered. Neither do I quite think that I am to be regarded, with reference to this matter, as one of the ordinary crowd. I show how in some places Hilary has been

---

[1] Letter of Erasmus to Anthony, Abbot of St. Bertin, Paris, March 16, 1501. Nichols, *op. cit.,* I, 313. This and the next quotation are by permission of Longmans, Green and Company.

[2] *Ibid.,* II, 324-30.

mistaken. So of Augustine, and Thomas Aquinas. And this I do, as it ought to be done, reverently and without contumely, so that, if they were themselves alive, they would thank me, whatever I might be, for setting them right in such a way. They were men of the highest worth, but they were men. Let my opponents prove that they were right, and refute me by argument, and I shall be greatly obliged to them. . . .

But they think it beneath them to descend to these small details of grammarians. For so they call those who have learned Good Letters, thinking the name of grammarian a severe reproach, as if it were a credit to a theologian not to know grammar. It is true that the mere knowledge of grammar does not make a theologian; still less does ignorance of it; and certainly some scholarship conduces to a knowledge of theology, while the want of it impedes such knowledge. Indeed it cannot be denied that Jerome, Ambrose and Augustine, on whose authority our theological system rests, belonged to the class of grammarians. For at that time Aristotle had not yet been received in the theological schools, and the Philosophy which is now in use there, was not yet born. But a modest man will not object to be set right by any one. "Though he be blind that shows the way, you still may pay him some regard," as Flaccus says. . . .

Neither indeed have any other theologians condemned our work. Only some have lamented that they did not learn Greek when they were boys, and that for them the book has come into the world too late. I might relate, what that venerable Prior of the Carthusians at Freiburg, Gregory Reisch, whose opinion has the weight of an oracle in Germany, and that eminent theologian, James Wimpfling, have thought of our edition; I might produce numberless letters of distinguished persons, in which they thank me, because they have been made both better and more learned by my lucubrations, and especially by what I have published on the New Testament.

3. The Reuchlin Controversy: "Letters of Obscure Men"

THE PLACE OF JOHN REUCHLIN (1455-1522)

One of the most brilliant satires of the Renaissance era was a product of a long and bitter literary duel between two men, John Pfefferkorn, a semi-literate Jewish thief who had taken "refuge in Christianity from the punishment which his crimes had merited from the hands of his countrymen" and thereafter led the van of anti-Jewish sentiment; and John Reuchlin (1455-1522), a man of great learning and high character who, during a long life as a jurist and man of affairs, pursued the study of philology and became one of the greatest Hebrew scholars of his day. The following estimate of Reuchlin is by a recent English scholar.

From CREIGHTON, *History of the Papacy* [1]

Reuchlin treated the text of the Hebrew Scriptures as a philologist, not as a theologian. He was concerned with the meaning of words, and the construction of sentences; with the literal meaning of a passage, not with the theological interpretation which had been hitherto put upon it. He went behind patristic exposition and corrected S. Augustin. He pointed out mistakes in the version of S. Jerome, and wrote, "Our text reads so, but the meaning of the Hebrew is other-

[1] Creighton, *A History of the Papacy*, I, 30. By permission of Longmans, Green and Company.

wise"; "we must more rightly translate"; "I do not know how our version has dreamed such a rendering." He spoke of other commentators as misled by the authority of holy doctors, and said that truth must be sought above all things. He deplored the "innumerable defects" of the Vulgate, and prayed that God might give him time to correct them all.

This work of Reuchlin revealed for the first time the strength of the new learning. Knowledge, pursued for its own sake, had brought the dim consciousness of a critical method, of an increasing command of the material of study. It had revealed laws of language, and taught a new sense of accuracy, with which came freedom from previous authority and a belief in the rightness of the conclusions of diligent investigation. Reuchlin was disturbing nothing; attacking nothing, proving nothing: he was merely engaged, to the best of his ability, in using all the knowledge which he possessed to get at the real meaning of the Hebrew text. But he unhesitatingly thought that his own work was capable of correcting errors, which had been made through haste or ignorance centuries ago, and which had been repeated without verification ever since. Though he had no doubts about the doctrine of the Church, he pointed out that the Old Testament Scriptures were by no means accurately understood; and by so doing was in a sense the founder of Biblical criticism and of all that followed from it.

THE "LETTERS OF OBSCURE MEN" (1515-1517)

Scholastic theologians, especially the Dominicans at Cologne, viewed Reuchlin's works with alarm. In their eyes the Hebrew scholar not only undermined scholastic theology but also he raised in importance Hebrew literature, the works of a people who had persecuted Christ and become outcasts from Christian society. Accordingly, when Pfefferkorn, the converted Jew, led an attack upon both Jews and Hebrew books, the Cologne scholastics joined forces with him. With this support, Pfefferkorn gained the approval of the Emperor, and, in 1509, armed with an imperial mandate, he went to Frankfurt-am-Main and began to seize and burn Hebrew books. Fortunately, the people of Frankfurt and the Archbishop of Mainz opposed Pfefferkorn's acts and appealed to the Emperor, saying that if it was really necessary to overhaul Jewish literature the task should be placed in the hands of men who knew something about it. During the stay in proceedings that followed, the Archbishop was asked to collect for the Emperor the opinions of informed men. Among those assembled, John Reuchlin's *Opinion* was especially judicious and illuminating. He held that Jewish writings which openly attacked Christianity should be suppressed but that the bulk of them should not only be preserved but also should be more diligently studied for the light they cast upon Christian learning.

When Reuchlin's opinion became known, he was bitterly attacked by Pfefferkorn and the Cologne Dominicans. In 1511 there appeared under Pfefferkorn's name (though doubtless Cologne scholars had helped write it) a pamphlet called *Handt Spiegel* (*The Mirror*) which so stung Reuchlin that he was led at once to prepare a defense, *Augenspiegel* (*Speculum Oculare,* in the Latin edition, meaning *"The Eyeglass"*). These booklets opened a controversy which lasted for many years and caused Reuchlin's humanist name to become linked with anti-Christian views, pagan opinions, and unrighteous motives. Amid such an atmosphere a group of humanist scholars, led by Crotus Rubianus (the pen name of John Jäger) and Ulrich von Hutten, came to Reuchlin's defense in the production of *Epistolae obscurorum virorum, Letters of Obscure Men* (1515-1517).

The *Letters* were intended to cast the withering force of ridicule upon Reuchlin's opponents. Accordingly, they pretended to have been written by scattered graduates of the University of Cologne to Ortwin Gratius, a Cologne professor who had assisted Pfefferkorn. By this means the foes of humanism were made to display themselves in the worst light, and the *Letters* aimed to make the Cologne professors, and all other opponents of the new learning, the laughingstock of Europe. Much of their brilliant satire is dulled in translation, but the following *Letters* will demonstrate, even in English, their forceful irony.

From *Letters of Obscure Men* (1515-1517) [1]

THE FIRST LETTER

Thomas Langschneider, *duly qualified, albeit unworthy, Bachelor in Theology, sendeth greeting to the supereminent and high-scientifical Herr Ortwin Gratius of Deventer, Poet, Orator, and Philosopher—Theologian too, and whatsoever else he listeth.*

Since, as *Aristotle* hath it, "To enquire concerning all and singular is not unprofitable" . . . I, therefore, am purposed to propound to your worship a question about which I have a doubt. . . .

Now, the aforesaid question arose after this manner:—The other day a *Feast of Aristotle* was celebrated here—the Doctors, the Licentiates, and the Magisters

[1] This and the following selections are from *Epistolae obscurorum virorum,* ed. by F. G. Stokes, 1925, 291-96, 352-54. By permission of Chatto and Windus, London.

were in high feather, and I too was present. To begin with, by way of a whet, we drank three bumpers of Malmsey, and for the first course we had fresh wastel-bread and made sops; and then we had six dishes of meat, and chickens, and capons and one of fish; and between courses we ceased not to drink Kotzberger and Rhine wine, and beer of *Eimbeck,* and *Torgau,* and *Naumburg;* and the Magistrates were full pleased, and vowed that the new-fledged graduates had acquitted themselves right well, and greatly to their credit.

Then began the Doctors over their cups to argue canonically concerning profundities. And the question arose, whether "magister nostrandus" or "noster magistrandus" is the fitter to denote a candidate eligible for the degree of Doctor in Divinity. . . .

Forthwith made answer Magister *Warmsemmel,* my compatriot—a right subtle Scotist, and a Master of eighteen years' standing. (He was, in his time, twice rejected and thrice impedited, for the Master's degree, and yet he resided until, for the honour of the University, he was graduated.)

He knoweth his business right well, and hath many pupils, high and low, young and old; and, speaking with ripeness of knowledge, he held that we should say "nostermagistrandus"—in one word—because "magistrare" signifies to make Master, and "baccalauriare" to make Bachelor, and "doctrare" to make Doctor. . . . Now Doctors in Divinity are not styled "Doctors," but on account of their humility and sanctity, and by way of distinction, are named and styled "Magistri Nostri," because in the Catholic Faith they stand in the room of our Lord *Jesus Christ,* who is the fount of life, and the "Magister" of us all: wherefore are they styled "Magistri Nostri" because it is for them to instruct us in the way of truth—and God is truth.

Rightly, he argued, are they called "our masters," for it is the bounden duty of us all, as Christians, to hearken to their preachments. . . . But "nostro-tras-trare" is not in use, and is found neither in the Vocabulary *Ex Quo,* nor in the *Catholicon,* nor even in the *Gemma gemmarum,* notwithstanding that this containeth many terms of art.

Thereupon uprose Magister *Andreas Delitzsch,* a very subtle scholar—on the one hand a Poet, and on the other, an Artsman, Physician, and Jurist—who lectureth in ordinary upon *Ovid* in his *Metamorphoses,* and explaineth all the fables allegorically and literally (I myself have attended his lectures) . . . and he held, in opposition to Magister *Warmsemmel,* that we should say "magister-nostrandus"; for, as there is a difference between "magisternoster" and "noster magister," so there is a like difference between "magisternostrandus" and "nostermagistrandus." Because "magisternoster" signifieth a Doctor of Divinity, and is one word, but "noster magister" consisteth of two words, and is used for a Master in any Liberal Science, whether it concern handicraft or braincraft. And it booteth not that "nostro-tras-trare" is not in use, for we may devise new words—and on this point he quoted *Horace.*

Then the company marvelled greatly at his subtilty, and a tankard of Naumburg beer was handed to him. Quoth he, "Now I wait awhile—but, with your leave!" and, laughing heartily, he touched his cap and pledged Master *Warmsemmel,* saying, "Marry, Herr Magister, think not that I am out with you!" He made but one draught of it, and bravely did Master *Warmsemmel* respond thereto, for the honour of the Silesian "Nation."

Then all the Magisters waxed merry, till at last the bell rang to Vespers.

I beseech your excellence, therefore, to set forth your opinion, seeing that you are mightily profound, and, as I said at the time, "Magister *Ortwin* will easily unfold the truth of the matter, for he was my teacher at *Deventer,* when I was in the third class."

Let me know, too, how standeth the strife between Doctor *Johann Reuchlin* and yourself. I have heard, indeed, that the scoundrel, albeit a Doctor and a Jurist, will not yet recant.

THE SECOND LETTER

Magister Johannes Pelzer, *to Magister Ortwin Gratius, Greeting.* Cordial greeting, and homage beyond belief. Reverend Herr Magister, since, as saith *Aristotle* in his *Categories,* to doubt concerning all and sundry is not unprofitable, know then that there is a matter that giveth me great searchings of heart.

I was lately at *Frankfurt* fair, and as I walked along the street with a certain Bachelor, two men met us, who, to all outward appearance, were reputable, and they wore black cassocks and great hoods with lappets. Now, heaven be my witness, I took them for two Doctors of Divinity, and I saluted them, taking off my cap. Thereupon the Bachelor nudged me, and said, "God-a-mercy! what doest thou? Those fellows are Jews, and thou uncoveredst to them!"

Then I was aghast, as though I had seen a devil! And I said, "Herr Bachelor, may the Lord forgive me, for in ignorance I did it! But how think you, is it a heinous sin?" And at first he said that it seemed to him that the sin was mortal, inasmuch as it fell under the head of idolatry, and broke the first commandment of the Ten—"Thou shalt believe in one God." "Because, when one payeth respect to a Jew or a heathen, as though he were a Christian, then he withstandeth

Christianity, and seemeth to be a Jew or a Pagan himself: the Jews, too, and the Pagans, say, 'Lo, ours is the better way, for the Christians do us reverence—and unless we were of the better way they would not do us reverence!' And thus they are confirmed in their own creed, and despise the Christian faith, and will not be baptized." Then I replied, "That is true enough, when the deed is done wittingly; but I did it in ignorance, and ignorance excuseth sin. For if I had known them to be Jews, and had nevertheless done them reverence, then I should have been deserving of the stake, for it would have been heresy. But, heaven knoweth, neither from word or gesture did I gather that they were Jews, but I thought that they were Doctors."

Still he declared that it was, nevertheless, a sin, . . . "Ignorance cannot excuse that sin, because you ought to have been vigilant, and the Jews always wear a round yellow patch on their cloaks in front, which you could have seen as well as I. . . ."

Now, seeing that you are a profound theologian, I beg of you, earnestly and humbly, that you will deign to resolve this my question, and tell me whether this sin is mortal or venial, and mine an ordinary, or an episcopal, or a papal case?

THE THIRTY-THIRD LETTER

Mammotrect Buntemantel, *Magister in the Seven Liberal Arts, sendeth right hearty greetings to Magister Ortwin Gratius, Philosopher, Orator, Poet, Jurist, and Theologian, of discretionary faculty.*

Right conscionable Herr Magister *Ortwin,* believe me in good sooth, you have been mine own dear heart from the days wherein I heard such discourse on Poetry from your worthiness at *Cologne,* where you overtop all others in that art. . . .

In all confidence, therefore, I desire to disclose somewhat to your reverence under seal of confession.

Reverend Herr Magister, I have become enamoured of a damsel here, *Margaret* by name, the daughter of a bell-ringer. Not long while ago she sat by your own side, to wit when the parson invited your worship to the feast. . . .

Her I love with such passion that I am beside myself. . . . I can neither eat nor sleep. Folk say to me, "Herr Magister, why so pale? For the love of God quit your books; you study over much; you should now and again seek some diversion, and drink deep. . . ."

But I am bashful, and cannot unfold my disorder. I have studied *Ovid,* "Of the Remedy of Love," which I annotated at *Cologne* under your worthiness, with many notabilia and moralisations in the margin—but it availeth not, for this love of mine waxeth from day to day.

Lately I danced with her thrice, at an evening junketing at the Mayor's house. The piper struck up the tune of "The Shepherds of Neustadt," and straightway all the dancers clasped their partners, as is the wont—so I also hugged mine right lovingly, with her bosom next my heart, and tightly did I squeeze her hand. Then she simpered, and said, "By my soul, Herr Magister, you are a sweet man, and you have softer hands than the others; you must not be a priest, you must take a wife!" Then she eyed me so amorously that I believe she loveth me—secretly. Her glance, in sooth, wounded my heart as though an arrow had pierced it, and straightway I went home with my servant, and flung myself upon my bed.

Then my mother fell a-weeping, because she thought I was sick of the plague. . . .

Now I beseech you, by all your bowels of mercy, give me a remedy for Love out of that little book of yours wherein is written "I have tried this." You once showed it to me, saying, "See, with this book I can make any woman love me!"

And unless you do this, Herr Magister, I shall die, and for grief my mother will die too.

Heidelberg.

4

THE REINTERPRETATION OF CLASSICAL SURVIVALS: ART

1. The Transition from Medieval to Renaissance Forms

The magnificent achievements of Renaissance art were largely the product of urban communities. A few noble possessors of great estates, using the resources of wide agrarian holdings, employed their wealth to patronize architects, painters, and sculptors for building and beautifying their manorial homes and chapels. But in comparison with urban achievements of similar nature, these manorial lords' accomplishments were of much less importance than those of wealthy merchants, princes, great ecclesiastics, and corporations that patronized the arts in cities. Renaissance art, then, developed simultaneously with the growth of cities in the late Middle Ages.

Evidences of a revival in artistic works date from the eleventh century in Europe. North of the Alps, in France, Spain, the Germanies, and England, the Gothic cathedral, mainly of French origin, marked new heights of achievement in architecture, sculpture, and stained-glass ornamentation. In Italy the Gothic style was less familiar because the Italians clung to Romanesque forms until the Renaissance

brought a revival of more purely classical design. Some evidence of this revival existed as early as 1016, when construction of the cathedral began at Pisa under direction of a gifted Greek named Buschetto. But it was the middle of the thirteenth century (about 1250) before the change to classical designs became significant. A Renaissance historian explains the reason for this change as follows: ". . . although those before them [that is, those artists of an earlier period] had seen remains of arches, of colossi, of statues, of urns, and of storied columns in the ages that came after the sackings, the destructions, and the burnings of Rome, and never knew how to make use of them or draw from them any benefit, up to the time mentioned above [1250], the minds that came after, discerning well enough the good from the bad and abandoning the old manners, turned to imitating the ancient with all their industry and wit."[1] It appears, then, that just as humanism drew its early inspiration from ancient writings so

[1] This and the following selections are reprinted from Giorgio Vasari, *Lives of the Most Eminent Painters, Sculptors, & Architects,* trans. by Gaston De Vere, 10 vols., 1912-15, London. The Medici Society, Ltd.; Boston and New York. By permission of Ralph T. Hale & Company. This selection is I, lvii (Preface by Vasari).

Renaissance art originated in a frank imitation of ancient architectural and sculptural remains. However, as Leonardo da Vinci wrote, "Poor is the pupil who does not surpass his master," and the Renaissance artists, after a preliminary period of imitation of ancient works, pushed on to more original —more individualistic—achievements. Furthermore, as there were few ancient remains in the field of painting, Renaissance painters turned to nature as their model. They studied anatomy and the proportions of the human body; they analyzed with new perfection the effects of light and shadow; they learned the importance of perspective; they experimented in the chemistry of paints, devised new materials, produced brilliant new colors.

Giorgio Vasari (1511-1574), himself a late Italian Renaissance painter and architect, has left a splendid—if sometimes legendary—account of the developments in his *Lives of the Most Eminent Painters, Sculptors, & Architects* (1550). Although a student of such masters as Michelangelo and Andrea del Sarto, Vasari was an indifferent painter and architect, and his fame is much greater as art historian than as artist. He traveled widely in Italy, knew many famous men of his day, collected information—and some misinformation —from a great variety of sources, and was sponsored in the preparation of his *Lives* by Duke Cosimo de' Medici. Vasari was profoundly ignorant of Gothic art and transalpine art in general and this fault, together with his occasional presentation of popular legend for historical fact, necessitates caution in reading his *Lives*. Nevertheless, Vasari's main emphasis still withstands critical assessment, and his narrative form is a monument to Renaissance literary style.

According to Vasari, five men, two in painting, two in sculpture, and one in architecture, took the lead in the production of the new art of the Renaissance. In painting, a Florentine, Giovanni Cimabue (1240-1300) was first of the new school but his work was completely overshadowed by the superior talents of his pupil, Giotto (1276-1336), who "became so good an imitator of nature that he banished completely that rude Greek manner and revived the modern and good art of painting, introducing the portraying well from nature of living people, which had not been used for more than two hundred years."[1] In sculpture, Andrea Pisano (?1270-1348) and his son Nino (?1315-1368?), who collaborated with him, produced wonderfully life-like effects; together they were "the first masters that were in Europe at that time." Nino was also an architect of merit. The first "modern" in architecture, however, was Arnolfo di Cambio (1232-1302), a Florentine who designed, among other works, the church of Santa Maria del Fiore at Florence, although the structure was completed by an even greater Renaissance architect, Brunelleschi. Vasari describes the achievements of these men and of their contemporaries as follows.

From VASARI, *Lives of the Painters* (1550)[2]

Is it not clearly seen how great improvement was acquired by architecture— to begin with one starting-point—from the time of the Greek Buschetto to that of . . . Arnolfo and of Giotto? See the buildings of those times, and the pilasters, the columns, the bases, the capitals, and all the cornices, with their ill-formed mem-

---

[1] *Ibid.*, I, 72.
[2] *Ibid.*, II, 80-87.

bers . . . wherein, excepting that little of the good which survived in the ancient fragments, there is nothing that has good order or form. But these men certainly improved it not a little, and under their guidance it made no small progress, seeing that they reduced it to better proportion, and made their buildings not only stable and stout, but also in some measure ornate, although it is true that their ornamentation was confused and very imperfect, and, so to speak, not greatly ornamental. For they did not observe that measure and proportion in the columns that the art required, or distinguish one Order from another, whether Doric, Corinthian, Ionic, or Tuscan, but mixed them all together with a rule of their own that was no rule, making them very thick or very slender, as suited them best; and all their inventions came partly from their own brains, and partly from the relics of the antiquities that they saw. . . .

The same do I say of sculpture, which, in that first age of its new birth, had no little of the good; for after the extinction of the rude Greek manner, which was so uncouth that it was more akin to the art of quarrying than to the genius of the craftsmen—their statues being entirely without folds, or attitudes, or movement of any kind, and truly worthy to be called stone images—when design was afterwards improved by Giotto, many men also improved the figures in marble and stone, as did Andrea Pisano and his son Nino and his other disciples, who were much better than the early sculptors and gave their statues more movement and much better attitudes. . . . It is seen, then, that during this time sculpture made a little progress, and that there was given a somewhat better form to the figures, with a more beautiful flow of folds in the draperies, and sometimes a better air in the heads and certain attitudes not so

stiff; and finally, that it had begun to seek the good, but was nevertheless lacking in innumerable respects, seeing that design was in no great perfection at that time and there was little good work seen that could be imitated. . . .

Nor did painting encounter much better fortune in those times, save that, being then more in vogue by reason of the devotion of the people, it had more craftsmen and therefore made more evident progress than the other two. Thus it is seen that the Greek manner, first through the beginning made by Cimabue, and then with the aid of Giotto, was wholly extinguished; and there arose a new one, which I would fain call the manner of Giotto, seeing that it was discovered by him and by his disciples, and then universally revered and imitated by all [see page 43]. By this manner, as we see, there were swept away the outlines that wholly enclosed the figures, and those staring eyes, and the feet stretched on tiptoe, and the pointed hands, with the absence of shadow and the other monstrous qualities of those Greeks; and good grace was given to the heads, and softness to the colouring. And Giotto, in particular, gave better attitudes to his figures, and revealed the first effort to give a certain liveliness to the heads and folds to his draperies, which drew more towards nature than those of the men before him; and he discovered, in part, something of the gradation and foreshortening of figures. Besides this, he made a beginning with the expression of emotions, so that fear, hope, rage, and love could in some sort be recognized; and he reduced his manner, which at first was harsh and rough, to a certain degree of softness; and although he did not make the eyes with that beautiful roundness that makes them lifelike, and with the tear-channels that complete them, and the hair soft, and the beards feathery, and the hands with their due joints and muscles, and the nudes true to life, let him find excuse in the difficulty of the art and in the fact that he saw no better painters than himself; and let all remember, amid the poverty of art in those times, the excellence of judgment in his stories, the observation of feeling, and the subordination of a very ready natural gift, seeing that his figures were subordinate to the part that they had to play. And thereby it is shown that he had a very good, if not a perfect judgment; and the same is seen in the others after him, as in the colouring of Taddeo Gaddi, who is both sweeter and stronger, giving better tints to the flesh and better colour to the draperies, and more boldness to the movements of his figures. . . .

And now that we have weaned these three arts, to use such a fashion of speaking, and brought them through their childhood, there comes their second age, wherein there will be seen infinite improvement in everything; invention more abundant in figures, and richer in ornament; more depth and more lifelike reality in design; some finality, moreover, in the works, which are executed thoughtfully and with diligence, although with too little mastery of handling; with more grace in manner and more loveliness in colouring, so that little is wanting for the reduction of everything to perfection and for the exact imitation of the truth of nature. Wherefore, with the study and the diligence of the great Filippo Brunelleschi, architecture first recovered the measures and proportions of the ancients, both in the round columns and in the square pilasters, and in the corner stones both rough and smooth; and then one Order was distinguished from another [see page 51], and it was shown what differences there were between them. It was ordained that all works should proceed by rule,

should be pursued with better ordering, and should be distributed with due measure. Design grew in strength and depth; good grace was given to buildings; the excellence of that art made itself known; and the beauty and variety of capitals and cornices were recovered in such a manner, that the ground-plans of his churches and of his other edifices are seen to have been very well conceived, and the buildings themselves ornate, magnificent, and beautifully proportioned. . . .

This I can also say of painting and sculpture, wherein very rare works of the masters of that second age may still be seen today, such as those in the Carmine by Masaccio, who made a naked man shivering with cold, and lively and spirited figures in other pictures; but in general they did not attain to the perfection of the third, whereof we will speak at the proper time, it being necessary now to discourse of the second, whose craftsmen, to speak first of the sculptors, advanced so far beyond the manner of the first and improved it so greatly, that they left little to be done by the third. They had a manner of their own, so much more graceful and more natural, and so much richer in order, in design, and in proportion, that their statues began to appear almost like living people, and no longer figures of stones, like those of the first age; and to this those works bear witness that were wrought in that new manner, as it will be seen in this Second Part, among which the figures of Jacopo della Quercia have more movement, more grace, more design, and more diligence; those of Filippo, a more beautiful knowledge of muscles, better proportion, and more judgment; and so, too, those of their disciples. But the greatest advance came from Lorenzo Ghiberti in the work of the gates of S. Giovanni, wherein he showed such invention, order, manner, and design, that his figures appear to move and to have souls. . . .

The same advance was made at this time by painting, from which that most excellent Masaccio [1401-1428] swept away completely the manner of Giotto in the heads, the draperies, the buildings, the nudes, the colouring, and the foreshortenings, all of which he made new, bringing to light that modern manner which was followed in those times and has been followed up to our own day by all our craftsmen, and enriched and embellished from time to time with better grace, invention, and ornament; as it will be seen more particularly in the Life of each master, wherein there will appear a new manner of colouring, of foreshortenings, and of natural attitudes, with much better expression for the emotions of the soul and the gestures of the body, and an attempt to approach closer to the truth of nature in draughtsmanship, and an effort to give to the expressions of the faces so complete a resemblance to the living men, that it might be known for whom they were intended. Thus they sought to imitate that which they saw in nature, and no more, and thus their works came to be better planned and better conceived; and this emboldened them to give rules to their perspectives and to foreshorten them in a natural and proper form, just as they did in relief; and thus, too, they were ever observing lights and shades, the projection of shadows, and all other difficulties, and the composition of stories with more characteristic resemblance, and attempted to give more reality to landscapes, trees, herbs, flowers, skies, clouds, and other objects of nature, insomuch that we may boldly say that these arts were not only reared but actually carried to the flower of their youth, giving hope of that fruit which afterwards appeared, and that, in short, they were about to arrive at their most perfect age.

2. *Vasari on the Painter Giotto* (*1276-1336*)

From VASARI, *Lives of the Painters* [1]

That very obligation which the craftsmen of painting owe to nature, who serves continually as model to those who are ever wresting the good from her best and most beautiful features and striving to counterfeit and to imitate her, should be owed, in my belief, to Giotto, painter of Florence, for the reason that, after the methods of good paintings and their outlines had lain buried for so many years under the ruins of the wars, he alone, although born among inept craftsmen, by the gift of God revived that art, which had come to a grievous pass, and brought it to such a form as could be called good. And truly it was a very great miracle that that age, gross and inept, should have had strength to work in Giotto in a fashion so masterly, that design, whereof the men of those times had little or no knowledge, was restored completely to life by means of him. And yet this great man was born at the village of Vespignano, in the district of Florence, fourteen miles distant from that city, in the year 1276, from a father named Bondone, a tiller of the soil and a simple fellow. He, having had this son, to whom he gave the name Giotto, reared him comformably to his condition; and when he had come to the age of ten, he showed in all his actions, although childish still, a vivacity and readiness of intelligence much out of the ordinary, which rendered him dear not only to his father but to all those also who knew him, both in the village and beyond. Now Bondone gave some sheep into his charge, and he, going about the holding, now in one part and now in another, to graze them, and impelled by a natural inclina-

[1] *Ibid.*, I, 71-75, 78-79, 92, 94.

tion to the art of design, was for ever drawing, on stones, on the ground, or on sand, something from nature, or in truth anything that came into his fancy. Wherefore Cimabue, going one day on some business of his own from Florence to Vespignano, found Giotto, while his sheep were browsing, portraying a sheep from nature on a flat and polished slab, with a stone slightly pointed, without having learnt any method of doing this from others, but only from nature; whence Cimabue, standing fast all in a marvel, asked him if he wished to go to live with him. The child answered that, his father consenting, he would go willingly. Cimabue then asking this from Bondone, the latter lovingly granted it to him, and was content that he should take the boy with him to Florence; whither having come, in a short time, assisted by nature and taught by Cimabue, the child not only equalled the manner of his master, but became so good an imitator of nature that he banished completely that rude Greek manner and revived the modern and good art of painting, introducing the portraying well from nature of living people, which had not been used for more than two hundred years. If, indeed, anyone had tried it, as has been said above, he had not succeeded very happily, nor as well by a great measure as Giotto, who portrayed among others, as is still seen today in the Chapel of the Palace of the Podestà at Florence, Dante Alighieri, a contemporary and his very great friend, and no less famous as poet than was in the same times Giotto as painter. . . .

The first pictures of Giotto were in the chapel of the high-altar in the Badia of Florence, wherein he made many works held beautiful, but in particular a Madonna receiving the Annunciation, for the reason that in her he expressed vividly the fear and the terror that the salutation of Gabriel inspired in Mary the Virgin, who appears, all full of the greatest alarm, to be wishing almost to turn to flight. By the hand of Giotto, likewise, is the panel on the high-altar of the said chapel. . . . These works finished, he betook himself to Assisi, a city of Umbria, being called thither by Fra Giovanni di Muro della Marca, then General of the Friars of S. Francis; where, in the upper church, he painted in fresco, under the gallery that crosses the windows, on both sides of the church, thirty-two scenes of the life and acts of S. Francis—that is, sixteen on each wall—so perfectly that he acquired thereby very great fame. And in truth there is seen great variety in that work, not only in the gestures and attitudes of each figure but also in the composition of all the scenes; not to mention that it enables us very beautifully to see the diversity of the costumes of those times, and certain imitations and observations of the things of nature. Among others, there is one very beautiful scene, wherein a thirsty man, in whom the desire for water is vividly seen, is drinking, bending down on the ground by a fountain with very great and truly marvellous expression, in a manner that it seems almost a living person that is drinking. . . . This whole work acquired for Giotto very great fame, by reason of the excellence of the figures and of the order, proportion, liveliness, and facility which he had from nature, and which he had made much greater by means of study, and was able to demonstrate clearly in all his works. And because, besides that which Giotto had from nature, he was most diligent and went on ever thinking out new ideas and wresting them from nature, he well deserved to be called the disciple of nature and not of others. . . .

Pope Benedict IX of Treviso sent one of his courtiers into Tuscany to see what sort of man was Giotto, and of what kind his works, having designed to have some pictures made in S. Pietro. This courtier, coming in order to see Giotto and to hear what other masters there were in Florence excellent in painting and in mosaic, talked to many masters in Siena. Then, having received drawings from them, he came to Florence, and having gone into the shop of Giotto, who was working, declared to him the mind of the Pope and in what way it was proposed to make use of his labour, and at last asked him for some little drawing, to the end that he might send it to His Holiness. Giotto, who was most courteous, took a paper, and on that, with a brush dipped in red, holding his arm fast against his side in order to make a compass, with a turn of the hand he made a circle, so true in proportion and circumference that to behold it was a marvel. This done, he smiled and said to the courtier: "Here is your drawing." He, thinking he was being derided, said: "Am I to have no other drawing but this?" " 'Tis enough and to spare," answered Giotto. "Send it, together with the others, and you will see if it will be recognized." The envoy, seeing that he could get nothing else, left him, very ill-satisfied and doubting that he had been fooled. All the same, sending to the Pope the other drawings and the names of those who had made them, he also sent that of Giotto, relating the method that he had followed in making his circle without moving his arm and without compasses. Wherefore the Pope and many courtiers that were versed in the arts recognized by this how much Giotto surpassed in excellence all the other painters of his time. This matter having afterwards spread abroad, there was born from it the proverb that is still wont to be said to men of gross wits: "Tu sei più tondo che l'O di Giotto" ("Thou art rounder than Giotto's circle"). . . .

Giotto, as it has been said, was very ingenious and humorous, and very witty in his sayings, whereof there is still vivid memory in that city; for besides that which Messer Giovanni Boccacio wrote about him, Franco Sacchetti, in his three hundred Stories, relates many of them that are very beautiful. . . .

It is said that Giotto, while working in his boyhood under Cimabue, once painted a fly on the nose of a figure that Cimabue himself had made, so true to nature that his master, returning to continue the work, set himself more than once to drive it away with his hand, thinking that it was real, before he perceived his mistake.

3. Leonardo da Vinci on the Art of Painting

In the footsteps of Giotto and Masaccio came a host of artists who carried Renaissance achievement to new and original heights. Such men as Fra Angelico (1387-1455), Fra Filippo Lippi (1406-1469), Sandro Botticelli (1444-1510), and Leonardo da Vinci (1452-1519) are but a few who perfected the naturalistic form and colorings of Italian painting. Of all these men, Leonardo da Vinci was the most extraordinary. A fine example of Renaissance versatility, Leonardo was not only a great painter but also sculptor, architect, mathematician, engineer, anatomist, inventor, and experimenter in almost all lines of scientific endeavor. His tremendous mind embraced practically all the intellectual activities then known to man. His unquenchable curiosity led him to explore, to experiment, and to analyze problems of perspective, proportion, facial expression, and other factors of the artists' technique. He took notes about everything, planned scores of books, wrote a few of them, made sketches and plans—in short, demonstrated a truly scientific spirit of inquiry about a multitude of interests. Among his "Aphorisms" he wrote, "The natural desire of good men is knowledge." But Leonardo was primarily a painter, and his studies tended to converge upon the painter's technique. "A good painter," he said, "has two chief objects to paint—man and the intention of his soul. The former is easy, the latter hard, for it must be expressed by gestures and movements of the limbs." Some of his observations on painting and related subjects are given below.

From LEONARDO, *Notebooks* (c. 1508) [1]

THE PAINTER'S NEED FOR ALERTNESS

The mind of the painter should be like a mirror which always takes the color of the thing that it reflects, and which is filled by as many images as there are things placed before it. Knowing therefore that you cannot be a good master unless you have a universal power of representing by your art all the varieties of the forms which nature produces—which indeed you will not know how to do unless you see them and retain them in your mind—look to it, O Painter, that when you go into the fields you give your attention to the various objects, and look carefully in turn first at one thing and then at another, making a bundle of different things selected and chosen from among those of less value. And do not after the manner of some painters who when tired by imaginative work, lay aside their task and take exercise by walking, in order to find relaxation, keeping, however, such weariness of mind as prevents them either seeing or being conscious of different objects.

[1] *The Notebooks of Leonardo da Vinci,* ed. by Edward MacCurdy, 2 vols., 1938, II, 235, 258, 260, 264. Reprinted by permission of Reynal & Hitchcock, Inc.

OF THE WAY TO FIX IN YOUR MIND THE FORM OF A FACE

If you desire to acquire facility in keeping in your mind the expression of a face, first learn by heart the various different kinds of heads, eyes, noses, mouths, chins, throats, and also necks and shoulders. Take as an instance noses: they are of ten types: straight, bulbous, hollow, prominent either above or below the centre, aquiline, regular, simian, round, and pointed. These divisions hold good as regards profile. Seen from in front, noses are of twelve types: thick in the middle, thin in the middle, with the tip broad, and narrow at the base, and narrow at the tip, and broad at the base, with nostrils broad or narrow, or high or low, and with the openings either visible or hidden by the tip. And similarly you will find variety in the other features; of which things you ought to make studies from nature and so fix them in your mind. Or when you have to draw a face from memory, carry with you a small note-book in which you have noted down such features, and then when you have cast a glance at the face of the person whom you wish to draw you can look privately and see which nose or mouth has a resemblance to it, and make a tiny mark against it in order to recognise it again at home. Of abnormal faces I here say nothing, for they are kept in mind without difficulty.

HOW IT IS NECESSARY FOR THE PAINTER TO KNOW THE INNER STRUCTURE OF MAN

The painter who has acquired a knowledge of the nature of the sinews, muscles, and tendons will know exactly in the movement of any limb how many and which of the sinews are the cause of it, and which muscle by its swelling is the cause of this sinew's contracting, and which sinews having been changed into most delicate cartilage surround and contain the said muscle. So he will be able in divers ways and universally to indicate the various muscles by means of the different attitudes of his figures; and he will not do like many who in different actions always make the same things appear in the arm, the back, the breast, and the legs; for such things as these ought not to rank in the category of minor faults.

OF THE CONFORMITY OF THE LIMBS

Further I remind you to pay great attention in giving limbs to your figures, so that they may not merely appear to harmonize with the size of the body but also with its age. So the limbs of youths should have few muscles and veins, and have a soft surface and be rounded and pleasing in color; in men they should be sinewy and full of muscles; in old men the surface should be wrinkled, and rough, and covered with veins, and with the sinews greatly protruding.

4. Michelangelo's Paintings in the Sistine Chapel at Rome

Among the artists of the "High Renaissance" period Michelangelo Buonarroti (1475-1564) was one of the greatest. Born in a Florentine family, Michelangelo turned to painting and design at an early age. When he was fourteen years old he was apprenticed to Domenico Ghirlandaio, but he soon surpassed his master, caught the eye of Lorenzo de' Medici ("The Magnificent"), and became his protégé until Lorenzo's death in 1492. Like Da Vinci, Michelangelo possessed varied talents. He was a sculptor, a painter, and an architect who, according to his admiring friend Vasari, aimed at nothing "but the portrayal of the human body in perfect proportions and most varied attitudes, together with the passions

and affections of the soul." One of Michelangelo's greatest accomplishments was the decoration of the Sistine Chapel, a task which he reluctantly accepted from Pope Julius II in 1508 and took four years to complete. A recent English writer's description of the work follows.

From VAUGHAN, *Italian Renaissance* (1930) [1]

The Sistine Chapel, one of the most famous shrines of art in the whole world, was built by Sisto Quarto, Pope Sixtus IV, uncle of Julius II, in 1473. It is not a beautiful structure, being merely a lofty rectangular hall, one hundred and thirty-three feet long and forty-five feet wide, with vaulted roof lit by fourteen rounded windows at a great height from the floor. One may compare the Sistine Chapel with a tall, oblong box with a slightly curved lid. Already, under Pope Sixtus IV, the huge interior wall-spaces had been largely covered with decoration by the Florentine and Umbrian artists of that day. There was a fine marble pavement, and a fine marble screen to divide the chapel into two unequal parts. Now Julius, obsessed with grandiose ideas, had already decided to make the adjoining basilica, or church of St. Peter's, the World's Cathedral, the seat of Western Christendom; he had planned to make the Vatican the central palace of the Pope, the spiritual Caesar of the Christian world; and he now intended to make of this large chapel built by his uncle Pope Sixtus an official chapel for the Pope and his Cardinals. It was to be the special seat of the inner circle and court attached to the Pope, and here papal elections and state receptions were to be held. It was, in short, intended to fill the office more of a throne-room than a

[1] Herbert M. Vaughan, *Studies in the Italian Renaissance*, 1930, 207-14. Reprinted by permission of Methuen & Co., Ltd.

chapel. At this time—the year 1508—the Sistine was adorned by a series of frescoes along its walls, midway between the windows and the floor, by Botticelli, Perugino, Luca Signorelli, Cosimo Rosselli, and other famous painters. . . .

Now the roof and its vaulting remained blank. This displeased Julius, and he determined to have the whole of this vast space, said to cover more than ten thousand square feet of surface, painted over, so as to render the Sistine Chapel still more beautiful and imposing. It was a grand conception on the Pope's part, and he bethought him of the only artist worthy of and equal to the stupendous task. This, I need hardly say, was Michelangelo, who was then busily engaged upon the statuary for the immense altar tomb that Julius intended to place in St. Peter's for himself and his successors in the papacy. As usual, there ensued a battle-royal between the Pope and the artist. Michelangelo was most unwilling to be taken away from Julius's own commission, that of the papal tomb. He declared he was a sculptor, not a painter; therefore the work proposed was not in his line of art. Julius would not listen to any of these reasons— one can hardly call them excuses. Michelangelo, and no other, must and shall decorate the roof of the Sistine. Finally, with a bad grace, the reluctant artist had to bow to the superior will of the Pope, and Michelangelo, after making due preparations for his gigantic task, arrived in Rome [1508]. . . .

Now let us take a survey of this famous and colossal masterpiece. Remember, it is a roof, and on entering the Sistine Chapel we cannot inspect it long without acute physical fatigue, and even pain. It can only be studied properly with the aid of large hand-mirrors. In the first place, the painting is made to fit into an architectural design, which was partly supplied by Michelangelo, and was partly enforced by the structure of the chapel. This being the case, Michelangelo, who was architect as well as sculptor, has treated his subject from an architectural standpoint. The whole work is, in fact, a combination of painting, architecture, and sculpture. The figures, said to be three hundred and forty-three in number, all fit into their proper places, as in some great plastic design; only in the long, flat space of the actual ceiling has the master a clear field for his inventions. Everything else had to be subordinated to the structural details of the chapel itself.

In the spaces over each of the twelve side-windows are shown five prophets and five sibyls of gigantic size. All these figures are seated; if they had been painted standing they would have been eighteen feet in height. The eastern end space over the altar is occupied by the prophet Jonah, a marvellous example of foreshortening, and the western end space by Zechariah. These colossal figures of seven prophets and five sibyls naturally stand out to the spectator with the greatest prominence from the elaborate composition, and give a peculiar air of majesty and mystery to the whole. They rank amongst the best known and most popular of the master's works, and with good reason. The Delphic and Cumaean and Persian sibyls are perhaps the grandest in conception of this superb group. Next in size and importance rank the lovely scenes depicted on the flat ceiling, the earliest-painted portion of the roof. These are, from west to east, that is, from the altar to the doorway, the Creation of the World, the Creation of Man, the Expulsion of Adam and Eve from Eden, and the Deluge. On either side of these four major scenes are five minor scenes from Genesis, of which the most beautiful is the Creation of Eve, occupying the exact centre of the whole composition. . . . The whole composition, intricate yet orderly in its marshalling, might fitly be termed "the Old Testament of Michelangelo." . . .

The colouring of the Sistine roof has often been described as sombre, but its present dingy tone is due to the lapse of four centuries and the constant action of candle-smoke and incense. The complete absence of all gilding, which at the time so disturbed Julius II, was no doubt an intentional omission on Michelangelo's part. In fact, the colouring is warm, soft, and harmonious, all the colours used being made subservient to the flesh tints of the many nude figures that the whole work contains. To emphasize these flesh tints there is an absence of any strong shade of red, the predominating colours used being yellow, blue, and green, that blend admirably with the general effect of silver-grey, which marks the composition throughout. The bronze colouring of the many classical medallions and of the figures of the genii above the points of the vaulting adds to the general softness of the colour scheme.

Yet it would be easy to show the revolution in contemporary art that such treatment as Michelangelo's wrought. Hitherto, the great painter Luca Signorelli alone had exhibited the tendency to avoid bright colour, and it is probable that Signorelli's work in the past to some extent influenced even so vast and original a mind as Michelangelo's. But the chorus of applause that greeted the unveiling of the Sistine roof may be called the death-knell of the beautiful and charming art of the *Quattrocento.* . . . The blue skies, the delicate trees, the flowery lawns, the birds, the beasts, the elegant if meaningless ornaments that had hitherto played so prominent a part in the pictures of the artists of the *Quattrocento,* are all missing in the Sistine roof. And far more than these adjuncts, there is lacking the true devotional spirit, which reached its zenith in Fra Angelico. . . . The frescoes of the Sistine Chapel form the great divide between the Early and the Late Renaissance; it might not be too much to say that they separate the medieval school from the modern. Art is progressive, and it had now run its race and reached its final goal in Michelangelo's masterpiece. There was nothing further to attain. Painting, sculpture, and architecture are all comprehended in this work, and it set a standard (as Vasari proudly declares) to the whole world which was henceforth adopted in its entirety.

5. *The Invention of Oil Painting and the Manner of Its Introduction to Italy*

An important defect in early Renaissance painting was the lack of good paints which would not crack or fade or be easily affected by dampness. Though continual experimentation went on, the best substance employed by early Renaissance artists was "distemper," or the white of eggs, to which pigments were added to gain a desired color. But this medium often lacked warmth in coloring, it rendered impossible the blending of colors and, as a picture must be varnished over after this "distemper" was dry, the varnish coating sometimes altered the original color scheme in an unpredictable manner. The perfection of the oil medium for painting culminated with the work of two Flemish artists, the brothers Hubert (about 1370-1426) and Jan van Eyck (about 1385-1440). Jan van Eyck, especially, brought to a climax generations of experiments with oil paints. But he guarded his secret well and the technique was not known in Italy until a wandering Italian, Antonello da Messina (1430-1479), learned it in Flanders and subsequently introduced it to Italy. Such, at any rate, is the story of Giorgio Vasari, who describes Van Eyck's discovery and Antonello's role in the following manner.

From VASARI, *Lives of the Painters* [1]

They [Renaissance painters] continued, then, to employ no other method of colouring save that of distemper for panels and for canvases, which method had been introduced by Cimabue in the year 1250, . . . although the craftsmen recognized clearly that pictures in distemper were wanting in a certain softness and liveliness, which, if they could be obtained, would be likely to give more grace to their designs, loveliness to their colouring, and greater facility in blending the colours together; . . . Many had made investigations and sought for something of the sort, yet no one had found any good method, either by the use of liquid varnish or by the mixture of other kinds of colours with the distemper. . . .

This same desire was felt by many lofty minds that were devoted to painting beyond the bounds of Italy—namely, by all the painters of France, Spain, Germany, and other countries. Now, while matters stood thus, it came to pass that, while working in Flanders, Johann [Jan van Eyck] of Bruges, a painter much esteemed in those parts by reason of the great mastery that he had acquired in his profession, set himself to make trial of various sorts of colours, and, as one who took delight in alchemy, to prepare many kinds of oil for making varnishes and other things dear to men of inventive brain, such as he was. Now, on one occasion, having taken very great pains with the painting of a panel, and having brought it to com-

pletion with much diligence, he gave it the varnish and put it to dry in the sun, as is the custom. But, either because the heat was too violent, or perchance because the wood was badly joined together or not seasoned well enough, the said panel opened out at the joinings in a ruinous fashion. Whereupon Johann, seeing the harm that the heat of the sun had done to it, determined to bring it about that the sun should never again do such great damage to his works. And so, being disgusted no less with his varnish than with working in distemper, he began to look for a method of making a varnish that should dry in the shade, without putting his pictures in the sun. Wherefore, after he had made many experiments with substances both pure and mixed together, he found at length that linseed oil and oil of nuts dried more readily than all the others that he had tried. These, then, boiled together with other mixtures of his, gave him the varnish that he—nay, all the painters in the world—had long desired. Afterwards, having made experiments with many other substances, he saw that mixing the colours with those oils gave them a very solid consistency, not only securing the work, when dried, from all danger from water, but also making the colour so brilliant as to give it lustre by itself without varnish; and what appeared most marvellous to him was this, that it could be blended infinitely better than distemper. Rejoicing greatly over such a discovery, as was only reasonable, Johann made a beginning with many works and filled all those parts with them, with incredible pleasure for others and very great profit for himself; and, assisted by experience from day to day, he kept on ever making greater and better works.

No long time passed before the fame of his invention, spreading not only throughout Flanders but through Italy and many other parts of the world, awakened in all

[1] This and the next selection are from Vasari. Reprinted by permission of Ralph T. Hale & Company. This is III, 59, 60-62.

craftsmen a very great desire to know by what method he gave so great a perfection to his works. These craftsmen, seeing his works and not knowing what means he employed, were forced to extol him and to give him immortal praise, and at the same time to envy him with a blameless envy, the rather as he refused for some time to allow himself to be seen at work by anyone, or to reveal his secret to any man. At length, however, having grown old, he imparted it to Roger of Bruges, his pupil, who passed it on . . . to the others. . . . But with all this, although merchants did a great business in his pictures and sent them all over the world . . . yet the knowledge did not spread beyond Flanders. . . .

Now there was one Antonello da Messina, a person of good and lively intelligence, of great sagacity, and skilled in his profession [painting], who, having studied design for many years in Rome, had first retired to Palermo, where he had worked for many years, and finally to his native place, Messina, where he had confirmed by his works the good opinion that his countrymen had of his excellent ability in painting. This man, then, going once on some business of his own from Sicily to Naples, heard that the said King Alfonso had received from Flanders the aforesaid panel by the hand of Johann of Bruges, painted in oil in such a manner that it could be washed, would endure any shock, and was in every way perfect. Thereupon, having contrived to obtain a view of it, he was so strongly impressed by the liveliness of the colours and by the beauty and harmony of that painting, that he put on one side all other business and every thought and went off to Flanders. Having arrived in Bruges, he became very intimate with the said Johann, making him presents of many drawings in the Italian manner and other things, insomuch that the latter, moved by this and by the respect shown

by Antonello, and being now old, was content that he should see his method of colouring in oil; wherefore Antonello did not depart from that place until he had gained a thorough knowledge of that way of colouring, which he desired so greatly to know. And no long time after, Johann having died, Antonello returned from Flanders in order to revisit his native country and to communicate to all Italy a secret so useful, beautiful, and advantageous.

6. *Filippo Brunelleschi (1378-1446), Renaissance Architect*

As is noted above (see page 42), Italian architecture was restored to classical purity and raised to new architectural triumphs by the study and genius of Filippo Brunelleschi. Filippo's chief interest was architecture, and he traveled widely in Italy making measurements of ancient Roman buildings, preparing architectural drawings of them, and studying Roman methods of construction. It was by virtue of his superior knowledge of such things that he succeeded in constructing the vast dome of the cathedral of Florence (Santa Maria del Fiore), a task which all other architects had given up as impossible. Filippo was a close friend of Donatello (1386-1466), the sculptor, and Vasari describes their association in discussing Filippo's work.

From VASARI, *Lives of the Painters* [1]

Filippo and Donatello, who were together, resolved to depart from Florence in company and to live for some years in Rome, to the end that Filippo might study architecture and Donatello sculpture; and

[1] *Ibid.*, II, 201-03.

this Filippo did from his desire to be superior both to Lorenzo and to Donatello, in proportion as architecture is held to be more necessary for the practical needs of men than sculpture and painting. After he had sold a little farm that he had at Settignano, they departed from Florence and went to Rome, where, seeing the grandeur of the buildings and the perfection of the fabrics of the temples, Filippo would stand in a maze like a man out of his mind. And so, having made arrangements for measuring the cornices and taking the ground-plans of those buildings, he and Donatello kept labouring continually, sparing neither time nor expense. There was no place, either in Rome or in the Campagna without, that they left unvisited, and nothing of the good that they did not measure, if only they could find it. And since Filippo was free from domestic cares, he gave himself over body and soul to his studies, and took no thought for eating or sleeping, being intent on one thing only—namely, architecture, which was now dead (I mean the good ancient Orders, and not the barbarous German, which was much in use in his time). And he had in his mind two vast conceptions, one being to restore to light the good manner of architecture, since he believed that if he could recover it he would leave behind no less a name for himself than Cimabue and Giotto had done; and the other was to find a method, if he could, of

raising the Cupola of S. Maria del Fiore in Florence, the difficulties of which were such that after the death of Arnolfo Lapi there had been no one courageous enough to think of raising it without vast expenditure for a wooden framework. . . . He had noted and drawn all the ancient vaults, and was for ever studying them; and if peradventure they had found pieces of capitals, columns, cornices, and bases of buildings buried underground, they would set to work and have them dug out, in order to examine them thoroughly. . . . Nor did he rest until he had drawn every sort of building—round, square, and octagonal temples, basilicas, aqueducts, baths, arches, colossea, amphitheatres, and every temple built of bricks, from which he copied the methods of binding and of clamping with ties, and also of encircling vaults with them; and he noted the ways of making buildings secure by binding the stones together, by iron bars, and by dovetailing; and, discovering a hole hollowed out under the middle of each great stone, he found that this was meant to hold the iron instrument . . . wherewith the stones are drawn up; and this he reintroduced and brought into use afterwards. He then distinguished the different Orders one from another—Doric, Ionic, and Corinthian; and so zealous was his study that his intellect became very well able to see Rome, in imagination, as she was when she was not in ruins.

5 | THE REVOLT FROM ACCEPTED AUTHORITIES: SCIENCE AND PHILOSOPHY

1. The Experimental Method: Roger Bacon (c. 1210-1292)

A characteristic of the late Middle Ages was the uncritical spirit of authoritarianism. Natural scientists and philosophers were prone to accept without question the words of men who, because of their sanctity or prestige, were believed to have known absolute truth. Broadly speaking, these "authorities" were in three categories: the Holy Scriptures, whose literal interpretation was generally accepted as revealed truth; the works of Christian saints, such as St. Augustine and St. Thomas Aquinas, whose great scholarship was valued next to the Scriptures; and such ancient writings as Aristotle's *Physics,* Strabo's and Ptolemy's astronomy and geography, Hippocrates' and Galen's medicine, and Virgil's *Georgics* (agriculture). So great was the authority of such men that quotation of their works generally constituted sufficient proof for any man, even though observed facts appeared to contradict them.

During the Renaissance, however, philosophers and students of natural science began to question these authorities. Objective experimentation in natural phenomena corrected many erroneous observations of the old "authorities" and led to the formulation of natural laws often contrary to the word of the ancients and to the church's interpretation of the Holy Scriptures. Similarly, critical comparison of manuscripts demonstrated such variants in scriptural texts and in the writings of saints that scholars were led to question and to correct many erroneous (but long accepted) opinions. Thus experimental science and critical scholarship were born. But before they gained wide credence or popular reception they suffered long and bitter opposition from smug scholastics and horrified churchmen. The "war between science and religion" was on.

One of the men first influential in the transition from the authoritarian age to the age of critical and experimental scholarship was Roger Bacon, a thirteenth-century English friar. Born sometime between 1210 and 1215, Bacon was trained at Oxford and Paris, entered the Franciscan order, and became a prominent philosopher. He wrote little until late in life and then he criticized current evils in education so severely that he was imprisoned during the last fourteen years of his life. His greatest work, the *Opus majus,* was an attempt both to correlate the learning of his day and to suggest more fruitful methods of study. But Bacon was not entirely free from the authoritarian viewpoint of his day. In the second part of his *Opus majus,* he wrote:[1] "I wish to show in this second part that there is one wisdom that is perfect and that this is contained in the Scriptures. From the roots of this wisdom all truth has sprung. I say, therefore, that one science is the mistress of the others, namely, theology, to which the remaining sciences are vitally necessary, and without which it cannot reach its end. The excellence of these sciences theology claims for her own law, whose nod and authority the rest of the sciences obey. Or better, there is only one perfect wisdom, which is contained wholly in the Scriptures, and is to be unfolded by canon law and philosophy." However, Bacon's belief in the whole and perfect wisdom of the Scriptures embraced also the notion that this wisdom "is to be unfolded by canon law and philosophy." And philosophy, in Bacon's opinion, includes experimentation— "experimental philosophy," as late Renaissance writers called it. And so, later in his book, Bacon unfolds clearly the methods of modern science.

From BACON, *Opus majus* (1267) [2]

I now wish to unfold the principles of experimental science, since without experience nothing can be sufficiently known. For there are two modes of acquiring knowledge, namely, by reasoning and experience. Reasoning draws a conclusion and makes us grant the conclusion, but does not make the conclusion certain, nor does it remove doubt so that the mind may rest on the intuition of truth, unless the mind discovers it by the path of experience; since many have the arguments relating to what can be known, but because they lack experience they neglect the arguments, and neither avoid what is harmful nor follow what is good. For if a man who has never seen fire should prove by adequate reasoning that fire burns and injures things and destroys them, his mind would not be satisfied thereby, nor would he avoid fire, until he placed his hand or some combustible substance in the fire, so that he might prove by experience that which reasoning taught. But when he has had actual experience of combustion his mind is made certain and rests in the full light of truth. Therefore reasoning does not suffice, but experience does. . . .

He therefore who wishes to rejoice without doubt in regard to the truths underlying phenomena must know how to devote himself to experiment. For authors write many statements, and people believe them through reasoning which they formulate without experience. Their reasoning is wholly false. . . .

Since this Experimental Science is wholly unknown to the rank and file of students, I am therefore unable to convince people of its utility unless at the same time I disclose its excellence and its proper signification. This science alone, therefore, knows how to test perfectly what can be done by nature, what by the effort of art, what by trickery, what the incantations, conjurations, invocations, deprecations, sacrifices, that belong to magic, mean and dream of, and what is in them, so that all falsity may be removed and the truth alone of art and nature may be retained. This science alone teaches us how to view the mad acts of magicians, that they may be not ratified but shunned, just as logic considers sophistical reasoning.

This science has three leading characteristics with respect to other sciences. The first is that it investigates by experiment the notable conclusions of all those sciences. For the other sciences know how to

---

[1] This and the next selection are from *The Opus Majus of Roger Bacon,* trans. by Robert Belle Burke, 2 vols., 1928. By permission of the University of Pennsylvania Press. This is I, 36.

[2] *Ibid.,* II, 583, 584, 587, 616, 627.

discover their principles by experiments, but their conclusions are reached by reasoning drawn from the principles discovered. But if they should have a particular and complete experience of their own conclusions, they must have it with the aid of this noble science. . . .

[Secondly, a readiness to believe the results of the experiment or in those who have made the experiment or] who have reliable information from experimenters, nor should he reject the truth, because he is ignorant of it, and because he does not arrive at it by reasoning. . . .

But there is a third dignity of this science. It arises from those properties through which it has no connection with the other sciences, but by its own power investigates the secrets of nature. This consists in two things; namely, in the knowledge of the future, the past, and the present, and in wonderful works by which it excels in the power of forming judgments, the ordinary astronomy dealing with judgments. For Ptolemy in the book introductory to the Almagest says that there is a more certain road than that through the ordinary astronomy, and this is the pathway of experiment, which follows the course of nature, to which many of the philosophers who are believers are turning.

2. Critical Scholarship: Lorenzo Valla (c. 1406-1457)

Roger Bacon's plea for the experimental method appeared to gain little support for a century and a half. Meanwhile, however, a host of unlettered men were revealing the errors and inadequacies of the old authorities. Merchants and sailors were demonstrating the faults of Ptolemaic geography; navigators, cartographers, and astronomers were questioning the old physics, astronomy, and mathematics; and as new drugs and new diseases kept pace with quickened commerce, physicians began to question and to improve upon accepted medical practice. Meanwhile, too, humanistic learning broke with scholasticism, revived the use of ancient languages, and gave rise to critical scholarship wherein, in the realms of law and history, men began to test accepted authorities by the measuring rods of the new learning.

One of the earliest of the critical scholars was the Italian humanist and papal secretary, Lorenzo Valla (about 1406-1457). In 1440, by a comparative study of texts, Valla definitively showed on philological grounds that the medieval document called the Donation of Constantine, upon which papal claims to supreme temporal authority were founded, was a complete forgery. Erasmus later exulted: "Valla, a man who with so much energy, zeal and labor, refuted the stupidities of the barbarians, saved half-buried letters from extinction, restored Italy to her ancient splendor of eloquence, and forced even the learned to express themselves henceforth with more circumspection." An American scholar's recent evaluation of Valla's work follows.

From SMITH, *Age of the Reformation* (1920) [1]

The papal claim to temporal supremacy in the Western world rested largely on a spurious document known as the Donation of Constantine. In this the emperor [Constantine] is represented as withdrawing from Rome in order to leave it to the pope, to whom, in return for being cured of leprosy, he gives the whole Occident.

[1] Preserved Smith, *The Age of the Reformation*, 1920, 48-50. Reprinted by permission of Henry Holt and Company.

An uncritical age had received this for-gery for five or six centuries without question. Doubt had been cast on it by Nicholas of Cusa and Reginald Peacock, but Valla demolished it. He showed that no historian had spoken of it; that there was no time at which it could have oc-curred; that it is contradicted by other contemporary acts; that the barbarous style contains expressions of Greek, Hebrew, and German origin; that the testimony of numismatics is against it; and that the author knew nothing of the antiquities of Rome, into whose council he introduced satraps. Valla's work was so thoroughly done that the document, embodied as were its conclusions in the Canon Law, has never found a reputable defender since. In time the critique had an im-mense effect. Ulrich von Hutten published it in 1517, and in the same year an English translation was made. In 1537 Luther turned it into German.

And if the legality of the pope's rule was so slight, what was its practical effect? According to Valla, it was a "barbarous, overbearing, tyrannical, priestly domina-tion." "What is it to you," he apostro-phizes the pontiff, "if our republic is crushed? You have crushed it. If our temples have been pillaged? You have pillaged them. If our virgins and matrons have been violated? You have done it. If the city is inundated with the blood of citizens? You are guilty of it all."

Valla's critical genius next attacked the schoolman's idol Aristotle and the hu-manist's demigod Cicero. More important were his *Annotations on the New Testa-ment,* first published by Erasmus in 1505. The Vulgate was at that time regarded, as it was at Trent defined to be, the authen-tic, or official form of the Scriptures. Tak-ing in hand three Latin and three Greek manuscripts, Valla had no difficulty in showing that they differed from one an-other and that in some cases the Latin had

no authority whatever in the Greek. He pointed out a number of mistranslations, some of them in passages vitally affecting the faith. In short he left no support stand-ing for any theory of verbal inspiration.

3. The Spirit of Experimentation Revived: Leonardo da Vinci

In the footsteps of Roger Bacon came that Italian genius of the High Renais-sance, Leonardo da Vinci. Leonardo (1452-1519), as is shown above [see page 45], was an artist with a distinctly scientific turn of mind. Though he was primarily a painter, he was one of the earliest Renaissance figures to accept the results of experiments when they contradicted the conclusions of scholas-tics or ancient authorities. Leonardo was capable of keen observations, and, as the following quotation demonstrates, gave great weight to experience.

From LEONARDO, *Notebooks* (*c.* 1508) [1]

They say that that knowledge is me-chanical which issues from *esperienza* [experience, or experimentation], and that is scientific which is born and ends in the mind. . . . But, as it seems to me, those sciences are vain and full of errors, which are not born of *esperienza,* mother of all certitude, and which do not termi-nate in cognition (*nota esperienza*), that is, whose origin or middle or end does not come through one of the five senses.

And if we have doubt of everything which comes through the senses, how much more should we doubt of things rebels to the senses, as the essence of God

[1] This and the next selection are from Henry Osborn Taylor, *Thought and Expression in the Sixteenth Century,* 2nd ed. rev., 2 vols. 1930. By permission of The Macmillan Company. This is II, 296n.

and the soul, and the like, about which one is always contending and disputing? And verily it always happens where reason fails, that clamor takes its place, which does not happen when things are certain. From which we say that where there is clamor there is not true knowledge (*vera scienza*), because truth has a single ending, and when that is made known, the contest is ended forever; . . .

But the true sciences (*vere scienze*) are those which *la sperienza* has caused to enter through the senses, silencing the tongue of the disputants, and not feeding its investigators upon dreams; but proceeds always upon true and known first principles step by step, and with true conclusions to the end; as is indicated in the elementary mathematical sciences, that is, number and measure, called arithmetic and geometry, which treat with absolute truth of discontinuous and continuous quantity.

4. Experimental Medicine

ANDREAS VESALIUS (1514-1564),
ANATOMIST

From TAYLOR, *Thought and Expression in the Sixteenth Century* (1930) [1]

A few years after Leonardo's death the method of direct examination of the pertinent physical facts was established in the most direct and simple form in that very science of anatomy to which he had set himself so zealously. Andreas Vesalius was the author of this achievement. Judging by results and their continuity, it was he, rather than Leonardo, who founded the modern method and science of anatomy, and prepared the way for physiology. He was born at Brussels in 1514, just as the

[1] *Ibid.*, II, 309-11.

bells were ringing out the old year. For generations his forbears had been doctors. He went to school at Louvain, and entered the university. But his constant and passionate occupation was the dissection of animals. In his eighteenth year he made his way to Paris to hear Jacobus Sylvius (Jacques Du Bois) the most famous master of anatomy at that time. Sylvius was a hard conservative, who taught after Galen [an ancient Greek physician, A.D. 130-200], and used dissections to illustrate that great authority rather than as independent means of gaining knowledge. Vesalius could not endure that Sylvius should lecture from a book while barbers clumsily cut up a human body or far more frequently a dog's. What knowledge could be gained from having the roughly extracted viscera shown to him? This masterful auditor insisted upon conducting the dissection himself. "I had to put my own hand to the business." Outside of the lecture-room, Vesalius dissected dogs, and haunted the cemeteries, where there were piles of human bones. He became so familiar with them that he could recognize any part of the human skeleton by touch, and name it with his eyes blindfolded.

After some three years of medical study in Paris, Vesalius returned to Louvain, and then went to Venice and soon to Padua, where at the end of the year 1537 he was made professor in the university. He was scarcely twenty-three.

Quickly casting aside "the ridiculous method of the schools," he demonstrated and dissected before his students, practicing also the vivisection of animals. But he used Galen in lecturing, at least until he became convinced that Galen had made his dissections and descriptions from apes, rather than from human bodies. After that, braving all opposition, he gradually freed himself and his demonstrations from the older author; and even used the bodies under dissection to show the many errors in Galen's descriptions when applied to the parts and organs of the human body. He was now demonstrating and lecturing from the facts alone, and from books no longer. He had five hundred students, and was already known beyond the university through his reputation and his *Anatomical Tables,* which circulated widely.

In order to establish the validity of his method before the learned world he set himself to the preparation of his great book, the *Humani Corporis Fabrica* [1543]. . . . The text presented careful and minute descriptions of the parts and organs of the body, and then compared Galen's defective accounts of the same. Thus while setting forth a corrected and improved anatomy, it demonstrated Galen's errors by appealing not to authority but to the facts carefully presented. . . . It was shown that Galen had made his descriptions from the dissection of apes and not of human bodies. Vesalius pointed to the Alexandrian physicians who centuries before Galen had really studied human bodies. By such arguments and biting sarcasm he sought to break the spell of Galen's infallibility. His polemic was directed as well against opponents, named and unnamed, who still relied upon authority in the face of facts. The attack was direct, the method incontestible; if only students could be prevailed upon to use their hands and eyes and reason.

This was the difficulty, since it meant a reversal of the long habit of seeing through others' eyes, and thinking in the forms of the traditional knowledge. Appeals to facts have proved futile quite as often as they have succeeded. But the time was ripe for the new method of investigation. Against storms of opposition, the book won such success that never more could professors at good universities read aloud from Galen, while barbers ignorantly cut up animals or even human bodies, and all present re-mained ignorant of the discrepancies between the facts before their eyes and the texts sounding in their ears. Vesalius's book was the foundation stone of a new anatomical science based upon dissection, and again dissection: the dissection of human bodies and the vivisection of living animals.

The last was to be of enormous importance. For Vesalius's book did not stop with strictly anatomical descriptions, but considered, none too successfully, the functions of the organs: in a word, it proceeded naturally from anatomy to physiology. Its tone and contents were in themselves an argument against the many superstitions touching the care of health and the cure of disease. Its preface set forth the long decline of medicine and the contempt into which it had fallen: all due to the ignorance of the human body which had prevailed ever since physicians ceased to make dissections with their own hands.

Vesalius was not yet thirty, and his work as the founder of modern anatomy was done. Angered by the abuse which followed the publication of his *Fabrica,* he burnt the records of his further investigations, and became court physician to the Emperor Charles V.

PARACELSUS (C. 1490-1541), PHYSICIAN

Contemporary with Vesalius, though somewhat older than he, was another medical man who rebelled against long-accepted medical authorities. This was the German-Swiss Theophrastus Bombast von Hohenheim, who is better known by his pen name, Paracelsus. Inclined toward medicine from his youth—his father was a physician and his mother a hospital superintendent—Paracelsus soon questioned the value of the formal education of his day and struck out for himself. He tried his hand at chemistry, learned much about ores, metals, and other minerals in the mines of Tyrol, studied nature and the diseases of man as he wandered over much of Europe, acquired a wide knowledge of practical medicine, and successfully introduced so many new drugs, especially minerals, into the pharmacopoeia that he is sometimes called the "father of pharmacy." But Paracelsus was blunt-spoken, and as lecturer at Basel (1527) he created a great row by criticizing the current medical learning and practices. His orthodox colleagues forced him out of town, pointed out that he held no degree, insisted that he was wholly unqualified to practice or to teach medicine, challenged his medical theories and novel treatments, and forced him from pillar to post during the last dozen years of his life. About 1537, Paracelsus published a defense of his career, entitled *Seven Arguments, Answering to Several of the Detractions of His Envious Critics,* wherein his contribution to medical theory and practice are well sampled.

From PARACELSUS, *Seven Arguments*
(c. 1537) [1]

Reader, give good heed so that I may inform you why I have written these arguments. In his time God laid well the foundation upon which the spirit of medicine had its beginnings, through Apollinus, Machaon, Podalirius and Hippocrates, allowing the light of nature to shine without any spirit of darkness. . . . But just as the wicked foe with his corn cockle and weeds would let nothing grow in the clean wheat ground, so medicine was obscured from the first spirit of nature and

fell prey to antimedical men. Accordingly it was jostled hither and yon by [persons and] sophistries, so much so that no one was able to come to the level of achievement reached by Machaon and Hippocrates; and in medicine that which is not tested in practice has lost its disputation and gains still less in debate. . . . Sophists would have it that the spirit of truth in medicine is but a clacking tongue. . . . But to let it be understood that a physician without works is nothing, and that a physician's works do not reside in tongue wagging, I have written these words to serve as instruction. . . .

I introduce in this work a new theory and physic, together with a new reasoning such as were never held before. . . . That is, I report as one who has proved to his own satisfaction that the doctrines and causes of death in the old school of thought have been inaccurately and ambiguously described. . . . I wish to apprise you of this, for I must adjudge it a great folly: When Heaven in the light of nature is constantly offering new ideas, new inventions, new arts, new cares, should not these be held valid? What profits the rain that fell a thousand years ago? Benefit comes from the rain that falls now. . . . Our concern should be for the present, not for the past, and every realm of thought is concerned with all the light of nature. . . . Accordingly from the power of the existing light of nature . . . I in my writings will go. . . .

We should have respect for authority which proves itself by works, even though we do not wish to believe the words. . . . That man is rare who can stand his ground with respect to a situation which he has not seen with his own eyes against one who has seen it with his own eyes. . . .

The outcry is . . . that the prescription I write is poisonous. . . . My first reply to such sham pretense and clamor . . . would be to ask if they know what is poison and what is not poison? Or is not a poison one of the mysteries of nature? For on these very points they lack knowledge and understanding of nature's forces. For what thing is there, created by God, which is not endowed with some great gift for the good of mankind? . . . Everything should be used for the purpose to which it is ordained and we should not stand in fear of it. . . . He who despises poison is ignorant of what resides therein. . . .

It is necessary for me to make some reply concerning my travels and concerning the fact that I have been so unsettled. . . . My travels up to the present time have taught me that, for good reason, no disciple finds a master growing in his own back yard, or an instructor in the chimney corner. Again, the arts are not confined to one native land, but are scattered the world over. They are not to be found in one man or place but they must be sought, collected, and accepted where they are. . . . Was it not well and proper for me to search out . . . what is effected in every person? If I were lacking in this I would not be true to . . . myself. . . .

Now they say that when I visit a patient I do not know at once what ails him but that I require time in which to learn it. That is true; the fact that they make immediate diagnosis is the fault of their own folly, for the off-hand judgment is wrong from the start and as days go by they know less and less the longer the time, and so they make themselves out as liars. But I seek day by day to arrive at the truth and the longer the time the more diligently I seek. For uncovering hidden diseases is not like recognizing colors. . . . What the eyes tell may be diagnosed at once but it is useless to diagnose that which is hidden from sight. . . . Take a miner as an example; no matter how good, how honest, how clever, how skilled he may be, when he sees an ore for the first

time he does not know what it contains and how he should treat it. . . . First he must analyze it through a course of testing and examination before he can see his way. . . . So it is also with obscure chronic diseases, for which quick diagnosis is impossible. . . . To consider the situation, to measure and make tests and to accord the tests their significance, that is not a matter for reproach; and having brought the proper art to bear, there is the adornment, the treasure which was sought. This is the way to proceed with such diseases. But those who . . . do not make their tests by experiment . . . go to books for their tests and trials. For this reason many . . . get away before they learn the truth and in that way they never learn it.

WILLIAM HARVEY'S EXPERIMENT ON THE HEART

One of the early triumphs of the experimental method was the demonstration by William Harvey (1578-1657) of the circulation of the blood and the function of the heart in that process. Harvey's work completely destroyed Galen's teachings about these things and opened wide the field for subsequent exploration of the chemical properties and uses of the blood, the study of the heart, and circulatory problems. Galen had taught that there were two kinds of blood in the human body. One carried "natural spirits" (that is, nutritive properties from the digestive tract) to body tissues, and it flowed through the veins; the other carried "vital spirits" (a kind of mystic, life-giving property) with which it was endowed by the heart, and it flowed through the arteries. The heart was supposed to be the source of all life and of all heat in the body. It imparted these "vital spirits" to the arterial blood by taking blood into the left ventricle and forcing it through invisible pores into the right ventricle, whence this blood imparted the "vital spirits" to the lungs and other tissues of the body.

Harvey dismissed the notion of "spirits," showed that there is but one single supply of blood, demonstrated the method of its circulation throughout the body, and explained clearly the role of the heart as a kind of central pumping station in the circulatory process. His work was the direct result of many dissections and long experimentation. Harvey himself was English-born, educated at Cambridge and at the famous medical school of Padua in Italy. He began medical practice in London in 1602, was made a member of the Royal College of Physicians in 1604, and was appointed Physician to St. Bartholomew's Hospital in 1609. Later he became Royal Physician to King Charles I, whom he loyally supported throughout the English Civil Wars. His most famous book, *An Anatomical Disquisition on the Motion of the Heart and Blood in Animals,* was first published in Latin in 1628.

From HARVEY, *On the Motion of the Heart* (1628) [1]

DEDICATION

I have already and repeatedly presented you, my learned friends, with my new views of the motion and function of the heart, in my anatomical lectures; but having now for nine years and more confirmed these views by multiplied demonstrations in your presence, illustrated them by arguments, and freed them from the objections of the most learned and skilful Anatomists, I at length yield to the requests, I might say entreaties, of many, and here present them for general consideration in this Treatise.

Were not the work indeed presented through you, my learned friends, I should scarcely hope that it could come out scatheless and complete; for you have been in general the faithful witnesses of almost all the instances from which I have either collected truth or confuted error; you have seen my dissections, and at my demonstrations of all that I maintain to be objects of sense, you have been accustomed to stand by and bear me out with your testimony. And as this book alone declares the blood to course and revolve by a new route, very different from the ancient and beaten pathway trodden for so many ages, and illustrated by such a host of learned and distinguished men, I was greatly afraid lest I might be charged with presumption . . . unless I had first proposed its subject to you, had confirmed its conclusions by ocular demonstrations in your presence, had replied to your doubts and objections, and secured the assent and support of our distinguished President. . . . True philosophers, who are only eager for truth and knowledge, never regard themselves as already so thoroughly informed, but that they welcome further information. . . . nor are they so narrowminded as to imagine any of the arts or sciences transmitted to us by the ancients, in such a state of forwardness or completeness, that nothing is left for the ingenuity and industry of others; very many, on the contrary, maintain that all we know is still infinitely less than all that still remains unknown; nor do philosophers pin their faith to others' precepts in such wise that they lose their liberty, and cease to give credence to the conclusions of their proper senses. Neither do they swear such fealty to their mistress Antiquity, that they openly, and in sight of all, deny and desert their friend Truth. . . .

[1] *The Works of William Harvey, M.D.,* trans. by Robert Willis. Printed for the Sydenham Society, London, 1847, 5-6, 9-11, 21-22, 68.

INTRODUCTION

As we are about to discuss the motion, action, and use of the heart and arteries, it is imperative on us first to state what has been thought of these things by others in their writings . . . in order that what is true may be confirmed, and what is false set right by dissection, multiplied experience, and accurate observation.

Almost all anatomists, physicians, and philosophers, up to the present time, have supposed, with Galen, that the object of the pulse was the same as that of respiration. . . . Whence it is affirmed, as by Hieronymus Fabricius of Aquapendente, in his book on "Respiration," which has lately appeared, that as the pulsation of the heart and arteries does not suffice for the ventilation and refrigeration of the blood, therefore were the lungs fashioned to surround the heart. From this it appears, that whatever has hitherto been said upon the systole and diastole, or on the movement of the heart and arteries, has been said with especial reference to the lungs:

But as the structure and movements of the heart differ from those of the lungs, and the motions of the arteries from those of the chest, so it seems likely that other ends and offices will thence arise, and that the pulsations and uses of the heart, likewise of the arteries, will differ in many respects from the heavings and uses of the chest and lungs. . . . Still further, although some affirm that the lungs, arteries, and heart have all the same offices, they yet maintain that the heart is the workshop of the spirits, and that arteries contain and transmit them; denying, however . . . that the lungs can either make or contain spirits; and then they assert, with Galen, against Erasistratus, that it is blood, not spirits, which is contained in the arteries.

These various opinions are seen to be so incongruous and mutually subversive, that every one of them is not unjustly brought under suspicion. That it is blood and blood alone which is contained in the arteries is made manifest by the experiment of Galen, by arteriotomy, and by wounds; for from a single artery divided, as Galen himself affirms in more than one place, the whole of the blood may be withdrawn in the course of half an hour, or less. . . .

OF THE MOTIONS OF THE HEART, AS SEEN IN THE
DISSECTION OF LIVING ANIMALS

When the chest of a living animal is laid open and the capsule that immediately surrounds the heart is slit up or removed, the organ is seen now to move, now to be at rest; there is a time when it moves, and a time when it is motionless.

These things are more obvious in the colder animals, such as toads, frogs, serpents, small fishes, crabs, shrimps, snails and shellfish. They also become more distinct in warm-blooded animals, such as the dog and hog, if they be attentively noted when the heart begins to flag, to move more slowly, and, as it were, to die: the movements then become slower and rarer, the pauses longer, by which it is made much more easy to perceive and unravel what the motions really are, and how they are performed. In the pause, as in death, the heart is soft, flaccid, exhausted, lying, as it were, at rest.

In the motion, and interval in which this is accomplished, three principal circumstances are to be noted:

1. That the heart is erected, and rises upwards to a point, so that at this time it strikes against the breast and the pulse is felt externally.

2. That it is everywhere contracted, but more especially towards the sides, so that it looks narrower, relatively longer, more drawn together. . . .

3. The heart being grasped in the hand, is felt to become harder during its action. Now this hardness proceeds from tension, precisely as when the forearm is grasped, its tendons are perceived to become tense and resilient when the fingers are moved.

4. It may further be observed in fishes, and the colder-blooded animals, such as frogs, serpents, &c., that the heart, when it moves, becomes of a paler colour, when quiescent of a deeper blood-red colour.

From these particulars it appeared to me evident that the motion of the heart consists in a certain universal tension— both contraction in the line of its fibres, and constriction in every sense. It becomes erect, hard, and of diminished size during its action; the motion is plainly of the same nature as that of the muscles when they contract in the line of their sinews and fibres; for the muscles, when in action, acquire vigour and tenseness, and from soft become hard, prominent and thickened: in the same manner the heart. . . .

CONCLUSION OF THE DEMONSTRATION OF THE
CIRCULATION

And now I may be allowed to give in brief my view of the circulation of the blood, and to propose it for general adoption.

Since all things, both argument and ocular demonstration, show that the blood passes through the lungs and heart by the action of the [auricles and] ventricles, and is sent for distribution to all parts of the body, where it makes its way into the veins and pores of the flesh, and then flows by the veins from the circumference on every side to the center, from the lesser to the greater veins, and is by them finally discharged into the vena cava and right auricle of the heart, and this in such a quantity or in such a flux and reflux thither by the arteries, hither by the veins, as cannot possibly be supplied by the in-gesta [food consumed], and is much greater than can be required for mere purposes of nutrition; it is absolutely necessary to conclude that the blood in the animal body is impelled in a circle, and is in a state of ceaseless motion; that this is the act or function which the heart performs by means of its pulse; and that it is the sole and only end of the motion and contraction of the heart.

5. The New Astronomy

NICHOLAS COPERNICUS AND HIS
HYPOTHESIS ABOUT THE UNIVERSE

The struggle for the acceptance of the Copernican theory well illustrates the difficulty of the new experimental science in gaining ground against the entrenched authorities of scholasticism and of the church. Copernicus himself believed his hypothesis to be fact, but he lacked sufficient data (obtainable only with better instruments) to prove his hypothesis conclusively; and, moreover, he and his friends feared excommunication and persecution for entertaining such heretical opinions. Accordingly, he set forth his opinions timidly, merely as an interesting hypothesis for which he lacked conclusive proofs.

Copernicus (1473-1543) was born in Prussia of Polish, or possibly German, parents. Well educated at Cracow, Bologna, Padua, and Ferrara under the watchful patronage of his uncle, the Bishop of Ermland, he followed the Renaissance ideal of versatility, became canon lawyer, physician, painter, ecclesiastic, mathematician, and astronomer. As professor of mathematics at Rome in 1500 and afterward, he became dissatisfied with the old explanations of the movements of heavenly bodies. Astronomical observations and mathematical calculations led him to adopt likelier explanations and to compound a new heliocentric theory of the universe, or the notion that the sun, not the earth, is the center of the universe about which other heavenly bodies revolve in regularized cycles. Prudence withheld him from publishing his work, but his ideas were circulated by letters among his friends, and people interested in astronomy knew them well. About 1530, when his theory was well matured in his mind, he prepared a *Commentariolus* (*Little Commentary*) for distribution in manuscript form among his friends. In this he laid down seven "assumptions" and proceeded to a more detailed description of the movements of the planets and the moon. In part, the *Commentariolus* ran as follows.

From COPERNICUS, *Commentaries* (*c.* 1530) [1]

Our ancestors assumed, I observe, a large number of celestial spheres for this reason especially, to explain the apparent motion of the planets by the principle of regularity. For they thought it altogether absurd that a heavenly body, which is a perfect sphere, should not always move uniformly. They saw that by connecting and combining regular motions in various ways they could make any body appear to move to any position.

Callippus and Eudoxus, who endeavored to solve the problem by the use of concentric spheres, were unable to account for all the planetary movements; they had to explain not merely the apparent revo-

[1] Reprinted from Edward Rosen, editor and translator, *Three Copernican Treatises*, pp. 57-59, Vol. XXX in the series *Records of Civilization: Sources and Studies*. Copyright 1939 by Columbia University Press.

lutions of the planets but also the fact that these bodies appear to us sometimes to mount higher in the heavens, sometimes to descend; and this fact is incompatible with the principle of concentricity. Therefore it seemed better to employ eccentrics and epicycles, a system which most scholars finally accepted.

Yet the planetary theories of Ptolemy and most other astronomers, although consistent with the numerical data, seemed likewise to present no small difficulty. For these theories were not adequate unless certain equants were also conceived; it then appeared that a planet moved with uniform velocity neither on its deferent nor about the center of its epicycle. Hence a system of this sort seemed neither sufficiently absolute nor sufficiently pleasing to the mind.

Having become aware of these defects, I often considered whether there could perhaps be found a more reasonable arrangement of circles, from which every apparent inequality would be derived and in which everything would move uniformly about its proper center, as the rule of absolute motion requires. After I had addressed myself to this very difficult and almost insoluble problem, the suggestion at length came to me how it could be solved with fewer and much simpler constructions than were formerly used, if some assumptions (which are called axioms) were granted me. They follow in this order.

ASSUMPTIONS

1. There is no one center of all the celestial circles or spheres.

2. The center of the earth is not the center of the universe, but only of gravity and of the lunar sphere.

3. All the spheres revolve about the sun as their mid-point, and therefore the sun is the center of the universe. . . .

4. The ratio of the earth's distance from the sun to the height of the firmament is so much smaller than the ratio of the earth's radius to its distance from the sun that the distance from the earth to the sun is imperceptible in comparison with the height of the firmament.

5. Whatever motion appears in the firmament arises not from any motion of the firmament, but from the earth's motion. The earth together with its circumjacent elements performs a complete rotation on its fixed poles in a daily motion, while the firmament and highest heaven abide unchanged.

6. What appear to us as motions of the sun arise not from its motion but from the motion of the earth and our sphere, with which we revolve about the sun like any other planet. The earth has, then, more than one motion.

7. The apparent retrograde and direct motion of the planets arises not from their motion but from the earth's. The motion of the earth alone, therefore, suffices to explain so many apparent inequalities in the heavens.

Having set forth these assumptions, I shall endeavor briefly to show how uniformity of the motions can be saved in a systematic way. However, I have thought it well, for the sake of brevity, to omit from this sketch mathematical demonstrations, reserving these for my larger work. But in the explanation of the circles I shall set down here the lengths of the radii; and from these the reader who is not unacquainted with mathematics will readily perceive how closely this arrangement of circles agrees with the numerical data and observations.

Accordingly, let no one suppose that I have gratuitously asserted, with the Pythagoreans, the motion of the earth; strong proof will be found in my exposition of the circles. For the principal arguments by which the natural philosophers attempt to establish the immobility of the earth rest for the most part on the appearances; it is particularly such arguments that collapse here, since I treat the earth's immobility as due to an appearance.

[The "larger work" to which Copernicus referred above was probably his *De revolutionibus orbium caelestium* (*On the Revolutions of the Heavenly Orbs*), 1543. In this work, Copernicus expounded his views more thoroughly, and showed clearly that he regarded the heliocentric system as truth, not as a mere hypothesis. But his friends worried about the results of publishing to the world such unorthodox views. In the Scriptures, they pointed out, Joshua had commanded the sun to stand still, and not the earth. So how could the earth move against such divine authority? To avoid the appearance of challenging this authority, Copernicus postponed publication of *De revolutionibus* and finally left it to a friend and pupil, Andreas Osiander, to oversee its printing. Osiander was a Lutheran theologian who feared the consequences of Copernicus' unorthodox teachings even more than Copernicus himself. So, in order to "mollify the peripatetics and theologians," Osiander suppressed Copernicus' "Introduction" to *De revolutionibus* and wrote one of his own which denied the truth of the Copernican theory, conflicted with the opinions expressed in the book that followed, and presented Copernicus' great work in such hypocritical fashion as to weaken it in the eyes of sympathetic readers and to increase the ridicule heaped upon it by scholastics and theologians. Unfortunately, Copernicus could do nothing to counteract the damage which his well-intentioned friend caused, for he died a short time after *De revolutionibus* appeared in print.]

GALILEO UPHOLDS (AND RECANTS) THE COPERNICAN THEORY

One of the most important supporters of the Copernican theory was Galileo Galilei (1564-1642). Born at Pisa, Galileo rebelled from the medical training his father wished him to pursue and turned to mathematics instead. A keen observer of natural phenomena, he discovered the law of the pendulum by watching a heavy lamp swinging in the cathedral at Pisa, and set forth the law of falling bodies by experimenting with objects dropped from the famous Leaning Tower of Pisa. In 1592 he left the University of Pisa, where he had been lecturer, to become professor of mathematics at Padua. Subsequently (1610), he moved to Florence. Endowed with limitless curiosity, he experimented with many things in physics, heard of the principle of the telescope, made one for his own use, and soon became engrossed in astronomy. With his telescope he described the rough surface of the moon, saw that the Milky Way consists of many small stars, and was first to discover the moons of Jupiter (1610). The sensational success of Galileo's work soon brought to a crisis the conflict between champions of Copernicus and defenders of the old system. In 1616, the ecclesiastical authorities at Rome summoned Galileo before the bar of the Inquisition and warned him "to forsake the opinion he had hitherto held, that the sun is the center of the sphere and immovable, and that the earth moves." Soon afterward, Galileo's books were placed on the Index of Prohibited Books. In 1623, however, Galileo was encouraged to write further in defense of Cópernicus by his close friend and admirer Barberini, who was now elevated to the Papacy as Pope Urban VIII. With such influential support, Galileo wrote and published in 1632 his most famous work, *Dialogue of Galileo Galilei . . . on the Two Principal Systems of the Universe, the Ptolemaic and the Copernican, Propounding, without Deciding for Either, the Natural and Philosophical Reasons in Favor of Each*. Of this a recent author has written:[1]

"The dialogue, divided into four days, is sustained by three interlocutors. The first, given the name of Salviati, a dear friend and disciple of the author, who had died in 1614, naturally advocates the Copernican system. Sagredo, another friend, though he is really also a Copernican, plays the part of an impartial seeker after truth. To the third speaker, the champion of Ptolemy and of Aristotle, is given the name of Simplicio, happily chosen as that of a real and noted medieval Peripatetic, and as at the same time suggesting, with fine malice, the mental quality of the anti-Copernicans. . . . However carefully the author may have guarded himself against summing up in favor of either side, when his book appeared it was at once hailed as the most powerful defence of Copernicus in existence."

So great was the stir created by this book that the church was roused to action. A papal commission reported not only that Galileo upheld the Copernican system but also that he had gained permission to publish the book by fraudulent misrepresentation. Accordingly, in the spring of 1633, Galileo, so ill that he had to be carried in a litter, was called again before the bar of the dreaded Roman Inquisition. Here he was convicted of heresy, forced by the threat of horrible torture to sign

[1] Preserved Smith, *A History of Modern Culture*, 2 vols., 1930-34, I, 50-51. Reprinted by permission of Henry Holt and Company.

a recantation, and sentenced to perpetual imprisonment and penance. However, the world knew that Galileo's recantation was forced and it had little influence upon scientific men. Galileo's personal opinion was unchanged and it was rumored that, as he rose from his knees after recantation, he muttered, *"Eppur si muove"*—"The earth does move, however." His sentence and recantation follow.

From *The Sentence of Galileo* (1633) [1]

We, Gasparo del titolo di S. Croce in Gierusalemme Gorgia; [. . . etc.] by the grace of God, cardinals of the Holy Roman Church, Inquisitors General, by the Holy Apostolic See specially deputed, against heretical depravity throughout the whole Christian Republic. . . .

Whereas you, Galileo, son of the late Vincenzo Galilei, Florentine, aged seventy years, were in the year 1615 denounced to this Holy Office for holding as true the false doctrine taught by many, that the sun is the centre of the world and immovable, and that the earth moves, and also with a diurnal motion. . . .

The proposition that the sun is the centre of the world and does not move from its place is absurd and false philosophically and formally heretical, because it is expressly contrary to the Holy Scripture.

Therefore by our order you were cited before the Holy Office, where, being examined upon your oath, you acknowledged the book to be written and published by you. . . .

And whereas it appeared to us that you had not stated the full truth with regard to your intention, we thought it necessary to subject you to a rigorous examination,

at which . . . you answered like a good Catholic. Therefore, having seen and maturely considered the merits of this your cause, together with your confessions and excuses above mentioned, all that ought justly to be seen and considered, we have arrived at the underwritten final sentence against you:

Invoking, therefore the most holy name of our Lord Jesus Christ and of His most glorious Mother and ever Virgin Mary . . . we say, pronounce, sentence, declare, that you, the said Galileo . . . have rendered yourself in the judgment of this Holy Office vehemently suspected of heresy . . . and that consequently you have incurred all the censures and penalties imposed and promulgated in the sacred canons and other constitutions, general and particular, against such delinquents. From which we are content that you be absolved, provided first, with a sincere heart, and unfeigned faith, you abjure, curse, and detest the aforesaid errors and heresies, and every other error and heresy contrary to the Catholic and Apostolic Roman Church in the form prescribed by us.

And in order that this your grave and pernicious error and transgression may not remain altogether unpunished, and that you may be more cautious for the future, and as an example to others, that they may abstain from similar delinquencies—we ordain that the book of the *Dialogues of Galileo Galilei* be prohibited by public edict.

We condemn you to the formal prison of the Holy Office during our pleasure, and by way of salutary penance, we enjoin that for three years to come you repeat once a week the seven penitential Psalms. . . .

So we the undersigned Cardinals pronounce.

F. Cardinalis de Asculo [*et al.*]

---

[1] Oliver J. Thatcher, ed., *The Library of Original Sources*, 10 vols., New York, 1907, V, 302-07.

From *The Recantation of Galileo* (1633) [1]

I, Galileo Galilei, son of the late Vincenzo Galilei, Florentine, aged 70 years, arraigned personally before this tribunal, and kneeling before you; most Eminent and Reverend Lord Cardinals, Inquisitors general against heretical depravity throughout the whole Christian Republic, having before my eyes and touching with my hands, the holy Gospels—swear that I have always believed, do now believe, and by God's help will for the future believe, all that is held, preached, and taught by the Holy Catholic and Apostolic Roman Church. But whereas—after an injunction had been judiciously intimated to me by this Holy Office, to the effect that I must altogether abandon the false opinion that the sun is the centre of the world and immovable, and that the earth is not the centre of the world, and moves, and that I must not hold, defend, or teach in any way whatsoever, verbally or in writing, the said doctrine, and after it had been notified to me that the said doctrine was contrary to the Holy Scripture—I wrote and printed a book in which I discuss this doctrine already condemned, and adduced arguments of great cogency in its favour; . . . and for this cause I have been pronounced by the Holy Office to be vehemently suspected of heresy, that is to say, of having held and believed that the sun is the centre of the world and immovable, and that the earth is not the centre and moves;

Therefore, desiring to remove from the minds of your Eminences, and of all faithful Christians, this strong suspicion, reasonably conceived against me, with sincere heart and unfeigned faith I abjure, curse, and detest the aforesaid errors and heresies, and generally every other error and sect whatsoever contrary to the said Holy Church; and I swear that in future I will never again say or assert, verbally

[1] *Ibid.*

or in writing, anything that might furnish occasion for a similar suspicion regarding me; but that should I know any heretic, or person suspected of heresy, I will denounce him to the Holy Office, or the Inquisitor, [and I] promise to fulfil and observe in their integrity all penances that have been, or that shall be, imposed upon me by this Holy Office. . . .

I, the said Galileo Galilei, have abjured, sworn, promised, and bound myself as above; and in witness of the truth thereof I have with my own hand subscribed the present document of my abjuration, and recited it word for word at Rome, in the Convent of Minerva, this twenty-second day of June, 1633.

I, Galileo Galilei, have abjured as above with my own hand.

6. *Francis Bacon, Lord Verulam* (*1560-1626*)

The revolt from accepted authorities was fairly complete by 1600. The experimental method was widely employed. Despite opposition from churches and conservative churchmen, critical scholarship was making headway in theology, politics, and philosophy. The Copernican theory had gained wide acceptance. Medical theory and practice were undergoing a gradual revolution. It was about this time that the classic statement of the experimental method was set forth together with grandiose plans for the systematic, cooperative exploitation of the secrets of nature by future generations of inquisitive scholars.

Both the statement and the plans were the work of Francis, Lord Bacon, an English lawyer, politician, and experimental philosopher. Lord Bacon is often called the father of the inductive method of reasoning. Yet the inductive method was not original with him (it is at least as old as Aristotle); Bacon merely restated it at a time and in such a manner as to demonstrate vividly its utility in a new age of experimental philosophy. Moreover, Bacon advocated plans whereby scholars endowed by the state and working co-operatively—in "Academies" or "Royal Societies" such as had existed in Italy and subsequently rose to prominence in seventeenth-century Europe—might attack the mysteries of nature, classify their results, and formulate laws of natural behavior. Bacon himself led the way by preparing "histories" of his observations, such as "The History of the Winds" and "On the Ebb & Flow of the Sea." He also drew up long lists of suggestions for further investigation and was among the first who urged the practical application of inventions and experimental discoveries to the enrichment of everyday life in this world or, as he stated it, "to endow the condition and life of man with new powers or works."

Bacon's published works fill several volumes. Best known are his *Essays* (1597), his *Advancement of Learning* (1605), his *Novum Organum* (*The New Organon: or, True Directions Concerning the Interpretation of Nature*) (1620), his *New Atlantis* (1627), and his *Instaurata magna* (*The Great Instauration*), left unfinished at his death. Below are selections which give the essence of Lord Bacon's contributions.

BACON ON SCIENTIFIC METHOD

From BACON, *Novum Organum* (1620) [1]

Those who have taken upon them to lay down the law of nature as a thing

---

[1] *The Works of Francis Bacon,* ed. by James Spedding, Robert L. Ellis, and Douglas D. Heath, 15 vols., Taggard and Thompson, Boston, 1861. Selections from the Second Book, "Preface" and "Aphorisms," VIII, 59-61, 115, 178-79, 358-60.

already searched out and understood, whether they have spoken in simple assurance or professional affection, have therein done philosophy and the sciences great injury. For as they have been successful in inducing belief, so they have been effective in quenching and stopping inquiry; and have done more harm by spoiling and putting an end to other men's efforts than good by their own. Those on the other hand who have taken a contrary course, and asserted that absolutely nothing can be known . . . have neither started from true principles nor rested in the just conclusion, zeal and affectation having carried them much too far. The more ancient of the Greeks (whose writings are lost) took up with better judgment a position between these two extremes—between the presumption of pronouncing on everything, and the despair of comprehending anything; and though frequently and bitterly complaining of the difficulty of inquiry and the obscurity of things, and like impatient horses champing the bit, they did not the less follow up their object and engage with Nature; thinking (it seems) that this very question—viz. whether or no anything can be known—was to be settled not by arguing, but by trying. And yet they too, trusting entirely to the force of their understanding, applied no rule, but made everything turn upon hard thinking and perpetual working and exercise of the mind.

Now my method, though hard to practise, is easy to explain; and it is this. I propose to establish progressive stages of certainty. The evidence of the sense, helped and guarded by a certain process of correction, I retain. But the mental operation which follows the act of sense I for the most part reject; and instead of it I open and lay out a new and certain path for the mind to proceed in, starting directly from the simple sensuous perception. The necessity of this was felt no doubt by those who attributed so much importance to Logic; showing thereby that they were in search of helps for the understanding, and had no confidence in the native and spontaneous process of the mind. But this remedy comes too late to do any good, when the mind is already, through the daily intercourse and conversation of life, occupied with unsound doctrines and beset on all sides by vain imaginations. And therefore that art of Logic, coming (as I said) too late to the rescue, and no way able to set matters right again, has had the effect of fixing errors rather than disclosing truth. There remains but one course for the recovery of a sound and healthy condition,—namely, that the entire work of the understanding be commenced afresh, and the mind itself be from the very outset not left to take its own course, but guided at every step; and the business be done as if by machinery. . . .

There remains simple experience; which, if taken as it comes, is called accident; if sought for, experiment. But this kind of experience is no better than a broom without its band, as the saying is— a mere groping, as of men in the dark, that feel all round them for the chance of finding their way; when they had much better wait for daylight, or light a candle, and then go. But the true method of experience on the contrary first lights the candle, and then by means of the candle shows the way; commencing as it does with experience duly ordered and digested, not bungling or erratic, and from it educing axioms, and from established axioms again new experiments; even as it was not without order and method that the divine word operated on the created mass. Let men therefore cease to wonder that the course of science is not yet wholly run, seeing that they have gone altogether astray; either leaving and abandoning experience entirely, or losing their way in

it and wandering round and round as in a labyrinth; whereas a method rightly ordered leads by an unbroken route through the woods of experience to the open ground of axioms. . . .

Now my directions for the interpretation of nature embrace two generic divisions; the one how to educe and form axioms from experience; the other how to deduce and derive new experiments from axioms. The former again is divided into three ministrations; a ministration to the sense, a ministration to the memory, and a ministration to the mind or reason.

For first of all we must prepare a *Natural and Experimental History,* sufficient and good; and this is the foundation of all; for we are not to imagine or suppose, but to discover, what nature does or may be made to do.

But natural and experimental history is so various and diffuse, that it confounds and distracts the understanding, unless it be ranged and presented to view in a suitable order. We must therefore form *Tables and Arrangements of Instances,* in such a method and order that the understanding may be able to deal with them.

And even when this is done, still the understanding, if left to itself and its own spontaneous movements, is incompetent and unfit to form axioms, unless it be directed and guarded. Therefore in the third place we must use *Induction,* true and legitimate induction, which is the very key of interpretation. . . .

Natural History, which in its subject (as I said) is threefold, is in its use twofold. For it is used either for the sake of the knowledge of the particular things which it contains, or as the primary material of philosophy and the stuff and subject-matter of true induction. And it is this latter which is now in hand; now, I say, for the first time. . . . And the chief part of the matter rests in this: that they who shall hereafter take it upon them to write natural history should bear this continually in mind—that they ought not to consult the pleasure of the reader, no, nor even the utility which may be derived immediately from their narrations; but to seek out and gather together such store and variety of things as may suffice for the formation of true axioms [natural laws]. Let them but remember this, and they will find out for themselves the method in which the history should be composed. For the end rules the method. . . .

And therefore there are three things upon which men should be warned to be sparing of their labour—as those which will immensely increase the mass of the work, and add little or nothing to its worth.

First then, away with antiquities, and citations or testimonies of authors; also with disputes and controversies and differing opinions; everything in short which is philological. Never cite an author except in a matter of doubtful credit: never introduce a controversy unless in a matter of great moment. And for all that concerns ornaments of speech, similitudes, treasury of eloquence, and such like emptinesses, let it be utterly dismissed. . . .

Secondly, that superfluity of natural histories in descriptions and pictures of species, and the curious variety of the same, is not much to the purpose. For small varieties of this kind are only a kind of sports and wanton freaks of nature; and come near to the nature of individuals. . . . The information they yield to the sciences is slight and almost superfluous.

Thirdly, all superstitious stories (I do not say stories of prodigies, when the report appears to be faithful and probable; but superstitious stories) and experiments of ceremonial magic should be altogether rejected.

6 THE GEOGRAPHICAL RENAISSANCE AND BEGINNINGS OF OVERSEAS EMPIRES

1. Expanding Geographical Knowledge

A number of Renaissance efforts combined to enlarge men's geographical knowledge, and culminated in the voyages of Christopher Columbus and Vasco da Gama. The revival of ancient literature reintroduced to Europeans the geographical knowledge of the ancients; commercial competition of western Europeans with the Italian cities which had monopolized trade with the Orient led to demands for new routes to the East; the prestige and wealth-seeking desires of national monarchs and of their adventurous subjects impelled them to seek new lands, new trade, and new allies; religious enthusiasm motivated both kings and clergy who sought to enlarge Christendom, to strengthen it against the infidel Turk, and to rescue pagan souls from eternal torment; and the inventions of several obscure navigators, sailors, and shipwrights so improved the seaworthiness of sailing craft and the art of open-sea navigation that such intrepid souls as Columbus could voyage afar and safely grope their way home again.

Ancient Greeks and Romans had had fairly accurate knowledge of a limited part of the world, the Mediterranean Basin. Almost without exception they believed the world to be spherical in shape, but theirs was a much smaller sphere than later generations learned to be the fact. Ancient geographical knowledge was summarized and transmitted to posterity by the works of Ptolemy (Claudius Ptolemaeus), a second-century Greco-Egyptian astronomer, mathematician, and geographer. But Ptolemy knew nothing about the New World, and his world map left no space for it. Instead, it extended Africa over the entire Southern Hemisphere in such a way as to render hopeless any attempt to sail around it to India. Moreover, Ptolemy's map showed the Arabian and the Malay peninsulas joined in such a way as to make the Indian Ocean a closed sea wholly unapproachable by way of the South Atlantic. Anyone who accepted Ptolemy's map would never have attempted to reach India by sailing west from Europe. The plan was unthinkable until scholars had found reason to dispute Ptolemy's accuracy, until reports of overland travelers to the East had cast doubt upon it further, and until European mariners had cautiously explored the west coast of Africa and found the way to sail around the Dark Continent into the Indian Ocean.

How and by whom some of this information was obtained is unknown. Italian sailors ventured out into the Atlantic; overland travelers, traders, and missionaries brought back information and rumor from the Orient; and gradually these stray bits of intelligence fitted together in the minds of practical seamen and demonstrated the inaccuracy and inadequacy of old maps. Renaissance scholars, by comparing ancient accounts, reached similar conclusions. For example, Roger Bacon (1210-1292, see page 53), in his *Opus majus,* demonstrated the feasibility—in opposition to Ptolemy—of reaching India by sailing west from Spain. About a century afterward, two sets of isolated events combined to accelerate greatly the geographical Renaissance. One set consisted of the publication of several important books in the decade 1410-1420, including a Latin translation of Ptolemy's *Geography* and the cosmographical works of Cardinal Pierre d'Ailly; the other was the beginning of the first systematic efforts of the Portuguese toward geographical exploration. The significance of Petrus de Aliaco, better known as Cardinal Pierre d'Ailly, Archbishop of Cambrai, is well summarized in the following account by an English scholar.

CARDINAL PIERRE D'AILLY (1330-1420)

From NEWTON, *Travellers of the Middle Ages* (1926) [1]

D'Ailly's work relating to geographical and astronomical speculations and the reform of the calendar is contained in a series of short treatises which are bound up with some of the writings of Jean Gerson in the unique edition which was printed at Louvain after 1480, but many MSS. copies of the treatise are extant showing how much they circulated in the fifteenth century. The most important treatise is the first in the published volume

[1] Arthur Percival Newton, ed., *Travel and Travellers of the Middle Ages,* 1926, 13-15, 18. Reprinted by permission of Alfred A. Knopf, Inc.

called *Tractatus de Imagine Mundi*. It was written in 1410 when d'Ailly knew the astronomical work of Ptolemy in his *Almagest*, but had not yet read his *Geography*, first translated into Latin in that year. Three years later in 1413 d'Ailly, having read the new translations, wrote another geographical work, the *Compendium Cosmographiae*, especially to summarize the useful things contained in Ptolemy's *Geographiae Syntaxis*, and he is therefore not only the last of medieval geographers before the Ptolemaic revival, but also the first of the Western scholars who began that revival and thus had so great an influence on thought. Besides these two treatises d'Ailly also drew a mappemonde to illustrate his geographical ideas and wrote a short explanatory note, the *Epilogus Mappe Mundi*, to accompany it. . . .

"The earth is spherical," he writes in the seventh chapter of his *Imago Mundi*, "and the Western ocean is relatively small. Aristotle pretends, contrary to Ptolemy, that more than a quarter of the whole globe is inhabited, and Averroes sustains the same opinion. The Stagyrite affirms also that the extent of sea is small between the coast of Spain in the West and the shores of India in the East. We are not concerned here with the actual Spain, but with the Further Spain, which is Africa. Seneca asserts that one can traverse that sea in a few days if the wind is favourable. Again, Pliny teaches us that ships from the Gulf of Arabia can arrive in a short time at Gades in the South of Spain. Whence we conclude that the sea is not big enough to cover three-quarters of the globe. Esdras affirms in his fourth book that six parts of the earth are habitable and inhabited and that the seventh part alone is covered by the waters. The authority of that work has been recognized by the saints, who have made use of it for confirming the sacred verities. Beyond

Thule, the last island of the Ocean, after one day's sail the sea is frozen and stiff. At the Poles there live great ghosts and ferocious beasts, the enemies of man. Water abounds there, because those places are cold, and cold multiplies humours [or vapours]."

In the forty-eighth chapter he tells us: "Thus the water runs from one Pole to the other forming a sea which extends between the extremity of Spain and the beginning of India, of small width, in such a way that the beginning of India comes to beyond the half of the equinoctial line [that is, in the other hemisphere], a situation very near to that which the end of our hemisphere occupies."

In the forty-ninth chapter he uses another argument that he had borrowed from Aristotle: "The west coast of Africa cannot be far removed from the east coast of India, for in both those countries elephants are found."

Now the greatest interest of these and similar extracts from d'Ailly is that they are of fundamental importance in governing the ideas of the last of the medieval travellers, Christopher Columbus. It has now been proved that practically the only books on cosmogony that were familiar to him were two—the *Imago Mundi* of d'Ailly, published between 1480 and 1487, and the *Historia rerum ubique gestarum* of Aeneas Silvius (Pope Pius II), published at Venice in 1477. There are still preserved in the Library of the Colombine at Seville the original copies of these books that were used by Christopher and his brother Bartholomew, and their margins are filled from end to end with remarks and notes in their own hands. . . .

The striking fact was . . . that the Cardinal [d'Ailly] had lifted this passage bodily and almost literally from Roger Bacon's treatise the *Opus Majus*. The demonstration is unmistakable and added to other evidence of a similar sort it shows us that the world of Columbus, who has long been credited in the popular view with a foremost position among the leaders of the Renaissance, was emphatically the world of the Middle Age. Columbus in 1498 cribbed his views from d'Ailly who wrote in 1410, d'Ailly cribbed from Roger Bacon whose work dates from 1267, Roger Bacon derives through the Arabs from the Greeks. The most famous of the explorers of the new age, in fact, drew none of his ideas directly from the newly recovered geographical literature of the Greeks as did the true Renaissance thinkers like Peter Martyr or Damian Goes. The discovery of a new world was accomplished not with Greek or modern geographical concepts but with medieval.

PRINCE HENRY, "THE NAVIGATOR" (1394-1460)

To Prince Henry of Portugal belongs the credit for the first systematic geographical exploration in the Renaissance era. Third son of King John I and his English Queen, Philippa of Lancaster, the Infant Henry was not likely to fall heir to the crown and, though he might have idled away his life, he chose to be a student and a seaman. Henry's interest was kindled when, in 1415, during the perennial struggle against the Moslem Moors, Portuguese forces captured Ceuta, on the north coast of Africa. At Ceuta, Henry learned of caravans which penetrated the interior of Africa to trade with non-Moslem peoples. A medieval legend told of the mighty Christian kingdom of Prester John [Abyssinia] to which Henry supposed these caravans went. Why not establish contacts by sea with these peoples, set up profitable trade relations, and ally with these Christians to drive the Moors from Africa? To this ambition, the Prince

added other motives: to find a sea route around Africa to India, to capture the profitable East Indian trade, to found a great Eastern empire for Portugal, and to carry the blessings of Christianity to African and Oriental pagans. Toward the realization of these ends, Prince Henry devoted nearly fifty years of his life. The following selection describes Prince Henry's achievements.

From BEAZLEY, *Prince Henry the Navigator* (1901) [1]

After the capture of Ceuta, in 1415, he planted himself in his Naval Arsenal at Sagres, close to Lagos town and Cape St. Vincent, and for more than forty years, till his death in 1460, he kept his mind upon the ocean that stretched out from that rocky headland to the unknown West and South. Twice only for any length of time did he come back into political life; for the rest, though respected as the referee of national disputes and the leader and teacher of the people, his time was mainly spent in thinking out his plans of discovery—drawing his maps, adjusting his instruments, sending out his ships, receiving the reports of his captains. . . . The old "Sacred Cape" of the Romans, then called Sagres, now the "Cape St. Vincent" of Nelson and modern maps, was his chosen home for the next forty years, though he seems to have passed a good deal of his time in his port of Lagos, close by.

In 1419 King John made him Governor for life of the Algarvos (the southern province of Portugal) and the new governor at once began to rebuild and enlarge the old naval arsenal, in the neck of the Cape, into a settlement that soon became the "Prince's Town." In Lagos, his ships were built and manned; and there, and in

[1] From C. Raymond Beazley, *Prince Henry the Navigator*, 1901, 138-39, 160-62, 170-75, 309-10. Courtesy of G. P. Putnam's Sons.

Sagres itself, all the schemes of discovery were thought out, the maps and instruments corrected, and the accounts of past and present travellers compared by the Prince himself. His results then passed into the instructions of his captains and the equipment of his caravels. The Sacred Cape, which he now colonised, was at any rate a good centre for his work of ocean voyaging. . . .

On this he now built himself a palace, a chapel, a study, an observatory—the earliest in Portugal—and a village for his helpers and attendants. "In his wish to gain a prosperous result for his efforts, the Prince devoted great industry and thought to the matter, and at great expense procured the aid of one Master Jacome from Majorca, a man skilled in the art of navigation and in the making of maps and instruments, and who was sent for, with certain of the Arab and Jewish mathematicians, to instruct the Portuguese in that science." So at least, says De Barros, the "Livy of Portugal." At Sagres was thus founded anew the systematic study of applied science in Christendom; it was better than the work of the old Greek "University" at Alexandria with which it has been compared, because it was essentially practical. From it "our sailors," says Pedro Nunes, "went out well taught and provided with instruments and rules which all mapmakers should know." . . . To Prince Henry's study and science two great improvements on this side may be traced: first in the art of map-making, secondly in the building of caravels and ocean craft. . . .

Bojador [on the west coast of Africa], the "paunch" or "bulging Cape," 180 miles beyond Cape Non, had been, since the days of the Laurentian Portulano (1351), and the Catalan and Portuguese voyages of 1341 and 1346, the southmost point of Christian knowledge. A long circuit was needed here, as at the Cape of Good Hope, to round a promontory that stretched, men said, fully one hundred miles into the ocean, where tides and shoals formed a current twenty miles across. It was the sight or the fancy of this furious surge which frightened Henry's crews, for it plainly forbade all coasting and compelled the seamen to strike into the open sea out of sight of land. And though the discovery of Porto Santo had proved the feasibility and the gain of venturing boldly into the Sea of Darkness, and though since that time (1418) the Prince had sent out his captains due west to the Azores and southwest to Madeira, both hundreds of miles from the continent, yet in rounding Bojador there were not only the real terrors of the Atlantic, but the legends of the tropics to frighten back the boldest.

Most mariners had heard it said that any Christian who passed Bojador would infallibly be changed into a black, and would carry to his end this mark of God's vengeance on his insolent prying. . . . And it was beyond the Cape which bounded their knowledge that the Saracen geographers had fringed the coast of Africa with sea-monsters and serpent rocks and water unicorns, instead of place names, and had drawn the horrible giant head of Satan raised above the waves to seize the first of his human prey that would venture into his den. . . . It was this ingrained superstition that Henry found his worst enemy, appearing as it did sometimes even in his most trusted and daring captains.

And then again, the legends of Tropical Africa, of the mainland beyond Bojador, were hardly less terrible than those of the Tropical Ocean. . . . Here only the northern parts could be lived in by man. In the south and central deserts, as we have heard from the Moslem doctors themselves, the sun poured down sheets of liquid flame upon the ground and kept the sea and the rivers boiling day and night with the fiery heat. So any sailors would of course be boiled alive as soon as they got near to the Torrid Zone.

It was this kind of learning, discredited but not forgotten, that was still in the minds of Gil Eannes and his friends when they came home in 1433, with lame excuses, to Henry's Court. The currents and south winds had stopped them, they said. It was impossible to get round Bojador.

The Prince was roused. He ordered the same captain to return the next year and try the cape again. His men ought to have learned something better than the childish fables of past time. "And if," said he, "there were even any truth in these stories that they tell, I would not blame you, but you come to me with the tales of four seamen who perhaps know the voyage to the Low Countries or some other coasting route, but, except for this, don't know how to use needle or sailing chart. Go out again and heed them not, for by God's help, fame and profit must come from your voyage, if you will but persevere." . . .

[And so Prince Henry] sent out Gil Eannes in 1434 under the strongest charge not to return without a good account of the Cape and the seas beyond. Running far out into the open, his caravel doubled Bojador, and coming back to the coast found the sea "as easy to sail in as the waters at home," and the land very rich and pleasant. They landed and discovered no trace of men or houses, but gathered plants, "such as were called in Portugal St. Mary's roses," to present to Don Henry. Not even the southern Cape of Tempests or Good Hope was so long and obstinate a barrier as Bojador had been, and the passing of this difficulty proved the salvation of the Prince's schemes. . . . Never again was there a serious danger of the failure of the whole movement through general opposition and discontent. . . . [The next year, 1435, Gil Eannes and

Alfonso Baldaya, Prince Henry's cup-bearer, sailed again beyond Bojador; and Baldaya returned the same year to land on the continent and, through "two young noble gentlemen" on horseback, to scour the immediate countryside.]

This first landing of Europeans on the coasts of unknown Africa, since the days of Carthaginian colonies, is one of the great moments in the story of Western expansion and discovery. For it means that Christendom on her Western side has at last got beyond the first circle of her enemies, the belt of settled Moslem ground, and has begun to touch the wider world outside, on the shore of the ocean as well as along the Eastern trade routes. . . .

THE RESULTS OF PRINCE HENRY'S WORK

Just as we cannot see how that work of his could have been done without each and every part of that many-sided preparation in the history of the past, so it is quite as difficult to see how the great achievements of the generation that followed him and of the century, that wonderful sixteenth century, which followed the age of Henry's courtiers and disciples, could have been realised without the impetus he had given and the knowledge he had spread.

For it was not merely that his seamen had broken down the middle wall of superstitious terror and had pierced through into the unknown South for a distance of nearly two thousand miles; it was not merely that between 1412 and 1460 Europeans passed the limits of the West and of the South, as legend had so long fixed them; not merely that the most difficult part of the African coast, between Bojador and the Gulf of Guinea, had been fairly passed and that the waterway to India was more than half found. . . .

But there was more than this. Henry did not only accomplish the first and most difficult steps of his own great central project, the finding of the way round

Africa to India; he not only began the conversion of the natives, the civilisation of the coast tribes and the colonisation of certain trading sites; he also founded that school of thought and practice which made all the great discoveries that have so utterly eclipsed his own.

From that school came Columbus, who found a western route to India, starting from the suggestion of Henry's attempt by south and east; Bartholomew Diaz, who reached and rounded the southernmost point of the old-world continent and laid open the Indian Ocean to European sailors [1486]; Da Gama, who was the first of those sailors to reap the full advantage of the work of ninety years, the first who sailed from Lisbon to Calicut and back again [1498]; Albuquerque, who founded the first colonial empire of Modern Europe, the first great out-settlement of Christendom, the Portuguese trade dominion in the East; Magellan, who finally proved what all the great discoverers were really assuming—the roundness of the world; the nameless adventurers who seem to have touched Australia some time before 1530; the draughtsmen who left us our first true map of the globe. So it is not in the actual things done by the Prince's efforts that we can measure his importance in history. It is because his work was infinitely suggestive, because he laid a right foundation for the onward movement of Europe and Christendom, because he was the leader of a true Renaissance and Reformation, that he is so much more than a figure in the story of Portugal.

2. The Portuguese Eastern Empire

After Prince Henry's death in 1460, the Portuguese monarchy continued the work of his "school." In 1486, Bartholomew Diaz, one of Prince Henry's students, rounded the Cape of Good Hope; and in 1498, Vasco da Gama, following Diaz's sailing instructions, reached India. Within a few years, under the leadership of Cabral, Almeida, and Albuquerque, a Portuguese empire was developed in the East Indies. This short-lived empire—short-lived because of shortsighted policies of Portuguese kings and because Portugal did not possess the resources to hold a vast empire in competition with other European states—is described in the following selection.

From LORD ACTON, *Lectures on Modern History* (1930) [1]

The Portuguese came to India as traders, not as conquerors, and desired not territory, but portable and exchangeable commodities. But the situation they found out there compelled them to wage war in unknown seas, divided from supports, and magazines, and docks by nearly half the globe. They made no attempt on the interior, for the Malabar coast was shut off by a range of lofty mountains. Their main object was the trade of the Far East, which was concentrated at Calicut. . . . But on the other side of the isthmus the carrying trade, all the way to the Pacific, was in the hands of Moors from Arabia and Egypt. . . . They possessed the monopoly of that which the Portuguese had come to take, and they were enemies of the Christian name. . . . A deadly conflict could not be avoided. . . . In 1509 their [the Moors'] fleet was defeated by the [Portuguese] Viceroy Almeida near Diu, off the coast of Kattywar. . . . It was his [Almeida's] last action before he surrendered power to his rival, the great Albuquerque. . . .

Almeida's successor, who had the eye of

[1] From *Lectures on Modern History by John Emerich Edward Dalberg-Acton*, ed. by J. N. Figgis and R. V. Laurence, 1930, 53-59. By permission of The Macmillan Company.

Alexander the Great for strategic points and commercial centres, was convinced that sea-power, at six months from home, rests on the occupation of seaports, and he carried the policy forward so far that Portugal possessed fifty-two establishments, commanding 15,000 miles of coast, and held them, nominally, with 20,000 men. . . . He made Goa the impregnable capital of his prodigious empire. . . .

The secret of Portuguese prosperity was the small bulk and the enormous market value of the particular products in which they dealt. In those days men had to do without tea, or coffee, or chocolate, or tobacco, or quinine, or cocoa, or vanilla, and sugar was very rare. But there were the pepper and the ginger of Malabar, cardamoms in the damp district of Tellicherry; cinnamon and pearls in Ceylon. Beyond the Bay of Bengal, near the equator, there was opium, the only conqueror of pain then known; there were frankincense and indigo; camphor in Borneo; nutmeg and mace in Amboyna; and in two small islands, only a few miles square, Ternate and Tidor, there was the clove tree, surpassing all plants in value. These were the real spice islands, the enchanted region which was the object of such passionate desire; and their produce was so cheap on the spot, so dear in the markets of Antwerp and London, as to constitute the most lucrative trade in the world. From these exotics, grown on volcanic soil, in the most generous of the tropical climates, the profit was such that they could be paid for in precious metals. When Drake was at Ternate in 1579, he found the Sultan hung with chains of bullion, and clad in a robe of gold brocade rich enough to stand upright. The Moluccas were of greater benefit to the Crown than to the Portuguese workman. About twenty ships, of 100 to 550 tons, sailed for Lisbon in the year. A voyage sometimes lasted two years, out and home,

and cost, including the ship, over £4000 [nearly $20,000]. But the freight might amount to £150,000. Between 1497 and 1612 the number of vessels engaged in the India trade was 806. Of these, ninety-six were lost. After the annexation by Philip II, Lisbon was closed to countries at war with Spain. Dutch and English had to make their own bargains in the East, and treated Portugal as an enemy. Their empire declined rapidly, and the Dutch acquired the islands long before the English succeeded on the mainland of India.

3. Columbus and the Beginnings of the Spanish Empire in America

For nearly a decade before 1492, Christopher Columbus (1451-1506) had been presenting his scheme of sailing westward to the Indies to European sovereigns without gaining their support. Columbus' experience embraced both practical navigation in the Portuguese service and the study of Cardinal Pierre d'Ailly's works [see page 72]. In vain he sought a royal sponsor, first in Portugal (1482), then in Spain, then in England. His plan was too bold, too expensive, and Columbus' terms were considered exorbitant, for he demanded all expenses, noble rank, the title of admiral, the viceroyalty of all lands discovered, and one tenth the value of their trade. Finally, however, after Ferdinand and Isabella had captured Granada and expelled the Moors from Spain (January, 1492), Columbus renewed his suit to them and, by a royal commission dated April 30, 1492, won the Spanish monarchs' support for his venture on the terms he had demanded.

Columbus began his first transatlantic voyage on August 3, 1492. He arrived in the West Indies on October 12, spent several months exploring the islands, which he was sure were bordering upon the empire of the Great Khan, and returned to Spain in March, 1493. Stopping at the Canary Islands on his voyage homeward, Columbus wrote (February 15, 1493) the following letter describing his discoveries to Luis de Santangel, Chancellor of the Aragon Exchequer. It is one of the earliest of a long series of accounts by European explorers who, anxious to impress their patrons back home, and misled by wishful interpretations of natives' "tall tales," misrepresent the nature of their discoveries and exaggerate the profits to be expected from them.

COLUMBUS' REPORT OF HIS FIRST VOYAGE (1493)

From COLUMBUS, Letter to Louis de Santangel (1493) [1]

SIR, Believing that you will take pleasure in hearing of the great success which our Lord has granted me in my voyage, I write you this letter, whereby you will learn how in thirty-three day's time I reached the Indies with the fleet which the most illustrious King and Queen, our Sovereigns, gave to me, where I found very many islands thickly peopled, of all which I took possession without resistance for their Highnesses by proclamation made and with the royal standard unfurled. To the first island that I found I gave the name of San Salvador, in remembrance of His High Majesty, who hath marvellously brought all these things to pass; the Indians call it Guanaham. To the second island I gave the name of Santa-Maria de Concepción; the third I called

Fernandina; the fourth, Isabella; the fifth, Juana; and so to each one I gave a new name. When I reached Juana, I followed its coast to the westward, and found it so large that I thought it must be the mainland—the province of Cathay; and, as I found neither towns nor villages on the sea-coast, but only a few hamlets, with the inhabitants of which I could not hold conversation, because they all immediately fled, I kept on the same route, thinking that I could not fail to light upon some large cities and towns. At length . . . I saw another island to the eastward at a distance of eighteen leagues from the former, to which I gave the name of La Española [Hispaniola]. Thither I went, and followed its northern coast. . . . This island, like all the others, is extraordinarily large. . . . In the interior there are many mines of metals and a population innumerable. Española is a wonder. Its mountains and plains, and meadows, and fields, are so beautiful and rich for planting and sowing, and rearing cattle of all kinds, and for building towns and villages. The harbours on the coast, and the number and size and wholesomeness of the rivers, most of them bearing gold, surpass anything that would be believed by one who had not seen them. There is a great difference between the trees, fruits, and plants of this island and those of Juana. In this island there are many spices and extensive mines of gold and other metals. The inhabitants of this and of all the other islands I have found or gained intelligence of, both men and women, go as naked as they were born, with the exception that some of the women cover one part only with a single leaf of grass or with a piece of cotton, made for that purpose. They have neither iron, nor steel, nor arms, nor are they competent to use them, not that they are not well-formed and of handsome stature, but because they are timid to a surprising

---

[1] Select Letters of Christopher Columbus, ed. by R. H. Major, 2nd ed., The Hakluyt Society, London, 1870, 1-18.

degree. . . . [When Columbus had reassured them and overcome their fear,
he entered into trading relations and
found them very gullible.] They are not
acquainted with any kind of worship,
and are not idolators; but believe that all
power and, indeed, all good things are
in heaven; and they are firmly convinced
that I, with my vessels and crews, came
from heaven, and with this belief received
me at every place at which I touched, after
they had overcome their apprehension.
. . . [Columbus describes rumors of other
islands with strange inhabitants "born
with a tail," of others who are cannibals,
of one island inhabited by women only,
and of a curious race of hairless people.]
Although I have taken possession of all
these islands in the name of their Highnesses, and they are all more abundant in
wealth than I am able to express . . .
yet there was one large town in *Española*
of which especially I took possession, situated in a locality well adapted for the
working of the gold mines, and for all
kinds of commerce, either with the main
land on this side, or with that beyond
which is the land of the great Khan, with
which there will be vast commerce and
great profit. To that city I gave the name
of *Villa de Navidad,* and fortified it with
a fortress, which by this time will be
quite completed, and I have left in it a
sufficient number of men with arms, artillery, and provisions for more than a year,
a barge, and a sailing master skilful in
the arts necessary for building others. I
have also established the greatest friendship with the king of that country, so
much so that he took pride in calling me
his brother, and treating me as such. Even
should these people change their intentions towards us and become hostile, they
do not know what arms are, but, as I have
said, go naked, and are the most timid
people in the world; so that the men I
have left could, alone, destroy the whole

country, and this island has no danger for
them, if they only know how to conduct
themselves. . . . Finally, and speaking
only of what has taken place in this
voyage, which has been so hasty, their
Highnesses may see that I shall give them
all the gold they require, if they will give
me but a very little assistance; spices also,
and cotton, as much as their Highnesses
shall command to be shipped; and mastic,
hitherto found only in Greece . . . slaves,
as many of these idolators as their Highnesses shall command to be shipped. I
think also I have found rhubarb and
cinnamon, and I shall find a thousand
other valuable things by means of the men
that I have left behind me. . . . Much
more I would have done if my vessels
had been in as good a condition as by
rights they ought to have been. . . . But
our Redeemer hath granted this victory to
our illustrious King and Queen and their
kingdoms, which have acquired great fame
by an event of such high importance, in
which all Christendom ought to rejoice,
and which it ought to celebrate with great
festivals and the offering of solemn thanks
to the Holy Trinity with many solemn
prayers, both for the great exaltation
which may accrue to them in turning so
many nations to our holy faith, and also
for the temporal benefits which will bring
great refreshment and gain, not only to
Spain, but to all Christians. This, thus
briefly, in accordance with the events.

Done on board the caravel, off the
Canary Islands, on the fifteenth of February, fourteen hundred and ninety-three.

At your orders.

The Admiral

HOW CORTEZ TOOK MONTEZUMA PRISONER (1519)

Hernando Cortez (1485-1547) arrived in Hispaniola in 1504 and announced to the Governor's secretary,

"I came to get gold, not to till the soil, like a peasant." These words aptly described the motives of the Spanish conquistadors. Cortez served the Governor in various military capacities, and in 1519 was appointed Captain General of an expedition to explore the coast of Central America. Landing in Mexico, he founded the city of Vera Cruz, double-crossed the Governor of Hispaniola by renouncing allegiance to him and by placing himself directly under the authority of the King of Spain, and sank his fleet so that his men could not turn back from Mexico. Then, by a cunning mixture of diplomacy and force, he gained entrance to what is now Mexico City as guest of Montezuma, the Aztec overlord of the Mexican Empire. The following is a contemporary account of how Cortez made a prisoner of his host. Subsequently, he ruled Mexico through Montezuma, filched the Emperor's vast treasures, and collected taxes in his name for the King of Spain. When Montezuma's outraged subjects rebelled and killed their erstwhile Emperor, Cortez, after many vicissitudes, conquered the whole of Mexico for Spain.

From GÓMARA, *The Pleasant Historie of the Conquest of the West Indies* (1519) [1]

Hernando Cortez and his company were five days in beholding and perusing the situation of the city [Mexico City] and secrets of the same. . . . They were often visited by Montezuma and the Gentlemen of his court, and abundantly provided of things necessary for his use. . . .

Likewise, his horses were cherished and

[1] Adapted from Francisco Lopez de Gómara's account as published in A. B. Hart, ed., *American History Told by Contemporaries*, 3 vols., 1929, I, 49-53. By permission of The Macmillan Company.

served with green barley and grass, whereof there is plenty all the year: likewise of corn, meal, roses, and of all things that their owners would request, in so much that beds of flowers were made for them in place of litter. But yet notwithstanding, although they were in this sort cherished, and also lodged in so rich a country where they might fill their purses, they were not yet all content and merry, but rather [beset] with great fear and care; especially Cortez, who had the sole responsibility as head and chief Captain for the defence of his fellows. He (I say) was pensive, noting the situation of the city, the infinite number of people, the state and majesty of Mexico, yea, and some disquietness of his own Company, who would come and lay unto his charge the snare and net that they were in, in thinking it a thing impossible that any of them could escape, if Montezuma were thereunto determined. . . . And to remedy the peril and danger that he stood in, he determined to apprehend Montezuma, and to build four forts to hold the lake in subjection, which he had before imagined; and without the apprehension of the King, he could not come by the Kingdom. . . .

The quarrel wherewith he had armed himself for that purpose was that the Lord Qualpopoca [one of Montezuma's vassals] had slain nine Spaniards; likewise he was driven to make good his boast to the Emperor Charles [Charles V], his king, to whom he had written that he would take Montezuma prisoner and dispossess him of his Empire. These causes considered, he took the letters of Pedro Hircio [from the garrison left at Vera Cruz], wherein was written how Qualpopoca was the cause of the death of nine Spaniards, put these letters in his pocket, and walking up and down his lodgings . . . full of care of the great enterprise that he had in hand . . . he chanced to espy one wall whiter than the rest, and beholding the same, he saw that it was a door làtely dammed up; and calling unto him two of his servants (for all the rest were asleep) . . . he opened that door and went in, and there found sundry halls, some with Idols, some with gallant feathers, Jewels, precious stones, plate, yea, and such an infinite quantity of gold that the sight thereof amazed him. . . . He shut this door again as well as he could, without touching any part of that treasure, because he would not make any uproar thereabout, nor yet to delay the imprisonment of Montezuma, for that treasure was always there to be had.

The next day in the morning came certain Spaniards unto him . . . saying that the Citizens did go about to conspire their death. . . . So that with this news, whether true or false, Cortez left the one half of his men to defend and keep his lodging, and at every cross street he planted men; and the residue he sent to the Court two by two and three by three, and he himself came to the palace, saying that he must talk with Montezuma on a matter of life and death. Cortez was secretly armed. Montezuma, hearing that Cortez attended him, came forth and received him, taking him by the hand, and placed him in his seat. Thirty Spaniards waited upon Cortez and the rest abode without the door.

Cortez saluted Montezuma according to his accustomed manner, and began to jest and talk merrily as he was wont to do. Montezuma, being unaware of the thing that Fortune had prepared against him, was also very merry and pleased with the conversation. He gave unto Cortez Jewels of gold, and one of his daughters, and other noble men's daughters to others of his company. Cortez received the gift, for otherwise it had been an affront unto Montezuma. But yet he informed him that he was a married man,

and that he could not marry with his daughter, for the Christian law did not permit it. . . .

After all this talk ended, Cortez took the letters of Pedro Hircio and caused them to be interpreted unto Montezuma, making his grievous complaint against Qualpopoca, who had slain so many Spaniards. . . .

Montezuma excused himself earnestly . . . saying that the report given out against his subjects was false, and as for Qualpopoca who had slain the Spaniards, he was innocent thereof; and in order that he should know the truth, he called certain of his servants and commanded them to fetch Qualpopoca before him as quickly as possible.

Cortez replied and said, "My Lord, your highness must go with me to my lodging and there abide until your messengers return with Qualpopoca and the certainty of the death of my men. In my lodging your highness shall rule and command as you do here in Court, your person shall be well used. . . ."

Montezuma was sore amazed, saying, "Sir, my person is not fit to be a prisoner; yea, and though I would permit the same, my subjects would not suffer it."

They abode arguing the matter nearly four hours, and at length Montezuma was content to go, being promised that he should rule and govern as he was wont to do. . . .

When it was blown abroad in the city that Montezuma was carried prisoner to the Spaniards, all the city was in an uproar; but yet Montezuma did comfort the Gentlemen that carried and followed him weeping, praying them to cease their lamentation, saying that he was not prisoner, nor yet went with the Christians against his will, but for his own pleasure. Cortez appointed a Spanish guard for him, with a Captain . . . and had Spaniards always in his company. . . . Cortez always entreated him to put off sadness, to be merry, permitting him to dispatch messengers, to deal in all affairs of his estate, and to commune and talk openly or secretly with his noblemen as he was wont to do; and that was only a bait to bring them to the hook. There was never Greek nor Roman, nor any other nation since the name of kings was ordained, did give the like enterprize as Hernando Cortez did, in taking Montezuma prisoner in his own house, being a most mighty King in a most strong fort among infinite people, he [Cortez] having but only 450 companions.

PIZARRO'S CONQUEST OF PERU
(1531-1532)

Francisco Pizarro (c. 1471-1541), a Spanish adventurer of illegitimate birth, turned up in Hispaniola in 1510. He was with Balboa in Panama and in 1524 began a series of expeditions by sea along the west coast of South America. In 1528, he went to Spain and gained a commission from Charles V to explore Peru and to govern it. Returning to Panama, he crossed the isthmus, sailed to Peru, crossed the Andes and, in imitation of Cortez's exploits in Mexico, seized Atahuallpa, ruler of the Inca monarchy, and made himself master of Peru. The treasure seized exceeded even that taken in Mexico. Pizarro's brother, Hernando, accompanied him on the expedition and gives the following account of it.

From PIZARRO, Letter to the Royal Audience of Santo Domingo (November, 1533) [1]

I arrived in this port of Yaguana on my way to Spain, by order of the Governor Francisco Pizarro, to inform his Majesty of what has happened in that government of Peru, to give an account of the country, and of its present condition. . . .

The Governor, in the name of his Majesty, found a town near the sea coast, which was called San Miguel. . . . Having left citizens there, and assigned the Indians in the district to them, he set out with sixty horse and ninety foot, in search of the town of Caxamalca, at which place he was informed that Atahuallpa then was. . . . After seven or eight marches, a Captain of Atahuallpa came to the Governor, and said that his Lord had heard of his arrival and rejoiced greatly at it, having a strong desire to see the Christians. . . . The Governor continued his march until he came to a town called La Ramada. Up to that point all the land was flat, while all beyond was very rugged, and obstructed by very difficult passes . . . and neither horse nor foot can cross these mountains except by the roads. The distance across them to Caxamalca is twenty leagues.

When we were half way, messengers arrived from Atahuallpa, and brought provisions to the Governor. They said that Atahuallpa was waiting for him at Caxamalca, wishing to be his friend. . . . Two days afterwards the Governor came in sight of Caxamalca, and he met Indians with food. He put the troops in order, and marched to the town. Atahuallpa was not there, but was encamped on the plain. . . . When the Governor saw that Atahuallpa did not come, he sent a Captain . . . and he desired him to come that they might be friends. . . . He replied that he would come to see him on the following morning. . . .

That night a good look-out was kept. In the morning he sent messengers to put off his visit until the afternoon; and these messengers, in conversing with some

[1] "Letter from Hernando Pizarro to the Royal Audience of Santo Domingo," ed. and trans. by Clements R. Markham, in *Reports on the Discovery of Peru*, printed for the Hakluyt Society, London, 1872, 113-27.

Indian girls in the service of the Christians, who were their relations, told them to run away because Atahuallpa was coming that afternoon to attack the Christians and kill them. . . . Atahuallpa set out from his camp at noon, and when he came to a place which was about half a quarter of a league from Caxamalca, he stopped . . . pitched his tents, and formed his men in three divisions. . . . The Governor had ordered his troops to be distributed in the three halls which were in the open courtyard, in form of a triangle; and he ordered them to be mounted and armed until the intentions of Atahuallpa were known. Having pitched his tents, Atahuallpa sent a messenger to the Governor to say that, as it was now late, he wished to sleep where he was, and that he would come in the morning. The Governor sent back to beg him to come at once. . . . The messengers came back to ask the Governor to send a Christian to Atahuallpa, that he intended to come at once, and that he would come unarmed. The Governor sent a Christian, and presently Atahuallpa moved, leaving the armed men behind him. He took with him about five or six thousand Indians without arms, except that, under their shirts, they had small darts and slings with stones.

He came in a litter, and before him went three or four hundred Indians in liveries, cleaning the straws from the road and singing. Then came Atahuallpa in the midst of his chiefs and principal men, the greatest among them being also borne on men's shoulders. . . . A Dominican Friar, who was with the Governor, came forward to tell him, on the part of the Governor, that he waited for him in his lodgings, and that he was sent to speak with him. The Friar then told Atahuallpa that he was a Priest, and that he was sent there to teach the things of the Faith, if they should desire to be Christians. He showed Atahuallpa a book . . . and told

him that that book contained the things of God. Atahuallpa asked for the book, and threw it on the ground, saying: "I will not leave this place until you have restored all that you have taken in my land. I know well who you are, and what you have come for. . . ." The Friar went to the Governor and reported what was being done, and that no time was to be lost. The Governor sent to me; and I had arranged with the Captain of the artillery that, when a sign was given, he should discharge his pieces, and that, on hearing the reports, all the troops should come forth at once. This was done, and as the Indians were unarmed, they were defeated without danger to any Christian. Those who carried the litter, and the chiefs who surrounded Atahuallpa, were all killed, falling round him. The Governor came out and seized Atahuallpa, and in protecting him, he received a knifecut from a Christian in the hand. The troops continued the pursuit as far as the place where the armed Indians were stationed, who made no resistance whatever, because it was night. All were brought into town, where the Governor was quartered.

Next morning the Governor ordered us to go to the camp of Atahuallpa, where we found forty thousand *castellanos* and four or five thousand *marcos*[1] of silver. . . . The Governor said that he had not come to make war on the Indians, but that our Lord the Emperor, who was Lord of the whole world, had ordered him to come that he might see the land, and let Atahuallpa know the things of our Faith. . . . The Governor also told him that that land, and all other lands, belonged to the Emperor, and that he must acknowledge him as his Lord. He replied that he was content, and, observing that the Christians had collected some gold, Atahuallpa said

[1] A castellano was worth about $3, equal to about $12 in present-day purchasing power. A marco was about 8 ounces.

to the Governor that they need not take such care of it, as if there was so little; for that he could give them ten thousand plates, and that he could fill the room in which he was up to a white line, which was the height of a man and a half from the floor. The room was seventeen or eighteen feet wide, and thirty-five feet long. He said he could do this in two months. [Two months passed, and the writer was sent out with troops "to hurry the arrival of the gold"; he plundered a village and a great temple—"Altogether I collected 85,000 *castellanos* and 3000 *marcos* of silver."]

After returning to Caxamalca . . . the Governor . . . ordered me to go to Spain and to give an account to his Majesty. . . . I took then, from the heap of gold, 100,000 *castellanos* for his Majesty, being the amount of his fifth. The day after I left Caxamalca, the Christians, who had gone to Cuzco . . . brought 1,500,000 of gold. . . . They say that a distribution of gold was made; and that the share of his Majesty, besides the 100,000 *pesos*[1] and the 5000 *marcos* of silver that I bring, was another 165,000 *castellanos,* and 7000 or 8000 *marcos* of silver.

4. Some Effects of the New World upon the Old: The Price Revolution

EFFECTS OF AMERICAN TREASURE

The discovery of the New World had far-reaching effects upon Europe. It greatly enhanced the prestige of those monarchies which developed overseas empires; it opened up dazzling new

opportunities for "get-rich-quick" adventurers, merchants, land speculators, and others who could manage to find transportation across the Atlantic; it gave to European society important new foods, the potato and maize especially, a variety of new drugs, and a few new diseases. But its most important *immediate* effect was the sudden vast expansion it gave to the European world's monetary supply—with all the economic and social readjustments which followed. So marked were these effects that historians refer to them as the "monetary [or price] revolution" of the sixteenth century.

Cortez, Pizarro, and their successors not only seized the treasures they found at hand; they also enslaved the Indians and forced them to work in the mines for the further enrichment of their masters. Complicated governmental machinery was set up at Seville to collect, protect, transport, and evaluate the gold and silver from the New World. Yearly "plate fleets" sailed from New Spain to Seville laden with the precious metals and other products and protected by convoys against English, French, and later, Dutch "hijacking" sea dogs who constantly attempted to snatch the prizes. But they rarely succeeded, and sizable quantities of gold and silver poured into Spain from the time of Cortez's conquest of Mexico (1521) until about 1650, as is shown in the table on next page.

From HAMILTON, *American Treasure and the Price Revolution* (1934)[2]

The highest average "general price level" attained in Spain, in 1601–1625, was 3.18

---

[1] A peso was identical with the castellano; that is, about $3 each; 100,000 pesos was about $300,000, which was equal to about $1,200,000 in present-day purchasing power.

[2] This selection and the table on next page are reprinted by permission of the publishers from Earl J. Hamilton, *American Treasure and the Price Revolution in Spain, 1501-1650,* Harvard University Press, 1934, 42, 44-45, 199, 207, 210.

TOTAL DECENNIAL IMPORTS OF FINE GOLD AND SILVER
(*in grams*)

PERIOD	Silver	Gold
1503-1510	......	4,965,180
1511-1520	......	9,153,220
1521-1530	148,739	4,889,050
1531-1540	86,193,876	14,466,360
1541-1550	177,573,164	24,957,130
1551-1560	303,121,174	42,620,080
1561-1570	942,858,792	11,530,940
1571-1580	1,118,591,954	9,429,140
1581-1590	2,103,027,689	12,101,650
1591-1600	2,707,626,528	19,451,420
1601-1610	2,213,631,245	11,764,090
1611-1620	2,192,255,993	8,855,940
1621-1630	2,145,339,043	3,889,760
1631-1640	1,396,759,594	1,240,400
1641-1650	1,056,430,966	1,549,390
1651-1660	443,256,546	469,430
Totals 1503-1660	16,886,815,303	181,333,180. . . .

[This rapid expansion in the supply of precious metals led to a rapid rise in prices, first in Spain and then, as Spain spent much of her treasure for goods and services in Europe at large, prices rose everywhere with bewildering rapidity. In Spain, between 1501 and 1550, prices rose on the average by more than 50 per cent. During the second half of the sixteenth century they continued to rise, as the following table shows.]

DECENNIAL AVERAGES OF INDEX NUMBERS OF COMMODITY PRICES
1551-1600
Base: 1571-1580

DECADES	Andalusia	New Castile	Old Castile-León	Valencia
1551-1560	72.85	68.21	78.74	78.06
1561-1570	92.48	89.41	92.96	87.32
1571-1580	98.24	100.00	99.44	99.83
1581-1590	110.14	110.26	105.59	111.79
1591-1600	121.26	118.77	121.78	124.28. . . .

times as high as a hundred years before, while the peak for France, in 1626-1650, was only 1.93 times as high as in 1501-1525.

The different modes of comparison uniformly indicate that the revolution of silver prices was considerably more violent in Spain than in France. The synchronism of the price movements in the two countries suggests that close commercial contacts were maintained, either directly or through the Spanish possessions in Italy and the Low Countries, in spite of the bitter political rivalry and protracted hostilities between the French kings and the house of Austria. . . .

The upward movement in other leading European countries continued into the seventeenth century. The data now available indicate that English prices commenced to rise at the opening of the sixteenth century and that the decennial averages increased rapidly, although irregularly, from 1540-1549 to 1643-1652, when they reached their zenith. From 1501-1510 to 1593-1602 commodity prices rose in the ratio of 1 to 2.56, and in 1643-1652 the commodity index was 3.48 times that of 1501-1510. . . .

The nineteenth- and twentieth-century annals of the leading countries of the Western World afford no example of a hundred-year price upheaval in terms of a fixed-weight monetary standard comparable to that which occurred in Spain during the first century of the Price Revolution. If we examine the period 1820-1920, for example, in order to include the peak of the Great War prices, we find that commodity index numbers in the United States rose considerably less than 100 per cent, or not half as much proportionately as did those of Spain in the sixteenth century. . . .

Let us examine briefly the effects of American treasure upon the motherland. For a season industry seems to have responded to the rise in prices precipitated by the influx of treasure. The resultant material prosperity, together with the effect of the specie on national psychology, played a part in the passage of Spain through her golden age of literature and art. But ultimately the importation of treasure (the exportation of which was retarded by legal restrictions) in exchange for goods sapped the economic vitality of the country and augmented the Price Revolution, which handicapped export industry. Historians have generally agreed that American gold and silver fanned the flames of Hapsburg imperialism, added to the zeal with which Spanish rulers defended the Catholic faith against Protestant and Mohammedan, furnished sinews of war, and, in short, constituted an important factor in Spain's aggressive foreign policy. . . . So gold and silver from the Indies were a factor in the shedding of the blood of Spain—sacrificed on altars of imperialism and religious fanaticism—on distant European battlefields. Other men, lured by the El Dorados of New Spain and the then Peru, emigrated at their most productive age. American treasure doubtless created the illusion of prosperity and thus fostered extravagance and vagrancy. One cannot escape the conclusion that the gold and silver drawn from the Indies ultimately had baneful effects upon the mother country.

Next let us turn to the effects of Spanish imports of gold and silver upon Hispanic America. One who examines the records of the House of Trade, especially for the early years, cannot fail to be impressed by the enormous part played by American gold in the exploration and development of the New World. The sailors who accompanied Columbus on his first voyage, including the heirs of the men left on Hispaniola, were paid in part with gold brought to Spain between 1513 and 1519. Treasure drawn from the Indies financed the memorable voyage of Magellan, which proved rich in scientific discovery and demonstrated to the lay mind the sphericity of the earth. It paid the salaries of such notable servants of Spain as Amerigo Vespucci and Sebastian Cabot; and it provided the means to purchase and to carry to America the seeds, plants, animals, tools, books, and scientific instruments of the Old World.

CONTEMPORARY OPINION ON RISING
PRICES: JEAN BODIN (1530-1596)

The rapid increase in prices occasioned much speculation and debate. One of the earliest writers to discern the principal cause was a Frenchman, Jean Bodin. More famous as a political theorist than as an economist, Bodin was trained in law, served the French Government, and become one of the greatest political writers of his day. In 1568 he wrote a *Reply to the Paradoxes of Malestroit Concerning the Dearness of All Things and the Remedy Therefor* in an effort to correct false impressions regarding the rising price levels. The substance of Bodin's explanations follows.

From BODIN, *Concerning the Dearness of All Things* (1568) [1]

I find that the high prices we see today are due to some four or five causes. The principal & almost the only one (which no one has referred to until now) is the abundance of gold & silver, which is today much greater in this Kingdom than it was four hundred years ago, to go no further back. . . . The second reason for the high prices arises in part from monopolies. The third is scarcity, caused partly by export & partly by waste. The fourth is the pleasure of kings & great lords, who raise the price of the things they like. The fifth has to do with the price of money, debased from its former standard. I will treat all these points briefly.

The principal reason which raises the price of everything, wherever one may be, is the abundance of that which governs the appraisal & price of things. . . . Now

[1] Reprinted by permission of the publishers from Arthur Eli Monroe, ed., *Early Economic Thought: Selections from Economic Literature Prior to Adam Smith,* Harvard University Press, 1924, 127-32.

it was not the scarcity of lands, which can neither increase nor diminish, or monopoly, which cannot exist in such a case: but it was the abundance of gold & silver which causes the depreciation of these & the dearness of the things priced . . . when the Spaniard made himself master of the new world, hatchets & knives were sold for much more than pearls & precious stones; for there were only knives of wood & stone, & many pearls. It is therefore abundance which causes depreciation. . . .

It is therefore necessary to demonstrate that there was not as much gold & silver in this Kingdom three hundred years ago . . . as there is now: which is evident at a glance. For if there is money in a country, it cannot be so well hidden that Princes will not find it, when they are in straits. Now the fact is that King John was unable to obtain a loan of sixty thousand *francs* (let us call them *escus*) in his extreme need. . . . Moreover, we read in our old histories that, because of a lack of silver, money was made of leather with a silver nail in it, which shows well the extreme need of gold & silver at that time in France.

Now if we come down to our own times, we shall find that in six months the King obtained in Paris, without going outside, more than three million four hundred thousand *livres,* besides the household charges, which were also obtained in Paris, as well as the subsidies & domainal revenues. . . .

But, someone will say, where did so much gold & silver come from since that time? . . .

Now the fact is that the Spaniard, who gets his subsistence only from France, being compelled by unavoidable necessity to come here for wheat, cloths, stuffs, dye-stuffs, paper, books, even joinery & all handicraft products, goes to the ends of the earth to seek gold & silver & spices to pay us with.

On the other hand, the English, the Scotch, & all the people of Norway, Sweden, Denmark, & the Baltic coast, who have an infinity of mines, dig the metals out of the center of the earth to buy our wines, our saffron, our prunes, our dye, & especially our salt, which is a manna that God gives us as a special favor, with little labor. . . . The other cause of the great amount of wealth that has come to us in the last hundred & twenty or thirty years is the huge population which has grown up in this Kingdom, since the civil wars between the houses of Orleans & Bourgogne were ended: which allowed us to experience the sweetness of peace, & enjoy the fruit thereof for a long time, down to the Religious troubles [of the present century]. . . .

Another cause of the riches of France is the trade with the Levant, which was opened to us as a result of the friendship between the house of France & the house of the Ottomans in the time of King Francis the first; so that French merchants since that time have done business in Alexandria, in Cairo, in Beirut, in Tripoli, as well as the Venetians & Geno-ese; & have as good standing at Fez & at Morocco as the Spaniard. . . .

Another cause of the abundance of gold & silver has been the bank of Lyons, which was opened, to tell the truth, by King Francis the first, who began to borrow money at the twelfth penny, & his successor at the tenth, then the sixth, & up to the fifth in emergencies. Suddenly the Florentines, Luccans, Genoese, Swiss, Germans, attracted by the high profit, brought a vast amount of gold & silver into France; & many settled here. . . .

These, Sir, are the means which have brought us gold & silver in abundance in the last two hundred years. There is much more in Spain & Italy than in France, owing to the fact that in Italy even the nobility engage in trade, & the people of Spain have no other occupation; & so everything is dearer in Spain & in Italy than in France, & dearer in Spain than in Italy. This is true even of servants & artisans, which attracts our Auvergnats & Limousins into Spain, as I learned from them myself, because they earn three times as much as they do in France. . . . It is therefore the abundance of gold & silver which causes, in part, the high prices of things.

The Beginnings of Modern-Mindedness

THE REFORMATION

| 7 | THE EVE OF THE PROTESTANT REVOLT |

The Reformation, or Protestant Revolt, as many scholars prefer to call it, marked the beginning of the "Great Schism," or of religious and ecclesiastical disunity—with the rise of Protestant churches—in western Christendom. It began early in the sixteenth century and led immediately to heated controversies, severe persecutions, and fanatically fought religious wars in many parts of western Europe. It ended in the mid-seventeenth century, with the close of the Thirty Years' War (1648), by which time the various factions were persuaded of their inability to destroy one another and, as a growing secularity had also cooled their religious fervor, they reluctantly gave in to an ever widening policy of religious toleration as a modus vivendi. In the meantime, however, a multitude of Christian sects had arisen—Lutherans, Presbyterians, Congregationalists, Baptists, Mennonites, Quakers, and others —whose existence has continued to the present day.

With reference to the Renaissance, the Reformation is paradoxical. On the one hand, the Reformation is clearly an extension of Renaissance individu-alism and revolt from "authority" into the realms of religious faith and forms of worship—as asserted by the Protestant appeal to the "right of private judgment" in matters of religion in contrast to the authoritarian orthodoxy of the Roman Catholic Church. On the other hand, the intense preoccupation with spiritual matters precipitated by the Protestant Revolt constituted a force opposed both to Renaissance secularism and to Renaissance man's faith in his own worldly powers. Thus to some scholars the Reformation appears as a continuation of the Renaissance— its invasion of the realm of religion; to others, the Reformation appears as the very opposite of the Renaissance—a revival of emphasis upon otherworldliness as opposed to worldliness.

Whether or not the Reformation retarded Renaissance worldliness, there is no doubt that it was a product of Renaissance forces. A glance at the biting humanist satires upon the church (see, for example, pages 10, 28, 30, 33, 34, 55) and the close interrelationship of later humanist scholars (for example, Erasmus, Reuchlin) with early Reformation leaders (Luther, Melanchthon) well demonstrates the contemporary assertion that "Erasmus laid the egg and Luther hatched it." Of course, some humanists, Erasmus in particular, refused to follow Luther in the latter's break with the Papacy. But that Luther was impelled to break with the church rather than continue to strive for its reform from within as other humanists had done was, at the outset, wholly foreign to his intention. Only the peculiar necessities of the new Emperor Charles V (1500-1558), the support of German princes (who saw in the religio-ecclesiastical dispute an opportunity to assert their own states' authority against that of the Emperor), the bungling tactics of the Papacy, and the bitter clash of such personalities as Martin Luther and the papal representatives sent to discipline him precipitated the revolt, furnished Luther with unexpected support, and made possible the survival of Protestantism.

The early events of the Protestant Revolt took place principally in the Holy Roman Empire, where the death of the Emperor Maximilian (1519) and the election of Charles V occasioned an interregnum which delayed action by anti-Lutheran forces. Further, the youthful inexperience of the new Emperor, the limitations set by his ignorance and opportunism, and the perplexities of his position all created an atmosphere favorable to the early growth of Lutheranism. Moreover, the Emperor Charles V's entire reign was colored by the danger of Turkish invasion. Mohammedan in religion and warlike in organization, the Turks threatened Europe from two directions, each of which pointed into the dominions of Charles V.

From Asia Minor the Turks had invaded the Balkan Peninsula, captured Constantinople (1453), and pushed on

against Austria and Hungary in the Holy Roman Empire; likewise they had expanded across northern Africa and constantly menaced Spain from across the Straits of Gibraltar. The Emperor's diplomacy and finance were greatly affected by the Ottoman threats, and his attentions and powers were so frequently diverted by them from internal imperial affairs that Protestantism was able to thrive on his weakness. A description of the Ottoman Turks, together with an analysis of their strength and weakness, is given below.

1. The Ottoman Turks: A Major Threat to Christendom

From RANKE, *The Ottoman and Spanish Empires* (1838) [1]

Humble indeed is the description the Ottomans give of their own origin. They relate that Othman, the founder of their empire and name, himself followed the plough with his servants, and that when he wished to break off from work at noon he used to stick up a banner as a signal to call them home. These servants and none besides were his first followers in war, and they were marshalled beneath the same signal. . . .

The new power that arose in Asia Minor having now established itself on its northern coasts, it chanced one day, as the story continues, that Soliman, the grandson of Othman, rode along the shores of the Hellespont, passing on through the ruins of ancient cities, and fell into a silent reverie. "What is my khan thinking of?" said one of his escort. "I am thinking," was the reply, "about

[1] Leopold von Ranke, *The Ottoman and the Spanish Empires in the Sixteenth and Seventeenth Centuries*, trans. by Walter K. Kelly, London, 1843, 5-24.

our crossing over to Europe." These followers of Soliman were the first who did cross over to Europe: they were successful; and Soliman's brother, Amurath I, was he who conquered Adrianople. . . .

Europe and Asia, both threatened by Bajazeth I [great-grandson of Othman], rose up to resist him. Europe however fell prostrate at Nicopolis; and though Asia . . . was victorious, still it did not destroy the dominion of Bajazeth. It was but fifty years after this defeat that Mahomet II [1451-81] took Constantinople. . . . The victor was not content with seeing the cities on the coasts of the Black Sea and the Adriatic own his supremacy; to bring the sea itself under subjection he built a fleet; he began to conquer the islands of the Aegean one after the other; and his troops showed themselves in Apulia.

There seemed to be no bounds to the career of victory. Though Bajazeth II [1481-1512] did not equal his predecessors in valour, still his cavalry swept Friuli, his infantry captured fortresses in the Morea, and his fleets rode victorious in the Ionian Sea. But he was far outstripped by his son Selim and his grandson Soliman. Selim [1512-20] overcame the Mamelukes of Cairo, who had often been victorious over Bajazeth. . . . Soliman [Solyman, or Suleiman II, "The Magnificent," 1520-66] effected far more than he. One battle made him master of Hungary, and thenceforth he trod in that kingdom as in his own house. In the far east he portioned out the territory of Bagdad. . . . With amazement and awe men reckoned up thirty kingdoms, and nearly 8000 miles of coast, that owned his sway. . . .

FOUNDATIONS OF OTTOMAN POWER

If we inquire what were the bases on which rested the essential strength and energy of this empire, and therewith the success of its efforts, our attention will be arrested by three things, viz. the feudal system, the institution of slavery, and the position of the supreme head.

Every country overrun by the Ottomans was immediately after its conquest parcelled out according to banners and scymitars into a multitude of fiefs. The design was, the protection of the country once well provided for within and without, to keep its original conquerors ever ready for new achievements. The great advantage of this system will be obvious, when it is considered that every possessor of the moderate income of 3000 aspers (sixty to a dollar) was required to hold a man and horse in constant readiness for war, and another mounted soldier was to be furnished for every additional 5000 aspers. . . . These fiefs conferred no title of nobility, neither were they properly entailed on sons. Soliman ordered that if a sandshakbeg [commander of the banners] with an income of 700,000 aspers left behind him a son, a minor, the latter should receive nothing but a timar [fief] of 5000 aspers, with the express obligation of maintaining a mounted soldier out of the proceeds. . . . "Therefore," says Barbaro [a contemporary Venetian chronicler], "there is among them neither nobility nor wealth; the children of men of rank, whose private treasures are taken possession of by other grandees, enjoy no personal distinction." . . . Every one was obliged to begin his career from the lowest grade. . . .

But a much more peculiar institution . . . was the education of stolen children for soldiers or statesmen in the service of the sultan.[1]

Every five years it was the practice to make a seizure of the children of the Christians in the empire. Small bands of soldiers, each under a captain . . .

[1] These were the famous Turkish janissaries. The name is a Europeanization of the Turkish name *yeni tscheri*, meaning "new troops."

marched from place to place. The captain was empowered to carry off all between the age of seven and that of manhood, who were distinguished for beauty or strength, or who possessed any peculiar talent or accomplishment. He brought them like a tithe, as it were, to the court of the grand signor. Others were carried thither from the campaigns. . . . Thus were there gathered together at the Porte children of various nations, the majority of them natives of the country. . . . They were divided into two classes. One of these . . . served among the peasants, and were trained up as Moslems; or they were kept in the serai [as menial slaves]. . . . But the others, those who appeared to give evidence of superior qualities . . . were visited by teachers . . . in reading the law and in writing . . . [and] became janissaries in process of time; those who were brought up in the serai were made either siphai [cavalry], (not feudatory but paid,) who served at the Porte, or higher state functionaries. . . .

Both classes were kept under strict discipline. . . .

Here is total separation, strict community, the formation as it were of a new principle of life. The youths thus brought up forgot their childhood, their parents, their homes, knew no native land but the serai, no lord and father but the grand signor, no will but his, no hope but of his favour; they knew no life but one passed in rigid discipline and unconditional obedience, no occupation but war in his service, no personal purposes unless it were plunder in this life, and in death the paradise thrown open to him who fought for Islam. . . .

This institution perfectly fulfilled its intentions. . . . Under their discipline brave and dignified men were produced. . . . It cannot be denied that in decisive engagements they alone preserved the empire. . . .

Hardly will . . . [an] example be found of one of these youths returning to the parents from whose arms he had been torn and to his old home. And how should they? There was no hereditary aristocracy to interpose their claims, and dispute with them the rewards of their valour or their talents; on the contrary they were themselves destined to fill all the highest dignities of the empire . . . not only the whole government of the country, but the command too of its armies was in their hands; every one saw before him a field of exertion, a career in life, with which before his eyes he might forget that he was a slave. . . .

Such was the institution of slaves. "It is in the highest degree remarkable," exclaims Barbaro, that "the wealth, the administration, the force, in short the whole body politic of the Ottoman empire reposes upon, and is intrusted to men born in the Christian faith, converted into slaves, and reared up Mahometans." On this institution depends the character and the form of government of the Turks. . . .

Now, taking into consideration all these facts, first, that all were slaves (and most so those who stood highest), trained unceasingly to unconditional obedience; that there was not a man among them possessed of any independent rights, of family property, jurisdiction, or retainers; that every career depended upon the beck of the sultan, from whom his slave expected either magnificent rewards, or degradation and death; and lastly, that the whole system was thoroughly military in its organization, that the state was warlike and its business war; taking all this into account, it is very clear that the sultan was the soul of this singularly constituted body, the origin of its very movement, and above all, that he too, if he would reign, must needs be of a warlike spirit. . . .

Whilst men thought thus, whilst they were filled with dismay and uttered gloomy forebodings as they compared the might and valour of the Ottomans with those of the western nations . . . just then alterations took place among the latter which produced an essential revolution in the condition of their empire.

The empire needed warlike sovereigns; it began to experience a dearth of them: it needed the unswerving discipline of its military institutions, and its slave education; this became corrupted: it needed continual conquests; they began to fail. Our purpose is to show how all this took place.

THE SULTANS

The contrast has long been remarked in the west, that subsisted between all the sultans before Soliman and all those after him . . . that all the sultans since Soliman were without exception fools or tyrants. . . . Selim II [1566-74] may be regarded as the first founder of this new line. . . . Selim, who preferred the society of eunuchs and of women, and the habits of the serai to the camp, who wore away his days in sensual enjoyments, in drunkenness and indolence. . . . With him begins the series of those inactive sultans, in whose dubious character we may trace one main cause of the decay of the Ottoman fortunes. . . .

There existed among the Ottomans an institution fitted to prevent the effects of incapacity in the sultan, the institution . . . of the grand vizier. This officer they were accustomed to style an unlimited deputy. . . . A great portion of the public weal depended on him . . . and when the sultan was incapable the whole executive power [was] in his hands. . . .

[Some of these, such as Mehemet, a Bosnian slave raised up under Selim II, were excellent and able men. But in time, especially under Amurath III (1574-95), the practice of selecting grand viziers only from among slaves was discarded and the sultan began to sell the offices, frequently turning out one grand vizier only to sell the office to his rival.]

The consequence of this new practice was that whilst the head of the government was constantly changed, the manner and course of the administration, and the principles and usuages of the higher functionaries were unsettled and subjected to no fewer changes. . . .

What constantly befalls Oriental despotisms occurred in this case likewise; here, too, caprice called up some one who was able to master it. A new system of government grew up, situated in the hands of favorites within the palace, such as the sultan's mother, or his wives, or his eunuchs. . . . In this way there arose, within the walls of the harem, an interest opposed to the vizier, and by which he was himself ruled, and placed and displaced; not a general interest of the empire, nor a personal one of the sultan, but an interest of women and of eunuchs, who now assumed the head of this warlike state. . . .

They began to cover their seats with cloth of gold; they slept in summer on the finest silk, and in winter wrapped in costly furs. . . . In lieu of the simple fare of Soliman's time they outdid all the delicacies of Italy . . . to do or suffer everything for gold. . . . Justice was venal; every office had its price. . . .

MILITARY FORCES

It is very well known how important the janissaries were in the beginning; it is no less known what they came to be at last. . . . It is less clear . . . how this decay took place. . . .

In the first place let us recollect that the janissaries were originally prohibited from marrying . . . but now marriage was allowed the janissaries. . . . This change alone must have produced no little mutation in the habits and way of thinking of the soldiery.

But another change immediately came forth from the first, and directly threatened the very vitality of the institution. The question was, what was to be done with the children of the janissaries? The fathers demanded that their sons should be received into their body. We learn . . . that they obtained this favour on the accession of Selim II to the throne. . . .

Now if it was constitutional with this body-guard to be made up of young people, who had lost all knowledge of their parental home, this principle was now decidedly violated. . . . Ere long the sons of the janissaries were seen in the ranks of that corps. It was impossible that they should have undergone the full rigour of discipline that had once been enforced.

It may readily be conceived that this facilitated the passage to a third innovation. . . . Admission was likewise granted to other native Turks, and to Musselmen of all nations, men unpractised, undisciplined, and incapable of all discipline. . . . Under Ahmed this warlike body was already brought to such a condition, that the privates when stationed through the country or on the frontiers began to ply in trades, to engage in commerce, and, satisfied with the advantage of their name, to think little of war and arms. . . . It passed soon into a proverb: The janissary has surely a good eye and good legs, the former to see if the cavalry waver, and the latter to run away with all speed thereupon. . . .

FRONTIERS

It is certain that under Soliman the Ottoman empire, as it surpassed all others in intrinsic strength, so likewise was it more threatening than any other power to the rest of the world.

It nevertheless appears from our investigations that under this very same Soliman the internal strength of this empire became afflicted with grave maladies.

Under him the influence of women in the harem first gained ascendancy; under him those edicts were issued that gave the chief occasion to change in the disposition of the timars; under him the janissaries began to have wives; through him it came to pass that the least worthy of his sons ascended the throne. Nor was this all. If a state has been founded on conquest, if it has hitherto known no pause to its progressive conquests, can any one doubt that the shock to it will be severe when the progress is stayed, and conquest ceases? Under Soliman, warlike and victorious as he was, the empire yet began to have boundaries. In the east he encountered in Persia a weak people indeed, that intrinsically was by no means able to cope with him, but still a people who venerated their shah as a god . . . that left their territory widely exposed to the foe, but not till they had first laid it waste, so that the assailants could never reach the fugitive defenders, and had enough to do to avoid being themselves assailed on their retreat. Christendom was Soliman's other foe, and it must be owned it was weakened by internal dissensions. Now if the establishment of the Austro-Spanish power [that is, the union of Spain and the Empire under Charles V] was in any point of view a fortunate thing for Christendom, it was inasmuch as it was fitted by circumstances, and had inherent strength enough, to resist the Turks at once in Africa, Italy, and Hungary. . . . It crossed and resisted both the directions taken by the Turkish power in its outspread westward, the continental and the maritime. . . .

When Selim II came to the throne [1566], two enterprises presented themselves to him, both in that maritime direction towards the west which Mahomet II [1451-81] had opened. The one was against Spain, the prime foe of the Mohammedan name . . . just then thrown into serious peril by the insurrection of the Moors. . . . The other enterprise was against Venice and Cyprus. The Venetians had been peaceful, compliant, almost submissive. . . . Cyprus was already half subdued. . . .

Sultan Selim did not ponder what were the manliest, the grandest enterprises. . . . He only considered what might be the easiest, the surest, and the nearest conquest. A landing could hardly be prevented in Cyprus . . . his army embarked, landed, conquered the capital, and took the island.

And now, strange to say, the easier undertaking proved to be attended with more dangerous consequences than could have ensued from the more difficult one.

Had Spain been attacked, Venice would never have resolved on lending that country her strenuous aid. . . . But when Venice was attacked, since it was the interest of Philip II [of Spain, 1556-98] to keep the war . . . in remote waters, the consequence was a confederation of the two maritime powers. It was joined by the pope; three fleets stood together to sea to meet the Turks. . . .

The Turks ruled the Mediterranean in war and piracy ever since that day in . . . 1538, when Chaireddin Barbarossa attacked with wonderful daring, and vanquished the far superior fleet of the Christians at Prevesa. They believed that the Christians would never venture again to stand before them in open fight. This superiority endured till the year 1571. . . . The Turks were now confronted by a youth who for daring, energy, fortune, and grand conceptions might well be compared with Chaireddin Barbarossa; this was Don John of Austria.[1] The

[1] Illegitimate son of Charles V and half-brother of Philip II of Spain. In 1571, Don John with a mixed Spanish, Genoese, and Venetian fleet, defeated the Turks in the naval battle of Lepanto and destroyed Turkish naval power in the western Mediterranean. See page 167.

Christians were victorious under his command . . . the day of Lepanto broke down the Ottoman supremacy [on the Mediterranean]. . . .

But as yet there was no cessation to their continental efforts. . . . Amurath embarked in two wars, the Persian and the Hungarian, that eventually exhausted the best energies of the empire. . . .

But if the sultan had some partial success in Persia, at least in the beginning, this was not the case in Hungary. The dreams of his commanders of carrying the dominion of the Porte into Germany and Italy, or at least of conquering Bohemia, were crossed by difficulties. . . . It is clear that the Ottoman conquests had met with that check, which it was foreseen even in Soliman's time they would one day sustain. The Persians and the Germans remained unvanquished.

2. Papal Ambition and Diplomacy

Besides the advantage gained by the Turkish threat, Protestantism also profited from the complicated diplomatic relations existing among the Emperor, the Papacy, and the King of France. In the first instance, these complications arose because of the secular ambitions of Renaissance popes. Late in the fifteenth century, as princes and city-states plotted to gain ascendancy in Italy, the Papacy came to desire to expand its temporal possessions in Italy. Pope Sixtus IV (1471-84) was the first deliberately to embark upon this policy, and Alexander VI (1492-1503), Julius II (1503-13), and Leo X (1513-21) continued with vigor but with unexpected —and, as things turned out, undesirable—results, as will be seen from the following account.

From RANKE, *History of the Popes* (1834) [1]

Whilst the Italian powers sought the one to overcome the others with the aid of foreign nations, they destroyed with their own hands the independence they had enjoyed during the fifteenth century, and exposed their country to be the common battle prize for the rest of Europe. A great share of this result must be imputed to the popes. They had now assuredly acquired a might, such as had never before been possessed by the Roman see; but they had not acquired it of themselves; they owed it to Frenchmen, Spaniards, Germans, and Swiss. But for his league with Louis XII [king of France, 1498-1515], Caesar Borgia would hardly have accomplished much. Enlarged as were the views of Julius II, heroic as were his achievements, he must have succumbed but for the aid of the Spaniards and the Swiss. . . . Julius II saw this clearly. His purpose was to maintain a certain balance among the other powers, and to make use only of the least potent among them, the Swiss, whom he might hope to lead.

But it proved otherwise. Two great powers grew up, and contended with each other, if not for universal dominion, at least for the supremacy in Europe, powers so mighty that a pope was far from being able to match them; and they fought out their quarrel on Italian ground.

First came the French. Not long after Leo's accession they appeared in greater force than they had ever before crossed the Alps, to reconquer Milan; at their head Francis I [1515-47], in the ardour of youth and chivalry. Everything hung on the question whether or not the Swiss would be able to resist them. The battle of

Marignano [1515] was therefore so important, because the Swiss were wholly routed, and because they never since that defeat have exercised an independent influence in Italy.

[When Pope Leo X learned of the French victory, he cried out in dismay], "We must throw ourselves into the king's arms, and cry him mercy."

In fact the French through this victory acquired the decided preponderance in Italy. Had they followed it up with resolution, neither Tuscany nor the States of the Church, both so easily moved to rebellion, would have been able to offer much resistance, and the Spaniards would have found it difficult to maintain themselves in Naples. . . . How much rested at that moment upon Leo! . . .

Against the advice of his cardinals he betook himself to Bologna, to have speech with the king. Here they concluded the concordat, in which they shared between them the rights of the Gallican church. Leo was forced to give up Parma and Placenza; but for the rest he succeeded in conjuring the storm, inducing the king to turn his steps homewards, and himself remaining secure in the possession of his dominions. . . .

Meanwhile, the second great power had become consolidated. . . . The power of Austria forthwith set itself against the preponderant influence of France. Charles V acquired through the imperial dignity a legitimate claim to paramount rank, at least in Lombardy. War arose without much delay out of these Italian circumstances.

The popes, as we have said, had hoped to attain to complete independence through the enlargement of their dominions. They now saw themselves hemmed in between two far superior powers. A pope was not so insignificant that he could remain neutral in a strife between them;

[1] Leopold von Ranke, *The History of the Popes, Their Church and State, in the Sixteenth and Seventeenth Centuries*, trans. by Walter Keating Kelly, London, 1843, 24-25.

nor on the other hand, was he strong enough to give a preponderance to the scale into which he cast his force: he could only look for safety to the dexterous use he made of events. Leo is reputed to have said, that when one had concluded terms with either party, he must not omit to treat with the other. So double-tongued a policy was the forced result of the position in which he was placed.

Leo nevertheless could hardly entertain any serious doubt as to which party it was his interest to adopt. . . . This was derived from religious considerations.

Throughout the whole period we are contemplating, there was nothing princes had so much at heart, in all their involved dealings with the Roman see, as to elicit a spiritual opposition against it. . . . When had a bolder or a more prosperous foe than Luther ever stood up against the pope? His mere appearance, his existence, gave him a weighty political importance. In this light [the Emperor] Maximilian viewed the matter; he would not have suffered any violence to befall the monk; he recommended him to the special protection of the elector of Saxony: "there might some time or other be need of him." From that time forth Luther's influence increased day by day.

3. The Indulgence Question

Though many social, economic, political, and religious discontents lay at the root of the Reformation, the *immediate* spark which set it off was the abuse of indulgences. As the term "indulgence" refers to a specific ecclesiastical concept of the Roman Catholic Church, it is necessary to define it clearly. In *theory,* indulgences are the same today as in the late Middle Ages, but the church has been very careful

to curb the *abuses* to which they were put in pre-Reformation days. The following is a recent explanation of indulgences by an approved Roman Catholic authority.

DEFINITION OF INDULGENCES

From *The Catholic Encyclopedia* (1913) [1]

What an Indulgence is not. To facilitate explanation, it may be well to state what an indulgence is not. It is not a permission to commit a sin, nor a pardon of future sin; neither could be granted by any power. It is not the forgiveness of the guilt of sin; it supposes that the sin has already been forgiven. It is not an exemption from any law or duty, and much less from the obligation consequent on certain kinds of sin, e.g., restitution; on the contrary, it means a more complete payment of the debt which the sinner owes to God. It does not confer immunity from temptation or remove the possibility of subsequent lapses into sin. Least of all is an indulgence the purchase of a pardon which secures the buyer's salvation or releases the soul of another from Purgatory. . . .

What an Indulgence is. An indulgence is the extra-sacramental remission of the temporal punishment due, in God's justice, to sin that has been forgiven, which remission is granted by the Church in the exercise of the power of the keys, through the application of the superabundant merits of Christ and of the saints, and for some just and reasonable motive. . . . In the Sacrament of Penance the guilt of sin is removed, and with it the eternal punishment due to mortal sin; but there still remains the temporal punishment required by Divine justice, and this require-

[1] *The Catholic Encyclopedia,* 15 vols., New York, 1913, VII, 783. Reprinted by permission of The Gilmary Society.

ment must be fulfilled either in the present life or in the world to come, i.e., in Purgatory. An indulgence offers the penitent the means of discharging this debt during his life on earth. . . . In granting an indulgence, the grantor (pope or bishop) . . . acts in his official capacity as having jurisdiction in the Church, from whose spiritual treasury he draws the means wherewith payment is to be made. The Church herself is not the absolute owner, but simply the administratrix, of the superabundant merits which that treasury contains [as a legacy from Christ and the Saints]. . . . By a plenary indulgence is meant the remission of the entire temporal punishment due to sin so that no further expiation is required in Purgatory. A partial indulgence commutes only a certain portion of the penalty.

PRE-REFORMATION ABUSE OF INDULGENCES

Widespread misuse of indulgences dated from the Crusades, when the popes assured soldiers and contributors that their services would be accepted in full discharge of the penance otherwise required of them. After the Crusades popes continued to grant indulgences for money payments, using the funds to further all sorts of pious works. In time, the benefits of indulgences were extended to souls in Purgatory, and living persons, upon payment of money, believed they could release the souls of their friends and relatives from torment. Many thoughtless, sinning souls overlooked the theoretical limitations of indulgences and supposed that they released the purchaser from all the consequences of his misdeeds. And indeed, overzealous priests, in their desire to raise money, often winked at this popular misconception. Thus, in the fifteenth and sixteenth centuries, traffic in indul-

gences often became harmful and demoralizing. On the one hand, the clergy used it to raise money for selfish ends, and on the other, the laity was led to substitute the mere payment of money for true penitence and amendment of life.

It was an attack upon abuses of this kind that started Martin Luther upon his career as a reformer.

Leo X proclaimed an indulgence in 1513 to build St. Peter's in Rome. A year later, after much costly political maneuvering, Archbishop Albert, a young Hohenzollern prince who already held two sees, gained the Archbishopric of Mainz. It cost him nearly 30,000 ducats for permission to hold two extra sees and for confirmation in the new post. Most of this money he borrowed. In order to repay the loan, he arranged to proclaim the extension of the indulgence of 1513 throughout his three ecclesiastical domains. Half of the proceeds was to be turned over to the pope; the other half was to be kept by Albert to discharge his debt. Thus an indulgence originally proclaimed for the pious purpose of building a church to St. Peter was employed for the crass purchase of a province for the Hohenzollern prince.

By 1517 all arrangements were made and Archbishop Albert issued the following instructions to his sub-commissioners. Their mercenary intent is amply evident.

From ARCHBISHOP ALBERT, *Instructions* (1517) [1]

Here follow the four principal graces and privileges, which are granted by the

[1] *Translations and Reprints from the Original Sources of European History,* II, No. 6. Published by the Department of History of the University of Pennsylvania, 1895, 4-9. Reprinted by permission of the University of Pennsylvania Press.

apostolic bull, of which each may be obtained without the other. In the matter of these four privileges preachers shall take pains to commend each to believers with the greatest care, and in-so-far as in their power lies, to explain the same.

The first grace is the complete remission of all sins; and nothing greater than this can be named, since man who lives in sin and forfeits the favor of God, obtains complete remission by these means and once more enjoys God's favor: moreover, through this remission of sins the punishment which one is obliged to undergo in Purgatory . . . is all remitted, and the pains of Purgatory completely blotted out. And although nothing is precious enough to be given in exchange for such a grace . . . yet in order than Christian believers may be the more easily induced to procure the same, we establish the following rules, to wit:

In the first place every one who is contrite in heart, and has made oral confession, or at all events has the intention of confessing at a suitable time, shall visit at least the seven churches indicated for this purpose . . . and in each church shall say devoutly five Paternosters and five Ave Marias in honor of the five wounds of our Lord Jesus Christ, whereby our salvation is won, or one *Miserere.* . . .

Respecting, now, the contribution to the chest, for the building of the said church of the chief of the apostles, the penitentiaries and confessors, after they have explained to those making confession the full remission and privileges, shall ask of them, for how much money or other temporal goods they would conscientiously go without the said most complete remission and privileges; and this shall be done in order that hereafter they may be brought the more easily to contribute. And because the conditions and occupations of men are so manifold and diverse . . . we have therefore concluded that the rates should be determined according to the recognized classes of persons.

Kings and Queens and their offspring . . . and other great rulers as well . . . shall pay at least five and twenty Rhenish guilders in gold. Abbots and the great prelates . . . counts, barons, and others of the higher nobility, together with their consorts, shall pay for each letter of indulgence ten such guilders. Other lesser prelates and nobles . . . and all others, who . . . enjoy a total yearly revenue of five hundred gold guilders, shall pay six such guilders. Other citizens and tradespeople and artisans, who have individual incomes and families of their own, shall pay one such guilder; others of less means only a half. . . . And those that have no money, they shall supply their contribution with prayer and fasting. . . .

In all the cases above indicated, however, some room shall be left for the exercise of discretion on the part of the sub-commissioners and confessors. . . .

The second signal grace is a confessional letter containing the most extraordinarily comforting and hitherto unheard of privileges. . . . First, the power to choose a qualified confessor . . . who shall absolve them . . . from all censures by whomsoever imposed; in the second place, from each and every crime, even the greatest, and as well from those reserved to the apostolic see, once in a lifetime and in the hour of death; third, in those cases which are not reserved, as often as necessary; fourth, the chosen confessor may grant him complete forgiveness of all sins once in life, and at the hour of death, as often as it may seem at hand . . . and, fifth, transform all kinds of vows, excepting alone those solemnly taken, into other works of piety (as when one has vowed to perform the journey to the Holy Land . . . to become a monk, or to take a vow of chastity); sixth, the confessor may administer to him the sacrament of the altar at all seasons, except on Easter day, and in the hour of death. . . .

[This letter is to be purchased for one fourth of a Rhenish gold guilder, or more if wealthy persons "be disposed to give more."]

The third most important grace [no extra charge] is . . . that contributors toward the said building, together with their deceased relations, who have departed this world in a state of grace, shall from now and for eternity, be partakers in all petitions, intercessions [and so on] . . . which have been brought forth or which shall be brought forth by the universal, most holy church militant or by any of its members. . . .

The fourth distinctive grace is for those souls which are in Purgatory, and is the complete remission of all sins, which remission the pope brings to pass through his intercession to the advantage of said souls, in this wise; that the same contribution shall be placed in the chest by a living person as one would make for himself. . . . It is furthermore not necessary that the persons who place their contributions in the chest for the dead should be contrite in heart and have orally confessed, since this grace is based simply on the state of grace in which the dead departed, and on the contribution of the living. . . . Moreover, preachers shall exert themselves to give this grace the widest publicity, since through the same, help will surely come to departed souls, and the construction of the Church of St. Peter will be abundantly promoted at the same time.

JOHN TETZEL (c. 1450-1519)

One of the Archbishop's chief agents for the sale of indulgences was a Dominican friar, John Tetzel of Leipsic. Tetzel was a man of considerable learn-

ing and a preacher with great popular appeal who had already proved his ability to raise money for the church. A modern historian has paraphrased an eyewitness's account of Tetzel's activities.

From SCHAFF, *The Reformation* (1888) [1]

Tetzel traveled with great pomp and circumstance through Germany, and recommended with unscrupulous effrontery and declamatory eloquence the indulgences of the Pope to the large crowds who gathered from every quarter around him. He was received like a messenger from heaven. Priests, monks, and magistrates, men and women, old and young, marched in solemn procession with songs, flags, and candles, under the ringing of bells, to meet him and his fellow-monks, and followed them to the church; the papal bull on a velvet cushion was placed on the high altar, a red cross with a silken banner bearing the papal arms was erected before it, and a large iron chest was put beneath the cross for the indulgence money. Such chests are still preserved in many places. The preachers, by daily sermons, hymns, and processions, urged the people, with extravagant laudations of the Pope's bull, to purchase letters of indulgence for their own benefit, and at the same time played upon their sympathies for departed relatives and friends whom they might release from their sufferings in purgatory "as soon as the penny tinkles in the box." [2]

[1] Philip Schaff, *History of the Reformation, I: The German Reformation, 1517-1530,* Scribner, 1888, I, 153-54.
[2] Tetzel placed an iron chest for the money beneath the cross in the front of the church, and he is said to have composed the following rhyme to move his hearers to action:
"*Sobald der Pfennig im Kasten klingt,*
  Die Seel' aus dem Fegfeuer springt."
[As soon as pennies in the money chest ring,
  The souls out of their Purgatory spring.]

The common people eagerly embraced this rare offer of salvation from punishment, and made no clear distinction between the guilt and punishment of sin; after the sermon they approached with burning candles the chest, confessed their sins, paid the money, and received the letter of indulgence which they cherished as a passport to heaven.

[Another recent writer has translated a short selection from one of Tetzel's rabble-rousing sermons. Tetzel is appealing to the emotions of his hearers in order to arouse them to purchase the fourth "grace" set forth in Archbishop Albert's instructions.]

Do you not hear your dead parents crying out "Have mercy upon us? We are in sore pain and you can set us free for a mere pittance. We have borne you, we have trained and educated you, we have left you all our property, and you are so hard-hearted and cruel, that you leave us to roast in the flames when you could so easily release us." [1]

8

LUTHER AND LUTHERANISM

1. Luther Initiates the Protestant Revolt: The Ninety-five Theses

By order of the Elector of Saxony, who feared that the church might relieve his subjects of too much money, John Tetzel and the other agents of Archbishop Albert were not permitted to hawk indulgences in electoral Saxony. But Tetzel operated at Jüterbogk, Eisleben, and other towns in ducal Saxony only a few miles from Wittenberg, where Martin Luther taught. Tetzel's activities aroused Luther to protest and to question the entire proceedings. In order to stimulate thought upon the matter—and in the pious hope of effecting reformation regarding the sale of indulgences—Luther posted his ninety-five theses as topics for debate, an act which sounded the tocsin of the

Reformation. He sent a copy of them, with an introductory letter to Archbishop Albert, as follows.

From LUTHER, *Ninety-five Theses* (October 31, 1517) [2]

DEDICATION

To the most Reverend Father in Christ and most illustrious Lord, Albert, Archbishop and Primate of the Churches of Magdeburg and Mentz, Marquis of Brandenburg, etc., his lord and pastor in Christ, most gracious and worthy of all fear and reverence—

Jesus.

The grace of God be with you, and whatsoever it is and can do.

Spare me, most reverend Father in Christ, most illustrious Prince, if I, the very dregs of humanity, have dared to think of addressing a letter to the eminence of your sublimity. The Lord Jesus

---

[1] Reprinted from *Martin Luther, The Man and His Work*, by A. C. McGiffert, 81. Copyright 1911 by The Century Company, 1939, by Gertrude H. McGiffert. By permission of D. Appleton-Century Company, Inc.

[2] *Luther's Primary Works*, trans. and ed. by Henry Wace and C. A. Buchheim, Hodder and Stoughton, London, 1896, 411-22.

is my witness that, in the consciousness of my own pettiness and baseness, I have long put off the doing of that which I have now hardened my forehead to perform, moved thereto most especially by the sense of that faithful duty which I feel that I owe to your most reverend Fatherhood in Christ. May your Highness then in the meanwhile deign to cast your eyes upon one grain of dust, and, in your pontifical clemency, to understand my prayer.

Papal indulgences are being carried about, under your most distinguished authority, for the building of St. Peter's. In respect of these I do not so much accuse the extravagant sayings of the preachers, which I have not heard, but I grieve at the very false ideas which the people conceive from them, and which are spread abroad in common talk on every side—namely, that unhappy souls believe that, if they buy letters of indulgences, they are sure of their salvation; also, that, as soon as they have thrown their contribution into the chest, souls forthwith fly out of purgatory; and furthermore, that so great is the grace thus conferred, that there is no sin so great—even, as they say, if, by an impossibility, any one had violated the Mother of God—but that it may be pardoned; and again, that by these indulgences a man is freed from all punishment and guilt. . . .

Why then, by these false stories and promises of pardon, do the preachers of them make the people to feel secure and without fear? since indulgences confer absolutely no good on souls as regards salvation or holiness, but only take away the outward penalty which was wont of old to be canonically imposed. . . .

This faithful discharge of my humble duty I entreat that your most illustrious Grace will deign to receive in a princely and bishoplike spirit—that is, with all clemency—even as I offer it with a most faithful heart, and one most devoted to your most reverend Fatherhood, since I too am part of your flock. May the Lord Jesus keep your most reverend Fatherhood for ever and ever. Amen.

From Wittenberg, on the eve of All Saints, in the year 1517.

If it so please your most reverend Fatherhood, you may look at these Disputations, that you may perceive how dubious a matter is that opinion about indulgences, which they disseminate as if it were most certain.

To your most reverend Fatherhood.
Martin Luther.

DISPUTATION OF DR. MARTIN LUTHER CONCERNING PENITENCE AND INDULGENCES

In the desire and with the purpose of elucidating the truth, a disputation will be held on the underwritten propositions at Wittenberg, under the presidency of the Reverend Father Martin Luther, Monk of the Order of St. Augustine, Master of Arts and of Sacred Theology, and ordinary Reader of the same in that place. He therefore asks those who cannot be present and discuss the subject with us orally, to do so by letter in their absence. In the name of our Lord Jesus Christ. Amen.

1. Our Lord and Master Jesus Christ, in saying "Repent ye," etc., intended that the whole life of believers should be penitence.

2. This word cannot be understood as sacramental penance, that is, of the confession and satisfaction which are performed under the ministry of priests.

3. It does not, however, refer solely to inward penitence; nay such inward penitence is naught, unless it outwardly produces various mortifications of the flesh.

4. The penalty thus continues as long as the hatred of self—that is, true inward penitence—continues: namely, till our entrance into the kingdom of heaven.

5. The Pope has neither the will nor the power to remit any penalties, except

those which he has imposed by his own authority, or by that of the canons. . . .

20. Therefore the Pope, when he speaks of the plenary remission of all penalties, does not mean simply of all, but only of those imposed by himself.

21. Thus those preachers of indulgences are in error who say that, by the indulgences of the Pope, a man is loosed and saved from all punishment. . . .

24. Hence the greater part of the people must needs be deceived by this indiscriminate and high-sounding promise of release from penalties. . . .

27. They preach man who say that the soul flies out of purgatory as soon as the money thrown into the chest rattles.

28. It is certain that, when the money rattles in the chest, avarice and gain may be increased, but the suffrage of the Church depends on the will of God alone. . . .

43. Christians should be taught that he who gives to a poor man, or lends to a needy man, does better than if he bought pardons.

44. Because, by a work of charity, charity increases and the man becomes better; while, by means of pardons, he does not become better, but only freer from punishment. . . .

PROTESTATION

I, Martin Luther, Doctor, of the Order of Monks at Wittenberg, desire to testify publicly that certain propositions against pontifical indulgences, as they call them, have been put forth by me. Now although, up to the present time, neither this most celebrated and renowned school of ours, nor any civil or ecclesiastical power has condemned me, yet there are, as I hear, some men of headlong and audacious spirit, who dare to pronounce me a heretic, as though the matter had been thoroughly looked into and studied. But on my part, as I have often done before, so

now too, I implore all men, by the faith of Christ, either to point out to me a better way, if such a way has been divinely revealed to any, or at least to submit their opinion to the judgment of God and of the Church. For I am neither so rash as to wish that my sole opinion should be preferred to that of all other men, nor so senseless as to be willing that the word of God should be made to give place to fables, devised by human reason.

2. Luther Breaks with the Church: the Leipsic Debate (July, 1519)

With reference to his *Theses,* Luther wrote: "I hoped the pope would protect me, for I had so fortified my theses with proofs from the Bible and papal decretals that I was sure he would condemn Tetzel and bless me. But when I expected a benediction from Rome, there came thunder and lightning instead, and I was treated like a sheep who had roiled the wolf's water. Tetzel went scot-free, and I must submit to be devoured."

From the princes and populace of Germany Luther won wide support at once. But from the church he was threatened with condemnation for heresy. Cardinal Cajetan, papal legate at the Diet of Augsburg before which Luther was summoned (October, 1518), refused to discuss the merits of the case and demanded unquestioning submission to papal authority. Luther appealed to the Scriptures as against papal infallibility and finally left Augsburg clandestinely. Back in Wittenberg he called for a hearing before a general church council—a clever stroke, especially as it brought to his side many opponents of papal absolutism in the church. But the next summer he was impelled to deny even the authority of church councils as against God's word as set forth in the Bible. The occasion for this revolutionary statement was his debate with John Eck at Leipsic.

Dr. John Eck, of the University of Ingoldstadt, was one of the ablest German Catholic theologians. Once a close friend of Luther, he now was a bitter critic and in the winter of 1518-19 he attacked Luther so that the latter felt obliged to answer him. Accordingly, they agreed upon a triangular public debate to be held in Leipsic between Eck, on the one hand, and, on the other, Andrew Carlstadt, one of Luther's Wittenberg colleagues, and Luther himself. One of Luther's biographers describes the debate as follows.

From MC GIFFERT, *Martin Luther* (1911) [1]

Peter Mosellan, a Leipsic professor of humanistic sympathies, gives us a vivid description of the participants in the debate. The following pen-picture of Luther, then thirty-five years old, is worth quoting:

"Martin is of medium height and slender form, with a body so wasted with cares and study that you can almost count his bones.[2] He is just in the prime of life, with a clear and penetrating voice. His learning and his knowledge of Scripture are admirable, and he has almost everything at command. He knows enough Greek and Hebrew to decide between different interpretations. Nor is he wanting in matter, for he has a great forest both of ideas and words. Judgment, perhaps, and discretion you might miss in him. In his life and manners he is polite and affable, not in the least stoical or supercilious, and he is able to adapt himself to all occasions. In company he is a gay and merry jester, alert and good-humored, everywhere and always with a bright and cheerful face, however terribly his enemies threaten him, so that you find it difficult to believe the man could undertake so arduous a task without divine aid. But there is one thing nearly all count a vice in him: he is a little more imprudent and biting in reproof than is either safe in one who goes new ways in theology or decorous in a theologian, a fault which I am sure does not attach to all that have learned late."

During the first week the debate was between Eck and Carlstadt, and Luther entered the fray only on the fourth of July. It was for this both Eck and the spectators had been eagerly waiting, and the disputation now assumed for the first time the aspect of a real and serious struggle. The disputants began at once with the fundamental question of the nature of papal authority. Luther was very careful and moderate in his utterances. He did not deny the supremacy of the pope. He claimed only that he ruled by human, not divine, right, and a Christian might therefore be saved even if he refused to submit to his authority. This, Eck at once declared, sounded very like the opinion of John Hus, who had been condemned by the Council of Constance and burned at the stake a hundred years before.

The spread of Hus's views in Bohemia, his native land, had led to civil war and cost Germany much blood and treasure. The Bohemian heresy had become the synonym of riot and revolution, and to accuse Luther of sympathy with it was to hold him up to general execration. He felt the gravity of the accusation, and at first repelled it angrily. "Never," he retorted, "have I taken pleasure in any schism whatsoever, nor will I to the end of time. The Bohemians have done wrong in voluntarily separating from our com-

---

[1] Reprinted from A. C. McGiffert, *op. cit.,* 140-45, by permission of D. Appleton-Century Company, Inc.

[2] Later in life, when most of Luther's portraits were made, he became heavy.

munion, even if they have divine right on their side; for the highest divine right is love and unity of the Spirit."

But after thinking the matter over, he declared, "It is certain that among the articles of John Hus and the Bohemians are many most Christian and evangelical, and these the universal church cannot condemn."

This was the climax of the debate. Luther's words were heard with horror by his enemies and with consternation by his friends. From the duke they elicited an angry oath audible to the whole assembly. Seeing the effect produced, Luther tried to qualify his statement and make it less offensive; but he had expressed his real opinion, as everybody saw, and explanation did not help the matter.

A couple of days later, in response to Eck's continued appeal to the authority of the Council of Constance, he declared: "I shall not be moved until the most excellent doctor proves that a council is unable to err, has not erred, and does not err. For a council cannot make divine right of what is not by its nature such, nor can it make that heresy which is not against divine right."

To which Eck replied: "The Reverend Father begs me to prove that a council cannot err. I am ignorant what he means by this unless he wishes to throw suspicion on the praiseworthy Council of Constance. This I say to you, Reverend Father, if you believe that a council lawfully assembled errs and has erred, you are to me as a heathen and a publican."

Eck was fully justified in taking this position, for to deny or doubt the infallibility of a general council was to reject the one ultimate authority depended upon for centuries by Catholic Christians. That Luther took his stand upon the Bible did not help the matter. According to Catholic belief, the church alone could properly interpret the Bible, and to set the teaching

of the one in opposition to the other was nothing less than heresy. . . .

The debate from Luther's point of view was not a success. He had hoped much from it, and returned home greatly disappointed. Despite his own and his supporters' claims, the victory was really Eck's, not his, and it was fairly won. No other outcome was possible, and the result might have been foreseen. Luther made a much better showing against the powerful and resourceful debater than Carlstadt, but even his skill was unequal to the task of defending an essentially indefensible position. He committed the mistake of supposing that the radical views reached under the influence of his own religious experience were in harmony with the faith of the church. It is a common mistake. Some men, when they find themselves out of sympathy with the prevailing beliefs of the institution wherein they have been born and bred, at once turn their backs upon it. Others of a more sanguine temperament, or with more of the reformer's instinct, read its faith in the light of their own opinions, and endeavor to call their fellows back to what they believe its real platform. When, as is very apt to happen, a conflict comes and they try to defend as orthodox what they were originally led to accept as true, they only invite defeat. Luther maintained at Leipsic not merely that his interpretation of the papacy was correct, but that it was orthodox, and in this, as Eck showed, he was wrong. There remained only the alternative of abandoning his interpretation and accepting the traditional view or of foregoing the claim of orthodoxy. Consciously and deliberately he chose the latter course, and in doing so broke decisively with all his past.

Eck repeatedly protested that he held all his opinions subject to correction by the ecclesiastical authorities, but Luther avowed submission to no one. Only to the clear teaching of the divine word would he bow, and he would read it with his own and not with other men's eyes. In his attack on indulgences he had appealed from the indulgence-venders to the pope; at Augsburg, from the pope-ill-informed to the pope-to-be-better-informed; and soon afterward from the pope to a council. Now, when the decision of a council was cited against him, he declined to be bound by it, and took his stand upon the sole authority of the Scriptures. But even this was not final. The Bible itself, he maintained, has to be used with discrimination, for parts of it do not teach Christian truth. He really substituted for all external authorities the enlightened conscience of the individual Christian. The Bible he read for himself and admitted the claim of no council or body of men to read it for him. This, in principle, though he never fully realized it, and seldom acted upon it, meant the right of private judgment in religious things, and in it lay the promise of a new age. . . .

The significance of the Leipsic debate for Luther's own development it is impossible to exaggerate. It meant the final parting of the ways. It showed him clearly where he stood and emancipated him once and for all from the delusion that he was in harmony with the papal Church and could remain permanently within it. His condemnation he saw must follow in due time, and while Miltitz was still hopeful, and was industriously laying plans for compromise and conciliation, Luther himself was preparing for the break he knew could not long be delayed.

3. The Core of Lutheran Doctrine

The Leipsic debate first demonstrated clearly to the world (and to Luther himself) the great gulf between Luther and the church. The inexorable logic of circumstances had driven the monk to deny first the authority of the pope, then that of church councils. Finally, he rested his case upon the Scriptures. But it was not the Scriptures as interpreted by the church; rather, it was the Scriptures as interpreted by the enlightened conscience of the individual Christian. In short, Luther denied the corporate judgment of the church and rested his case upon the private judgment of educated Christians. This shocking unorthodoxy jarred Luther, but it did not deter him. Convinced of the righteousness of his cause, he set out immediately to clarify and, with many appeals to the Bible, to justify his position. Even while the church prepared the Bull *Exsurge Domine* (June 15, 1520) which excommunicated him and condemned his writings, Luther was preparing written defenses and expositions of his opinions. During the summer of 1520 he published three treatises which, taken together, constitute the core of Lutheranism. The first, his *Address to the Christian Nobility of the German Nation Respecting the Reformation of the Christian Estate,* is an appeal to the temporal authorities —to those German princes who were eager to enlarge their state powers at imperial expense—to defy the church and to institute much-needed religious, social, and political reform—an appeal, in short, to the state as against the church; the second, *On the Babylonian Captivity of the Church,* attacks the sacramental system of the church and argues particularly against transubstantiation; and the third, a magnificent essay, *Concerning Christian Liberty,* sets forth the essence of Protestant theology, justification by faith. Excerpts from each of these treatises follow.

From LUTHER, *Address to the Christian Nobility* (1520) [1]

The time for silence is gone, and the time to speak has come, as we read in Ecclesiastes (iii, 7). I have, in conformity with our resolve, put together some few points concerning the reformation of the Christian estate, with the intent of placing the same before the Christian nobility of the German nation, in case it may please God to help His Church by means of the laity, inasmuch as the clergy, whom this task rather befitted, have become quite careless. . . .

It is not out of mere arrogance and perversity that I, an individual poor man, have taken upon me to address your lordships. The distress and misery that oppress all the Christian estates, more especially in Germany, have led not only myself, but every one else, to cry aloud and to ask for help, and have now forced me too to cry out and to ask if God would give His Spirit to any one to reach a hand to His wretched people. Councils have often put forward some remedy, but it has adroitly been frustrated, and the evils have become worse, through the cunning of certain men. Their malice and wickedness I will now, by the help of God, expose, so that, being known, they may henceforth cease to be so obstructive and injurious. God has given us a young and noble sovereign, and by this has aroused great hopes in many hearts; now it is right that we too should do what we can, and make good use of time and grace. . . .

The Romanists have, with great adroitness, drawn three walls round themselves, with which they have hitherto protected themselves, so that no one could reform them, whereby all Christendom has fallen terribly.

Firstly, if pressed by the temporal power,

[1] *Luther's Primary Works,* trans. and ed. by Wace and Buckheim, 159, 161-239.

they have affirmed and maintained that the temporal power has no jurisdiction over them, but, on the contrary, that the spiritual power is above the temporal.

Secondly, if it were proposed to admonish them with the Scriptures, they objected that no one may interpret the Scriptures but the Pope.

Thirdly, if they are threatened with a council, they pretend that no one may call a council but the Pope. . . .

Now may God help us, and give us one of those trumpets that overthrew the walls of Jericho, so that we may blow down these walls of straw and paper, and that we may set free our Christian rods for the chastisement of sin, and expose the craft and deceit of the devil, so that we may amend ourselves by punishment and again obtain God's favour.

THE FIRST WALL
THAT THE TEMPORAL POWER HAS NO JURISDICTION OVER THE SPIRITUALITY. . . .

It has been devised that the Pope, bishops, priests, and monks are called the *spiritual estate,* princes, lords, artificers, and peasants are the *temporal estate.* This is an artful lie and hypocritical device, but let no one be made afraid by it, and that for this reason: that all Christians are truly of the spiritual estate, and there is no difference among them, save of office alone. . . .

Since, then, the temporal power is baptised as we are, and has the same faith and Gospel, we must allow it to be priest and bishop, and account its office an office that is proper and useful to the Christian community. . . .

It follows, then, that between laymen and priests, princes and bishops, or, as they call it, between spiritual and temporal persons, the only real difference is one of office and function, and not of estate, for they are all of the same spiritual estate, true priests, bishops, and popes, though their functions are not the same—just as among priests and monks every man has not the same functions. . . . Therefore I say, Forasmuch as the temporal power has been ordained by God for the punishment of the bad and the protection of the good, therefore we must let it do its duty throughout the whole Christian body, without respect of persons, whether it strike popes, bishops, priests, monks, nuns, or whoever it may be.

THE SECOND WALL
THAT NO ONE MAY INTERPRET THE SCRIPTURES BUT THE POPE

The second wall is even more tottering and weak: that they alone pretend to be considered masters of the Scriptures; although they learn nothing of them all their life. They assume authority, and juggle before us with impudent words, saying that the Pope cannot err in matters of faith, whether he be evil or good, albeit they cannot prove it by a single letter. . . . But not to fight them with our own words, we will quote the Scriptures. St. Paul says, "If anything be revealed to another that sitteth by, let the first hold his peace" (1 Cor. xiv. 30). What would be the use of this commandment, if we were to believe him alone that teaches or has the highest seat? Christ Himself says, "And they shall be all taught of God" (St. John vi. 45). Thus it may come to pass that the Pope and his followers are wicked and not true Christians, and not being taught by God, have no true understanding, whereas a common man may have true understanding. Why should we then not follow him? Has not the Pope often erred? Who could help Christianity, in case the Pope errs, if we do not rather believe another who has the Scriptures for him?

Therefore it is a wickedly devised fable—and they cannot quote a single letter to confirm it—that it is for the Pope alone to interpret the Scriptures or to confirm the interpretation of them. They have assumed the authority of their own selves. And though they say that this authority was given to St. Peter when the keys were given to him, it is plain enough that the keys were not given to St. Peter alone, but to the whole community.

THE THIRD WALL
THAT NO ONE MAY CALL A COUNCIL BUT THE POPE

The third wall falls of itself, as soon as the first two have fallen; for if the Pope acts contrary to the Scriptures, we are bound to stand by the Scriptures, to punish and to constrain him, according to Christ's commandment, "Moreover, if thy brother shall trespass against thee, go and tell him his fault between thee and him alone; if he shall hear thee, thou hast gained thy brother. But if he will not hear thee, then take with thee one or two more, that in the mouth of two or three witnesses every word may be established. And if he shall neglect to hear the Church, let him be unto thee as a heathen man and a publican" (St. Matt. xviii. 15-17). Here each member is commanded to take care for the other; much more then should we do this, if it is a ruling member of the community that does evil, which by its evil-doing causes great harm and offence to the others. If then I am to accuse him before the Church, I must collect the Church together. . . .

Therefore when need requires, and the Pope is a cause of offence to Christendom, in these cases whoever can best do so, as a faithful member of the whole body, must do what he can to procure a true free council. This no one can do so well as the temporal authorities. . . .

Let us now consider the matters which should be treated in the councils, and with which popes, cardinals, bishops, and all learned men should occupy themselves day and night, if they love Christ and His Church. . . .

1. It is a distressing and terrible thing to see that the head of Christendom, who boasts of being the vicar of Christ and the successor of St. Peter, lives in a worldly pomp that no king or emperor can equal. . . .

2. What is the use in Christendom of the people called "cardinals"? I will tell you. In Italy and Germany there are many rich convents, endowments, fiefs, and benefices, and as the best way of getting these into the hands of Rome, they created cardinals, and gave them the sees, convents, and prelacies, and thus destroyed the service of God. That is why Italy is almost a desert now. . . .

Now that Italy is sucked dry, they come to Germany and begin very quietly; but if we look on quietly Germany will soon be brought into the same state as Italy. . . .

What has brought us Germans to such a pass that we have to suffer this robbery and this destruction of our property by the Pope? If the kingdom of France has resisted it, why do we Germans suffer ourselves to be fooled and deceived? . . .

Long ago the emperors and princes of Germany allowed the Pope to claim the *annates* from all German benefices; that is, half of the first year's income from every benefice. The object of this concession was that the Pope should collect a fund with all this money to fight against the Turks and infidels, and to protect Christendom, so that the nobility should not have to bear the burden of the struggle alone, and that the priests should also contribute. The popes have made such use of this good simple piety of the Germans that they have taken this money for more than one hundred years, and have now made of it a regular tax . . . [for] posts and offices at Rome. . . .

Whenever there is any pretence of fighting the Turks, they send out some com-

mission for collecting money, and often send out indulgences under the same pretext of fighting the Turks. They think we Germans will always remain such great and inveterate fools that we will go on giving money to satisfy their unspeakable greed, though we see plainly that neither *annates,* nor absolution money, nor any other—not one farthing—goes against the Turks, but all goes into the bottomless sack. . . .

Now though I am too lowly to submit articles that could serve for the reformation of these fearful evils, I will yet sing out my fool's song, and will show, as well as my wit will allow, what might and should be done by the temporal authorities or by a general council.

1. Princes, nobles, and cities should promptly forbid their subjects to pay the *annates* to Rome and should even abolish them altogether. For the Pope . . . has forfeited his right to them, and deserves punishment. . . .

3. It should be decreed by an imperial law that no episcopal cloak and no confirmation of any appointment shall for the future be obtained from Rome. The order of the most holy and renowned Nicene Council must again be restored, namely that a bishop must be confirmed by the two nearest bishops or by the archbishop. . . .

9. The Pope should have no power over the Emperor, except to anoint and crown him at the altar, as a bishop crowns a king. . . .

10. The Pope must withdraw his hand from the dish, and on no pretence assume royal authority over Naples and Sicily. He has no more right to them than I. . . .

14. We see also . . . how many a poor priest is encumbered with a woman and children and burdened in his conscience, and no one does anything to help him . . . therefore I say, According to the ordinances of Christ and His Apostles, every

town should have a minister or bishop, as St. Paul plainly says (Titus i.), and this minister should not be forced to live without a lawful wife, but should be allowed to have one, as St. Paul writes, saying that "a bishop then must be blameless, the husband of one wife . . . having his children in subjection with all gravity" (1 Tim. iii.). . . .

24. It is high time to take up earnestly and truthfully the cause of the Bohemians, to unite them with ourselves and ourselves with them, so that all mutual accusations, envy, and hatred may cease. I will be the first, in my folly, to give my opinion, with all due deference to those of better understanding.

First of all, we must honestly confess the truth, without attempting self-justification, and own one thing to the Bohemians, namely that John Huss and Jerome of Prague were burnt at Constance in violation of the papal, Christian, and imperial oath and safe-conduct. . . .

25. The universities also require a good, sound reformation. I must say this, let it vex whom it may. The fact is that whatever the papacy has ordered or instituted is only designed for the propagation of sin and error. . . .

Physicians I would leave to reform their own faculty; lawyers and theologians I take under my charge, and say firstly that it would be right to abolish the canon law entirely. . . . We are taught quite sufficiently in the Bible how we ought to act; all this study only prevents the study of the Scriptures. . . .

The civil law, too, good God! what a wilderness it is become! It is, indeed, much better, more skilful, and more honest than the canon law. . . . Still there is far too much of it. . . .

27. Let this be enough about the faults of the spiritual estate . . . we must now consider the defects of the temporal estates. In the first place, we require a general law and consent of the German nation against profusion and extravagance in dress, which is the cause of so much poverty among the nobles and the people. Surely God has given to us, as to other nations, enough wool, fur, flax, and whatever else is required for the decent clothing of every class; and it cannot be necessary to spend such enormous sums for silk, velvet, cloth of gold, and all other kinds of outlandish stuff.

From LUTHER, *On the Babylonian Captivity of the Church* (1520) [1]

CONCERNING THE LORD'S SUPPER

There are two passages which treat in the clearest manner of this subject, at which let us look: the statements in the Gospels respecting the Lord's Supper and the words of Paul (1 Cor. xi.). Matthew, Mark, and Luke agree that Christ gave the whole Sacrament to all His disciples; and that Paul delivered both parts of it is so certain that no one has yet been shameless enough to assert the contrary. Add to this that, according to the relation of Matthew, Christ did not say concerning the bread, "Eat ye all of this," but did say concerning the cup, "Drink ye all of this." Mark also does not say, "They all ate," but "They all drank of it." Each writer attaches the mark of universality to the cup, not to the bread, as if the Spirit foresaw the schism that should come, which would forbid to some that communion in the cup which Christ would have common to all. . . .

The first bondage, then, of this Sacrament is as regards its substance or completeness, which the tyranny of Rome has wrested from us. Not that they sin against Christ who use one kind only, since Christ has not commanded the use of any, but has left it to the choice of each individual,

[1] *Ibid.,* 302-13.

saying, "This do ye, as oft as ye shall do it, in remembrance of Me"; but they sin who forbid that both kinds should be given to those who desire to use this freedom of choice, and the fault is not in the laity, but in the priests. The Sacrament does not belong to the priests, but to all; nor are the priests lords, but servants, whose duty it is to give both kinds to those who seek them, as often as they seek them. . . .

There is, however, very much to be said for my opinion; in the first place this: that no violence ought to be done to the words of God, neither by man nor by angel, but that as far as possible they ought to be kept to their simplest meaning, and not to be taken, unless the circumstances manifestly compel us to do so, out of their grammatical and proper signification, that we may not give our adversaries any opportunity of evading the teaching of the whole Scriptures. . . . So in the present case, since the Evangelists write clearly that Christ took bread and blessed it, and since the book of Acts and the Apostle Paul also call it bread, real bread and real wine must be understood, just as the cup was real. For even these men do not say that the cup is transubstantiated. Since then it is not necessary to lay it down that a transubstantiation is effected by the operation of Divine power, it must be held as a figment of human opinion; for it rests on no support of Scripture or of reason. . . .

The Church, however, kept the right faith for more than twelve centuries, nor did the holy Fathers ever or anywhere make mention of this transubstantiation (a portentous word and dream indeed) until the counterfeit Aristotelian philosophy [scholasticism] began to make its inroads on the Church within these last three hundred years, during which many other erroneous conclusions have also been arrived at.

From LUTHER, *A Treatise on Christian Liberty* (1520) [1]

A Christian man is the most free lord of all, and subject to none; a Christian man is the most dutiful servant of all, and subject to every one.

Although these statements appear contradictory, yet, when they are found to agree together, they will make excellently for my purpose. They are both the statements of Paul himself, who says, "Though I be free from all men, yet have I made myself servant unto all" (1 Cor. ix. 19). . . .

Let us examine the subject on a deeper and less simple principle. Man is composed of a twofold nature, a spiritual and a bodily. As regards the spiritual nature, which they name the soul, he is called the spiritual, inward, new man; as regards the bodily nature, which they name the flesh, he is called the fleshly, outward, old man . . . the fact being that in the same man these two men are opposed to one another; the flesh lusting against the spirit, and the spirit against the flesh (Gal. v. 17).

We first approach the subject of the inward man, that we may see by what means a man becomes justified, free, and a true Christian; that is, a spiritual, new, and inward man. . . .

To preach Christ is to feed the soul, to justify it, to set it free, and to save it, if it believes the preaching. For faith alone, and the efficacious use of the word of God, bring salvation. "If thou shalt confess with thy mouth the Lord Jesus, and shalt believe in thine heart that God hath raised Him from the dead, thou shalt be saved" (Rom. x. 9); and again, "Christ is the end of the law for righteousness to every one that believeth" (Rom. x. 4), and "The just shall live by faith" (Rom. i. 17). For the word of God cannot be received and honoured by any works, but by faith

[1] *Ibid.*, 256-74.

alone. Hence it is clear that as the soul needs the word alone for life and justification, so it is justified by faith alone, and not by any works. For if it could be justified by any other means, it would have no need of the word, nor consequently of faith. . . .

But you ask how it can be the fact that faith alone justifies, and affords without works so great a treasure of good things, when so many works, ceremonies, and laws are prescribed to us in the Scriptures? I answer, Before all things bear in mind what I have said: that faith alone without works justifies, sets free, and saves, as I shall show more clearly below.

Meanwhile it is to be noted that the whole Scripture of God is divided into two parts: precepts and promises. The precepts certainly teach us what is good, but what they teach is not forthwith done. For they show us what we ought to do, but do not give us the power to do it. . . .

Now when a man has through the precepts been taught his own impotence, and become anxious by what means he may satisfy the law . . . then, being truly humbled and brought to nothing in his own eyes, he finds in himself no resource for justification and salvation.

Then comes in that other part of Scripture, the promises of God, which declare the glory of God, and say, "If you wish to fulfil the law, and, as the law requires, not to covet, lo! believe in Christ, in whom are promised to you grace, justification, peace, and liberty." All these things you shall have, if you believe, and shall be without them if you do not believe. For what is impossible for you by all the works of the law, which are many and yet useless, you shall fulfil in an easy and summary way through faith, because God the Father has made everything to depend on faith, so that whosoever has it has all things, and he who has it not has nothing. . . . Thus the promises of God give that which the precepts exact, and fulfil what the law commands; so that all is of God alone, both the precepts and their fulfilment. . . .

Now, since these promises of God are words of holiness, truth, righteousness, liberty, and peace, and are full of universal goodness, the soul, which cleaves to them with a firm faith, is so united to them, nay, thoroughly absorbed by them, that it not only partakes in, but is penetrated and saturated by, all their virtues. . . . In this way therefore the soul, through faith alone, without works, is from the word of God justified, sanctified, endued with truth, peace, and liberty, and filled full with every good thing. . . .

From all this it is easy to understand why faith has such great power, and why no good works, nor even all good works put together, can compare with it. . . . Faith alone and the word reign in it; and such as is the word, such is the soul made by it, just as iron exposed to fire glows like fire, on account of its union with the fire. It is clear then that to a Christian man his faith suffices for everything, and that he has no need of works for justification. But if he has no need of works, neither has he need of the law; and if he has no need of the law, he is certainly free from the law, and the saying is true, "The law is not made for a righteous man" (1 Tim. i. 9). This is that Christian liberty, our faith, the effect of which is, not that we should be careless or lead a bad life, but that no one should need the law or works for justification and salvation. . . .

And now let us turn to the other part: to the outward man. Here we shall give an answer to all those who, taking offence at the word of faith and at what I have asserted, say, "If faith does everything, and by itself suffices for justification, why then are good works commanded? Are we then to take our ease and do no works, content with faith?" Not so, impious men, I reply; not so. That would indeed really be the case, if we were thoroughly and completely inner and spiritual persons; but that will not happen until the last day, when the dead shall be raised. As long as we live in the flesh, we are but beginning and making advances in that which shall be completed in a future life. On this account the Apostle calls that which we have in this life the first fruits of the Spirit (Rom. viii. 23). . . . To this part belongs the fact I have stated before: that the Christian is the servant of all and subject to all. For in that part in which he is free he does no works, but in that in which he is a servant he does all works. Let us see on what principle this is so.

Although . . . a man is amply enough justified by faith . . . still he remains in this mortal life upon earth, in which it is necessary that he should rule his own body and have intercourse with men. Here then works begin; here he must not take his ease; here he must give heed to exercise his body by fastings, watchings, labour, and other regular discipline, so that it may be subdued to the spirit, and obey and conform itself to the inner man and faith, and not rebel against them nor hinder them, as is its nature to do if it is not kept under. For the inner man, being conformed to God and created after the image of God through faith, rejoices and delights itself in Christ, in whom such blessings have been conferred on it, and hence has only this task before it: to serve God with joy and for nought in free love. . . .

These works, however, must not be done with any notion that by them a man can be justified before God . . . but solely with this purpose: that the body may be brought into subjection, and be purified from its evil lusts. . . . Thus it comes that, from the requirements of his own body, a man cannot take his ease, but is compelled on its account to do many good works, that he may bring it into subjec-

tion. Yet these works are not the means of his justification before God; he does them out of disinterested love to the service of God; looking to no other end than to do what is well-pleasing to Him whom he desires to obey most dutifully in all things.

On this principle every man may easily instruct himself in what measure, and with what distinctions, he ought to chasten his own body. He will fast, watch, and labour, just as much as he sees to suffice for keeping down the wantonness and concupiscence of the body. But those who pretend to be justified by works are looking, not to the mortification of their lusts, but only to the works themselves; thinking that, if they can accomplish as many works and as great ones as possible, all is well with them, and they are justified.

4. The Growth of Lutheran Churches

RISE OF THE "PROTESTANT" PARTY

From SMITH, *Age of the Reformation* (1920) [1]

Having overthrown much of the doctrine and discipline of the old church Luther addressed himself with admirable vigor and great success to the task of building up a substitute for it. In this the combination of the conservative and at the same time thoroughly popular spirit of the movement manifested itself. In divine service the vernacular was substituted for Latin. New emphasis was placed upon preaching, Bible-reading and hymn-singing. Mass was no longer incomprehensible, but was an act of worship in which all could intelligently participate; bread and wine were both given to the

[1] Preserved Smith, *The Age of the Reformation*, 112-15. Reprinted by permission of Henry Holt and Company.

laity, and those words of the canon implying transubstantiation and sacrifice were omitted. Marriage was relegated from the rank of a sacrament to that of a civil contract. Baptism was kept in the old form, even to the detail of exorcizing the evil spirit. Auricular confession was permitted but not insisted upon.

The problems of church government and organization were pressing. Two alternatives were theoretically possible, congregationalism or state churches. After some hesitation, Luther was convinced . . . that the latter was the only practicable course. The governments of the various German states and cities were now given supreme power in ecclesiastical matters. They took over the property belonging to the old church and administered it generally for religious or educational or charitable purposes. A system of church-visitation was started, by which the central authority passed upon the competence of each minister. Powers of appointment and removal were vested in the government. The title and office of bishop were changed in most cases to that of "superintendent," though in some German sees and generally in Sweden the name bishop was retained.

How genuinely popular was the Lutheran movement may be seen in the fact that the free cities, Nuremberg, Augsburg, Strassburg, Ulm, Lübeck, Hamburg, and many others, were the first to revolt from Rome. In other states the government led the way. Electoral Saxony evolved slowly into complete Protestantism. . . . The neighboring state of Hesse was won about 1524, though the official ordinance promulgating the evangelical doctrine was not issued until 1526. A very important acquisition was Prussia. Hitherto it had been governed by the Teutonic Order, a military society like the Knights Templars. Albert of Brandenburg became Grand Master in 1511, and fourteen years later saw the opportunity of aggrandizing his personal power by renouncing his spiritual ties. He accordingly declared the Teutonic Order abolished and himself temporal Duke of Prussia. . . .

The growth of Lutheranism unmolested by the imperial government was made possible by the absorption of the emperor's energies in his rivalry with France and Turkey and by the decentralization of the Empire. Leagues between groups of German states had been quite common in the past, and a new stimulus to their formation was given by the common religious interest. The first league of this sort was that of Ratisbon, between Bavaria and other South German principalities; its purpose was to carry out the Edict of Worms. This was followed by a similar league in North Germany between Catholic states, known as the League of Dessau, and a Protestant confederation known as the League of Torgau.

The Diet held at Spires in the summer of 1526 witnessed the strength of the new party, for in it the two sides treated on equal terms. Many reforms were proposed, and some carried through against the obstruction by Ferdinand, the emperor's brother and lieutenant. The great question was the enforcement of the Edict of Worms, and on this the Diet passed an act, known as a Recess, providing that each state should act in matters of faith as it could answer to God and the emperor. In effect this allowed the government of every German state to choose between the two confessions, thus anticipating the principle of the Religious Peace of Augsburg of 1555.

The relations of the two parties were so delicate that it seemed as if a general religious war were imminent. . . .

The Diet which met at Spires early in 1529 endeavored to deal as drastically as possible with the schism. The Recess passed by the Catholic majority on April 7 was most unfavorable to the Reformers, repealing the Recess of the last Diet in their favor. Catholic states were commanded to execute the persecuting Edict of Worms, although Lutheran states were forbidden to abolish the office of the (Catholic) mass, and also to allow any further innovations in their own doctrines or practices until the calling of a general council. The princes were forbidden to harbor the subjects of another state. The Evangelical members of the Diet, much aggrieved at this blow to their faith, published a Protest taking the ground that the Recess of 1526 had been in the nature of a treaty and could not be abrogated without the consent of both parties to it. . . . The Protest and the appeal were signed by the Elector of Saxony, the Landgrave of Hesse, a few smaller states, and fourteen free cities. From the Protest they became immediately known as "the Protesting Estates," and subsequently, the name Protestant was given to all those who left the Roman communion.

THE SPREAD OF LUTHERANISM: AN EXAMPLE FROM WEST PRUSSIA

From THE BISHOP OF POMERANIA, *Program of Reforms* (1525) [1]

1. Hitherto you have held seven sacraments, but not rightly. Henceforward faith must be before all things the foundation of your salvation, and you must have no more sacraments than Christ ordained; namely, Holy Communion and Holy Baptism.

2. Henceforward no ban shall hold good which burdens the conscience without ground in God's Word, and is of force only by human institution.

3. Henceforward no confession (auric-

ularis scilicet confessio) shall be made to the priest, whereby a man is bound to make known all his sins.

4. Henceforward there shall be no pilgrimages nor wanderings to holy places, since they aid no man's salvation. . . .

6. Henceforward no ringing nor singing nor Masses nor Vigils for the dead are to be held: for they are of no use, and of no avail.

7. Henceforward no water, salt, ashes, palms, tapers, greenery, and the like are to be hallowed: for it is all nonsense and no good. . . .

9. There are to be no more Orders, neither monks nor nuns; but only such Orders as war against unbelievers and heathen, like the Teutonic Order.

10. Bishops shall continue and remain; not anointing-bishops nor ordaining-bishops, but such as preach and teach and expound the pure word of God and preside over the Church.

11. Henceforward there are to be no superstitious distinctions made of days and seasons, with all sorts of Feast Days; it conduces to God's dishonour. Holy Baptism is to be administered in German, without chrism and oil. . . .

16. Pictures in houses and churches are not to be prayed to, nor to have any candles lit before them. . . .

19. The daily Mass is an abomination to God: so henceforward it is not to be observed in any church or anywhere.

20. When a man desires to go to Holy Communion, he must cause the priest, his confessor, to inform him out of God's Word, and must also inform himself, how he should receive and take the bread and wine according to Christ's institution in both kinds.

21. If any one thinks that he can make satisfaction for his sins himself or can save himself apart from the merits of Christ, *anathema esto,* let him be damned!

[1] This and the next two selections are from B. J. Kidd, ed., *Documents Illustrative of the Continental Reformation,* 1911. By permission of The Clarendon Press, Oxford. This is No. 92, 189-91.

22. All priests and monks and nuns are at liberty to leave their orders and marry.

THE LEAGUE OF SCHMALKALDEN (1531)

In 1530, at an Imperial Diet in Augsburg, the Lutherans, having lent assistance to Charles V against the Turks, hoped to win imperial recognition by a show of moderation. Accordingly, a Confession of Faith, carefully drawn up by Melanchthon, was presented to the Emperor "in order that in this matter of religion the opinions and judgments of diverse parties may be heard in each other's presence . . . [and] harmonized." But for the opposition of orthodox princes and papal representatives, Charles might have accepted the Augsburg Confession. Instead, he denounced it as contrary to the Catholic faith, and the Confession remained merely as a mature statement of Lutheran principles.

The Emperor's rejection of the Augsburg Confession was followed by resolutions to execute the Edict of Worms (whereby, in 1521, Luther had been declared an outlaw by the Imperial Diet) and to restore church properties confiscated by Lutheran princes. For the latter purpose, the Imperial Court of Appeals (*Reichskammergericht*) was reconstituted to obstruct secularization of church property and to aid in suppressing Lutheranism. To combat this legal attack and to prepare against the possible use of force by the Emperor, Lutheran leaders assembled at Schmalkalden. In the course of negotiations from December, 1530, until a year later, the Lutheran princes concluded an armed union known as the League of Schmalkalden. One of the early agreements signed (February 27, 1531) during these negotiations follows.

From the Schmalkaldic *Agreement for Mutual Assistance* (1531) [1]

We, John, by the grace of God, Arch-marshal and Elector of the Holy Roman Empire and John Frederick, father and son, Dukes of Saxony &c.; Philip, Otto, and the brothers Ernest and Francis, all Dukes of Brunswick and Lüneburg; Philip, Landgrave of Hesse, &c.; Wolfgang, Prince of Anhalt, &c.; the brothers Gebhard and Albert, Counts of Mansfeld; and the Burgomaster and Council of the under-mentioned cities of Upper Germany, Saxony, and the Sea, viz., Strassburg, Ulm, Constance, Reutlingen, Memmingen, Lindau, Biberach, Isny, Lübeck, Magdeburg and Bremen, do all men to wit:

Whereas it is altogether likely that those who have the pure Word of God preached in their territory, and thereby have abolished many abuses, are to be prevented by force from continuing this service so pleasing to God;

And whereas it is the duty of every Christian government not only to have the Word of God preached to its subjects but also, as far as possible, to prevent their being compelled to fall away from it;

Now we, solely for the sake of our own defence and deliverance, which both by human and divine right is permitted to every one, have agreed that whenever any one of us is attacked on account of the Word of God and the doctrine of the Gospel, or anything connected therewith, all the others shall immediately come to his assistance, as best they can, and help to deliver him.

THE RELIGIOUS PEACE OF AUGSBURG (SEPTEMBER 25, 1555)

The existence of the League of Schmalkalden essentially divided the

[1] *Ibid.*, No. 124, 301.

Holy Roman Empire into two armed camps, the imperial and the Lutheran. But until the Emperor could compose his external differences with the Turk and with Francis I of France, he had no opportunity to march against the Lutherans within his borders. That opportunity came in 1546 and the internal struggles known as the Schmalkaldic Wars lasted, with some uneasy respites, until 1555. In that year, at an imperial diet at Augsburg, Catholic and Lutheran princes negotiated a treaty which gave legal recognition to Lutheranism in Germany on the narrow principle of *cuius regio eius religio* [whosoever rules the territory, his religion shall prevail]. The core of the treaty is set forth in the following excerpts; that it was little more than a truce is evident from the wording of article 20.

From *The Peace of Augsburg* (1555) [1]

15. In order to bring peace into the holy Empire of the Germanic Nation between the Roman Imperial Majesty and the Electors, Princes, and Estates: let neither his Imperial Majesty nor the Electors, Princes, &c., do any violence or harm to any estate of the Empire on account of the Augsburg Confession, but let them enjoy their religious belief, liturgy and ceremonies as well as their estates and other rights and privileges in peace; and complete religious peace shall be obtained only by Christian means of amity, or under threat of the punishment of the imperial ban.

16. Likewise the Estates espousing the Augsburg Confession shall let all the Estates and Princes who cling to the old religion live in absolute peace and in the enjoyment of all their estates, rights and privileges.

17. However, all such as do not belong to the two above-named religions shall not

1 *Ibid.*, No. 149, 363-64.

be included in the present peace but be totally excluded from it.

18. And since it has proved to be matter of great dispute what was to happen with the bishoprics, priories, and other ecclesiastical benefices of such Catholic priests as would in course of time abandon the old religion, we have in virtue of the powers of Roman Emperors ordained as follows: Where an archbishop, bishop or prelate or any other priest of our old religion shall abandon the same, his archbishopric, bishopric, prelacy, and other benefices, together with all their income and revenues which he has so far possessed, shall be abandoned by him without any further objection or delay. The chapters and such as are entitled to it by common law or the custom of the place shall elect a person espousing the old religion, who may enter on the possession and enjoyment of all the rights and incomes of the place without any further hindrance and without prejudging any ultimate amicable settlement of religion.

19. Some of the abbeys, monasteries, and other ecclesiastical estates having been confiscated and turned into churches, schools, and charitable institutions, it is herewith ordained that such estates as their original owners had not possessed at the time of the treaty of Passau [1552] shall be comprised in the present treaty of peace.

20. The ecclesiastical jurisdiction over the Augsburg Confession, doctrine, appointment of ministers, church usages, orders, and ceremonies hitherto practised (but apart from all the rights of the Electors, Princes and Estates, Colleges and Monasteries, to taxes in money or tithes) shall from now cease, and the Augsburg Confession shall be left to the free and untrammelled enjoyment of their religion, ceremonies, appointment of ministers, as is stated in a subsequent separate article, until the final settlement of religion shall take place.

9 CALVINISM

1. "Institutes of the Christian Religion" (1536)

After Martin Luther, the greatest Protestant figure of the Reformation was John Calvin (1509-1564). Born in France and educated in law and humanistic learning, Calvin was impelled toward theology late in his university career. In the course of 1534, the cruel treatment of French Protestants by Francis I led Calvin to seek refuge in Switzerland. Arriving at Basel early in 1535, he devoted the early months of his exile to the completion of his greatest work, *Institutes of the Christian Religion,* first published in 1536.

Primarily, the *Institutes* was an exposition of the Bible which, as Calvin always insisted, constituted the whole and perfect Word of God—the complete law and discipline for Christian man. Yet, by the nature and timing of the book, it was much more. Its dignified tone, judicious nature, and learned contents marked its young author as the ablest interpreter of Christian doctrine that Protestantism had produced. Also, its bold though respectful "Prefatory Address" to King Francis I of France betrayed Calvin as a passionate defender of a persecuted cause and placed him at the head of French reformers.

Calvin's greatest contributions were the *systematization* of the whole body of Protestant divinity and the *practical application* of scriptural law to civil society at Geneva. He was not highly original. He merely built upon the theological and ecclesiastical structure of his predecessors, especially Luther, whom he greatly admired. Still, in at least two important particulars Calvinism came to bear the peculiar stamp of its creator. The first of these was Calvin's emphasis upon predestination [see page 121]; the second (which, as will be seen, followed from the first) was Calvin's unusual concept of the church both as to its ecclesiastical organization and as to its relation to the state. Calvin held that the church was a dual concept, the *Visible Church* and the *Invisible Church* [see pages 121, 125]. The Visible Church was the church actually organized by men, containing both saints and sinners, sincere Christians and hypocrites; the Invisible Church consisted of all the Elect of God, whether members of a Visible Church or not. Only God knew the exact boundaries of the Invisible Church, which was the Church Universal, giving that unity to Christendom which Roman Catholics maintained the Reformation had destroyed. But it was the duty of the Visible Church, by a careful and constant scrutiny of its members, to identify itself as closely as humanly possible with the Invisible Church. The attempts of the members of Visible Churches to exclude hypocrites and to confine their membership to the elect goes far to explain the strictness of Calvinists in manners and morals. And as they believed eternal salvation to be the most important aim of man, they insisted that the power of the state must ever be directed toward this goal in co-operation with the Visible Churches. To a considerable degree Calvin's insistence upon the co-operation of the state made the state coterminous with, and subservient to, the church. Accordingly, the government of Geneva was known as a "theocracy," and Calvin, because he meddled in politics, became known among his adversaries as the "Pope of Geneva."

The *Institutes* was revised several times and passed through many editions before Calvin's death. The following extracts illustrate the tone, the style, and some of the tenets of Calvin's work.

From CALVIN, *Institutes* (1536) [1]

[PREFATORY ADDRESS TO KING FRANCIS I
(DATED "BASLE, IST AUGUST, 1536")]

Sire, When I first engaged in this work, nothing was farther from my thoughts than to write what should afterwards be presented to your Majesty. My intention was only to furnish a kind of rudiments, by which those who feel some interest in religion might be trained to true godliness. And I toiled at the task chiefly for the sake of my countrymen the French, multitudes of whom I perceived to be hungering and thirsting after Christ, while very few seemed to have been duly imbued with even a slender knowledge of him. That this was the object which I had in view is apparent from the work itself, which is written in a simple and elementary form adapted for instruction.

But when I perceived that the fury of certain bad men had risen to such a height in your realm, that there was no place in it for sound doctrine, I thought it might be of service if I were in the same work both to give instruction to my countrymen, and also lay before your Majesty a Confession, from which you may learn what the doctrine is that so inflames the rage of those madmen, who are this day, with fire and sword, troubling your kingdom. For I fear not to declare, that what I have here given may be regarded as a summary of the very doctrine which, they vociferate, ought to be punished with confiscation, exile, imprisonment, and flames, as well as exterminated by land and sea. . . .

Let it not be imagined that I am here framing my own private defence, with the view of obtaining a safe return to my native land. Though I cherish towards it the feelings which become me as a man, still, as matters now are, I can be absent from it without regret. The cause which I plead is the common cause of all the godly, and therefore the very cause of Christ—a cause which, throughout your realm, now lies, as it were, in despair, torn and trampled upon in all kinds of ways, and that more through the tyranny of certain Pharisees than any sanction from yourself. . . .

Your duty, most serene Prince, is, not to shut either your ears or mind against a cause involving such mighty interests as these: how the glory of God is to be maintained on the earth inviolate, how the truth of God is to preserve its dignity, how the kingdom of Christ is to continue amongst us compact and secure. The cause is worthy of your ear, worthy of your investigation, worthy of your throne. . . .

Our adversaries, indeed, clamorously maintain that our appeal to the word of God is a mere pretext—that we are, in fact, its worst corrupters. How far this is not only malicious calumny, but also shameless effrontery, you will be able to decide, of your own knowledge, by reading our Confession. . . . The true religion which is delivered in the Scriptures, and which all ought to hold, they [our adversaries] readily permit both them-

[1] *Institutes of the Christian Religion,* trans. by Henry Beveridge, *Works of John Calvin,* 52 vols., Calvin Translation Society, Edinburgh, 1843-1855, L, 3-19; LI, 529-46, 385-90; LII, 10-11, 19-22.

selves and others to be ignorant of, to neglect and despise; and they deem it of little moment what each man believes concerning God and Christ, or disbelieves, provided he submits to the judgment of the Church with what they call implicit faith; nor are they greatly concerned though they should see the glory of God dishonoured by open blasphemies, provided not a finger is raised against the primacy of the Apostolic See and the authority of holy mother Church. Why, then, do they war for the mass, purgatory, pilgrimage, and similar follies, with such fierceness and acerbity, that though they cannot prove one of them from the word of God, they deny godliness can be safe without faith in these things—faith drawn out, if I may so express it, to its utmost stretch? Why? Just because their belly is their God, and their kitchen their religion. . . . He, accordingly, who is most anxious about his stomach, proves the fiercest champion of his faith. In short, the object on which all to a man are bent, is to keep their kingdom safe or their belly filled; not one gives even the smallest sign of sincere zeal. . . .

The hinges on which the controversy turns are these: first, in their contending that the form of the Church is always visible and apparent; and, secondly, in their placing this form in the see of the Church of Rome and its hierarchy. We, on the contrary, maintain, both that the Church may exist without any apparent form, and, moreover, that the form is not ascertained by that external splendour which they foolishly admire, but by a very different mark, namely, by the pure preaching of the word of God, and the due administration of the sacraments. . . .

But to return, Sire. Be not moved by the absurd insinuations with which our adversaries are striving to frighten you into the belief that nothing else is wished and aimed at by this new gospel (for so

they term it) than opportunity for sedition and impunity for all kinds of vice. Our God is not the author of division, but of peace; and the Son of God, who came to destroy the works of the devil, is not the minister of sin.

[PREDESTINATION]

The covenant of life is not preached equally to all, and among those to whom it is preached, does not always meet with the same reception. This diversity displays the unsearchable depth of the divine judgment, and is without doubt subordinate to God's purpose of eternal election. But if it is plainly owing to the mere pleasure of God that salvation is spontaneously offered to some, while others have no access to it, great and difficult questions immediately arise, questions which are inexplicable, when just views are not entertained concerning election and predestination. To many this seems a perplexing subject, because they deem it most incongruous that of the great body of mankind some should be predestinated to salvation, and others to destruction. How causelessly they entangle themselves will appear as we proceed. . . . Paul declares that it cannot be known unless God, throwing works entirely out of view, elect those whom he has predestined. His words are, "Even so then at this present time also, there is a remnant according to the election of grace. And if by grace, then it is no more of works: otherwise grace is no more grace. But if it be of works, then it is no more grace: otherwise work is no more work," (Rom. xi. 6.) If to make it appear that our salvation flows entirely from the good mercy of God, we must be carried back to the origin of election, then those who would extinguish it, wickedly do as much as in them lies to obscure what they ought most loudly to extol, and pluck up humility by the very roots. . . .

But before I enter on the subject, I have

some remarks to address to two classes of men. . . . First, then, when they inquire into predestination, let them remember that they are penetrating into the recesses of the divine wisdom, where he who rushes forward securely and confidently, instead of satisfying his curiosity will enter an inextricable labyrinth. For it is not right that man should with impunity pry into things which the Lord has been pleased to conceal within himself, and scan that sublime eternal wisdom which it is his pleasure that we should not apprehend but adore, that therein also his perfections may appear. Those secrets of his will, which he has seen it meet to manifest, are revealed in his word—revealed in so far as he knew to be conducive to our interest and welfare.

"We have come into the way of faith," says Augustine: "let us constantly adhere to it. It leads to the chambers of the king, in which are hidden all the treasures of wisdom and knowledge. For our Lord Jesus Christ did not speak invidiously to his great and most select disciples when he said, 'I have yet many things to say unto you, but ye cannot hear them now,' (John xvi. 12.) We must walk, advance, increase, that our hearts may be able to comprehend those things which they cannot now comprehend.". . . Let us not be ashamed to be ignorant in a matter in which ignorance is learning. Rather let us willingly abstain from the search after knowledge, to which it is both foolish as well as perilous, and even fatal to aspire. If an unrestrained imagination urges us, our proper course is to oppose it with these words, "It is not good to eat much honey: so for men to search their own glory is not glory," (Prov. xxv. 27.) There is good reason to dread a presumption which can only plunge us headlong into ruin. . . .

I admit that profane men lay hold of the subject of predestination to carp, or cavil, or snarl, or scoff. But if their petulance frightens us, it will be necessary to conceal all the principal articles of faith, because they and their fellows leave scarcely one of them unassailed with blasphemy. . . .

The predestination by which God adopts some to the hope of life, and adjudges others to eternal death, no man who would be thought pious ventures simply to deny; but it is greatly cavilled at, especially by those who make prescience its cause. We, indeed, ascribe both prescience and predestination to God; but we say, that it is absurd to make the latter subordinate to the former. When we attribute prescience to God, we mean that all things always were, and ever continue, under his eye; that to his knowledge there is no past or future, but all things are present, and indeed so present, that it is not merely the idea of them that is before him (as those objects are which we retain in our memory,) but that he truly sees and contemplates them as actually under his immediate inspection. This prescience extends to the whole circuit of the world, and to all creatures. By predestination we mean the eternal decree of God, by which he determined with himself whatever he wished to happen with regard to every man. All are not created on equal terms, but some are preordained to eternal life, others to eternal damnation; and, accordingly, as each has been created for one or other of these ends, we say that he has been predestinated to life or to death. . . .

Many controvert all the positions which we have laid down, especially the gratuitous election of believers, which, however, cannot be overthrown. For they commonly imagine that God distinguishes between men according to the merits which he foresees that each individual is to have, giving the adoption of sons to those whom he foreknows will not be unworthy of his grace, and dooming those to destruction whose dispositions he perceives will be prone to mischief and wickedness. Thus by interposing foreknowledge as a veil, they not only obscure election, but pretend to give it a different origin. Nor is this the commonly received opinion of the vulgar merely, for it has in all ages had great supporters. This I candidly confess, lest any one should expect greatly to prejudice our cause by opposing it with their names. The truth of God is here too certain to be shaken, too clear to be overborne by human authority. Others, who are neither versed in Scripture, nor entitled to any weight, assail sound doctrine with a petulance and improbity which it is impossible to tolerate. Because God of his mere good pleasure electing some passes by others, they raise a plea against him. But if the fact is certain, what can they gain by quarrelling with God? We teach nothing but what experience proves to be true, viz., that God has always been at liberty to bestow his grace on whom he would. . . .

Wherever this good pleasure of God reigns, no good works are taken into account. The Apostle, indeed, does not follow out the antithesis, but it is to be understood, as he himself explains it in another passage, "Who hath called us with a holy calling, not according to our works, but according to his own purpose and grace, which was given us in Christ Jesus before the world began," (1 Tim. ii. 9.) We have already shown that the additional words, "that we might be holy," remove every doubt. If you say that he foresaw they would be holy, and therefore elected them, you invert the order of Paul. You may, therefore, safely infer, If he elected us that we might be holy, he did not elect us because he foresaw that we would be holy. . . . Assuredly divine grace would not deserve all the praise of election, were not election gratuitous; and it would not be gratuitous,

did God in electing any individual pay regard to his future works. Hence, what Christ said to his disciples is found to be universally applicable to all believers, "Ye have not chosen me, but I have chosen you," (John xv. 16.) Here he not only excludes past merits, but declares that they had nothing in themselves for which they could be chosen, except in so far as his mercy anticipated. And how are we to understand the words of Paul, "Who hath first given to him, and it shall be recompensed unto him again"? (Rom. xi. 35.) His meaning obviously is, that men are altogether indebted to the preventing goodness of God, there being nothing in them, either past or future, to conciliate his favour.

[GOOD WORKS]

[In the eyes of his enemies, especially of Catholics, Calvin's emphasis upon predestination appeared to destroy any obligation on the part of Christians to perform good works. Calvin rejected these charges with vigor.]

Our last sentence may refute the impudent calumny of certain ungodly men, who charge us, first, with destroying good works, and leading men away from the study of them, when we say, that men are not justified, and do not merit salvation by works; and, secondly, with making the means of justification too easy, when we say that it consists in the free remission of sins, and thus alluring men to sin to which they are already too much inclined. These calumnies, I say, are sufficiently refuted by that one sentence; however, I will briefly reply to both. The allegation is, that justification by faith destroys good works. I will not describe what kind of zealots for good works the persons are who thus charge us. We leave them as much liberty to bring the charge, as they take license to taint the whole world with the pollution of their lives. They pretend to lament that when faith is so highly extolled, works are deprived of their proper place. But what if they are rather ennobled and established? We dream not of a faith which is devoid of good works, nor of a justification which can exist without them: the only difference is, that while we acknowledge that faith and works are necessarily connected, we, however, place justification in faith, not in works. How this is done is easily explained, if we turn to Christ only, to whom our faith is directed, and from whom it derives all its power. Why, then, are we justified by faith? Because by faith we apprehend the righteousness of Christ, which alone reconciles us to God. This faith, however, you cannot apprehend without at the same time apprehending sanctification; for Christ "is made unto us wisdom, and righteousness, and sanctification, and redemption," (1 Cor. i. 30.) Christ, therefore, justifies no man without also sanctifying him. These blessings are conjoined by a perpetual and inseparable tie. Those whom he enlightens by his wisdom he redeems; whom he redeems he justifies; whom he justifies he sanctifies. . . . Would ye then obtain justification in Christ? You must previously possess Christ. But you cannot possess him without being made a partaker of his sanctification: for Christ cannot be divided. Since the Lord, therefore, does not grant us the enjoyment of these blessings without bestowing himself, he bestows both at once, but never the one without the other. Thus it appears how true it is that we are justified not without, and yet not by works, since in the participation of Christ, by which we are justified, is contained not less sanctification than justification.

It is also most untrue that men's minds are withdrawn from the desire of well-doing when we deprive them of the idea of merit. Here, by the way, the reader must be told that those men absurdly infer merit from reward, as I will afterwards more clearly explain. They thus infer, because ignorant of the principle that God gives no less a display of his liberality when he assigns regard to works, than when he bestows the faculty of well-doing. This topic it will be better to defer to its own place. At present, let it be sufficient merely to advert to the weakness of their objection. This may be done in two ways. For, *first,* they are altogether in error when they say that, unless a hope of reward is held forth, no regard will be had to the right conduct of life. For if all that men do when they serve God is to look to the reward, and hire out or sell their labour to him, little is gained: he desires to be freely worshipped, freely loved: I say he approves the worshipper who, even if all hope of reward were cut off, would cease not to worship him. . . . Can there by a stronger incentive to holiness than when we are told . . . by Paul, "Having, therefore, these promises, dearly beloved, cleanse yourselves from all filthiness of the flesh and spirit;" or when we hear our Saviour hold forth himself as an example to us that we should follow his steps? . . .

All the Apostles abound in exhortations, admonitions, and rebukes, for the purpose of training the man of God to every good work, and that without any mention of merit. Nay, rather their chief exhortations are founded on the fact, that without any merit of ours, our salvation depends entirely on the mercy of God. . . .

But the most futile calumny of all is, that men are invited to sin when we affirm that the pardon in which we hold that justification consists is gratuitous. Our doctrine is, that justification is a thing of such value, that it cannot be put into the balance with any good quality of ours; and, therefore could never be obtained unless it were gratuitous: moreover, that it is gratuitous to us, but not also to Christ, who paid so dearly for it; namely, his own most sacred blood, out of which there was no price of sufficient value to pay what was due to the justice of God. . . . They pretend that God is appeased by their frivolous satisfactions; in other words, by mere dross. We maintain that the guilt of sin is too heinous to be so frivolously expiated; that the offence is too grave to be forgiven to such valueless satisfactions; and therefore, the forgiveness is the prerogative of Christ's blood alone. They say that righteousness, wherever it is defective, is renewed and repaired by works of satisfaction. We think it too precious to be balanced by any compensation of works, and, therefore, in order to restore it, recourse must be had solely to the mercy of God.

OF CHURCHES AND CHURCH UNITY

When in the Creed we profess to believe the Church, reference is made not only to the visible Church of which we are now treating, but also to all the elect of God, including in the number even those who have departed this life. . . . But as they are a small and despised number, concealed in an immense crowd, like a few grains of wheat buried among a heap of chaff, to God alone must be left the knowledge of his Church, of which his secret election forms the foundation. Nor is it enough to embrace the number of the elect in thought and intention merely. By the unity of the Church we must understand an unity into which we feel persuaded that we are truly ingrafted. For unless we are united with all the other members under Christ our head, no hope of the future inheritance awaits us. Hence the Church is called Catholic or Universal, for two or three cannot be invented without dividing Christ; and this is impossible. All the elect of God are so joined together in Christ, that as they depend on one head, so they are as it were compacted into one body, being knit together like its different members; made truly one by living together under the same Spirit of God in one faith, hope, and charity, called not only to the same inheritance of eternal life, but to participation to one God and Christ. For although the sad devastation which everywhere meets our view may proclaim that no Church remains, let us know that the death of Christ produces fruit, and that God wondrously preserves his Church, while placing it as it were in concealment. . . .

I have observed that the Scriptures speak of the Church in two ways. Sometimes when they speak of the Church they mean the Church as it really is before God—the Church into which none are admitted but those who by the gift of adoption are sons of God, and by the sanctification of the Spirit true members of Christ. In this case it not only comprehends the saints who dwell on the earth, but all the elect who have existed from the beginning of the world. Often, too, by the name of Church is designated the whole body of mankind scattered throughout the world, who profess to worship one God and Christ, who by baptism are initiated into the faith; by partaking of the Lord's Supper profess unity in true doctrine and charity, agree in holding the word of the Lord, and observe the ministry which Christ has appointed for the preaching of it. In this Church there is a very large mixture of hypocrites, who have nothing of Christ but the name and outward appearance: of ambitious, avaricious, envious, evil-speaking men, some also of impurer lives, who are tolerated for a time, either because their guilt cannot be legally established, or because due strictness of discipline is not always observed. Hence, it is necessary to believe the invisible Church, which is manifest to the eye of God only, so we are also enjoined to regard this Church which is so called with reference to man, and to cultivate its communion.

Accordingly, inasmuch as it was of importance to us to recognise it, the Lord has distinguished it by certain marks, and as it were symbols. It is, indeed, the special prerogative of God to know those who are his. . . . And doubtless it has been so provided as a check on human rashness, the experience of every day reminding us how far his secret judgments surpass our apprehension. For even those who seemed most abandoned, and who had been completely despaired of, are by his goodness recalled to life, while those who seemed most stable often fall. . . . For he knows, and has his mark on those who know neither him nor themselves. . . . On the other hand, foreseeing that it was in some degree expedient for us to know who are to be regarded by us as his sons, he has in this matter accommodated himself to our capacity. But as here full certainty was not necessary, he has in its place substituted the judgment of charity, by which we acknowledge all as members of the Church who by confession of faith, regularity of conduct, and participation in the sacraments, unite with us in acknowledging the same God and Christ. . . .

Hence the form of the Church appears and stands forth conspicuous to our view. Wherever we see the word of God sincerely preached and heard, wherever we see the sacraments administered according to the institution of Christ, there we cannot have any doubt that the Church of God has some existence, since his promise cannot fail, "Where two or three are gathered together in my name, there am I in the midst of them," (Matth. xviii. 20.) But that we may have a clear summary of this subject, we must proceed by the following steps:—The Church universal is the multitude collected out of all nations, who, though dispersed and far distant from each other, agree in one truth of divine doctrine, and are bound together by the tie of a common religion. In this way it comprehends single churches, which exist in different towns and villages, according to the wants of human society, so that each of them justly obtains the name and authority of the Church; and also comprehends single individuals, who by a religious profession are accounted to belong to such churches, although they are in fact aliens from the Church, but have not been cut off by a public decision. . . . Thus we both maintain the Church universal in its unity, which malignant minds have always been eager to dissever, and deny not due authority to lawful assemblies distributed as circumstances require.

2. The Genevan Model of a Christian Commonwealth

In July, 1536, Calvin, returning to Basel from a hurried business trip to France, paused overnight at Geneva. When his presence became known to the eloquent Genevan reformer William Farel, the latter urged him to remain and further the cause of reformation there. So persuasive was Farel that Calvin felt "as if God had stretched forth His hand upon me from on high to arrest me," and he at once made the fateful decision to stay.

Few cities had a stormier history than Geneva during the decade before Calvin's arrival. It had just won an uncertain independence from rival neighbors which had dominated it, Freiburg, Bern, and the Duke of Savoy. It was torn internally by rival lay and ecclesiastical authorities and its citizens had just (May, 1536) sworn to uphold Farel's Reformed Church, although a powerful Catholic party still resided there. Moreover, as the city was a crossroads of commerce between France, Germany, and Italy, and a pleasant place of retirement for wealthy men, it was cosmopolitan, bustling, prosperous, and given to riotous living—gambling, immorality, loose songs and dances, vices of every kind. William Farel had need of a strong ally for reformation of the city's morality as well as its religion.

Calvin was soon busy denouncing sinful practices and suggesting reforms to the town council. With Farel, he drew up articles for church government, a catechism for Christian instruction, and a confession of faith for the entire community. A biographer of Calvin describes the articles and their effects as follows.

CALVIN'S ARTICLES ON CHURCH GOVERNMENT (JANUARY, 1537)

From WALKER, *John Calvin* (1909) [1]

The Articles begin with a declaration that good churchly order demands the frequent and dignified observance of the Lord's Supper. Calvin's prime thought is evidently religious. As in the first edition of the *Institutes,* he advocates its observance at least every Sunday, yet "because the weakness of the people is such that there is danger that this holy and most excellent mystery may be despised if so often celebrated," he recommends its maintenance, for the present, once a month. The dignity of this central feature of worship demands the exclusion of those of unworthy life and contemptuous conduct; and this consideration brings Calvin

[1] From Williston Walker, *John Calvin: The Organiser of Reformed Protestantism, 1509-1564,* 1909, 186-91. Courtesy of G. P. Putnam's Sons.

to the most significant element of the Articles—their provision for church discipline. "For this reason our Lord has established in his Church the correction and discipline of excommunication."

The Articles then propose a systematic establishment of discipline. . . .

"To accomplish this we have decided to ask of you [the government] that your pleasure may be to appoint and choose certain persons of upright life and good reputation among all the faithful, likewise of firmness and not easily corruptible, who being divided and distributed in all the quarters of the city, shall have an eye to the life and conduct of each one; and if they see any notable fault to censure in any person they shall communicate with some one of the ministers to admonish the one in fault and exhort him fraternally to reform. And if it appears that such remonstrances are of no avail, he shall be informed that his obstinacy will be reported to the Church. And if he confesses, there is already a great profit in this discipline. But if he will not hear, it will be time for the minister, being informed by those who have this charge, to declare publicly in the assembly the effort which has been made to bring him to amendment and how all has been of no avail. When it is apparent that he wishes to persevere in hardness of heart, then it will be time to excommunicate him, that is to say, he shall be held as rejected from the company of Christians. . . . Such seems to us a good way to re-establish excommunication in our Church and to maintain it in its entirety; and beyond this admonition the Church cannot go. But if there are those of such insolence and so abandoned to all wickedness that they only laugh at being excommunicated and do not concern themselves about living and dying in such exclusion, it will be for you to judge whether you will suffer such conduct long to continue and leave unpunished such contempt and such mockery of God and of His Gospel."

With this recommendation was coupled another of well-nigh equal importance:

"It is certain that there is no greater division than concerning faith; and if those who agree in faith with us ought, nevertheless, to be excommunicated by reason of their ill deeds, with much more reason they ought not to be endured in the Church who are wholly contrary to us in religion. The remedy that we have thought of for this situation is to ask you that all the inhabitants of your city shall make confession and give account of their faith, so that it may be understood who of them agree with the Gospel, and who love better to be of the kingdom of the Pope than of the kingdom of Jesus Christ. It would therefore be an act becoming Christian magistrates if you, Gentlemen of the Council, each one for himself, would make confession in your council by which it may be understood that the doctrine of your faith is truly that whereby all the faithful are united in one Church. For by your example you would show what each one should do in imitation of you; and afterwards you should appoint certain of your body, who, being joined with some minister, should require each person to do the same. This should be for this time only, since it cannot yet be seen what doctrine each person holds, which is the right beginning of a Church."

Besides this sifting process by which those really in sympathy with the Evangelical cause could be distinguished among the inhabitants of Geneva, and the maintenance of the purity of the Church by discipline, Calvin and his associates proposed the training of the young in religious truth as a third important means of securing the spiritual welfare of the city:

"There should be a brief and easy outline of the Christian faith, which should be taught to all children, and at certain seasons of the year they should come before the ministers to be questioned and examined, and to receive more ample explication according as there shall be need in proportion to the capacity of each, until they are approved as sufficiently instructed. But may your pleasure be to order parents to exercise care and diligence that their children learn this outline and present themselves to the ministers at the time appointed."

Here then was a program of far-reaching significance, and of the utmost boldness as applied to a city like Geneva. All inhabitants were to be sifted by a creed test, which in the conditions of the sixteenth century life meant something different from such a test today. It was almost impossible to be non-partisan between Protestantism and Romanism, and Calvin intended that it should be absolutely impossible. Each inhabitant must choose one side or the other with all its consequences. He must live "according to the Gospel," or according to the Papacy. But all inhabitants who accepted the Evangelical side, were, by right of their acceptance, as well as of their baptism, members of the Genevan Church. Calvin does not say what shall be done with inhabitants who refuse Protestantism. He did not need to say. The Genevan authorities had already taken the position, in the month of Calvin's arrival, and without influence from him, that they must leave the city.

This Church thus established must be maintained in purity not merely by education, but by discipline; and this discipline was to be applied not, as in most American religious bodies, to that relatively small portion of the population who have made a profession of Christian experience and have "joined a church," but to all inhabitants who professed adherence to the Evangelical side, that is to all dwellers in Geneva after the sifting process should be completed. There was nothing novel in the idea of a strict watch by the civil government over the manners and morals of the citizens. . . . Calvin's contribution was two-fold, however. He would secure the appointment of lay inspectors, who should work in conjunction with the ministry—a real Consistory, if still in undeveloped form; and, even more important, he would make the work of the inspectors a function of the Church, not of the State. To the point of excommunication, which he deemed the limit of spiritual functions, these inspectors and the ministers, though appointed by the government, should act as spiritual, not as civil, officers. The independent self-government of the Church was thus Calvin's aim. That self-government was far from complete as presented in these Articles; but it was real. When discipline had done its utmost, and not till then, was the State to exercise its authority over the hopelessly incorrigible. The chief peculiarity of Calvin's recommendation is not therefore its regulation of private conduct—that had existed before his work was begun—but this provision for an independent exercise of ecclesiastical discipline in a Church which was largely the creature of the State and over which the State exercised control. It was the first step toward the restoration, in a new and Protestant form, of that ancient ecclesiastical independence which the Reformation had almost universally sacrificed to its need of State support. Calvin's motive in thus asserting the principle of independent discipline was primarily pastoral, not theoretical, and grew out of his conception of the care of souls. As he declared in 1538, in his Preface to the Genevan Catechism:

"Whatever others may think, we certainly do not regard our office as bound in so narrow limits that when the sermon is delivered we may rest as if our task were done. They whose blood will be required of us, if lost through our slothfulness, are to be cared for much more closely and vigilantly."

It was an independent discipline, aided by the civil government when discipline had done its utmost, that there might be a trained and conscientious Christian community—the ideal of a Puritan State—that Calvin planned, but to believe that Geneva could become such a state required high idealism, intense determination to secure the result which seemed logically desirable, and a persuasive capacity to win others to his point of view.

CALVIN ESTABLISHES THE PRESBYTERIAN SYSTEM AT GENEVA

The Genevan council was not yet ready to adopt and enforce Calvin's plan of excommunication and his system of censors. A heterogeneous group of Catholic sympathizers and worldly-minded individuals disliked Calvin and Farel and their Protestant influences. These "liberals," as they were called, regained control of the town council in 1538 and banished both Calvin and Farel from the city. Within three years, however, the "liberals" lost popularity, and in October, 1540, Calvin received a letter begging him "on the part of the Little, Great, and General Councils . . . to return to your former place and ministry . . . seeing that our people greatly desire you among us, and promise to behave themselves to you in a way with which you will be content." In September, 1541, Calvin returned to Geneva, and this time found the council ready to adopt his plan of church government, which he submitted in a series of "Ordonnances" ["Regulations"] (September-November, 1540). The "Ordonnances" held that, according to the Scriptures, there should be four orders of officials in the government of the church: pastors, teachers, elders (or presbyters), and deacons. It was the' elders who constituted Calvin's most important contribution to the development of church government. The Greek form of their title, presbyters, has become the stem to the name of the Presbyterian Church. Calvin described their duties as follows.

From Genevan Church *Regulations* (1541) [1]

The office of the elders is to watch over the conduct of every individual, to admonish lovingly those whom they see doing wrong or leading an irregular life. When there is need, they should lay the matter before the body deputed to inflict paternal discipline [i.e., the consistory], of which they are members. As the Church is organized, it is best that the elders be chosen, two from the small council, four from the council of sixty, and six from the council of two hundred [these councils constituted the city government in Geneva]; they should be men of good life and honest, without reproach and beyond suspicion, above all God-fearing and endowed with spiritual prudence. And they should be so chosen that they be distributed in each quarter of the city, so that they can have an eye on everything. . . .

The elders, who have been described, shall assemble once a week with the ministers, namely Thursday morning, to see if there be any disorders in the Church and discuss together such remedies as shall be necessary. . . . If any one shall in contempt refuse to appear before them, it

shall be their duty to inform the council, so that it supply a remedy.

EXAMPLES OF CALVINIST ORDINANCES FOR THE CONDUCT OF GENEVANS (1547)

Geneva in Calvin's time gave up its dissolute ways of living and became such a model of a Christian community that thousands of Protestants from all over Europe went there to observe its ways, to partake of Calvin's ministry, or to attend the splendid Genevan college. Some of the rigid rules governing the conduct of the community are seen in the following excerpts from ordinances drawn up for the village churches in the territory of Geneva.

From the Genevan *Ordinances* (1547) [2]

BLASPHEMY

Whoever shall have blasphemed, swearing by the body or by the blood of our Lord, or in similar manner, he shall be made to kiss the earth for the first offence; for the second to pay 5 sous, and for the third 6 sous, and for the last offence be put in the pillory for one hour.

DRUNKENNESS

1. That no one shall invite another to drink under penalty of 3 sous.

2. That taverns shall be closed during the sermon, under penalty that the tavern-keeper shall pay 3 sous, and whoever may be found therein shall pay the same amount.

3. If any one be found intoxicated he shall pay for the first offence 3 sous and shall be remanded to the consistory; for

[1] James Harvey Robinson, ed., *Readings in European History*, 2 vols., 1906, II, 133. Reprinted by permission of Ginn and Company.

[2] *Translations and Reprints from the Original Sources of European History*, for the Department of History of the University of Pennsylvania, 1902, III, No. 3, 10-11. Reprinted by permission of the University of Pennsylvania Press.

the second offence he shall be held to pay the sum of 6 sous, and for the third 10 sous and be put in prison.

4. That no one shall make *roiaumes* ["wild parties"] under penalty of 10 sous.

SONGS AND DANCES

If any one sing immoral, dissolute or outrageous songs, or dance the *virollet* or other dance, he shall be put in prison for three days and then sent to the consistory.

USURY

That no one shall take upon interest or profit more than five per cent. upon penalty of confiscation of the principal and of being condemned to make restitution as the case may demand.

10
THE REFORMATION IN ENGLAND

1. Henry VIII and the Nationalization of the English Church

Many factors combined to make the English Reformation exceedingly complex. England's insularity, her distance from Rome, and her increasing concern for her national interest had long rendered her orthodoxy questionable. The popular appeal of John Wyclif (d. 1384) and of the Lollard movement, together with later nationalist tendencies and the influence of such humanists as Erasmus, Colet, and More, led the English people to be singularly receptive to Reformation tenets. Nevertheless, the English Church remained officially Roman Catholic until the dispute arose between Henry VIII and Pope Clement VII over the King's divorce from his first Queen, Catherine of Aragon, in the 1520's and 1530's. Even then the break with Catholicism was incomplete. Henry despised Luther, and for years the English Church remained essentially Roman Catholic in creed and ceremonies [see page 137], the only important change being the substitution of the king for the pope as supreme head. In short, the English Church was nationalized without, at first, becoming Protestantized.

Gradually, however, Protestant reformers made headway until, in 1553, the death of Henry's only son, Edward VI, and the accession of Mary, Roman Catholic daughter of Catherine of Aragon, temporarily reversed the course of events, reunited the English Church to Rome, and forced into martyrdom or exile the English Protestant leaders. Queen Mary's marriage to Philip II of Spain (1554) gave Catholics additional cause for rejoicing, but the Queen's early death in 1558 and the accession of her half-sister, Elizabeth, Protestant daughter of Anne Boleyn, cut short their satisfaction, for the new Queen soon made clear her Protestant sympathies. The English Protestants exiled by Mary (the "Marian exiles") returned from the German and Swiss towns on the Continent re-inforced in their Protestantism and especially indoctrinated with Calvinism. As some of these men took part in the Elizabethan church settlement, the English Church was tinctured by Calvinist doctrines even though its ecclesiastical organization was not a Presbyterian form. Indeed, the failure of the Elizabethan church to free itself entirely from ceremonies of Catholic origin led some English reformers to protest against it, to refuse to conform to it unless it be "purified" further of popish remains in ceremonies; and from their demands for demands for greater "purity" in worship they gained the name of "Puritans."

The readings which follow illustrate some of the factors in this complex pattern of the English reformation. The first is an account of Henry VIII and Queen Catherine as seen in 1519 by Sebastian Giustinian, the Venetian ambassador to England.

HENRY VIII IN 1519

From a Report of the Venetian Ambassador (1519) [1]

King Henry was 29 years old, and much handsomer than any other Sovereign in Christendom—a great deal handsomer than the King of France. He was very fair, and his whole frame admirably proportioned. Hearing that King Francis wore a beard, he allowed his own to grow, and as it was reddish, he had then got a beard which looked like gold. He was very accomplished and a good musician; composed well; was a capital horseman, and a fine jouster; spoke good French, Latin, and Spanish; was very religious; heard three masses daily when he hunted, and sometimes five on other days, besides hearing the office daily in the Queen's chamber, that is to say, vespers and compline. He was extremely fond of hunting, and never took that diversion without tiring eight or ten horses, which he caused to be stationed beforehand along the line of country he meant to take. He was also fond of tennis, at which game it was the prettiest thing in the world to see him play; his fair skin glowing through a shirt of the finest texture. He gambled with the French hostages to the amount, occasionally, it was said, of from 6,000 to 8,000 ducats in a day.

He was affable and gracious; harmed no one; did not covet his neighbour's goods, and was satisfied with his own dominions, having often said to the ambassador, *"Domine Orator,* we want all potentates to content themselves with their own territories; we are satisfied with this island of ours." He seemed extremely desirous of peace.

He was very rich. His father left him ten millions of ready money in gold, of which he was supposed to have spent one half in the war against France, when he had three armies on foot; one crossed the Channel with him; another was in the field against Scotland; and the third remained with the Queen in reserve.

His revenues amounted to about 350,000 ducats annually, and were derived from estates, forests, and meres, the customs, hereditary and confiscated property, the duchies of Lancaster, York, Cornwall, and Suffolk, the county palatine of Chester and others, the principality of Wales, the export duties, the wool staple, the Great Seal, the annates yielded by church benefices, the Court of Wards, and from new years' gifts; for on the first day of the year it is customary for his Majesty to make presents to everybody, but the value of those he receives in return greatly exceeds his own outlay. . . .

He was the best dressed sovereign in the world. His robes were very rich and superb, and he put on new clothes every holiday.

The Queen (Catherine) was the sister

[1] Rawdon Brown, ed., *The Calendar of State Papers . . . Venetian, 1509-1519,* 28 vols. London, 1864—, II, 559-61.

of the mother of the King of Spain (Joanna of Castile), now styled King of the Romans. She was 35 years old, and not handsome, though she had a very beautiful complexion. She was religious, and as virtuous as words could express.

THE SIGNIFICANCE OF THE ROYAL DIVORCE QUESTION

The ostensible cause of the quarrel between Henry VIII and the Papacy was the King's desire, arising at first from political considerations and then from Henry's infatuation with Anne Boleyn, to be divorced from Queen Catherine. To obtain this, proceedings before a papal court were necessary. The case was knotty, not only because of the international complications involved, but also because Catherine of Aragon had formerly (1501) been married to Henry's elder brother, Prince Arthur, after whose death (1502) she became Henry's bride (1509); a papal dispensation permitted the marriage with a deceased brother's wife—for according to ecclesiastical law no such marriage is permissible without a dispensation. Divorce proceedings began in England in the spring of 1529, but Catherine's appeal to the Pope carried the case to Rome where Clement VII, for political reasons, sought to postpone a decision and gradually brought himself to refuse the King's demand. Meanwhile, as the question hung fire, English sentiment, skillfully directed by the King, expressed itself in increasingly antipapal terms until, by the Act of Supremacy of 1534, Parliament declared the King to be "the only supreme head in earth of the Church of England." In five years a kind of institutional revolution had occurred in England the nature and significance of which are ably set forth in the following excerpt of an essay by A. F. Pollard, the late English historian.

From POLLARD, "Henry VIII" (1935) [1]

The King, indeed, was not in search or in need of a mistress, or even of a wife, so much as of a son to succeed him, carry on the Tudor succession, and avert a recrudescence of the Wars of the Roses. That was his engrossing problem throughout almost the whole of his reign; and it was only solved in the end by an Act of Parliament, to the terms of which—in spite of religious passions and rival claims —England stood staunch so long as a Tudor remained to fufil them. Catherine of Aragon, whom he had not chosen himself, failed him: one miscarriage or stillborn child succeeded another, and in 1514, after five years of parental misfortune Henry—or Wolsey—petitioned Leo X to annul the marriage with his brother's wife which another pope had sanctioned, doubting the validity of his own dispensation. Then in 1516 came Mary, who was welcomed, not for her own sake, but as an earnest of the son to follow. No woman had yet reigned in England. . . . The expected heir never followed Mary, and by 1527 it was certain that Henry VIII would have no legitimate son so long as Catherine remained his wife. He ceased to cohabit, though not to live, with her from that date, and fell a victim to the one grand passion of his life. It might provide a better hope for the succession than the *mariage de convenance* with Catherine. He was the second English king to marry for love and nothing else, and its ripe and refreshing fruit was Queen Elizabeth. But for five years he waited; the child must be legitimate, and a divorce from Catherine was confidently expected from Clement

[1] A. F. Pollard, "Henry VIII" in *The Great Tudors,* ed. by Katharine Garvin, 1935, 24-30. Reprinted by permission of Ivor Nicholson and Watson, London.

VII in 1529. It was refused: if, wrote the Pope's secretary, it is granted, "The Church cannot escape utter ruin, as it is entirely in the power of the Emperor's servants." Charles V's armies had almost turned Italy into a province of Spain; Catherine was his aunt, and Mary his cousin whose succession to the English throne he was bent on securing.

The Papacy was immovable: so was Henry on the question of the succession to his throne. So, too, was the Queen: her honor was involved, the legitimacy of her child, that child's prospects of a crown, and the Spanish alliance of which they were the emblems and the agents. The women of England supported her on the grounds of morality and sentiment; their husbands opposed on those of national policy. It was not yet a question of religion or the faith: the Lutherans and Tyndale, the Protestant martyr, denounced the divorce; and, could Clement VII have been constrained or persuaded to grant it, there might have been no immediate breach with Rome and no Act of Supremacy. France, for the sake of the English alliance and her ambitions in Italy, supported Henry, and the diplomatic struggle raged for three years. But, meanwhile, the Reformation Parliament assembled in November 1529 and gave voice to the anti-clerical tide which Wolsey had dammed for fifteen years. It overflowed, swept away some of the more notorious privileges and abuses, and enabled Henry to extort from the Church itself a reluctant admission of his supremacy. . . . The Act of Annates [1532] robbed the Papacy of its revenues from English benefices, and the Acts of Appeals [1533] made England independent of its jurisdiction. Henry married Anne Boleyn about the end of January 1533, in the confidence born of her pregnancy, and on September 7, she gave birth to the future queen, Elizabeth. Finally, in 1534, the Royal Supremacy was enshrined in a Parliamentary statute, where it has remained ever since, save for Mary's Catholic reign and the Puritan regime a century later.

Never was revolution more skilfully draped as reform; it was made respectable, like treason, by success. Its path had, indeed, been prepared by centuries of struggle between Church and State, in which the Church had grown weaker and the monarchy stronger through the decline of ecclesiastical unity and the rise of secular nationalism; and the Church in England had already proved too weak to resist the royal demand that it should become the Church of England. Nevertheless, Henry VIII was the parent of what Lord Acton justly termed "a new polity." Hitherto there had been no "State" in England, but various Estates, of which the ecclesiastical were subject to papal, and the secular to royal, sovereignty. The Act of Supremacy brought all under one Sovereign and created out of them a single, novel State which also claimed to be an Empire, independent alike of Holy Roman Emperor and Holy Roman Pope; and, what was more, the emancipator became dictator and the father of all the Fascists in the world. The Middle Ages passed away in child-birth, and its child was what Michelet calls *"le nouveau Messie, le Roi"* ["the new Messiah, the King"].

Happily, the Middle Ages had also left in England another child, born before the decadence and still surviving . . . and, with equal good fortune, Parliament found in Henry a foster-father who did not, like other Fascists, strangle the offspring left by the Middle Ages on the doorstep of modern despots. He nursed it, because he discerned its promise as a sure shield and weapon for his own defence and that of the realm. "He has always fortified himself by the consent of Parliament," wrote the Emperor's ambassador with an envious wish that Charles V could do the same. Of all the legends about Henry VIII, the most extravagant is that he sought to weaken Parliament. In truth he gave it and its acts a prestige and authority they had never possessed before; he enhanced its power and extended its sphere of authority; and critics in 1540 were jeering at "this newfound article of our creed, that Parliament cannot err." All his great acts were Acts of Parliament, and they fill in the statute-book more space than all the earlier Acts of Parliament put together.

This invitation to Parliament to share his work and strengthen his hands constitutes Henry's chief claim to statesmanship. It may be that he had no choice, and that Parliament was the only means at hand adequate to his purpose. But that implies that Parliament was the dominant factor in the situation, and that is a view which is not easily reconcilable with the decline of parliamentary institutions elsewhere. . . . It is truer to say that Henry VIII felt the national impulse, discerned possibilities which were not yet explicit, and saw in Parliament the means of effecting his own particular objects. Only a national legislature could effect the breach with Rome, eradicate foreign jurisdiction, and make England the exclusive and common property of Englishmen. Wolsey's gaze was riveted on Rome; Henry's after 1529 on what he called his little island. That did not mean that he could not see beyond it. England herself was not an island; Wales and even Calais were brought within its Parliamentary system, and during his later years most of his attention was devoted to Ireland and Scotland: England for the English was to be expanded into Britain for the British.

But England was the core of the situation when theological dissension was rending Europe and precipitating it into a century of Wars of Religion. So long as she was united, said Henry . . . she could not be conquered; the problem was to keep it united and English Catholics and Protestants at peace with one another. His last speech to Parliament, a lay sermon on

charity, summed up Henry's position. He denounced Catholics for calling Protestants heretics and anabaptists, and Protestants for calling Catholics papists, hypocrites, and pharisees, and asked "how can poor souls live in concord when you preachers sow amongst them in your sermons debate and discord?" . . . The balance he strove to maintain and the *via media* he sought to follow could only be achieved by supporting now the one and now the other disputant. . . . Henry seemed bent for the rest of his life on showing that Catholicism was safer in essence but more capable of practical reform under his royal supremacy than under papal jurisdiction. It was a position which history showed that none but he could maintain. . . .

That was no disservice to the Church in England, however obnoxious it might seem to the Church abroad. But Henry was a nationalist and therefore a schismatic; Popes and Councils having failed in their efforts at reform, he determined to attempt it himself in his own dominions, hoping that others would follow suit. So far as England is concerned, his anti-ecclesiastical character has been exaggerated. He secured the concurrence of Convocation in all his measures; and instead of exasperating the medieval conflict between Church and State, he brought it to an end. Whatever might happen elsewhere, he was determined that England should be united, self-sufficient, and independent. Within its borders there was to be no jurisdiction to rival that of the Crown in Parliament. But he did not contemplate the purely secular modern State: he was himself Head of the Church and a theologian of no mean learning; he took his unction at coronation seriously, and composed anthems still occasionally sung in our cathedrals. . . .

This national reconciliation under the Crown in Parliament substituted a single for a dual control of the life and liberty, the faith, the law, and property of English people. It imposed upon them self-reliance; henceforth they could look to no appeals at Rome, to no papal censures or excommunications to remove a tyrant or chastise an heretical king. They must seek their remedies at home and realize that they are responsible for their own government. Some sought a remedy in rebellion. . . . The rebellions were all against Parliament as well as against the Crown; and, while Parliament might rebel with success against the Crown, no rebellion against Parliament in England has ever succeeded. If the English had been taught to look to themselves for their own remedies, they had also learnt that remedies were not to be found by means of force imposed upon their own representatives. While other European countries were dispensing with representative systems and falling into the arms of despots or the abyss of civil war, Henry VIII wound round his royal carcase and the Tudor State a garment more effective than coats of armor. Had his constitution of Church and State been overthrown, Parliament would have died before becoming the mother of Parliaments scattered all over the world, upon whose vitality depends today the freedom of mankind. The New World would have been a mere replica of the Old, and government of the people, for the people, by the people, might have perished from the earth.

2. The English Church during the Reign of Henry VIII

DISSOLUTION OF THE MONASTERIES

Soon after passage of the Act of Supremacy (1534), Henry VIII appointed a commission, headed by Thomas Cromwell, to visit churches, monasteries, and other religious houses in England and report on their condition. On the basis of the reports submitted, which demonstrated more of relaxation of discipline, decay of high religious feeling, and general secularization than they did of "vicious, carnal, and abominable living," Henry determined to suppress the smaller religious houses. Subsequently (in 1539) all the religious houses were suppressed. The acts of dissolution essentially confiscated the properties for the Crown, and Henry employed much of the money and lands either to endow a new nobility of his own creation or to found schools and colleges, which thus multiplied greatly in his reign.

An unknown Catholic writer set down, about 1591, an account of the suppression of the religious houses as he had heard it told by his father and his uncle. Part of this account, showing the greed of the royal visitors and some of the hardships and pain caused by them, follows.

From a Sixteenth-Century Account [1]

In the plucking down of which Houses for the most part this order was taken: that the Visitors should come suddenly upon every House unawares (for they never looked to be visited out of the doors, seeing they had pleased the King so well with the ready money bestowed of him, in good hope of the standing thereof, as is aforesaid), to the end to take them napping, as the Proverb is; least if they should have had so much as any inkling of their coming, they would have made conveyance of some part of their own goods to help themselves withal, when they were

[1] From the Cole Manuscripts, XII, 1-49, in the British Museum, as quoted in Sir Henry Ellis, ed., Original Letters Illustrative of English History, 3d ser., 4 vols., London, 1846, III, 32-34.

turned forth of their houses: and both reason and nature might well have moved them so to have done, although it will be said all was given to the King before by Act of Parliament; and so they had neither goods, houses, nor possessions. . . . So soon as the Visitors were entered within the gates, they called the Abbot and other Officers of the House, and caused them to deliver up to them all their keys, and took an inventory of all their goods, both within doors and without: for all such beasts, horses, sheep, and such cattle as were abroad in pastures or grange places, the Visitors caused to be brought into their presence: and when they had so done, turned the Abbot with all his convent and household forth of the doors.

Which thing was not a little grief to the Convent, and all the Servants of the House departing one from another, and especially such as with their conscience could not break their profession: for it would have made an heart of flint to have melted and wept to have seen the breaking up of the House, and their sorrowful departing; and the sudden spoil that fell the same day of their departure from the House. And every person had every thing good cheap; except the poor Monks, Friars, and Nuns, that had no money to bestow of any thing. .. . But such persons as afterward bought their corn and hay or such like, found all the doors either open, or the locks and shackles plucked away, or the door itself taken away, went in and took what they found, filched it away.

Some took the Service Books that lied in the Church. . . . For the Church was the first thing that was put to the spoil; and then the Abbot's lodging, dorter, and Frater, with the cloister and all the buildings thereabout, within the Abbey walls. .. . It would have pitied any heart to see what tearing up of the lead there was,

and plucking up of boards, and throwing down of the sparres; and when the lead was torn off and cast down into the Church, and the tombs in the Church all broken (for in most Abbeys were divers noble men and women, yea and in some Abbeys Kings, whose tombs were regarded no more than the tombs of all other inferior persons: for to what end should they stand, when the Church over them was not spared for their cause), and all things of price either spoiled, carped away, or defaced to the uttermost.

THE SIX ARTICLES (1539)

The dissolution of the monasteries and other acts served well to nationalize the English Church and to make it independent of Rome. But they did almost nothing to alter the creed or the ceremonies of the church. This fact caused much dissatisfaction among Lutherans and other Protestants in England, all of whom clamored for reformation now that the pope's authority had been cast out. But Henry resisted these demands and in 1539 procured passage of the Six Articles Act which required uniformity in doctrine and ceremonies in the English Church, reasserted several fundamental Catholic beliefs and practices, and established death penalties for nonconformity. Protestants reviled the Six Articles as "the whip of Six Strings" and complained that the "Reformation goes backwards" in England.

From "The Six Articles" (1539) [1]

First, that in the most blessed Sacrament of the altar, by the strength and

[1] This and the next two quotations are from Henry Gee and William John Hardy, eds., *Documents Illustrative of English Church History*, 1896. Reprinted by permission of The Macmillan Company. This is 305-06.

efficacy of Christ's mighty word (it being spoken by the priest), is present really, under the form of bread and wine, the natural body and blood of our Saviour Jesus Christ, conceived of the Virgin Mary; and that after the consecration there remaineth no substance of bread or wine, nor any other substance, but the substance of Christ, God and man. [This article, of course, reaffirms transubstantiation. Opposition to it is here made punishable by burning as a heretic and confiscation of property.]

Secondly, that communion in both kinds is not necessary *ad salutem,* by the law of God, to all persons; and that it is to be believed, and not doubted of, but that in the flesh, under the form of bread, is the very blood; and with the blood, under the form of wine, is the very flesh; as well apart, as though they were both together.

Thirdly, that priests after the order of priesthood received, as afore, may not marry, by the law of God.

Fourthly, that vows of chastity or widowhood, by man or woman made to God advisedly, ought to be observed by the law of God; and that it exempts them from other liberties of Christian people which without that they might enjoy.

Fifthly, that it is meet and necessary that private masses be continued and admitted in this the king's English Church and congregation, as whereby good Christian people, ordering themselves accordingly, do receive both godly and goodly consolations and benefits; and it is agreeable also to God's law.

Sixthly, that auricular confession is expedient and necessary to be retained and continued, used and frequented in the Church of God. [Opposition to Articles II-VI is punishable by death and confiscation of property, as for felony.]

3. Examples of the Growth of Protestantism in the Reign of Edward VI, 1547-1553

Under the boy king Edward VI Protestants made considerable headway in "reforming" the English Church and purging it of Roman beliefs and ceremonies. Some of the provisions of the Six Articles [see page 137] were reversed.

From "The Act for Receiving Communion in Both Kinds" (1547) [1]

And forasmuch as it is . . . more conformable to the common use and practice both of the Apostles and of the primitive Church, by the space of 500 years and more after Christ's ascension, that the said blessed Sacrament should be ministered to all Christian people under both the kinds of bread and wine, than under the form of bread only, and . . . that the people being present should receive the same with the priest . . . therefore be it enacted by our said sovereign lord the king, with the consent of the Lords spiritual and temporal, and the Commons, in this present Parliament assembled, and by the authority of the same, that the said most blessed Sacrament be hereafter commonly delivered and ministered unto the people within the Church of England and Ireland, and other the king's dominions, under both the kinds, that is to say, of bread and wine, except necessity otherwise require.

From "The Act Legalizing the Marriage of Priests" (1549) [2]

Although it were not only better for the estimation of priests, and other ministers in the Church of God, to live chaste,

[1] *Ibid.,* 327.
[2] *Ibid.,* 367-68.

sole, and separate from the company of women and the bond of marriage, but also thereby they might the better intend to the administration of the gospel, and be less intricated and troubled with the charge of household. . . .

Yet forasmuch as the contrary has rather been seen, and such uncleanness of living, and other great inconveniences, not meet to be rehearsed, have followed of compelled chastity . . . it were better . . . that those which could not contain, should . . . live in holy marriage, than feignedly abuse with worse enormity outward chastity or single life:

Be it therefore enacted by our sovereign lord the king, with the assent of the Lords spiritual and temporal, and the Commons in this present Parliament assembled, and by the authority of the same, that all and every law and laws positive . . . heretofore made by the authority of man only, which do prohibit or forbid marriage to any ecclesiastical or spiritual person or persons . . . which by God's law may lawfully marry . . . shall be utterly void and of none effect.

From "Instructions Issued for the Regulation of Ceremonies and Creed" (1549) [1]

For an uniformity, that no minister do counterfeit the popish mass, as to kiss the Lord's table; washing his fingers at every time in the communion; blessing his eyes with the paten, or sudary; or crossing his head with the paten; shifting of the book from one place to another; laying down and licking the chalice of the communion; holding up his fingers, hands, or thumbs, joined towards his temples; breathing upon the bread or chalice; shewing the sacrament openly before the distribution of the communion; ringing of sacrying

bells; or setting any light upon the Lord's board at any time; and finally to use no other ceremonies than are appointed in the king's book of common prayers, or kneeling, otherwise than is in the said book. . . .

That no man maintain purgatory, invocation of saints, the six articles, beadrolls, images, relics, lights, holy bells, holy beads, holy water, palms, ashes, candles, sepulchres, paschal, creeping to the cross, hallowing of the font of the popish manner, oil, chrism, altars, beads, or any other such abuses, and superstitions, contrary to the King's Majesty's proceedings.

4. Roman Interlude: The Reign of Mary, 1553-1558

AN EYEWITNESS'S DESCRIPTION OF QUEEN MARY IN 1557

From a Report of the Venetian Ambassador (1557) [2]

Queen Mary, the daughter of Henry VIIIth. and of his Queen Catherine daughter of Ferdinand the Catholic, King of Aragon, is a Princess of great worth. In her youth she was rendered unhappy by the event of her mother's divorce; by the ignominy and threats to which she was exposed after the change of religion in England, she being unwilling to bend to the new one; and by the dangers to which she was exposed by the Duke of Northumberland, and the riots among the people when she ascended the throne. She is of short stature, well made, thin and

[1] Edward Cardwell, ed., Documentary Annals of the Reformed Church of England, 2 vols., Oxford, 1844, I, 75-76.

[2] From the "Report of the Signor Giovanni Michele on his Return from England, A.D. 1557," as given in Henry Ellis, ed., Original Letters Illustrative of English History, 2d ser., 4 vols., London, 1827, II, 218-42. Giovanni Michele was Venetian Ambassador to England in the early part of Mary's reign.

delicate, and moderately pretty; her eyes are so lively that she inspires reverence and respect, and even fear, wherever she turns them; nevertheless she is very short sighted. Her voice is deep, almost like that of a man. She understands five languages, English, Latin, French, Spanish, and Italian, in which last, however, she does not venture to converse. She is also much skilled in ladies' work, such as producing all sorts of embroidery with the needle. She has a knowledge of music, chiefly on the lute, on which she plays exceedingly well. As to the qualities of her mind, it may be said of her that she is rash, disdainful, and parsimonious rather than liberal. She is endowed with great humility and patience, but withal high spirited, courageous, and resolute; having during the whole course of her adversity been guiltless of any the least approach to meanness of comportment; she is, moreover, devout and staunch in the defence of her religion. Some personal infirmities under which she labours are the causes to her of both public and private affliction; to remedy these recourse is had to frequent blood-letting, and this is the real cause of her paleness and the general weakness of her frame. These have also given rise to the unfounded rumour that the Queen is in a state of pregnancy. The cabal she has been exposed to, the evil disposition of the people towards her, the present poverty and the debt of the Crown, and her passion for King Philip from whom she is doomed to live separate, are so many other causes of the grief by which she is overwhelmed. She is, moreover, a prey to the hatred she bears my Lady Elizabeth, and which has its source in the recollection of the wrongs she experienced on account of her mother, and in the fact that all eyes and hearts are turned towards my Lady Elizabeth as successor to the Throne.

MARIAN POLICIES AND ENGLISH PROTESTANTS

Although Queen Mary proclaimed at her accession that she adhered to "that religion which God and the world know she has ever professed from her infancy," she did not, at the outset, anticipate the persecution of Protestants which soon followed. The persecutions, in some measure at least, resulted from the contumacy of the Protestants themselves—although the Queen's marriage (1554) to Philip of Spain aroused bitter English opposition against the foreign king, alienated France (whose Gallic finger could often be seen stirring up trouble against Mary both in England and abroad), and placed a convenient political tool in the hands of English Protestants. The ensuing riots and rebellions by Mary's religious and political enemies, as well as the Queen's own loyalty to the Roman Church, led her to repeal the church legislation of Edward's reign and to erase that of Henry VIII's. Thus she restored England to the ecclesiastical position which had existed before 1529, except that she could find no practicable means to give back the confiscated church properties. A recent explanation of Mary's ecclesiastical policies, and the conditions which prompted them, is given in the following selection.

From PRESCOTT, *A Spanish Tudor* (1940) [1]

She believed firmly that English Protestantism was no more than the temporary aberration of a few, and she intended to

[1] Reprinted from H. F. M. Prescott, *A Spanish Tudor: The Life of "Bloody Mary,"* pp. 232-34, 375-79, 383-84. Copyright 1940 by Columbia University Press and Constable and Company, Ltd., London.

use no compulsion against those who differed from her in religion.

That startling intention she solemnly announced to the Council on August 12th [1553] in a declaration which she bade them publish, a declaration ". . . which was that, albeit her Grace's conscience is stayed in matters of religion, yet she meaneth graciously not to compel or constrain other men's consciences, otherwise than God shall (she trusteth) put into their hearts a persuasion of the truth that she is in, through the opening of his word unto them by godly, virtuous, and learned preachers. . . ."

In hoping for reconciliation she totally mistook the temper of the Protestant party. Did she totally mistake its numbers? Just how wide-spread was Protestantism? How deeply was it rooted . . . ?

These were the questions that perplexed many minds at the time, and received many answers. Each side—Catholic and Protestant—was frequently appalled, to the pitch of despair, by the numerical strength of the enemy, and it is hard for us now to judge the validity of their fears. London was, by nearly all foreign observers, judged to be riddled with heresy, yet when the Queen first came to the city an Italian saw how the little images of the Virgin or of Saints, which had been carefully hidden away, were set up again in many and many a window. Nor must it be forgotten that many of the most earnest, or at least most vocal, Protestants were not Englishmen at all, but French, Dutch, even Polish refugees. These, and the effects of their influence, were to be found largely in the eastern counties . . . or in Kent and Sussex. . . . The North and North-West were, and for years yet continued, almost solid for Catholicism. . . . The South-West, which had risen in 1549 against the Prayer Book, was soon to be an anxiety to the Catholic Queen

. . . but the trouble was not religion, it was the Queen's marriage.

Mary hoped, when she spoke to the Council on August 12th, that it only needed persuasion to turn the hearts of the opponents of the old ways. But already that history of violence and disorder had begun which was to contradict all her hopes and force her to use methods the opposite of what she intended. . . .

To modern minds, accustomed by the passage of time to a variety of creeds, the penalty of death, and a terrible death, for difference in a matter of dogma, is offensive. Yet in the middle of the sixteenth century none on either side, except a few speculative souls, felt any qualms at the application, in principle, of such a penalty. The reply to the challenge of heresy was the same from either party—"Burn the heretic." What Catholic sovereigns did to Protestants, Protestants did to Anabaptists. . . .

And there was at that time more than a little justification for the application of such a desperate expedient. By the middle years of the century it seemed as though Protestantism, like a bursting grenade, would split itself into slivers, losing in its disruption all trace of its original form. . . . Even Protestant writers, Protestant leaders, admitted how far many Protestants had strayed from the common and fundamental truths of Christianity, held by both Catholics and the moderates of their own side. "There were now," says Strype, speaking of the year 1556, "abundance of sects and dangerous doctrines; whose maintainers shrouded themselves under the professors of the gospel. Some denied the divinity of Christ; some denied his manhood; others denied the godhead of the Holy Ghost, original sin, the descent of Christ into Hell . . . the baptism of infants. Some condemned the use of all indifferent things in religion." There were "schismatical spirits" who had imbibed the principles of Pelagianism, Arianism, and Anabaptism.

Faced with a crop of heresies old and new, sober and moderate Protestants were aghast. . . . If Protestants were distressed by the strange religious company in which they had to fight their battle against the Mass, old-fashioned Catholics hardly knew whether to hate or to despise their adversaries. "Remember," said Weston, answering Latimer at Oxford, "Remember who were the beginners of your doctrine: a few flying apostates, running out of Germany for fear of the faggot. Remember what they were who have set forth your doctrine in this realm; fling-brains and light heads, never constant in one thing, as might be seen in turning the table one day west, one day east, one that way, another this way, when like a sort of apes they could not tell which way to turn their tails. . . ."

This was what in Edward's and Mary's reign Protestant doctrines had seemed, to the Catholic, to mean. But in Mary's reign they also wore another habit, which made them equally obnoxious to those who cared more for peace and order than for theological truth. As Sir Thomas More had said: "Heresies breed disorders, and fear of these have been the causes that princes and peoples have been constrained to punish heretics by terrible death. . . ."

There were, of course, loyal and peaceable Protestants, but from the first day of the reign to the last the Protestant cause was inexplicably confused, both in fact and in estimation, with disobedience, sedition, disloyalty, and foreign intrigue. . . .

Three days after Mary's arrival in London, in July 1553, John Rogers, in the pulpit at Paul's Cross threw down the gage, "confirming such true doctrine as he and others had taught in King Edward's days, exhorting the people constantly to remain in the same, and to beware of all pestilent popery, idolatry, and superstition." That challenge had been repeated by the Archbishop in the next month and, when the Queen had prohibited any but licenced preaching, by many an unlicenced Protestant preacher. Such protests might be wrung from the speaker by an overwhelming sense of duty to witness to the truth, but they were, for all that, after the Queen's proclamation, illegal, and what was worse, inflammatory. The verbal challenge of the preachers, from the country parson to Archbishop, was reinforced by every form of violence from arson to rebellion. The earlier attacks on the Queen's preachers had been followed up by rioting all over the South and East of England. A priest in Kent had his nose cut off. A church in Suffolk was set on fire while Mass was being sung. . . .

It was this huge and growing force of disorder and rebellion that Mary, her husband, her Council, and her Bishops, had to face. It was the same which Charles V in the Netherlands, Henri II in France, must also face. The alarm and apprehension of all these rulers was extreme, but no harder to understand than the panic which the ruling and propertied classes of the rest of Europe suffered after the French Revolution in the 18th century and the Russian Revolution in the 20th. To stem the rising tide which threatened their dykes and breakwaters, and whose high water mark they could in no wise prophesy, the Catholic sovereigns of the middle of the sixteenth century, all over Europe, fell back upon the same remedy, the old and barbarous method of burning heretics.

THE MARIAN EXILES

Queen Mary's persecution of Protestants earned for her the discreditable title of "Bloody Mary." Several hundred men and women were executed as heretics, often by burning at the stake, and they promptly became—in the eyes of their fellows—Protestant "martyrs." About eight hundred others fled to the Continent, where, by their studies and by their contacts with Continental leaders, they imbibed such pregnant ideas of church reformation that when, a few years later, they returned to Elizabethan England, they promptly emerged as leaders in the Elizabethan church. Some took a prominent part in effecting the Elizabethan church settlement, lending it a somewhat Calvinistic tone in creed if not in polity; others, pressing on for yet further reformation, became prominent among the founders of English Puritanism. Daniel Neal, a puritan historian of a later day, described these "Marian Exiles."

From NEAL, *The Puritans* (1738) [1]

Many escaped the fury of the persecution by withdrawing from the storm and flying into foreign countries. Some went into France and Flanders, some to Geneva, and others into those parts of Germany and Switzerland where the Reformation had taken place; as Basil, Frankfort, Embden, Strasburgh, Doesburgh, Arrow, and Zurich, where the magistrates received them with great humanity, and allowed them places for public worship. But the uncharitableness of the Lutherans on this occasion was very remarkable: they hated the exiles because they were Sacramentarians, and when any English came among them for shelter, they expelled them from their cities; so that they found little hospitality in Saxony and other places of Germany where Lutheranism was professed. Philip Melancthon interceded with the Senate on their behalf, but the clergy were so zealous for their consubstantiation, that they irritated the magistrates

---

[1] Daniel Neal, *The History of the Puritans*, ed. by John O. Choules, 2 vols., New York, 1871, I, 66-68.

everywhere against them. The number of the refugees is computed at above eight hundred; the most considerable of whom have been mentioned, as the Bishops of Winchester, Bath, and Wells, Chichester, Exeter, and Ossory; the Deans of Christ Church, Exeter, Durham, Wells, and Chichester; the Archdeacons of Canterbury, Stowe, and Lincoln; with a great many other very learned divines. . . .

The exiles were most numerous at Frankfort, where that contest and division began which gave rise to the Puritans, and to that separation from the Church of England which continues to this day. . . .

The more learned clergymen, and some younger divines, settled at Strasburgh, Zurich, and Basil, for the benefit of the libraries of those places, and of the learned conversation of the professors, as well as in hopes of some little employment in the way of printing. . . .

Mr. Fox, the martyrologist, with a few more, went to Basil; and the rest to Geneva, where they were received with great humanity, and having a church appointed them, they chose Mr. Knox and Goodman their pastors. Here they set up the Geneva discipline, which they published in English, under the title of The Service, Discipline, and Form of Common Prayers and Administration of Sacraments used in the English Church of Geneva, with a dedication to their brethren in England and elsewhere, dated from Geneva, February 10th, 1556. The liturgy is too long to be inserted in this place, but is agreeable to that of the French [Calvinist] churches. In their dedication, they say, "that their discipline is limited within the compass of God's Word, which is sufficient to govern all our actions. That the dilatory proceedings of the bishops in reforming church discipline and removing offensive ceremonies is one cause of the heavy judgments of God upon the land. That the late service-book of King Edward being now set aside by Parliament according to law, it was in no sense the established worship of the Church of England, and, consequently, they were under no obligation to use it, any farther than it was consonant to the Word of God. Being, therefore, at liberty, and in a strange land, they had set up such an order as, in the judgment of Mr. Calvin and other learned divines, was most agreeable to Scripture, and the best Reformed Churches."

5. The Elizabethan Church Settlement

ELIZABETH AND HER CHURCH SETTLEMENT, 1558-1559

The following pen portrait of Queen Elizabeth, together with an analysis of the delicate circumstances in which she found herself at the threshold of her reign, is the work of a present-day scholar and shows promise of becoming a classic on "Good Queen Bess" and her times.

From BLACK, The Reign of Elizabeth (1936) [1]

"Elizabethan England" was, in a very real sense, Elizabeth's England. She it was who nursed it into being, and by her wisdom made possible its amazing development. Her characteristic virtues and defects, her sympathies and antipathies, her very whims and caprices are writ large across its political firmament. She inspired its patriotism, its pageantry, its heroisms, stimulated its poetry, and shaped its destiny. And when she died she left behind her a kingdom that had won a command-

[1] From J. B. Black, The Reign of Elizabeth 1558-1603, in The Oxford History of England, ed. by G. N. Clark, 1936, pp. 1-8, 13-14. By permission of The Clarendon Press, Oxford.

ing position among the great powers of Europe.

On 17 November 1558, when she succeeded her half-sister, Mary, on the throne, there was no glimmering of the splendid future in store for her. England was "ragged and torn with misgovernment"; the treasury was empty; the principal fortresses at Portsmouth and Berwick were falling into ruin; the country was bare of munitions; and a huge debt of more than £266,000 had to be liquidated. . . . The French king, Henry II, bestrode the realm like a Colossus, with one foot in Calais and the other in Edinburgh; and the alliance with Spain had played itself out with the loss of England's last continental possession. The prospect was rendered gloomier by the uncertainty of the young queen's title, and the probability that the Stuart claim, barred by Henry VIII, would be revived by the French dauphiness, Mary Stuart. So insecure did the state of affairs appear that few expected the new regime to last, and many calculated on its speedy downfall. . . .

As for the queen, what contemporaries saw was a tall, "comely rather than handsome" woman of twenty-five summers, with fair hair, "fine" eyes, and a delicate "olive" complexion. While, in some respects, she took after her mother, Anne Boleyn, her temperament and bearing were those of her imperious father, in whom, we are told, she "gloried." Close beneath her winsome, debonair exterior lay the terribilità of the Tudor "lion." Her character, however, was largely an unknown quantity, and her capacity for government altogether untried. Few probably realized, and time alone would show, that this slip of a woman, ignorant as yet of the technique of statesmanship, had already graduated in the hard school of experience, and was, in all essential respects, mistress of her destiny.

Wisdom, indeed, had come early to

Elizabeth. Fate had deprived her of a mother at the tender age of two years and eight months; but, as a sort of compensation for the loss, had developed in her a remarkable precocity of intellect. She became an observant, introspective child, apt to learn from books and from life. . . . She ripened quickly, almost too quickly to preserve that balance between emotion and restraint which is the glory of true womanhood. At the age of fifteen, an unsavoury but harmless love-affair with Admiral Seymour, which cost the admiral his life and involved the princess herself in public disgrace, had given her a first bitter taste of the power of scandal, and shown her the importance of keeping a tight hold over her natural impulses. It was, in fact, the fiery crucible in which all that remained of irresponsible childhood was remorselessly burnt to dross and ashes: out of it came a woman with a purpose, schooled to self-repression, prudence, and mistrust. Following upon this crude awakening came the five momentous years of her sister's reign, when, as heir presumptive to the throne, she became willy nilly the center of every plot against the existing regime, and had to pick her steps with care between the calculated malice of her enemies and the pitfalls dug by her friends. . . . Danger had sharpened her wits; she had learnt to screen her thoughts from others, to prevaricate, to dissimulate, to deceive, and to overcome difficulties less by vanquishing them than by circumventing them. Circumstances had bred in her a hard, self-regarding type of mind, not particularly sensitive to fine issues, nor open in its acceptance of life, but strong in the grain and pliant as steel. She was wise with this world's wisdom—resourceful, self-reliant, cautious, and morally courageous in moments of stress. But she had lived too long in an atmosphere of plot and intrigue to cultivate the virtue of magnanimity—it was a luxury she could ill afford; and suspicion was a second nature to her. . . . Of religious feeling, in the ordinary sense of the word, she probably had little. Her cold, entirely humanist outlook, nourished by classical study, kept her apart from the deeper spiritual current of her time. Moreover she had seen too much of the ravages of fanaticism, both protestant and catholic, to set any store by the dogmatic formularies of either side. The only religious faith she can be said to have held with any degree of conviction was a belief in an over-ruling Providence—the refuge of all distressed human beings. Her culture, on the other hand, was considerable. In an age that could boast of such feminine prodigies as Jane Grey, Mildred Cecil, and the accomplished daughters of Sir Thomas More, Elizabeth was notable for her learning. Her schoolmaster, Roger Ascham, tells us that she could speak French and Italian fluently, Latin readily and well, and Greek moderately. Above all, she had realized, while still quite young, that the stability of her throne would depend upon the success with which she interpreted national aspirations and gave them articulation—the very point, be it noted, on which her sister had blundered so badly. . . . The future policy of the country would be based upon its vital needs. Thus did Elizabeth strike the keynote to a new age when she resolved to identify herself with her people, and become, in fact as well as in name, the "most English woman in England.". . .

From the first day of her arrival in the capital, 23 November, to her coronation day, 15 January, the young queen revelled in the enthusiastic loyalty of her subjects, feasting their eyes with equipages through the city and on the Thames. The popular rejoicing reached a climax on the eve of the coronation, when the glittering royal procession wound its way from the Tower to Westminster. . . . More striking, perhaps, than the popular rejoicing was the affability of the queen: she entered into the spirit of the celebration with a frankness that disconcerted at least one foreign spectator, who thought that she exceeded the bounds of gravity and decorum. But there was method in this wooing of the people. Elizabeth's first care was to show that she had their interests at heart, and thereby to recover for the Crown the favor her sister had so recklessly squandered.

Meanwhile signs of an impending revolution in national policy were beginning to be visible in the political world; and one of the first to notice them was the Count de Feria, Philip II's ambassador. . . . This proud Spaniard had journeyed down to Hatfield to inform her [Elizabeth] that her succession was assured, and that she owed her good fortune to the kind services of his master. To his chagrin he was firmly but politely told that in this matter her gratitude was due solely to her people. . . . It was a gesture to the world that English policy was henceforth to be modelled on English interests and not as the Spaniard should dictate.

In regard to religion changes were also imminent, but here the signs were more difficult to discern. This was due to the fact that the political question of the queen's personal and dynastic security took precedence over all other matters. Doubtless if the throne could have been secured by means of a concordat with Rome, involving concessions on both sides, this would have been the method employed. The queen herself, despite outward friendliness to protestantism, had no vested interest in the movement, nor was she in favor—rather the reverse—of the prevailing Calvinism of the time. . . . Extreme caution was the only feasible line to follow. Matters must not be brought to a crisis until the new government was properly in the saddle, and until a religious policy had been formulated that would secure the allegiance of as many of the queen's subjects as possible. . . .

Thus, for example, the first important proclamation of the reign forbade, under severe penalties, "all manner our subjects of every degree" to attempt of their own authority any alteration of the established order of religion. Ostensibly the purpose was to quieten the Catholics, but observant critics, reading between the lines, came to the conclusion that, as the proclamation bound only subjects, it reserved to the Crown the right to make any innovation it pleased, and was really an announcement to that effect. . . . It was also observed that the royal title which the queen affected omitted all reference to the supreme headship, Elizabeth being content to style herself simply "Queen of England, France, and Ireland, etc." But the use of the "etc." left her the loop-hole to restore the obnoxious phrase if she saw fit to do so. It was no ordinary brain that devised so clever a subterfuge. . . .

The work of parliament, which received the queen's approval on 8 May [1559], may now be conveniently summarized. By the Act of Supremacy the whole of Mary's reactionary legislation was swept away, the anti-papal statutes of Henry VIII revived in all essential points, and the supreme power over the national church vested for ever in the Crown. At the same time the Act of Uniformity restored the second Edwardian prayer book, slightly modified, as the directory of public worship. Both of these acts carried their penal codes. Refusal to take the oath of supremacy was punishable with loss of office, and any attempt to maintain by "writing, printing, teaching, preaching, express words, deed or act" the authority of a foreign prince prelate, or potentate, within her majesty's dominions, exposed the offender, on the third committal, to death for high treason. The oath was compulsory for all clergy, judges, justices, mayors, royal officials, and persons taking orders or receiving degrees at the universities. The provisions of the Act of Uniformity, on the other hand, applied to the entire community, clerical and lay alike: clerical offenders against the prayer book being liable, on the third committal of the offence, to imprisonment for life, and the laity to a fine of 12d. for every absence from church.

THE PURITANS' DISSATISFACTION

That Elizabeth's church settlement was even more conservative than that at the end of Edward's reign was a source of grave dissatisfaction to most of those Protestants who had been in exile or in hiding in England during Mary's reign. Schooled in the tenets of the Continental reformers, Marian exiles who returned to England so consistently resisted the English Church forms that, as early as 1564, the term "Puritan" was given to those who desired a purer form of worship and discipline in the church. Had the Puritans been united in their demands they might have wielded telling force; but they were united negatively only, in their opposition to the Elizabethan church. In their positive demands for further reformation they were divided into a multitude of opinions which only gradually congealed into two main groups near the end of Elizabeth's reign—Presbyterians and Congregationalists. In 1564, however, they were still widely disorganized; their chief points at issue with Elizabeth's church have been outlined by Daniel Neal.

From NEAL, *The Puritans* [1]

The hierarchy being now at its standard, it may not be improper to set before the reader in one view the principles upon which it stands; with the different sentiments of the Puritans, by which he will discover the reasons why the Reformation proceeded no farther:

1. The court-reformers apprehended that every prince had authority to correct all abuses of doctrine and worship within his own territories. From this principle, the Parliament submitted the consciences and religion of the whole nation to the disposal of the king; and in case of a minority, to his council; so that the king was sole reformer, and might, by commissioners of his own appointment, declare and remove all manner of errors, heresies, &c., and model the doctrine and discipline of the Church as he pleased, provided his injunctions did not expressly contradict the statute law of the land. . . .

The Puritans disowned all foreign authority and jurisdiction over the Church as much as their brethren, but could not admit of that extensive power which the crown claimed by the supremacy, apprehending it unreasonable that the religion of a whole nation should be at the disposal of a single lay person. . . .

2. It was admitted by the court-reformers that the Church of Rome was a true church, though corrupt in some points of doctrine and government; that all her ministrations were valid, and that the pope was a true Bishop of Rome, though not of the universal Church. . . .

But the Puritans affirmed the pope to be antichrist, the Church of Rome to be no true church, and all her ministrations to be superstitious and idolatrous; they renounced her communion, and durst not risk the validity of their ordinations upon

[1] Neal, *The History of the Puritans*, I, 78-79.

an uninterrupted line of succession from the apostles through their hands.

3. It was agreed by all that the Holy Scriptures were a perfect rule of faith; but the bishops and court-reformers did not allow them a standard of discipline or church government, but affirmed that our Saviour and his apostles left it to the discretion of the civil magistrate, in those places where Christianity should obtain, to accommodate the government of the Church to the policy of the state.

But the Puritans apprehended the Holy Scriptures to be a standard of church discipline, as well as doctrine; at least, that nothing should be imposed as necessary but what was expressly contained in, or derived from them by necessary consequence. . . .

4. The court-reformers maintained that the practice of the primitive Church for the first four or five centuries was a proper standard of church government and discipline, and in some respects better than that of the apostles, which, according to them, was only accommodated to the infant state of the Church while it was under persecution, whereas theirs was suited to the grandeur of a national establishment. . . .

Whereas the Puritans were for keeping close to the Scriptures in the main principles of church government, and for admitting no church officers or ordinances but such as are appointed therein. . . .

5. Our Reformers maintained that things indifferent in their own nature, which are neither commanded nor forbidden in the Holy Scriptures, such as rites, ceremonies, habits, &c., might be settled, determined, and made necessary by the command of the civil magistrate; and that in such cases it was the indispensable duty of all subjects to observe them.

But the Puritans insisted that those things which Christ had left indifferent ought not to be made necessary by any human laws, but that we are to stand fast in the liberty wherewith Christ has made us free; and farther, that such rites and ceremonies as had been abused to idolatry, and manifestly tended to lead men back to popery and superstition, were no longer indifferent, but to be rejected as unlawful.

6. Both parties agreed too well in asserting the necessity of a uniformity of public worship, and of using the sword of the magistrate for the support and defence of their respective principles, which they made an ill use of in their turns whenever they could grasp the power into their hands.

11

THE CATHOLIC REFORMATION

1. The Council of Trent (1545-63)

No informed, honest Catholic denied all of the charges leveled by Protestant reformers against the Church of Rome. But Catholics preferred to eradicate abuses which had crept into the church rather than to break with it. Most

Catholics agreed that the best means to reform the church was by a General Council, though while the Protestant Revolt grew in force a variety of factors combined to prevent its assembly. Mundane popes, jealous of their authority, postponed calling a council lest it limit their powers and thwart their ambitions; churchmen feared that political enemies of the Papacy, especially the Emperor, might employ a Council to weaken papal prestige and authority; and the constant threats from the Turks [see page 91] and from the Protestants made difficult and unpropitious an assembly of Roman Catholic Christendom. By the 1530's, however, the demand for a Council could no longer be ignored. In 1534, when Paul III became pope, he began preparations for it. After much dispute over the place of meeting and other details, the long-awaited Council assembled for its first session at Trent, December 13, 1545. Even then, Lutherans refused to attend, Calvinists were not invited, the king of France refused to permit his subjects to participate, and only a few Englishmen, disloyal to their king, were present. Spaniards and Italians were most numerous in the Council, and Italians dominated it. Of 225 prelates who signed the Council's official acts, 189 were Italians—and the Italians were largely controlled by representatives of the Curia, thus permitting Roman forces to protect the Papacy against those who might wish to assert the Council's supremacy over the pope.

The Council of Trent experienced many interruptions and postponements, largely occasioned by the delicate state of international affairs, and its final sessions were not held until December, 1563. Not all of its meetings were orderly. The secretary recorded such occasions as when "the Bishop of La Cava seized the beard of the Bishop of Chironia with both hands, and plucked out several hairs, without saying a word." In the end, however, the Council did much to revivify the Catholic cause. By 1560, before the Council of Trent had finished its work, Protestantism had reached its zenith of power on the Continent and a reaction toward Catholicism was beginning to become apparent. One of the principal reasons for this turn in the religious tide was the work of the Council of Trent. This fell into three categories: Definition of Roman Catholic doctrine with defenses against Protestant objections; anathemas against specific heretical opinions and practices; and reforms designed to eradicate abuses and establish a more rigid discipline among the Catholic clergy. Examples of each of these types of decrees are given below.

From *The Canons and Decrees of the Council of Trent* (1566) [1]

DEFINITION OF DOCTRINE—DECREES CONCERNING INDULGENCES AND JUSTIFICATION BY FAITH

Whereas the power of conferring Indulgences was granted by Christ to the Church; and she has, even in the most ancient times, used the said power, delivered unto her of God; the sacred holy Synod teaches, and enjoins, that the use of Indulgences, for the Christian people most salutary, and approved of by the authority of sacred Councils, is to be retained in the Church; and It condemns with anathema those who either assert, that they are useless; or who deny that there is in the Church the power of granting them. In granting them, however, It

---

[1] *The Canons and Decrees of the Sacred and Oecumenical Council of Trent,* trans. by the Rev. J. Waterworth, London, 1848, 277-78 and 36-37; and 44-47, 54, 82, and 174 respectively.

desires that, in accordance with the ancient and approved custom in the Church, moderation be observed; lest, by excessive facility, ecclesiastical discipline be enervated. And being desirous that the abuses which have crept therein, and by occasion of which this honourable name of Indulgences is blasphemed by heretics, be amended and corrected, It ordains generally by this decree, that all evil gains for the obtaining thereof,—whence a most prolific cause of abuses amongst the Christian people has been derived—be wholly abolished. But as regards the other abuses which have proceeded from superstition, ignorance, irreverence, or from whatsoever other source, since, by reason of the manifold corruptions in the places and provinces where the said abuses are committed, they cannot conveniently be specially prohibited; It commands all bishops, diligently to collect, each in his own church, all abuses of this nature, and to report them in the first provincial Synod; that, after having been reviewed by the opinions of the other bishops also, they may forthwith be referred to the Sovereign Roman Pontiff, by whose authority and prudence that which may be expedient for the universal Church will be ordained; that thus the gift of holy Indulgences may be dispensed to all the faithful, piously, holily, and incorruptly.

IN WHAT MANNER IT IS TO BE UNDERSTOOD, THAT THE IMPIOUS IS JUSTIFIED BY FAITH, AND GRATUITOUSLY

And whereas the Apostle saith, that man is *justified by faith* and *freely,* those words are to be understood in that sense which the perpetual consent of the Catholic Church hath held and expressed; to wit, that we are therefore said to be *justified by faith,* because faith is the beginning of human salvation, the foundation, and the root of all Justification; *without which it is impossible to please God,* and to come unto the fellowship of His sons: but we are therefore said to be justified *freely,* because that none of those things which precede justification—whether faith or works—merit the grace itself of justification. For, *if it be a grace, it is not now by works,* otherwise, as the same Apostle says, *grace is no more grace.*

AGAINST THE VAIN CONFIDENCE OF HERETICS

But, although it is necessary to believe that sins neither are remitted, nor ever were remitted save gratuitously by the mercy of God for Christ's sake; yet is it not to be said, that sins are forgiven, or have been forgiven, to any one who boasts of his confidence and certainty of the remission of his sins, and rests on that alone; seeing that it may exist, yea does in our day exist, amongst heretics and schismatics; and with great vehemence is this vain confidence, and one alien from all godliness, preached up in opposition to the Catholic Church. But neither is this to be asserted—that they who are truly justified must needs, without any doubting whatever, settle within themselves that they are justified, and that no one is absolved from sins and justified, but he that believes for certain that he is absolved and justified; and that absolution and justification are effected by this faith alone. . . . For even as no pious person ought to doubt of the mercy of God, of the merit of Christ, and of the virtue and efficacy of the sacraments, even so each one, when he regards himself, and his own weakness and indisposition, may have fear and apprehension touching his own grace; seeing that no one can know with a certainty of faith, which cannot be subject to error, that he has obtained the grace of God.

ANATHEMAS AGAINST SPECIFIC
HERETICAL OPINIONS AND PRACTICES

ON JUSTIFICATION

Canon I.—If any one saith, that man may be justified before God by his own works, whether done through the teaching of human nature, or that of the law, without the grace of God through Jesus Christ; let him be anathema. . . .

Canon IX.—If any one saith, that by faith alone the impious is justified; in such wise as to mean, that nothing else is required to co-operate in order to the obtaining the grace of Justification, and that it is not in any way necessary, that he be prepared and disposed by the movement of his own will; let him be anathema. . . .

Canon XIV.—If any one saith, that man is truly absolved from his sins and justified, because that he assuredly believed himself absolved and justified; or, that no one is truly justified but he who believes himself justified; and that, by this faith alone, absolution and justification are effected; let him be anathema.

Canon XV.—If any one saith, that a man, who is born again and justified, is bound of faith to believe that he is assuredly in the number of the predestinate; let him be anathema. . . .

Canon XIX.—If any one saith, that nothing besides faith is commanded in the Gospel; that other things are indifferent, neither commanded nor prohibited, but free; or, that the ten commandments nowise appertain to the Christian; let him be anathema.

Canon XX.—If any one saith, that the man who is justified and how perfect soever, is not bound to observe the commandments of God and of the Church, but only to believe; as if indeed the Gospel were a bare and absolute promise of eternal life, without the condition of observing the commandments; let him be anathema.

ON THE SACRAMENTS IN GENERAL

Canon I.—If any one saith, that the sacraments of the New Law were not all instituted by Jesus Christ, our Lord; or, that they are more, or less, than seven, to wit, Baptism, Confirmation, the Eucharist, Penance, Extreme Unction, Order, and Matrimony; or even that any one of these seven is not truly and properly a sacrament; let him be anathema.

Canon II.—If any one saith, that these said sacraments of the New Law do not differ from the sacraments of the Old Law, save that the ceremonies are different, and different the outward rites; let him be anathema.

Canon III.—If any one saith, that these seven sacraments are in such wise equal to each other, as that one is not in any way more worthy than another; let him be anathema.

Canon IV.—If any one saith, that the sacraments of the New Law are not necessary unto salvation, but superfluous; and that, without them, or without the desire thereof, men obtain of God, through faith alone, the grace of justification—though all (the sacraments) are not indeed necessary for every individual; let him be anathema.

ON THE SACRAMENT OF ORDER

Canon VI.—If any one saith, that, in the Catholic Church there is not a hierarchy by divine ordination instituted, consisting of bishops, priests, and ministers; let him be anathema.

Canon VII.—If any one saith, that bishops are not superior to priests; or, that they have not the power of confirming and ordaining; or, that the power which they possess is common to them and to priests; or, that orders, conferred by them, without the consent, or vocation of the people, or of the secular power, are invalid; or, that those who have neither been rightly ordained, nor sent, by ecclesiastical and canonical power, but come from elsewhere, are lawful ministers of the word and of the sacraments; let him be anathema.

Canon VIII.—If any one saith, that the bishops, who are assumed by authority of the Roman Pontiff, are not legitimate and true bishops, but are a human figment; let him be anathema.

ON THE MOST HOLY SACRAMENT OF THE EUCHARIST

Canon I.—If any one denieth, that, in the sacrament of the most holy Eucharist, are contained truly, really, and substantially, the body and blood together with the soul and divinity of our Lord Jesus Christ, and consequently the whole Christ; but saith that He is only therein as in a sign, or in figure, or virtue; let him be anathema.

Canon II.—If any one saith, that, in the sacred and holy sacrament of the Eucharist, the substance of the bread and wine remains conjointly with the body and blood of our Lord Jesus Christ, and denieth that wonderful and singular conversion of the whole substance of the bread into the Body, and of the whole substance of the wine into the Blood— the species only of the bread and wine remaining—which conversion indeed the Catholic Church most aptly calls Transubstantiation; let him be anathema.

REFORMS OF THE CLERGY [1]

It is to be desired that those who undertake the office of bishop should understand what their portion is, and compre-

hend that they are called, not to their own convenience, not to riches or luxury, but to labors and cares, for the glory of God. For it is not to be doubted that the rest of the faithful also will be more easily excited to religion and innocence if they shall see those who are set over them not fixing their thoughts on the things of this world, but on the salvation of souls and on their heavenly country. Wherefore this holy Council, being minded that these things are of the greatest importance towards restoring ecclesiastical discipline, admonishes all bishops that, often meditating thereon, they show themselves conformable to their office by their actual deeds and the actions of their lives; which is a kind of perpetual sermon; but, above all, that they so order their whole conversation that others may thence be able to derive examples of frugality, modesty, continency, and of that holy humility which so much commends us to God.

Wherefore, after the example of our fathers in the Council of Carthage, this Council not only orders that bishops be content with modest furniture, and a frugal table and diet, but that they also give heed that in the rest of their manner of living, and in their whole house, there be nothing seen which is alien to this holy institution, and which does not manifest simplicity, zeal toward God, and a contempt of vanities.

It strictly forbids them, moreover, to strive to enrich their own kindred or domestics out of the revenues of the Church, seeing that even the canons of the apostles forbid them to give to their kindred the property of the Church, which belongs to God; but if their kindred be poor, let them distribute to them thereof as poor, but not misapply or waste the Church's goods for their sakes: Yea, this holy Council, with the utmost earnestness, admonishes them completely to lay aside all this human and carnal affection to-

---

[1] Robinson, *Readings in European History*, II, 160-61. Reprinted by permission of Ginn and Company.

wards brothers, nephews, and kindred, which is the seed plot of many evils in the Church. And what has been said of bishops, the same is to be observed by all who hold ecclesiastical benefices, whether secular or regular, each according to the nature of his rank.

THE MANNER OF PROCEEDING AGAINST CLERICS WHO KEEP CONCUBINES IS PRESCRIBED [1]

How shameful a thing, and how unworthy it is of the name of clerics who have devoted themselves to the service of God, to live in the filth of impurity, and unclean bondage, the thing itself doth testify, in the common scandal of all the faithful, and the extreme disgrace entailed on the clerical order. To the end, therefore, that the ministers of the Church may be recalled to that continency and integrity of life which becomes them; and that the people may hence learn to reverence them the more, that they know them to be more pure of life: the holy Synod forbids all clerics whatsoever to dare to keep concubines, or any other woman of whom any suspicion can exist, either in their own houses, or elsewhere, or to presume to have any intercourse with them: otherwise, they shall be punished with the penalties imposed by the sacred canons, or by the statutes of the (several) churches.

2. The Rise of Religious Orders

Another important feature of the Catholic Reformation was the organization, among women as well as among men, of new religious orders which expended their energies to strengthen the Catholic Church and to combat Protestant heresies. The new orders arose, often spontaneously, in Italy and

in Spain about the same time Lutheranism developed in the Germanies.

A GENERAL DESCRIPTION

From KIDD, *The Counter-Reformation* (1933) [2]

The Oratory of Divine Love was a pious sodality, of which mention is first made during the pontificate of Leo X, 1513-21. It was founded, *c.* 1517, by some distinguished men, remarkable both for learning and piety. They met in the church of St. Silvester and St. Dorothea in the Trastevere, of which one of the members, Giuliano Dati, was the parish priest. They were not bound by vows; for they had not constituted themselves an Order; nor prayed for the requisite sanction. But, as divine service was negligently, and even irreverently, performed, they united themselves, in number about sixty, to restore its dignity and due observance; and by special exercises and devotions to reawaken the spiritual life. Among them were Jacopo Sadoleto, Bishop of Carpentras, 1517-40 (d. 1547); Giovanni Matteo Giberti, Bishop of Verona 1524-43; Giovanni Pietro Caraffa, Bishop of Chieti 1505-24—afterwards Cardinals and the last Pope Paul IV, 1555-59; with Gaetano di Tiene 1480-1547, one day to be canonised, and Luigi Lippomano, Bishop of Verona, 1548-58. This was the first stage of the movement when all its adherents were actuated by a common purpose but had, as yet, manifested no diversity of opinion. . . .

With the exception of Caraffa, who was a conservative in theology though eager for reform in practice, most of these men displayed some sympathy with evan-

[1] *Canons and Decrees of the . . Council of Trent*, 270.

[2] B. J. Kidd, *The Counter-Reformation, 1550-1600*, 1933, 11-22. Reprinted by permission of the Society for the Promotion of Christian Knowledge.

gelical doctrine. There is no evidence of direct connexion between them and the Lutheran movement. But it is certain that the works of the reformers were circulated in Italy at an early period, and read with avidity. Contarini and his friends had no little sympathy with the doctrine of justification by faith; and henceforward "Lutheranism" had its attraction for friends, as well as foes, of the Church in Italy. . . .

New Religious Orders began to appear about the same time as the Oratory of Divine Love. They were a second sign of the revival; and obtained recognition before the Cardinals presented their *Consilium*. Two of them were new only in the sense that they were the fruit of a new spirit, revivifying Orders already in existence. But others—Theatins, Somaschi, Barnabites and Oratorians—were new foundations altogether. So too were the Jesuits: but they demanded a chapter to themselves. . . .

Orders of women also grew up concurrently with Orders of men.

In 1538 Maria Laurentia Longo, d. 1542, instituted the Capucines at Naples; and framed their rule upon the model of the Poor Clares, which St. Clare, d. 1253, had received from St. Francis in 1224.

In 1544 Paul III confirmed the well-known Order of Ursulines. They had been founded, 1535, by Angela Merici, 1474-1540, of Brescia, for the care of the sick, and for teaching young girls. It was the first teaching Order of women established in the Church: and, in 1900, had 100 communities, in 8 provinces: besides many large and important communities which retain their independence.

Again, in 1562, St. Teresa, 1515-82, became the foundress of the Discalced Carmelitesses, in order to recall the Carmelite nuns to the ideals of their earlier days: as her friend, St. Peter of Alcantara, 1499-1562, had attempted to revive the

devotion of the Franciscans by founding, in 1555, the Order of the Barefooted Friars. Both Orders received the approval of Pius IV: the Friars in February 1562 and the nuns in July 1565. Their founders drew their inspiration from the soil of Spanish mysticism, and fructified it in their turn: St. Peter by his "golden book" and *Prayer and Meditation*, 1560: and St. Teresa by the history of her inner *Life*, written 1563-6.

THE SOCIETY OF JESUS: ITS CONSTITUTION

Of especial importance among the new religious orders was the Society of Jesus, founded by St. Ignatius Loyola, a Spanish soldier and mystic. The society began when Loyola formed a league with his two roommates of the University of Paris, Peter Faber and Francis Xavier. Soon others joined the Society. In 1537, calling themselves the Company of Jesus, and organized like a small army to make war upon Satan, they went on a pilgrimage to Venice. Later, they went to Rome, where they attracted favorable attention from Pope Paul III, who approved their constitution by a bull issued September 27, 1540. The powers of the society were enlarged by later bulls (1543, 1546, and 1549), but the nature of the society is shown by the first bull, portions of which follow.

From *The Constitution of the Society of Jesus* (1540) [1]

The plan of the proposed rule follows and is this:

In our society, which we wish to be called by the name Jesus, let whoever desires to fight under the sacred banner

[1] Oliver J. Thatcher, ed., *The Library of Original Sources*, 10 vols., New York, 1907, V, 180-83.

of the Cross, and to serve only God and the Roman pontiff, His vicar on earth, after a solemn vow of perpetual chastity—let him keep in mind that he is part of a society, instituted for the purpose of perfecting souls in life and in Christian doctrine, for the propagation of the faith through public preaching, ministering the word of God, spiritual macerations, works of charity, and especially through the teaching of the young and uninstructed in the Christian precepts; and lastly for giving consolation to believers in hearing their confessions. Let him think first of God, then of the rule of this order, which is the way to Him; and let him follow after the end proposed by God with all his strength. Let each one, nevertheless, rest in the grace given him by the Holy Spirit, and in the proper grade of his calling, and lest anyone use zeal but not discretion, let the deciding of the grade of each, of the offices, and whole arrangement be in the hands of the general or prelate selected through us, in order that the harmony so necessary in all well-governed institutions may be preserved.

Let this general, with the council of his associates, have the power in council to draw up rules suitable for the end proposed, the majority of all voters of the society always having the right of deciding. Let it be understood that there be consultation in regard to the more important or permanent questions, the majority of the whole society, that can conveniently be convoked; in the case of less important or transient matters, all those that are present where the general lives. The right of carrying out laws, however, belongs only to the general.

Let all members know, and let it be not only at the beginning of their profession, but let them think over it daily as long as they live, that the society as a whole, and each of them, owes obedience to our most holy lord, the pope, and the other Roman pontiffs, his successors, and to fight with faithful obedience for God. And however much he may be learned in the Gospel, and however we may be taught in the orthodox faith, let all Christians profess themselves under the Roman pontiff as leader, and vicar of Jesus Christ. For the greater humility of our society, and toward the complete self-mortification of each one, and in order to aid the abnegation of our own wills to the greatest extent, let each one, besides that common obligation, be devoted to this by special vow. So that whatever the present or other Roman pontiffs order that concerns the saving of souls and the spread of the faith, and to whatever provinces he shall wish to send us, this let us strive to accomplish as far as in us lies, without any turning back or excuse, whether he shall send us to the Turks, or to any other infidels, even those living in the lands that are called the Indies; or to any heretics or schismatics, or unbelievers, whatever. Wherefore let those that are about to join us consider long and well, before they put their shoulders to this task, whether they have enough grace for good deeds to mount this citadel at the command of their superiors. . . .

Let each vow to be obedient to the general of the society in all things that concern the fulfillment of these our regulations.

Let him command what he knows to be opportune for the advancement of the ends proposed by God and the society. In issuing these commands, he shall always keep the memory of the kindness, gentleness, and love of Christ, Peter, and Paul, before him, whose example in this rule let the council carefully follow.

Let them have charge especially over the education of children and of the heathen in the Christian doctrine of the ten commandments, and like rudiments, whatever seems suitable to the circumstances of the individuals, and of time and place. . . .

Since we know by experience that no life is happier, purer, or more apt to aid its fellow than the one most removed from all contagion of avarice, and close to holy poverty, and since we know that our Lord Jesus Christ provides necessary food and clothing for his servants seeking the kingdom of God, let each and all vow eternal poverty. . . .

Let them have the power, however, to have a college or colleges at the Universities, having census returns, revenues, or possessions, to be applied to the use and necessities of the students; the thing held to be under control of the general, and the society in accordance with the common government.

3. The Italian Inquisition and the Index

Two other instruments employed by the Catholic Church to arrest the growth of Protestantism, the Supreme Tribunal of the Inquisition and the Index of Prohibited Books, were revivals of methods long employed against heretics. To a degree, as the account below indicates, the two were interrelated, although they subsequently became separate institutions within the church. In point of time, the Inquisition was reorganized first, fashioned after the famous Spanish model which since its establishment in 1478 had been very effective in producing religious unity in Spain [see page 160]. The rigor of its officials, the frequent use of torture, and the unfairness of its trials (judged by more recent standards) have caused the Inquisition to be severely denounced. But it was extraordinarily efficient in rooting out heresies, espe-

cially in Italy and in Spain. The Supreme Tribunal of the Inquisition was authorized by Pope Paul II, July 21, 1542, with joyful support from the new Society of Jesus. Its organization and operation in Italy are described below.

From RANKE, *History of the Popes* (1843) [1]

It [the bull which established the Inquisition] names six cardinals, among whom Caraffa [Cardinal Pietro Caraffa, later Pope Paul IV, 1555-1559] and Toledo [Cardinal Juan Alvarez de Toledo] stood first, to be commissioners of the apostolic see, general and universal inquisitors on this side the Alps and beyond them. It bestows on them the right to delegate ecclesiastics with similar power, to all such places as it shall seem good to them, to determine absolutely all appeals against the acts of the latter, and even to proceed without the participation of the ordinary spiritual courts. Every man, without a single exception, without any regard whatever to station or dignity, shall be subject to their jurisdiction; the suspected shall be thrown into prison, the guilty shall be punished even capitally, and their property confiscated. One restriction is imposed on the court. To punish shall be its function: the pope reserves to himself the right of pardoning the guilty who become converted. Thus shall everything be done, ordered, and accomplished, to suppress and uproot the errors, that have broken out among the Christian community.

Caraffa lost not a moment in putting this bull into execution. He was not over rich, but upon this occasion he would have regarded it as a loss, had he waited for a payment from the apostolic chamber: he immediately hired a house, fitted up the rooms for officers and the prisons at his own cost; provided them with bars

[1] Ranke, *The History of the Popes,* trans. by Kelly, 55-57.

and strong locks, with blocks, chains, and bonds, and all the horrible utensils of his office. He then named commissioners general for the several countries. The first, as far as I can discover, for Rome, was his own chaplain, Teofilo di Tropea, of whose severity cardinals, such as Pole, had soon reason to complain.

"The following rules," says the MS. biography of Caraffa, "were conceived by the cardinal to be the best directed to the end in view.

"Firstly, In matters of faith, not a moment's delay must be made, but upon the least suspicion, measures must immediately be taken with the utmost rigour.

"Secondly, No respect must be shown to any prince or prelate, however high his station.

"Thirdly, Extraordinary and extreme severity must be used, against such as shall seek to defend themselves through the protection of any potentate; only whoso confesses, shall be treated mildly and with fatherly compassion.

"Fourthly, We must not debase ourselves to any sort of toleration towards heretics, and especially towards Calvinists."

All, we see, is rigour, unrelenting, unscrupulous rigour, till the confession has been worked out. Horrible, especially at a moment when opinions were not yet fully developed, when many were seeking to conciliate the profounder doctrines of Christianity with the institutions of the existing Church. The weaker gave way and submitted; those of stronger mould, on the contrary, now first decidedly embraced the tenets of opposition, and sought to withdraw themselves from violence. . . .

Everywhere throughout Italy, persecution and terrors broke out. The rancour of contending factions seconded the designs of the inquisitors. How often, after long waiting in vain other opportunity of revenge, was a man's enemy known to have recourse to the charge of heresy. Of two parties that cherished an equal degree of rancorous hate against each other, the monks of the old school, and all that host of men of talent, who had been led by their literary labours to a religious tendency, the former had now got weapons in their hands, and condemned their antagonists to perpetual silence. "It is hardly possible," exclaims Antonio dei Pagliarici, "to be a Christian and die in one's bed." . . . Literature in general, was subjected to the severest scrutiny. In the year 1543, Caraffa gave orders that for the future no book, whatever were its contents, whether it were old or new, should be printed without the permission of the inquisitors: booksellers were also to send them in catalogues of their stock, and were not to sell any more books without their permission: the customs' officers of the Doguna received orders not to deliver to its address any package of MS. or printed books without first having laid it before the Inquisition. By degrees the index of forbidden books came to be published; the first example had been set in Louvain and Paris.

In Italy Giovanni della Casa, who was on terms of the closest intimacy with the house of Caraffa, printed the first catalogue of about seventy numbers in Venice. More lengthened lists appeared in 1552 at Florence, in 1554 at Milan, and the first drawn up in what was afterwards the usual form at Rome, in 1559. It contains works of the Cardinals, and the poems of that same della Casa himself. Not only were these laws imposed on printers and booksellers, but it was made an obligation of conscience upon private persons to denounce forbidden books, and to contribute to their destruction. The rule was applied with incredible strictness. Many as were the thousands of copies circulated of the book on "The Benefits bestowed by

Christ," it wholly vanished, and is no longer to be found. In Rome, whole piles of confiscated copies were burnt.

[After the list of 1559 was set forth, the Council of Trent took up the matter, appointed a committee which drafted rules to guide judges in the future, and left it to the Pope to prepare a new list. A new Index was published by Pope Pius IV. In 1571, Pius V created at Rome the Congregation of the Index, an institution apart from the Inquisition, to examine all suspected books, revise the list of prohibited books from time to time, and, in general, to keep the Index abreast of the new age of printing and Protestantism. The Congregation of the Index functioned until 1917, when its work was assumed directly by the office of the popes.]

12 | SPAIN IN REFORMATION DAYS: THE BEGINNINGS OF DECLINE

The Spanish monarchy, which blossomed quickly in the early 1500's into a vast empire with widespread overseas possessions [see page 78], was showing unmistakable signs of decay by 1600. The treasure which poured in from the New World, instead of being invested in the development of Spanish internal economy, was largely frittered away by Charles V and his son, Philip II, in expensive efforts to defend Catholic Christendom from its opponents, both Turk and Protestant. Moreover, before the sixteenth century ended, Spain had lost the Dutch provinces in the Netherlands, had suffered manifold indignities at the hands of English seamen culminating in the defeat of the famous "Invincible" Armada in 1588, and had won its only major success against the infidel Turk at Lepanto in 1571. The policies which wrought such damage to Spanish wealth and prestige were inaugurated by Charles V and extended with stubborn fanaticism by Philip II.

1. Philip II, King of Spain, 1556-1598

From CREIGHTON, *Age of Elizabeth* (1876) [1]

Philip had been brought up in Castile, and was Spanish in character, in manner, in appearance, in language. His coldness, haughtiness, and pride vexed the Flemings; his reserve seemed to them to be contemptuous. Yet they were loyal to Philip at first. It was the troops of the Netherlands that won for him the decisive battle of St. Quentin and enabled him to make with France the Peace of Cateau Cambrésis (1559).

When this had been concluded Philip returned to Spain, which he never left again. Charles V had not ruled in the interest of any one of the countries under his power. He had had no capital, but moved about from place to place according as the necessities of the times demanded.

[1] Mandell Creighton, *The Age of Elizabeth* New York, 1921 (*Epochs of Modern History*), 84-87, 223-24. Reprinted by permission of Longmans, Green and Company, Inc.

But Philip II first gave to the power which he had inherited a fixed seat in Castile; he founded a Spanish Empire, with Madrid as its capital. From Madrid he himself would govern his dominions. The countries over which he ruled were to be regarded as provinces of Spain; they should be cared for by Spanish viceroys, and be treated as members of a great administrative system. This change in the political relations of the countries which formed the dominions of Philip II came gradually. When once it had been made it was most important for the destinies of Europe. If one man were to wield absolutely all the resources of these scattered provinces, if he were to infuse into all these peoples the daring, fierce, fanatical spirit of the Spaniards, if he were to combine them to fight for Spain and Catholicism, the control of the future of Europe would be in his hands.

Philip II was profoundly ambitious. Like his ancestors, he believed that to his house belonged the rule of the world. But he was obliged to adapt his method to his own individual character and capacity. He was no military leader who could inspire his soldiers by his presence, nor was he a vigorous and genial prince, whose winning and affable manners might create enthusiasm for his rule. But he was a diligent, industrious, calm, and calculating politician. The personal disadvantages and ill-health which prevented him from taking a brilliant part in the affairs of the world might make him more fit to take a decisive one. Alone, in quietness, unswayed by the passions of combatants and undisturbed by the tumult of discordant advice, he might, as from a height of contemplation, look down upon the complicated affairs of Europe and shape them to his own ends. This was Philip's ideal of life. In the seclusion of his gloomy residence of the Escurial, he aimed at

pulling the threads which were to move the course of Europe. From morning to night he sat alone in his cabinet and received the despatches which poured in from every quarter. All communications were carried on with him by writing, and he was his own chief minister. The despatches were read and read again, they were marked and underlined and analysed and commented on in their margin. They were laid aside and carefully weighed and compared laboriously with others; their truth and the integrity of their writers were tested by every means which the ingenuity of a suspicious nature without a spark of affection or sympathy could suggest. At last the conclusion drawn from all this careful thought and comparison of contradictory authorities slowly took shape as a definite plan. All was calmly and deliberately done; when a plan was once formed it was deliberately carried out, and no exultation followed its success, no complaint its failure. Philip was an admirable and conscientious man of business. He set about the task of governing the world as though it had been a trade, and if the world could have been governed by the industry of a painstaking clerk, Philip would have succeeded admirably.

Philip never trusted anyone, but regarded his ministers as instruments for carrying out his schemes. Habitually reserved himself, he listened to everything that was told him without betraying his own feelings. Rival ministers poured out to him their accusations against one another; he listened without being carried away. He allowed a plan to be carried out, but judged it solely by its success, and if it failed he at once abandoned its contriver. None of his ministers were sure of his continued favour. If he distrusted a man, he gave no sign of it till he had gradually detached him from the business in which he was employed, and had deprived him of all means of being harmful; then he suddenly dismissed him.

Philip felt that the weakness of his political position was its unattractiveness and want of interest in the eyes of ordinary men. This interest he secured by completely identifying himself and his policy with the cause of Catholicism. In so doing he was no hypocrite, for he was sincerely religious. But he saw the advantage to be gained by making his own interests coincide with those of the old religion. As the champion of Catholicism he interfered in the affairs of Europe in such a way that the gain of Catholicism must in every case lead to an increase in the power of Spain. It was for this purpose that he identified his government with Spain, which had still fresh in its memory the crusades against the Moors, and where Protestant opinions were regarded as a sure token of the taint of Jewish or Moorish blood.

Thus, under Philip, Spain became enthusiastically Catholic. The Castilians felt their pride gratified at seeing their country made the seat of Philip's power, and they were willing to be taxed for its maintenance. Their chivalrous spirit was enlisted on the side of their religion. Round Philip's person, as being the champion of that religion, was thrown the glamour of a passionate loyalty, such as was far removed from the old Spanish spirit. Philip had been wise in identifying himself with Spain. . . . It remained for Philip to establish the spirit of Spain in the other parts of his dominions, especially in the Netherlands. . . .

Philip could not, however, prosecute his designs. He died in September [1598], after a most painful illness, which he endured with Christian fortitude. "I die like a good Catholic, in faith and obedience to the holy Roman Church," were his last words. He was seventy-one years old, and had ruled the Spanish monarchy for forty years. He was a sincere fanatic, who had identified his own interests with those of Catholicism. We have seen how wide were his plans and how far-reaching was his policy. His great schemes failed one by one, and left him hopelessly bankrupt. In 1597 he repudiated his debts, and ruined many of the chief commercial houses in Europe. His enterprises aimed solely at extending his own influence and the power of his house. His possessions were taxed to the utmost to supply funds for these great undertakings, and his peoples' industry was stopped by unwise taxes. Castile, as being the seat of his government, suffered most. The fall of Spain from its high position in Europe was gradual, but the causes of its decay were financial. It had to pay for the great plans of Charles V and Philip II, and it received no national advantage to recompense it for the injurious results of their failure. Philip II left to his successor a high position, an impoverished exchequer, and a ruinous system of government. It required only a few years for the last two legacies to destroy the first.

2. The Spanish Inquisition

Originally organized in the time of Ferdinand and Isabella to eradicate Jews and Moors from Spain, the Spanish Inquisition extirpated all heresies, effectively discouraged the growth of Protestantism, and cruelly tortured and executed those Protestants discovered in Spanish dominions. Creation of the Spanish Inquisition as a vigilant and efficient arm peculiar to the Spanish Government has been described in the selection which follows.

ORIGIN AND ORGANIZATION OF THE
SPANISH INQUISITION

From LEA, *The Inquisition of Spain* (1906) [1]

It was inevitable that there should have been a prolonged struggle in the court before the drastic remedy of the Inquisition was adopted. . . . There seems at first to have been a kind of compromise adopted, under which Pedro Fernández de Solis, Bishop of Cadiz, who was Provisor of Seville, with the Assistente Diego de Merlo, Fray Alfonso de Hojeda and some other frailes were commissioned to take charge of the matter, with power to inflict punishment. This resulted in a report by the commissioners to the sovereigns that a great portion of the citizens of Seville were infected with heresy, that it involved men high in station and power, and that it spread throughout not only Andalusia but Castile, so that it was incurable save by organization of the Inquisition. . . . At last the victory was won. Ferdinand and Isabella resolved to introduce the Inquisition in the Castilian kingdoms and their ambassadors to the Holy See, the Bishop of Osma and his brother Diego de Santillan, were ordered to procure the necessary bull from Sixtus IV. . . .

Sixtus can have been nothing loath to accomplish the introduction of the Inquisition in Castile, which his predecessors had so frequently and so vainly attempted. . . . If the request of the Castilian sovereigns, therefore, was not immediately granted it . . . [was] because Ferdinand and Isabella desired, not the ordinary papal Inquisition, but one which should be under the royal control and should pour into the royal treasury the resultant confiscations. Hitherto the appointment

of inquisitors had always been made by the Provincials of the Dominican or Franciscan Orders according as the territory belonged to one or to the other, with occasional interference on the part of the Holy See, from which the commissions emanated. It was a delegation of the supreme papal authority and had always been held completely independent of the secular power, but Ferdinand and Isabella were too jealous of papal interference in the internal affairs of their kingdoms to permit this, and it is an evidence of the extreme desire of Sixtus to extend the Inquisition over Castile that he consented to make so important a concession. . . .

The bull as finally issued bears date November 1, 1478, and is a very simple affair which, on its face, bears no signs of its momentous influence in moulding the destinies of the Spanish Peninsula. After reciting the existence in Spain of false Christians and the request of Ferdinand and Isabella that the pope should provide a remedy, it authorizes them to appoint three bishops or other suitable men, priests either regular or secular, over forty years of age, masters or bachelors in theology or doctors or licentiates of canon law, and to remove and replace them at pleasure. These are to have the jurisdiction and faculties of bishops and inquisitors over heretics, their fautors [protectors] and receivers. . . .

The various provinces of Castile thus became provided with the machinery requisite for the extermination of heresy, and at an early period in its development it was seen that, for the enormous work before it, some more compact and centralized organization was desirable than had hitherto been devised. The Inquisition which had been so effective in the thirteenth and fourteenth centuries was scattered over Europe; its judges were appointed by the Dominican or Franciscan Provincials, using a course of procedure and obeying in-

[1] This and the next selection are from Henry Charles Lea, *A History of the Inquisition of Spain*, 4 vols., 1906-07. By permission of The Macmillan Company. This is I, 156-59, 172-74.

structions which emanated from the Holy See. The papacy was the only link between them; they were not subjected to visitation or inspection and it was, if not impossible, a matter of difficulty to call them to account for the manner in which they might discharge their functions. Such was not the conception of Ferdinand and Isabella who intended the Spanish Inquisition to be a national institution, strongly organized and owing obedience to the Crown much more than to the Holy See. The measures which they adopted with this object were conceived with their customary sagacity, and were carried out with their usual vigor and success.

At this period they were earnestly engaged in reorganizing the institutions of Castile, centralizing the administration and reducing to order the chaos resulting from the virtual anarchy of the preceding reigns. In effecting this they apportioned, in 1480, with the consent of the Córtes of Toledo, the affairs of government among four royal councils, that of administration and justice, known as the Concejo Real de Castella, that of Finance, or Concejo de Hacienda, the Concejo de Estado and the Concejo de Aragon, to which was added a special one for the Hermandades. These met daily in the palace for the despatch of business and their effect in making the royal power felt in every quarter of the land and in giving vigor and unity to the management of the state soon proved the practical value of the device. The Inquisition was fast looming up as an affair of state of the first importance, while yet it could scarce be regarded as falling within the scope of either of the four councils; the sovereigns were too jealous of papal interference to allow it to drift aimlessly, subject to directions from Rome, and their uniform policy required that it should be kept as much as possible under the royal superintendence. That a fifth council should be created for the pur-

pose was a natural expedient, for which the assent of Sixtus IV was readily obtained, when it was organized in 1483 under the name of the *Concejo de la Suprema y General Inquisición*—a title conveniently abbreviated to *la Suprema*—with jurisdiction over all matters connected with the faith. To secure due subordination and discipline over the whole body it was requisite that the president of this council should have full control. . . . It thus became necessary to create a new office, unknown to the older Inquisition—an inquisitor-general who should preside over the deliberations of the council. The office evidently was one which would be of immense weight and the future of the institution depended greatly on the character of its first chief. By the advice of the Cardinal Archbishop of Toledo, Pedro González de Mendoza, the royal choice fell on Thomás de Torquemada, the confessor of the sovereigns. . . .

The selection of Torquemada justified the wisdom of the sovereigns. Full of pitiless zeal, he developed the nascent institution with unwearied assiduity. Rigid and unbending, he would listen to no compromise of what he deemed to be his duty, and in his sphere he personified the union of the spiritual and temporal swords which was the ideal of all true churchmen. Under his guidance the Inquisition rapidly took shape and extended its organization throughout Spain and was untiring and remorseless in the pursuit and punishment of the apostates.

THE SPANISH INQUISITION IN ACTION

Protestantism made little headway in Spain. Until 1558 only 105 cases were recorded by the Inquisitors, thirty-nine native Spaniards and sixty-six foreigners. But early in the reign of Philip II two groups of Protestants were uncovered, one at Seville and one at

Valladolid, and impressive autos-da-fé (acts of faith) were organized by the Inquisitor-General, Valdés.

From LEA, *The Inquisition of Spain* [1]

Nothing was spared to enhance the effect of the auto-de-fé of Trinity Sunday, May 21, 1559, in which the first portion of the Valladolid prisoners were to suffer. It was solemnly proclaimed fifteen days in advance, during which the buildings of the Inquisition were incessantly patrolled, day and night, by a hundred armed men, and guards were stationed at the stagings in the Plaza Mayor, for there were rumors that the prison was to be blown up and that the stagings were to be fired. Along the line of the procession palings were set in the middle of the street, forming an unobstructed path for three to march abreast. . . . Every house-front along the line and around the plaza had its stagings; people flocked in from thirty and forty leagues around and encamped in the fields. . . .

The procession was headed by the effigy of Leonor de Vivero, who had died during trial, clad in widow's weeds and bearing a mitre with flames and appropriate inscriptions, and followed by a coffin containing her remains to be duly burnt. Those who were to be relaxed in person numbered fourteen, of whom one, Gonzalo Baez, was a Portuguese convicted of Judaism. Those admitted to reconciliation, with penance more or less severe, were sixteen in number, including an Englishman variously styled Anthony Graso or Bagor—probably Baker—punished for Protestantism, like all the rest, excepting Baez. When the procession reached the plaza, Agustin Cozalla was placed in the highest seat, as the conspicuous chief of the heresy, and next to him his brother, Francisco de Vivero. Melchor Cano at once commenced

the sermon, which occupied an hour, and then Valdés and the bishops approached the Princess Juana and Prince Carlos, who were present, and administered to them the oath to protect and aid the Inquisition, to which the multitude responded in a mighty roar, "To the death!" Cozalla, his brother and Alonso Pérez, who were in orders, were duly degraded from the priesthood, the sentences were read, those admitted to reconciliation made the necessary adjurations and those condemned to relaxation were handed over to the secular arm. Mounted on asses, they were carried to the Plaza de la Puerta de Campo, where the requisite stakes had been erected, and there they met their end. . . .

Of these there were only two or three who merit special consideration. Cozalla, on his trial, had at first equivocated and denied that he had dogmatized, asserting that he had only spoken of these matters to those already converted. As a rule, all the prisoners eagerly denounced their associates; he may have been more reticent at first, for he was sentenced to torture *in caput alienum,* but when stripped he promised to inform against them fully, which he did, including Carranza among those who had misled him as to purgatory. He recanted, professed conversion and eagerly sought reconciliation. . . . He declared that, when opportunity offered in the auto, he would curse and detest Lutheranism and persuade everyone to do the same, with which purpose he took his place in the procession.

So great was his emotional exaltation that he fulfilled this promise with such exuberance during the auto that he had to be checked. . . . On the way to the brasero he continued to exhort the people and directed his efforts especially to the heroic Herrezuelo, who had steadfastly refused to abandon his faith and was to be burnt alive. . . .

It was otherwise with Herrezuelo, the

[1] *Ibid.,* III, 437-42, 411.

only martyr in the group. He avowed his faith and resolutely adhered to it, in spite of all effort to convert him and of the dreadful fate in store for him. On their way to the brasero, Cozalla wasted on him all his eloquence. He was gagged and could not reply, but his stoical endurance showed his unyielding pertinacity. When chained to the stake, a stone thrown at him struck him in the forehead, covering his face with blood but, as we are told, it did him no good. Then he was thrust through the belly by a pious halberdier, but this moved him not and, when the fire was set, he bore his agony without flinching and, to the general surprise, he thus ended diabolically. Illescas, who stood so near that he could watch every expression, reports that he seemed as impassive as flint but, though he uttered no complaint and manifested no regret, yet he died with the strangest sadness in his face, so that it was dreadful to look upon him as on one who in a brief moment would be in hell with his comrade and master, Luther. . . .

The remainder of the Valladolid reformers were reserved for another celebration, October 8th, honored with the presence of Philip II, who obediently took the customary oath, with bared head and ungloved hand. It was, if possible, an occasion of greater solemnity than the previous one. A Flemish official, who was present, estimates the number of spectators at two hundred thousand and, though he must have been hardened to such scenes at home, he could not repress an expression of sympathy with the sufferers. Besides a Morisco who was relaxed, a Judaizer reconciled and two penitents for other offences, there were twenty-six Protestants. The lesson was the same as in the previous auto, that few had the ardor of martyrdom. Thirteen had made their peace in time to secure reconciliation or penance. Even Juana Sánchez, who had managed to bring with her a pair of scissors and had

cut her throat, recanted before death, but her confession was considered imperfect and she was burnt in effigy. . . . Only in two cases did this withstand the test of fire. Carlos de Seso was unyielding to the end and, when we are told that he had to be supported by two familiars to enable him to stand when hearing his sentence, we can guess the severity of the torture endured by him. Juan Sánchez was likewise pertinacious; when the fire was set it burnt the cord fastening him to the stake; he leaped down and ran in flames; it was thought that he wanted to confess but, when a confessor was brought, he refused to listen to him; one account says that the guards thrust him back into the flames, another, that he looked up and saw Carlos de Seso calmly burning and himself leaped back into the blazing pile. . . . Thus was exterminated the nascent Protestantism of Valladolid.

There never was the slightest real danger that Protestantism could make such permanent impression on the profound and unreasoning religious convictions of Spain in the sixteenth century, as to cause disturbance in the body politic; and the excitement created in Valladolid and Seville, in 1558 and 1559, was a mere passing episode leaving no trace in popular beliefs. Yet, coming when it did, it exercised an enduring influence on the fortunes of the Inquisition, and on the development of the nation. At the moment, the career of the Holy Office might almost seem to be drawing to a close, for it had nearly succeeded in extirpating Judaism from Spain . . . and its operations against the Moriscos of Valencia were suspended. The panic, skilfully excited at the appearance of Lutheranism, raised it to new life and importance and gave it a claim on the gratitude of the State, which enabled it to dominate the land during the seventeenth century. . . . Yet more important even than all this was the dread inspired of heresy, which served as a reason for isolating Spain from the rest of Europe, excluding all foreign ideas, arresting the development of culture and of science, and prolonging medievalism into modern times.

3. Circumstances Leading to the Dutch Revolt

SPANISH SEVERITIES

A long chain of unhappy circumstances produced the revolt of the Dutch provinces from Spain, the principal links of which can be summarized as follows: 1. Philip's unpopularity was enhanced by his continual absence from the Netherlands after 1559, by his preoccupation with Spanish affairs, by his attempts to subject the Low Countries to the needs of Spain, and by his assignment of the administration of the Low Countries to regents, first to his half-sister, Margaret, Duchess of Parma, then to the Duke of Alva, and then to others—all supported by garrisons of Spanish soldiers. 2. The discontent of native nobles, especially William of Orange and the Count of Egmont, because the regents gave them no voice in affairs—a discontent which led them to form a league (1562) to support the interests of the Low Countries (the league came to be known as the *Gueux,* or "Beggars," a title given them by Margaret's advisers and quickly appropriated as a patriotic cry). 3. The severe treatment of Dutch Protestants—Lutherans, Calvinists, and Anabaptists—by clerical authorities supported by Spanish arms. 4. The union of patriotic nobles with Protestant commoners into the party of the Gueux to resist Spain by force of arms, with occasional assistance from Protestants in France,

Germany, and later England. 5. Division of the seventeen provinces [1] into two groups, the ten southern provinces remaining under Spanish influence, the seven northern provinces uniting (Union of Utrecht, 1579) and declaring their independence from Spain by an Act of Abjuration drawn up at The Hague (1581). [2] After 1566 these events were punctuated by almost constant warfare in the Low Countries and, though the United Netherlands declared their independence in 1581, that independence was not given full international recognition until 1648, by the Treaties of Westphalia. Primarily, the Dutch conflict with Spain was a religious conflict—the bitter clash of fanatical Catholicism reinvigorated by the Catholic Reformation with the equally fanatical Protestantism of the Dutch. An example of Spanish severity is seen in the following Edict of 1550, known also as a "Placard," which was re-enacted as soon as Philip II acceded to the throne (1555).

From MOTLEY, *The Dutch Republic* (1856) [3]

"No one," said the edict, "shall print, write, copy, keep, conceal, sell, buy or

[1] Four duchies: Brabant, Limburg, Luxemburg, Gelderland; seven counties: Flanders, Artois, Hainault, Namur, Zeeland, Holland, Zütphen; five lordships: Friesland, Groningen, Overyssel, Utrecht, Mechlin; and one marquisate: Antwerp.

[2] The seven northern provinces which won independence were: Holland, Zeeland, Utrecht, Gelderland, Overyssel, Friesland, and Groningen. The remaining ten provinces formed what was known as the Spanish Netherlands until 1713. For the remainder of the eighteenth century they were the Austrian Netherlands, and in the nineteenth century they became the independent state of Belgium (1830). The northern provinces became predominantly Calvinist (the Dutch Reformed Church), while the southern area was made, under Spanish influence, into one of the most decided Roman Catholic countries in Europe.

[3] John Lothrop Motley, *The Rise of the Dutch Republic,* 3 vols., London (Everyman's Library), I, 228-30. Reprinted by permission of E. P. Dutton and Company, Inc.

give in churches, streets, or other places, any book or writing made by Martin Luther, John Ecolampadius, Ulrich Zwinglius, Martin Bucer, John Calvin, or other heretics reprobated by the Holy Church . . . nor break, nor otherwise injure the images of the holy virgin, or canonized saints . . . nor in his house hold conventicles, or illegal gatherings, or be present at any such in which the adherents of the above-mentioned heretics teach, baptize, and form conspiracies against the Holy Church and the general welfare. . . . Moreover, we forbid all lay persons to converse or dispute concerning the Holy Scriptures, openly or secretly, especially on any doubtful or difficult matters, or to read, teach, or expound the Scriptures, unless they have duly studied theology and been approved by some renowned university . . . or to preach secretly, or openly, or to entertain any of the opinions of the above-mentioned heretics . . . on pain, should any one be found to have contravened any of the points above mentioned, as perturbators of our state and of the general quiet, to be punished in the following manner." The edict went on to provide:

"That such pertubators of the general quiet are to be executed, to wit: the men with the sword and the women to be buried alive, if they do not persist in their errors; if they do persist in them, then they are to be executed with fire; all their property in both cases being confiscated to the crown. . . .

"We forbid," continued the decree, "all persons to lodge, entertain, furnish with food, fire, or clothing, or otherwise to favour any one holden or notoriusly suspected of being a heretic . . . and any one failing to denounce any such we ordain shall be liable to the above-mentioned punishments. . . .

"All who know of any person tainted with heresy are required to denounce and give them up to all judges, officers of the bishops, or others having authority on the premises, on pain of being punished according to the pleasure of the judge. Likewise, all shall be obliged, who know of any place where such heretics keep themselves, to declare them to the authorities, on pain of being held as accomplices, and punished as such heretics themselves would be if apprehended."

In order to secure the greatest number of arrests by a direct appeal to the most ignoble, but not the least powerful, principle of human nature, it was ordained "that the informer, in case of conviction, should be entitled to one-half the property of the accused, if not more than one hundred pounds Flemish; if more, then ten per cent. of all such excess."

Treachery to one's friends was encouraged by the provision "that if any man being present at any secret conventicle, shall afterwards come forward and betray his fellow members of the congregation, he shall receive full pardon."

PROTESTANT OUTRAGES

In order more effectively to enforce the above edict, Philip II petitioned the Pope for a larger ecclesiastical force in the Netherlands. Accordingly, by a bull of May 18, 1559, Paul IV created three new archbishoprics, fifteen new bishops, and nine prebends to each new bishop, "who were to assist him in the matter of the inquisition throughout his bishopric, two of whom were themselves to be inquisitors." This clerical force, backed by Spanish soldiers, was an efficient body to root out heresy in the Netherlands. The inquisitors, however, only aggravated Protestants and strengthened their spirit of revolt. Soon mobs were taking revenge. An eyewitness's story of the plundering of the

Cathedral of Notre Dame in Brussels in August, 1566, follows.

From Richard Clough, Letter to Sir Thomas Gresham (August 21, 1566) [1]

When they [the priests] should have begun their service, there was a company began to sing psalms, at the beginning being but a company of boys; whereupon the Margrave, and other [of] the Lords came to the church, and rebuked them. But all in vain; for that as soon as they turned their backs, they did it again; and the company increased, being begun in our Lady Church: so that, about 6 of the clock, they broke up the choir, and went and visited all the books; whereof, as it is said, some they saved, and the rest [they] utterly destroyed and broke.

After that, they begun with the image of our Lady, which had been carried about the town on Sunday last, and utterly defaced her and her chapel; and after, the whole church, which was the costliest church in Europe; and have so spoiled it, that they have not left a place to sit on in the church. And from thence, part went to the parish churches, and part to the houses of Religion, and made such dispatch as I think the like was never done in one night; and not so much to be wondered at of the doing, but that so few people dared or could do so much: for that when they entered into some of the houses of Religion, I could not perceive in some churches above 10 or 12 that spoiled —all being boys and rascals; but there were many in the church lookers-on, (as some thought, setters-on).

This thing was done so quiet and so still, as if there had been nothing ado in the churches; all men standing before their doors in harness, looking upon these fellows passing from church to church,

[1] John William Burgon, *The Life and Times of Sir Thomas Gresham, Knt.,* 2 vols., London, 1839, II, 137-41.

who as they passed through the streets, required all men to be quiet, and cried *vyve la gowsse,* [*vivent les gueux*—"long live the Beggars"]. So that, after I saw that all should be quiet, I, with above 10 thousand more, went into the churches to see what stir was there; and coming into our Lady Church, it looked like a hell: where were above 1000 torches burning, and such a noise! as if heaven and earth had gone together, with falling of Images and beating down of costly works; in such sort, that the spoil was so great that a man could not well pass through the church. So that, in fine, I cannot write you in 10 sheets of paper the strange sight I saw there—organs and all, destroyed! and from thence I went, (as the rest of the people did,) to all the houses of religion, where was the like stir—breaking and spoiling all that there was. Yet, they that this did, never looked towards any spoil, but broke all in pieces, and let it lie underfoot. So that, to be short, they have spoiled and destroyed all the churches, so well nunneries as other; but as I do understand they neither said nor did any thing to the nuns: but when all was broken, left it there, and so departed. So that, by estimation, they that spoiled, meddled with nothing, but let it lie; and before it was 3 of the clock in the morning, they had done their work, and all [were] home again, as if there had been nothing done: so that they spoiled this night between 25 and 30 churches.

4. Reduction of the Turkish Threat: The Battle of Lepanto (1571)

Partially to offset the losses to Spain and to Catholic Christendom by the defection of the Dutch provinces, the Turkish menace to Christian Europe [see page 91] was greatly reduced by the naval victory of Lepanto, October, 1571. In 1571, Pope Pius V organized the "Holy League" of Spain, Venice, and Genoa. Don John of Austria (1547-1578), illegitimate son of Charles V and half-brother of Philip II, was given supreme command of the fleet formed by the League. The Battle of Lepanto, described in a newsletter given below, broke the sea power of the Turks in the western Mediterranean.

From *The Fugger News-Letters* (1571) [1]

As soon as the Christian Armada arrived at 6 o'clock in the evening in the little channel of Cephalonia, it was at once espied by the crafty Turkish Armada, which lay in the Gulf of Lepanto. . . . Thereupon, the wind being very favourable, the Turkish Commander began preparations for battle with great joy, and took on board twelve thousand men over and above the soldiery he had in the Armada. Thus, thanks to divine Providence and Fate, he robbed himself of an advantage, contrary to all usage of sea warfare. Don Juan of Austria also set sail with his Armada and sent ahead several galleys to inspect the enemy. Moreover, he sent forth six galleons from the harbour. These reported that the Turkish Armada was already nearing, and not far from Cephalonia. Thereupon Don Juan attired himself in a light suit of armour and boarded a small ship, called a frigate. Holding a crucifix in his hand, he visited one galley after the other, appointing to each its proper place in the battle and exhorting the crew to fight valiantly against the arch-enemy of the Christian Faith. Not he, but Christ, who had died for us upon the Cross, was the Father of all, and

the Patron of this Armada, and he hoped that they would find help and sustenance in His mercy. Thereupon the whole soldiery sent forth great shouts of jubilation and forthwith placed themselves in battle formation. Whereafter the above mentioned Don Juan of Austria again entered his galley and went out to meet the Turkish Armada. Then the sea became quite still and the galleasses, which had sailed ahead, opened with heavy fire which brought great damage and terror to the Turks, causing them to cry: "Maom, Maom!" which means in their language "Big ships, big ships with big cannon!" Thus the Turkish Armada, which had been sailing ship to ship in half-moon formation, fell into disorder and was split into three parts. The first and largest part attacked the left wing of the Christian Armada, the second the centre and the third the right wing, which was led by Don Andreas Doria, who had lost almost all his fighters on ten of his galleys at the outset of the fight, although they had put up a most valiant and brave defence. It would have fared ill with him had not several galleys from the centre squadron come to his rescue, which help instilled fresh courage into his men, so that they forced the enemy again to withdraw. The left wing also put up a brave and gallant fight, but it also would have been in a sorry plight had not the rear, led by the Marques de Santa Cruz, come to relieve it, attacking the enemy in such fashion that the scales of victory turned completely in our favour. There also sprang up a wind to our assistance. In the smoke of battle Uluch Ali [Viceroy of Algiers] escaped. It is unknown whether he has fled to Africa or to the Gulf of Lepanto. Of forty of the principal galleys, of which we captured twenty-nine, one only was he able to save. Our general, Don Juan of Austria

[1] From *The Fugger News-Letters,* ed. by Victor von Klarwill, trans. by Pauline de Chary, 1925, 14-17. Courtesy of G. P. Putnam's Sons.

—whose achievements I should have reported first of all—rammed with his galley that of the Turkish commander, finally captured it, cut off the head of the Turkish Pasha with his own hand and placed it at the end of a spear of his own galley. The galley of Don Vittorio Colonna was attacked by two Turkish ones, fore and amidships, but he defended himself valiantly and was finally rescued, and thus was victorious. The Venetian Chief, Venier by name, who is seventy years of age, appeared, clad in light armour, on his own galley, at the head of all and fought right valiantly alongside his men, so that he captured Ali Pasha and his vessel. Don Barbarigo also carried himself like a true knight in this battle. An arrow pierced his right eye and he died in great pain and greatly to the sorrow of those near to him. . . .

The battle began on the 7th day of this month [October], two hours after daybreak, and within five hours the Christians had achieved victory with the help of the Lord. Almost all the Turkish nobles and nearly eighteen thousand men were killed, ten thousand taken prisoner, and fifteen thousand Christians, who had been slaves on the Turkish galleys, were set free. These latter caused the Turks much harm when the battle began. On several galleys there were also found a large number of Sultanas and Zechines and on Caragoggia's galley a beautiful young woman, a Christian. She was daintily and richly attired and her neck adorned with large pearls and other precious stones and jewels. She offered to buy her release with 60,000 ducats.

As far as can be gathered in all haste, on our side twenty Venetian noblemen and several thousand men lost their lives. One hundred Turkish galleys are captured, sixty have been sent to the bottom.

5. The Failure of the Spanish Armada (1588)

ELIZABETHAN SEA DOGS

Relations between England and Spain grew steadily worse after the death of Queen Mary in 1558. Religious differences, commercial rivalries, diplomatic differences, and the clash of personalities between Queen Elizabeth and Philip II all conspired to produce unpleasant repercussions. Philip was guided by a persistent desire to bring England back into the Catholic Church. To accomplish this purpose, he repeatedly tried to negotiate a marriage with Elizabeth, fostered Jesuit attempts, centering about Mary Queen of Scots, to incite rebellion against the English Queen, let the Inquisition have its way with English merchants caught in Spanish territories, and finally decided, when all else had failed and Elizabeth had been formally excommunicated by the Pope (1570), to launch a great naval attack upon England. Elizabeth countered these attempts with consummate skill. She toyed with Philip's marriage offers until he was exasperated; she imprisoned Mary Queen of Scots, and later (1587) had her executed; she treated Jesuits and other Catholics in England with great severity; she built up alliances with Protestants everywhere, assisted the Huguenots in the French civil wars (Philip aided the Catholics), and lent aid to the Dutch in their revolt against Spain. Moreover, Elizabeth winked at numerous attempts of her subjects to force an entrance, in opposition to Spanish laws, into Spanish colonial ports to trade in slaves and other commodities and to capture the fabulous plate fleets [see page 85] on their return voyages from the Spanish Main. These semipiratical voyages of Elizabethan seamen were often conducted with English naval vessels by such romantic figures as Sir John Hawkins and Sir Francis Drake. These Elizabethan "sea dogs" combined a lust for profits with national patriotism and religious fervor, hoping to revenge their Queen, expand English commerce and geographical discovery, weaken Spain, and fill their pockets at the expense of Catholicism's foremost champion. A contemporary account of one of Sir Francis Drake's escapades in 1578 illustrates these facts.

From HAKLUYT, *Voyages* (1589) [1]

We kept our course . . . along the coast of Nueva Espanna [New Spain], until we came to the Haven and Town of Guatulco, which (as we were informed) had but seventeen Spaniards dwelling in it. . . .

As soon as we were entered this Haven we landed, and went presently to the town, and to the Town house, where we found a Judge sitting in judgement, he being associate with three other officers, upon three Negroes that had conspired the burning of the Town: both which Judges, and prisoners we took, and brought them a-shipboard, and caused the chief Judge to write his letter to the Town, to command all the Townsmen to avoid, that we might safely water there. Which being done, and they departed, we ransaked the Town, and in one house we found a pot of the quantitie of a bushell full of royals of plate, which we brought to our ship.

[1] Richard Hakluyt, *The Principal Navigations, Voyages, Traffiques and Discoveries of the English Nation,* 12 vols., 1903-1905, IX, 319-20. Reprinted by permission of Jackson, Son & Company (Booksellers) Ltd., Glasgow.

And here one Thomas Moone one of our company, took a Spanish gentleman as he was flying out of the Town, and searching him, he found a chaine of Gold about him, and other jewels, which we took and so let him go. . . .

Our General at this place and time thinking himself both in respect of his private injuries received from the Spaniards, as also of their contempts and indignities offered to our Countrey and Prince in general, sufficiently satisfied, and revenged: and supposing that her Majesty at his return would rest contented with this service, purposed to continue no longer upon the Spanish coasts, but began to consider and to consult of the best way [to go] for his Countrey.

THE DEFEAT OF THE ARMADA

Philip's preparations for a naval descent upon England were frequently postponed because of a shortage of funds and supplies and the crippling effects of English raids upon Spanish ports. Finally, in July, 1588, the "Invincible" Armada set sail, consisting of about 120 ships and perhaps 24,000 men —far below the 586 ships and 85,000 men originally proposed for the task. The Spanish admiral, the Duke of Medina-Sidonia, a political appointee wholly inexperienced in naval affairs, expected to collect additional troops held in readiness under the Duke of Parma in the Spanish Netherlands. Against this force, the English could muster about 197 vessels with approximately 16,000 men under command of Lord Howard of Effingham assisted by such experienced men as Sir John Hawkins, Sir Francis Drake, and Sir Martin Frobisher. The English vessels were smaller but swifter and more mobile, and they carried a gun power far greater than the Spanish vessels—

though they lacked sufficient quantities of ammunition and foodstuffs. From the first meeting of the opposing fleets in the western waters of the English Channel (July 21, 1588), the English outmaneuvered the Spanish and drove them eastward. One of the commanders in the English fleet, Thomas Fenner, tells the rest of the story in a letter he wrote (August 4) to the English Secretary, Sir Francis Walsingham, and given below. Defeat of the Armada was a mortal blow to Spanish control of the seas and it freed England from further serious danger of militant Catholicism.

From FENNER, Letter to Walsingham (1588) [1]

Right Honourable: I assure myself you are ascertained of our encounters with the enemy on Monday, the 29th of July, in long continuance and great force of shot on both sides; many of their ships wonderfully spoiled and beaten, to the utter ruin of three of the greatest sort, beside the cutting off the galleass, the enemy thereby greatly weakened.

A thing greatly to be regarded, that the Almighty hath stricken them with a wonderful fear; in that I hardly have seen any of their companies succoured of their extremities which befell them after their fights, but left at utter ruin, without regard, bearing always as much sail as possible they might, holding the rest of their army together. Our want of powder, and shot, and victual hath hindered much service which otherwise might have been performed in continuance with them, to their utter subversion in keeping them from water. There were many ships in our fleet not possessed with three days' victuals.

The causes aforesaid considered in council . . . it was thought meet for the safety of men's lives and shipping, the wind being southerly, to shape our course for the Frith in Scotland, to relieve our wants with water and such other things as the benefit of that place would yield, thereby to attain that place for the better regard both of England and Scotland. . . .

Two pinnaces were left to follow the fleet afar off, until the Spaniards were beyond the Isles of Orkneys and Shetland, unto which place they continued their courses. And if, by any change of wind, they shaped their course otherwise, then, if wind would permit, the pinnaces [were] to advertise us at the Firth; and not finding us there, to come alongst our own coast with the advertisement. . . .

I verily believe that unless great extremity force them they will not behold England in sight again. By all that I can gather, they are weakened of eight of their best sorts of shipping, which contained many men; as also many wasted in sickness and slaughter. Their masts and sails much spoiled; their pinnaces and boats, many cast off and wasted; wherein they shall find great wants when they come to land and water, which they must do shortly or die; and where or how, my knowledge cannot imagine. As the wind serveth, no place but between the Foreland and Hull. Considering the shallows and sands not greatly to be doubted, the hugeness and great draught of water in their ships considered, and otherwise the wind as it is at North-West, they have no place to go withal, but for the Scaw in Denmark, which were an hard adventure as the season of the year approacheth. If the wind by change suffer them, I verily believe they will pass about Scotland and Ireland to draw themselves home; wherein, the season of the year considered, with the long course they have to run and their

[1] State Papers Relating to the Defeat of the Spanish Armada Anno 1588, ed. by John Knox Laughton, 2d ed., 2 vols., London, 1895, II, 37-42.

sundry distresses, and—of necessity—the spending of time by watering, winter will so come on as it will be to their great ruin.

God hath mightily protected her Majesty's forces with the least losses that ever hath been heard of, being within the compass of so great volleys of shot, both small and great. I verily believe there is not three score men lost of her Majesty's forces. God make us and all her Majesty's good subjects to render hearty praise and thanks unto the Lord of Lords therefor. . . .

God mightily defend my gracious mistress from the raging enemy; not doubting but that all the world shall know and see that her Majesty's little army, guided by the finger of God, shall beat down the pride of his enemies and hers, to his great glory; unto whom I betake your Honour. From aboard the good ship of her Majesty the Nonpareil, this 4th of August, 1588.

Your Honour's in all love and duty for ever to command,

Thomas Fenner

Within two hours after the writing of this letter the wind came up at South-West, so as thereby the enemy was able neither to make England, Ireland, Scotland, Flanders, and hardly the out isles of Scotland. This 4th day and 5th, especially at night, continued very great storm at South-West, [we] being forced to ride out in the sea the extremity thereof. . . . Mine opinion is they are by this time so distressed, being so far thrust off, as many of them will never see Spain again; which is the only work of God, to chastise their malicious practices, and to make them know that neither the strengths of men, nor their idolatrous gods can prevail, when the mighty God of Israel stretcheth out but his finger against them. God make all her Majesty's good subjects thankful.

Thomas Fenner

13

THE REFORMATION IN FRANCE (TO 1598)

1. The Rise of the Huguenots

THE YEAR OF THE PLACARDS (1534)

Protestantism existed in France in the 1520's, its growth only slightly curtailed at first by sporadic suppressions by the King. Francis I, supported by scholastics in the Sorbonne and judges in the *parlement* of Paris, insisted upon religious unity in France on the basis of his nationalistic motto,

Une foi, une loi, un Roi (One faith, one law, one king—much like the principle of *cuius regio eius religio* later set up in the Empire by the Peace of Augsburg, 1555); but Francis also hoped to win support of German Lutherans in his struggles with the Emperor and the Pope [see page 96]. Moreover, his sister, Margaret of Navarre, his friend, the great French humanist Jacques Le Fèvre d'Etaples (1455-1536), and others in high stations were favorable toward

Protestantism. Accordingly, the King's policy alternated leniency with severity. One of the most severe periods was the Year of the Placards (1534), the year in which John Calvin determined to leave France [see page 119]. After 1534, the course of Protestantism in France was increasingly difficult. The reasons will become clear from the following account.

From BAIRD, *Rise of the Huguenots* (1879) [1]

For many months the street-walls of Paris had been employed by both sides in the great controversies of the day, for the purpose of giving publicity to their views. Under cover of night, placards, often in the form of pasquinades [cartoons], were posted where they would be likely to meet the eyes of a large number of curious readers. . . .

The success of this method of reaching the masses, who could never be induced to read a formal treatise or book, suggested to some of the more ardent "Lutherans" of Paris the idea of preparing a longer placard, which should boldly attack the cardinal errors of the papal system of religion. But, the press being closely watched in the French capital, it was thought best to have the placard printed in Switzerland, where, indeed, the most competent and experienced hands might be found for composing such a paper. The messenger employed was a young man named Féret, an apprentice of the king's apothecary. . . .

Féret, having on his return eluded detection at the frontiers, reached Paris in safety. He brought with him a large number of copies of a broadside headed, *"True Articles respecting the horrible, great and insupportable Abuses of the Papal Mass."*

[1] Henry M. Baird, *History of the Rise of the Huguenots of France,* 2 vols., Scribner, 1879, I, 163-68.

Among those to whom the paper was secretly submitted, there were some who, more prudent than the rest, decidedly opposed its publication. It was too violent, they said. The writer's ill-advised severity would answer no good purpose. The tract would alienate the sympathy of many, and thus retard, instead of advancing, the cause it advocated. Remonstrance, however, proved futile.

Early on the morning of the eighteenth of October, 1534, a placard was found posted upon the walls in all the principal thoroughfares of the metropolis. Everywhere it was read with horror and indignation, mingled with rage; and loud threats and curses were uttered against its unknown author.

The document that called for these expressions and was the occasion of more important commotions in the sequel, had so direct and potent an influence upon the fortunes of the Reformation in France that it cannot be passed over without a brief reference to the general character of its contents. It began with a solemn address: "I invoke heaven and earth in testimony of the truth, against that proud and pompous papal mass, through which (if God remedy not speedily the evil) the world will be wholly desolated, destroyed, and ruined. For therein is our Lord so outrageously blasphemed and the people so blinded and seduced, that it ought no longer to be suffered or endured." Every Christian must needs be assured that the one sacrifice of Christ, being perfect, demands no repetition. Still the world has long been, and now is, flooded with wretched sacrificing priests, who yet proclaim themselves liars, inasmuch as they chant every Sunday in their vespers, that Christ is a priest forever after the order of Melchisedek. Wherefore not only every man of sound understanding, but "they themselves, in spite of themselves, must admit that the Pope and all his brood of cardinals, bishops, monks, and canting mass priests, with all who consent thereunto, are false prophets, damnable deceivers, apostates, wolves, false shepherds, idolaters, seducers, liars and execrable blasphemers, murderers of souls, renouncers of Jesus Christ, of his death and passion, false witnesses, traitors, thieves, and robbers of the honor of God, and more detestable than devils." After citing from the book of Hebrews some passages to establish the sufficiency of Christ, the writer addresses his opponents: "I demand then of all sacrificing priests, whether their sacrifice be perfect or imperfect? If imperfect, why do they deceive the poor people? If perfect, why need it be repeated? Come forward, priests, and reply if you can!" . . .

[The Placard continued with a bitter tirade against the doctrine of transubstantiation.] Closing with a vivid contrast between the fruits of the mass and those of the true Supper of our Lord, the writer finally exclaims of his opponents, "Truth fails them, Truth threatens and pursues them, Truth terrifies them; by which their reign shall shortly be destroyed forever."

It would be difficult to exaggerate the effect produced upon the populace of Paris by this intemperate handbill. If any part of the ceremonial of the church was deeply rooted in the devotion of the common people, it was the service of the mass. And in attacking the doctrine of the Real Presence, the authors of this libel, distributed under cover of darkness, had, in the estimation of the rabble, proved themselves more impious and deserving a more signal punishment than that sacrilegious Jew whose knife had drawn drops of miraculous blood from the transubstantiated wafer. Not the parish priests, nor the doctors of the Sorbonne, could surpass the infuriated populace in loud execrations of the wretch for whom burning alive seemed too mild a punishment. [When an auda-cious Huguenot tacked a copy of the Placard upon the door of the royal bedchamber, Francis I was so indignant that further official clemency toward Huguenots was impossible.]

THE RELIGIOUS CONDITION OF FRANCE ABOUT 1561

Upon the death of Francis I, his successor, Henry II (1547-59) dealt with Protestantism with increased severity. A special court, the Chambre Ardente, was created (October, 1547) to try persons suspected of heresy and a series of royal edicts culminating in the Edict of Compiègne (July, 1557) left judges no option but to inflict the death penalty upon persons found guilty. But persecution only fanned the flames of Protestant zeal. By this time, too, John Calvin was directing the course of the Reformation in France. In 1560, a Venetian ambassador reported that:

From the city of Geneva, the chief seat and abode of those who have alienated themselves from the Catholic religion, many persons are accustomed to go forth into divers parts of Christendom to preach their doctrine. In France, for a long while, forty of the ministers from Geneva have remained permanently, and dividing the country amongst themselves by virtue of their assumed authority they had the daring to usurp the title of bishops, and as such they were acknowledged amongst themselves and by their followers, being favored and assisted by some of the chief personages in France whose faith had been already corrupted.[1]

[1] Report of Paulo Tiepolo, March 25, 1560, *Calendar of State Papers and Manuscripts Relating to English Affairs Existing in . . . Venice . . . , 1558-1580,* ed. by Rawdon Brown and G. Cavendish Bentinck, London, 1890, VII, 169-70.

In 1555, a Calvinist church was organized in Paris, and in 1559 representatives of more than seventy French Calvinist churches met at Paris, set forth a Confession of Faith, and adopted an ecclesiastical constitution centered in a National Synod. Two years later, the Venetian ambassador, Signor Giovanni Michiel, predicted that France faced imminent civil war over religion.

From a Report of the Venetian Ambassador (1561) [2]

Unless it otherwise pleases the Almighty, religious affairs will soon be in an evil case in France, because there is not one single province uncontaminated. Indeed in some provinces, such as Normandy, almost the whole of Britany, Touraine, Poitou, Gascony, and a great part of Languedoc, of Dauphiny, and of Provence, comprising three-fourths of the kingdom, congregations and meetings, which they call assemblies, are held; and in these assemblies they read and preach, according to the rites and uses of Geneva, without any respect either for the ministers of the King or the commandments of the King himself. This contagion has penetrated so deeply that it affects every class of persons, and, what appears more strange, even the ecclesiastical body itself. I do not mean only priests, friars, and nuns, for there are but few monasteries that are not corrupted, but even bishops and many of the principal prelates; who hitherto had not shown any such disposition; and it is only on account of the rigorous execution of the law that other persons besides the populace have not disclosed themselves, because they have restrained themselves for the time being from fear of the loss of their property and lives. But your Serenity must learn that while the people and the populace show fervent devotion by frequenting the churches and observing the Catholic rites, all other classes are supposed to be disaffected, and the nobility perhaps more than any other class, and, particularly, persons of forty years of age and under. If these disaffected individuals continue to attend mass and the Divine offices, and externally to practise Catholic rites, they do so for show and from fear; because when they either are, or believe themselves to be, unobserved, they avoid and even fly from the mass above all things, and also from the churches as far as they are able, and more so since it became known that by imprisonment, chastisement, and burnings, no remedy was found. It has now been determined not to proceed against any disaffected persons unless they venture to preach, persuade, and to take part publicly in congregations and assemblies. All other such persons are allowed to live, and some have been set at liberty, and released from the prisons of Paris and of other parts of the kingdom. A great number of these last have still remained in the kingdom, preaching and speaking publicly, and boasting that they have gained their cause against the Papists, as they delight to style their adversaries; so that, now, every one of them is assured against the fear of being questioned; and there exists thus a silent truce, because whilst formerly all suspected persons had to quit the kingdom, and to retire some to Geneva, some to Germany, and some to England, now they not only do not leave the country, but a large number of those who had already emigrated have returned. . . . Your Serenity will hardly believe the influence and the great power which the principal minister of Geneva, by name Calvin, a Frenchman, and a native of Picardy, possesses in this kingdom; he is a man of extraordinary authority, who by his mode of life, his doctrines, and his writings, rises superior

[2] Ibid., 322-23.

to all the rest; and it is almost impossible to believe the enormous sums of money which are secretly sent to him from France to maintain his power. It is sufficient to add that if God does not interfere, there is great and imminent danger that one of two things will happen in this kingdom: either that the truce, which is desired and sought publicly, will end by the heretics having churches wherein they can preach, read, and perform their rites, according to their doctrine, without hindrance, and in like manner as they obtained churches by command of the late King, given at Fontainebleau, at the end of August, in compliance with a petition presented to him by the Admiral [Coligny]; or, else, that we shall see an obedience to the Pope and to the Catholic rites enforced, and shall have resort to violence and imbrue our hands in noble blood. For these reasons I foresee a manifest and certain division in the kingdom, and civil war as a consequence; and this will be the cause of the ruin both of the kingdom and of religion, because upon a change in religion a change in the State necessarily follows.

2. The Religious Wars in France

CATHERINE DE' MEDICI AND HER FAMILY

In 1559, while French Calvinists perfected their National Synod, King Henry II, accidentally wounded in a tournament, died. For the next thirty years—a period of almost constant religious wars—his Italian Queen, Catherine de' Medici, ruling through her young and sickly sons, held decisive political authority in France. Something of her appearance and character is given in the following description.

From BATIFFOL, *The Renaissance* (1913) [1]

Queen Catherine de' Medici could hardly be called an attractive woman. She was the same age as her husband, her birthday falling barely a fortnight later than his. She was afflicted with a fat, coarse face, crowned by black hair, large goggle eyes, heavy eyebrows, a big nose, loose, pouting lips, surmounting a body which lost its shape very early in life. The *bourgeoise* granddaughter of Florentine bankers and merchants, she was distinctly ugly. But to counterbalance this, she became a great lady of high importance when she was very young. She was intelligent, possessed considerable discrimination and prudence, and, moreover, displayed the impenetrable reserve of an Italian woman who has suffered and thought much. From the first, during the reign of Francis I, when she felt that she was unwelcome on account of her origin, she had studied to achieve an attitude of modest retirement and to please every one by her agreeable manners. And she had succeeded. Francis I, with whom she used to ride out to the hunt, appreciated her intelligent firmness, and was fond of her; whilst she won the sympathy of . . . all who had influence at Court. But she kept a very strict watch over her own conduct.

As soon as she became Queen, however, she was transformed into an accomplished hostess, who received a great deal. Her amiability was unstinted, and she made herself charming and attractive to everybody. People were enchanted with her, and the whole Court considered her perfection itself. She dressed as a rule simply and in a severe style; but on reception days she wore extremely rich and elegant clothes, covered with numberless chased ornaments, for the designs of which she

[1] From Louis Batiffol, *The Century of the Renaissance,* trans. by E. F. Buckley, 1916 (The National Library of France), 121-24. Courtesy of G. P. Putnam's Sons.

herself gave instructions to her goldsmiths. She conferred incomparable order and brilliancy upon Court gatherings, and as she inherited vast wealth from her family, she spared no outlay in order to increase the success of her receptions. Her table was abundantly supplied. She attached to her person a host of ladies-in-waiting and maids-of-honour in order to make sure that the composition of her gatherings should be in accordance with her wishes. She was generous in her distribution of costly gifts to those about her, and showed herself very kind-hearted in finding husbands and providing dowries for young girls, spending a great deal on clothes for her dependents and giving generous help to one and all. This conduct was not calculated on her part. For her husband was young and strong, and she had nothing to expect or to fear. But she was a woman of the world who loved to receive, and as she was in a position to do so, she indulged lavishly in her favourite pastime.

The Court became the centre of a society which was one of the most brilliant that has ever existed. Fair ladies and young lords full of life formed the magnetic nucleus attracting the best people in the kingdom, who flocked from all quarters. An uninterrupted succession of balls, musical evenings, and banquets took place. "The Court of Catherine de' Medici," wrote Brantôme, "was a veritable earthly paradise and a school for all the chivalry and flower of France. Ladies shone there like stars in the sky on a fine night." The Queen presided over everything with grace and dignity. "You alone are Queen," Pietro Aretino told her, "you are both woman and goddess!" Much more intelligent than her husband, she extended her patronage to artists and men of letters. She employed Della Robbia and Léonard Limosin, the enamellist, chose Amyot as a tutor for her children, and arranged performances of the works of Mellin de Saint-Gelais. Later on in the seventeenth century she was credited—as a matter of fact erroneously—with the introduction of refinement into the French Court by the inculcation of Italian manners. Surrounded by charming princesses—her sister-in-law Margaret, a dainty and distinguished personality who presented Ronsard to her, and encouraged du Bellay—her son's little wife, Mary Stuart, and her own daughters, she directed this life of luxury and pleasure with tact and discrimination.

For her husband, that distinguished, somewhat cold, but extremely fascinating prince, she had a real passion. She worshipped him and was terrified of displeasing him, though she was fully aware that Henry II felt nothing but respect for her. . . .

The royal couple were long without children. They had none for ten years, and Catherine began to despair. There was some talk of annulling the marriage. Catherine threw herself in tears at the feet of Francis I, offering to sacrifice herself, and consenting to retire into a convent. Francis I, with his usual gallantry, raised her up, and kissing her, told her that she was his daughter-in-law and was to remain so. Subsequently she had ten children in thirteen years, thus giving rise to some little consternation. "As their Majesties are yet young," wrote one of the ambassadors, "they are afraid of having more children than they ought, for the King is desirous of leaving to each one of them a heritage in keeping with the greatness of his name." Catherine was a very good mother. She was sedulous in her attention to the smallest details in the lives of the young princes, and, when she was separated from them, wrote every day to their governess, Madame d'Humières. Her two daughters, Elisabeth and Claude, she decided to bring up herself.

Three out of the ten children, a boy and twins, died in infancy. The seven others consisted of four sons and three daughters. Elisabeth, the oldest girl, eventually became Queen of Spain; the second, Claude, was given to the Duke of Lorraine, whilst the third, Margaret, was the vivacious, intelligent and sparkling Margaret of Valois, the wife of Henry IV. "Queen Margot," as she was called, whose life was so gay and so brilliant. Of the four sons, the youngest, Francis, Duke of Alençon, died young, and the three others were the last three Kings of the House of Valois—Francis II, Charles IX, and Henry III, the feeble scions of an exhausted race, dying out amidst the pleasures, the festivities and bloodstained dramas of an involved policy.

THE EDICT OF 1562

In 1561, Catherine de' Medici held an assembly of French churchmen at Poissy (the ill-fated "Colloquy of Poissy") to which were invited Huguenots (as French Protestants, for reasons unknown, were now being called) as well as Catholics. Calvin himself was invited to attend, but as Protestants feared for his safety, the learned and eloquent Theodore Beza went in his stead. If the Queen had hoped for a reconciliation between the opposing factions, she was greatly disappointed. Beza greatly impressed the Queen and the court by his reasonableness, but when he presented articles of compromise they were scorned by the Catholic party and the assembly finally was dismissed in an atmosphere of approaching violence. The Huguenots, however, had won temporary favor in the Queen's eyes and, as Philip II of Spain was threatening military interference on behalf of French Catholics, the harassed Queen issued, January 17, 1562, the ill-advised Edict of Toleration—an Edict which displeased both parties and, because it and its successors were neither

observed nor enforced, led directly to the religious wars of the next forty years.

The Queen issued the edict of January "in order to keep our subjects at peace until such time as God will do us the grace to be able to reunite them in one fold." It was wholly inconsistent inasmuch as it provided: first, that Huguenots were forbidden to assemble within city limits, publicly or privately, by day or night; and second, that they were authorized to meet by day, outside city limits, to worship according to their own convictions. According to the Chancellor, "the only purpose of the restrictions was to avoid the disorders arising from large assemblies in the cities." The dissatisfaction produced by the Edict of Toleration is explained by the following account.

From BAIRD, *Rise of the Huguenots* [1]

The Edict of January was on its very face a compromise, and as such rested on no firm foundation. Inconsistent with itself, it fully satisfied neither Huguenot nor Roman Catholic. The latter objected to the toleration which the edict extended; the former demanded the unrestricted freedom of worship which it denied. If the existence of two diverse religions was compatible with the welfare of the state, why ignominiously thrust the places of Protestant worship from the cities into the suburbs? If the two were irreconcilable, why suffer the Huguenots to assemble outside the walls?

Yet there was this difference between the attitude assumed by the rival parties with reference to the edict: while the Roman Catholic leaders made no secret of their intention to insist upon its repeal, the Huguenot leaders were urgent in their

[1] Henry M. Baird, *History of the Rise of the Huguenots of France*, II, 3-7.

advice to the churches to conform strictly to its provisions, restraining the indiscreet zeal of their more impetuous members, and exhibiting due gratitude to Heaven for the amelioration of their lot. . . . And so Beza and other prominent men of the Protestant Church, after obtaining from Chancellor L'Hôpital some further explanations on doubtful points, addressed to their brethren in all parts of France a letter full of wholesome advice. "God," said they, "has deigned to employ new means of protecting His Church in this kingdom, by placing those who profess the Gospel under the safeguard of the king, our natural prince, and of the magistrates and governors established by him. This should move us so much the more to praise the infinite goodness of our Heavenly Father, who has at length answered the cry of His children, and lovingly to obey the king, in order that he may be induced to aid our just cause." . . . The letter produced a deep impression, and its salutary advice was followed scrupulously, if not cheerfully, even in southern France, where the Huguenots, in some places, outnumbered the adherents of the Romish Church.

The papal party was less ready to acquiesce. The Edict of January was, according to its representative writers, the most pernicious law for the kingdom that could have been devised. By forbidding the magistrates from interfering with the Protestant conventicles held in the suburbs, by permitting the royal officers to attend, by conferring upon the ministers full liberty of officiating, a formal approval was, for the first time, given to the new sect under the authority of the royal seal. The pulpits resounded with denunciations of the government. The King of Navarre and the queen mother were assailed under scriptural names, as favoring the false prophets of Baal. Scarcely a sermon was preached in which they did not figure as Ahab and

Jezebel. A single specimen of the spirited discourses in vogue will suffice. A Franciscan monk—one Barrier . . . after reading the royal ordinance in his church of Sainte-Croix, in Provins, remarked: "Well now, gentlemen of Provins, what must I, and the other preachers of France, do? Must we obey this order? What shall we tell you? What shall we preach? 'The Gospel,' Sir Huguenot will say. . . . Bidding you beware of their teaching, bidding you refuse to listen to them, or read their books; telling you that they only seek to stir up sedition, murder, and robbery, as they have begun to do in Paris and numberless places in the realm—is not this preaching 'the Gospel'? But some one may say: 'Pray, friar, what are you saying? You are not obeying the king's edict; you are still talking of Calvin and his companions; you call them and those who hold their sentiments *heretics* and *Huguenots;* you will be denounced to the courts of justice, you will be thrown into prison —yes, you will be hung as a seditious person.' I answer, *that* is not unlikely, for Ahab and Jezebel put to death the prophets of Baal. 'Stop, friar, you are saying too much, you will be hung.' Very well, then there will be a gray friar hung! Many others will therefore have to be hung, for God, by His Holy Spirit, will inspire the pillars of His church to uphold the edifice, which will never be overthrown until the end of the world, whatever blows may be struck at it."

The parliaments *parlements*] exhibited scarcely less opposition to the edict than did the pulpits of the Roman Catholic churches. One—the Parliament of Dijon —never registered it at all; while that of Paris instituted a long and decided resistance. . . . It was not possible until March to obtain a tardy assent to the reception of the January Edict into the legislation of the country, and then only a few of the judges vouchsafed to take part in the act. The delay served to inflame yet more the passions of the people.

[On Sunday, March 1, occurred an incident which precipitated the first civil war. At Vassy, the Duke of Guise, accompanied by armed retainers, happened to discover a Huguenot service being conducted in a barn. When the Duke attempted to break up the meeting, stones flew, shots were fired, and sixty of the Huguenots were killed. Similar incidents elsewhere led to open warfare within a month.]

THE MASSACRE OF ST. BARTHOLOMEW'S DAY (AUGUST 24, 1572)

Three ugly civil wars occurred in France between 1562 and 1570, the third ending with the Peace of St. Germain, by which the Huguenots were granted a limited toleration not unlike that provided by the Edict of Toleration of January, 1562, except that they were granted full possession of four cities as places of safety and their leader, Admiral Gaspard de Coligny, was made a member of the royal council. Coligny soon gained much favor in the eyes of the young King, Charles IX. In an effort to heal the breach between the rival factions in France, the King and the Admiral endorsed a plan to marry the King's sister, Margaret, a Catholic, to Henry of Navarre, who, after Coligny, was the leader of the Huguenots, and successor to the French throne in the event Queen Catherine's sons had no heirs. The marriage was celebrated August 18, 1572. Meanwhile, Catherine de' Medici had become jealous of Coligny because of the influence he had gained over her son, Charles IX; and Catholic nobles, led by the Guise faction, were disturbed by the favor shown to Huguenots at the court.

These factors combined to produce the plot, made without the King's knowledge, to assassinate Admiral Coligny. A hired assassin made the attempt on August 22, but failed. The angry reaction of the Huguenots led to muttered threats against the entire royal family. Civil war was imminent in Paris. Accordingly, the Queen Mother and the Catholic faction, in utter terror, prevailed upon the King to order a wholesale execution of Huguenots. Only after hours of passionate pleading by his mother and the Catholic noblemen had the King finally given way with the cry: "Well, then, kill them all, that not a single man may be left to reproach me!" The Catholic intentions were guarded with great secrecy until early in the morning of St. Bartholomew's Day (August 24, 1572) when, by a prearranged signal, the massacre began. The Duke of Guise with about 300 men made for Admiral Coligny's lodgings at once. Accounts follow of the murder of the already wounded Admiral, together with the experiences of the young Maximilian de Béthune, later Duke of Sully, during the three-day massacre of the Huguenots—an event which opened the fourth religious war.

THE DEATH OF COLIGNY

From *Histoire de M. de Thou* (c. 1580) [1]

Meanwhile Coligny awoke and recognized from the noise that a riot was taking place. Nevertheless he remained assured of the king's good will, of which he was

[1] Merrick Whitcomb, ed., *Period of the Later Reformation* (*Translations and Reprints from the Original Sources of European History*, III, No. 3, rev. ed., 1902, 24-26. The quotation is translated from the *Histoire de M. de Thou des choses arrivées de son temps* (Paris, 1659), III, 660-62. Reprinted by permission of the University of Pennsylvania Press.

persuaded by his credulity or by Teligny, his son-in-law; and he believed the populace had been stirred up by the Guises and that quiet would be restored as soon as it was seen that soldiers of the guard under the command of Cosseins had been detailed to protect him and guard his property.

But when he perceived that the noise increased and that some one had fired an arquebuse in the courtyard of his dwelling, then at length conjecturing what it might be, but too late, he arose from his bed and having put on his dressing-gown he said his prayers, leaning against the wall. Labonne held the key of the chamber, and when Cosseins commanded him in the king's name to open the door he obeyed at once without fear and apprehending nothing. But scarcely was Cosseins in the room when Labonne, who stood in his way, was killed with a dagger-thrust. The Swiss, who were in the courtyard, when they saw this, fled into the house and closed the door, piling against it tables and all the furniture they could find. It was in the first scrimmage that a Swiss was killed with a ball from an arquebuse fired by one of Cosseins' people. But finally the conspirators broke through the door and mounted the stairway, Cosseins, Attin, Corberan de Cordillac, Seigneur de Sarlabous, first captains of the regiment of the guards, Achilles Petrucci of Siena, all armed with cuirasses, and Besme the German, who had been brought up as a page in the house of Guise; for the duke of Guise was lodged at court, together with the great nobles and others who accompanied him.

After Coligny had said his prayers with Merlin the minister, he said without any appearance of alarm to those who were present, and almost all were surgeons, for few of them were of his retinue: "I see clearly that which they seek, and I am ready steadfastly to suffer that death which I have never feared and which for a long time past I have pictured to myself. I consider myself happy in feeling the approach of death and in being ready to die in God, by whose grace I hope for the life everlasting. I have no further need of human succor. Go then from this place, my friends, as quickly as you may, for fear lest you shall be involved in my misfortune, and that some day your wives shall curse me as the author of your loss. For me it is enough that God is here, to whose goodness I commend my soul, which is so soon to issue from my body." After those words they ascended to an upper room whence they sought safety in flight here and there upon the tiles.

Meanwhile the conspirators, having burst through the door of the chamber, entered, and when Besme, sword in hand, had demanded of Coligny, who stood near the door, "Are you Coligny?" Coligny replied, "Yes, I am he," with fearless countenance. "But you, young man, respect these white hairs. What is it you would do? You cannot shorten by many days this life of mine." As he spoke Besme gave him a sword thrust through the body, and having withdrawn his sword, another thrust in the mouth, by which his countenance was disfigured. So Coligny fell, killed with many thrusts. Others have written that Coligny in dying pronounced as though in anger these words: "Would that I at least might die at the hands of a soldier and not a valet." But Attin, one of the murderers, has reported as I have written, and added that he never saw any one less afraid in so great a peril, nor die more steadfastly.

Then the duke of Guise inquired of Besme from the courtyard if the thing were done, and when Besme answered him that it was, the duke replied that the Chevalier d'Angoulême was unable to believe it unless he saw it; and at the same time that he made the inquiry they threw the body through the window into the courtyard, disfigured as it was with blood. When the Chevalier d'Angoulême, who could scarcely believe his eyes, had wiped away with a cloth the blood which overran the face and finally had recognized him, some say that he spurned the body with his foot. However this may be, when he left the house with his followers he said: "Cheer up, my friends! Let us do thoroughly that which we have begun. The king commands it." He frequently repeated these words and as soon as they had caused the palace clock to strike, on every side arose the cry "To arms," and the people ran to the house of Coligny. After his [Coligny's] body had been insultingly treated in every way, they threw it into a neighboring stable and finally cut off his head, which they sent to Rome. They also cut off his privates and his hands and feet and dragged his body through the streets to the bank of the Seine. . . .

As the children were throwing the body into the river, it was dragged out and placed upon the gibbet of Montfaucon, where it hung by the feet [legs?] in chains of irons; and then they built a fire beneath, by which he was burned without being consumed; so that he was, so to speak, tortured with all the elements, since he was killed upon the earth, thrown into the water, placed upon the fire, and finally put to hang in the air. After he had served for several days as a spectacle to gratify the hate of many and arouse the just indignation of many others, who reckoned that this fury of the people would cost the king of France many a sorrowful day, François de Montmorency, who was nearly related to the dead man, and still more his friend, and who moreover had escaped in time the danger, had him taken by night from the gibbet by trusty men and carried to Chantilly, where he was buried in the chapel.

M. DE BÉTHUNE (LATER DUKE OF SULLY) AND THE MASSACRE

From the DUKE OF SULLY, Memoirs (1638) [1]

I was in bed, and awaked from sleep three hours after midnight, by the sound of all the bells, and the confused cries of the populace. My governor St. Julian, with my valet de chambre, went hastily out to know the cause; and I never afterwards heard more of these men, who without doubt were amongst the first that were sacrificed to the public fury. I continued alone in my chamber dressing myself, when in a few moments I saw my landlord enter, pale, and in the utmost consternation: he was of the reformed religion, and having learned what the matter was, had consented to go to mass, to save his life, and preserve his house from being pillaged. He came to persuade me to do the same, and to take me with him. I did not think proper to follow him, but resolved to try if I could gain the college of Burgundy, where I had studied: though the great distance between the house where I then was, and the college, made the attempt very dangerous. Having disguised myself in a scholar's gown, I put a large prayer-book under my arm, and went into the street. I was seized with horror inexpressible, at the sight of the furious murderers, who, running from all parts, forced open the houses, and cried aloud, "Kill, kill, massacre the Huguenots!" The blood which I saw shed before my eyes redoubled my terror. I fell into the midst of a body of guards; they stopped me, interrogated me, and were beginning to use me ill, when, happily for me, the book that I carried was perceived, and served me for a passport. Twice after this I fell into the same danger, from which I extricated myself with the same good for-

[1] Memoirs of Maximilian de Béthune, Duke of Sully, trans. by Charlotte Lennox, 3 vols., London, 1761, I, 27-29.

tune. At last I arrived at the college of Burgundy, where a danger still greater than any I had yet met with, waited me. The porter having twice refused me entrance, I continued standing in the midst of the street, at the mercy of the furious murderers, whose numbers increased every moment, and who were evidently seeking for their prey, when it came into my mind to ask for La Faye, the principal of this college, a good man, by whom I was tenderly beloved. The porter, prevailed upon by some small pieces of money which I put into his hand, admitted me; and my friend carried me to his apartment, where two inhuman priests, whom I heard mention Sicilian vespers, wanted to force me from him, that they might cut me in pieces, saying the order was, not to spare even infants at the breast. All the good man could do was to conduct me privately to a distant chamber, where he locked me up. Here I was confined three days, uncertain of my destiny; and saw no one but a servant of my friend's, who came from time to time to bring me provisions.

At the end of these three days, the prohibition for murdering, and pillaging any more of the protestants, being published, I was suffered to leave my cell; and immediately after I saw . . . two soldiers of the guard, who were my father's creatures, enter the college. They were armed, and came, without doubt, to rescue me by force wherever they should find me. They gave my father a relation of what had happened to me; and eight days afterwards I received a letter from him, in which he expressed the fears he had suffered on my account, and advised me to continue in Paris, since the prince I served [Henry of Navarre] was not at liberty to quit it. He added, that to avoid exposing myself to an evident danger, it was necessary I should resolve to follow that prince's example, and to go to mass. In effect, the king of Navarre had found no other means of saving his life.

THE CATHOLIC LEAGUE (1576)

In February, 1576, Henry of Navarre fled from the French court, publicly declared he was a Calvinist despite his enforced conformity to Catholicism while at court, and immediately assumed leadership of the Huguenot faction. The Queen, seeing the court destitute of funds and fearing civil war, issued an edict (the Edict of Beaulieu, May, 1576) conceding greater toleration to Huguenots than ever before. The edict amazed the entire kingdom, and Catholics, convinced that the Crown would not defend their cause, determined to take matters into their own hands. The result was the formation, under leadership of Henry, Duke of Guise, of the Catholic League, designed to nullify the Edict of Beaulieu. Some of the articles of the League follows.

From *Articles of the Catholic League* (1576) [1]

In the name of the Holy Trinity, Father, Son, and Holy Ghost, our only true God, to whom be glory and honor.

I. The association of Catholic princes, lords and gentlemen is intended to be and shall be formed for the purpose of establishing the law of God in its entirety; to restore and maintain the holy service of the same according to the form and manner of the holy Catholic Apostolic church, abjuring and renouncing all errors to the contrary.

II. To maintain king Henry, third of this name, by the grace of God, and his successors, very Christian kings, in the state, splendor, authority, duty, service and

[1] Merrick Whitcomb, ed., *Period of the Later Reformation*, 26-28. Reprinted by permission of the University of Pennsylvania Press.

obedience which are due him from his subjects. . . .

III. To restore to the provinces of this kingdom and the Estates of the same the ancient rights, prerogatives, franchises and liberties, such as they were in the time of Clovis, the first Christian king, and still better and more profitable, if such are to be found, under the protection above named.

IV. In case there be any hindrance, opposition or rebellion against that which has been stated above, let it come from whatsoever source it may, the said associates shall be bound and obliged to make use of all their possessions and means, and their very selves, even to death, in order to punish, chastise and fall upon those who have sought to constrain and hinder them. . . .

VI. If it should come to pass that any of the associates, after having sworn an oath to the said association, should wish to retire or withdraw from the same under any pretext whatsoever (which may God forbid), such persons, falling away from their agreements, shall be injured in person and possessions, in all ways which may be devised, as enemies of God, rebels, violators of the public peace. . . .

VII. The said associates shall swear absolute and ready obedience and service to the head who shall be selected. . . .

VIII. Notice shall be given to all Catholics in incorporated towns and villages and they shall be summoned secretly by the local governors to enter into the said association and to furnish their due proportion of arms and men for the purpose of the same, each according to his power and ability.

IX. That those who are unwilling to enter into the said association shall be considered enemies of the same. . . .

XII. I swear by God the Creator, upon the Gospels, and upon penalty of anathema and eternal damnation, that I have entered into this holy Catholic association according to the form of the agreement which has now been read to me, loyally and sincerely, be it to command, to obey, or to serve; and I promise upon my life and my honor, not to spare myself up to the last drop of my blood; and that I will not oppose the association or withdraw from it on account of any command, pretext, or excuse, whatever may be the occasion.

FRANCE DURING THE CIVIL WARS

Ogier Ghiselin de Busbecq, ambassador from the Emperor to France, well describes the effects of the religious wars in France. One of his letters follows.

From BUSBECQ, *Letters* (1575) [1]

Ever since the commencement of the civil wars which are distracting the country, there has been a terrible change for the worse. So complete is the alteration, that those who knew France before would not recognise her again. Everywhere are to be seen shattered buildings, fallen churches, and towns in ruins; while the traveller gazes horror-stricken on spots which have but lately been the scenes of murderous deeds and inhuman cruelties. The fields are left untilled: the farmer's stock and tools have been carried off by the soldier as his booty, he is plundered alike by Frenchman and by foreigner. Commerce is crippled; the towns lately thronged with merchants and customers are now mourning their desolation in the midst of closed shops and silent manufactories. Meanwhile, the inhabitants, ground down by ceaseless exactions, are crying out at the immense sums which are being

[1] Charles Thornton Forster and F. H. Blackburne Daniell, *The Life and Letters of Ogier Ghiselin de Busbecq,* 2 vols., London, 1881, II, 38-43.

squandered for nought, or applied to purposes for which they were never intended. They demand a reckoning in tones which breathe a spirit of rebellion. Men of experience, members of the oldest families in France, are in many cases regarded with suspicion, and either not allowed to come to Court, or left to vegetate at home. Besides the two parties into which Frenchmen are divided by their religious differences, there are also feuds and quarrels which affect every grade of society.

In the first place, the feeling against the Italians who are in the French service is very strong; the high promotion they have received and the important duties with which they have been intrusted, arouse the jealousy of men who consider them ignorant of French business, and hold that they have neither merit, services, nor birth to justify their appointment. Birague, as Chancellor, holds one of the highest offices in the kingdom; Comte de Tetz is a Maréchal; Strozzi is in command of the infantry of France; Guadagni is Seneschal of Lyons; and in the same way other Italians occupy most important posts, while Frenchmen murmur.

Again, Italians farm nearly all the taxes, and exact their dues so rigidly as to drive the natives, who are unaccustomed to such extortion, to the very verge of rebellion; there will be another Saint Bartholomew if they do not take care, and they will be the victims.

The feuds which separate the leading families of France are more bitter than those described in ancient tragedy; this is the state of feeling which exists between the Houses of Guise, Vendôme and Bourbon, not to mention that of Montmorency, which, through its alliances and connections, has a considerable party of its own.

The Bourbons are the strongest; the Guises have most influence at Court, but this is an advantage which they may lose any day by the death of the King, and then their fall is inevitable.

By his nearest relations the King [Henry III] is feared rather than loved, for, knowing the designs they entertained before the death of his brother [Charles IX], they have no confidence in his mercy and forgiveness, though he professes to have pardoned them, and think that his vengeance is only deferred for a time. His companions are wild young men, the tone of French society is licentious, and he listens to selfish intriguers who are seeking their own advantage; under such circumstances, who can say that he will not go astray? Both he and his brother (Alençon [1]) are of a weakly constitution and not likely to be long-lived.

THE MURDER OF HENRY III, 1589

From *The Fugger News-Letters* (1589) [2]

On the first day of the month of August [1589], a young Dominican friar [Jacques Clément] betook himself to St. Cloud where the late King sojourned, with a passport from the Count de Brienne, who is kept imprisoned in Paris. On his arrival he informed the guard that he had something which he wished to communicate to the King. The King ordered that he might be permitted to deliver his message on the following day. The Provost-Marshal gave the monk quarters at the King's request and entertained him right nobly. The monk said he was minded to do the King a great service. The following day the Provost-Marshal led the monk to the King's chamber. But, as there were several persons present, the monk demanded that the King might receive him

[1] François, Duke of Alençon and Anjou, youngest son of Catherine de' Medici. His death in 1584 left Henry III the last of the Valois line of French kings.
[2] From *The Fugger News-Letters*, 135-37. Courtesy of G. P. Putnam's Sons.

alone. He led him into his cabinet and read various scripts which the monk handed to him. When the King had perused the last, he asked the monk whether he had any more. The latter thereupon replied "Yes," and, in place of the script, drew forth from his sleeve a short knife, the width of two fingers, which he thrust into the King's abdomen below the navel. He left it sticking in the wound. The King pulled it out himself and thus enlarged the wound. He then himself inflicted a stab upon the monk. At his calls for help several people came into the room, among them La Bastida, who helped to murder the late Guise [Henry, Duke of Guise, murdered December 23, 1588], and he with his dagger slashed at the monk. Also one of the halberdiers thrust his halberd into the monk so that he was mortally wounded. He said that he had not hoped to come off so easily. After his death his corpse was dragged along the streets, rent asunder by four horses, and publicly burnt. The King did not expect to die of his wound. He walked up and down his room, and showed himself to his servants and to the soldiery at the window. But at four o'clock in the evening he felt great pains and when the doctors visited him they found the injury to be most grievous. They gave him an enema, and discovered that the intestine had been injured. The wound turned black and the King was informed of his perilous condition. He did not at first believe this, because he was feeling fairly well. But by and by he became weaker and a Capuchin was sent for to comfort him. But when he arrived the King no longer spoke. He died upon the 2nd day of this month at midnight. The body has not been interred as yet, and has been taken to Senlis. It is said that he has asked the King of Navarre not to take revenge for his death on the city of Paris. The story goes that the monk had delivered discourses not far from Paris and had then said that he would take the King's life. Even though he be burnt and quartered, he would feel no pain. The King of Navarre [now Henry IV] is still in St. Cloud and is besieging Paris to the extent of his power. He has made himself King of France and is thus acclaimed by his followers. He tries all ways and means in order to win to his side both the nobility and the common people. The Council of Paris has declared the Cardinal of Bourbon, who is held a prisoner in the castle of Chion, to be king. The King of Navarre intends to go to Rheims to be crowned there and to gain possession of the three royal cities.

3. The Edict of Nantes (1598)

The murder of Henry III left Henry of Navarre, except for the continued opposition of the Catholic League, uncontested king in France. But the League still held Paris and some other cities, and they had support from Spain and from the Papacy. Moreover, though the Huguenots were in a strong military position, they constituted a minority among the people of France and it was very doubtful whether a Calvinist king could ever gain acceptance of the majority of the populace—particularly as long as the Catholic League existed to foment armed opposition. Consideration of these facts, together with the exhausted condition of France, now in its ninth civil war since 1562, led Henry IV to adopt the Catholic faith in 1593. The act destroyed much of the reason for continued resistance from the Catholic League, and in 1594 Paris fell into his hands. The whole kingdom was his. Within the next four years foreign opposition was likewise crushed. Spain sued for peace (signed at Vervins, May, 1598), and the long religious wars in France were at an end. But what of the Huguenots, the King's companions-in-arms for twenty-five years? To provide for their toleration, their civil rights, and their security against further Catholic persecution (as well as Catholic security against them), Henry IV issued, April 13, 1598, the Edict of Nantes. The edict was a long document of ninety-five public articles, fifty-six "secret" articles, and a supplement of twenty-three articles attached later. Because of Catholic opposition, it was not registered by the *parlement* of Paris until February 25, 1599. At that time it became part of the fundamental law of France, "an Edict perpetual and irrevocable." As such, with few modifications, it established religious peace in France for eighty-seven years—until its ill-advised revocation by Louis XIV in 1685. A few of its more important provisions follow.

From *The Edict of Nantes* (1598) [1]

III. We ordain that the Catholic Apostolic and Roman religion shall be restored and reëstablished in all places and localities of this our kingdom and countries subject to our sway, where the exercise of the same has been interrupted, in order that it may be peaceably and freely exercised, without any trouble or hindrance. Forbidding very expressly all persons of whatsoever estate, quality or condition . . . from troubling, molesting or disturbing ecclesiastics in the celebration of divine service, in the enjoyment or perception of tithes, fruits or revenues of their benefices, and all other rights and dues belonging to them; and that all those who during

[1] Merrick Whitcomb, ed., *Period of the Later Reformation,* 30-32. Reprinted by permission of the University of Pennsylvania Press.

the troubles have taken possession of churches, houses, goods or revenues belonging to the said ecclesiastics, and who retain and occupy the same, shall surrender to them entire possession and peaceable enjoyment of such rights, liberties and sureties as they had before they were deprived of them. Forbidding thus very expressly to those of the said religion called Reformed [Huguenots] to have preaching or perform other exercises of the said religion in churches, houses and habitations of the said ecclesiastics.

VI. And in order to leave no occasion for troubles or differences between our subjects we have permitted and herewith permit those of the said religion called Reformed to live and abide in all the cities and places of this our kingdom and countries of our sway, without being annoyed, molested or compelled to do anything in the matter of religion contrary to their consciences, nor for this reason to be subject to visitation in houses and places where they desire to dwell, upon condition that they comport themselves in other respects according to that which is contained in this our present edict.

VII. It is permitted to all lords, gentlemen and other persons ["their families and subjects"], natives and others as well, making profession of the said religion called Reformed . . . to enjoy in their houses . . . which they shall be required to name before our bailiffs and seneschals, each one in his jurisdiction, as their principal domiciles, the exercise of the said religion, so long as they there reside; and in their absence their wives, or indeed their family, or any part of the same. . . .

VIII. In houses of fiefs, where those of the said religion have not . . . [noble rank], the exercise of the said religion may be enjoyed for the family alone. It is not however intended, in case there should happen to arrive other persons, up to the number of thirty outside of the family, whether it be upon the occasion of a baptism, visits of friends or otherwise, that this should be cause for investigation: provided also that the said houses shall not be within the cities, towns or villages belonging to Catholic lords other than ourselves, having the right of high justice, in which the said Catholic lords shall have their houses. In which case those of the said religion shall not be able to enjoy said exercise in said towns or villages, unless by permission and leave of said lords high justices, and not otherwise.

IX. We also permit those of the said religion to make and continue the exercise of the same in all villages and places of our dominion where it was established by them and publicly enjoyed several and divers times in the year 1597, up to the end of the month of August, notwithstanding all decrees and judgments to the contrary.

XIII. We very expressly forbid to all those of the said religion the exercise . . . of all that concerns religion, otherwise than in the places permitted and granted by the present Edict.

XIV. As well from performing any function of the said religion in our court or retinue, or equally in our lands and territories beyond the mountains, or in our city of Paris or within five leagues of the said city: at the same time those of the said religion who live in the said lands and territories beyond the mountains and in our said city, and for five leagues thereabout, may not be investigated in their houses, nor constrained to do anything in respect to religion con-

trary to their consciences, providing they comport themselves in other respects according to . . . our present Edict.

XV. And it will not be allowed to exercise the said religion in the armies, except in the quarters of those chiefs who may be of that confession, not however in those quarters wherein our own person is lodged.

XVIII. We also forbid all our subjects of whatever quality and condition, from carrying off by force or persuasion, against the will of their parents, the children of the said religion, in order to cause them to be baptised or confirmed in the Catholic Apostolic and Roman church: and the same is forbidden to those of the said religion called Reformed, upon penalty of being punished with especial severity.

XXI. Books concerning the said religion called Reformed may not be printed and publicly sold, except in cities and places where the public exercise of the said religion is permitted. And as for the other books, which may be printed in other cities, they shall be examined and investigated . . . as it is prescribed in our ordinances. We forbid very expressly the printing, publishing and sale of all books, pamphlets and writings of a defamatory character upon the penalty indicated.

XXII. We ordain that there shall be no difference or distinction made in respect to the said religion, in receiving pupils to be instructed in universities, colleges and schools; nor in receiving the sick and poor into hospitals, retreats and public charities.

THE THIRTY YEARS' WAR (1618-1648): LAST INTERNATIONAL WAR OF RELIGION

1. Origins of Conflict

The Thirty Years' War is a term loosely applied to a series of wars which occurred in Europe between 1618 and 1648. Fundamentally, the war was a religious struggle born of the inadequacies of the Religious Peace of Augsburg [see page 117], which had provided for Lutherans in the Empire without recognizing Calvinism or other Protestant sects. From the outset, however, the religious motive was not clear-cut, for on the one hand, the Protestants were divided among themselves into Lutheran and Calvinist camps, and on the other, Lutheran, Calvinist, and Catholic princes endeavored to strengthen their forces by making alliances outside the Empire—the Lutherans with Denmark and Sweden, the Calvinists with England, the Dutch Netherlands, and France, and the Catholics with the Papacy and Spain. As these allies were drawn into the conflict, the initial religious impulse came to be replaced by territorial designs, so that the Thirty Years' War, beginning as an internal religious struggle in the Holy Roman Empire, ended as a vast international dynastic conflict between the French Bourbons and the Austro-Spanish Hapsburgs. In this respect, too, the Thirty Years' War at once symbolizes the entire transition period of the Renaissance-Reformation era and marks the end of the transition.

After 1648, the European world witnessed no further international wars for religion's sake; and while matters of an economic and political nature usurped the modern scene, toleration of a variety of creeds and churches (and even of individuals who professed no creed and belonged to no church) gradually became the *practice,* if not the *law,* in the Western world.

RELIGIOUS CONDITIONS IN THE EMPIRE AFTER THE PEACE OF AUGSBURG, 1555-1618

From SCHILLER, *The Thirty Years' War* (1793) [1]

The seizure of ecclesiastical benefices, the powerful motive which impelled so many Protestant princes to embrace Lutheranism, was no less powerful after the Peace of Augsburg than before. . . . All of lower Germany was already secularized, and if it was otherwise in upper Germany it was because of the stubborn resistance of Catholics who maintained the preponderance there. Each party, wherever it held the power, oppressed the other; the ecclesiastical princes, as the most defenseless members of the Empire, were constantly tormented by their ambitious Protestant neighbors. Those who were too weak to meet force with force

[1] Johann Christoph Friedrich von Schiller, *Geschichte des dreissigjährigen Kriegs,* in *Schiller's sämmtliche Werke,* 2 vols., Stuttgart, 1840, II, Pt. I, Bk. I, 883-84.

flew to the law courts for justice; the legal judgments piled up against Protestants in the Imperial Chamber, which willingly gave verdicts but found too little support to carry them into effect. The peace, which provided religious freedom for princes of the Empire, had also made provision for the subject by enabling him to leave the state in which the exercise of his religion was forbidden. But from the violence which the sovereign might inflict upon an obnoxious subject, from the nameless oppressions by which he might harass an emigrant, from the artful snares in which subtility combined with power might entangle him—from these the dead letter of the treaty offered no protection. The Catholic subject of Protestant princes complained loudly of violations of the religious peace; the Lutherans even more loudly of the oppressions which they experienced at the hands of Catholic overlords. The rancor and quarrelsomeness of the theologians poisoned every event, however unimportant, and inflamed the spirit of the people. How happy would it have been had this theological hatred exhausted itself on the common enemies of religion without setting adherents of a kindred faith at each others' throats!

Unanimity among Protestants as a whole might, by establishing a better balance between the opposing parties, have prolonged the peace. But, as if to complete the confusion, this harmony was quickly broken. The doctrines which had been promulgated by Zwingli in Zürich and by Calvin in Geneva soon won adherents in Germany, and divided Protestants so that they had no union among themselves save their common hatred of the papacy. Protestants of this time had little resemblance to those who, fifty years before, had drawn up the Augsburg Confession [1530], and the reason for this change is to be sought in that Confession

itself. The Confession had established a fixed boundary to the Protestant belief before the newly awakened spirit of inquiry had satisfied itself as to the limits it should set, and, in this manner, Protestants unwittingly forfeited part of the advantage won by their rejection of popery. Common complaints against the Romish hierarchy, against papal ecclesiastical abuses, and against Catholic dogmas furnished an adequate basis for union among Protestants; but they sought a further rallying point in the promulgation of a new and positive creed in which they placed the discriminations, the privileges, and the essence of *their* church; and under cover of this creed they sought to combat the Catholics. As adherents to this Confession [the Augsburg Confession] they had acceded to the Treaty [of Augsburg], and only those who subscribed to this creed could participate in the benefits of the peace. This fact became embarrassing to adherents of the Confession [Lutherans]; for if blind obedience were given to the Confession the spirit of inquiry was limited to fixed bounds, but if, on the other hand, anyone dissented from the formula agreed upon the point of union was lost. Unfortunately, both things occurred, and from both evil results followed. One party [the Lutherans] adhered stubbornly to the original creed, and another, the Calvinists, adopted a similar creed with the same exclusiveness.

Nothing could have furnished the common enemy a more credible defense of his cause than this Protestant dissension; no spectacle could have been more gratifying to him than the rancor with which Protestants persecuted one another. . . . But the division created even more serious embarrassments for the Protestants. The religious peace applied only to adherents of the Augsburg Confession, and the Catholics, insisting upon clear definition, demanded to know who were to be recognized as adherents to that creed. The Lutherans could not, without offending their consciences, include Calvinists in their communion, and they could not exclude them without turning much needed friends into dangerous enemies. This unfortunate difference provided a way for the machinations of Jesuits to plant distrust in both parties and to destroy the unity of their measures. Thus, bound by the double fear of Catholics and their own divisions, the Protestants failed to place their church on an equal footing with the Romish church.

LEADERS AND LEAGUES IN THE EMPIRE

From GARDINER, *The Thirty Years' War* (1886) [1]

Two men stood forward to personify the elements of strife—Maximilian, the Catholic Duke of Bavaria, and the Calvinist Prince Christian of Anhalt, whilst the warmest advocate of peace was John George, the Lutheran Elector of Saxony. Maximilian of Bavaria was the only lay prince of any importance on the side of the Catholics. He had long been known as a wise administrator of his own dominions. No other ruler was provided with so well-filled a treasury, or so disciplined an army. No other ruler was so capable of forming designs which were likely to win the approbation of others, or so patient in waiting till the proper time arrived for their execution. . . .

Such a man was not likely to take up the wild theories which were here and there springing up, of the duty of uprooting Protestantism at all times and all places, or to declare, as some were declaring, that the Peace of Augsburg was

[1] Samuel Rawson Gardiner, *The Thirty Years' War, 1618-1648,* 7th ed., London, Longmans, Green and Co., 1886 (Epochs of Modern History), 14-22.

invalid because it had never been confirmed by the Pope. To him the Peace of Augsburg was the legal settlement by which all questions were to be tried. What he read there was hostile to the Protestant administrators and the secularising princes. Yet he did not propose to carry his views into instant action. He would await his opportunity. But he would do his best to be strong, in order that he might not be found wanting when the opportunity arrived. . . .

Such an opponent, so moderate and yet so resolute, was a far more dangerous enemy to the Protestants than the most blatant declaimer against their doctrines. Naturally, the Protestants regarded his views as entirely inadmissible. They implied nothing less than the forcible conversion of the thousands of Protestants who were inhabitants of the administrators' dominions, and the occupation by the Catholic clergy of points of vantage which would serve them in their operations upon the surrounding districts. It is true that the change, if effected, would simply replace matters in the position which had been found endurable in 1552. But that which could be borne when the Catholics were weak and despondent might be an intolerable menace when they were confident and aggressive.

Resistance, therefore, became a duty, a duty to which the princes were all the more likely to pay attention because it coincided with their private interest. In the bishoprics and chapters they found provision for their younger sons, from which they would be cut off if Protestants were hereafter to be excluded.

The only question was in what spirit the resistance should be offered. The tie which bound the Empire together was so loose, and resistance to law, or what was thought to be law, was so likely to lead to resistance to law in general, that it was the more incumbent on the Protestants to choose their ground well. And in North Germany, at least, there was not likely to be any hasty provocation to give Maximilian an excuse for reclaiming the bishoprics. Far removed from the danger, these northern Lutherans found it difficult to conceive that there was any real danger at all. The states of the south, lying like a wedge driven into the heart of European Catholicism, were forced by their geographical position to be ever on the alert. They knew that they were the advanced guard of Protestantism. On the one flank was the Catholic duchy of Bavaria, and the bishoprics of Würzburg and Bamberg. On the other flank were the ecclesiastical electorates on the Rhine and the Moselle, the bishoprics of Worms, Spires, and Strasburg, the Austrian lands in Swabia and Alsace, and the long line of the Spanish frontier in Franche Comté and the Netherlands garrisoned by the troops of the first military monarchy in Europe. What wonder if men so endangered were in haste to cut the knot which threatened to strangle them, and to meet the enemy by flying in his face rather than by awaiting the onslaught which they believed to be inevitable.

Under the influence of this feeling the princes of these southern regions for the most part adopted a religion very different from the courtly Lutheranism of the north. If Würtemberg continued Lutheran under the influence of the University of Tübingen, the rulers of the Palatinate, of Hesse Cassel, of Baden-Durlach, of Zwei-Brücken, sought for strength in the iron discipline of Calvinism, a form of religion which always came into favour when there was an immediate prospect of a death-struggle with Rome.

Unhappily, German Calvinism differed from that of Scotland and the Netherlands. Owing to its adoption by the princes rather than by the people, it failed in gaining that hardy growth which made it invincible on its native soil. It had less of the discipline of an army about it, less resolute defiance, less strength altogether. And whilst it was weaker it was more provocative. Excluded from the benefits of the Peace of Augsburg, which knew of no Protestant body except the Lutheran, the Calvinists were apt to talk about the institutions of the Empire in a manner so disparaging as to give offence to Lutherans and Catholics alike.

Of this Calvinist feeling Christian of Anhalt became the impersonation. The leadership of the Calvinist states in the beginning of the seventeenth century would naturally have devolved on Frederick IV, Elector Palatine. But Frederick was an incapable drunkard, and his councillors, with Christian at their head, were left to act in his name.

Christian of Anhalt possessed a brain of inexhaustible fertility. As soon as one plan which he had framed appeared impracticable, he was ready with another. He was a born diplomatist, and all the chief politicians of Europe were intimately known to him by report, whilst with many of them he carried on a close personal intercourse. His leading idea was that the maintenance of peace was hopeless, and that either Protestantism must get rid of the House of Austria, or the House of Austria would get rid of Protestantism. Whether this were true or false, it is certain that he committed the terrible fault of underestimating his enemy. Whilst Maximilian was drilling soldiers and saving money, Christian was trusting to mere diplomatic finesse. . . . In order to give to Protestantism that development which in Christian's eyes was necessary to its safety, it would be needful to overthrow the authority of the Emperor and of the Diet. And if the Emperor and the Diet were overthrown, what had Christian to offer to save Germany from anarchy? If his plan included, as there is little doubt that it did, the seizure of the lands of the neighbouring bishops, and a fresh secularisation of ecclesiastical property, even Protestant towns might begin to ask whether their turn would not come next. A return to the old days of private war and the law of the strongest would be welcome to very few.

In 1607 an event occurred which raised the alarm of the southern Protestants to fever heat. In the free city of Donauwörth the abbot of a monastery saw fit to send out a procession to flaunt its banners in the face of an almost entirely Protestant population. Before the starting-point was regained mud and stones were thrown, and some of those who had taken part in the proceedings were roughly handled. The Imperial Court (*Reichskammergericht*), whose duty it was to settle such quarrels, was out of working order in consequence of the religious disputes; but there was an Imperial Council (*Reichshofrath*), consisting of nominees of the Emperor, and professing to act out of the plenitude of imperial authority. By this council Donauwörth was put to the ban of the Empire without due form of trial, and Maximilian was appointed to execute the decree. He at once marched a small army into the place, and, taking possession of the town, declared his intention of retaining his hold till his expenses had been paid, handing over the parish church in the meanwhile to the Catholic clergy. It had only been given over to Protestant worship after the date of the Convention of Passau, and Maximilian could persuade himself that he was only carrying out the law.

It was a flagrant case of religious aggression under the name of the law. The knowledge that a partial tribunal was ready to give effect to the complaints of Catholics at once threw the great Protestant cities of the South—Nüremberg, Ulm, and Strasburg—into the arms of the neighbouring princes of whom they had hitherto been jealous. . . .

On May 14, 1608, the Protestant Union, to which Lutherans and Calvinists were alike admitted, came into existence under the guidance of Christian of Anhalt. It was mainly composed of the princes and towns of the south. Its ostensible purpose was for self-defence, and in this sense it was accepted by most of those who took part in it. Its leaders had very different views.

A Catholic League was at once formed under Maximilian. It was composed of a large number of bishops and abbots, who believed that the princes of the Union wished to annex their territories. Maximilian's ability gave it a unity of action which the Union never possessed. It, too, was constituted for self-defence, but whether that word was to include the resumption of the lands lost since the Convention of Passau was a question probably left for circumstances to decide.

Whatever the majority of the princes of the [Protestant] Union may have meant, there can be no doubt that Christian of Anhalt meant aggression. He believed that the safety of Protestantism could not be secured without the overthrow of the German branch of the House of Austria, and he was sanguine enough to fancy that an act which would call up all Catholic Europe in arms against him was a very easy undertaking. . . .

The third party, the German Lutherans, looked with equal abhorrence upon aggression on either side. Their leader, John George, Elector of Saxony, stood aloof alike from Christian of Anhalt, and from Maximilian of Bavaria. He was attached by the traditions of his house as well as by his own character to the Empire and the House of Austria. But he was anxious to obtain security for his brother Protestants. He saw there must be a change; but he wisely desired to make the change as slight as possible. In 1612, therefore, he proposed that the highest jurisdiction should still be retained by the Imperial Council, but that the Council, though still nominated by the Emperor, should contain an equal number of Catholics and Protestants. Sentences such as that which had deprived Donauwörth of its civil rights would be in future impossible.

Unhappily, John George had not the gift of ruling men. He was a hard drinker and a bold huntsman, but to convert his wishes into actual facts was beyond his power. When he saw his plan threatened with opposition on either side he left it to take care of itself. In 1613 a Diet met, and broke up in confusion, leaving matters in such a state that any spark might give rise to a general conflagration.

BOHEMIAN BEGINNINGS, 1617-18

From RUSHWORTH, *Historical Collections* (1659) [1]

The clouds gather thick in the German sky; jealousies and discontents arise between the Catholics and the Evangelics, or Lutherans of the Confession of Augsburg. Both parties draw into confederacies, and hold assemblies; the one seeking by the advantage of power to incroach and get ground, the other to stand the ground, and hold their own. The potency of the House of Austria, a house devoted to the persecution of the Reformed Religion, became formidable. The old Emperor Matthias declared his cousin germane, the Archduke Ferdinand, to be his adopted son and successor, and caused him to be chosen and crowned king of Bohemia and Hungary; yet reserving to himself the sole exercise of kingly power during his life. . . .

The Bohemian troubles took their first rise from the breach of the edict of peace concerning religion, and the accord made by the Emperor Rudolph, whereby the Protestants retained the free exercise of their religion, enjoyed their temples, colleges, tithes, patronages, places of burial, and the like; and had liberty to build new temples, and power to choose defenders to secure those rights, and to regulate what should be of service in their churches. Now the stop of building certain churches on lands within the lordships of the Catholic clergy, (in which places the Evangelics conceived a right to build) was the special grievance and cause of breach.

On the twenty-third of May [1618], the Chief of the Evangelics went armed into the castle of Prague, entered into the Council-chamber, and opened their grievances; but enraged by opposition, threw Slabata the chief justice, and Smesantius one of the council, and Fabritius the secretary, from an high window into the castle ditch; others of the council temporising in this tumult, and seeming to accord with their demands, were peaceably conducted to their own houses. Hereupon the assembly took advice to settle the town and castle of Prague with new guards; likewise to appease the people, and to take an oath of fidelity. They chose directors, governors, and counsellors provincial to govern affairs of state, and to consult of raising forces against the enemies of God and the King, and the edicts of his Imperial Majesty. They banished the Jesuits throughout all Bohemia: Moreover to defend their own cause, and to give an account of their late proceedings, and present posture, a declaration was drawn up, and sent, with letters, to the estates of Moravia, Silesia, and Lusatia, and to all the princes and states, their allies,

---

[1] John Rushworth, ed., *Historical Collections,* 6 vols., London, 1721, I, 5-8, 11.

throughout the Empire, with request of aid in case of need. . . .

Forthwith a pernicious war, and all confusion breaks out. The Emperor raised forces under the conduct of divers commanders. . . . The Evangelics raise two armies under Count de Thorne, and Count Mansfelt. Moravia, Silesia, and Lusatia, with all the estates Protestant, Germans, and neighbours of Bohemia, (very few excepted) assist the Evangelics with counsel, men and money: likewise the Prince of Orange, and the states of the United Provinces, promised to aid them with their forces. The electors and princes Protestant favouring the Bohemians, whose country the imperialists destroy with fire and sword, persuade the Emperor to stop the rage of civil war, the success whereof is doubtful, and the end ever miserable. The Emperor propounded an arbitration of these differences. . . . The Evangelics consent to the arbitration . . . but new actions of war made the overtures of peace more difficult. . . .

In the beginning of the year one thousand six hundred and nineteen, the Emperor Matthias died; but immediately before his death, to engage persons of honour in the service of the Empire, he instituted knights of several orders, for the defence of the Catholic religion; who were bound by oath to be faithful to the Apostolic See, and to acknowledge the Pope their chief protector. The Count Palatine of Rhine, who in the interregnum is chief vicar of the Empire, published his right, by the Golden Bull, to govern in chief, till a new Emperor be chosen, and, by advice, assumed the power, requiring the people to demean themselves peaceably under his government.

King Ferdinand, in his broken estate, propounded a cessation of arms, and offered fair terms of peace; but was not answered, for the breach would not be made up. The Bohemians declared, that

their kingdom was elective, not hereditary; that the states-general ought to have the free election of their king, who always ought to be one of the royal house of Bohemia: that Ferdinand took the government upon him, by virtue of his coronation in the Emperor's life time, and had thereby made the kingdom a donative. . . .

The Archbishop of Mentz, the representers of the Duke of Saxony, and the other electors, Brandenburg, Cullen [Cologne], and Tryers, met at Frankfort, to choose the emperor.

Upon the twenty-eighth day of August [1619], Ferdinand was chosen king of the Romans; and upon the nineteenth of September had the imperial crown set upon his head. Ambassadors from the Elector Palatine came to oppose Ferdinand, but were denied entrance at Frankfort; the Bohemians disclaimed the said election, and being assembled for that purpose, with the consent of their confederates, elected for their king, Count Frederick Palatine of Rhine.

2. Some Events of the Thirty Years' War

THE EDICT OF RESTITUTION (1629)

By 1629, the Emperor's forces under Tilly and Wallenstein, together with Spanish and Italian aid, not only had defeated the Protestants of the Empire but also had crushed the forces of Christian IV of Denmark, who had invaded the Empire on behalf of the Protestants. For a moment, it seemed as if the war had come to an end with the Catholics and Imperials everywhere successful. But at this point, the Emperor Ferdinand II overreached himself. On March 6, 1629, he issued the Edict of Restitution, which required all ecclesiastical properties that had been seized since the Treaty of Passau (July 29, 1552) to be restored to the church, definitely excluded Calvinists from the religious peace, and left Catholics a free hand in the work of reconversion. The edict inspired German Protestants to new resistance and was a direct cause of the entry of Sweden into the war. Part of the Edict follows.

From *The Edict of Restitution* (1629) [1]

We are determined for the realisation both of the religious and profane peace to despatch our imperial commissioners into the Empire; to reclaim all the archbishoprics, bishoprics, prelacies, monasteries, hospitals and endowments which the Catholics had possessed at the time of the treaty of Passau (1552) and of which they have been illegally deprived; and to put into all these Catholic foundations duly qualified persons so that each may get his proper due. We herewith declare that the religious peace (of 1555) refers only to the Augsburg Confession as it was submitted to our Ancestor Emperor Charles Vth twenty-fifth of June 1530; and that all other doctrines and sects, whatever names they may have, not included in the Peace are forbidden and cannot be tolerated. We therefore command to all and everybody under punishment of the religious and the land ban that they shall at once cease opposing our ordinance and carry it out in their lands and territories and also assist our commissioners. Such as hold the archbishoprics and bishoprics, prelacies, monasteries, hospitals &c., shall forthwith return them to our imperial commissioners with all their appurtenances. Should they

[1] Emil Reich, ed., *Select Documents Illustrating Mediaeval and Modern History*, 1915, 234-35. Reprinted by permission of Staples Press, Ltd., London.

not carry out this behest they will not only expose themselves to the imperial bar and to the immediate loss of all their privileges and rights without any further sentence on commendation, but to the inevitable real execution of that order.

THE BATTLE OF LÜTZEN AND DEATH OF GUSTAVUS ADOLPHUS (1632)

The armies of Gustavus Adolphus achieved the first considerable successes which the Protestants enjoyed in the Thirty Years' War. The Emperor's determined attempts to enforce the Edict of Restitution [see page 195] led German Protestant princes to lay aside their dissensions and apathy and to rally around the King of Sweden, who, with great military genius and a splendidly disciplined army of his own, was soon recognized as the champion of Protestantism. At Breitenfeld (September, 1631), Gustavus inflicted upon Tilly's imperial army its first defeat. In a series of subsequent victories the Swedes revenged the Elector Frederick, recovered much of the Palatinate, and were in a fair way to become masters of the Empire. At the Battle of the Lech (April, 1632), Tilly was seriously wounded, and died shortly afterwards. At Lützen, near Leipsic, in November, 1632, Gustavus came to blows with Wallenstein, with whom he had been sparring for an advantage for several months. A terrific battle followed with heavy losses on both sides. But the Swedes stood firm while Wallenstein's men retired from the field at nightfall —not, however, without leaving the mangled body of Gustavus himself among the dead. Many accounts of the battle exist, and so few agree that exact details of the struggle cannot be known. The following description is probably not entirely accurate, but its outlines are as good as any. It was written by an Imperialist and published in Munich, 1632—accordingly it throws as favorable light as it can upon the imperialist accomplishments in the battle.

From A Contemporary Report (1632) [1]

On the aforementioned Tuesday [November 16, 1632] in the morning about ten o'clock the shooting from the pieces began with great seriousness and according to the words of the Royal Swedes themselves a very great damage was done by the Imperials, so that horses and men frequently fell over each other. Whereupon the King had his pieces fired repeatedly but no especially great damage was done. Meanwhile, his Ducal Grace [Wallenstein] had the Field-Marshal, Count Pappenheim, attack the King's forces with several regiments on horseback, and the aforementioned Count attacked with great ferocity. However he encountered powerful resistance, and he was met with such fire that his troops, and particularly the life-guard, suffered severe damage. Also the Count himself was so wounded with a falconet and three musket-balls that soon after he had retired and the General inquired after his condition he fell from his horse. He was put into a litter, lived about two hours longer, and that same evening was brought to Leipsic. He had confessed early on the morning before and even while he was on the litter he asked for his confessor but he could not say anything else. His body will shortly be brought to Prague.

1 "A thorough & detailed Report how & in what manner the bloody battle between his Imperial Majesty, General Duke von Mecklenberg & Friedland, and the King of Sweden at Lützen . . . took place," translated from the reprint in G. von Droysen, "Gedruckte Relationen über die Schlacht bei Lützen. 1632," in Materialen zur neueren Geschichte, 2 Druck, Halle, 1881-1903, 9-12.

These and other circumstances brought about among the imperial cavalry such a panic that several Croatian as well as some German and other well known cavalrymen took to their heels in a hurry. The main attack was given up as lost and the Imperials' own baggage wagons were plundered.

At this point the King of the Swedes lost no time. Rather, he set upon the Imperials with great ferocity and, although the infantry resisted him splendidly, he nevertheless soon took possession of several pieces. These he had fired repeatedly upon the imperial regiments so that they were in considerable danger and were ready to flee. At this time, while the imperial infantry still knew nothing of the death of Count Pappenheim, it was heard that the soldiers cried out with a loud voice, "Where can Pappenheim be that he does not come to help us with his cavalry?"

However, the Almighty gave the imperial infantry such heroic valor and the soldiers were so inspired by Wallenstein's presence and by his eager encouragement that with the aid of a good part of the cavalry not only three pieces were recovered but also 42 pennants and coronets were taken from the enemy. However, because of the lack of artillery horses that had been unhitched earlier, they had to leave some pieces on the battlefield and the Swedish forces likewise had to leave some of theirs there.

The battle lasted from 10 o'clock on into the dark of night and neither side retreated until the night fell between the two armies. The regiments on foot were so close to each other that they could fight with their pikes and got mixed up into each other's forces. The Swedish soldiers failed to capture a single troop of imperial infantry much less a regiment, although they did get five or six coronets, among them the coronet with the wheel belong-

ing to the troops of Mainz. The King of
Sweden received about ten wounds, so
that soon thereafter he died, expiring in
the arms of Duke Franz Albert of Saxony.
. . . And such irreparable harm was done
to the Royal Swedes that the Armada,
particularly the infantry, was almost completely split up and the two best Swedish
regiments, the blue and the yellow, were
so decimated that few got away alive.
And those who stood fast were beaten to
death with muskets. The quarter was
bought very dearly by the Swedes. Neither
side lost outstanding officers by capture,
except that the imperial army captured a
lieutenant-colonel, two sergeant-majors of
cavalry, a captain of horse, and several
other captains. In short, time did not permit further capturing, as they had their
hands full with the butchering of the
enemy. If the above-mentioned [Count
Galas's] five imperial infantry regiments
had arrived two hours earlier, they would
have finished off the Swedish forces, God
willing, but the Swedish forces retired to
Weissenfels and Naumburg and the imperial forces retired to Leipsic. From
Leipsic the Imperials proceeded on to
Chemnitz not out of fear of the Swedes,
since their army was ruined, but rather so
that his Grace [Wallenstein] could join
with himself Field Marshal Count Galas
who still had about 10,000 fresh men with
him. The purpose being that he could cut
off the Saxon Field Marshal Arnheim,
who had arrived near the Elbe from
Silesia. For had the latter joined with the
Swedish army prior to the Duke's juncture
with Count Galas and cut off the Imperials' passage, it would not have been
difficult to imagine how things would
have turned out.

All day long there was beautiful bright
sunshine and a clear day at Leipsic and
its vicinity, but in the area of the battle
there was such a thick, heavy fog that
one could not see a pistol shot away the
whole time; which also accounts for the
fact that some of the Imperials' own regiments fired on each other now and then.

When the above-mentioned five regiments got close to the field of battle, the
fog suddenly lifted and it became bright.
But as soon as they got in sight of the
enemy it became foggy again. Furthermore, night fell so that both forces withdrew, and neither followed the other. . . .

The dead were piled up in great piles,
and it is believed that in all over 6000
Swedes remained on the field of battle.
The Imperials were also hard hit, having
lost about 3000 men. . . . Not a single
infantry regiment was cut off and, be it
repeated once more with amazement, no
infantry troop fell into the enemy's hands.

3. The Peace of Westphalia, 1648

The Thirty Years' War continued
for years after Gustavus Adolphus
passed from the scene, with France,
which had been subsidizing the Swedes
since 1630, gradually assuming a more
prominent role until, in 1638, she formally declared war upon the Empire.
By 1640, however, the sufferings entailed upon the peoples and properties
of the Empire by the endless ravages of
troops led German princes to press the
Emperor for a peace settlement. Finally,
at the close of a diet held at Ratisbon
(1640-41), there was made by France,
Sweden, and the Empire a preliminary
agreement (December 25, 1641) in
which it was determined that negotiations should be opened in 1643 at Münster and at Osnabrück in Westphalia,
the two assemblies being considered as
one peace congress. At Münster, the
Spanish treated with the Dutch and the
Emperor treated with both France and
the Princes of the Empire—the Papacy

and the Seigniory of Venice serving as mediators; at Osnabrück, the Emperor treated with Sweden, Christian IV of Denmark serving as mediator. Because not all the plenipotentiaries arrived on time, actual negotiations were carried on only from the early summer of 1645 until the treaties were signed in 1648. When one considers the complexity of the questions to be determined, the multiplicity of negotiators (every major power in Europe was represented except England, Poland, Russia, and Turkey), and the slowness of communications at the time, it is not surprising that the treaty required more than three years to conclude. The reconstitution of the entire Empire was effected, every detail of each of the three hundred German states had to be discussed with reference to territorial claims, religious controversies, and political reconstruction, and in addition to these internal affairs of the Empire, the demands of neighboring states likewise required settlement. No one felt that the settlement of the internal problems of the Holy Roman Empire would be lasting, yet no further general reconstitution occurred until the Congress of Vienna in 1815. Nevertheless, the effects of the Peace of Westphalia were to weaken the Empire by transferring powers to individual princes and states at the expense of the Emperor and of the Imperial Diet. Moreover, neighboring states, especially Sweden and France, acquired territories at the expense of the Empire and, as guarantors of the peace, gained a right to meddle in imperial affairs. By accident of circumstances, however, the religious settlement of the treaties proved to be the final solution of religious problems raised by the Reformation. For though the peace did not establish liberty of conscience and it positively forbade the exercise of any religion within the Empire save Catholicism, Lutheranism, and Calvinism, nevertheless memories of the Thirty Years' War and the growing indifference to religious controversies resulted in relatively few instances of religious persecution either within the Empire or in Europe at large after 1648. Finally, the Peace of Westphalia sank piles in the quicksands of European international relations upon which was erected a shadowy "States System" for the maintenance of peace—a "system" which, though repeatedly challenged and frequently modified, gradually assumed distinct outlines in the European "Concert" of the nineteenth century [see page 462] and the League of Nations and the United Nations of the twentieth [see page 984]. R. B. Mowat, the late English historian and diplomatic adviser, has described these aspects of the Peace of Westphalia.

From MOWAT, *European States System* (1923) [1]

The Peace of Westphalia . . . is the first of the grand settlements of modern European history. Of these there have been four [prior to World War II]— Westphalia, 1648, ending the Thirty Years' War; Utrecht, 1713, ending the Spanish Succession War [see page 264]; Vienna, 1815, ending the Napoleonic War [see page 457]; and Versailles, 1919, ending the "Great War" [see page 742]. The Peace of Westphalia may be said to have reconstructed the European system which had been in dissolution since the beginning of the Reformation. The three subsequent settlements reconstructed the system after an outbreak of general European war had temporarily destroyed it.

The Peace of Westphalia consisted of

[1] R. B. Mowat, *The European States System,* 1923 (The World's Manuals), 14-19. Reprinted by permission of the Clarendon Press, Oxford.

three treaties: one between Spain and the Dutch, dated at Münster, on the 30th January 1648; a second between the Emperor, the King of France, and the Princes of the Empire, at Münster, on the 24th October of the same year; and thirdly a treaty between the Empire and Sweden, also dated the 24th October, but signed at Osnabrück. These three treaties established, among other matters, three things which henceforth may be considered as fundamental, as vital parts of the structure of the European States System. The first thing was a clear adjustment of relations between Catholics and Protestants and the establishing of a *modus vivendi* between them which has endured till this day, and has prevented any further religious wars. This *modus vivendi* was recognized by Article V of the Osnabrück treaty:

"That there be an exact and reciprocal equality amongst all the Electors, Princes and States of both Religions, conformably to the State of the Commonweal, the Constitution of the Empire, and the present Convention: so that what is just of one side shall be so of other, all violence and force between the two Parties being for ever prohibited."

Mutual toleration of Catholic and Protestant thus became the law of the Empire; and although the treaty only referred to the Empire, that is, to the States of Germany, the principle which it contained became a pattern for all northern and, ultimately, for western Europe.

The second thing, which is fundamental to the European System and which was established at Westphalia, was the independence of the Dutch (the United Netherlands or Holland), in the Münster Treaty of the 30th January. Belgium—known then as the Spanish Netherlands—was not independent but remained under the Crown of Spain. Consequential to the establishing of Dutch independence was the fixing of the frontier between the United Netherlands and the Spanish (Belgian) Netherlands.

"Each shall remain effectively in the possession and enjoyment of the countries. towns, forts, lands and dominions which he holds and possesses at present (Art. 3)."

Thus the Belgo-Dutch frontier was established, such as it has, with small modifications, existed to the present day, with the Dutch holding the south side of the estuary of the Scheldt as well as the north side. In addition to this permanent fact in Belgo-Dutch relations, another provision —only temporary, although it lasted for 167 years—was introduced by Article 14.

"The river of the Scheldt, as also the canals of Sas, Zwyn, and other mouths of rivers disemboguing themselves there, shall be kept shut on the side of the Lords of the States."

This is the famous "Closure of the Scheldt" which prevented any sea-borne trade from coming to Antwerp throughout the rest of the seventeenth and the eighteenth centuries.

The third fundamental part of this European settlement was the acquisition in full sovereignty by France of a large part of Alsace, and also of Lorraine as a "sphere of influence" (it was actually annexed in 1739). The Alsace-Lorraine terms are contained in Articles 72-6 of the Münster treaty of the 24th October. Acts more particularly relating to Lorraine are the Treaty of the Pyrenees, 1659 (Arts. 68-9), and the Treaty of Bar, 1661. It cannot seriously be questioned now, that it is essential to any stable European system that France should have a firm eastern frontier.

The Treaty of the Pyrenees must be included, as being a kind of pendant to the Peace of Westphalia. Two of the Powers which had engaged in the Thirty Years' War did not conclude peace with each other in 1648. These were France and Spain (with Spain's ally, the Duchy of Lorraine). Their war went on till 1659, when Cardinal Mazarin and Don Louis Mendez de Haro signed articles of peace on the Isle of Pheasants in the Bidassoa river, on the confines of the Pyrenees, on the 7th November 1659. Article 42 defined the frontier between the two countries as the Pyrenees:

"The Pyrenean Mountains, which anciently hath divided the Gauls from Spain, shall also make henceforth the division of both the said kingdoms."

The territories "that be in the said Pyrenean Mountains towards Spain" were to be in Spanish jurisdiction, while the mountains towards France were to be French. In practice this method of division meant the adoption of the watershed: rivers flowing into Spain water Spanish territory, rivers flowing towards France water the French territory. The Treaty of the Pyrenees has provided the most stable frontier in the European System. . . .

The Peace of Westphalia established the modern European States System. It recognized a division of religious power which has, on the whole, been found to be satisfactory. According to this division North Germany and Holland retained their freedom to worship as Protestants; and with these countries Great Britain and the Scandinavian Powers may be considered as being included, having been involved in the struggle, and being vitally interested in the result. The rest of Europe, except Russia, the Balkans, and Switzerland, was Catholic. Thus by the Peace of Westphalia both the Reformation and the Counter Reformation ceased to be militant. It is true that there were subsequent outbursts of persecution, in France under Louis XIV, and in Salzburg in 1731; yet on the whole, in Europe, the two religions agreed to live and let live. Since then there has been no religious war, and there never will be any (between Catholics and Protestants at any rate) unless the balance of religious power, as established at Westphalia, be seriously disturbed. . . .

The States System of Europe depends upon an equipoise, a balance of power, so adjusted that each State can keep what it already possesses, and that no one State or group of States shall be able to coerce and despoil the rest. In the absence of any super-State, of any international League or Society of Nations, this balance of power has necessarily been attended to and maintained by the States which themselves make up the States System. Normally each State can look after its own interests, and preserve its independence and its territory. Even a State that has little or no material resources can in normal times rest securely upon the accepted principles of International Law, and be certain that no other State will without provocation assail its independence or rob it of its territories.

Thus for years at a time the European System goes on existing happily enough. Each State keeps what it has, lives at peace with its neighbors, and consumes or exchanges the fruits of its labor. But this halcyon period is unstable: it is always liable to be broken into by some State that takes upon itself to assault the system. This assault comes about, either because a whole people waxes fat and arrogant, or because one or more persons within it become ambitious of conquest, and form designs to extend their State by force. Indeed this ambition to make conquests is not necessarily limited to one State at a time; it may exist in the breasts of men of several States. Yet, as far as can be discerned, till the present day [1923] only one man, set of persons or State has had in any one period both the will and the power to make an assault on the European system.

History shows that since the Peace of Westphalia the States of Europe have enjoyed periods of equilibrium and therefore periods of peace (or of relative peacefulness), which, however, have been every now and then threatened and sometimes destroyed by a Disturber. The appearance of such a Disturber (or of a Disturbing State) has, in turn, always provoked the other States of Europe (or some of them) to band together to defend the system and to check the aggressor. The end of each struggle has usually been that the aggressor has been overcome, and that the European system has been re-established by some general peace-settlement, some treaty on the grand scale, continuing, with the modifications which the struggle has made necessary, the settlement of Westphalia.

4. Some Effects of the Thirty Years' War in the Empire

A CONTEMPORARY NOVEL,
"SIMPLICISSIMUS"

For thirty years the Holy Roman Empire was a vast battleground across which both foreign soldiers and native troops marched, countermarched, foraged, plundered, murdered, and destroyed. Scattered records and reports which survive that era amply demonstrate the enormous loss of life, property, and popular morale. One very revealing account is the semiautobiographical novel, The Adventurous Simplicissimus, published in 1668 by Hans Jacob Christoffel von Grimmelshausen, himself a soldier during the war. Simplicissimus was an innocent peasant boy turned out in the world by marauding soldiers—a kind of seventeenth-century Parsifal whose wanderings portray a realistic picture of German life during the Thirty Years' War. Chapter Four (Book I) relates what happened when a band of soldiers came upon his father's peasant dwelling (humorously called a "palace"). It is a story which could have been repeated by thousands of German householders during the era, 1618-1648.

From GRIMMELSHAUSEN, Simplicissimus
(1668) [1]

HOW SIMPLICISSIMUS'S PALACE WAS STORMED, PLUNDERED, AND RUINATED, AND IN WHAT SORRY FASHION THE SOLDIERS KEPT HOUSE THERE

Although it was not my intention to take the peaceloving reader with these troopers to my dad's house and farm, seeing that matters will go ill therein, yet the course of my history demands that I should leave to kind posterity an account of what manner of cruelties were now and again practised in this our German war. . . .

The first thing these troopers did was, that they stabled their horses: thereafter each fell to his appointed task: which task was neither more nor less than ruin and destruction. For though some began to slaughter and to boil and to roast so that it looked as if there should be a merry banquet forward, yet others there were who did but storm through the house above and below stairs. Others stowed together great parcels of cloth and apparel and all manner of household stuff, as if they would set up a frippery market. All that they had no mind to take with them they cut in pieces. Some thrust their

[1] Simplicissimus the Vagabond, trans. by A. T. S. Goodrick, 1912 (Broadway Translations), 8-10. Reprinted by permission of E. P. Dutton and Company, Inc.

swords through the hay and straw as if they had not enough sheep and swine to slaughter: and some shook the feathers out of the beds and in their stead stuffed in bacon and other dried meat and provisions as if such were better and softer to sleep upon. Others broke the stove and the windows as if they had a never-ending summer to promise. Houseware of copper and tin they beat flat, and packed such vessels, all bent and spoiled, in with the rest. Bedsteads, tables, chairs, and benches they burned, though there lay many cords of dry wood in the yard. Pots and pipkins must all go to pieces, either because they would eat none but roast flesh, or because their purpose was to make there but a single meal.

Our maid was so handled in the stable that she could not come out; which is a shame to tell of. Our man they laid bound upon the ground, thrust a gag into his mouth, and poured a pailful of filthy water into his body: and by this, which they called a Swedish draught, they forced him to lead a party of them to another place where they captured men and beasts, and brought them back to our farm, in which company were my dad, my mother, and our Ursula.

And now they began: first to take the flints out of their pistols and in place of them to jam the peasants' thumbs in and so to torture the poor rogues as if they had been about the burning of witches: for one of them they had taken they thrust into the baking oven and there lit a fire under him, although he had as yet confessed no crime: as for another, they put a cord round his head and so twisted it tight with a piece of wood that the blood gushed from his mouth and nose and ears. In a word each had his own device to torture the peasants, and each peasant his several torture. But as it seemed to me then, my dad was the luckiest, for he with a laughing face confessed what others must out with in the midst of pains and miserable lamentations: and such honour without doubt fell to him because he was the householder. For they set him before a fire and bound him fast so that he could neither stir hand nor foot, and smeared the soles of his feet with wet salt, and this they made our old goat lick off, and so tickle him that he well nigh burst his sides with laughing. And this seemed to me so merry a thing that I must needs laugh with him for the sake of fellowship, or because I knew no better. In the midst of such laughter he must needs confess all that they would have of him, and indeed revealed to them a secret treasure, which proved far richer in pearls, gold, and trinkets than any would have looked for among peasants. Of the women, girls and maidservants whom they took, I have not much to say in particular, for the soldiers would not have me see how they dealt with them. Yet this I know, that one heard some of them scream most piteously in divers corners of the house; and well I can judge it fared no better with my mother and our Ursel than with the rest. Yet in the midst of all this miserable ruin I helped to turn the spit, and in the afternoon to give the horses drink, in which employ I encountered our maid in the stable, who seemed to me wondrously tumbled, so that I knew her not, but with a weak voice she called to me, "O lad, run away, or the troopers will have thee away with them. Look to it well that thou get hence: thou seest in what plight. . . ." And more she could not say.

AN ASSESSMENT OF IMPERIAL LOSSES IN THE THIRTY YEARS' WAR

From GARDINER, *The Thirty Years' War* [1]

Whatever life there was under that deadly blast of war had been attracted to

[1] Samuel Rawson Gardiner, *The Thirty Years' War*, 212-16.

the camps. The strong man who had lost his all turned soldier that he might be able to rob others in turn. The young girl, who in better times would have passed on to a life of honourable wedlock with some youth who had been the companion of her childhood in the sports around the village fountain, had turned aside, for very starvation, to a life of shame in the train of one or other of the armies by which her home had been made desolate. In the later years of the war it was known that a body of 40,000 fighting men drew along with it a loathsome following of no less than 140,000 men, women, and children, contributing nothing to the efficiency of the army, and all of them living at the expense of the miserable peasants who still contrived to hold on to their ruined fields. If these were to live, they must steal what yet remained to be stolen; must devour, with the insatiable hunger of locusts, what yet remained to be devoured. And then, if sickness came, or wounds—and sickness was no infrequent visitor in those camps —what remained but misery or death? Nor was it much better with the soldiers themselves. No careful surgeons passed over the battlefield to save life or limb. No hospitals received the wounded to the tender nursing of loving, gentle hands. Recruits were to be bought cheaply, and it cost less to enroll a new soldier than to cure an old one.

The losses of the civil population were almost incredible. In a certain district of Thuringia which was probably better off than the greater part of Germany, there were, before the war cloud burst, 1,717 houses standing in nineteen villages. In 1649, only 627 houses were left. And even of the houses which remained many were untenanted. The 1,717 houses had been inhabited by 1,773 families. Only 316 families could be found to occupy the 627 houses. Property fared still worse. In the same district 244 oxen alone remained of 1,402. Of 4,616 sheep, not one was left. Two centuries later the losses thus suffered were scarcely recovered.

And, as is always the case, the physical decline of the population was accompanied by moral decadence. Men who had been accustomed to live by the strong arm, and men who had been accustomed to suffer all things from those who were strong, met one another, even in the days of peace, without that mutual respect which forms the basis of well-ordered life. Courts were crowded with feather-brained soldiers whose highest ambition was to bedeck themselves in a splendid uniform and to copy the latest fashion or folly which was in vogue at Paris or Versailles. In the country districts a narrow-minded gentry, without knowledge or culture, domineered over all around, and strove to exact the uttermost farthing from the peasant in order to keep up the outward appearance of rank. The peasant whose father had been bullied by marauding soldiers dared not lift up his head against the exactions of the squire. The burthen of the general impoverishment fell heavily upon his shoulders. The very pattern of the chairs on which he sat, of the vessels out of which he ate and drank, assumed a ruder appearance than they had borne before the war. In all ranks life was meaner, poorer, harder than it had been at the beginning of the century. . . .

As far as national institutions were concerned the Thirty Years' War made a clean sweep in Germany. Nominally, it is true, Emperor and Empire still remained. Ferdinand III. was still according to his titles head of all Christendom, if not of the whole human race. The Diet still gathered to discuss the affairs of the Empire. The imperial court, re-established on the principle of equality between the two religions, still met to dispense justice between the estates of the Empire. But from these high-sounding names all reality had fled. The rule over German men had passed for many a long day into the hands of the princes. It was for the princes to strive with one another in peace or war under the protection of foreign alliances; and by and by, half consciously, half unconsciously, to compete for the leadership of Germany by the intelligence and discipline which they were able to foster under their sway.

Part Two

THE ERA OF ENLIGHTENED DESPOTISM (c. 1648-1815)

The Era of Enlightened Despotism
(c. 1648-1815)

15	SOME GENERAL CHARACTERISTICS OF THE ERA OF ENLIGHTENED DESPOTISM

A HIGH DEGREE OF SIMILARITY appears in the development of European states between the end of the Thirty Years' War (1648) and the outbreak of the French Revolution (1789). For, in spite of ever present differences in geography, population, climate, language, and cultural traditions, the governments and peoples of Europe generally subscribed to certain common principles and, with due regard to local circumstances, they employed similar methods in the solution of political, economic, and social problems. Like most periods in history, the era was marked by a progressive decay of some states and by the emergence of others to unprecedented heights of power and prestige. The Hapsburg powers in Spain, Italy, and the Holy Roman Empire, the prestige of Sweden, Poland, and the Ottoman Turks—all these became relatively unimportant beside more aggressively successful neighbors, especially France, Russia, Prussia, and England. New dynastic families came to the fore. The Bourbons, who had replaced the Valois in France in 1589, outshone all the crowned heads in Europe in the reign of Louis XIV (1643-1715); the Romanovs, succeeding the Ruriks (1613), made Russia an important member of the European family of nations; the Hohenzollerns, already established as margraves of Brandenburg and electors in the Empire, suddenly inherited new territories, became dukes and later kings of Prussia, and, in the time of Frederick the Great (1740-86), rose to be head of one of the first states of Europe; and when the last Tudor, Queen Elizabeth, died, she was succeeded on the English throne first by the Stuarts (1603-1714) and then by the Hanoverian kings (1714 to the present).

Possibly some significance is attached to the fact that these new ruling houses were anxious to make their respective marks upon the European scene—just as the older dynasties sought to keep theirs bright. But it is of far greater significance that they all faced somewhat similar situations. Nearly every absolutist king inherited a state whose laws were an unsystematized jumble of feudal customs and modern statutes, whose tax system was obsolete and corrupt, whose army was a strange mixture of mercenary soldiers and impressed nationals, and whose governmental administration creaked with delays and confusion caused by decentralization. Moreover, nearly every king found his authority challenged by a jealous, recalcitrant nobility and a wealthy, powerful clergy. Further, nearly every ruler attempted to reform his government through greater concentration of authority in his hands as king—to bring the nobility and the clergy under greater royal subjection, to codify the laws, and to centralize administration in regard to the tax system, the army, and the judiciary. And finally, nearly every enlightened despot, even while he attempted to seize his neighbor's territory and to reduce him to political ashes, studied his neighbor's policies, read his literature, corresponded with him, subscribed to political and economic ideas similar to his, and imitated him on every suitable occasion.

These facts account, in large part at least, for that similarity in development mentioned above. Its chief characteristics can be classified under five main heads: 1. The theory of the divine right of kings and its opponents. 2. The economic, social, and political pressures of a rising middle class. 3. The theory and practice of mercantilism. 4. Territorial expansion and conflict. 5. The influence of rationalism. These five characteristics were often closely interrelated. Each is discussed briefly in the paragraphs that follow, and the readings of this entire section are mainly devoted to the illustration of these five characteristics from nation to nation in the era under survey.

The Theory of the Divine Right of Kings and Its Opponents

Briefly stated, the theory of the divine right of kings maintained that governments originated among men by the direct institution of God; that God created the *office* (not the person) of kingship; that kings, having thus derived their authority from heaven, possessed supreme power, subject to no checks by man-made constitutions or parliaments; that rebellion against such divinely instituted authority was rebellion against God's will; that the king, as God's vicegerent, owned the lands and the persons of his state, and therefore whatever use people made of the properties as well as whatever liberty was allowed to the subjects were grants from the king's grace, ever liable to modification or recall; that kings were instituted among men for mankind's own benefit, but a bad king must be tolerated without revolt as a visitation of divine wrath upon a people for their sins.

The theory was not new. Christian philosophy had long subscribed to the divine origin of "the power of the two swords," ecclesiastical and civil. Modern kings simply elevated the idea to justify their authority, first in struggles against the popes and then in conflicts with their own subjects. It became the theoretical justification for despotic absolutism as exemplified by such statements as Louis XIV's famous remark, *"L'état, c'est moi"* [I am the state] and the choleric claims of Frederick William I of Prussia that "Salvation belongs to the Lord; everything else is my affair." In several instances, it is apparent that subscription to the theory of the divine right of kings made monarchs keenly aware of their enormous responsibilities. To wield such vast powers required training, intelligence of a high order, and much hard work. The "divine-right" monarch, if he was conscientious, tended to become not only an absolutist but also an "enlightened" king; for the identification of the state with the monarch meant that the advancement of the one enriched the other. The king became the chief servant as well as the master of his people.

In time, certain defects became apparent in the application of this theory. The organization of the state tended to become a vast hierarchy of bureaucratic officials each dependent upon the king himself, so that few kings were physically or intellectually able to manage such a huge structure without fatal errors and serious delays. A miracle man was necessary to fill such a position. Such miracle men were few in number (if, indeed, they existed at all), and, finally, there was no guarantee that they would beget miracle sons to carry on their exacting tasks.

Even before these defects were recognized, however, the theory of the divine right of kings had been challenged again and again. Protestants in France and in the Netherlands, Puritans and parliamentarians in England, English colonists in America—all protested against the theory and appealed to another ancient theory of the origin of the state; namely, that civil power was *man-made,* that it derived from the *consent* of the people given in a kind of *contract* between the governors and the governed. This contract, written or unwritten, erected governments, defined limits to their power, established rights of the people, and whenever a governor overstepped the bounds of this "constitution," the governed possessed the right of rebellion against him.

Throughout the Era of Enlightened Despotism, in nearly every state in Europe, these two theories at one time or another came into conflict. Civil wars were fought and pamphlet wars raged in an effort to establish the ascendancy of one or the other. By 1750, such "enlightened despots" as Frederick the Great in Prussia and Joseph II in the Holy Roman Empire had adopted the contract theory and held that they were kings by contract—but that by the terms of the contract they had been invested with absolute powers! Even the French Revolution did not entirely eradicate the theory of the divine right of kings from the minds of important European statesmen.

The Economic, Social, and Political Pressures of a Rising Middle Class

Fundamentally, pressures arose because of two facts: The "privileged classes" of European society, the clergy and the nobility, no longer performed such socially useful tasks as to warrant their privileged positions in society and government; and a new class of merchants and professional men, the bourgeoisie, was developing in such numbers and social importance as to demand greater privileges than they had legally and socially been permitted to enjoy. In general, the kings of European states were caught between these two opposing factions and while they disciplined the privileged classes, they were forced to surrender great concessions to the rising bourgeoisie.

As a rule, the nobility resisted the royal extensions of authority in the collection of taxes, the organization of the army, and the administration of justice, standing upon the precedents of their customary, feudal privileges; while the kings, by virtue of their divine-right claims to absolutism and in the interests of greater national unity and efficiency, sought to reorganize and centralize their controls. Evidences of this conflict between the "localism" of the nobility and the centralization of the monarchs will be seen in almost every state—in the Fronde troubles of France and the elaborate pains of Louis XIV to lessen the power of the nobility, in the reorganizations of the state at the hands of Prussian monarchs, in the conflicts between the Russian monarchs and the boyars, and in the futile efforts of Joseph II to modernize the administration of the Empire.

Similarly, the clergy, though they sometimes possessed enormous areas of land in the kingdom, insisted upon retaining exemption from taxation, upon the right to be tried in their own ecclesiastical courts without interference from civil authorities, and upon the privilege of selecting their own ecclesiastical officers without governmental interference—even though these officers sometimes exerted a powerful influence over matters of a political and civil nature, such as control of education, of marriage and divorce laws, of vital statistics, and of probate records. Like the nobility's claims, the clergy's stubborn grasp upon these privileges, inherited from the medieval age, constituted a threat to the absolutism of kingly powers, and everywhere, to some degree, the conflict between the royal power and the clergy is evident. Again, although the French Revolution swept aside the pretensions of the clergy in most of Europe, the problems of "clericalism," especially in the control of education, arose to plague civil authorities in the nineteenth and twentieth centuries.

Lastly, the rising middle class demanded a larger recognition and share in political control. Unlike the clergy, it was disorganized; unlike the nobility, it could lay few claims to legal precedents; but it possessed an all-powerful weapon in the eyes of a harassed king, the power of the purse. It controlled the industry, the trade, the financial structure of the nation. A monarch was compelled either to assume control of the economic affairs of his state as a governmental monopoly (as the Russian monarchs did, and thus there developed no powerful independent middle class in Russia), or to depend upon the bourgeoisie for most of his financial credit (as was generally true elsewhere in Europe). That monarch who did not meet the demands of the middle classes faced, in time, bankruptcy, revolution, or both. This circumstance goes far to explain many of the concessions granted by "absolute" kings to their merchant subjects, to explain many of their internal improvements in roads, harbors, canals, and the like, and to explain the existence of bankers and merchants in the inner councils of the kings. Of course, co-operation was mutually beneficial, inasmuch as a prosperous middle class accompanied a wealthy and powerful kingdom.

The Theory and Practice of Mercantilism

A compelling feature in the interrelationships of monarchs and their middle-class subjects was the widespread acceptance in Europe of a set of economic ideas generally called mercantilism. To be sure, mercantilist economics was not everywhere accepted (the Dutch, for example, gave little attention to it), nor was it applied in the same fashion in every European state. But the policies of most states were colored by mercantilism in regard to internal economic matters, colonial relations, and foreign affairs.

Mercantilist economics centered about a peculiar concept of wealth called *bullionism,* a belief that the wealth of a nation was measured solely in terms of gold, silver, and precious gems. To increase a nation's wealth, then, it was necessary merely to augment the supply of these items. As few European states possessed important gold and silver mines with which to add to their wealth, it was possible to increase the supply of gold and silver by manipulating commerce so as to have perennially a favorable balance of trade; that is, to export more than was purchased abroad, so that the difference could be received in gold and silver. The attempts to maintain a favorable balance of trade led, in turn, to a high degree of state regulation and control of national economy, a policy which fitted well into the absolutism of divine-right despotism. Accordingly, the state kept a close check upon the supplies of gold and silver, forbade their exportation either as cash or as manufactured wares, established new industries and curtailed old ones in the interests of national economic self-sufficiency, became interested in colonial ventures in an effort both to gain control over raw materials not available at home and to expand markets and the carrying trade of the nation, and carefully regulated the quantities and qualities of goods which figured importantly in international trade in order to extend sales and forbid purchases abroad as much as possible. In the interests of easier control, it became customary for states to center industries and commerce in individuals or companies which possessed a chartered monopoly of a stated industry or trade. In time, these methods tended to "freeze" technological improvements and forbid private ventures, so that both illicit commerce and demands for "free trade" and individual enterprise arose. It is important to note that mercantilism was concerned chiefly with wealth as a basis of *state power,* rather than wealth as an asset to *individuals.* Before the Era of Enlightened Despotism had drawn to a close, whole new schools of economic thought had arisen, in opposition to the state-regulated economy of mercantilism, emphasizing the importance of wealth to individuals and proclaiming advantages in technique and vastly greater wealth-multiplying powers through freedom of trade and of individual enterprise.

Territorial Expansion and International Conflicts

A regrettable feature of the absolutist king was his tendency to seek prestige by force of arms, to evaluate his own and his neighbor's worth by the wealth of territory and populations controlled rather than by the quality of his justice or the standards of living enjoyed by his subjects. Circumstances combined to produce this situation in nearly every state. Added to the personal ambitions and dynastic jealousies of monarchs was the stupid adulation of peoples for a military conqueror. Constant shifts in the European balance of power necessitated new alliances and new strategically valuable territorial acquisitions in the interests of greater national security. Moreover, the requirements of mercantilistic economics led to territorial aggrandizement and international struggles for raw materials, markets, port facilities, for commercially important rivers or other centers of trade, and for overseas colonies. Accordingly, the Era of Enlightened Despotism is a period of almost continual warfare with the points in dispute no longer matters of religious concern but primarily dynastic, economic, and material in nature.

The Influence of Rationalism

Renaissance man had emphasized the worth and capacities of man in this world by proclaiming that "Man can do all things if he will." Furthermore, by means of the new experimental, inductive method, Renaissance scholars had discovered enough that was new in the realms of physics, astronomy, medicine, and geography to undermine the old authoritarian attitudes and to gain a wide hearing for the new "experimental philosophy." Now, in the seventeenth and eighteenth centuries, as concern for religion was increasingly displaced by secular ambition, men came more and more to rely upon their own rational powers of observation and induction, and the new science found all but universal favor. Kings fostered it by means of national academies and grants of money for experimental purposes, universities adopted it in their curricula, and literary men praised it in prose and poetry.

Fundamental to these developments was a new faith in the rational powers of man. Human reason came to be looked upon as the key to all knowledge. Scientists identified reason with experimental science; philosophers identified it with the law of nature; political theorists identified it with the law of nations; and theologians identified it with the law of God. "Sweet reasonableness" became the final test of all things. Scientists and philosophers rescued one after another of the laws of nature from the wild speculations of Aristotle and other ancient authorities and molded them, upon the basis of experiments and observations, into rational patterns. Political writers ignored the dross of customs and legal precedents and reconstructed constitutions and the laws of states upon the basis of rationalism. Theologians even toyed with the idea of "natural religion," and Deists, by ruling out miracles as irrational, constructed a "rational faith" so unorthodox that clerics of all denominations condemned it bitterly.

Such was the Age of Reason, a phase of European intellectual history embraced within the Era of Enlightened Despotism. Before the middle of the seventeenth century it was well developed in England, where it ran its course for nearly a century. It spread to France about 1700 and enveloped the Continent during most of the eighteenth century. Before the French Revolution, however, a reaction had set in against the omnipotence of reason and, in the realm of literature in particular, a new age of romanticism displaced the rule of reason.

16   THE ENGLISH STRUGGLE OVER PREROGATIVE

Throughout most of the seventeenth century England was torn by political and constitutional conflicts. Basically, these conflicts centered about two problems. The first was the question of prerogative, that is, whether the elements of supreme political power in England belonged to the King or to the Parliament. In this struggle, both parties to the conflict made extravagant claims to power which went far beyond the accepted constitutional theory and practice of English polity. The Stuart kings (especially James I, 1603-25, and Charles I, 1625-49) rested their case principally upon the theory of the divine right of kings. James, though he said that a king "leaves to be a king and degenerates into a tyrant as soon as he leaves off to rule according to his laws" (that is, "the fundamental laws of his kingdom"), nevertheless likened his powers to those of a god: "kings . . . make and unmake their subjects; they have the power of raising, and casting down; of life, and of death: judges over their subjects, and in all causes, and yet accountable to none but God only." And he made sure that the courts of England interpreted the "fundamental laws" in accord with his claims. Parliament countered these royal pretensions with equally extravagant claims of its own, and all England divided on the issue, one faction supporting the King, another, the Parliament. As a whole, Puritans, who inclined toward representative institutions in government, and who were outraged at James's policy of making them conform to the English Church or he "would harry them out of the land," supported the parliamentary faction.

The second major problem concerned Puritans and the church. Broadly speaking, two puritan groups existed, each with an ecclesiastical policy unacceptable to the King and his supporters. One group, the Presbyterians, sought to make over the Church of England into a new state church on a presbyterian pattern, vaguely resembling the Kirk of Scotland and with a policy of stern intolerance and extirpation toward dissenting sects. The other group, the Independents, was a coalition group of Congregationalists, Baptists, and others, who wished to separate Church and State, place the church on a voluntary basis, and throw open the doors of religious toleration to a variety of sects. In effect, these issues boiled down to the question of religious toleration for those sects that dissented from the state church.

Two bloody civil wars were fought over these issues (1642-46 and 1647-49), a king (Charles I) was beheaded (1649), and a bloodless "Glorious Revolution" took place (1688-89) before these issues were permanently settled in England in favor of parliamentary supremacy and toleration for a selected group of sects. Meanwhile, in the midst of these bitter conflicts, a number of opinions were set forth and a few important private and state papers emerged which greatly enlarged the English tradition of liberty, permanently colored English political thinking, and pointed up to some of the opinions expressed by Americans at the time of the American Revolution. In an era of growing absolutism, England preserved constitutional liberty by reasserting limits to arbitrary government, by setting forth the rights of individuals, and by extending the powers of a representative Parliament.

1. King James on the Divine Right of Kings

Some of the most extreme statements of the divine right of kings theory were made by James I (1603-25). As James VI of Scotland, before he succeeded Elizabeth to the English throne, he had set forth the doctrine in a book, *The True Law of Free Monarchies* (1598). To his first English Parliament in 1603 he proclaimed, "I am the husband, and the whole isle is my lawful wife; I am the head, and it is my body." Later, on March 21, 1609, he enlarged further upon the theory in a speech before the houses of Parliament.

From *The Works of James I* (1609) [1]

The state of monarchy is the supremest thing upon earth; for kings are not only God's lieutenants upon earth, and sit upon God's throne, but even by God himself they are called gods. There be three principal similitudes that illustrate the state of

[1] *The Works of the Most High and Mightie Prince, James . . . King of Great Britaine,* London, 1616, 529, 537.

monarchy: one taken out of the word of God; and the two other out of the grounds of policy and philosophy. In the Scriptures kings are called gods, and so their power after a certain relation compared to the divine power. Kings are also compared to fathers of families: for a king is truly *Parens patriae,* the politique father of his people. And lastly, kings are compared to the head of this microcosm of the body of man.

Kings are justly called gods, for that they exercise a manner or resemblance of divine power upon earth: for if you will consider the attributes to God, you shall see how they agree in the person of a king. God hath power to create or destroy, make or unmake at his pleasure, to give life or send death, to judge all and to be judged nor accountable to none; to raise low things and to make high things low at his pleasure, and to God are both soul and body due. And the like power have kings: they make and unmake their subjects, they have power of raising and casting down, of life and of death, judges over all their subjects and in all causes and yet accountable to none but God only. They have power to exalt low things and abase high things, and make of their subjects like men at the chess, a pawn to take a bishop or a knight, and to cry up or down any of their subjects, as they do their money. And to the king is due both the affection of the soul and the service of the body of his subjects. . . . I would wish you to be careful to avoid three things in the matter of grievances:

First, that you do not meddle with the main points of government; that is my craft . . . to meddle with that were to lesson [teach] me. I am now an old king; for six and thirty years have I governed in Scotland personally, and now have I accomplished my apprenticeship of seven years here; and seven years is a great time for a king's experience in government. . . . I must not be taught my office.

Secondly, I would not have you meddle with such ancient rights of mine as I have received from my predecessors, possessing them, *more majorum;* such things I would be sorry should be accounted for grievances. All novelties are dangerous as well in a politic as in a natural body, and therefore I would be loath to be quarreled in my ancient rights and possessions; for that were to judge me unworthy of that which my predecessors had and left me.

And lastly, I pray you beware to exhibit for grievance anything that is established by a settled law, and whereunto (as you have already had a proof) you know I will never give a plausible answer; for it is an undutiful part in subjects to press their king, wherein they know beforehand he will refuse them.

2. *King James's Dislike of Puritans: The Hampton Court Conference (1604)*

English Puritans, having suffered greatly because of their discontent with the Elizabethan church settlement [see page 144], held high hopes at the accession of King James. In Scotland James had appeared friendly toward Presbyterians, and when he arrived in England the Puritans eagerly presented him with a petition (called the Millenary Petition because it reputedly bore a thousand signatures) setting forth their demands for further reformation of the English Church. But James had borne with Scottish reformers out of necessity, and he had no intention of permitting English Puritans to challenge his authority as head of the Anglican Church.

At a conference of churchmen held at Hampton Court (January, 1604), James treated puritan ministers with abrupt severity, as the following account demonstrates.

From NEAL, *The Puritans* (1738) [1]

The place of conference was the drawing-room within the privy-chamber at Hampton Court; the disputants on both sides were nominated by the king. For the Church there were nine bishops, and about as many dignitaries. . . .

For the Puritans were only four ministers: Dr. John Raynolds, Dr. Thomas Sparks, professors of divinity in Oxford; Mr. Chadderton and Mr. Knewstubs, of Cambridge. . . .

The conference continued three days, viz., January the 14th, 16th, and 18th; the first was with the bishops and deans alone, January 14th, the Puritan ministers not being present, when the king made a speech in commendation of the hierarchy of the Church of England, and congratulated himself that "he was now come into the promised land; that he sat among grave and reverend men, and was not a king, as formerly, without state, nor in a place where beardless boys would brave him to his face. He assured them he had not called this assembly for any innovation, for he acknowledged the government ecclesiastical, as now it is, to have been approved by manifold blessings from God himself; but because he had received some complaints of disorders, he was willing to remove them if scandalous, and to take notice of them if but trifling. . . ."

The second day's conference was on Monday, January 16th, when the four ministers were called in. . . . Whereupon Dr. Raynolds, in the name of his brethren,

[1] Daniel Neal, *The History of the Puritans,* I, 230-32.

humbly requested: 1. That the doctrine of the Church might be preserved pure, according to God's Word. 2. That good pastors might be planted in all churches to preach the same. 3. That the Book of Common Prayer might be fitted to more increase of piety. 4. That Church government might be sincerely ministered according to God's Word. . . .

But the doctor's chief objections were to the service-book and church government. Here he complained of the late subscriptions, by which many were deprived of their ministry who were willing to subscribe to the doctrinal articles of the Church, to the king's supremacy, and to the statutes of the realm. He excepted to the reading the Apocrypha; to the interrogatories in baptism, and to the sign of the cross; to the surplice, and other superstitious habits; to the ring in marriage; to the churching of women by the name of purification. He urged that most of these things were relics of popery; that they had been abused to idolatry, and therefore ought, like the brazen serpent, to be abolished. Mr. Knewstubs said these rites and ceremonies were at best but indifferent, and therefore doubted whether the power of the Church could bind the conscience without impeaching Christian liberty.

Here his majesty interrupted them, and said that he apprehended the surplice to be a very comely garment; that the cross was as old as Constantine, and must we charge him with popery. . . . "But as to the power of the Church in things indifferent," says his majesty, "I will not argue that point with you, but answer as kings in Parliament, *Le Roy s'avisera*. This is like Mr. John Black, a beardless boy, who told me, the last conference in Scotland, that he would hold conformity with me in doctrine, but that every man as to ceremonies was to be left to his own liberty,

but I will have none of that; I will have one doctrine, one discipline, one religion in substance and ceremony: never speak more to that point, how far you are bound to obey."

Dr. Raynolds . . . desired that the clergy might have assemblies once in three weeks; that in rural deaneries they might have the liberty of prophesyings . . . that those cases which could not be resolved there might be referred to the archdeacon's visitation, and from thence to the diocesan synod, where the bishop with his presbyters should determine such points as were too difficult for the other meetings. Here the king broke out into a flame, and instead of hearing the doctor's reasons, or commanding his bishops to answer them, told the ministers that he found they were aiming at a Scots presbytery, "which," says he, "agrees with monarchy as well as God and the devil; then Jack and Tom, Will and Dick, shall meet, and at their pleasure censure both me and my council. Therefore, pray stay one seven years before you demand that of me, and if then you find me pursy and fat, and my windpipe stuffed, I will perhaps hearken to you; for let that government be up, and I am sure I shall be kept in breath; but till you find I grow lazy, pray let that alone." . . . Then turning to the bishops, he put his hand to his hat and said, "My lords, I may thank you that these Puritans plead for my supremacy, for if once you are out and they in place, I know what would become of my supremacy, for, No bishop, no king. Well, doctor, have you anything else to offer?" Dr. Raynolds: "No more, if it please your majesty." Then rising from his chair, the king said, "If this be all your party have to say, I will make them conform, or I will harry them out of this land, or else worse"; and he was as good as his word.

3. Some Fruits of Stuart Policies Early in the Reign of Charles I

THE PETITION OF RIGHT (1628)

Besides their claims to divine-right absolutism and their severe treatment of Puritans, the first two Stuart kings (James I and Charles I) pursued other policies disliked by large sections of English people. Their foreign policies were vastly disapproved. James followed a pacific policy, not only to the extent of making an unpopular peace with Catholic Spain, but also of seeking to marry his son and heir to the Spanish Infanta. And when this effort failed, James arranged for Charles to marry the haughty, devoutly Catholic daughter of France, Henrietta Maria, whose imperious ways were a constant irritant to English Protestants. Moreover, the monarchs failed to offer material aid to the German Protestants in the Thirty Years' War, although James's daughter (and Charles's sister) was wife of one of the German Protestant leaders, Frederick, Elector of the Palatinate [see page 195], and English public opinion ran far ahead of the kings' in favoring his cause.

The kings' internal policies were even more distasteful. Partly because of lavish grants to court favorites and partly because of an unavoidable growth of expenses, James and Charles often found themselves in financial difficulties. Accordingly, they resorted to extraordinary means to raise money, and the Parliaments, always jealous of their constitutional rights in financial matters, protested. Lawyers questioned the legality of the kings' acts; merchants objected to new and unusual duties on their commerce; both groups challenged the monarchs' right to raise money without parliamentary grant. As a consequence, the kings encountered increasingly stiff parliamentary opposition until Parliament countered each royal demand for money with requests for guarantees of the rights of subjects and Puritans added their bid for "reformation" in Church and State. Puritans, moreover, were further embittered by the Declaration of Sports (1618) wherein James declared, "for his people's lawful recreations, his pleasure was that, after the end of Divine service, they should not be disturbed . . . or discouraged from lawful recreations, such as dancing either of men or women, archery for men, leaping, vaulting, or any such harmless recreations; nor from having May games, Whitsun ales, or morris dances, and setting up of May-poles, or other sports therewith used, so as the same be had in due and convenient time, without impediment . . . of Divine service." Puritans objected to this Declaration—which Charles I ill-advisedly reissued in 1633—because many of the sports seemed to desecrate the Sabbath, because the dancing often appeared lascivious and immoral, and because Maypoles were considered pagan in origin and popish in nature.

After 1625, Charles I repeatedly dismissed Parliaments only to find the next more exacting in its demands. When his third Parliament assembled (March, 1628), Charles ominously threatened to "use those other means which God hath put in my hands" unless his fiscal demands were promptly met. But Parliament ignored the threat and fell to airing "their just grievances" until Charles—never a firm, unfaltering hand—sought to placate it with a verbal promise "That he holdeth the Statute of Magna Carta and the other six statutes insisted upon for the subjects' liberty to be all in force, and assureth you that he will maintain all his subjects in the just freedom of their persons and safety of their estates."

But Parliament was still dissatisfied, and Sir Edward Coke demanded: "Was it ever known that general words were a sufficient satisfaction to particular grievances? Was ever a verbal declaration of the King a law of the land? When grievances be, parliament is to redress them. . . . Let us put up a Petition of Right: not that I distrust the King, but that I cannot take his trust but in a parliamentary way." The petition which Sir Edward demanded was soon drawn up and presented to Charles (June 7, 1628). By its appeal to Magna Carta and its bold assertion of the rights of the people against royal prerogative, it constituted an important document in defining the rights and liberties of English-speaking peoples everywhere.

From *The Petition of Right* (1628) [1]

TO THE KING'S MOST EXCELLENT MAJESTY

Humbly show unto our Sovereign Lord the King, the Lords Spiritual and Temporal, and Commons in Parliament assembled, that whereas it is declared and enacted by a statute made in the time of the reign of King Edward the First, commonly called *Statutum de Tallagio non concedendo,* that no tallage or aid shall be laid or levied by the King or his heirs in this realm, without the goodwill and assent of the Archbishops, Bishops, Earls, Barons, Knights, Burgesses, and other the freemen of the commonalty of this realm: and by authority of Parliament holden in the five and twentieth year of the reign of King Edward the Third, it is declared and enacted, that from thenceforth no person

shall be compelled to make any loans to the King against his will, because such loans were against reason and the franchise of the land; and by other laws of this realm it . . . [appears that] your subjects have inherited this freedom, that they should not be compelled to contribute to any tax, tallage, aid, or other like charge, not set by common consent in Parliament:

Yet nevertheless, of late divers commissions directed to sundry Commissioners in several counties with instructions have issued, by means whereof your people have been in divers places assembled, and required to lend certain sums of money unto your Majesty, and many of them upon their refusal so to do . . . have been constrained to become bound to make appearance and give attendance before your Privy Council . . . and others of them have been therefore imprisoned, confined, and sundry other ways molested and disquieted. . . .

And where also by the statute called, "The Great Charter of the Liberties of England," it is declared and enacted, that no freeman may be taken or imprisoned or be disseized of his freeholds or liberties, or his free customs, or be outlawed or exiled; or in any manner destroyed, but by the lawful judgment of his peers, or by the law of the land:

And in the eight and twentieth year of the reign of King Edward the Third, it was declared and enacted by authority of Parliament, that no man of what estate or condition that he be, should be put out of his lands or tenements, nor taken, nor imprisoned, nor disherited, nor put to death, without being brought to answer by due process of law:

Nevertheless, against the tenor of the said statutes, and other the good laws and statutes of your realm, to that end provided, divers of your subjects have of late been imprisoned without any cause showed. . . .

[1] Samuel Rawson Gardiner, *The Constitutional Documents of the Puritan Revolution,* 3d ed., rev., 1906, 66-70. By permission of The Clarendon Press, Oxford.

And whereas of late great companies of soldiers and mariners have been dispersed into divers counties of the realm, and the inhabitants against their wills have been compelled to receive them into their houses, and there to suffer them to sojourn, against the laws and customs of this realm, and to the great grievance and vexation of the people. . . .

They [the Parliament] do therefore humbly pray your Most Excellent Majesty, that no man hereafter be compelled to make or yield any gift, loan, benevolence, tax, or such like charge, without common consent by Act of Parliament; and that none be called to make answer, or take such oath, or to give attendance, or be confined, or otherwise molested or disquieted concerning the same, or for refusal thereof; and that no freeman, in any such manner as is before-mentioned, be imprisoned or detained; and that your Majesty will be pleased to remove the said soldiers and mariners, and that your people may not be so burdened in time to come; and that the foresaid commissions for proceeding by martial law, may be revoked and annulled. . . .

All which they most humbly pray of your most Excellent Majesty, as their rights and liberties according to the laws and statutes of this realm.

[Less than a year after the presentation of the above Petition, Charles I, after tumultuous scenes in Parliament, dissolved it and vowed that he would call no more Parliaments until they would do his bidding. For eleven years thereafter (1629-40) the King governed without a Parliament, a period often called "The Personal Government of Charles I."]

THE PURITAN EMIGRATIONS

Even before Charles I's dismissal of Parliament seemed to close all hopes of reformation in Church or in State, many Puritans had sought safety abroad. At first most of them emigrated to the Dutch Netherlands, where broad religious toleration and prosperous commerce made possible their existence. That group is probably best known which, under care of their pastor, John Robinson, left Scrooby in Yorkshire and settled in Holland for a dozen years; finally, in 1620, a portion of them founded the puritan colony of New Plymouth in America. But others followed, and soon Plymouth Plantation was enveloped by her more populous and prosperous neighbor, the Massachusetts Bay Colony (1630), offshoots from which established Connecticut and Rhode Island (1636). Indeed, in the decade 1630-40, during the personal government of Charles I, about twenty thousand puritan emigrants settled in New England, most of them leaving old England because of political and religious dissatisfaction. John Winthrop (1588-1649), repeatedly chosen governor of the Massachusetts Bay Colony, left a summary of the chief reasons for this migration, as he understood them.

From WINTHROP, "Reasons for Going to New England" (1629) [1]

1. It will be a service to the Church of great consequence to carry the Gospel into those parts of the world . . . & to raise a bulwark against the kingdom of Antichrist which the [French and Spanish] Jesuits labor to rear up in those parts.

2. All other churches of Europe are brought to desolation . . . & who knows, but that God hath provided this place to

[1] "Reasons to be considered for justifying the undertakers of the intended Plantation in New England & for incouraging such whose hearts God shall move to join with them in it."—R. C. Winthrop, *Life and Letters of John Winthrop*, 2 vols., Boston, 1864, I, 309-13.

be a refuge for many whom he means to save out of the general calamity, & seeing the Church hath no place left to fly into but the wilderness, what better work can there be, than to go & provide tabernacles & food for her against she comes thither.

3. This land grows weary of her inhabitants. . . . All towns complain of the burden of their poor, though we have taken up many unnecessary, yea, unlawful trades to maintain them, & we use the authority of the law to hinder the increase of our people, as by urging the Statute against cottages, & inmates, & thus it is come to pass, that children, servants & neighbors, especially if they be poor, are counted the greatest burdens, which if things were right would be the chiefest earthly blessings.

4. The whole earth is the Lord's garden & he hath given it to the sons of men with a general commission: Gen. 1:28: increase & multiply, & replenish the earth & subdue it . . . the end is double & natural, that man might enjoy the fruits of the earth, & God might have his due glory from the creature: why then should we stand striving here for places of habitation . . . & in the mean time suffer a whole continent as fruitful & convenient for the use of man to lie waste without any improvement?

5. We are grown to that height of intemperance in all excess of riot, as no man's estate almost will suffice to keep sail with his equals: & he who fails herein, must live in scorn & contempt. Hence it comes that all arts & trades are carried in that deceitful & unrighteous course, as it is almost impossible for a good & upright man to maintain his charge & live comfortably in any of them.

6. The fountains of learning & religion are so corrupted as (besides the unsupportable charge of their education) most children (even the best wits & of fairest hopes) are perverted, corrupted, & utterly overthrown by the multitude of evil examples & the licentious government of those seminaries. . . .

7. What can be a better work, & more honorable & worthy a Christian than to help raise & support a particular church while it is in the infancy, & to joyn his forces with such a company of faithful people, as by a timely assistance may grow strong & prosper, & for want of it may be put to great hazard, if not wholly ruined? . . .

9. It appears to be a work of God for the good of his church, in that he hath disposed the hearts of so many of his wise & faithful servants, both ministers & others, not only to approve of the enterprise but to interest themselves in it.

4. The Clash of Parliament and King: The Nineteen Propositions

Late in the 1630's, Charles I sought to extend the English Church into Presbyterian Scotland. The effort provoked stubborn resistance which soon developed into war. Financial necessities growing out of the Scottish War forced Charles to call a Parliament (April, 1640). But Parliament refused to vote money unless the King came to terms with the Scots, and Charles angrily dismissed it after three weeks— hence its name, the "Short Parliament." Before the summer ended, however, Charles could not avoid issuing writs for another Parliament, which, meeting in November, 1640, did not dissolve for nearly twenty years (though often "purged" and temporarily replaced by Cromwell's assemblies), and is known, accordingly, as the "Long Parliament." From the first it adopted a thoroughly defiant attitude toward the King. It demanded revolutionary reforms in the Church, passed such acts as the Triennial Act, requiring Parliaments at least every three years, an "Act against Dissolving Parliament without Its Own Consent," and acts which abolished the Star Chamber, the Court of High Commission, and Ship-Money; it presented (December 1, 1641) a "Grand Remonstrance" which listed over two hundred items of protest against the abuse of royal power by the King's "evil advisors." Meanwhile, the Irish, taking advantage of English disorders, arose in bloody rebellion in October, 1641. To deal with them an army was needed, but an army in the King's hands could also be used to subdue Parliament. Accordingly, Parliament passed an ordinance (March 15, 1642) appointing its own officers of the militia—an act which directly challenged the King's authority as commander in chief of armed forces. Both parties to the dispute had long since overstepped the bounds of English constitutional authority. The question was whether King or Parliament was to be sovereign, as the following ultimatum sent by Parliament to the King, June 1, 1642, will demonstrate.

From the "Nineteen Propositions" (June 1, 1642) [1]

Your Majesty's most humble and faithful subjects, the Lords and Commons in Parliament, having nothing in their thoughts and desires more precious and of higher esteem, next to the honour and immediate service of God, than the just and faithful performance of their duty to your Majesty and this kingdom, and being very sensible of the great distractions and distempers, and of the imminent dangers and calamities which those distractions and distempers are like to bring

[1] *Journals of the House of Lords,* London, 1767 ff., V, 97-99.

upon your Majesty and your subjects . . . do in all humility and sincerity present to your Majesty their most dutiful petition and advice, that . . . you will be pleased to grant and accept these their humble desires and propositions as the most necessary effectual means, through God's blessing, of removing those jealousies and differences which have unhappily fallen betwixt you and your people, and procuring both your Majesty and them a constant course of honour, peace, and happiness.

1. That the Lords and others of your Majesty's Privy Council, and such great officers and Ministers of State, either at home or beyond the seas, may be put from your Privy Council, and from those offices and employments, excepting such as shall be approved of by both Houses of Parliament; and that the persons put into the places and employments of those that are removed may be approved of by both Houses of Parliament; and that the Privy Councillors shall take an oath for the due execution of their places, in such form as shall be agreed upon by both Houses of Parliament.

2. That the great affairs of the kingdom may not be concluded or transacted by the advice of private men, or by any unknown or unsworn councillors, but that such matters as concern the public, and are proper for the High Court of Parliament, which is your Majesty's great and supreme council, may be debated, resolved and transacted only in Parliament and not elsewhere. . . .

3. That the Lord High Steward of England, Lord High Constable, Lord Chancellor, or Lord Keeper of the Great Seal, Lord Treasurer, Lord Privy Seal, Earl Marshall, Lord Admiral, Warden of the Cinque Ports, Chief Governor of Ireland, Chancellor of the Exchequer, Master of the Wards, Secretaries of State, two Chief Justices and Chief Baron may al-

ways be chosen with the approbation of both Houses of Parliament. . . .

4. That he, or they, unto whom the government and education of the King's children shall be committed shall be approved by both Houses of Parliament. . . .

5. That no marriage shall be concluded or treated for. any of the King's children with any foreign prince, or any person whatsoever, abroad or at home, without the consent of Parliament. . . .

6. That the laws in force against Jesuits, priests, and Popish recusants be strictly put into execution, without any toleration or dispensation to the contrary. . . .

7. That the votes of Popish lords in the House of Peers may be taken away so long as they continue Papists; and that your Majesty will consent to such a Bill as shall be drawn for the education of the children of Papists by Protestants in the Protestant religion. . . .

8. That your Majesty will be pleased to consent that such a reformation be made of the Church government and liturgy as both Houses of Parliament shall advise, wherein they intend to have consultations with divines . . . and that your Majesty will be pleased to give your consent to laws for the taking away of innovations and superstition, and of pluralities, and against scandalous ministers.

9. That your Majesty will be pleased to rest satisfied with that course that the Lords and Commons have appointed for ordering of the militia until the same shall be further settled by a Bill. . . .

10. That such members of either House of Parliament as have . . . been put out of any place and office may be either restored to that place and office, or otherwise have satisfaction for the same, upon petition of that House whereof he or they are members.

11. That all Privy Councillors and Judges may take an oath, the form whereof to be agreed on and settled by Act of Parliament, for the maintaining of the Petition of Right and of certain statutes made by the Parliament which shall be mentioned by both Houses of Parliament. . . .

12. That all the Judges, and all the officers placed by approbation of both Houses of Parliament, may hold their places *quamdiu bene se gesserint* [during good behavior].

13. That the justice of Parliament may pass upon all delinquents . . . and that all persons cited by either House of Parliament may appear and abide the censure of Parliament.

14. That the general pardon offered by your Majesty may be granted with such exceptions as shall be advised by both Houses of Parliament.

15. That the forts and castles of this kingdom may be put under the command and custody of such persons as your Majesty shall appoint with the approbation of your Parliament. . . .

16. That the extraordinary guards and military forces now attending your Majesty may be removed and discharged; and that for the future you will raise no such guards . . . but according to the law. . . .

17. That your Majesty will be pleased to enter into a more strict alliance with the States of the United Provinces and other neighbour princes and states of the Protestant religion, for the defense and maintenance thereof. . . .

19. That your Majesty will be graciously pleased to pass a Bill for restraining peers made hereafter from sitting or voting in Parliament unless they be admitted thereunto with the consent of both Houses of Parliament.

And these our humble desires being granted by your Majesty, we shall forthwith apply ourselves to regulate your present revenue in such sort as may be for your best advantage . . . and cheerfully employ to the uttermost of our power and endeavour in the real expression and performance of our most dutiful and loyal affections, to the preserving and maintaining the royal honour, greatness, and safety of your Majesty and your posterity.

THE KING'S REACTION

Acceptance of the above propositions would have meant, as Charles clearly recognized, government by Parliament instead of government by King. An account of Charles' reaction follows.

From FIRTH, *Oliver Cromwell* (1902) [1]

"These being passed," he answered, "we may be waited upon bareheaded, we may have our hand kissed, the style of majesty continued to us, and the King's authority declared by both Houses of Parliament may still be the style of your commands, we may have swords and maces carried before us, and please ourselves with the sight of a crown and sceptre, but as to true and real power we should remain but the outside, but the picture, but the sign of a king."

On the other side, their demand, as it presented itself to the minds of the Parliamentarians, was rather defensive than aggressive in its intention. Without this transference of sovereignty, they held it impossible to transmit to their descendants the self-government they had received from their ancestors.

"The question in dispute between us and the King's party," says Ludlow, "was, as I apprehended, whether the King should govern as a god by his will and the nation be governed by force like beasts; or whether the people should be governed by laws made by themselves,

and live under a government derived from their own consent."

Only the sword could decide. On July 4th [1642], Parliament appointed a Committee of Safety; on July 6th, they resolved to raise ten thousand men; on July 9th, they appointed the Earl of Essex their general. The King set up his standard at Nottingham on August 22nd.

5. Revolutionary Parties and Principles, 1642-1660

Between the outbreak of war (August 22, 1642) and the execution of Charles I (January 30, 1649), two distinct civil wars occurred in England. The first was between King and Parliament, and it ended (1646) when Charles I was made a prisoner pending a satisfactory treaty settlement. Until 1645, however, the King's forces had been generally successful, and not until Parliament organized its "New Model" army (winter, 1644-45) under the command of General Thomas Fairfax and Lieutenant General Oliver Cromwell were the fortunes of war reversed in Parliament's favor. Between Parliament and the New Model army, however, dissensions soon arose. The Long Parliament was dominated by Presbyterians who, with Scottish connivance, sought to remold the English Church in an exclusive Presbyterian pattern. The New Model, on the other hand, was dominated by Independents, a motley crowd of sectaries led chiefly by Congregationalists, who demanded, as their minimum requirement, a toleration for the religious sectaries (excluding Catholics) in England. As neither side trusted the other in its negotiations with the fallen King, the second civil war began (1647), the New Model army of Independents (with the

[1] Sir Charles Firth, *Oliver Cromwell and the Rule of the Puritans in England,* ed. by Evelyn Abbott, 1902 (Heroes of the Nations), 67-68. Courtesy of G. P. Putnam's Sons.

King in its hands) against the Presbyterian Parliament and its Scottish allies. Victory fell to the New Model and its brilliant leader, Oliver Cromwell, who immediately purged the Parliament of Presbyterian members (the famous Pride's Purge, December, 1648) and, feeling they could not trust the King, erected an extraordinary court which found him guilty of high treason and sentenced him to death.

Naturally, as thousands of books and documents of the time demonstrate, feelings ran high during these years. Especially significant were the ideas relative to the state, for the Independents appealed to the theory of contract as a check upon absolutism and also set forth a reform program along the general lines of which the English government reconstructed itself during the next two hundred years. The following selections are broadly illustrative of the English Civil War era.

RICHARD BAXTER DESCRIBES THE NEW MODEL ARMY

The Reverend Richard Baxter was one of the saintliest puritan ministers of England. A mild Presbyterian, he spent most of his long life (1615-1691) trying to harmonize the discordant religious elements of England. Two days after the battle of Naseby (June 14, 1645), one of the earliest successes of the New Model army against the King, he visited the army. His impressions are representative of moderates of the time.

From BAXTER, *Narrative of His Life* (1645) [1]

Naseby not being far from Coventry where I was, and the noise of the victory

[1] Matthew Sylvester, *Reliquiae Baxterianae: or, Mr. Richard Baxter's Narrative of . . . His Life and Times,* London, 1696, 50-51.

being loud in our ears, and I having two or three that of old had been my intimate friends in Cromwell's Army, whom I had not seen of above two years, I was desirous to go see whether they were dead or alive; and so to Naseby field I went two days after the fight, and thence by the army's quarters before Leicester to seek my acquaintance. When I found them, I stayed with them a night, and I understood the state of the Army much better than ever I had done before. We that lived quietly in Coventry did keep our old principles, and thought all others had done so too, except a very few inconsiderable persons. We were unfeignedly for king and parliament. We believed that the war was only to save the parliament and kingdom from papists and delinquents, and to remove the dividers that the king might again return to his parliament, and that no changes might be made in religion but by the laws which had his free consent. We took the true happiness of king and people, church and state, to be our end. . . . And when the Court-Newsbook told the world of the swarms of Anabaptists in our armies, we thought it had been a mere lie, because it was not so with us, nor with any of the garrison or county forces about us. But when I came to the army among Cromwell's soldiers, I found a new face of things which I never dreamt of. I heard the plotting heads very hot upon that which intimated the intention to subvert both church and state. . . .

Abundance of the common troopers, and many of the officers I found to be honest, sober, orthodox men, and others tractable ready to hear the truth, and of upright intentions. But a few proud, self conceited, hot-headed sectaries had got into the highest places and were Cromwell's chief favorites, and by their very heat and activity bore down the rest, or carried them along with them, and were the soul of the army, though much fewer in number than the rest. . . .

I perceived that they took the King for a tyrant and an enemy, and really intended absolutely to master him, or to ruin him; and they thought if they might fight against him, they might kill or conquer him; and if they might conquer, they were never more to trust him further than he was in their power. . . . They plainly showed me that they thought God's Providence would cast the trust of religion and the kingdom upon them as conquerers. They made nothing of all the wise and godly in the armies and garrisons that were not of their way. *Per fas aut nefas,* by law or without it, they were resolved to take down, not only Bishops and Liturgy and Ceremonies, but all that did withstand their way. They were far from thinking of a moderate episcopacy; or of any healing way between Episcopal and the Presbyterians. They most honored the Separatists, Anabaptists, and Antinomians; but Cromwell and his council took on them to join themselves to no party, but to be for the liberty of all.

A PROPOSED CONSTITUTION FOR ENGLAND

In its efforts to achieve a satisfactory peace in England, the New Model army became a political as well as a military organization. Many of its political demands had a sound not unlike those of the Americans of '76, especially those of a group of radicals in the army known as Levellers, whose chief spokesman was John Lilburne. Among the Levellers' proposals was a new, *written constitution* for England known as the *Agreement of the People.* The gist of the *Agreement* is presented below, together with records of part of the debates in the army over its provisions. Four significant features stand out in

this document: 1. It is proposed as a written constitution, to replace the unwritten, customary "fundamental laws" theretofore forming the English constitution. 2. It implies that the government originates in an "Agreement," or contract, among the people, not upon any divine-right theories, and it states specifically that the power of the government rests upon the consent of the governed. 3. It proposes a representative body (Parliament) proportioned "according to the number of the inhabitants." 4. It declares that the rights of Englishmen are *native rights* (that is, *natural* rights?), not, as Magna Carta and the Petition of Right had stated, the "ancient" (that is, customary) rights and liberties of Englishmen. Moreover, in perusing the army debates over the *Agreement,* the student, if he is familiar with nineteenth-century struggles in democratic states between *personal* rights and *property* rights in the extension of the franchise, will see Colonel Thomas Rainborough and Commissary General Henry Ireton (Cromwell's son-in-law) representing points of view similar to those of Jefferson and Hamilton respectively in the early political struggles of the United States.

From *An Agreement of the People for a Firm and Present Peace upon Grounds of Common Right* (October 28, 1647) [1]

Having by our late labours and hazards made it appear to the world at how high a rate we value our just freedom, and God having so far owned our cause as to deliver the enemies thereof into our hands, we do now hold ourselves bound in mutual duty to each other to take the best care we can for the future to avoid both the danger of returning into a slavish

[1] Gardiner, *The Constitutional Documents of the Puritan Revolution,* 333-35. By permission of The Clarendon Press, Oxford.

condition and the chargeable remedy of another war. . . . In order whereunto we declare:

That the people of England, being at this day very unequally distributed by Counties, Cities, and Boroughs for the election of their deputies in Parliament, ought to be more indifferently proportioned according to the number of the inhabitants. . . .

That the people do, of course, choose themselves a Parliament once in two years. . . .

That the power of this, and all future Representatives of this Nation, is inferior only to theirs who choose them, and doth extend, without the consent or concurrence of any other person or persons, to the enacting, altering, and repealing of laws, to the erecting and abolishing of offices and courts, to the appointing, removing, and calling to account magistrates and officers of all degrees, to the making war and peace, to the treating with foreign States, and, generally, to whatsoever is not expressly or impliedly reserved by the represented to themselves:

Which are as followeth.

That matters of religion and the ways of God's worship are not at all entrusted by us to any human power. . . .

That in all laws made or to be made every person may be bound alike, and that no tenure, estate, charter, degree, birth, or place do confer any exemption from the ordinary course of legal proceedings whereunto others are subjected. . . .

That as the laws ought to be equal, so they must be good, and not evidently destructive to the safety and well-being of the people.

These things we declare to be our native rights, and therefore are agreed and resolved to maintain them with our utmost possibilities against all opposition whatsoever.

ARMY REACTION TO "THE AGREEMENT OF THE PEOPLE"

In the army debates, General Ireton and Colonel Rainborough disputed the nature of the franchise proposed in the above *Agreement* as follows.

From *The Army Debates* (1647) [1]

Ireton: The exception that lies in it is this. It is said, they are to be distributed according to the number of the inhabitants: "The people of England," &c. And this doth make me think that the meaning is, that every man that is an inhabitant is to be equally considered, and to have an equal voice in the election of those representers, the persons that are for the general Representative; and if that be the meaning, then I have something to say against it. . . .

Rainborough: I desired that those that had engaged in it might be included. For really I think that the poorest man that is in England hath a life to live, as the greatest man; and therefore truly, sir, I think it's clear, that every man that is to live under a government ought first by his own consent to put himself under that government; and I do think that the poorest man in England is not at all bound in a strict sense to that government that he hath not had a voice to put himself under. . . .

Ireton: That's the meaning of this, "according to the number of the inhabitants"?

Give me leave to tell you, that if you make this the rule I think you must fly for refuge to an absolute natural right, and you must deny all civil right; and I am sure it will come to that in the conse-

[1] Adapted from A. S. P. Woodhouse, *Puritanism and Liberty: Being the Army Debates (1647-9) from the Clarke Manuscripts with Supplementary Documents*, London, 1938, 52-56. Reprinted by permission of J. M. Dent and Sons, Ltd.

quence. . . . For my part, I think it is no right at all. I think that no person hath a right to an interest or share in the disposing of the affairs of the kingdom, and in determining or choosing those that shall determine what laws we shall be ruled by here—no person hath a right to this, that hath not a permanent fixed [property] interest in this kingdom, and those persons together are properly the represented of this kingdom, and consequently are also to make up the representers of this kingdom, who taken together do comprehend whatsoever is of real or permanent interest in the kingdom. . . . Truly by birthright there is thus much claim. Men may justly have by birthright, by their very being born in England, that we should not seclude them out of England, that we should not refuse to give them air and place and ground, and the freedom of the highways and other things, to live amongst us—not any man that is born here, though by his birth there come nothing at all (that is part of the permanent interest of this kingdom) to him. That I think is due to a man by birth. But that by a man's being born here he shall have a share in that power that shall dispose of the lands here, and of all things here, I do not think it a sufficient ground. . . .

Rainborough: Truly, sir, I am of the same opinion I was, and am resolved to keep it till I know reason why I should not. . . . I do hear nothing at all that can convince me, why any man that is born in England ought not to have his voice in election of burgesses. It is said that if a man have not a permanent interest, he can have no claim; and that we must be no freer than the laws will let us be, and that there is no law in any chronicle will let us be freer than that we now enjoy. Something was said to this yesterday. I do think that the main cause why Almighty God gave men reason, it was that they should make use of that reason, and that

they should improve it for that end and purpose that God gave it them. And truly . . . I think there is nothing that God hath given a man that any one else can take from him. And therefore I say; that either it must be the Law of God or the law of man that must prohibit the meanest man in the kingdom to have this benefit as well as the greatest. I do not find anything in the Law of God, that a lord shall choose twenty burgesses, and a gentleman but two, or a poor man shall choose none: I find no such thing in the Law of Nature, nor in the Law of Nations. But I do find that all Englishmen must be subject to English laws, and I do verily believe that there is no man but will say that the foundation of all law lies in the people, and if it lie in the people, I am to seek for this exemption. . . .

And therefore I do think, and am still of the same opinion, that every man born in England cannot, ought not, neither by the Law of God nor the Law of Nature, to be exempted from the choice of those who are to make laws for him to live under, and for him, for aught I know, to lose his life under.

CROMWELL AS A POLITICIAN

After the New Model army had defeated the parliamentary forces in the Second Civil War, it purged the Long Parliament of its Presbyterian and other anti-Independent members (December, 1648), leaving a "Rump," as the purged body was called. This done, the question of what to do with the King arose and, as no one could place any confidence in him, the Independent leaders reluctantly determined to bring him to trial. Charged with "a wicked design to erect and uphold in himself an unlimited and tyrannical power to rule according to his will, and to overthrow the rights and liberties of the people," Charles I was tried by a special court set up by the Rump Parliament, condemned, and, to the horror of all Europe, executed (January 30, 1649). Thereupon the Rump appointed a Council of State to manage affairs, passed an "Act Abolishing the Office of King" (March 17), "An Act Abolishing the House of Lords" (March 19), and "An Act Declaring England to be a Commonwealth." The new government was forced to defend itself at once, first in Ireland (1649-50), where Cromwell's army subjected the Irish to savage slaughter and imposed upon the Irish a harsh settlement which deprived them of their religion and their best lands; and then in Scotland (1650-51), where Prince Charles (later Charles II) sought, with Scottish aid, to regain the English throne. After Cromwell and the "army of saints," as they called themselves, had subdued these elements, the Rump proved unruly, and Cromwell dissolved it, assumed the title of Lord Protector of England (December, 1653), and announced his intention to rule according to a written constitution known as the *Instrument of Government.* This, the first written constitution in English history, was a conservative modification of the *Agreement of the People,* and Cromwell tried vainly to establish an acceptable civil regime in accordance with its provisions. An estimate of his efforts follows.

From FIRTH, *Oliver Cromwell* [1]

Cromwell wished to govern constitutionally. No theory of divine right . . . blinded his eyes to the fact that self-government was the inheritance and right of the English people. He accepted in the main the first principle of democracy, the doctrine of the sovereignty of the people,

[1] From Firth, *Oliver Cromwell,* 483-86. Courtesy of G. P. Putnam's Sons.

or, as he phrased it, "that the foundation of supremacy is in the people and to be by them set down in their representatives." More than once he declared that the good of the governed was the supreme end of all governments, and he claimed that his own government acted "for the good of the people, and for their interest, and without respect had to any other interest." But government for the people did not necessarily mean government by the people. "That's the question," said Cromwell, "what's for their good, not what pleases them," and the history of the Protectorate was a commentary on this text. Some stable government was necessary to prevent either a return to anarchy or the restoration of the Stuarts. Therefore Cromwell was determined to maintain his own government, with the assistance of Parliament if possible, without it if he must. If it became necessary to suspend for a time the liberties of the subject or to levy taxes without parliamentary sanction, he was prepared to do it. In the end the English people would recognise that he had acted for their good. "Ask them," said he, "whether they would prefer the having of their will, though it be their destruction, rather than comply with things of necessity?" He felt confident the answer would be in his favour.

• England might have acquiesced in this temporary dictatorship in the hope of a gradual return to constitutional government. What it could not accept was the permanent limitation of the sovereignty of the people in the interest of the Puritan minority whom Cromwell termed the people of God. Yet it was at this object that all the constitutional settlements of the Protectorate aimed. . . .

Puritanism was spending its strength in the vain endeavour to make England Puritan by force. The enthusiasm which had undertaken to transform the world was being conformed to it. A change was coming over the party which supported the Protector; it had lost many of the "men of conscience"; it had attracted many of the time-servers and camp-followers of politics; it was ceasing to be a party held together by religious interests, and becoming a coalition held together by material interests and political necessities. Cromwell once rebuked the Scottish clergy for "meddling with worldly policies and mixtures of worldly power" to set up that which they called "the kingdom of Christ," and warned them that "the Sion promised" would not be built "with such untempered mortar." He had fallen into the same error himself, and the rule of Puritanism was founded on shifting sands. So the Protector's institutions perished with him and his work ended in apparent failure. Yet he had achieved great things. Thanks to his sword absolute monarchy failed to take root in English soil. Thanks to his sword Great Britain emerged from the chaos of the civil wars one strong state instead of three separate and hostile communities. Nor were the results of his action entirely negative. The ideas which inspired his policy exerted a lasting influence on the development of the English state. Thirty years after his death the religious liberty for which he fought was established by law. The union with Scotland and Ireland, which the statesmen of the Restoration undid, the statesmen of the eighteenth century effected. The mastery of the seas he had desired to gain, and the Greater Britain he had sought to build up became sober realities. Thus others perfected the work which he had designed and attempted.

6. The Restoration (1660-1685)

After Cromwell's death (1658), the Protectorate quickly fell to pieces. Cromwell's son, Richard, who succeeded as Protector, could not command

respect of the army, and discordant factions soon threatened renewal of civil war. Finally, one Cromwellian officer, General George Monk, called together the remnants of the Long Parliament, persuaded it to dissolve itself (March 15, 1660) in favor of a newly elected "convention" Parliament, and the latter, in turn, invited the Stuart heir in exile, Charles II, to reassume the English throne (1660). A contemporary's description of the King follows.

GILBERT BURNET'S DESCRIPTION OF
CHARLES II

From BURNET, History of His Own Time
(1723-34) [1]

The king was then thirty years of age, and, as might have been supposed, past the levities of youth and the extravagance of pleasure. He had a very good understanding. He knew well the state of affairs both at home and abroad. He had a softness of temper that charmed all who came near him, till they found how little they could depend on good looks, kind words, and fair promises; in which he was liberal to excess, because he intended nothing by them, but to get rid of importunities, and to silence all farther pressing upon him. He seemed to have no sense of religion: both at prayers and sacrament, he, as it were, took care to satisfy people, that he was in no sort concerned in that about which he was employed. So that he was very far from being a hypocrite, unless his assisting at those performances was a sort of hypocrisy (as no doubt it was): but he was sure not to increase that, by any the least appearance of religion. . . . He disguised his popery to the last. But when he talked freely, he could not help letting himself out against the liberty, that, under the reformation, all men took of inquiring

[1] Bishop Burnet's History of His Own Time. London, 1839, 61.

into matters of religion: for, from their inquiring into matters of religion, they carried the humour farther, to inquire into matters of state. He said often, he thought government was a much safer, and easier thing, where the authority was believed infallible, and the faith and submission of the people was implicit: about which I had once much discourse with him. He was affable and easy, and loved to be made so by all about him. The great art of keeping him long was, the being easy, and the making every thing easy to him. He had made such observations on the French government, that he thought a king who might be checked, or have his ministers called to an account by a parliament, was but a king in name. He had a great compass of knowledge, though he never was capable of much application or study. He understood mechanics and physic; and was a good chemist, and much set on several preparations of mercury, chiefly the fixing it. He understood navigation well: but above all he knew the architecture of ships so perfectly, that in that respect he was exact rather more than became a prince. . . . He thought that nobody did serve him out of love: and so he was quits with all the world, and loved others as little as he thought they loved him. He hated business, and could not be easily brought to mind any: but when it was necessary, and he was set to it, he would stay as long as his ministers had work for him. The ruin of his reign, and of all his affairs, was occasioned chiefly by his delivering himself up at his first coming over to a mad range of pleasure.

THE "CLARENDON CODE"

A new Parliament was elected in May, 1661, which sat for nearly eighteen years. Known as the Cavalier Parliament, it was as Anglican and monarchical in sympathies as the old Long Parliament had been Puritan and anti-monarchical. Some of its early acts known as the Clarendon Code are described below.

From TREVELYAN, *England under the Stuarts* (1904) [1]

By the Restoration settlement the land-owners bore rule in England, as against Puritan and soldier, Bishop and King. The Cavalier squires, however loyal they might be in profession or even in feeling, were so enchanted by the sweets of power tasted during the early years of their Parliament, that they set themselves steadily to maintain and enlarge their own supremacy, and to enforce upon all other classes the type of religion and politics with which it was now associated. This was the policy afterwards known as Toryism; till the rise of the Whigs fifteen years later there was no one to oppose Tory supremacy, except the King and the Catholics of the Palace. By the "Clarendon Code" the squires closed the ranks of their class, imposing on all the shibboleths of Anglicanism, which few, at any rate of the upper ranks of society, ventured to refuse.

In the first five years of its hot youth the Cavalier Parliament passed the great Code, called in history after the name of Chancellor Hyde, now Earl of Clarendon—those Penal Laws which broke forever the pretensions of Puritanism to political supremacy, reduced the quantity and purified the quality of its religious influence, confined its social sphere to the middle and lower classes, and created the division of England into Church and Dissent.

By the Corporation Act (1661) the membership of the municipal bodies who ruled the towns and usually controlled the elections of their Parliamentary repre-

[1] From *England under the Stuarts* by G. M. Trevelyan, ed. by C. W. C. Oman, in *A History of England*, New York, 1904, V, 340-42. Courtesy of G. P. Putnam's Sons.

sentatives, was confined to those who would receive the Communion by the rites of the Church of England.

By the Act of Uniformity (1662) 2,000 Puritan clergy were expelled from livings in the Established Church, for refusing to assert their "unfeigned consent and assent" to everything in the Prayer-book.

By the Conventicle Act (1664) attendance at meetings for religious rites, other than those of the Established Church, were punished by imprisonment for the first and second offence, and transportation for the third, on pain of death if the criminal returned.

By the Five Mile Act (1665) no clergyman or schoolmaster was to come within five miles of a city or corporate town, unless he declared that he would not "at any time endeavour any alteration of Government either in Church or State." As the Puritan congregations were principally seated in the towns, the great body of dissenters were hereby cut off from even private education or domestic encouragement in their faith. The Act must have hastened the great decline in the numbers of Puritanism and the consequent decay of religious zeal in England, which was so evident when the century closed. And perhaps it had a worse effect upon educational progress than anything the Puritans ever did.

These terrible laws were not left suspended, a mere threat to restrain activity of propaganda, as the yet more terrible laws against Catholics had been suspended by the action of Charles I. Under his son, Parliament had power to insist that the statutes which it framed should be executed without Royal mercy or Court favour. Until the Revolution of 1689, with a few brief intervals, the Clarendon Code was vigorously enforced. . . . Some magistrates spent a good part of their lives surprising midnight conventicles; trapping teachers and clergymen who had strayed out of bounds; crowding the plague-stricken gaols with hundreds of priests and prophets, and thousands of men and women; creating day by day the martyrology of dissent.

MERCANTILIST THEORY IN ENGLAND

Mercantilism, that form of economic nationalism which became so much a part of the policies of absolutist kings, was given an important theoretical justification in England by Thomas Mun (1571-1641). Mun was an English merchant of wide experience. He wrote several economic tracts, but his most important one was published posthumously in 1664 at the hands of his son. The gist of his arguments follows.

From MUN, *England's Treasure* (1664) [1]

Although a Kingdom may be enriched by gifts received, or by purchase taken from some other Nations, yet these are things uncertain and of small consideration when they happen. The ordinary means therefore to encrease our Wealth and Treasure is by *Forraign Trade,* wherein we must ever observe this Rule; to sell more to strangers yearly than we consume of theirs in value. For suppose that when this Kingdom is plentifully served with the Cloth, Lead, Tinn, Iron, Fish and other native Commodities, we doe yearly export the overplus to forraign Countries to the value of twenty two hundred thousand pounds; by which means we are enabled beyond the Seas to buy and bring in forraign Wares for our use and Consumptions, to the value of twenty hundred thousand pounds; By this order duly kept in our trading, we may rest assured that the Kingdom shall be enriched

[1] Thomas Mun, *England's Treasure by Forraign Trade; or, the Ballance of Our Forraign Trade Is the Rule of Our Treasure,* London, 1669, 10-13, 14-29.

yearly two hundred thousand pounds, which must be brought to us in so much Treasure; because that part of our stock which is not returned to us in Wares must necessarily be brought home in Treasure.

For in this case it cometh to pass in the stock of a Kingdom, as in the estate of a private man; who is supposed to have one thousand pounds yearly revenue and two thousand pounds of ready money in his Chest: If such a man through excess shall spend one thousand five hundred pounds *per annum,* all his ready money will be gone in four years; and in the like time his said money will be doubled if he take a Frugal course to spend but five hundred pounds *per annum;* which rule never faileth likewise in the Commonwealth, but in some cases (of no great moment) which I will hereafter declare. . . .

The Revenue or Stock of a Kingdom by which it is provided of forraign Wares is either *Natural* or *Artificial.* The Natural wealth is so much only as can be spared from our own use and necessities to be exported unto strangers. The Artificial consists in our Manufactures and industrious trading with forraign Commodities, concerning which I will set down such particulars as may serve for the cause we have in hand.

1. First, Although this Realm be already exceeding rich by nature, yet might it be much encreased by laying the waste grounds (which are infinite) into such employments as should no way hinder the present Revenues of other manured Lands, but hereby to supply our selves and prevent the importations of Hemp, Flax, Cordage, Tobacco and divers other things which now we fetch from Strangers to our great impoverishing.

2. We may likewise diminish our importations, if we would soberly refrain from excessive Consumption of forraign Wares in our Diet and Rayment, with such often change of Fashions as is used. . . . Yet might they easily be amended by enforcing the observation of such good Laws as are strictly practised in other Countries against the said excesses. . . .

3. In our Exportations we must not onely regard our own superfluities, but also we must consider our Neighbours necessities, that so upon the Wares which they cannot want, nor yet be furnished thereof elsewhere, we may (besides the vent of the Materials) gain so much of the manufacture as we can, and also endeavour to sell them dear, so far forth as the high price cause not a lesse vent in the quantity. . . .

4. The value of our Exportations likewise may be much advanced when we perform it our selves in our own Ships, for then we get not onely the price of our Wares as they are worth here, but also the Merchants gains, the Charges of ensurance, and fraight to carry them beyond the Seas. . . .

12. Lastly, In all things we must endeavour to make the most we can of our own, whether it be *Natural* or *Artificial;* And forasmuch as the people which live by the Arts are far more in number than they who are Masters of the fruits, we ought the more carefully to maintain those endeavours of the multitude, in whom doth consist the greatest strength and riches both of King and Kingdom: for where the people are many, and the Arts good, there the Traffique must be great, and the Countrey rich.

[Legislation to give reality to such theories as Thomas Mun maintained was frequent. Prominent examples in England were the Navigation Acts designed to give English ships and merchants a monopoly of colonial trade. The first Navigation Laws were passed in 1645; others followed in the 1650's, in 1660, and later.]

7. The Victory of Constitutional Monarchy in England: The Glorious Revolution of 1688

James II, who, in 1685, succeeded his brother, Charles II, had two major objectives in England: to be an absolute monarch by virtue of the theory of the divine right of kings and to re-establish the Roman Catholic Church. Accordingly, he appointed Roman Catholics to high positions in his government and, in 1687, in defiance of Parliament, he issued a Declaration of Indulgence which proclaimed a wish "that all the people of our dominions were members of the Catholic Church," "that conscience ought not to be constrained nor people forced in matters of mere religion," and "that it is our royal will and pleasure that from henceforth the execution of all and all manner of penal laws in matters ecclesiastical, for not coming to church, or not receiving the Sacrament, or for any other nonconformity to the religion established, or for or by reason of the exercise of religion in any manner whatsoever, be immediately suspended." A toleration had long been desired by Protestant dissenters, but neither they nor the Anglicans desired it to be extended to Catholics. Accordingly, a few months later, when a male heir was born to the throne, thereby giving prospect of a whole line of Catholic kings, prominent Englishmen invited William of Orange, who by both blood and marriage held claims to the English succession, to invade England. The invasion was rendered bloodless by the flight of James II (December, 1688), and a convention Parliament proclaimed William and Mary, his Queen, to be joint rulers of England (February 13, 1689).

THE ENGLISH BILL OF RIGHTS, 1689

The new monarchs' acceptance of the crown at the hands of Parliament, on the theory that water cannot rise above its source, proclaimed the supremacy of Parliament over the King. But the Bill of Rights, read before the King and Queen at the time of their acceptance of the crown and subsequently confirmed by a regular Parliament (December, 1689), made the tenure of the crown strictly conditional. Thus the long English struggle over prerogative ended with the assertion of the supremacy of Parliament and a limited, constitutional monarchy.

From The Bill of Rights (1689) [1]

Whereas the said late King James II having abdicated the government, and the throne being thereby vacant, his highness the Prince of Orange (whom it hath pleased Almighty God to make the glorious instrument of delivering this kingdom from popery and arbitrary power) did (by the advice of the Lords spiritual and temporal, and divers principal persons of the Commons) cause letters to be written to the Lords spiritual and temporal, being Protestants; . . . for the choosing of such persons to represent them, as were of right to be sent to Parliament, to meet and sit at Westminster upon the two-and-twentieth day of January, in this year 1688, in order to such an establishment, as that their religion, laws, and liberties might not again be in danger of being subverted: upon which letters, elections have been accordingly made:

And thereupon the said Lords spiritual and temporal, and Commons, pursuant to

[1] From Henry Gee and W. J. Hardy, eds., *Documents Illustrative of English Church History*, 646-50. By permission of The Macmillan Company.

their respective letters and elections, being now assembled in a full and free representative of this nation, taking into their most serious consideration the best means for attaining the ends aforesaid, do in the first place (as their ancestors in like case have usually done), for the vindicating and asserting their ancient rights and liberties, declare:

1. That the pretended power of suspending of laws, or the execution of laws, by regal authority, without consent of Parliament, is illegal.

2. That the pretended power of dispensing with laws, or the execution of laws, by regal authority, as it has been assumed and exercised of late, is illegal.

3. That the commission for erecting the late Court of Commissioners for Ecclesiastical Causes, and all other commissions and courts of like nature, are illegal and pernicious.

4. That levying money for or to the use of the crown, by pretence of prerogative, without grant of Parliament, for longer time, or in other manner than the same is or shall be granted, is illegal.

5. That it is the right of the subjects to petition the king, and all commitments and prosecutions for such petitioning are illegal.

6. That the raising or keeping a standing army within the kingdom in time of peace, unless it be with consent of Parliament, is against law.

7. That the subjects which are Protestants may have arms for their defence suitable to their conditions, and as allowed by law.

8. That election of members of Parliament ought to be free.

9. That the freedom of speech, and debates or proceedings in Parliament, ought not to be impeached or questioned in any court or place out of Parliament.

10. That excessive bail ought not to be required, nor excessive fines imposed, nor cruel and unusual punishments inflicted.

11. That jurors ought to be duly empanelled and returned, and jurors which pass upon men in trials for high treason ought to be freeholders.

12. That all grants and promises of fines and forfeitures of particular persons before conviction are illegal and void.

13. And that for redress of all grievances, and for the amending, strengthening, and preserving of the laws, Parliaments ought to be held frequently.

And they do claim, demand, and insist upon all and singular the premises, as their undoubted rights and liberties; and that no declarations, judgments, doings, or proceedings to the prejudice of the people in any of the said premises, ought in any wise to be drawn hereafter into consequence or example. . . .

Having therefore an entire confidence, that his said highness the Prince of Orange will perfect the deliverance so far advanced by him, and will still preserve them from the violation of their rights, which they have here asserted, and from all other attempts upon their religion, rights, and liberties:

The said Lords spiritual and temporal, and Commons, assembled at Westminster, do resolve that William and Mary, prince and princess of Orange, be, and be declared, King and Queen of England, France, and Ireland, and the dominions thereunto belonging, to hold the crown and royal dignity of the said kingdoms and dominions to them the said prince and princess during their lives, and the life of the survivor of them . . . and for default of such issue to the Princess Anne of Denmark, and the heirs of her body; and for default of such issue to the heirs of the body of the said Prince of Orange. And the Lords spiritual and temporal, and Commons, do pray the said prince and princess to accept the same accordingly. . . .

Upon which their said majesties did accept the crown and royal dignity of the kingdoms of England, France, and Ireland, and the dominions thereunto belonging, according to the resolution and desire of the said Lords and Commons contained in the said declaration.

THE TOLERATION ACT (MAY 24, 1689)

Toleration for Puritans and other dissenters from the Church of England, excepting Roman Catholics, was established by an Act of Parliament in 1689. Gilbert Burnet, who had recently been appointed Bishop of Salisbury, described it as follows.

From BURNET, *History of His Own Time* [1]

The bill of toleration passed easily. It excused dissenters from all penalties for their not coming to church, and for going to their separate meetings. There was an exception of Socinians; but a provision was put in it, in favour of quakers; and, though the rest were required to take the oaths to the government, they were excused upon making in lieu thereof a solemn declaration. They were to take out warrants for the houses they met in; and the justices of peace were required to grant them. . . .

The clergy began now to shew an implacable hatred to the nonconformists, and seemed to wish for an occasion to renew old severities against them; but wise and good men did very much applaud the quieting the nation by the toleration. It seemed to be suitable, both to the spirit of the Christian religion, and to the interest of the nation. It was thought very unreasonable, that, while we were complain-

[1] *Bishop Burnet's History of His Own Time,* 530-31.

ing of the cruelty of the church of Rome, we should fall into such practices among ourselves; chiefly, while we were engaging in a war, in the progress of which we would need the united strength of the whole nation.

This bill gave the king great content. He in his own opinion always thought, that conscience was God's province, and that it ought not to be imposed on; and his experience in Holland made him look on toleration as one of the wisest measures of government: he was much troubled to see so much ill humour spreading among the clergy, and by their means over a great part of the nation. He was so true to his principle herein, that he restrained the heat of some who were proposing severe acts against papists. He made them apprehend the advantage which that would give the French, to alienate all the papists of Europe from us; who from thence might hope to set on foot a new catholic league, and make the war a quarrel of religion; which might have very bad effects. Nor could he pretend to protect the protestants in many places of Germany, and in Hungary, unless he could cover the papists in England from all severities on the account of their religion. This was so carefully infused into many, and so well understood by them, that the papists have enjoyed the real effects of the toleration, though they were not comprehended within the statute that enacted it.

LOCKE'S THEORETICAL JUSTIFICATION OF THE ENGLISH REVOLUTIONARY SETTLEMENT

John Locke (1632-1704), the great English philosopher, had lived during most of the English struggles over prerogative. Although not wholly satisfied with the English revolutionary settlement in 1688-89, he wrote widely in justification of it. His *Two Treatises of*

Government (1689) gave a somewhat more liberal interpretation of the Glorious Revolution than the actual settlement deserved, but it was a classic statement of the contract theory of government and obviously derived from the same climate of opinion which had prevailed in the New Model army (see page 228). Locke's first *Treatise* is given wholly to a denial of the divine origin of government; the second is "concerning the true original, extent, and end of civil government."

From LOCKE, *Two Treatises of Government* (1689) [1]

To understand political power right, and derive it from its original, we must consider what state all men are naturally in, and that is a state of perfect freedom to order their actions and dispose of their possessions and persons as they think fit, within the bounds of the law of nature, without asking leave or depending upon the will of any other man.

A state also of equality [exists], wherein all the power and jurisdiction is reciprocal, no one having more than another. . . .

But though this be a state of liberty, yet it is not a state of license; though man in that state have an uncontrollable liberty to dispose of his person or possessions, yet he has not liberty to destroy himself or so much as any creature in his possession but where some nobler use than its bare preservation calls for it. The state of nature has a law of nature to govern it, which obliges every one; and reason, which is that law, teaches all mankind who will but consult it that, being all equal and independent, no one ought to harm another in his life, health, liberty, or possessions. . . .

[1] *The Works of John Locke,* 10 vols., London, 1823, V, 339-41, 351, 394-96, 411-12, 414-15.

The natural liberty of man is to be free from any superior power on earth, and not to be under the will or legislative authority of man, but to have only the law of nature for his rule. The liberty of man in society is to be under no other legislative power but that established by consent in the commonwealth; nor under the dominion of any will or restraint of any law but what that legislative shall enact according to the trust put in it. Freedom, then, is . . . to have a standing rule to live by, common to every one of that society and made by the legislative power erected in it; a liberty to follow my own will in all things where the rule prescribes not; and not to be subject to the inconstant, uncertain, unknown, arbitrary will of another man, as freedom of nature is to be under no other restraint but the law of nature.

This freedom from absolute, arbitrary power is so necessary to and closely joined with a man's preservation that he cannot part with it but by what forfeits his preservation and life together; for a man not having the power of his own life cannot, by compact, or with his own consent, enslave himself to any one nor put himself under the absolute, arbitrary power of another to take away his life when he pleases. Nobody can give more power than he has himself; and he that cannot take away his own life cannot give another power over it. . . .

Men being, as has been said, by nature all free, equal, and independent, no one can be put out of this estate and subjected to the political power of another without his own consent. The only way whereby one divests himself of his natural liberty and puts on the bonds of civil society is by agreeing with other men to join and unite into a community for their comfortable, safe, and peaceable living one amongst another in a secure enjoyment of their properties and a greater security against any that are not of it. This any number of men may do because it injures not the freedom of the rest; they are left as they were in the liberty of the state of nature. When any number of men have so consented to make one community or government, they are thereby presently incorporated and make one body politic wherein the majority have a right to act and conclude the rest. . . .

And thus every man, by consenting with others to make one body politic under one government, puts himself under an obligation to every one of that society to submit to the determination of the majority, and to be concluded by it, or else this original compact whereby he with others incorporate into one society would signify nothing and be no compact. . . .

Whosoever therefore out of a state of nature unite into a community must be understood to give up all the power necessary to the ends for which they unite into society to the majority of the community, unless they expressly agreed in any number greater than the majority. And this is done by barely agreeing to unite into one political society, which is all the compact that is, or needs be, between the individuals that enter into or make up a commonwealth. And thus that which begins and actually constitutes any political society is nothing but the consent of any number of freemen capable of a majority to unite and incorporate into such a society. And that is that, and that only which did or could give beginning to any lawful government in the world. . . .

If a man in the state of nature be so free as has been said, if he be absolute lord of his own person and possessions, equal to the greatest and subject to nobody, why will he part with his freedom, why will he give up his empire and subject himself to the dominion and control

of any other power? To which it is obvious to answer that though in the state of nature he hath such a right, yet the enjoyment of it is very uncertain and constantly exposed to the invasion of others . . . the enjoyment of the property he has in this state is very unsafe, very insecure. This makes him willing to quit a condition which, however free, is full of fears and continual dangers: and it is not without reason that he seeks out and is willing to join in society with others who are already united, or have a mind to unite, for the mutual preservation of their lives, liberties, and estates which I call by the general name property. . . .

But though men, when they enter into society, give up the equality, liberty, and executive power they had in the state of nature into the hands of the society to be so far disposed of by the legislative as the good of society shall require; yet it being only with an intention in every one the better to preserve himself, his liberty and property (for no rational creature can be supposed to change his condition with an intention to be worse), the power of the society, or legislative constituted by them, can never be supposed to extend farther than the common good, but is obliged to secure every one's property. . . . And so whoever has the legislative or supreme power of any commonwealth is bound to govern by established standing laws, promulgated and known to the people, and not by extemporary decrees; by indifferent and upright judges who are to decide controversies by these laws; and to employ the force of the community at home only in the execution of such laws, or abroad to prevent or redress foreign injuries and secure the community from inroads and invasion. And all this to be directed to no other end but the peace, safety, and public good of the people.

17

THE AGE OF LOUIS XIV IN FRANCE

1. Preparations for a Great Age

One of the most important phases of the Era of Enlightened Despotism was the ascendancy in European affairs won by France during the long reign (1643-1715) of Louis XIV. To a considerable extent the golden age of the "Sun King" represented, in miniature, the entire age of the enlightened despots, and France became the model imitated by nearly every European monarch in matters of statecraft, diplomacy, art, letters, music, and costumes. While this supremacy was effected in large part by the extraordinary character and abilities of Louis XIV himself, it cannot be denied that it was also the culmination of careful preparations which reached back as far as the reign of Louis's grandfather, the first Bourbon king of France, Henry IV [see page 186]. After Henry's assassination (1610), a period of disorder intervened until, in 1624, the colorless Louis XIII had the wisdom to place control of public affairs in the hands of Cardinal Richelieu. Richelieu (1624-42) and his hand-picked successor, Cardinal Mazarin (1642-61), adhered consistently to policies designed to develop greater national unity at home and to achieve greater prestige abroad. To the first end they strove to make the King supreme over all rival influences in France; to the second they engaged in dynastic wars to extend French boundaries and prestige. Richelieu left a series of writings, known as his "Political Testament," to explain and justify his acts. The portion of it which follows outlines the conditions which determined his policies at the opening of his ministry (1624).

CARDINAL RICHELIEU'S ACCOUNT OF CONDITIONS WHICH DETERMINED HIS POLICIES

From RICHELIEU, *Political Testament* (c. 1640) [1]

At the time when your Majesty (Louis XIII) resolved to admit me both to your council and to an important place in your confidence for the direction of your affairs, I may say that the Huguenots shared the state with you; that the nobles conducted themselves as if they were not your subjects, and the most powerful governors of the provinces as if they were sovereign in their offices.

I may say that the bad example of all of these was so injurious to this realm that even the best regulated *parlements* [2] were

[1] From Robinson, *Readings in European History*, II, 268-70. By permission of Ginn and Company.

[2] The thirteen French *parlements* were the highest courts of law and must be carefully distinguished from the English Parliaments, which had become primarily *lawmaking* bodies. Medieval practices permitted the *parlements* to register royal edicts before they had the force of law in France, thereby giving them precedents for encroaching upon the king's authority by refusing to register his edicts and pretending that unregistered ones had no legality.

affected by it, and endeavored, in certain cases, to diminish your royal authority as far as they were able in order to stretch their own powers beyond the limits of reason.

I may say that every one measured his own merit by his audacity; that in place of estimating the benefits which they received from your Majesty at their proper worth, all valued them only in so far as they satisfied the extravagant demands of their imagination. . . .

I may also say that the foreign alliances were unfortunate, individual interests being preferred to those of the public; in a word, the dignity of the royal majesty was so disparaged, and so different from what it should be, owing to the malfeasance of those who conducted your affairs, that it was almost impossible to perceive its existence.

It was impossible, without losing all, to tolerate longer the conduct of those to whom your Majesty had intrusted the helm of state; and, on the other hand, everything could not be changed at once without violating the laws of prudence, which do not permit the abrupt passing from one extreme to another. . . .

Thoughtful observers did not think that it would be possible to escape all the rocks in so tempestuous a period; the court was full of people who censured the temerity of those who wished to undertake a reform; all well knew that princes are quick to impute to those who are near them the bad outcome of the undertakings upon which they have been well advised; few people consequently expected good results from the change which it was announced that I wished to make, and many believed my fall assured even before your Majesty had elevated me.

Notwithstanding these difficulties which I represented to your Majesty, knowing how much kings may do when they make good use of their power, I ventured to promise you, with confidence, that you would soon get control of your state, and that in a short time your prudence, your courage, and the benediction of God would give a new aspect to the realm.

I promised your Majesty to employ all my industry and all the authority which it should please you to give me to ruin the Huguenot party, to abase the pride of the nobles, to bring back all your subjects to their duty, and to elevate your name among foreign nations to the point where it belongs.

THE INTENDANCIES

As Richelieu pointed out, the nobility threatened French unity and royal absolutism by clinging to feudal privileges "as if they were sovereign in their offices." To lessen this danger, Richelieu persuaded Louis XIII to issue an edict (1626) ordering all feudal castles—fortresses from which unruly nobles often defied the king—to be demolished. Shortly afterward, the Cardinal instituted a new and more centralized administrative system to deprive the nobles of their local administrative functions. Lawyers known as "masters of petitions" had long been employed by the royal council. Occasionally they had been sent into the provinces as temporary agents to oversee local police, justice, or finance. Now Richelieu made this office a regular part of the machinery of local government. The royal agents became known as "intendants," and Mazarin later increased their authority and gave them fixed posts within territorial units called "intendancies." In time, thirty-four of these intendants were created, and so great was their authority, under the King, that they became known as the "thirty tyrants of France." Louis XIV was careful to appoint commoners to the posts so that, as he wrote in his *Memoirs,* "the public could judge, by the rank of those whom I employed, that I had no intention of sharing authority with them, and that they themselves, knowing what they were, would not entertain higher hopes than those I would grant them." A writer in the latter part of Louis XIV's reign gave the following account of the intendants.

From SAINT-SIMON, *Memoirs* (1739-51) [1]

The intendants were few, powerless, and little used before this reign. The king, and still more his ministers of the same character as the intendants, have multiplied them little by little, establishing new districts and increasing their powers. They used them first to counterbalance, then to overshadow, and finally to annihilate the power of the governors, of the commanders, and of the lieutenant-governors of the provinces, and also with much more reason, the power which the seigniors, powerful by birth and prestige, had acquired in the country. They bridled the temporal power of the bishops within their dioceses; they forced the cities to submission. Their financial power was so extended that they decided disputes about taxes and rights, and they determined the price of offices. Their power of granting protection to the nobles and commoners or of withdrawing it at pleasure from them, of raising up some at the expense of others, has depopulated gradually the provinces of the most important families, who could not brook this new kind of persecution nor accustom themselves to paying court to the intendants in order to avoid affronts and insults.

The assessment of the *taille* and of other imposts, which rests entirely in their hands, makes them masters of oppression or of relief to parishes and individuals. When suits, arising between individuals, seigniors or others, nobles or commoners, which are not carried to the court of justice, are appealed to the court and are assigned to the office of the Secretary of the State or of Finances, they are always returned to the intendants for their opinion, which is invariably followed, unless a miracle intervenes. They have thus acquired an authority over all kinds of affairs, which are no longer left to the seigniors or to individuals. All who have had the means, have therefore deserted their estates to come to Paris, in order to watch from a distance the decline of their influence, and to attempt to build up at court such credit and protection, as will compel the intendants to treat them with consideration.

The governors of the provinces became indignant on account of their continual defeats in the contests with the intendants over their duties and personal dignity and accustomed themselves to remaining away from their provinces, until they gradually lost the right to visit them without the permission of the king; and this is seldom given.

The frequent shifting of intendants from one district to another breaks all connections, which they may form within the district. . . . This extreme servitude of the intendants is some compensation for their power. They tremble before the ministers and even before the principal clerks and the farmers general and the great *partisans.*

The first ambition of an intendant is to be placed over one of the five or six great financial districts; and the second is to enter one of the councils of state, or perhaps the ministry. . . . These officials, all powerful in the provinces, are without power in the hands of the ministers and

[1] Translated from *Ecrits inédits de Saint-Simon,* in Clarence W. Alvord, ed., *Documents Illustrating French History in the Seventeenth Century,* Champaign, Ill., n.d., 10-11.

are always fearful of being crushed just like reeds. Such has been the means used to annihilate the magnates, the seigniors, the nobles, the individuals. Men of no power in themselves have accomplished this.

RICHELIEU AND THE FOUNDING OF THE FRENCH ACADEMY (1635)

The pre-eminence of the French language in diplomacy, science, polite literature, and aristocratic society dates from the reign of Louis XIV. The superior eloquence of the tongue has been consciously fostered by the French Academy, the chief function of which, according to its "Statutes and Regulations" was "to devote all possible care and diligence to establish definite rules for our language and to render it pure, eloquent, and capable of treating the arts and sciences." The organization of the Academy has been admirably described by Paul Pellison-Fontanier, one of its early members.

From PELLISON-FONTANIER, *History of the French Academy* (1652) [1]

About the year 1629 some gentlemen lodging in several places in Paris, and finding nothing more inconvenient in that great city than to go many times to seek one another to no avail, resolved to meet one day a week at some one of their lodgings. They were all men of letters and of extraordinary merit: [among others,] M. [Antoine] Godeau, now Bishop of Grasse . . . M. [Valentin] Conrart . . . and M. [Claude] de Malleville. They met at M. Conrart's, whose lodgings were the most commodious to receive them, and in the heart of the city from whence all the others

[1] Paul Pellison-Fontanier, *Histoire de l'Académie Française* (1652), in M. Ch.-L. Livet, ed., *Histoire de l'Académie Française par Pellison et D'Olivet*, 2 vols., Paris, 1858, I, 8-34.

were almost equally distant. There they entertained themselves familiarly, as is usual in an ordinary visit, with all kinds of things, affairs, news, and belles-lettres. If any one of the company had composed a work, as they often did, he voluntarily communicated it to the others, who freely gave him their opinions of it. . . . Thus they continued three or four years, and as I have heard many of them say, with great pleasure and incredible profit. . . .

They had made it a rule not to speak of these meetings to anybody, and that was very exactly observed for a time. The first that failed in it was M. de Malleville—for there is no harm in accusing him of a fault which has been erased by the happiness of its outcome. He said something to M. [Nicolas] Faret, who had just printed his *Honest Man* and who, having obtained leave to be at one of their conferences, brought a copy of his book which he gave them. He returned with very great satisfaction both with the opinions they had given of his book and with all that had passed in the rest of the conversation. But when a secret is once told, it is difficult to prevent its becoming public. . . . M. [Jean] Desmarests and M. [François de Métel] de Boisrobert learned of the meetings by M. Faret. M. Desmarests attended several times . . . M. de Boisrobert also desired to attend and there was no reason at all to deny him admittance, for besides his being a friend to most of the gentlemen, his fortune procured him some authority and considerable prestige. He was admitted, then; and when he observed how they examined literary works and understood that it was not a matter of compliments and flatteries where each one delivered eulogies in order to receive them, but that they boldly and freely criticized even the smallest faults, he was filled with joy and admiration. He was then in his greatest favor with the Cardinal Richelieu, and his chief care was to recreate his master's spirits after the noise and perplexities of public business by relating pleasant stories and telling all the gossip of the court and town. . . .

Among these familiar discourses, M. de Boisrobert did not fail to give a favorable account of the little assembly which he had seen and of the persons who composed it. And the Cardinal—who had a soul naturally carried into great things, and who loved above all the French tongue in which he wrote exceedingly well himself—after he had commended the design, asked M. de Boisrobert whether these gentlemen would form a society and assemble regularly under public authority. M. de Boisrobert having responded that in his opinion this proposition would be received with joy, the Cardinal commanded him to make it and to offer to these gentlemen his protection for their company, which he would establish by letters patent. . . .

When these offers had been made and the question was to decide what answer they should return, there was hardly any of the gentlemen who did not express displeasure and regret because the honor which was done them would disturb the sweetness and familiarity of their gatherings. . . . Finally, however, when they considered that they had to do with a man who was extravagant in his desires, and who is not accustomed to opposition or, if he does meet it, not to suffer it unpunished; that the Cardinal might feel affronted if they refused his protection, and might take revenge for it upon each of them in particular; that, at least, since the laws of the realm forbade all kinds of assemblies made without authority from the Prince, he might if he pleased easily put an end to their meetings and so break up the society which each of them desired to be eternal. Upon these considerations it was resolved, "That M. de Boisrobert

should return most humble thanks to M. the Cardinal for the honor which he had accorded them and to assure him that, although they had never had any such ambitious thoughts and were much surprised at His Eminence's design, they were fully resolved to follow his wishes." The Cardinal received their reply with great satisfaction and, giving many testimonies of his pleasure, he commanded: "that they should assemble as they were wont, and that they should augment their company as they should see fit, and that they should consider among themselves what form and what laws they would like to have for the future."

Things passed thus in the beginning of the year 1634. . . . Thereafter they began . . . to think seriously, according to the intention of the Cardinal, about the establishment of the Academy.

[In the following months the society formally organized, selected officers, added new members, and adopted the name of "The French Academy." The Cardinal gave his approval and persuaded the King to issue letters patent, January 2, 1635, which constituted the French Academy under royal authority to foster eloquence as a means of furthering arts and sciences in France, "with a view of establishing fixed rules for the language . . . and render the French language not only elegant but also capable of treating all the arts and sciences." The letters patent concluded: "We have of our special grace, full power, and royal authority, permitted, approved, and authorized, and by these presents, signed with our hand, do permit, approve, and authorize the said assemblies and conferences. We will that they be continued henceforth in our good city of Paris under the name of the French Academy; that our said cousin [Richelieu] have liberty to style himself the head and protector of it; that the number of members be limited to forty persons."]

2. The Divine-Right-of-Kings Theory in France

BISHOP BOSSUET ON THE DIVINE RIGHT OF KINGS

Louis XIV's remark, *L'état, c'est moi,* "I am the state," is a statement of absolutism more famous than James I's exposition of the divine right of kings [see page 216]. But that French absolutism, like the English Stuarts', was of divine origin is well demonstrated in the writings of Jacques Bénigne Bossuet (1627-1704), the most prominent French churchman of his day. Bossuet became preacher in ordinary to Louis XIV in 1666, and in 1670 the King entrusted him with the education of the Dauphin. A decade later he was appointed Bishop of Meaux. Bossuet was an eloquent preacher and a vigorous writer in defense of French Catholicism. In 1678, while still tutor, Bossuet wrote for the Dauphin's education a book entitled *Politics Drawn from the Words of Holy Scripture.* Intended to impress upon the heir to the French throne the loftiness of his position and the heavy responsibilities of it, the book is a superb statement, bristling with scriptural references, of the divine origins of monarchical authority. After maintaining that all civil societies were created by God from the earliest creation of man, Bossuet praised monarchy as the best form of government and imputed "four elements or essential qualities to royal authority: first, royal authority is sacred; second, it is paternal; third, it is absolute; fourth, it is in accordance with reason." He continued as follows.

From BOSSUET, *Politics Drawn from the Words of the Holy Scripture* (1678) [1]

We have already seen that all power is of God.[2] The ruler, adds St. Paul, "is the minister of God to thee for good. But if thou do that which is evil, be afraid; for he beareth not the sword in vain: for he is the minister of God, a revenger to execute wrath upon him that doeth evil." [3] Rulers then act as the ministers of God and as his lieutenants on earth. It is through them that God exercises his empire. Think ye "to withstand the kingdom of the Lord in the hand of the sons of David"? [4] Consequently, as we have seen, the royal throne is not the throne of a man, but the throne of God himself. The Lord "hath chosen Solomon my son to sit upon the throne of the kingdom of the Lord over Israel." [5] And again, "Solomon sat on the throne of the Lord." [6]

Moreover, that no one may assume that the Israelites were peculiar in having kings over them who were established by God, note what is said in Ecclesiasticus: "God has given to every people its ruler, and Israel is manifestly reserved to him." . . .[7]

It appears from all this that the person of the king is sacred, and that to attack him in any way is sacrilege. God has the kings anointed by his prophets with the holy unction in like manner as he has

---

[1] Robinson, *Readings in European History,* II, 273-77. By permission of Ginn and Company.
[2] Referring to St. Paul's words (Romans 13:1-2): "Let every soul be subject unto the higher powers. For there is no power but of God: the powers that be are ordained of God. Whosoever therefore resisteth the power, resisteth the ordinance of God: and they that resist shall receive to themselves damnation."
[3] See Rom. 13:4.
[4] II Chron. 13:8.
[5] I Chron. 28:5.
[6] I Chron. 29:23.
[7] Ecclesiasticus 17:17.

bishops and altars anointed. But even without the external application in thus being anointed, they are by their very office the representatives of the divine majesty deputed by Providence for the execution of his purposes. Accordingly God calls Cyrus his anointed.[1] . . . Kings should be guarded as holy things, and whosoever neglects to protect them is worthy of death. . . .

But kings, although their power comes from on high, as has been said, should not regard themselves as masters of that power to use it at their pleasure . . . they must employ it with fear and self-restraint, as a thing coming from God and of which God will demand an account. "Hear, O kings, and take heed, understand, judges of the earth, lend your ears, ye who hold the peoples under your sway, and delight to see the multitude that surround you. It is God who gives you the power. Your strength comes from the Most High, who will question your works and penetrate the depths of your thoughts, for, being ministers of his kingdom, ye have not given righteous judgments nor have ye walked according to his will. He will straightway appear to you in a terrible manner, for to those who command is the heaviest punishment reserved. The humble and the weak shall receive mercy, but the mighty shall be mightily tormented. For God fears not the power of any one, because he made both great and small and he has care for both."[2] . . .

Kings should tremble then as they use the power God has granted them; and let them think how horrible is the sacrilege if they use for evil a power which comes from God. . . . What profanation, what arrogance, for the unjust king to sit on God's throne to render decrees contrary to his laws and to use the sword which God

has put in his hand for deeds of violence and to slay his children! . . .

The royal power is absolute. With the aim of making this truth hateful and insufferable, many writers have tried to confound absolute government with arbitrary government. But no two things could be more unlike, as we shall show when we come to speak of justice.

The prince need render account of his acts to no one. "I counsel thee to keep the king's commandment, and that in regard of the oath of God. Be not hasty to go out of his sight: stand not on an evil thing; for he doeth whatsoever pleaseth him. Where the word of a king is, there is power: and who may say unto him, what doest thou? Whoso keepeth the commandment shall feel no evil thing."[1] Without this absolute authority the king could neither do good nor repress evil. It is necessary that his power be such that no one can hope to escape him, and, finally, the only protection of individuals against the public authority should be their innocence. This conforms with the teaching of St. Paul: "Wilt thou then not be afraid of the power? do that which is good."[2]

I do not call majesty that pomp which surrounds kings or that exterior magnificence which dazzles the vulgar. That is but the reflection of majesty and not majesty itself. Majesty is the image of the grandeur of God in the prince. . . .

Look at the prince in his cabinet. Thence go out the orders which cause the magistrates and the captains, the citizens and the soldiers, the provinces and the armies on land and on sea, to work in concert. He is the image of God, who, seated on his throne high in the heavens, makes all nature move. . . .

So great is this majesty that it cannot reside in the prince as in its source; it is borrowed from God, who gives it to him

[1] Isa. 45:1.
[2] Wisd. of Sol. 6:1-7.

[1] Eccles. 8:2-5. [2] Rom. 13:3.

for the good of the people, for whom it is good to be checked by a superior force. Something of divinity itself is attached to princes and inspires fear in the people. The king should not forget this. "I have said"—it is God who speaks—"I have said, Ye are gods; and all of you are children of the Most High. But ye shall die like men, and fall like one of the princes." [1] "I have said, Ye are gods"; that is to say, you have in your authority, and you bear on your forehead, a divine imprint. "You are the children of the Most High"; it is he who has established your power for the good of mankind. But, O gods of flesh and blood, gods of clay and dust, "ye shall die like men, and fall like princes." Grandeur separates men for a little time, but a common fall makes them all equal at the end.

O kings, exercise your power then boldly, for it is divine and salutary for human kind, but exercise it with humility. You are endowed with it from without. At bottom it leaves you feeble, it leaves you mortal, it leaves you sinners, and charges you before God with a very heavy account.

LOUIS XIV'S ADVICE TO HIS SON

In the early years of his reign Louis XIV composed some *Memoirs* filled with advice for the Dauphin and based upon his own experiences as King of France. Hoping that his *Memoirs* might become "the sole place where young princes can find a thousand truths without a trace of flattery," Louis tried to be practical, to emphasize the need for self-discipline and hard work, and to explain some of his own motives. Consequently, the *Memoirs* illustrate the absolute monarch in action, shorn of much of the glamour and glitter of

[1] Ps. 82:6-7.

courtly show. Excerpts from the King's writings follow.

From LOUIS XIV, *Memoirs* (c. 1668) [2]

THE NECESSITY OF WORK

As for work, my son, it is very likely that you may begin to read these memoirs at an age when you are more accustomed to fear work than to like it. You are very happy because you have escaped the subjection of tutors, schoolmasters, regimented routine, and long arduous study. I hereby say to you that it is not only by work that one rules, but also for work that one rules. . . .

Nothing will ever be more laborious for you than idleness if you have the misfortune to become addicted to it. If you allow yourself to become lazy, you will first be displeased with the affairs of state, then with pleasure, and then with yourself. . . . I have a strict rule to work two times a day and to work two or three hours each time with various persons, without counting the hours that I spend alone nor the time that I devote to extraordinary affairs when they come up unexpectedly. . . .

THE IMPORTANCE OF BEING WELL INFORMED

In a word, my son, it is most necessary to have your eyes open, watchful over all parts of the world. It is essential to learn the news of all the provinces and nations, the secrets of every court, the temper and weakness of each prince and of all the foreign ministers. We must be informed of an infinite number of things that people generally believe we do not know and see that which is hidden with great care from us. . . .

USE OF MINISTERS

As regards the persons who must assist me in my work, I was resolved above all

[2] *Mémoires pour l'instruction du dauphin*, in *Œuvres de Louis XIV*, 6 vols., Paris, 1806, I, 19-44.

things not to secure a first minister [such as Richelieu and Mazarin had been]. If you take my advice, my son, and all your successors after you, the office of first minister shall be abolished forever in France, there being nothing more unworthy than visualizing on one side the executive head, and on the other the sale of kingly offices. For this plan it was absolutely necessary that I share my confidence and the execution of orders with others without giving full authority in anything to a single person. I placed various persons in different kinds of work and directed their special skills, which is, perhaps, the first and greatest talent of princes.

In order that I might better succeed as king, as there were a great many affairs where our occupations and dignity did not ordinarily permit us to descend, I resolved, when I had made choice of my ministers, to confer several times with each one. When he expected the least to happen he suddenly found matters of business thrust upon him. . . .

In regard to the art of knowing your men, which is so important to you, I tell you, my son, that it is possible to learn but more difficult to teach it. In general, it is undoubtedly right to consider their general reputation and established place in society, because the public has no interest in these and is greatly imposed on in these matters. It is wise to listen to everybody, but believe nobody other than the good which they are constrained to recognize in their enemies, which they are loath to admit, or the bad qualities which they see in their friends, which they try to excuse. . . . But in arriving at conclusions, one learns the talents, the inclinations, and the courage of each one by studying each one and pleasing each one. . . .

If the more important occupations and duties allow the time, you will not do badly to be present at times in order to excite and animate your judiciaries by your presence. . . . From these men one ordinarily selects provincial intendants, army intendants, ambassadors, or higher officers. . . .

ON ARRIVING AT DECISIONS

The most clever persons, in their own interest, take advice from other clever persons. What would kings be like who, having the public interest in their hands and possessing the power of good or evil throughout the earth, did not take advice? One must not form any important decisions without having called upon, if possible, all the sources of knowledge, wisdom, and reason of our subjects. . . .

Our rank, my son, estranges us in a certain manner from our people, to which our ministers are the nearest which we are capable of consulting. They attend to a thousand details which we ignore—for which, however, we must make decisions and take action. We must not overlook the age, experience, study, and liberty of them that have been greater than all our capacities. This wisdom of our inferiors we must borrow and accept from persons of highest to lowest degree.

But in the important occasions, when all evidence and contrary reasons have been brought to our attention, the decisive action, my son, is up to us; for we decide that which we must enforce. And in this choice, I tell you that we must lack neither sense nor courage.

3. Colbert and French Mercantilism

"Colbertism" is a term sometimes used interchangeably with "mercantilism." It derives from Jean Baptiste Colbert (1619-1683), a son of French tradespeople who, upon Mazarin's recommendation, rose in the King's service and who, in Louis XIV's own words, was "a man in whom I had all possible confidence because I knew that he possessed a great deal of industry, intelligence, and probity." Colbert held many offices during his career, but it was as Finance Minister—first as intendant (1661) and then as Controller General (1665)—that he won his greatest fame. Colbert's conception of financial administration embraced not only the tax system but also the entire economic and social structure of the state. He was an indefatigable worker and his broad views led him to take a hand in many phases of Louis's government. Besides financial reform, Colbert encouraged industry and set up minute regulations and an army of officers to regulate the kind, quantity, and quality of French products; he improved roads, built canals and harbors, rehabilitated the French Navy (chiefly to enlarge commerce), founded trading companies for overseas and colonial ventures, patronized arts, letters, and sciences, established the Academy of Sciences, the Royal Observatory, and other learned institutions. Except for his peculiar attitude toward world trade, which led him to support a "war of money," Colbert's policies were peaceful. He went far to create, in the early part of Louis's reign, that prosperity which made possible the grandeur of the court, the expensive wars, and the extravagance of the Sun King.

ASPECTS OF COLBERTISM

A striking feature of Colbert's mercantilism was his belief in the essentially static condition of European economic society—in an unchanging level of population and the standards of living. In a "Dissertation on the Question Whether, of Two Alliances, One with France or One with Holland Can Be of Greater Advantage to England" Colbert discusses European commerce.

From COLBERT, "Dissertation on Two Alliances" (1669) [1]

From all our knowledge and after a very exact examination it can be stated with certainly that the trade of all Europe is carried on with about 20,000 ships of all sizes; and it is easy to understand that this number cannot be increased, since the populations and the consumption of all the states remains the same; and of this number of 20,000 vessels, the Dutch possess 15,000 to 16,000, the English 3,000 to 4,000, and the French 500 to 600. . . .

After setting forth this information, which is reliable, it is necessary to return to our first consideration; namely, that England seeks by this alliance primarily to increase her trade. That increase cannot be gained except by providing greater employment for English ships and by increasing their number. Such an increase cannot occur without the discovery of some new, hitherto unknown, commerce, or by a decrease in the number of ships of one of the other nations. The discovery of new trade is very uncertain, and it is not safe to found an argument upon such an accidental base, or rather it is better to say that such an accident simply will not occur. And even if it did occur, it would not bring about any new consumption of necessities or luxuries, but only make it easier for one nation rather than another to attract those goods which are already being consumed and which constitute a part of the general consumption of all Europe. Any increase in English trade must, therefore, take place only by a corresponding decrease in the number of vessels of other nations. . . .

[1] *Lettres, instructions, et mémoires de Colbert,* ed. by Pierre Clément, 8 vols., Paris, 1861-73, VI, 260-70.

It must be added that commerce causes a perpetual combat in peace and in war among the nations of Europe in an effort to see who shall win the greatest share. . . . The Dutch, the English, and the French are the chief contestants.

But that which is of paramount importance is that commerce is a perpetual and peaceable war of wit and industry among all the nations. It is carried on by 20,000 vessels, and this number cannot be increased. Each nation works incessantly to maintain its legitimate share or to gain an advantage over its neighbors. At present, the Dutch fight this war with 15,000 or 16,000 vessels, with a government of merchants whose entire thoughts and power are directed solely toward the preservation and increase of their commerce, and with much more care, industry, and economy than any other nation. The English fight with 3,000 or 4,000 ships, and with less industry, care, and economy than the Dutch. The French fight with 500 or 600 ships. These last two cannot increase their commerce except by increasing their number of vessels, and they cannot increase this number except by controlling a larger proportion of the total of 20,000 ships which carry all the commerce, and consequently they cannot increase their commerce without decreasing the 15,000 or 16,000 ships controlled by the Dutch.

COLBERT'S BULLIONISM AND THE "WAR OF MONEY"

Like other mercantilists, Colbert was a bullionist: "I believe this principle will be readily accepted," he declared, "that it is only the abundance of money in a state which makes the difference in its greatness and power." To add to the nation's store of money, Colbert hoped to prevent its export from the realm, to give Frenchmen an opportunity to make profits from money in the kingdom, and to increase the quantity of money in France by attracting it from other lands. In a "Memoir to the King on Finances" Colbert enlarges upon these three points.

From COLBERT, "Memoir on Finances" (1670) [1]

In these three points consist the greatness and the power of the state and the magnificence of the king through all the expenditures which large revenues permit. And this magnificence is greater still because, at the same time, it abases all the neighboring states, inasmuch as there is only a given quantity of money which circulates in Europe and this quantity is increased from time to time by what comes in from the West Indies. It is certain and clear that if there are only 150,000,000 livres which circulate publicly in France, one cannot increase it by 20,000,000, 30,000,000 and 50,000,000 without at the same time taking the same quantity from neighboring states, a fact which explains the double elevation which has been seen to go on so notably in the past few years: the one augmenting the power and greatness of your Majesty, the other lowering that of your enemies and those envious of you. . . .

I beg your Majesty to permit me to say that it appears to me that since you have taken charge of the administration of finances, you have undertaken a war of money [*une guerre d'argent*] against all the states of Europe. You have already conquered Spain, Italy, Germany, England, and some others in which you have caused great misery and want, and by despoiling them you have enriched yourself, whereby you have gained the means to do all the great things which you have done and still continue to do every day. Only Holland is left, and it fights with

[1] *Ibid.*, VII, 239, 250-51.

great resources. . . . Your Majesty has formed companies which, like armies, attack them everywhere. In the North, the company has already a capital of a million livres and 20 vessels; in Guinea, there are 6 French vessels which have begun their trading; in the West, your Majesty has excluded them from all the islands under your authority, and the company which you have formed already furnishes the entire kingdom with sugar, tobacco, and other merchandise which is sold in northern Italy and other foreign countries. In the Orient, your Majesty has 20 vessels employed. . . . Those trading in the Levant have a capital of 12,000,000 livres and 12 vessels. Your manufactures, your canal for navigation between the seas, and all the other new establishments which your Majesty makes are so many reserve corps that your Majesty creates to do their duty in this war, in which your Majesty can see clearly that he is winning every year some great advantage.

4. Louis XIV and the Church

Although his personal life was hardly unspotted, Louis XIV was outwardly always an exceedingly pious and devout Catholic. His religious enthusiasm, however, never led him to forget that he was king, and any diminution of his authority, even at the hands of churchmen, excited stubborn resistance. At the beginning of his reign, two conditions existed in French Christianity which, in Louis's opinion, required reform. The first consisted of encroachments by the Papacy upon the "Gallican Liberties" of the French church; that is, upon the royal claim to infallible authority in the temporal affairs of France. The second was the disunity in the French church caused by the toleration of the

French Huguenots [see page 186]. In regard to the former, in 1682, the King summoned at Paris a general council of Catholic churchmen to formulate in unequivocal terms the privileges of the French church. Dominated by Bossuet [see page 245], the assembly drew up the following "Declaration of the Gallican Church" (1682). Though bitterly assailed by Pope Innocent XI, the Declaration was upheld by Louis XIV, who thereby reaffirmed his divinely created absolutism by asserting freedom from papal interference in the temporal affairs of his kingdom.

REAFFIRMATION OF THE GALLICAN LIBERTIES

From "Declaration of the Gallican Church" (1682) [1]

There are many who labor to subvert the decrees of the Gallican Church and its liberties which our ancestors defended with so much zeal and which rest upon the sacred canons and the traditions of the Fathers. . . . With a view to remedy these evils, we, the archbishops and bishops assembled at Paris by the king's order, representing, together with other deputies, the Gallican Church, have judged it advisable, after mature deliberation, to make the regulations and declarations which follow:

Article 1. St. Peter and his successors, vicars of Jesus Christ, and likewise of all the church itself, have received from God power in things spiritual and pertaining to salvation, but none whatever in things temporal and civil, inasmuch as Jesus himself tells us that his kingdom is not of this world and, in another place, that one should render unto Caesar that which is

[1] This and the next selection are from Emil Reich, ed., *Select Documents Illustrating Mediaeval and Modern History,* 1915. By permission of Staples Press, Ltd., London. This is 379-81.

Caesar's and unto God that which is God's. . . . Consequently, we declare that kings and princes are not by the law of God subject to any ecclesiastical power in temporal things; that neither directly nor indirectly can they be deposed by the leaders of the Church; that their subjects cannot be released from submission and obedience to them, nor be absolved from the oath of allegiance. . . .

Article 2. The plenitude of power in things spiritual, which resides in the Apostolic See and the successors of St. Peter . . . approved as they are by the Holy See and the practice of the entire Roman Catholic Church, and religiously observed by the Gallican Church, remain in full force. . . .

Article 3. It follows, then, that the Apostolic power must be regulated by the canons enacted by the Spirit of God and consecrated by the reverence of the whole world. The ancient rules, customs, and institutions of the Gallican Church likewise remain inviolable. . . .

Article 4. The Pope has the principal part in deciding questions of faith, and his decrees extend to all the churches and to each particular church; yet his judgment is not irreversible unless confirmed by consent of the church.

REVOCATION OF THE EDICT OF NANTES

In his "Memoirs for the Instruction of the Dauphin," Louis XIV wrote: "As for the great number of my subjects who adhere to the reformed religion, which I have always looked upon with misfortune and still regard with sadness, I have formed this plan of conduct . . . to subdue little by little the Huguenots in my realm." The Revocation of the Edict of Nantes was, then, merely the culmination of a whole series of repressive acts directed against the Huguenots after Louis assumed personal charge of the French monarchy. Its timing, however, is significant: It was issued after the death of Colbert (1683), who had opposed persecution of the Huguenots; after Louis had become intimate with Madame de Maintenon, who was an exceedingly devout Catholic and who may have hastened Louis's decision; and after the Declaration of the Gallican Clergy, who deserved a reward for their loyalty to the royal authority and who may have wished to conciliate the Pope for the loss of his privileges in France effected by the Declaration. It is probable, too, that Louis wished to make a good impression on the Spanish, an ultra-Catholic people; for the succession to the Spanish throne [see page 265] was already an open question. The royal decree revoking the Edict of Nantes was published October 22, 1685.

From LOUIS XIV, Decree of Revocation (1685) [1]

King Henry the Great, our grandfather of glorious memory, being desirous that the peace which he had procured for his subjects after the great losses they had suffered on account of civil and foreign wars, should not be troubled on account of the *Religion Prétendue Reformée* ["the religion which pretended to be reformed," a derisive term commonly employed by French Catholics in referring to Huguenots] as had happened in the reigns of his predecessors, by his edict, granted at Nantes in the month of April, 1598, regulated the procedure to be adopted with regard to those of the said religion . . . so as to be in a better position to work, as he had resolved to do, for the reunion to the Church of those who had so lightly withdrawn from it.

As the intention of the king, our grand

[1] *Ibid.,* 381-86.

father, was frustrated by his sudden death, and as the execution of the said edict was interrupted during the minority of the late king, our most honored lord and father of glorious memory, by new encroachments on the part of the adherents of the said *Religion Prétendue Reformée,* which gave occasion for their being deprived of divers advantages accorded to them by the said edict; nevertheless the king, our late lord and father, with his usual clemency, granted them yet another edict at Nîmes, in July, 1629, by means of which, tranquillity being established anew, the said late king, animated by the same spirit and the same zeal for religion as the king, our said grandfather, had resolved to take advantage of this repose to attempt to put his said pious design into execution. But foreign wars interfered soon after. . . . God having at last permitted that our people should enjoy perfect peace, we . . . are able to profit by this truce (which we have ourselves facilitated), and devote our whole attention to the means of accomplishing the designs of our said grandfather and father, which we have kept before us since our succession to the crown. We now see, with thankful recognition of our debt to God, that our endeavors have attained their proposed end, inasmuch as the better and the greater part of our subjects of the said *Religion Prétendue Reformée* have embraced the Catholic faith. And since by this fact the execution of the Edict of Nantes and of all that has ever been ordained in favor of the said *Religion Prétendue Reformée* has become useless, we have determined that we can do nothing better . . . than entirely to revoke the said Edict of Nantes. . . .

Art. I. Be it known that for these causes and others which move us hereunto . . . we have, by this present perpetual and irrevocable edict, suppressed and revoked, and do suppress and revoke, the edict of our said grandfather given at Nantes in

April, 1598 . . . and the edict given at Nîmes in July, 1629. We declare them null and void, together with all concessions, of whatsoever nature . . . in favor of the said *Religion Prétendue Reformée.* . . . And, in consequence, we desire, and it is our pleasure, that all the temples of those of the said *Religion Prétendue Reformée* situated in our kingdom, countries, territories, and the lordships under our crown, shall be demolished without delay.

Art. II. We forbid our subjects of the *Religion Prétendue Reformée* further to assemble in any place or private house for the exercise of the said religion. . . .

Art. III. We likewise forbid all noblemen, of what condition soever, to hold such religious exercises in their houses or fiefs. . . .

Art. IV. We enjoin all ministers of the said *Religion Prétendue Reformée,* who do not desire to become converts and to embrace the Catholic, Apostolic, and Roman religion to leave our kingdom and the territories subject to us within fifteen days of the publication of our present edict, without leave to reside therein beyond that period, or, during the said fifteen days, to engage in any preaching, exhortation, or any other function, on pain of being sent to the galleys. . . .

Art. VII. We forbid private schools for the instruction of children of the said *Religion Prétendue Reformée,* and in general all things whatever that can be held as a concession of any kind in favor of the said religion. . . .

Art. IX. And to extend our clemency towards those of our subjects of the said *Religion Prétendue Reformée* who, before the publication of our present edict, have emigrated from our kingdom, lands, and territories subject to us, it is our will and pleasure that in case they return within four months from the day of the said publication, it shall be lawful for them and they may take possession again of their property; [otherwise, their property will be confiscated]. . . .

Art. X. We repeat our most express prohibition to all our subjects of the said *Religion Prétendue Reformée,* together with their wives and children, against leaving our kingdom, lands, and territories subject to us, or transporting their goods and effects therefrom under penalty, as respects the men, of being sent to the galleys, and as respects the women, of imprisonment and confiscation of their goods. . . .

As for the rest of the *Religion Prétendue Reformée,* liberty is granted to them, pending the time when it shall please God to enlighten them as well as others, to remain in the cities and places of our kingdom, lands, and territories subject to us, and there to continue their commerce, and to enjoy their possessions, without being subjected to molestation or hindrance on account of the said *Religion Prétendue Reformée,* on condition, as is said, that they do not exercise the said religion, or assemble under pretext of prayers or religious services, of whatever nature these may be, under the penalties above mentioned of imprisonment and confiscation.

SOME EFFECTS OF THE REVOCATION OF THE EDICT OF NANTES

Louis XIV's persecution of the Huguenots, culminating in the Revocation of the Edict of Nantes, permanently exiled between 300,000 and 500,000 Frenchmen to Switzerland, Germany, the Dutch Netherlands, Great Britain, the English colonies in America, and elsewhere. The population of some entire provinces—Normandy, for instance —was greatly diminished, and commerce and manufactures languished for lack of shippers, master workmen, and other skilled operatives, nullifying almost at a stroke of the pen much of the constructive work of Colbert. The Duke of Saint-Simon, a contemporary critic of Louis's reign, described the effects.

From SAINT-SIMON, *Memoirs* [1]

The revocation of the edict of Nantes, without the slightest pretext or necessity, and the various proscriptions that followed it, were the fruits of a frightful plot, in which the new spouse [Madam de Maintenon] was one of the chief conspirators, and which depopulated a quarter of the realm, ruined its commerce, weakened it in every direction, gave it up for a long time to the public and avowed pillage of the dragoons, authorised torments and punishments by which so many innocent people of both sexes were killed by thousands; ruined a numerous class; tore in pieces a world of families; armed relatives against relatives, so as to seize their property and leave them to die of hunger; banished our manufactures to foreign lands, made those lands flourish and overflow at the expense of France, and enabled them to build new cities; gave to the world the spectacle of a prodigious population proscribed, stripped, fugitive, wandering, without crime, and seeking shelter far from its country; sent to the galleys, nobles, rich old men, people much esteemed for their piety, learning, and virtue, people well off, weak, delicate, and solely on account of religion; in fact, to heap up the measure of horror, filled all the realm with perjury and sacrilege, in the midst of the echoed cries of these unfortunate victims of error, while so many

[1] *Memoirs of Louis XIV and His Court and of the Regency,* trans. by Bayle St. John, in *Memoirs of the Courts of Europe,* 3 vols., 1910, II, 913-15. Reprinted by permission of P. F. Collier and Son Corporation, New York.

others sacrificed their conscience to their wealth and their repose, and purchased both by simulated abjuration, from which without pause they were dragged to adore what they did not believe in, and to receive the divine body of the Saint of Saints whilst remaining persuaded that they were only eating bread which they ought to abhor! Such was the general abomination born of flattery and cruelty. . . .

The King received from all sides news and details of these persecutions and of these conversions. It was by thousands that those who had abjured and taken the communion were counted; ten thousand in one place; six thousand in another— all at once and instantly. The King congratulated himself on his power and his piety. . . . All France was filled with horror and confusion; and yet there never was so much triumph and joy—never such profusion of laudations! The monarch doubted not of the sincerity of this crowd of conversions; the converters took good care to persuade him of it and to beatify him beforehand. He swallowed their poison in long draughts. He had never yet believed himself so great in the eyes of man, or so advanced in the eyes of God, in the reparation of his sins and of the scandals of his life. He heard nothing but eulogies, while the good and true Catholics and the true bishops, groaned in spirit to see the orthodox act towards error and heretics as heretical tyrants and heathens had acted against the truth, the confessors, and the martyrs. They could not, above all, endure this immensity of perjury and sacrilege. They bitterly lamented the durable and irremediable odium that detestable measure cast upon the true religion, whilst our neighbours, exulting to see us thus weaken and destroy ourselves, profited by our madness, and built designs upon the hatred we should draw upon ourselves from all the Protestant powers.

5. Society, Art, and Letters at the Court of Louis XIV

VERSAILLES AND ITS FUNCTIONS

On May 6, 1682, Louis XIV and all his court moved to the newly constructed palace of Versailles. Thousands of men and horses were still engaged in work on the palace and parks—a work which, as additions were made to the palace and grounds, continued almost to the end of Louis's reign. This enormous establishment, planned by the architects Le Vau and Mansart and personally supervised by the King himself, was constructed by herculean efforts on the barren site of an old château of Louis XIII at a total cost, in present-day currency, of about a billion dollars. It became the envy of all the crowned heads of Europe and the symbol of the might and magnificence of the Sun King. But it was not all tinsel display. Louis conceived it not only as a work due the vanity and pride of a divine-right monarch, but also as a means of depriving the nobility, without destroying its social position, of its political power in the kingdom—a feudal residue which had constantly threatened the unity of France and the paramount authority of the King. A recent writer has described this policy and its effectiveness.

From FARMER, *Versailles* (1906) [1]

The policy begun by Louis in 1661 was well established and had borne fruit by the time Versailles became the seat of government. Throughout France there was not a single estate of any size the

[1] James Eugene Farmer, *Versailles and the Court under Louis XIV*, 1906, 337-39. Reprinted by permission of D. Appleton-Century Company, Inc., New York.

proprietor of which was not at court. The new hotels of the nobility lined the streets near the royal palace, and their owners filled its salons and formed each day a cortege for the king. . . . Each morning when the king went to mass, an obsequious nobility awaited him in the gallery of Versailles. . . .

But such concentration imposed a heavy load upon the sovereign; it was the price he had to pay for his absolutism. As Taine has well said, "A nobility for useful purposes is not transformed with impunity into a nobility for ornament. . . . The king is expected to keep the entire aristocracy busy, consequently to make a display of himself, to pay back with his own person at all hours. It is the life of an actor who is on the stage the entire day."

The nobility had their price to pay. The cost of living at court ate up their incomes; their continued absence from their estates made their revenues diminish, left their châteaux neglected, and much of their land uncultivated; high play plunged them into debt. A few years brought the inevitable, and they became dependent on the royal bounty. . . . The last traces of their independence vanished.

They numbered in all some 160,000 persons, some 25,000 or 30,000 noble families in a nation of 25,000,000 people, upon whom they looked haughtily and indifferently, by whom they were disliked, and from whom they still demanded feudal tribute though they themselves had ceased to render feudal service. Thus they took something and gave nothing in return, an evil which in succeeding generations would bring catastrophe. But the day of ruin was distant and undreamed of. Absorbed in the etiquette and intrigues of Versailles, the *noblesse de cour* had neither time nor inclination to think of anything else. State affairs were not for them, but for the monarch and his ministers, in councils from which they were excluded. With the establishments they

had to maintain, their valets and lackeys, their equipages, their costumes, their high play, they were always in debt, and the poverty in the provinces affected them in so far only as it reduced their incomes. They very rarely came in contact with the peasants on their estates, and had therefore little personal interest in them. . . . Duties at Versailles, on the other hand, were real and pressing. One was hoping to get the post of gentleman usher to the Duc de Bourgogne, but Madame de Maintenon had never smiled on him, and so he was hurrying hither and thither to find some person with influence enough to vin her over; another was all upset because somebody had taken precedence of her at the king's supper, and was trying o make her husband complain to the king; a third was wondering if he would get the royal candlestick at the *coucher*. . . There were hundreds of others busy about just such matters, and all these things were vital. Versailles produced its type, the grand seigneur, "polished but hard as marble." He was master of his features and his emotions; he smiled alike on friends and enemies; he concealed his thoughts and disguised his passions; he knew when to speak and when to sigh and when to be silent; he was alert and on his guard; he had wit and charm; his pose and manners were perfect; he measured them to the fraction of an inch and appeared only with those from whom something was to be gained. But, above all, he had the court air. "The court air is contagious," says La Bruyère. "It pervades Versailles as the Norman accent pervades Rouen or Falaise. It appears in the lackeys, in the grooms of the Stables, in the people of the Fruit-loft."

THE ROUTINE OF LOUIS XIV AND HIS COURT

Louis de Rouvroy, Duke of Saint-Simon (1675-1755), was born at Versailles and spent most of his early life at court. An active collector of gossip, he wrote a heterogeneous but vastly entertaining mass of memoirs which contain some of our best word pictures of the Sun King and his court—although he disliked Louis XIV intensely, partly because the latter repressed the nobility. His description of the King's daily life follows.

From SAINT-SIMON, *Memoirs* [1]

At eight o'clock the chief *valet de chambre* on duty, who alone had slept in the royal chamber, and who had dressed himself, awoke the King. The chief physician, the chief surgeon, and the nurse (as long as she lived), entered at the same time. The latter kissed the King; the others rubbed [him] and often changed his shirt, because he was in the habit of sweating a great deal. At the quarter, the grand chamberlain was called (or, in his absence, the first gentleman of the chamber), and those who had what was called the *grandes entrées*. The chamberlain (or chief gentleman) drew back the curtains which had been closed again, and presented the holy-water from the vase, at the head of the bed. These gentlemen stayed but a moment, and that was the time to speak to the King, if any one had anything to ask of him; in which case the rest stood aside. . . . Then all passed into the cabinet of the council. A very short religious service being over, the King called, they re-entered. The same officer gave him his dressing-gown; immediately after, other privileged courtiers entered, and then everybody, in time to find the King putting on his shoes and stockings, for he did almost everything himself and with address and grace. Every other day we saw

[1] Louis de Rouvroy, Duke of Saint-Simon, *Memoirs of Louis XIV and His Court and of the Regency,* in *Memoirs of the Courts of Europe,* III, 935-43. By permission of P. F. Collier & Son Corporation.

him shave himself; and he had a little short wig in which he always appeared, even in bed, and on medicine days. . . .

As soon as he was dressed, he prayed to God, at the side of his bed, where all the clergy present knelt, the cardinals without cushions, all the laity remaining standing; and the captain of the guards came to the balustrade during the prayer, after which the King passed into his cabinet.

He found there, or was followed by all who had the *entrée,* a very numerous company, for it included everybody in any office. He gave orders to each for the day; thus within a half a quarter of an hour it was known what he meant to do; and then all this crowd left directly. . . .

All the Court meantime waited for the King in the gallery, the captain of the guard being alone in the chamber seated at the door of the cabinet. . . . During this pause the King gave audiences when he wished to accord any, spoke with whoever he might wish to speak secretly to, and gave secret interviews to foreign ministers in presence of Torcy. They were called "secret" simply to distinguish them from the uncommon ones by the bedside.

The King went to mass, where his musicians always sang an anthem. . . . The King amused himself a little upon returning from mass and asked almost immediately for the council. Then the morning was finished.

On Sunday, and often on Monday, there was a council of state; on Tuesday a finance council; on Wednesday council of state; on Saturday finance council. Rarely were two held in one day or any on Thursday or Friday. Once or twice a month there was a council of despatches on Monday morning; but the order that the Secretaries of State took every morning between the King's rising and his mass, much abridged this kind of business. . . .

Thursday morning was almost always blank. It was the day for audiences that the King wished to give—often unknown to any—backstair audiences.. . . . At Fontainebleau on the mornings when there was no council, the King usually passed from mass to Madame de Maintenon's, and so at Trianon and Marly. It was the time for their *tête-à-tête* without interruption. Often on the days when there was no council the dinner hour was advanced, more or less for the chase or the promenade. The ordinary hour was one o'clock; if the council still lasted, then the dinner waited and nothing was said to the King.

The dinner was always *au petit couvert,* that is, the King ate by himself in his chamber upon a square table in front of the middle window. It was more or less abundant, for he ordered in the morning whether it was to be "a little," or "very little" service. But even at this last, there were always many dishes, and three courses without counting the fruit. The dinner being ready, the principal courtiers entered. . . .

Upon leaving the table the King immediately entered his cabinet. That was the time for distinguished people to speak to him. He stopped at the door a moment to listen, then entered; very rarely did any one follow him, never without asking him for permission to do so; and for this few had the courage. If followed he placed himself in the embrasure of the window nearest to the door of the cabinet, which immediately closed of itself, and which you were obliged to open yourself on quitting the King. This also was the time for the bastards and the valets.

The King amused himself by feeding his dogs, and remained with them more or less time, then asked for his wardrobe, changed before the very few distinguished people it pleased the first gentleman of the chamber to admit there, and immediately went out by the back stairs into the court of marble to get into his coach. From the bottom of that staircase to the coach, any one spoke to him who wished. . . .

As he was but little sensitive to heat or cold, or even to rain, the weather was seldom sufficiently bad to prevent his going abroad. He went out for three objects: stag-hunting, once or more each week; shooting in his parks (and no man handled a gun with more grace or skill), once or twice each week; and walking in his gardens for exercise, and to see his workmen. Sometimes he made picnics with ladies, in the forest at Marly or at Fontainebleau, and in this last place, promenades with all the Court around the canal, which was a magnificent spectacle. . . .

Upon returning home from walks or drives, anybody, as I have said, might speak to the King from the moment he left his coach till he reached the foot of his staircase. He changed his dress again, and rested in his cabinet an hour or more, then went to Madame de Maintenon's, and on the way any one who wished might speak to him.

At ten o'clock his supper was served. The captain of the guard announced this to him. A quarter of an hour after the King came to supper, and from the antechamber of Madame de Maintenon to the table again, any one spoke to him who wished. This supper was always on a grand scale, the royal household (that is, the sons and daughters of France) at table, and a large number of courtiers and ladies present, sitting or standing. . . .

The King, wishing to retire, went and fed his dogs; then said goodnight, passed into his chamber to the *ruelle* of his bed, where he said his prayers, as in the morning, then undressed. . . .

He was always clad in dresses more or less brown, lightly embroidered, but never at the edges, sometimes with nothing but a gold button, sometimes black velvet. He wore always a vest of cloth, or of red, blue, or green satin, much embroidered. He used no ring; and no jewels, except in the buckles of his shoes, garters, and hat, the latter always trimmed with Spanish point, with a white feather. He had always the *cordon bleu* outside, except at fêtes, when he wore it inside, with eight or ten millions of precious stones attached.

NICOLAS BOILEAU-DESPRÉAUX AND "THE ART OF POETRY"

French literature, especially poetry, was profoundly affected by the writings of Nicolas Boileau-Despréaux (1636-1711), a poet and critic who in 1677 became historiographer to the King. One of his works, *L'art poétique* (1674), written in imitation of the *Ars Poetica* of Horace, set forth rules which not only governed French verse but also established maxims of esthetic appreciation which affected all forms of art. Selections from Boileau's maxims follow.

From BOILEAU, *The Art of Poetry* (1674) [1]

Whate're you write of Pleasant or Sublime,
Always let Sense accompany your Rhyme:
Vainly they seem two different ways to
   draw,
Rhyme must be made to close with Rea-
   son's Law.
And when to conquer her you bend your
   Force,
The Mind will Triumph in the Noble
   Course;
To Reason's Yoke she quickly will in-
   cline,
Which, far from hurting, renders her Di-
   vine:
But, if neglected, will as quickly stray,
And master Reason, which she should
   Obey.
Love Reason then: and let what e're you
   Write

[1] *The Works of Boileau*, 3 vols. London, 1712, I, 85-93, Canto I.

Borrow from her its Beauty, Worth and
   Light.
Most Writers, mounted on a resty Muse,
Extravagant, and Senseless Objects chuse;
They Think they err, if in their Verse they
   fall
On any Thought that's Plain, or Natural:
Fly this Excess; and let *Italians* be
Vain Authors of false glitt'ring Poesie;
All ought to aim at Sense; but most in vain
Strive the hard Pass and slipp'ry Height
   to gain:
You're lost, if you the right or left prefer;
Reason has but one way, and cannot
   Err. . . .
A frozen Stile, that neither Ebbs or Flows,
Instead of pleasing, makes us gape and
   doze.
Those tedious Authors are esteem'd by
   none
Who tire us, Humming the same heavy
   Tone. . . .
In all you Write, be neither Low nor Vile:
The meanest Theme may have a proper
   Stile. . . .
Take Time for thinking; never work in
   haste;
And value not your self for writing fast.
A rapid Poem, with such Fury writ,
Shews want of Judgment, not abounding
   Wit. . . .
Polish, repolish, every Colour lay,
And sometimes add; but oft'ner take
   away. . . .
One perfect whole, of all the Pieces join'd.
Keep to your Subject close, in all you say;
Nor for a sounding Sentence lose the Way.
The publick Censure for your Writings
   fear,
And to your self be Critic most severe.

PAINTING, LITERATURE, AND COSTUMES

Boileau's emphasis upon reason and good sense established truth as the end of all art. But the strict etiquette of the

French court, designed to pamper the pompous dignity of the King, choked imagination so as to impair the quality of much of the art patronized by the Sun King. In the selection given below, a recent Austrian writer discusses art in the Age of Louis XIV. He begins with a treatment of the paintings of Nicolas Poussin (1594-1665).

From FRIEDELL, *A Cultural History* (1931) [1]

It is characteristic of him that he learnt drawing from classical reliefs. His figures have only types of faces, they are mere specimens of a genus like plants in a herbarium. We never have, as in so many of the figures of Renaissance art, the impression of a personal acquaintance with them. Poussin was a learned painter, an accurate connoisseur of the classical. He did the great service of bringing the landscape into the picture, but he did it as an archaeologist: it is invariably a classical scene that he paints. . . .

Poussin saw everything mathematically: trees, with their exquisitely fine but geometrical silhouettes; rocks, with their magnificently clear and harmonious edges and surfaces modelled according to crystal-like structure; circular lakes, clean-angled mountain chains, even cloud-formations, and the lines of human bodies systematically disposed as ornament. Yet with all this he was, strange to say, a mighty master of mood: a true Baroque painter, and the most forceful pioneer for the subtle Claude Lorrain [also known as Claude Gellée, 1600-1687] and his virtuosity of light-treatment and foregrounds. With him nature is genuine nature, but he paints her only in her domesticated, well-behaved, drawing-room moments. . . . Then there is Rigaud [Hyacinthe Rigaud,

1659-1743], chamberlain and master-of-the-robes-in-chief, as it were, of the age. He paints his men with the "correct" facial expressions and posture, coiffure and costume. They must stand, lean, and sit just so; stretch out their hands, carry their swords, clutch their cloaks with exactly the right effect and sense of proportion, with majesty and self-respect, masters of themselves as of others: every one a miniature Louis XIV. . . .

Music was devoted chiefly to the service of drama. Jean Baptiste Lully (a Florentine, whose name was really Lulli) was the creator of grand opera, the *tragédie lyrique*. His librettist was Philippe Quinault, whose art ranked him about the great tragic dramatists in the public mind. Lully contrived to create a positive monopoly of opera for himself by obtaining a royal warrant forbidding any theatres except his own to employ more than two singers and six stringed instruments. He was not merely composer, but director, conductor, producer, and stage-manager into the bargain. . . . The chorus, which had sunk to being a mere accessory, was restored by him to its full significance. He gave the rhythmic element precedence over the melodic and used music solely to strengthen the effect of the word and to lend it emotional richness and depth. . . . It was fundamentally designed for recitation, without coloratura or true arias, but on the other hand with a magnificent equipment of scenery, ballet, costumes, women's and men's choruses in many parts (even behind the scenes), musical descriptions of storms at sea, battles, thunderstorms, volcanic eruptions, and the torments of hell. The *tragédie classique* was already music in a sense, responding as it did to the rhythmic currents which bore it along and moulded it; but in opera the will-to-style of the period reached its summit: there everything was ordered and clear,

[1] Egon Friedell, *A Cultural History of the Modern Age,* trans. by Charles Francis Atkinson, 3 vols., 1931, II, 97-103. Reprinted by permission of Alfred A. Knopf, New York.

sonorous and pure, brightly and pleasantly cadenced. . . .

If the age of Louis XIV were to be judged by its operas and tragedies, its buildings and paintings, its dissertations and sermons, the impression gained would be that of a race of heroes striding across the earth, grandiose but very dull heroes, bigger than life, but lacking souls. To find out what these people were really like we must go to the second category of their art and literature, their caricatures, lampoons, and satires, memoirs, anecdotes, and aphorisms. . . . Out of the mass of these expressions of real life we will single out the one which speaks for all: the *Maxims* of the Duc de La Rochefoucauld.

La Rochefoucauld is the first real aphorist of modern times. His short sentences are compressed moral and psychological treatises. In them too there lives the *esprit géométrique,* which is seen in their razor-sharp antithesis, their crystallographic phrasing. He is none the less the man of the world and of the salon, even in point of style. His sketches are not merely witty, but also pleasing and graceful, elegant as drops of a choice perfume, the strong extract of the fragrance left by many thousands of minor experiences. The author's philosophical system is very simple. Just as psycho-analysis explains everything on sexual grounds, so he derives all human actions from a single motive: namely, *l'orgueil, la vanité, l'amour-propre* (pride, vanity, self-love): "many as are the discoveries that have been made in the realm of self-love, it still holds many an unexplored country"; "selfishness speaks all languages and plays all roles, even that of unselfishness"; and "even virtue would not get so far did not vanity keep her company." And, because he is ever on the alert for the secret under-layer of vanity, he succeeds in rooting it out of its last hiding-place and catching and holding its most delicate nuances: "we should rather hear

evil spoken of us than nothing at all"; "to decline praise is to ask for it twice over"; "we often pardon those whom we find tedious, but never those who find us tedious"; "whether philosophers regard life with affection or indifference is merely a matter of the direction taken by their vanity." Virtue, too, is only a form of vice: "the virtues lose themselves in selfishness as rivers in a sea"; "we are often only prevented from giving ourselves up to a particular vice because we possess several varieties"; "when the vices desert us, we flatter ourselves that we have shaken them off"; "old people give good advice by way of consoling themselves for no longer being able to give bad examples." . . . Yet La Rochefoucauld is no cynic, but a sceptic full of secret aspirations. He is convinced that intellect cannot for long play the part of soul, and that the real *politesse de l'esprit* rests in "thinking nobly and delicately," that cunning and treachery arise solely from ineptitude, and that the surest way of being deceived is to believe oneself more artful than other people. A large number of his *bons mots* are distinguished by extreme delicacy, as, for instance: "It is a greater disgrace to mistrust our friends than to be deceived by them"; "To be in too great a hurry to clear off a debt is a sort of ingratitude"; "We are easily consoled for a friend's misfortunes when they give us an opportunity to show our love for him." This blending of frivolity and nobleness, harsh materialism and sensitive tactfulness, makes La Rochefoucauld the finest bloom of all the intellectual flora which sprang to life around Louis XIV. His saying: "Ridicule is more shaming than shame," mirrors the whole world of Versailles with all its light and shade, and he once summed up the whole of this culture in the words: "Every member of every class of society adopts a particular look and posture which shall make him appear what he wishes to be regarded as; we may say, therefore, that the world is made up of nothing but attitudes." And in fact we scan this race in vain for faces and spontaneous movements; wherever we look there is nothing but pose and gesture.

The costume of the period illustrates this very clearly. It is exclusively for salon wear, designed for parade occasions, for persons perpetually "on show." The doublet disappears under the *justaucorps,* a richly embroidered gala coat, reaching to the knees, with wide sleeves, long cuffs, and enormous buttons. Ladies wore the full robe with tight bodice, a train— whose length might be six to forty feet according to the wearer's rank—and the *cul de Paris,* a padded bustle suggesting abnormal development behind. Boots gave way to buckled shoes, and gloves of fine white leather were indispensable for both sexes. The chief article of external apparel was, however, the *allonge* or large state wig, which was introduced in 1625 and universally worn by 1655. . . . The feminine counterpart to the *allonge* was the *fontange,* a towering head-dress made of lace, ribbons, ruchings, and false hair, which not infrequently rose to a height of nearly five feet.

6. The Foreign Policy and Wars of Louis XIV

Louis XIV was born (1638) before the Thirty Years' War had ended, and from his earliest childhood he thirsted after military glory commensurate with his pretensions to absolute power. His foreign policies are separated, however, into two distinct parts. In 1661, when he assumed personal direction of France, until 1700, he continued the policies of Richelieu and Mazarin and enlarged upon them as opportunity offered. In this era, Louis sought to extend the French frontiers to the Rhine and to the Scheldt rivers, to enlarge the colonial empire overseas, to usurp the Emperor's position as temporal leader of the Catholic Church, and, if possible to secure the imperial title for himself. After 1700, and to the end of his reign in 1715, Louis directed his policies in a single-minded effort to set up his grandson over the Spanish Empire and through close alliance with Spain to secure Bourbon supremacy in Europe. The following chart provides a summary of the wars of his entire reign:

A SUMMARY OF THE PRINCIPAL WARS AND TREATIES IN THE REIGN OF LOUIS XIV

The Wars	Principal Contestants	Peace Treaties and a Résumé of French Gains
1. Thirty Years' War (French phase, 1635-48)	France, Sweden and lesser allies *vs.* the Empire and Spain	Treaty of Westphalia, 1648 [see page 198]. France gained from the Emperor the bishoprics of Metz, Toul, and Verdun; all Upper and Lower Alsace, including the Sundgau, except the bishoprics of Basel and Strasbourg; the fortress of Breisach and the right to garrison Philippsburg, on the right bank of the Rhine; the prefec-

A SUMMARY OF THE PRINCIPAL WARS AND TREATIES IN THE REIGN OF LOUIS XIV (Cont'd)

The Wars	Principal Contestants	Peace Treaties and a Résumé of French Gains
		tures of ten imperial cities; and Pinerolo, in Italy. War with Spain continued.
2. Spanish War (continued from Thirty Years' War until 1659)	France (with English aid after 1657) vs. Spain	Treaty of the Pyrennes, 1659. France gained from Spain Roussillon and Cerdagne, most of Artois, part of Flanders, of Hainault, of Luxembourg, and of Lorraine. Louis XIV agreed to marry the Spanish Infanta, Maria Theresa, who renounced her claims upon the Spanish throne for herself and her heirs (but this renunciation was made dependent upon Spanish payment of a huge dowry and when Spain failed to pay, Louis denounced as invalid the renunciation of his wife's claims upon the Spanish throne).
3. War of Devolution, 1667-68	France vs. Spain	Treaty of Aix-la-Chapelle (Aachen), 1668. France gained Charleroi, Lille, Tournay, and eight other towns in Flanders and Brabant.
4. The Dutch War, 1672-78	France (with English support until 1674) vs. the Dutch Netherlands, the latter aided by a coalition of the Empire, Spain, Sweden, Denmark, and others	Treaty of Nimwegen, 1678. France won from Spain the Franche Comté and important fortresses along the Spanish Netherlands frontier. The Dutch lost nothing.
5. War of the Palatinate (also known as War of the League of Augsburg), 1688-97.	France vs. the League of Augsburg, formed in 1686 and consisting of the Holy Roman	Treaty of Ryswick, 1697. France lost Breisach and other possessions on the right bank of the Rhine, but retained Strasbourg

A SUMMARY OF THE PRINCIPAL WARS AND TREATIES IN THE REIGN
OF LOUIS XIV (*Cont'd*)

The Wars	*Principal Contestants*	*Peace Treaties and a Résumé of French Gains*
	Empire, Spain, Brandenburg, Sweden, Holland, and others. England also joined (1689) after William of Orange succeeded to the English throne	and the rest of Alsace and Landau; granted commercial concessions to the Dutch and rights for them to garrison "barrier fortresses" at Ypres, Menin, Namur, and elsewhere; recognized William III as rightful King of England. As this war also took place between England and France in overseas colonies ("King William's War" in America), the treaty also provided that France regain Pondicherry in India and Nova Scotia (Acadia) in America, but return Fort Albany, Hudson's Bay, to England.
6. War of Spanish Succession, 1701-13	France and Spain (with Bavaria, some other small German states, and, until 1703, Savoy and Portugal) *vs.* the Grand Alliance, formed 1701, of Austria, most of the German states, Prussia, England, and the Dutch Netherlands (aided by Denmark and Sweden and, after 1703, by Savoy and Portugal, who changed sides in the contest in that year)	The Treaty of Utrecht, a series of treaties signed April 11, 1713, the terms of which can be summarized as follows: 1. The powers recognized Philip of Anjou as King of Spain and the Spanish colonies overseas on condition that the crowns of France and Spain should never be united. 2. Naples, Sardinia, Milan, and the Spanish Netherlands (hereafter known as the "Austrian Netherlands") were ceded to the Emperor. 3. Sicily, together with the French provinces, Savoy and Nice, were granted to the Duke, now recognized as King, of Savoy. 4. The Dutch won commercial concessions from France, a monopoly of trade on the Scheldt River and the right to garrison, with

A SUMMARY OF THE PRINCIPAL WARS AND TREATIES IN THE REIGN
OF LOUIS XIV (*Cont'd*)

The Wars	Principal Contestants	Peace Treaties and a Résumé of French Gains
		financial aid from the Austrian Netherlands, a series of barrier fortresses against France, including Furnes, Ypres, Menin, Ghent, Tournay, Mons, Charleroi, and Namur. 5. The Elector of Brandenburg, having assumed the title of King in Prussia (1701), was confirmed in that title and given Rhenish additions to his territory, including Spanish Guelderland. 6. England gained from *Spain:* Gibraltar, Minorca, preferential tariffs for her imports into Cadiz, the Asiento (monopoly of the slave trade in Spanish colonies), and the right to send each year one shipload of English goods into the Spanish colonies; from *France:* recognition of George I as lawful heir to the English throne, permanent demolition of the fortifications at Dunkirk, and, as this war too had been fought in overseas colonies ("Queen Anne's War" in America), England won Newfoundland (subject to some French fishing reservations), Nova Scotia (French "Acadia"), the Island of St. Kitts, and undisputed possession of the Hudson Bay region.

PRECURSORS OF THE WAR OF SPANISH
SUCCESSION

Charles II, last Hapsburg King of Spain (1665-1700), was frail all his life. Twice married, he had no direct heirs, and as his death was constantly expected, his neighbors began to negotiate among themselves for the partition of his empire more than thirty years before he finally expired. By the end of the War of the Palatinate (1697), three men had become prominent candidates for the Spanish throne: the Archduke Charles, second son of the Emperor Leopold; Joseph Ferdinand, electoral prince of Bavaria; and Louis, son of Louis XIV, Dauphin of France. The genealogical chart below illustrates each candidate's relationship upon which his claim was based.

Between 1697 and the outbreak of the War of Spanish Succession (1701), the following chain of events took place: 1. On October 11, 1698, unknown to the ailing Spanish monarch, was signed at The Hague the First Partition Treaty wherein France, England, Holland, and Austria agreed to partition the Spanish dominions upon the death of Charles II. Joseph Ferdinand, the Electoral Prince of Bavaria, the principal heir, was to have Spain proper, the Spanish colonies, and the Spanish Netherlands; the Italian possessions of

Spain were to be divided between the Archduke Charles and the Dauphin. 2. When Charles II learned about this treaty, he was enraged and, in an effort to preserve his kingdom intact, he signed a will, November 14, 1698, which granted all his possessions to Joseph Ferdinand of Bavaria. 3. On February 5, 1699, Joseph Ferdinand died of smallpox, upsetting all the plans both of the partitioners and of the King of Spain. 4. England, Holland, and France signed a Second Partition Treaty (March 25, 1700) whereby the Archduke Charles was to succeed to Spain, the Spanish Netherlands, and the colonies, leaving the Dauphin of France the Spanish possessions in Italy—but the Emperor refused to sign this treaty, hoping to inherit all the Spanish possessions. 5. On October 3, 1700, Charles II of Spain made a new will which, thanks to the recommendations of the pope

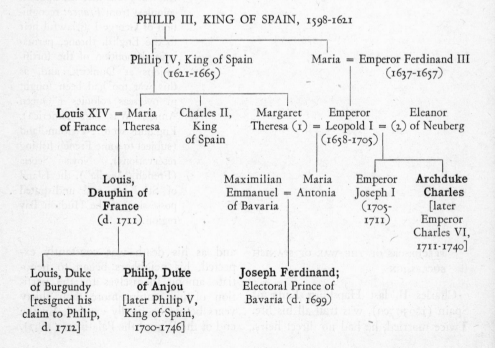

PHILIP III, KING OF SPAIN, 1598-1621

Philip IV, King of Spain (1621-1665)
Maria = Emperor Ferdinand III (1637-1657)

Louis XIV = Maria Theresa
of France
Charles II, King of Spain
Margaret Theresa (1) = Leopold I = (2) Eleanor of Neuberg (1658-1705)

Louis, **Dauphin of France** (d. 1711)
Maximilian Emmanuel of Bavaria = Maria Antonia
Emperor Joseph I (1705-1711)
Archduke Charles [later Emperor Charles VI, 1711-1740]

Louis, Duke of Burgundy [resigned his claim to Philip, d. 1712]
Philip, Duke of Anjou [later Philip V, King of Spain, 1700-1746]
Joseph Ferdinand; Electoral Prince of Bavaria (d. 1699)

and clever French diplomacy, granted all his possessions to Philip of Anjou, second son of the French Dauphin and grandson of Louis XIV. On November 1 following, the King of Spain died. 6. Louis XIV decided to accept the will of the Spanish monarch, thereby ignoring the Second Partition Treaty which he had signed, and in less than a year war had begun and the Grand Alliance was formed against the Bourbons (September 7, 1701). Saint-Simon wrote the following relation of Louis XIV's carefully considered action upon receipt of the news from Spain.

From SAINT-SIMON, *Memoirs* [1]

The news arrived at Court (Fontainebleau) in the month of November [1700]. The King was going out shooting that day; but, upon learning what had taken place, at once countermanded the sport, announced the death of the King of Spain, and at three o'clock held a council of ministers in the apartments of Madame de Maintenon. This council lasted until past seven o'clock in the evening. Monseigneur [the Dauphin], who had been out wolf-hunting, returned in time to attend it. On the next morning, Wednesday, another council was held, and in the evening a third, in the apartments of Madame de Maintenon. However accustomed persons were at Court to the favor Madame de Maintenon enjoyed there, they were extremely surprised to see two councils assembled in her rooms for the greatest and most important deliberation that had taken place during this long reign, or indeed during many others.

The King, Monseigneur, the Chancellor, the Duc de Brinvilliers, Torcy, and Madame de Maintenon were the only persons

who deliberated upon this affair. Madame de Maintenon preserved at first a modest silence; but the King forced her to give her opinion after everybody had spoken except herself. The council was divided. Two were for keeping to the [Second Partition] treaty that had been signed with King William [of England], two for accepting the [King of Spain's] will.

Monseigneur . . . to the great surprise of the King and his assistants, when it was his turn to speak . . . expressed himself with force in favor of accepting the testament. Then, turning towards the King in a respectful but firm manner, he said that he took the liberty of asking for his inheritance, that the monarchy of Spain belonged to the Queen his mother, and consequently to him; that he surrendered it willingly to his second son for the tranquillity of Europe; but that to none other would he yield an inch of ground. . . .

The King did not yet declare himself. He said that the affair might well be allowed to sleep for four-and-twenty hours, in order that they might ascertain if the Spaniards approved the choice of their King. . . .

At last, on Tuesday, the 16th of November, the King publicly declared himself. The Spanish ambassador had received intelligence which proved the eagerness of Spain to welcome the Duc d'Anjou as its King. There seemed to be no doubt of the matter. The King, immediately after getting up, called the ambassador into his cabinet, where M. le Duc l'Anjou had already arrived. Then, pointing to the Duke, he told the ambassador he might salute him as King of Spain. The ambassador threw himself upon his knees after the fashion of his country, and addressed to the Duke a tolerably long compliment in the Spanish language. Immediately afterwards, the King, contrary to all custom,

[1] Saint-Simon, *Memoirs,* in *Memoirs of the Courts of Europe,* I, 239-42. By permission of P. F. Collier and Son Corporation.

opened the two folding doors of his cabinet, and commanded everybody to enter. It was a very full Court that day. The King, majestically turning his eyes towards the numerous company, and showing them M. le Duc d'Anjou said—"Gentlemen, behold the King of Spain. His birth called him to that crown: the late King also has called him to it by his will; the whole nation wished for him, and has asked me for him eagerly; it is the will of heaven. I have obeyed it with pleasure." And then, turning towards his grandson, he said, "Be a good Spaniard, that is your first duty; but remember that you are a Frenchman born, in order that the union between the two nations may be preserved; it will be the means of rendering both happy, and of preserving peace in Europe."

7. Some Contemporary Critics of Louis XIV's Reign

FÉNELON

Contemporary critics of the Sun King and his reign seldom breathed freely once their criticisms had been made known. A few outspoken ones existed, however—mostly in the latter part of Louis's reign, when his extravagant manners and costly wars weighed increasingly heavily upon the French people. One of these critics was Fénelon (François de Salignac de La Mothe-, Archbishop of Cambrai, 1651-1715), the famous French author and tutor (1689-97) of the young Duke of Burgundy. About 1694 Fénelon addressed an anonymous letter to Louis XIV consisting of "Remonstrances to That Prince upon Various Points of His Administration." Part of the letter follows.

From FÉNELON, "Remonstrances" (c. 1694) [1]

Sire, the person who takes the liberty to write this letter to you has no ax to grind. . . . If he speaks strongly to you, do not be astonished; for the truth is free and strong. You have not been accustomed to hear it. . . .

For nearly thirty years, your principal Ministers have destroyed and reversed all the ancient maxims of the state in order to raise your authority to its highest pitch, an authority which has become theirs because they have it in their own hands. They no longer speak of the state and of its constitution; they only speak of the King and of his royal pleasure. They have pushed your revenues and your expenses to unprecedented heights. They have raised you up to the sky in order, they say, to outshine the grandeur of all your predecessors; that is to say, in order to impoverish the whole of France for the introduction of monstrous and futile luxuries at the court. They have wished to establish you upon the ruin of all the state, as if you could be great in ruining all your subjects, upon whom your true greatness rests. It is true that you have been jealous of authority, perhaps even too much so in little things; but, at bottom, each Minister has been master in the conduct of his own administration. You have believed yourself governor because you have regulated the limits of those who govern. They have well demonstrated their power to the public, and they have done it only too completely. They have been harsh, haughty, unjust, violent, of bad faith. They have recognized no other rule, either in the administration of internal affairs or in foreign relations, but to threaten, to crush, and to destroy all who resist them. . . . They have rendered your name odious, and the whole French nation intolerable

[1] Œuvres de Fénelon, ed. by Aimé Martin, 3 vols. Paris, 1870, III, 425-28.

to all our neighbors. They have kept none of our ancient allies, because they only want slaves. They have caused almost twenty years of bloody wars. . . .

Meanwhile, your people, whom you should love as your children, and who until now have been so eager to support you, die of hunger. The cultivation of the soil is almost abandoned; the towns and the countryside are depopulated; all business enterprise is stagnant, and no longer offers employment to workingmen. All commerce is destroyed. As a result, you have ruined half of the real forces within your state in order to make and defend vain conquests outside. Instead of taking money from these poor people, one should give them alms and feed them. All France is nothing more than a great poorhouse, desolate and without provisions. . . .

The people themselves, it should be said, who hitherto have loved you and had confidence in you, are beginning to lose love, confidence, and even respect. Your victories and your conquests no longer cause them to rejoice; they are full of bitterness and despair. Sedition is kindled little by little everywhere. They believe that you love only your authority and your glory. . . .

There, Sire, is the state of things. You live as one whose eyes are fatally blinded.

VAUBAN

A second informed critic of Louis's administration was the famous military engineer and marshal of France, Sébastien le Prestre de Vauban (1633-1707). Vauban's work had taken him into all parts of France, and his observations led him to believe that the poverty-stricken, tax-burdened peasantry could be relieved and the kingdom vastly improved by altering the tax system. He advocated a single tax, a royal tithe, patterned after that of the church, whereby the peasantry might pay one-tenth of their agricultural products while merchants and manufacturers paid one-tenth of their money incomes, the tax to be payable by all classes, with few exemptions. Vauban wrote his book in 1698 but delayed its publication until 1707. It was quickly suppressed by order of Louis XIV, and Vauban died soon afterward, brokenhearted because of the royal disfavor. The introduction to his treatise, including his reasons for writing, ran as follows.

From VAUBAN, *Project for a Royal Tithe* (1698) [1]

I say it with all imaginable Sincerity, that it is not out of any fondness of my own abilities, nor any inclination to arrogate to my self any thing above my merit, or to attract any additional esteem, that I have set about this work. I am neither a scholar, nor one concerned in the revenues; and should I attempt to acquire honour or profit by things that do not belong to my profession, I should do it with a very ill grace. I am a *French* man, well affected to my country, and very sensible of the distinguishing marks of favour the King has been pleased for a long time to heap upon me. . . .

The wandering life I have led for above forty years has given me opportunities of seeing and observing, often and in different manners, the most part of the provinces of this kingdom. . . . The state and condition of the people, whose poverty having often moved my compassion, has put me upon an enquiry into the causes of it. . . .

During the several years that I have made it my business to enquire into that matter, by all I can observe and find, in these late times, near a tenth part of the

[1] *A Project for a Royal Tithe, or General Tax*, London, 1708, Preface, i-ii, iii-iv, viii.

people are actually reduced to beggary; that of the other nine parts, not five of them are in a condition to give alms to that tenth, by reason of the miserable condition they are reduced to, and the small pittance that is left them. That of the four other parts of the people, three are in hard circumstances, by reason of their great debts, and the inextricable law-suits they are intangled in; and that of the other tenth part, in which I comprehend the gentlemen of the sword (as they're called), those of the robe, both clergy and laity, the nobility of all sorts, all those who bear civil or military offices, the rich merchants and burghers that have estates, and others who are pretty well to pass; I say, of all those there cannot be reckoned above a hundred thousand families. And I should not be much out of the way if I averred, that, great and small together, there are not ten thousand of them whose circumstances are easy; and if you will abstract from those the farmers of the revenues, under-farmers, collectors, &c. and all their associates and adherents, open and secret,

and those the King maintains by his favour, some few merchants, &c., I am very sure the remainder would be small.

Though the causes of the misery of the people of this kingdom be well known [inequalities and corruption in the tax system] . . . it would be a thing of great use and importance to find out some substantial remedy for this evil, now while we enjoy a peace, which promises us a long continuance. . . .

In effect, the establishment of a Royal Tithe, laid upon all the fruits of the earth, on one hand, and on all that produces yearly incomes on the other, seems to me to be the most equal and proportionable of all other; because the one goes always with the land, which yields increase according to its fertility; and the other goes according to the evident and unquestionable incomes. This scheme is of all other the least liable to corruption, because it is subject only to its own regulations, and does no way depend on the will and pleasure of any man.

18 | HOHENZOLLERN *vs.* HAPSBURG: THE RISE OF BRANDENBURG-PRUSSIA TO 1786

1. The Accomplishments of Frederick William, the "Great Elector" (1640-88)

The story of the rise of Brandenburg-Prussia as a first-rate European power is one of territorial enlargement and population growth, of administrative reform and centralization of authority in the hands of the Electors of Branden-

burg (who, in 1618, became dukes and later (1701) kings in East Prussia), and of economic improvement and expansion. All of these accomplishments occurred under the direction of members of the House of Hohenzollern which in 1412 acquired the Mark of Brandenburg, then a weak and unprosperous buffer state in the Holy Roman Empire. Considerations of policy as well as conviction led the Hohenzollerns to become Lutherans (1539), Calvinists (1613), and early proponents of religious freedom (1614). When, by shrewd politics and fortunate legacy, John Sigismund, Elector of Brandenburg (1608-19), won Cleves, Mark, and Ravensberg (1614) and inherited (as fief of the King of Poland) the Duchy of East Prussia (1618), Brandenburg-Prussia was on the threshold of greatness. Though it partook greatly of the general devastation caused by the Thirty Years' War, it added new territories (East Pomerania, Halberstadt, Minden, Magdeburg, and Cammin) by the Treaty of Westphalia and, under the prudent administration of Frederick William, the "Great Elector" (1640-88), first achieved prominence. The following excerpt is from an old account of the Great Elector's reign.

A SURVEY OF THE GREAT ELECTOR'S ADMINISTRATION

From *Memoirs of the House of Brandenburg* (*c.* 1690) [1]

There would have been an end of Brandenburg forever if Frederick William, who began to reign in 1640, had not taken such immense pains to retrieve it. His prudence and resolution, together with time, overcame all those obstacles; he concluded a peace, and immediately set about a new creation.

Brandenburg, in fact, became a new country, formed of a mixture of all nations, who afterwards intermarried with those few of the ancient inhabitants that had escaped destruction. . . . [2]

---

[1] Adapted from *Memoirs of the House of Brandenburg . . . by the Hand of a Master*, translated from the Berlin Copy, London, 1751, 226-32.

[2] In all his territories, the Great Elector had a population of only about 600,000 in 1640; by the end of his reign (1688), the population had grown to about 1,500,000.

The first colony that came to settle in the electorate were Dutch [1649]. These revived the several handicraft trades and formed a project for selling timber, with which the country abounded; for thirty years had turned almost all the soil into a forest. The sale of this timber constituted afterwards one of the principal branches of our commerce. The Elector gave leave to some Jewish families to settle in his dominions, the neighborhood of Poland rendering them very useful for vending in that kingdom the refuse of our frippery.

Not long after a favourable event ensued which considerably promoted the designs of the Great Elector. Louis XIV revoked the Edict of Nantes in 1685, upon which occasion at least 300,000 French quitted the kingdom. Those who had most money retired to England and Holland, but the most industrious part of them, to the number of 20,000 or thereabouts, took shelter in the country of Brandenburg. These helped to repeople our deserted villages and brought all sorts of manufactures amongst us, which we wanted. . . .

At the accession of Frederick William to the regency, there was no manufacture in this country, either of hats, stockings, serges, or any kind of woollen stuffs. We are indebted to the industry of the French for all these manufactures: they erected fabrics of cloths, serges, stuffs, felts, crepes, caps, woven stockings, all sorts of hats, and dyeing in different colors. Some of those refugees turned shop-keepers and retailed the several wares that were fabricated by their countrymen. Berlin now had goldsmiths, jewellers, watchmakers, and carvers. The French who settled in open country planted tobacco and a variety of fruits and excellent pulse were seen to grow in a sandy soil which, by their careful cultivation, was become an admirable kitchen garden. . . .

Thus the Electorate was in a more

flourishing condition under the administration of Frederick William than it had
been under any of his ancestors. The great
improvement of the manufactures increased the different branches of commerce, which was afterwards confined
chiefly to our corn, timber, woollen manufactures, and salt. The use of post-houses,
hitherto unknown in Germany, was introduced by the Great Elector throughout
all his dominions. . . . The cities before
that time paid arbitrary taxes, which were
suppressed, and an excise was substituted
in their stead. The cities began to be
civilized, the streets were paved, and
lanthorns were set up at proper distances
to light the inhabitants. . . .

Frederick William was the first Elector
that kept a regular body of disciplined
troops in his service. . . .

The continual wars, together with the
mixture of new inhabitants, had already
made a change in ancient manners. A
great many of the French and Dutch customs were adopted by our people, but the
predominant vices were [still] drunkenness and avarice.

THE GREAT ELECTOR WELCOMES
HUGUENOT REFUGEES

The extraordinary liberality of the
Great Elector's provisions for French
refugees mirrors his eagerness to improve his realm. His edict of welcome
was issued at Potsdam.

From FREDERICK WILLIAM, Edict Concerning
    Huguenot Refugees (1685) [1]

As the persecutions and severe punishments which have been exercised repeatedly against confessors of the reformed

[1] Franz Zurbonsen, *Quellenbuch zur brandenburgisch-preussischen Geschichte,* in *Geschicht-
liche Repetitionsfragen und Ausführungen,* 4 Tiel.,
2nd ed., Berlin, 1906, No. 97; 120-22.

religion in France have forced many families to emigrate from that kingdom and
to seek refuge in foreign lands, we have
been pleased, out of the righteous sympathy which we feel for those who suffer for
the sake of the Evangelical Religion and
the purity of that faith to which we adhere, by means of the present edict signed
by our own hand, to offer them a free and
safe admission to all our lands and provinces, and to declare further to them what
rights, privileges, and advantages we shall
permit them to enjoy, as follows:

1. In order that all those who shall determine to settle in our state may remove
thither with the greatest convenience, we
have commanded all our extraordinary
envoys to the States General of the United
Netherlands and to our consul in Amsterdam [or agents at Frankfurt-am-Main] to
furnish at our expense necessary ships and
provisions to all those of the Reformed
Religion who apply to them, in order to
transport their families and their goods
from Holland to Hamburg. In the latter
city, they will obtain from our agents to
the lower Saxon district all conveyance
which they need in order to reach any city
or province of our state in which they
choose to live. . . .

4. The goods, furniture, merchandise,
and provisions which they bring with
them shall be admitted duty-free. . . .

5. In case there should be in the towns,
villages, and hamlets where the above-
mentioned refugees are going to settle, any
empty, forsaken, or dilapidated houses
whose proprietors are financially unable
to put them in good repair, we shall give
to the immigrants such houses in full title
and reimburse the previous owners in
proportion to the value of the properties,
and we shall relieve them of all other obligations, be they mortgages or other debts.
We shall also supply the immigrants with
wood, stone, plaster, brick, and other ma-

terials necessary for the repair of these houses; and these houses shall be free from all taxes, quartering of soldiers, and other public burdens, save payment of excise, for a period of six years. . . .

7. As soon as they have definitely settled in any town or village of our state, they shall be accorded full civic rights and permission to join those guilds and corporations for which they are eligible—in short, they may enjoy the same rights and privileges as our native-born subjects.

8. All those who desire to set up manufactures, be it textiles, cloth, hats, or other things, will be endowed not only with all special privileges, considerations, and freedom which they might desire, but also we shall support them with money and other supplies so that their projects may become successful enterprises.

9. The farmers and others who wish to settle in the country will be given a certain piece of land for cultivation, and they will be supplied with all necessary things at the beginning in the same manner as has already been done with a considerable number of Swiss immigrants.

10. As for the legal side of life and the administration of justice among the above-mentioned French Reformed brethren, we permit that in towns where several families of them are settled, they may choose a magistrate of their own who may settle their difficulties peaceably, without any recourse to courts. If differences arise between Germans and French, these are to be settled mutually by the German authorities and the French magistrates, and this procedure shall also be followed in case of French troubles which are not settled peaceably among themselves.

11. In every town we shall employ a clergy and shall designate a suitable place so that the immigrants may worship in the French language and according to their customary ceremonies.

THE GREAT ELECTOR'S POLITICAL TESTAMENT FOR HIS SON

Frederick William prepared for his son a list of "secret advices" which, as they reflect his own experiences, illustrate his policies. Though not as extensive as the "Advice" written by Louis XIV for the Dauphin [see page 247], the Great Elector's suggestions are comparable, especially with reference to the relations with the nobility and the necessity of full knowledge of administrative details.

From FREDERICK WILLIAM, "Secret Advices to His Son" (1667) [1]

You should conduct yourself as a good father of your realm, love your subjects regardless of their religious persuasions, and seek to advance their welfare at all times. Labor to stimulate commerce everywhere, and be mindful of the increase of the population of the Mark of Brandenburg. Call in the clergy and the nobility frequently in order to discuss affairs with them; be interested and gracious to all of them, as behooves one in your position; recognize merit, because by so doing you will increase the love and affection of your subjects toward you. However, at all times, you must observe moderation so as not to jeopardize your position and lose respect, and against those of your own kind [the nobility] you must in no way give in to them as far as precedence and all that to which you are entitled is concerned, but hold fast to that pre-eminence which pertains to your superior position, because with too great pomp and too great a show on the part of the courtiers it can happen that one loses his pre-eminent position, as examples have shown.

Take a keen interest in the administration of justice throughout your land, and

[1] Zurbonsen, *Quellenbuch zur brandenburgisch-preussischen Geschichte*, No. 102; 128-30.

see to it that it be administered to the poor as well as to the rich without discrimination among persons and that lawsuits are carried out speedily, without prolongation, for such a policy solidifies the position of the ruler. . . . [Be careful to select incorruptible, wise judges; administer strict punishments to wrongdoers, as examples to others; and always be sure to hear all the arguments on both sides of a case before giving a decision.]

At all times, seek to have friendly relations with the princes and nobility of the Empire. Hold active correspondence and friendship with them, and give them no cause for ill will; be careful not to evoke envy or animosity, but be sure that you are always in a strong position in order to lend weight in case of disputes. . . . And in case there should be war, be sure that good order obtains at home, and that the people are not oppressed, because the outcome of the war rests upon them.

Alliances are all right, but your own strength is better, because you can rely on it. Without the means and the people, the ruler is in no strong position. It is these, God be praised, which have made me powerful since the time I began to have them. I regret that in the beginning of my reign I forsook this policy and followed the advice of others [the Swedes] against my will.

2. The First Two Kings of Prussia (1701-40)

Between the immediate successor of the Great Elector, Frederick III (who in 1701 became *King* Frederick I), and his son, Frederick William I (1713-40), there was a violent contrast in personalities and policies—a contrast which has been compared to the differences between ancient Athens and Sparta. For Frederick was weak and deformed in body, excessively vain in spirit, possessed a love of elaborate pomp and extravagant ceremony (meticulously patterned after the court of Louis XIV), and was a liberal patron of arts and sciences; whereas Frederick William was a hard-working, ill-tempered tyrant who despised all that his father held dear at court, was economical to the point of parsimony, and devoted his enormous energies to the militarization of the administration, economy, and all the forces of the Prussian state. The selections below will serve to illustrate this contrast.

FREDERICK III, THE ELECTOR, BECOMES FREDERICK I, THE KING, 1701

"What was undertaken as an act of vanity became a great stroke of policy" —thus wrote Frederick the Great of his grandfather's accession to kingship. No one will deny the vanity of the proceedings, and as a stroke of policy it was but the culmination, shrewdly timed when Europe tottered on the brink of the War of Spanish Succession, of a century's work on the part of Electors of Brandenburg—a symbol of the new unity and prestige of Brandenburg-Prussia. A recent historian has written the following account of it.

From HENDERSON, *History of Germany* (1902) [1]

There is a twofold marvel connected with Frederick's extravagances and with his excessive demands on the people. On the one hand, although in addition to money payments constant contributions were required for his court festivals, his subjects were fond of him, and sincerely

[1] From Ernest F. Henderson, *A Short History of Germany*, 2 vols., 1902, II, 31-37. By permission of The Macmillan Company, New York.

mourned when he died. His very profusion endeared him to them, and many found occupation in carrying out his pageants and public works. But still more remarkable is the circumstance that at the end of his reign there was no very alarming deficit in the treasury. This is due to the fact that for his war expenses he had received large subsidies from Austria and other powers, while the regular Brandenburg revenues, administered along the lines laid down by the Great Elector, had considerably increased. The most expensive of Frederick's hobbies, costing him in all some six million thalers, was the attainment of the royal crown. . . . It was his own work from beginning to end; his councillors and ministers were almost all against the project, and the difficulties in the way were very great; but he would not be daunted, and politically, as the event proved, he acted wisely and well. . . .

Everything turned on this consent of the House of Austria and of the Holy Roman Empire, but it was difficult to obtain. . . . The Austrian ministers were opposed to the project, chiefly on the ground that the aggrandisement of an elector would weaken the imperial authority; already electors were beginning to dispute with his Majesty on questions of etiquette. There was a religious side to the matter, too, which weighed heavily with Leopold. Should he, the natural defender of the Catholic church, help to set up a Protestant monarchy? . . .

Leopold remained firm for almost a year; the correspondence on the subject fills twenty-one folio volumes. The last straw that broke his resistance was the partition treaty of March 25, 1700, between France, England, and Holland, by which Austria considered herself scandalously treated, not having been consulted on any point. Father Wolf [a Jesuit priest at the Imperial Court who had had a part in the negotiations] was allowed to send a message to Berlin to the "most serene elector, and *soon, soon to be* most mighty king." The final treaty was signed only two days before the death of the childless King of Spain. . . .

It remained to give an outward expression to the new honor the emperor had "accorded," and to prepare a grander and more sumptuous coronation than anything that had yet been seen. Frederick had been very impatient for this event, had "sighed for it ceaselessly and could not sleep," wrote the French ambassador, Des Alleurs. The crown, sceptre, and mantle had been made ready months before the time. . . . All points of ceremonial had been carefully studied from books of etiquette and from the usages observed in Denmark and Poland. . . . There are learned discussions in the Prussian archives as to how the new king should receive the envoys of foreign countries less important than his own. . . . The procession that set out from Berlin to Königsberg, in December, 1700, was of great size and magnificence; it was obliged to move in relays, as the towns through which it passed could otherwise not have stood the burden. Thirty thousand horses had been requisitioned, in addition to those from the royal stables. The journey lasted twelve days, and the ceremonies four more; on the 15th of January four heralds-at-arms proclaimed through all the streets the elevation of Prussia to a kingdom. . . .

On January 18 took place the coronation itself, the ceremonial of which was copied from that of the imperial coronation at Frankfort, with the exception, however, that the religious element was kept in the background. Frederick did, indeed, in order that he might be called "his sacred Majesty," create for the occasion two Protestant bishops—one Lutheran, one Calvinist; but he significantly placed the crown on his own head, and afterward with his own hands on that of his queen, the episcopal functions being confined to the consecration with the holy oil.

Frederick's second wife, Sophie Charlotte, did much to assist him in making Berlin a cultural center. Charming and inquisitive, she attracted many learned men to the court, among them the famous philosopher-scientist Leibnitz. Such influences intensified Frederick's natural bent to patronize arts and sciences and led him to establish a new university at Halle (1694), the Academy of Arts (1696), and the Academy of Sciences (1701). To Frederick, who wanted to make Berlin a Versailles of the North, these acts were as much for ostentation as for intelligent patronage, and under his hard-bitten successor they fell into decay for a generation. His grandson, Frederick the Great, appreciated them to the full and described them in the following letter.

From FREDERICK THE GREAT, Letter to Voltaire (1737) [1]

Frederic I king of Prussia, who was a prince of very confined genius, but well disposed and docile, caused the arts to flourish under his reign. He delighted much in grandeur and magnificence, and was liberal even to profusion. Feeling emulation at all the praises which he heard bestowed on Louis XIV, he imagined that by choosing this monarch for his model, he could not fail in like manner to be praised. The court of Berlin was soon seen to ape that of Versailles; the imitation extended to every thing; ceremonies, harangues, the stately step, the

[1] Frederick II to Voltaire, July 6, 1737, in *Posthumous Works of Frederick II,* trans. from the French by Thomas Holcroft, 13 vols., London, 1789, IV, 134-38.

measured phrase, tall musketeers, light horse, &c. . . . .

Queen Charlotte, the consort of Frederic, was a princess who, added to all the gifts of nature, had received an excellent education. She was daughter to the duke of Lunenburg, afterward elector of Hanover. This princess had been intimately acquainted with Leibnitz, at the court of her father, who had taught her the principles of philosophy, and particularly of metaphysics. The queen highly respected Leibnitz; she kept up a correspondence with him, and this occasioned him to make frequent journeys to Berlin. The philosopher naturally was a lover of all the sciences, and was acquainted with them all. M. de Fontenelle, speaking of him, very wittily says that, by decomposing him, materials enough might have been found to have formed several men of learning. The attachment Leibnitz had for the sciences never suffered him to lose sight of an endeavour to procure their establishment. He conceived the design of instituting an academy at Berlin, on the model of that at Paris, introducing however some trifling changes. He communicated his purpose to the queen, who was charmed with it, and promised to aid him with all her influence. Care was taken to introduce the name of Louis XIV. The astronomers affirmed they should discover an infinity of stars, of which the king was to be the god-father; the botanists and physicians dedicated their talent to him. How was it possible to resist such various persuasion! The effects accordingly became evident; an observatory was presently constructed, an anatomical theatre was opened, and the academy, being formed, found Leibnitz its protector. . . .

There is one difficulty, however, which will continually prevent us from having good books in our language; and this consists in our not having any fixed use of words. Germany is divided into so many princes that no means ever can be found to induce them to submit to the decisions of an academy [compare page 243]. Our men of learning, therefore, have no other resource than that of writing in foreign languages [usually in French]; and as it is exceedingly difficult perfectly to possess these, it is much to be feared our literature will never make any great progress.

FREDERICK WILLIAM I (1713-40)

Frederick William I believed in absolutism. "Salvation belongs to the Lord; everything else is my affair," he said, and he applied the principle literally. He possessed, in strange contrast to his predecessor, a choleric temper and a passion for detail; he bullied his family and fired office clerks whom he found loafing on the job. "At the table," wrote his daughter, "nothing else was talked of but economy and soldiers." The first was to contribute to the second, for Frederick William went far toward the militarization of the modern Prussian state. But in his stern, efficient discipline, and in his militarism, he did not neglect the economic welfare of his people; and he appears, in general retrospect, like an ill-tempered Great Elector, for his works, as will be seen below, were singularly like those of his grandfather.

From RANKE, *House of Brandenburg* (1848) [1]

On coming to the throne, Frederick William fixed his chief attention on these two points—the increase and right organization of his army. During the very first months of his reign he altered everything connected with the care and maintenance, dress and lodging, of the army. . . . Soon

[1] Leopold von Ranke, *Memoirs of the House of Brandenburg,* trans. by Sir Alexander and Lady Duff Gordon, 3 vols., London, 1849, I, 142-46, 440-42.

after he promulgated his articles of war; which were a fresh version of those of the great Elector, but still more severe as to discipline. Whosoever should resist, were it only by word of mouth, the commands of his corporal or sergeant, was to run the gauntlet; and if anyone should offer forcible resistance, he was to suffer death. . . .

In the pursuit of this one object, he looked upon every other expenditure of money as mere extravagance.

Besides, a court like that of his father was quite contrary to all his tastes and ideas. Lords of the bedchamber, lords in waiting, and many others attached to the court, were immediately dismissed in a body, and the salaries of those retained were considerably reduced. . . .

To the expenditure of the court the King sustituted the wants of the army, which he resolved should be equipped in native materials, manufactured entirely by native industry. He entirely adopted Colbert's system, which then spread over Europe: he forbade the exportation of wool, and the importation of foreign cloth. . . . As yet, the native manufacture . . . was exceedingly imperfect, [but the King] induced better workmen to come, [and] in due course of time he succeeded in producing cloth of such fine texture and at the same time so cheap that it not only drove the foreign manufacture out of the market, but even found its way into other countries. . . .

In November, 1721, he ordered that in eight months from that date no one of either sex or of any class . . . should wear cottons either fine or coarse, under penalty of a fine of a hundred reichsthalers. He understood the art of enforcing obedience; and in seven years from that time we are assured that nobody even thought of foreign wares, which were completely superseded by the woollen and linen goods of the country. . . .

In order that all these restrictions might not expose the country to be overrun with bad manufactures, he subjected them to a vigilant inspection. The clothmakers were instructed how to clean their wool, to sort it, make it soft and supple, to comb it, and . . . [so on]; in the same manner Colbert gave the French workmen the most elaborate technical rules. The Prussian inspectors likewise swore accurately to examine the cloths when they came out of the loom . . . and to denounce any defects to condign punishment. . . .

There is no doubt that these measures produced, on the whole, favourable results. The home manufactures were soon able to support the competition of neighbouring nations; the blue cloths of Berlin acquired a certain celebrity in Europe. A more important advantage to the country was that the town population . . . had increased . . . in the course of the whole reign probably a half.

GOVERNMENTAL REORGANIZATION: THE GENERAL DIRECTORY

In January, 1723, Frederick William set forth a new "Instruction" to consolidate, in the interests of greater unity in government, under a single board the war commissariat (which administered war taxes) and the finance department (which managed the royal domains). The new General Supreme Finance War and Domains Directory—called for short the General Directory—consisted of five departments whose heads reported to the King on certain days of each week. The "Instruction" itself well reflects the King's great vigilance in order to combat laxity or corruption in office, the centralization and militarization of the Prussian state, and the royal capacity for detail. It consisted of thirty-five articles of which part of Article I follows.

From FREDERICK WILLIAM I, "Instruction" (1723) [1]

1. We have found it necessary to reorganize our administration, to abolish our former General War Commissariat and General Finance Directory, and to institute in their places a General Directory over Finance, War, and Domains and to entrust it with the supervision of all affairs which until now were supervised by the former General War Commissariat and General Finance Directory. We hereby declare that we ourselves shall take over the presidency of the new Directory in order to give it more prestige, authority, and weight and, at the same time, to show that special care and exact attention which, because of their extreme importance, we observe constantly and untiringly toward the affairs of the realm. . . .

3. We hold further that the five Ministers appointed are each responsible to us alone for whatever takes place in the General Directory. . . .

7. They [the *local* administrative officers] must be the most capable persons that can be found unquestionably Calvinist or Lutheran in religion—truthful, honest, intelligent—persons who understand management and have been active in it themselves, those who are well informed about commerce, manufactures, and all related matters, and above all things, they must be native subjects. . . .

9. The councilors in the provincial commissariats shall be good, efficient persons with good health and common sense and who since youth have been associated with commerce, manufacturing, excise, and other things related to these departments.

10. In the provisional chambers must be employed good managers who them-

[1] Friedrich Förster, *Friedrich Wilhelm I, König von Preussen*, 3 vols. Potsdam, 1834-35, II, 173-79.

selves had a good reputation . . . as good managers and officers, who can write and understand arithmetic, and who are vigilant and healthy persons.

11. . . . It is our most gracious intention that no persons shall be suggested for employment in provincial chambers and commissariats who were born in the province in which they are to serve.

12. As small or unimportant officers are appointed in our provincial chambers, they must be selected from men who have been honorably discharged from their military service. . . .

17. We command the General Directory to investigate thoroughly whether in the provincial chambers and commissariats, which employ so many assistants, some officers could not be removed and various services combined so as to reduce costs of maintenance. . . .

19. The instructions for provincial chambers and commissariats are to include specific orders that the presidents of commissariats are to visit the towns under their supervision frequently to inform themselves most completely about their condition, the state of their commerce and public life, of their manufactures; their citizens and other inhabitants, and their supplies of provisions, so that the towns of their departments may be as well known to them as we require a captain in our army to know his company. . . .

21. Furthermore, it must be included in instructions that the provincial chambers and commissariats be ordered to assemble for business every day with the exception of Sundays, Christmas Day, Easter, Whitsuntide, and the first two festival days . . . and to be there promptly at 7 A.M. in summer and 8 A.M. in winter. The session shall end at 11:30, resume at 2 P.M., and continue until 6 P.M. so that by the observation of such industry and application our services and our highest interest may be properly advanced in all places.

FREDERICK WILLIAM I'S INSTRUCTIONS FOR THE EDUCATION OF HIS SON, LATER FREDERICK THE GREAT

Frederick the Great passed a most unhappy youth. He was a willful, luxury-loving lad, and his short-tempered father, in an effort to make him an "upright fellow," caned him, degraded him, taunted him, drove him into flight and, when he was caught, imprisoned him, executed his friend and confidant before his eyes, and threatened to execute Frederick himself. Later, in hopes of "settling" Frederick, his father forced him into a marriage which he abhorred. With such a background, it is not surprising that Frederick became hard, dissimulating, scornful of all mankind and of mankind's conventions. In 1721, when Frederick was ten, his father drew up the following directions for his tutors to observe.

From FREDERICK WILLIAM I, "Instructions for His Son's Tutor" (1721) [1]

On Sunday he [Frederick] is to get up at seven o'clock in the morning; as soon as he has put on his slippers, he is to fall down on his knees by the bedside and briefly pray to God, and loud enough that everyone in the room can hear it. The prayer must be learned by heart and shall be as follows: "Lord God, holy Father! I thank Thee from my heart that Thou hast so graciously preserved me through this night; make me useful for Thy holy will and keep me from doing anything today or all the days of my life that could separate me from Thee, for the sake of our Lord Jesus my Redeemer, Amen!" And then follow with the Lord's Prayer.

As soon as this is done, he is to dress himself quickly and expeditiously, wash properly, and tie up his queue, and pow-

[1] *Ibid.*, I, 357-59.

der; and dressing and the short prayer must be finished in a quarter of an hour, so it is then a quarter past seven. When this is done, then all his servants and Duhan [the French tutor] shall come in to recite the great prayer on their knees; thereupon Duhan shall read a chapter out of the Bible, and sing some good hymn, till it is a quarter to eight. Then all the servants shall go out again, and Duhan shall read the Gospel of the Sunday with my son, briefly explain it, and by these means demonstrate what is true Christianity; also he shall repeat something out of the catechism of Noltenius [the court chaplain], and this is to continue till nine o'clock. Then he is to come down to me with my son and go with me to church and then to eat; but the rest of the day is for my son. In the evening he must say good night to me at half-past nine, then go at once to his room, undress very quickly, wash his hands, and as soon as that is done, Duhan shall recite a prayer on his knees, sing a hymn, at which all his servants shall again be present; thereupon my son must immediately go to bed, so as to be in bed by half-past ten.

Monday he is to be awakened at six o'clock and as soon as this is done he shall be required, without grumbling or turning round once more, to get up quickly and immediately, and he must then kneel down and say a short prayer, as on Sunday morning. As soon as he has done this, he shall, as rapidly as possible, put on his shoes and gaiters, also wash his face and hands, but not with soap; further he shall put on his jacket, comb out his hair, and have his queue tied but not powdered. While he is combed and his queue is tied he shall take tea and breakfast at the same time, so that this is all one job, and all this must be finished before half-past six o'clock. Then Duhan and all his servants shall come in, and the great prayer will be recited, a chapter read out of the Bible,

and a hymn sung, as on Sunday—all of which lasts till seven o'clock, when the servants must also go out again. From seven to nine o'clock Duhan shall work at history with him; at nine o'clock Noltenius shall come, and he must instruct him in Christianity till a quarter to eleven. At a quarter to eleven he shall wash his face quickly with water and his hands with soap, dress himself in white, powder, and put on his coat, and come to the King at eleven o'clock; there he stays till two o'clock; whereupon he at once returns to his room. Duhan shall also be there at once, to describe maps to him from two to three o'clock; and to explain to him therewith the power and the weakness of all European states, together with the size, wealth, and poverty of the towns. From three till four o'clock he is to work at morality, from four till five o'clock Duhan shall write German letters with him and see to it that he acquires a good style. At five o'clock he shall go to the King, ride and divert himself in the fresh air and not indoors, and do what he likes, as long as it is not against God.

On Tuesday he shall do exactly as he did on Monday except that from nine until ten thirty Panzendorf shall come instead of Noltenius, to teach him fencing, and in the afternoon he shall do arithmetic instead of letter-writing. Wednesday like Monday except that from seven till half-past nine Duhan is only to work at history with him and make him learn something by heart, so that his memory will be strengthened. At half-past nine he is to dress quickly and come to the King. The rest of the day belongs to little Fritz. [And so on, until Saturday.] . . .

On Saturday morning till half-past ten o'clock everything which he learned during the whole week in history, in writing and reckoning, also in morality, is to be repeated so as to see whether he has profited, and the General Count Finken-

stein and the Colonel von Kalkstein shall
be present; if he has profited, then the
afternoon is for Fritz, but if he has not
profited, he must from two till six o'clock
repeat everything which he has forgotten
in the preceding days.

In undressing and dressing you must
accustom him to get out of and into his
clothes as quickly as is humanly possible.
You are also to see to it that he learns to
undress and dress by himself, and that he
becomes tidy and clean, and not be so
dirty.

3. The Opening of the War of Austrian Succession

THE IMPERIAL PRAGMATIC SANCTION (1713-40)

Leopold I, Holy Roman Emperor,
1658-1705, had two sons, Joseph and
Charles (the latter being a Hapsburg
candidate for the Spanish crown in
1700; see page 266). Neither son had
male heirs, and when Joseph, having
succeeded to the imperial throne in
1705, died (1711), the office passed to
his younger brother, who became Emperor Charles VI (1711-40). In 1713,
after the War of Spanish Succession,
Charles, in order to meet the altered
condition of Europe, changed the
family agreement made by his father
(1703) for succession to the Hapsburg
throne. The new family agreement,
known as the Pragmatic Sanction, was
kept secret until 1718, when the Emperor, despairing of a male heir, made
it public by soliciting guarantees to respect it from the princes of the Holy
Roman Empire and neighboring states.
The Pragmatic Sanction and its role in
imperial policy are described in the
following passage.

From COXE, *The House of Austria* (1807) [1]

According to the family compact formed
by Leopold [in 1703], and confirmed by
Joseph and Charles, the succession was
entailed on the daughters of Joseph in
preference to the daughters of Charles,
should they both die without issue male.
Charles, however, had scarcely ascended
the throne, though at that time without
children, than he reversed this compact,
and settled the right of succession, in default of his male issue, first on his own
daughters, then on the daughters of
Joseph, and afterwards on the queen of
Portugal and the other daughters of Leopold. Since the promulgation of that
decree, the empress had borne a son who
died in his infancy, and three daughters,
Maria Theresa, Maria Anne, and Maria
Amelia. With a view to insure the succession of these daughters, and to obviate the
dangers which might arise from the
claims of the Josephine archduchesses, he
published the Pragmatic Sanction, and
compelled his nieces to renounce their
pretensions on their marriages with the
electors of Saxony and Bavaria. Aware,
however, that the strongest renunciations
are disregarded, he obtained from the different states of his extensive dominions
the acknowledgment of the Pragmatic
Sanction, and made it the great object of
his reign, to which he sacrificed every
other consideration, to procure the guaranty of the European powers. . . .

Having obtained the guaranty of the
Pragmatic Sanction from Spain, Prussia,
Russia, England, and Holland, the emperor directed all his efforts to procure
the accession of the other European powers, particularly the states of the German
empire. In pursuing this object he experienced extreme difficulty, from the religious
disputes between the Catholic and Protes-

[1] William Coxe, *History of the House of Austria,* 3d ed., 3 vols., Bohn, London, 1847, III,
109-53.

tant bodies, and from the discordant views of the German princes. . . .

The emperor also renewed [1731] his promises of favouring the claims of Frederick William [Frederick William I, King of Prussia, who, in 1726, had signed a treaty guaranteeing the Pragmatic Sanction providing the Emperor would support his claims to the succession of Juliers, Berg, and other small Rhenish territories] on the succession of Juliers, which, in consequence of the advanced age of Philip William, Elector Palatine, seemed likely to become vacant.

FREDERICK THE GREAT STATES HIS REASONS FOR UNDERTAKING THE SILESIAN WARS

On May 31, 1740, Frederick William I died, leaving a well-filled treasury, a prosperous state, and a splendid army for his successor, Frederick II, later known as "the Great." On the following October 20, the Emperor Charles VI died, leaving his throne to his eldest daughter, Maria Theresa, by the terms of the Pragmatic Sanction. The new King of Prussia, though protesting friendship to the Empress, ignored the Prussian guarantee of the Pragmatic Sanction, seized possession of Silesia, and began a series of wars known as the War of Austrian Succession (1740-48). At first Frederick tried to excuse his action by claiming that the Emperor Charles had not carried out his part of the treaty by turning over Juliers, Berg, and other Rhenish provinces to Prussia. Later, he exposed his real reasons with surprising candor, as follows.

From FREDERICK THE GREAT, *History of My Times* (1775) [1]

The emperor Charles VI ended his days on October 20, 1740. That news arrived

[1] *Histoire de mon temps*, in *Œuvres de Frédéric le Grand*, 30 vols., Berlin, 1846, II, 54-56.

at Rheinsberg where the King [Frederick II] was suffering an attack of quartan fever. The doctors, infatuated with ancient maxims, would not give him quinine, but he took it in spite of them because he proposed to do things more important than nursing a fever. He resolved to lay claim at once to the territories of Silesia, to which his house had undeniable rights, and to prepare himself to support those claims by force of arms, if necessary. That project fulfilled all his political desires: It was a means of acquiring reputation, of increasing the power of his state, and of terminating all that concerned the litigious question of the Berg-Jülich succession. However, before he made up his mind completely, the King weighed the risks there were in undertaking such a war and the advantages that were to be hoped for from it.

On the one side, there was the powerful house of Austria, which, with vast territories, did not lack resources; there was the daughter of the Emperor attacked, who would probably find allies in the King of England, in the Dutch Republic, and in most of the princes of the empire, since they had signed the Pragmatic Sanction. The Duke of Courland, who was then governing in Russia, was engaged with the court of Vienna; besides, the young Queen of Hungary could attract Saxony to her interests by ceding it some districts of Bohemia; and as for details of executing the trick, the scanty harvests of 1740 made it difficult to provision troops.

On the other hand, a host of reflections revived the hopes of the King. The situation of the court of Vienna after the death of the Emperor was very unpleasant: the finances were in disorder; the army was shattered and discouraged by the ill success which it had had against the Turks; the Ministry was disunited; and when one considered that, in addition to these factors, there was at the head of the government a young, inexperienced princess who had to defend a disputed succession, the result was that that government could not appear formidable. Besides, it was not possible that the King would lack allies. The rivalry which existed between France and England necessarily assured the King the assistance of one or the other of these powers; and the many pretenders to the Austrian throne ought to unite their interests with those of Prussia. The King could bargain with his electoral vote; he could barter with his claims upon the Duchy of Berg either with France or with Austria; and finally, the war which he proposed to undertake in Silesia was especially favorable geographically for offensive action, as Silesia bordered upon Prussia and the Oder River supplied an ever ready means of communication.

That which tipped the balance in favor of the war was the death of Anne, Czarina of Russia, following soon after that of the Emperor. By her decease, the Russian crown fell to young Ivan, Grand Duke of Russia, son of a princess of Mecklenburg and of Prince Antoine-Ulric of Brunswick, a good friend of the King of Prussia. It appeared that during the minority of the young czar Russia would be well occupied in maintaining order at home, without supporting the Pragmatic Sanction— a fact which could not fail to be reflected in Germany. Add to these reasons an army all ready to go, supplies all gathered together, and perhaps the desire of making a name for oneself—all this was the cause of the war which the King declared upon Maria Theresa of Austria.

4. The Seven Years' War (1756-63)

Between the end of the War of Austrian Succession (1748) and the beginning of the Seven Years' War (1756), there occurred one of the most surprising diplomatic reversals in history. England, which had been the Holy Roman Empire's only important ally at the opening of the war in 1740, now allied with Prussia; and France, Prussia's ally in the former war, joined with her oldest enemy, the Empire. How this "Diplomatic Revolution" came about is described below.

THE DIPLOMATIC REVOLUTION OF 1756

From COXE, *The House of Austria* [1]

In the course of the negotiations for the peace of Aix-la-Chapelle [1748], the empress-queen had attempted to conciliate France, and [Count] Kaunitz had even secretly offered the cession of part of the Low Countries, provided Louis would assist in recovering Silesia. The empress-queen, not disconcerted at the rejection of this proposal, renewed her overtures to Blondel, chargé d'affaires at Vienna, and afterwards to the marquis d'Hautefort, the French ambassador; and at the same time Kaunitz was despatched to Paris with instructions to promote this great object.

During his embassy he laboured with continual assiduity and address to soften the inveterate enmity of the French court, and to loosen the connection between France and Prussia. He insinuated to the ministers that the aggrandizement of Prussia was their work, and that they had hitherto received no other return than ingratitude from a sovereign who was governed solely by his own interest. To strengthen these impressions, which gradually began to take effect, he paid assiduous court to the marchioness of Pompadour, with whom he had opened a correspondence during the negotiation for the peace of Aix-la-Chapelle, and employed every

[1] Coxe, *History of the House of Austria*, III, 352-65.

species of flattery to induce her to second his views. . . . [Meanwhile, France and England had gone to war over colonial affairs in America and the East Indies.]

Frederic [of Prussia] had long been disgusted with the haughty and contemptuous tone of superiority assumed by the court of Versailles; he was not unacquainted with the intrigues of the imperial minister; he was alarmed at the evasive conduct of France, when pressed to renew the alliance which expired in May, 1756, and was apprehensive of being exposed singly to the arms of Russia and Austria. He therefore readily entered into engagements with the king of England, and on the 16th of January, 1756, a convention of neutrality was concluded, to prevent the contests in America from disturbing the peace of Germany, and for that purpose only to resist the entrance of foreign troops into the empire. By the two secret articles the Austrian Netherlands were excepted from the operations of this treaty; and England agreed to indemnify the Prussian merchants for the capture of vessels during the preceding war.

The empress and her minister beheld the conclusion of this convention, not only without regret, but with extreme satisfaction. They had already matured their plan for the alliance with France. . . .

This whole transaction had been conducted with so much secrecy, that only vague suspicions were entertained of those negotiations which had passed in September and October; and the Prussian treaty was alleged by the court of Vienna, as the sole and operating cause which had compelled the house of Austria to quit her ancient allies, and to renounce that system which she had invariably followed for the last century. The empress-queen and her minister therefore received the communication of the treaty of London with as much affected surprise and indignation, as if no previous overture had been made to the court of Versailles. . . .

[The British ambassador attempted to persuade the Empress that the English-Prussian alliance was inoffensive, intended merely to maintain the peace of the Empire. But Maria Theresa accused England of coming to terms with her inveterate enemy, and in audiences with the British ambassador, she said:]

"I and the king of Prussia are incompatible; and no consideration on earth shall ever induce me to enter into any engagement of which he is a party. . . . Why should you be surprised, if, following your example in concluding a treaty with Prussia, I should enter into an engagement with France? . . . I have truly but two enemies whom I really dread, the king of Prussia and the Turks; and while I and the empress of Russia continue on the same good terms as now subsist between us, we shall, I trust, be able to convince Europe that we are in a condition to defend ourselves against those adversaries, however formidable."

The empress gave this audience on the 13th of May, and the treaty with France [Treaty of Versailles] had been already signed on the 1st. In imitation of the convention of London, the two sovereigns agreed, by an act of neutrality, to prevent the contest in America from disturbing their mutual harmony; and a treaty of alliance, purely defensive, renewed all former engagements since the treaty of Westphalia. The empress-queen promised to defend the French dominions in Europe, if attacked, except during the present war with England; while the king of France was to aid the house of Austria without any exception. The two powers also stipulated to assist each other with a mutual succour of 24,000 men in case of invasion, the present war excepted.

THE CLOSE OF THE SEVEN YEARS' WAR
(1763)

The Seven Years' War (1756-63) strained Prussia's powers to the limit. Frederick's only ally, England, was engaged simultaneously in a great naval and colonial struggle with France (the French and Indian War in America), and assisted Prussia mainly with subsidies. The tremendous odds against Prussia, and her military reverses, several times threw Frederick into the depths of despair. "Who could foresee or imagine," he wrote later, "that Prussia, attacked by the powers of Austria, Russia, France, Sweden, and all the Holy Roman Empire, should withstand a league so formidable, and in a war wherein everything predicted ruin, should lose not one of its possessions?" The saving factor was the defection of Russia upon the death of the Czarina Elizabeth Petrovna in 1762, "with whom," said Frederick, "was buried the Austrian alliance." A contemporary observer wrote the following account of the last years of the war.

From WRAXALL, *Memoirs* (1779) [1]

Towards the close of 1761 another campaign, according to all appearances, must have laid him [Frederick] entirely at the mercy of the vast combination which had determined his destruction. Maria Theresa, mistress of Schweidnitz and Glatz, already anticipated the restoration of all Silesia; while the various Princes and States of Germany, whom Frederick had either injured or attacked, impatiently waited for the accomplishment of their respective expectations in the division of his dominions. Such was the critical and almost hopeless condition of his affairs, when the death of Elizabeth, Empress of Russia, took place.

That Princess, Frederick's implacable enemy, expired at Petersburg, of a distemper accelerated by her intemperance, on the fifth of January, 1762. Her nephew and successor, Peter the Third, who had secretly labored during several years to impede the progress of the Russian armies, instantly manifested, without disguise, the violent predilection that he had long nourished for his Prussian Majesty, a partiality which rose to adoration. Not content with separating his forces from those of Maria Theresa, he acted as her avowed enemy, and as the auxiliary of Frederick. His reign was indeed short, and its termination tragical [see page 310], but the great principle of political connection between Muscovy and Austria, which had subsisted under Elizabeth, was none the less dissolved. Catherine the Second, who succeeded Peter, though she by no means adopted the intemperate zeal of her husband in favour of Prussia, was too wise as well as magnanimous to resume the personal animosities of Elizabeth. She withdrew her troops altogether from the contest almost as soon as she ascended the throne [July, 1762]. Sweden, wearied with a war in which she had lost her military reputation without reaping the smallest augmentation of territory, had previously concluded a separate peace with the Court of Berlin.

Thus liberated from two of his numerous opponents, the King, in 1762, became superior to Daun [the Austrian commander] in the field. . . . In face of the Austrian army, Frederick even ventured to lay regular siege to Schweidnitz, which, after a long and gallant defense, protracted to the last extremity, surrendered, notwithstanding every effort made for its relief. With the battle of Freiburg terminated

[1] N. William Wraxall, *Memoirs of the Courts of Berlin, Dresden, Warsaw, and Vienna*, 3d ed., 2 vols., London, 1806, I, 206-11.

the seventh and last campaign of this long and sanguinary war; an action in which neither the King, nor Daun, nor Landhohn, had any share. The honor of the day was exclusively reserved for Prince Henry of Prussia, to whom his brother [Frederick] constantly entrusted the arduous task of repelling the enemy on the Saxon frontier. . . .

The Prussian troops, elevated by their advantages, once more re-entered Bohemia, from which they had been so long expelled; while detached parties ravaged the circle of Nuremberg and spread consternation over every part of the German empire. In this situation, Maria Theresa, abandoned by Russia and by Sweden, deriving little or no assistance from France, and unable to extend protection to her own dominions, was necessitated to have recourse to negotiation. After seven campaigns, and after sustaining the rudest shocks of adverse fortune, Frederick was still not only capable of resistance, but in a state to act everywhere offensively. Of all their conquests, Glatz alone, together with a portion of the Duchy of Cleves, remained in possession of the Austrians. It was requisite to sacrifice them in order to induce the enemy to evacuate Saxony, which unfortunate country had severely suffered for the political connections of its sovereign and his steady adherence to the House of Austria. These considerations imperiously dictated the peace of Hubertsburg, which restored tranquillity to the north of Europe in the beginning of 1763. Silesia, the principal object of contest, remained entire to the Prussian monarchy; and scarcely a foot of territory was lost or gained on either side by a war which had not only caused so vast an effusion of blood, but which threatened more than once the subversion of the present political system of Europe.

5. West Prussia Is Acquired by Frederick the Great: The First Partition of Poland (1772)

On October 5, 1763, Augustus III, King of Poland and Elector of Saxony, died. The question of his succession immediately became an international issue, for Poland had been in the process of political disintegration for more than a century, and the Polish nobility, having shorn their kings of power, had fallen into dissensions that invited foreign interference. Now, upon the death of Augustus, the new Czarina of Russia, Catherine II (later known as "the Great"), urged the election of her former lover, Prince Stanislas Poniatowski, to the Polish throne—expecting, through him, practically to rule Poland herself. By supporting the Russian candidate, Frederick the Great hoped to win Catherine's goodwill and to protect his own lands. Accordingly, on April 11, 1764, Frederick and Catherine agreed to support Poniatowski's election and to prevent any reforms in Poland which might strengthen that state's impotent political institutions. Thus were made the early steps toward the first partition of Poland, which was finally effected in 1772. William Wraxall, an Englishman intimately acquainted with the courts of northern Europe during these years, wrote the following account of Poland's initial dismemberment.

From WRAXALL, Memoirs [1]

The plan unquestionably originated in the cabinet of Prussia; but not with the King, nor with any of his ministers. His brother Prince Henry's deep and capacious mind is said to have first seized, digested,

[1] Ibid., II, 20-29.

and ripened the plan in silence. . . . He brought over the King to his opinion; and they began in concert the train of measures requisite for its completion. The first step taken, was artfully to flatter the new Empress of Russia, to awaken her vanity, and to represent to her the honor, as well as the advantage, of giving a sovereign to Poland, after having placed herself on the throne of the czars. Catherine listened with complacency to suggestions so well calculated to make impression on a mind like hers, anxious for every species of glory. Impelled by her partiality for Count Poniatowski, and probably likewise induced by her perfect knowledge of his character, she signified to Frederick her intention of elevating that nobleman to the crown. The choice being approved at Berlin, on the decease of Augustus, Catherine's forces and treasures overcame all oppositions. Stanislaus was elected by violence; while the Russian ambassador, Prince Repnin, as the delegate and representative of the Empress, became in fact the despot and the oppressor of the Poles. The unfortunate King, who retained little more of royalty than the name, was only an engine in the hands of the court of Petersburg.

Frederick, attentive to the accomplishment of his primary objects, and who by no means intended that Poland should sink virtually into a Russian province, next fomented the discontents of the great Polish nobility. By means of his emissaries, he secretly stimulated them to throw off so ignominious a yoke, and to dethrone a prince illegally elected, as well as unable to afford them protection against the tyranny of Catherine. His insinuations were successful; confederations were formed in various provinces, and Poland soon became a theatre of civil war, of insurrection, and devastation. In order to maintain Stanislaus on the throne, Muscovites and Cossacks were quartered in all the principal cities; while Warsaw resembled rather a Russian garrison, than the capital of an independent republic. It was not difficult for Frederick to excite the jealousy of the Turks at such an interference; and to represent to them, that under pretence of reducing the Polish rebels to obedience, Catherine in effect rendered the country a province of her empire. At the same time he encouraged and exhorted the court of Petersburg to engage in hostilities with the Porte. No exertions were omitted in order to inflame the two sovereigns and governments, already irritated against each other. War ensued between them, and was prosecuted with various success, in Asia as well as in Europe.

The object to which his policy had so long tended was now in some measure attained. Frederick . . . turned his attention next to the court of Vienna. Nothing could be effected without the Austrian consent and co-operation. With a view of studying the character of Joseph the Second, he therefore artfully caused a proposition to be made on his part for an interview between them. The Emperor accepted it; and the two princes met at Neiss in Silesia, towards the end of August, 1769. But, though the state of Poland might there have been mentioned in general terms . . . it was not till the following autumn, in 1770, that after previously sounding the imperial cabinet, the subject was fully discussed in the second interview of Frederick and Joseph, at Neustadt in Moravia. . . . Joseph, young, ambitious, and eager to extend the dominions of the House of Austria, was not difficult to be persuaded. It may more naturally excite our astonishment, that a minister such as Prince Kaunitz allowed himself to be convinced either of the policy, or of the necessity, of the measure. As little can we conceive how so pious and circumspect a princess as Maria Theresa could have been induced to lend her aid to a measure so repugnant to every principle of justice or rectitude. Such, however, was the fact. Frederick and Joseph spread before them the map of Poland, agreed on their respective shares, and fixed on the tract of country to be offered to the Empress of Russia, as her portion. These preliminaries being adjusted, the two sovereigns parted.

In the course of the ensuing year appeared the fruits of the interview. By command of their respective courts, the Austrian and Prussian ambassadors at Petersburg signified to Catherine the determination of the cabinets of Berlin and Vienna. . . . Catherine had no alternative left except acquiescence. After a proper delay therefore, necessary in order to prepare manifestos, the armies of the three powers, which had previously approached the frontiers of Poland, marched into the country, and sequestered the territories respectively allotted to them. They then compelled the unfortunate Stanislaus to convoke a diet, in which he ratified his own degradation, and that of his subjects, by giving to their usurpations the mock sanction of legislative and deliberative consent. . . .

Which of the three sovereigns has been the greatest gainer by the division? . . . Unquestionably it was not Catherine, since she might be considered as already mistress of all Poland. . . . The portion which has been assigned to her, is indeed a fertile, extensive, and important tract of country, contiguous to her own dominions on the west, and including a great part of Lithuania, as well as Polish Livonia; but, comparatively estimated, it adds little to her revenues, power, or political consideration.

The Austrian share, locally as well as financially considered, is indeed more valuable. By its position it covers Hungary and Moravia, while it extends the Imperial frontier on that side, far beyond the Carpathian Mountains, to the distant confines of Podolia and Moldavia. The mines of Vielicza, which may enable the Empress Queen to supply all Poland with salt, form a considerable permanent source of revenue; and the population cannot be estimated in those provinces, at a smaller number than two millions.

But these advantages, great as they must be separately allowed in themselves, sink on a comparison with the political benefits derived to Prussia from the partition of Poland. . . . It suffices to look at its geographical position, in order to be convinced of the fact in all its force. Though less in mere extent than the Austrian and Russian shares, it far exceeds them in fertility of soil, in the number of cities, industry, and faculties of raising pecuniary supplies. Not only the Vistula, from the gates of Thorn to those of Dantzic, together with the whole commerce of that river, are become Prussian. The circumstance which renders them inestimable to Frederick, is, that he has joined his electoral dominions of Brandenburg and the Duchy of Pomerania, to his kingdom of Prussia.

6. The Enlightenment in the Germanies: Frederick the Great and Joseph II

During the reign of Frederick the Great the Enlightenment captured the imaginations of several European despots, of whom the King of Prussia was one of the most prominent. As the Enlightenment meant different things to different people, it is difficult to define; but, in general, it meant the reform of European society so that political, economic, and social institutions would conform to reason and the natural laws formulated by the new sciences [see page 349]. Demands for reform appeared in the writings of philosophers all over Europe, especially in the works of such French *philosophes* as Voltaire, Rousseau, Diderot, Montesquieu, and D'Alembert. These men advocated that "philosopher-princes" should establish religious freedom, abolish privilege, grant freedom of speech and of the press, develop an honest and efficient administrative corps, and improve justice by abolishing torture, by codifying the laws, and by establishing equality before the law. Only an absolute monarch could accomplish such beneficent reforms in a short space of time without revolution, and those who made some attempts at it came to be known as "benevolent" or "enlightened" despots. Most of these corresponded with the philosopher-reformers themselves, supported them at their courts or patronized them liberally, and even wrote philosophical treatises themselves. Frederick the Great was one of the most indefatigable proponents of the "Enlightenment." Considering himself the "first servant of the state," he wrote to Voltaire, "My chief occupation is to fight the ignorance and the prejudices of the country. . . . I must enlighten my people, cultivate their manners and morals, and make them as happy as human beings can be." The following excerpts from Frederick's own works, originally written in French, which Frederick always favored as a literary medium, will illustrate his attitudes and activities.

FREDERICK THE GREAT ON ENLIGHTENED DESPOTISM

From FREDERICK THE GREAT, "Essay on Forms of Government and the Duties of Sovereigns" (1777) [1]

Let it be carefully remembered that the preservation of the laws was the sole reason which induced men to allow of, and to elect, a superior; because this is the true origin of sovereign power. The magistrate, thus appointed, was the first servant of the state. . . .

Princes and monarchs, therefore, are not invested with supreme authority that they may, with impunity, riot in debauchery and voluptuousness. They are not raised by their fellow citizens in order that their pride may pompously display itself, and contemptuously insult simplicity of manners, poverty and wretchedness. Government is not intrusted to them that they may be surrounded by a crowd of useless people, whose idleness engenders every vice. . . .

The sovereign is attached by indissoluble ties to the body of the state; hence it follows that he, by repercussion, is sensible of all the ills which afflict his subjects; and the people, in like manner, suffer from the misfortunes which affect their sovereign. There is but one general good, which is that of the state. If the monarch lose his provinces, he is no longer able as formerly to assist his subjects. If misfortune has obliged him to contract debts, they must be liquidated by the poor citizens; and, in return, if the people are not numerous, and if they are oppressed by poverty, the sovereign is destitute of all resource. These are truths so incontestable that there is no need to insist on them further.

I once more repeat, the sovereign repre-

[1] *Posthumous Works of Frederick II*, V, 8-25; *Œuvres de Frédéric le Grand*, IX, 196-206.

sents the state; and he and his people form but one body, which can only be happy as far as united by concord. The prince is to the nation he governs what the head is to the man; it is his duty to see, think, and act for the whole community, that he may procure it every advantage of which it is capable. If it be intended that a monarchical should excel a republican government, sentence is pronounced on the sovereign. He must be active, possess integrity, and collect his whole powers, that he may be able to run the career he has commenced. Here follow my ideas concerning his duties.

He ought to procure exact and circumstantial information of the strength and weakness of his country, as well relative to pecuniary resources as to population, finance, trade, laws, and the genius of the nation whom he is appointed to govern. If the laws are good they will be clear in their definitions; otherwise, chicanery will seek to elude their spirit to its advantage, and arbitrarily and irregularly determine on the fortunes of individuals. Law-suits ought to be as short as possible, to prevent the ruin of the appellants, who consume in useless expenses what is justly and duly their right. . . . It is perhaps superfluous to add that the penalty ought never to exceed the crime; that violence never ought to supersede law; and that it were better the sovereign should be too merciful than too severe. . . .

No government can exist without taxation, which is equally necessary to the republic and to the monarchy. . . . This money must all be necessarily levied on the people; and the grand art consists in levying so as not to oppress. That taxes may be equally and not arbitrarily laid on, surveys and registers should be made, by which, if the people are properly classed, the money will be proportionate to the income of the persons paying. . . .

The state of manufactures and of trade,

and article no less important, next presents itself. For the country to be preserved in prosperity, it is indubitably necessary that the balance of trade should be in its favour. If it pay more for importation than it gains by exportation, the result will be that it be annually impoverished. . . . The means to avoid incurring any such loss are to work up all raw material of which the country is in possession, and to manufacture foreign raw materials that the price of labour may be gained in order to procure a foreign market.

THE ENLIGHTENMENT IN PRACTICE

From FREDERICK THE GREAT, *History of the Seven Years' War* (1764) [1]

Justice, ill administered during the preceding reign . . . called loudly for reform; as well in the persons of the judges, advocates, and attornies, as in the laws themselves, which it was necessary to render more clear. . . .

The king committed this labour to his great chancellor [Baron Samuel] Cocceji, a man of integrity, whose virtue and probity were worthy of the noble ages of the Roman republic. . . . This sage of the laws undertook the painful and delicate work with so much zeal that, after one year's assiduous industry, the sovereign courts of justice, purged of those men by whom they had been disgraced, were supplied with virtuous magistrates; a new code of laws, for all the provinces under the Prussian dominion, was finished; and, after it had been approved by the states, promulgated. The prospect was extended to futurity; and, as experience teaches us that the best institutions decline, or become useless, if they are left in neglect, and if not restored to those first principles on which they were founded, a rule was

[1] *The History of the Seven Years' War*, in *Posthumous Works of Frederick II*, II, 2-7.

made that there should be a general visitation, of the sovereign courts of justice, once in three years; that observation of the new laws might be enforced, and such officers of justice as were discovered to have been guilty of prevarication punished. This new order, introduced in the administration of justice, enforced the happiness of the people; and secured to each family its possessions. Every individual lived under the safeguard of the laws, for they were absolute.

However great the cares of the late king in regulating and arranging the finances had been, he had not effected all it was possible to effect. He had neither the time nor the means for concluding a work so great; and the improvements that still might be made were immense; as well respecting lands that were to be cleared as the establishment of manufactories, the extending of trade, and the encouraging of industry. The first years of the king's reign were appropriated to war; nor could he turn his attention to interior government, till he had first insured tranquillity. Along the Oder, from Swinemunde to Kustrin, were vast marshes; which perhaps had, in all ages, lain uncultivated. A plan for clearing this country was formed. A canal was dug, from Kustrin to Wrietzen, by which these marshy lands were drained, and two thousand families were there settled. These settlements were continued from Schwedt to beyond Stettin, where twelve hundred additional families found ease and plenty. Thus was a small province gained, by industry, from ignorance and idleness.

The woollen manufactory, which was rather considerable, was in want of spinners. These were brought out of foreign countries, and were settled in different villages of two hundred families each. It had been a custom, time immemorial, in the duchy of Magdeburg, for the inhabitants of Vogtland to come and gather in the harvest; after which they returned home. The king gave these people settlements in the duchy; and thus procured the state of a number of these foreigners.

By such various operations, the kingdom, during peace, acquired two hundred and eighty new villages. Nor did the care of the country occasion the towns to be neglected. A new town was built on the Swine, after which it was called Swinemunde, and was at the same time made a port, by digging the channel deeper, and cleansing the basin at the mouth of the Oder. The city of Stettin thus gained the tolls that had formerly been paid to the Swedes, in passing to Wolgast down the Peene, which greatly contributed to render its trade flourishing, and to attract foreigners. New manufactories were established in all the towns. Those for rich stuffs and velvets were found most suitable to the city of Berlin. Light velvets and plain stuffs were made at Potsdam. Splittgerber supplied all the provinces with the sugar which he refined at Berlin. A dimity manufactory rendered the city of Brandenbourg flourishing. Russian leather was dressed at Frankfort, on the Oder. Silk stockings and handkerchiefs were made at Berlin, Magdeburg, and Potsdam. The Wegely manufactory was doubled. The planting of mulberry trees was encouraged throughout all the provinces. The clergy gave an example to the husbandmen, and taught them to rear that precious insect which originally comes from the Indies, and from the down of which silk is obtained. In places where wood was plentiful . . . iron foundries were established, which soon supplied the fortresses and the army with cast cannon, bullets, and bombs. In the principality of Minden and the county of Marck, new salt pits were discovered, and the salt was refined. The pits of Halle were brought to perfection, by the construction of buildings for the gradation of the salt, which saved wood. In a word, industry was encouraged in the capital and in the kingdom.

The king enforced the right of market tolls, which the Saxons had disputed with the town of Magdeburg; and, by the means of duties established on the frontiers, the trade of the Prussian provinces was almost on a par with that of Saxony. The Embden company established an important trade with China. By diminishing the exportation duties at Stettin, Königsberg, and Colberg, the revenues of these places were almost doubled. The result of these various operations of finance was, without including the revenues of Silesia and East Friseland, or loading the people with any new tax whatever, that the crown had acquired an increase of revenue, in 1756, of twelve hundred thousand crowns; and, after the inhabitants of all the provinces had been numbered, the sum total was found to amount to five millions of souls. Thus, since the riches of a state consist in the number of its inhabitants, Prussia might be estimated twice as powerful as it had been, during the latter part of the reign of Frederic William, the father of the king.

JOSEPH II AS AN ENLIGHTENED DESPOT

Maria Theresa was not untouched by the Enlightenment. She made improvements in educational facilities, established hospitals, fostered scientific medicine, and promoted agriculture. But her son, Joseph, who became coRegent in 1765 and Emperor (1780-1790), partook liberally of enlightened sentiments. Even before he became coRegent, Joseph wrote: "The inner force, good laws, an honest judiciary, an orderly finance, an imposing military force, a progressive industry, a ruler held in esteem are more worthy of a great European Court than festivals, parades, expensive clothes, diamonds,

golden halls, precious vessels, and brilliant sleighing parties." And when he became Emperor he wrote, "Since I have ascended the throne and wear the first diadem in the world, I have made philosophy the legislator of my empire." Joseph was sincere and indefatigable. "His toilette," wrote a contemporary observer, "is that of a common soldier, his wardrobe that of a sergeant, business his recreation, and his life perpetual motion." Nevertheless, because of undue haste, highhanded and inexpedient methods, and bitter resistance, Joseph failed in most of his projected reforms and is reputed to have said on his deathbed that he would have engraved on his tomb, "Here lies a sovereign who with the best of intentions never carried a single project into execution." Even so, his stated objectives, some of which are given in his letters printed below, are among the best examples of Enlightened Despotism.

From "Letters of Joseph II" [1]

GENERAL OBJECTIVES: JOSEPH II TO THE MAGISTRATES OF OFEN, IN HUNGARY, WHO HAD RAISED A MONUMENT TO HIM (1780)

I thank the magistrates and the citizens for the honor they intend me by erecting a statue to me in one of their principal public places. . . .

When, however, I shall have succeeded in making the whole of Hungary understand what the real relations between the king and the subjects are; when I shall have removed all ecclesiastical and civil abuses; when I shall have awakened the inhabitants to activity and industry; when I shall have caused commerce to flourish, and shall have provided the country from one end to the other with roads and navigable canals, as I hope will be the case;

[1] "Letters of Joseph II," in *The Pamphleteer,* London, XIX (1822), 279-90.

if the nation will then erect a monument to me, I may then, perhaps, have deserved it, and will acknowledge the honor with gratitude.

MERCANTILIST DECREES: JOSEPH II TO COUNT KOLLOWRAT, GRAND CHANCELLOR OF BOHEMIA (1784)

For the encouragement of home productions, and in order to check the progress of luxury and fashion, my commands respecting a general prohibition of foreign merchandise have been made known.

The Austrian commerce has become passive in consequence of the increasing consumption of foreign productions, and the funds of the state, which has thereby lost more than twenty-four millions annually, would by this time have been nearly exhausted but for the produce of our excellent mines. It has been hitherto, one would almost think, the particular object of the Austrian government to benefit the manufactures and the merchants of the French, English, and Chinese, and to deprive itself of all the advantages the state must necessarily enjoy when it provides for the national wants by national industry.

I know what sensations the prohibition caused among the merchants of the capital, and I have conversed with Prince Kaunitz on the subject, but I granted them nothing except that I prolonged the term for their disposing of the foreign merchandise; and more they do not deserve; they are merely the commissioners of the other European merchants.

TAX REFORM: JOSEPH II TO TOBIAS PHILIP, BARON VON GEBLER, VICE-CHANCELLOR OF BOHEMIA (1785)

The present system of taxation in my dominions, and the inequality of the taxes which are imposed on the nation, form a subject too important to escape my attention. I have discovered that the principles on which it is founded are unsound, and have become injurious to the industry of the peasant; that there is neither equality, nor equity. . . .

With this view I give you the necessary orders to introduce a new system of taxation, by which the contribution, requisite for the wants of the state, may be effected without augmenting the present taxes, and the industry of the peasant, at the same time, be freed from all impediments.

Make these arrangements the principal object of your care, and let them be made conformably to the plan which I have proposed. . . .

Adieu, Gebler! Hasten everything that brings me nearer to the accomplishment of my plans for the happiness of my people.

RELIGIOUS TOLERATION: JOSEPH II TO VON SWIETEN (1787)

Till now the Protestant religion has been opposed in my states; its adherents have been treated like foreigners; civil rights, possession of estates, titles, and appointments—all were refused them. I determined from the very commencement of my reign to adorn my diadem with the love of my people, to act in the administration of affairs according to just, impartial, and liberal principles; consequently, I granted toleration [1781], and removed the yoke which had oppressed the protestants for centuries.

Fanaticism shall in future be known in my states only by the contempt I have for it; nobody shall any longer be exposed to hardships on account of his creed; no man shall be compelled in future to profess the religion of the state if it be contrary to his persuasion. . . .

Tolerance is an effect of that beneficent increase of knowledge which now enlightens Europe and which is owing to philosophy and the efforts of great men; it is a

convincing proof of the improvement of
the human mind, which has boldly re-
opened a road through the dominions of

superstition . . . and which, fortunately
for mankind, has now become the highway of monarchs.

---

19 | THE EXPANSION AND EUROPEANIZATION OF RUSSIA

1. Russia before Peter the Great

The transition of Russia from a medieval Muscovite community which still
retained its Oriental characteristics to a
more unified modern state with European connections occurred to a considerable extent in the reign of Ivan III
("the Great"), 1462-1505. The following
account of Ivan's reign is by a nineteenth-century French historian.

THE REIGN OF IVAN THE GREAT,
"BINDER OF THE RUSSIAN LANDS"
(1462-1505)

From RAMBAUD, *History of Russia* (1877) [1]

At the death of Vassili the Blind [Ivan's
father], Russia was all but stifled between
the great Lithuanian empire and the vast
possessions of the Mongols. To the north,
she had two restless neighbors, the Livo-
nian Order and Sweden. In spite of the
labors of eight Muscovite princes, the little
Russian State could not yet make its unity
a fact. . . . It was, however, the time
when the nations of the West began to be
organized. Charles VII and Louis XI in
France, Ferdinand and Isabella in Spain,
the Tudors in England, Frederick III and

[1] Alfred Rambaud, *The History of Russia from
the Earliest Times to 1877*, trans. by Leonora B.
Lang, 2 vols., New York, 1886, I, 161-73.

Maximilian in Austria, labored to build up
powerful States from the ruins of feudal
anarchy. European civilization made unheard of strides; the Renaissance began,
printing spread, Christopher Columbus
and Vasco de Gama discovered new
worlds. Was not Russia also going to
achieve her unity, to take part in the great
European movement? The man who was
to restore her to herself, to free her from
the Mongol yoke, to put her into relations with the West—this man was
expected. . . .

Ivan III, whose reign of forty-three
years was to permit him to realize the
expectations of Russia, was a cold, imperious, calculating prince. . . . Disliking
war, he allowed doubts to be thrown upon
his courage. He was victorious in Lithuania, in Livonia and Siberia almost
without leaving the Kremlin. . . . Ivan
exhausted his enemies by negotiations and
delay, and never employed force till it was
absolutely necessary. His devotion was
mixed with hypocrisy. He wept for his
relatives whom he put to death, as Louis
XI bewailed the Duc de Guienne. Born a
despot, "he had," says Karamsin, "penetrated the secret of autocracy, and became
a formidable deity in the eyes of the Russians." His glance caused women to faint.
When he slept after his meals, it was
wonderful to see the frightened aspect of

the boyards [nobles] for the sleep of the master. He inflicted cruel punishments and tortures on all rebels, even on those of highest rank; he mutilated the counsellors of his son, whipped Prince Oukhtomski and the archimandrite of a powerful monastery, and burned alive two Poles in an iron cage on the Moskowa, for having conspired against him. . . .

Ivan's first effort was directed against Novgorod the Great. The republic of the Ilmen was dying in the anarchy of the aristocracy, the dissensions of the people, the Church, and especially of the boyards. . . . They thought themselves able to despise the authority of a new prince, and had the impudence to neglect the complaints and suggestions made in a tolerably moderate tone by Ivan III. . . . He had a large party in Novgorod, but the opposing faction was the bolder. Marfa, the widow of the possnadnik [lieutenant] Boretski, mother of two grown-up sons, put herself at the head of the anti-Muscovite party. . . . At last Ivan decided to begin the war. . . . At the battle of the Chelona, 5000 Muscovites defeated 30,000 Novgorodians. At Rousa the Grand Prince caused many boyards to be beheaded, one of whom was the son of Marfa, and sent others as prisoners to Muscovy. Ivan III always advanced, fighting and negotiating. Novgorod submitted, paid a war indemnity, and, if she still remained a republic, she was a republic dependent on the good pleasure of the Prince (1470). . . .

Whilst he was destroying the liberty of Novgorod, Ivan deprived her of her colonies, and undertook on his own account the conquest of Northern Russia. By this time Muscovy extended as far as Finland, the White Sea, and the Icy Ocean, and had already obtained a footing in Asia. . . . In 1489, Viatka, which had fallen for a short time into the power of the Tartars of Kazan, was reconquered. . . . In 1499 the voïevodes [governors] of

Oustiougue, of the Dvina and of Viatka, advanced as far as the Pechora, and built a fortress on the banks of the river. In the depths of winter, in sledges drawn by dogs, they passed the defile of the Urals [into Siberia], in the teeth of wind and snow, slew 50 of the Samoyedes, and captured 200 reindeer; invaded the territory of the Vogouls and Ugrians, the Finnish brethren of the Magyars; took 40 enclosures of palisades, made 50 princes prisoners, and returned to Moscow, after having reduced this unknown country, supposed by the geographers of antiquity to be the home of so many wonders and monsters. Russia, like the maritime nations of the West, had discovered a new world. . . .

[In 1480, Ivan III freed Russia from further vassalage to the Mongols by defeating the Khan of the Golden Horde; in 1487, he captured Kazan; and about this same time he advanced westward against Poland and Lithuania, though with less success.]

The acquisition of the Novgorodian possessions and the appanages, the capture of Kazan, the fall of the Horde, and the conquest of Lithuania up to the Soja [tributary of the Dnieper], had doubled the extent of the Grand Duchy of Muscovy, even without reckoning the immense territory it had gained on the north. An event not less important in its consequences was the marriage of Ivan III with a Byzantine princess. Thomas Paleologus, a brother of the last [Eastern] Emperor, had taken refuge at the court of Rome [after Constantinople fell to the Turks in 1453]. There he died, leaving a daughter named Sophia. The Pope wished to find her a husband, and the Cardinal Bessarion, who belonged to the Eastern Rite, advised Paul II to offer her hand to the Grand Prince of Russia. . . . Ivan and his boyards accepted the proposal with enthusiasm; it was God, no doubt, who had given him so illustrious a wife; "a branch of the imperial tree which formerly overshadowed all orthodox Christianity." . . . This daughter of emperors was destined to have an enormous influence on Ivan. It was she, no doubt, who taught him to "penetrate the secret of autocracy." She bore the Mongol yoke with less patience than the Russians, who were accustomed to servitude. She incited Ivan to shake it off. "How long am I to be the slave of the Tartars?" she would often ask. With Sophia a multitude of Greek emigrants came to Moscow, not only from Rome, but from Constantinople and Greece. . . . They gave to Russia statesmen, diplomatists, engineers, artists, and theologians. They brought her Greek books, the priceless inheritance of ancient civilization. . . .

Ivan III was the heir of the Emperors of Byzantium and the Roman Caesars. He took for the new arms of Russia the two-headed eagle. . . . Moscow succeeded to Byzantium as Byzantium had succeeded to Rome. Having become the only metropolis of orthodoxy, it was incumbent on her to protect the Greek Christians of the entire East, and to prepare the revenge against Islamism for the work of 1453. With the Greeks came Italians: Aristotele Fioraventi of Bologna, who was Ivan III's architect, military engineer, and master of artillery; Marco Ruffo, his ambassador to Persia; Pietro Antonio, who built his imperial palace; the metal-founder, Paul Bossio, besides architects and arquebusiers.

Ivan entered into relations with Venice . . . [and] whether to secure himself allies against Poland or to obtain from Germany artists and handicraftsmen, he exchanged more than one embassy with Frederick III and Maximilian of Austria, Mattias of Hungary, and the Pope. When attacked by Sweden, he negotiated an alliance with Denmark [an alliance which, with periodical renewals, lasted about

three hundred years and which, with the other diplomatic relations cited above, ended the isolation of Russia and brought her into closer contact with western Europe].

RUSSIAN INSTITUTIONS AND MANNERS BEFORE PETER THE GREAT

Beginning in the sixteenth century, western Europeans, especially Dutch, English, and German merchants, engaged increasingly in commerce with Russia. Many of them wrote descriptions of the Muscovites. The following account was composed in the early eighteenth century and, as it was based almost entirely upon the observations of such witnesses, it serves as a composite of their accounts.

From BANKS, *Czar Peter the Great* (1740) [1]

The constitution of Muscovy is entirely monarchical. Unity in religion, the absolute power of the Czars, and the profound submission of their subjects all contribute to maintain this form of government. . . . They [the Czars] are not only the source of all authority, but used to be respected as the center of all knowledge; and to hinder any inquisitive person from endeavouring to penetrate into the mysteries of their government, they entirely banished sciences from their dominions, and forbad the profession of them under severe penalties. They would not permit the establishment of any college for the instruction of youth, that none of their subjects might know more than they themselves. . . . It was then common with the Muscovites, when they spoke of anything secret or hard to comprehend, to say, *God and the Czar only know it.* As for their own parts,

[1] John Banks, *A New History of the Life and Reign of the Czar Peter the Great,* London, 1740, 13-24.

the utmost of their learning was to write and read. Christianity itself, which imposes on the priests, at least, a sort of necessity of learning, did yet leave the Russian clergy as ignorant as the laity. All they knew was that they were of the Greek profession and must therefore mortally hate the Latins. Not a doctor among them was able to make a sermon, even to such auditors as the poor Russians. It was not sufficient that books were not read, but in Russia scarce any could be found, even in the richest and most ancient monasteries.

No subject of Muscovy could travel without the Czar's permission, and his ordinances were very severe against those who infringed this regulation. The conversation of strangers, according to these princes, would render them too knowing and teach them to live with greater liberty. The grandees were not even suffered to retire from Court. . . . Obedience to these severe injunctions was become so habitual, that we shall find it one of the Czar Peter's most difficult works to introduce a more natural freedom. The Sovereign himself, in those times, never married a foreign wife, but chose one from among his nobility, and sometimes the common people. . . .

The Muscovites were a clownish, ignorant people, destitute of politeness and even civility; which was owing to their being denied the use of the sciences and liberty of travelling. They were very irregular in their manners, regardless of faith, treaties, and oaths; most excessive drinkers; but hardy, and able upon occasion to bear hunger, cold, and all the fatigues of war. They did not want natural vivacity and penetration, being expert imitators of whatever they saw; but then all industry was entirely suppressed among them. The peasants, born in slavery to their merciless lord, were content with a rude sort of agriculture, which just brought them sufficient to live on. Rich they could not grow, nor durst they if able: even the nobles were afraid to appear so. But Arts are the children of riches and lenity of government; no wonder then if they were strangers in Russia.

In religion, they use the ceremonies and discipline of the Greek Church. Their Patriarch, the Supreme in all Ecclesiastical Affairs, was elected by the Metropolitans, the Archbishops, the Bishops, and the inferior clergy from among the monks of St. Basil. His election was confirmed by the Czar with the ceremony of delivering to him a pastoral staff. Anciently he depended on the See of Constantinople. . . . His successors were contented with that title till 1588, when Job assumed the rank of Patriarch. . . . The successor of Job, jealous of his new-acquired title, bought off the dependence of it for a sum of money which he had the address to raise from the Muscovites under the pretence of releasing them from all foreign authority in matters of religion, and that it was their interest and honour to become a separate church. There were, besides, reasons of state in this alteration. The Czar, looking on all those Turks who were sent to him by the Patriarch of Constantinople, as so many spies, to avoid this inconvenience, which might be attended with dangerous consequences, he thought a separation was the most infallible means. . . .

But among all their ridiculous and superstitious customs, the Muscovites had some significant and instructive. They put a crown of wormwood upon the heads of new-married persons to represent the bitterness of marriage; and as a token of fecundity, sprinkled them with hops. They covered the woman's eyes with a veil to signify that she ought not to see the faults of her husband. Their laws did not prohibit bigamy; yet those who committed it were never respected after, but looked upon as the shame and dishonour of their families. They believed no women to be honest unless they entirely refrained the conversation of men, and kept themselves prisoners in their houses. Virtue, according to them, consisted in being confined within four walls, and the more savage and unpolished, the better wife. Husbands might kill their wives by way of correction without incurring the penalty of the law; they might also repudiate them for sterility, and force them to retire into a Convent. And yet, what is hardly credible, it was usual for a wife to be proud of her husband's jealousy and ill-nature. It was not till towards the beginning of the Czar Peter's reign that it became customary for fathers in marriage contracts to article that their daughters should be used according to their quality, fed with good victuals, and not cudgelled on every slight occasion. . . .

As the Muscovites are more submissive than even the Turks, they glory in calling themselves slaves to their Prince. His will, which they always regard as the will of God, is the only rule of their actions. . . . They would confess that they had nothing of their own, but that their lives and possessions were all from his bounty and no longer theirs than he was pleased to permit. The Czars, for their parts, made their advantage of this credulity, and drew from their subjects whatever they pleased. Besides the traffic in Siberian furs, the customs, the taxes upon brandy-shops and other public-houses, the property of baths and stoves, the duty upon entry and departure in the port of Archangel (amounting alone to above 600,000 crowns), the imposts on the Caviar of Astrakan, upon ichthyol and agaric, the profits made of the Persian and Armenian merchandises, the commerce of skins, wax, honey, and hemp; besides all these, and what they levied on their officers, the Czars were, and still continue, the lawful and sole heirs of all who die intestate, or have been accused of any crime, and the absolute

masters of all their subjects' effects, which they usually surrender to the next of blood upon their paying a considerable fine. . . .

To sum up the character of these people: there reigned everywhere an extreme depravation, both of manners and sentiments, which was not, as in other places, so much as concealed under a modest outside, or dressed in the appearance of wit and superficial humor. Yet, as pride is the perfection of ignorance, this same people was superlatively haughty and full of contempt for everything they did not understand. The Muscovite nation, knowing nothing, and little known by any of its neighbours, made a sort of peculiar people which did not enter into the system of Europe.

2. Peter the Great (1682-1725): The Man

A PEN PORTRAIT

The personality of Peter the Great is one of the most striking in history. It was brilliantly portrayed by a nineteenth-century Polish writer, Kazimierz Waliszewski, whose pen portrait follows.

From WALISZEWSKI, Peter the Great (1896) [1]

Peter may be described, physically, as a fine man, exceedingly tall (his exact height was 6 feet, 8½ inches), dark—"extremely dark, as if he had been born in Africa," says one of his contemporaries—powerful in frame, with a good deal of majesty about him, marred by certain faults of deportment, and a painful infirmity, which spoilt the general effect. He dressed care-

[1] Kazimierz Waliszewski, Peter the Great, trans. from the French by Lady Mary Lloyd, 1898, 106-10. Reprinted by permission of the publishers, William Heinemann, Ltd., London.

lessly, put on his clothes awry, frequently appeared in a most untidy condition, was always changing his garments, military or civil, and would occasionally select a garb of the most grotesque description. He had no sense whatever of propriety in dress. He showed himself to the Danes, at Copenhagen, in 1716, with a green cap on his head, a black military cravat tightly buckled round his neck, and his shirt collar fastened by a big silver button, set with mock stones, such as his own officers were in the habit of wearing. A brown overcoat with horn buttons, coarse worsted stockings, full of darns, and very dirty shoes, completed his costume. He agreed to wear a wig, but insisted on its being short, so that he might be able to thrust it into his pocket; and his own hair [very long and thick], which he rarely cut, showed far below it. . . .

The sovereign's intimate circle frequently saw him in his shirt sleeves, for, even at table, he never scrupled to take off his coat if he was too hot. Restraint, of any kind, he never would endure. . . .

His whole nature appears utterly at variance with the surroundings into which he was born. He has no prejudices, and his Russian subjects brim over with them. They are fanatics in their own religion; he is almost a Free-thinker. They look askance at novelty; he is never weary of innovations. They are fatalists; he, an originating force. They worship form and ceremony; he views all such things with an almost cynical scorn. Finally, and above all, they are indolent, lazy, emotionless—frozen, as it were, into a perpetual winter, or slumbering in some everlasting dream. He, driven by the feverish love of movement and of labour . . . wakes them roughly from their torpor, and their sluggish inactivity, with downright blows, falling on them with sticks, and, not unfrequently, with axes. It would be interesting to follow his perpetual comings and goings, even during the space of a few months. Cast a mere glance over the list of his correspondence with Catherine [his wife]—some 223 letters, published, in 1861, by the Ministry for Foreign Affairs. The various dates—from Lemberg in Galicia, from Marienwerder in Prussia, from Tsaritsin on the Volga, in the south of his empire, from Vologda, in the north, from Berlin, Paris, Copenhagen—make the brain reel. One moment he is in the depths of Finland inspecting forests; then again in the Urals inspecting mines. Soon he is in Pomerania, taking part in a siege; in the Ukraine, where he is occupied in breeding sheep; at the brilliant Court of some German prince, where he acts as his own Ambassador; and then, suddenly, in the Bohemian mountains, where he enacts the part of a private tourist. . . . And so on, year in and year out, from the beginning to the end of his life. He is always in a hurry: he makes his coachman drive full gallop; when he is on foot he never walks —he runs.

When did he take his rest, then? It is not easy to conceive. He would sit far into the night, glass in hand, but even then he was discussing, holding forth, trying his guests sorely, from time to time, with his sudden changes from gaiety to ill-humour, his sallies, his ill-bred jokes, and fits of fury; and he would give audiences at four o'clock in the morning. This was the hour for which he summoned his two Ambassadors, Ostermann and Boutourlin, before sending them to Stockholm, after the conclusion of peace with Sweden, in 1721. He received them, garbed in a short dressing-gown, below which his bare legs were exposed, a thick nightcap, lined with linen on his head—for he perspired violently—and his stockings dropped down over his slippers. According to his orderly officer, he had been walking about for a considerable time, awaiting the arrival of the two gentlemen. Forthwith he fell upon them, questioned them closely, and in every direction, to make sure they thoroughly knew what they were about, and then, having dismissed them, dressed hastily, swallowed a glass of vodka, and hurried off to his dockyards.

Even the pleasures he permitted himself —banquets, illuminations, masquerades— imposed extra labor on him; he took more pains than actual relaxation, letting off his own fireworks, directing the order of processions, beating the big drum—for he was drum-major among other things—and leading the dancers. . . .

But indeed his favourite occupation, even in the hours of recreation, was work, perpetual work. Thus he engraved on copper, and turned in ivory. In May, 1711, the French envoy Baluze, to whom he had granted audience at Jaworow, in Poland, found him in the garden, in the company of a fair lady. He was pushing his suit with a charming Pole, Madame Sieniawska, and meanwhile, saw and plane in hand, he was busily engaged in building a boat!

HOW PETER BECAME INTERESTED IN THE NAUTICAL ARTS

The circumstances of Peter's boyhood caused him to receive a haphazard, mostly informal education. When his father, Czar Alexis, died in 1676, he left two sons, Theodore and Ivan, and several daughters by his first wife, and one son, Peter, by his second wife. Theodore succeeded to the throne (1676-82), but upon his death Peter was elected Czar by the nobles, who passed over Ivan, Peter's elder half-brother, because he was nearly blind and almost idiotic. Peter's election excited the jealousy of Sophia, the strongest of Ivan's sisters, who fomented revolt among the royal guards (the Streltsi) and executed a coup d'état whereby Ivan was pro-

claimed joint ruler with Peter and Sophia was proclaimed Regent during their minorities (1682). There was much bloodshed, and Peter—then only ten years old—witnessed the cruel murder of his mother's relatives in the royal palace, events which may explain the bloodthirsty impulses of Peter's mature years. From 1682 to 1689, however, Sophia was virtual ruler in Russia. Peter was sent away to a country villa, Preobrozhenskoe, where, neglected by the court, he was permitted to amuse himself after his own fashion. It was during these years that he played soldier—so seriously that he organized paid "play" battalions which formed the nucleus of a new Russian army later on—and took up with members of a near-by "German colony" (mostly Dutch and German merchants) where he made many friends and acquired predilections for "Western" ways. During these years, too, he became so enamored of ships and sailing that he afterward startled the world by his manual efforts and earned the title "Father of the Russian Navy." It began in 1688, when Peter was barely sixteen.

From SCHUYLER, *Peter the Great* (1890) [1]

He had heard somewhere that abroad, in foreign parts, people had an instrument by which distances could be measured without moving from the spot. When Prince Jacob Dolgorúky was about to start on his mission to France, and came to take his leave, Peter told him of this wonderful instrument, and begged him to procure him one abroad. . . . On Dolgorúky's return in May, 1688, the first question of Peter was whether he had fulfilled his promise; and great was the excitement as

[1] Eugene Schuyler, *Peter the Great, Emperor of Russia*, 2 vols., 1890, I, 110-13. By permission of Charles Scribner's Sons, New York.

the box was opened and a parcel containing an astrolabe and a sextant was eagerly unwrapped; but, alas! when they were brought out no one knew the use of them. Dolgorúky scratched his head, and said that he had brought the instrument, as directed, but it had never occurred to him to ask how it was used. In vain Peter sought for someone who knew its use. At last his new doctor, Zacharias von der Hulst, told him that in the German suburb he knew of a man with a notion of mechanics—Franz Timmermann, a Dutch merchant, who had long ago settled in Moscow, and who had a certain amount of education. Timmermann was brought next day. He looked at the instrument, and, after a long inspection, finally said he could show how it should be used. Immediately he measured the distance to a neighboring house. A man was at once sent to pace it, and found the measurement correct. Peter was delighted, and asked to be instructed in the use of the new instrument. Timmermann said: "With pleasure; but you must first learn arithmetic and geometry." Peter had once begun studying arithmetic, but was deficient in its full knowledge. He did not even know how to subtract or divide. He now set to work with a will, and spent his leisure time, both day and night, over his copybooks. These are still preserved at St. Petersburg [Leningrad], and we find there many problems, written in the hand of Timmermann, with Peter's efforts at solution. . . .

From this time Timmermann became one of Peter's constant companions, for he was a man from whom something new could always be learned. A few weeks later, in June, 1688, as Peter was wandering about one of his country estates near the village of Ismaílovo, he pointed to an old building in the flax-yard and asked one of his attendants what it was. "A storehouse," replied the man, "where all the rubbish was put that was left after the death of Nikíta Ivánovitch Románof, who used to live here." This Nikíta was an own cousin of the Czar Michael Románof, and in that way the estate had descended to Peter. With the natural curiosity of a boy, Peter had the doors opened, went in, and looked about. There, in one corner, turned bottom upward, lay a boat, yet not in any way like those flat-bottomed, square-sterned boats which he had seen on the Moskvá or the Yaúza.

"What is that?" he asked.

"That is an English boat," said Timmermann.

"What is it good for? Is it better than our boats?" asked Peter.

"If you had sails to it, it would go not only with the wind, but against the wind," replied Timmermann.

"How against the wind? Is it possible? Can it be possible?"

Peter wished to try it at once. But, after Timmermann had looked at the boat on all sides, it was found to be too rotten for use; it would need to be repaired and tarred, and, beside that, a mast and sails would have to be made. Timmermann . . . sent to Ismaílovo a certain Carsten Brandt, who had been brought from Holland about 1660 by the Czar Alexis, for the purpose of constructing vessels on the Caspian Sea. . . . The old man looked over the boat, caulked it, put in the mast and arranged the sail, and launched it on the river Yaúza. There, before Peter's eyes, he began to sail up and down the river, turning now to the right and then to the left. Peter's excitement was intense. He called out to him to stop, jumped in, and began himself to manage the boat under Brandt's directions. "And mighty pleasant it was to me," he writes in the preface to his "Maritime Regulations," where he describes the beginning of the Russian navy. . . .

[Subsequently, Peter sought a larger

body of water on which to sail. He found it nearly fifty miles away, at Lake Plescheyevo, too far to transport the English boat.] Anxiously he asked Brandt whether it were not possible to build some boats there.

"Yes, sire," said Brandt, "but we shall require many things."

"Ah, well! that is of no consequence," said Peter. "We can have anything."

And he hastened back to Moscow with his head full of visions of shipbuilding.

PETER'S TRAVELS IN EUROPE, 1697-98

In 1697, Peter undertook a trip into western Europe primarily to learn at first hand the trade of shipbuilding and secondarily to unite Christian states against Turkey. In order to avoid formalities and give the Czar greater freedom of action, the journey was disguised as an extraordinary embassy with Peter traveling incognito as "Mr. Peter Mikháilof"—with a train of 250 servants, associates, and students! Setting out March 20, 1697, Peter visited Riga, the Prussian court at Königsberg, Holland (where he stayed over four months working in shipyards and observing many other phases of Dutch life), England, and the Imperial Court at Vienna. Everywhere Peter aroused widespread interest and comment. The brilliant Sophia Charlotte [see page 276] met him at Koppenbrügge and found him shy and guilty of bad table manners. But his conversation pleased her, and she wrote amusedly that in dancing the Muscovites "took the whalebones of our corsets for our bones, and the Czar showed his astonishment by saying that the German ladies had devilish hard bones." Peter was in England from January to April, 1698, and his visit was excellently described by Bishop Burnet, although the good Bishop said nothing

about the damage the Czar and his party did to John Evelyn's house at Deptford, where they resided. Evelyn's servant described them as "right nasty," and Evelyn wrote in his famous diary: "I went to Deptford to see how miserably the Czar had left my house after three months making it his Court. I got Sir Christopher Wren, the King's surveyor, and Mr. London, his gardener, to go and estimate the repairs, for which they allowed £150." Burnet's account follows.

From BURNET, *History of His Own Time* (1723-34) [1]

I mentioned in the relation of the former year, the czar's coming out of his own country, on which I will now enlarge: he came this winter over to England, and stayed some months among us; I waited often on him, and was ordered, both by the king, and the archbishop and bishops, to attend upon him, and to offer him such informations of our religion and constitution, as he was willing to receive: I had good interpreters, so I had much free discourse with him. He is a man of a very hot temper, soon inflamed, and very brutal in his passion; he raises his natural heat by drinking much brandy, which he rectifies himself with great application: he is subject to convulsive motions all over his body, and his head seems to be affected with these; he wants not capacity, and has a larger measure of knowledge than might be expected from his education, which was very indifferent: a want of judgment, with an instability of temper, appear in him too often, and too evidently; he is mechanically turned, and seems designed by nature rather to be a ship carpenter than a great prince; this was his chief study and exercise while he stayed here; he wrought much with his own hands, and made all

[1] *Bishop Burnet's History of His Own Time*, 655.

about him work at the models of ships: he told me he designed a great fleet at Azoff [Azov], and with it to attack the Turkish empire; but he did not seem capable of conducting so great a design, though his conduct in his wars since this, has discovered a greater genius in him than appeared at that time. He was desirous to understand our doctrine, but he did not seem disposed to mend matters in Muscovy; he was indeed resolved to encourage learning, and to polish his people, by sending some of them to travel in other countries, and to draw strangers to come and live among them. He seemed apprehensive still of his sister's [Sophia's] intrigues. There was a mixture both of passion and severity in his temper. He is resolute, but understands little of war, and seemed not at all inquisitive that way. After I had seen him often, and had conversed much with him, I could not but adore the depth of the Providence of God that had raised up such a furious man to so absolute an authority over so great a part of the world. . . .

He went from hence to the court of Vienna . . . but he was called home sooner than he had intended, upon a discovery or a suspicion of intrigues managed by his sister: the strangers to whom he trusted most were so true to him, that those designs were crushed before he came back; but on this occasion he let loose his fury on all whom he suspected; some hundreds of them were hanged all round Moscow, and it was said, that he cut off many heads with his own hand.

3. Peter the Great: Reformer

All the reforms of Peter the Great appear to have been subordinate to one major end: to improve Russian capacity for war. In part, this objective was forced upon the Czar by warlike neighbors; in part, it was an inevitable corollary of Peter's ambitions. To realize this aim, it was necessary to improve Russian efficiency; and it was with this in view that Peter undertook to "Westernize" his people in costume, manners, education, and thought; to inaugurate ecclesiastical reforms which subjected the Church wholly to the State; to make noble rank dependent upon military, naval, or civil service; to reorganize, re-equip, and discipline the army; to build a navy; to improve industry, agriculture, and commerce in the interests of greater national self-sufficiency and greater national wealth; to reorganize the revenue and judicial administrations in an effort to reduce corruption—all these things Peter attempted. If royal edicts and tyrannical benevolence could have changed a people in a generation, Russia would have become a new nation during Peter's reign. But at every step Peter met with the fearful superstition, widespread ignorance, and stubborn resistance of the Russian people. In the end, few of Peter's social reforms had lasting effect outside court circles. Russia simply did not have the cultural resources necessary for the full absorption of the Czar's reforms. Some of his attempts are described as follows by a contemporary admirer.

From BANKS, *Czar Peter the Great* [1]

The general habit of the Russians was a long vestment, hanging down almost to their ankles, and gathered up in plaits at the hips, like a woman's petticoat. The Czar resolved to have this changed, and gave orders first to his boyards, and all who came to court, that they should furnish themselves, according to their several

[1] Banks, *A New History of . . . the Czar Peter the Great,* 107-13.

abilities, with handsome clothes, after the English [or west-European] mode, the wealthiest of them with gold or silver trimming. He also commanded that suits of clothes in the English fashion should be hung up at all the gates of the city of Moscow, and that all persons, except the peasants who brought in provisions, should dress themselves after those patterns. Whoever disobeyed this order was obliged to pay 2 grevens (about twenty pence of our money) at passing the gates, or submit to kneel down and have their skirts cropt, so as just to touch the ground in that posture. Many hundreds of garments were to be seen thus curtailed; and as the whole was done in good humor, it soon reconciled people to the new fashion, which was found the most commodious.

The women too, especially the ladies about the court, were ordered to reform their dress according to the English manner. . . . To make this go down the better with the fair, he abrogated the custom of keeping them in apartments by themselves, and admitting them only once to come into any company, present a dram of brandy round, and retire; ordering that for the future they should be present at all public entertainments, and converse freely with the men, especially at weddings. . . .

I before took notice of the retrenchment of beards, as well as of habits. The Russians wore long ones, hanging down on their bosoms, and nicely combed out. . . . To reform this foolish custom, the Czar laid a heavy tax on all his subjects, exclusive of the priests and peasants, for the wearing of beards. The very common people were obliged to pay a copeck, for entering any city or town with a beard, and an officer waited at the gate to receive it. But such was their veneration for this piece of natural ornament, as they esteemed it, that they looked upon the Czar as guilty of a grievous sin, and this injunction passed for a terrible persecution.

Indeed it was rigorously put in force on some of the most obstinate, who had their beards plucked up by the roots for non-compliance. Some were so superstitious as to save the hair when taken off, in order to have it put in their coffin, that they might give an account of it to St. Nicholas. Libels were writ on this occasion, and dropped about the streets, charging his Majesty with heathenism and tyranny. But the women liking their husbands and sweethearts the better, most of the men by degrees were reconciled to this depilation of their chins.

In the first book of this history I mentioned the Muscovite Religion, and in particular the grandeur and authority of the patriarch. The Czar had been in England, and seen what advantage accrued to the sovereign from being the chief in ecclesiastical affairs. He resolved to be so himself in Muscovy, but would not attempt to depose the prelate in possession, though he sometimes took the liberty to curb the excess of his priestly power. . . .

This prelate, who was a very old man, dying about the time we are upon [1700], the Czar refused to have any other elected, and took upon himself to be head of the church. . . .

The other reformations he made were of different kinds, but none of them more remarkable than those which related to matrimony. Matches, till now, were always made up by the parents. . . . But the Czar, observing that marriages in Russia were often remarkably unhappy, very justly attributed it to this cause. He therefore ordered, that no young couple should be married without their own free consent, nor till after a correspondence of at least six weeks. This new regulation had a very good effect. Husbands before would beat their wives so inhumanly that they often died of the blows, and the man never suffered for the murder, which was interpreted as done by way of correction. But these barbarities, in a great measure, were now prevented. . . .

There had been a printing-house erected in Moscow, by the approbation of one of the former Czars: but not long after it was set on fire in the night, and the press and letters burnt, as was thought by the procurement of the priests, who looked upon all books, but the legends of their saints, the history of their own country, and the exploits of their czars, to be as bad as witchcraft. As they had no university, nor any school worthy of notice, it was unlikely they should have any taste for literature. . . . But things began now to put on a new face in Russia; books were printed, schools were erected, the mathematics were studied, even astronomy itself. . . .

I before mentioned that the Russians began their year upon the first of September, because the world, they imagined, was created in autumn, when the fruits of the earth were in perfection; and very fond they were of an argument, which they thought unanswerable. But the Czar Peter had often shown his boyards a map of the globe, and merrily gave them to understand that Russia was not all the world. . . . He had so far inculcated these remonstrances that at the beginning of the present century, a period the most happy for beginning a new succession of time, he resolved to make his subjects conform to what the wisest of them could not but be convinced was very rational. With this view he proclaimed a jubilee on the first of January, 1700 . . . and then ordered that no person, from that time forwards, should make use of any other date, under a severe penalty, than what was followed by the other nations of Europe. . . .

While these civil regulations were on foot, the army and navy had not been neglected. All the troops were now disciplined, and regularly clothed, according to what was practised in other nations: for till now

every soldier, except those on Le Fort's establishment, was dressed according to his own fancy. And that no man in his dominions might want employment, the Czar ordered lists to be taken of such gentlemen as had none, and commanded some of them to enter as volunteers, giving the rest appointments in different stations, either about the navy or in the frontier garrisons.

4. Peter the Great and the Expansion of Russia

CONFLICT WITH SWEDEN

The acquisition of satisfactory ports on the open seas has been a major desideratum in Russian foreign relations throughout the modern age. Prior to his European tour, Peter had, after two attempts, captured Azov from the Turks (1696). The port was of little use as long as the Sultan controlled the Dardanelles. Moreover, the problems of Spanish succession (see page 265) loomed too large in western Europe for Peter to have any success in creating a league against the Turks. Accordingly, when opportunity offered, Peter signed a treaty with the Turks (Carlowitz, 1699), and undertook the exploitation of Swedish territory in order to gain a "window on the Baltic." A French historian has written the following description of these actions.

From RAMBAUD, *History of Russia* [1]

Peter I had navigated the White Sea, and conquered a port on the Sea of Azov; but by the Baltic alone could he secure rapid and regular communication with

[1] Alfred Rambaud, *The History of Russia*, II, 9-21.

the nations of the West. It was only by taking up a position on the Baltic that Russia could cease to be an Oriental State, and could form part of Europe. The Baltic at this time belonged to Sweden, whose possessions on the coasts—Finland, Carelia, Ingria, Esthonia, Livonia, and Pomerania—made it a Swedish Mediterranean. Stockholm was situated in the center of the monarchy of the Vasas, instead of lying, as it does at present, on its maritime frontier. To "open a window" into the West, it was necessary to break in some point the chain of Swedish possessions. The opportunity seemed favorable. . . . It was . . . proposed to Augustus of Saxony, King of Poland, a scheme by which Sweden was to be attacked simultaneously by all her neighbors. Poland was to take from her Livonia and Esthonia, Russia was to conquer Ingria and Carelia, Denmark was to invade Holstein, which belonged to a brother-in-law of Charles XII. Peter accepted the overtures of the King of Poland; he desired nothing better than to carry out the designs of Ivan the Terrible and of his father Alexis. The youth of the new King of Sweden [Charles XII], and his reputed incapacity [which proved to be without foundation] led Peter to expect rapid success. . . .

The coalition was almost immediately smitten by two unexpected blows. The King of Denmark, threatened in Copenhagen, had been forced to sign the Treaty of Traventhal, and at the approach of the Swedes the King of Poland had been forced to raise the siege of Riga. Without waiting to pursue the Poles, Charles turned against the Russians [at Narva]. . . .

The latter [the Swedes] had hardly 8430 men; the Russians amounted to 63,500, of whom only 40,000 took part in the action. The army was composed of regular troops, besides streltsi, Cossacks,

and men raised in haste. In the absence of the Tsar, who had quitted the camp on the previous evening to hasten the arrival of reënforcements, it was placed under the command of an old general of the Emperor of Germany, the Duc de Croï, whom the troops suspected from the fact of his being a stranger. . . .

On the 19th of November, 1700, the battle began by a cannonade that lasted till two in the afternoon. At that time the Swedes reached the foot of the entrenchmens under cover of a snow-storm, which prevented the Russians from seeing twenty paces in front. In an instant the Swedes had crossed the fosse and the parapet, and the Russian camp was seized with panic. "The Germans have betrayed us," cried the soldiers, and began to stab the foreign officers.

[So the Swedes, despite heavy odds, won the battle of Narva and the Czar's army was disgraced. Had Charles XII followed up his victory, he might have forever ruined Peter's military pretensions. Instead, he turned against the King of Poland, plotted for his dethronement, and, after more than five years of intrigue, Charles XII set up his own puppet, Stanislaus Leszczynski, on the Polish throne. Meanwhile, Peter reorganized his humiliated troops, seized Swedish provinces along the Baltic, and began his new capital, St. Petersburg, near the mouth of the Neva River. "Let the Tsar tire himself with founding new towns," exclaimed Charles XII, "We will keep for ourselves the honor of taking them later." Not until 1708 was Charles ready to attack the Russians, and now the latter slowly retreated until the Swedes were forced to spend the winter in Russia. Late the following spring, the most decisive battle of Peter's career was fought at Poltava.]

The Tsar arrived (15th June, 1709) with 60,000 men, whom he covered by an entrenchment raised during a single night. Charles's army was now reduced to 29,000 men, who lacked everything, suffered as much from the extreme heat as they had formerly done from the extreme cold, and were exhausted by suffering and privations. He had only four field-pieces against seventy-two guns of the Tsar. In one of his nightly sallies, when he was trying to harass the enemy's vanguard, Charles received a wound in his heel which necessitated a cruel operation, and on the day of the famous battle (8th July, 1709) he had to be carried in a litter. . . .

The Russian fire on the front of the Swedes was so violent that the horses harnessed to Charles's litter were killed; his drabans [halbardiers] then took it in turns to carry him, but twenty-one out of the twenty-four were left where they fell. The Russian cavalry rallied, and the Russian infantry which was now put in motion broke the Swedish line. Attacked in front by Peter, and in the rear by Menchikof [a Russian general], the Swedes were speedily thrown into disorder. They fled, and Charles was placed on horseback by his guards, and obliged to go with the stream. He hardly escaped being taken. . . .

Poltava marks a new era in universal history. Sweden, which under Gustavus Adolphus, and again under Charles XI, had played in Europe the part of a great power, which had even obtained an importance out of all proportion with her actual resources, was suddenly relegated to the third rank among states. The place she left vacant in the North was taken by a nation which had at its disposal far larger resources, besides a greater power of expansion. The shores of the Baltic were to pass into its hands. Already Russia declared herself, not only a power of the North, but a power of Europe. Muscovy, which had been formerly held in check by little Sweden, by anarchic Poland, by decrepit Turkey, or even by the Khan of the Tartars, was destined to become formidable to France, to England, and to the house of Austria. . . . Finally, Poltava was not only a victory, it was proof of the regeneration of Russia; it justified the Tsar, his foreign auxiliaries, his regular army; it left his hands free to reform, gave to the empire a new capital, and promised to Europe a new civilized people.

THE PEACE OF NYSTADT (AUGUST 20, 1721)

After Poltava, Charles XII fled to Turkey, where he succeeded in drawing the Sultan into war against Russia. The Czar lost Azov, but after the death of Charles XII in 1718, he concluded The Treaty of Nystadt, which completed the dismemberment of the Swedish empire. The principal article of this treaty follows.

From The Treaty of Nystadt (1721) [1]

In the name of the holy and undivided Trinity.

Let it herewith be published and known, that, since between His Royal Majesty of blessed memory, the most illustrious, the most powerful King and Lord, Charles the Twelfth, of the Swedes, Goths, and Vandals King, &c., and Her Royal Majesty his successor on the Swedish throne, the most illustrious and powerful Queen and Lady, Queen Ulrica Leonora, of the Swedes, Goths, and Vandals Queen, &c., &c., and the most illustrious and mighty King and Lord, King Frederick the First

[1] Reich, *Select Documents Illustrating Mediaeval and Modern History,* 678-82. By permission of Staples Press, Ltd.

of the Swedes, Goths, and Vandals King, &c., &c., and the kingdom of Sweden on the one hand, and His Majesty the Czar, the most illustrious and mighty Czar and Lord, the Czar Peter the Great, autocrat of all the Russians, &c., &c., and the Russian Empire on the other, a Grievous and destructive war has already since several years arisen and been waged, both High Parties on the impulse of a spirit of conciliation well pleasing to God, have become thoughtful as to how an end may be set to the protracted shedding of blood, the land-wasting scourge the earlier, the better be removed; thus by the Divine providence it has come about, that ministers plenipotentiary from both High Parties, have been sent together . . . who by mutual agreement met at the place of Nystadt, in Finland, named and fixed for the Congress and negotiation, and . . . agreed and arrived at the following everlasting and durable peace in the name of both High Parties and by the grace and goodwill of the Almighty. . . .

Article IV. His Majesty the King of Sweden cedes hereby for himself and for his heirs and successors upon the Swedish throne, and for the Kingdom of Sweden, to His Majesty the Czar and his heirs and successors to the Russian Empire, the complete and irrevocable possession and propriety of the provinces of Livonia, Esthonia, Ingermannland, and the portion of Carelia with Wiburgs-Lehn conquered by the arms of His Majesty the Czar from the Crown of Sweden during the present war, and which are hereunder specified and described in the article on frontier delimitation, together with the towns and fortresses of Riga, Dünamunde, Pernau, Reval, Dorpt, Narva, Wiburg, Kexholm and all other towns, fortresses, havens, fortified places, districts, shores belonging to the provinces mentioned, together with the islands of Oesel, Dagoe, Moen, and all

other islands on the Courland frontier laying off the shores of Livonia, Esthonia, and Ingermannland to the east, with all towns and places, inhabitants and dwellings, and all appurtenances, defences, authorities, rights, and uses in the aforementioned islands, without any exception as they have been possessed, employed, and enjoyed by the Crown of Sweden. . . . Likewise all archives, documents and letters concerning those lands and carried out of them during this war to Sweden, shall be traced and faithfully delivered up to the plenipotentiaries appointed to this end by His Majesty the Czar.

5. The Accession of Catherine II, "the Great" (1762)

CATHERINE AS WIFE OF THE GRAND DUKE PETER

Peter the Great, having executed his only son for opposition to his policies, left the succession in such uncertainty that for thirty-seven years after his death the Russian crown became an object of court intrigues and revolutions. During the reign of Peter's younger daughter, Elizabeth (1741-1762), the Grand Duke Peter, Elizabeth's nephew, married Sophia Augusta Frederica, Princess of Anhalt-Zerbst, the precocious, calculating daughter of a petty north-German prince. This princess, who was rechristened Catherine by the Orthodox Church, spent her early married years in wretchedness and boredom, for the Grand Duke was a drunken, lascivious, undeveloped booby who played with dolls. Catherine, however, adopted the Russian religion, became adept in the Russian tongue, and, as her *Memoirs* quoted below show, was from the first aware of her opportunity.

From CATHERINE THE GREAT, *Memoirs*
(c. 1780) [1]

Now the Grand Duke had about as much discretion as a cannon ball, and, when his mind was full of anything, he could not rest until he had unburdened it to the persons he was in the habit of talking with, never for a moment considering to whom it was he spoke. Consequently, he used to tell me all these things, with the utmost frankness, the first time he saw me afterwards. He always fancied that everyone was of his opinion, and that nothing could be more reasonable than all this. I took good care not to speak of these things to any one; but they made me reflect very seriously upon the fate which awaited me. I determined to husband carefully the confidence of the Grand Duke, in order that he might at least consider me as a person of whom he felt sure, and to whom he could confide everything without the least inconvenience to himself; and in this I succeeded for a long time. Besides, I treated every one in the best way I could, and studied how to gain the friendship, or at least to lessen the enmity of those whom I any way suspected of being badly disposed to me. I showed no leaning to any side, nor meddled with anything; always maintained a serene air, treated every one with great attention, affability, and politeness, and, as I was naturally very gay, I saw with pleasure that from day to day I advanced in the general esteem, and was looked upon as an interesting child, and one by no means wanting in mind. I showed great respect for my mother, a boundless obedience for the Empress, and the most profound deference for the Grand Duke; and I sought with the most anxious care to gain the affection of the public. . . .

At last the Empress fixed the 21st of August [1744] for the [wedding] cere-

mony. As the day came nearer, I became more and more melancholy. My heart predicted but little happiness; ambition alone sustained me. In my inmost soul there was a something which never allowed me to doubt for a single moment that sooner or later I should become the sovereign Empress of Russia in my own right. . . .

Generally speaking, we were all dreadfully tired of the dull life we led. . . . Since my marriage I read a great deal. The first book I read after my marriage was a novel called *Tiran the Fair* (*Tiran le blanc*), and for a whole year I read nothing but novels. But I began to tire of these. I stumbled by accident upon the letters of Madame de Sévigné, and was much interested by them. When I had devoured these, the works of Voltaire fell into my hands. After reading them, I selected my books with more care. . . .

I saw . . . that three paths almost equally perilous presented themselves for my choice: first, to share the fortunes of the Grand Duke, be they what they might; secondly, to be exposed every moment to everything he chose to do either for or against me; or, lastly, to take a path entirely independent of all eventualities; to speak more plainly, I had to choose the alternative of perishing with him, or by him, or to save myself, my children, and perhaps the empire also, from the wreck of which all the moral and physical qualities of this Prince made me foresee the danger. This last choice appeared to me the safest. I resolved, therefore, to the utmost of my power to continue to give him on all occasions the very best advice I could for his benefit, but never to persist in this, as I had hitherto done, so as to make him angry; to open his eyes to his true interests on every opportunity that presented itself; and, during the rest of the time, to maintain a gloomy silence; and, on the other hand, to take care of my own inter-

[1] *Memoirs of the Empress Catherine II Written by Herself*, ed. by A. Herzen, New York, 1859, 45-46, 75, 255-56.

ests with the public, so that in the time of need they might see in me the saviour of the commonwealth.

THE COUP D'ETAT OF JULY, 1762

The Czarina Elizabeth died in January, 1762, and the Grand Duke, now Peter III, reigned long enough (January-July, 1762) to reverse Russia's alliances and save his hero, Frederick the Great of Prussia, from humiliating defeat in the Seven Years' War (see page 285). But in July, Catherine, conspiring with the nobility and the army, was proclaimed Empress, and the astounded Peter, seeking to drown his troubles in liquor, was murdered, probably at the instigation of the new Czarina. Catherine described the circumstances of her seizure of the throne to her favorite, Poniatowski, who later figured in the First Partition of Poland (see page 286).

From CATHERINE THE GREAT, *Memoirs* [1]

Peter III had lost the small share of sense which naturally belonged to him; he openly offended all parties; he wished to dismiss the guards, and was on the point of leading them into the country for this purpose, intending to replace them by his Holstein troops, who were to be stationed in the city; he wished also to change the religion of the country, marry Elizabeth Voronzoff, repudiate me, and place me in confinement.

On the occasion of the celebration of peace with the King of Prussia, after having publicly insulted me at table, he gave, in the evening, an order for my arrest. My uncle, Prince George, had the order retracted, and it was only from this time that I listened to the proposals which

[1] *Memoirs of the Empress Catherine II*, Appendix, 301-08.

had been made to me since the death of the Empress Elizabeth. It was intended to seize him in his room, and imprison him, as had formerly been done in the case of the Princess Anne and her children. He went to Oranienbaum. We had in our interest a great number of captains in the regiments of the guards. The fate of the secret was in the hands of the three brothers Orloff, the elder of whom Osten remembers to have seen following me everywhere, and perpetrating a thousand follies; his passion for me was notorious, and everything he has done has been inspired by it. All three are men of great determination, and very much beloved by the soldiery. . . . The minds of the guards were prepared, and, towards the end, some thirty or forty officers and nearly ten thousand men were in the secret. In this number there was not a single traitor during the space of three weeks. . . . I was at Peterhoff; Peter III was residing and carousing at Oranienbaum. It had been agreed that, in case of treason, they would not await his return, but at once assemble the guards and proclaim me. Their zeal for me did what treason would have effected. A report was spread on the 27th that I had been arrested. The soldiers became excited; one of our officers quieted them. Then came a soldier to a captain, named Pacik, the head of a party, and told him that I was certainly lost. Pacik assured him that he had just heard from me. The man, still alarmed for my safety, went to another officer and told him the same story. This person was not in the secret; terrified at learning that an officer had dismissed the man without arresting him, he went to the major; the latter had Pacik arrested, and sent, during the night, a report of the arrest to Oranienbaum. Instantly the whole regiment was in commotion, and our conspirators in alarm. . . .

At six o'clock on the morning of the 28th, Alexis Orloff entered my room awoke me, and said very quietly, "It is time to get up; everything is prepared for proclaiming you." I asked for details. He replied, *"Pacik has been arrested."* I no longer hesitated, but dressed hastily, without waiting to make any toilet, and entered the carriage which he had brought with him. . . . I went to the new Winter Palace, where the synod and senate had assembled. The manifesto and oath were drawn up in haste. Thence I descended, and made, on foot, the inspection of the troops; there were more than fourteen thousand men, guards and country regiments. The instant I appeared the air was rent with shouts of joy, which were caught up and repeated by an innumerable multitude. I then proceeded to the old Winter Palace, to take the necessary measures for completing our work. There a council was held, and it was determined that I should go at the head of the troops to Peterhoff, where Peter III was to dine. Posts were stationed on all the roads, and we received information from moment to moment. I sent Admiral Taliezsin to Cronstadt. Then came the Chancellor Voronzoff to reprove me for having left Peterhoff. He was led to the church to swear fealty to me; that was my answer. Next came Prince Troubetzkoy and Count Alexander Schouvaloff, also from Peterhoff: they came to assure themselves of the fidelity of the regiments, and put me to death. They also were quietly led away to take the oath. . . .

Peter III renounced the empire at Oranienbaum, in full liberty, surrounded by fifteen hundred Holstein troops, and came to Peterhoff. . . . Terror had brought on a dysentery, which continued for three days, and stopped on the fourth. He drank to excess on that day, for he had everything he wanted except his liberty. He had, however, asked me for nothing but his mistress, his dog, his negro, and his violin; but, for fear of scandal, and not

wishing to increase the general excitement, I sent him only the three last named. The hemorrhoidal cholic again came on, accompanied by delirium; he was two days in this condition, which was followed by excessive weakness, and, notwithstanding the efforts of the physicians, he at last sunk, demanding a Lutheran clergyman. I was afraid the officers might have poisoned him, so much was he hated. I had him opened, but not a trace of poison could be discovered. . . .

Such, pretty nearly, is our history. The whole was managed, I confess, under my immediate direction, and towards the end I had to check its progress . . . everything, in fact, was more than ripe a fortnight beforehand.

6. Catherine and Her Government in 1778

The following observations on the nature and circumstances of Catherine's reign as of 1778 were made by Sir James Harris, later the first Earl of Malmesbury, who was English Ambassador to Russia from 1777 to 1784.

From MALMESBURY, *Diaries* (July 31, 1778) [1]

The immense extent of the Russian empire, and the security of its frontiers, doubtless render it a desirable ally, and almost an inaccessible enemy. The various articles of commerce the rest of Europe must necessarily fetch from hence, and the very few which this country need receive from them, insures its independence and wealth. Russia, therefore, incontestably stands very high among the European powers; but it may be controverted whether it can come up to the high repu-

[1] *Diaries and Correspondence of James Harris, First Earl of Malmesbury,* ed. by his grandson, 4 vols. London, 1844, I, 203-07.

tation it enjoys, or to the superiority it assumes. The advantages just mentioned are merely the effects of situation; they existed before this people were civilized, and will remain with them if they ever should return to that state of barbarity from which they have so recently emerged. To give an empire pre-eminence abroad, its political system should be uniform, wise, and steady. To make it respectable at home, fixed rules of interior policy should be established, and their administration should be secure and uncorrupted. I must confess, my Lord, since my residence here, my researches after such a system and such rules have been fruitless; and it is in vain that I have attempted to discover on what those high-flown encomiums of this government, which everywhere met my ear, were founded.

In an absolute monarchy, everything depends on the disposition and character of the Sovereign: my principal object, therefore, has been to investigate that of the Empress, and as well from my own observations, as from the relations of unprejudiced and well-informed men, it appears to me that she has a masculine force of mind, obstinacy in adhering to a plan, and intrepidity in the execution of it; but she wants the more manly virtues of deliberation, forbearance in prosperity, and accuracy of judgment, while she possesses, in a high degree, the weakness vulgarly attributed to her sex—love of flattery, and its inseparable companion, vanity; an inattention to unpleasant but salutary advice; and a propensity to voluptuousness, which leads her to excesses that would debase a female character in any sphere of life.

If we recapitulate the events of the sixteen years which have elapsed since her accession, they will, I believe, on a fair and candid inquiry appear to be in great measure the effects of such a character. On tracing her operations in Poland, we shall find that, after having given a King to that country, on no very laudable motive, she, by sometimes supporting his measures too violently, and, at others, by not supporting them at all, reduced that republic to a state of despair and anarchy; which, in the first instance, brought on herself the Turkish war, and, in its consequences, forced her into a connection that induced her to make a most unjustifiable treaty, which, besides leaving an indelible blot on her reign, has added force to the only two powers from whom she had anything to apprehend, and left them in future an influence in the Polish affairs equal to her own. What other evils the Turkish war may produce, it is difficult to foresee: the events are still depending; and that peace, which at first appeared as glorious as it was unexpected, has only proved an armed truce, and given time to the sinews of this country to relax and be enervated.

The turn affairs have taken in Sweden proves the Russian measures there to have been equally ill-concerted and ill-conducted. . . . Sweden, from being considered as a dependent state, is now become an object of fear and jealousy.

To counterbalance these facts, Her Imperial Majesty has concluded two alliances; the one with Denmark, the other with Prussia. From the first, no advantages have yet arisen; from the latter, this Court has been held for several years in a state of implicit obedience to that of Berlin, and now finds itself under the greatest distress, in order either to evade the purport of the treaty, or to fulfil it without increasing the evils which threaten this state. . . .

If we turn our reflections to the interior administration of Government, I fear the result of them will not be more advantageous. A mistaken lenity, arising either from fear or indolence, has subverted the great purposes of law and justice. The great men oppress their inferiors wantonly; the inferiors pilfer and steal in security. From a conviction of this remissness, and from the specious pretext of the cruelty of their lords, we have seen a rebellion [of serfs and Cossacks, in 1771-1775, led by Emilyan Ivanovich Pugachev, a Cossack who claimed to be Peter III] break out in the heart of the empire; which, had it been led by men of judgment or courage, would have shaken it to its foundations. No troops were ready to make head against it; a panic had seized half the country; and the same spirit of sedition which animated Pugatscheff, had infected the rest. He was within a few days' march of Moscow, and the Court was near retreating to Riga, when, from want of resolution and conduct, he was defeated, and tranquillity restored to the empire. The sparks of discontent, however, are not yet extinguished; and it is much to be apprehended, that, in case of any national calamity, they would blow out afresh. The want of proper attention in the civil magistrates, joined to the avidity of the officers in sending home their booty from the army, occasioned the plague to break out at Moscow in 1771. A hundred and forty thousand people perished. . . .

In opposition to these facts we may place the establishment of several colonies of emigrants from Germany, the institution of many useful seminaries for the youth of both sexes, and a very great generosity and munificence.

The code of laws, sketched out by the Empress herself in really a masterly manner, has never yet been digested; it remains as a deposit at the Academy, and many reasons render its being put in execution impracticable.

Such, I can venture to assert, is the real state of this empire. A thriving commerce and increasing revenue, owing to its unexhausted resources, and to the progress of civilization in its remoter quarters, would, under a wise administration, very soon restore it to its force and vigour. The vanity of the Empress, however, throws an obstacle in the way of this amelioration: having been taught by flatterers that Russia is the greatest empire in the world, and confirmed in this idea by the most fortunate successes, she never can be brought to see the situation of her country in its true light.

7. Catherine the Great and the Enlightenment

Like her contemporaries, Frederick the Great, Joseph II, and others (see pages 288-294), Catherine subscribed to theories of the Enlightenment. During her early married life she had begun reading works of the philosophers (see page 309). Later she engaged in active correspondence with many of them, purchased the library of the French encyclopedist Diderot, and renewed support to Russian academies of art and science which had fallen into neglect since the time of Peter I. Early in her reign, Catherine determined to reform and codify the laws of Russia on the basis of enlightened principles. Great preparations were made, and Catherine herself spent two years preparing *The Instructions to the Commissioners for Composing a New Code of Laws* (1767). Despite all this thoughtful preparation, very little was actually done. The first Turkish war, the Partition of Poland, the Pugachev Rebellion—all these forced the Empress to turn to other things. Subsequently, the American Revolution and the French Revolution inclined her toward more conservative policies, and the reform of the law was permanently dropped. Nevertheless, *The Instructions* serve excellently to illustrate the Enlightenment, which, at the hands of all its apostles, promised more than it was ever able to perform. As the Russian historian, Kluchevsky, has said, *The Instructions* were Catherine's "political confession . . . a feature in the biography of the document's composer." Researches have shown that Catherine borrowed large sections of *The Instructions* from Montesquieu's *Spirit of the Laws* (1748) and from Cesare Beccaria's *On Crime and Punishment* (1764). Catherine herself wrote of the encyclopedist D'Alembert, "I shall soon be sending him a manuscript to show him how serviceable the works of writers of genius may prove to them who will put them to use." In its revised form, *The Instructions* consisted of about six hundred fifty paragraphs.

From CATHERINE THE GREAT, *Instructions* (1767) [1]

1. The Christian Law teaches us to do mutual Good to one another, as much as possibly we can.

2. Laying this down as a fundamental Rule prescribed by that Religion, which has taken, or ought to take Root in the Hearts of the whole People; we cannot but suppose, that every honest Man in the Community is, or will be, desirous of seeing his native Country at the very Summit of Happiness, Glory, Safety, and Tranquillity.

3. And that every Individual Citizen in particular must wish to see himself protected by Laws, which should not distress him in his Circumstances, but, on the Contrary, should defend him from all Attempts of others, that are repugnant to this fundamental Rule.

4. In order therefore to proceed to a speedy Execution of what *We* expect from

[1] *Documents of Catherine the Great,* ed. by W. F. Reddaway, 1931, 215-55. By permission of Cambridge University Press, Cambridge, England.

such a general Wish, *We,* fixing the Foundation upon the above first-mentioned Rule, ought to begin with an Inquiry into the natural Situation of this Empire.

5. For those Laws have the greatest Conformity with Nature, whose particular Regulations are best adapted to the Situation and Circumstances of the People, for whom they are instituted.

This natural Situation is described in the three following Chapters.

CHAP. I

6. Russia is an European State.

7. This is clearly demonstrated by the following Observations: The Alterations which *Peter the Great* undertook in Russia succeeded with the greater Ease, because the Manners, which prevailed at that Time, and had been introduced amongst us by a Mixture of different Nations, and the Conquest of foreign Territories, were quite unsuitable to the Climate. *Peter the First,* by introducing the Manners and Customs of Europe among the European People in his Dominions, found at that Time such Means as even he himself was not sanguine enough to expect. . . .

9. The Sovereign is absolute; for there is no other Authority but that which centers in his single Person, that can act with a Vigour proportionate to the Extent of such a vast Dominion.

10. The Extent of the Dominion requires an absolute Power to be vested in that Person who rules over it. It is expedient so to be, that the quick Dispatch of Affairs, sent from distant Parts, might make ample Amends for the Delay occasioned by the great Distance of the Places. . . .

13. What is the true End of Monarchy? Not to deprive People of their natural Liberty; but to correct their Actions, in order to attain the *supreme Good.*

14. The Form of Government, therefore, which best attains this End, and at

the same Time sets less Bounds than others to natural Liberty, is that which coincides with the Views and Purposes of rational Creatures, and answers the End, upon which we ought to fix a steadfast Eye in the Regulations of civil Polity.

15. The Intention and the End of Monarchy, is the Glory of the Citizens, of the State, and of the Sovereign.

16. But, from this Glory, a Sense of Liberty arises in a People governed by a Monarch; which may produce in these States as much Energy in transacting the most important Affairs, and may contribute as much to the Happiness of the Subjects, as even Liberty itself. . . .

33. The Laws ought to be so framed, as to secure the Safety of every Citizen as much as possible.

34. The Equality of the Citizens consists in this; that they should all be subject to the same Laws.

35. This Equality requires Institutions so well adapted, as to prevent the Rich from oppressing those who are not so wealthy as themselves, and converting all the Charges and Employments intrusted to them as Magistrates only, to their own private Emolument.

36. General or political Liberty does not consist in that licentious Notion, *That a Man may do whatever he pleases.*

37. In a State or Assemblage of People that live together in a Community, where there are Laws, Liberty can only consist *in doing that which every One ought to do, and not to be constrained to do that which One ought not to do.*

38. A Man ought to form in his own Mind an exact and clear Idea of what Liberty is. *Liberty is the Right of doing whatsoever the Laws allow:* And if any one Citizen could do what the Laws forbid, there would be no more Liberty; because others would have an equal Power of doing the same. . . .

96. Good Laws keep strictly a just Medium: They do not always inflict pecuniary, nor always subject Malefactors to corporal, Punishment.

All Punishments, by which the human Body might be maimed, ought to be abolished. . . .

240. It is better to *prevent* Crimes, than to *punish* them.

241. To *prevent* Crimes is the *Intention,* and the *End* of every *good* Legislation; which is nothing more than the Art of conducting People to the *greatest* Good, or to leave the *least* Evil possible amongst them, if it should prove impracticable to *exterminate* the whole. . . .

243. Would you *prevent* Crimes? order it *so,* That the laws might rather favour every *Individual,* than any particular Rank of Citizens, in the Community. . . .

245. Would you prevent Crimes? order it so, that the *Light of Knowledge* may be *diffused* among the people. . . .

248. Finally, the *most sure,* but, at the same Time, the *most difficult* Expedient to mend the Morals of the People, is a perfect System of Education.

20

STRUGGLES FOR COLONIAL SUPREMACY

1. The Desire for Colonies

The success of the Spanish western and the Portuguese eastern empires not only had profound effects upon European economy (see pages 85-89) but also fired the ambition of neighboring states. Late in the sixteenth century, when rivalry ran high between Elizabethan English and Hapsburg Spanish, Sir Humphrey Gilbert and his half-brother, Sir Walter Raleigh, undertook to establish English colonies in North America. To enlist royal support they engaged a brilliant preacher, Richard Hakluyt, later famous for his compilations of accounts about voyages of discovery, to prepare "Certain reasons to induce Her Majesty [Queen Elizabeth] and the state to take in hand the western voyage and the planting therein." In 1584, Hakluyt presented to the Queen in Raleigh's name (Gilbert having been drowned), a *Particular Discourse on the Western Planting*. Written on the threshold of vast new colonial enterprises on the part of several European states, particularly of England and France, Hakluyt's *Discourse,* although colored somewhat by the immediate struggles between England and Spain, sets forth the motives and intentions of nearly all the colonizers of Europe, whether English, French, Dutch, Swedish, or other. The gist of his arguments is presented in the following extracts.

From HAKLUYT, *Discourse on Western Planting* (1584) [1]

Seeing that the people of that part of America from 30 degrees in Florida northward to 63 degrees (which is yet in no Christian princes actual possession) are idolaters . . . it remains to be thoroughly weighed and considered by what means and by whom this most godly and Christian work may be performed of enlarging the glorious gospel of Christ, and reducing of infinite multitudes of these simple people that are in error into the right and perfect way of their salvation. . . . Now the means to send such as shall labor effectually in this business is by planting one or two colonies . . . where they may remain in safety and first learn the language of the people near adjoining . . . and little by little acquaint themselves with their manner, and so with discretion and mildness distill into their purged minds the sweet and lively liquor of the gospel. . . .

The next thing is that now I declare unto you the commodities of this new western discovery, and what merchandize are there to be had, and from thence to be expected. . . . The countries therefore of America where unto we have just title, as being first discovered by Sebastian Cabot, at the cost of that prudent King, Henry VII, from Florida northward to 67 degrees (and not yet in any Christian princes ac-

[1] *Documentary History of the State of Maine,* ed. by Charles Deane, in *Collections of the Maine Historical Society,* 2d ser., II, Cambridge, 1877, 7-160.

tual possession), being answerable in climate to Barbary, Egypt, Syria, Persia, Turkey, Greece, all the islands of the Levant Sea, Italy, Spain, Portugal, France, Flanders, High Germany, Denmark, Eastland, Poland, and Muscovy, may presently or within a short space afford us, for little or nothing, and with much more safety, either all or a great part of the commodities which the aforesaid countries do yield us at a very dear hand and with manifold dangers. . . . [Hakluyt here cites "many printed testimonies" of persons who had visited the American shores and reported that the country afforded precious metals and gems "in abundance," spices and drugs, silk, cotton, furs and skins, dyestuffs, fishes, fowls, salt, wines, citrus fruits, lumber, shipbuilding materials of all kinds, and so on.]

Many thousands of idle persons are within this realm, which, having no way to be set on work, are either mutinous and seek alteration in the state, or, at least, very burdensome to the commonwealth, and often fall to pilfering and thieving and other lewdness, whereby all the prisons of the land are daily pestered and stuffed full of them, where either they pitifully pine away, or else at length are miserably hanged, even twenty at a clap out of some one jail. Whereas if this voyage were put in execution, these petty thieves might be condemned for certain years in the western parts . . . in sawing and felling of timber . . . in burning of firs and pine trees to make pitch, tar, rosin, and soap ashes . . . in setting them to work in mines . . . in dragging for pearls and coral, in planting of sugar canes . . . [etc.]

Besides this, such as by any kind of infirmity cannot pass the seas thither, and now are chargeable to the realm at home, by this voyage shall be made profitable members, by employing them in England in making a thousand trifling things which will be very good merchandize for those countries where we shall have most ample vent thereof.

In sum, this enterprise will minister matter for all sorts and states of men to work upon; namely, all several kinds of artificers, husbandmen, seamen, merchants, soldiers, captains, physicians, lawyers, divines, cosmographers, hydrographers, astronomers, historiographers—yea, old folks, lame persons, women, and young children, by many means which hereby shall still be ministered unto them, shall be kept from idleness, and be made able by their own honest and easy labor to find themselves without surcharging others. . . .

Whatsoever cloth we shall vent on the tract [of that colony] . . . all these clothes, I say, are to pass out of this realm full wrought by our natural subjects in all degrees of labor. . . . And then consequently it followeth that the like number of people . . . shall be set on work in England of our poor subjects more than hath been. . . . And on the other side we are to note that all the commodities we shall bring thence we shall not bring them wrought . . . but shall receive them all substances unwrought, to the employment of a wonderful multitude of the poor subjects of this realm in return. And so to conclude, what in the number of things to go out wrought, and to come in unwrought, there need not one poor creature to steal, to starve, or to beg as they do. . . .

And this is the greatest fear that the Spaniards have, to wit, our planting in those parts and joining with those savages, their neighbors, in Florida. . . . Which thing an Englishman, Captain Muffett, who is now in France, told divers times this last winter in my hearing and others of credit, namely, that when he was in Spain, prisoner, not long since, he heard the treasurer of the West Indies say, that there was no such way to hinder his master

[Philip II] as to plant upon the coast near Florida. . . . And entering into the consideration of how this Philip may be abased, I mean first to begin with the West Indies, as there to lay a chief foundation for his overthrow. . . . If you touch him in the Indies, you touch the apple of his eye; for take away his treasure . . . which he hath almost [all] out of his West Indies, his old bands of soldiers will soon be dissolved, his purposes defeated, his power and strength diminished, his pride abated, and his tyranny utterly suppressed. . . .

By these colonies the north west passage to Cathay and China may easily, quickly, and perfectly be searched out as well by river and overland as by sea.

2. New European Advances into India

The Portuguese monopoly of European trade with India (see page 77) lasted almost exactly a century, 1500-1600. By 1600, the English, the Dutch, and the French were making almost simultaneous preparations to challenge Portuguese control. In 1600, Queen Elizabeth chartered the English East India Company; in 1602, the Dutch organized a similar company; and in 1604, Henry IV followed suit in France. Thus, while the French company was relatively inactive till Colbert's time, the stage was set for bitter conflict over control of Indian trade and, ultimately, of India herself. In 1615, the English company, in conjunction with King James I, sent an ambassador, Sir Thomas Roe, to the court of Jahangir, "Conqueror of the World," Great Mogul (1605-27). Sir Thomas found the Indians proud and untrustworthy, their minds poisoned against the English by the Por-

tuguese; but he managed, after three years, to obtain concessions as shown in the following articles whereby English trade to India was approved by the Mogul.

THE FRUITS OF SIR THOMAS ROE'S EMBASSY (1615-18)

From the Treaty of Amity and Commerce (1617) [1]

1. That the Prince had received the English nation into his protection and favor, and had concluded peace and amity with them, according to the command of the great king, and hereby doth give notice to all his Governor, Lieutenant and other officers of Suratt and all his other Signories, to publish the same and to obey it.

2. In consideration of this treaty, and that the Portugals are common enemies to their peace and traffic, it shall be lawful for the English to land with their arms and to pass with them for defence of their persons and goods. . . .

3. That it should be lawful for the English to buy or hire any house in his ports, where they might quietly dwell and no man to disturb or displace them; and therein house their goods. . . .

4. That the Governor of Suratt and other officers should receive and dispeed the English Ambassador with honor and courtesy, and see him well housed during his stay in Suratt. . . .

6. That it should be lawful for the said English to land any sort of goods and to relade, at their pleasure; and upon the land in any part to trade, traffic, buy and sell according to their own will. . . .

7. That the said English might live in their own houses and among themselves

[1] William Foster, *The Embassy of Sir Thomas Roe to the Court of the Great Mogul*, in The Hakluyt Society *Works*, 2d ser., I-II, London, 1894-1899, II, 506-08. By permission of The Hakluyt Society.

according to their own religion and laws. . . .

8. That if any quarrel or other controversy whatsoever did arise among the English, that the Governors nor any other officers should not intermeddle, but leave it wholly to the President of their own nation. . . .

9. That the linguist and brokers serving the English should have free liberty to speak and deliver anything in the behalf of their masters, and should have licence to bargain, traffic, sell, or buy for them, and to do them any other service. . . .

11. That in all causes of complaint or controversy the Governors and *Cazies* of the place should do them speedy justice and protect them from all injuries or oppressions whatsoever, and should aid and entreat them as friends with curtesy and honor; for that so it is the command of the Great King.

COLBERT ON WAYS TO DRIVE THE DUTCH FROM INDIAN TRADE

In 1664, Colbert, as part of his mercantilist program (see pages 248-251), created a new French East India Company and strove to enlarge that phase of French commerce. As one of his objects was to break the Dutch commercial supremacy in Europe and as the Dutch had already gained a large share in Indian trade, Colbert strove to weaken them in the East, practically ignoring English competition in the same field. Colbert proposed to accomplish his aim by persuading the Portuguese, whose Indian empire was now greatly decayed, to join with the French East India Company against the Dutch. The following instructions to the French ambassador to Portugal, Saint-Romain, summarize Colbert's views.

From COLBERT, *Instructions* (1669) [1]

His lordship of Saint-Romain is well informed of the care which his Majesty has taken to organize the East India Company, of the powerful protection which he gives it, and of the great sums of money which he has furnished from the royal treasury for its establishment and for the support of the great losses . . . which all enterprises of this kind meet at their beginning. . . .

It is certain that of the four great nations of Europe who at present trade in the Indies, namely, the French, the English, the Portuguese, and the Dutch, the Portuguese for a long time have held sole possession of this commerce. . . . But this great power has notably decayed since the Dutch have begun to trade in these same countries, and Portugal finds herself at present reduced to the places only at Goa, Diu, and some others less important on the Coromandel coast.

The Dutch are at present masters of all the isles and even of all the countries which produce spices; and their effort to monopolize that trade is such that they destroy and depopulate all the spice countries, either because of the difficulty of becoming absolute masters there, or because they think it advantageous to their commerce that there should not be such an abundance. And if their efforts in this succeed, they will go farther and, if possible, drive out all the other nations and become masters of everything. The ill treatment they gave the English . . . all the measures they have taken to win from the Portuguese the island of Ceylon and all the other islands, even the villages of Cochin and Cananore, seized in violation of treaties; and, in general, all that the Dutch have done in these countries since they have brought in their avarice and

[1] *Lettres, Instructions et Mémoires de Colbert,* ed. by Pierre Clément, II [2], 456-59.

tyranny, of which the Portuguese are only too well informed, are conclusive proofs that they aim at nothing short of the complete destruction of the Portuguese as soon as, by force or by even more dangerous means, they believe they can accomplish this end. And if one considers the state of the Dutch and the advantages which the public and private individuals of their nation enjoy from this trade, together with the state of the Portuguese, one can easily see that the complete expulsion of the latter is imminent, unless they employ prompt and effective countermeasures.

It is certain that the fleets which arrive yearly in Holland carry merchandise to the value of 10 to 12 million livres which they distribute in all the realms of Europe and gain thereby the money which gives them their power; that the company which produces this advantage to the Dutch public maintained at its own expense as many as 30 vessels during the last war with England; that this same company has more than 150 vessels in the Indies; that it made and sustained the war against the Portuguese with the advantages cited above; that it has continued it against various kings of the same country, and always with success; that it maintains in the same Indies an army of 10 to 12 thousand men and a navy of 40 to 50 vessels; that it is mistress of all the isles, and has alone established its commerce in China and in Japan, and it might well be said in all the Indies, since the merchandise carried by the English is of little consequence.

And, on the contrary, the Portuguese have neither vessels nor troops, and there remain to them only Goa, Diu, and some other places of little importance.

This enormous difference in the two powers, and the effort of the Dutch to preserve and increase their strength, make clear to the Portuguese the necessity of a powerful and effective remedy in order to avoid complete ruin. The only remedy for the Portuguese consists in joining with another commercial power and perhaps even in dividing the areas and places under their control with one of the other nations which, having the same interests, might join its force with theirs so as to render themselves formidable to the Dutch, and to gain a condition whereby, through their combined efforts, they may not only keep the Dutch within their present limits but also be able to take from them part of the trade and some of the places they have usurped by force.

Only the French are capable of procuring this great advantage to the Portuguese in giving them, by firm treaties which could be made between their kings, a share in the settlements and commerce which remain to them, inasmuch as the religion of the English does not permit the Portuguese to call upon them.

In order to effect this result, his Majesty desires that his said lordship of Saint-Romain, instructed in all the arguments contained in this document, together with all those which his capacity, his experience, and the information that he may be able to get from the Portuguese may furnish him, should suggest them on every opportunity to the mind of the prince, of the queen, and of all their ministers, and work incessantly to bring them to treat with his Majesty about some one of their places in the Indies, and also to create a commercial union between the French and the Portuguese on conditions of mutual advantage to the two nations.

3. The Weaknesses of the Mogul's Empire

The European advance into India was facilitated not only by the weakness of the Portuguese but also by the decay of the government of the Indian emperors. Since 1525, India had been ruled by a dynasty of Mohammedan emperors called Moguls. Akbar the Great (1556-1605) and Shah Jahan (1628-58) raised the Mogul Empire to great size and magnificence, but the sons of Shah Jahan fell to fighting even before their father died. The third son, Aurangzeb, seized the throne in 1658, murdered his brothers, and ruled until his death in 1707, after which the Mogul Empire declined rapidly—and European power in India rose accordingly. A French physician, François Bernier, spent almost a decade (1659-69) at Aurangzeb's court and was one of the few Europeans who looked beneath the rich exterior of the Mogul's government to discern the true weaknesses of his empire. In a letter to Colbert, Bernier described these weaknesses.

From BERNIER, Letter to Colbert (c. 1670) [1]

The *Great Mogol,* lord and master of the greater part, must necessarily be in the receipt of an immense revenue, and possess incalculable wealth. But there are many circumstances to be considered, as forming a counterpoise to these riches.

First. Of the vast tracts of country constituting the empire of *Hindustan,* many are little more than sand, or barren mountains, badly cultivated, and thinly peopled; and even a considerable portion of the good land remains untilled from want of labourers; many of whom perish in consequence of the bad treatment they experience from the Governors. . . .

Second. The empire of the *Great Mogol* comprehends several nations, over which he is not absolute master. Most of them still retain their own peculiar chiefs or

[1] *Travels in the Mogul Empire,* ed. by Archibald Constable, 2nd ed. rev. by Vincent A. Smith, 1914, 205-27. By permission of Oxford University Press, London.

sovereigns, who obey the *Mogol* or pay him tribute only by compulsion. In many instances this tribute is of trifling amount; in others none is paid; and I shall adduce instances of nations which, instead of paying, receive tribute. . . .

Third. It is material to remark that the *Great Mogol* is a Mahometan . . . who, believing with the Turks that Osman was the true successor of *Mahomet,* are distinguished by the name of *Osmanlys.* The majority of his courtiers, however, being Persians, are of the party known by the appellation of *Chias,* believers in the real succession of *Aly.* Moreover, the *Great Mogol* is a foreigner in *Hindustan,* a descendant of *Tamerlan,* a chief of those *Mogols* from *Tartary* who, about the year 1401, overran and conquered the *Indies.* Consequently he finds himself in an hostile country, or nearly so. . . . To maintain himself in such a country, in the midst of domestic and powerful enemies, and to be always prepared against any hostile movement on the side of *Persia* or *Usbec,* he is under the necessity of keeping up numerous armies, even in the time of peace. These armies are composed either of natives, such as *Ragipous* and *Patans,* or of genuine *Mogols* and people who, though less esteemed, are called *Mogols* because white men, foreigners, and *Mahometans.* . . .

Rajas bear an equal rank with the foreign and Mahometan *Omrahs,* whether employed in the army which the King retains at all times near his person, or in those stationed in the provinces. . . . There are many reasons why the *Mogol* is obliged to retain *Rajas* in his service. First. Ragipous are not only excellent soldiers, but, as I have said, some *Rajas* can in any one day bring more than twenty thousand to the field. Second. They are necessary to keep in check such *Rajas* as are not in the *Mogol's* pay; to reduce to submission those who take up arms rather than pay tribute, or refuse to join the army when summoned by the *Mogol.* Third. It is the King's policy to foment jealousy and discord amongst the *Rajas,* and by caressing and favouring some more than others, he often succeeds, when desirous of doing so, in kindling wars among them. Fourth. They are always at hand to be employed against the *Patans,* or against any rebellious *Omrah* or governor. . . .

The *Mogol* is also compelled to engage *Patans* in his service by reasons very similar to those I have assigned for employing *Ragipous.* . . .

It is also important to remark the absolute necessity which exists of paying the whole of this army every two months, from the *Omrah* to the private soldier; for the King's pay is their only means of sustenance. . . .

But I have not enumerated all the expenses incurred by the *Great Mogol.* He keeps in *Dehly* and *Agra* from two to three thousand fine horses, always at hand in case of emergency: eight or nine hundred elephants, and a large number of baggage horses, mules, and porters, intended to carry the numerous and capacious tents, with their fittings, his wives and women, furniture, kitchen apparatus, *Ganges'-water,* and all the other articles necessary for the camp, which the *Mogol* has always about him, as in his capital, things which are not considered necessary in our kingdoms in Europe.

Add to this, if you will, the enormous expenses of the *Seraglio,* where the consumption of fine cloths of gold, and brocades, silks, embroideries, pearls, musk, amber and sweet essences, is greater than can be conceived.

Thus, although the *Great Mogol* be in the receipt of an immense revenue, his expenditure being much in the same proportion, he cannot possess the vast surplus of wealth that most people seem to imagine. . . .

Before I conclude, I wish to explain how it happens that, although this Empire of the *Mogol* is such an abyss for gold and silver, as I said before, these precious metals are not in greater plenty here than elsewhere; on the contrary, the inhabitants have less the appearance of a moneyed people than those of many other parts of the globe.

In the first place, a large quantity is melted, re-melted, and wasted, in fabricating women's bracelets, both for the hands and feet, chains, ear-rings, nose and finger rings, and a still larger quantity is consumed in manufacturing embroideries; *alachas,* or striped silken stuffs; *touras,* or fringes of gold lace, worn on turbans; gold and silver cloths; scarfs, turbans, and brocades. The quantity of these articles made in *India* is incredible. . . .

In the second place, the *King,* as proprietor of the land, makes over a certain quantity to military men, as an equivalent for their pay. . . . Similar grants are made to governors, in lieu of their salary, and also for the support of their troops, on condition that they pay a certain sum annually to the King out of any surplus revenue that the land may yield. . . .

The persons thus put in possession of the land . . . have an authority almost absolute over the peasantry, and nearly as much over the artisans and merchants of the towns and villages within their district; and nothing can be imagined more cruel and oppressive than the manner in which it is exercised. . . .

This debasing state of slavery obstructs the progress of trade and influences the manners and mode of life of every individual. There can be little encouragement to engage in commercial pursuits, when the success with which they may be attended, instead of adding to the enjoyments of life, provokes the cupidity of a neighbouring tyrant possessing both power and inclination to deprive any man of the fruits of his industry. When wealth is acquired, as must sometimes be the case, the possessor . . . studies the means by which he may appear indigent: his dress, lodging and furniture, continue to be mean, and he is careful, above all things, never to indulge in the pleasures of the table. In the meantime, his gold and silver remain buried at a great depth in the ground; agreeable to the general practice among the peasantry, artisans and merchants, whether *Mahometans* or *Gentiles,* but especially among the latter, who possess almost exclusively the trade and wealth of the country, and who believe that the money concealed during life will prove beneficial to them after death. . . .

The facts I have mentioned are sufficient to account for the rapid decline of the *Asiatic* states.

4. French-English Competition for Eastern Empire

The supreme contest for European control in India centered about competition between the French and the English, a competition which broke into open warfare during the War of Austrian Succession in Europe. Two commanding figures dominated this struggle, one French, Joseph François Dupleix (1696-1764), and one English, Robert Clive (1725-1774), and, though Clive ultimately won, the basis of his policy—and that finally adopted by the English in India—was furnished by Dupleix. Dupleix went to India in 1721 as a fortune-hunter. He remained to become one of France's greatest empire-builders. Experience showed him that a European commercial company with only coastal trading posts in India— posts which required constant military and naval defense against both natives and European competitors—could not become a profitable enterprise without local Indian revenues which, in turn, required conquest and political control over the country. Such local revenues were, in Dupleix' view, the only means of stopping the yearly export from France of millions of livres for the defense of the Company's posts. This line of reasoning led Dupleix to undertake military conquests in India, a line of action which the French company was not prepared to support. Dupleix, in hopes of making such conquests as would supply enough local revenues to justify his policy, ignored the Company's orders and finally, in 1754, was recalled in bitter disgrace. Before his recall, he prepared a long *Mémoire* for the Company to explain his conduct.

DUPLEIX'S POLICY

From DUPLEIX, *Mémoire* (1753) [1]

The divergency of opinion, which I perceive exists among my compatriots and which is shared even by those responsible for the management of the East India Company, concerning what is happening in India makes me want to expose fully certain truths which a long experience has impressed on me, and the evidence for which I must lay before you. These truths are: that no commercial company whatsoever can subsist solely on the profits derived from its commerce, but that a fixed and assured revenue is essential, especially when such a Company maintains a large number of trading centers; and that, secondly, such a Company must avoid as far as possible the exportation of gold and silver.

[1] Virginia McLean Thompson, *Dupleix and His Letters,* Ballou, 1933, 801-22. Reprinted by permission of Virginia McLean Thompson.

These two points form the subject matter of this *mémoire*. . . .

All the Company's commerce in India is shared with the English, the Dutch, the Portuguese and the Danes. . . . This division of trade, or rather this rivalry, has served to raise considerably the price of merchandise here and has contributed quite a little toward cheapening the quality—two unfortunate circumstances which, of course, further reduce the price and profits in Europe. . . . Our Company can hope for no monopoly in the Indian trade. We shall always share whatever we deal in with other countries. We can, therefore, hope for no other profits than those being made at present. We should even anticipate that instead of increasing, they are likely to decline and that very soon, if we force the trade beyond a certain point. . . . The only possible way of making profits on inferior merchandise would be to have a large and regular revenue; then the losses could be offset by our income. Those of our rivals who did not have such a resource would be obliged to give up this branch of commerce, or else restrict themselves to their national market. . . .

I think that I have shown the truth of the first point of this memorandum, and the complete proof can be found in the Company's books. I pass now to the second truth, which is that every commercial company should avoid the exportation of bullion from the kingdom. It is a maxim long established that the more the specie circulates in a state, the more flourishing is the state's condition, and the more the state can be helped and sustained by it. It is, then, good policy to seek every means of preventing its exportation. But it is very hard, not to say impossible, to trade in China and India without exporting specie. . . . Since it is obviously impossible to keep all our specie in France, we should neglect nothing to reduce to a minimum its exportation to India, whence it will never flow back to Europe. Our manufactures in wool, gilt, etc., can diminish such exportation, but not to the extent we desire; we need something else, and this can only be found in a fixed, constant, and abundant local revenue. Permit me, kindly, to give you a brief illustration.

Let us suppose that the Company is obliged yearly to send twelve millions to India. Wool, cloth, and other exported manufactures amount to two millions, so there remains ten millions to be sent in specie, a large sum and one exported only too frequently. It could be reduced by at least half, and might even entirely cease, if the local revenue amounted to ten millions. . . .

These are the motives which have led me to sacrifice everything to attain this end. I have been deprived myself of the rest to which my long years of work have entitled me. . . . This work . . . would have been already accomplished, if I had been better supported, not only here but in my native land, which has looked upon the benefits I have acquired for it with too great indifference. . . . I shall content myself by saying that, in spite of all the obstacles, I have succeeded in procuring for my nation a revenue of at least five millions. My intention was to raise it to ten millions, and I would have succeeded. . . . Yes, I can truly say that if what has arrived this year had been drawn from France's regular troops, all the fighting would now be over and the Company would be enjoying more than ten millions in revenue.

THE BATTLE OF PLASSEY AND ITS RESULTS (JUNE-JULY, 1757)

Dupleix's ambitions to establish a French colonial empire in India led to conflicts with England, both the French and the English espousing rival Indian princes in an effort to extend their own political power through the agency of native puppets. Thus, despite the Peace of Aix-la-Chapelle in Europe (1748), war arose in India even before the Seven Years' War broke out in Europe. Clive captured Arcot (1751) and the English became masters of the Carnatic while the French held the Deccan. In 1756, Aliverdi Khan, native governor of Bengal, died. His grandson, Siraj-ud-daula, succeeded him and, with French aid, determined to drive the English from Bengal. In June, 1756, he captured Calcutta and murdered many English prisoners in the infamous "Black Hole." Immediately, Clive, with force far inferior in numbers, marched against Siraj-ud-daula and met his forces at Plassey near the end of June, 1757. Clive himself wrote the following account of the battle and its results— results which marked the beginning of the British Empire in India after a pattern similar to that envisioned by Dupleix.

From CLIVE, Report on the Battle of Plassey (1757) [1]

I gave you an account of the taking of Chandernagore [on the way to Plassey, March, 1757]; the subject of this address is an event of much higher importance, no less than the entire overthrow of Nawab Siraj-uddaula, and the placing of Mir Jafar on the throne. I intimated, in my last, how dilatory Siraj-uddaula appeared in fulfilling the articles of the treaty. This disposition not only continued but increased, and we discovered that he was designing our ruin, by a conjunction with the French. . . .

About this time some of his principal officers made overtures to us for dethron-

[1] Quoted in Ramsay Muir, *The Making of British India,* London, 1915, No. 9, 53-57, and No. 11, 58-59. By permission of Longmans, Green & Co., Inc.

ing him. At the head of these was Mir Jafar, then Bakhshi [paymaster] to the army, a man as generally esteemed as the other was detested. As we had reason to believe this disaffection pretty general, we soon entered into engagements with Mir Jafar to put the crown on his head. All necessary preparations being completed with the utmost secrecy, the army, consisting of about one thousand Europeans, and two thousand sepoys, with eight pieces of cannon, marched from Chandernagore on the 13th, and arrived on the 18th at Katwa Fort, which was taken without opposition. The 22nd, in the evening, we crossed the river, and landing on the island, marched straight for Plassey Grove, where we arrived by one in the morning. At daybreak we discovered the Nawab's army moving towards us, consisting, as we since found, of about fifteen thousand horse, and thirty-five thousand foot, with upwards of forty pieces of cannon. They approached apace, and by six began to attack with a number of heavy cannon, supported by the whole army, and continued to play on us very briskly for several hours, during which our situation was of the utmost service to us, being lodged in a large grove, with good mud banks. . . . Their horse exposing themselves a good deal on this occasion, many of them were killed, and among the rest four or five officers of the first distinction, by which the whole army being visibly dispirited and thrown into some confusion, we were encouraged to storm both the eminence and the angle of their camp, which were carried at the same instant, with little or no loss. . . . On this a general rout ensued, and we pursued the enemy six miles, passing upwards of forty pieces of cannon they had abandoned, with an infinite number of *hackeries,* and carriages filled with baggage of all kinds. Siraj-uddaula escaped on a camel, and reaching Murshidabad early next morning, despatched away what jewels and treasure he conveniently could, and he himself followed at midnight, with only two or three attendants.

It is computed there are killed of the enemy about five hundred. Our loss amounted to only twenty-two killed, and fifty wounded. . . .

As, immediately on Siraj-uddaula's flight, Mir Jafar found himself in peaceable possession of the palace, I encamped without, to prevent the inhabitants from being plundered or disturbed. . . . The same evening I waited on Mir Jafar, who refused seating himself on the *masnad* [throne] till placed on it by me; which done, he received homage as Nawab from all his courtiers. The next morning he returned my visit; when, after a good deal of discourse on the situation of his affairs, I recommended him to consult Jagat Seth [a rich Bengal merchant] on all occasions, who being a man of sense, and having by far the greatest property among all his subjects, would give him the best advice for settling the kingdom in peace and security.

On this, he proposed that we should immediately set out together to visit him, which being complied with, solemn engagements were entered into by the three parties, for a strict union and mutual support of each other's interests. Jagat Seth then undertook to use his whole interest at Delhi (which is certainly very great), to get the Nawab acknowledged by the Mogul, and our late grants confirmed. . . .

The substance of the treaty with the present Nawab [Mir Jafar] is as follows:

1. Whatever Articles were agreed upon in the time of peace with the Nawab Siraj-uddaula . . . I agree to comply with.

2. The enemies of the English are my enemies, whether they be Indians or Europeans.

3. All the effects and factories belonging to the French, in the Provinces of Bengal (the Paradise of Nations), Behar and Orissa, shall remain in the possession of the English, nor will I ever allow them any more to settle in the three Provinces.

4. In consideration of the losses which the English Company have sustained by the capture and plunder of Calcutta, by the Nawab, and the charges occasioned by the maintenance of the forces, I will give them one *crore* of Rupees [£1,000,-000]. . . .

7. For the effects plundered from the . . . inhabitants of Calcutta, I will give the sum [totaling 77 *lacs* of Rupees— about £770,000]. The distribution of the sums allotted the natives, English inhabitants, Hindus, and Mussulmans, shall be left to the Admiral, and Colonel Clive . . . and the rest of the Council, to be disposed of by them to whom they think proper.

8. Within the ditch, which surrounds the borders of Calcutta, are tracts of land, belonging to several Zemindars; besides this I will grant the English Company six hundred yards without the ditch.

9. All the land lying to the south of Calcutta, as far as Kalpi, shall be under the Zemindari of the English Company; and all the Officers of those parts shall be under their jurisdiction. The revenues to be paid by them (the Company) in the same manner with other Zemindars.

10. Whenever I demand the English assistance, I will be at the charge of the maintenance of them. . . .

It is impossible as yet to form a judgment how much the granted lands will produce you, as the Europeans are quite ignorant of the extent of the country between the river and lake; but, in order to give you some idea of the value, I'll estimate it at 10 lacs *per annum* [£100,-000]. An officer on the part of the Nawab is already despatched to Calcutta to begin the survey, in company with one of ours. . . .

The present Nawab has every appearance of being firmly and durably seated on the throne . . . so that this great revolution, so happily brought about, seems complete in every respect. I persuade myself the importance of your possessions now in Bengal will determine you to send out, not only a large and early supply of troops and good officers, but of capable young gentlemen for the civil branches of your business.

5. French-English Competition for Western Empire

Concurrent with the contests for Far Eastern empires, similar struggles took place in the West Indies and North America. The Spanish Empire (see pages 78-89) never extended far inland north of the Gulf of Mexico and in the seventeenth century, English, French, Dutch, and Swedish settlements arose along the Atlantic seaboard. Of all these, the English were the most numerous, and before the end of the seventeenth century they had driven out or absorbed the Dutch and the Swedes. Thus, along the Atlantic coast, from Maine to Georgia, there arose between 1607 and 1732 the English "Thirteen Colonies"—with some of the West Indies, notably Bermuda, Jamaica, and some lesser sugar islands likewise under English control. The English colonies on the mainland were compact and relatively heavily populated. While they were developing, the French, beginning at Quebec in 1608, had established scattered trading posts and some colonies up the St. Lawrence Valley, around the Great Lakes, and down the Mississippi Valley to the Gulf of Mexico. By 1700, the English, with the Spanish in the Floridas and the

French in the St. Lawrence-Great Lakes-Mississippi basins, found themselves surrounded by their enemies. Attempts were made to pierce the French encirclement by a conjunction of the English in Hudson Bay with the English in New York, but little came of it. Raids and counter-raids occurred along the borders from Nova Scotia to Albany during the War of the Palatinate (1689-97) and the War of Spanish Succession (1702-13); and by the Treaty of Utrecht (1713) the English gained commercial advantages in the New World which, in conjunction with their industrial and maritime development, ultimately enabled them to outbid the French for control of the interior of North America (see pages 335-336). Within five years after the Treaty of Utrecht, Colonel Alexander Spotswood, who had been appointed Deputy Governor of Virginia (1710) after valiant service under Marlborough in the War of Spanish Succession, wrote to the English Board of Trade the following warning against the French danger.

ENGLISH DANGERS FROM FRENCH ENCIRCLEMENT IN NORTH AMERICA (1718)

From SPOTSWOOD, *Official Letters* (1718) [1]

Having a long time endeavoured to inform myself of the situation of the French to the westward of us, and the advantages they reap by an uninterrupted communication along the lake, I shall here take the liberty of communicating my thoughts to Your Lordships, both of the dangers to which his Majesty's plantations may be exposed by this new acquisition of our neighbours, and how the same may be

[1] *The Official Letters of Alexander Spotswood,* ed. by R. A. Brock, in *Collections of the Virginia Historical Society,* new ser., II, Richmond, 1885, 295-97.

best prevented. I have often regretted that after so many years as these countries have been seated, no attempts have been made to discover the sources of our rivers, nor to establishing correspondence with those nations of Indians to the westward of us, even after the certain knowledge of the progress made by French in surrounding us with their settlements. . . .

Having also informed myself of that extensive communication which the French maintain by means of their water carriage from the River St. Lawrence to the mouth of the Mississippi, I shall here set down the route from Montreal (a place well known and distinguished in the ordinary maps) to Maville, their chief town in their new settlement of Louisiana, according to the account given me by three French men, who had often travelled that way, and were taken in a late expedition under the command of the Gov'r and L't-Gov'r's Sons, of Montreal, and is as follows:

French Leagues

From Montreal up St. Lawrence River, to Fort Frontenac, at the entrance of Lake Ontario, is	60
The length of Lake Ontario, which is navigable	60
Up the river to the Falls of Niagara, where there is a necessity of land carriage	3
From Niagara to the Lake Erie	100
Up the River Mic. [Maumee] which falls into Lake Erie	60
From the River Mic. to the River Occabacke [Wabash] a land carriage of ..	3
Down the River Occabacke till it falls into the River Mississippi	200
Thence down Mississippi to Maville	360

By this communication and the forts they have already built, the British plantations are in a manner surrounded by their commerce with the numerous nations of Indians seated on both sides of the lakes; they may not only engross the whole skin trade, but may, when they please, send out such bodies of Indians on the back of these plantations as may greatly distress his Majesty's subjects here, and should they multiply their settlements along these lakes, so as to join their dominions of Canada to their new colony of Louisiana, they might even possess themselves of any of these plantations they pleased. Nature, 'tis true, has formed a barrier for us by that long chain of mountains which run from the back of South Carolina as far as New York, and which are only passable in some few places, but even that natural defence may prove rather destructive to us, if they are not possessed by us before they are known to them. To prevent the dangers which threaten his Majesty's dominions here from the growing power of these neighbours, nothing seems to me of more consequence than that now while the nations are at peace, and while the French are yet uncapable of possessing all that vast tract which lies on the back of these plantations, we should attempt to make some settlements on the lakes, and at the same time possess our selves of those passes of the great mountains, which are necessary to preserve a communication with such settlements.

As the Lake Erie lies almost in the center of the French communication, and, as I observed before, not above 5 days' march from the late discovered passage of our great mountains, that seems the most proper for forming a settlement on, by which we shall not only share with the French in the commerce and friendship of those Indians inhabiting the banks of the lakes, but may be able to cut off or disturb the communication between Canada and Louisiana, if a war should happen to break out. If such a settlement were once made, I can't see how the French could dispute our right of possession, the law of nations giving a title to the first occupant, and should they think fit to dispossess us by force, we are nearer to support than they to attack.

THE FRENCH PROPOSE A LINE OF FORTS FROM THE GREAT LAKES TO THE OHIO RIVER (1750)

In 1726, the English established a trading post at Oswego on Lake Ontario, thereby, as Colonel Spotswood had foreseen, threatening French trade and French communications between the St. Lawrence and the Mississippi. Each side labored for twenty years thereafter to gain its desires without war, but by the end of the War of Austrian Succession (1748) peace in America was no longer possible, notwithstanding the status of affairs between the European mother countries. The following "Memoir" depicts clearly the French action to stem the tide of English westward expansion from New York, Pennsylvania, and Virginia.

From "Memoir on the French Colonies in North America" (1750) [1]

The interior of Canada is traversed by the River St. Lawrence, and the Lakes which supply the waters of that great stream.

Its navigation and trade can be interrupted more easily than people suppose. . . . One of the principal means to avoid this misfortune is to strengthen, still further, not only Quebec and Montreal, but also Fort St. Frederic [Crown Point], at which place it would be essential to settle a large, well fortified French village, in time of peace, and to attract thither an Indian village in time of war. All that will cost little, if at the same time we take care to settle some farmers on Lake Champlain, and form some villages there.

[1] *Documents Relative to the Colonial History of the State of New York,* ed. by E. B. O'Callaghan, 15 vols., Albany, 1858, X, 227-30.

It would be proper, also, to fortify, but discreetly, the post established in 1748 on the River St. Lawrence by Mr. Picquiet near La Galotte, Fort Frontenac and to settle some villages in the vicinity.

Fort Frontenac [now Kingston, Ontario] is at the outlet of Lake Ontario, on which the English have established a port or fort called Chouaguen [Oswego]; an usurpation the most flagrant, and at the same time the most pernicious to Canada.

This post, located on ground, and on the borders of a lake, always in the possession of the French, has not been erected by the English until a number of years after the Treaty of Utrecht [1726], and in a period of profound peace. The Governor of Canada then confined himself to protests, and the post has continued, and remains, when it ought to have been pulled down in the beginning by force. . . .

We must not omit observing that this post, which has been almost regarded as an object of trifling importance, is capable of causing the entire ruin of Canada, and has already inflicted on it the greatest injury.

There it is that the French often carry on a fraudulent trade which transmits to England profits the most unquestionable, that Canada ought to afford to France.

There it is that the English scatter rum among the Indians, the use of which had been forbidden them by the King's Ordinances, because it set them crazy.

In fine, it is there that the English entice all the Indian Nations, and endeavor by force of presents, not only to debauch them, but also to induce them to assassinate the French traders dispersed throughout the vast extent of the forests of New France.

As long as the English will possess Chouaguen there will be a perpetual distrust of Indians the most loyal to the

French; twice more troops than the state of the Colony requires, or comports with its condition, will have to be maintained in times of the most profound peace; forts will have to be established and kept in an infinite number of places, and very numerous and very expensive detachments sent almost every year, to restrain the different Nations of Indians. The navigation of the lakes will be always exposed to be disturbed; agriculture will not advance, except very slowly, and cannot be pursued except in the heart of the Colony; in fine, matters will be always in a situation possessing all the inconveniences of war, even without any of its advantages.

Nothing, then, must be left undone to destroy this dangerous post, on the first occasion for reprisals the English will offer by some of those hostilities they are but too much accustomed to commit in time of peace; supposing that its cession, by common consent, cannot be obtained, for some equivalent.

What has been observed already in the course of this Memoir . . . shows the absolute necessity of the free and certain communication from Canada to the Mississippi. This chain, once broken, would leave an opening of which the English would doubtless take advantage. . . . That of the River Oyo [Ohio], otherwise called the Beautiful river, is the most interesting in this relation. It rises near the country at present partly occupied by the Iroquois, runs southwardly, falls into the Wabash, and with that river into the Mississippi.

This last has been discovered by Sieur De la Salle, who took possession of it in the King's name; and it would perhaps today be full of French settlements, had not the Governors of Canada been deterred from establishing permanent posts there by the apprehension that a counterband trade between the French traders and the English would be the consequence.

Neither have the English any posts there, nor did they come to that quarter to trade, except clandestinely, until the last war, when the revolt of some neighboring nations against the French, encouraged them to come more boldly.

They have been summoned since the peace, to retire, and if they do not do so, there is no doubt but the Governor of Canada will constrain them thereto by force, otherwise the case would be the same as at Chouaguen, and this misfortune would be still more disastrous, for a post on the Beautiful river would possess more opportunities to do damage than Chouaguen alone.

1st. They would have much greater opportunities there than at Chouaguen to seduce the Indian nations.

2nd. They would possess more facilities to interrupt the communication between Canada and Louisiana, for the Beautiful river affords almost the only route for the conveyance from Canada to the River Mississippi, of detachments capable of securing that still feeble Colony against the incursions of the neighboring Indians of Carolina, whom the English are unceasingly exciting against the French. . . .

4th. By it alone will they also be able to attack, with any considerable force, and any hope of success, the Illinois posts and all those which will be established along the River St. Louis, otherwise, Mississippi.

5th. It is, moreover, by that route that they can attack the post of the Miamis, which, again, cuts off one of our best communications with the River Mississippi, and involves the loss of Detroit, an important post. . . .

The establishment of some posts on the Beautiful river is considered, then, one of the most urgent expenses.

ENGLISH ORDERS TO RESIST THE FRENCH

In 1753-54 the French plan to establish a line of forts from Lake Erie to the upper Ohio Valley was realized with the erection of Fort Presque Isle, Fort Le Bœuf, Fort Venango, and Fort Duquesne. The English were quick to retaliate, and in August, 1753, the Earl of Holdernesse, English Secretary of State, issued the following orders to all the governors and commanders of British forces in North America.

From HOLDERNESSE, *Orders*
(August 28, 1753) [1]

His Majesty having received information of the march of a considerable number of Indians not in alliance with the King, supported by some regular European troops, intending as it is apprehended, to commit some hostilities on parts of his Majesty's dominions in America, I have the King's commands to send you this intelligence, and to direct you to use your utmost diligence, to learn, how far the same may be well grounded, and to put you upon your guard, that you may, at all events, be in a condition to resist any hostile attempts that may be made upon any parts of His Majesty's dominions within your government; and to direct you in the King's name, that in case the subjects of any foreign prince or state, should presume to make any incroachment on the limits of His Majesty's dominions, or to erect forts on His Majesty's land, or commit any other act of hostility, you are immediately, to represent the injustice of such proceeding, and to require them forthwith to desist from any such unlawful undertaking; but if notwithstanding your requisition, they should still persist, you are then to draw

[1] *Ibid.,* VI, 794-95.

forth the armed force of the province, and to use your best endeavours, to repel force by force. But as it is His Majesty's determination not to be the aggressor, I have the King's commands, most strictly to enjoin you, not to make use of the armed force under your direction, excepting within the undoubted limits of his Majesty's dominions.

And whereas it may be greatly conducive to His Majesty's service, that all his provinces in America should be aiding and assisting each other, in case of any invasion . . . it is his Royal will and pleasure, that you should keep up an exact correspondence with all His Majesty's Governors on the continent; and in case you shall be informed by any of them, of any hostile attempts, you are immediately to assemble the general assembly within your government, and lay before them, the necessity of a mutual assistance, and engage them to grant such supplies as the exigency of affairs may require.— I have wrote by this conveyance to all his Majesty's Governors to the same purpose.

BRADDOCK'S FAILURE AT FORT DUQUESNE (JULY, 1755)

In a vain effort to dissuade the French, Lieutenant Governor Robert Dinwiddie of Virginia dispatched Major George Washington to Fort Le Bœuf in the winter of 1753-54. The French commander was polite but adamant, and the soldiers told Washington that "it was their absolute design to take possession of the Ohio" and "by God they would do it," as the region rightfully belonged to France. The following summer (1754), Washington returned, intending to build a British fort where the Allegheny and Monongahela rivers join to form the Ohio. But before the project was finished, the

English were overwhelmed by the French, who at once built Fort Duquesne (Pittsburgh) on the spot. War was inevitable, and the English letter-writer Horace Walpole said, "a volley fired by a young Virginian in the back-woods of America set the world on fire." In the spring of 1755, British regulars and colonial militiamen set out under Major General Edward Braddock to capture Fort Duquesne. Disaster overtook Braddock and his troops within seven miles of the fort.

From a French Version of Braddock's
    Defeat (1755) [1]

M. de Contrecœur, Captain of Infantry, Commandant of Fort Duquesne, on the Ohio, having been informed that the English were taking up arms in Virginia for the purpose of coming to attack him, was advised, shortly afterwards, that they were on the march. He dispatched scouts, who reported to him faithfully their progress. On the 17th instant he was advised that their army, consisting of 3000 regulars from Old England, were within six leagues of this fort. That officer employed the next day in making his arrangements; and on the ninth detached M. de Beaujeu, seconded by Messrs. Dumas and de Lignery, all three Captains, together with four Lieutenants, 6 Ensigns, 20 Cadets, 100 Soldiers, 100 Canadians and 600 Indians, with orders to lie in ambush at a favorable spot, which he had reconnoitred the previous evening. The detachment, before it could reach its place of destination, found itself in presence of the enemy within three leagues of that fort. M. de Beaujeu, finding his ambush had failed, decided on an attack. This he made with so much vigor as to astonish the enemy, who were waiting for us in the best possible order; but their artillery, loaded with

grape, having opened its fire, our men gave way in turn. The Indians, also, frightened by the report of the cannon rather than by any damage it could inflict, began to yield, when M. de Beaujeu was killed. M. Dumas began to encourage his detachment. He ordered the officers in command of the Indians to spread themselves along the wings so as to take the enemy in flank, whilst he, M. de Lignery and the other officers who led the French, were attacking them in front. This order was executed so promptly that the enemy, who were already shouting their "Long live the King," thought now only of defending themselves. The fight was obstinate on both sides and success long doubtful; but the enemy at last gave way. Efforts were made, in vain, to introduce some sort of order in their retreat. The whoop of the Indians, which echoed through the forest, struck terror into the hearts of the entire enemy. The rout was complete. We remained in possession of the field with six brass twelves and sixes, four howitz-carriages of 50, 11 small royal grenade mortars, all their ammunition, and, generally, their entire baggage. Some deserters, who have come in since, have told us that we had been engaged with only 2000 men, the remainder of the army being four leagues further off. These same deserters have informed us that the enemy were retreating to Virginia, and some scouts, sent as far as the height of land, have confirmed this by reporting that the thousand men who were not engaged, had been equally panic-stricken and abandoned both provisions and ammunition on the way. On this intelligence, a detachment was dispatched after them, which destroyed and burnt everything that could be found. The enemy have left more than 1000 men on the field of battle. They have lost a great portion of the artillery and ammunition, provisions, as also their General, whose name was Mr. Braddock,

---

[1] *Ibid.*, X, 303-04.

and almost all their officers. We have had 3 officers killed; 2 officers and 2 cadets wounded. Such a victory, so entirely unexpected, seeing the inequality of the forces, is the fruit of M. Dumas' experience, and of the activity and valor of the officers under his command.

THE ENGLISH CAPTURE OF QUEBEC (1759)

The French and Indian War, which began so unfavorably for the English in Braddock's defeat, ended even more unfavorably for the French. One of the most severe blows to France was the loss of Quebec to General James Wolfe in September, 1759. Nearly every schoolboy has read of the brilliant attack of General Wolfe and the brave defense of the French commander, Montcalm. The following description is that of a participant in the struggle, John Knox, a lieutenant in General Wolfe's army.

From KNOX, *The Campaigns in North America* (1769) [1]

Thursday, September 13, 1759

Before day-break this morning we made a descent upon the north shore [of the St. Lawrence], about half a quarter of a mile to the eastward of Sillery; and the light troops were fortunately, by the rapidity of the current, carried lower down, between us and Cape Diamond; we had, in this debarkation, thirty flat-bottomed boats, containing about sixteen hundred men. This was a great surprise on the enemy, who, from the natural strength of the place, did not suspect, and consequently were not prepared against, so bold an attempt. . . . This grand enterprise was conducted and executed with

[1] John Knox, *An Historical Journal of the Campaigns in North America for the Years 1757, 1758, 1759, and 1760*, 2 vols. London, 1769, II, 67-84.

great good order and discretion; as fast as we landed, the boats put off for reinforcements, and the troops formed with much regularity. The General [Wolfe], with Brigadiers Monckton and Murray, were a-shore with the first division. We lost no time here, but clambered up one of the steepest precipices that can be conceived, being almost a perpendicular, and of an incredible height [about 180 feet]. As soon as we gained the summit, all was quiet, and not a shot was heard, owing to the excellent conduct of the light infantry under Colonel Howe; it was by this time clear day-light. Here we formed again, the river and the south country in our rear, our right extending to the town, our left to Sillery, and halted a few minutes. The General then detached the light troops to our left to route the enemy from their battery, and to disable their guns, except they could be rendered serviceable to the party who were to remain there; and this service was soon performed. We then faced to the right, and marched towards the town by files, till we came to the plains of Abraham, an even piece of ground which Mr. Wolfe had made choice of while we stood forming upon the hill. . . . About six o'clock the enemy first made their appearance upon the heights, between us and the town; whereupon we halted, and wheeled to the right, thereby forming the line of battle. . . . The enemy had now likewise formed the line of battle, and got some cannon to play on us with round and canister-shot; but what galled us most was a body of Indians and other marksmen they had concealed in the corn opposite to the front of our right wing, and a coppice that stood opposite to our center, inclining towards our left; but the Colonel Hale, by Brigadier Monckton's orders, advanced some platoons, alternately, from the forty-seventh regiment, which, after a few rounds, obliged these skulkers to retire: we were now ordered to lie down, and remained some time in this position. About eight o'clock we had two pieces of short brass six-pounders playing on the enemy, which threw them into some confusion, and obliged them to alter their disposition, and Montcalm formed them into three large columns; about nine the two armies moved a little nearer each other. The light cavalry made a faint attempt upon our parties at the battery of Sillery, but were soon beat off, and Monsieur de Bougainville, with his troops from Cape Rouge, came down to attack the flank of our second line, hoping to penetrate there, but, by a masterly disposition of Brigadier Townshend, they were forced to desist, and the third battalion of Royal Americans was then detached to the first ground we had formed on after we gained the heights, to preserve the communication with the beach and our boats. About ten o'clock the enemy began to advance briskly in three columns, with loud shouts and recovered arms, two of them inclining to the left of our army, and the third towards our right, firing obliquely at the two extremities of our line . . . until they came within forty yards; which our troops withstood with the greatest intrepidity and firmness. . . . This uncommon steadiness, together with the havoc which the grape-shot from our field-pieces made among them, threw them into some disorder, and was most critically maintained by a well-timed, regular, and heavy discharge of our small arms, such as they could no longer oppose; hereupon they gave way and fled with precipitation . . . and, profiting by the advantage we had over them, [we] pursued them almost to the gates of the town, and the bridge over the little river, redoubling our fire with great eagerness, making many officers and men prisoners. . . . The Highlanders chased them vigorously towards Charles's river, and the fifty-eighth to the suburb

close to John's gate, until they were checked by the cannon from the two hulks; at the same time, a gun which the town had brought to bear upon us with grape-shot galled the progress of the regiments to the right, who were likewise pursuing with equal ardor, while Colonel Hunt Walsh, by a very judicious movement, wheeled the battalions of Bragg and Kennedy to the left and flanked the coppice where a body of the enemy made a stand, as if willing to renew the action; but a few platoons from these corps completed our victory. Then it was that Brigadier Townshend came up, called off the pursuers, ordered the whole line to dress, and recover their former ground. Our joy at this success is inexpressibly dampened by the loss we sustained of one of the greatest heroes which this or any other age can boast of —General James Wolfe, who received his mortal wound, as he was exerting himself at the head of the grenadiers of Louisbourg. . . . The Officers who are prisoners say that Quebec will surrender in a few days; some deserters who came to us in the evening agree in that opinion, and inform us that the Sieur de Montcalm is dying in great agony of a wound he received today in their retreat. . . .

[September 14] The Sieur de Montcalm died last night; when his wound was dressed and he settled in bed, the surgeons who attended him were desired to acquaint him ingenuously with their sentiments of him, and, being answered that his wound was mortal, he calmly replied, "he was glad of it." His Excellency then demanded, "whether he could survive it long, and how long?" He was told, "about a dozen hours, perhaps more, peradventure less." "So much the better," rejoined this eminent warrior, "I am happy I shall not live to see the surrender of Quebec.". . .

After our late worthy General, of renowned memory, was carried off wounded to the rear of the front line, he desired those who were about him to lay him down; being asked if he would have a surgeon? he replied, "it is needless; it is all over with me." One of them then cried out, "they run, see how they run." "Who runs?" demanded our hero, with great earnestness, like a person roused from sleep. The Officer answered, "The enemy, Sir; Egad, they give away everywhere." Thereupon the General rejoined, "Go one of you, my lads, to Colonel Burton; tell him to march Webb's regiment with all speed down to Charles's river to cut off the retreat of the fugitives from the bridge." Then, turning to his aide, he added, "Now, God be praised, I will die in peace": and thus expired. . . .

[September 17] The capital of Canada having this day surrendered to his Britannic Majesty's arms, upon terms honorable to our victorious army, all acts of violence, pillage, or cruelty, are strictly forbidden. The garrison to have the honours of war; the inhabitants to lay down their arms, and are, by the capitulation, intitled thereupon to his Majesty's protection.

6. The Treaty of Paris (1763)

Such victories as those of Robert Clive at Plassey, in East India, and of General Wolfe at Quebec, in Canada, reenforced by subsequent British successes in both hemispheres, and by equally important conquests by the British Navy in both the East and the West Indies, left England, at the close of the Seven Years' War in Europe, the dominant colonial power of the world. The Treaty of Paris, whereby peace was re-established between England, France,

and Spain in 1763, clearly confirmed England's colonial gains.

From The Treaty of Paris, February 10, 1763 [1]

IV. His most Christian Majesty [of France] renounces all pretensions which he has heretofore formed, or might form, to Nova Scotia, or Acadia, in all its parts, and guarantees the whole of it, and with all its dependencies, to the king of Great Britain: moreover, his most Christian majesty cedes and guarantees to his said Britannic majesty, in full right, Canada, with all its dependencies, as well as the island of Cape Breton, and all the other islands and coasts in the gulf and river of St. Lawrence, and, in general, everything that depends on the said countries, lands, islands, and coasts, with the sovereignty, property, possession, and all rights acquired by treaty or otherwise, which the most Christian king, and the Crown of France, have had. . . . His Britannic majesty, on his side, agrees to grant the liberty of the Catholic religion to the inhabitants of Canada. . . . His Britannic majesty further agrees that the French inhabitants, or others, who had been the subjects of the most Christian king in Canada, may retire with all safety and freedom wherever they shall think proper, and may sell their estates, provided it be to subjects of his Britannic majesty, and bring away their effects, as well as their persons, without being restrained in their emigration, under any pretence whatsoever, except that of debts, or of criminal prosecutions. . . .

V. The subjects of France shall have the liberty of fishing and drying on a part of the coasts of the island of Newfoundland, such as is specified in the 13th article of the Treaty of Utrecht . . . and the liberty of fishing in the gulf of

1 "State Papers," in The Annual Register . . . for the Year 1762, 8th ed., London, 1810, 235-41.

St. Lawrence, on condition that the subjects of France do not exercise the said fishery but at the distance of three leagues from all the coast belonging to Great Britain. . . .

VI. The king of Great Britain cedes the islands of St. Pierre and Miquelon, in full right, to his most Christian majesty, to serve as a shelter to the French fishermen; and his said Christian majesty engages not to fortify the said islands. . . .

VII. The limits of the British and French territories on the Continent of America . . . shall be fixed irrevocably by a line drawn along the middle of the river Mississippi, from its source to the river Iberville, and from thence, by a line drawn along the middle of this river, and the lake Maurepas and Pontchartrain, to the sea; and for this purpose the most Christian king cedes, in full right, and guarantees to his Britannic majesty, the river and port of Mobile, and everything which he possesses, or ought to possess, on the left side the river Mississippi, except the town of New Orleans, and the island in which it is situated, which shall remain to France; provided that the river Mississippi shall be equally free, as well to the subjects of Great Britain as to those of France, in its whole breadth or length. . . .

VIII. The king of Great Britain shall restore to France the islands of Guadaloupe, of Marie Galante, of Desirade, of Martinico, and of Belleisle. . . .

XI. In the East Indies, Great Britain shall restore to France . . . the different factories which that crown possessed, as well as the coast of Coromandel and Orixa as that of Malabar, as also in Bengal, at the beginning of the year 1749. . . . His most Christian majesty shall restore, on his side, all that he may have conquered

from Great Britain in the East Indies during this present war; and will expressly cause Nattal and Tapanoully, in the island of Sumatra, to be restored; he engages further, not to erect fortifications, or to keep troops, in any part of the dominions of the Subah of Bengal. And in order to preserve future peace on the coast of Coromandel and Orixa, the English and the French shall acknowledge Mahomet Ali Khan for the lawful nabob of the Carnatic and Salabat Jing for lawful Subah of the Deccan [both of whom were British candidates]. . . .

XII. The island of Minorca shall be restored to his Britannic majesty. . . .

XVI. His Britannic majesty shall cause to be demolished all the fortifications which his subjects shall have erected in the bay of Honduras, and other places of the territory of Spain . . . and his Catholic majesty [of Spain] shall not permit his Britannic majesty's subjects, or their workmen, to be disturbed or molested . . . in their occupation of cutting, loading, and carrying away logwood [in Honduras]. . . .

XIX. The king of Great Britain shall restore to Spain all the territory which he has conquered in the island of Cuba, with the fortress of Havana. . . .

XX. In consequence of the restitution stipulated in the preceding article, his Catholic majesty cedes and guarantees in full right to his Britannic majesty, Florida, with fort St. Augustine, and the bay of Pensacola, as well as all that Spain possesses on the Continent of North America to the east or to the south-east of the river Mississippi. . . . His Britannic majesty agrees, on his side, to grant to the inhabitants of the countries above ceded, the liberty of the Catholic religion.

21

INTELLECTUAL DEVELOPMENTS: WIDENING THE RENAISSANCE MIND

1. Pleas and Programs for Reform in Government and Political Economy

The Age of Enlightenment produced many writers in the fields of government and political economy who advocated reform of existing institutions and policies. Certain characteristics were common to most of these writers (or *philosophes,* as they were sometimes called). They demanded religious freedom, abolition of privilege (of the nobility and clergy), freedom of speech, freedom of the press, an honest and efficient administrative corps in government, and improvements of the machinery of justice by eradicating torture, by codifying the laws of a nation, and by establishing equality before the law; they advocated reform in the tax structure and in the economic and social policies in an effort to make them consonant with human reason and the laws of nature (which they often identified); and they scorned the divine-right-of-kings theory, considered governments to be the works of man, usually subscribed to the contract theory of the origin of civil society, and hoped to discover—just as scientists were discovering in the realms of physics, chemistry, botany, and medicine—the true and perfect "natural" laws for the governance of mankind. Collectively, the *philosophes* encompassed the whole of political, ethical, and moral philosophy and set forth a program of reform for the American and French revolutionists.

England, by virtue of her seventeenth-century struggles, already had established some of these things. As the English were very proud of their political accomplishments and boasted of their liberty and stable government, and as these political achievements had been closely followed by unparalleled commercial power and economic prosperity, Continental Europeans began first to admire and then to study the English example. The writings of John Locke (see pages 237-239) especially attracted attention, for Locke was widely known on the Continent. Indeed, it would be only a slight exaggeration to say that John Locke was the literary channel through which the ideas of seventeenth-century English social and political idealists were conveyed to the minds of Continental "enlightened" philosopher-reformers.

VOLTAIRE'S "PHILOSOPHICAL LETTERS ON THE ENGLISH"

François Marie Arouet (1694-1788), better known by his pen name, Voltaire,[1] was one of the cleverest of the French *philosophes*. A contemporary admirer wrote that "Voltaire expressed everybody's thoughts better than anybody." Among his numerous works are the *Lettres philosophiques sur les Anglais* published in 1733, shortly after Voltaire returned from three years' exile in England. The *Lettres* created quite a stir in France, and were publicly burned because, under pretense of a panegyric on the English, Voltaire leveled criticisms at nearly everything in France.

From VOLTAIRE, *Philosophical Letters* (1733)[2]

It has not been without some difficulty that liberty has been established in England, and the idol of arbitrary power has been drowned in seas of blood; nevertheless, the English do not think they have purchased their laws at too high a price. Other nations have shed as much blood; but then the blood they spilled in defence of their liberty served only to enslave them the more.

That which rises to a revolution in England is no more than a sedition in other countries. . . . The civil wars of France lasted longer, were more cruel, and productive of greater evils, than those of England: but none of these civil wars had a wise and becoming liberty for their object.

In the detestable times of Charles IX and Henry III the whole affair was only, whether the people should be slaves to the Guises. As to the last war of Paris [the Fronde], it deserves only to be hooted at. It makes us think we see a crowd of schoolboys rising up in arms against their master, and afterward being whipped for it. . . . Our civil wars under Charles VI were bloody and cruel, those of the League execrable, and that of the Frondeurs ridiculous. . . .

THE ENGLISH CONSTITUTION

This mixture of different departments in the government of England, this harmony between the King, Lords, and Commons has not always subsisted. England was for a long time in a state of slavery, having, at different periods, worn the yoke of the Romans, Saxons, Danes, and, last of all, the Normans. William the Conqueror, in particular, governed them with a rod of iron. . . .

Happily, in those shocks which the quarrels of kings and great men gave to empires, the chains of nations have been relaxed more or less. Liberty in England has arisen from the quarrels of tyrants. . . .

Here is no such things as the distinction of high, middle, and low justice in France; nor of the right of hunting on the lands of a citizen, who has not the liberty of firing a single shot of a musket on his own estate.

A peer or nobleman in this country pays his share of the taxes as others do, all of which are regulated by the House of Commons; which house, if it is second only in rank, is first in point of credit. The lords and bishops, it is true, may reject any bill of the commons, when it regards the raising of money; but are not entitled to make the smallest amendment in it: they must either pass it or throw it out, without any restriction whatever. When the bill is confirmed by the lords, and approved by the king, then every person is to pay his quota without distinction; and that not according to his rank or quality, which would be absurd, but in proportion to his revenue. Here is no *taille,* or arbitrary poll-tax, but a real tax on lands; all of which underwent an

---

[1] The name "Voltaire" is supposed to have been an anagram on "Arouet l.j., Arouet le jeune" ("the younger"—corresponding to the English Arouet, Jr.).

[2] *The Works of Voltaire,* 42 vols., E. R. Du Mont, 1901 (La Vérité Edition), XXXIX, 7-16.

actual valuation under the famous William III. The taxes remain always the same, notwithstanding the fact that the value of lands has arisen; so that no one is stripped to the bone, nor can there be any ground of complaint; the feet of the peasant are not tortured with wooden shoes; he eats the best wheaten bread, is well and warmly clothed, and is in no apprehension on account of the increase of his herds and flocks, or terrified into a thatched house, instead of a convenient slated roof, for fear of an augmentation of the *taille* the year following. There are even a number of peasants, or, if you will, farmers, who have from five to six hundred pounds sterling yearly income, and who are not above cultivating those fields which have enriched them, and where they enjoy the greatest of all human blessings, liberty.

MONTESQUIEU'S "SPIRIT OF LAWS"

Charles Louis de Secondat, Baron de la Brède et de la Montesquieu (1689-1775), was a French nobleman of distinguished family. As a *philosophe,* he wrote one of the earliest and most popular satires on French civilization, the *Persian Letters* (1721). But he achieved more enduring fame as author of *The Spirit of Laws* (1748), one of the most influential books in eighteenth-century political philosophy. A long treatise of thirty-five tersely written books, moderate in tone, *The Spirit of Laws* was a searching analysis of the nature of political authority which did much to clarify—if not to oversimplify—the executive, judicial, and legislative functions of political power and, in the interests of liberty, to advocate the separation of powers and a system of checks and balances among the three divisions of sovereign authority. In these things, *The Spirit of Laws* ex-

erted a vital influence upon American constitutionalism in its formative period. A few pertinent excerpts from the treatise follow:[1]

Montesquieu held that *"The united strength of individuals . . . constitutes what we call the body politic,"* and that "the strength of individuals cannot be united without a conjunction of their wills. *The conjunction of those wills . . . is what we call the* CIVIL STATE." As "law in general is human reason, inasmuch as it governs all the inhabitants of the earth, the political and civil laws of each nation ought to be only the particular cases in which human reason is applied." These laws "should be adapted . . . to the people for whom they are framed . . . in relation to the nature and principle of each government . . . to the climate of each country, to the quality of its soil, to its situation and extent, to the principal occupation of the natives . . . to the degree of liberty which the constitution will bear, to the religion of the inhabitants, to their inclinations, riches, numbers, commerce, manners, and customs. In fine, they have relations to each other, as also to their origin, to the intent of the legislator, and to the order of things on which they are established; in all of which different lights they ought to be considered." This, continues Montesquieu, "is what I have undertaken to perform in the following work. These relations I shall examine, since all these together constitute what I call the *Spirit of Laws.* . . . I do not pretend to treat of laws,

[1] *The Spirit of the Laws,* trans. by Thomas Nugent, new ed. rev. by J. V. Pritchard, 2 vols., 1906 (Bohn's Standard Library), Bk. I, Chap. 3, 6-7; Bk. II, Chaps. I, 8; Bk. XI, Chaps. 3-4, 161-62; Chap. 6, 163, 165-67, 169, 172-73; Bk. XII, Chap. 1, 196; Chap. 2, 197; Chaps. 3-4, 198. Reprinted by permission of G. Bell & Sons, Ltd., Publishers.

but of their spirit." After a discussion of the various forms of government ("republican," in which the body of the people possess the supreme power; "aristocracy," in which the nobility only possess it; "monarchy," in which *a single person governs by fixed and established laws"*; and despotism, *"in which a single person directs everything by his own will and caprice*), the author treats "Of the Laws Which Establish Political Liberty with Regard to the Constitution" in the following words.

From MONTESQUIEU, *The Spirit of Laws* (1748)

Political liberty does not consist in an unlimited freedom. In governments, that is, in societies directed by laws, liberty can consist only in the power of doing what we ought to will, and in not being constrained from doing what we ought to will.

We must have continually present in our minds the difference between independence and liberty. Liberty is a right of doing whatever the laws permit, and if a citizen could do what they forbid he would be no longer possessed of liberty, because all his fellow-citizens would have the same power. . . .

Political liberty is to be found only in moderate governments; and even in these it is not always found. It is there only when there is no abuse of power. But constant experience shows us that every man invested with power is apt to abuse it. . . . To prevent this abuse, it is necessary from the very nature of things that power should be a check to power. A government may be so constituted, as no man shall be compelled to do things to which the law does not oblige him, nor forced to abstain from things which the law permits. . . .

In every government there are three sorts of power: the legislative; the executive in respect to things dependent on the law of nations; and the executive in regard to matters that depend on the civil law.

By virtue of the first, the prince or magistrate enacts temporary or perpetual laws, and amends or abrogates those that have been already enacted. By the second, he makes peace or war, sends or receives embassies, establishes the public security, and provides against invasions. By the third, he punishes criminals, or determines disputes that arise between individuals. The latter we shall call the judiciary power, and the other simply the executive power of the state.

The political liberty of the subject is a tranquillity of mind arising from the opinion each person has of his safety. In order to have this liberty, it is requisite the government be so constituted as one man need not be afraid of another.

When the legislative and executive powers are united in the same person, or in the same body of magistrates, there can be no liberty; because apprehensions may arise lest the same monarch or senate should enact tyrannical laws, to execute them in a tyrannical manner.

Again, there is no liberty if the judiciary power be not separated from the legislative and executive. Were it joined with the legislative, the life and liberty of the subject would be exposed to arbitrary control; for the judge would be then the legislator. Were it joined to the executive power, the judge might behave with violence and oppression. . . .

As in a country of liberty every man who is supposed a free agent ought to be his own governor, the legislative power should reside in the whole body of the people. But since this is impossible in large states, and in small ones is subject to many inconveniences, it is fit the people should transact by their representatives what they cannot transact by themselves. . . .

All the inhabitants of the several districts ought to have a right of voting at the election of a representative, except such as are in so mean a situation as to be deemed to have no will of their own. . . .

In such a state there are always persons distinguished by their birth, riches, or honours; but were they to be confounded with the common people, and to have only the weight of a single vote like the rest, the common liberty would be their slavery, and they would have no interest in supporting it, as most of the popular resolutions would be against them. The share they have, therefore, in the legislature ought to be proportioned to their other advantages in the state; which happens only when they form a body that has a right to check the licentiousness of the people, as the people have a right to oppose any encroachment of theirs.

The legislative power is therefore committed to the body of the nobles, and to that which represents the people, each having their assemblies and deliberations apart. . . .

The executive power ought to be in the hands of a monarch, because this branch of government, having need of despatch, is better administered by one than by many: on the other hand, whatever depends on the legislative power is oftentimes better regulated by many than by a single person. . . .

It is fit . . . that the executive power should regulate the time of meeting [of the legislature], as well as the duration of those assemblies, according to the circumstances and exigencies of a state known to itself.

Were the executive power not to have a right of restraining the encroachments of the legislative body, the latter would become despotic. . . .

But it is not proper, on the other hand, that the legislative power should have a right to stay the executive. . . . But if the legislative power in a free state has no right to stay the executive, it has a right and ought to have the means of examining in what manner its laws have been executed. . . .

The armies . . . should consist of the people, and have the same spirit as the people. . . . When once an army is established, it ought not to depend immediately on the legislative, but on the executive, power; and this from the very nature of the thing, its business consisting more in action than in deliberation. . . . As soon as the troops depend entirely on the legislative body, it becomes a military government. . . .

It is not sufficient to have treated of political liberty in relation to the constitution; we must examine it likewise in the relation it bears to the subject. . . .

The constitution may happen to be free, and the subject not. The subject may be free, and not the constitution. . . .

It is the disposition only of the laws, and even of the fundamental laws, that constitutes liberty in relation to the constitution. But as regards the subject: manners, customs, or received examples may give rise to it, and particular civil laws may encourage it. . . .

Political liberty consists in security, or, at least, in the opinion that we enjoy security.

This security is never more dangerously attacked than in public or private accusations. It is, therefore, on the goodness of criminal laws that the liberty of the subject principally depends. . . . When the subject has no fence to secure his innocence, he has none for his liberty.

Those laws which condemn a man to death on the deposition of a single witness are fatal to liberty. . . . Liberty is in perfection when criminal laws derive each punishment from the particular nature of the crime. There are then no arbitrary decisions; the punishment does not flow from the capriciousness of the legislator, but from the very nature of the thing; and man uses no violence to man.

ROUSSEAU'S "SOCIAL CONTRACT"

Jean Jacques Rousseau (1712-1778), the Genevan philosopher, though he exerted an influence against divine-right absolutism in similar fashion, was hardly in full sympathy with contemporary *philosophes*. Sensitive to a fault, impulsive, and highly emotional, Jean Jacques was on the way to becoming a romantic, and he represents a transitional phase in literature and thought from rationalism to romanticism. While he retained a high regard for reason, he idealized nature. His literary career culminated in 1762 with publication of *Emile,* a treatise on education, and *The Social Contract; or, Principles of Political Right,* a classic treatment of the contract theory of the state. Unlike Montesquieu, who "took laws as they were, and saw what sort of men they made," Rousseau took "man as the basis, and regards him as giving himself what laws he pleases . . . making the will of the members the sole basis of every society." He tried to set forth a civil society based upon "pure right." "All power comes from God, I admit," wrote Rousseau, "so does all sickness; does that mean we are forbidden to call in the doctor?" His own medicine for the ills of society was prescribed in the following words.

From ROUSSEAU, *Social Contract* (1762) [1]

Man is born free; and everywhere he is in chains. One thinks himself the master

[1] *The Social Contract & Discourses,* ed. by Ernest Rhys, 1932 (Everyman's Library), Bk. I, Chap. 1, 5-6; Chap. 2, 7; Chap. 3, 8-9; Chap. 6, 14-16; Chap. 8, 18-19; Chap. 9, 21-22; Bk. II, Chap. 6, 32-34. By permission of E. P. Dutton and Company, Inc.

of others, and still remains a greater slave than they. How did this change come about? I do not know. What can make it legitimate? That question I think I can answer.

If I took into account only force, and the effects derived from it, I should say: "As long as a people is compelled to obey, and obeys, it does well; as soon as it can shake off the yoke, and shakes it off, it does still better; for, regaining its liberty by the same right as took it away, either it is justified in resuming it, or there was no justification for those who took it away." But the social order is a sacred right which is the basis of all other rights. Nevertheless, this right does not come from nature, and must therefore be founded on conventions. . . .

[Here Rousseau treats of primitive civil societies, holding that the family was "the first model of political societies" and "all, being born free and equal, alienate their liberty only for their own advantage." Persons who remain in slavery have only themselves to blame: "Nothing can be more certain than that every man born in slavery is born for slavery. Slaves lose everything in their chains, even the desire of escaping from them. . . . If then there are slaves by nature, it is because they have been slaves against nature. Force made the first slaves, and their cowardice perpetuated the condition. . . . Force is a physical power, and I fail to see what moral effect it can have. To yield to force is an act of necessity, not of will—at the most, an act of prudence. In what sense can it be a duty? . . . Let us then admit that force does not create right, and that we are obliged to obey only legitimate powers." No man, then, has a natural authority over his fellows, and as force creates no right, all legitimate political authority is man-made and based upon human convention. This convention is, says Rousseau, "the Social Compact," which he discusses as follows:]

I suppose men to have reached the point at which the obstacles in the way of their preservation in the state of nature show their power of resistance to be greater than the resources at the disposal of each individual for his maintenance in that state. That primitive condition can then subsist no longer; and the human race would perish unless it changed its manner of existence.

But, as men cannot engender new forces, but only unite and direct existing ones, they have no other means of preserving themselves than the formation, by aggregation, of a sum of forces great enough to overcome the resistance. . . . This sum of forces can arise only where several persons come together: but as the force and liberty of each man are the chief instruments for self-preservation, how can he pledge them without harming his own interests, and neglecting the care he owes to himself? This difficulty . . . may be stated in the following terms—

"The problem is to find a form of association which will defend and protect with the whole common force the person and goods of each associate, and in which each, while uniting himself with all, may still obey himself alone, and remain as free as before." This is the fundamental problem of which the *Social Contract* provides the solution.

The clauses of this contract are so determined by the nature of the act that the slightest modification would make them vain and ineffective; so that, although they have perhaps never been formally set forth, they are everywhere the same and everywhere tacitly admitted and recognized, until, on the violation of the social compact, each regains his original rights and resumes his natural liberty, while losing his conventional liberty in favour of which he renounced it.

These clauses, properly understood, may be reduced to one—the total alienation of each associate, together with all his rights, to the whole community; for, in the first place, as each gives himself absolutely, the conditions are the same for all; and, this being so, no one has any interest in making them burdensome to others.

Moreover, the alienation being without reserve, the union is as perfect as it can be, and no associate has anything more to demand. . . . Finally, each man, in giving himself to all, gives himself to nobody; and as there is no associate over whom he does not acquire the same right as he yields others over himself, he gains an equivalent for everything he loses, and an increase of force for the preservation of what he has.

If then we discard from the social compact what is not of its essence, we shall find that it reduces itself to the following terms—

"*Each of us puts his person and all his power in common under the supreme direction of the general will, and, in our corporate capacity, we receive each member as an indivisible part of the whole.*"

At once, in place of the individual personality of each contracting party, this act of association creates a moral and collective body, composed of as many members as the assembly contains votes, and receiving from this act its unity, its common identity, its life, and its will. This public person, so formed by the union of all other persons, formerly took the name of *city,* and now takes that of *Republic* or *body politic;* it is called by its members *State* when passive, *Sovereign* when active, and *Power* when compared to others like itself. Those who are associated in it take collectively the name of *people,* and severally are called *citizens,* as sharing in the sovereign power, and *subjects,* as being under the laws of the State. . . .

The passage from the state of nature to the civil state produces a very remarkable change in man. . . . What man loses by the social contract is his natural liberty and an unlimited right to everything he tries to get and succeeds in getting; what he gains is civil liberty and the proprietorship of all he possesses. . . . We must clearly distinguish natural liberty, which is bounded only by the strength of the individual, from civil liberty, which is limited by the general will; and possession, which is merely the effect of force or the right of the first occupier, from property, which can be founded only on a positive title. . . .

I shall end this chapter and this book [Book I of four] by remarking on a fact on which the whole social system should rest: *i.e.* that, instead of destroying natural inequality, the fundamental compact substitutes, for such physical inequality as nature may have set up between men, an equality that is moral and legitimate, and that men, who may be unequal in strength or intelligence, become every one equal by convention and legal right. . . .

By the social compact we have given the body politic existence and life; we have now by legislation to give it movement and will. For the original act by which the body is formed and united still in no respect determines what it ought to do for its preservation. . . .

All justice comes of God, who is its sole source; but if we knew how to receive so high an inspiration, we should need neither government nor laws. Doubtless, there is a universal justice emanating from reason alone; but this justice, to be admitted among us, must be mutual. Humanly speaking, in default of natural sanctions, the laws of justice are ineffective among men: they merely make for the good of the wicked and the undoing of the just, when the just man observes them toward everybody and nobody observes them towards him. Conventions and laws are therefore needed to join rights to duties, and refer justice to its object. . . .

The object of laws is always general, I mean that law considers subjects *en masse* and actions in the abstract, and never a particular person or action. . . . No function which has a particular object belongs to the legislative power.

On this view, we at once see that it can no longer be asked whose business it is to make laws, since they are acts of the general will; nor whether the prince is above the law, since he is a member of the State; nor whether the law can be unjust, since no one is unjust to himself. . . .

I therefore give the name "Republic" to every State that is governed by laws, no matter what the form of its administration may be: for only in such a case does the public interest govern, and the *res publica* rank as a *reality*.

THE PHYSIOCRATS: QUESNAY

François Quesnay (1694-1774) was a physician-surgeon to Louis XV of France who became interested in economic affairs and founded one of the earliest scientific "schools" of political economy. In 1757, Quesnay, who had already contributed articles to Diderot's *Encyclopedia* on economic matters, had an interview with Victor Riqueti, the Marquis de Mirabeau, already a popular writer on the same subjects, and from this meeting arose the "school" which, by 1767, met weekly at "receptions" held in the Marquis's home. Composed of many men of letters and science, including Jean C. M. V. de Gournay and Pierre Samuel Dupont de Nemours, the school gained disciples in all parts of Europe, published the *Journal of Agriculture* (edited by Dupont de Nemours), and strove to translate their ideas for reform into political action—a policy which was partially realized when one of their number, Turgot, became Minister of Finance under Louis XVI. The Physiocrats represented a reaction against Colbertism and mercantilism in general. They objected to the mercantilist concept of wealth (see Chapter 15 and pages 233, 248), to the emphasis on commerce and industry at the expense of agriculture, to the intricate regulations of all enterprise and trade; and they recommended reforms in the interests of free trade, free enterprise, and greater equality in taxation. In 1758, Quesnay, probably with the collaboration of others in the group, composed *General Maxims of the Economical Government in an Agricultural Realm,* patterned after a memoir which the Duke of Sully had presented to Henry IV in 1604. Some of these *Maxims,* as illustrative of Physiocratic opinion, follow.

From QUESNAY, *Maxims* (1758) [1]

III. The sovereign and the nation should never lose sight of the fact that the earth is the only source of all wealth, and that it is agriculture which multiplies riches. For the augmentation of riches assures that of the population; men and wealth cause agriculture to prosper, extend commerce, animate industry, multiply and perpetuate wealth. . . .

IV. Landed property and movable wealth should be assured to those who are their legitimate possessors. For the security of property is the essential foundation of the economic order of society. . . .

V. Taxes should not be destructive or disproportionate to the total income of the nation. Their increase should follow increases in income. They should be assessed upon the immediate net product of lands, and not on the wages of man, nor on commodities, where they multiply the costs of collection, become prejudicial to commerce, and annually destroy a portion of the wealth of the nation. . . .

IX. A nation which has large territory to cultivate and facilities to carry on a large commerce in the land's produce should not use too much of the people's money for the manufacture and trade of luxuries to the prejudice of workers and agricultural investments; for, above all, the kingdom ought to be a people of rich agriculturalists. . . .

XI. The emigration of inhabitants who take their wealth with them to the loss of the kingdom should be prevented.

XII. The children of rich farmers should establish themselves in the country in order to perpetuate the labor supply there. For if vexations cause them to abandon the country and determine them to retire into cities they take with them the wealth of their fathers which was employed in agriculture. . . .

XIII. Each one should be free to cultivate in his field those products which his interest, his faculties, and the nature of the soil suggest to him will produce the greatest possible returns. . . . The precedent which favors the abundance of products of greatest need, in preference to other productions, irrespective of the sale value of one or the other, is inspired by a shortsighted view which does not comprehend the effects of reciprocal foreign commerce, and which fixes the price of products which each nation can cultivate with the most profit. . . .

XVI. Foreign commerce in the products of the land should not be prevented in any way, for it is the demand which regulates production.

[1] *Œuvres économiques et philosophiques de F. Quesnay,* ed. by Auguste Oncken, Frankfort, 1888, 331-37.

XVII. The facilities for export and the means of transportation for the products and merchandise of manual labor should be improved by the repair of roads and the navigation of canals, rivers, and seas. For the more that is saved in commerce, the more is added to the income of the nation. . . .

XX. The comfort of the lowest classes of citizens should not be diminished; for they must assist in the consumption of goods in the country, if reproduction and the income of the nation are not to be lowered. . . .

XXIV. No one should be deceived by an apparent advantage in reciprocal commerce with foreigners in judging simply by the balance of money without examining the gain or loss of profits which result from the merchandise which one has sold and the merchandise which one has bought. For often the loss is to that nation which has received a surplus in money; and that loss redounds to the prejudice of the distribution and the reproduction of revenues.

XXV. There should be complete liberty in commerce. For the policy which is the surest, most exact, and most profitable to the nation and to the state with reference to internal and foreign trade consists of the greatest possible freedom in competition. . . .

XXVII. The government should be concerned less with its expenditures than with those operations necessary for the prosperity of the realm; for the very large expenses will cease to appear excessive with the increase of wealth.

ADAM SMITH'S "WEALTH OF NATIONS"

The Scottish philosopher Adam Smith (1723-1790), who wrote the famous book, *An Inquiry into the Nature and Causes of the Wealth of Nations,* had for his objectives ends similar to those of the Physiocrats. Of Quesnay, whom Smith knew personally, he wrote that the Frenchman's system of political economy, "with all its imperfections," was "the nearest approximation to truth that had yet been published on the principles of that science." Smith's system varied from the Physiocrats' in that he gave more place to labor and less to land as the source of wealth; but like the Physiocrats, he denounced mercantilist regulation and upheld the principles of free trade and untrammeled enterprise as those most conducive to prosperity in a state. *The Wealth of Nations* is a long treatise, consisting of five books, only small portions of which are given below. Present-day students will, in the main, find Smith's economics more consonant with their own ideas previously received than they will the political economy of earlier writers, inasmuch as *The Wealth of Nations* became a classic statement of the system of economy underlying the capitalistic system of the nineteenth and early twentieth centuries.

From SMITH, *Wealth of Nations* (1776) [1]

INTRODUCTION

The annual labour of every nation is the fund which originally supplies it with all the necessaries and conveniences of life which it annually consumes, and which consist always either in the immediate produce of that labour, or in what is purchased with that produce from other nations.

According, therefore, as this produce, or what is purchased with it, bears a greater or smaller proportion to the number of those who are to consume it, the

[1] Adam Smith, *An Inquiry into the Nature and Causes of the Wealth of Nations,* 2 vols. London, I, Grant Richards, 1904; II, Henry Frowde, n.d.), (*The World's Classics* LIV, LIX) I, 1, 5, 7, 9, 15. 421, 453-55; II, 2, 4, 8-9, 12, 24-25, 72, 289

nation will be better or worse supplied with all the necessaries and conveniences for which it has occasion.

But this proportion must in every nation be regulated by two different circumstances: first, by the skill, dexterity, and judgment with which its labour is generally applied; and, secondly, by the proportion between the number of those who are employed in useful labour, and that of those who are not so employed. Whatever be the soil, climate, or extent of territory of any particular nation, the abundance or scantiness of its annual supply must, in that particular situation, depend upon those two circumstances. . . .

OF THE DIVISION OF LABOUR

The greatest improvements in the productive powers of labour, and the greater part of the skill, dexterity, and judgment, with which it is anywhere directed, or applied, seem to have been the effects of the division of labour. . . .

This great increase in the quantity of work, which, in consequence of the division of labour, the same number of people are capable of performing, is owing to three different circumstances; first, to the increase of dexterity in every particular workman; secondly, to the saving of the time which is commonly lost in passing from one species of work to another; and, lastly, to the invention of a great number of machines which facilitate and abridge labour, and enable one man to do the work of many. . . .

This division of labour, from which so many advantages are derived, is not originally the effect of any human wisdom, which foresees and intends that general opulence to which it gives occasion. It is the necessary, though very slow and gradual, consequence of a certain propensity in human nature, which has in view no such extensive utility; the propensity to truck, barter, and exchange one thing for another. . . .

OF THE NATURAL PROGRESS OF OPULENCE

The great commerce of every civilized society is that carried on between the inhabitants of the town and those of the country. It consists in the exchange of rude for manufactured produce, either immediately, or by the intervention of money, or of some sort of paper which represents money. The country supplies the town with the means of subsistence and the materials of manufacture. The town repays this supply, by sending back a part of the manufactured produce to the inhabitants of the country. The town, in which there neither is nor can be any reproduction of substances, may very properly be said to gain its whole wealth and subsistence from the country. We must not, however, upon this account, imagine that the gain of the town is the loss of the country. The gains of both are mutual and reciprocal, and the division of labour is in this, as in all other cases, advantageous to all the different persons employed in the various occupations into which it is subdivided. . . .

The increase and riches of commercial and manufacturing towns contributed to the improvement and cultivation of the countries to which they belonged, in three different ways:

First, by affording a great and ready market for the rude produce of the country, they gave encouragement to its cultivation and further improvement. . . .

Secondly, the wealth acquired by the inhabitants of cities was frequently employed in purchasing such lands as were to be sold, of which a great part would frequently be uncultivated. . . .

Thirdly, and lastly, commerce and manufactures gradually introduced order and good government, and with them the liberty and security of individuals, among the inhabitants of the country, who had before lived almost in a continual state of war with their neighbours, and of servile dependency upon their superiors. . . .

OF THE PRINCIPLE OF THE COMMERCIAL OR
MERCANTILE SYSTEM

That wealth consists in money, or in gold and silver, is a popular notion which naturally arises from the double function of money, as the instrument of commerce, and as the measure of value. . . . A rich country, in the same manner as a rich man, is supposed to be a country abounding in money; and to heap up gold and silver in any country is supposed to be the readiest way to enrich it. . . .

In consequence of those popular notions, all the different nations of Europe have studied, though to little purpose, every possible means of accumulating gold and silver in their respective countries. . . .

A country that has no mines of its own, must undoubtedly draw its gold and silver from foreign countries, in the same manner as one that has no vineyards of his own must draw its wines. It does not seem necessary, however, that the attention of government should be more turned towards the one than towards the other object. A country that has wherewithal to buy wine, will always get the wine which it has occasion for; and a country that has wherewithal to buy gold and silver, will never be in want of those metals. . . .

It would be too ridiculous to go about seriously to prove, that wealth does not consist in money, or in gold and silver; but in what money purchases, and is valuable only for purchasing. Money, no doubt, makes always a part of the national capital; but it has already been shown that it generally makes but a small part, and always the most unprofitable part of it. . . .

It is not by the importation of gold and silver that the discovery of America has enriched Europe. By the abundance of the American mines, those metals have become cheaper. A service of plate can now be purchased for about a third part of the corn, or a third part of the labour, which it would have cost in the fifteenth century. . . . The discovery of America, however, certainly made a most essential [change in the state of Europe]. By opening a new and inexhaustible market to all the commodities of Europe, it gave occasion to new divisions of labour and improvements of art, which in the narrow circle of the ancient commerce could never have taken place, for want of a market to take off the greater part of their produce. The productive powers of labour were improved, and its produce increased in all the different countries of Europe, and together with it the real revenue and wealth of the inhabitants. . . .

Nothing, however, can be more absurd than this whole doctrine of the balance of trade, upon which, not only these restraints, but almost all the other regulations of commerce, are founded. When two places trade with one another, this doctrine supposes that, if the balance be even, neither of them either loses or gains; but if it leans in any degree to one side, that one of them loses, and the other gains, in proportion to its declension from the exact equilibrium. Both suppositions are false. A trade, which is forced by means of bounties and monopolies, may be, and commonly is, disadvantageous to the country in whose favour it is meant to be established, as I shall endeavour to show hereafter. But that trade which, without force or constraint, is naturally and regularly carried on between any two places, is always advantageous, though not always equally so, to both. . . .

It can never be the interest of those landed nations, if I may call them so, to discourage or distress the industry of such mercantile states, by imposing high duties upon their trade, or upon the commodities which they furnish. Such duties, by rendering those commodities dearer, could serve only to sink the real value of the surplus produce of their own land, with which, or, what comes to the same thing, with the price of which those commodities are purchased. Such duties could only serve to discourage the increase of that surplus produce, and consequently the improvement and cultivation of their own land. The most effectual expedient, on the contrary, for raising the value of that surplus produce, for encouraging its increase, and consequently the improvement and cultivation of their own land, would be to allow the most perfect freedom to the trade of all such mercantile nations.

2. Extending the New Science

The Era of Enlightened Despotism witnessed an enormous scientific development, primarily the result of brilliant extensions of the "experimental method" set forth in Renaissance times (see pages 53-71). This period was one marked by vast collection, precise observation, and accurate classification of data, all leading to the earliest formulation of the basic laws which govern natural phenomena. A variety of factors contributed to these achievements. The New World quickened interest with its new geographical and geological information, its new plants and animals; newly perfected instruments (themselves scientific accomplishments) furthered accurate work—the telescope, the microscope, the prism, the barometer, the thermometer, and the pendulum clock; societies fostered scientific cooperation, and museums and botanic gardens were founded as repositories for the preservation and study of specimens; wealthy merchants, princes, and

kings offered encouragement and financial patronage. These aids, combined with the genius of a host of scholars, led to many important discoveries, such as Kepler's laws and the velocity of light in astronomy; logarithms and the calculus in mathematics; smallpox inoculation and vaccination, the isolation of bacteria, and other advances in medicine; the atomic theory, discovery of oxygen, hydrogen, chlorine, and other elements, the theory of the indestructibility of matter, and other important beginnings in modern chemistry; Boyle's law, the law of gravitation, the laws of motion, spectrum analysis, electricity and the electric battery in physics; the accurate classification of plant species, sexuality in plants, and the beginnings of plant chemistry in botany; the origin of historical geology, modern physiology, and other scientific fields. Of these vast accomplishments, of course, only a small sampling can be illustrated below.

THE ROLE OF SCIENTIFIC SOCIETIES: THE ROYAL SOCIETY OF LONDON (1662)

Among the factors which fostered scientific achievement were the worldwide activities of a number of scientific academies and societies which were organized during the seventeenth and eighteenth centuries, usually chartered and patronized by the national monarchs. Academies of art and of science had existed in several Italian cities during the Renaissance, and after these examples were patterned a variety of seventeenth-century organizations, two of which, the Royal Society of London, chartered by Charles II (1662), and the French *Académie des Sciences*, sponsored by Colbert and chartered by Louis XIV (1666), were extraordinarily influential and themselves became models for similar organizations in northern

Europe and in America. Each of these societies sprang up spontaneously among scientifically inclined men some years before they became chartered organizations. In England, Francis Bacon had advocated co-operative efforts among scholars as early as 1617, and during the English Civil Wars (1640's), a group of Oxford and London pioneers, including Robert Boyle, John Wallis, John Evelyn, Christopher Wren, and William Petty, began the "Invisible College" in London and a similar society at Oxford, which, after the Restoration (1660), combined and were chartered in 1662 as the Royal Society of London. Charles II's charter well states the Society's purpose.

From the Charter of the Royal Society
(1662) [1]

We have long and fully resolved with Ourself to extend not only the boundaries of the Empire, but also the very arts and sciences. Therefore we look with favour upon all forms of learning, but with particular grace we encourage philosophical studies, especially those which by actual experiments attempt either to shape out a new philosophy or to perfect the old. In order, therefore, that such studies, which have not hitherto been sufficiently brilliant in any part of the world, may shine conspicuously amongst our people, and that at length the whole world of letters may always recognize us not only as the Defender of the Faith, but also as the universal lover and patron of every kind of truth:

Know ye that we, of our special grace and of our certain knowledge and mere motion, have ordained, established,

granted, and declared . . . that from henceforth for ever there shall be a Society, consisting of a President, Council, and Fellows, which shall be called and named The Royal Society . . . whose studies are to be applied to further promoting by the authority of experiments the sciences of natural things and of useful arts. . . .

And further, for the improvement of the experiments, arts, and sciences of the aforesaid Royal Society . . . we have given and granted . . . that they and their successors from time to time may and shall have full power and authority, by letters or epistles under the hand of the aforesaid President . . . to enjoy mutual intelligence and knowledge with all and all manner of strangers and foreigners, whether private or collegiate, corporate or politic, without any molestation, interruption, or disturbance whatsoever: Provided nevertheless, that this our indulgence, so granted as it is aforesaid, be not extended to further use than the particular benefit and interest of the aforesaid Royal Society in matters or things philosophical, mathematical, or mechanical.

[In the Original Statutes of the Royal Society of London (1663), the purpose of its meetings was outlined as follows: [2]]

The business of the Society in their ordinary Meetings shall be, to order, take account, consider, and discourse of philosophical experiments and observations; to read, hear, and discourse upon letters, reports, and other papers, containing philosophical matters; as also to view, and discourse upon, rarities of nature and art: and thereupon to consider, what may be deduced from them, or any of them; and how far they, or any of them, may be improved for use or discovery.

[1] This and the next selection are from *The Record of the Royal Society of London,* 3d ed., rev., 1912. Reprinted by permission of The Royal Society, London. This is 59, 67-68.

[2] *Ibid.,* 119.

THE ROLE OF SCIENTIFIC SOCIETIES: SCIENTIFIC PUBLICATIONS

The Royal Society maintained curators of experiments, one of whom, Robert Hooke, was an important scientist and inventor; it developed a large "repository of rarities," or museum of specimens; it organized committees for corresponding with scientific men all over the world; it supplied observers in the colonies and elsewhere with telescopes, barometers, and other instruments for the collection of scientific data of all kinds; it solicited the cooperation of ship captains, commercial companies, missionaries, and others to obtain scientific information about geography, geology, oceanography, botany, medicine, astronomy, and many other things, so that, as one of its early admirers wrote, "there will scarce a Ship come up the Thames that does not make some return of *Experiments* as well as of *Merchandize*." In 1669, the Society's secretary, Henry Oldenburg, wrote to Rome "to procure for the Royal Society such observations of a philosophical nature as have been made by those persons that have been and are still sent from Rome into the remotest parts of the world, the East and West Indies, Mogol, China, Persia, Turkey, Egypt, Arabia, Mexico, Peru, Brazil, Hispaniola, Cuba, &c." The vast materials collected by the Royal Society enabled its members to experiment with and to classify data drawn from all parts of the world, to exchange ideas and criticisms not only with one another but also with scientists in other parts of the world, and, upon such experiments, classifications, and criticisms, to construct fundamental laws of natural phenomena. To these achievements of the Royal Society of London, the French Academy of Sciences, and their sister institutions later organized in Berlin, St. Petersburg, Stockholm, Dublin, Madrid, Lisbon, and Philadelphia, was added yet another important service to the development of experimental science: the publication of scientific journals. Both the French and the English societies began scientific publications in 1665. The French, in January, began the *Journal des Sçavans,* and the English, in March, put forth the *Philosophical Transactions.* The purposes of the two journals were similar, and in the first number of the latter, Henry Oldenburg made these purposes clear.

From OLDENBURG in the *Philosophical Transactions* (March 6, 1664/5) [1]

Whereas there is nothing more necessary for promoting the improvement of Philosophical Matters than the communicating to such as apply their Studies and Endeavours that way, such things as are discovered or put in practice by others; It is therefore thought fit to employ the *Press* as the most proper way to gratifie those whose engagement in such Studies and delight in the advancement of Learning and profitable Discoveries doth entitle them to the knowledge of what this Kingdom, or other parts of the World, do, from time to time, afford, as well of the Progress of the Studies, Labours, and attempts of the Curious and Learned in things of this kind, as of their complete Discoveries and Performances: To the end that such Productions being clearly and truly communicated, desires after solid and useful knowledge may be further entertained, ingenious endeavours and undertakings cherished, and those addicted to and conversant in such matters

[1] *Philosophical Transactions,* I, London, 1665, No. 1, 1-2.

may be invited and encouraged to search, try, and find out new things, impart their knowledge to one another, and contribute what they can to the Grand Design of improving Natural Knowledge and perfecting all *Philosophical Arts and Sciences.* All for the Glory of God, the Honour and Advantage of these Kingdoms, and the Universal Good of Mankind.

SIR ISAAC NEWTON (1642-1727) AND HIS "PRINCIPIA" (1687)

Fundamental to the development of natural sciences in modern times were the achievements of Sir Isaac Newton in mathematics, physics, astronomy, and mechanics. A prodigy from his youth, Newton had discovered the binomial theorem before he had finished college, worked out the principles of the integral calculus (independently of Leibnitz, who did the same thing), made valuable contributions to the theory of light, invented the reflecting telescope (1668), and—his greatest achievement—discovered the law of gravity. Moreover, Newton's great work on the laws of motion and gravity, the *Principia,* was a model of lucidity in the new scientific literature. Newton became a member of the English Royal Society in 1672 and was greatly assisted in his work by that body, as the following account of his major work attests.

From BREWSTER, *Isaac Newton* (1855) [1]

It was doubtless in . . . 1666, or perhaps in the autumn of 1665, that Newton's mind was first directed to the subject of Gravity. He appears to have left Cambridge some time before the 8th of August, 1665, when the College was "dis-

[1] Sir David Brewster, *Memoirs of the Life, Writings, and Discoveries of Sir Isaac Newton,* 2 vols. Edinburgh, 1855, I, 25-26, 291-94, 320-22.

missed" on account of the Plague, and it was therefore in the autumn of that year . . . that the apple is said to have fallen from the tree at Woolsthorpe, and suggested to Newton the idea of gravity. When sitting alone in the garden, and speculating on the power of gravity, it occurred to him that as the same power by which the apple fell to the ground, was not sensibly diminished at the greatest distance from the centre of the earth to which we can reach, neither at the summits of the loftiest spires, nor on the tops of the highest mountains, it might extend to the moon and retain her in her orbit, in the same manner as it bends into a curve a stone or a cannon ball, when projected in a straight line from the surface of the earth. If the moon was thus kept in her orbit by gravitation to the earth, or, in other words, its attraction, it was equally probable, he thought, that the planets were kept in their orbits by gravitating towards the sun. Kepler had discovered the great law of the planetary motions, that the squares of their periodic times were as the cubes of their distances from the sun, and hence Newton drew the important conclusion that the force of gravity or attraction, by which the planets were retained in their orbits, varied as the square of their distances from the sun. Knowing the force of gravity at the earth's surface, he was, therefore, led to compare it with the force exhibited in the actual motion of the moon, in a circular orbit; but having assumed that the distance of the moon from the earth was equal to sixty of the earth's semi-diameters, he found that the force by which the moon was drawn from its rectilineal path in a second of time was only 13.9 feet, whereas at the surface of the earth it was 16.1 in a second. This great discrepancy between his theory and what he then considered to be the fact [together with other difficulties], induced him to abandon the subject. . . .

Some years after he had laid aside his former thoughts, "a letter from Dr. [Robert] Hooke [the Royal Society's curator of experiments] put him on inquiring what was the real figure in which a body, let fall from any high place, descends, taking the motion of the earth round its axis into consideration"; and that this gave occasion to his resuming his former thoughts concerning the moon, and determining, from Picard's measures, that "the moon appeared to be kept in her orbit purely by the power of gravity.". . . It was, therefore, in 1684, that Newton discovered that the moon's deflexion in a minute was sixteen feet, the same as that at the earth's surface. . . .

Sir Christopher Wren and Hooke and [Edmond] Halley [the famous astronomer] had each of them, from independent considerations, concluded that "the centripetal force decreased in the proportion of the squares of the distances reciprocally." . . . [But none of them had been able to produce the demonstration of it.] It is therefore to Newton alone that we owe the demonstration of the great truth, that the moon is kept in her orbit by the same power by which bodies fall on the earth's surface. . . . If the force of the earth's gravity bends the moon into her orbit, the satellites of the other planets must be guided by the same power in their primaries, and the attractive force of the sun must in like manner control the movements of the comets and the planets which surround him. . . .

[Newton was assisted in applying his theory of gravity to the motions of the planets by the observations and co-operation of the English astronomer-royal at Greenwich, John Flamsteed; and in the actual publication of his great work, *The Mathematical Principles of Natural Phil-*osophy, commonly known by its Latin short title, the *Principia,* Edmond Halley did the editing and paid the expenses of printing. The work was published in 1687, in three books, of which the first two treat "On the Motion of Bodies," and the third "On the System of the World." The *Principia* is a highly technical work which few laymen can read with comprehension. But out of the mass of mathematical figures and demonstrations emerged the fundamental laws of movement familiar to nearly every schoolboy today; that is, 1. That every body remains in a state of rest or moves uniformly in a given direction unless it is compelled to change by impressed force. 2. That the change of motion of a body is proportional to the impressed force and takes place in the straight line by which that force is impressed. 3. To every action there is an equal and opposite reaction. But Newton's contributions in the *Principia* went farther:]

The great discovery which characterizes the *Principia* is that of the principle of universal gravitation, *that every particle of matter in the universe is attracted by, or gravitates to, every other particle of matter, with a force inversely proportional to the squares of their distances.* In order to establish this principle, Newton begins by considering the curves which are generated by the composition of a direct impressed motion with a gravitation or tendency towards a centre; and, having demonstrated that in all cases the areas described by the revolving body are proportional to the times of their description, he shows how to find, from the curves described, the law of the force. . . . In order to determine whether the force or gravity resided in the centres of the sun and planets, or in each individual particle of which they are composed, Newton demonstrated that if a spherical body acts upon a distant body with a force varying as the distance of this body from the centre of the sphere, the same effect will be produced as if each of its particles acted upon the distant body according to the same law. And hence it follows, that the spheres, whether [or not] of uniform density . . . will act upon each other in the same manner as if their force resided in their centre alone. But as the bodies of the solar system are very nearly spherical, they will all act upon one another . . . as if they were so many centres of attraction; and therefore we obtain the law of gravity which subsists between spherical bodies, namely, that one sphere will act upon another with a force directly proportional to their quantities of matter, and inversely, as the square of the distance between the centres of the spheres. From the equality of action and reaction, to which no exception can be found, Newton concluded that the sun gravitated to the planets, and the planets to their satellites, and the earth itself to the stone which falls upon its surface; and consequently that the two mutually gravitating bodies approached to one another with velocities inversely proportional to their quantities of matter.

Having established this universal law, Newton was enabled not only to determine the weight which the same body would have at the surface of the sun and the planets, but even to calculate the quantity of matter in the sun and in all the planets that had satellites, and even to determine the density or specific gravity of the matter of which they were composed—results which Adam Smith pronounced to be "above the reach of human reason and experience." In this way he found that the weight of the same body would be twenty-three times greater at the surface of the sun than at the surface of the earth, and that the density of the earth was four times greater than that of the sun.

FRANCESCO REDI (1626-1697): "EXPERIMENTS ON THE GENERATION OF INSECTS" (1668)

Until the seventeenth century, European mankind believed that insects were generated spontaneously in putrefying flesh. Aristotle had taught this notion, the Old Testament, in the story of Samson and the lion (Judges 14:5-9), seemed to support the view, and Virgil's *Georgics,* the medieval and early modern handbook in agriculture and husbandry, confirmed it (Book IV, lines 538-43, Dryden's translation). The first scientific treatment of the question was at the hands of an Italian, Francesco Redi, who published the results of his experiments in 1668—experiments which showed conclusively that insects could be produced only through parent forms.

From REDI, *Experiments* (1668) [1]

Through many observations repeatedly made by me, I am inclined to believe that the earth . . . has never produced by herself any plant, tree, or animal, perfect or imperfect; and that all living things born in times past and born now come from the true seed of the plants and animals, which, by means of their own seed, conserve their species. . . . I feel inclined to believe that all those worms generate from the parental seed, and that meat, herbs, and other putrid things do nothing else in the generation of insects except to provide a place, or a nest, in which animals in the time of their giving birth are carried, and to supply sufficient nourishment. And in order . . . that you can see well

[1] Francesco Redi, *Esperienze intorno alla generazione degl' insetti,* Florence, 1668, 14-27. I am indebted to my colleague, Dr. Mary Lucille Shay, for the translation of Redi's work.

the truth of what I say, I shall talk now minutely of a few of these insects. . . .

At the beginning of June I had three serpents killed. As soon as they were dead I put them in an open box to decay. Not long after, I noticed they were all covered with worms which looked like shellfish without legs. Even the naked eye could see the worms grow larger as they devoured the meat. From one day to another, as I could observe, the number increased. All were like shellfish, but not of the same size, being born on different days; but after eating all except the bones, all escaped through a little hole that I made, without my finding where they went. On June 11, I put in three others of the same snakes. After three days, I saw worms which increased in numbers and size, but, however, not of the same figure, because they were not all the same color. . . . After they had consumed the flesh they sought to escape, but I had closed all the crevices. I observed on the nineteenth of the same month that some of the large and small ones had commenced to become immobile and had taken a form similar to an egg. On the twenty-first all had taken that form. All were white at the beginning, then they became rather red. Some remained red, others became dark. . . . The difference between the red and the black eggs made me more curious. It seemed that they were made of rings joined together, but the rings were more apparent in the black than in the red. The latter appeared at first almost smooth and did not have, like the black, a small concavity at one end similar to the lemon or other fruits when they are taken from the branch. I separated the red eggs and put them in glass vases well covered with paper, and on the eighth day from every red egg came a fly . . . of a vivid green and marvelously bright. . . . From the black eggs after fourteen days came large and black

striped flies, with hairy stomachs and red skins, of the type which we see daily buzzing about meat. . . .

That such different moths came from one cadaver did not satisfy me, but rather stimulated me to make new experiments. I took six boxes without lids. In the first I put two of the snakes, in the second a large pigeon, in the third two pounds of veal, in the fourth a large piece of horse meat, in the fifth a chicken, in the sixth a sheep's heart; and all in little over twenty-four hours were covered with worms. After five or six days they transformed themselves as usual into eggs; from those in the snake box all were red without a concavity and were hatched on the twelfth day, some blue flies and some violet ones. The eggs in the pigeon box were red and black; from the red on the eighth day were hatched green flies, and from the black on the fourteenth day, having broken the shell at the end where there was no concavity, were hatched black flies striped with white. Similar flies striped with white were seen hatched at the same time from all the other eggs in the boxes containing veal, horse meat, chicken, and the sheep's heart. . . . I continued to make similar experiments many other times [with many kinds of flesh, fish, and fowl, both cooked and uncooked]; the flies appeared, always indifferently, now the one then the other of the aforesaid species; sometimes from one animal all those together; other times many black flies, some of which were so small it was painful to the eye to follow them. . . .

I began to wonder if all the worms were not derived from the flies only, and not from the putrid flesh; and I was confirmed by those hatched by the fact that I had always seen on the meats before they were infected flies of the same species that afterward were hatched. But my wondering would have been in vain if experimenting had not confirmed it. In the middle of July I put in four flasks a snake, some fish, four eels of the Arno, and a cut of veal, and covered the mouths well with paper and string and sealed tightly; then in bottles I put the same meats and left the mouths open. Not much time passed until the fish and meat of these second bottles became infested, and in these could be seen flies entering and leaving at will; but in the closed bottles I have not seen a worm.

THE INTRODUCTION OF SMALLPOX INOCULATION (1714)

The greatest advance in preventive medicine during the Era of the Enlightenment—and a beautiful example of the Royal Society's function—was the introduction into the Western world of the practice of inoculation with smallpox, then a pandemic and fearfully mortal disease. The method was first made known to the Royal Society of London by Dr. John Woodward, who learned of it from Dr. Emanuel Timonius, a Greek physician of Constantinople who had studied in England. Woodward communicated Timonius' account to the Society, and it was published in the Philosophical Transactions in the spring of 1714. At first it attracted little attention, but a copy of it fell into the hands of a colonial physician, Dr. Zabdiel Boylston of Boston, who, with the encouragement of the great Puritan minister, Cotton Mather, resolved to give it a trial at the earliest opportunity. When a smallpox epidemic broke out in Boston in 1721, Boylston, following Timonius' instructions as set forth by Woodward in the Philosophical Transactions, began inoculation. He kept careful record of the results and was able to show that only about 2 per cent of the persons inoculated died of the smallpox, whereas

among those who acquired the disease by ordinary means upward of 15 per cent expired. These results Boylston communicated to the Royal Society and, as by this time some prominent English persons were also advocating the practice, the control of smallpox by inoculation soon spread widely over Europe.[1] Until 1798, when Edward Jenner had perfected the smallpox vaccine to immunize persons by the less dangerous method of vaccination, inoculation for smallpox went far to reduce the mortality of a disease formerly extremely virulent in European society. Extracts from Timonius' letter to Dr. Woodward as published in the Philosophical Transactions follow.

From WOODWARD in the Philosophical Transactions (1714) [2]

The writer of this ingenious Discourse [Timonius] observes in the first place that the Circassians, Georgians, and other Asiatics have introduced this practice of procuring the smallpox by a sort of inoculation for about . . . forty years among the Turks and others at Constantinople. That although at first the more prudent were very cautious in the use of this practice, yet the happy success it has been found to have in thousands of subjects for these eight years past has now put it out of all suspicion and doubt, since the operation having been performed on persons of all ages, sexes, and different temperaments, and even in the worst constitution of the air, yet none have been found to die of the smallpox; when at the same time it was very mortal when it seized the patient the common way,

[1] In 1768, Catherine the Great of Russia imported a prominent English physician to inoculate herself, the Grand Duke, and others of the Russian aristocracy, and planned methods for extending inoculation "through the whole Russian Empire."

[2] Philosophical Transactions, XXIX, No. 339 (London, April-June, 1714), 72-82.

of which half the affected died. This he attests upon his own observation. Next he observes, they that have this inoculation practised upon them are subject to very slight symptoms, some being scarce sensible they are ill or sick, and what is valued by the fair [sex], it never leaves any scars or pits in the face.

The method of the operation is this. Choice being made of a proper contagion, the matter of the pustules is to be communicated to the person proposed to take the infection, whence it has, metaphorically, the name of incision or inoculation. For this purpose they make choice of some boy, or young lad, of a sound, healthy temperament, that is seized with the common smallpox . . . on the twelfth or thirteenth day from the beginning of his sickness; with a needle they prick the tubercles . . . and press out the matter coming from them into some convenient vessel of glass, or the like. . . . A convenient quantity of this matter being thus collected, it is to be stopped close and kept warm in the bosom of the person that carries it and, as soon as may be, brought to the place of the expecting future patient.

The patient therefore being in a warm chamber, the operator is to make several little wounds with a needle in one, two, or more places of the skin till some drops of blood follow, and immediately drop out some drops of the matter in the glass and mix it well with the blood issuing out. One drop of the matter is sufficient for each place pricked. These punctures are made indifferently in any of the fleshy parts, but succeed best in the muscles of the arm. . . . The needle is to be a three-edged surgeon's needle. . . . The wound is covered with half of a walnut shell, or the like concave vessel, and bound over so that the matter be not rubbed off by the garments, [the bandage being] removed in a few hours. The patient is to take care of his diet. . . .

The smallpox begins to appear sooner in some than in others, in some with greater [and] in others with lesser symptoms [severity], but with happy success in all. . . . It was observed, in a year when the common smallpox was very mortal, that those by incision were also attended by greater symptoms. . . . At other times the symptoms are distinct, few, and scattered; commonly 10 or 20 pustules break out; here and there one has but 2 or 3; few have 100. There are some in whom no pustule rises but in the places where the incision was made, which swell up into purulent tubercles; yet these have never had the smallpox afterwards in their whole lives, though they have cohabited with persons having it. . . .

If this inoculation be made on persons who have before had the smallpox, they find no alteration, and the places pricked presently dry up, except in an ill habit of body, where possibly a slight inflammation and exulceration may happen for a few days.

BENJAMIN FRANKLIN DEMONSTRATES THAT LIGHTNING IS ELECTRICITY (1752)

Benjamin Franklin (1706-1790), the great Philadelphian printer, literary man, scientist, and diplomat, sometimes called the "First American," became interested in electrical experiments in 1746, when Peter Collinson, a wealthy London Quaker and patron of science, sent the Library Company of Philadelphia (of which Franklin was a leading member) a Leyden jar, a species of electrical condenser, or battery, discovered at Leyden in the previous year. At this time electricity was a scientific toy about which little was known. It was known to be created by rubbing rods, or balls, of sulphur, resin, or glass ("static electricity"), but its properties and the laws governing its conduct were undiscovered. In the decade after 1746, Franklin made important contributions to the knowledge of the subject. He discovered the fluid quality of electricity, distinguished between positive and negative electric currents, proved that pointed rods would pick up or give off electric charges (the basic idea of lightning rods, which Franklin invented in 1753), and, in a dangerous experiment with a kite in a thunderstorm in the summer of 1752, proved that lightning and electricity are identical. His account of this latter experiment follows. It was read before the Royal Society of London, which gave Franklin its Copley prize in 1753 and elected him to membership in 1756.

From FRANKLIN, Letter to Peter Collinson (October 19, 1752 [Philadelphia]) [1]

Sir,

As frequent mention is made in public papers from *Europe* of the success of the *Philadelphia* experiment for drawing the electric fire from clouds by means of pointed rods of iron erected on high buildings &c. [lightning rods], it may be agreeable to the curious to be informed, that the same experiment has succeeded in *Philadelphia,* though made in a different and more easy manner, which is as follows:

Make a small cross of two light strips of cedar, the arms so long as to reach to the four corners of a large thin silk handkerchief when extended; tie the corners of the handkerchief to the extremities of the cross, so you have the body of a kite; which being properly accommodated with a tail, loop, and string, will rise in the air, like those made of paper;

but this being of silk, is fitter to bear the wet and wind of a thunder-gust without tearing. To the top of the upright stick of the cross is fixed a very sharp-pointed wire, rising a foot or more above the wood. To the end of the twine, next the hand, is to be tied a silk ribbon, and where the silk and twine join, a key may be fastened. This kite is to be raised when a thunder-gust appears to be coming on, and the person who holds the string must stand within a door or window, or under some cover, so that the silk ribbon may not be wet; and care must be taken that the twine does not touch the frame of the door or window. As soon as any of the thunder-clouds come over the kite, the pointed wire will draw the electric fire from them, and the kite, with all the twine, will be electrified, and the loose filaments of the twine will stand out every way, and be attracted by an approaching finger. And when the rain has wet the kite and twine, so that it can conduct the electric fire freely, you will find it stream out plentifully from the key on the approach of your knuckle. At this key the phial [battery] may be charged; and from electric fire thus obtained, spirits may be kindled, and all the other electric experiments be performed, which are usually done by the help of a rubbed glass globe or tube, and thereby the sameness of the electric matter with that of lightning completely demonstrated.

B. Franklin

3. Philosophy and Religion

RENÉ DESCARTES AND CARTESIAN THOUGHT

Philosophy, during the Era of Enlightened Despotism, was profoundly affected by the multiplicity of new sci-

[1] From *The Writings of Benjamin Franklin,* ed. by Albert Henry Smyth, 10 vols., 1905-07, III (1905), 99-100. By permission of The Macmillan Company.

entific discoveries. Having scarcely shaken themselves free from scholasticism and older forms of authoritarianism, philosophers were forced to recognize the powers of human reason as demonstrated by the new "experimental philosophers." But they were seldom in agreement about the *nature* of reason or of the human mind upon which, or through which, reason acted. Moreover, before the era ended, some philosophers began to rebel against the omnipotence of reason, to hold that, outside the realm of pure reason, there were influences of an emotional nature which vitally affect the conduct and the thought of man.

One of the earliest influential philosophers of the era was the Frenchman, René Descartes (1596-1650), from whose latinized surname, Cartesius, derived the title of his philosophy, Cartesianism. Descartes became dissatisfied with the state of learning in his day, and sought, by a study of himself and the world about him, to find the right method for obtaining solid knowledge. Mathematics attracted him, principally because the method of analytical geometry seemed to lead to certainty, and he felt that the mathematical pattern of thought might be applied to other fields. Reason, said Descartes, which is the power to distinguish truth from error, is the chief attribute which separates man from brutes. As it is the property of every man, Descartes determined to employ it as the guiding light of his life. That decided, he sought "the Method which each ought to follow for the right conduct of his Reason" —a method which would at least serve his own purposes. This method he describes in an autobiographical treatise, *Discourse on the Method of Rightly Conducting the Reason and Seeking Truth in the Sciences.*

From DESCARTES, *Discourse on Method* (1637) [1]

Among the branches of Philosophy, I had, at an earlier period, given some attention to Logic, and among those of the Mathematics to Geometrical Analysis and Algebra—three Arts or Sciences which ought, as I conceived, to contribute something to my design. But, on examination . . . I was induced to seek some other Method which would comprise the advantages of the three and be exempt from their defects. . . . I believed that the four following would prove perfectly sufficient for me. . . .

The *first* was never to accept anything for true which I did not clearly know to be such; that is to say, carefully to avoid precipitancy and prejudice, and to comprise nothing more in my judgment than what was presented to my mind so clearly and distinctly as to exclude all ground of doubt.

The *second,* to divide each of the difficulties under examination into as many parts as possible, and as might be necessary for its adequate solution.

The *third,* to conduct my thoughts in such order that, by commencing with objects the simplest and easiest to know, I might ascend little by little, and, as it were, step by step, to the knowledge of the more complex; assigning in thought a certain order even to those objects which in their own nature do not stand in a relation of antecedence and sequence.

And the *last,* in every case to make enumerations so complete, and reviews so general, that I might be assured nothing was omitted.

The long chains of simple and easy reasonings by means of which geometers are accustomed to reach the conclusions of their most difficult demonstrations, had

[1] *The Method, Meditations, and Selections from the Principles of Descartes,* trans. by John Veitch, 10th ed., Edinburgh, 1890, 18-20.

led me to imagine that all things, to the knowledge of which man is competent, are mutually connected in the same way, and that there is nothing so far removed from us as to be beyond our reach, or so hidden that we cannot discover it, provided only we abstain from accepting the false for the true, and always preserve in our thoughts the order necessary for the deduction of one truth from another.

In a later work, *Meditations on the First Philosophy in Which the Existence of God and the Immortality of the Soul Are Demonstrated* (1641), Descartes carried his thoughts farther. Knowing, as he says, that he had formerly held many opinions which were false, he tried to divest himself of all former opinions, to doubt everything which his senses told him, for he had observed that the senses sometimes misled. He found that he could doubt many things—his own sanity, his consciousness, even God—but one thing he could not doubt: the fact that he doubted. But what is doubting? It is thinking. *"Cogito, ergo sum,"* "I think, therefore, I am." This triumphant conclusion furnished a certitude upon which, without appeal to other authorities, Descartes founded his system of philosophy. Cartesianism contained dualisms which Descartes was unable to avoid. One was the dualism which Descartes felt existed between intellectual perception and sensual perception, between mind and matter (as illustrated in the discussion of the nature of wax below); the other was the dualism that exists because of the finite (limited) powers of man and the infinite (unlimited) powers of God. And lastly, a distinctive feature of Cartesianism was its author's belief in the existence of innate ideas in the human mind. The following excerpts from the *Meditations* illustrate some of these characteristics.

From DESCARTES, *Meditations* (1641) [1]

OF THE NATURE OF THE HUMAN MIND

Let us now accordingly consider the objects that are commonly thought to be the most easily, and likewise the most distinctly known, viz., the bodies we touch and see. . . . Take, for example, this piece of wax; it is quite fresh, having been but recently taken from the beehive; it has not yet lost the sweetness of the honey it contained; it still retains somewhat of the odor of the flowers from which it was gathered; its color, figure, size, are apparent (to the sight); it is hard, cold, easily handled; and sounds when struck upon with the finger. In fine, all that contributes to make a body as distinctly known as possible, is found in the one before us. But, while I am speaking, let it be placed near the fire—what remained of the taste exhales, the smell evaporates, the color changes, its figure is destroyed, its size increases, it becomes liquid, it grows hot, it can hardly be handled, and, although struck upon, it emits no sound. Does the same wax still remain after this change? It must be admitted that it does remain. . . . What, then, was it I knew with so much distinctness in the piece of wax? Assuredly, it could be nothing of all that I observed by means of the senses, since all the things that fell under taste, smell, sight, touch, and hearing are changed, and yet the same wax remains. It was perhaps what I now think, viz., that this wax was neither the sweetness of honey, the pleasant odor of flowers, the whiteness, the figure, nor the sound, but only a body that a little before appeared to me conspicuous under these forms, and which is now perceived under others. But,

[1] *Ibid.*, 110-31.

to speak precisely, what is it that I imagine when I think of it in this way? . . . There certainly remains nothing, except something extended, flexible, and moveable. . . . I must, therefore, admit that I cannot even comprehend by imagination what the piece of wax is, and that it is the mind alone [as distinguished from the senses] which perceives it. . . . The perception of it is neither an act of sight, of touch, nor of imagination, and never was either of these, though it might formerly seem so, but is simply an intuition of the mind. . . . It is now manifest to me that bodies themselves are not properly perceived by the senses nor by the faculty of imagination, but by the intellect alone. . . .

OF GOD: THAT HE EXISTS

I will now close my eyes, I will stop my ears, I will turn away my senses from their objects, I will even efface from my consciousness all the images of corporeal things; or at least, because this can hardly be accomplished, I will consider them empty and false; and thus, holding converse only with myself, and closely examining my nature, I will endeavour to obtain by degrees a more intimate and familiar knowledge of myself. I am a thinking (conscious) thing, that is, a being who doubts, affirms, denies, knows a few objects, and is ignorant of many. . . . Now, as I am endeavouring to extend my knowledge more widely, I will use circumspection, and consider with care whether I can still discover in myself anything further which I have not hitherto observed. I am certain that I am a thinking thing; but do I not therefore likewise know what is required to render me certain of a truth? In this first knowledge, doubtless, there is nothing that gives me assurance of its truth except the clear and distinct perception of what I affirm . . . and accordingly it seems to me that I may now

take as a general rule, that all that is very clearly and distinctly apprehended (conceived) is true. . . .

It is necessary at this stage to divide all my thoughts into certain classes, and to consider in which of these classes truth and error are . . . to be found. Of my thoughts some are, as it were, images of things, and to these alone properly belongs the name *idea*. . . . Others, again, have certain other forms; as when I will, fear, affirm, or deny . . . and of this class of thoughts some are called volitions or affections, and others judgments.

Now, with respect to ideas, if these are considered only in themselves, and are not referred to any object beyond them, they cannot, properly speaking, be false; for, whether I imagine a goat or a chimera, it is not less true that I imagine the one than the other. Nor need we fear that falsity may exist in the will or affections. . . . There thus only remain our judgments, in which we must take diligent heed that we be not deceived. . . .

But, among these ideas, some appear to me to be innate, others adventitious, and others to be made by myself (factitious) . . . for I have not yet clearly discovered their true origin; and what I have here principally to do is to consider, with reference to those that appear to come from certain objects without me, what grounds there are for thinking them like these objects.

The first of these grounds is that it seems to me I am so taught by nature; and the second that I am conscious that those ideas are dependent on my will, and therefore not on myself, for they are frequently presented to me against my will—as at present, whether I will or not, I feel heat; and I am thus persuaded that this sensation or idea of heat is produced in me by something different from myself. . . .

And in proportion to the time and care with which I examine all those matters, the conviction of their truth brightens and becomes distinct. But, to sum up, what conclusion shall I draw from it all? It is this—if the objective reality of any one of my ideas be such as clearly to convince me, that this same reality exists in me neither formally nor eminently, and if, as follows from this, I myself cannot be the cause of it, it is a necessary consequence that I am not alone in the world, but that there is besides myself some other being who exists as the cause of that idea. . . . [This External Cause, Descartes calls God.] By the name God, I understand a substance infinite, eternal, immutable, independent, all-knowing, all-powerful, and by which I myself, and every other thing that exists, if any such there be, were created. . . .

There remains only the inquiry as to the way in which I received this idea from God; for I have not drawn it from the senses, nor is it even presented to me unexpectedly . . . it is not even a pure production or fiction of my mind, for it is not in my power to take from or add to it; and consequently there but remains the alternative that it is innate, in the same way as is the idea of myself . . . that God, at my creation, implanted this idea in me.

JOHN LOCKE AND THE SCIENCE OF HUMAN NATURE

John Locke (1632-1704), the English philosopher whose justification of the "Glorious Revolution" of 1688 has been cited above (page 237) contributed further to philosophy *An Essay Concerning Human Understanding* (1690), which was the earliest extensive effort to develop the science of human nature and, as such, remains still a valuable pioneer work in modern psychology. Locke disagreed with Descartes on the notion of innate ideas, and his empha-sis upon *experience* as the basis of knowledge both set empiricism in competition with rationalism and furnished splendid philosophical justification for Newtonian science in the eighteenth century.

From LOCKE, *Human Understanding* (1690) [1]

I know it is a received doctrine that men have native ideas and original characters stamped upon their minds, in their very first being. This opinion I have at large examined already [in Book I, wherein Locke proved to his own satisfaction that there are no innate ideas or principles]; and I suppose what I have said in the foregoing Book will be much more easily admitted when I have shown whence the understanding may get all the ideas it has, and by what ways and degrees they may come into the mind; for which I shall appeal to every one's own observation and experience.

Let us then suppose the mind to be, as we say, white paper, void of all characters, without any ideas; how comes it to be furnished? Whence comes it by that vast store, which the busy and boundless fancy of man has painted on it with an almost endless variety? Whence has it all the materials of reason and knowledge? To this I answer, in one word, from experience: In that, all our knowledge is founded; and from that it ultimately derives itself. Our observation employed either about external sensible objects or about the internal operations of our minds, perceived and reflected on by ourselves, is that which supplies our understandings with all the materials of thinking. These two are the fountains of knowledge, from whence all the ideas we have, or can naturally have, do spring.

[1] John Locke, *An Essay Concerning Human Understanding*, 17th ed., 2 vols., London, 1775, I, Bk. II, 67-69, 79; II, Bk. IV, 121, 262-64, 288, 308-09, 315-16.

First, our senses, conversant about particular sensible objects, do convey into the mind several distinct perceptions of things according to those various ways wherein those objects do affect them: And thus we come by those ideas we have of yellow, white, heat, cold, soft, hard, bitter, sweet, and all those which we call sensible qualities; which when I say the senses convey into the mind, I mean they from external objects convey into the mind what produces there those perceptions. This great source of most of the ideas we have, depending wholly upon our senses, and derived by them to the understanding, I call sensation.

Secondly, the other fountain from which experience furnisheth the understanding with ideas is the perception of the operations of our own mind within us, as it is employed about the ideas it has got: which operations when the soul comes to reflect on and consider do furnish the understanding with another set of ideas, which could not be had from things without; and such are perception, thinking, doubting, believing, reasoning, knowing, willing, and all the different actings of our own minds; which we being conscious of, and observing in ourselves, do from these receive into our understandings as distinct ideas, as we do from bodies affecting our senses. This source of ideas every man has wholly in himself: and tho' it be not sense, as having nothing to do with external objects, yet it is very like it, and might properly enough be called internal sense. But as I call the other sensation, so I call this reflection; the ideas it affords being such only as the mind gets by reflecting on its own operations within itself. . . . These two, I say, viz., external, material things, as the objects of sensation, and the operations of our own minds within, as the objects of reflection, are to me the only originals from whence all our ideas take their beginnings. . . .

Follow a child from its birth, and observe the alterations that time makes, and you shall find, as the mind by the senses comes more and more to be furnished with ideas, it comes to be more and more awake; thinks more, the more it has matter to think on. . . . So we may observe how the mind . . . advances to the exercise of those other faculties of enlarging, compounding, and abstracting its ideas, and of reasoning about them, and reflecting upon all these. . . .

Since the mind, in all its thoughts and reasonings, hath no other immediate object but its own ideas, which it alone does or can contemplate, it is evident that our knowledge is only conversant about them.

Knowledge then seems to me to be nothing but the perception of the connection and agreement, or disagreement and repugnancy, of any of our ideas. In this alone it consists. Where this perception is, there is knowledge; and where it is not, there, though we may fancy, guess, or believe, yet we always come short of knowledge. . . .

We must therefore, if we will proceed as reason advises, adapt our methods of enquiry to the nature of the ideas we examine, and the truth we search after. . . .

In our search after the knowledge of substances, our want of ideas that are suitable to such a way of proceeding obliges us to a quite different method. We advance not here as in the other (where our abstract ideas are real as well as nominal essences) by contemplating our ideas, and considering their relations and correspondences; that helps us very little . . . the want of ideas of their real essences sends us from our own thoughts to the things themselves, as they exist. Experience here must teach me what reason cannot: and it is by trying alone that I can certainly know what other qualities co-exist with those of my complex idea. . . .

The word reason, in the English language, has different significations: sometimes it is taken for true and clear principles; sometimes for clear and fair deductions from those principles; and sometimes for the cause and particularly the final cause. But the consideration I shall have of it here is in a signification different from all these; and that is, as it stands for a faculty in man, that faculty whereby man is supposed to be distinguished from beasts, and wherein it is evident he much surpasses them. . . .

From these things thus premised I think we may come to lay down the measures and boundaries between faith and reason: the want whereof may possibly have been the cause, if not of great disorders, yet at least of great disputes, and perhaps mistakes in the world: For, till it be resolved how far we are to be guided by reason, and how far by faith, we shall in vain dispute, and endeavour to convince one another in matters of religion.

I find every sect, as far as reason will help them, make use of it gladly; and where it fails them, they cry out, It is matter of faith and above reason. And I do not see how they can argue with any one, or ever convince a gainsayer who makes use of the same plea without setting down strict boundaries between faith and reason, which ought to be the first point established in all questions where faith has any thing to do.

Reason therefore here, as contradistinguished to faith, I take to be the discovery of the certainty or probability of such propositions or truths which the mind arrives at by deduction made from such ideas which it has got by the use of its natural faculties, *viz.* by sensation or reflection.

Faith, on the other side, is the assent to any proposition not thus made out by the deductions of reason, but upon the credit of the proposer, as coming from God, in some extraordinary way of communica-

tion. This way of discovering truths to men we call revelation. . . .

If the provinces of faith and reason are not kept distinct by these boundaries, there will, in matters of religion, be no room for reason at all; and those extravagant opinions and ceremonies, that are to be found in the several religions of the world, will not deserve to be blamed. For, to this crying up of faith in opposition to reason we may, I think, in a good measure, ascribe those absurdities that fill almost all the religions which possess and divide mankind. For men having been principled with an opinion, that they must not consult reason in the things of religion, however apparently contradictory to common sense, and the very principles of all their knowledge, have let loose their fancies and natural superstition and have been by them led into so strange opinions and extravagant practices in religion that a considerate man cannot but stand amazed at their follies and judge them so far from being acceptable to the great and wise God, that he cannot avoid thinking them ridiculous and offensive to a sober good man.

KANT'S MODIFICATION OF RATIONALISM AND EMPIRICISM

Until the last quarter of the eighteenth century, rationalism and empiricism, with some additions or exceptions (such as David Hume's skepticism), dominated European thought. During the latter part of the century, however, these modes of thinking began to be questioned, modified, and, in some cases, rejected completely. In the realm of literature, for example, writers rebelled against the cold, unimaginative qualities of the prevailing philosophy, and inaugurated attempts to express individual emotions and aesthetic, irrational beauty—to write from the heart as well as the head; and thus arose a literature which has been called "romantic." Philosophers produced a corollary to the general literary trend, a movement in which they began to question the adequacy of experience as the sole source of ideas and to hold that something more than reason is necessary for real knowledge. One of the first important writers in this new school was Immanuel Kant (1724-1804), A German physicist and philosopher, whose *Critique of Pure Reason* (1781) helped disentangle metaphysics (philosophy) from physics (natural science), reallocated to each a specific sphere of activity, and thereby gave to each a new sense of importance. Kant's work transformed contemporary thought and inaugurated some of the fundamental tendencies of the following century.

From KANT, *Critique of Pure Reason* (1781) [1]

OF THE DIFFERENCE BETWEEN PURE AND EMPIRICAL KNOWLEDGE

That all our knowledge begins with experience there can be no doubt. . . .

But though all our knowledge begins with experience, it by no means follows that all arises out of experience. For, on the contrary, it is quite possible that our empirical knowledge is a compound of that which we receive through impressions, and that which the faculty of cognition supplies from itself (sensuous impressions giving merely the *occasion*), an addition which we cannot distinguish from the original element given by sense, till long practice has made us attentive to, and skilful in separating it. It is, therefore, a question which requires close investigation, and is not to be answered at first

[1] Immanuel Kant, *Critique of Pure Reason,* trans. by J. M. D. Meiklejohn, London, 1913, 1-2, 15-17, 483-86, 503-14. Reprinted by permission of G. Bell and Sons, Ltd., Publishers.

sight—whether there exists a knowledge altogether independent of experience, and even of all sensuous impressions? Knowledge of this kind is called *a priori,* in contradistinction to empirical knowledge, which has its sources *a posteriori,* that is, in experience. . . .

By the term "knowledge *a priori,*" therefore, we shall in the sequel understand, not such as is independent of this or that kind of experience, but such as is absolutely so of *all* experience. . . . Knowledge *a priori* is either pure or impure. Pure knowledge *a priori* is that with which no empirical element is mixed up. . . .

From all that has been said, there results the idea of a particular science, which may be called the *Critique of Pure Reason.* For reason is the faculty which furnishes us with the principles of knowledge *a priori.* Hence, pure reason is the faculty which contains the principles of cognizing any thing absolutely *a priori.* An Organon of pure reason would be a compendium of those principles according to which alone all pure cognitions *a priori* can be obtained. The completely extended application of such an organon would afford us a system of pure reason. As this, however, is demanding a great deal, and it is yet doubtful whether any extension of our knowledge be here possible, or if so, in what cases; we can regard a science of the mere criticism of pure reason, its sources and limits, as the propaedeutic [introduction] to a system of pure reason. Such a science must not be called a Doctrine, but only a Critique of Pure Reason; and its use, in regard to speculation, would be only negative, not to enlarge the bounds of, but to purify our reason, and to shield it against error—which alone is no little gain. I apply the term *transcendental* to all knowledge which is not so much occupied with objects as with the mode of our cognition of these objects, so far as this mode of cognition is possible *a priori*. A system of such conceptions would be called *Transcendental Philosophy*. But this, again, is still beyond the bounds of our present essay. . . .

Transcendental philosophy is the idea of a science, for which the Critique of Pure Reason must sketch the whole plan architectonically, that is, from principles, with a full guarantee for the validity and stability of all the parts which enter into the building. It is the system of all the parts which enter into the building. It is the system of all the principles of pure reason. If this Critique itself does not assume the title of transcendental philosophy, it is only because, to be a complete system, it ought to contain a full analysis of all human knowledge *a priori*. . . .

To the Critique of Pure Reason, therefore, belongs all that constitutes transcendental philosophy; and it is the complete idea of transcendental philosophy, but still not the science itself; because it only proceeds so far with the analysis as is necessary to the power of judging completely of our synthetical knowledge *a priori*.

OF THE ULTIMATE END OF THE PURE USE OF REASON

There exists in the faculty of reason a natural desire to venture beyond the field of experience. . . .

The transcendental speculation of reason relates to three things: the freedom of the will, the immortality of the soul, and the existence of God. . . .

All the powers of reason, in the sphere of what may be termed pure philosophy, are, in fact, directed to the three above-mentioned problems alone. These again have a still higher end—the answer to the question, *what we ought to do,* if the will is free, if there is a God, and a future world. Now, as this problem relates to our conduct, in reference to the highest aim of humanity, it is evident that the ultimate intention of nature, in the constitution of our reason, has been directed to the *moral* alone.

THE ARCHITECTONIC OF PURE REASON

By the term *Architectonic* I mean the art of constructing a system. . . .

Reason cannot permit our knowledge to remain in an unconnected and rhapsodistic state, but requires that the sum of our cognitions should constitute a system. It is thus alone that they can advance the ends of reason. By a system I mean the unity of various cognitions under one idea. This idea is the conception—given by reason—of the form of a whole, in so far as the conception determines *a priori* not only the limits of its content, but the place which each of its parts is to occupy. . . .

Our purpose at present is merely to sketch the plan of the *Architectonic* of all cognition given by pure reason; and we begin from the point where the main root of human knowledge divides into two, one of which is *reason*. By reason I understand here the whole higher faculty of cognition, the *rational* being placed in contradistinction to the *empirical*. . . .

All rational cognition is, again, based either on conceptions, or on the construction of conceptions. The former is termed philosophical, the latter mathematical. . . . But it is remarkable that mathematical knowledge, when committed to memory, is valid, from the subjective point of view, as rational knowledge also, and that the same distinction cannot be drawn here as in the case of philosophical cognition. The reason is, that the only way of arriving at this knowledge is through the essential principles of reason, and thus it is always certain and indisputable: because reason is employed *in concreto*—but at the same time *a priori*—that is, in pure, and therefore, infallible intuition; and thus all causes of illusion and error are excluded. Of all the *a priori* sciences of reason, therefore, mathematics alone can be learned. Philosophy—unless it be in an historical manner—cannot be learned; we can at most learn to *philosophize*. . . .

The mathematician, the natural philosopher, and the logician—how far soever the first may have advanced in rational, and the two latter in philosophical knowledge —are merely artists, engaged in the arrangement and formation of conceptions; they cannot be termed philosophers. Above them all, there is the ideal teacher, who employs them as instruments for the advancement of the essential aims of human reason. Him alone can we call philosopher; but he nowhere exists. But the idea of his legislative power resides in the mind of every man, and it alone teaches us what kind of systematic unity philosophy demands in view of the ultimate aims of reason. This idea is, therefore, a cosmical conception.

In view of the complete systematic unity of reason, there can only be one ultimate end of all the operations of the mind. To this all other aims are subordinate, and nothing more than means for its attainment. This ultimate end is the destination of man, and the philosophy which relates to it is termed Moral Philosophy. The superior position occupied by moral philosophy, above all other spheres for the operations of reason, sufficiently indicates the reason why the ancients always included the idea—and in an especial manner—of Moralist in that of Philosopher. . . .

The above is the general idea of Metaphysics, which, as more was expected from it than could be looked for with justice, and as these pleasant expectations were unfortunately never realised, fell into general disrepute. Our Critique must have fully convinced the reader, that, although metaphysics cannot form the foundation of religion, it must always be one of its most important bulwarks, and that human

reason, which naturally pursues a dialectical course, cannot do without this science, which checks its tendencies towards dialectic, and, by elevating reason to a scientific and clear self-knowledge, prevents the ravages which a lawless speculative reason would infallibly commit in the sphere of morals as well as in that of religion. We may be sure, therefore, whatever contempt may be thrown upon metaphysics by those who judge a science not by its own nature, but according to the accidental effects it may have produced, that it can never be completely abandoned, that we must always return to it as to a beloved one who has been for a time estranged, because the questions with which it is engaged relate to the highest aims of humanity, and reason must always labour either to attain to settled views in regard to these, or to destroy those which others have already established.

Metaphysics, therefore—that of nature, as well as that of ethics, but in an especial manner the criticism which forms the propaedeutic to all the operations of reason—forms properly that department of knowledge which may be termed, in the truest sense of the word, philosophy. The path which it pursues is that of science, which, when it has once been discovered, is never lost, and never misleads. Mathematics, natural science, the common experience of men, have a high value as means, for the most part, to accidental ends—but at last also, to those which are necessary and essential to the existence of humanity. But to guide them to this high goal, they require the aid of rational cognition on the basis of pure conceptions, which, be it termed as it may, is properly nothing but metaphysics.

RATIONAL RELIGION: DEISM

As the Age of Reason permeated the entire intellectual life of man, it invaded the realm of faith, and attempts to make religion conformable to human reason were known as Deism. Deism was an intellectual movement, not a church. It arose as a rationalists' protest against the alleged irrationalism of Christianity—its miracles, its "inspired" religious writings, its rituals, its multiplicity of bitter sects and jealous creeds. Deists were violently anticlerical in that they charged that churches existed mainly because of the vested interests of priests and the political interests of rulers. As they viewed the success of natural scientists in discovering the laws of nature (which they identified with the laws of God), they concluded that God was a force which chose to work through specific laws and that in the elucidation of the laws of nature, man learned more and more of the laws of God. Moreover, as they compared the religions of the Orient and of the New World with Christianity, they felt that if mankind could only rise above narrow sectarianism, the principles of a universal religion which would embrace all the peoples of the world might be found. Few common people knew anything of Deism; it was mainly a movement among the upper classes and the intelligentsia, including many of the natural scientists and most of the *philosophes*. One of its earliest and most constructive advocates was an Englishman, Edward, Lord Herbert of Cherbury (1583-1648). In his first religious treatise, *De Veritate, "Concerning Truth"* (1624), Lord Herbert wrote: "Now this party, now that, loudly proclaims the truth of its own doctrines, and calls the rest plagiarists, liars, and impostors. The opposing school contests its case with equal heat; nor could I find any refuge for my spirit. . . . Finally, I am even commanded to abandon my reason and, if I hesitate, I am offered according to some

of these doctrines nothing less than the prospect, whichever way I may turn, of everlasting damnation. But . . . I sought no other hold but that of God. . . . I . . . addressed myself to the construction of my own idea of truth; and these, the product both of Nature and of Grace, I herewith present to the public." Among his posthumous papers, Lord Herbert left a simple statement of what he considered the fundamental truths of universal religion in *A Dialogue between a Tutor and His Pupil.* The five points set forth therein were the same as he had set forth in *De Veritate,* and they gained wide adherence among Deists as their basic creed.

From LORD HERBERT, *Dialogue* (*c.* 1630) [1]

Pupil. I have so much profitted in my studies that I conceive myself able to distinguish between truth and falsehood according to the ordinary rules of logic taught in our universities. . . . I pray tell me how far the use of these doctrines extends, and particularly, whether logic be not limited to such and such sciences and arts . . . but elsewhere defective and of little or no advantage.

Tutor. Why do you ask this question?

Pupil. Because I find not only in the pulpit but in our divinity schools, that in the matter of theology, or religious worship, I am commanded to renounce my reason and to cleave wholly to a certain faith they teach us, being yet so diverse from the grounds and principles of reason that this their faith can neither be derived from nor consistent with any demonstration. . . . Our divines would have me begin at faith and afterwards come to reason.

[1] Edward, Lord Herbert of Cherbury, *A Dialogue between a Tutor and His Pupil,* London, 1768, 1-8.

Tutor. You may answer them, that if there be a reason for this their opinion, that you will embrace it; howsoever, unless they produce such a faith as may be clear and evident to all mankind, that no scruple can remain about it, it would not pass for much more than particular tradition . . . so that unless the intrinsic value bear it out, *i.e.* the wise and good precepts for living well, do in a sort authorize the narrative or historical part, the faith will be but little worth and perchance be thought no better than as an holy legend or allegorical history . . . besides if this argument be good, that we must begin at faith before we come to reason, what absurd faith hath been heretofore or is now anywhere extant, which may not pretend to assert itself out of this hypothesis? . . . and here you must understand that I speak of faiths in general, that have been, or are, in Asia, Europe, Africa, or America; so that you must not limit my words to any one single faith, and especially to that which is piously received among us. . . .

Pupil. But our divines everywhere tell us that we must reject all faiths but theirs. . . .

Tutor. You ought to consider whether such a postulatum, or demand, is just and rational in itself; and whether it doth not at least preclude the way to find out which among the several religions in the world is purest, chastest, and best. . . .

Pupil. I shall, by your good help, consider whether it be possible for me to find out and learn all the several religions in the world, even if in my whole life I did nothing else? What would you have me do in this case?

Tutor. I should advise you in the first place to shake off and cast away all terrors, and, according to the true maxims of fortitude (which is one of the cardinal virtues) to keep yourself upright, free and undaunted every way till your reason convince you of some imminent danger appearing. Next I would comfort yourself with assurance that the true God whom they all pretend to serve, is *communis pater,* even by their own confession, and therefore the God of all mankind; and that the articles which are so disputed amongst them cannot be so discrepant from, or repugnant to, one another, but that some amongst them, at least, must be found catholic or universal; it being impossible otherwise to assert or establish that universal providence which is God's highest and truest attribute. These articles, therefore, which yet you find to be but few, I would have you select and put in order the best you can, that so at least you may find some truths whereon to fix and repose yourself. For which purpose it would be necessary, in every proposition or article they offer, to examine how much of it is common reason, and how much is particular faith, reducing still these articles to common reason and universal consent. 1. That there is a supreme God. 2. That a chief worship is to be given unto him. 3. That the best worship of him consists in virtue, piety, and charity conjoined with faith in and love of God. 4. That if we transgress or fall from the rules hereof, we must repent from the bottom of our heart and return to the right way, since without it repentance will be but vain. 5. That there is both reward and punishment here and hereafter. Religion being thus stated, according to common reason and universal consent, you may descend afterwards to the particular faiths taught each where (for they all move about these five centers), and then consider [1.] whether their additions are consistent with these common principles; for anything that contradicts the said principles must not by any means be admitted upon what pretence soever of faith. 2. If the said articles depend not on common reason, but on tradition or authority, whether the same be sufficiently averred or proved to you. 3. If sufficient proof be wanting, and the said articles be such only as cannot easily be disproved, whether they be proposed as necessary unto salvation or as only credible, possible, or probable truths, which might piously be embraced by well-disposed persons. 4. Whether (all these ways of proof being laid aside) the said articles did depend upon revelations pretended to be made to others in some former ages, and, if so, whether the same can be evidently notified to you, unless some revelation, made immediately to you by the supreme God, do confirm the same. 5. Whether the said articles of faith, though not sufficiently proved, be such yet as may dispose men the rather to make their way to God by goodness and virtue, and not such as may form so easy a hope of pardon for their faults as they will not fear to sin again. 6. Whether they be not controverted by foreign nations, among whom other faiths are received. 7. Whether the believing of, or holding the said articles of faith, hinder the establishment of common peace and concord throughout the world. [And so, having "settled religion, as far as it appears to be catholic and universal, and stated it in the five articles before mentioned," the pupil and his tutor begin a long conversation to discover the origin of religion and some of the peculiar forms of religious worship.]

EVANGELICAL RELIGION: THE WESLEYS AND THE RISE OF METHODISM

In strong contrast to Deism were a series of evangelical movements which passed over the Western world in the eighteenth century, reactions against Deism, atheism, and religious apathy similar to the literary escape from rationalism as found in romanticism. The new evangelicalism assumed many forms: Pietism in the Germanies,

intensified Jansenism (a kind of French Puritanism within the Gallican church), the "Great Awakening" in the English American colonies, and the rise of Methodist Societies in England. The last were the work of John Wesley (1703-1791), his brother Charles (1707-1788), and a small group of associated ministers. The prime actor was John Wesley (though Charles contributed about 6,500 hymns to the cause!), who, in 1729, while student and Greek lecturer at Oxford, began at Christ Church a "Holy Club" of pious fellow students. "The exact regularity of their lives," Wesley wrote afterward, "as well as their studies, occasioned a young gentleman of Christ-Church to say, 'Here is a new set of Methodists sprung up,' alluding to some ancient physicians who were so-called [from the methodical manner of their lives]. The name was new and quaint; so it took immediately, and Methodists were known all over the University." After a brief sojourn in Georgia (1735-36) and a series of inward religious experiences not unlike those of Martin Luther two centuries before, Wesley formed his first Methodist "Society" in London, May 1, 1738. "We see on every side," wrote Wesley, "either men of no religion at all, or men of a lifeless, formal religion. We are grieved at the sight, and should greatly rejoice if by any means we might convince some that there is a better religion to be attained . . . a religion of love, joy, and peace, having its seat in the heart, in the inmost soul . . . spreading virtue and happiness all around it." Wesley was a forceful preacher, a splendid writer, and a brilliant organizer, and soon Methodist Societies grew up all over the British Isles. The movement began strictly *within* the Church of England; but in time Wesley ran afoul the English bishops for the use of his own version of the Psalms and the like without Anglican approval and for "ordination" of ministers without episcopal authority. As a consequence, Methodists joined the ranks of "dissenting" English sects. There was nothing new in Methodism except the great zeal of its founders and the enthusiasm of their converts. It was a revival of personal religion "to spread Scriptural holiness over the land." As such it gained considerable support, especially from the lower classes, and, though it has divided into several separate groups, Wesleyanism remains today an important Protestant sect. The following selection gives Wesley's definition of his movement.

From WESLEY, "The Character of a Methodist" (c. 1750) [1]

The distinguishing marks of a Methodist are not his opinions of any sort. . . . We believe, indeed, that all Scripture is given by the inspiration of God, and herein we are distinguished from Jews, Turks, and Infidels. We believe the written word of God to be the only and sufficient rule, both of Christian faith and practice; and herein we are fundamentally distinguished from those of the Romish church. We believe Christ to be the eternal, supreme God; and herein we are distinguished from the Socinians and Arians. But as to all opinions which do not strike at the root of Christianity, we think and let think. So that whatsoever they are, whether right or wrong, they are no distinguishing marks of a Methodist.

Neither are words or phrases of any sort. We do not place our Religion . . . in being attached to any peculiar mode of speaking, any quaint or uncommon set of expressions [as the Quakers used]. . . .

Nor do we desire to be distinguished by *actions, customs,* or *usages,* of an *indifferent* nature. Our Religion . . . does not lie in the form of our apparel, in the posture of our body, or the covering of our heads; nor yet abstaining from marriage, nor from meats and drinks, which are good if received with thanksgiving. . . .

"What then is the *mark?* Who is a *Methodist* according to your own account?" I answer: A Methodist is one who has "the love of God shed abroad in his heart by the Holy Ghost given unto him." One who "loves the Lord his God with all his heart, and with all his soul, and with all his mind, and with all his strength." God is the joy of his heart, and the desire of his soul. . . . He is therefore happy in God, yea always happy, as having in him "a well of water springing up into everlasting life, and overflowing his soul with peace and joy." . . . Yea, this his joy is full, and all his bones cry out, "Blessed be the God and Father of our Lord Jesus Christ, who, according to his abundant mercy hath begotten me again to a living hope, of an inheritance incorruptible, undefiled, and that fadeth not away, reserved in heaven for me."

And he who hath this *hope,* thus full of *immortality,* in *every thing gives thanks:* as knowing that *this* (whatsoever it is) *is the will of God in Christ Jesus concerning him.* From him therefore he *cheerfully* receives all, saying "Good is the will of the Lord!" and whether the Lord giveth or taketh away, equally "blessing the Name of the Lord." . . . He prays "without ceasing." It is given him "always to pray, and not to faint." . . . And while he thus always exercises his love to God, by praying without ceasing, rejoicing evermore, and in every thing giving thanks, this commandment is written in his heart, that he who loveth God, love his brother also. And he accordingly loves his

[1] *The Works of the Rev. John Wesley,* 17 vols., London, 1809-13. VI, 392-400.

neighbour as himself; he loves every man as his own soul. . . . All the commandments of God he accordingly keeps, and that with all his might. For his obedience is in proportion to his love, the source from whence it flows. . . . He continually presents his soul and body a living sacrifice, holy, acceptable to God; entirely and without reserve, devoting himself, all he has, and all he is, to his glory. . . .

These are the *principles* and *practices* of our *sect;* these are the *marks* of a true Methodist. By these alone do those who, in derision so-called, desire to be distinguished from other men. If any man say, "Why, these are only the common, fundamental principles of Christianity!" *Thou hast said* [it]; So I mean. This is the very truth; I know they are no other; and I would to God both thou and all men knew, that I, and all who follow my judgment, do vehemently refuse to be distinguished from other men by any but the common principles of Christianity. The plain, old Christianity that I teach, renouncing and detesting all other marks of distinction. . . . By these *marks,* by these fruits of a living faith, do we labour to distinguish ourselves from the unbelieving world, from all those whose minds or lives are not according to the gospel of Christ. But from real Christians, of whatsoever denomination they be, we earnestly desire not to be distinguished at all.

22
THE FRENCH REVOLUTION

1. Some Aspects of the Old Regime: French Society

If the immediate circumstance which led to the French Revolution was the impending bankruptcy of the Bourbon monarchy, the remote causes of the upheaval were the inequalities, injustices, and inefficiencies resulting from the Old Regime in France. The "Old Regime" is a term employed to describe the forms of society, the institutions, and the practices of eighteenth-century Europe, many of which had been centuries in the making. Most of the evils of the Old Regime were the products of inertia, of the failure of governments and of social systems to cast off vestigial remains of feudal institutions and practices as they assumed both the centralized administration of modern national states and the commercial and industrial aspects of modern societies. The evils of the Old Regime pervaded every corner of Europe. It was against evils of the Old Regime that the *philosophes* declaimed (see pages 337-349), and both they and their contemporaries, the "Enlightened Despots" (pages 288-294), endeavored to eradicate some of the obvious defects in eighteenth-century European government and society. Taken altogether, however, they accomplished little more than to set forth a program of reform—a program which was scarcely undertaken in France until the accession of Louis XVI in 1774, and then with such vacillation and indecision that revolution overtook the bewildered Bourbons before anything of consequence had been accomplished.

Many volumes have been written to describe the complicated nature of society and government during the Old Regime. Necessarily, therefore, the materials below are illustrative of only selected aspects of the Old Regime in France, namely, of the structure and condition of society; of governmental administration, of the royal family, and of the financial difficulties of the Bourbon government.

THE FIRST ESTATE: A HOUSE DIVIDED

The French clergy, the first estate, were sharply divided in sentiment at the outbreak of the Revolution. The upper clergy—archbishops, bishops, vicar-generals, canons, abbots, and so on—consisted mostly of nobles and their relatives and retainers, totaling about 10,000, and they held a lion's share of the vast income of the church; whereas the lower clergy—the parish priests, monks, and nuns, numbering, in all, about 120,000—were drawn largely from the third estate and eked out a bare existence. A recent writer has commented on this division and its effects.

From MONTAGUE, "The Government of France" (1904) [1]

In judging the character of the French priesthood during the eighteenth century, we must distinguish between the higher and the lower ranks. . . . The superior clergy, taken in the gross, were courtiers and men of the world. Some notoriously disbelieved the religion which they were supposed to teach; and some were disso-

[1] F. C. Montague, "The Government of France," in *The Cambridge Modern History*, 13 vols., 1934, VIII, 55-56 (Cambridge University Press). By permission of The Macmillan Company.

lute in their conduct. Yet the majority, even under Louis XV, observed outward decorum; and here and there was to be found a prelate of sterling piety and benevolence. . . .

The inferior clergy offered a glaring contrast to their chiefs. Drawn mostly from a humble middle class, or even from the peasantry, since their office had so few worldly allurements, and condemned to poverty and a monotonous routine, they were rarely men of wide culture or polished manners; but they were usually regular and edifying in their lives. In spite of occasional scandals, such as will occur in every large body of professional men, the parish priests appear to have generally deserved and enjoyed the goodwill of their flocks. They felt for the people from whom they sprang and amid whom they laboured; and they often entertained democratic opinions. They had indeed their own grievances, and they might be pardoned if they felt some bitterness in reflecting on what stamp of divine the richest preferments of the Church were so often lavished. Many of them regarded their Bishop as the common soldier regarded his noble colonel, and as the peasant regarded the lord of the manor. The abuses of the French system tended to alienate those whom both duty and interest should have drawn together; and the privileged orders, a mere handful among discontented millions, were themselves rent into hostile factions. In the first stage of the Revolution, the sympathy of the parish priests ensured the victory of the Third Estate over the nobles and the prelates.

A PRIVILEGE OF THE SECOND ESTATE: "CAPITAINERIES"

Among the privileges of the nobility were their hunting rights, a source of much loss to the peasantry of France.

Arthur Young, an English agricultural expert who traveled widely in France in the years 1787, 1788, and 1789 to observe the methods and the state of agriculture, commented severely upon the effects of these privileges.

From YOUNG, *Travels in France* (1792) [1]

The *Capitaineries* were a dreadful scourge on all the occupiers of land. By this term is to be understood the paramountship of certain districts, granted by the king to princes of the blood by which they were put in possession of the property of all game, even on lands not belonging to them; and, what is very singular, on manors granted long before to individuals; so that the erecting of a district into a *capitainerie*, was an annihilation of all manorial rights to game within it. This was a trifling business in comparison to other circumstances; for, in speaking of the preservation of the game in these *capitaineries*, it must be observed that by game it must be understood whole droves of wild boars and herds of deer not confined by any wall or pale, but wandering at pleasure over the whole country to the destruction of crops, and to the peopling of the gallies by the wretched peasants who presumed to kill them in order to save that food which was to support their helpless children. The game in the *capitainerie* of Montceau, in four parishes only, did mischief to the amount of 184,263 liv. per annum. No wonder then that we should find the people asking, "We loudly demand the destruction of the *capitaineries* and of all sorts of game." And what are we to think of demanding, as a favour, the permission "to harvest their grain, to mow their meadows, and to remove the stubble without regard to partridges and other game." Now, an English reader will scarcely understand it without being told that there were numerous edicts for preserving game which prohibited weeding and hoeing, lest the young partridges should be disturbed; steeping seed, lest it injure the game; manuring with night soil, lest the flavour of the partridges should be injured by feeding on the corn so produced; mowing hay, &c., before a certain time, so late as to spoil many crops; and taking away the stubble, which would deprive the birds of shelter. The tyranny exercised in these *capitaineries*, which extended over 400 leagues of country, was so great that many *cahiers* demanded the utter suppression of them.

THE THIRD ESTATE

In 1788, Emmanuel Joseph Sieyès (1748-1836), better known as the Abbé Sieyès, wrote a pamphlet, *Qu'est-ce que le Tiers Etat?* (*What Is the Third Estate?*). He began his reply with these words: "Everything. What has it been hitherto in the political order? Nothing. What does it desire? To be something." The pamphlet was widely read, and its author was elected (1789) to the Estates General, where he took a prominent part in the early phase of the French Revolution. As the revolution became more radical, Sieyès dropped from public view (1790), but he reappeared as a Director in 1799, and as architect of the coup d'état of 1799 which overthrew the Directory and elevated Napoleon as First Consul. Representative selections from his book follow.

From SIEYÈS, *What Is the Third Estate?* (1788) [2]

What is necessary that a nation should subsist and prosper? Individual effort and public functions.

[1] *Arthur Young's Travels in France during the Years 1787, 1788, 1789,* ed. by M. Betham-Edwards, London, 1909, 316-17. By permission of G. Bell and Sons, Ltd., Publishers.

[2] *Qu'est-ce que le Tiers Etat?* Paris, 1839, 33-41.

All individual effort can be embraced in four classes: 1. As the earth and the waters supply crude products for the needs of man, the first class, in logical sequence, will be that of all families who devote themselves to agricultural labor. 2. Between the first sale of products and their consumption or use, new processes, more or less repeated . . . perfect the gifts of nature. . . . Such are the efforts of the second class. 3. Between production and consumption, as well as among the various stages of production, a group of intermediary agents . . . merchants and brokers . . . are charged with distribution, in final analysis, either at wholesale or retail. This species of utility characterizes the third class. 4. Outside these three classes of productive and useful citizens . . . there is also need in society of a series of efforts and pains whose objects are directly useful or agreeable to the individual. This fourth class embraces all those who stand between the most distinguished and liberal professions and the less esteemed services of domestics.

Such are the efforts which sustain society. Who puts them forth? The Third Estate.

Public functions may be classified equally well, in the present state of affairs, under four recognized heads: the sword, the robe, the church, and the administration. It would be superfluous to consider them one by one for the purpose of showing that everywhere the Third Estate attends to nineteen-twentieths of them, with this exception: that it is laden with all that is really painful, with all the burdens which the privileged classes refuse to carry. . . .

It is sufficient to have made clear that a privileged order's pretended utility for public service is nothing more than a chimera; that with it all that is burdensome in this service is performed by the Third Estate; that without it the superior places would be infinitely better filled; that they naturally ought to be the lot and the recompense of ability and recognized service; and that if privileged persons have come to usurp all the lucrative and honorable posts, it is a hateful injustice to the rank and file of citizens and at the same time a treason to the public weal.

Who then shall dare to say that the Third Estate has not within itself all that is necessary for the formation of a complete nation? . . . If the privileged order should be abolished, the nation would be nothing less, but something more. Therefore, what is the Third Estate? Everything. But an everything shackled and oppressed. What would it be without the privileged order? Everything. But an everything free and flourishing. Nothing can succeed without it; everything would be infinitely better without the others. . . .

[The author goes on to argue that the nobility is not only of no utility but also that, by its indolence, this class is estranged from the nation. He continues:]

What is a nation? A body of associates, living under a common law, and represented by the same legislature, and so on.

Is it not evident that the noble order has privileges and expenditures which it dares to call its rights, but which are separate from the rights of the great mass of citizens? It departs there from the common order, from the common law. So its civil rights make it an isolated people in the midst of the great nation. This is truly *imperium in imperio* [a state within the state]. . . .

The Third Estate embraces, then, all that belongs to the nation; and all that which is not of the Third Estate cannot be regarded as being of the nation. What is the Third Estate? It is the whole.

THE BOURGEOISIE

Among the various groups of which the Third Estate was constituted—bourgeoisie, peasants, artisans, laborers—the bourgeoisie was rising rapidly in importance. Of them a contemporary nobleman, cousin of Lafayette, wrote as follows.

From BOUILLÉ, *Memoirs* (1801) [1]

That which the clergy and the nobility had lost in consideration, in riches, and in power, had been acquired by the third estate since the reign of Henry IV and since the last meeting of the States-General in 1614. France had founded colonies in America; she had established a maritime commerce; she had created manufactures; she had, so to say, rendered all Europe and part of the world tributary to her industry. The immense riches brought to the kingdom were distributed only to the plebeians, the prejudices of the nobles excluding them from commerce and from all the mechanical and liberal arts. Even this increase in wealth, in augmenting the currency, had contributed to their impoverishment, and that of proprietors in general. But the cities were considerably enlarged; commercial centers were established, such as Lyon, Nantes, Bordeaux, and Marseille, becoming as important and as rich as the capitals of some neighboring states. Paris had increased in a terrific manner. . . . All the little provincial towns had become more or less commercial; almost all had manufactures of some particular commercial product. All were peopled with *petits bourgeois,* who were richer and more industrious than the nobles, and who had found the way, themselves or their fathers, to enrich themselves in the administration or in the leasing of the fiefs and lands of the great lords and nobles, or even in their service. . . . They had received, in general, an education which had become more necessary to them than to the nobles, of which some, by their birth and by their wealth, obtained the leading places in the state without merit and without talents. . . . Thus at Paris and in the large cities the bourgeoisie was superior in riches, in talents, and in personal merit. In the provincial towns it had the same superiority over the country nobility; it felt this superiority and yet was humiliated everywhere; it found itself excluded by the military regulations from places in the army; it was, in some manner, from the higher clergy. . . . The high magistracy rejected it likewise, and most of the sovereign courts admitted only nobles to their company.

THE PEASANTRY

Of the French peasantry, Arthur Young, the English agricultural expert who traveled widely in France, gave many vivid descriptions.

From YOUNG, *Travels in France* [2]

[In western France, June, 1787.] All the country, girls and women, are without shoes or stockings; and the ploughmen at their work have neither sabots nor feet to their stockings. This is a poverty that strikes at the root of national prosperity; a large consumption among the poor being of more consequence than among the rich: the wealth of a nation lies in its circulation and consumption; and the case of poor people abstaining from the use of manufactures of leather and wool ought to be considered as an evil of the first magnitude. It reminded me of the misery of Ireland. . . .

[1] François-Claude-Amour, Marquis de Bouillé, *Mémoires,* Paris, 1822, 52-54, as trans. in E. L. Higgins, in *The French Revolution as Told by Contemporaries,* Boston, 1938, 23. By permission of Houghton Mifflin Company.

[2] Arthur Young, *Travels during the Years 1787, 1788, and 1789,* 2 vols., Dublin, 1793, I, 37-38, 176-77, 280-81.

[In Brittany, September, 1788.] The poor people seem poor indeed; the children terribly ragged, if possible worse clad than if with no clothes at all; as to shoes and stockings, they are luxuries. A beautiful girl of six or seven years playing with a stick, and smiling under such a bundle of rags as made my heart ache to see her: they did not beg, and when I gave them any thing seemed more surprized than obliged. One third of what I have seen of this province seems uncultivated, and nearly all of it in misery. What have kings, ministers, and parliaments, and states, to answer for their prejudices, seeing millions of hands that would be industrious, idle and starving, through the execrable maxims of despotism, or the equally detestable prejudices of a feudal nobility. . . .

[In northern France (Champagne), July, 1789.] Walking up a long hill to ease my mare, I was joined by a poor woman who complained of the times, and that it was a sad country; demanding her reasons, she said her husband had but a morsel of land, one cow, and a poor little horse, yet they had a *franchar* (42 lbs.) of wheat, and three chickens, to pay as a quit-rent to one Seigneur; and four *franchar* of oats, one chicken, and 1 sou to pay to another, besides very heavy tailles and other taxes. She had seven children, and the cow's milk helped to make the soup. But why, instead of a horse, do not you keep another cow? Oh, her husband could not carry his produce so well without a horse; and asses are little used in the country. It was said, at present, that *something was to be done by some great folks for such poor ones, but she did not know who nor how,* but God send us better, *for the tailles and the dues are crushing us.* This woman, at no great distance, might have been taken for sixty or seventy, her figure was so bent, and her face so furrowed and hardened by labour—but she said she was only twenty-eight. . . . The country-women of France . . . work harder than the men, and this, united with the more miserable labour of bringing a new race of slaves into the world, destroys absolutely all symmetry of person and every feminine appearance.

2. Some Aspects of the Old Regime: French Government

CONSTITUTIONAL SHORTCOMINGS

The French monarchy suffered gravely from the want of constitutional definition. As it had grown into a national state with increasing centralization, there had arisen new administrative officials—such as the intendants [see pages 241-243]—while the administrative agents of former times were only partially displaced. As older instruments challenged the authority of the newer ones (and vice versa), uncertainties of constitutional authority arose, creating administrative confusion, delay, unnecessary expense, and opportunities for petty tyranny—the inevitable results of a multiplicity of authorities with overlapping and ill-defined jurisdictions. In her posthumous work, *Considerations on the Principal Events of the French Revolution,* Madame de Staël (1766-1817), daughter of the Finance Minister, Necker, commented on this constitutional melee.

From MME. DE STAËL, *Considerations* (*c.* 1790) [1]

Of all the monarchies of modern times, France certainly has been the most arbitrary and unsettled in its political institutions. Perhaps the successive additions of provinces to the crown is one cause of this.

---

[1] *Considérations sur les principaux événemens de la Révolution Française,* ed. by M. le Duc de Broglie and M. le Baron de Staël, 3 vols. Paris, 1818, I, 129-32, 141, 142.

Each of the provinces brought with it its own customs and peculiar claims; the government cleverly played off old provinces against new ones, and the country was only gradually unified.

Whatever may have been the reason, there is no law, however fundamental, which has not been questioned at some time or other. There is nothing which has not been challenged. Were the kings the lawmakers of the realm, or no? And might they raise taxes of their own free will, or no? Or were the Estates General, as representatives of the people, solely invested with the taxing power? And how should the Estates General be composed? Should the privileged orders, who had two votes out of three, be considered as separate nations who vote their taxes separately, and might thereby vote none—thus requiring the common people to bear all the burden of necessary taxes? What were the privileges of the clergy, who sometimes claimed to be independent of the king, sometimes of the Pope? What were the powers of the nobles who sometimes, as during the minority of Louis XIV, believed themselves entitled to reclaim their rights by force of arms and by alliances with foreign powers [during the Fronde], and, at other times, acknowledged the king as an absolute monarch? What should be the status of the third estate, emancipated by the kings, admitted to the Estates General by Philip the Fair, and yet condemned to be always in the minority, inasmuch as it was granted only one vote out of three . . . ?

What ought to be the proper political power of the *parlements,* which now declared themselves to be the courts of justice and again called themselves the Estates General in miniature—as representatives of the representatives of the people? These same *parlements* did not acknowledge the jurisdiction of the intendants, administrators of provinces in the name of the king. . . .

The history of France would furnish us a mass of other examples of this lack of fixity, both in the smallest and in the most important affairs; but it will suffice to cite some of the deplorable results of this absence of fixed rules. Individuals accused of state offenses have almost always been deprived of their natural judges; and many of them have passed their entire lives in prison, where the government had sent them on its own authority without trial. The code of terror against Protestants, cruel punishments, and torture of various kinds existed up to the Revolution. . . .

Imprisonment or exile has become the fate of all who would dispute the power of the kings; and the despotism of ministers—the habitual tools of the throne—has been made complete by the inconceivable maxim, "If it pleases the king, it is according to law," as the unique political institution of France. . . .

The Estates General has been convoked only eighteen times between 1302 and 1789, that is, during almost five centuries, and this despite the fact that the Estates General ought to have the sole right to levy taxes . . . but the kings have often disputed this as their prerogative, and have taxed arbitrarily. . . . France has been governed by customs, often by caprice, and never by the laws.

ADMINISTRATIVE DEFECTS

French constitutional inconsistencies might have been of little moment had the central government, especially the royal council, adhered to consistent policies. But vacillation appeared to be the only constant in the royal government. Alexis de Tocqueville (1805-1859), in his brilliant analysis, *The Old Regime and the Revolution,* discussed these de-

fects and clearly pointed out their inevitable results.

From TOCQUEVILLE, *The Old Regime* (1856) [1]

It [the central government of France]
seldom undertook, or soon abandoned
projects of useful reform which demanded
perseverance and energy, but it was incessantly engaged in altering the laws.
Repose was never known in its domain.
New rules followed each other with such
bewildering rapidity that its agents never
knew which to obey of the multifarious
commands they received. Municipal officers complained to the comptroller-general
of the extreme instability of minor laws.
"The financial regulations alone," say
they, "vary so constantly that it would
require the whole time of a municipal
officer, holding office for life, to acquire
a knowledge of the new regulations as
they appear from time to time."

When the substance of the laws was
allowed to remain the same, their execution varied. Those who have not studied
the actual working of the old régime in
the official records it left behind can form
no idea of the contempt into which the
laws fall, even in the minds of their administrators, when there are no political
meetings or newspapers to check the capricious activity and set bounds to the
arbitrary tendencies of government officials. . . .

Complaints are heard that Frenchmen
show contempt for law. Alas! when could
they have learned to respect it? It may be
broadly said that, among the men of the
old régime, the place in the mind which
should have been occupied by the idea of
law was vacant. Petitioners begged that
established rules might be departed from
in their case as seriously and as earnestly

as if they had been insisting on the honest
execution of the law; nor were they ever
referred to the law unless government
intended to give them a rebuff. Custom,
rather than volition, still inculcated submission to authority on the part of the
people; but whenever they did break
loose, the least excitement gave rise to
violent acts, which were themselves met,
not by the law, but by violence on the
other side, and arbitrary stretches of
power.

Though the central power had not acquired in the eighteenth century the
strong and healthy constitution it has since
possessed, it had, notwithstanding, so
thoroughly destroyed all intermediate authorities, and left so wide a vacant space
between itself and the public, that it
already appeared to be the mainspring of
the social machine, the sole source of
national life.

Nothing proves this more thoroughly
than the writings of its assailants. During
the period of uneasiness which preceded
the Revolution, a host of schemes for new
forms of society and government were
brought to light. These schemes sought
various ends, but the means by which they
were to be reached were invariably identical. All the schemers wanted to use the
central power for the destruction of the
existing system, and the substitution of
their new plan in its stead: that power
alone seemed to them capable of accomplishing so great a task. They all assumed
that the rights and powers of the state
ought to be unlimited, and that the only
thing needed was to persuade it to use
them aright. . . .

Nobody expected to succeed in any
enterprise unless the state helped him.
Farmers, who, as a class, are generally
stubborn and indocile, were led to believe
that the backwardness of agriculture was
due to the lack of advice and aid from
the government. . . .

[1] Alexis de Tocqueville, *The Old Régime and
the Revolution,* trans. by John Bonner, New York,
1856, 88-89, 90-93.

The masses were quite satisfied that the government alone could preserve the public peace. The mounted police alone commanded the respect of the rich, and inspired terror among the people. Both viewed that force rather as the incarnation of public order than as one of its chief instruments. . . .

Government having assumed the place of Providence, people naturally invoked its aid for their private wants. Heaps of petitions were received from persons who wanted their petty private ends served, always for the public good.

THE ROYAL FAMILY: THE KING

Madame Roland (1754-1793), Girondist apologist, wrote the following account of Louis XVI.

From MME. ROLAND, *Appeal to Posterity* (1793) [1]

This man was not precisely what he was depicted by those who took a pleasure in vilifying him. He was neither the brutish blockhead, who was held up to the contempt of the people, nor was he the honest, kind, and sensible creature whom his friends extolled to the skies. Nature had endowed him with ordinary faculties, which would have done well in an obscure station; but he was depraved by his princely education and ruined by his mediocrity in difficult times, when his safety could be effected only by the union of genius and virtue. A common understanding, educated for the throne, and taught dissimulation from earliest infancy, has a great advantage in dealing with mankind. The art of showing to each person only what is proper for him to see is, *in him*, no more than a habit, the practice of which gives him the appearance of ability; but a man must be born an idiot to appear a fool in similar circumstances. Louis XVI had, besides, an excellent memory and an active turn of mind; was never idle, and read a great deal. He had also a ready recollection of the various treaties existing between France and the neighbouring nations; was well versed in history, and was the best geographer in the kingdom. His knowledge of the names, and his application of them to the faces, of all the persons about the court to whom they belonged, as well as his acquaintance with the anecdotes peculiar to each, had been extended to all the individuals who had distinguished themselves in any manner during the revolution; so that it was impossible to present to him a candidate for any place, concerning whom he had not formed an opinion founded on particular facts. But Louis XVI, without elevation of soul, energy of mind, or firmness of character, had suffered his views to be still further contracted, and his sentiments to be twisted, if I may use the expression, by religious prejudices and jesuitical principles. . . . If he had been born two centuries before, and his wife had been a rational woman, he would have made no more noise in the world than so many other princes of the Capetian line who have "fretted their hour upon the stage" without doing either much good or much harm.

THE ROYAL FAMILY: THE QUEEN

From MME. DE STAËL, *Considerations* [2]

The Queen of France, Marie Antoinette, was one of the most amiable and gracious persons who had been seen on the throne. Nothing prevented her from keeping the

---

[1] *An Appeal to Impartial Posterity, by Citizeness Roland, trans. from the French*, London, 1795, Pt. II, 8-10.

[2] *Considérations sur les principaux événemens de la Révolution Française*, I, 46.

love of the French, because she had done nothing to lose it. The personal characters of the Queen and the King were entirely worthy of attachment; but the arbitrary nature of the French government, as the centuries had made it, accorded so badly with the spirit of the times that even the virtues of princes disappeared in the vast ensemble of abuses with which they were encompassed. When people feel the need of political reform, the private qualities of the monarch do not suffice to arrest the force of this impulsion. An unhappy chance placed the reign of Louis XVI in an era when great talents and high aspirations were essential to struggle with the spirit of the century, or to make—which might have been better—a reasonable compromise with that spirit.

[A Swiss officer at the court of Louis XVI, Baron Pierre-Victor de Besenval de Bronstadt (1722-1791), gave a less favorable picture of the Queen.]

From BESENVAL, *Memoirs* (c. 1785) [1]

The Queen is far from lacking spirit, but her education, as far as instruction is concerned, has been neglected. Except novels, she has never opened a book, and has not even sought the ideas that society can give; as soon as conversation takes a serious turn, a look of boredom comes over her face and chills the atmosphere. Her conversation is desultory, constantly shifting from subject to subject. Without spontaneous gaiety, she amuses herself with the day's gossip, with little liberties cleverly toned down, and, above all, with the scandal of the court; that is what pleases her. Approachable, not hard to please, but without depth of feeling, she knew nothing of friendship.

[1] Besenval, *Mémoires,* 4 vols. Paris, 1805-06, III, 332-33.

FINANCIAL TROUBLES

The financial disorders prevalent at the end of Louis XIV's reign [see pages 268-270] were not corrected in the years that followed. Indeed, the debts grew so large and the taxes so inadequate, despite their oppressive inequalities, that Louis XVI, when he ascended the throne in 1774, immediately undertook financial reforms. His appointment of Anne Robert Jacques Turgot (1727-1781) as comptroller general in 1774 aroused great hopes, because Turgot had already served as intendant of Limoges (1761-1774), where he had made an enviable record. Turgot's policies as comptroller general were admirably summed up in a letter to the King.

From TURGOT, Letter to Louis XVI
(August 24, 1774) [2]

Sire, Having just come from the private interview with which your Majesty has honoured me, still full of the anxiety produced by the immensity of the duties now imposed upon me, agitated by all the feelings excited by the touching kindness with which you have encouraged me, I hasten to convey to you my respectful gratitude and the devotion of my whole life.

Your Majesty has been good enough to permit me to place on record the engagement you have taken upon you to sustain me in the execution of those plans of economy which are at all times, and today more than ever, of an indispensable necessity. I would have desired the opportunity of developing to you the reflections suggested to me by the present position of finances; but time does not permit. . . .

[2] W. Walker Stephens, *The Life and Writings of Turgot,* London, 1895, 85-89. By permission of Longmans, Green and Company, Inc.

At this moment, Sire, I confine myself to recall to you these three policies:

No Bankruptcy.

No Increase of Taxes.

No Loans.

No *bankruptcy,* either avowed or disguised by illegal reductions.

No *increase of taxes;* the reason for this being in the condition of your people, and, still more, in that of your Majesty's own generous heart.

No *loans;* because every loan diminishes always the free revenue and necessitates, at the end of a certain time, either bankruptcy or the increase of taxes. In times of peace it is permissible to borrow only in order to liquidate old debts, or in order to redeem other loans contracted on less advantageous terms.

To meet these three points there is but one means. It is to reduce expenditure below revenue, and sufficiently below it to insure each year a saving of twenty millions, to be applied in redemption of the old debts. Without that, the first gunshot will force the State to bankruptcy. . . .

[Turgot urged the King to reduce his financial favors to courtiers, to cut down concessions and profits to tax farmers and other financiers.]

It may reasonably be hoped by the improvement of cultivation, by the suppression of abuses in the collection of the taxes, and by their more equitable assessment, that a substantial relief of the people can be attained without diminishing greatly the public revenue; but without economy being the first step all reforms are impossible. . . .

I foresee that I shall be alone in fighting against abuses of every kind, against the power of those who profit by these abuses, against the crowd of prejudiced people who oppose themselves to all reform, and who are such powerful instruments in the hands of interested parties for perpetuating the disorder. I shall have to struggle even against the natural goodness and generosity of your Majesty, and of the persons who are most dear to you. I shall be feared, hated even, by nearly all the court, by all who solicit favours. . . .

Your Majesty will remember that it is upon the faith of your promises made to me that I charge myself with a burden perhaps beyond my strength, and it is to yourself personally, to the honest man, the just and good man, rather than to the King, that I give myself.

[Turgot did not overestimate the power of his enemies. Within two years, pressures upon the King, applied by the Queen and others, led to his dismissal, and he retired with prophetic words of warning: "Never forget, Sire, that it was weakness which brought the head of Charles I to the block." After a few months, Louis XVI called upon Necker, the Genevese financier, to take charge of finances (1776-81). Within five years, Necker was attempting vainly to defend himself against his foes by publishing the *Compte rendu au roi* (1781), a work which first showed the French public the enormous sums paid yearly as pensions and gifts to courtiers. But the entrenched forces were too great for him. His fall is related by his daughter, Madame de Staël, as follows.]

From MME. DE STAËL, *Considerations* [1]

The second-class courtiers declared against M. Necker. The great lords, having no fears as to their positions or their fortunes, were in general more independent in their views than that obscure swarm that holds to favor in order to obtain

[1] *Considérations sur les principaux événemens de la Révolution Française,* I, 90-101.

some new gift on each new opportunity. M. Necker made some retrenchments in the King's household, in the sums allotted to pensions, in financial charges, and in the gratuities accorded to people of the court on these charges. This economic system was not at all acceptable to all those who had formed the habit of being paid by the government, and of practicing the trade of solicitation as a means of livelihood. . . .

But the partisans of the princes and the financiers were violently against him. A memoir which he sent to the King about the establishment of provincial assemblies had been indiscreetly published, and the *parlements* had noted that he gave as one reason for this institution the weight of public opinion which it might lend against the *parlements* themselves if the latter acted as ambitious corporations and not according to national views. This was enough to lead these magistrates, jealous of a political authority already contested, to call M. Necker an innovator. But, of all the innovations, that which the courtiers and the financiers detested most was economy. . . .

M. de Maurepas caused it to be secretly circulated that it would please the King to attack his Minister. . . . M. Necker was content to require a sign of royal favor to discourage his libelers. He desired that they be removed from the household of Monseigneur le Comte d'Artois in which they held posts, and that he be granted an entree to the council of state from which he had been removed on the pretext that he was a Protestant. . . .

M. Necker offered his resignation if the conditions asked were not granted. M. de Maurepas, who had urged him to take this step, foresaw with certainty the result. . . .

The next day M. Necker returned from Versailles, having ceased to be a Minister.

INFLUENCES OF THE AMERICAN REVOLUTION

"The American Revolution has laid the foundations of another in France," said Arthur Young, "if government does not take care of itself." To avenge herself against the English, France had spent more than a billion livres which she could ill afford; and, of even greater import, thousands of Frenchmen imbibed the spirit of American democratic thought. The selection which follows presents the views of Joseph Weber, foster brother of Marie Antoinette, on the effects of the American Revolution upon France.

From WEBER, *Memoirs* (1822) [1]

That republic [the United States] was formed by the subjects of one king who had been aided in their revolt by another king. . . . All those warriors in the prime of life who had run to fight in the New World had departed Frenchmen and returned Americans. They had sought only perils and military glory; they brought back systems and patriotic enthusiasm. They returned to the midst of a court, bearing on their breasts wounds sustained in the cause of liberty, and on their coats were the external signs of a republican decoration. Lafayette, who had made himself an ally of the Americans before his King did, and who with the ardor and prodigality of all strong passions, but with a secretiveness and perseverance incomprehensible at his age, had armed a vessel for the American cause, had loaded it with munitions of all kinds to the value of nearly a million, and had stolen away from his family to sail without anyone having discovered his secret; Lafayette, who had commanded an army of insurg-

[1] *Mémoires de Weber, concernant Marie-Antoinette,* 2 vols. Paris, 1822, I, 128-29.

ents, who had conquered with them, whom the United States had adopted as a citizen, and whom Washington for six years had called his son; Lafayette returned to his native land full of a burning desire and of vain illusions of an exotic liberty which, transplanted to France, would produce there fruits so different from those which he expected. He had, it was said, in his back cabinet at Paris a cardboard mounted in a brilliant frame and divided into two columns: in one could be read the *Declaration of Rights* proclaimed by the Anglo-Americans; the other was blank, and appeared to await the same declaration by the French. His own rapture was even less astonishing than that which it excited. The monarchy had neither enough cheers to celebrate nor enough favors to repay this young champion of *la liberté républicaine.*

THE GATHERING CLOUDS OF REVOLUTION IN FRANCE

Necker's immediate successors, Charles Alexandre de Calonne (1783-87) and Etienne Charles Loménie de Brienne (1787), exhausted the credit of the French government. Only reform of the entire system of administration and taxation, with removal of the tax exemptions enjoyed by the privileged classes, could avert bankruptcy. But recommendations to these ends met with the firm opposition of the *parlement* of Paris which, refusing to register royal edicts for tax reform, declared: "The nation alone, in Estates General assembled, can give the necessary consent to a permanent tax [on the privileged classes]." Thus, with the cry of "Taxation without representation is tyranny," the privileged classes sought to defend their privileges. Arthur Young, after a dinner on October 17, 1787, with a party "whose conversation was entirely politi-

cal," made the following observations in his diary.

From YOUNG, *Travels in France* [1]

One opinion pervaded the whole company, that they are on the eve of some great revolution in the government: that everything points to it: the confusion in the finances great; with a *deficit* impossible to provide for without the states-general of the kingdom, yet no ideas formed of what would be the consequence of their meeting; no minister existing, or to be looked to in or out of power, with such decisive talents as to promise any other remedy than palliative ones: a prince on the throne, with excellent dispositions, but without resources of a mind that could govern in such a moment without ministers: a court buried in pleasure and dissipation; and adding to the distress, instead of endeavouring to be placed in a more independent situation: a great ferment amongst all ranks of men, who are eager for some change without knowing what to look to or to hope for: and a strong leaven of liberty, increasing every hour since the American revolution; altogether form a combination of circumstances that promise e'er long to ferment into motion if some master hand of very superior talents and inflexible courage is not found at the helm to guide events, instead of being driven by them. It is very remarkable that such conversation never occurs but a bankruptcy is a topic: the curious question on which is, *would a bankruptcy occasion a civil war, and a total overthrow of the government?* The answers that I have received to this question appear to be just: such a measure conducted by a man of abilities, vigour, and firmness, would certainly not occasion either one or the other. But the same measure, attempted by a man of a different character,

[1] Young, *Travels,* I, 136-38.

might possibly do both. All agree that the states of the kingdom cannot assemble without more liberty being the consequence; but I meet with so few men that have any just ideas of freedom, that I question much the species of this new liberty that is to arise.

3. The First Phase of Revolution: Reforms of the Constitutional Monarchy

SPECIFIC REFORMS DEMANDED

From the convocation of the Estates General (August, 1788) until proclamation of the first French Republic (September, 1792), the most basic reforms of the revolution were effected. A group of "Patriots" persuaded the King to permit the Third Estate a "double" representation, that is, as many representatives as the other two orders combined. During the hard winter, 1788-89, elections were held and, in accordance with ancient custom, the voters drew up *cahiers,* or lists of grievances and instructions for their Deputies. Some eight hundred of these *cahiers* are still extant, and they constitute one of the best expressions of the French people's desires on the eve of revolution. Extracts *"Of the grievances, complaints and remonstrances of the members of the third estate of the bailliage of Versailles"* illustrate the nature and contents of the *cahiers* as a whole. Significantly, as the *cahiers* almost universally demanded that France be reconstructed as a constitutional monarchy, the following document is divided into two parts, on the "Constitution" (Articles 1-65) and on "General Demands" (Articles 66-102).

From a *Cahier* by the Third Estate (1789) [1]

Art. 1. The power of making laws resides in the king and the nation.

Art. 2. The nation, being too numerous for a personal exercise of this right, has confided its trust to representatives freely chosen from all classes of citizens. These representatives constitute the national assembly.

Art. 3. Frenchmen should regard as laws of this kingdom those alone which have been prepared by the national assembly and sanctioned by the king. . . .

Art. 6. That affairs of the kingdom may not suffer neglect and delay, the States General shall be convoked at least every two or three years. . . .

Art. 11. Personal property, proprietary rights, and the security of citizens shall be established in a clear and irrevocable manner. All *lettres de cachet* shall be abolished forever. . . .

Art. 12. The jury system shall be introduced in all criminal cases, and in civil cases for the determination of fact, in all the courts of the realm. . . .

Art. 15. A wider liberty of the press shall be accorded, with this provision alone: that all manuscripts sent to the printer shall be signed by the author, who shall be obliged to disclose his identity and bear the responsibility for his work . . . no writing shall be held a libel until it is so determined by twelve jurors. . . .

Art. 16. Letters shall never be opened in transit. . . .

Art. 17. All distinctions in penalties shall be abolished; and crimes committed by citizens of the different orders shall be punished irrespectively, according to the same forms of law and in the same manner. . . .

[1] *Typical Cahiers of 1789,* ed. by Merrick Whitcomb, in *Translations and Reprints from the Original Sources of European History,* 1898, IV, No. 5, 23-34. By permission of the University of Pennsylvania Press.

Art. 18. Penalties shall in all cases be moderate and proportionate to the crime. All kinds of torture, the rack and the stake, shall be abolished. . . .

Art. 19. Civil and criminal laws shall be reformed. . . .

Art. 21. No tax shall be legal unless accepted by the representatives of the people and sanctioned by the king.

Art. 22. Since all Frenchmen receive the same advantage from the government, and are equally interested in its maintenance, they ought to be placed upon the same footing in the matter of taxation.

Art. 23. All taxes now in operation are contrary to these principles. . . . They ought to be abolished as soon as possible, and replaced by others common to the three orders . . . without exception. . . .

Art. 30. The exact debt of the government shall be established by the States General, and after verification it shall be declared the national debt. . . .

Art. 36. A statement of pensions shall be presented to the States General; they shall be granted only in moderate amounts, and then only for services rendered. . . . A list of pensions should be printed and made public each year. . . .

Art. 43. A new subdivision shall be made of the provinces of the realm; provincial estates [assemblies] shall be established, members of which . . . shall be elected.

Art. 44. The constitution of the provincial estates shall be uniform throughout the kingdom. . . .

Art. 45. All members of the municipal assemblies of towns and villages shall be elected. . . .

Art. 46. All offices and positions, civil, ecclesiastical and military, shall be open to all orders; and no humiliating and unjust exceptions (in the case of the third estate) . . . shall be perpetuated. . . .

Art. 49. All relics of serfdom, agrarian or personal, still remaining in certain provinces, shall be abolished. . . .

Art. 51. The three functions, legislative, executive, and judicial, shall be separated and carefully distinguished [see pages 339-342].

The communes of the bailliage of Versailles have already expressed themselves in respect to the necessity of adopting the form of deliberation *per capita* in the coming States General [see pages 387-389]. The reform of the constitution will be one of their principal duties. . . .

Art. 66. The deputies . . . shall be instructed to unite themselves with the deputies of other provinces in order to join with them in securing, as soon as possible, the following abolitions: Of the *taille;* of the *gabelle;* of the *aides;* of the *corvée* . . . [etc.]

Art. 67. We demand also the abolition of the royal preserves (*capitaineries*); of the game laws . . . of tolls; of useless authorities and governments in cities and provinces. . . .

Art. 70. We demand, for the benefit of commerce, the abolition of all exclusive privileges: the removal of customs barriers to the frontiers; the most complete freedom in trade. . . .

Art. 72. The States General are entreated to devise means for abolishing guild organizations. . . .

Art. 93. Since clergymen in general ought not to occupy themselves with worldly affairs, there ought to be provided for bishops, archbishops, and all holders of benefices a decent income and one suitable to their dignity; accordingly the property of the church in each province ought to be sold under the supervision of the provincial estates, which shall assume the duty of paying to holders of benefices the sums accorded to them by the States General [see pages 395-396].

FROM ESTATES GENERAL TO NATIONAL
ASSEMBLY: THE TENNIS COURT OATH

Although the "communes of the bailliage of Versailles" had already gone on
record in favor of *per capita* voting in
the Estates General (see Article 51
above), the nobility, the clergy, and
the court were not of that opinion. Six
weeks expired after the meeting of the
Estates (May 1, 1789) before the Third
Estate, judging "that it can no longer
follow the privileged classes in their in-
action without sinning against the nation," declared that it was the "urgent
duty" of all the Deputies to organize an
active assembly at once. As the two upper estates, with royal support, insisted
upon voting separately, by orders, the
Third Estate finally took matters into
its own hands. Jean-Sylvain Bailly
(1736-1793), scientist, man of letters,
leader of the Third Estate in the National Assembly and, after the fall of
the Bastille, mayor of Paris, wrote the
following account of the organization
of the National Assembly.

From BAILLY, *Memoirs* (1789) [1]

[June 17] This day is forever memorable. This is the day on which the Assembly is constituted; this is the day when it
announces the rights of the nation, and
when it demonstrates, for the first time,
the resolute and judicious bearing which
belongs to its representatives and to the
trustees of its authority. . . .

A *yes* and *no* vote was made by roll
call, and the motion of the Abbé Sieyès
was adopted by a large majority [491 to
90]. Here is the resolution which was
adopted and which is the first constitutional act:

[1] *Mémoires de Bailly,* ed. by MM. Berville and
Barrière, 3 vols., Paris, 1821-22, I, 156-61, 180-99,
249.

"The Assembly, deliberating upon the
verification of powers, recognizes that it
is already composed of representatives
sent directly by at least ninety-six hun-
dredths of the nation. . . . Such a mass
of Deputies could not remain inactive
because of the absence of Deputies of
certain bailiwicks, or of some classes of
citizens; for the absent, *who have been
called,* cannot prevent those present from
the exercise of the plentitude of their
rights, especially when the exercise of
these rights is an urgent and imperative
duty. . . .

Moreover, as it belongs only to the verified representatives to concur in the national will, and as all the verified representatives ought to be in that Assembly,
it is further indispensable to conclude that
it belongs to it, and to it alone, to interpret
and to represent the general will of the
nation. . . .

There cannot exist between the throne
and the Assembly any veto, any negative
power.

The Assembly declares, therefore, that
the general work of national restoration
can and ought to be begun by the Deputies present, and that they ought to
prosecute it without interruption or impediment. . . .

The Assembly will never lose hope of
embracing in its midst all the Deputies
who are today absent; it will not cease to
call them to fulfill the obligation imposed
ipon them to concur in the holding of
the Estates General. At whatever moment
the absent Deputies present themselves
during the session that is about to be
opened, it declares in advance that it will
be prepared to receive them, and to share
with them, after verification of their
powers, the series of great tasks which
ought to procure the regeneration of
France. . . ."

[June 20] This is the second memorable
day which ought to be inscribed in the

memory of the nation. About six-thirty in the morning one of my friends . . . came to my house and told me that, having gone to the assembly room, as he had been doing for days, he had been refused entrance. . . . I sent to the hall and was informed that it was surrounded by guardsmen and a placard read: *"By order of the King."* I no longer doubted that it was a question of a royal session: "The King having resolved to hold a royal session of the Estates General on the twenty-second of June, preparations to be made in the three halls which serve as meeting places for the orders require that these meetings be suspended until after the holding of the said session. His Majesty will make known by a new proclamation the hour at which he will meet the Assembly of the States on Monday.". . .

[This method of notifying members of the Third Estate was highly irregular and created delicate problems for the self-styled National Assembly.]

In the avenue we met a large number of Deputies: all were of the opinion that the Assembly should meet for deliberation in a situation so delicate, and, consequently, should search out a suitable place. M. Guillotin suggested the Tennis Court; they resolved to go there. I marched at the head of this crowd of Deputies; and, for fear that some political reason might close the entrance to us, I asked five or six Deputies to go on ahead and take possession of it. The master of the Tennis Court received us gladly, and hastened to obtain for us all the conveniences that he could; having no guard, I asked two Deputies to stand by the door to prevent strangers from entering. . . .

The Deputies arrived successively, and each one, conscious of the stroke which

the Ministry had wished to make, congratulated us upon meeting again and upon finding ourselves reunited. . . . A member had the idea of the oath, and instantly there arose a cry of general approbation; after a short discussion, the Assembly made the following resolution, so simple and yet so firm:

"The National Assembly, considering itself called to establish the constitution of the kingdom, to effect the regeneration of public order, and to maintain the true principles of the monarchy, can in no way be prevented from continuing its deliberations in whatever place it may be forced to establish itself; and wherever its numbers are forgathered, there is the National Assembly.

"Be it resolved, that all the members of this Assembly immediately take a solemn oath never to separate, and to reassemble wherever circumstances require, until the constitution of the kingdom shall be established and fixed upon firm foundations; and that the said oath being taken, all the members, and each of them in particular, shall confirm this irrevocable resolve by their signatures." [Only one Deputy opposed, to the great indignation of the Assembly. Two days later (June 22), the clergy sent a deputation which announced, "Gentlemen, the majority of the order of the clergy having resolved to unite for the verification of powers, we come to announce it to you and to ask of you our place in the Assembly." A few nobles joined the same day. The King, many of the nobility, and the upper clergy resisted the action of the Third Estate until June 27. On that day, as even the soldiers had begun to show disaffection to the King, Louis ordered both the upper estates to join with the National Assembly to "apply themselves to objects of national interest." From a medieval Estates General which had voted by orders was formed a National Assembly which voted per capita and claimed to represent the entire nation. The victory of the Third Estate was complete.]

THE ABOLITION OF FEUDALISM (AUGUST 4-11, 1789)

About the time of the fall of the Bastille (July 14), sinister rumor and persistent anxiety, added to the woeful ignorance and widespread poverty of the peasantry, produced that curious mass delusion known as the Great Fear. The high hopes which had pervaded rural France when the peasants had elected their Deputies to the Estates General were giving way to bitterness as May and June passed with nothing done. Starving farm hands pillaged crops as they began to ripen, and the rumor got around that they were "brigands" sent by the nobility to punish the peasantry for daring to hope for reforms. News of Bastille Day increased their fear of retaliation and, mistaking their fear for reality, peasants began to fall upon their feudal landlords, to murder, pillage, and burn. By the end of July, anarchy reigned in many provinces. On August 4, Arthur Young, the English traveler, reported from west central France (Autun):[1]

"The reports here of *brigands,* and burning and plundering, are as numerous as before; and when it was known at the inn that I came from Burgundy and Franche Compté, I had eight or ten people introducing themselves, in order to ask for news. The rumour of *brigands* here had got to 1600 strong. They were much surprized to find, that I gave no credit to the existence of *brigands,* as I was well persuaded, that all the outrages that had been committed, were the work of the peas-

ants only, for the sake of plundering. This they had no conception of, and quoted a list of châteaus burnt by them; but on analysing these reports, they plainly appeared to be ill-founded."

The peasant uprisings interrupted the constitutional debates of the Assembly. A committee appointed to consider the question recommended repressive measures, but liberal noblemen, led by the Viscount of Noailles and the Duke of Aiguillon, the latter one of the largest landholders, proposed that all feudal rights and dues be surrendered at once. The proposals, made in the course of a session of the National Assembly during the night of August 4-5, precipitated a "frenzy of sacrifice," with noblemen vying with one another to renounce their feudal privileges. Bailly has vividly described the scene.

From BAILLY, *Memoirs*[2]

During the evening, M. Target [for the committee] read a draft of the proclamation which had been prepared to stop the pillage and burning of châteaux and to require payment of taxes, rents, and feudal dues which no longer were voluntarily paid. This proclamation occasioned a majestic debate and a truly grand scene, interesting and forever memorable. It was declared that both the refusal to pay feudal dues and the burning of title deeds originated in hatred of the feudal regime and the burdens it placed upon the peasantry. At this point, the Viscount of Noailles made the motion wherein he declared that the taxes ought to be borne equally by all, that the Assembly, at the same time, should decree that seigneurial corvées and personal servitude should be abolished without indemnification, and that feudal rights, at the desire of the peasants, should be redeemable according to rates which

[1] Young, *Travels,* I, 324-25.

[2] *Mémoires de Bailly,* II, 212-16.

shall be established. The Duke of Aiguillon, in seconding the motion, added that the privileges of all bodies, villages, communities, and individuals should be abolished. The Duke of Châtelet approved and demanded that the tithes be converted into dues and made redeemable at will. M. Cotin proposed the abolition of seigneurial courts; the Bishop of Chartres, that of hunting rights, and the recognition of the rights of all proprietors to kill game on their own lands. . . . Many of the barons of Languedoc, and others . . . sacrificed either their baronies or their rights of representation in the estates. . . . Finally, nothing was lacking for the regeneration of all things and for the prompt relief of the rural inhabitants. Never before had so many groups and individuals at one time, by most generous renunciation and with great unanimity, voted such sacrifices. . . . The feudal regime, which for centuries had weighed so heavily upon the people, was instantaneously destroyed by a single stroke.

[A week later (August 11), the National Assembly passed a decree giving the force of law to the enthusiastic gestures of the night of August 4-5. The decree of August 11, by abolishing many institutions of the Old Regime in France, made necessary future social, economic, and religious reconstruction and reform. It read, in part, as follows.]

From "Decree Abolishing Feudalism,"
August 11, 1789 [1]

Article I. The National Assembly completely abolishes the feudal regime. It decrees that among the rights and dues that are feudal as well as rental, those which derive from real or personal mort-

[1] *Collection complète des lois,* ed. by J. B. Duvergier, 2nd ed., 31 vols., Paris, 1834 ff., I, 33-34.

main and from personal servitude . . . shall be abolished without compensation. All other dues are declared redeemable, and the amount and the method shall be fixed by the National Assembly. . . .

III. The exclusive right of hunting and of maintaining open warrens is likewise abolished, and every landowner has the right to destroy, or to have destroyed, on his own land, all kinds of game. . . . All *capitaineries,* including royal ones, and all hunting preserves under whatever denomination, are likewise abolished. . . .

IV. All manorial courts are suppressed without compensation. . . .

V. Tithes of all kinds . . . are abolished; on condition, however, that some other provision be made to defray the expenses of divine worship . . . for assistance to the poor . . . and for the support of all institutions, seminaries, schools, colleges, hospitals, [etc.]. . . . Until such provision is made . . . the said tithes shall continue.

VI. All perpetual ground rents, payable either in kind or in money, of whatever kind or origin . . . shall be redeemable. . . .

VII. The sale of judicial and municipal offices is hereby suppressed. . . .

IX. Pecuniary privileges, real or personal, in matters of taxation are abolished forever. Taxes shall be collected from all citizens, and from all property, in the same manner and form. . . .

X. As a national constitution and public liberty are of greater advantage to the provinces than the privileges which some of them enjoy, and as the sacrifice of these is necessary for the intimate union of the realm, it is declared that all the peculiar privileges of provinces . . . [etc.] are forever abolished, and shall be incorporated into the law common to all Frenchmen.

XI. All citizens, without distinction of birth, can be admitted to all offices and dignities, be they ecclesiastical, civil, or military. . . .

THE DECLARATION OF THE RIGHTS OF MAN AND THE CITIZEN (AUGUST 26, 1789)

The National Assembly faced a twofold task: to serve as a legislative body and to act as a Constituent Assembly in the preparation of a new constitution for France. In its latter capacity, the Assembly labored more than two years, and the constitution, in its final form, was not enacted until September 3, 1791. However, on August 26, 1789, one of the first fruits of the Assembly's deliberations was set forth, the "Declaration of the Rights of Man and the Citizen." Modeled closely after bills of rights included in the American state constitutions, the "Declaration" had a threefold purpose: to set forth principles upon which the entire constitution of France was to be founded; to outlaw specific practices of the Old Regime in France; and to serve as a preamble for the completed constitution of 1791. The "Declaration" was widely imitated by subsequent constitution makers in various parts of the world.

From "The Declaration of the Rights of Man" (1789) [1]

The representatives of the French people, constituted as a National Assembly, considering that ignorance, forgetfulness, or contempt of the rights of man are the sole causes of public misery and the corruption of governments, have resolved to set forth in a solemn declaration the natural, inalienable, and sacred rights of man, in order that this declaration, constantly before all the members of the social body, may remind them continually of their

[1] *Ibid.*, III, 240.

rights and their duties; in order that the acts both of the legislative and of the executive power may be compared at each instant with the aims of all political institutions and thus become more respected; and finally, in order that the grievances of citizens, founded hereafter on simple and incontestable principles, shall tend always to the maintenance of the constitution and to the happiness of all.

Accordingly, the National Assembly recognizes and declares, in the presence and under the auspices of the Supreme Being, the following rights of man and of the citizen:

Article I. Men are born and remain free and equal in rights. Social distinctions can be founded only upon common utility.

II. The aim of all political association is the conservation of the natural and imprescriptible rights of man. These rights are liberty, property, security, and resistance to oppression.

III. The principle of all sovereignty resides essentially in the nation. No body, no individual, can exercise any authority which does not expressly emanate from it.

IV. Liberty consists in freedom to do all that does not injure others; thus the exercise of natural rights of each man has no limits other than those which assure other members of society the enjoyment of these same rights. These limits can be determined only by law.

V. The law has the right to prohibit only those actions harmful to society. All that is not prohibited by law cannot be forbidden, and no one can be forced to do anything that it does not ordain.

VI. Law is the expression of the general will. All citizens have the right to assist personally, or by their representatives, in its formation. It should be the same for all, whether it protects or punishes. All citizens, being equal in the eyes of the law, are equally admissible to all dignities, places, and public employments according to their capacity, and without distinctions other than their virtue and talents.

VII. No man can be accused, arrested, or detained except in cases determined by law. . . . Every citizen, when summoned or seized by virtue of the law, ought to obey instantly; he renders himself culpable by resistance.

VIII. The law should establish only such punishments as are strictly and evidently necessary; and no one can be punished except by virtue of a law established and promulgated previous to the offense and legally applied.

IX. As every man is presumed innocent until he has been declared guilty, when it is deemed indispensable to make an arrest, all severity not necessary for securing the prisoner should be severely repressed by law.

X. No one should be disturbed because of his opinions, even in religion, provided their manifestation does not disturb public order as established by law.

XI. The free communication of thoughts and opinions is one of the most precious rights of man; thus every citizen can speak, write, and publish freely; but in cases determined by law he shall be responsible for the abuse of this liberty.

XII. Guarantee of the rights of man and of the citizen necessitates a public force. This force, then, is instituted for the advantage of all, and not for the particular use of those to whom it is confided.

XIII. For the maintenance of a public force, and for the expenses of administration, a common contribution is essential. It ought to be equally distributed among all citizens according to their means.

XIV. Each citizen has the right, either by himself or through his representative, to ascertain the necessity of the public contribution, to consent to it without compulsion, to follow up its use, and to determine the quota, assessment, collection, and duration.

XV. Society has the right to demand from every public agent an account of his administration.

XVI. A society in which a guarantee of rights is not assured, nor the separation of powers determined, has no constitution at all.

XVII. Property being a sacred and inviolable right, no one can be deprived of it except when public necessity, lawfully ascertained, clearly demands it, and then only upon condition of a just and previous indemnification.

THE RISE OF JACOBINISM

The Jacobins possessed a dual significance. Not only did they form an organized political group which, in the early years of the revolution, gained an ascendancy over other political groups, but also they set forth a political faith which, growing progressively more radical as the revolution advanced, persisted long after the Jacobin Clubs had ceased to exist, and exerted a powerful influence in the French—and in the entire European—political outlook. Jacobin Clubs arose almost spontaneously after the National Assembly got under way. It was inevitable that like-minded Deputies should gravitate toward one another, and at Versailles a group of radical members formed a caucus called the Club Breton. Later, at Paris, members of this club formed the Society of the Friends of the Constitution, better known as the Jacobin Club, after the convent in which the Paris "mother club" sat. In time, this club affiliated with provincial literary societies and Masonic clubs which, as the revolution approached, had assumed a political complexion. One of the early Jacobins, Count Alexandre T. V. de Lameth, wrote the following story of the origin of the Jacobins.

From LAMETH, *History of the Constituent Assembly* (1790) [1]

After the transfer of the Assembly to Paris [effected Oct. 6, 1789, by the March of the Women on Versailles], the Deputies from provinces distant from the capital and who, for the most part, had never been there (for traveling was not so easy then as it is now) underwent a sort of terror at the idea of being alone and, so to speak, lost in the midst of this great city. Accordingly, they nearly all sought to lodge as close as possible to the Assembly, which then sat near the Feuillants (at the intersection of the Rue Rivoli and the Rue Castiglione) in order that they might be easily found in case of need. But they also desired a place where they might meet to determine upon the direction of public affairs. They consulted residents of the capital in whom they had confidence. After searching in the vicinity of the Assembly, they leased, for two hundred francs a year, the refectory of the Convent of the Jacobins; and for a like sum the necessary furniture, which consisted of chairs and tables for the committee, was obtained.

At the first meeting about one hundred Deputies were present, the next day double that number. They elected the Baron de Menou as president, and Target, Barnave, Alexandre Lameth, Le Chapelier, and Adrien du Port were chosen secretaries, together with three others whose names I cannot recall. A committee was appointed, with Barnave as chairman, to draw up a list of regulations. The society decided to call itself Friends of the Constitution. They determined to admit all the members of the Assembly, but only such other persons who had published useful works. The first to be thus received were Con-

dorcet, the Marquis de Casotte, a distinguished economist, the Abbé Lecamus, a mathematician, and a small number of other savants or publicists.

The aim of the Society of the Friends of the Constitution was to discuss questions which were already on or were about to be placed on the calendar of the National Assembly. It cannot be denied that inasmuch as the non-Deputies exercised no influence in the Assembly, these discussions often had more force and greater brilliancy than in the Assembly itself, where one found himself hindered by the violent contradictions of the right wing, and often intimidated by the crowd of spectators. These preliminary considerations cast much light upon the discussions. It was a great advantage for the popular party to determine, by preliminary ballots within the society itself, the nominees for president, secretaries, and the committees of the Assembly. For from that time the elections were almost always carried by the left wing, although up to that time they had been almost entirely controlled by the right. Camus, a canon lawyer, then president and since become a republican, had been elected by the aristocracy.

The number of Deputies who customarily frequented the Society of the Friends of the Constitution soon rose to nearly four hundred. The number of writers also increased in a marked proportion. But soon afterward the requirement of having published a useful book was discarded as a basis for admission, and it was decided that it was sufficient to have been recommended by six members. The meeting then grew considerably larger, and no longer possessed the same high quality in its composition. Very soon the place of meeting became insufficient, and permission was obtained of the friars of the convent to meet in their library and later in their church.

[1] Translated from the quotation in F. A. Aulard, *La Société des Jacobins*, 6 vols., Paris, 1889, I, xix-xx.

About the month of December, 1789, many leading inhabitants of the provinces, having come to Paris either on private business or to attend more closely the course of public affairs, were presented to the society and expressed the desire to establish similar organizations in the chief cities of France. For they felt that these associations of citizens intent upon the defense of the cause of public interest would constitute an efficient means of counteracting the violent opposition of the aristocracy, which had not yet lost the power which it had so long exercised.

[Thus, many of the existing literary societies and Masonic clubs became affiliated with the "mother club" in Paris, and the Jacobins possessed a nation-wide network of political clubs. On February 8, 1790, the Paris society adopted a constitution and bylaws, the preamble of which began with the following statement.]

From *Rules of the Friends of the Constitution* (1790) [1]

Members of the Society . . . animated by a most ardent zeal for the rights of men . . . saw in these associations a means of establishing among good citizens a uniformity of view, of principles, and of conduct which would consummate in the most prompt and peaceable manner the happy revolution which they all desired. When the constitution prepared by the National Assembly is placed in execution in all the kingdom, it is necessary that the principles upon which it is founded shall be universally understood. . . . A society established near the National Assembly and including a large number of Deputies from various provinces can offer a common center to those organizations established throughout the kingdom; it will

[1] *Ibid.,* xxviii-xxx.

receive their instructions and transmit to them the views which result from the conjunction of insight and interest; it will transmit to them, above all, the spirit of the decrees of the National Assembly, for the execution of which all the societies shall be particularly dedicated.

Designed to spread the truth, to defend liberty and the constitution, the means employed shall be as pure as the objects which they set forth. Publicity shall be the guarantee of all their measures. To write and to speak openly, to profess their principles without deterrents, to dedicate their works, their views, and their hopes—these shall be the frank ways by which they shall seek to obtain the goodwill of the public; for these alone can have force and utility. Fidelity to the constitution, devotion to its defense, respect for and submission to the powers which shall be established—these will be the primary laws imposed upon those who seek admission to these societies. Their claims to membership shall be above all the love of equality and a profound respect for the rights of men. . . .

Art. I. The object of the Society of the Friends of the Constitution is: First, to discuss in advance the questions which ought to be decided in the National Assembly. Second, to work for the firm establishment of the constitution after the manner set forth in the preamble above. Third, to correspond with other societies of the same kind which may organize in the kingdom. . . .

IV. Whenever a member of the society shall be convicted of having manifested, either orally or in writing . . . principles clearly contrary to the constitution, the rights of men, and, in a word, the spirit of the society, he shall be, according to the gravity of the case, reprimanded by the president or, as determined by a majority vote, excluded from the society.

NATIONALIZATION OF THE CHURCH

The financial crisis which had precipitated revolution in France grew worse as time went on. The need for new collateral for state loans led to confiscation of church property as, on November 2, 1789, the National Assembly decreed "that all ecclesiastical estates are at the disposal of the nation." The bonds issued upon this new national domain were the ill-fated assignats, later made legal tender, and overissued until they became embarrassingly depreciated. Meantime, the French clergy was deprived of its sources of income and, in an effort to remedy this situation, on July 12, 1790, the National Assembly issued the famous "Civil Constitution of the Clergy." By this document ·the clergy of France became elected civil servants of the state—a condition very satisfactory to those who wanted the church made wholly subservient to the state and entirely independent of papal control. But the Pope denounced it; the King signed it with reluctance (his bad conscience in the matter was one of the chief impulses leading to the disastrous flight to Varennes, June, 1791); the lower clergy and devout Catholics everywhere resisted it; and, because of it, the Vendée became both a reservoir of pious Catholics alienated from the revolutionary cause and the center of the fiercest armed counterrevolutionary movement in France. Extracts of some of the most controversial points of this "constitution" are given below.

From "The Civil Constitution of the Clergy" (July 12, 1790) [1]

The National Assembly, after having heard the report of its Ecclesiastical Com-

[1] Duvergier, ed., *Collection complète des lois,* i, 242-48.

mittee, has decreed and does decree the following as constitutional articles:

TITLE I. ECCLESIASTICAL OFFICES

Article I. Each department shall form a single diocese, and each diocese shall have the same extent and the same limits as the department. [As there were 83 departments, there became 83 coterminous bishoprics.] . . .

IV. No church or parish of France nor any French citizen may recognize upon any occasion or upon any pretext whatsoever the authority of an ordinary bishop or archbishop whose see shall be under the supremacy of a foreign power, nor that of its representatives residing in France or elsewhere; all this without prejudice, however, to the unity of the faith and the communion which shall be maintained with the Visible Head of the Universal Church, as hereafter provided. . . .

TITLE II. ELECTION TO OFFICE

Article I. From the day of publication of the present decree there shall be but one method of choosing bishops and parish priests; namely, that of election.

II. All elections shall be decided by ballot and by the absolute majority of the votes. . . .

VII. In order to be eligible for a bishopric, a man shall have fulfilled, for fifteen years at least, the duties of the ecclesiastical ministry in the diocese as a parish priest, curate, vicar, head vicar, or directing vicar of the seminary. . . .

XVII. The archbishop or senior bishop of the province shall have the right to examine the bishop-elect in the presence of his council upon his doctrine and his character. If he deems him fit for the position, he shall give him the canonical institution. . . .

XVIII. The bishop of whom confirmation is asked shall not exact of the person elected any form of oath except that he makes profession of the Apostolic Roman Catholic religion.

XIX. The new bishop cannot address the Pope for any form of confirmation; but he shall write to him as the Visible Head of the Universal Church as a testimony to the unity of faith and communion which he should maintain with him. . . .

XXI. Before the ceremony of consecration begins, the bishop-elect shall take, in the presence of the municipal officers, the people, and the clergy, a solemn oath to guard with care the faithful of his diocese who are confided to him, to be loyal to the Nation, the Law and the King and to support with all his power the constitution decreed by the National Assembly and accepted by the King. . . .

TITLE III. EMOLUMENTS OF MINISTERS OF THE RELIGION

Article I. The ministers of religion, exercising the first and most important functions of society, and obliged to live continuously in the place of service to which they have been called by the confidence of the people, shall be supported by the nation. . . .

II. Each bishop, priest, and officiating clergyman in a chapel of ease shall be furnished with a suitable dwelling on condition that he make all the current repairs. . . . Salaries shall be assigned to each as indicated below. [Bishops, 12,000 to 50,000 livres, according to location; parish priests, 1,200 to 6,000 livres, according to location. All salaries payable quarterly, in advance, by the treasurer of the district. Priests and others shall perform all episcopal and priestly duties without charge.] . . .

TITLE IV. THE LAW ON RESIDENCE

Article I. The law of residence shall be strictly observed. . . .

II. No bishop may absent himself from his diocese more than fifteen consecutive days during the year, except in case of

real necessity and with the consent of the Directory of the Department. . . .

III. In the same manner, the parish priests and the curates may not absent themselves from the place of their duties beyond the term fixed above.

4. Foreign Attitudes toward the Revolution

EDMUND BURKE

After the March of the Women upon Versailles (October 5-6, 1789) forced the government to move to Paris and practically made prisoners of the royal family, foreign opinion of the French Revolution, especially at courts of neighboring kings, became increasingly hostile. One of the most severe—and influential—criticisms of the Revolution came, in 1790, from the pen of Edmund Burke, the English statesman and writer. Although he had befriended Americans in their revolt from England, Burke deplored the illegalities perpetrated by the National Assembly and the excesses of that body in its treatment of the King and Queen, of property rights, and of religion. A selection from his essay, *Reflections on the Revolution in France . . . Intended to Have Been Sent to a Gentleman in Paris, 1790,* follows.

From BURKE, *Revolution in France* (1790) [1]

When all the frauds, impostures, violences, rapines, burnings, murders, confiscations, compulsory paper currencies, and every description of tyranny and cruelty employed to bring about and to uphold

[1] *The Works of the Right Honorable Edmund Burke,* 4th ed., 12 vols., Boston, 1871, III, 395-407, 449-54.

this Revolution have their natural effect, that is, to shock the moral sentiments of all virtuous and sober minds, the abettors of this philosophic system immediately strain their throats in a declamation against the old monarchical government of France. When they have rendered that deposed power sufficiently black, they then proceed in argument, as if all those who disapprove of their new abuses must of course be partisans of the old; that those who reprobate their crude and violent schemes of liberty ought to be treated as advocates of servitude. I admit that their necessities do compel them to this base and contemptible fraud. . . . It is nothing but plain impudence. Have these gentlemen never heard, in the whole circle of the worlds of theory and practice, of anything between the despotism of the monarch and the despotism of the multitude? . . .

I do not know under what description to class the present ruling authority in France. It affects to be a pure democracy, though I think it in a direct train of becoming shortly a mischievous and ignoble oligarchy. . . .

Your government in France, though usually, and I think justly, reputed the best of the unqualified or ill-qualified monarchies,[1] was still full of abuses. These abuses accumulated in a length of time, as they must accumulate in every monarchy not under the constant inspection of a popular representative. I am no stranger to the faults and defects of the subverted government of France. . . . But the question is not now of the vices of that monarchy, but of its existence. Is it then true, that the French government was such as to be incapable or undeserving of reform; so that it was of absolute necessity that the whole fabric should be at once pulled down, and the area cleared for the erection of a theoretic, experimental edifice in

its place? All France was of a different opinion in the beginning of the year 1789. The instructions to the representatives to the states-general, from every district in that kingdom, were filled with projects for the reformation of that government, without the remotest suggestion of a design to destroy it. Had such a design been then even insinuated, I believe there would have been but one voice, and that voice for rejecting it with scorn and horror. . . . In the interval between the instructions and the Revolution, things changed their shape; and, in consequence of that change, the true question at present is, whether those who would have reformed, or those who have destroyed, are in the right.

To hear some men speak of the late monarchy of France you would imagine that they were talking of Persia bleeding under the ferocious sword of Thamas Kouli Khân . . . where the finest countries in the most genial climates in the world are wasted by peace more than any countries have been worried by war; where arts are unknown, where manufactures languish, where science is extinguished. . . . Was this the case of France? I have no way of determining the question but by a reference to facts. Facts do not support this resemblance. . . .

[Burke notes that estimates of French population for the era 1700 to 1789 show a very considerable increase, and that as the government of the Old Regime, "amidst the inconstancy and fluctuation natural to courts," made "an earnest endeavour towards the prosperity and improvement of the country . . . so far from refusing itself to reformation, that government was open, with a censurable degree of facility, to all sorts of projects and projectors on the subject."]

Whether the system, if it deserves such a name, now built on the ruins of that

[1] That is, of the *unlimited* or *poorly limited* monarchies.

ancient monarchy, will be able to give a better account of the population and wealth of the country, which it has taken under its care, is a matter very doubtful. Instead of improving by the change, I apprehend that a long series of years must be told, before it can recover in any degree the effects of this philosophic revolution, and before the nation can be replaced on its former footing. . . .

I have taken a view of what has been done by the governing power in France. I have certainly spoken of it with freedom. Those whose principle it is to despise the ancient, permanent sense of mankind, and to set up a scheme of society on new principles, must naturally expect that such of us who think better of the judgment of the human race than of theirs should consider both them and their devices, as men and schemes upon their trial. They must take it for granted that we attend much to their reason, but not at all to their authority. . . .

I can never consider this Assembly as anything else than a voluntary association of men, who have availed themselves of circumstances to seize upon the power of the state. They have not the sanction and authority of the character under which they first met. They have assumed another of a very different nature; and have completely altered and inverted all the relations in which they originally stood. They do not hold the authority they exercise under any constitutional law of the state. . . . They have created the arbitrary republic of Paris. With them defects in wisdom are to be supplied by the plenitude of force. . . . The difficulties, which they rather had eluded than escaped, meet them again in their course; they multiply and thicken on them; they are involved, through a labyrinth of confused detail, in an industry without limit, and without direction; and, in conclusion, the whole

of their work becomes feeble, vicious, and insecure.

THE DUKE OF BRUNSWICK'S MANIFESTO

After failure of the royal family's attempted flight to Varennes (June, 1791), the Emperor Leopold II, led on by intrigues of *émigrés* and by appeals from his sister, Marie Antoinette, dispatched to leading European monarchs the "Padua Circular" (July, 1791). In this document, the Emperor held that the "honor of sovereigns" had been compromised by the French revolutionists and urged a union of kings for "counsel, co-operation, and measures in order to restore the liberty and honor" of the French royal family and "to put limits to the dangerous extremities of the French Revolution." The appeal was ignored by all save the King of Prussia, who on August 27, 1791, united with the Emperor in the joint "Declaration of Pillnitz," wherein the two monarchs declared "the present situation of the King of France" to be "of common interest to all the sovereigns of Europe," and solicited the aid of all "to place the King of France in a position to establish, with the most absolute freedom, the foundations of a monarchical form of government . . . in harmony with the rights of sovereigns and promote the welfare of the French nation. . . . In the meantime, they will give such orders to their troops as are necessary in order that these may be in a position to be called into active service." Leopold died shortly afterward, but on April 20, 1792, the National Assembly declared war upon his successor, Francis I, declaring that he granted "open protection to the French rebels [*émigrés*]" and that he plotted against "the independence and security of the French nation." On July 25 following, the Duke of

Brunswick, as commander of the united armies of Prussia and the Empire, set forth a manifesto which enraged the French revolutionists and hastened the final overthrow of the French monarchy.

From the DUKE OF BRUNSWICK, "Manifesto" (July 25, 1792) [1]

Their Majesties, the Emperor and the King of Prussia, having committed to me the command of the united armies which they have caused to assemble on the frontiers of France, I have wished to announce to the inhabitants of this kingdom the motives which have determined the measures of the two sovereigns and the intentions which guide them.

After having arbitrarily suppressed the rights and possessions of the German princes in Alsace and Lorraine, disturbed and overthrown good order and legitimate government in the interior; exercised against the sacred person of the king and his august family outrages and brutalities which are still carried on and renewed day by day; those who have usurped the reins of the administration have at last completed their work by declaring an unjust war against His Majesty the Emperor and by attacking his provinces situated in the Low Countries. . . .

To these great interests is added another aim equally important and very dear to the hearts of the two sovereigns; it is to put an end to the anarchy in the interior of France, to stop the attacks carried on against the throne and the altar, to re-establish the legal power, to restore to the king the security and liberty of which he is deprived, and to put him in a position

[1] Frank Maloy Anderson, ed., *The Constitutions and Other Select Documents Illustrative of the History of France 1789-1907,* 2nd ed. rev., Minneapolis, 1908, 119-22. By permission of Frank Maloy Anderson.

to exercise the legitimate authority which is his due. . . .

It is in accordance with these views that I, the undersigned, the General, commanding in chief the two armies, declare:

1. That . . . the two allied courts propose to themselves no other aim than the welfare of France [no conquests intended]. . . .

2. That they do not intend to meddle with the internal government of France, but that they merely wish to deliver the king, the queen, and the royal family from their captivity. . . .

3. That the combined armies will protect . . . [all who submit to the king and assist in the re-establishment of order].

4. That the national guard will be called upon to watch provisionally over the peace . . . until the arrival of the troops of their Imperial and Royal Majesties . . . that on the contrary, those of the national guard who shall fight against the troops of the two allied courts, and who shall be taken with arms in their hands, will be treated as enemies and punished as rebels to their king. . . .

6. That the members of the departments, of the districts and municipalities shall likewise answer with their heads and their goods for all offences, fires, murders, pillaging, and acts of violence, which they shall allow to be committed. . . .

8. The city of Paris and all its inhabitants without distinction shall be required to submit at once and without delay to the king, to put that prince in full and perfect liberty . . . their Imperial and Royal Majesties declare personally responsible with their lives for all events, to be tried by military law and without hope of pardon, all the members of the National Assembly, of the department, district, municipality, and national guard of Paris . . . their Majesties also declare . . . that if the château of the Tuileries be entered by force or attacked, if the

least violence or outrage be offered to their Majesties, the king, queen, and royal family, if their preservation and their liberty be not immediately provided for, they will exact an exemplary and ever-memorable vengeance, by delivering the city of Paris over to a military execution and to complete ruin, and the rebels guilty of these outrages to the punishments they shall have deserved. . . .

Given at the head-quarters at Coblentz, July 25, 1792.

Signed, Charles-William Ferdinand, Duke of Brunswick-Lunebourg

THE FRENCH APPEAL TO FOREIGN PEOPLES

The Duke of Brunswick's manifesto provoked the revolutionists to new extremities. The King was suspended (August 10, 1792), a new convention was called (August 11), a decree abolished the monarchy (September 21), and the First French Republic was proclaimed (September 22, 1792). The following December, the National Convention, in an effort to spread revolution against neighboring monarchs, proclaimed "the Liberty and Sovereignty of all the peoples to whose Homeland they have carried and are carrying their arms."

From a Proclamation of the National Convention (December 15, 1792) [1]

THE NATIONAL CONVENTION . . . DECREES

Article I. In the countries which are or shall be occupied by the armies of the Republic, the generals shall proclaim immediately, in the name of the French nation, the soveignty of the people, the suppression of all established authorities . . . the abolition of the tithe, of feudal-

[1] Duvergier, ed., *Collection complète des lois,* V, 82, 84.

ism, of seigneurial rights . . . of real and personal servitude, of hunting and fishing privileges, of the corvées, and generally of all privileges. . . . [And they distributed among the peoples of occupied countries the following handbill:]

THE FRENCH PEOPLE TO THE . . . PEOPLE

Brothers and friends, we have won liberty and we shall keep it. We offer to cause you to enjoy this inestimable blessing. . . .

We have driven out your tyrants; show yourselves free men and we will secure you from their vengeance, their plots, and their return.

From this moment the French nation proclaims the sovereignty of the people, the suppression of all civil and military authorities which have governed you up to this day . . . the abolition of the tithe, of feudalism, of seigneurial rights . . . [etc.]. You are from this moment brothers and friends, all citizens, all equal in rights, and all equally called to govern, to serve, and to defend your fatherland.

Form yourselves at once into primary and communal assemblies. . . . The agents of the French Republic will co-operate with you in order to assure your welfare and the brotherhood which ought hereafter to exist among us.

5. *The Terror* (*1793-94*)

"Let us," said Danton in the new National Convention, "cast down before Europe, as the gauntlet of battle, the head of a king." While all Europe looked on in horror, Louis XVI was tried, convicted "of conspiring against the liberty of the nation and of attempts against the general safety of the state," and executed (January 21, 1793). By this act, the revolutionists multiplied their enemies outside France and intensified opposition within. Recognition of the former was given by a declaration of war against England and Holland (February 1, 1793); and a series of measures was taken to deal with counterrevolutionary efforts at home. An Extraordinary Criminal Tribunal was created (March 10) to deal with "every counterrevolutionary enterprise"; another act (March 21) authorized the organization in each commune of a Revolutionary Committee to check on the doings of the populace; and, on April 6, the Convention established a Committee of Public Safety "to take, under urgent circumstances, measures of external and internal defense." Meanwhile, between the leading factions of the Convention, Jacobins and Girondins, there had developed a serious rupture. The Jacobins, now often referred to as the "Mountain" in the Convention, had grown increasingly radical since the organization of their society (now, since August, 1792, officially called The Society of Friends of Liberty and Equality; see pages 392-394. The Mountain tended to represent the urban, Parisian, propertyless sans-culotte interests; the Girondins the rural, propertied classes. The Mountain wished to carry the revolution on to further achievements; the Girondins hoped to stop it where it was. Bitter personal antipathies boiled between leaders of the two groups and when the Girondins showed hesitancy during the King's trial, the Mountain leaders charged them with promonarchical sympathies. Finally, by an appeal to force, the Mountain purged the Convention of Girondins (May 31-June 2, 1793), thereby gaining complete mastery of a "rump" Convention. Shortly afterward (July 27), the Committee of Public Safety was reorganized with Robespierre its dominating figure and, as dangers from without and within France necessitated firm, unwavering control, the Committee became all powerful, determined to put down "enemies of the revolution" wherever found. A series of extraordinary measures followed, one of the most significant of which was the decree which conscripted the entire nation for war, the *Levée en Masse*. By means of its provisions, Carnot, Minister of War, earned the glorious title "Organizer of Victory"; and the reorganized French armies, fired with revolutionary ardor, not only repelled the enemies from the borders but also overran enemy territory. Extracts from this famous decree follow.

MOBILIZATION AGAINST THE FOREIGN ENEMIES

From the *Levée en Masse* (August 23, 1793) [1]

Article I. From this moment until that in which the enemies shall have been driven from the territory of the Republic, all Frenchmen are permanently requisitioned for service in the armies.

Young men shall go forth to battle; married men shall forge weapons and transport munitions; women shall make tents and clothing, and shall serve in hospitals; children will make lint from old linen; and old men shall be brought to public places to arouse the courage of soldiers and preach the hatred of kings and the unity of the Republic.

II. Public buildings shall be converted into barracks, public squares into workshops for arms. . . .

IV. Saddle horses are requisitioned to complete the cavalry corps; draught horses, except those employed in agriculture, will haul the artillery and provisions.

[1] *Ibid.*, VI, 107.

V. The Committee of Public Safety is charged to take all measures necessary to set up without delay an extraordinary manufactory of arms of all kinds to correspond to the spirit and energy of the French people. It is authorized, therefore, to set up all the establishments . . . necessary for the accomplishment of this work, and to requisition throughout the Republic the craftsmen and workers that can co-operate in making this a success. . . .

VI. The representatives of the people sent to execute the present law shall have the power of enforcement in their respective districts in concert with the Committee of Public Safety. . . .

VII. No one can furnish a substitute for the place to which he has been requisitioned. . . .

VIII. The levy shall be general. Unmarried citizens and childless widowers between the ages of eighteen and thirty-five shall be called first. . . .

MOBILIZATION AGAINST THE DOMESTIC ENEMIES

Just as the *Levée en Masse* was designed against foreign enemies of the Revolution, so the Law of Suspects was directed against the counterrevolutionaries within France. And as Carnot's armies marched against the foreign foes, so the Committee of Public Safety, working through the revolutionary committees in every commune, rounded up "suspects" at home.

From the "Law of Suspects"
(September 17, 1793) [1]

Article I. Immediately after publication of the present decree, all suspect people

[1] *Ibid.*, VI, 172.

still at liberty within the territory of the Republic shall be placed under arrest.

II. Those considered to be suspect are: 1. Those who by their conduct, relations, speech, or writings have shown themselves the partisans of tyranny or federalism, and enemies of liberty. 2. Those who cannot after the manner prescribed by the law of March 21 last justify their means of existence and the performance of their civic duties. 3. Those to whom certificates of civism have been refused. . . . 5. Those of the former nobles, including husbands, wives, fathers, mothers, sons, daughters, brothers, sisters, and agents of émigrés who have not constantly manifested their attachment to the revolution. 6. Those who have emigrated during the interval between July 1, 1789, to . . . April 8, 1792, even if they have returned to France within the period fixed by law.

III. The committees of surveillance established by the decree of March 21 last, or those which have been substituted for them . . . are charged to prepare lists of suspects in their respective districts, issue warrants of arrest against them, and seal their papers.

WAGES AND PRICE CONTROL

The Mountain's responsiveness to demands of the Parisian masses is well illustrated by the Law of the Maximum. Since the outbreak of the revolution, crop failures, currency depreciation, and profiteering had led to a general advance in prices which bore heavily upon the propertyless sans-culottes. As a kind of wartime rationing and defense of the poor against speculators, the Mountain-controlled Convention passed a series of price-fixing measures of which the most inclusive was the following Law of the Maximum.

From the "Law of the Maximum"
(September 29, 1793)[1]

Art. 1. The articles which the National Convention has judged to be of prime necessity and for which it has believed that it should fix the maximum, or the highest price, are: fresh meat, salt meat and bacon, butter, sweet oil, cattle, salt fish, wine, brandy, vinegar, cider, beer, firewood, charcoal, coal, candles, lamp oil, salt, soda, sugar, honey, white paper, leather, iron, brass, lead, copper, hemp, linen, wool, woolens, fabrics, the materials which serve to make fabrics, sabots, shoes, cabbages and turnips, soap, potash, and tobacco.

2. For the articles listed above, the *maximum* price for firewood of the first quality, of charcoal and of coal, are the same as in 1790, plus a twentieth of the price. . . .

The *maximum,* or the highest price, of tobacco in rolls is twenty sous per pound (of eight ounces); that of smoking tobacco is ten sous; that of salt is two sous per pound; that of soap is twenty-five sous.

3. The *maximum* price of all the other commodities and goods included in Article 1, for the whole extent of the Republic, until the month of September next, shall be the price which each of them had in 1790, such as is established by the official price lists or the market price of each department, and a third over and above this same price, deduction being made of fiscal and other duties to which they were then subject, under whatsoever denomination they may have existed. . . .

7. All persons who buy or sell the goods listed in Article 1 above the *maximum* of the price determined and posted in each department shall pay to the municipal police a fine double the value of the article sold, the fine payable to the informer;

[1] *Ibid.,* VI, 193-95.

they shall be enrolled upon the list of suspected persons and treated as such. The purchaser shall not be subject to the above penalties if he denounces the offense of the seller; and each merchant shall be required to have a list in his shop bearing the *maximum* or highest prices of his goods.

8. The *maximum* or the highest price belonging to salaries, wages, and manual labor by the day in each place shall be fixed, to commence from the publication of this law until the month of September next, by the general councils of the communes at the same amount as in 1790, to which there shall be added half of that price in addition.

9. The municipalities shall put into requisition and punish, according to circumstances, with three days' imprisonment the workingmen, factory operatives, and other laboring persons who refuse without legitimate cause to engage in their usual labors. . . .

[Great care is exercised in Articles 9-20, Article 17 excepted, to ensure prompt and effective enforcement of the law of the maximum. Article 17 provided:]

17. During the war, all exportation of goods or merchandise of prime necessity, under whatsoever name or commission, is prohibited at all frontiers, salt excepted.

ROBESPIERRE'S AIMS FOR THE COMMITTEE OF PUBLIC SAFETY (FEBRUARY 5, 1794)

Opinion of Maximilien Robespierre (1758-1794), the provincial lawyer who came to dominate the Terror, has varied widely. He has been treated as though he had been practically insane; he has been charged with having had a particularly bloodthirsty desire for dictatorial power; and he has been considered as a fanatical idealist whose unfortunate zeal led him to adopt methods which precluded realization of his dreams. In the main, the verdict of recent students tends toward the last view, not because it is kinder, but because it best squares with the facts of Robespierre's life and the circumstances of France during the Terror. For Robespierre was certainly not mad, and while he strove for dictatorial powers, he clearly considered dictatorship as a temporary phase of the revolution, necessary but not desirable. By the end of 1793, the newly organized republican armies had driven the foreigners from the borders of France. The foreign threat, though not entirely removed, was under control. The immediate need of revolutionary France, as the Committee of Public Safety now saw it, was to establish the Republic on a firm foundation. It was with this end in view that Robespierre made the following speech on February 5, 1794, a "Report [to the Committee of Public Safety] on the Principles of Political Morality Which Ought to Guide the National Convention in the Internal Administration of the Republic." This report is probably the best single statement of Robespierre's views, and it goes far to explain the perpetuation of the Terror until his death (July 27, 1794). The "Incorruptible" set forth *virtue* as the fundamental principle of the Republic. "Virtues," said he on another occasion, "are simple, modest, poor, often ignorant, sometimes gross; they are the appanage of misfortune and the patrimony of the people. Vices are surrounded with riches, adorned by the charms of pleasure and the snares of perfidy, escorted by all the dangerous talents, by crime." Robespierre held that "the people is

sublime," that the mass of Frenchmen was virtuous, that only the virtuous could be citizens in the Republic. Others, lacking virtue, were not citizens —were, indeed, enemies of the Republic who must be wiped out. Such a Republic must inevitably remain at war with a large part of its own population. And so, in the name of virtue, Robespierre employed implacable Terror against the "enemies of the Republic." The idealistic concepts which impelled his fateful actions are portrayed in the speech which follows.

From ROBESPIERRE, Speech of February 5, 1794 [1]

It is time to mark clearly the aim of the Revolution and the end toward which we wish to move; it is time to take stock of ourselves, of the obstacles which we still face, and of the means which we ought to adopt to attain our objectives. . . .

What is the goal for which we strive? A peaceful enjoyment of liberty and equality, the rule of that eternal justice whose laws are engraved, not upon marble or stone, but in the hearts of all men.

We wish an order of things where all low and cruel passions are enchained by the laws, all beneficent and generous feelings aroused; where ambition is the desire to merit glory and to serve one's fatherland; where distinctions are born only of equality itself; where the citizen is subject to the magistrate, the magistrate to the people, the people to justice; where the nation safeguards the welfare of each individual, and each individual proudly enjoys the prosperity and glory of his fatherland; where all spirits are enlarged by the constant exchange of republican sentiments and by the need of earning

[1] P. J. B. Buchez and P. C. Roux, eds., *Histoire parlementaire de la Revolution Française,* 40 vols., Paris, 1834-38, XXXI, 268-76.

the respect of a great people; where the arts are the adornment of liberty, which ennobles them; and where commerce is the source of public wealth, not simply of monstrous opulence for a few families.

In our country we wish to substitute morality for egotism, probity for honor, principles for conventions, duties for etiquette, the empire of reason for the tyranny of customs, contempt for vice for contempt for misfortune, pride for insolence, the love of honor for the love of money . . . that is to say, all the virtues and miracles of the Republic for all the vices and snobbishness of the monarchy.

We wish in a word to fulfill the requirements of nature, to accomplish the destiny of mankind, to make good the promises of philosophy . . . that France, hitherto illustrious among slave states, may eclipse the glory of all free peoples that have existed, become the model of all nations. . . . That is our ambition; that is our aim.

What kind of government can realize these marvels? Only a democratic government. . . . But to found and to consolidate among us this democracy, to realize the peaceable rule of constitutional laws, it is necessary to conclude the war of liberty against tyranny and to pass successfully through the storms of revolution.

Such is the aim of the revolutionary system which you have set up. . . .

Now what is the fundamental principle of democratic, or popular government—that is to say, the essential mainspring upon which it depends and which makes it function? It is virtue: I mean public virtue . . . that virtue which is nothing else but love of fatherland and its laws. . . .

The splendor of the goal of the French Revolution is simultaneously the source of our strength and of our weakness: our strength, because it gives us an ascendancy of truth over falsehood, and of public rights over private interests; our weakness, because it rallies against us all vicious men, all those who in their hearts seek to despoil the people. . . . It is necessary to stifle the domestic and foreign enemies of the Republic or perish with them. Now in these circumstances, the first maxim of our politics ought to be to lead the people by means of reason and the enemies of the people by terror.

If the basis of popular government in time of peace is virtue, the basis of popular government in time of revolution is both virtue and terror: virtue without which terror is murderous, terror without which virtue is powerless. Terror is nothing else than swift, severe, indomitable justice; it flows, then, from virtue.

23

NAPOLEON AND THE FRENCH IMPERIUM

1. The Rise of Napoleon Bonaparte

Napoleon Bonaparte (1769-1821), born in Corsica of Florentine ancestry, left his native island when he was nine years old to study in France. Sullen, morose, and unpopular among his French schoolfellows, and early torn between Corsican patriotism and French opportunity, he excelled in mathematics and finished military school to become a sublieutenant in the French army. For a time he was enthusiastic for the *philosophes,* and when the French Revolution began he supported the Jacobin faction until the excesses of the Terror cooled his ardor. In 1793, at the siege of Toulon, he attracted attention by his extraordinary military dispositions and mastery of artillery. Later, he won recognition of the Directory, first by dispelling with a "whiff of grape-shot" a Parisian mob which threatened the Convention (October 5, 1795); then by submitting promising plans for the conduct of the war in Italy, where two French commanders, first Kellermann and then Schérer, had failed to meet the Directory's expectations; and finally by marrying (March 9, 1796) a friend of one of the Directors, Josephine, widow of Alexandre de Beauharnais. Shortly before his marriage, Napoleon had won the long-coveted appointment as commander of the French army of Italy. On March 12 he set out for Italy, where he found his troops in a deplorable condition—ragged, ill-fed, and dispirited. Yet it was with this army that, within twenty days after he opened the campaign, Napoleon drove the Austrian troops across the Po River and forced the King of Sardinia to sign an armistice.

NAPOLEON'S EARLIEST PROCLAMATIONS
TO THE FRENCH ARMY OF ITALY
(1796)

Napoleon's unusual capacity to arouse his soldiers is seen in his earliest proclamations to the army. His first words to the army in Italy, couched in his usual clipped, forceful style, ran as follows.

From NAPOLEON, First Proclamation (1796) [1]

General Headquarters, Nice, 7 Germinal,
Year IV [March 27, 1796]

Soldiers, you are naked, ill-fed; the Government owes you much, it can give you nothing. Your patience, and the courage which you have shown in the midst of these rocky crags, are admirable; but they have won you no glory; no glamour clings about you. I wish to lead you into the most fertile plains of the world. Rich provinces, great cities, will be in your power; you will find honor, glory, and riches there. Soldiers of Italy! do you lack courage or constancy?

[A month later, having thrice defeated the Austrians, and forced the Sardinians to the point of surrender, Napoleon issued a second stirring proclamation to his troops.]

From NAPOLEON, Second Proclamation
(1796) [2]

Headquarters at Cherasco, 7th Floréal,
Year IV [April 26, 1796]

Soldiers:

In fifteen days you have won six victories, taken twenty-one standards, fifty-five pieces of artillery, many fortified places, and conquered the richest part of Piedmont; you have made fifteen thousand prisoners and killed or wounded more than ten thousand men.

Until now you have fought for sterile rocks, made famous by your courage but useless to the fatherland; now your services place you on an equality with the armies of Holland and of the Rhine. Without resources you have supplied everything. Without cannon you have

[1] *Correspondance de Napoléon Ier,* 32 vols., Paris, 1858-70, I, 107 (No. 91).
[2] *Ibid.,* I, 187-88 (No. 234).

won battles, without bridges you have crossed rivers, without shoes you have made forced marches, without brandy and often without bread you have pitched camp. Only republican phalanxes, soldiers of liberty, are capable of enduring what you have suffered. Thanks should be given to you, soldiers! Your country will owe its prosperity to you. . . .

But, soldiers, you have done nothing as yet compared with what you have still to do. Neither Turin nor Milan belongs to you. . . . You were destitute of everything at the beginning of the campaign; now you are abundantly provided. Numerous supplies have been taken from the enemy; artillery for siege and for the field has arrived.

Soldiers, your fatherland has the right to expect great things of you. Will you justify its faith? The greatest obstacles are undoubtedly overcome; but you still have battles to fight, cities to take, rivers to cross. Which of you lacks courage? Which of you prefers to return across the summits of the Apennines and the Alps to bear patiently the insults of that slavish soldiery? No, there is no one among the conquerors of Montenotte, of Dego, of Mondovi. Everyone is burning to extend the glory of the French people; everyone wishes to humiliate those haughty kings who dare contemplate binding us in fetters. Everyone wishes to dictate a glorious peace. . . . Everyone wants to return to his native village and be able to say proudly, "I was with the conquering army of Italy!"

Friends, I promise you this conquest; but there is one condition which you must swear to fulfill: that is to respect the people whom you deliver, to repress the horrible pillage which certain scoundrels, incited by our enemies, commit. Without this you will not be deliverers of the people, but their scourge; you will not do honor to the French people, but will disgrace them. . . . As for me and the generals who have your confidence, we would blush to command an army without discipline or restraint, which recognizes no law but force. . . . Pillagers will be shot without mercy; several have been already. . . .

Peoples of Italy, the French army comes to break your chains. The French people is the friend of all peoples. Come to them with confidence. Your property, your religion, and your customs will be respected. We are making war as generous enemies, and we bear no grudge save against the tyrants who oppress you.

Bonaparte

NAPOLEON INTERFERES IN THE DIRECTORY'S FOREIGN POLICY: THE TREATY OF CAMPO FORMIO (OCTOBER 17, 1797)

It was during his first Italian campaign that Napoleon began to betray large political ambitions. In keeping with earlier revolutionary policy [see page 400], the Directory sought to propagate republicanism in Italy. Napoleon, too, fell in with this design, as the last paragraph of the proclamation above will show; but he also proposed to bend the policy to suit his own purposes. While he posed to the Italian people as a liberator against Austrian tyranny, he bled them for guns, men, supplies, and money which rendered the Army of Italy independent of support from the Directory and actually filled French coffers with Italian spoils. Thus, he could appear to the French nation as a conqueror independent of Directory policy and support. Napoleon's appeals to Italian peoples went far to awaken them from their torpor and create in them a nationalist longing for liberty. "It is time," he wrote to the people of Reggio, "that

Italy should be counted among the free and powerful nations." And so, without the assent of the Directory, he committed France to the recognition of an Italian Republic made up of Reggio, Modena, Ferrara, and Bologna. Again, when he found it inexpedient with the forces at his command to prosecute the war against Austria further, he negotiated a treaty—an action for which he held no lawful authority and an action, moreover, which reversed the Directory's foreign policy and reduced the Directory to a subordinate role in French affairs. "From the date of this proceeding," wrote Madame de Staël,[1] "there no longer existed in the government of France the slightest respect for any political doctrine, and the reign of one man began when the dominion of principle was at an end. Bonaparte made himself remarkable by his character and capacity as much as by his victories, and the imagination of the French was beginning to attach itself warmly to him. His proclamations to the Cisalpine and Ligurian republics were quoted. In the one this phrase was remarked, *You were divided, and bent down by tyranny; you were not in a situation to conquer liberty.* . . . In his style there reigned a spirit of moderation and dignity which formed a contrast with the revolutionary bitterness of the civil leaders of France. The warrior then spoke like a magistrate, while magistrates expressed themselves with military violence. . . . The nation was so weary of oppressors who borrowed the name of liberty, and of oppressed persons who regretted the loss of arbitrary power, that admiration knew not what to attach itself to, and Bonaparte seemed to unite all that was fitted to take it captive." Louis Antoine Fauvelet

de Bourrienne, a former schoolmate whom Napoleon called to Italy to serve as his secretary, wrote the following description of the motives which led Bonaparte to sign the Treaty of Campo Formio whereby the Emperor recognized the Cisalpine Republic "as an independent power," ceded the Austrian Netherlands and certain Italian and Rhenish territories to France, and terminated the war begun against the Emperor in 1792.

From BOURRIENNE, *Memoirs* (1823) [2]

Some of the general's friends wrote to him from Paris, and for my part I never ceased repeating to him, that the peace, the power of making which he had in his own hands, would render him far more popular than the renewal of hostilities. . . .

The early appearance of bad weather precipitated his determination. On the 13th of October, at daybreak, on opening my window, I perceived the mountains covered with snow. . . . I proceeded, as I always did, at seven o'clock in the morning to the general's chamber. I woke him, and told him what I had seen. He feigned at first to disbelieve me, then leaped from his bed, ran to the window, and, convinced of the sudden change [of weather], he calmly said, "What! Before the middle of October! What a country this is! Well, we must make peace!" While he hastily put on his clothes, I read the journals to him, as was my daily custom. He paid but little attention to them. Shutting himself up with me in his closet, he reviewed with the greatest care all the returns from the different corps of the army. "Here are," said he, "nearly eighty thousand effective men. I feed, I pay them: but I can bring but sixty thousand into the

---

[1] *Considérations sur les principaux événemens de la Revolution Française,* II, 195-96.

[2] *Memoirs of Napoleon Bonaparte,* 4 vols., London, 1836, I, 104-06.

field on the day of battle. I shall gain it, but afterwards my force will be reduced twenty thousand men—by killed, wounded, and prisoners. Then how oppose the Austrian forces that will march to the protection of Vienna? It would be a month before the armies of the Rhine could support me, if they should be able; and in a fortnight all the roads and passages will be covered deep with snow. It is settled—I will make peace. Venice will pay for the expense of the war, and the boundary of the Rhine: let the Directory and the lawyers say what they like."

He wrote to the Directory in the following words: "The summits of the hills are covered with snow; I cannot, on account of the stipulations agreed to for the commencement of hostilities, begin before five-and-twenty days, and by that time we shall be overwhelmed with snow. . . ."

It is well known that, by the treaty of Campo Formio, the two belligerent powers made peace at the expense of the republic of Venice, which had nothing to do with the quarrel in the first instance, and which only interfered at a late period, probably against her inclination, and impelled by the force of inevitable circumstances. But what has been the result of this great political spoliation? A portion of the Venetian territory was adjudged to the Cisalpine republic: it is now in the possession of Austria. Another considerable portion, and the capital itself, fell into the lot of Austria in compensation for the Belgic provinces [the Austrian Netherlands] and Lombardy [which were ceded to France]. . . .

The Directory was far from being satisfied with the treaty of Campo Formio, and with difficulty resisted the temptation of not ratifying it. A fortnight before the signature, the Directors wrote to General Bonaparte that they would not consent to

give to the emperor Venice, Friuli, Padua, and the *terra firma* with the boundary of the Adige. "That," said they, "would not be to make peace, but to adjourn the war. We shall be regarded as the beaten party, independently of the disgrace of abandoning Venice, which Bonaparte himself thought so worthy of freedom. France ought not, and never will wish, to see Italy delivered up to Austria. The Directory would prefer the chances of a war to changing a single word of its ultimatum, which is already too favourable to Austria." But all this was said in vain. Bonaparte made no scruple of disregarding his instructions.

THE COUP D'ETAT OF 18-19 BRUMAIRE, YEAR VII (NOVEMBER 9-10, 1799)

The government which Napoleon flouted in 1797 consisted, according to the constitution of the Year III (August 22, 1795), of an executive of five Directors appointed by a legislative body of two houses, a Council of Ancients, and a Council of Five Hundred. This government, known as the Directory, was constantly assailed, either by Jacobins or by monarchists, and it was repeatedly in danger of being overthrown. After the Treaty of Campo Formio, Napoleon toyed with the notion of seizing power; but as the time did not appear ripe, he embarked upon a campaign in Egypt (1798-99) in the hope of seizing a new empire for France and striking a new blow against England. Meanwhile, a new coalition formed with England, Russia, Austria, Naples, Portugal, and Turkey arrayed against France, fresh royalist uprisings threatened the Directory at home, and the Abbé Sieyès, elected to the Directory in May, 1799, was plotting with the Viscount Paul F. J. N. de Barras, another Director, for the overthrow of the Directory government. As Napoleon's Egyptian campaign proved to be a fruitless adventure, the General, with a few members of his staff, deserted the Egyptian army (August 21, 1799) and returned to France. He was welcomed as the only possible savior of France. After a cautious survey of the state of politics, he cast in his fortune with Sieyès and Barras and plotted to seize political control of France. The projected coup d'état was carefully planned. J. Holland Rose, in his biography of Napoleon, has described its execution.

From ROSE, *Napoleon I* (1901) [1]

The army and most of the generals were also ready for some change, only Bernadotte and Jourdan refusing to listen to the new proposals; and the former of these came "with sufficiently bad grace" to join Bonaparte at the time of action. The police was secured through that dexterous trimmer, the regicide Fouché, who now turned against the very men who had recently appointed him to office. Feeling sure of the soldiery and police, the innovators fixed the 18th of Brumaire as the date of their enterprise. . . .

Meanwhile in the legislative Councils there was a feeling of vague disquiet. The Ancients were, on the whole, hostile to the Directory, but in the Council of Five Hundred the democratic ardor of the younger deputies foreboded a fierce opposition. Yet there also the plotters found many adherents, who followed the lead now cautiously given by Lucien Bonaparte. This young man, whose impassioned speeches had marked him out as an irreproachable patriot, was now President of that Council. No event could have been more auspicious for the conspirators. With Sieyès, Barras, and Ducos, as traitors

in the Directory, with the Ancients favorable, and the junior deputies under the presidency of Lucien, the plot seemed sure of success.

The first important step was taken by the Council of Ancients, who decreed the transference of the Councils to St. Cloud. The danger of a Jacobin plot was urged as a plea for this motion. . . . The Ancients then appointed Bonaparte to command the armed forces in and near Paris. The next step was to insure the abdication of Gohier and Moulin [the remaining Directors]. . . . The Directory was doomed; for the two defenders of the institution had not the necessary quorum for giving effect to their decrees. . . .

Meanwhile, accompanied by a brilliant group of generals, Bonaparte proceeded to the Tuileries, where the Ancients were sitting; and by indulging in a wordy declamation he avoided taking the oath to the constitution required of a general on entering upon a new command. In the Council of Five Hundred, Lucien Bonaparte stopped the eager questions and murmurs, on the pretext that the session was only legal at St. Cloud.

There, on the next day (19th Brumaire or 10th November), a far more serious blow was to be struck. The overthrow of the Directory was a foregone conclusion. But with the Legislature it was far otherwise, for its life was still whole and vigorous. . . .

Despite the adhesion of most of the Ancients to his plans, Bonaparte on appearing before them, could only utter a succession of short, jerky phrases which smacked of the barracks rather than of the Senate. Retiring in some confusion, he regains his presence of mind among the soldiers outside, and enters the hall of the Five Hundred, intending to intimidate them not only by threats, but by armed force. At the sight of the uniforms at the door, the republican enthusiasm of the younger deputies catches fire. They fiercely

[1] John Holland Rose, *The Life of Napoleon I*, 2 vols. in 1, 1924, I, 204-10. By permission of Harcourt, Brace and Company, Inc., New York.

assail him with cries of "Down with the tyrant! down with the Dictator! outlaw him!" In vain Lucien Bonaparte commands order. Several deputies rush at the general, and fiercely shake him by the collar. He turns faint with excitement and chagrin; but Lefebvre and a few grenadiers rushing up drag him from the hall. He comes forth like a somnambulist (says an onlooker), pursued by the terrible cry, "Outlaw him!" Had the cries at once taken form in a decree, the history of the world might have been different. One of the deputies, General Augereau, fiercely demands that the motion of outlawry be put to the vote. Lucien Bonaparte refuses, protests, weeps, finally throws off his official robes, and is rescued from the enraged deputies by grenadiers whom the conspirators send in for this purpose. Meanwhile Bonaparte and his friends were hastily deliberating when one of their number brought the news that the deputies had declared the general an outlaw. The news chased the blood from his cheek until Sieyès, whose *sangfroid* did not desert him in these civilian broils, exclaims, "Since they outlaw you, they are outlaws." This revolutionary logic recalls Bonaparte to himself. He shouts, "To arms!" Lucien, too, mounting a horse, appeals to the soldiers to free the Council from the menaces of some deputies armed with daggers, and in the pay of England [as he claims], who are terrorizing the majority. The shouts of command, clinched by the adroit reference to daggers and English gold, cause the troops to waver in their duty; and Lucien, pressing his advantage to the utmost, draws a sword, and, holding it towards his brother, exclaims that he will stab him if ever he attempts anything against liberty. Murat, Leclerc, and other generals enforce this melodramatic appeal by shouts for Bonaparte, which the troops excitedly take up. The drums sound for an advance, and the troops forthwith enter the hall. In vain the deputies raise the shout, *"Vive la République,"* and invoke the constitution. Appeals to the law are overpowered by the drum and by shouts for Bonaparte; and the legislators of France fly pell-mell from the hall through doors and windows. . . .

At the close of that eventful day, the 19th of Brumaire, Lucien Bonaparte gathered about him in the deserted hall at St. Cloud some score or so of the dispersed deputies known to be favorable to his brother, declaimed against the Jacobins, whose spectral plot had proved so useful to the real plotters, and proposed to this "Rump" of the Council the formation of a commission who should report on measures that were deemed necessary for the public safety. The measures were found to be the deposition of the Directory, the expulsion of sixty-one members from the Councils, the nomination of Sieyès, Roger Ducos, and Bonaparte as provisional Consuls, and the adjournment of the Councils for four months. The consuls accordingly took up their residence in the Luxembourg Palace, just vacated by the Directors, and the drafting of a constitution was confided to them and to an *interim* commission of fifty members chosen equally from the two Councils.

[Late the same day, Napoleon issued the following proclamation which shows, as Bourrienne said, "how much Bonaparte excelled in the art of twisting the truth to his own advantage."]

From NAPOLEON, Proclamation to the French People (1799) [1]

Paris, 19 Brumaire, Year VIII
[November 10, 1799] 11 P.M.

On my return to Paris, I found division among all authorities, and agreement on just one fact, that the constitution was

---

[1] *Correspondance de Napoléon Ier*, VI, 5 (No. 4389).

half destroyed and could not save liberty.

Every party came to me, confided to me their designs, imparted their secrets, and requested my support; But I refused to be the man of any party.

The Council of Ancients appealed to me; I responded to their appeal. A plan of general restoration had been made by men whom the nation has become accustomed to regard as defenders of liberty, equality, and property. This plan required calm examination, free of all influence and of all fear. As a result, the Council of Ancients resolved to remove the legislative bodies to St. Cloud. They placed me in charge of the force necessary to their independence. I believed myself bound, out of duty to my fellow citizens, to the soldiers perishing in our armies, and to the national honor acquired at the price of so much blood, to accept the command.

The Councils assembled at St. Cloud. Republican troops guaranteed their safety from without; but from within assassins created terror. Many Deputies of the Council of Five Hundred, armed with stilettos and pistols, endangered all about them with the menace of death.

The plans which ought to have been matured were withheld. The majority of the Councils was disorganized, the boldest orators were disconcerted, and the futility of the entire plan proposed was evident.

I went to the Council of Ancients with indignation and sorrow. I begged them to push through their original plans. I reminded them of the evils of the nation which had caused them to make these plans. They united in giving me fresh proofs of their determination.

I presented myself to the Council of Five Hundred, alone, without arms, my head uncovered, just as the Ancients had received and applauded me. I went to recall the majority to firmness and to assure it of its authority.

The stilettos which had menaced the Deputies were instantly raised against their deliverer. Twenty assassins rushed at me and aimed at my breast. The grenadiers of the legislative body whom I had left at the door of the hall ran forward and placed themselves between me and the assassins. One of these grenadiers was struck by a stiletto which pierced his clothes. They bore me out. At the same moment, cries of "Outlaw him!" were raised against the defender of the law. It was the horrid cry of assassins against the power destined to repress them. They pressed about the president [Lucien Bonaparte], hurling threats, arms in their hands. They commanded him to declare me outlawed. I confirmed this. I ordered him to be rescued from their fury, and six grenadiers of the legislative body brought him out. Immediately afterward, some grenadiers of the legislative body charged the hall and cleared it.

The seditious ones, thus intimidated, dispersed and fled. The majority, freed of their assailants, returned freely and peaceably into the hall, attended to the propositions which had already been set forth for the public safety, deliberated, and drew up the salutory resolution which ought to become the new and provisional law of the Republic.

Frenchmen, without doubt you will recognize in this conduct the zeal of a soldier of liberty, of a citizen devoted to the Republic. Conservative, protective, and liberal ideas have resumed their sway by the dispersion of those factions which oppressed the Councils and which, by such acts, have proved themselves the most odious and contemptible of men.

Bonaparte

NAPOLEON'S SECOND PEACE WITH THE EMPEROR (1801)

In the spring of 1800, Napoleon, having consolidated his position as First

Consul in France, set out upon his second Italian campaign, once more to dissolve Austrian adhesion to the new coalition which had been formed against France. At the battle of Marengo (June 14, 1800), the First Consul defeated the Imperial forces, but the Emperor was unwilling to consider peace terms separately from his English ally, and the war went on. Again, at Hohenlinden (December 2, 1800), the French Army of the Rhine, under General Moreau, administered defeat upon the Austrians and, in the following February, a treaty was signed at Lunéville. The new treaty confirmed many articles of the Treaty of Campo Formio [see page 407], but it placed France in a more improved position and forced the Emperor's withdrawal from the Second Coalition.

From The Treaty of Lunéville
(February 9, 1801) [1]

His Majesty the Emperor, the King of Hungary and of Bohemia [Francis I], and the First Consul of the French Republic, in the name of the French people, induced by a common desire to put an end to the evils of war, have resolved to proceed to the conclusion of a definitive treaty of peace and amity. His said Imperial and Royal Majesty desiring no less sincerely to extend the benefits of peace to the German Empire, and the existing conditions not affording the necessary time for consulting the Empire, or permitting its representatives to take part in the negotiations, has resolved, in view of the concessions made by the Deputation of the Empire at the recent Congress of Rastadt [1797-99] to treat in the name of the German Union, as has happened before under similar circumstances.

Hence the contracting parties have named the following as their plenipoten-

tiaries [for Austria, Louis, Count of Cobenzl; for France, Joseph Bonaparte, Napoleon's elder brother]. . . . These, having exchanged their credentials, have agreed upon the following Articles:

I. Peace, amity, and a good understanding shall hereafter exist forever between His Majesty the Emperor, King of Hungary and of Bohemia, acting both in his own name and in that of the German Empire, and the French Republic; His Majesty agreeing that the said Empire shall ratify the present treaty in due form [which was done March 7, 1801, at an Imperial Diet at Regensberg]. . . .

II. The cession of the former Belgian Provinces to the French Republic, stipulated in Article III of the Treaty of Campo Formio, is renewed here in the most solemn manner. His Majesty the Emperor and King therefore renounces for himself and his successors, as well on his own part as on that of the German Empire, all right and title to the above specified provinces, which shall be held in perpetuity by the French Republic in full sovereignty and proprietary right. . . .

III. Moreover, in confirmation of Article VI of the Treaty of Campo Formio, His Majesty the Emperor and King shall possess in full sovereignty and proprietary right the countries enumerated below, to wit: Istria, Dalmatia and the Islands of the Adriatic, formerly belonging to Venice, dependent upon them; the Mouths of the Cattaro, the City of Venice, the Lagoons, and the territory included between the hereditary States of His Majesty the Emperor and King; the Adriatic Sea and the Adige from the point where it leaves Tyrol to that where it flows into the Adriatic. . . .

[As the above article established the Adige River, north and east of the Po, as the farthest extent of Imperial territory in northern Italy, Articles IV and V provided for the removal from Italy of

[1] *Translations and Reprints from the Original Sources of European History,* II, No. 2, 8-12. By permission of the University of Pennsylvania Press.

the Duke of Modena and the Grand Duke of Tuscany. The Duke of Modena's territory was incorporated in the Cisalpine Republic—under French influence—and the Duke was indemnified with Breisgau, at the Emperor's expense; similarly, the Grand Duchy of Tuscany was turned over to Louis, the infant Duke of Parma, and called the Kingdom of Etruria, while the erstwhile Grand Duke "shall receive a complete and full indemnity in Germany for the loss of his states in Italy."]

VI. His Majesty the Emperor and King consents not only on his part but upon the part of the German Empire that the French Republic shall hereafter possess in full sovereignty and proprietary right the territory and domains lying on the left bank of the Rhine and forming a part of the German Empire, so that . . . the *Thalweg* [channel] of the Rhine shall hereafter form the boundary between the French Republic and the German Empire from that point where the Rhine leaves Helvetian [Swiss] territory to the point where it reaches Batavian territory. In view of this, the French Republic formally renounces all possessions whatsoever upon the right bank of the Rhine. . . . [German princes dispossessed by the cession made to France on the left bank of the Rhine shall be provided "an indemnity within the Empire."]

XI. The present treaty . . . is declared to be common to the Batavian, Helvetian, Cisalpine, and Ligurian Republics. The contracting parties mutually guarantee the independence of the said republics and the freedom of the inhabitants of the said countries to adopt such form of government as they shall see fit. . . .

Done and signed at Lunéville, February 9, 1801 (The 20th Pluviôse of the Year IX of the French Republic).

(Signed) Louis, Count of Cobenzl

Joseph Bonaparte

NAPOLEON'S PEACE WITH ENGLAND (1802)

Not long after the Treaty of Lunéville, Napoleon found it expedient to make peace with England. Preliminaries were signed at London on October 1, 1801, and the definitive treaty was concluded five months later at Amiens. By the Treaty of Amiens France won the only breathing spell in the war which had begun in 1792 and was destined to open again in May, 1803, and to continue until 1814. Napoleon outwitted gouty old Lord Cornwallis at Amiens, and the treaty was a deep disappointment to the English. England appeared to have made all the concessions; the absence of any commercial provisions left French-controlled Continental markets closed to British goods; a number of the provisions were vague—Article XVIII, for example; and, as French domination of the Continent was tacitly admitted, Napoleon not only gratified the French desire for a victorious peace, but also lifted his own popularity and prestige to new heights. Chief provisions of the Treaty of Amiens follow.

From The Treaty of Amiens
(March 27, 1802) [1]

His Majesty the King of the United Kingdom of Great Britain and Ireland, and the First Consul of the French Republic, in the name of the French people, being animated with an equal desire to put an end to the calamities of war, have laid the foundations of Peace in the Preliminary Articles signed at London, the 1st of October, 1801 (9th Vendémiaire, Year X). And as by the fifteenth Article of the said Preliminaries, it has been stipulated that Plenipotentiaries should be

[1] "State Papers," in *The Annual Register* . . . *for the Year 1802*, London, 1802, 307-14.

named on each side, who should proceed to Amiens for the purpose of concluding a Definitive Treaty, in concert with the Allies of the Contracting Powers. . . . [Names plenipotentiaries, as follows: for England, Marquis Cornwallis; for France, Joseph Bonaparte; for Spain, Don Joseph Nicholas de Azara; and for the Batavian Republic, Roger John Schimmelpeninck. These representatives met and agreed upon the following articles:]

I. There shall be peace, friendship, and good understanding between his Majesty the King of the United Kingdom of Great Britain and Ireland, his heirs and successors, on the one part; and the French Republic, his Majesty the King of Spain, his heirs and successors, and the Batavian Republic, on the other part. . . .

III. His Britannic Majesty restores to the French Republic, and her Allies, namely, his Catholic Majesty and the Batavian Republic, all the possessions and colonies which belonged to them respectively, and which had been occupied or conquered by the British forces in the course of the war, with the exception of Trinidad, and the Dutch possessions in the island of Ceylon. . . . [These latter possessions are ceded in full to Great Britain.]

VI. The Cape of Good Hope remains in full sovereignty to the Batavian Republic, as it was before the war. The ships of every description belonging to the other Contracting Parties shall have the right to put in there, and to purchase supplies. . . .

VIII. The territories, possessions, and rights of the Ottoman Porte [Egypt, Syria, and territories invaded by the French in 1798-99] are hereby maintained in their integrity, such as they were previous to the war.

IX. The Republic of the Seven Islands is hereby acknowledged. . . . [In Article X Malta and some other Mediterranean islands are restored to the order of St. John of Jerusalem which is declared a neutral power "entirely independent of each of the powers," its neutrality guaranteed in perpetuity by Great Britain, France, Austria, Russia, Spain and Prussia.]

XI. The fisheries on the coast of Newfoundland . . . are replaced on the same footing on which they were previous to the war. . . .

XVIII. The Branch of the House of Nassau [Orange], which was established in the republic formerly called the Republic of the United Netherlands, and now the Batavian Republic, having suffered losses there . . . an adequate compensation shall be procured for the said Branch of the House of Nassau for the said losses.

XIX. The present Definitive Treaty of Peace is declared common to the Sublime Ottoman Porte, the Ally of his Britannic Majesty; and the Sublime Porte shall be invited to transmit its act of accession thereto in the shortest delay possible.

NAPOLEON AS EMPEROR OF THE FRENCH: A CONTEMPORARY PEN PORTRAIT

The First Consul's popularity after the Treaty of Amiens led the French Tribunate to "express the wish," on May 7, 1802, that General Bonaparte be given "a striking token of national recognition." Four days later (May 11), the Senate, considering that Napoleon has "filled the world with his renown, has preserved France from the horrors of anarchy which were menacing it, broken the revolutionary sickle, dispersed the factions," and so on, re-elected him "First Consul of the French Republic for the ten years which shall immediately follow the ten for which he has been appointed." On the same day, the Consuls ordered, upon Napoleon's initiative, that "The French people shall be consulted upon this question: Shall Napoleon Bonaparte be Consul for life?" A plebiscite followed and the results, published August 2, 1802, showed a vote of 3,572,329 to 2,569 in favor of the proposition. Two days afterward (August 4), by a senatus-consultum, a new constitution was in fact set forth which declared that "The Consuls are for life" and that Napoleon, as First Consul, should nominate not only his own successor but also, upon the death of the other Consuls, their successors as well. In all but name, Napoleon was absolute monarch of the French "Republic." But the First Consul's ambition was still unsatisfied. In 1804, after the European war had been renewed, royalist plots against Napoleon's life were discovered. "They seek to destroy the Revolution," said Bonaparte, "by attacking my person: I will defend it, for I am the Revolution." These words, so reminiscent of Louis XIV's "I am the state," were accompanied by a new constitution—the "constitution of the Year XII" (May 18, 1804)—wherein the complaisant Senate decreed that "The government of the French Republic is entrusted to an emperor, who takes the title of Emperor of the French. . . . Napoleon Bonaparte, present First Consul of the Republic, is Emperor of the French." The throne was declared hereditary, to pass to the "natural and legitimate" male heir of Napoleon "by order of primogeniture." A new order of nobility was set up and, on December 2, 1804, at the Cathedral of Notre Dame in the presence of the Pope and a cheering populace, a flashy coronation service was held. But after the Pope anointed Emperor and Empress with the holy oil, gave them his pontifical blessing, and offered up prayers on their behalf, Na-

poleon gently waved His Holiness aside, placed the crown on his head himself, and then crowned the Empress. "We have done better than we intended," declared the defiant leader of the royalist conspirators, "We came to give France a King and we have given her an Emperor." Madame de Rémusat, a friend of Josephine de Beauharnais before the latter married Napoleon, became a lady in waiting to the new Empress. In this capacity she came to know the Emperor intimately and in her *Memoirs* she left the following sketch of him.

From MME. DE RÉMUSAT, *Memoirs* (c. 1809) [1]

Napoleon Bonaparte is of low stature, and ill-made; the upper part of his body is too long in proportion to his legs. He has thin chestnut hair, his eyes are greyish blue, and his skin, which was yellow whilst he was slight, has become of late years a dead white without any color. His forehead, the setting of his eye, the line of his nose—are all beautiful, and remind one of an antique medallion; his mouth, which is thin-lipped, becomes pleasant when he laughs; the teeth are regular; his chin is short, and his jaw heavy and square; he has well-formed hands and feet: I mention them particularly, because he thought a good deal of them.

He has an habitual slight stoop; his eyes are dull, giving to his face a melancholy and meditative expression when in repose. When he is angry his looks are fierce and menacing. Laughter becomes him; it makes him look more youthful, and less formidable. When he laughs, his countenance improves. He was always simple in his dress, and generally wore the

[1] *Memoirs of Madame de Rémusat,* ed. by Paul de Rémusat, trans. from the French by Mrs. Caskel Hoey and Mr. John Lillie, 2 vols., London, 1880, I, 1-16.

uniform of his own guard. He was cleanly rather from habit than from a liking for cleanliness; he bathed often, sometimes in the middle of the night, because he thought the practice good for his health. Otherwise, the precipitation with which he did everything did not admit of his clothes being put on carefully; and on gala days and full-dress occasions, his attendants were obliged to consult together as to when they might snatch a moment to dress him.

He could not endure the wearing of ornaments; the slightest constraint was insupportable to him. He would tear off or break anything that gave him the least annoyance, and the poor valet who had occasioned him a passing inconvenience would receive violent proofs of his anger. I have said there was fascination in the smile of Bonaparte; but during all the time when I was in the habit of seeing him constantly, he rarely put forth that charm. Gravity was at the bottom of his character; not the gravity of a dignified and noble manner, but that which arises from profound thought. In his youth he was a dreamer, later in life he became moody, and, later still, an habitually ill-tempered man. . . .

Bonaparte was deficient in education and in manners; it seemed as if he must have been destined either to live in a tent where all men are equal, or upon a throne where everything is permitted. He did not know how either to enter or to leave a room; he did not know how to make a bow, how to rise, or how to sit down. His questions were abrupt, and so also was his manner of speech. Spoken by him, Italian loses all its grace and sweetness. Whatever language he speaks, it always sounds like a foreign tongue; he appears to force it to express his thoughts. . . . He would never yield to grammar. . . .

In trying to depict Bonaparte, it would

be necessary, if one were to follow the analytical forms of which he was so fond, to separate into three distinct parts his soul, his heart, and his mind, for no one of these ever blended completely with the others. Although remarkable for certain intellectual qualities, no man, it must be allowed, was ever less lofty of soul. There was no generosity, no true greatness in him. I have never known him to admire, I have never known him to comprehend, a fine action. He always regarded every indication of good feeling with suspicion; he did not value sincerity, and he did not hesitate to say that he recognized the superiority of a man by the greater or less dexterity with which he practised the art of lying. . . .

Bonaparte's methods of government were all selected from among those which have a tendency to debase men. He dreaded ties of affection; he endeavoured to isolate every one; he never sold a favour without awakening a sense of uneasiness, for he held that the true way to attach the recipient to himself was by compromising him, and often even blasting him in public opinion. He could not pardon virtue until he had succeeded in weakening its effect by ridicule. He cannot be said to have truly loved glory, for he never hesitated to prefer success; thus, although he was audacious in good fortune, and pushed it to its utmost limits, he was timid and troubled when threatened with reverses. . . .

According to the order I have laid down, I ought now to speak of Bonaparte's heart; but if it were possible to believe that a being, in every other way similar to ourselves, could exist without that portion of our organization which makes us desire to love and to be loved, I should say that in his case the heart was left out. Perhaps, however, the truth was that he succeeded in suppressing it completely. He was always too much engrossed by himself to be influenced by any sentiment of affection, no matter of what kind. . . . Notwithstanding his habitual hardness, Bonaparte was not entirely without experience of love. But, good heavens! what manner of sentiment was it in his case? A sensitive person forgets self in love, and becomes almost transformed, but to a man of the stamp of Bonaparte it only meant an additional object of despotism. The Emperor despised women, and contempt cannot exist together with love. He regarded their weakness as an unanswerable proof of their inferiority. . . . On this account Bonaparte was under restraint in the society of women; and as every kind of restraint put him out of humour, he was awkward in their presence, and never knew how to talk to them. . . .

The intellect of Bonaparte was most remarkable. It would be difficult, I think, to find, among men, a more powerful or comprehensive mind. It owed nothing to education; for, in reality, he was ignorant. He read but little, and that hurriedly; but he quickly seized upon the little he had learnt, and his imagination developed it so extensively that he might easily have passed for a well-educated man.

His intellectual capacity seemed to be vast, from the number of subjects he could take in and classify without fatigue. With him one idea gave birth to a thousand, and a word would lift his conversation into elevated regions of fancy, in which strict logic did not indeed keep him company, but in which his intellect never failed to shine.

It was always a great pleasure to me to hear him talk, or rather to hear him hold forth, for his conversation was generally composed of long monologues; not that he objected to replies when he was in a good humour, but, for many reasons, it was not always easy to answer him. . . . Any individual undertaking to refute him,

or to carry on a dialogue with him, felt like an actor before an audience. I have said that he spoke badly, but his language was generally animated and brilliant; his grammatical inaccuracies sometimes gave his sentences an unexpected strength, which well became the originality of his ideas. He required no interlocutor to warm him up. He would dash into a subject, and go on for a long time, but he was careful to notice whether he was listened to, and pleased with those who comprehended and applauded him. . . . I remember well that, because he interested me very much when he spoke, and I listened to him with pleasure, he proclaimed me a woman of intellect, although at the time I had not addressed two consecutive sentences to him.

2. Mastering the Revolution: Napoleonic Measures for the Construction of Imperial France

NAPOLEON MUZZLES THE PRESS

The era of the Consulate (1800-04) and the first years of the Empire were the most constructive of the Napoleonic regime. "We have done with the romance of the Revolution," said the First Consul, "We must now commence its history. We must have eyes only for what is real and practicable in the application of principles, and not for the speculative and hypothetical." To consolidate the political forces of France and to preserve the appearance of being a man of no party, Napoleon enlisted in the government of the Consulate men of all political colors from Jacobins to Royalists. Moreover, by an indulgent policy towards émigrés, rebels, and others alienated from the Revolution, the First Consul placated many discordant groups, restored order, and embarked upon a series of reform measures which, for a time, seemed to vindicate his boast, "I am the Revolution." The price of order, however, was the restraint of freedom. On January 17, 1800, under the guise of "security" in time of war but actually in order to ensure friendly public opinion, political newspapers in Paris were reduced in number from seventy-three to thirteen by the following consular order.

From Consular Order, January 17, 1800 [1]

The Consuls of the Republic, considering that a part of the newspapers which are printed in the department of the Seine are instruments in the hands of the enemies of the Republic; that the government is particularly charged by the French people to look after their security, orders as follows:

1. The minister of police shall permit to be printed, published, and circulated during the whole course of the war only the following newspapers. . . . [Here follow the names of thirteen newspapers] and newspapers devoted exclusively to science, arts, literature, commerce, announcements and notices.

2. The minister of the general police shall immediately make a report upon all the newspapers that are printed in the other departments.

3. The minister of the general police shall see that no new newspaper be printed. . . .

4. The proprietors and editors of the newspapers preserved by the present order shall present themselves to the minister

of the police in order to attest their character. . . .

5. All newspapers which shall insert articles opposed to the respect that is due to the social compact, to the sovereignty of the people and the glory of the armies, or which shall publish invectives against the governments and nations who are friends or allies of the Republic, even when these articles may be extracts from foreign periodicals, shall be immediately suppressed.

6. The minister of the general police is charged with the execution of the present order.

FOUCHÉ ON THE SECRET POLICE

"I was like a rider on an unruly horse who always wanted to swerve either to the right or to the left; and to make him keep a straight course I was obliged to let him feel the bridle occasionally." So spoke Napoleon at St. Helena. One curb constantly employed was, as Josephine called it, "a vile system of espionage." As Minister of Police, Napoleon employed, during most of his regime, the infamous Joseph Fouché (1763-1820), a former pedagogue turned into a demagogue, profiteer, and spy. "Bonaparte's natural mistrust," wrote Pasquier, "warned him not to repose entire confidence in such a man and that it would be necessary to set a watch on the man who was about to be entrusted with the duty of watching others. It was from that day that he began to employ several police systems exercising a respective check on each other, always trying to surpass each other in zeal." Fouché "had seen everything, known everything. I add that he cared seriously for nothing. Without affection for anybody, of a duplicity and of a perfidy never equalled," he spied even upon Napoleon and Jose-

[1] Anderson, ed., *The Constitutions and Other Select Documents Illustrative of the History of France 1789-1907*, 282. By permission of Frank Maloy Anderson.

phine. How much we can believe of what Fouché wrote of his Napoleonic Gestapo is difficult to tell. Reputedly he wrote the following boasts.

From FOUCHÉ, *Memoirs* (1809-10) [1]

It will not be doubted that I had salaried spies in all ranks and orders; I had some of both sexes, hired at the rate of a thousand or two thousand francs per month, according to their importance and their services. I received their reports directly in writing, having a conventional mark. . . .

I also had my foreign spies. It was in my cabinet, also, that the foreign gazettes, prohibited to the perusal of the French people, were collected, abstracts of which were made for my own use. By that means, I held in my hands the most important strings of foreign politics. . . .

I was thus far from limiting my duties to espionage. All the state prisons were under my control, as well as the *gendarmerie*. The delivery of the visa of passports belonged to me. To me was assigned the duty of watching amnestied individuals and foreigners. I established general commissariats in the principal towns of the kingdom, which extended the network of the police over the whole of France, and especially our frontiers. . . .

I confess that such an establishment was expensive; it swallowed up several millions, the funds of which were secretly provided from taxes laid upon gambling and prostitution, and from the granting of passports. Notwithstanding all that has been said against gambling, reflecting and firm minds must allow, that in the actual state of society, the legal converting of vice into profit is a necessary evil. . . . Under the empire . . . it became necessary to organize the gambling-houses upon a much larger scale, for the produce of them was not solely destined to reward my moving phalanxes of spies. I nominated as superintendent-general of the gambling-houses in France, Perrein the elder, who already farmed them, and who, after the coronation, extended his privilege over all the chief towns of the empire, upon condition of paying fourteen millions yearly, independently of three thousand francs daily to the minister of the police [Fouché himself!] which, however, did not remain entirely in his hands.

All these elements of an immense power did not reach my cabinet there to expire without utility. As I was informed of all, it became my duty to centre in myself the public complaints, in order to make known to the head of the government the discomforts and sufferings of the state.

I will not therefore dissemble that it was in my power to act upon the fear or terror which either more or less constantly agitated the possessor of an unlimited power. The great searcher into the state, I could complain, censure, and condemn for the whole of France. . . .

In my second ministry, I succeeded much more by the force of remonstrances and of apprehension, than by restraint and the use of coercive measures. I revived the ancient police maxim, namely, that three persons could not meet and speak indiscreetly upon public affairs, without its coming the next day to the ears of the minister of police. Certain it is, that I had the address to make it universally believed that wherever four persons assembled, there, in my pay, were eyes to see and ears to hear. . . . Such then was this vast and terrific machine called the general police of the empire. It may easily be conceived, that without neglecting the details, I was chiefly engaged with its *ensemble* and results.

[1] *Memoirs of Joseph Fouché*, London, 1894 (Memoir Library), 189-92.

REORGANIZATION OF LOCAL ADMINISTRATION

One of Napoleon's earliest measures for the political reconstruction of France was an act for the reorganization of French local government. In the existing confusion and urgent need for orderly administration, the First Consul found little opposition to the centralization of all local powers in his own hands. Indeed, the new system, which substituted local government by the central power for local self-government and made each prefect and subprefect a kind of First Consul in miniature, functioned so satisfactorily that subsequent governments retained it, with only minor readjustments, until the fall of France in 1940. Basic provisions of the Napoleonic act are given herewith.

From the Act of February 17, 1800 [1]

I. DIVISION OF TERRITORY

The European territory of the Republic shall be divided into departments and communal districts [*arrondissements*] as set forth in the table annexed below. . . . [This table lists 98 departments into which France was divided, and each department was subdivided into from 3 to 6 *arrondissements*.]

II. ADMINISTRATION

Section 1. Departmental Administration

There shall be in each department a prefect, a council of prefecture [of from 3 to 5 members], and a department general council [of from 16 to 24 members], which shall discharge the functions now performed by the administrations. . . .

The prefect alone shall be charged with the administration.

The council of prefecture shall determine: upon the petitions of individuals seeking to escape or to reduce their share of the direct taxes . . . [and other matters, such as disputes between contractors for public works, claims of individuals for indemnities, litigation over public lands, etc.].

The departmental general council shall meet each year, as determined by the government, and its sessions shall not exceed fifteen days in duration. . . .

It shall make the division of the direct taxes among the communal districts of the department . . . [etc.].

Section 2. Communal Administration

In each communal district there shall be a subprefect and a district council composed of eleven members.

The subprefect shall perform the duties now performed by the municipal administrations and the cantonal commissioners, with the exception of those which are hereafter assigned to the district council and the municipalities.

The district council shall meet each year . . . [and] shall make the division of the direct taxes among the cities, towns, and villages of the district. . . .

Section 3. Municipalities

In cities, towns, and other places for which there are now a municipal agent and Deputy, and whose population shall not exceed two thousand five hundred inhabitants, there shall be a mayor and a deputy. . . . [From 2,500 to 5,000, a mayor and two Deputies; from 5,000 to 10,000, a mayor, two Deputies, and a police commissioner; from 10,000 up, a Deputy for each 20,000 in excess, and a commissioner for each 10,000 in excess.]

Section 4. Of the Appointments

The First Consul shall appoint the prefects, the councilors of prefecture, the

[1] Duvergier, ed., *Collection complète des lois,* XII, 78-98.

members of the general councils of the departments, the general secretary for the prefecture, the subprefects, the members of the district councils, the mayors and Deputies of cities of more than five thousand inhabitants, the commissioners general of police and prefects of police in the cities in which they shall be established. . . . [Mayors and Deputies in towns of less than 5,000 shall be appointed by the prefect of the department.]

THE NAPOLEONIC CHURCH SETTLEMENT

"All was calculation with Bonaparte," said Bourienne, "To produce effect was his highest gratification." No better illustration of this fact exists than Napoleon's Concordat with Pope Pius VII. "In every country," the First Consul said, "religion is useful to the government, and those who govern ought to avail themselves of it to influence mankind. . . . Many persons have urged me to found a Gallican church, and make myself its head: but they do not know France. If they did, they would know that the majority of the people would not like a rupture with Rome." In this spirit of political aggrandizement, Napoleon undertook to reach a settlement with Rome and to quiet the religio-political discords which had followed upon confiscation of church lands in 1789 and the Civil Constitution of the Clergy in 1790 [see page 395]. Even so, the Concordat, together with subsequent legislation providing for toleration of Protestant sects, established a church settlement in France which lasted for more than a century. More immediately, it ended the religious disorder which had prevailed in France since 1789, and re-established the Catholic Church in France; it terminated the schism with Rome and restored the spiritual authority of the pope in the Gallican Church; it validated the titles to lands purchased from the confiscated church properties; and it rendered the French church submissive to the state. The Concordat was signed July 15, 1801, but not proclaimed by Napoleon until April 8, 1802.

From The Concordat (July 15, 1801-April 8, 1802) [1]

CONVENTION BETWEEN THE FRENCH GOVERNMENT AND HIS HOLINESS PIUS VII

The government of the French Republic recognizes that the Roman Catholic and apostolic religion is the religion of the great majority of French citizens.

His Holiness likewise recognizes that this same religion has derived and at this moment again expects the greatest benefit and prestige from the establishment of the Catholic worship in France and from the particular profession of it which is made by the Consuls of the Republic.

In consequence, after this mutual recognition, as well for the benefit of religion as for the maintenance of internal tranquillity, they have agreed as follows:

1. The Catholic apostolic and Roman religion shall be freely exercised in France; its worship shall be made public, in conformity to those police regulations which the government shall deem necessary for public tranquillity.

2. In concert with the government, the Holy See shall make a new division of French dioceses.

3. His Holiness shall declare to the titular French bishops that [they shall resign and] . . . provision shall be made for the government of the bishops of the new division by new titularies in the following manner:

4. The First Consul of the Republic shall make appointments, within the three

[1] Ibid., XIII, 89-91.

months which shall follow the publication of the bull of His Holiness, to the archbishoprics and bishoprics of the new division. His Holiness shall confer the canonical institution, following the forms established in relation to France before the change of government.

5. Nominations to the bishoprics which shall be vacant in the future shall likewise be made by the First Consul, and canonical institution shall be given by the Holy See, as in the preceding article.

6. Before entering upon their functions, bishops shall take directly at the hands of the First Consul, the oath of fidelity which was in use before the change of government, expressed in the following terms:

"I swear and promise to God, upon the Holy Scriptures, to remain in obedience and fidelity to the government established by the constitution of the French Republic. I also promise to have no intercourse, nor to aid by any counsel, nor to support any league, either within or without, which is inimical to the public tranquillity; and if, within my diocese or elsewhere, I learn that anything to the prejudice of the state is being contrived, I will make it known to the government."

7. Ecclesiastics of the second rank shall take the same oath at the hands of civil authorities designated by the government.

8. The following form of prayer shall be repeated at the end of divine service in all the Catholic churches of France: *Domine, salvam fac Rempublicam; Domine, salvos fac Consules.* . . .

12. All the metropolitan, cathedral, parochial, and other nonalienated churches needed for worship shall be again placed at the disposal of the bishops.

13. His Holiness, in the interest of peace and the happy re-establishment of the Catholic religion, declares that neither he nor his successors will disturb in any manner the purchasers of the alienated ecclesiastical properties, and that, in consequence, the ownership of these same properties, with all rights and revenues attached to them, shall remain incontestably in their hands and those of their assigns.

14. The government shall settle a suitable stipend upon the bishops and priests whose dioceses and parishes shall be included in the new division. . . .

16. His Holiness recognizes in the First Consul of the French Republic the same rights and prerogatives which belonged to the old government.

17. It is agreed between the contracting parties that in case any one of the successors of the First Consul shall not be Catholic, the rights and prerogatives mentioned in the above article and the nomination of bishops shall be regulated, as regards him, by a new convention.

THE CATECHISM OF THE FRENCH EMPIRE (APRIL 4, 1806)

At the time the Concordat was proclaimed (April 8, 1802), the Consulate set forth—without consulting the Papacy and, indeed, much to the Pope's disapproval—a series of "Organic Articles" for the Catholic Church in France designed further to make the church servant to the state. One of the "Organic Articles" provided that "There shall be only one liturgy and one catechism for all the Catholic churches of France." In the interests of religious unity this provision appeared harmless; but four years later, after Napoleon had become Emperor, a new catechism was drawn up under the Emperor's direction for the use of all French Catholics. The new *Catéchisme de l'Empire Français* was modeled closely after the *Catéchisme de Bossuet* of Louis XIV's day [see page 251]. Like its predecessor, it ascribed divine sanctions to the imperial power, as the following excerpts illustrate.

From the Napoleonic *Catechism* (1806) [1]

Question: What are the duties of Christians with reference to their governing princes, and what in particular are our duties toward Napoleon I, our Emperor?

Answer: Christians owe to the princes who govern them, and we owe in particular to our Emperor, Napoleon I, love, respect, obedience, fidelity, military service, and the taxes levied for the preservation and defense of the empire and of his throne. We also owe him fervent prayers for his safety and for the spiritual and temporal prosperity of the state.

Q. Why are we held to all these duties toward our Emperor?

A. First, because God, who has created empires and distributed them according to His will, has, by blessing our Emperor with gifts in both peace and war, established him as our sovereign and made him the agent of His power and His image upon earth. *To honor and to serve our Emperor is, then, to honor and to serve God Himself.* Secondly, because our Lord Jesus Christ Himself, both by His teachings and by His examples, has taught us what we owe to our sovereigns. Even at His birth He obeyed the edict of Caesar Augustus; He paid the established tax; and while He commanded us to render unto God those things which belong unto God, He also commanded us to render unto Caesar those things which are Caesar's.

Q. Are there not particular motives which should attach us more closely to Napoleon I, our Emperor?

A. Yes. For it is he whom God has raised up in trying times to re-establish

the public worship of the holy religion of our fathers and to be its protector. He has restored and preserved public order by his profound and active wisdom; he defends the state by his mighty arm; he has become the anointed of the Lord by the consecration which he received from the sovereign pontiff, head of the Universal Church.

Q. What ought we to think of those who are wanting in their duties toward the Emperor?

A. According to the Apostle Paul, they are resisting the order established by God Himself and thereby they render themselves worthy of eternal damnation.

Q. Do we owe toward the legitimate successors as established by the constitution of the Empire the same duties as toward the Emperor himself?

A. Undoubtedly yes. For we read in the sacred Scriptures that God, Lord of the Heavens and of the earth, by a dispensation of His Supreme Will and by His Goodness, grants empires not only to one person in particular, but also to his family.

THE LAW CODES

Reformers of the Old Regime had stressed the need of substituting for the confused mass of inherited judicial procedures and legislation a simple, unified code of laws. The abolition, early in the Revolution, of ancient statutes and obsolete institutions had cleared the ground, but no legislative committee had succeeded in completing legal codification. In August, 1800, Napoleon appointed a committee to prepare a civil code. A draft was completed within a year, debated and amended by the First Consul and the Council of State, and finally enacted in 1804. A Code of Civil Procedure was set forth in 1806, a Commercial Code in 1807, a Criminal Code

---

[1] Pierre Larousse, *Grande dictionnaire universel du XIXᵉ siècle,* 20 vols., Paris, 1865-90, III, 567, under "Catéchisme de l'Empire français."

in 1808, and a Penal Code in 1810. Taken together, these codes were the most comprehensive effort ever made in France to achieve legal unity. They outlived the Emperor and remained, with some ameliorations, the law of France until 1940. Moreover, during the Napoleonic era, they took root in such imperial conquests as Italy, Switzerland, the Netherlands, and parts of Germany, as well as in the former French settlements of Louisiana. An American historian has recently analyzed the codes as follows.

From BRUUN, *The French Imperium* (1938) [1]

In four important particulars the new code preserved the social aims of the Revolution, for it affirmed the equality of all citizens before the law, the right of the individual to choose his profession, the supremacy of the lay state, and the freedom of the individual conscience. But the concern which had been manifested earlier in the Revolution for the rights and liberties of minors and dependents was notably diminished. The wife was subordinated to the husband's authority and even her property was at his disposal. The father of a family regained the power to place an adolescent in confinement for a period not exceeding six months, and a testator could dispose at will of one-half or less of his estate, depending upon the number of his children. Bastards were denied a claim to any part of their parents' inheritance unless they had been legally acknowledged, and even then their share was less than that of legitimate children. The retention of divorce by mutual consent, and of the practice of legal adoption, both of which Bonaparte advocated,

have been cited as evidence that he sometimes yielded to private reasons in his decisions, but no proof that his personal marital problems influenced him at this juncture can be definitely adduced.

The civil code protected the interests of the new society, dominated by the propertied classes, which had risen to supremacy through the Revolution. As land was still the most important form of wealth, the regulations governing mortgages and liens, and the transfer or inheritance of landed estates, were traced in detail, but the sections covering the newer forms of industrial wealth were inadequate, and the attempt to fix a legal rate of interest reflected Napoleon's hostility towards the financiers. To the disinherited classes, the wage-earners and those without possessions, the code offered little save the guarantee of civil liberty. . . . The state assumed no responsibility towards the unemployed; workers were forbidden to organize for collective bargaining (law of April 12, 1803); the testimony of the employer was preferred to that of the worker in wage disputes. With the introduction of police regulations compelling each employee to carry a card relating his vocational vicissitudes, and the official comments thereon, the subjugation of the working classes was assured. . . .

The code of civil procedure (1806) revived in substance the court methods of the old regime, but retained the provision, dear to the revolutionary idealists with their faith in right reason, that litigants must make a final effort at conciliation before the case opened. The code of criminal procedure and penal law (1810) buttressed the growing despotism of the imperial government by augmenting the penalties for crimes against persons and property, and particularly for political offenses. . . . The accused was still permitted public trial by jury, but the jurors were to be selected by the prefect, and a

[1] Geoffrey Bruun, *Europe and the French Imperium,* in *The Rise of Modern Europe,* ed. by William L. Langer, 1938, 27-29. Copyright, 1938, by Harper & Brothers, and reprinted with their permission.

simple majority vote sufficed for a verdict. The ball and chain, branding, and the barbarous custom of striking off a parricide's hand before execution were reintroduced, and some lighter forms of judicial torture condoned. . . .

In their totality the codes well represent that compromise settlement which Napoleon imposed upon France. They recognized and embodied, in principle at least, the leading demands of the revolutionary program, the profound aspiration for order, for a unified national system of secular legislation, for civil equality, religious liberty, and a soil freed from feudal encumbrances. They recognized no privileges of birth, opened all careers to men of industry and talent, promoted the distribution of property and discouraged the accumulation of large landed estates. In this sense they were a summary of the Revolution, and were so regarded in neighboring states which attacked or adopted them.

The abuses of the old regime had engendered among its critics a spirit of hostility towards all constituted authority. The work of demolition carried through in the first years of the Revolution was inspired by a deep conviction that it was necessary to limit the powers of government in the interests of individual liberty. Resistance against oppression was listed as one of the natural and imprescriptible rights of man, orators assured insurgent multitudes that "the voice of reason and the voice of the people are the same thing," and mob violence was dignified as "the sacred right of insurrection." For such anarchical postulates and their sanguinary conclusions Napoleon had a soldier's contempt. The spirit of his codes is the antithesis of the liberal philosophy, for they are dedicated, not to the principle that government must be restricted in the interests of liberty, but that liberty must be restricted in the interests of government. In this sense the Napoleonic laws were a

prefiguration of the mood which was to dominate the European courts after 1815. In this sense they were reactionary.

3. The French Imperium in Europe

THE THIRD COALITION AGAINST FRANCE: ALLIANCE OF GREAT BRITAIN AND RUSSIA (APRIL 11, 1805)

"Well, well!" Napoleon said after signing the Peace of Amiens, "What a beautiful fix we are in now. Peace has been declared." The treaty was never more than a truce. From the first it was unsatisfactory to the English [see pages 414-415], and when Napoleon refused to follow it with commercial agreements and exerted every effort to close the Continent to British trade, the English became increasingly apprehensive. This apprehension was intensified as it was observed how Napoleon's ambitions soared and how he labored to make secure his upstart position by meddling in the affairs of neighboring states—in Holland, Switzerland, Italy, the Empire, and even in Turkish dominions. Moreover, the First Consul strove to reconstruct a colonial empire in the West Indies, renewed threats against English interests in India, and collected men and materials for an invasion of England itself. Great Britain could not view such acts without protective measures, and when war between France and England recommenced in May, 1803, the English sought to construct a new alliance of Continental powers against the French. The first important result of this diplomatic maneuvering was an alliance between Great Britain and Russia, the treaty for which, signed April 11, 1805, not only became the core of the Third Coalition

(Austria adhered to it in August) but also foreshadowed the European settlement of 1815 after Napoleon's downfall [see pages 434-445].

From the Treaty of Alliance
(April 11, 1805) [1]

His Majesty the Emperor of all the Russias and His Majesty the King of the United Kingdom of Great Britain and Ireland, animated by the desire to secure for Europe the peace, independence and well being of which it is deprived through the unmeasured ambition of the French government and the degree of influence out of all proportion which it tends to arrogate to itself, have resolved to employ all the means which are in their power, in order to obtain this salutary aim and to prevent the renewal of such distressing circumstances. . . .

1. As the state of suffering in which Europe finds itself demands prompt remedies, their Majesties . . . have agreed to consult upon the means of causing its cessation, without waiting for the case of further encroachments on the part of the French government. They have agreed, in consequence, to employ the most prompt and efficacious measures in order to form a general league of the states of Europe, and to bind them to accede to the present concert and to gather, for the purpose of fulfilling the aim, a force which, independent of that which His Britannic Majesty shall furnish, shall amount to 500,000 effective men and to employ them with energy in order to bring the French government by inclination or by force to assent to the re-establishment of the peace and the equilibrium of Europe.

2. This league shall have for its aim

the accomplishment of that which is proposed by the present concert, to wit:

A. The evacuation of the country of Hanover and of the north of Germany.

B. The establishment of the independence of the republics of Holland and Switzerland.

C. The re-establishment of the King of Sardinia in Piedmont. . . .

D. The future security of the Kingdom of Naples and the entire evacuation of Italy . . . by the French forces.

E. The establishment of an order of things which guarantees effectively the security and independence of the different states and presents a solid barrier against future usurpations.

3. His Britannic Majesty . . . agrees to contribute to the common efforts by the employment of his land and sea forces. . . . He will aid, besides, the different powers which shall accede thereto by subsidies . . . in the proportion of 1,250,000 pounds sterling per annum for each hundred thousand men of regular troops. . . .

[In subsequent articles, Their Majesties agree not to make a separate peace with France without consent of all the powers of the league, not to interfere "with the national will in France relative to the form of government," and, "Finally, to assemble at the end of the war a general congress, in order to discuss and settle upon the most precise foundations . . . the precepts of international law, and to assure the observance of them by the establishment of a federative system based upon the situation of the different states of Europe."]

AUSTRIA WITHDRAWS FROM THE THIRD COALITION: THE TREATY OF PRESSBURG (DECEMBER 26, 1805)

When news of Austrian adhesion to the Third Coalition reached Napoleon

[1] Anderson, ed., *The Constitutions and Other Select Documents Illustrative of the History of France*, 371-74. By permission of Frank Maloy Anderson.

at Boulogne, where he was preparing to invade England, he addressed these words to his soldiers: "Brave soldiers of the Camp of Boulogne, you will not go to England. English gold has seduced the Emperor of Austria, who has just declared war against France. . . . Soldiers, new victories await you beyond the Rhine. Let us hasten to defeat once more the enemies whom you have already conquered." Quickly turning his "Grand Army" against Austria, Napoleon surrounded an Austrian army at Ulm and forced its surrender (October 17, 1805) before Russian aid had arrived. Six weeks later, he defeated combined Austrian and Russian forces at Austerlitz (December 2)—"the most splendid [battle] of all I have fought," said Napoleon proudly—and forced upon Austria the disastrous Treaty of Pressburg. This treaty, after the usual declaration of peace and amity "forever" between the two Emperors, provided:

From The Treaty of Pressburg
     (December 26, 1805) [1]

2. France shall continue to possess in complete ownership and sovereignty the duchies . . . [etc.] which were, prior to the present treaty, united or incorporated with the French Empire or ruled by French laws and administrations. . . .

4. His Majesty the Emperor of Germany and Austria renounces . . . the portion of the states of the Republic of Venice ceded to him in the treaties of Campo Formio and Lunéville, which shall be united forever with the Kingdom of Italy [which had been created by Napoleon, March 17, 1805, with himself as king].

5. His Majesty the Emperor of Germany and of Austria recognizes His

Majesty the Emperor of the French as King of Italy. But it is agreed that . . . the crowns of France and Italy shall be separated forever, and they can no longer in any case be united upon the same head.

6. The present treaty of peace is declared common to . . . the electors of Bavaria, Württemberg, and Baden, and to the Batavian Republic, allies . . . of His Majesty the Emperor of the French, King of Italy.

7. The electors of Bavaria and of Württemberg having taken the title of king, without however ceasing to belong to the Germanic Confederation, His Majesty the Emperor of Germany and of Austria recognizes them in that capacity. . . . [And to each of them, as well as to the Elector of Baden, the Holy Roman Emperor surrendered a number of German principalities totaling about 28,000 square miles and 3,000,000 inhabitants, thereby enlarging Napoleonic puppet states and diminishing his own area and prestige.]

DISSOLUTION OF THE HOLY ROMAN EMPIRE (JULY-AUGUST, 1806)

Napoleon's repeated defeats of Austria had shattered the Holy Roman Empire. The Treaty of Lunéville, by indemnifying within the Empire those princes dispossessed west of the Rhine, necessitated internal imperial readjustments, and the reduction of many small states, especially of free towns and ecclesiastical states—thus simplifying the map of Germany. The Treaty of Pressburg, by recognizing the rulers of Bavaria and Württemberg as kings who, together with the Elector of Baden, were guaranteed "the plentitude of sovereignty" by Napoleon, thereby destroyed the dependence of these states upon the Holy Roman Emperor and rendered doubtful the further existence of the age-old empire. Immediately

[1] Ibid., 375-78. By permission of Frank Maloy Anderson.

afterward, Napoleon intimidated the anxious German princes and urged upon them the necessity of seeking "protection" against a rancorous Austria. After they had concluded a series of separate treaties with France, Napoleon presented them (July 12, 1806) with a collective text which set up the Confederation of the Rhine "forever separated from the territory of the Germanic Empire, and united among themselves by a separate confederation" with the French Emperor as "Protector." Fifteen states were admitted to the Confederation at first, though by 1808 the total had grown to thirty-eight. Their common interests were dealt with in a diet, held at Frankfurt, and each state was bound by an alliance to furnish a stated number of soldiers to France in the event of war. Napoleon, as Protector of the Confederation, was empowered to appoint the successor to each prince primate upon the latter's decease. Having thus gained control over the South German states, the Emperor of the French dispatched a message to the Imperial Diet insolently denying the further existence of the Holy Roman Empire.

From NAPOLEON, Message to the Imperial Diet (August 1, 1806) [1]

The undersigned, *chargé d'affaires* of His Majesty the Emperor of the French and King of Italy at the general Diet of the German Empire, has received orders from His Majesty to make the following declarations to the Diet:

Their Majesties the Kings of Bavaria and of Württemberg, the Sovereign Princes of Regensburg, Baden, Berg, Hesse-Darmstadt and Nassau, as well as the other leading princes of the south and west of Germany have resolved to form a confederation between themselves which shall secure them against future emergencies, and have thus ceased to be states of the Empire.

The position in which the Treaty of Pressburg has explicitly placed the courts allied to France, and indirectly those princes whose territory they border or surround, being incompatible with the existence of an empire, it becomes a necessity for those rulers to reorganize their relations upon a new system and to remove a contradiction which could not fail to be a permanent source of agitation, disquiet and danger.

France, on the other hand, is directly interested in the maintenance of peace in Southern Germany and . . . cannot but regard the confederation that they have formed as a natural result and a necessary sequel to that treaty.

For a long period successive changes have, from century to century, reduced the German constitution to a shadow of its former self. Time has altered all the relations . . . which originally existed among the various members of the confederation. . . .

The Diet has no longer a will of its own. The sentences of the superior courts can no longer be executed. Everything indicates such serious weakness that the federal bond no longer offers any protection whatever and only constitutes a source of dissension and discord between the powers. . . . The Treaty of Pressburg assures complete sovereignty to their Majesties the Kings of Bavaria and of Württemberg and to His Highness the Elector of Baden. This is a prerogative which the other electors will doubtless demand, and which they are justified in demanding; but this is in harmony neither with the letter nor the spirit of the constitution of the Empire.

[1] *Translations and Reprints from the Original Sources of European History*, II, No. 2, 13-17. By permission of the University of Pennsylvania Press.

His Majesty the Emperor and King is, therefore, compelled to declare that he can no longer acknowledge the existence of the German Constitution, recognizing, however, the entire and absolute sovereignty of each of the princes whose states compose Germany today, maintaining with them the same relations as with the other independent powers of Europe.

[Five days later, Francis II abdicated as Holy Roman Emperor, finding that "the results of certain articles of the Treaty of Pressburg . . . as well as the events which, as is generally known, have taken place in the German Empire, have convinced us that it would be impossible under these circumstances farther to fulfill the duties which we assumed by the conditions of our election . . . we owe it to our principles and to our honor to renounce a crown . . . [and] we proclaim, accordingly, that we consider the ties which have hitherto united us to the body politic of the German Empire as hereby dissolved; that we regard the office and dignity of the imperial headship as extinguished by the formation of a separate Union of the Rhenish States, and regard ourselves as thereby freed from all our obligations toward the German Empire; herewith laying down the imperial crown which is associated with these obligations, and relinquishing the imperial government which we have hitherto conducted." Thus was dissolved the Holy Roman Empire. But Francis, as Francis I, remained as "Emperor and hereditary ruler of the Austrian lands" until his death in 1835.]

THE "CONTINENTAL SYSTEM"

Close upon Napoleon's triumph over the Austrians at Ulm (October 17, 1805), the British Admiral Nelson defeated the combined French and Spanish fleets off Trafalgar (October 21). Napoleon, no longer able seriously to menace the shores of Great Britain, sought to compensate for his lack of naval power by striking at British commerce through the boycott of British goods on the Continent. By this extreme application of protectionist principles, the Emperor hoped both to bankrupt English commercial houses, causing the "nation of shopkeepers" to sue for peace, and to force the Continent to become economically self-sufficing. Neither aim was realized, and the hardships wrought upon the French, their subject peoples, and their allies were among the fundamental causes for Napoleon's downfall. Napoleon's first major step in setting up the Continental System was his Berlin Decree, November 21, 1806, issued after England (in May) had *announced*— though only partially *enforced*—a blockade of the coast from the river Elbe to Brest.

From NAPOLEON, Berlin Decree (1806) [1]

The Imperial Camp at Berlin,
November 21, 1806

Napoleon, Emperor of the French, King of Italy, etc., considering,

1. That England never recognizes the international law universally followed by all civilized peoples;

2. That she regards as an enemy every individual belonging to the enemy state, and consequently makes prisoners of war not only of the crews of armed ships of war but also of ships of commerce and merchantmen, and even of commercial agents and of merchants traveling on business. . . .

4. That she extends to unfortified towns and commercial ports and the mouths of rivers, the right of blockade, which, in accordance with reason and with the prac-

[1] *Correspondance de Napoléon Ier*, XIII, 555-57 (No. 11283).

tice of all civilized states, is applicable only to fortified places; that she declares places under blockade before which she has not a single vessel of war. . . .

5. That this monstrous abuse of the right of blockade has no other aim than to prevent communications among the nations and to raise up the commerce and industry of England upon the ruin of that of the Continent;

6. That, as this is the obvious aim of England, whoever on the Continent deals in English goods thereby favors and himself becomes an accomplice of her designs. . . .

8. That it is a natural right to oppose an enemy with the arms which he himself employs, and to fight in the same way that he fights. . . .

We have consequently decreed and do decree that which follows:

1. The British Isles are declared to be in a state of blockade.

2. All commerce and all correspondence with the British Isles are forbidden. . . .

3. Every individual English subject, of whatsoever state or condition, who shall be found in any country occupied by our troops or by those of our allies shall be made a prisoner of war.

4. All warehouses, merchandise, or property of whatever nature belonging to an English subject shall be regarded as lawful prize.

5. Trade in English goods is prohibited, and all goods belonging to England or coming from her factories or her colonies are declared lawful prize.

6. Half of the product arising from confiscation of goods and possessions declared lawful prize by the preceding articles shall be used to indemnify the merchants for the losses which they have sustained by the capture of merchant vessels taken by English cruisers. . . .

10. The present decree shall be communicated by our Minister of Foreign Affairs to the Kings of Spain, Naples, Holland, and Etruria, and to our other allies whose subjects, like our own, are victims of the injustice and barbarity of English maritime legislation.

[England retaliated to the above decree, first by an Order in Council of January 10, 1807, which declared illegal all trade between French ports and those of French allies, and then by a second Grand Order in Council of November 11, 1807, which declared "all ports and places of France, and her allies, or of any other country at war with His Majesty, and all other ports or places in Europe, from which, although not at war with His Majesty, the British flag is excluded, and all ports or places in the colonies belonging to His Majesty's enemies, shall, from henceforth, be subject to the same restrictions in point of trade and navigation . . . as if the same were actually blockaded by His Majesty's naval forces, in the most strict and rigorous manner"—thereby creating an undisguised "paper blockade" of all Britain's enemies, and at the same time practically forbidding neutral trade. On December 17 following, Napoleon extended the Continental System by issuing the Milan Decree.]

From NAPOLEON, Milan Decree (1807) [1]

The Royal Palace at Milan,
December 17, 1807

Napoleon, Emperor of the French, King of Italy, Protector of the Confederation of the Rhine. In view of the measures adopted by the British government on the eleventh of November last . . . We have decreed and do decree that which follows:

1. Every vessel of whatever nation which shall submit to a search by an English vessel or shall consent to a voyage to England, or shall pay any tax imposed by

[1] *Ibid.,* XVI, 192-93 (No. 13391).

the English government is, by such act, declared denationalized, has lost the protection afforded by its flag, and has become English property.

2. Vessels thus denationalized by the arbitrary acts of the English government, should they enter our ports or those of our allies, or fall into the hands of our ships of war or of our privateers, shall be regarded as good and lawful prizes.

3. The British Isles are declared to be in a state of blockade on the sea and on the land. Every vessel, of whatever nation, no matter what its cargo may be, that sails from the ports of England or those of English colonies or of countries occupied by English troops, or is bound for England or for any of the English colonies or any country occupied by English troops, is a lawful prize [if captured].

4. These measures, which are only a just retaliation against the barbarous system adopted by the English government, which imitates the Algerian pirates in its methods, shall cease to have any effect upon those nations which shall force the English to respect their flags.

THE TREATIES OF TILSIT (JULY 7-9, 1807)

After Pressburg [page 428], England sought new allies against Napoleon and, in the course of 1806, Prussia and Russia combined with her to form the Fourth Coalition. It was short-lived. At Jena and Auerstädt (October 14), Napoleon overpowered the decadent armies of Prussia and marched triumphantly into Berlin, while the Prussian King, Frederick William III, fled to East Prussia to seek the protection of advancing Russian forces. In late November, shortly after issuing the Berlin Decree which inaugurated the Continental System, Napoleon followed. At Eylau (February 8, 1807) and at Friedland

(June 14), the French armies defeated the Russians and were upon the point of crossing the Niemen River into Russian territory when an armistice (June 21) closed the operations and cleared the way for treaty-making. The treaties that followed raised Napoleon's fortunes to full tide; one, with Russia, dissolved the Fourth Coalition and formed an alliance between the Czar and the Emperor against Great Britain; the other, with Prussia, considerably reduced the latter's territory and subjected the Prussian King to other humiliations unthinkable in the days of Frederick the Great. Napoleon and Czar Alexander I met on a raft in the Niemen River and, while the King of Prussia wandered sadly on the bank anxiously seeking a means to join the conference, the two Emperors—who found unexpected pleasure in each other's company —prepared to divide the continent of Europe and to work in concert for either the pacification or destruction of England.

From The Franco-Russian Treaty (1807) [1]

His Majesty the Emperor of the French, King of Italy, Protector of the Confederation of the Rhine, and His Majesty the Emperor of all the Russias, animated with the same interest in putting an end to the devastation of war, have . . . agreed upon the following articles:

1. From the day of the exchange of ratifications of the present treaty, there shall be perfect peace and amity between H. M. the Emperor of the French . . . [etc.] and H. M. the Emperor of all the Russias. . . .

4. Out of esteem for H. M. the Emperor of all the Russias, and to afford him proof

---

[1] G. F. and the Baron Charles de Martens, eds., *Recueil des principaux traités . . . de l'Europe*, 2nd ed. rev., 8 vols., Göttingen, 1835, VIII (1803-1808), 637-43.

of his sincere desire to unite both nations in the bonds of immutable confidence and friendship, H. M. the Emperor Napoleon consents to restore to H. M. the King of Prussia, the ally of H. M. the Emperor of all the Russias, all the conquered countries, towns, and territories as named hereinafter, to wit: that part of the Duchy of Magdeburg on the right bank of the Elbe . . . the middle and new Mark of Brandenburg . . . the Duchy of Pomerania; upper, lower, and new Silesia. . . . Lastly, the Kingdom of Prussia as it was on the 1st of January, 1772. . . .

5. Those provinces which, on January 1, 1772, formed a part of the former Kingdom of Poland and since have been at different times under Prussian domination (with the exception of the countries named in the preceding article . . .), shall be possessed in full ownership and sovereignty of H. M. the King of Saxony, under the title of the Duchy of Warsaw. . . .

6. The city of Dantzig, with an area of two leagues about it, is restored to its independence under the protection of H. M. the King of Prussia and H. M. the King of Saxony. . . .

12. Their Serene Highnesses the Dukes of Saxe-Coburg, Oldenburg, and Mecklenburg-Schwerin shall each be restored to the complete and peaceable possession of his states; but the ports of the Duchies of Oldenburg and Mecklenburg shall continue to be occupied by French garrisons until exchange of ratifications of the future definitive treaty of peace between France and England.

13. H. M. the Emperor Napoleon accepts the mediation of H. M. the Emperor of all the Russias for the purpose of negotiating and concluding a definitive treaty of peace between France and England, providing that this mediation shall be accepted by England in one month after the ratification of the present treaty. . . .

[In Articles 14-15, 18-19, the Czar recognizes: 1. "H. M. the King of Naples, Joseph Napoleon." 2. "H. M. the King of Holland, Louis Napoleon." 3. "The Confederation of the Rhine, the actual state of possession of each of the sovereigns who compose it and the titles given to several of them . . . [and] the sovereigns who shall subsequently become members of the Confederation." 4. "His Imperial Highness, Prince Jerome Bonaparte as King of Westphalia," this kingdom to be "composed of provinces on the left of the Elbe ceded by H. M. the King of Prussia and other states actually possessed by H. M. the Emperor Napoleon."]

17. The present treaty of peace and amity is declared common to Their Majesties the Kings of Naples and of Holland and to the Confederated Sovereigns of the Rhine, allies of H. M. the Emperor Napoleon. . . .

23. H. M. the Emperor of all the Russias accepts the mediation of H. M. the Emperor of the French . . . for the purpose of negotiating a peace [between Russia and Turkey]. . . .

Done at Tilsit, July 7, 1807

[Simultaneously, the two Emperors signed a secret treaty of alliance wherein they agreed "to make common cause, by land or by sea, or both by land and sea, in every war which France or Russia may find it necessary to undertake against any European power." They contracted to carry on all operations in such wars in concert, and neither party would "in any case" treat for peace without the consent of the other. Russia further agreed that if England did not accept the Czar's mediation for peace with France by November 1, recognizing that "all the powers should enjoy an equal and complete independence upon the seas" and restoring to

France and her allies all conquests made since 1805, Russia should then "make common cause with France" against Great Britain. Likewise, in case England refused to make peace, the two Emperors undertook "to act in concert" to require Denmark, Sweden, Portugal, and Austria "to close their ports to the English," and to declare war upon England—or risk war with the allied empires. Moreover, in case the Ottoman Turks refused French mediation for peace with Russia, France agreed to join Russia against the Turks.

Frederick William III of Prussia was bitterly aggrieved at the Czar's desertion of him, and when Napoleon adopted such a lofty tone with the Prussian King the latter was induced to call his Queen, Louisa, for whom the French Emperor had expressed admiration, to win more generous treatment. Napoleon saw the Queen but refused to talk of anything but "dress, fashions, jewelry, or the like," and the French treaty with Prussia cost the latter, besides heavy indemnities, much of her most precious territories and half her population. The King was forced to accede to Prussian boundaries as set forth in Articles 4-6 of the treaty with Russia, to recognize Napoleonic puppets as in Articles 14-15 and 18-19 above, and to accept the following additional articles:]

From The Franco-Prussian Treaty (1807) [1]

7. H. M. the King of Prussia cedes in full ownership and sovereignty to the kings, grand dukes, dukes, or princes who shall be designated by H. M. the Emperor of the French . . . all territorial property of whatever kind, or by whatever title possessed . . . between the Rhine and the Elbe at the beginning of the present war. . . .

[1] *Ibid.*, VIII (1803-1808), 663-68.

13. H. M. the King of Prussia renounces forever possession of all the provinces which formerly constituted parts of the Kingdom of Poland and which at different periods subsequent to January 1, 1772, came under the dominion of Prussia, with the exception of Ermeland and the countries situated to the west of old Prussia, to the east of Pomerania and the new mark . . . [and some other small areas which] shall continue to be possessed in full ownership and sovereignty of H. M. the King of Prussia.

14. H. M. the King of Prussia likewise renounces forever the possession of the city of Dantzig.

15-16. [Recognizes the Duchy of Warsaw, as in Article 5 of the treaty with Russia, and agrees:] To secure communication between the Kingdom of Saxony and the Duchy of Warsaw, H. M. the King of Saxony shall be granted free use of a military road through the states of H. M. the King of Prussia. . . .

27. Until . . . the ratifications of the future definitive treaty of peace between France and England, all the countries under the domination of H. M. the King of Prussia . . . shall be closed to the navigation and commerce of the English. . . .

Done at Tilsit, July 9, 1807

[In a series of secret articles, the King of Prussia further agreed to join France against England in case England had not made a peace satisfactory to France by December 1, 1807.]

4. The Fall of Napoleon

After Tilsit, Napoleon's ambition seemed to know no bounds. Considering himself master of the Continent, with the Czar Alexander as a junior partner, Napoleon strove to combine all Europe in a grand boycott of Great Britain. "I will not allow a single British envoy in Europe," he declared, "I will declare war against any power which has one two months from now. I have three hundred thousand Russians at my disposal, and with such a powerful ally I can do anything. Since the English have declared that they will no longer respect neutrals on the sea, I will not recognize them on land." In accordance with this policy, the French Emperor attacked Portugal (October, 1807) and, induced by Spanish internal weaknesses, then seized the Spanish throne for his brother Joseph (May, 1808)—thus arousing a bitter Spanish opposition which, encouraged by English aid, remained in active revolt until Napoleon's downfall. The Spanish war encouraged Austria to renew her struggle with France (April, 1809). But at Wagram, outside Vienna, Napoleon again defeated the Austrians (July 5-6, 1809), and, at the Peace of Schönbrunn (October 14, 1809), the French Emperor signed his last peace as a conqueror. Meanwhile, in May, 1809, he had proclaimed the Papal States "reunited" to France and made a prisoner of Pope Pius VII. In 1810, with the annexation of Holland and the German Hanse towns, Napoleon's empire reached its widest extent. But the seeds of its destruction were already well sprouted. Within France, the people were growing weary of war and some of the Emperor's closest advisers—notably his erstwhile Foreign Minister, Talleyrand —had turned against him. In Spain, guerrilla warfare had swollen, with English aid, into the Duke of Wellington's "Peninsular Campaigns." In the Germanies, a rising tide of nationalism conspired against the French dominion, unchecked by Napoleon's espousal of the Austrian Archduchess, Marie Louise, now Empress of France. And in Russia, Czar Alexander, who, significantly, had not lifted a finger to aid his French partner in the Austrian war of 1809, ceased, after December, 1810, to cooperate in the enforcement of the Continental System. During the year 1811, the two Emperors prepared for war and, on June 23, 1812, Napoleon led his Grand Army across the Niemen River into Russia.

THE RUSSIAN CAMPAIGN OF 1812

Napoleon's chief valet, Constant, has related that at Erfurt in 1808, after a day's conference with Czar Alexander, Napoleon had a fearful nightmare and that, after he had been awakened, he said, "Ah, my friend, I have had a frightful dream; a bear was tearing open my breast, and devouring my heart." Later the Emperor recalled this omen which, with others,[1] augured ill for him in his relations with the Russians; and surely the Russian Bear in 1812 did devour the heart of Napoleon's imperium—his Grand Army! The Emperor entered Russia with nearly 600,000 men, bent upon his usual practice: to meet the enemy in a great battle or two, defeat him, and dictate peace terms. How the Russians foiled his plans is described below by Napoleon's own Master of the Horse, General Marquis Armand A. L. de Caulaincourt, who had served as French ambassador to Russia after Tilsit.

[1] On the first day of the campaign, Napoleon's horse shied at a rabbit and threw the Emperor to the ground.

From CAULAINCOURT, *Memoirs* (1812-13) [2]

The Emperor was so anxious for a battle that he pressed forward the movements of the army with all his energy and all the brilliance of his genius. The battle of Ostrovno [July 25] . . . was quite costly, and sufficiently advantageous, but it was nevertheless only a rear-guard action in which the enemy really obtained the result he desired, in that he hindered our movement, forced us to make fresh dispositions, and in consequence delayed us for several hours.

The Russians were pushed as far as the Lutchesia, a stream that flows into the Düna a short distance from Vitebsk. During the night all the corps and artillery reserves were hurried forward, and everything was got ready in the hope that on the morrow, or at latest the following day, the great battle would be fought which had so long been the goal of all the Emperor's wishes and hopes. . . .

It is impossible to give any idea of the general disappointment—especially the Emperor's disappointment—when, at daybreak [July 28, the 27 having been dissipated in skirmishes] the certainty was borne in upon us that the Russian army had vanished and abandoned Vitebsk. There were no inhabitants to be found, no prisoners to be taken, not a single straggler to be picked up. There were no spies. We were in the heart of inhabited Russia and yet, if I may be permitted the comparison, we were like a vessel without a compass in the midst of a vast ocean, knowing nothing of what was happening around us. At last it was learned from two peasants who were caught that the Russian army was far ahead of us, and that

it had been on the move for four days. . . . The certainty that the Russian army was going to escape him, and that he would not, for some time, obtain the battle he desired so keenly, cast the Emperor into deep gloom. . . .

Our cavalry and artillery had already suffered severely. A very large number of horses had died. Many were lagging behind, wasting away, wandering at the rear; others followed their corps, to whom they were but a useless embarrassment. A considerable number of ammunition wagons and other vehicles had been abandoned one after the other. One-third of the horses were missing; not more than half of those we had had at the beginning of the campaign were still in service. . . .

On his return to Vitebsk the Emperor's first care was for provisions and hospitals. . . . The unfortunate men were in the direst want, lying on the ground . . . without even straw beneath them. . . . The surgeons and doctors, far too few in number, were unable to cope with the needs of the service; besides they were without requisites; there was neither linen nor medicine. . . . It had been hoped to obtain some supplies at Vitebsk, but the place was practically deserted. Moreover, the capital cities of these great Russian provinces were of less use than the smallest towns in Germany. Too much accustomed to relying upon the resources of the country, we had reckoned on being able to do the same in Russia. . . .

[Napoleon remained at Vitebsk until August 12, hoping that the Russian army would attack him. Then he marched after the Czar's forces. When the latter evacuated Smolensk and left the city in flames, Napoleon was delighted. "Before the month is out we shall be in Moscow," he said, "In six weeks we shall have peace." For he felt that if Moscow fell into French hands the Czar would be forced to sue for

[2] From *With Napoleon in Russia* (*Memoirs of General de Caulaincourt, Duke of Vicenza, 1812-1813*), trans. by Hamish Miles, ed. by Jean Hanoteau, 2 vols., 1935, I, 139-43, 147, 212-19, 229-30, 315-17, 360-77. Copyright 1935 by William Morrow & Co., Inc., by permission of William Morrow & Co., Inc.

peace. By mid-September, the Grand Army entered Moscow.]

As was the case in most of the private palaces, nothing had been disturbed in the Kremlin; even the clocks were still going, as though the rightful owners were still in occupation. . . . [But] the better-to-do inhabitants had fled; all the authorities had left the place, which was entirely deserted. . . . No one remained but a few *outchitets* (French tutors), a few foreign shopkeepers, the servants in some of the hotels, and for the rest, people of the lowest classes of society. . . .

About eleven o'clock in the evening, news came that the Bazaar was on fire. The Duke of Treviso and Count Durosnel went to the spot, but in the darkness it was impossible to cope with the conflagration, for there was nothing at hand, and no one knew where to find pumps and hoses. The inhabitants and soldiers pillaged such shops as they had time to enter. . . . [The next day] At eight oclock in the evening flames broke out in one of the suburbs. Assistance was sent, without more attention being paid to the matter, for it was still attributed to the carelessness of the troops.

The Emperor retired early; everyone was fatigued and as anxious to rest as he was. At half-past ten my valet . . . woke me up with the news that for three-quarters of an hour the city had been in flames. I had only to open my eyes to realize that this was so, for the fire was spreading with such fierceness that it was light enough to read in the middle of my room. . . . About four o'clock in the morning the conflagration was so widespread that we judged it necessary to wake up the Emperor, who at once sent more officers to find out what was actually happening and discover whence these fires could be starting. . . . From different houses officers and soldiers brought *bou-*

tecknicks (street constables) and *moujiks* (peasants) who had been taken in the act of firing imflammable material into houses for the purpose of burning them down. The Poles reported that they had already caught some incendiaries and shot them, and they added, moreover, that from these men and from other inhabitants they had extracted the information that orders had been given by the governor of the city and the police that the whole city should be burned during the night. . . . A great portion of the city was reduced to ashes; the northern district, nearest the Kremlin, had been saved by the wind shifting to the west; some isolated districts to windward had not suffered at all. . . .

[As he was accustomed to dictate peace on his arrival at the palaces of the sovereigns whose principal cities he had conquered, Napoleon was amazed that the Czar, to whom he had made overtures of peace, remained silent at St. Petersburg. Meanwhile, supplies ran low in the French army; communications with France were frequently intercepted by the Russians; Cossacks raided the outskirts of Moscow, endangering foraging parties; and winter was about to close in. After much hesitation, Napoleon decided to retire from Moscow, shorten his lines of communications, and renew the struggle in the spring. The French left Moscow on October 23, after blowing up part of the Kremlin, and immediately the Russians fell upon their rear. Of this retreat, Caulaincourt wrote:]

The carriages, drawn by tired and underfed horses, were travelling fourteen and fifteen hours of the twenty-four. They kept to the road, and found no place that afforded them any supplies. . . . The country on either hand of our route had been marched over, eaten out, and left bare. . . . The plight of the carriages can be imagined. Having left Moscow with us, already full of refugees, women and children, they had had to take up the men wounded at . . . Maloyaroslavets . . . and Mojaisk. They were put on the top-seats of the carts, on the fore-carriage, behind the trunks, on the seats, in the fodder-carts. . . . At the least jolt those who were most insecurely placed fell; the drivers took no care. The driver following . . . for fear of stopping and losing his place (in the line) . . . would drive pitilessly on over the body of the wretch who had fallen. . . . Every man thought of himself, and of himself alone. . . .

Cossacks kept up perpetual raids along the road, which they constantly crossed between one division and another, even, where there was a gap, between one regiment and another. Three determined men armed with rifles, however, were sufficient to keep them at a respectful distance; but wherever there was no shooting to fear, wherever transport wagons were moving along in disorder, or unarmed stragglers making their way as best they could, the Cossacks improvised sudden attacks, wounding and robbing all those whose lives they spared, and looting wagons and carriages when they came upon them. . . .

From Tolotchine to Bobr, where we arrived on the 23rd [of November], the road was even more thickly covered with dead horses than on preceding marches. There were also a certain number of human corpses; and at all the bivouacs a large number of men died from asphyxiation due to their having gone too near the fire, being already frost-bitten and nearly frozen. The others groaned, but could not drag themselves away. . . . This horrible sight made a profound impression on everyone. It was impossible to convince a poor wretch numbed with cold that fire was fatal to him, that the only remedy was movement, dry friction, and even better for the hands and feet, friction with snow.

[By the time the French army crossed the Beresina River on November 26, the retreat had become a rout. The leaders lost their heads, panic-stricken fugitives scurried helter-skelter, and little discipline remained. On December 5, Napoleon left the army and hurried to Paris to repair his political fences and to assemble a fresh army for the following year. When Murat, to whom the Emperor had confided command, took stock of the stragglers at Kovno, on the Niemen, he found about 100,000 ragged, half-starved, frost-bitten men. A half million others, the flower of the Grand Army, had perished, deserted, or become Russian prisoners. The first act in the drama of Napoleon's downfall was finished. In mid-January, 1813, the Czar's army crossed the Niemen into Prussian territory to pass from defensive to offensive tactics against the French.]

PREPARATIONS FOR THE "WAR OF LIBERATION": PRUSSIAN REGENERATION

Frederick William III, of Prussia, was much embarrassed by the Russian approach in 1813, for he had been too timid not to support Napoleon against the Czar. That Prussia was now able and ready, despite the King's pusillanimity, to join with Russia in a "War of Liberation" was traceable in large part to internal reforms and a great upsurge of nationalistic feeling after the disaster of Jena and the humiliation of Tilsit. One of the chief instruments of reform was Heinrich Friedrich Karl, Baron von Stein, a Nassau nobleman who had moved to Prussia and twice served as a Minister of State. "We started," wrote Stein, "from the fundamental idea of rousing a moral, religious, patriotic spirit in the nation, of inspiring it anew with courage, self-confidence, readiness for every sacrifice in the cause of independence of the foreigner, and of national honor, and of seizing the first favorable opportunity of beginning the bloody and hazardous struggle for both." One of the foremost acts in Prussian regeneration was Stein's abolition of serfdom and certain restrictions on landholding. This ordinance, set forth only a few months after Tilsit, was similar to—though not as thorough as—the French act in 1789 [pages 389-391].

From the Prussian Reform Ordinance
(October 9, 1807) [1]

We, Frederick William, by the grace of God King of Prussia, &c., &c., make known hereby and give to understand: Since the beginning of the peace we have been before all things occupied with the care for the depressed condition of our faithful subjects, and the speediest restoration and greatest improvement of it. We have herein considered that in the universal need it passes the means at our command to furnish help to each individual . . . and it accords equally with the imperative demands of justice and with the principles of a proper national economy, to remove all the hindrances which hitherto prevented the individual from attaining the prosperity which, according to the measure of his powers, he was capable of reaching; further, we have considered that the existing restrictions, partly on the possession and enjoyment of landed property, partly on the personal condition of the agricultural laborer, specially thwart our benevolent purpose and disable a great force which might be applied to the restoration of cultivation, the former by their prejudicial influence on the value of landed property and the credit of the proprietor, the latter by diminishing the value of labor. We pur-

[1] J. R. Seeley, *Life and Times of Stein; or, Germany and Prussia in the Napoleonic Age,* 2 vols., Boston, 1879, I, 295-97.

pose, therefore, to reduce both within the limits required by the common well-being, and accordingly ordain as follows:

I. Freedom of Exchange of Land. Every inhabitant of our State is competent, without any limitation on the part of the State, to possess either as property or pledge landed estates of every kind, and the citizen and peasant to possess not only citizen, peasant, and other non-noble but also noble, pieces of land, without the one or the other needing any special permission for any acquisition of land whatever, although, henceforward as before, each change of possession must be announced to the authorities.

II. Free Choice of Occupation. Every noble is henceforth permitted without any derogation from his position to exercise citizen occupations; and every citizen or peasant is allowed to pass from the peasant into the citizen class, or from the citizen into the peasant class. . . .

IV. Division of Lands. Owners of estates and lands of all kinds, in themselves alienable either in town or country, are allowed . . . to separate the principal estate from its parts, and in general to alienate piecemeal. . . .

IX. Extinction of Feudal Relations, Family Settlements, and Entails, by Family Resolution. Every feudal connection not subject to a chief proprietor, every family settlement and entail may be altered at pleasure or entirely abolished by a family resolution. . . .

X. Abolition of Villainage. From the date of this Ordinance no new relation of serfdom, whether by birth, or marriage, or acquisition of a villain holding, or by contract, can come into existence.

XI. With the publication of the present Ordinance the existing condition of serfdom of those serfs with their wives and children who possess their peasant holdings by hereditary tenures of whatever kind ceases entirely both with its rights and duties.

XII. From Martinmas, 1810, ceases all serfdom in our entire states. From Martinmas, 1810, there shall be only free persons . . . free persons, however, still subject, as a matter of course, to all the obligations which bind them as free persons by virtue of the possession of an estate or by virtue of a special contract. . . .

Authentically, under our royal signature. Given at Memel, Oct. 9th, 1807.

[Such ordinances as that above led, in the years between Tilsit and War of Liberation, to a social and economic revolution in Prussia. Similarly, a series of acts especially sponsored by General Gerhard Johann David von Scharnhorst reformed the Prussian army and redesigned it as a *national* army on the principle that "It is every citizen's duty to defend the State." Meanwhile, a new German literature infused Prussians with an intensely patriotic spirit. The writings of Herder, Goethe, Lessing, and Schiller already had served effectively to weld together the diverse peoples of Germany—to arouse in them the consciousness of common language, traditions, and nationality. Now, in the writings of Ernst Moritz Arndt (1769-1860), a patriotic history professor, reformer, and poet, appeared bitter protests against Napoleonic oppression and appeals to Prussia to liberate all Germans from the French tyrant. A sample of the works of this most "German of all Germans" follows.]

From ARNDT, "What Is the German's Fatherland?" (1812) [1]

What is the German's fatherland?
Is it Prussia, or the Swabian's land?

[1] From the translation in Charles Dudley Warner, ed., *Library of the World's Best Literature,* 30 vols., Peale and Hill, 1896, II, 814-16.

Is it where the grape glows on the Rhine?
Where sea-gulls skim the Baltic's brine?
  Oh no! more grand
Must be the German's fatherland!

What is the German's fatherland?
Bavaria, or the Styrian's land?
Is it where the Master's cattle graze?
Is it the Mark where forges blaze?
  Oh no! more grand
Must be the German's fatherland! . . .

What is the German's fatherland?
Now name for me that mighty land!
Ah! Austria surely it must be,
So rich in fame and victory.
  Oh no! more grand
Must be the German's fatherland!

What is the German's fatherland?
Tell me the name of that great land!
Is it the land which princely hate
Tore from the Emperor and the State?
  Oh no! more grand
Must be the German's fatherland!

What is the German's fatherland?
Now name at last that mighty land!
"Where'er resounds the German tongue,
Where'er its hymns to God are sung!"
  That is the land,
Brave German, that thy fatherland! . . .

That's the German's fatherland!
Where scorn shall foreign triflers brand,
Where all are foes whose deeds offend,
Where every noble soul's a friend:
  Be this the land,
All Germany shall be the land!

All Germany that land shall be:
Watch o'er it, God, and grant that we,
With German hearts, in deed and thought,
May love it truly as we ought,
  Be this the land,
All Germany shall be the land!

[The fruits of such patriotic appeals were recognized when, in March, 1813, the King of Prussia joined with the Russian Czar in "an invitation to the Princes and the peoples (of Germany) to co-operate in the liberation of their country." The Prussian King also addressed an unprecedented "Appeal to My People" (*"An mein Volk"*) wherein he explained his reasons for declaring war against France and urged German people everywhere to rise up against the oppressor.]

From FREDERICK WILLIAM III, "Appeal to My People" (1813) [1]

There is no need of explaining to my loyal subjects, or to any German, the reasons for the war which is about to begin. They lie plainly before the eyes of awakened Europe. We succumbed to the superior force of France. The peace which followed deprived me of my people and, far from bringing us blessings, it inflicted upon us deeper wounds than the war itself, sucking out the very marrow of the country. Our principal fortresses remained in the hand of the enemy, and agriculture, as well as the highly developed industries of our towns, was crippled. The freedom of trade was hampered and thereby the sources of commerce and prosperity cut off. The country was left a prey to the ravages of destitution. . . .

Brandenburgers, Prussians, Silesians, Pomeranians, Lithuanians! You know what you have borne for the past seven years; you know the sad fate that awaits you if we do not bring this war to an honorable end. Think of the times gone by—of the Great Elector, the great Frederick! Remember the blessings for which your forefathers fought under their leadership and which they paid for with their

[1] From the translation in Robinson, ed., *Readings in European History*, 522-23. By permission of Ginn and Company.

blood—freedom of conscience, national honor, independence, commerce, industry, learning. Look at the great example of our powerful allies, the Russians; look at the Spaniards, the Portuguese. For such objects as these even weaker peoples have gone forth against mightier enemies and returned in triumph. Witness the heroic Swiss and the people of the Netherlands. . . .

Faith in God, perseverance, and the powerful aid of our allies will bring us victory as the reward of our honest efforts. Whatever sacrifices may be required of us as individuals, they will be outweighed by the sacred rights for which we make them, and for which we must fight to a victorious end unless we are willing to cease to be Prussians or Germans. This is the final, the decisive struggle; upon it depends our independence, our prosperity, our existence. There are no other alternatives but an honorable peace or a heroic end. You would willingly face even the latter for honor's sake, for without honor no Prussian or German could live.

However, we may confidently await the outcome. God and our own firm purpose will bring victory to our cause and with it an assured and glorious peace and the return of happier times.

Frederick William

Breslau, March 17, 1813

THE FINAL ALLIANCE AGAINST NAPOLEON

The combined armies of Prussia and Russia met the Napoleonic forces in two indecisive battles in May, 1813 (Lutzen, May 2; Bautzen, May 20), after which the French Emperor, probably to gain time to bring up Italian forces and ascertain the Austrian attitude, signed an armistice for seven weeks (June 4). During this interim,

Austria joined the allies (June 24) and Great Britain followed suit the next day. The armistice ended with both sides jockeying for positions and, after several lesser struggles, the allies closed in upon Napoleon at Leipzig (October 16-19). From this "Battle of the Nations" Napoleon was forced to retire. In November, when he crossed the Rhine into France, he had left nearly 200,000 French soldiers in Germany, and the allies were still advancing. In the following March (1814), after the allied forces had invaded France, Great Britain, Austria, Prussia, and Russia signed the following alliance against Napoleon, an alliance some of the provisions of which forecast the shape of the post-Napoleonic European settlement.

From The Treaty of Chaumont
(March 1, 1814) [1]

His Imperial Majesty and Royal Highness the Emperor of Austria, King of Hungary and Bohemia, H. M. the Emperor of all the Russias, H. M. the King of the United Kingdom of Great Britain and Ireland, H. M. the King of Prussia, having forwarded to the French government proposals for the conclusion of a general peace, and desiring, in case France should refuse the conditions of that peace, to draw closer the bonds which unite them for the vigorous prosecution of a war undertaken with the salutary purpose of putting an end to the misfortunes of Europe by assuring future repose through the re-establishment of a just equilibrium of the powers . . . have agreed to sanction by a solemn treaty . . . this double engagement. . . .

1. The high contracting parties above

[1] This and the next selection are from Anderson, *The Constitutions . . . Illustrative of the History of France.* By permission of Frank Maloy Anderson. This is 440-42.

named solemnly engage by the present treaty, and in the event of France refusing to accede to the conditions of peace now proposed, to apply all the means of their respective states to the vigorous prosecution of the war against that power, and to employ them in perfect concert, in order to obtain for themselves and for Europe a general peace, under the protection of which the rights and liberties of all nations shall be established and secured. . . . [Toward this end, each state agrees to keep in the field "150,000 effective men, exclusive of garrisons."]

2. The high contracting parties reciprocally engage not to treat separately with the common enemy, nor to sign peace, truce, nor convention, but with common consent. They, moreover, engage not to lay down their arms until the object of the war, mutually understood and agreed upon, shall have been attained.

3. In order to contribute in the most prompt and decisive manner to fulfill this great object, His Britannic Majesty engages to furnish a subsidy of £5,000,000 for the service of the year 1814, to be divided in equal proportions amongst the three powers. . . . [To be renewed in 1815 if the war still goes on.]

5. The high contracting parties . . . have also determined to enter without delay into defensive engagements for the protection of their respective states in Europe against every attempt which France might make to infringe the order of things resulting from such pacification.

6. To effect this, they agree that in the event of one of the high contracting parties being threatened with an attack on the part of France, the others shall employ their most strenuous efforts to prevent it, by friendly interposition. [Other powers "most exposed to a French invasion" are invited "to accede to the present treaty of defensive alliance."]

7. In case of these endeavours proving

ineffectual, the high contracting parties promise to come to the immediate assistance of the power attacked, each with a body of 60,000 men. . . .

16. The present treaty of defensive alliance having for its object to maintain the equilibrium of Europe, to secure the repose and independence of its states, and to prevent the invasions which during so many years have desolated the world, the high contracting parties have agreed to extend the duration of it to twenty years, to take date from the day of its signature. . . .

Secret Articles

1. The re-establishment of an equilibrium of the powers and a just distribution of forces among them being the aim of the present war, their Imperial and Royal Majesties obligate themselves to direct their efforts toward the actual establishment of the following system in Europe, to wit:

Germany composed of sovereign princes united by a federative bond which assures and guarantees the independence of Germany.

The Swiss Confederation in its former limits and in an independence placed under the guarantee of the great powers of Europe, France included.

Italy divided into independent states, intermediaries between the Austrian possessions in Italy and France.

Spain governed by King Ferdinand VII in its former limits.

Holland, free and independent state, under the sovereignty of the Prince of Orange, with an increase of territory and the establishment of a suitable frontier.

NAPOLEON'S ABDICATION

On March 31, 1814, after the allies had occupied Paris and Napoleon was hesitating at Fontainebleau, torn between ambition and despair, the allies set forth, over the signature of Czar Alexander, a proclamation declaring that, in the interests of European security, they would not treat with Bonaparte or any member of his family. They further promised to respect the integrity of old France "as it was under its legitimate kings," and urged the French Senate to create a provisional government and to prepare a constitution "appropriate for the French people." Four days later, Napoleon, hoping to salvage as much as possible from the wreck of his empire, abdicated in favor of his son; but neither the Senate nor the allies would accept this action and, on April 11, Napoleon signed a second abdication. On the same day, he acceded to the Treaty of Fontainebleau with the allies, the first article of which repeated the essence of his second renunciation of the throne.

From The Treaty of Fontainebleau
(April 11, 1814) [1]

1. His Majesty the Emperor Napoleon renounces for himself, his successors and descendants, as well as for all the members of his family, all right of sovereignty and dominion, as well to the French Empire and the Kingdom of Italy as to every other country.

2. Their Majesties the Emperor Napoleon and the Empress Maria Louisa shall retain their titles and ranks, to be enjoyed during their lives. The mother, brothers, sisters, nephews and nieces of the Emperor shall retain, wherever they may be, the title of princes of his family.

3. The island of Elba, adopted by His Majesty the Emperor Napoleon as the place of his residence, shall form, during his life, a separate principality, which shall be possessed by him in full sover-

[1] *Ibid.*, 450-51.

eignty and ownership. There shall be given besides, in full property, to the Emperor Napoleon, an annual revenue of 2,000,000 francs in *rentes* upon the ledger of France of which 1,000,000 shall be in reversion to the Empress. . . .

5. The Duchies of Parma, Piacenza, and Guastalla shall be given in full ownership and sovereignty to Her Majesty the Empress Maria Louisa. They shall pass to her son, and to his descendants in the direct line. The prince, her son, shall take from this moment the title of Prince of Parma, Piacenza and Guastalla.

NAPOLEON ON ST. HELENA

In March, 1815, just as the powers assembled at Vienna had about settled the affairs of post-Napoleonic Europe, Napoleon returned to France, proclaimed himself Emperor, and threatened the entire settlement of Vienna. The allies declared (March 13) that "In thus violating the convention which established him in the island of Elba, Bonaparte destroyed the only legal title for his existence . . . he has cut himself off from the protection of the law." Thus outlawed, Napoleon, defeated at Waterloo in June, threw himself into the hands of the English, who kept him as a prisoner in exile at St. Helena until his death in 1821. One of his few French companions, the Count de Las Cases, compiled a *Mémorial de Sainte-Hélène*, or a record of his experiences and conversations with Napoleon in exile.

From LAS CASES, *Memoirs* (1821-23) [1]

Aug. 10. This day we cleared the Channel, and lost sight of land. We

[1] Count E. A. D. de Las Cases, *Memoirs of the Life, Exile, and Conversations of the Emperor Napoleon*, 4 vols., New York, 1879, I, 54, 57, 163-64.

had now entered upon the dreary unknown course to which fate had doomed us. . . . Thus, in less than six weeks, had the Emperor abdicated his throne, and placed himself in the hands of the English who were now hurrying him to a barren rock in the midst of a vast ocean! . . .

[Napoleon landed upon St. Helena on October 16. Pending repairs at Longwood, the spacious colonial residence designed for his abode, Napoleon stayed nearly two months in a merchant's summer house called the Briars. It is the latter to which Las Cases refers below, although Longwood was little better—larger, but rat-infested.]

Oct. 23-24. The Emperor Napoleon, who but lately possessed such boundless power, and disposed of so many Crowns, now occupies a wretched hovel, a few feet square, perched upon a rock, unprovided with furniture, and without either shutters or curtains to the windows. This place must serve him for bed-chamber, dressing-room, dining-room, study, and sitting-room; and he is obliged to go out when it is necessary to have this one apartment cleaned. His meals, consisting of a few wretched dishes, are brought to him from a distance, as though he were a criminal in a dungeon. He is absolutely in want of the necessaries of life: the bread and wine are not such as we have been accustomed to, and are so bad that we loathe to touch them. . . .

Assuredly, if the Sovereigns of Europe decreed this exile, private enmity has directed its execution. . . . We were all assembled round the Emperor; and he was recapitulating these facts with warmth: "For what infamous treatment are we reserved!" he exclaimed. "This is the anguish of death! To injustice and violence, they now add insult and protracted torment. If I were so hateful to them, why did they not get rid of me? . . . How can the monarchs of Europe permit the sacred character of sovereignty to be violated in my person? Do they not see that they are, with their own hands, working their own destruction at St. Helena? I entered their capitals victorious, and had I cherished such sentiments, what would have become of them? They styled me their brother; and I had become so by the choice of the people, the sanction of victory, the character of religion, and the alliances of their policy and their blood. Do they imagine that the good sense of nations is blind to their conduct? and what do they expect from it? At all events, make your complaints, gentlemen; let indignant Europe hear them! Complaints from me would be beneath my dignity and character; I must command, or be silent."

Part Three

THE TRIUMPH OF THE BOURGEOISIE, 1815-1914

The Triumph of the Bourgeoisie, 1815-1914

24 | THE NINETEENTH CENTURY, 1815-1914: SOME GENERAL TRENDS

THE FRENCH REVOLUTION marked the beginning of the end to privilege in European society. As a result of the internal convulsions in France and the ensuing international wars most of the traces of the feudal era, especially the powers and privileges of the nobility, of the clergy, and of the guilds, were destroyed in France, and the French example set in motion attempts which were continued throughout the nineteenth century to modify or to destroy these institutions elsewhere in Europe. Gradually the structure of European society was altered from a society of birth to a society of status; that is, from a society in which power and prestige depended upon noble descent to one in which power and prestige depended principally upon wealth. Consequently, as power slipped from the grasp of the former privileged groups it was seized by the wealthy, property-holding middle class—the bourgeoisie. Simultaneously, the Industrial Revolution improved the position of the middle class by increasing their numbers and by multiplying their wealth. Thus enlarged and possessed of political and economic power, the middle class rested, of course, on a broader base than had the privileged classes of the Old Regime; and because power in the new society depended primarily upon wealth, the middle class was in a state of constant flux as wealthy persons lost their property and as propertyless persons enriched themselves, and became both propertied and powerful. Herein lay a source of strength in bourgeois society, for while the middle class sought to exclude propertyless people from positions of power, the "lower" classes nevertheless had an avenue to wealth and hence to power through good management, thrift, superior ability, and hard work. For so long as these attributes offered a reasonable opportunity for the successful political and social metamorphosis of the "lower" classes, society was fluid, "class consciousness" was virtually non-existent, and the middle class, constantly recruited from below, possessed dominant authority. By 1914, the new political and social structure inaugurated by the French Revolution had spread over most of Europe, save possibly in Spain, Russia, and the Turkish Empire, where decadent nobility and reactionary clergy still clung precariously to privilege.

The middle class, however, did not achieve and maintain its newly won power unchallenged. The French Revolution, during which the middle class won its first taste of power against fearful opposition, went to such extremes in change and bloodshed that it infected nineteenth-century Europe with a fear of revolution similar to the twentieth century's terror born of the Russian Revolutions in 1917. Accordingly, the middle class was long tainted with the charge of "radicalism" by its embittered opponents, the former privileged classes; and these tended everywhere to coalesce into "reactionary," or clerical, parties in support of monarchical institutions founded upon the divine right of kings and an established church with sole control of education and social policies. Until 1848, and in some instances longer, the "reactionaries" went far to retard the full expression of middle-class power. Meanwhile, from the Industrial Revolution arose another group to challenge the middle class. As the factory system spread from industry to industry and from nation to nation, the number of wage-earners multiplied. Generally propertyless and poor, they possessed at first neither political nor economic power, and they were often so meanly exploited by middle-class factory-owners and managers that their hope of economic betterment, of the opportunity to become themselves propertied persons endowed with a measure of political power and social prestige, appeared nonexistent. At this point they tended to become acutely class-conscious, organized labor unions, challenged the political and economic control of the middle class, demanded free public education, the right to vote, and other means for the enlargement of their own power and prestige. In some cases, too, they threatened revolution "to the Left" to establish the rule of the "proletariat" in place of bourgeois control. Challenges to middle-class power arose, then, from two sides: from the "Right," by monarchists and clergy, and from the "Left," from organized labor and the rising proletariat. Out of this three-cornered struggle developed most of the political contests, the civil strife, and, to a lesser extent, the international wars of the nineteenth century.

Each of the three parties proclaimed a "philosophy," or "system of society," designed to justify and to explain its bid for power. That of the middle class came to be known as "Liberalism," that of the wage-earners, "Socialism," and that of the monarchists and clergy went under various names indicative of its dual composition, such as "Royalism," "Ultramontanism" (meaning papal, or clerical, supremacy), and "Reactionism."

The last-named party, the extreme Right, or the party of reaction, was a two-winged group, consisting of a secular faction which pinned its faith to divine right, nationalist kings, and a clerical faction which demanded a return to unity in Church and State under the banner of the Papacy at Rome. Both wings opposed the doctrine of the rights of man, the contractual concept of the state, constitutionalism, representative government, and the notion of ministerial responsibility to popular assemblies.

The Emperor Francis II of Austria (1792-1835) so hated constitutions that when, in 1822, his physician commented—"This cough, although harassing, does not alarm me, as I have known your Majesty so long. There is, after all, nothing like a good constitution."—"What do you say?" cried the Emperor. "We have known each other very long, Stifft; but let me never hear that word again: say robust health, or, if you like, a strong bodily system; but there is no such thing as a good constitution. I have no constitution, and will never have one." And most of the royalty of Europe agreed. "No power on earth," said Frederick William IV of Prussia on the eve of the Revolutions of 1848, "shall ever persuade me to exchange the natural relation between prince and people for a contractual and constitutional relation; or to countenance the insertion, between our Lord in Heaven and this country, of a piece of written paper; like a second Providence, to rule by its paragraphs and to take the place of ancient sacred loyalty." Clerical reactionaries, however, including such men as Viscount Louis G. A. de Bonald and Count Joseph Marie de Maistre, held that all revolutionary impulses in modern society, from the Protestant Revolt to the French Revolution, were grounded in religious disunity; that national monarchies had arisen from the breakup of the religious universalism of the Middle Ages, either by resort to the Protestant secession (as in England) or by claiming a partial ecclesiastical freedom through such devices as the Gallican Liberties (as in France). Against the differentiation of national states and religious disunity, the clericals proclaimed a return to unity with the Pope at Rome as the rightful head of civilization and the church as the perfect world monarchy, combining infallibility in the spiritual realm with undivided sovereignty in the temporal sphere; against the rights of man they advocated the rights of God; and against the divine right of kings they set forth the supereminence of the Papacy. Thus the party of reaction, though solidly united against Liberalism and Socialism, was often torn asunder over the relation of temporal to spiritual authority, and the nineteenth century witnessed, in contrast to the friendly relations usually existing between the old monarchical governments and the Roman Catholic Church, a new order of temporal states with the church in conspiracy against them all. The reactionaries labored manfully to refurbish the old ideas of divine-right monarchy and ecclesiastical authoritarianism to combat the militant claims of their new-found challengers, but the divisions in their ranks and the obsolescence of their demands left them a poor third in the nineteenth-century triad of parties.

Liberalism, the term applied to the rising philosophy of the middle class in the nineteenth century, is singularly familiar to Americans, because the United States was born proclaiming its basic ideology, has nurtured liberal tenets as it grew powerful, and is still the stronghold of liberal philosophy. It is important to remember, however, that Liberalism was dynamic; that it was never static; that it became modified in the face of new circumstances, generally broadening its tenets as radicals, especially socialists, forced concessions in matters of policy and of practice; and that nineteenth-century Liberalism was a philosophy apart from what is often called liberalism today, as today's liberalism is strongly tinctured with evolutionary Socialism, giving rise to a confusion of terms whereby nineteenth-century Liberalism is today often labeled "Conservatism." That which follows refers exclusively to nineteenth-century Liberalism, a title conferred at the time upon certain principles of constitutional liberty and representative government widely sponsored in various European states by "liberal" political parties.

The Liberal creed was an application and extension of the program of the reformers of the Enlightenment [see pages 337-349]. For purposes of analysis, it can be separated into interrelated groups of tenets which, for convenience, will be labeled political, economic, and social demands.

In the political sphere, liberals sought to avoid the excesses of democracy and to disguise the newly acquired privilege of the propertied middle class with protestations of the sovereignty of the people, governments based upon consent of the people as expressed in written constitutions, representative government, the natural rights of man, and other tenets lifted from the writings of eighteenth-century reformers. In practice, however, "the people" were generally limited to the property-holders by constitutional provisions setting up property qualifications, literacy tests, and the like for voters and officeholders. But the principles were extendable, and as the nineteenth century wore on, labor organizations, socialists, and other radical groups forced a gradual democratization of the franchise by lowering qualifications for voting and officeholding until Liberalism and democracy became reluctantly identified. Except insofar as economic limitations operated against the propertyless individual, the doctrine of the natural rights of man generally granted full civil rights to all citizens, established equality before the law, trial by jury, freedom from false arrest, the right to property, and the sanctity of contract. A final political tenet of Liberalism with far-reaching international effects was the ideal of nationalism; that is, the right of a people who believe themselves to be a nation to become independent, self-governing states. This liberal notion found nineteenth-century expression in the independence of Greece, of Belgium, of united Italy, of Prussianized Germany, of Norway, and of the Balkan States—not to detail liberals' sympathy for the nationalistic efforts of Poles, Magyars, and others, nor to elucidate the Wilsonian doctrine of self-determination of peoples, which is still a potent principle in world affairs.

The economic tenets of Liberalism were postulated upon a capitalistic organization of society, borrowed heavily from the teachings of Adam Smith [see page 346], held axiomatic the principle that the interest of the individual coincides in the long run with the over-all interests of society, and thus subscribed to "economic freedom," a term which summarized economic Liberalism. Economic freedom included a number of economic "rights," such as the rights of individual enterprise and private ownership of property, of freedom of contract and sanctity of contract, of free trade and laissez faire. Each of these "rights" became subject to modification as the nineteenth century passed. For example, the right of individual enterprise became the right of *lawful* individual enterprise, with curbs upon narcotics, liquors, and other items; private ownership of property became subject to public rights of eminent domain; the freedom and sanctity of contracts were modified to protect workers, especially women and children, by state regulation of the hours and conditions of labor and a gradual acceptance of collective bargaining. Free trade was never wholly realized, nor indeed seriously desired by liberals in the *international* sphere (Great Britain excepted), but in the *internal* trade of nations free trade became almost universally realized as tolls and excise barriers were removed or hidden. Finally, laissez faire was always a unilateral demand of liberals, in that they demanded freedom from state restrictions upon economic enterprise but usually welcomed state aids in the form of free public lands, freedom to exploit mineral and forest resources, mail subsidies, patent monopolies, and the like. Moreover, as monopoly and combination movements in industry threatened private enterprise, liberals often demanded state interference to preserve freedom of individual enterprise.

In its social tenets Liberalism achieved its greatest heights. Liberals recognized religion to be a private matter, and consequently they demanded religious freedom and the separation of Church and State, a separation, however, which usually reduced the church to a position inferior to that of the state; they believed in intellectual freedom—that is, the free and untrammeled intercommunication of any and all ideas and opinions without censorship in speech or in press, save to exclude obscenities; they subscribed to policies designed to effect just legal procedures, "to make the punishment fit the crime" in criminal law, to effect prison reform, to give scientific care to the insane, and to establish better methods for assistance and care of the poor. And finally, liberals accepted the idea of progress as an axiom of human society, a fact that led them easily and often thoughtlessly into "social Darwinism" after the theory of evolution was set forth in the mid-nineteenth century. Darwin's biological theories of natural selection, of the struggle for existence, and of the survival of the fittest dovetailed beautifully into Liberalism's belief in individualism, private enterprise, laissez faire, and progress, and seemed to give scientific justification to the liberals' political, economic, and social program.

Liberalism meant different things to different men and, as has been seen, it underwent considerable modification and development during the nineteenth century. By 1914, however, it was a mature and widely held philosophy of constitutional liberty and representative government. It recognized that men are free, that a man's acts are his own, that they spring from his own inner personality, and that they cannot be coerced. Whether or not "man is born free," he should be able to acquire freedom through discipline and moral development. Liberalism aimed to assist man to discipline himself and to achieve moral progress, but it sought to avoid the two opposite errors of either forcing upon him a development for which he was inwardly unprepared or of leaving him alone, deprived of those aids to progress which a political system well designed and wisely administered might furnish. Thus Liberalism regarded the state not as a vehicle of superhuman wisdom and power, but as an organ through which a people might express whatever political ability it could find and develop within itself. This was not necessarily democracy, or the rule of the mere majority; neither was it authoritarianism, or the irresponsible rule of those who, for whatever reason and by whatever means, hold power at the moment. It was something between the two, democratic in its respect for human liberty, authoritarian in its insistence upon skillful and practiced government; but it was no mere compromise, for it had its own principles, as set forth above.

Socialism, the philosophy of the rising class of wage-earners, or the proletariat, is difficult to describe. This is true chiefly because Socialism began with the independent teachings of a number of men who, firm in their beliefs and sometimes unaware of one another's efforts, seldom composed their differences. Later, with the philosophy of Karl Marx, Socialism found a coherent body of doctrine, but socialists soon divided over the meaning and the method of Marx, broke up into a variety of splinter groups, and wrangled among themselves until the term "Socialism" covered a variety of extreme Leftist groups who rarely presented a united front. Broadly speaking, the tenets of Socialism were divided into two groups, Pre-Marxian, or Utopian, Socialism, and Marxian, or "Scientific," Socialism. Utopian Socialism gave birth to some of the tenets of Marxism, although the objectives and the methods of the two groups differed materially.

The earliest socialists, the Utopians, and indeed Marx himself, sprang from the middle class and included a sprinkling of the nobility and the clergy; not until the mid-century did Socialism sink deeply into the consciousness of the masses and become the creed of the proletariat. Out of compassion for the wage-earners, out of new economic and social theories, and out of applied Christianity, Utopian socialists devised experimental industrial communities and sought a new basis for the social order. Thus, Claude Henri Rouvroy, Count de Saint-Simon, proposed reconstruction based upon the social teachings of Jesus and designed to bring plenty to all mankind; François Marie Charles Fourier hoped to reform the social order through a world federation of small co-operative communities (the *phalange*) and a redistribution of income; and Robert Owen experimented with an ideal industrial community at his New Lanark cotton mill, urged factory legislation, trade-unionism, and industrial co-operation, and indulged in wide philanthropy on behalf of the poor. All of these early Utopian socialists emphasized the insufficiency of the individual in isolation, proposed co-operation as a panacea, and hoped to set an example which the world would follow to effect a new and better economic, social, and political society. Meanwhile, labor was becoming organized and pressed for higher wages, factory legislation to improve working conditions, free public education, and extension of the franchise to wage-earners. Simultaneously, too, economists and other social philosophers were setting forth new economic and social theories which socialists seized upon as their own. David Ricardo propounded his concept of surplus value, wherein he held that all value is created by labor—a concept adopted by William Thompson (and later by Marx), who drew the logical deduction that if all value is created by labor, then laborers should receive all the returns. Pierre Joseph Proudhon attacked private property and advocated the distribution of income upon the basis of the amount of labor performed. Louis Blanc and others proposed a new "natural right" for the proletariat—the right to work—and maintained that it was a function of the state to provide employment for all. Blanc and Ferdinand Lassalle also urged workers to help themselves by union organization and by resort to political activity. But nearly all of the pre-Marxian socialists sought bases for the reconstruction of all classes of society, not for the benefit of the proletariat alone; they hoped to motivate production for social welfare, not merely for private profit; they pioneered in experimental co-operative communities to set examples upon which social reconstruction might be modeled; most of them accepted the prevailing moral and religious values of society; and they expected to effect their ends by peaceful education and parliamentary means. While antiliberal in appearance, they sought in reality to bring into existence a wider Liberalism. And so they appeared impractical, undemocratic, too little concerned with the welfare of the proletariat alone, and too content with halfway measures to satisfy the Marxists.

Karl Marx and his alter ego, Friedrich Engels, combined, and added to the above socialist tenets to produce the classical body of socialist doctrine sometimes called "Scientific Socialism" in contrast to the catch-as-catch-can tenets of the Utopian socialists and out of respect for the scholarly manner in which Marx marshaled his data. In essence, Marx stressed only a few concepts. He was an economic determinist; that is, he believed that in all history the successive economic systems of production and distribution of wealth—the pastoral, the agrarian, and the capitalist systems—determined the accompanying social and cultural institutions. He held the labor theory of value—the belief that labor creates all value—and, having pointed out the difference between the totality of value produced and the fractional proportion received by labor, he held that the difference is the surplus value produced by labor out of which it is cheated by capitalists in the form of rent, interest, and profit. From this alleged unfairness arose an inevitable, omnipresent, and irreconcilable class struggle between the proletariat and the capitalists. This struggle, prophesied Marx, will inevitably end in the overthrow of capitalist society, because capitalism is being constantly weakened by the concentration of wealth, by repeated and disastrous economic depressions, and by the excesses of economic imperialism, while at the same time the proletariat is growing in strength through unionization, political organization, and the extension of the franchise. In time, thought Marx, wage-earners will secure enough power to rise up, expropriate their capitalistic oppressors, and set up a regime of collectivism under a dictatorship of the proletariat. This dictatorship would then seek to wrest all capital from the bourgeoisie and concentrate all production in the hands of the state, whereby, said Marx, the proletariat will have "swept away the conditions for the existence of class antagonisms, and of classes generally, and will thereby have abolished its own supremacy as a class. In place of the old bourgeois society, with its classes and class antagonisms, we shall have an association in which the free development of each is the condition for the free development of all." The movement was to be uncompromising, sweeping before it all bourgeois institutions, including churches, religion ("the opiate of the people"), and bourgeois philosophy, and it was to be international, embracing the victory of Socialism on a world-wide basis. Whether the proletarian state should be ushered in by violence or by democratic and constitutional means, in which order, and to what extent, the facilities of production should be collectivized, and the basis upon which workers' incomes should be determined in the proletarian state—these became items bitterly debated by Marx's disciples. Out of their differences arose the above-mentioned splinter groups which fragmentize and weaken Socialism to this day.

While clashes among conservatives, liberals, and socialists determined, in the main, the internal politics and policies of nations throughout the nineteenth century, such vast changes occurred in international relations and in ways of living as to amount to a revolution in each of these spheres of human affairs.

In the realm of international affairs, the French Revolution so outraged and terrified the ruling castes of Europe that in the early part of the century every effort was bent upon curbing France and upon stamping out the reform movements and nationalistic impulses engendered by the French example. The Concert of Europe, given reality by the Quadruple Alliance and the Holy Alliance, labored valiantly to preserve the settlement made at Vienna in 1815 and to salvage as much of the Old Regime as was politically and socially practicable; but within a generation the efforts failed, although the Concert idea retained its vitality throughout the century. The twin viruses of nationalism and reform, clothed in the growing philosophy of Liberalism, infected all Europe, and gradually found means to evade every effort of the watchdogs of conservatism. The Concert of Europe lost its effectiveness as the allies became suspicious of one another, as they became themselves overwhelmed by demands for liberal reform, and as Great Britain resumed "the course of empire" which had been interrupted by the American Revolution. And new nations rose to such unity and power as to render the settlement at Vienna in 1815 and the ideals of the old alliances obsolete and meaningless. During the nineteenth century four new nations rose to the first rank in international affairs, and two former great states emerged with even greater potentialities: Italy was proclaimed an independent kingdom in 1861 and won control over the entire Italian Peninsula by 1870. The German Empire was proclaimed upon the Prussian defeat of France in 1871. Japan was shaken from her isolation in 1854, reorganized her government, industrialized her society along Western lines, and by her victories over China (1895) and Russia (1905) emerged as a Great Power with dangerous ambitions. The United States of America marched across a continent, preserved its union despite bloody civil war, and appeared, after its easy victory over Spain in 1898, as a nation of the first magnitude. Meanwhile, Russia had expanded in southeastern Europe and across Asia to the Pacific, embracing one-sixth of the earth's surface and a vast population; and Great Britain had extended imperialistic control until Britishers boasted that the sun never set on their empire. With these shifts in international relations, preservation of the settlement at Vienna faded gradually from diplomatic view. France, decisively defeated by Prussia in 1870, no longer appeared the bête noire of Europe. Germany, fearful of French revenge, built up alliances for protection against her, and France retaliated with a series of alliances and loose ententes against Germany. But while Europe became aligned into two hostile, armed coalitions of powers, to the original Franco-German enmity were added a number of additional sources of conflict, arising out of the desire for colonies, commercial concessions, raw materials, and market outlets on the part of some of the "new" states, especially Italy and rapidly industrialized Germany and Japan; out of the scramble for control over the territories of "decadent" states, particularly the Austrian Empire, the Turkish Empire, and China; and out of nationalistic fervor screwed up to chauvinism and giving rise to international ill will, the propaganda of hatred, armament races, and all the other points of conflict which culminated in World War I.

In this melee of political and international conflict, the "new" science born in the sixteenth century began to bear such extraordinary fruits in the realms of learning and invention that the ways of thinking and the ways of living were transformed between 1789 and 1914. In this era alone, to mention but a few of the items, the steamboat, the steam railway, the electric tram, the automobile, and the airplane revolutionized transportation; the telegraph, the telephone, and the wireless revolutionized communication; the electric light, the photograph, the phonograph, the "movies," and a host of other gadgets revolutionized everyday life, especially in urban communities; and in the various fields of science scholars probed deeply to discover far more about the nature of the physical world than was known to any other age of man.

It is inevitable, then, if possibly regrettable, that the selections which follow can include only a small segment of the vast materials illustrative of this complex and fruitful era of European history.

25 REACTION AND REVOLUTION, 1815-1830

1. The Congress of Vienna: Social and Diplomatic Aspects

The Treaty of Paris, May 30, 1814, restored Louis XVIII as Bourbon King in France, and the allies declared French boundaries to be "as they existed on the 1st of January, 1792." In Article XXXII of the treaty the allies further agreed that "all the powers engaged on either side in the present war shall, within the space of two months, send Plenipotentiaries to Vienna for the purpose of regulating, in General Congress, the arrangements which are to complete the provisions of the present treaty." The chief object of the Congress was "The disposal of the Territories given up by His Most Christian Majesty [Louis XVIII] . . . and the relations from whence a system of real and permanent Balance of Power in Europe is to be derived." It was the clear intention of the four Great Powers—Great Britain, Russia, Austria, and Prussia—that all major decisions should be made by the "Four" themselves, and the Congress of Vienna was proposed merely as a ratifying instrument of these decisions. But to the lesser princes and peoples of

Europe the idea of a Congress fired the imagination. Princes dispossessed during the revolutionary era looked to the Congress to restore their "legitimate rights." Germans, Italians, Poles, and others whose nationalism had been quickened were eager to win that nationhood which Napoleon had promised. And so there assembled at Vienna, in the autumn of 1814, an enormous concourse of princes, potentates, and plenipotentiaries.

With such a membership and in such surroundings as Vienna, it was natural that the Congress should become a brilliant social event. The old Prince Marshal Charles Joseph von Ligne said, "The Congress has legs to dance—but not to walk." Another bon mot asserted that "The Emperor of Russia loves for them all, the King of Prussia thinks for them all, the King of Denmark speaks for them all, the King of Bavaria drinks for them all, the King of Württemberg eats for them all, and the Emperor of Austria pays for them all." A contemporary French man of letters has left a splendid account of the social setting at the Congress.

ROYALTY ON PARADE

From COMTE DE LA GARDE-CHAMBONAS, *The Congress of Vienna* (1815) [1]

Doubtless, at no time of the world's history had more grave and complex interests been discussed amidst so many fêtes. A kingdom was cut into bits or enlarged at a ball; an indemnity was granted in the course of a dinner; a constitution was planned during a hunt; now and again a cleverly placed word or a happy and pertinent remark cemented a treaty. . . .

The number of strangers attracted to Vienna by the Congress was estimated at close upon a hundred thousand. It ought to be said that for this memorable gathering no other city would have answered so well. Vienna is in reality the centre of Europe; at that time it was its capital. A Viennese who had happened to leave the city for a few months before would have had some difficulty in identifying himself and his familiar surroundings amidst that new, gilded, and titled population which crowded the place at the time of the Congress. All the sovereigns of the North had come thither; the West and the East had sent their most notable representatives. The Tsar Alexander, still young and brilliant; the Tsarina Elizabeth, with her winning though somewhat melancholy grace, and the Grand Duke Constantine represented Russia. Behind these were grouped a mass of ministers, princes, and generals . . . all of whom were marked out from that hour to play important parts in the political debates of Europe. . . . the King of Prussia was accompanied by the Princes William and August. . . . The King of Denmark, Frederick VI . . . the Kings of Bavaria and Württemberg, the Dukes of Saxe-Coburg, Hesse-Darm-

stadt, and Hesse-Cassel—in short, all the heads and princes of the reigning houses of Germany—were there . . . [except] the King of Saxony [who, having remained loyal to Napoleon,] was only represented at the Congress by his plenipotentiaries. The representatives of France were the Duc de Dalberg, the Comte Alexis de Noailles, M. de la Tour-du-Pin, and the Prince de Talleyrand. The last-named maintained his high reputation with great dignity under difficult circumstances and perhaps conspicuous justice has never been done him. The English plenipotentiaries were Lords Clancarty and Stewart, and Viscount Castlereagh. . . .

The Kings of Württemberg and Denmark arrived before any of the others. The Emperor Francis proceeded as far as Schönbrunn to welcome each of them. The interview between those princes was exceedingly cordial, and free from diplomatic reserve; but the ceremony which by its pomp and splendor was evidently intended to crown the series of wonders of the Congress was the solemn entry of Tsar Alexander and the King of Prussia. . . .

From that moment Vienna assumed an aspect which was as bright as it was animated. Numberless magnificent carriages traversed the city in all directions [the imperial stables held fourteen hundred horses at the disposal of the royal guests]. . . . The promenades and squares teemed with soldiers of all grades, dressed in the varied uniforms of all the European armies. Added to these were the swarms of the servants of the aristocracy in their gorgeous liveries. . . . When night came, the theatres, the cafés, the public resorts were filled with animated crowds, apparently bent on pleasure only. . . . In almost every big thoroughfare there was the sound of musical instruments discoursing joyous tunes. Noise and bustle everywhere. . . .

[1] Comte A. de la Garde-Chambonas, *Anecdotal Recollections of the Congress of Vienna,* ed. by the Comte Fleury, 1902, 1-3, 12, 29. By permission of Chapman and Hall, Ltd., London.

In order to convey an idea of the expenses of the Austrian Court, it will suffice to say that the imperial table cost fifty thousand florins per day [nearly $25,000]. This was keeping "open table" with a vengeance. Hence it is not surprising that the extraordinary expenses of the fêtes of the Congress, during the five months of its [social] duration, amounted to forty millions of francs [about $8,000,000].

THE CONGRESS OF VIENNA: SOME DIPLOMATIC ASPECTS

How Talleyrand Made France a Party to the "Real Congress of Vienna"

The intention of the Four to determine decisions at the Congress of Vienna was balked by differences among themselves. Prussia demanded all of Saxony and Russia required Poland, neither of which claims, in the interests of "equilibrium," was admissible by Great Britain and Austria. To enable the Four to settle their differences, the Congress was postponed until October 1, but even then the Four had arrived at no decision save "that the conduct of the business must practically rest with the leading powers." The "leading powers" were interpreted to be the Four plus France and Spain (the "Six"), and on September 22, the Four agreed that they should have the "initiative" (meaning the decision), and that they would "communicate" with France and Spain. But no plans were made for the organization and function of the Congress as a whole. An astute diplomat might widen the breach among the Four, champion the cause of the lesser powers at Vienna, and force his way into the central committee of the Congress. Such, in brief, was the role played by the French plenipotentiary, Charles Maurice de Talleyrand-Périgord, Prince de Bénévent—a role made doubly difficult by the fact that France was viewed with hatred and suspicion by most of the powers at the Congress.

Though on the surface Talleyrand's career appears singularly inconsistent and indecently opportunistic, underneath there was an unbroken strand of loyalty and patriotism to France. He had been a bishop under the Bourbons, an ambassador under the Girondins, an émigré during the Terror, Minister of Foreign Affairs under the Directory, Foreign Minister and Grand Chamberlain under Napoleon, advocate of the Bourbon restoration in 1814, and now, as Foreign Minister to Louis XVIII, he had written his own instructions and headed the French delegation at the Congress of Vienna! Such suppleness demonstrated unusual gifts in political perception and in powers of persuasion and intrigue. How Talleyrand employed these gifts to inject into the Congress of Vienna the political catchword "legitimacy," and to regain for France a seat among the Great Powers, is described in his own words below.

From TALLEYRAND, *Memoirs* (c. 1830) [1]

I arrived at Vienna September 23, 1814. . . . The day after my arrival, I presented myself at the houses of members of the diplomatic corps. They all seemed to me rather surprised at the little advantage they had derived from the capitulation of Paris. They had just traversed countries that had been ravaged by war for many years, in which they had heard, they said, but words of hatred and vengeance against France. . . . I therefore did not find them

[1] From *Memoirs of the Prince de Talleyrand,* ed. by the Duc de Broglie, trans. by R. L. de Beaufort and Mrs. Angus Hall, 5 vols., 1891-92, II, 199-205, 209. Courtesy of G. P. Putnam's Sons, New York.

very enthusiastic over the satisfaction to be derived from generosity. . . . How could they make up their minds to admit to the council of Europe the very power against which Europe had been in arms during twenty years? . . .

It remained for me to hope that there would be among the powers some divergence of opinion, when they came to distribute the numerous territories that the war had put at their disposal. . . .

The opening of congress had been fixed for the 1st of October. I had been at Vienna since September 23, but I had been preceded there by several days by the ministers who, having directed the war, and repented of peace, wished to take up their advantages again at the congress. It was not long before I was informed that they had already formed a committee [the Four], and were holding conferences among themselves, of which a protocol had been prepared. Their object was to decide alone, what ought to be submitted to the deliberations of the Congress, and that, too, without the assistance of either France, Spain, or any power of the second order; to these, however, they would afterwards communicate, in the form of a proposition, what would in reality be a resolution. . . . I made no remonstrances. I continued to see them, without speaking of business. I limited myself to communicating to the ministers of the secondary powers, who had a common interest with me, the dissatisfaction I felt. . . . They very soon looked upon me as their support, and once assured of their assent in all that I was about to do, I officially pressed the opening of the congress. . . . A few replies, evasive at first, caused me to repeat my entreaties. I even went so far as to complain a little, but was finally obliged to make use of the personal influence that I had fortunately acquired in the previous negotiations, over the principal personages of the congress. Prince Metternich, and the

Count Nesselrode, not wishing to be disobliging to me, both had me invited to a conference which was to have been held at the office of the minister of foreign affairs. Count de Labrador, minister of Spain, with whom I had the honor to support a common cause in the deliberations of the congress, received the same invitation.

I went to the office of the minister of state at the hour indicated, and found there, Lord Castlereagh, Prince von Hardenberg, Herr von Humboldt [the latter two being Prussian representatives], and Herr von Gentz, a man of distinguished talents, who fulfilled the functions of secretary. The protocol of the preceding sittings was on the table. I mention all the details of that first sitting, because it decided the position of France at the Congress. Prince Metternich opened it by a few sentences on the duty of the congress to give solidity to the peace which had just been restored to Europe. The Prince von Hardenberg added, that in order to consolidate the peace it was indispensable that the engagements that followed perforce from the war should be religiously kept, and such was the intention of the allied powers. . . .

I remarked that the Prince von Hardenberg had let fall an expression that appeared to me to belong to other times, for that they had both of them spoken of the intentions of the *allied powers*. I declared that *allied powers,* and a *congress* in which powers that were not allied were to be found, were in my eyes very little able to arrange affairs loyally together. I repeated with some astonishment and even warmth, the words *allied powers* . . . "allied," I said, "and against whom? It is no longer against Napoleon—he is on the isle of Elba. . . . It is no longer against France, for peace has been made. . . . It is surely not against the King of France; he is a guarantee of the duration of that peace.

Gentlemen, let us speak frankly; if there are still *allied powers,* I am one too many here." I perceived that I had produced some impression, and especially on Herr von Gentz. I continued: "And nevertheless if I were not here, I should decidedly be missed. Gentlemen, I am perhaps the only one who asks nothing. Great esteem is all I would have for France. . . . I want nothing, I repeat it, but I bring you a great deal. The presence of a minister of Louis XVIII consecrates here the principle upon which all social order rests. The first need of Europe is to banish for ever the opinion that right can be acquired by conquest alone, and to cause the revival of that sacred principle of legitimacy from which all order and stability spring. To show today that France troubles your deliberations would be to say that true principles are no longer the only ones that guide you, and that you are unwilling to be just. . . . When does the general congress open? When do the conferences begin? These are questions posed by all those whose interests bring them here. If, as is already rumoured, some privileged powers would exercise a dictatorial authority over the congress, I must say that, confining myself to the terms of the treaty of Paris, I could not consent to recognize in this assembly any supreme power in questions that the congress is competent to treat, and that I should heed no proposal that proceeded from them."

After a few moments' silence, Count Labrador made, in his proud and piquant language, a declaration almost identical with my own. Embarrassment was depicted on every face. They denied and explained in the same breath all that had taken place before this meeting. I profited by this moment. . . . I said that in an assembly as numerous as the congress . . . it was very difficult, nay even impossible, to reach any result by treating of all these subjects in general assemblies, but that some means of distributing and classifying all the business could be found without wounding either the interest or the dignity of the powers. . . . Herr von Gentz drew up the protocols of the previous sittings, and arranged one for that day. That protocol constituted the reports of the first sitting, and, in order to officially date our arrival at the congress, I signed it. From that time there was no conference among the great powers in which France did not take a part. . . .

Thus, at the end of the month of October, 1814, I was able to write to Paris, that the house of Bourbon, which had only returned to France five months ago, and France herself, who had been conquered five months previously, found themselves already replaced to their proper place in Europe, and had again regained that influence that belonged to them in the most important deliberations of the Congress.

[Once in the inner circle of the congress, Talleyrand conveniently forgot the demands of the lesser powers for an assembly of the congress as a whole. Indeed, the "Committee of Five"—Great Britain, Austria, Prussia, Russia, and France—replaced the Four and became the "real Congress of Vienna"; for an official plenary session of all the powers was never held. As a member of the Five, Talleyrand widened the breach between Prussia and Russia on the one hand, and between Great Britain and Austria on the other (over the disposition of Saxony and Poland), so that by January 3, 1815, France, Great Britain, and Austria had signed a defensive alliance against Prussia and Russia. The latter states then gave way, and the questions of Saxony and Poland were settled by compromise. "In this way," concluded Talleyrand, "France, who had but just ceased to be an object of dread to all Europe, became, in a measure, her arbitrator and moderator."]

The Concert of Europe: The Holy Alliance
and the Quadruple Alliance

The Congress of Vienna was another peace settlement on a grand scale, like the Peace of Westphalia in 1648 [see page 198]. Like the latter, also, the Congress of Vienna sought, besides the details of boundaries, political reconstruction, and the like, to create machinery which would both safeguard the peace settlement itself and preserve European peace for the future. To these ends was erected the Concert of Europe, a new phase in the European States System [page 199], and an extension of the alliance of Chaumont [page 442]. The Concert rested, at the outset, upon two international agencies, the Holy Alliance and the Quadruple Alliance. Unfortunately, both of these agencies were relatively ineffective and short-lived, principally because the statesmen at Vienna, who were generally conservatively inclined, made the mistake of directing their forces strongly against *all* movements which threatened the Vienna settlement, unhappily including those directed toward liberal constitutional reforms. But they hit upon a most promising means by which to maintain peace; namely, by concerted action of the powers of Europe, meeting together and exchanging views whenever the general peace seemed to be threatened. Until 1848 the Concert maintained the general peace, and the idea was employed again at Paris in 1856, after the Crimean War, and at Berlin in 1878, after the Russo-Turkish War of 1877-78.

The Holy Alliance was set forth by Czar Alexander I and, though signed by the Austrian Emperor and the King of Prussia, was looked upon as a harmless brainstorm of the Czar. Metternich described it as "nothing more than a philanthropic aspiration disguised under the cloak of religion. . . . A moral gesture . . . simply an expression of the Emperor Alexander's mystical feelings." Great Britain coyly refused to accede, and Castlereagh privately declared that the Holy Alliance was nothing but hollow verbiage. Still, the alliance possessed some moral force, and it contained the working principles—reasserted shortly in the more potent Quadruple Alliance —upon which the powers designed the suppression of the revolutionary movements that followed close upon the heels of the Congress of Vienna.

From The Holy Alliance (1815) [1]

In the name of the Most Holy and Indivisible Trinity. Their Majesties, the Emperor of Austria, the King of Prussia, and the Emperor of Russia, having, in consequence of the great events which have marked the course of the three last years in Europe, and especially of the blessings which it has pleased Divine Providence to shower down upon those States which place their confidence and their hope on it alone, acquired the intimate conviction of the necessity of settling the steps to be observed by the Powers, in their reciprocal relations, upon the sublime truths which the Holy Religion of our Saviour teaches. They solemnly declare . . . their fixed resolution . . . to take for their sole guide the precepts of that Holy Religion, namely the precepts of Justice, Christian Charity, and Peace . . . as being the only means of consolidating human institutions and remedying their imperfections. In consequence their Majesties have agreed on the following Articles:

Art. I. Conformedly to the words of the Holy Scriptures, which command all men

[1] E. Hertslet, ed., *The Map of Europe by Treaty*, I, 317-19.

to consider each other as brethren, the three contracting monarchs will remain united by the bonds of a true and indissoluble fraternity, and considering each other as fellow-countrymen, they will, on all occasions and in all places, lend each other aid and assistance . . . to protect Religion, Peace, and Justice.

Art. II. In consequence, the sole principle of force, whether between the said Governments or between their Subjects, shall be that of doing each other reciprocal service, and of testifying by unalterable good will the mutual affection with which they ought to be animated, to consider themselves all as members of one and the same Christian nation . . . thus confessing that the Christian world, of which they and their people form a part, has in reality no other Sovereign than Him to whom alone power really belongs, because in Him alone are found all the treasures of love, science, and infinite wisdom, that is to say, God, our Divine Saviour. . . .

Art. III. All the Powers who shall choose solemnly to vow the sacred principles which have dictated the present Act . . . will be received with equal ardour and affection into this Holy Alliance.

Done in triplicate, and signed at Paris, the year of Grace, 1815, 14/26 September.

(*Signed*) Francis. Frederick William. Alexander.

[On November 20, 1815, the same day of the conclusion of the new Treaty of Paris between the allies and France (wherein, as punishment for Napoleon's "Hundred Days," French boundaries were reduced to the limits of 1790, France was required to pay an indemnity of 700,000,000 francs and to support an army of occupation as a guarantee of payment), there was signed a "Treaty of Alliance

and Friendship between Great Britain, Austria, Prussia, and Russia." This compact, a renewal of the alliance of Chaumont [see page 442], was the basis of the powerful Quadruple Alliance which for several years after the Congress of Vienna sought to enforce the settlements by international action and, by the same means, to suppress any threat to the general peace of Europe.]

From The Quadruple Alliance (1815) [1]

In the name of the Most Holy Undivided Trinity . . . Their Majesties . . . considering that the repose of Europe is essentially interwoven with the confirmation of the order of things founded on the maintenance of the Royal Authority and of the Constitutional Charter [of France], and wishing to employ all their means to prevent the general tranquillity . . . from being again disturbed . . . have resolved to give the principles solemnly laid down in the Treaties of Chaumont of the 1st of March, 1814, and of Vienna of the 25th of March, 1815, the application the most analogous to the present state of affairs, and to fix beforehand by a solemn treaty the principles which they propose to follow, in order to guarantee Europe from dangers by which she may still be menaced; for which purpose the High Contracting Parties have . . . [concluded] the conditions of this Treaty, namely. . . .

Art I. The High Contracting Parties reciprocally promise to maintain, in its force and vigour, the treaty signed this day with His Most Christian Majesty, and to see that the stipulations of the said treaty . . . shall be strictly and faithfully executed. . . .

Art. II. [The powers emphasize that Napoleon and his family "have been for ever excluded from Supreme Power in France."] And as the same revolutionary

[1] *Ibid.*, I, 372-75.

principles which upheld the last criminal usurpation, might again, under other forms, convulse France, and thereby endanger the repose of other states . . . the High Contracting Parties solemnly . . . engage, in case so unfortunate an event should again occur, to concert amongst themselves, and with His Most Christian Majesty . . . for the general tranquillity of Europe. . . .

Art. VI. To facilitate and to secure the execution of the present treaty, and to consolidate the connections which at the present moment so closely unite the Four Sovereigns for the happiness of the world, the High Contracting Parties have agreed to renew their meetings at fixed periods, either under the immediate auspices of the Sovereigns themselves, or by their respective ministers, for the purpose of consulting upon their common interests, and for the consideration of measures which at each of those periods shall be considered the most salutary for the repose and prosperity of nations, and for the maintenance of the peace of Europe.

2. The Pattern of Conservatism

THE GOVERNMENT OF THE RESTORED BOURBONS IN FRANCE

After Napoleon's abdication [see page 443] the allies agreed to restore the Bourbons in France "with constitutional guarantees." These guarantees, embraced in the French constitution, at once illustrate the permanent gains of the French Revolution and the strict limits set to protect monarchical interests. Set forth by Louis XVIII in June, 1814, the Charter was maintained, with some modifications in 1830, until 1848. It read in part as follows.

From the French Charter of 1814[1]

Divine Providence in recalling us to our estates after a long absence has imposed grave responsibilities upon us. Peace was the first necessity of our subjects. . . . That peace so essential to France and to the rest of Europe has been signed. A constitutional charter was demanded by the existing condition of the Kingdom, we promised this and now publish it. We have taken into consideration the fact that although the whole authority in France resides in the person of the king, our predecessors have not hesitated to modify the exercise of this in accordance with the differences of the time. . . . We, like the kings our predecessors, have had to consider the ever increasing progress of knowledge, the new relations which this progress has introduced into society, the direction given to the public mind during half a century and the serious troubles resulting therefrom. We have perceived that the wish of our subjects for a constitutional charter was the expression of a real need, but in yielding to this wish we have taken every precaution that this charter should be worthy of us and of the people whom we are proud to rule. . . . While we recognize that the expectations of enlightened Europe ought to be gratified by a free monarchical constitution, we have had to remember that our first duty towards our peoples was to preserve for their own interest the rights and prerogatives of our crown. We hope that, taught by experience, they may be convinced that the supreme authority can alone give to institutions which it establishes the power, permanence and dignity with which it is itself clothed. . . .

We have sought the principles of the

[1] James Harvey Robinson, ed., Restoration and Reaction, 1814-20 (in Translations and Reprints from the Original Sources of European History, I, No. 3), 2-5. By permission of the University of Pennsylvania Press, Philadelphia.

constitutional charter in the French character and in the venerable monuments of past centuries. Thus we perceived in the revival of the peerage a truly national institution which binds memories to hope, by uniting ancient and modern times. We have replaced by the chamber of deputies . . . those chambers of the third estate which so often exhibited at once proof of their zeal for the interests of the people, and fidelity and respect for the authority of kings. In thus endeavoring to renew the chain of time which fatal excesses had broken, we effaced from our memory, as we would we might blot out from history, all the evils which have afflicted the country during our absence. . . .

Confident in our intentions, strong in our conscience, we engage ourselves before the assembly which listens to us to be faithful to this Constitutional Charter, with the intention of swearing to maintain it with added solemnity before the altars of Him who weighs in the same balance kings and nations.

For these reasons we have voluntarily and by the free exercise of our royal authority granted and do grant, concede and accord, as well for us as for our successors forever, the Constitutional Charter as follows:

PUBLIC RIGHTS OF THE FRENCH

Article 1. The French are equal before the law, whatever may be their title or rank.

2. They contribute without distinction to the impositions of the State in proportion to their fortune.

3. They are all equally eligible to civil and military positions.

4. Their personal liberty is likewise granted. No one can be prosecuted or arrested except in the cases and in the manner prescribed by the law.

5. All may with equal liberty make profession of their religion and enjoy the same protection for their form of worship.

6. Nevertheless the Roman Catholic and Apostolic religion is the religion of the State.

7. The ministers of the Roman Catholic and Apostolic religion and those of other Christian forms of worship only receive subsidies from the royal treasury.

8. The French have the right to publish and cause their opinions to be printed, if they conform to the laws destined to check the abuse of this liberty.

9. All property is inviolable, that known as *national* property forming no exception. . . .

10. The State may demand the surrender of property in the cause of the public interest when this is legally certified, but only with previous indemnification.

11. All investigation of opinions expressed or of votes cast previous to the Restoration is prohibited. . . .

12. The conscription is abolished. The method of recruiting . . . shall be determined by law.

FORM OF GOVERNMENT OF THE KING

13. The person of the King is inviolable and sacred. His ministers are responsible. In the King alone is vested the executive power.

14. The King is the supreme head of the state, he has command of the land and naval forces, declares war, concludes treaties of peace, alliance and commerce, appoints all the officials of the public administration and issues the regulations and ordinances necessary for the execution of the laws and the safety of the State.

15. The legislative power is exercised jointly by the King, the Chamber of Peers [appointed by the King], and the Chamber of Deputies of the Departments [indirectly elected by a franchise sharply limited by age and property qualifications].

16. The right of initiating legislation belongs to the King.

17. Proposed laws are submitted, at the option of the King, either to the Chamber of Peers or to the Chamber of Deputies, except laws for raising taxes, which must be submitted to the Chamber of Deputies first.

18. Every law must be discussed and passed freely by a majority of each of the two houses.

19. The chambers have the right to petition the King to submit a law relating to any subject and to indicate what they deem the law should contain.

THE GERMANIC CONFEDERATION AS CONSTITUTED AT VIENNA

German liberals who hoped for a "regenerated," unified national state with constitutional government were sorely disappointed with the German settlement at the Congress of Vienna. Metternich, writing of the considerations which impelled the powers to constitute the Germanic Confederation, explained it as follows: "To the question: *Ought the German political unity be revived?* a single reply was possible: Yes; but to the further inquiry, *Ought the Holy Roman Empire of earlier days be restored to life?* we could only respond without hesitation, No. For in Germany . . . the elements necessary for the reconstitution of the Empire under its old form have disappeared. . . . The [Napoleonic] Confederation of the Rhine was in the hands of princes of confederated states whose sovereign rights, under the Holy Roman Empire, had resided in the *Emperor* and in the *Empire*. It would be necessary to restore these rights to the chief of the resuscitated Empire; and the moral conse-quences of that violence would throw the former Empire into interminable conflict—that is, between the chief sov-

ereign and the heads of particular states. . . . For these reasons, we could not wish for the re-establishment of a German Empire, and of an Empire having that unity; and the formation of a *Germanic Confederation* was the only practical solution in our eyes." The resultant Bund was a loose union of sovereign princes created by a treaty among the powers, signed at Vienna, June 9, 1815. This constitution obtained in Germany until 1866.

From The Constitution of the Germanic Confederation (1815) [1]

Art. LIII. The sovereign princes and free towns of Germany, under which denomination, for the present purpose, are comprehended . . . the Emperor of Austria and the King of Prussia, for all their possessions which anciently belonged to the German Empire; The King of Denmark, for the Duchy of Holstein; and the King of the Netherlands, for the Grand Duchy of Luxemburg; establish among themselves a perpetual Confederation, which shall be called "The Germanic Confederation."

Art. LIV. The object of this Confederation is the maintenance of the external and internal safety of Germany, and of the Independence and Inviolability of the Confederated States.

Art. LV. The members of the Confederation, as such, are equal with regard to their rights; and they all equally engage to maintain the act which constitutes their union.

Art. LVI. The affairs of the Confederation shall be confided to a Federative Diet in which all the members shall vote by their plenipotentiaries, either individually or collectively, in the following manner, with prejudice to their rank:

[1] Hertslet, *op. cit.,* I, 243-48.

Votes

1. Austria 1
2. Prussia 1
3. Bavaria 1
4. Saxony 1
5. Hanover 1
6. Württemberg 1
7. Baden 1
8. Electoral Hesse [Hesse-Cassel] 1
9. Grand Duchy of Hesse [Hesse-Darmstadt] 1
10. Denmark, for Holstein 1
11. The Netherlands, for Luxemburg 1
12. Grand-Ducal and Ducal Houses of Saxony 1
13. Brunswick and Nassau. 1
14. Mecklenburg-Schwerin and Strelitz 1
15. Holstein-Oldenburg, Anhalt, and Schwartzburg 1
16. Hohenzollern, Liechtenstein, Reuss, Schaumberg-Lippe, Lippe, and Waldeck 1
17. The free towns of Lübeck, Frankfurt, Bremen, and Hamburg 1
   Total 17

Art. LVII. Austria shall preside at the Federative Diet. . . .

[Art. LVIII provides that whenever fundamental laws of the Confederation are to be enacted or amended, or the present constitution amended, the Diet shall form itself into a general assembly (*Plenum*) in which the votes are distributed so that the larger states have proportionately greater voting power. Thus, Austria, Prussia, Saxony, Bavaria, Hanover, and Württemberg have *four* votes each; Baden, Electoral Hesse, Grand Duchy of Hesse, Holstein, and Luxemburg have *three* votes each: Brunswick, Mecklenburg-Schwerin, and Nassau have *two* votes each: and the remainder of the thirty-eight states in the Confederation— Saxe-Weimar, Saxe-Gotha, Saxe-Coburg, Saxe-Meiningen, Saxe-Hildburghausen, Mecklenburg-Strelitz, Holstein-Oldenburg, Anhalt-Dessau, Anhalt-Bernburg, Anhalt-Cöthen, Schwarzburg - Sondershausen, Schwarzburg-Rudolstadt, Hohenzollern-Hechingen, Liechtenstein, Hohenzollern-Sigmaringen, Waldeck, Reuss (Elder Branch), Reuss (Younger Branch), Schaumberg-Lippe, Lippe, and the free towns of Lübeck, Frankfurt, Bremen, and Hamburg—have *one* vote each (a total of 69 votes for the 38 states)].

Art. LXI. The Diet shall assemble at Frankfurt-on-the-Main. The first meeting is fixed for the 1st of September, 1815. . . .

Art. LXIII. The states of the Confederation engage to defend not only the whole of Germany, but each individual state of the union, in case it should be attacked. . . . When war shall be declared by the Confederation, no member can open a separate negotiation with the enemy, nor conclude an armistice, without the consent of the other members.

The Confederated States engage, in the same manner, not to make war against each other, on any pretext . . . but to submit . . . [their differences] to the Diet, which will attempt a mediation by means of a Commission. If this should not succeed, and judicial sentence becomes necessary, recourse shall be had to a well-organized Austregal Court [Court of Arbitration] to the decision of which the contending parties are to submit without appeal.

FERDINAND VII REJECTS THE SPANISH CONSTITUTION (1814)

When Ferdinand VII was restored to Spain in 1814, he bitterly rejected the Spanish constitution which had been drawn up by Spanish liberals in 1812.

From FERDINAND VII, Manifesto (1814) [1]

This form of legislation, so foreign to the Spanish nation, consigns to oblivion the laws which have rendered it so happy and respected in former times. In fact, all the foundations of the ancient monarchical constitution are overturned, while all the revolutionary and democratic principles of the French Constitution of 1791 have been copied. . . . Thus are set forth, not the fundamental laws of a limited monarchy, but those of a popular government presided over by a chief or magistrate who is only a clerk, not a king. . . .

In order to dispose the minds of men to receive without suspicion such dangerous innovations . . . use is made of some of the newspapers with which most of the deputies in the Cortes are themselves connected. The attempt is made to render the royal power odious by giving to all of the rights of the crown the name of despotism, by regarding the titles of king and despot as synonymous, and by calling tyrants kings. At the same time those who have the courage to combat these innovations and object to this monarchical and seditious language are persecuted in the most cruel manner. Wherever democracy appears, it changes all that recalls the name of king; the armies, the institutions which for a long time have been honoured by the title of royal, are called "national," and thus the people are deceived, who, nevertheless, in spite of so many perfidious intrigues, have preserved their natural loyalty and nobleness of character.

I have learned of all this since my happy return to the realm, both from my own observations and from the newspapers in which many articles have been impudently printed up till this very day about my character and return. . . . Unexpected insults have also filled my heart with bitter-

[1] British and Foreign State Papers 1812-1814, London, 1841, I, Pt. ii, 1096-99 (translation).

ness. I have been consoled only by the evidences of the love of my faithful subjects. . . . I promise you and I swear to you, true and loyal Spaniards, that since I sympathize with the evils which you have suffered, you will not be in the least deceived in your hopes. Your sovereign wishes to live for you; he makes his glory consist in being the sovereign of a heroic nation. . . . I detest, I abhor despotism; it cannot be reconciled either with civilization or with the enlightenment of the nations of Europe. Kings have never been despots in Spain. Neither the kings nor the constitution of the realm have ever authorized despotism, although unfortunately we have seen at times, here as everywhere, certain abuses of power which no human constitution could ever entirely prevent. But if these have occurred in Spain, it was not the fault of the constitution but of persons and circumstances. . . .

Conforming myself to the general demonstration of good will on the part of my people, which I believe to be well founded, I declare that my royal intention is not only to refuse to swear to or accept their constitution or any decree of the General and Extraordinary Cortes and of the ordinary Cortes now actually assembled; and particularly the decrees which attack the rights and prerogatives of my sovereignty established by the constitution and the laws which have governed the nation for so long a time; but also to declare their constitution and their decrees null and void now and for ever; that my subjects, of whatsoever rank or condition, are not bound to observe them; and that those who seek to uphold them in opposition to my royal intentions in this matter shall be regarded as having made an attack on the prerogatives of my sovereignty and the well-being of the nation.

I declare guilty of lèse-majesty, and as such punishable by death, whoever ventures either by act, by writing, or by word of mouth to excite or engage any one to observe or execute the decrees and constitution. . . .

I declare that whoever opposes the execution of the present decree in any way whatsoever is guilty of lèse-majesty and as such is punishable by death.

[In July following Ferdinand VII restored the tribunal of the Inquisition [see page 160], which Napoleon had suppressed. The object, as stated in the royal decree, was to enforce conformity to the Roman Catholic religion by rooting out "the wicked" and the "many pernicious opinions" which gave rise to, and were a product of, "the past disturbances."]

THE PRINCIPLES OF CONSERVATISM: PRINCE METTERNICH'S "POLITICAL FAITH"

The principles and policies of Conservatism in the era 1815 to 1848 have become identified with the influential Austrian Minister, Prince Metternich. Metternich often claimed to be a liberal, and certainly he was not as reactionary as the Emperor Francis I or Ferdinand VII of Spain. But he sought to set limits to "ultraliberalism" as attributed to French revolutionary principles; and as he lacked courage to insist upon even those reforms which he felt desirable, he won the reputation of being the personification of Conservatism and reactionary policies. Metternich's was essentially an eighteenth-century mind, unable to estimate accurately post-Napoleonic forces, especially liberal nationalism, which he opposed bitterly, partly on principle and partly because he sensed that it would be fatal to Austria's position in Germany and Italy—as, indeed, it was in time. In 1820, at the Conference of Troppau, Metternich

drew up, at Czar Alexander's request and with Emperor Francis's approval, the following illuminating statement of his "Political Faith"—that is, the principles which underlay his political acts, for Metternich stoutly denied that he clung to any specific system.

Metternich began with the assertion that "Man's nature is immutable. The first needs of society are and remain the same." Local differences arise from natural causes, such as diversity of climate. Similarly, "It is . . . with institutions as with everything else. . . . Conforming to the law of man's nature, they have . . . their infancy, their youth, their age of strength and reason, and their age of decay." But, "two elements alone remain in all their strength. . . . These are the precepts of morality, religious as well as social, and the necessities created by locality." Whenever men try to "swerve from these bases . . . society suffers from a *malaise* [sickness]." Never has "an evil of this nature" spread over such a vast area as at the present time. "The Causes are natural" —arising, states Metternich, from the impact on the moral world of the invention of printing and of gunpowder, of the discovery of the New World, and of the Reformation. "From that time the face of the world was changed."

From Metternich, *Memoirs* (1820) [1]

The progress of the human mind has been extremely rapid in the course of the last three centuries. This progress having been accelerated more rapidly than the growth of wisdom (the only counterpoise to passions and to error); a revolution prepared by the false systems, the fatal errors into which many of the most illustrious

[1] *Memoirs of Prince Metternich*, ed. by Prince Richard Metternich, trans. by Mrs. Alexander Napier, 5 vols., N. Y., 1880-82, III, 458-75.

sovereigns of the last half of the eighteenth century fell [the Enlightenment], has at last broken out in a country advanced in knowledge and enervated by pleasure, in a country [Italy] inhabited by a people whom one can only regard as frivolous, from the facility with which they comprehend and the difficulty they experience in judging calmly.

Having now thrown a rapid glance over the first causes of the present state of society, it is necessary to point out in a more particular manner the evil which threatens to deprive it, at one blow, of the real blessings, the fruits of genuine civilization, and to disturb it in the midst of its enjoyments. This evil may be described in one word—presumption; the natural effect of the rapid progression of the human mind towards the perfecting of so many things. This it is which at the present day leads so many individuals astray, for it has become an almost universal sentiment.

Religion, morality, legislation, economy, politics, administration, all have become common and accessible to everyone. Knowledge seems to come by inspiration; experience has no value for the presumptuous man; faith is nothing to him; he substitutes for it a pretended individual conviction, and to arrive at this conviction, he dispenses with all inquiry and with all study; for these means appear too trivial to a mind which believes itself strong enough to embrace at one glance all questions and all facts. Laws have no value for him, because he has not contributed to make them. . . . Power resides in himself. . . . That which, according to him, was required in an age of weakness cannot be suitable in an age of reason and vigour, amounting to universal perfection, which the German innovators designate by the idea, absurd in itself, of the Emancipation of the People!

. . . Presumption makes every man the guide of his own belief, the arbiter of laws according to which he is pleased to govern himself, or to allow some one else to govern him and his neighbours; it makes him, in short, the sole judge of his own faith, his own actions, and the principles according to which he guides them. . . .

It is principally the middle classes of society which this moral gangrene has affected, and it is only among them that the real heads of the party are found.

For the great mass of the people it has no attraction and can have none. The labours to which this class—the real people—are obliged to devote themselves are too continuous and too positive to allow them to throw themselves into vague abstractions and ambitions. The people know what is the happiest thing for them: namely, to be able to count on the morrow, for it is the morrow which will repay them for the cares and sorrows of today. The laws which afford a just protection to individuals, to families, and to property, are quite simple in their essence. The people dread any movement which injures industry and brings new burdens in its train. . . .

There is besides scarcely any epoch which does not offer a rallying cry to some particular faction. This cry, since 1815, has been *Constitution*. But do not let us deceive ourselves: this word, susceptible of great latitude of interpretation, would be but imperfectly understood if we supposed that the factions attached quite the same meaning to it under different *régimes*. Such is certainly not the case. In pure monarchies it is qualified by the name of "national representation." In countries which have lately been brought under the representative *régime* it is called "development," and promises charters and fundamental laws. In the only State which possesses an ancient national representation it takes "reform" as its object. Everywhere it means change and trouble. . . .

The Governments, having lost their balance, are frightened, intimidated, and thrown into confusion by the cries of the intermediary class of society, which, placed between the Kings and their subjects, breaks the sceptre of the monarch, and usurps the cry of the people. . . . The evil is plain. . . .

We are convinced that society can no longer be saved without strong and vigorous resolutions on the part of the Governments still free in their opinions and actions. . . . By this course the monarchs will fulfil the duties imposed upon them by Him who, by entrusting them with power, has charged them to watch over the maintenance of justice and the rights of all. . . .

The first principle to be followed by the monarchs, united as they are by the coincidence of their desires and opinions, should be that of maintaining the stability of political institutions against the disorganized excitement which has taken possession of men's minds; the immutability of principles against the madness of their interpretation; and respect for laws actually in force against a desire for their destruction. . . .

The first and greatest concern for the immense majority of every nation is the stability of the laws and their uninterrupted action—never their change. Therefore let the Governments govern, let them maintain the groundwork of their institutions. . . .

Let them announce this determination to their people, and demonstrate it by facts. . . .

Let them be just, but strong; beneficent, but strict.

Let them maintain religious principles in all their purity, and not allow the faith to be attacked and morality interpreted according to the *social contract* or the visions of foolish sectarians.

Let them suppress Secret Societies, that gangrene of society.

In short, let the great monarchs strengthen their union, and prove to the world that if it exists, it is beneficent, and ensures the political peace of Europe . . . that the principles which they profess are paternal and protective, menacing only the disturbers of public tranquillity.

3. Conflicts with Liberal Aspirations

THE GERMAN "BURSCHENSCHAFTERS"

Disappointment of German liberals in the Confederation found expression in the Burschenschaft movement, ultra-patriotic societies of students who agitated for a united Fatherland with constitutional representative government. In October, 1817—the three-hundredth anniversary of Luther's theses [see page 102] and the fourth anniversary of the Battle of Leipsic—the patriots held a national festival at Wartburg, scene of Luther's alleged encounter with the Devil, where some eight hundred representatives of German youth staged protests against the Conservative settlement. Franz Hegewisch, a Kiel physician, drew up a "Confession of Faith of Those Who Protest against Tyrants," which he hoped the assembly would adopt as an official statement of principles. His proposals well illustrate the ideals of German liberals. A few of his twenty-seven "fundamental principles" follow.

From HECEWISCH, "Confession of Faith" (1817) [1]

(1) Germany is, and shall remain, ONE. We cannot accept the belief that Germany is composed of thirty-eight islands. We Germans are brothers; we desire to be friends. . . .

(2) We do not forget those who have fallen in the struggle for German freedom. . . . It is the duty of every honorable and pious German man, of every honorable and pious German prince, to celebrate the eighteenth day of October [day of the victory at Leipsic in 1813].

(3) The doctrine that Germany is split up into North Germany and South Germany is false and erroneous; it is the doctrine of a malicious enemy. We mutually pledge one another to fight against this doctrine . . . and to suppress all similar, false ideas which may contribute to an artificial disintegration of Germany. . . .

(7) We render homage to the just and noble grand duke of Weimar. . . . He, before all others, has redeemed the pledge given in Vienna, in days of danger, by the German princes, and has introduced an improved constitution into his own land, a constitution which contains so much that is exemplary for all German lands. We, contemporaries, shall daily echo the saying: "God bless Blücher and Weimar!". . .

(10) We declare ourselves unable and unwilling to associate with the word "sovereignty," which derives from the Confederation of the Rhine, the concept of despotism. We declare further that we know no other desirable equality than equality before the law, such as has long existed in England. . . .

[1] Heinrich von Treitschke, *History of Germany in the Nineteenth Century,* trans. by Eden and Cedar Paul, 5 vols., 1917, III, Appendix, 613-17. By permission of Robert M. McBride and Company, New York.

(11) We express our conviction of the truth of that principle established in the early days of Germany that TAXES ARE NOT BURDENS BUT GIFTS; and we are equally convinced of the truth that popular approval of taxes can be accorded solely by ELECTED representatives of the people. . . .

(17) We pledge ourselves that should any of us at any future date enter official service, not one of us will accept any kind of office which subserves the purposes of a secret police . . . nor any office connected with the censorship of printed books. . . .

(18) We pledge ourselves that should we ever occupy official positions, we will do all in our power to introduce freer communal administration . . . and to bring about the establishment in Germany of a universally valid coinage, a universal system of weights and measures, better roads, and a better postal system.

THE CARLSBAD DECREES (1819)

The Wartburg Festival was held under the close scrutiny of the Bund's officers. Prince Metternich had little fear of the Burschenschaft movement, which he characterized as "an unpractical puppet-show." Nonetheless, he recognized that by such organizations "a whole generation of revolutionaries must be formed unless the evil is restrained." In 1819, after Karl Ludwig Sand, an earnest Burschenschafter, had assassinated August F. F. von Kotzebue, a reactionary spy in the pay of the Czar, Metternich called a conference of the larger states of the Confederation at Carlsbad in Bohemia. Here a series of resolutions were drawn which, on September 20, were ratified by the Diet and became known as the Carlsbad Decrees. These decrees were designed to ferret out liberal conspirators and to check the free expression of liberal opinions.

From The Carlsbad Decrees (1819) [1]

SUPERVISION OF UNIVERSITIES

. The sovereign shall make choice for each university of an extraordinary commissioner. . . .

The duty of this commissioner shall be to watch over the most rigorous observation of the laws and disciplinary regulations; to observe carefully the spirit with which the professors and tutors are guided in their public and private lectures; to endeavour, without interfering directly in the scientific courses, or in the method of instruction, to give the instruction a salutary direction, suited to the future destiny of the students. . . .

2. The governments of the states . . . reciprocally engage to remove from their universities and other establishments of instruction, the professors and other public teachers against whom it may be proved, that in departing from their duty, in overstepping the bounds of their duty, in abusing their legitimate influence over the minds of youth, by the propagation of pernicious dogmas, hostile to order and public tranquillity, or in sapping the foundation of existing establishments, they have shown themselves incapable of executing the important functions entrusted to them. . . .

3. The laws long since made against secret or unauthorized associations at the universities shall be maintained in all their force and vigour, and shall be particularly extended with so much the more severity against the well-known society formed some years ago under the name of the General Burschenschaft. . . .

1 "Appendix to the Chronicle," *The Annual Register . . . for the Year 1819*, London, 1820, 159-62.

PRESS CENSORSHIP

1. As long as the present decree shall be in force, no writing appearing in the form of a daily paper or periodical pamphlet, which does not contain more than 20 printed leaves, shall be issued from the press without the previous consent of the public authority. . . .

4. Each government of the confederation is accountable for the writings published under its jurisdiction. . . .

6. The Diet will proceed also . . . of its own authority, against every publication comprised in Article I in whatever state of Germany it may be published, if . . . it may have compromised the dignity of the Germanic body, or the internal peace of Germany. . . .

COMMITTEE OF INVESTIGATION

1. In 15 days . . . an extraordinary commission of inquiry, appointed by the Diet and composed of 7 members . . . shall assemble in the city of Mayence. . . .

2. The object of this commission is to make careful and detailed inquiries respecting the facts, the origin, and the multiplied ramifications of the secret revolutionary and demagogic associations directed against the political constitution and internal repose, as well of the Confederation in general as of the individual members thereof.

THE ERA OF THE CONGRESSES (1815-1825): EARLY DISPUTES IN POLICY

The decision of the powers of the Quadruple Alliance "to renew their meetings at fixed periods" led to a unique series of international congresses within the next decade—at Aix-la-Chapelle (1818), Troppau (1820), Laibach (1821), and Verona (1822)—each concerned with specific problems or crises in European affairs. At Aix-la-Chapelle in 1818, the powers were concerned with French affairs, ending with the admission of France to the Quadruple Alliance as an equal, thus turning it into the Quintuple Alliance. By 1820, a series of violent acts galvanized European conservative circles and led them to seek safety in further repressive measures. In January, revolution began in Spain, and on March 1, Ferdinand VII was forced to accept the constitution which he had rejected in 1814; on February 13, Henri, Duke of Berry, heir to the Bourbon crown in France, was assassinated; on February 23, a bloodthirsty plot (the "Cato Street Conspiracy") was uncovered in London just in time to prevent the murder of the entire Tory Cabinet; in June, a revolution broke out in the Kingdom of Naples; and in August the Portuguese rebelled and demanded a constitutional regime. To the conservative forces of the Quintuple Alliance, prompt measures seemed obligatory. Even Czar Alexander, who had oscillated between sentimental liberalism and religious conservatism, demanded severe repressive measures, and he wrote an expiatory letter to Metternich saying: "Today I deplore all that I said and did between the years 1815 and 1818. I regret the time lost; we must study to retrieve it. You have correctly judged the condition of things. Tell me what you want and what you want of me, and I will do it." Not all the members of the Quintuple Alliance, however, were so amenable. Lord Castlereagh was unwilling to commit England to assist the alliance in forcible interference in the internal affairs of other states; and France, too, was hesitant. Accordingly, at the Conference of Troppau (October-December, 1820) a rift appeared among the powers in the alliance, and the following "Circular Respecting the Affairs of Spain, Portugal, and Naples" was signed only by the Austrian Prussian, and Russian sovereigns.

From *The Troppau Circular*
(December 8, 1820) [1]

The Events which occurred on the 8th of March in Spain, on the 2nd July at Naples, and the Portuguese catastrophe, have naturally led to a feeling of great anxiety and sorrow in all persons who are under the obligation of watching over the Tranquillity of States, but at the same time revealing to them the necessity of assembling together and deliberating on the means of preventing all the evils which threatened to fall upon Europe.

It was natural that these feelings should especially create a lively impression on the Powers which had recently stifled Revolution, and which saw it again raising its head. It was not less natural that those Powers, in order to battle with it for the third time, should have recourse to the same means which they had adopted with so much success in that memorable struggle which delivered Europe from the yoke which she had endured for 20 years.

Everything led to the hope that that Alliance, founded under the most critical circumstances, crowned with the most brilliant success, affirmed by the Conventions of 1814, 1815, and 1818 . . . would also be in a position to put a curb on a force no less tyrannical and no less detestable, that of Revolution and Crime. Such were the motives and the end of the meeting at Troppau. . . .

The Powers have exercised an undeniable right in concerting together upon means of safety against those States in which the overthrow of a Government caused by revolution could only be con-

[1] E. Hertslet, *The Map of Europe by Treaty*, I, 658-60.

sidered as a dangerous example, which could only result in an hostile attitude against constitutional and legitimate Governments. The exercise of this right became still more urgent when those who had placed themselves in that position sought to communicate to neighbouring States the misfortune into which they had themselves plunged, and to propagate revolution and confusion around them. . . .

As the Revolution of Naples daily takes deeper root, that no other imperils the tranquillity of neighbouring States to a danger so certain and so imminent, and that it is not possible to act so immediately and so promptly upon any other, they have come to the conviction of the necessity of proceeding according to the above principles, towards the kingdom of the Two Sicilies.

In order to prepare measures of conciliation for that purpose, the Monarchs assembled at Troppau invited the King of the Two Sicilies to join them at Laybach [in January, 1821], a step the object of which was solely to deliver the will of His Majesty from all external constraint, and to constitute that Monarch mediator between his erring peoples, and the States whose tranquillity they threatened. The Allied Monarchs being determined not to recognise a Government created by open revolt, could only negotiate with the person of the King. . . .

France and England have been invited to take part in this movement, and it is hoped that they will not refuse to give their assent, the principle upon which that invitation is founded being in perfect harmony with the Treaties which they have previously agreed to [an interpretation which Castlereagh denied]. . . .

There is nothing new in the system followed by Austria, Prussia, and Russia; it rests upon the same maxims as those which served as bases of the Treaties upon which the Alliance of the European States was founded. The intimate Union between the Courts which are in the very heart of this Alliance, can thereby only gain more strength and durability.

THE ERA OF THE CONGRESSES (1815-1825) : THE BREACH IN THE QUINTUPLE ALLIANCE

The rift which appeared among the powers at the Conference of Troppau widened into an irreparable breach by 1825. Italian affairs were settled at the Conference of Troppau and Laibach, and allied troops restored the King of Naples to his throne, thereby "protecting the free exercise of legitimate authority." In 1822, at the Congress of Verona, the revolution in Spain and the revolt of Spanish American colonies were the chief concerns of the powers. Despite the Czar's enthusiasm for armed intervention, the other powers hesitated. Metternich felt that it was impossible to regain the Spanish colonies by force; the new English Foreign Minister, George Canning, reasserted the British stand that the guarantees of 1815 related only to territorial settlements, not to the domestic disturbances of European states. To the Duke of Wellington, who represented England at Verona, Canning gave instructions: ". . . there is entertained by the Allies a determined project of interference by force, or by menace, in the present struggle in Spain. . . . I am to instruct your Grace at once frankly and peremptorily to declare, that to any such interference, come what may, His Majesty will not be a party." Wellington's adherence to these instructions marked the failure of the Congress of Verona and, as later became evident, inflicted a severe setback to the Concert of Powers inaugurated at Vienna. In 1823, however, the French Bourbon

Louis XVIII sent troops to "free" the Spanish Bourbon Ferdinand VII from the revolutionists. Britain watched jealously lest France remain permanently in Spain, lest France invade Portugal, and lest France appropriate for herself any part of the Spanish colonies. The last factor particularly concerned England because of the profitable commercial relations which she had established with the revolted Spanish colonies, which she wished to see neither returned to the exclusive monopoly of Spain nor to be restricted in French hands. In October, 1823, as it became apparent that French arms would overthrow the Spanish constitutionalists, Canning held several interviews with the French ambassador, August J. A. M., Prince de Polignac, in order to clarify the intent of the two nations, especially to make clear that England would tolerate no European interference in Spanish America which would imperil Britain's trade there. The results of these conferences were published in "The Polignac Memorandum," parts of which appear below. As the reader will see, it ended all question of European interference by force in the New World.

From "The Polignac Memorandum"
    (October, 1823) [1]

The Prince de Polignac having announced to Mr. Canning that His Excellency was now prepared to enter with Mr. Canning into a frank explanation of the views of his Government respecting the question of Spanish America in return for a similar communication which Mr. Canning had previously offered to make to the Prince de Polignac on the part

[1] Harold Temperley and Lillian M. Penson, eds., *Foundations of British Foreign Policy,* 1938, No. 8,. 70-73. By permission of the Cambridge University Press, Cambridge, England.

of the British Cabinet; Mr. Canning stated. . . .

That the British Government were of opinion that any attempt to bring Spanish America again under its ancient submission to Spain must be utterly hopeless— that all negotiation for that purpose would be unsuccessful; and that the prolongation or renewal of War for the same object would be only a waste of human life. . . .

That the British Government would, however, not only abstain from interposing any obstacle, on their part, to any attempt at negotiation which Spain might think proper to make, but would aid and countenance such negotiation, provided it were founded upon a basis which appeared to them to be practicable, and that they would, in any case, remain strictly neutral in a war between Spain and the Colonies. . . . But that the junction of any foreign power in an enterprise of Spain against the Colonies would be viewed by them as constituting an entirely new question; and one upon which they must take such decision as the interest of Great Britain might require.

That the British Government absolutely disclaimed not only any desire of appropriating to itself any portion of the Spanish Colonies; but any intention of forming a political connection with them, beyond that of Amity and Commercial Intercourse.

That, in these respects, so far from seeking an exclusive preference for its Subjects over those of other foreign States, it was prepared, and would be contented, to see the Mother Country (by virtue of an amicable arrangement) in possession of that preference; and to be ranked, after her, equally with others, only on the footing of the most favoured Nation.

That, completely convinced that the ancient system of the colonies could not be restored, the British Government could not enter into any stipulation binding itself either to refuse or to delay its recognition of their Independence.

That the British Government has had no desire to precipitate that recognition, so long as there was any reasonable chance of an accommodation with the Mother Country . . . and that it would consider any foreign interference by force . . . as a motive for recognizing the latter [the colonies] without delay. . . .

The Prince de Polignac declared that his Government believed it to be utterly hopeless to reduce Spanish America to the state of its former relation to Spain; that France disclaimed, on her part, any intention or desire . . . to appropriate to herself any part of the Spanish possessions in America; or to obtain for herself any exclusive advantages; and that, like England, she would willingly see the Mother Country in possession of superior commercial advantages, by amicable arrangement; and would be contented, like her, to rank, after the Mother Country, among the most favoured nations. Lastly, that she abjured, in any case, any design of acting against the colonies by force of arms.

[Two years later, Great Britain accorded full political recognition to the Latin American states. In the meantime, in December, 1824, Canning refused to attend a congress of the powers called by the Czar to discuss Turkish problems. The meeting broke up in May, 1825, without results. It was the last of the congresses of the type inaugurated by the Vienna settlement. Thereafter England—and, to a lesser extent, France—tended to join the forces of liberal, constitutional states in opposition to conservative, despotic ones; whereas in 1833, by a convention signed at Berlin, Austria, Russia, and Prussia reaffirmed the Troppau Protocol [see page 474], creating thereby a league of autocratic states against revolutionary outbursts of all kinds.]

AMERICA REJECTS EUROPEAN CONSERVATISM: THE MONROE DOCTRINE (1823)

The United States of America was vitally concerned in European events of the early 1820's. Russia, now champion of conservatism in the congresses, was an American power, claiming exclusive commercial and fishing privileges for Alaska—the extent·of which ran, according to the Czar, from the Bering Strait to Vancouver; Great Britain disputed possession of the Columbia River area with the United States, and it was feared had designs on Cuba; and the European powers were threatening to employ force, not only to recover Spanish colonies, but also, possibly, to extend despotic institutions into the New World. To combat these dangers, President James Monroe issued a warning to European states in his Message to Congress in December, 1823. Had it been put to the test, the United States could have offered no more effective powers of resistance than the Quintuple Alliance could have demonstrated in aggression. But American statesmen were well aware how closely Great Britain's policy paralleled their own; and, with this knowledge, they determined to follow an independent policy. The message, which was neither a law nor a treaty obligation, came to be known as the Monroe Doctrine.

From PRESIDENT MONROE, Message to Congress (1823) [1]

At the proposal of the Russian Imperial Government, made through the minister of the Emperor residing here, a full power and instructions have been transmitted to the minister of the United States at St.

[1] *A Compilation of the Messages and Papers of the Presidents, 1789-1897*, ed. by James D. Richardson, 10 vols., Government Printing Office, Washington, D. C., 1896-99, II (1896), 209, 217-19.

Petersburg to arrange by amicable negotiation the respective rights and interests of the two nations on the northwest coast of this continent. A similar proposal had been made by His Imperial Majesty to the Government of Great Britain, which has likewise been acceded to. The Government of the United States has been desirous by this friendly proceeding of manifesting the great value which they have invariably attached to the friendship of the Emperor and their solicitude to cultivate the best understanding with his Government. In the discussions to which this interest has given rise and in the arrangements by which they may terminate, the occasion has been judged proper for asserting, as a principle in which the rights and interests of the United States are involved, that the American continents, by the free and independent condition which they have assumed and maintain, are henceforth not to be considered as subjects for future colonization by any European powers. . . .

It was stated at the commencement of the last session that a great effort was then making in Spain and Portugal to improve the condition of the people of those countries, and that it appeared to be conducted with extraordinary moderation. It need scarcely be remarked that the result has been so far very different from what was then anticipated. Of events in that quarter of the globe, with which we have so much intercourse and from which we derive our origin, we have always been anxious and interested spectators. The citizens of the United States cherish sentiments the most friendly in favor of the liberty and happiness of their fellow-men on that side of the Atlantic. In the wars of the European powers in matters relating to themselves we have never taken any part, nor does it comport with our policy so to do. It is only when our rights are invaded or seriously menaced that we resent injuries or make preparation for our defense. With the movements in this hemisphere we are of necessity more immediately connected, and by causes which must be obvious to all enlightened and impartial observers. The political system of the allied powers is essentially different in this respect from that of America. This difference proceeds from that which exists in their respective Governments; and to the defense of our own, which has been achieved by the loss of so much blood and treasure, and matured by the wisdom of their most enlightened citizens, and under which we have enjoyed unexampled felicity, this whole nation is devoted. We owe it, therefore, to candor and to the amicable relations existing between the United States and those powers to declare that we should consider any attempt on their part to extend their system to any portion of this hemisphere as dangerous to our peace and safety. With the existing colonies or dependencies of any European power we have not interfered and shall not interfere. But with the Governments who have declared their independence and maintained it, and whose independence we have, on great consideration and on just principles, acknowledged, we could not view any interposition for the purpose of oppressing them, or controlling in any other manner their destiny, by any European power in any other light than as the manifestation of an unfriendly disposition toward the United States. . . .

The late events in Spain and Portugal show that Europe is still unsettled. Of this important fact no stronger proof can be adduced than that the allied powers should have thought it proper, on any principle satisfactory to themselves, to have interposed by force in the internal concerns of Spain. To what extent such interposition may be carried, on the same principle, is a question in which all inde-

CONFLICTS WITH LIBERAL ASPIRATIONS

pendent powers whose governments differ from theirs are interested, even those most remote, and surely none more so than the United States. Our policy in regard to Europe, which was adopted at any early stage of the wars which have so long agitated that quarter of the globe, nevertheless remains the same, which is, not to interfere in the internal concerns of any of its powers; to consider the government *de facto* as the legitimate government for us; to cultivate friendly relations with it, and to preserve those relations by a frank, firm, and manly policy, meeting in all instances the just claims of every power, submitting to injuries from none. But in regard to those continents circumstances are eminently and conspicuously different. It is impossible that the allied powers should extend their political system to any portion of either continent without endangering our peace and happiness; nor can anyone believe that our southern brethren, if left to themselves, would adopt it of their own accord. It is equally impossible, therefore, that we should behold such interposition in any form with indifference.

4. *The Revolution of 1830*

THE JULY REVOLUTION IN FRANCE

Charles X, who succeeded the easygoing Louis XVIII to the French throne in 1824, chafed exceedingly under the Constitutional Charter of 1814. The new King wanted to enlarge the position of the clergy, "to support the monarchy by the Church," and thereby threw liberals into opposition; he desired to supervise more closely the liberty of the press, to exercise greater control over the Chamber of Deputies, and to restrict the franchise to the con-

servative classes—a series of items which struck deeply at the Constitutional Charter itself. On July 25, 1830, upon the recommendation of his conservative and clerical advisers, Charles issued three ordinances, one to accomplish each of the above-stated desires.

From the "July Ordinances" (1830) [1]

I. ORDINANCE FOR SUSPENDING LIBERTY OF THE PRESS. . . .

We have ordained and do ordain as follows: 1st. The liberty of the periodical press is suspended. . . .

In consequence, no newspaper or periodical or semiperiodical publication, established or to be established, without discrimination as to their contents, shall appear . . . except by virtue of an authorization . . . obtained from us.

This authorization must be renewed every three months. It can be revoked. . . .

4th. Newspapers and works published in contravention of Article 2 shall be seized immediately.

5th. No work of less than twenty printed pages can appear without authorization of our Minister-Secretary of State of the Interior of Paris, and of the prefects in the departments. Any work of more than twenty printed pages which does not constitute a connected work, shall also be subject to the necessity of authorization. . . .

II. ORDINANCE FOR DISSOLVING THE CHAMBER OF DEPUTIES. . . .

Being informed of the maneuvers which have been practiced in our kingdom to deceive and mislead the electors during the recent operations of the electoral colleges . . . We have ordained and do ordain as follows: 1st. The Chamber of Deputies of the departments is dissolved. . . .

[1] Duvergier, ed., *Collection complète des lois*, XXX, 74-78.

III. ORDINANCE UPON THE ELECTIONS. . . .

Having resolved to prevent the recurrence of the maneuvers which have exercised a pernicious influence during the late proceedings of the electoral bodies; wishing, therefore, to reform, in accordance with the principles of the Constitutional Charter, the rules of election of which experience has made inconveniences felt, we have recognized the necessity of making use of the right which belongs to us to provide, by acts proceeding from us, for the safety of the state and for the repression of any enterprise attacking the dignity of our Crown. [There follow thirty articles to restrict the franchise by tightening up property qualifications for voters and by providing strict rules for the conduct of elections.]

LOUIS PHILIPPE IS MADE KING (1830)

Charles X's ordinances brought down the wrath of France upon his head. Within a fortnight Charles was overthrown by Paris uprisings, and the Chamber of Deputies, which he had "dissolved," declared the throne vacant and offered it to Louis Philippe in the following declaration.

From the Declaration of the Chamber of Deputies (August 7, 1830) [1]

The Chamber of Deputies, in view of the imperative necessity resulting from the events of July 26, 27, 28, 29, and the days following and the general situation of France because of the violation of the Constitutional Charter; and considering also that, in consequence of that violation and of the heroic resistance of the Paris citizens, His Majesty Charles X . . . and all the members of the elder branch of the royal house have now left French territory, declares that the throne is vacant

[1] *Ibid.*, XXX, 93-101.

in fact and in right, and that it is indispensable to provide therefor.

The Chamber of Deputies declares secondly that, in accord with the wish and in the interest of the French people, the preamble of the Constitutional Charter is suppressed, as wounding the national dignity, as it appears to *grant* to Frenchmen the rights which are inherently theirs, and that the following articles of the same charter must be suppressed or modified in the manner indicated below. . . . [Here follows a series of alterations in the charter designed to prevent such illiberal constructions as Charles X had sought to effect.]

On condition of the acceptance of these arrangements and provisions, the Chamber of Deputies declares that the universal and pressing interest of the French people calls to the throne His Royal Highness Louis Philippe of Orléans, Duke of Orléans, Lieutenant General of the Kingdom, and his descendants in perpetuity, from male to male, by order of primogeniture, to the perpetual exclusion of women and their descendants. Consequently, His Royal Highness Louis Philippe d'Orléans shall be invited to accept and swear to the clauses and engagements set forth above, to the observation of the Constitutional Charter and the modifications indicated, and after having done this before the assembled chambers, to take the title of King of the French.

THE JULY REVOLUTION OUTSIDE FRANCE

The July Revolution in France rekindled the revolutionary fires of many discontented European peoples, although in most cases their revolutionary impulses were restrained or held in abeyance until the outbreaks of 1848. Louis Blanc (1811-1882), a French Socialist leader of considerable weight, a severe critic of Louis Philippe's regime and a prominent politician in the French Revolution of 1848, wrote the *Histoire de dix ans, 1830-1840* (*History of Ten Years*), first published in 1841. His book included the following account of the revolutionary sentiments as of about 1830 among some of his contemporaries in Italy, Belgium, and Poland.

From BLANC, *History of Ten Years* (1841) [1]

Italy palpitated under the sway of Austria, of which her princes were little more than the prefects; a sway the more abhorred for that it was exercised by means of diplomacy. Deprived of the right of freely traversing their native land—tracked by spies, even to their household circles . . . the Italians were watching with swelling impatience for the moment to shake off their chains. . . . It is certain that the love of Italian independence existed everywhere, even among the lowest of the populace, if not in the shape of opinion, yet at least in that of instinct and sentiment. . . . And again, those who were naturally called to place themselves at the head of the movement looked for the achievement of independence only to the achievement of unity. In fact, though Italy was yet parted into fragments, and the memory of the federative struggles of the middle ages was perhaps not yet quite extinct there, Palermo and Naples were the only two cities between which there subsisted a deep spirit of enmity. . . . Only let France lend them her aid, let her hinder the Austrians from crossing the Alps, and Italy was free. Rome would then readily open her gates to the insurrection advancing from Bologna; the pope, stripped of his temporal power, would preserve his spiritual authority intact; Italy, in fine, would be politically constituted after inscribing on her banners the word *Unity*. Such were the projects of the Italian patriots. . . .

Belgium was scarcely less agitated than Italy, though its situation was different. In a physical point of view it had never been more prosperous than since its union with Holland. The Dutch colonies afforded important and necessary outlets for its productions. The monarch who ruled it was, moreover, a man of sound head. . . . But William was a thorough Dutchman at heart. He remembered but too well that Belgium had been united in 1815 to Holland, only as an *accession of territory*. Hence, offensive preferences, and a revolting partiality in the distribution of public employments. . . . Add to this, that the two people did not speak the same language, did not profess the same religion, had not the same habits and manners; that four millions of Belgians sent no greater number of representatives to the States-general than two millions of Dutch; that William had insisted on introducing the use of one common language into the public documents and the proceedings of the law courts; and that, in fine, he had . . . aroused against him the jealous and unforgiving power of the Belgian clergy. . . . [Hence, the establishment of an independent Belgium in 1830.]

The situation of Poland, like that of Belgium, contained within it numerous germs of revolution. The forward, warlike nobility of Poland had submitted with fierce resentment to the treaties of 1815, and had more than once endeavoured to cast off their yoke. . . . A conspiracy was on the point of breaking out in Warsaw upon the Coronation of Nicolas [1825]; it failed only through the timidity of some members of the diet. . . . It cannot be said that the revolution which seemed in preparation had not to contend with rude

[1] Louis Blanc, *The History of Ten Years, 1830-1840*, 2 vols., London, 1844, 260-63.

obstacles. Brutalized by the hereditary serf-dom . . . the Polish peasants knew little of the pride of independence, for their hearts had never beaten for liberty. And as for the nobles, those alone of them ardently longed for an unknown future whose privileges were reduced to a mere name, and who vegetated in penury; for among the nobles who possessed along with the authority of high title that of fortune likewise, hatred of the stranger's yoke was combated by the fear of anarchy. Moreover, by the side of that noblesse, whose patriotism was timid, though sincere, there was the watchful Polish aristoc-racy; that is to say, that class of felon nobles who had accepted from Russia the titles of dukes, counts, barons, and princes. . . . In spite of all this a revo-lution in Poland was a thing easy to foresee, and events like those of July [in France] could not but render it inevi-table. [Revolution actually began in Po-land in 1830, but it was severely repulsed by Russia in 1831; the Polish constitution set forth by Alexander I in 1815 was abro-gated and replaced by an organic statute whereby Poland lost her political rights and retained only a small degree of ad-ministrative autonomy.]

26

THE INDUSTRIAL REVOLUTION

1. The Nature of the Industrial Revolution

"The division of labor," wrote Adam Smith in *The Wealth of Nations,* "is limited by the extent of the market." This law, of the contemporary opera-tion of which Smith was only vaguely aware, holds good in nearly all stages of economic development. And it was, at base, the rapid expansion of market outlets and demands which produced the Industrial Revolution in the latter half of the eighteenth century, result-ing in a new division and organization of labor in the factory system. An in-creasing population (including over-seas areas, particularly the prosperous English colonies in America), a rising standard of living, and improving means of transportation and communi-cation—these led to market demands which expanded so rapidly that existing means of production failed to supply the quantities of goods salable. Natu-rally, enterprising men, aware of the opportunities for gain, sought new means to meet the demands. An end-less chain of ingenious inventions began which, when applied by resourceful businessmen to the practical problems of the moment, swiftly started a revo-lution in the methods of production, which goes on to this day. Without slighting the inventors or their remark-able creations, it seems likely, however, that the greatest "invention" of them all was the factory system of produc-tion, that tightly knit organization of the means of production whereby the endless chain of inventions has been combined with disciplined workers to produce goods in quantity for an ever expanding world market.

TOYNBEE ON THE INDUSTRIAL REVOLUTION

About 1880, Arnold Toynbee, an English student of economics, history, philosophy, and religion, gave one of the best early descriptions of the circumstances and conditions which led to the Industrial Revolution in England and to the emergence of the factory system. Toynbee's facts and figures have been improved upon, and more recent research has made his contrast between agrarian and industrial England appear much less abrupt, showing a more gradual industrialization than he depicts. Nevertheless, Toynbee's account has become a classic of economic history and is still a useful source.

From TOYNBEE, *Industrial Revolution* (1884) [1]

Previous to 1760 the old industrial system obtained in England; none of the great mechanical inventions had been introduced; the agrarian changes were still in the future. It is this industrial England which we have to contrast with the industrial England of today. For determining the population of the time we have no accurate materials. There are no official returns before 1801. . . . In this absence of trustworthy data all sorts of wild estimates were formed. . . . According to Mr. Finlaison, the population of England and Wales was, in 1700, 5,134,516, in 1750, 6,039,684, an increase of not quite a million, or between 17 and 18 per cent in the first half of the century. In 1801 the population of England and Wales was

[1] Arnold Toynbee, *Lectures on the Industrial Revolution of the 18th Century in England,* New York, n.d., pp. 32-34, 46, 49-54, 56-57, 87-88, 90-93.

9,187,176, showing an increase of three millions, or more than 52 per cent in the second half. The difference in the rates of increase is significant of the great contrast presented by the two periods. In the former, England, though rapidly increasing in wealth owing to her extended commercial relations, yet retained her old industrial organization; the latter is the age of transition to the modern industrial system, and to improved methods of agriculture.

The next point to consider is the distribution of population. A great difference will be found here between the state of things at the beginning of the eighteenth century, or in Adam Smith's time, and that prevailing now. . . . If we consider as the counties north of the Trent Northumberland, Durham, Yorkshire, Cumberland, Westmoreland, Lancashire, Cheshire, Derbyshire, Nottinghamshire, and Staffordshire (about one-third of the total area of England), we shall find on examination that in 1700 they contained about one-fourth of the population, and in 1750 less than one-third, while in 1881, they contained more than two-fifths; or, taking only the six northern counties, we find that in 1700 their population was under one-fifth of that of all England, in 1750 it was about one-fifth, in 1881 it was all but one-third. . . .

Among the manufactures of the time the woollen business was by far the most important. "All our measures," wrote Bishop Berkeley in 1737, "should tend towards the immediate encouragement of our woollen manufactures, which must be looked upon as the basis of our wealth." In 1701 our woollen exports were worth £2,000,000, or "above a fourth part of the whole export trade." In 1770 they were worth £4,000,000, or between a third and a fourth of the whole. The territorial distribution of the manufacture was much the same as now. . . .

Next in importance was the iron trade, which was largely carried on, though by this time a decaying industry, in the Weald of Sussex, where in 1740 there were ten furnaces, producing annually 1400 tons. The trade had reached its chief extent in the seventeenth century, but in 1724 was still the principal manufacturing interest of the county. . . . In 1755 an ironmaster named Anthony Bacon had got a lease for ninety-nine years of a district eight miles in length, by five in breadth, at Merthyr-Tydvil, upon which he erected iron and coal works. In 1709 the Coalbrookdale works in Shropshire were founded, and in 1760 Carron iron was first manufactured in Scotland. Altogether, there were, about 1737, fifty-nine furnaces in eighteen different counties, producing 17,350 tons annually. It has been computed that we imported about 20,000 tons. In 1881 we exported 3,820,315 tons of iron and steel, valued at £27,590,908, and imported to the value of £3,705,332.

The cotton trade was still so insignificant as to be mentioned only once, and that incidentally, by Adam Smith. It was confined to Lancashire, where its headquarters were Manchester and Bolton. In 1760 not more than 40,000 persons were engaged in it, and the annual value of the manufactures was estimated at £600,000. The exports, however, were steadily growing; in 1761 they amounted to £23,253, in 1751 to £45,986, in 1764 to £200,354. . . . But even in 1764 our exports of cotton were still only one-twentieth of the value of wool exports. . . .

The mechanical arts were still in a very backward state. In spite of the fact that the woollen trade was the staple industry of the country, the division of labour in it was in Adam Smith's time "nearly the same as it was a century before, and the machinery employed not very different." . . . The reason why division of labour was carried out to so small an extent, and invention so little regarded, is given by Adam Smith himself. Division of labour, as he points out, is limited by the extent of the market, and, owing chiefly to bad means of communication, the market for English manufactures was still a very narrow one. Yet England, however slow the development of her manufactures, advanced nevertheless more rapidly in this respect than other nations. One great secret of her progress lay in the facilities for water-carriage afforded by her rivers, for all communication by land was still in the most neglected condition. A second cause was the absence of internal customs barriers, such as existed in France, and in Prussia until Stein's time. The home trade of England was absolutely free. . . .

When we turn to investigate the industrial organization of the time, we find that the class of capitalist employers was as yet but in its infancy. A large part of our goods were still produced on the domestic system. Manufactures were little concentrated in towns, and only partially separated from agriculture. The "manufacturer" was, literally, the man who worked with his own hands in his own cottage. Nearly the whole of the cloth trade of the West Riding, for instance, was organized on this system at the beginning of the century.

An important feature in the industrial organization of the time was the existence of a number of small master-manufacturers, who were entirely independent, having capital and land of their own, for they combined the culture of small freehold pasture-farms with their handicraft. Defoe has left an interesting picture of their life. The land near Halifax, he says, was "divided into small Enclosures from two Acres to six or seven each, seldom more. . . . At every considerable house was a manufactory. . . . Every clothier keeps one horse, at least, to carry his

Manufactures to the Market; and every one, generally, keeps a Cow or two or more for his Family. By this means the small Pieces of enclosed Land about each house are occupied, for they scarce sow Corn enough to feed their Poultry. . . . The houses are full of lusty Fellows, some at the Dye-vat, some at looms, others dressing the Cloths; the women and children carding or spinning; being all employed from the youngest to the oldest." . . .

This system, however, was no longer universal in Arthur Young's time. That writer found at Sheffield a silk-mill employing 152 hands, including women and children; at Darlington "one master-manufacturer employed above fifty looms"; at Boynton there were 150 hands in one factory. So, too, in the West of England cloth-trade the germs of the capitalist system were visible. The rich merchant gave out work to labourers in the surrounding villages, who were his employees, and were not independent. In the Nottingham hosiery trade there were, in 1750, fifty manufacturers; known as "putters out," who employed 1200 frames; in Leicestershire 1800 frames were so employed. In the hand-made nail business of Staffordshire and Worcestershire, the merchant had warehouses in different parts of the district, and gave out nail-rod iron to the nail-master, sufficient for a week's work for him and his family. In Lancashire we can trace, step by step, the growth of the capitalist employer. At first we see, as in Yorkshire, the weaver furnishing himself with warp and weft, which he worked up in his own house and brought himself to market. By degrees he found it difficult to get yarn from the spinners; so the merchants at Manchester gave him out linen warp and raw cotton, and the weaver became dependent on them. Finally, the merchant would get together thirty or forty looms in a town. This was the near-

est approach to the capitalist system before the great mechanical inventions. . . . The old simple conditions of production and exchange were on the eve of disappearance before the all-corroding force of foreign trade.

The home trade was still indeed much greater in proportion than now; but the exports had grown from about £7,000,000 at the beginning of the century to £14,500,000 in 1760. During the interval great changes had taken place in the channels of foreign commerce. In 1700 Holland was our greatest market, taking more than one-third of all our exports, but in 1760 the proportion was reduced to about one-seventh. Portugal, which in 1703 took one-seventh, now took only about one-twelfth. The trade with France was quite insignificant. On the other hand, the Colonies were now our chief markets, and a third of our exports went there. In 1770 America took three-fourths of all the manufactures of Manchester. In 1767 the exports to Jamaica were nearly as great as they had been to all the English plantations together in 1704. The shipping trade had doubled, and the ships themselves were larger. In 1732 ships of 750 tons were considered remarkable; in 1770 there were many in Liverpool of 900 tons; but in this as in other branches of business progress was still slow, partial, local, thus presenting a striking contrast to the rapid and general advance of the next half-century. . . .

Coming to the facts of the Industrial Revolution, the first thing that strikes us is the far greater rapidity which marks the growth of population. Before 1751 the largest decennial increase, so far as we can calculate from our imperfect materials, was 3 per cent. For each of the next three decennial periods the increase was 6 per cent; then between 1781 and 1791 it was 9 per cent; between 1791 and 1801, 11 per cent; between 1801 and 1811, 14 per cent;

between 1811 and 1821, 18 per cent. . . .

Next we notice the relative and positive decline in the agricultural population. In 1811 it constituted 35 per cent of the whole population of Great Britain; in 1821, 33 per cent; in 1831, 28 per cent. And at the same time its actual numbers have decreased. . . . In 1851 the whole number of persons engaged in agriculture in England was 2,084,153 . . . in 1871 it was 1,657,138. Contemporaneously with this change, the center of density of population has shifted from the Midlands to the North; there are at the present day [1881] 458 persons to the square mile in the counties north of the Trent, as against 312 south of the Trent. . . .

Passing to manufactures, we find here the all-prominent fact to be the substitution of the factory for the domestic system, the consequence of the mechanical discoveries of the time. Four great inventions altered the character of the cotton manufacture; the spinning-jenny, patented by Hargreaves in 1770; the water-frame, invented by Arkwright the year before; Crompton's mule introduced in 1779, and the self-acting mule, first invented by Kelly in 1792, but not brought into use till Roberts improved it in 1825. None of these by themselves would have revolutionized the industry. But in 1769—the year in which Napoleon and Wellington were born—James Watt took out his patent for the steam-engine. Sixteen years later it was applied to the cotton manufacture. In 1785 Boulton and Watt made an engine for a cotton-mill at Papplewick in Notts, and in the same year Arkwright's patent expired. These two facts taken together mark the introduction of the factory system. But the most famous invention of all, and the most fatal to domestic industry, the power-loom, though also patented by Cartwright in 1785, did not come into use for several years, and till the power-loom was introduced the workman was hardly injured.

. . . In fifteen years the cotton trade trebled itself; from 1788 to 1803 has been called "its golden age"; for, before the power-loom but after the introduction of the mule and other mechanical improvements by which for the first time yarn sufficiently fine for muslin and a variety of other fabrics was spun, the demand became such that "old barns, cart-houses, out-buildings of all descriptions were repaired, windows broke through the old blank walls, and all fitted up for loomshops; new weavers' cottages with loomshops arose in every direction, every family bringing home weekly from 40 to 120 shillings per week." At a later date, the condition of the workman was very different. Meanwhile, the iron industry had been equally revolutionized by the invention of smelting by pit-coal brought into use between 1740 and 1750, and by the application in 1788 of the steam-engine to blast furnaces. In the eight years which followed this latter date, the amount of iron manufactured nearly doubled itself.

A further growth of the factory system took place independent of machinery, and owed its origin to the expansion of trade, an expansion which was itself due to the great advance made at this time in the means of communication. The canal system was being rapidly developed throughout the country. In 1777 the Grand Trunk canal, 96 miles in length, connecting the Trent and Mersey, was finished; Hull and Liverpool were connected by one canal while another connected them both with Bristol; and in 1792, the Grand Junction canal, 90 miles in length, made a waterway from London through Oxford to the chief Midland towns. Some years afterwards, the roads were greatly improved under Telford and Macadam; between 1818 and 1829 more than a thousand additional miles of turnpike road were constructed; and the next year, 1830, saw the opening of the first railroad. These improved means of communication caused an extraordinary increase in commerce, and to secure a sufficient supply of goods it became the interest of merchants to collect weavers around them in great numbers, to get looms together in a workshop, and to give out the warp themselves to the work-people. To these latter this system meant a change from independence to dependence; at the beginning of the century the report of a committee asserts that the essential difference between the domestic and the factory system is, that in the latter the work is done "by persons who have no property in the goods they manufacture." Another direct consequence of this expansion of trade was the regular recurrence of periods of over-production and of depression, a phenomenon quite unknown under the old system, and due to this new form of production on a large scale for a distant market. . . .

The new class of great capitalist employers made enormous fortunes, they took little or no part personally in the work of their factories, their hundreds of workmen were individually unknown to them; and as a consequence, the old relations between masters and men disappeared, and a "cash nexus" was substituted for the human tie. The workmen on their side resorted to combination, and Trades-Unions began a fight which looked as if it were between mortal enemies rather than joint producers. The misery which came upon large sections of the working people at this epoch was often, though not always, due to a fall in wages, for, as I said above, in some industries they rose. But they suffered likewise from the conditions of labour under the factory system, from the rise of prices, especially from the high price of bread before the repeal of the corn-laws, and from those sudden fluctuations of trade, which, ever since production has been on a large scale, have exposed them to recurrent periods of bitter distress. The effects of the Industrial Revolution prove that free competition may produce wealth without producing well-being. We all know the horrors that ensued in England before it was restrained by legislation and combination.

RICHARD ARKWRIGHT, "FATHER" OF THE FACTORY SYSTEM

The "substitution of the factory for the domestic system" of production was the keynote of the Industrial Revolution. No doubt, as in the case of most of the inventions of the era, many hands took part in the creation of the factory. One of the most prominent was Richard Arkwright, a description of whose career follows.

From MANTOUX, *Industrial Revolution* (1928) [1]

Richard Arkwright was born at Preston on December 23rd, 1732, the youngest of a large and poor family. While still quite young, he was apprenticed to a barber and wig-maker, and just found time in which to learn to read and write. At fifty, he was taking lessons in grammar and spelling. In 1750, he set up at Bolton, a few miles from his native town, where for a long time he plied his trade of barber, first of all in a basement, and then in a very humble shop. He was twice married. His first wife came from Leigh, between Warrington and Bolton—a detail of some interest. The second brought him some money, which enabled him to leave his shop and to go in for a more paying occupation, that of a dealer in hair. He attended markets, and visited farms in order to buy the hair of country girls. He then treated it with a dye of his own making

[1] Paul Mantoux, *The Industrial Revolution in the Eighteenth Century,* rev. ed., trans. by Marjorie Vernon, n.d., 225-29, 237-39. By permission of Harcourt, Brace and Company, New York.

and resold it to the wig-makers who, in that century of wigs, were ready buyers.

This story of Arkwright's early life is not only interesting in itself, but gives us an insight into his character and thus helps us to judge of the part he actually played. We must first note that there is nothing about him which suggested an inventor's career. He had no technical experience, for he was not a weaver like John Kay and Hargreaves, or a carpenter and mechanic like Wyatt. He must have learnt everything he knew of the textile industry . . . through conversations in his barber's shop or during his rounds in Lancashire villages. On the other hand, he displayed very early those qualities which explain his success. He was anxious to better himself, he had fertile brains for devising means of rising in the world, and he knew how to drive a good bargain. . . .

The origins of his main invention are wrapped in curious obscurity. . . . No end of ridiculous and conflicting stories, which he was careful never to deny, were circulated during his lifetime by his admirers. According to some people, the principle of the spinning machine had been suggested to him by a cylindrical wire-drawing machine. . . . According to others, he had studied at Derby the working of the silk-throwing machines, or, in his barber's shop, he had overheard a sailor describe a machine used by the Chinese. . . . While the history of the invention is so obscure, the story of Arkwright's ventures is clear and easy to follow. The machine was made, in 1768, in a room adjoining the Free Grammar School at Preston. Arkwright had enlisted the help of a Warrington clockmaker, a namesake of Kay the inventor of the fly shuttle. As we shall see, this collaboration accounts for many things. Apparently Arkwright had great difficulty in raising the necessary funds. He first turned to a scientific-instrument-maker,

who refused to take him seriously, and then to one of his friends, a publican called John Smalley. The next year [1769] he took out his patent of invention, valid for fourteen years.

We can not only read the text of this patent, but also see the original model of the machine itself, preserved at the South Kensington Museum [London]. It is made entirely of wood, and is about thirty-two inches high. As far as we can judge, it is very like the machine invented in 1733 by John Wyatt, and improved by Lewis Paul. A wheel sets in motion four pairs of rollers of increasing rapidity of rotation. The top cylinder of each pair is covered with leather, whilst the lower one is ribbed or grooved lengthwise. After it has gone through the rollers, whose progressive acceleration stretches it more and more, the thread is twisted and wound on vertical spindles. Generally speaking, this machine only differs in its details from that of Wyatt. These trifling differences cannot explain Arkwright's triumphal success in a line where more ingenious men than he had been hopeless failures. His success was due to his business capacity, of which he gave proof almost at once.

It was, above all, necessary to raise capital. Smalley was not rich enough, and Arkwright already dreamed of big business. For this reason . . . he migrated to Nottingham. We know that this town was the center of the stocking-frame industry, in which a capitalistic organization had followed the development of mechanical equipment. Arkwright succeeded in interesting in his schemes the local bank of Wright Brothers. . . . But profits no doubt did not follow rapidly . . . for at the end of a year the Wrights withdrew their support. Arkwright knew how to extricate himself from his difficulties. In 1771 he entered into a contract with two rich hosiers, Need of Nottingham and

Strutt of Derby. Need and Strutt belonged to the class of merchant manufacturers. They employed a large number of workers in their own homes, and also had workshops where stockings were knitted on frames. Thus it was a system of production akin to "manufacture," if not on "manufacture" itself, that the factory system was grafted. . . .

The first workshop set up by Arkwright at Nottingham was hardly larger than the one Wyatt and Paul had established in Birmingham thirty years before. It had but a few machines, which were worked by horses. It was in 1771, the year he joined forces with Need and Strutt, that Arkwright settled at Cromford, near Derby . . . on the Derwent [where water power was available]. . . . In a few years the Cromford spinning mill had grown up, and by 1779 it contained several thousand spindles and employed three hundred workmen.

That which made the success of the undertaking quite certain was not only the rapidity but the quality of the production. The new machine (the water frame as it was called, to distinguish it from the jenny, which was worked by hand) produced a much stronger thread than the most skilled spinner. . . . Instead, therefore, of weaving materials which were partly linen and only partly cotton, it became possible to weave pure cotton goods, which were as perfect, in every respect, as their Indian models. At first the Cromford factory was only an appendage to those of Need and Strutt. All the thread it spun was used solely for making stockings. But in 1773, Arkwright and his partners set up weaving workshops in Derby, where, for the first time, pure cotton calicoes were made. . . .

[Here Arkwright ran into trouble. Jealous competitors appealed to the Act of 1735, which forbade the manuracture of pure cotton goods for excise reasons. Arkwright was forced to defend his industry before Parliament. Soon after this obstacle was overcome (1774), he ran into patent difficulties. One Thomas Highs charged that Arkwright had stolen his spinning machine from one he had made in 1767; John Kay, the clockmaker who had assisted Arkwright in his first model, testified on Highs's behalf. Highs, a born inventor without business acumen, came from Leigh, the home of Arkwright's first wife, and Arkwright had known him for years. The case continued until June, 1785, when the court condemned Arkwright and declared his patent to have lapsed. Thus it appears "that Arkwright's chief invention, to which he owed most of his wealth and fame, was not really his."]

This trial, together with the judgment, would have utterly crushed any other man than Arkwright. But he was not so easily daunted. Deprived of his patent, he was still the richest cotton-spinner in England, and his factories were the most numerous, the most important and the best run. He went on developing his undertakings. In 1784, with David Dale [Robert Owen's father-in-law], he founded the New Lanark spinning mills, which derived their power from the falls of the Clyde. He set up others at Wirksworth and Bakewell near Cromford, and he did not neglect the old ones . . . in Nottingham . . . he first made use of the steam engine. Honors too became his portion. In 1786 . . . he was knighted . . . [and became] Sheriff of the County of Derby. He died in 1792, leaving a capital of half a million. One of his factories, that at Bakewell, brought his heirs in £20,000 a year . . . big figures, in days when great millionaire manufacturers had not yet been heard of. . . .

His success, in fact, best illustrates what

he really achieved, and what his place in economic history should be. He was no inventor. At the most he arranged, combined and used the inventions of others, which he never scrupled to appropriate for his own ends. . . . He was the first who knew how to make something out of other men's inventions, and who built them up into an industrial system. In order to raise the necessary capital for his undertakings, in order to form and dissolve those partnerships which he used successively as instruments with which to make his fortune, he must have displayed remarkable business ability, together with a curious mixture of cleverness, perseverance and daring. In order to set up large factories, to engage labor, to train it to a new kind of work, and to enforce strict discipline in the workshops, he needed an energy and an activity not often met with. These were qualities which most inventors never had, and without which their inventions could not have resulted in the building up of a new industrial system. It was Arkwright who . . . really created the modern factory. He personified the new type of great manufacturer, neither an engineer nor a merchant, but adding to the main characteristics of both, qualifications peculiar to himself: those of a founder of great concerns, an organizer of production, and a leader of men. Arkwright's career heralded a new social class and a new economic era.

THE CUMULATIVE EFFECT OF THE MACHINE IN INDUSTRY

Karl Marx, who resided in England from 1848 to his death in 1883, was a keen observer and close student of industrial matters. In his famous book *Das Kapital* he commented as follows on the tendency of industry to mechanize its processes.

From MARX, *Capital* (1867) [1]

A radical change in the mode of production in one sphere of industry involves a similar change in other spheres. This happens at first in such branches of industry as are connected together by being separate phases of a process, and yet are isolated by the social division of labour in such a way that each of them produces an independent commodity. Thus spinning by machinery made weaving by machinery a necessity, and both together made the mechanical and chemical revolution that took place in bleaching, printing, and dyeing, imperative. So, too, on the other hand, the revolution in cotton-spinning called forth the invention of the gin, for separating the seeds from the cotton fibre; it was only by means of this invention that the production of cotton became possible on the enormous scale at present required. But more especially, the revolution in the modes of production of industry and agriculture made necessary a revolution in the general conditions of the social process of production, *i.e.*, in the means of communication and transport. In a society whose pivot . . . was agriculture on a small scale, with its subsidiary domestic industries and the urban handicrafts, the means of communication and transport were so utterly inadequate to the productive requirements of the manufacturing period . . . that they became in fact revolutionized. . . . Hence, apart from the radical changes introduced in the construction of sailing vessels, the means of communication and transport became gradually adapted to the modes of production of mechanical industry, by the creation of a system of river steamers, railways, ocean steamers, and telegraphs. But the huge masses of iron that had now to be forged,

[1] Karl Marx, *Capital: A Critical Analysis of Capitalist Production,* ed. by Frederick Engels, translated by Samuel Moore and Edward Aveling, London, 1900, 379-82.

welded, cut, bored, and shaped demanded, on their part, cyclopean machines for the construction of which the methods of the manufacturing period were utterly inadequate.

Modern Industry had therefore itself to take in hand the machine, its characteristic instrument of production, and to construct machines by machines. It was not till it did this, that it built up for itself a fitting technical foundation, and stood on its own feet. Machinery, simultaneously with the increasing use of it in the first decades of this century appropriated, by degrees, the fabrication of machines proper. But it was only during the decade preceding 1866 that the construction of railways and ocean steamers on a stupendous scale called into existence the cyclopean machines now employed in the construction of prime movers [that is, motors or power plants].

The most essential condition to the production of machines by machines was a prime mover capable of exerting any amount of force and yet under perfect control. Such a condition was already supplied by the steam-engine. But at the same time it was necessary to produce the geometrically accurate straight lines, planes, circles, cylinders, cones, and spheres, required in the detailed parts of the machines. This problem Henry Maudsley solved in the first decade of this century by the invention of the slide rest, a tool that was soon made automatic, and in a modified form was applied to other constructive machines besides the lathe, for which it was originally intended. This mechanical appliance replaces, not some particular tool, but the hand itself, which produces a given form by holding and guiding the cutting tool along the iron or other material operated upon. Thus it became possible to produce the forms of the individual parts of machinery with a degree of ease, accuracy, and speed, that

no accumulated experience of the hand of the most skilled workman could give.

If we now fix our attention on that portion of the machinery employed in the construction of machines . . . we find the manual implements reappearing, but on a cyclopean scale. The operating part of the boring machine is an immense drill driven by a steam-engine; without this machine . . . the cylinders of large steam-engines and of hydraulic presses could not be made. The mechanical lathe is only a cyclopean reproduction of the ordinary foot-lathe; the planing machine, an iron carpenter, that works on iron with the same tools that the human carpenter employs on wood; the instrument that on the London wharves cuts the veneers is a gigantic razor; the tool of the shearing machine, which shears iron as easily as a tailor's scissors cut cloth, is a monster pair of scissors; and the steam hammer works with an ordinary hammer head, but of such a weight that not Thor himself could wield it. . . . It is mere child's play for it to crush a block of granite into powder, yet it is no less capable of driving, with a succession of light taps, a nail into a piece of soft wood. The implements of labour, in the form of machinery, necessitate the substitution of natural forces for human force, and the conscious application of science instead of the rule of thumb.

2. Some Social Effects of the Industrial Revolution

In addition to the factory system, the Industrial Revolution gave rise to vast new social problems. The middle class, or bourgeoisie, which had slowly grown in numbers and in influence since the Renaissance, was suddenly enlarged and enriched far beyond its former limits; and the wage-earners, or proletariat, who had enjoyed a large measure of independence under the earlier systems of production, were not only suddenly increased in numbers but also became almost wholly dependent upon their employers for their means of livelihood. The maladjustments and conflicts between these newly enlarged classes of society have colored the European social, political, and economic scene since the Industrial Revolution. Daniel Defoe, famous alike for *Robinson Crusoe* and his observations upon English society in his day, early noticed the growing importance of the rising middle class in England.

THE IMPORTANCE OF ENGLISH TRADESPEOPLE

From DEFOE, *English Tradesmen* (1726-27) [1]

As to the wealth of the nation, that undoubtedly lies chiefly among the trading part of the people; and though there are a great many families raised within few years, in the late war by great employments and by great actions abroad, to the honour of the English gentry, yet how many more families among the tradesmen have been raised to immense estates, even during the same time, by the attending circumstance of war, such as the clothing, the paying, the victualling, and the furnishing, etc., both army and navy? And by whom have the prodigious taxes been paid, the loans supplied, and money advanced upon all occasions? By whom are the banks and companies carried on, and on whom are the customs and excises levied? Have not the trade and tradesmen borne the burden of the war? And do they not still pay four millions a year interest for the public debts? . . . Is not trade the inexhausted fund of all funds, and upon which all the rest depend?

[1] Daniel Defoe, *The Compleat English Tradesmen*, 2 vols., London, 1732, I, 307-11, 315-16.

As is the trade, so in proportion are the tradesmen; and how wealthy are tradesmen in almost all the several parts of England as well as in London? How ordinary is it to see a tradesman go off of the stage, even from mere shopkeeping, with from ten to forty thousand pounds' estate to divide among his family? When, on the contrary, take the gentry in England from one end to the other, except a few here and there, what with excessive high living, which is of late grown so much into a disease, and the other ordinary circumstances of families, we find few families of the lower gentry, that is to say, from six or seven hundred a year downwards, but they are in debt and in necessitous circumstances, and a great many of greater estates also.

On the other hand, let any one who is acquainted with England look but abroad into the several counties, especially near London, or within fifty miles of it; how are the ancient families worn out by time and family misfortunes, and the estates possessed by a new race of tradesmen, grown up into families of gentry, and established by the immense wealth gained, as I may say, behind the counter; that is, in the shop, the warehouse, and the counting house? . . .

How many noble seats, superior to the palaces of sovereign princes (in some countries) do we see erected within few miles of this city by tradesmen, or the sons of tradesmen, while the seats and castles of the ancient gentry, like their families, look worn out and fallen into decay! Witness the noble house of Sir John Eyles, himself a merchant at Giddyhall, near Romford; Sir Gregory Page on Blackheath, the son of a brewer; Sir Nathanael Mead near Weal Green, his father a linen-draper; with many others, too long to repeat; and to crown all, the Lord Castlemain's, now earl of Tilney, at Wanstead, his father, Sir Josiah Child, originally a tradesman. . . .

This being the case in England, and our trade being so vastly great, it is no wonder that the tradesmen in England fill the lists of our nobility and gentry; no wonder that the gentlemen of the best families marry tradesmen's daughters, and put their younger sons apprentices to tradesmen; and how often do these younger sons come to buy the elder sons' estates and restore the family, when the elder and head of the house, proving rakish and extravagant, has wasted his patrimony and is obliged to make out the blessing of Israel's family, where the younger son bought the birthright and the elder was doomed to serve him?

Trade is so far here from being inconsistent with a gentleman that, in short, trade in England makes gentlemen, and has peopled this nation with gentlemen; for, after a generation or two, the tradesman's children, or at least their grandchildren, come to be as good gentlemen, statesmen, parliament men, privy counsellors, judges, bishops, and noblemen as those of the highest birth and most ancient families, and nothing too high for them. . . . Nor do we find any defect either in the genius or capacities of the posterity of tradesmen, arising from any remains of mechanic blood, which, it is pretended, should influence them. . . .

We see the tradesmen of England, as they grow wealthy, coming every day to the herald's office to search for the coats-of-arms of their ancestors, in order to paint them upon their coaches and engrave them upon their plate . . . and how often do we see them trace the registers of their families up to the prime nobility or the most ancient gentry of the kingdom? In this search we find them often qualified to raise new families, if they do not descend from old; as was said of a certain tradesman of London, that if he could not find the ancient race of gentlemen from which he came, he would begin a new race, who should be as good gentlemen as any that went before him. . . .

These things prove abundantly that the rising greatness of the British nation is not owing to war and conquests, to enlarging its dominions by the sword, or subjecting the people of other countries to our power; but it is all owing to trade, to the increase of our commerce at home and the extending it abroad. It is owing to trade that new discoveries have been made in lands unknown, and new settlements and plantations made, new colonies planted, and new governments formed in the uninhabited islands and the uncultivated continent of America; and those plantings and settlements have again enlarged and increased the trade, and thereby the wealth and power of the nation by whom they were discovered and planted.

THE CONDITION OF THE INDUSTRIAL WORKERS

Early in the nineteenth century the condition of workers, especially of women and children, in English factories and mines became so scandalous as to provoke a series of parliamentary inquiries, the results of which shocked Parliament into factory legislation. In 1832, Michael Sadler was chairman of a committee set up to investigate the conditions of textile workers. Some of the evidence heard by the Sadler Committee follows.

From the Sadler Committee's *Report* (1832) [1]

MR. MATTHEW CRABTREE, CALLED IN; AND EXAMINED

What age are you?—Twenty-two.

What is your occupation?—A blanket manufacturer.

[1] "Report of Committee on Factory Children's Labour," in *Parliamentary Papers, 1831-32*, XV, 95-97, 192-94.

Have you ever been employed in a factory?—Yes.

At what age did you first go to work in one?—Eight.

How long did you continue in that occupation?—Four years.

Will you state the hours of labour at the period when you first went to the factory, in ordinary times?—From 6 in the morning to 8 at night.

Fourteen hours?—Yes.

With what intervals for refreshment and rest?—An hour at noon.

When trade was brisk what were your hours?—From 5 in the morning to 9 in the evening.

Sixteen hours?—Yes. . . .

How far did you live from the mill?—About two miles.

Was there any time allowed for you to get your breakfast in the mill?—No.

Did you take it before you left your home?—Generally.

During those long hours of labour could you be punctual; how did you awake?—I seldom did awake spontaneously; I was most generally awoke or lifted out of bed, sometimes asleep, by my parents.

Were you always in time?—No.

What was the consequence if you had been too late?—I was most commonly beaten.

Severely?—Very severely, I thought.

In those mills is chastisement towards the latter part of the day going on perpetually?—Perpetually.

So that you can hardly be in a mill without hearing constant crying?—Never an hour, I believe.

Do you think that if the overlooker were naturally a humane person it would be still found necessary for him to beat the children, in order to keep up their attention and vigilance at the termination of those extraordinary days of labour?—Yes; the machine turns off a regular quantity of cardings, and of course they must keep as regularly to their work the whole of the day; they must keep with the machine, and therefore however humane the slubber may be, as he must keep up with the machine or be found fault with, he spurs the children to keep up also by various means but that which he commonly resorts to is to strap them when they become drowsy.

At the time when you were beaten for not keeping up with your work, were you anxious to have done it if you possibly could?—Yes; the dread of being beaten if we could not keep up with our work was a sufficient impulse to keep us to it if we could.

When you got home at night after this labour, did you feel much fatigued?—Very much so.

Had you any time to be with your parents, and to receive instruction from them?—No.

What did you do?—All that we did when we got home was to get the little bit of supper that was provided for us and go to bed immediately. If the supper had not been ready directly, we should have gone to sleep while it was preparing.

Did you not, as a child, feel it a very grievous hardship to be roused so soon in the morning?—I did.

Were the rest of the children similarly circumstanced?—Yes, all of them; but they were not all of them so far from their work as I was.

And if you had been too late you were under the apprehension of being cruelly beaten?—I generally was beaten, when I happened to be too late; and when I got up in the morning the apprehension of that was so great, that I used to run, and cry all the way as I went to the mill.

THE EVIDENCE OF SAMUEL COULSON

At what time in the morning, in the brisk time, did those girls go to the mills?—In the brisk time, for about six weeks, they have gone at 3 o'clock in the morning, and ended at 10, or nearly half-past, at night.

What intervals were allowed for rest or refreshment during those nineteen hours of labour?—Breakfast a quarter of an hour, and dinner half an hour, and drinking a quarter of an hour. . . .

Had you not great difficulty in awakening your children to this excessive labour? —Yes, in the early time we had them to take up asleep and shake them, when we got them on the floor to dress them, before we could get them off to their work; but not so in the common hours.

Supposing they had been a little too late, what would have been the consequence during the long hours?—They were quartered in the longest hours the same as in the shortest time.

What do you mean by quartering?—A quarter taken off.

If they had been how much too late?— Five minutes.

What was the length of time they could be in bed during those long hours?—It was near 11 o'clock before we could get them into bed after getting a little victuals, and then at morning my mistress used to stop up all night, for fear we could not get them ready for the time; sometimes we have gone to bed, and one of us generally awoke.

What time did you get them up in the morning?—In general me or my mistress got up at 2 o'clock to dress them.

So that they had not above four hours sleep at this time?—No, they had not.

For how long together was it?—About six weeks it held; it was done only when the throng was very much on; it was not often that.

The common hours of labour were from 6 in the morning till half-past eight at night?—Yes.

With the same intervals for food?—Yes, just the same.

Were the children excessively fatigued by this labour?—Many times; we have cried often when we have given them the little victualling we had to give them; we had to shake them, and they have fallen asleep with the victuals in their mouths many a time.

Had any of them any accident in consequence of this labour?—Yes, my eldest daughter . . . the cog caught her forefinger nail and screwed it off below the knuckle, and she was five weeks in the Leeds infirmary.

Has she lost that finger?—It is cut off at the second joint.

Were her wages paid during that time?—As soon as the accident happened the wages were totally stopped; indeed, I did not know which way to get her cured. . . .

Did this excessive term of labour occasion much cruelty also?—Yes, with being so much fatigued the strap was very frequently used.

Have any of your children been strapped?—Yes, every one; the eldest daughter; I was up in Lancashire a fortnight, and when I got home I saw her shoulders, and I said, "Ann, what is the matter?" She said, "the overlooker has strapped me; but," she said, "do not go to the overlooker, for if you do we shall lose our work." . . . Her back was beat nearly to a jelly. . . .

What was the wages in the short hours? —Three shillings a week each.

When they wrought those very long hours what did they get?—Three shillings and sevenpence halfpenny.

For all that additional labour they had only 7½ pence a week additional?—No more.

[As a consequence of such evidence as that shown above, Parliament passed a Factory Act in 1833 limiting hours of employment for children in textile work. But conditions in mines were still intolerable, as is evidenced in another parliamentary inquiry in 1842, by a committee headed by Lord Ashley. As a consequence of the testimony gathered by Lord Ashley's Committee, some of which follows, Parliament passed the Mines Act of 1842 to forbid employment of women and of boys under thirteen in mines.]

From the *Report* of Lord Ashley's Committee (1842) [1]

THE EVIDENCE OF ISABEL WILSON, 38 YEARS OLD, A COAL PUTTER

When women have children thick [often] they are compelled to take them down early, I have been married 19 years and have had 10 bairns; seven are in life. When on Sir John's work was a carrier of coals, which caused me to miscarry five times from the strains, and was very ill after each. Putting is not so oppressive; last child was born on Saturday morning, and I was at work on the Friday night.

Once met with an accident; a coal brake my cheek-bone, which kept me idle some weeks.

I have wrought below 30 years, and so has the guid man; he is getting touched in the breath now.

None of the children read, as the work is no regular. I did read once, but no able to attend to it now; when I go below lassie 10 years of age keeps house and makes the broth or stir-about.

Nine sleep in two bedsteads; there did not appear to be any beds, and the whole of the other furniture consisted of two chairs, three stools, a table, a kail-pot and a few broken basins and cups. Upon asking if the furniture was all they had, the

[1] "Report of Children's Employment Commission, Mines, 1842," in *Parliamentary Papers, 1842,* XV-XVII, Appendix I, 461; Appendix II, 107.

guid wife said, furniture was of no use, as it was so troublesome to flit wit.

THE EVIDENCE OF PATIENCE KERSHAW, AGED 17, "AN IGNORANT, FILTHY, RAGGED, AND DEPLORABLE-LOOKING OBJECT"

My father has been dead about a year; my mother is living and has ten children, five lads and five lassies; the oldest is about thirty, the youngest is four; three lasses go to mill; all the lads are colliers, two getters and three hurriers; one lives at home and does nothing; mother does nought but look after home.

All my sisters have been hurriers, but three went to the mill. Alice went because her legs swelled from hurrying in cold water when she was hot. I never went to day-school; I go to Sunday-school, but I cannot read or write; I go to pit at five o'clock in the morning and come out at five in the evening; I get my breakfast of porridge and milk first; I take my dinner with me, a cake, and eat it as I go; I do not stop or rest any time for the purpose; I get nothing else until I get home, and then have potatoes and meat, not every day meat. I hurry in the clothes I have now got on, trousers and ragged jacket; the bald place upon my head is made by thrusting the corves [trucks]; my legs have never swelled, but sisters' did when they went to mill; I hurry the corves a mile and more under ground and back; they weigh 300 cwt; I hurry 11 a-day; I wear a belt and chain at the workings to get the corves out; the getters that I work for are naked except their caps; they pull off all their clothes; I see them at work when I go up; sometimes they beat me, if I am not quick enough, with their hands; they strike me upon my back; the boys take liberties with me, sometimes they pull me about; I am the only girl in the pit; there are about 20 boys and 15 men; all the men are naked; I would rather work in a mill than in a coal-pit.

3. Patterns of Bourgeois Thought

MALTHUS ON THE PRINCIPLE OF POPULATION

Thomas Robert Malthus (1766-1834), an English economist, as a result of discussions with his father about the perfectibility of human society, published in 1798 *An Essay on the Principle of Population as It Affects the Future Improvement of Society*. Malthus held, as against the supporters of Utopia, that the tendency of population to increase faster than the means of subsistence gives rise to suffering, vice, and misery which constantly hinders the realization of a truly happy society. The argument, while it somewhat embarrassed the liberal proponents of the idea of progress, seemed to explain the perennial existence of poverty, to make it plain that poverty is unavoidable, to show that the poor are the cause of their own poverty, and to hold that, as poverty is unavoidable, social reform is futile and that wars, pestilence, and famine might be beneficial as checks on the growth of population. Malthus's *Essay* exerted wide influence on nineteenth-century opinion, and Darwin borrowed from it in arriving at the theory of evolution [see page 518]; but the increasing efficiency of the means of production and distribution have since weakened Malthus's argument. He enlarged his *Essay* in 1803, and it passed through six editions before his death. The following extract is from the revised edition of 1803.

From MALTHUS, *Essay on Population* (1803) [1]

In an inquiry concerning the future improvement of society, the mode of

[1] T. R. Malthus, *An Essay on the Principle of Population*, London, 1803, 1-3, 5, 7-13, 16.

conducting the subject which naturally presents itself is: 1. An investigation of the causes that have hitherto impeded the progress of mankind towards happiness; and, 2. An examination into the probability of the total or partial removal of these causes in the future.

To enter fully into this question, and to enumerate all the causes that have hitherto influenced human improvement, would be much beyond the power of an individual. The principal object of the present essay is to examine the effects of one great cause intimately united with the very nature of man, which, though it has been constantly and powerfully operating since the commencement of society, has been little noticed by the writers who have treated this subject. . . .

The cause to which I allude is the constant tendency in all animated life to increase beyond the nourishment prepared for it.

It is observed by Dr. Franklin that there is no bound to the prolific nature of plants or animals, but what is made by their crowding and interfering with each other's means of subsistence. . . . In plants and animals the view of the subject is simple. They are all impelled by a powerful instinct to the increase of their species; and this instinct is interrupted by no reasoning or doubts about providing for their offspring. Wherever, therefore, there is liberty, the power of increase is exerted; and the superabundant effects are repressed afterwards by want of room and nourishment, which is common to plants and animals; and among animals by their becoming the prey of each other.

The effects of this check on man are more complicated. Impelled to the increase of his species by an equally powerful instinct, reason interrupts his career, and asks him whether he may not bring beings into the world for whom he cannot provide the means of support. If he attend to this natural suggestion, the restriction too frequently produces vice. If he hear it not, the human race will be constantly endeavouring to increase beyond the means of subsistence. But as by that law of our nature which makes food necessary to the life of man, population can never actually increase beyond the lowest nourishment capable of supporting it; a strong check on population, from the difficulty of acquiring food, must be constantly in operation. This difficulty must fall somewhere; and must necessarily be severely felt in some or other of the various forms of misery, or the fear of misery, by a large portion of mankind.

That population has this constant tendency to increase beyond the means of subsistence, and that it is kept to its necessary level by these causes, will sufficiently appear from a review of the different states of society in which man has existed. But before we proceed to this review, the subject will perhaps be seen in a clearer light if we endeavour to ascertain what would be the natural increase in population if left to exert itself with perfect freedom; and what might be expected to be the rate of increase in the productions of the earth, under the most favourable circumstances of human industry. A comparison of these two rates of increase will enable us to judge of the force of that tendency in population to increase beyond the means of subsistence, which has been stated to exist. . . .

[Here Malthus, upon reviewing available evidence, concludes:]

It may safely be pronounced therefore that population, when unchecked, goes on doubling itself every twenty-five years, or increases in a geometrical ratio [1, 2, 4, 8, 16, etc. Whereas:]

It may be fairly pronounced therefore that, considering the present average state of the earth, the means of subsistence, under circumstances the most favourable to human industry, could not possibly be made to increase faster than in an arithmetical ratio [1, 2, 3, 4, 5, etc.]. . . . In two centuries the population would be to the means of subsistence as 256 to 9; in three centuries as 4096 to 13. . . .

The checks to population, which are constantly operating . . . and keep down the number to the level of the means of subsistence, may be classed under two general heads; the preventive and the positive checks.

The preventive check is peculiar to man, and arises from that distinctive superiority in his reasoning faculties which enables him to calculate distant consequences. . . . Man cannot look around him and see distress which frequently presses upon those who have large families . . . without feeling a doubt whether, if he follow the bent of his inclinations, he may be able to support the offspring which he will probably bring into the world. . . . Will he not lower his rank in life . . . be unable to transmit to his children the same advantages . . . that he had himself possessed? . . . These considerations . . . prevent a great number of persons in all civilized nations from pursuing the dictate of nature in an early attachment to one woman. If this restraint do not produce vice . . . it must be allowed to produce a certain degree of temporary unhappiness. . . . When the restraint produces vice, as it does most frequently among men . . . the evils which follow are but too conspicuous [a social evil, which also hinders realization of the perfect society]. . . .

The positive checks to population are extremely various and include every cause, whether arising from vice or misery, which in any degree contribute to shorten the natural duration of human life . . . unwholesome occupations, severe labour and exposure to the seasons, extreme poverty, bad nursing of children . . . wars, pestilence, plague, and famine.

On examining these obstacles to the increase of population . . . it will appear that they are all resolvable into moral restraint, vice, and misery. . . .

These effects, in the present state of society, seem to be produced in the following manner. . . . The constant effort towards population . . . increases the number of people before the means of subsistence are increased. . . . The poor consequently must live much worse . . . the price of labour must tend to fall; while the price of provisions would at the same time tend to rise. . . . During this season of distress, the discouragements to marriage . . . are so great that population is nearly at a stand. In the meantime, the cheapness of labour . . . [and the dearness of provisions] encourage cultivators to employ more labour . . . to turn up fresh soil . . . till ultimately the means of subsistence may become in the same proportion to the population. . . . The situation of the labourer being then again tolerably comfortable, the restraints to population are in some degree loosened; and, after a short period, the same retrograde and progressive movements, with respect to happiness, are repeated. . . .

But without attempting to establish in all cases these progressive and retrograde movements in different countries . . . the following propositions are proposed to be proved:

1. Population is necessarily limited by the means of subsistence.

2. Population invariably increases, where the means of subsistence increase, unless prevented by some very powerful and obvious checks.

3. These checks . . . are all resolvable into moral restraint, vice, and misery.

RICARDO ON POLITICAL ECONOMY

David Ricardo (1772-1823) leaned heavily upon Malthus, as will be seen, in his *Principles of Political Economy and Taxation,* published in 1817. Ricardo had become estranged from his Jewish parents by marrying a Gentile and joining the English Church. Deprived of his birthright, he proceeded to make a fortune on the London stock exchange and to become a member of Parliament, where liberals looked upon him as a wizard in political economy. Ricardo's theories regarding value, rent, and wages had a wide influence in the nineteenth century. The value of a commodity, he said, depends on the relative quantity of labor which is necessary for its production.

From RICARDO, *Political Economy* (1817) [1]

It is according to the division of the whole produce of the land . . . between the three classes of landlord, capitalist, and labourer, that we are to judge of the rise or fall of rent, profit, and wages, and not according to the value at which that produce may be estimated in a medium which is confessedly variable.

It is not by the absolute quantity of produce obtained by either class that we can correctly judge of the rate of profit, rent, and wages, but by the quantity of labour required to obtain that produce. . . .

ON RENT . . .

Rent is that portion of the produce of the earth, which is paid to the landlord for the use of the original and indestructible powers of the soil. . . . If all land had the same properties, if it were un-

[1] *The Works of David Ricardo,* ed. by J. R. McCulloch, London, 1852, 31, 34-36, 50-53, 55, 57-58.

limited in quantity, and uniform in quality, no charge could be made for its use, unless where it possessed peculiar advantages of situation. It is only, then, because land is not unlimited in quantity and uniform in quality, and because in the progress of population, land of an inferior quality, or less advantageously situated, is called into cultivation, that rent is ever paid for the use of it. When in the progress of society, land of a second degree of fertility is taken into cultivation, rent immediately commences on that of the first quality, and the amount of that rent will depend on the difference in the quality of these two portions of land. When land of the third quality is taken into cultivation, rent immediately commences on the second, and it is regulated as before, by the difference in their productive powers. At the same time, the rent of the first quality will rise. . . . With every step in the progress of population, which shall oblige a country to have recourse to land of a worse quality to enable it to raise its supply of food, rent, on all the more fertile land, will rise. . . .

ON WAGES

Labour, like all other things which are purchased and sold, and which may be increased or diminished in quantity, has its natural and its market price. The natural price of labour is that price which is necessary to enable the labourers, one with another, to subsist and to perpetuate their race, without either increase or diminution. . . . With a rise in the price of food and necessaries, the natural price of labour will rise; with the fall in their price, the natural price of labour will fall. . . .

The market price of labour is the price which is really paid for it, from the natural operation of the proportion of the supply to the demand; labour is dear when it is scarce, and cheap when it is plentiful. However much the market price of labour

may deviate from its natural price, it has, like commodities, a tendency to conform to it.

It is when the market price of labour exceeds its natural price that the condition of the labourer is flourishing and happy, that he has it in his power to command a greater proportion of the necessaries and enjoyments of life, and therefore to rear a healthy and a numerous family. When, however, by the encouragement which high wages give to the increase of population, the number of labourers is increased, wages again fall to their natural price, and indeed from a reaction sometimes fall below it.

When the market price of labour is below its natural price, the condition of the labourers is most wretched. . . . It is only after their privations have reduced their number, or the demand for labour has increased, that the market price will rise to its natural price, and that the labourer will have the moderate comforts which the natural rate of wages will afford.

Notwithstanding the tendency of wages to conform to their natural rate, their market rate may, in an improving society, for an indefinite period, be constantly above it; for no sooner may the impulse, which an increased capital gives to a new demand for labour be obeyed, than another increase of capital may produce the same effect; and thus, if the increase of capital be gradual and constant, the demand for labour may give a continued stimulus to an increase of people.

Capital is that part of the wealth of a country which is employed in production and consists of food, clothing, tools, raw materials, machinery, etc., necessary to give effect to labour. . . .

Thus, then, with every improvement of society, with every increase in its capital, the market wages of labour will rise; but the permanence of their rise will depend on the question whether the natural price of wages has also risen; and this again will depend on the rise in the natural price of those necessaries on which the wages of labour are expended. . . . It appears, then, that wages are subject to a rise or fall from two causes:

1st. The supply and demand of labourers.

2ndly. The price of the commodities on which the wages of labour are expended.

In different stages of society, the accumulation of capital, or the means of employing labour, is more or less rapid, and must in all cases depend on the productive powers of labour. The productive powers of labour are generally greatest when there is an abundance of fertile land: at such periods accumulation is often so rapid that labourers cannot be supplied with the same rapidity as capital. . . .

In new settlements . . . it is probable that capital has a tendency to increase faster than mankind: and if the deficiency of labourers were not supplied by more populous countries, this tendency would very much increase the price of labour. In proportion as these countries become populous, and the land of a worse quality is taken into cultivation, the tendency to an increase of capital diminishes . . . for, the land being limited in quantity, and differing in quality, with every increased portion of capital employed on it there will be a decreased rate of production, whilst the power of population continues always the same. . . .

It appears then, that the same cause which raises rent, namely, the increasing difficulty of providing an additional quantity of food with the same proportional quantity of labour, will also raise wages; and therefore if money be of an unvarying value, both rent and wages will have a tendency to rise with the progress of wealth and population.

But there is this essential difference between the rise of rent and the rise of wages. The rise in the money value of rent is accompanied by an increased share of the produce; not only is the landlord's money rent greater but his corn rent also. . . . The fate of the labourer will be less happy; he will receive more money wages, it is true, but his corn wages will be reduced; and not only his command of corn, but his general condition will be deteriorated by his finding it more difficult to maintain the market rate of wages above their natural rate. While the price of corn rises 10 per cent, wages will always rise less than 10 per cent, but rent will always rise more; the condition of the labourer will generally decline, and that of the landlord will always be improved. . . .

These then are the laws by which wages are regulated, and by which the happiness of far the greatest part of every community is governed. Like all other contracts, wages should be left to the fair and free competition of the market, and should never be controlled by the interference of the legislature.

The clear and direct tendency of the poor laws is in direct opposition to these obvious principles. . . . This pernicious tendency of these laws is no longer a mystery since it has been fully developed by the able hand of Mr. Malthus; and every friend of the poor must ardently wish for their abolition. . . . It is a truth which admits not a doubt that the comforts and well-being of the poor cannot be permanently secured without some regard on their part, or some effort on the part of the legislature, to regulate the increase of their numbers, and to render less frequent among them early and improvident marriages. The operation of the poor laws has been directly contrary to this. They have rendered restraint superfluous, and have invited imprudence by offering it a portion of the wages of prudence and industry.

The nature of the evil points out the

remedy. By gradually contracting the sphere of the poor laws; by impressing on the poor the value of independence, by teaching them that they must look not to systematic or casual charity, but to their own exertions for support, that prudence and forethought are neither unnecessary nor unprofitable virtues, we shall by degrees approach a sounder and more healthful state.

No scheme for the amendment of the poor laws merits the least attention which has not their abolition for its ultimate object.

4. Some Beginnings of the Proletarian Movement

ENGLISH CHARTISM

English law long regarded trade combinations, whether of workers or employers, as "conspiracies in restraint of trade": "the strike was a crime, and the trade union was an unlawful association." In 1824, in a burst of laissez-faire enthusiasm, Parliament repealed all Acts against trade combinations, but the series of violent strikes which followed led to hasty revision in 1825. By the Combination Act of 1825 the common law of conspiracy was reaffirmed, but limited rights of combination were conceded. The general effect was to render trade-unions nonlegal, but also noncriminal, organizations, or, in point of fact, to recognize trade-unions but to deny them the right to strike. Not until 1871 were trade-unions conceded legal existence in England. Meanwhile, the wage-earning class turned to politics for amelioration of their condition. Among other organizations, there was organized at London in 1838 the Workingmen's Association, which drew up for

parliamentary attention a People's Charter of six points; namely, universal manhood suffrage, annual Parliaments, vote by ballot, no property qualifications for voting, payment of members of Parliament, and equal voting districts. Mostly, the Chartists, as they were called, agitated by peaceful means, although the fiery Feargus Edward O'Connor urged the use of more revolutionary methods. Chartism died out about 1850, partly crushed by reactionary forces in the Revolution of 1848, partly by the loss of leaders through death or emigration, and partly because, in the latter half of the century, its program was gradually accepted. Their first petition was presented in 1838.

From the Chartists' First Petition (1838) [1]

Humbly Sheweth,—

That we, your petitioners, dwell in a land whose merchants are noted for their enterprise, whose manufacturers are very skilful, and whose workmen are proverbial for their industry. The land itself is goodly, the soil rich, and the temperature wholesome. It is abundantly furnished with the materials of commerce and trade. It has numerous and convenient harbours. In facility of internal communication it exceeds all others. For three and twenty years we have enjoyed a profound peace. Yet, with all the elements of national prosperity, and with every disposition and capacity to take advantage of them, we find ourselves overwhelmed with public and private suffering. . . . We have looked on every side; we have searched diligently in order to find out the causes of distress so sore and so long continued. We can discover none in nature or in Providence. . . . But the foolishness of our rulers has made the goodness of God

[1] R. G. Gammage, History of the Chartist Movement, 1837-1854, London, 1894, 87-90.

of none effect. The energies of a mighty kingdom have been wasted in building up the power of selfish and ignorant men, and its resources squandered for their aggrandisement. The good of a part has been advanced at the sacrifice of the good of the nation. The few have governed for the interest of the few, while the interests of the many have been sottishly neglected, or insolently and tyrannously trampled upon. It was the fond expectation of the friends of the people that a remedy for the greater part, if not for the whole of their grievances, would be found in the Reform Act of 1832. They regarded that Act as a wise means to a worthy end, as the machinery of an improved legislation, where the will of the masses would be at length potential. They have been bitterly and basely deceived. . . . The Reform Act has effected a transfer of power from one domineering faction to another, and left the people as helpless as before. Our slavery has been exchanged for an apprenticeship to liberty, which has aggravated the painful feelings of our social degradation, by adding to them the sickening of still deferred hope. We come before your honourable house to tell you, with all humility, that this state of things must not be permitted to continue. That it cannot long continue, without very seriously endangering the stability of the throne, and the peace of the kingdom, and that if, by God's help, and all lawful and constitutional appliances, an end can be put to it, we are fully resolved that it shall speedily come to an end. We tell your honourable house, that the capital of the master must no longer be deprived of its due profit; that the labour of the workman must no longer be deprived of its due reward. That the laws which make food dear, and the laws which make money scarce, must be abolished. . . . That the good of the many, as it is the only legitimate end, so must it be

the sole study of the government. As a preliminary essential to these and other requisite changes—as the means by which alone the interests of the people can be effectually vindicated and secured, we demand that those interests be confided to the keeping of the people. . . . We perform the duties of freemen; we must have the privileges of freemen. Therefore, we demand universal suffrage. The suffrage, to be exempt from the corruption of the wealthy and the violence of the powerful, must be secret. The assertion of our right necessarily involves the power of our uncontrolled exercise. We ask for the reality of a good, not for its semblance, therefore we demand the ballot. . . . To public safety, as well as public confidence, frequent elections are essential. Therefore, we demand annual parliaments. With power to choose, and freedom in choosing, the range of our choice must be unrestricted. We are compelled, by the existing laws, to take for representatives men who are incapable of appreciating our difficulties, or have little sympathy with them. . . . The labours of a representative who is sedulous in the discharge of his duty are numerous and burdensome. It is neither just, nor reasonable, nor safe, that they should continue to be gratuitously rendered. We demand that in the future election of members of your honourable house, the approbation of the constituency shall be the sole qualification, and that to every representative so chosen, shall be assigned out of the public taxes, a fair and adequate remuneration for the time which he is called upon to devote to the public service. . . . May it therefore please your honourable house, to take this our petition into your most serious consideration, and to use your utmost endeavours, by all constitutional means, to have a law passed, granting to every male of lawful age, sane mind, and unconvicted of crime, the right of voting for members of parliament, and directing all future elections of members of parliament to be in the way of secret ballot, and ordaining that the duration of parliament, so chosen, shall in no case exceed one year, and abolishing all property qualifications in the members, and providing for their due remuneration while in attendance on their parliamentary duties.

PRE-MARXIAN SOCIALIST REFORMERS: SAINT-SIMON AND FOURIER

As the Industrial Revolution invaded the Continent, carrying with it the problems of the wage-earners, social reformers began to speculate upon new social organizations to ameliorate the condition of the proletariat and to effect "social justice." Most of these speculations, though marked by widely different approaches, set forth a form of Socialism as the panacea. The "systems" proposed by two of them, Claude Henri de Rouvroy, Count de Saint-Simon (1760-1825), sometimes regarded as the "Father of French Socialism," and François Marie Charles Fourier (1772-1837), appealed to many thoughtful persons. Fourierism, in particular, led to many experimental communities, including the famous Brook Farm in Massachusetts. An account of their proposals follows, beginning with Saint-Simonianism.

From DICKINSON, *Revolution and Reaction* (1892) [1]

SAINT-SIMON

Men were divided into three classes, Priests (or Artists), "Savants" and "Industriels": the function of the first was to appeal to the imagination in the inter-

[1] G. Lowes Dickinson, *Revolution and Reaction in Modern France*, London, 1892, 142-49.

est of religion, or, more precisely, in the interest of those general ideas which were the basis of the bond of the whole society. . . . "We designate by the name of priest the man who, by his thoughts and acts, by the morality of his whole life, inspires generous sentiments and awakens sympathies. He is the organizer of others and the bond of union between them . . . he is the priest according to the order of St. Simon." Those whom the Priest is to harmonize and inspire are the two subordinate classes, the "Savants" and "Industriels": science, henceforth, is to work in the interest of industry, and industry to develop under the direction of science . . . the Savants, then, must be defined not merely as men of science, but as men of science in touch with practical tendencies and needs; their organization, like that of the whole society, will be threefold; on the one hand will be the men of research—the "Perfectionnants," on the other the teaching staff—the "Enseignants"; and above these two groups, to co-ordinate and inspire their labours, will be placed a group of philosophers impressed with the conception of society as a whole, intent on the general direction and the aim of all knowledge, and synthesizing to a common end the diversity of its special branches. . . .

The complement of science was industry, and the "Industriels" like the "Savants" must be brought under the direction of the Priests: even more patent than the anarchy of science was the anarchy of trade . . . it was, in fact, the primary aim of the St. Simonians to "ameliorate as quickly and as completely as possible the moral and physical existence of the most numerous class;" this they regarded as the modern reading of the precept, "love thy neighbour as thyself:" their remedy was a form of Socialism: the State was to own the means of production, and organize industry on the principle indicated by the motto, "to each according to his capacity and to each capacity according to its works:" the "Industriels" were to be divided into communities, each directed by a mayor, and all grouped together under a central authority; the production of each community, and of each department of industry, would be regulated by statistical information as to the probable needs of consumers, and the distribution would be regulated by the services of each producer; there would be promotion for merit and pensions for old age and this, it was thought, would be sufficient to provide a motive to work. . . .

As the St. Simonians never formed a compact political party, they were never able to press their proposals upon the country; their scheme remained a suggestion, but a faithful and interesting one, and one that has influenced, indirectly, the tendency of modern thought.

FOURIER

From St. Simon and his followers we pass to Fourier. His system is based on a fantastic and elaborate cosmology: the law of the world is universal attraction, which manifests itself in five forms, material, organic, intellectual, animal, and social, corresponding to the five classes of phenomena, inorganic matter, life, mind, magnetism, and society; attraction, in general, is good; therefore, in particular, every desire and passion of man is good; if then, as appears to be the case, there is such a thing as evil, this must be ascribed not to the indulgence of the passions, but to the circumstances under which they are indulged: thus distinction between right and wrong is merely the result of artificial conditions; expansion, not repression, love, not duty, is the law of a natural society; and the problem of the reformer is so to arrange the various relations of men that every passion may find a vent and contribute its force to the common good.

From this position Fourier is led to an analysis of the passions: he divides them into three classes; those that are concerned with the satisfaction of the senses, those that are concerned with association in groups, and those that are concerned with the association of the groups in a unity; on this classification is based the arrangement of the perfect society; individuals will organize themselves in groups, the groups in series, and the series in phalansteries; all the associations will be voluntary, the members of the group will be attracted by some one or other of the passions that tend to that particular form of union—ambition, friendship, family affection, or love; similarly, the groups will be connected by the passions that urge to larger combinations; and the result will be a harmonious organization comprehending, in the end, the whole of mankind. In the new society all will be workers, for work will be congenial to all; each will be directed by his dominant passion to some particular task, and it is from the conjunction of several individuals having the same natural bent that the associations in groups will arise; any member of one group may become a member of another, and thus avoid the monotony attending a single task. . . . A single example will illustrate the way in which the system was supposed to work:—"Imagine," says Fourier, "a mass of about 600 people, half men and half women, all inspired with a passion for the same branch of industry. Let us take the series for the cultivation of pears; these 600 people will be divided into groups which will devote themselves to the production of one or two kinds of pears. Thus there will be a group of the sectaries of the butter pear, another of the sectaries of the russet pear, &c. And when every one has been enrolled in the groups attached to his favourite pears (for he may belong to several), there will be perhaps thirty groups. . . . The result of this mechanism will be that each group will produce the most magnificent fruit conceivable. Similar competitions and similar alliances arise among the various groups of a division. . . . It may be imagined that the pear-series will be a vigorous rival of the apple-series, while, on the other hand, it will enter into alliance with the cherry-series, since the pear and the cherry are not sufficiently akin to excite to jealousy their respective cultivators."

This passage is not only an illustration but a criticism of the whole system; everything depends on the assumption that people will be born into the world who will have a consuming passion for the cultivation of, say, "melting" pears; and by analogy, others, who will be driven by their natural bent to the scavenging of streets or the flushing of the main sewers: this assumption admitted, the difficulty is solved at once; society will organize itself as soon as the idea is grasped. . . . The scheme, in fact, may be described as one of spontaneous co-operation; instead of solving the problem, it assumes that it will solve itself: this, however, has not yet occurred; and the phalansteries of Fourier are remembered only as a curious and suggestive speculation.

THE BEGINNINGS OF MARXIAN SOCIALISM

In 1847, the international Communist League, a radical organization dominated largely by a German secret workingmen's organization of the same name, held a Congress in London. At this gathering the league commissioned two of its members, Karl Marx and Friedrich Engels, to prepare a statement of the party program to be pub-

lished to the world. The document was prepared, principally by Marx (whose later unfinished volume, *Das Kapital,* was little more than an enlargement and documentation of the *Manifesto*), in January, 1848, on the eve of the revolutions which swept over most of Europe in the course of that year. As a consequence of these revolutions, the Communist League was dissolved and its members scattered; but the *Manifesto* survived, to be taken up by later radical proletariat organizations and parties and gradually to become the clarion call of extreme Leftist groups the world over. As the *Manifesto* sharply castigated the pre-Marxian socialists for their impractical Utopias and halfway measures, and as Utopian Socialism tended to die out after 1848, the *Communist Manifesto* marked a clear-cut division between Utopian Socialism and Marxian, or Scientific, Socialism. Intended, as Engels said, to emancipate "society at large from all exploitation, oppression, class-distinction and class-struggle," the *Communist Manifesto* has exerted a tremendous influence in the world since its first publication nearly a century ago. In a condensed form, it read as follows.

From the *Communist Manifesto* (1848) [1]

A spectre is haunting Europe—the spectre of Communism. All the Powers of old Europe have entered into holy alliance to exorcise this spectre; Pope and Czar, Metternich and Guizot, French Radicals and German police-spies.

Where is the party in opposition that has not been decried as communistic by

[1] *Capital, The Communist Manifesto, and Other Writings by Karl Marx,* ed. by Max Eastman, 1932 (The Modern Library), 320-31, 334-35, 337, 340, 342-43, 335. By permission of Random House, New York.

its opponents in power? Where the Opposition that has not hurled back the branding reproach of Communism against the more advanced opposition parties, as well as against its reactionary adversaries?

Two things result from this fact.

I. Communism is already acknowledged by all European Powers to be itself a Power.

II. It is high time that Communists should openly, in the face of the whole world, publish their views, their aims, their tendencies, and meet this nursery tale of the spectre of Communism with a Manifesto of the party itself.

To this end, Communists of various nationalities have assembled in London and sketched the following Manifesto, to be published in the English, French, German, Italian, Flemish and Danish languages. . . .

The history of all hitherto existing society is the history of class struggles. Freeman and slave, patrician and plebian, lord and serf, guild-master and journeyman, in a word, oppressor and oppressed, stood in constant opposition to one another, carried on uninterrupted, now hidden, now open fight, a fight that each time ended, either in a revolutionary re-constitution of society at large, or in the common ruin of the contending classes. . . .

Our epoch, the epoch of the bourgeoisie, possesses, however, this distinctive feature; it has simplified the class antagonisms. Society as a whole is more and more splitting up into two great hostile camps. . . . Bourgeoisie and Proletariat. From the serfs of the middle ages sprang the chartered burghers of the earliest towns. From these burgesses the first elements of the bourgeoisie were developed. . . . We see, therefore, how the modern bourgeoisie is itself the product of a long course of development. . . . The bourgeoisie has at last, since the establishment

of Modern Industry and of the world-market, conquered for itself, in the modern representative State, exclusive sway. The executive of the modern State is but a committee for managing the common affairs of the whole bourgeoisie. . . . The bourgeoisie . . . has left no other nexus between man and man than naked self-interest, than callous "cash payment.". . . It has converted the physician, the lawyer, the priest, the poet, the man of science, into its paid wage labourers. . . .

The bourgeoisie cannot exist without constantly revolutionizing the instruments of production, and thereby the relations of production, and with them the whole relations of society. . . . The need of a constantly expanding market for its products chases the bourgeoisie over the whole surface of the globe. . . . In place of the old local and national seclusion and self-sufficiency, we have intercourse in every direction, universal interdependence of nations. And as in material, so also in intellectual production . . . from the numerous national and local literatures there arises a world-literature. . . . The bourgeoisie has subjected the country to the rule of the towns. . . . It has made barbarian and semi-barbarian countries dependent on civilized ones, nations of peasants on nations of bourgeois, the East on the West. . . . Modern bourgeois society . . . is like the sorcerer who is no longer able to control the powers of the nether world whom he has called up by his spells. . . . It is enough to mention the commercial crises that by their periodical return put on its trial, each time more threateningly, the existence of the entire bourgeois society. . . . How does the bourgeoisie get over these crises? On the one hand by enforced destruction of a mass of productive forces; on the other, by the conquest of new markets, and by the more thorough exploitation of the old ones. That is to say, by paving the way for more extensive and more destructive crises, and by diminishing the means whereby crises are prevented. . . .

Not only has the bourgeoisie forged the weapons that bring death to itself; it has also called into existence the men who are to wield these weapons—the modern working-class—the proletarians . . . a class of labourers who live only so long as they find work, and who find work only so long as their labour increases capital. . . . The lower strata of the middle class—the small tradespeople, shopkeepers and retired tradesmen generally, the handicraftsmen and peasants—all these sink gradually into the proletariat . . . because their diminutive capital does not suffice for the scale on which modern industry is carried on. . . . Thus the proletariat is recruited from all classes of the population. . . . With the development of industry the proletariat not only increases in number; it becomes concentrated in greater masses, its strength grows and it feels that strength more. . . . The bourgeoisie finds itself involved in a constant battle. . . . In all these battles it sees itself compelled to appeal to the proletariat, to ask for its help, and thus, to drag it into the political arena. The bourgeoisie itself, therefore, supplies the proletariat with its own elements of political and general education; in other words, it furnishes the proletariat with weapons for fighting the bourgeoisie. . . . What the bourgeoisie therefore produces, above all, are its own grave-diggers. Its fall and the victory of the proletariat are equally inevitable. . . .

The immediate aim of the Communists is . . . formation of the proletariat into a class, overthrow of the bourgeois of supremacy, conquest of political power by the proletariat. . . . The distinguishing feature of Communism is not the abolition of property generally, but the abolition of bourgeois property. But modern bourgeois private property is the final and most complete expression of the system . . . that is based on class antagonism, on the exploitation of the many by the few. In this sense, the theory of the Communists may be summed up in a single sentence: Abolition of private property. . . . Communism deprives no man of the power to appropriate the products of society; all that it does is to deprive him of the power to subjugate the labour of others by means of such appropriation. . . . Communists are further reproached with desiring to abolish countries and nationalities. The working-men have no country. We cannot take from them what they don't possess. . . . National differences and antagonisms between peoples are daily more and more vanishing. . . . The supremacy of the proletariat will cause them to vanish still faster. United action, of the leading civilized countries . . . is one of the first conditions for the emancipation of the proletariat. . . .

The proletariat will use its political supremacy to wrest, by degrees, all capital from the bourgeoisie, to centralize all instruments of production in the hands of the State, *i.e.,* of the proletariat organized as ruling class; and to increase the total productive forces as rapidly as possible. Of course, in the beginning, this cannot be effected except by means of despotic inroads on the rights of property, and on the conditions of bourgeois production; by means of measures, therefore, which appear economically insufficient and untenable. . . . These measures will of course be different in different countries. . . . In the most advanced countries the following will be pretty generally applicable: 1. Abolition of property in land and application of all rents to public purposes. 2. A heavy progressive or graduated income tax. 3. Abolition of all right of inheritance. 4. Confiscation of the property of all emigrants and rebels. 5. Centralization of credit in the hands . . . of a national bank with State capital and an exclusive monopoly. 6. Centralization of the means of communication and transport in the hands of the State. 7. Extension of factories and instruments of production owned by the State. . . . 8. Equal liability of all to labour. . . . 9. . . . A more equal distribution of the population over the country. 10. Free education for all children in the public schools. . . .

When . . . all production has been concentrated in the hands of a vast association of the whole nation, the public power will lose its political character. . . . The proletariat . . . will . . . have swept away the conditions for the existence of class antagonism, and of classes generally, and will thereby have abolished its own supremacy as a class. In place of the old bourgeois society, with its classes and class antagonisms, we shall have an association in which the free development of each is the condition for the free development of all. . . .

Communists everywhere support every revolutionary movement against the existing social and political order of things. . . .

Communists disdain to conceal their views and aims. They openly declare that their ends can be attained only by the forcible overthrow of all existing social conditions. Let the ruling classes tremble at a Communistic revolution. The proletarians have nothing to lose but their chains. They have a world to win.

Working-men of all countries, unite!

---

27 SCIENCE, RELIGION, AND PHILOSOPHY IN THE NINETEENTH CENTURY

The "New Science," which was born in Renaissance times and reached fruitful adolescence during the Era of Enlightened Despotism, became of age in the nineteenth century. So vast and so complex were the achievements of science in the last century that it becomes impossible to illustrate more than a few of the principal accomplishments, and some of these tend to become somewhat technical for the nonscientific reader. In the fields of physics and chemistry, the atomic theory and the periodic table were among major developments.

1. Physics and Chemistry

JOHN DALTON AND THE ATOMIC THEORY OF MATTER (1808)

The nature of matter has been an age-old source of speculation. Since the ancient Greeks, scholars had held the hypothesis that matter consists of tiny particles joined together by some curious attraction. But until the early nineteenth century, no acceptable scientific proof of the hypothesis existed. This proof was the work of John Dalton

(1766-1844), an English Quaker of humble origin who in 1793 became a teacher of mathematics and philosophy at New College, Manchester. In the early 1800's, after a series of experiments with the combination of gases, Dalton came to believe that gases combine with each other in definite proportions. To explain this phenomenon, he resorted to the atomic hypothesis, soon applied it to chemical combinations in general, and pointed out that chemical combinations can be represented as a union of specific particles with definite weights characteristic of each element, and that the measurement of the relative weights in which chemical elements combine will give the relative weights of the constituent atoms. Thus the age-old hypothesis became a demonstrable theory, the atomic theory, which has since become accepted as one of the great laws of nature. A section of Dalton's *New Systems of Chemical Philosophy* (1808) illustrates his method of proof, although it contains some errors of detail inevitable at the time.

From DALTON, *Chemical Philosophy* (1808) [1]

ON THE CONSTITUTION OF BODIES

There are three distinctions in the kinds of bodies, or three states, which have more especially claimed the attention of philosophical chemists; namely, those which are marked by the terms elastic fluids [gases], liquids, and solids. A very familiar instance is exhibited to use in water, of a body which, in certain circumstances, is capable of assuming all the three states. In steam we recognise a perfectly elastic fluid, in water a perfect

[1] Oliver J. Thatcher, ed., *The Ideas That Have Influenced Civilization in Original Documents*, 10 vols., Robert Manchester Publishing Company, 1902, VIII, 368-72.

liquid, and in ice a complete solid. These observations have tacitly led to the conclusion which seems universally adopted, that all bodies of sensible magnitude, whether liquid or solid, are constituted of a vast number of extremely small particles, of atoms of matter bound together by a force of attraction, which is more or less powerful according to circumstances, and which as it endeavours to prevent their separation, it is very properly called . . . attraction of cohesion . . . or more simply, affinity. . . .

Whether the ultimate particles of a body, such as water, are all alike, that is, of the same figure, weight, etc., is a question of some importance. From what is known, we have no reason to apprehend a diversity in these particulars: if it does exist in water, it must equally exist in the elements constituting water, namely hydrogen and oxygen. Now it is scarcely possible to conceive how the aggregates of dissimilar particles should be so uniformly the same. If some of the particles of water were heavier than others, if a parcel of the liquid on any occasion were constituted principally of these heavier particles, it must be supposed to affect the specific gravity of the mass, a circumstance not known. Similar observations may be made on other substances. Therefore we may conclude that the ultimate particles of all homogeneous bodies are perfectly alike in weight, figure, etc. In other words, every particle of water is like every other particle of water; every particle of hydrogen is like to every other particle of hydrogen, etc. . . .

ON CHEMICAL SYNTHESIS

When any body exists in the elastic [gaseous] state, its ultimate particles are separated from each other to a much greater distance than in any other state. . . . When we attempt to conceive the number of particles in an atmosphere, it is somewhat like attempting to conceive the number of stars in the universe. We are confounded with the thought. But if we limit the subject, by taking a given volume of any gas, we seem persuaded that, let the divisions be ever so minute, the number of particles must be finite. . . .

Chemical analysis and synthesis go no farther than to the separation of particles one from another, and to their reunion. No new creation or destruction of matter is within the reach of chemical agency. . . . All the changes we can produce, consist in separating particles that are in a state of cohesion or combination, and joining those that were previously at a distance.

In all chemical investigations, it has justly been considered an important object to ascertain the relative weights of the simples which constitute a compound. But unfortunately the enquiry has terminated here; whereas from the relative weights in the mass, the relative weights of the ultimate particles or atoms of the bodies might have been inferred, from which their number and weight in various other compounds would appear, in order to assist and to guide future investigations and to correct their results. Now it is the one great object of this work, to show the importance and advantage of ascertaining the relative weights of the ultimate particles, both of simple and compound bodies, the number of simple elementary particles which constitute one compound particle, and the number of less compound particles which enter into the formation of one more compound particle. . . . [Here follow technical rules regarding chemical synthesis.]

From the application of these rules to the chemical facts already well ascertained, we deduce the following conclusions: 1st. That water is a binary compound of hydrogen and oxygen, and the relative weights of the two elementary atoms are as 1:7, nearly; 2d. That ammonia is a binary compound of hydrogen and azote [nitrogen], and the relative weights of the two atoms are as 1:5, nearly; 3d. That nitrous gas is a binary compound of azote and oxygen, the atoms of which weigh 5 and 7 respectively; that nitric acid is a binary or ternary compound according as it is derived, and consists of one atom of azote and two of oxygen, together weighing 19 . . . &c. In all these cases the weights are expressed in atoms of hydrogen, each of which is denoted by unity.

In the sequel, the facts and experiments from which these conclusions are derived will be detailed; as well as a great variety of others from which are inferred the constitution and weight of the ultimate particles of the principal acids, the alkalies, the earths, the metals, the metallic oxides and sulphurets, the long train of neutral salts, and in short, all the chemical compounds which have hitherto obtained a tolerably good analysis.

THE PERIODIC LAW (1869)

Dmitri Ivanovich Mendeleev (1834-1907), born in Tobolsk, Russia, became professor of chemistry at St. Petersburg in 1866. Shortly afterward he engaged in a study of the close relations between the atomic weights of chemical elements. In 1869, he set forth a table of the distribution of elements in order of ascending atomic weights whereby it appeared that the elements grouped into related families, and Mendeleev was able to correct some of the atomic weights then accepted. Even more significant, he was able to predict the existence of other elements formerly unknown, predictions which have been fulfilled in surprising accord with his descriptions as new elements have been isolated. In a lecture before the Fellows of the Chemical Society of London in

1889, Mendeleev gave an account of his discovery.

From MENDELEEV, *Faraday Lecture* (1889) [1]

The high honor bestowed by the Chemical Society in inviting me to pay a tribute to the world-famed name of Faraday by delivering this lecture has induced me to take for its subject the Periodic Law of the Elements—this being a generalization in chemistry which has of late attracted much attention. . . . It was in March, 1869, that I ventured to lay before the then youthful Russian Chemical Society the ideas upon the same subject which I had expressed in my just written "Principles of Chemistry."

Without entering into details, I will give the conclusions I then arrived at in the very words I used:

1. The elements, if arranged according to their atomic weights, exhibit an evident *periodicity* of properties.

2. Elements which are similar as regards their chemical properties have atomic weights which are either nearly the same value (*e.g.,* platinum, iridium, osmium) or which increase regularly (*e.g.,* potassium, rubidium, caesium).

3. The arrangement of the elements, or of groups of elements, in the order of their atomic weights, corresponds to their so-called *valencies,* as well as, to some extent, to their distinctive chemical properties—as is apparent, among other series, in that of lithium, beryllium, barium, carbon, nitrogen, oxygen, and iron.

4. The elements which are most widely diffused have small atomic weights.

5. The magnitude of the atomic weight determines the character of the element, just as the magnitude of the molecule determines the character of a compound.

6. We must expect the discovery of many yet unknown elements—for ex-

ample, elements analogous to aluminum and silicon, whose atomic weight would be between 65 and 75.

7. The atomic weight of an element may sometimes be amended by a knowledge of those of the contiguous elements. Thus, the atomic weight of tellurium must be between 123 and 126, and cannot be 128.

8. Certain characteristic properties of the elements can be foretold from their atomic weights. . . .

Today, twenty years after the above conclusions were formulated, they may still be considered as expressing the essence of the now well known periodic law.

Reverting to the epoch terminating with the [eighteen] sixties, it is proper to indicate three series of data without the knowledge of which the periodic law could not have been discovered, and which rendered its appearance natural and intelligible.

In the first place, it was at that time that the numerical value of atomic weights became definitely known. . . . Secondly, it had become evident during the period 1860-70, and even during the preceding decade, that the relations between the atomic weights of analogous elements were governed by some general and simple laws. Cooke, Cremers, Gladstone, Gmelin, Lenssen, Pettenkofer, and especially Dumas, had already established many facts bearing on that view. . . . A third circumstance which revealed the periodicity of chemical elements was the accumulation, by the end of the sixties, of new information respecting the rare elements, disclosing their many-sided relations to the other elements and to each other. The researches of Marignac on niobium, and those of Roscoe on vanadium, were of special moment. . . . The law of periodicity was thus a direct outcome of the stock of generalizations and established facts which had accumulated by the end

[1] *Ibid.,* X, 255-60.

of the decade 1860-70; it is an embodiment of those data in a more or less systematic expression.

2. Medicine

PERCUSSION

In 1761, Leopold Auenbrugger, a Viennese physician, published a little volume which set forth for the first time the method and value of percussion of the chest and furnished a new, objective method for diagnosis of chest disorders. A model of scientific clarity, Auenbrugger began: "I here present the Reader with a new sign I have discovered for detecting diseases of the chest. This consists in the Percussion of the human thorax, according to the character of the particular sounds thence elicited, an opinion is formed of the internal state of that cavity."

From AUENBRUGGER, "Observations" (1761) [1]

First Observation: Of the natural sound of the chest, and its character in different parts.
I. The thorax of a healthy person sounds, when struck. . . .
II. The sound thus elicited from the healthy chest resembles the stifled sound of a drum covered with a thick woollen cloth or other envelope.
III. This sound is perceptible on different parts of the chest. . . . [These are described.]
Second Observation: On the method of Percussion.
IV. The thorax ought to be struck,

slowly and gently, with the points of the fingers, brought close together and at the same time extended. . . .
VI. During the application of percussion the patient is first to go on breathing in the natural manner, and then is to hold his breath after a full inspiration. The difference of sound during inspiration, expiration, and the retention of the breath. is important in fixing our diagnosis. . . .
Third Observation: Of the preternatural or morbid sound of the chest, and its general import. . . .
X. To be able justly to appreciate the value of the various sounds elicited from the chest in cases of disease, it is necessary to have learned by experience on many subjects, the modifications of sound, general or partial, produced by the habit of the body . . . inasmuch as these various circumstances [size, degree of fleshiness, and so on] modify the sound very considerably.
XI. If, then, a distinct sound, equal on both sides, and commensurate to the degree of percussion, is not obtained from the sonorous regions above mentioned, a morbid condition of some of the parts within the chest is indicated. . . .
XII and XIII. If a sonorous part of the chest, struck with the same intensity, yields a duller sound than natural, disease exists in that part.

THE STETHOSCOPE

From percussion to the stethoscope was a logical, but at first accidental, step by René Théophile Hyacinthe Laënnec (1781-1826), a Paris clinician, who thus described his discovery.

From LAËNNEC, "On Mediate Auscultation" (1819) [2]

In 1816 I was consulted by a young woman presenting general symptoms of

[1] This and the next selection are from Logan Clendening, ed., Source-Book of Medical History, 1942, copyright, 1942, by Paul B. Hoeber, Inc., New York, and reprinted with their permission. This is 306-11.

[2] Ibid., 315-19.

disease of the heart. Owing to her stoutness little information could be gathered by application of the hand and percussion. The patient's age and sex did not permit me to resort to the kind of examination I have just described [that is, direct application of the ear to the chest]. I recalled a well-known acoustic phenomenon: namely, if you place your ear against one end of a wooden beam the scratch of a pin at the other extremity is most distinctly audible. It occurred to me that this physical property might serve a useful purpose in the case with which I was then dealing. Taking a sheaf of paper I rolled it into a very tight roll, one end of which I placed over the praecordial region, whilst I put my ear to the other. I was both surprised and gratified at being able to hear the beating of the heart with much greater clearness and distinctness than I had ever done before by direct application of my ear.

I saw at once that this means might become a useful method for studying, not only the beating of the heart, but likewise all movements capable of producing sound in the thoracic cavity, and that consequently it might serve for the investigation of respiration, the voice, râles and even possibly the movements of a liquid effused into the pleural cavity or pericardium.

With this conviction, I at once began and have continued to the present time, a series of observations at the Hospital Necker. As a result I have obtained many new and certain signs, most of which are striking, easy of recognition, and calculated perhaps to render the diagnosis of nearly all complaints of the lungs, pleurae and heart both more certain and circumstantial. . . .

The first instrument employed by me consisted of a cylinder or roll of paper. . . .

Substances of medium density, such as paper, wood and cane, are those which have always appeared to me preferable to all others. . . .

I consequently employ at the present time a wooden cylinder with a tube three lines in diameter [2.256 mm.] bored right down its axis; it is divisible into two parts by means of a screw and is thus more portable. One of these parts is hollowed out at its end into a wide funnel-shaped depression 1½ in. deep leading into the central tube. . . .

Suffice it to say for the moment that in all cases the stethoscope should be held like a pen, and that the hand must be placed quite close to the patient's chest in order to make sure that the instrument is properly applied.

The end of the instrument intended to rest on the patient's chest . . . should be very slightly concave; it is then less liable to wobble, and as this concavity is easily filled by the skin it in no case leaves an empty space even when placed on the flattest part of the chest. . . .

Some of the signs obtained by mediate auscultation are very easy to distinguish, and if they have been heard once there will be no difficulty in again recognizing them. . . .

Mediate auscultation must not, however, lead us to neglect Auenbrugger's method [or others]; to which it gives, on the contrary, an entirely new importance, extending its use to numerous maladies in which percussion alone would be of no help or might positively lead to error.

THE GERM THEORY OF DISEASE: PASTEUR

Minute organisms only visible with the microscope were observed in the seventeenth century; their possible role in disease was conceived in the eighteenth century; but it was not until the nineteenth century that it was proved that contagions are due to microbes and that each germ disease has a particular microbe all its own. This new concept resulted primarily from the works of Louis Pasteur (1822-1895) and Robert Koch (1843-1910). Pasteur combined great genius with hard work and a sunny personality. In studies of fermentation he discovered, during the 1860's, the bacteria responsible for the process, proved they were not spontaneously generated (a notion that died hard, see page 354), and showed that the application of properly controlled heat would kill them (pasteurization). Subsequently, in a study of the silkworm disease which crippled French industry, he showed how to control it by systematic examination of ova with the elimination of those found to be diseased; and he went on to prove the existence of other bacilli and, in the 1880's, to develop preventive vaccination against rabies (hydrophobia). An example of Pasteur's work, in his own words, follows.

From PASTEUR, "Inoculation for Hydrophobia" (1885-86) [1]

We have found that the virus of rabies develops itself invariably in the nervous system, brain, and spinal cord, in the nerves, and in the salivary glands; but it is not present at the same moment in every one of those parts. . . . If an animal is killed whilst in the power of rabies, it may require a pretty long search to discover the presence here or there in the nervous system, or in the glands, of the virus of rabies. We have been fortunate enough to ascertain that in all cases, when death has been allowed to supervene naturally, the swelled-out portion, or bulb, of the medulla oblongata nearest to the brain . . . is always rabid. When an animal has died of rabies (and the disease always ends in death), rabid matter can

with certainty be obtained from its bulb, capable of reproducing the disease in other animals when inoculated into them, after trephining, in the arachnoid space of the cerebral meninges. . . .

Those two great results, the constant presence of the virus in the bulb at the time of death, and the certainty of the reproduction of the disease by inoculation into the arachnoid space, stand out like experimental axioms, and their importance is paramount. . . . But, however solid those experimental bases, they were, nevertheless, incapable in themselves of giving us the faintest notion as to some method of vaccination against rabies. In the present state of science the discovery of a method of vaccination against some virulent malady presupposes:

1. That we have to deal with a virus capable of assuming diverse intensities, of which the weaker ones can be put to vaccinal or protective uses.

2. That we are in possession of a method enabling us to reproduce those diverse degrees at will.

At the present time, however, science is acquainted with one sort of rabies only— viz., dog rabies. Rabies, whether in dog, man, horse, ox, wolf, fox, etc., comes originally from the bite of a mad dog. It is never spontaneous, neither in the dog nor in any other animal. . . .

In fine, then, the first question to be solved on our way towards the prophylaxis of rabies is that of knowing whether the virus of that malady is susceptible of taking on varying intensities, after the manner of the virus of fowl-cholera or of splenic fever. . . . Might we . . . make use of the duration of incubation as a means of estimating the intensity of our virus? . . . [This method, tried under carefully controlled conditions of artificial inoculation in dogs, rabbits, and guinea pigs, developed a virus of *increasing* virulence, a fact in itself embarrassing, except

[1] *The Ideas That Have Influenced Civilization*, X, 324-27, 331-35.

that it indicated that varying degrees of intensity existed in rabies. The problem became one of altering the approach to discover a diminution in intensity. Pasteur continues:]

Jenner [Edward Jenner, who discovered vaccination for smallpox in 1798] was the first to introduce into current science the opinion that the virus which he called the grease of the horse, and which we call now more exactly horse-pox, probably softened its virulence, so to speak, in passing through the cow and before it could be transferred to man without danger. It was therefore natural to think of a possible diminution of the virulence of rabies by a number of passages through the organisms of some animal or other, and the experiment was worth trying. A large number of attempts were made, but the majority of the animal species experimented on exalted the virulence after the manner of rabbits and guinea-pigs; fortunately, however, it was not so with monkeys.

On December 6, 1883, a monkey was trephined and inoculated with the bulb of a dog. . . . The monkey took rabies eleven days later, and when dead served for inoculation into a second monkey, which also took the disease on the eleventh day. A third monkey . . . showed the first symptoms on the twenty-third day, etc. The bulb of each one of the monkeys was inoculated . . . into two rabbits each time. The rabbits inoculated from the first monkey developed rabies between thirteen and sixteen days, those from the second monkey between fourteen and twenty days, those from the third monkey between twenty-six and thirty days, those from the fourth monkey both of them after the twenty-eighth day, those from the fifth monkey after twenty-seven days, those from the sixth monkey after thirty days.

It cannot be doubted after that, that successive passages through monkeys, and

from the several monkeys to rabbits, do diminish the virulence of the virus for the latter animals; they diminish it for dogs also. The dog inoculated with the bulb of the fifth monkey gave an incubation of no less than fifty-eight days. . . . We were therefore actually in possession of a method by means of which we could attenuate the virulence of rabies. . . .

The practical application of those facts gives us a method for the vaccination of dogs against rabies. As a starting point, make use of one of the rabbits inoculated from a monkey sufficiently removed from the first animal of the monkey series for the inoculation . . . not to be mortal for a new rabbit. The next vaccinal inoculations are made with the bulbs of rabbits derived by successive passage from that first rabbit. . . .

I do not speak of the micro-organism of rabies. We have not got it. The process for isolating it is still imperfect. . . . Long still will the art of preventing diseases have to grapple with virulent maladies the micro-organic germs of which will escape our investigations. It is, therefore, a capital scientific fact that we should be able, after all, to discover the vaccination process for a virulent disease without yet having at our disposal its special virus and whilst yet ignorant of how to isolate or to cultivate its microbe.

As soon as the method for the vaccination of dogs was firmly established, and we had in our possession a large number of dogs which had been rendered refractory to rabies, I had the idea of submitting to a competent committee those of the facts which appeared destined in future to serve as a basis for the vaccination of dogs against rabies. . . . [Thus Pasteur persuaded the Minister of Public Instruction to appoint a Rabies Commission, the first report of which Pasteur summarizes as follows:]

The Rabies Commission have, therefore,

experimented on thirty-eight dogs alto-gether—namely, nineteen refractory dogs and nineteen control dogs susceptible of taking the disease. . . . The Commission . . . find that out of the nineteen control dogs six were bitten, of which six three have taken rabies. Seven received intra-venous inoculations, of which five have died of rabies. Five were trephined and inoculated on the brain; the five have died of rabies.

On the other hand, not one of the nine-teen vaccinated dogs [though similarly bitten and inoculated] has taken rabies.

THE GERM THEORY OF DISEASE: KOCH

From CASTIGLIONI, *History of Medicine* (1936) [1]

The one who brought one of the great-est contributions to the young science of microbiology and gave a new impetus to its advancement was a young district phy-sician in a small Prussian town, Robert Koch (1843-1910). Born at Klausthal (Hanover), Koch was graduated in medi-cine in 1866 at Göttingen. . . . After serv-ing through the Franco-Prussian War, he became District Physician at Wollstein (1872), where in addition to his routine of country work he began his immortal bacteriological studies. Already in 1873 he had begun the study of the anthrax bacil-lus, having observed the frequent grave manifestations of that disease in his local-ity. He was able, for the first time in his-tory, to work out the complete life cycle of the bacillus, transmitting it through many generations of mice and always producing the disease. He was also able to grow it on artificial media. His study of its spores threw new light on the question of how

[1] Arturo Castiglioni, *A History of Medicine,* trans. and ed. by E. B. Krumbhaar, 1941, 808-10. By permission of Alfred A. Knopf, Inc., New York.

the infection occurred and how long it might last.

Koch's success in this work, confirmed by further experiments of Pasteur . . . led him in 1876 to seek an interview with Ferdinand Cohn, Professor of Botany at Breslau, to demonstrate his observations. Cohn and his colleagues and pupils, Auer-bach, Weigert, Cohnkeim, Welch, Traube, became at once delighted supporters of Koch's views. . . . Following the publi-cation of this work [1878], which was of fundamental importance in the problem of surgical infection, Koch was given an important post in the Imperial Health De-partment, with Loeffler and Gaffky as his assistants. There he continued his studies that resulted in the constant improvement of technical methods—pure cultures, stain-ing and microscopic examination of bac-teria, and so on—work which he had first written about in 1877. With his technical innovations and photographic reproduc-tion of bacterial preparations and unremit-ting search for further improvements, and with utilization of such advances in the microscope as the oil immersion lens, he complemented the work of Pasteur in placing the new science on a firm basis. His ability as a patient and methodical investigator also found expression in his use of *transparent and solidifiable media,* such as gelatin and agar, which can be liquefied at temperatures sufficiently low not to harm the bacteria, yet solidify at room temperature. With suitable dilution single bacteria could thus be isolated and colonies grown in pure culture. By the use of this method most of the pathogenic bacteria were isolated and their properties gradually learned. In 1882, an outstanding date in the history of medicine, Koch pre-sented to the Berlin Physiological Society his discovery of the tubercle bacillus, which was also cultivated by him. This discovery definitely established the infectiousness of tuberculosis. . . . The pathological picture of tuberculosis was now established in its broad lines. In this article also Koch first announced his famous Postulates . . . outlining the four steps necessary to prove that a given organism was the cause of a given disease. . . . Koch's .investigations covered most of the field of bacteriology— malaria, recurrent fever, rinderpest, and so on. . . .

Robert Koch was one of the most famous men of his time and one of Germany's greatest scientists. By physicians, scientific institutes, and governments throughout the world he was given the highest honors and the most distinguished scientific awards. He gathered about him pupils who occupy illustrious positions in the history of bacteriology. . . .Though possessed of esteem and admiration of his colleagues, he did not acquire the popularity of Pasteur, partly because of his austere, distant manner, partly perhaps because of certain episodes in his private life which alienated the sympathy of many of his colleagues. Nevertheless, his great accomplishments, in bacteriology and in hygiene, the vastness of his knowledge, and the importance of his investigations ensure him permanently a leading role in the history of bacteriology.

3. The Darwin Theory of Evolution

Probably no idea of modern times has affected men's thinking more, or led to more controversy, than the Darwin theory of evolution. Its author, Charles Darwin (1809-1882), devoted the whole of his adult life to its substantiation and exposition. Shipping as a naturalist on H.M.S. *Beagle* in 1831, he spent five years in the southern Atlantic and Pacific areas collecting, classifying, and studying all kinds of living creatures— plants, fishes, animals, and natives. After he returned to England, he continued his studies with experiments in pigeon breeding and with domestic plants and animals. He developed a tentative theory of evolution as early as 1844, but withheld publication pending further proofs. The principal results of his work are contained in two books, *The Origin of Species,* first published in 1859, and *The Descent of Man,* published in 1871. The first, as Darwin said, is "one long argument," the main features of which are: 1. Nature gives birth to more individuals of every species than can survive. 2. Therefore, within each species, among the various species, and between the individual and the conditions of its life, there is a constant struggle for existence. 3. Variation, or differences between members of the same species, makes some individuals better adapted to their environment than others, and accordingly better fitted to survive. 4. This brings into operation the law of natural selection between the more and the less adaptable individuals. 5. The result is the survival of the fittest. Darwin's second book is but a specific application of his theory to consider "firstly, whether man, like every other species, is descended from some pre-existing form; secondly, the manner of his development; and thirdly, the value of the differences between the so-called races of man." Darwin's work rested squarely on that of his predecessors and contemporaries. The idea of evolution was very old, but not until the flora and fauna of. the world had been fairly well classified, not until after the beginnings of geology, archaeology, and anthropology, could Darwin's work be done.

From DARWIN, *The Origin of Species* (1859) [1]

INTRODUCTION

When on board H.M.S. "Beagle," as naturalist, I was much struck with certain facts in the distribution of the organic beings inhabiting South America, and in the geological relations of the present to the past inhabitants of that continent. These facts, as will be seen in the latter chapters of this volume, seemed to throw some light on the origin of species—that mystery of mysteries, as it has been called by one of our greatest philosophers. On my return home, it occurred to me, in 1837, that something might perhaps be made out on this question by patiently accumulating and reflecting on all sorts of facts which could possibly have any bearing on it. After five years' work I allowed myself to speculate on the subject, and drew up some short notes; these I enlarged in 1844 into a sketch of the conclusions, which then seemed to me probable: from that period to the present day I have steadily pursued the same object. I hope that I may be excused for entering on these personal details, as I give them to show that I have not been hasty in coming to a decision.

My work is now (1859) nearly finished; but as it will still take me many more years to complete it, and as my health is far from strong, I have been urged to publish this Abstract. I have more especially been induced to do this, as Mr. [Alfred Russell] Wallace, who is now studying the natural history of the Malay archipelago, has arrived at almost exactly the same general conclusions that I have on the origin of species. . . .

In considering the Origin of Species, it is quite conceivable that a naturalist, re-

flecting on the mutual affinities of organic beings, on their embryological relations, their geographical distribution, geological succession, and other such facts, might come to the conclusion that species had not been independently created, but had descended, like varieties, from other species. Nevertheless, such a conclusion, even if well founded, would be unsatisfactory, until it could be shown how the innumerable species inhabiting this world have been modified, so as to acquire that perfection of structure and coadaptation which justly excites our admiration. Naturalists continually refer to external conditions, such as climate, food, etc., as the only possible cause of variation. In one limited sense, as we shall hereafter see, this may be true; but it is preposterous to attribute to mere external conditions, the structure, for instance, of the woodpecker, with its feet, tail, beak, and tongue, so admirably adapted to catch insects under the bark of trees. In the case of the mistletoe, which draws its nourishment from certain trees, which has seeds that must be transported by certain birds, and which has flowers with separate sexes absolutely requiring the agency of certain insects to bring pollen from one flower to another, it is equally preposterous to account for the structure of this parasite, with its relations to several distinct organic beings, by the effects of external conditions, or of habit, or of the volition of the plant itself.

It is, therefore, of the highest importance to gain a clear insight into the means of modification and coadaptation. At the commencement of my observations it seemed to me probable that a careful study of domesticated animals and of cultivated plants would offer the best chance of making out this obscure problem. Nor have I been disappointed; in this and in all other perplexing cases I have invariably found that our knowledge, imperfect though it be, of variation under domes-

[1] This and the next selection are from Charles Darwin, *The Origin of Species* . . . and *The Descent of Man*, n.d. (*The Modern Library*). By permission of Random House, New York. This is 11-13, 367-68, 373-74.

tication, afforded the best and safest clue. . . .

From these considerations, I shall devote the first chapter of this Abstract to Variation under Domestication. We shall thus see that a large amount of hereditary modification is at least possible; and what is equally or more important, we shall see how great is the power of man in accumulating by his Selection successive slight variations. I will then pass on to the variability of species in a state of nature . . . to discuss what circumstances are most favourable to variation. In the next chapter the Struggle for Existence amongst all organic beings throughout the world, which inevitably follows from the high geometrical ratio of their increase, will be considered. This is the doctrine of Malthus, applied to the whole animal and vegetable kingdoms. As many more individuals of each species are born than can possibly survive; and as, consequently, there is a frequently recurring struggle for existence, it follows that any being, if it vary however slightly in any manner profitable to itself, under the complex and sometimes varying conditions of life, will have a better chance of surviving, and thus be *naturally selected*. From the strong principle of inheritance, any selected variety will tend to propagate its new and modified form.

This fundamental subject of Natural Selection will be treated at some length in the fourth chapter; and we shall then see how Natural Selection almost inevitably causes much Extinction of the less improved forms of life, and leads to what I have called Divergence of Character. In the next chapter I shall discuss the complex and little known laws of variation. In the five succeeding chapters, the most apparent and gravest difficulties in accepting the theory will be given; namely, first, the difficulties of transitions, or how a simple being or a simple organ can be changed and perfected into a highly developed being or into an elaborately constructed organ; secondly, the subject of Instinct, or the mental powers of animals; thirdly, hybridism, or the infertility of species and the fertility of varieties when intercrossed; and fourthly, the imperfection of the Geological Record. In the next chapter I shall consider the geological succession of organic beings throughout time; in the twelfth and thirteenth, their geographical distribution throughout space; in the fourteenth, their classification or mutual affinities, both when in mature and in an embryonic condition. In the last chapter I shall give a brief recapitulation of the whole work, and a few concluding remarks. . . .

CONCLUSION

I have now recapitulated the facts and considerations which have thoroughly convinced me that species have been modified, during a long course of descent. This has been effected chiefly through the natural selection of numerous successive, slight, favourable variations; aided in an important manner by the inherited effects of the use and disuse of parts; and in an unimportant manner, that is, in relation to adaptive structures, whether past or present, by the direct action of external conditions, and by variations which seem to us in our ignorance to arise spontaneously. It appears that I formerly underrated the frequency and value of these latter forms of variation, as leading to permanent modifications of structure independently of natural selection. But as my conclusions have lately been much misrepresented, and it has been stated that I attribute the modification of species exclusively to natural selection, I may be permitted to remark that in the first edition of this work, and subsequently, I placed in the most conspicuous position—namely, at the close of the Introduction—the following words:

"I am convinced that natural selection has been the main but not the exclusive means of modification." . . .

I see no good reason why the views given in this volume should shock the religious feelings of any one. It is satisfactory, as showing how transient such impressions are, to remember that the greatest discovery ever made by man, namely, the law of the attraction of gravity, was also attacked by Leibnitz, "as subversive of natural, and inferentially of revealed, religion." A celebrated author and divine has written to me that "he has gradually learnt to see that it is just as noble a conception of the Deity to believe that He created a few original forms capable of self-development into other and needful forms, as to believe that He required a fresh act of creation to supply the voids caused by the action of His laws." . . .

It is interesting to contemplate a tangled bank, clothed with many plants of many kinds, with birds singing on the bushes, with various insects flitting about, and with worms crawling through the damp earth, and to reflect that these elaborately constructed forms, so different from each other, and dependent upon each other in so complex a manner, have all been produced by laws acting around us. These laws, taken in the largest sense, being Growth with Reproduction; Inheritance which is almost implied by reproduction; Variability from the indirect and direct action of the conditions of life, and from use and disuse; a Ratio of Increase so high as to lead to a Struggle for Life, and as a consequence to Natural Selection, entailing Divergence of Character and the Extinction of less-improved forms. Thus, from the war of nature, from famine and death, the most exalted object which we are capable of conceiving, namely, the production of higher animals, directly follows. There is grandeur in this view of life, with its several powers, having been originally breathed by the Creator into a few forms or into one; and that, whilst this planet has gone cycling on according to the fixed law of gravity, from so simple a being endless forms most beautiful and most wonderful have been, and are being evolved.

From DARWIN, *The Descent of Man* (1871) [1]

GENERAL SUMMARY

The main conclusion here arrived at, and now held by many naturalists who are competent to form a sound judgment, is that man is descended from some less highly organized form. The grounds upon which this conclusion rests will never be shaken, for the close similarity between man and the lower animals in embryonic development, as well as in innumerable points of structure and constitution, both of high and of the most trifling importance—the rudiments which he retains, and the abnormal reversions to which he is occasionally liable—are facts which cannot be disputed. They have long been known, but until recently they told us nothing with respect to the origin of man. Now when viewed by the light of our knowledge of the whole organic world, their meaning is unmistakable. The great principle of evolution stands up clear and firm, when these groups or facts are considered in connection with others, such as the mutual affinities of the members of the same group, their geographical distribution in past and present times, and their geological succession. It is incredible that all these facts should speak falsely. He who is not content to look, like a savage, at the phenomena of nature as disconnected, cannot any longer believe that man is the work of a separate act of creation. He will be forced to admit that the close resemblance of the embryo of man to that,

[1] *Ibid.*, 909-11, 919-20.

for instance, of a dog—the construction of his skull, limbs, and whole frame on the same plan with that of other mammals, independently of the uses to which the parts may be put—the occasional re-appearance of various structures, for instance of several muscles, which man does not normally possess, but which are common to the Quadrumana—and a crowd of analogous facts—all point in the plainest manner to the conclusion that man is the co-descendant with other mammals of a common progenitor.

We have seen that man incessantly presents individual differences in all parts of his body and in his mental faculties. These differences or variations seem to be induced by the same general causes, and to obey the same laws as with the lower animals. . . .

Through the means just specified, aided perhaps by others as yet undiscovered, man has been raised to his present state. But since he attained to the rank of manhood, he has diverged into distinct races, or as they may be more fitly called, sub-species. . . . Nevertheless all the races agree in so many unimportant details of structure and in so many mental peculiarities that these can be accounted for only by inheritance from a common progenitor; and a progenitor thus characterized would probably deserve to rank as man.

It must not be supposed that the divergence of each race from the other races, and of all from a common stock, can be traced back to any one pair of progenitors. On the contrary, at every stage in the process of modification, all the individuals which were in any way better fitted for their conditions of life, though in different degrees, would have survived in greater numbers than the less well-fitted. The process would have been like that followed by man, when he does not intentionally select particular individuals, but breeds from all the superior individuals, and neglects the inferior. He thus slowly but surely modifies his stock, and unconsciously forms a new strain. So with respect to modifications acquired independently of selection, and due to variations arising from the nature of the organism and the action of the surrounding conditions, or from changed habits of life, no single pair will have been modified much more than the other pairs inhabiting the same country, for all will have been continually blended through free intercrossing. . . .

CONCLUSION

The main conclusion arrived at in this work, namely, that man is descended from some lowly organized form, will, I regret to think, be highly distasteful to many. But there can hardly be a doubt that we are descended from barbarians. The astonishment which I felt on first seeing a party of Fuegians on a wild and broken shore will never be forgotten by me, for the reflection at once rushed into my mind—such were our ancestors. . . . He who has seen a savage in his native land will not feel much shame, if forced to acknowledge that the blood of some more humble creature flows in his veins. . . . Man may be excused for feeling some pride at having risen, though not through his own exertions, to the very summit of the organic scale. . . . But we are not here concerned with hopes or fears, only with the truth as far as our reason permits us to discover it; and I have given the evidence to the best of my ability. We must, however, acknowledge, as it seems to me, that man with all his noble qualities, with sympathy which feels for the most debased, with benevolence which extends not only to other men but to the humblest living creature, with his god-like intellect which has penetrated into the movements and constitutions of the solar system—with all these exalted powers—Man still bears in his bodily frame the indelible stamp of his lowly origin.

4. Social Darwinism: Herbert Spencer on "Progress: Its Law and Cause"

Darwin was concerned with biology and natural history; he was cautious about extending the theory of evolution to social, political, and economic matters. But his contemporaries were not so reticent. Soon the evolutionary concept was applied to all society; "progress" became an inevitable "evolution"; "competition" became the economic area in which the law of natural selection—the survival of the fittest—operated; the concepts of laissez faire, individual freedom, and other tenets of Liberalism appeared justified as ways to avoid interference in the operation of a natural law of society. Foremost in the extension of the evolutionary concept to social affairs was Herbert Spencer (1820-1903), an English engineer who became a social philosopher interested in synthesizing and explaining the scientific achievements of his own day to his own generation. Spencer was one of the first to accept Darwin's theory; to him it explained all existence, organic and inorganic. In a series of enthusiastic—but sometimes shallow—articles and books, Spencer flooded the reading public for forty years with the philosophy of evolution. A liberal himself, he endeared himself to the triumphant bourgeoisie, who saw in "social Darwinism" a logical and emphatic defense of laissez faire and a scientifically constructed weapon against Socialism. Spencer explained "Progress" in one of his early articles.

From SPENCER, "Progress" (1867) [1]

The current conception of progress is shifting and indefinite. Sometimes it comprehends little more than simple growth—as of a nation in the number of its members and the extent of territory over which it spreads. Sometimes it has reference to quantity of material products—as when the advance of agriculture and manufactures is the topic. . . . Not only, however, is the current conception of progress more or less vague, but it is in great measure erroneous. It takes in not so much the reality of progress as its accompaniments—not so much the substance as the shadow. . . . Social progress is supposed to consist in the making of a greater quantity and variety of articles required for satisfying men's wants; in the increasing security of person and property; in widening freedom of action; whereas, rightly understood, social progress consists in those changes of structure in the social organism which have entailed these consequences. . . . Rightly to understand progress, we must learn the nature of these changes, considered apart from their interests. . . .

In respect to that progress which individual organisms display in the course of their evolution, this question has been answered by the Germans. The investigations of Wolff, Goethe, and von Baer, have established the truth that the series of changes gone through during the development of a seed into a tree, or an ovum into an animal, constitute an advance from homogeneity of structure to heterogeneity of structure. . . . This is the history of all organisms whatever. It is settled beyond dispute that organic progress consists in a change from the homogeneous to the heterogeneous.

Now, we propose in the first place to

[1] *Westminster Review*, N.S., XI (April, 1867), 445-56, 465-67.

show that this law of organic progress is the law of all progress. Whether it be in the development of the earth, in the development of life upon its surface, in the development of society, of government, of manufactures, of commerce, of language, literature, science, art, this same evolution of the simple into the complex, through successive differentiations, holds throughout. . . .

Let us descend to a more certain order of evidence. It is now generally agreed among geologists and physicists that the earth was at one time a mass of molten matter. If so, it was at that time relatively homogeneous in consistence and : . . in temperature. . . . [As it cooled, solidified, stratified, and so on it became less simple.] Thus, between our existing earth . . . and the molten globe out of which it evolved, the contrast in heterogeneity is extreme. When from the earth itself we turn to plants and animals which have lived, or still live, upon its surface, we find ourselves in some difficulty from lack of facts. [Darwin helped greatly to supply this deficiency.] That every existing organism has been developed out of the simple into the complex, is indeed the first established truth of all; and that every organism which existed in past times was similarly developed, is an inference no physiologist will hesitate to draw. . . . Nevertheless we cannot but think, scanty as they are, the facts, taken altogether, tend to show both that the more heterogeneous organisms have been evolved in the later geologic periods, and that life in general has been more heterogeneously manifested as time has advanced. . . . Whether an advance from the homogeneous to the heterogeneous is or is not displayed in the biological history of the globe, it is clearly enough displayed in the progress of the latest and most heterogeneous creature—man. It is true alike that, during the period in which the earth has been peopled, the human organism has grown more heterogeneous among the civilized divisions of the species; and that the species as a whole has been growing more heterogeneous in virtue of the multiplication of races and the differentiation of these races from each other. . . .

On passing from humanity under its individual form, to humanity as socially embodied, we find the general law still more variously exemplified. The change from the homogeneous to the heterogeneous is displayed in the progress of civilization as a whole, as well as in the progress of every nation; and is still going on with increasing rapidity. As we see in existing barbarous tribes, society in its first and lowest form is a homogeneous aggregation of individuals having like powers and like functions: the only marked difference of function being that which accompanies difference of sex. Every man is warrior, hunter, fisherman, tool-maker, builder; every woman performs the same drudgeries. Very early, however, in the course of social evolution, there arises an incipient differentiation between the governing and the governed. . . . Gradually, as the tribe progresses, the contrast . . . grows more decided. Supreme power becomes hereditary in one family; the head of that family . . is served by others . . . there has been arising a co-ordinate species of government—that of religion. . . . For a long time these connate forms of government—civil and religious—remain closely associated. . . . Each of these is itself subject to successive differentiations. In the course of ages there arises, as among ourselves, a highly complex political organization of monarch, ministers, lords and commons [and so on]. . . . By its side there grows up a highly complex religious organization, with its various grades of officials . . . to all of which must be added the ever-multiplying independent sects, each with its general and local authorities. . . . Simultaneously there has been going on a second differentiation . . . that, namely, by which the mass of the community has been segregated into distinct classes and orders of workers. . . . It has been an evolution which . . . ends with a civilized community whose members severally perform different actions for each other; and an evolution which has transformed the solitary producer of any one commodity into a combination of producers who, united under a master, take separate parts in the manufacture of such a commodity. . . . So that, beginning with a barbarous tribe, almost if not quite homogeneous in the functions of its members, the progress has been, and still is, towards an economic aggregation of the whole human race; growing ever more heterogeneous in respect of the separate functions assumed by separate nations . . . by the local sections of each nation . . . by the many kinds of makers and traders in each town, and . . . by the workers united in producing each commodity.

The law thus clearly exemplified in the evolution of the social organism is exemplified with equal clearness in the evolution of all products of human thought and action; whether concrete or abstract, real or ideal. . . . [Here Spencer illustrates by the growth of language (philology), literature, art, religion, and science, each of which displays an "advance from the homogeneous to the heterogeneous."]

And now . . . does not the universality of the law imply a universal cause? . . . We may suspect a priori that in some universal law of change lies the explanation of this universal transformation of the homogeneous into the heterogeneous. Thus much premised, we pass at once to the statement of the law, which is this: Every active force produces more than one change—every cause produces more than one effect. . . . Universally the effect is more complex than the cause.

Doubtless the reader already foresees the course of our argument. This multiplica-tion of effects, which is displayed in every event of today, has been going on from the beginning; and it is true of the grandest phenomena of the universe as of the most insignificant. From the law that every active force produces more than one change, it is an inevitable corollary that during the past there has been an ever-growing complication of things. Throughout creation there must have gone on, and must still go on, a never-ceasing transformation of the homogeneous into the heterogeneous.

5. *The Church* vs. *Liberalism*

Liberalism and its implementation in the nineteenth century early aroused opposition from churches. The reactionaries at Vienna, in France, in Spain, and in Italy, opposed it on religious grounds [see page 468]; and in England, John Henry Newman, John Keble, Edward Pusey, and other leaders of the Oxford Movement, in their *Tracts for the Times* (1833-41), denounced Liberalism's freedom of speech, subjection of Church to State, materialism, and tendencies "to destroy the basis of revealed religion, and ultimately all that can be called religion at all," and many of the Oxford Movement leaders ended up by embracing the Roman Catholic faith. Within the Roman Church itself, especially in France, an effort was made to "liberalize" the church or, more accurately, to catholicize Liberalism; "You tremble before Liberalism," wrote Félicité Robert de Lamennais, "catholicize it and the world will be saved." But the efforts were vain; neither the church nor the liberals would bridge the chasm which separated them. Pius IX (1846-78), to be sure, had a preliminary liberal fling, but the revolutions of 1848 condemned

Liberalism in his eyes, and he began at once to strengthen the position of the Roman Church against its liberal and socialist enemies. As a matter of doctrinal strength, the Immaculate Conception of the Mother of God was defined by a bull issued December 8, 1854. Meanwhile, an ecclesiastical commission was set up (1852) to define the errors of the times. After long preliminaries, a congregation of Cardinals formulated the *Syllabus of the Principal Errors of Our Time, Which Are Stigmatized in the Consistorial Allocutions, Encyclicals, and Other Apostolical Letters of Our Most Holy Father, Pope Pius IX,* which was issued by the Pope in 1864. Consisting of eighty-one propositions, in its cumulative effect it reads like an indictment of contemporary civilization. In reading the following extracts, the reader must remember that each statement is the *exact opposite* of the belief sanctioned by the Pope.

From the *Syllabus of Errors* (1864) [1]

I. PANTHEISM, NATURALISM, AND ABSOLUTE RATIONALISM

1. There exists no supreme, all-wise, most provident divine Being, distinct from the universe; God and nature are one, and God is therefore subject to change; actually, God is produced in man and in the world; God and the world are identical, as are spirit and matter, true and false, good and evil, just and unjust. . . .

3. Human reason, without any regard whatsoever to God, is the sole judge of the true and the false, of good and evil; it is a law unto itself, and suffices by its natural powers to secure the welfare of men and nations.

[1] This and the next selection are from the translation in Raymond Corrigan, *The Church and the Nineteenth Century.* By permission of The Bruce Publishing Company, Milwaukee. This is 289-95.

4. All truths of religion derive from the natural force of human reason; hence reason is the principle rule by which man can and should attain the knowledge of all truths of whatever kind. . . .

6. Faith in Christ is opposed to human reason; and divine revelation is not only unprofitable, but is even harmful to the perfection of man.

7. Prophecies and miracles, set forth and narrated in Holy Scripture, are poetical fictions; the mysteries of Christian faith are the results of philosophic investigations; in the books of both Testaments are contained mythical inventions; and Jesus Christ Himself is a mythical fiction. . . .

II. MODERATE RATIONALISM . . .

9. Without exception, all the dogmas of the Christian religion are the object of natural science or philosophy; and human reason, developed solely by history, can by its own natural strength and principles arrive at the true knowledge of even the more abstruse dogmas, provided these dogmas be proposed as the object of reason. . . .

III. INDIFFERENTISM, LATITUDINARIANISM

15. Every man is free to embrace and profess that religion which, guided by the light of reason, he shall believe true.

16. Men may, in any religion, find the way of eternal salvation and attain eternal salvation. . . .

18. Protestantism is nothing but another form of the same true Christian religion, in which it is equally possible to please God as in the Catholic Church.

IV. SOCIALISM, COMMUNISM, SECRET SOCIETIES, BIBLICAL SOCIETIES, CLERICO-LIBERAL SOCIETIES

Plagues of this variety are reprobated in the strongest terms in various Encyclicals.

V. ERRORS CONCERNING THE CHURCH AND HER RIGHTS

19. The Church is not a true, perfect and entirely free society, nor does she enjoy peculiar and perpetual rights conferred upon her by her Divine Founder; it belongs to the civil power to define what are the rights of the Church and the limits within which she can exercise them.

20. The Ecclesiastical power must not exercise its authority without the permission and assent of civil government.

21. The Church has not the power of defining dogmatically that the religion of the Catholic Church is the only true religion. . . .

24. The Church has no right to employ force, nor any direct or indirect temporal power. . . .

27. The ministers of the Church and the Roman Pontiff ought to be absolutely excluded from all care and dominion over temporal things. . . .

VI. ERRORS CONCERNING CIVIL SOCIETY CONSIDERED BOTH IN ITSELF AND IN ITS RELATION TO THE CHURCH

39. The commonwealth is the origin and source of all rights, and enjoys rights which are not circumscribed by any limits. . . .

42. In the case of conflicting laws of the two powers, civil law prevails. . . .

45. The entire direction of public schools in which the youth of any Christian state are educated, except to some extent in the case of episcopal seminaries, may and must belong to the civil power; and this in such a way that no other authority whatsoever shall be recognized as having any right to interfere in the discipline of the schools, the direction of studies, the conferring of degrees, and the choice and approval of teachers. . . .

47. The best theory of civil authority demands that the public schools which are open to the children of all classes, and in general all public institutions intended for the education of youth in letters and higher learning, shall be free from all ecclesiastical authority, government, and interference, and shall be completely subjected to the civil and political authority according to the desires of the rulers and the opinions of the age. . . .

49. The civil authority may prevent Bishops and the faithful from free and mutual communication with the Roman Pontiff.

50. Civil authority has in itself the right of presenting Bishops and can demand that they take over their dioceses before they have received canonical institution and the apostolic letters from the Holy See. . . .

53. The laws which pertain to the protection of religious bodies and of their rights and duties should be abrogated; moreover, the civil government can assist all those who wish to abandon the religious life and to break their solemn vows; likewise the government can suppress religious bodies, collegiate churches, and simple benefices, even those of private patronage, and take over their goods and revenues to be administered and disposed of by the civil power. . . .

55. The Church should be separated from the State, and the State from the Church. . . .

VII. ERRORS CONCERNING NATURAL AND CHRISTIAN ETHICS . . .

57. The science of philosophy and morals, and likewise of civil laws, may and should be withdrawn from divine and ecclesiastical authority. . . .

59. Rights consist in the mere material fact, and all human duties are an empty name, and every human deed has the force of right.

60. Authority is nothing but the result of numerical superiority and material force. . . .

63. It is lawful to refuse obedience to legitimate princes, and even to rebel against them. . . .

VIII. ERRORS CONCERNING CHRISTIAN MARRIAGE

65. The teaching that Christ elevated marriage to the dignity of a sacrament can in no way be admitted. . . .

67. The marriage bond is not indissoluble according to the natural law, and in certain cases divorce, properly so called, may be sanctioned by civil authority. . . .

73. A civil contract can constitute true marriage among Christians; and it is false to affirm either that the marriage contract was always sacramental or that there is no contract if the sacrament be excluded. . . .

X. ERRORS CONCERNING LIBERALISM OF THE DAY

77. In our times it is no longer necessary that the Catholic religion should be the only religion of the State to the exclusion of all others whatsoever.

78. Hence it has been wisely provided by law that in certain regions, Catholic in name, immigrants shall be allowed the public exercise of their own forms of religion. . . .

80. The Roman Pontiff can and should reconcile and align himself with progress, liberalism, and modern civilization.

THE DOCTRINE OF PAPAL INFALLIBILITY (1870)

Six years after publication of the *Syllabus of Errors,* a Vatican Council, composed of nearly eight hundred ecclesiastics from all over the world, set forth the doctrine of papal infallibility which, in the face of rising constitutionalism and democracy, declared the Roman Church to be a divine-right monarchy (July 18, 1870). But the power of the pope was not an arbitrary power, for the bishops also claimed their position by divine right, and no pope could dispense with their co-operation in the government of the church. The declaration settled, however, the question, which had plagued the church since the Middle Ages, as to whether pope or church council is supreme; for, the council held, "none may reopen the judgment of the Apostolic See, than whose authority there is none greater," and further stated that "they err . . . who assert that it is lawful to appeal from the judgments of the Roman pontiffs to an ecumenical council, as to an authority higher than that of the Roman Pontiff." The Council concluded with the famous doctrine of infallibility, as follows: [1]

Wherefore, faithfully adhering to the tradition handed down from the beginning, for the glory of God our Savior, for the exaltation of the Catholic Religion, and the salvation of Christian peoples, with the approbation of the Sacred Council, we teach and we define the divinely revealed dogma that: when the Roman Pontiff speaks *ex cathedra,* that is, when in the discharge of his office as Doctor and Pastor of all Christians, in virtue of his supreme Apostolic authority, he defines a doctrine concerning faith or morals to be held by the whole Church, he enjoys, by the divine assistance promised him in Blessed Peter, that infallibility with which the divine Redeemer willed that His Church should be endowed for the purpose of defining doctrines concerning faith or morals.

6. *The Roman Church Opposes Socialism*

Although the *Syllabus of Errors* had denounced Socialism, Pope Leo XIII (1878-1903), who issued many encyclicals on social affairs, found it advisable

[1] *Ibid.,* 199.

to clarify the position of the Church—or at least of Pope Leo XIII—on labor problems. In an Encyclical Letter dated May 15, 1891, Leo XIII stated his objections to Socialism and urged means to ameliorate the lot of the working classes.

From LEO XIII, *Encyclical,* "On the Condition of Labor" (1891) [1]

The ancient workmen's Guilds were destroyed in the last century, and no other organization took their place. Public institutions and the laws have repudiated the ancient religion. Hence by degrees it has come to pass that Working Men have been given over, isolated and defenseless, to the callousness of employers and the greed of unrestrained competition. . . . And to this must be added the custom of working by contract, and the concentration of so many branches of trade in the hands of a few individuals, so that a small number of very rich men have been able to lay upon the masses of the poor a yoke little better than slavery itself.

To remedy these evils the *Socialists,* working on the poor man's envy of the rich, endeavor to destroy private property, and maintain that individual possessions should become the common property of all, to be administered by the State or by municipal bodies. They hold that, by thus transferring property from private persons to the community, the present evil state of things will be set to rights, because each citizen will then have his equal share of whatever there is to enjoy. But their proposals are so clearly futile for all practical purposes, that if they were carried out the working man himself would be among the first to suffer. Moreover they are emphatically unjust, because they would rob the lawful possessor, bring the State into

a sphere that is not its own, and cause complete confusion in the community.

PRIVATE OWNERSHIP

It is surely undeniable that, when a man engages in remunerative labor, the very reason and motive of his work is to obtain property, and to hold it as his own private possession. . . . Thus, if he lives sparingly, saves money, and invests his savings, for greater security, in land, the land in such a case is only his wages in another form; and, consequently, a working man's little estate thus purchased should be as completely at his own disposal as the wages he receives for his labor. But it is precisely in this power of disposal that ownership consists, whether the property be land or movable goods. The *Socialists,* therefore, in endeavoring to transfer the possessions of individuals to the community, strike at the interests of every wage earner, for they deprive him of the liberty of disposing of his wages, and thus of all hope and possibility of increasing his stock and of bettering his condition in life.

What is of still greater importance, however, is that the remedy they propose is manifestly against justice. For every man has by nature the right to possess property as his own. . . . The authority of the Divine Law adds its sanction, forbidding us in the gravest terms even to covet that which is another's: "Thou shalt not covet thy neighbor's wife; nor his house, nor his field, nor his man-servant, nor his maid-servant, nor his ox, nor his ass, nor anything which is his." . . .

Thus it is clear *that the main tenet of Socialism, the community of goods, must be utterly rejected;* for it would injure those whom it is intended to benefit, it would be contrary to the natural rights of mankind, and it would introduce confusion and disorder into the commonwealth. Our first and most fundamental principle,

[1] *Five Great Encyclicals,* 1939, 2-3, 5, 7-8, 10. By permission of the Paulist Press, New York.

therefore, when We undertake to alleviate the condition of the masses, must be the inviolability of private property. This laid down, We go on to show where we must find the remedy that We seek. . . .

The great mistake that is made in the matter now under consideration, is to possess oneself of the idea that class is naturally hostile to class; that rich and poor are intended by nature to live at war with one another. So irrational and so false is this view, that the exact contrary is the truth. Just as the symmetry of the human body is the result of the disposition of the members of the body, so in a State it is ordained by nature that these two classes should exist in harmony and agreement, and should, as it were, fit into one another, so as to maintain the equilibrium of the body politic. Each requires the other; capital cannot do without labor, nor labor without capital. Mutual agreement results in pleasantness and good order; perpetual conflict necessarily produces confusion and outrage. Now, in preventing such strife as this, and in making it impossible, the efficacy of Christianity is marvelous and manifold. First of all, there is nothing more powerful than Religion (of which the Church is the interpreter and guardian) in drawing rich and poor together, by reminding each class of its duties to the other, and especially of the duties of justice. Thus Religion teaches the laboring man and the workman to carry out honestly and well all equitable agreements freely made, never to injure capital, nor to outrage the person of an employer; never to employ violence in representing his own cause, nor to engage in riot and disorder; and to have nothing to do with men of evil principles, who work upon the people with artful promises, and raise foolish hopes which usually end in disaster and in repentance when too late. Religion teaches the rich man and the employer

that their work people are not their slaves; that they must respect in every man his dignity as a man and as a Christian; that labor is nothing to be ashamed of, if we listen to right reason and to Christian philosophy, but is an honorable employment, enabling a man to sustain his life in an upright and creditable way; and that it is shameful and inhuman to treat men like chattels to make money by, or to look upon them merely as so much muscle or physical power. Thus, again, Religion teaches that, as among the workmen's concerns are Religion herself, and things spiritual and mental, the employer is bound to see that he has time for the duties of piety; that he be not exposed to corrupting influences and dangerous occasions; and that he be not led away to neglect his home and family or to squander his wages. Then, again, the employer must never tax his work-people beyond their strength, nor employ them in work unsuited to their sex or age. His great and principal obligation is to give to every one that which is just. Doubtless before we can decide whether wages are adequate many things have to be considered; but rich men and masters should remember this—that to exercise pressure for the sake of gain, upon the indigent and destitute, and to make one's profit out of the need of another, is condemned by all laws, human and divine. To defraud anyone of wages that are his due is a crime which cries to the avenging anger of Heaven. . . . Finally, the rich must religiously refrain from cutting down the workman's earnings, either by force, fraud, or by usurious dealing; and with the more reason because the poor man is weak and unprotected, and because his slender means should be sacred in proportion to their scantiness.

Were these precepts carefully obeyed and followed would not strife die out and cease?

But the Church, with Jesus Christ for its Master and Guide, aims higher still. It lays down precepts yet more perfect, and tries to bind class to class in friendliness and good understanding.

7. The Impact of Romanticism upon Literature and Thought

THE GENESIS OF ROMANTICISM

The present-day cultural heritage of the European world derives immediately from the Romantics who, in the realms of art, literature, politics, and philosophy, affected or produced many important phases of nineteenth and twentieth century thought. Yet the term "Romanticism" has such a diversity of meanings that it defies accurate definition. Writers infected with the Romantic spirit appear to have mounted their temperamental hobbies and to have ridden off in all directions. Discernible among the writers of the Romantic Age are a wide variety of apparently unrelated features, such as glorification of uncorrupted nature, individualism intense to the point of demanding the destruction of every barrier to individual growth, revolutionary fervor inspired by nationalistic ideals of unity and liberty, deep religious feeling, and flights of fancy, imagination, and mysticism. At base, however, Romanticism was a reaction against rationalism, science, and materialism—against the rationalists' attempts to explain all human experience in terms of reason alone (see pages 259-262, 364-370).

The Romantics held that man possesses a faculty higher than reason, his imagination, by which, in flashes of intuitive insight, he discerns truths which engulf and transcend the mere physical facts revealed by science and reason. Man may be bound up with the world of the senses, yet he is essentially a spiritual being, determining the material world rather than being determined by it. Regardless of the doubts and criticisms which had swept away traditional and sectarian faiths, man's inner consciousness appeared wholly trustworthy still. Here, then, is a basis for a new religious belief, a belief that it is possible to serve God only by serving man, for man is perfectible, he is advancing slowly toward perfection, and that perfection is divine. The divine, then, is the final goal of life, not its pre-existing cause. The Romantics saw man poised between two worlds, the one a world of ideal truth, goodness, and beauty—an eternal, infinite, and genuine world; the other a world of appearances, of falsehood, ignorance, evil, and wretchedness—a finite world. Through the eyes of his imagination man can see the first world, the real world toward which he is striving. And it becomes the highest function of the arts and literature to portray to man this world in all its beauty. By this means man finds hope in a "Slough of Despond," sees beauty in the midst of ugliness, finds happiness in the prospect of his own perfectibility and ultimate oneness with the divine.

The Romantic Era did not emerge abruptly as a sharply defined reaction against the Age of Reason. A considerable number of "Pre-Romantics" presaged the new movement during the eighteenth century—Rousseau, Samuel Richardson, Laurence Sterne, Oliver Goldsmith, Thomas Gray, Johann Gottfried Herder, Immanuel Kant, and a host of others. Nor was Romanticism opposed to reason: the Romantics simply felt that man was endowed with imagination as well as with reason and that, in the search for truth and beauty, both faculties should be employed—but they allotted to imagination a higher role than they allowed to reason.

That Romanticism was, in the first instance, a reaction against the aesthetic and philosophical limits prescribed by the Age of Reason is well illustrated from the autobiography of Johann Wolfgang von Goethe (1749-1832). About 1770, while Goethe was still a student at Strasbourg, he and his friends began to take exceptions to French rationalism, to Voltaire, the Encyclopedists, and especially to one Encyclopedist, the Baron Holbach, whose atheistic materialism as set forth in his *System of Nature* (1770) was too extreme even for some of the *philosophes* of the Enlightenment (in as much as both Voltaire and Frederick the Great wrote in refutation of it). Goethe, whose works trumpeted the Romantic revolution in German literature, commented as follows.

From GOETHE, *Autobiography* (1811) [1]

To us youths, before whom . . . honesty towards ourselves and others hovered as the best guide both in life and learning, the factious dishonesty of Voltaire and the perversion of so many worthy subjects became more and more annoying, and we daily strengthened ourselves in our aversion from him. He could never have done with degrading religion and the sacred books for the sake of injuring priestcraft, as they called it, and had thus produced in me many an unpleasant sensation. But when I now learned that, to weaken the tradition of a deluge, he had denied all

[1] *The Autobiography of Goethe. Truth and Poetry: From My Own Life,* trans. by John Oxenford, 2 vols., London, 1874, I, Bk. XI, 419-22, 424-26.

petrified shells, and only admitted them as *lusus naturæ* [a sport of nature], he entirely lost my confidence; for my own eyes had, on the Baschberg, plainly enough shown me that I stood on the bottom of an old dried-up sea, among the *exuviae* [shells] of its original inhabitants. These mountains had certainly been once covered with waves, whether before or after the deluge did not concern me; it was enough that the valley of the Rhine had been a monstrous lake . . . out of this I was not to be talked. . . .

French literature, then, had grown old and genteel in itself, and through Voltaire [to whom it had become subjugated]. . . .

If we heard the Encyclopaedists mentioned, or opened a volume of their monstrous work, we felt as if we were going between the innumerable moving spools and looms in a great factory, where, what with the mere creaking and rattling— what with all the mechanism, embarrassing both eyes and noses—what with the mere incomprehensibility of an arrangement, the parts of which work into each other in the most manifold way—what with the contemplation of all that is necessary to prepare a piece of cloth, we feel disgusted with the very coat which we wear upon our backs. . . .

All this, and much else, right and foolish, true and half-true, operating upon us as it did, still more perplexed our notions; we were driven astray through many byways and roundabout ways, and thus on many sides was prepared that German literary revolution, of which we were witnesses, and to which, consciously or unconsciously, willingly or unwillingly, we unceasingly contributed.

We had neither impulse nor tendency to be illumined and advanced in a philosophical manner; on religious subjects we thought we had sufficiently enlightened ourselves, and therefore the violent contest of the French philosophers with the priesthood was tolerably indifferent to us. Prohibited books condemned to the flames, which then made a great noise, produced no effect upon us. I mention as an instance, to serve for all, the *Système de la Nature,* which we took in hand out of curiosity. We did not understand how such a book could be dangerous. It appeared to us so dark, so Cimmerian, so deathlike, that we found it a trouble to endure its presence, and shuddered at it as at a spectre. The author fancies he gives his book a peculiar recommendation, when he declares in his preface, that as a decrepit old man, just sinking into the grave, he wishes to announce the truth to his cotemporaries and to posterity.

We laughed him out; for we thought we had observed that by old people nothing in the world that is loveable and good is in fact appreciated. "Old churches have dark windows; to know how cherries and berries taste, we must ask children and sparrows." [1] These were our gibes and maxims; and thus that book, as the very quintessence of senility, appeared to us as unsavoury, nay, absurd. "All was to be of necessity," so said the book, "and therefore there was no God." But could there not be a God by necessity too? asked we. We indeed confessed, at the same time, that we could not withdraw ourselves from the necessities of day and night, the seasons, the influence of climate, physical and animal condition; but nevertheless we felt that within us something that appeared like perfect freedom of will, and again something which sought to counterbalance this freedom. . . .

None of us had read the book through;

[1] Compare Wordsworth's "The Prelude," Bk. xi:
". . . Youth maintains,
In all conditions of society,
Communion more direct and intimate
With Nature,—hence, ofttimes, with reason too—
Than age or manhood, even."

for we found ourselves deceived in the expectations with which we had opened it. A system of nature was announced; and therefore we had hoped to learn really something of nature—our idol. Physics and chemistry, descriptions of heaven and earth, natural history and anatomy, with much else, had now for years, and up to the last day, constantly directed us to the great adorned world; and we would willingly have heard both particulars and generals about suns and stars, planets and moons, mountains, valleys, rivers and seas, with all that live and move in them. That in the course of this, much must occur which would appear to the common man as injurious, to the clergy as dangerous, and to the state as inadmissible, we had no doubt; and we hoped that the little book had not unworthily stood the fiery ordeal. But how hollow and empty did we feel in this melancholy, atheistical halfnight, in which the earth vanished with all its images, heaven with all its stars. There was to be a matter in motion from all eternity, and by this motion, right and left and in every direction, without anything further, it was to produce the infinite phenomena of existence. Even all this we should have allowed to pass, if the author, out of his moved matter, had really built up the world before our eyes. But he seemed to know as little about nature as we did; for, having set up some general ideas, he quits them at once, for the sake of changing that which appears as higher than nature, or as a higher nature within nature, into material, heavy nature, which is moved, indeed, but without direction or form—and thus he fancies he has gained a great deal.

If, after all, this book did us any mischief, it was this—that we took a hearty dislike to all philosophy, and especially metaphysics, and remained in that dislike; while, on the other hand, we threw ourselves into living knowledge, experience, action, and poetising, with all the more liveliness and passion.

Thus, on the very borders of France, we had at once got rid and clear of everything French about us. The French way of life we found too defined and genteel, their poetry cold, their criticism annihilating, their philosophy abstruse, and yet insufficient, so that we were on the point of resigning ourselves to rude nature, at least by way of experiment, if another influence had not for a long time prepared us for higher and freer views of the world, and intellectual enjoyments as true as they were poetical, and swayed us, first moderately and secretly, but afterwards with more and more openness and force.

[The other "influence" to which Goethe refers was that of William Shakespeare, whose works, only then recently translated into German, brought from Goethe's "Strasbourg society" first admiration and then imitation. "I revere the rhythm as well as the rhyme," said Goethe, and the inspiration he received from the English master went far to hasten that "German literary revolution" of which Goethe was a principal part.]

EXAMPLES OF ROMANTIC LITERATURE

GOETHE

As the entire literary production of the Romantics fills scores of volumes, only a very small sample of the whole can be included in this volume. We shall begin with excerpts from Goethe's greatest work, *Faust,* even though Goethe turned from Romanticism to an increasing Classicism in his later years. The story of *Faust,* conceived in Goethe's youth but not completed until his old manhood, is that of a learned man striving for complete understanding. A compound of idealist and base

realist (as represented in the drama by Faust and Mephistopheles), Faust turns away from barren knowledge to nature and action—to life—to discover, after many trials and grievous errors (into which Mephistopheles leads him), that only by striving for the happiness of others—for mankind—can he avoid evil and ignorance and acquire "the highest bliss." At the outset, in his discontent, Faust says: [1]

Alas! I have explored
Philosophy, and Law, and Medicine;
And over deep Divinity have pored,
Studying with ardent and laborious zeal;
And here I am at last, a very fool,
With useless learning curst,
No wiser than at first!
Here am I—boast and wonder of the
    school;
Magister, Doctor, and I lead
These ten years past, my pupils' creed;
Winding, by dexterous words, with ease,
Their opinions as I please.
And now to feel that nothing can be
    known!
This is a thought that burns into my heart.
I have been more acute than all these
    triflers,
Doctors and authors, priests, philosophers;
Have sounded all the depths of every
    science.
Scruples, or the perplexity of doubt,
Torment me not, nor fears of hell or devil.
But I have lost all peace of mind:
Whate'er I knew, or thought I knew,
Seems now unmeaning or untrue.
The fancy too has died away,
The hope, that I might, in my day,
Instruct, and elevate mankind.
Thus robbed of learning's only pleasure,
Without dominion, rank, or treasure,
Without one joy that earth can give,
Could dog—were I a dog—so live? . . .

[1] *Faust,* Part I, trans. by John Anster, Leipzig, 1867, 23-24, 41, 65-66.

Every thing fails me—every thing—
These instruments, do they not all
Mock me? lathe, cylinder, and ring,
And cog and wheel—in vain I call
On you for aid, ye keys of Science,
I stand before the guarded door
Of Nature; but it bids defiance
To latch or ward: in vain I prove
Your powers—the strong bolts will not
    move.
Mysterious, in the blaze of day,
Nature pursues her tranquil way:
The veil she wears, if hand profane
Should seek to raise, it seeks in vain,
Though from her spirit thine receives,
When hushed it listens and believes,
Secrets—revealed, else vainly sought,
Her free gift when man questions not,—
Think not with levers or with screws
To wring them out if she refuse. . . .

In my breast
Alas! two souls dwell—all there is unrest;
Each from the other strives for mastery,
Each from the other struggles to be free.
One to the fleshy joys the coarse earth
    yields,
With clumsy tendrils clings, and one
    would rise
In native power and vindicate the fields,
Its own by birthright—its ancestral skies.

WORDSWORTH

William Wordsworth (1770-1850),
the great English Romantic poet, echoed
some of Goethe's thoughts and carried
the "Romantic revolution" to new
heights of poetic achievement and philosophic revolt, especially in the exaltation of nature. In his autobiographical
poem, "The Prelude; Or, Growth of
A Poet's Mind," he wrote (Bk. xiii):

From Nature doth emotion come, and
    moods
Of calmness equally are Nature's gift:

This is her glory; These two attributes
Are sister horns that constitute her
    strength.

Excerpts from two of his other poems
follow:

Lines Composed a few miles above Tintern Abbey (July 13, 1798)

        . . . For I have learned
To look on Nature, not as in the hour
Of thoughtless youth; but hearing often-
    times
The still, sad music of humanity,
Nor harsh nor grating, though of ample
    power
To chasten and subdue. And I have felt
A presence that disturbs me with the joy
Of elevated thoughts; a sense sublime
Of something far more deeply interfused,
Whose dwelling is the light of setting suns,
And the round ocean and the living air,
And the blue sky, and in the mind of
    man:
A motion and a spirit, that impels
All thinking things, all objects of all
    thought,
And rolls through all things. Therefore
    am I still
A lover of the meadows and the woods,
And mountains; and of all that we behold
From this green earth; of all the mighty
    world
Of eye and ear, both what they half create,
And what perceive; well pleased to recog-
    nize
In Nature and the language of the sense,
The anchor of my purest thoughts, the
    nurse,
The guide, the guardian of my heart, and
    soul
Of all my moral being.

The Tables Turned
Books! 't is a dull and endless strife:
Come, hear the woodland linnet,

How sweet his music! On my life,
There's more of wisdom in it.

And hark! how blithe the throstle sings!
He, too, is no mean preacher:
Come forth into the light of things,
Let Nature be your teacher.

She has a world of ready wealth,
Our minds and hearts to bless—
Spontaneous wisdom breathed by health,
Truth breathed by cheerfulness.

One impulse from a vernal wood
May teach you more of man,
Of moral evil and of good,
Than all the sages can.

Sweet is the lore which Nature brings;
Our meddling intellect
Mis-shapes the beauteous forms of
  things:—
We murder to dissect.

Enough of Science and of Art;
Close up those barren leaves;
Come forth and bring with you a heart
That watches and receives.

KEATS

For one who died so young, John
Keats (1795-1821) produced some
lovely examples of English Romantic
poetry, especially poems of imagination
and fancy. Parts of two of his poems
follow.

Fancy

Ever let the Fancy roam,
Pleasure never is at home:
At a touch sweet Pleasure melteth,
Like to bubbles when rain pelteth;
Then let winged Fancy wander
Through the thought still spread beyond
  her:
Open wide the mind's cage door,
She'll dart forth, and cloudward soar. . . .

Sit thee there, and send abroad,
With a mind self-overawed,
Fancy, high-commission'd:—send her!
She has vassals to attend her:
She will bring, in spite of frost,
Beauties that the earth hath lost;
She will bring thee, all together,
All delights of summer weather;
All the buds and bells of May,
From dewy sward or thorny spray;
All the heaped Autumn's wealth,
With a still, mysterious stealth:
She will mix these pleasures up
Like three fit wines in a cup,
And thou shalt quaff it: . . .

Break the mesh
Of the Fancy's silken leash;
Quickly break her prison-string,
And such joys as these she'll bring.—
Let the winged Fancy roam,
Pleasure never is at home.

Ode on a Grecian Urn

Thou still unravish'd bride of quietness!
  Thou foster-child of Silence and slow
    Time,
Sylvan historian, who canst thus express
  A flowery tale more sweetly than our
    rhyme
What leaf-fringed legend haunts about
    thy shape
  Of deities or mortals, or of both,
    In Tempe or the dales of Arcady?
  What men or gods are these? what
    maidens loath?
What mad pursuit? What struggle to
    escape?
    What pipes and timbrels? What wild
    ecstasy?

Heard melodies are sweet, but those un
    heard
  Are sweeter; therefore, ye soft pipes,
    play on;
Not to the sensual ear, but, more en-
    dear'd,
  Pipe to the spirit ditties of no tone:

Fair youth, beneath the trees, thou canst
not leave
  Thy song, nor ever can those trees be
  bare;
    Bold Lover, never, never, canst thou
    kiss,
Though winning near the goal—yet, do
not grieve;
  She cannot fade, though thou hast
  not thy bliss,
For ever wilt thou love, and she be fair!

Ah, happy, happy boughs! that cannot
shed
  Your leaves, nor ever bid the Spring
  adieu;
And, happy melodist, unwearied,
  For ever piping songs for ever new.
More happy love! more happy, happy
love!
  For ever warm, and still to be enjoy'd,
    For ever panting and for ever young;
All breathing human passion far above,
  That leaves a heart high sorrowful and
  cloy'd
    A burning forehead, and a parching
    tongue. . . .

O Attic shape! Fair attitude! with brede
  Of marble men and maidens over-
  wrought,
With forest branches and the trodden
weed;
  Thou, silent form! dost tease us out of
  thought.
As doth eternity: Cold Pastoral!
  When old age shall this generation
  waste,
    Thou shalt remain, in the midst of
    other woe.
Than ours, a friend to man, to whom
  thou say'st,
"Beauty is truth, truth beauty,"—that
is all
  Ye know on earth, and all ye need
  to know.

COLERIDGE

Samuel Taylor Coleridge (1772-1834),
widely known for his "Rime of the Ancient Mariner" and that delightful fragment, "Kubla Khan," also wrote—still
in the Romantic vein—about religion
and the French Revolution. Selections
from his poems on both these latter
topics follow.

Religious Musings

There is one Mind, one Omnipresent
  Mind,
Omnific. His most holy name is Love.
Truth of subliming import! with the
  which
Who feeds and saturates his constant soul,
He from his small particular orbit flies,
With blest outstarting. From himself he
  flies,
Stands in the sun, and with no partial
  gaze,
Views all creation; and he loves it all,
And blesses it, and calls it very good!
This is indeed to dwell with the Most
  High!
Cherubs and rapture-trembling Seraphim
Can press no nearer to the Almighty's
  throne.
But that we roam unconscious, or with
  hearts
Unfeeling of our universal Sire,
And that in his vast family no Cain
Injures uninjured (in her best-aimed blow
Victorious murder a blind suicide)
Haply for this some younger Angel now
Looks down on human nature: and, be-
  hold!
A sea of blood bestrewed with wrecks,
  where mad
Embattling interests on each other rush
With unhelmed rage!

      'Tis the sublime of man,
Our noontide majesty, to know ourselves

Parts and proportions of one wondrous
    whole!
This fraternizes man, this constitutes
Our charities and bearings. But 'tis God
Diffused through all, that doth make all
    one whole; . . .

I will raise up a mourning, O ye Fiends!
And curse your spells, that film the eye of
    Faith,
Hiding the present God: whose presence
    lost,
The moral world's cohesion, we become
An anarchy of Spirits! Toy-bewitched,
Made blind by lusts, disherited of soul,
No common centre Man, no common sire
Knoweth! A sordid solitary thing. . . .

        Believe thou, O·my soul,
Life is a vision shadowy of Truth;
And vice, and anguish, and the wormy
    grave,
Shapes of a dream! The veiling clouds
    retire,
And lo! the Throne of the redeeming God,
Forth flashing unimaginable day,
Wraps in one blaze earth, heaven, and
    deepest hell.
  Contemplant Spirits! ye that hover o'er
With untired gaze the immeasurable fount
Ebullient with creative Deity! .
And ye of plastic power, that interfused
Roll through the grosser and material
    mass
In organizing surge! Holies of God!
(And what if Monads of the infinite
    mind?)
I haply journeying my immortal course
Shall sometime join your mystic choir.
    Till then
I discipline my young and novice thought
In ministries of heart-stirring song,
And aye on Meditations heaven-ward
    wing
Soaring aloft I breathe the empryeal air
Of Love, omnific, omnipresent Love,

Whose day-spring rises glorious in my
    soul,
As the great Sun, when he his influence
Sheds on the frost-bound waters—The
    glad stream
Flows to the ray and warbles as it flows.

France. An Ode (1797)

II

When France in wrath her giant-limbs
    upreared,
    And with that oath, which smote air,
        earth, and sea,
    Stamped her strong foot and said she
        would be free,
Bear witness for me, how I hoped and
    feared!
With what a joy my lofty gratulation
    Unawed I sang, amid a slavish band:
And when to whelm the disenchanted
    nation,
    Like fiends embattled by a wizard's
        wand,
    The Monarchs marched in evil day,
    And Britain joined the dire array:
    Though dear her shores and circling
        ocean,
Though many friendships, many youthful
    loves
    Had swol'n the patriot emotion
And flung a magic light o'er all her hills
    and groves;
Yet still my voice, unaltered, sang defeat
    To all that braved the tyrant-quelling
        lance,
And shame too long delayed and vain
    retreat!
For ne'er, O Liberty! with partial aim
I dimmed thy light or damped thy holy
    flame;
    But blessed the paeans of delivered
        France,
And hung my head and wept at Britain's
    name. . . .

IV

Forgive me, Freedom! O forgive those
dreams!
I hear thy voice, I hear thy loud
lament,
From bleak Helvetia's icy cavern
sent—
I hear thy groans upon her blood-stained
streams!
Heroes, that for your peaceful coun-
try perished,
And ye that, fleeing, spot your mountain-
snows
With bleeding wounds; forgive me,
that I cherished
One thought that ever blessed your cruel
foes!
To scatter rage, and traitorous guilt,
Where Peace her jealous home had
built;
A patriot-race to disinherit
Of all that made their stormy wilds so
dear;
And with inexpiable spirit
To taint the bloodless freedom of the
mountaineer—
O France, that mockest Heaven, adulter-
ous, blind,
And patriot only in pernicious toils,
Are these thy boasts, Champion of human
kind?
To mix with Kings in the low lust
of sway,
Yell in the hunt, and share the mur-
derous prey;
To insult the shrine of Liberty with
spoils
From freemen torn; to tempt and to
betray?

V

The Sensual and the Dark rebel in
vain,
Slaves by their own compulsion! In
mad game

They burst their manacles and wear the
name
Of Freedom, graven on a heavier
chain!
O Liberty! with profitless endeavour
Have I pursued thee, many a weary hour;
But thou nor swell'st the victor's strain,
nor ever
Didst breathe thy soul in forms of human
power.
Alike from all, howe'er they praise thee,
(Nor prayer, nor boastful name delays
thee)
Alike from Priestcraft's harpy min-
ions,
And factious Blasphemy's obscener
slaves,
Thou speedest on thy subtle pinions,
The guide of homeless winds, and play-
mate of the waves!
And there I felt thee!—on that sea-cliff's
verge
Whose pines, scarce travelled by the
breeze above,
Had made one murmur with the distant
surge!
Yes, while I stood and gazed, my temples
bare,
And shot my being through earth, sea,
and air,
Possessing all things with intensest love,
O Liberty! my spirit felt thee there.

ROMANTICISM AND PHILOSOPHY

The results of the impact of the ideas
of Romanticism upon the course of
human thought in the nineteenth and
twentieth centuries, inasmuch as they
are still an active leaven in the philosophical loaf, are difficult to evaluate.
The following selection is an analysis
of "The Meaning of Romanticism for
the Historian of Ideas." Written by a
present-day scholar, it attempts to portray a few of the principal "new ideas"

set forth by philosophers of the Romantic Period and to indicate their significance, especially in the realm of politics, to the current twentieth-century scene.

From LOVEJOY, "Meaning of Romanticism" (1940) [1]

In the last quarter of the eighteenth century, especially in the 1780's and 1790's, there were discovered, invented or revived, chiefly in Germany, a large number of ideas which had been relatively, though not always absolutely, unfamiliar or uninfluential through most of the seventeenth and eighteenth centuries; and . . . the total impact of what we may call, for short, the new ideas of the 1780's and 1790's (including revivals of old ideas under "new"), as they developed, ramified, and were diffused during the following decades, profoundly altered the habitual preconceptions, valuations, and ruling catchwords of an increasingly large part of the educated classes in Europe, so that there came into vogue in the course of the nineteenth century and in our own a whole series of intellectual fashions—from styles in poetry and styles in metaphysics to styles in government—which had no parallels in the preceding period. . . . The "newness" of these ideas of (*e.g.*) the 1790's was, for the most part, not an absolute newness; it lies in the contrast with the dominant ideas of the immediately antecedent age, and with what may be called the "old ideas" of the 1790's, exemplified, on the political side, in the French Revolution. For, roughly, in that decade two revolutions were taking place —one, external and political, in France, which was the culmination of the *Aufklärung*, the other, primarily in the realm of abstract ideas, mainly in Germany, which was only somewhat later to manifest its political consequences—some of them, indeed, only in our own unhappy day.

To call these new ideas of the 1780's and 1790's "Romanticism" is confusion-breeding and productive of historical error, above all because it suggests that there was only one such idea, or, if many, that they were all implicates of one fundamental "Romantic" idea, or, at the least, that they were harmonious *inter se* and formed a sort of systematic unity. None of these things are true. The new ideas of the period—even when held, as they often were, by the same individual minds —were in large part heterogeneous, logically independent, and sometimes essentially antithetic to one another in their implications, though their full implications were not always at once discerned; and some writers traditionally labelled "Romantic" were influenced by some of them, others by others, and yet others, I suspect, by none. But though there is no such thing as Romanticism, there emphatically *was* something which—for lack of any other brief name—may still be called a Romantic period; and one may perhaps speak of—not a, but several, Romantic movements: the period in which this array of new or newly energized ideas emerged into prominence. . . . For my own part, at any rate, I am—in a spirit of compromise—willing to speak of such a period and of such movements—meaning, approximately, the half-century 1780-1830, but especially its second decade, and the movements in which any one or more of these ideas conspicuously manifested themselves. . . .

Now the question: What were the new, or newly *active* and peculiarly influential, ideas of the 1790's and what were their vicissitudes and developments in the subsequent decades? . . .

[1] Arthur O. Lovejoy, "The Meaning of Romanticism for the Historian of Ideas." Reprinted from the *Journal of the History of Ideas*, II, No. 3 (June, 1941), 260-64, 270-78, with the permission of the author.

It is, I suppose, commonly recognized that *one* of the relatively new phenomena of the Romantic period was a new or, at all events, a much wider and intensified, vogue of the highly abstract and equivocal term "infinite." It is notorious that such phrases as *Streben ins Unendliche* ["striving endlessly"] or *Sehnsucht nach dem Unendlichen* ["longing for endlessness"] or *Annäherung zu einer unendlichen Grösse* ["approximating an endless largeness"], were peculiarly dear to the German *Frühromantiker* ["early romanticist"] as expressions of their ideal of life or of art. . . . The "infinite," whatever positive meaning might be connected with the word, meant at least the not-limited or not-completed. . . . And the sanctity of the word in most of the new writers of the period was evidence of a tendency to a new presupposition about what is excellent or valuable—and also about the nature of things, the constitution of the universe or the course of history. It was a presupposition contrary to a feature of what may be fairly called the main—not the only—earlier tradition of European thought, at least in value-judgments of all kinds, and not in these alone. There were important opposing strains in the older tradition, but the most prevalent and orthodox tendency had been to think in terms of finites, and to regard limitation as an essential element of excellence, at least for mortals. In logic and science, the first thing needful was to have precisely *defined* concepts and terms; in a work of art, the first essential was that it should have one limited theme, and a clear-cut and readily recognizable "form" . . . in literary style, the supreme merit was the clarity that comes from using words which immediately convey clear and distinct ideas, express exact and therefore limited meanings; and in human character and conduct, the mark of excellence was to observe metes and bounds and to be moderate in all one's desires, ambitions, and pretensions. The historic process, too, in the Christian tradition . . . was conceived as a finite thing, having a beginning, a middle and an end. . . . Now the German Romantics of the 1790's were in conscious and zealous—though not in consistent or unwavering—revolt against all these assumptions, but first of all in the theory of art. They conceived and proclaimed themselves to be the prophets of a new, a "modern," art—and "modern" is what *they* primarily meant by "Romantic"—which should be a *Kunst des Unendlichen* [an "art of the infinite"]. The new valuation, the revolt against "the finite," speedily passed over into other provinces . . . [and] has had many and far-reaching consequences. . . .

Most of the slight illustrations hitherto given . . . of the Romantic period have not been obviously pertinent to political or social history. They have had to do with seemingly non-political notions, belonging initially to the fields of literary criticism, aesthetics, or quasi-aesthetic valuations, or religion, or metaphysics. The reason for this lies in a fact which the political historian needs to bear in mind—namely, that most of the new ideas of the 1780's and 1790's *were* originally aesthetic or religious or metaphysical ideas. But they are not on that account less pertinent to political history. For they were the sort of ideas that, when accepted and developed, could modify men's general ways of thinking profoundly, and because profoundly, widely—in many diverse fields, including the political. And if one were to consider the "meaning," in the sense of the historic significance, of—not "Romanticism," but certain ideas of the Romantic period—from the point of view of 1940, their political consequences may well be regarded as the most significant. For a particular group of these ideas, continuously at work on the minds of the educated and reading public for fifteen decades, have produced in our own time a sort of culminating joint-effect, which is at least an essential and conspicuous part of the monstrous scene presented by Germany and by Europe today [1940]. That the revolutionary—or counter-revolutionary—political events of the past twenty years would not have occurred but for these earlier alterations in fashions of thought, it would be hazardous to maintain. For most of these events are merely new instances of familiar types of historical phenomena which seem to repeat themselves in ages or among peoples whose ruling ideologies are extremely dissimilar. The rise of dictatorships, for example, is an old story. . . . I am, therefore, far from suggesting that the rise of dictatorships and the return of an era of wars of territorial aggrandizement in Europe have their sufficient condition in the changes in ideas which marked the Romantic period; and I recognize that there is room for question whether those changes were even among the necessary conditions for the present recrudescence of those ancient evils. Nevertheless, it is certain—and notorious—that all these contemporary revolutions have had distinctive ideologies—i.e., idea-complexes—associated with them, and that their leaders—some of whom are past masters of practical political psychology—seem to regard the inculcation of these ideologies as indispensable to the success of their revolutionary enterprises and the permanence of the "new orders" they wish to establish. The ideologies may be, in great part they indubitably are, only "rationalizations" of the ambitions, or delusions of grandeur, of the leaders or of the passions of their followers; but even so, the rationalizations are found necessary, before these ambitions are converted into deeds of those latent passions into mass-action. A Hitler or a Mussolini is not more sedulous in the strengthening of his armaments than in the propagating of his ideas—the ideas which, on the one hand, serve his purpose, but on the other, can appeal to the minds of his followers because those minds have already been "conditioned" for their reception.

Now, out of the many "new ideas of the 1780's and 1790's," there were three which—though at the outset they were not political at all in their reference—were destined to be transferred to the domain of political thought and sentiment; to which the German—and in less degree the general European—mind was increasingly conditioned by a series of influential nineteenth-century writers; and the *fusion or combination* of which, I suggest, has been a factor in the production of the state of mind upon which the totalitarian ideologies depend for their appeal. These three are by no means the only ones of which the same might be said; but they are, I incline to think, the most fundamental and most important, though the estimate is certainly debatable. They consist in a sort of apotheosis of conceptions associated with three words: the German words are for the present purpose the most appropriate: *das Ganze* [the whole, totality], *Streben* [striving for], and *Eigentümlichkeit* [the quality of being heterogeneous]. If terms ending in -ism must be had to designate these ideas, they may be called holism or organicism, voluntarism or "dynamism," and diversitarianism.

1. The first—which is now familiar enough—was a relatively new idea about the relation of the individual to the whole —the idea of organism, in its logical or metaphysical sense. The political liberalism of the seventeenth and eighteenth centuries had, it need hardly be recalled, usually conceived the individual as primary. This is the essence of the doctrine of natural rights; it is not really less characteristic of the presuppositions of political utilitarianism. The reality with which

politics was concerned was the human person, conceived as a possessor of intrinsic rights, or as a claimant for the means of happiness. He had, admittedly, relations to other individuals, and—at least in the natural rights theory—moral obligations towards them. But the relations and obligations were *between* individuals as such; and though the interests or instincts of the individuals required them to combine in organized aggregates, such as the State, these were secondary, derivative, and merely instrumental to the assurance and adjustment of individual rights or the satisfaction of individual needs and desires. The whole was just the aggregate of its parts, and apart from them was nothing; and the dominant conception of scientific method, like the dominant political theory, proceeded, in its investigation of any complex thing, by an "analysis" . . . of it into its ultimate component parts. To understand *it,* you had to take it to pieces, to know the parts and *their* characteristics and the laws of their action, and how many of them there were in the given complex—and your problem was solved. But a strain of German thought in the late eighteenth century . . . tended increasingly towards a reversal of this whole way of thinking —towards giving primacy and a mystical sanctity to what was called "the Idea of the Whole," as defined by Kant in the *Critique of Judgment:* "An Idea [of something] which must determine *a priori* all that is contained *in* it"—of a "product of nature" in which, "just as every part of it exists *through* all the others, so every part is also thought as existing *for* all the others and for the sake of the Whole . . . that is, as a tool or organ." . . . Kant was talking about a natural organism—a tree; but, as is well known, the conception was speedily carried over into the provinces of metaphysics, or morals, and especially, of politics. The "Idea of the Whole" came

increasingly to mean, in its practical application, the idea of the political State. . . . The general result of the repetition of this conception, by many greater and lesser teachers, in diverse forms and with or without qualifications, was the conditioning of the mind of individuals to think of themselves (to a degree perhaps unprecedented in history) as *mere* members of *das Ganze,* as "tools or organs" of the national State . . . and as finding the interest and value of their existence in the realization of the ends of the State, which are by no means merely the summation of the private ends even of all its members. Without a long prior conditioning, then, to this idea, among others, the totalitarian ideology would not, I suggest, have the potency that it has, either in Germany or Italy. . . .

2. But the practical tendency of this idea is profoundly modified by its fusion with another idea of the 1790's. This is the assumption of the primacy, in reality and in value, of process, striving, cumulative becoming, over any static consummation—the dislike of finality . . . and in particular, the peculiar sensibility to the pathos of struggle, which is, by necessary implication, a struggle *against* something or somebody. . . . *Streben,* as everyone knows, was one of the most sacred words of the German Romantics—and it was necessarily, for them, a *Streben ins Unendliche,* a striving without a terminus. . . . The notion of *Streben* was originally . . . an ideal for the individual. But it too, naturally enough, has been converted into a political idea. . . . But as a political idea, this second notion has been fused with the first. The individual, as essentially an organ of *das Ganze,* the State, does his striving through the State, which is the embodiment of the Will to Power. If it is to be effective in this capacity, it must be completely integrated; it can permit no struggles within itself,

between its parts—for example, no class-struggle and no party conflicts. The parts must be strictly regimented . . . for the service of the whole. But the nation or State takes on the role of the insatiable Romantic hero—in which its members can, indeed, vicariously share. It must ever strive for expansion, external power, and yet more power, not as a regrettably necessary means to some final rationally satisfying goal, but because continuous self-assertion, transcending of boundaries, triumph over opposition, is its vocation. . . .

3. One of the most revolutionary of the ideas of the 1790's was an assertion of the value of diversity in human opinions, characters, tastes, arts and cultures. . . . It was revolutionary because it reversed a presupposition that had been dominant for some two centuries: the presupposition which may be called uninformitarianism. By this term I do not mean the assumption that individuals and peoples are *in fact* identical in their characters and beliefs and ways of living. It was evident . . . that they are not. Uniformitarianism is the assumption that what is most important, most valuable, normal, in men consists in what is the same in all men, and that their actual diversities in opinion and cultures and forms of government are evidences of departures from the norm of human life. And this was a natural and seemed an obvious inference from a very common assumption concerning the nature of truth. . . . What is rational is uniform; and what is not uniform is *eo ipso* not rational; and diversity is therefore the easily recognizable mark of error. . . .

But to the Romantics of the 1790's (following Herder) it appeared that the diversity of men and ages and peoples, in their ways of thinking and feeling and expressing themselves in arts and institutions, is "natural" and necessary, and also supremely desirable and right. And from this pregnant premise they drew two opposite consequences, of which the second was to prevail over the first. The assumption made initially for tolerance and catholicity. All the historic manifestations of human nature are good, and the cultivated man will train himself to appreciate and enjoy them all. But the other inference was that it is the first duty of an individual or a people to cherish and intensify the differentness . . . with which nature has endowed him or it. This, like the ideal of *Streben,* was, at the outset, applied largely to the individual, especially to the artist; but it also tended to be applied, and in the end to be chiefly applied, to the nation or race. So applied, it eventually destroyed, in many minds, the conception of a universal standard of human conduct and the sense of a common human destiny. . . . It tended to substitute for the piety towards humanity as such an exclusive piety towards one's own folk and its peculiarities. . . . When combined with that "permanent affective element of human nature," the collective . . . it was easily transformed into a conviction of the superiority of what is distinctive of one's own people—its "blood," its *Volksgeist,* traditions, *mores* and institutions—and of its right to dominate all lesser breeds.

Of these three among the ideas of the 1790's, any one, by itself, might have worked out to historic issues quite different from those that actually resulted—and, in fact, when not combined with the others, did so. For example, if the first had not been combined with the third, the "whole" to which the individual is to subordinate himself and whose ends he is to seek might have been construed as humanity—which is, in fact, the only real social totality—and a tendency towards this interpretation may be seen in Novalis's *Die Christenheit oder Europa;* and the second and third, when taken as ideals for the individual, have always been at variance with the first. But when, and in so far as, these three ideas are (however incongruously) combined, one may discern, I think, an important part (though, assuredly, far from all) of the pattern of ideas behind—or associated with—the fateful political events of our own time: the idea of a national State whose members are but instruments of its own vaster ends; in which, therefore, no internal opposition or disagreements in individual opinion can be permitted; which, however, is itself dedicated to a perpetual struggle for power and self-enlargement, with no fixed goal or terminus, and is animated by an intense and obsessing sense of differentness of its own folk, of their duty of *keeping* different and uncorrupted by any alien elements, and by a conviction of the immeasurable value of their supposedly unique characteristics and culture.

28 | FRANCE, 1848-1914

1. The Revolution of 1848

THE WEAKNESSES OF THE JULY MONARCHY

From GUÉRARD, *French Civilization* (1914) [1]

The July monarchy, established through a series of skilful intrigues, ratified by a minority of deputies without any constitutional rights, never submitted to the vote of the country as a whole, rested on insecure foundations. From first to last it was called by good observers "a compromise," a "truce," a "bridge"—anything but a permanent settlement. The Legitimists could not but feel that Louis-Philippe had tricked his young cousin out of his throne. The Bonapartists were able to claim that Napoleon's Constitution alone had been ratified by the people. The Republicans realized that their blood had

been shed for a cause not their own. . . . The Duke [of Orléans, Louis Philippe] . . . was the elect of a handful of bourgeois politicians. . . . Unvarnished plutocracy prevailed. In the eyes of the law, 200,000 electors were the whole country (*le pays légal*), and the July monarchy steadily refused to enlarge these narrow limits.

For a few months Louis-Philippe had to pay for his elevation by stooping to flatter, not merely the bourgeoisie, but the populace. It was a time when any rabble of loafers could call their new King to his balcony and have him smile, bow, and sing the "Marseillaise"—abominably out of tune. . . . But the King was waiting for his opportunity; he soon got rid of his radical Ministers, and Casimir Périer assumed control.

Casimir Périer's ministry was cut short by death, but it remains the type of the "government with a grip." The victors of 1830 had already split into two factions, the party of resistance and the party of

[1] Albert Léon Guérard, *French Civilization in the Nineteenth Century*, 1914, 102-05. Reprinted by permission of D. Appleton-Century Company, Inc., New York.

movement. The one considered the Revolution as closed, and meant to restore discipline; the other looked upon the "Three Glorious Days" of July as merely the beginning of indefinite reforms. Casimir Périer belonged emphatically to the former. Eminently successful in spite of his overbearing manners, he perished a victim of the cholera in 1831. The King, whom he had reduced to a mere figurehead whilst making his throne secure, wondered whether the loss of such a masterful servant were not a blessing in disguise.

Then followed, after an interregnum of a few months . . . another efficient Cabinet in which Thiers, Guizot, de Broglie formed a trinity of talent, ably supported by specialists like Humann and de Rigny. It was during this period that the Republicans made a last desperate stand and that the romantic dash of the Duchess of Berry from Versailles to Vendée ended in failure, betrayal, and the whole unsavoury scandal of the prison of Blaye. But on the whole order was maintained, the ruins of 1830 repaired, and progress resumed its normal course. The most creditable achievement of this Ministry was Guizot's law on primary education, the first determined effort in that line.

From 1836 to 1840 the political see-saw was at its worst; Thiers, Molé, Guizot alternate in power, fighting tremendous word-battles in which their personal positions alone were at stake, striking immoral alliances, and resorting to every kind of political trickery. Finally . . . Guizot became the actual head of the administration destined to last as long as the monarchy.

Guizot is a commanding figure in French history. "Journalist, professor, historian, administrator, Cabinet Minister, Premier, dictator of the Huguenots, there is hardly any branch of human activity in which he did not play a prominent part. But he was as unpopular as he was admired and respected; as selfish for his class as he was distinguished for himself; as blind to the state of the country at large as he was clear-sighted in his bourgeois Parliament; austere, but relying, like Walpole, on political conscience-jobbing; high-minded, but flourishing before the electorate the motto *'Enrichissez-vous!'* ['Get rich'] a great historian, but a poor prophet, who explained with assumed infallibility the progress of civilization, and, not long before the Revolution of 1848, declared, 'The day of universal suffrage will never come'; a great intellect, but with blinkers; a great heart, but outwardly cold; a great leader who wrecked his party; a great conservative who, through sheer blundering and obstinacy, plunged his country into a revolution."

For over seven years Guizot worked in closest harmony with Louis-Philippe—without any subserviency on his part, for both were agreed on a policy of conservation: peace at any price abroad, inertia at home. The opposition summed up the achievements of the Ministry in the oft quoted *"Rien, rien, rien!"* ["Nothing, nothing, nothing!"] Lamartine complained that France was "bored to death." The régime was threatened with "the revolution of contempt." But Guizot manipulated his 250,000 electors and the State officials in the Chamber were entirely at his mercy. General elections and parliamentary debates gave him handsome majorities. This upper bourgeoisie was legally the whole country; the rest of France he would ignore.

Meanwhile scandals were breaking out in the closed oligarchy of wealth: a peer was condemned for murder, two Ministers arraigned for corrupt practices. Yet the extension of the franchise to lesser capitalists (paying 100 francs in direct taxes) and to men who had received a superior education was systematically refused. A campaign of political banquets created an extraordinary stir in the country. Lamartine, hitherto unattached to any party, took the lead in the reform movement. His *History of the Girondists* idealized certain aspects of the Revolution and was as popular as any novel. The last of these banquets was interdicted by the Government. A demonstration took place, however, which soon assumed ominous proportions. A timely sacrifice could still save the régime. Whilst the King, long wavering, finally dismissed Guizot, the first shot had been fired, the agitation had turned into a riot, and the riot into a revolution.

TOCQUEVILLE ON THE CAUSES OF THE FEBRUARY REVOLUTION

Alexis de Tocqueville (1805-1859) entered politics during Louis Philippe's reign. A Frenchman of unusual penetration in social and political affairs, he wrote the following account of the February Revolution soon after the event.

From TOCQUEVILLE, *Recollections* (c. 1850) [1]

And so the Monarchy of July was fallen, fallen without a struggle, and before rather than beneath the blows of the victors, who were as astonished at their triumph as were the vanquished at their defeat. I have often, since the Revolution of February, heard M. Guizot and even M. Molé and M. Thiers declare that this event should only be attributed to a surprise and regarded as a mere accident, a bold and lucky stroke and nothing more. . . . It was difficult for them to admit that it was the King's bad government which had prepared the catastrophe. . . .

As for me, I have not the same motives

[1] *The Recollections of Alexis de Tocqueville,* ed. by the Comte de Tocqueville, trans. by Alexander Teixeira de Mattos, London, 1896, 79-87.

for forming an opinion, and I could hardly persuade myself to be of theirs. I am not prepared to say that accidents played no part in the Revolution of February; on the contrary, they played a great one; but they were not the only thing. . . .

The Revolution of February, in common with all other great events of this class, sprang from general causes, impregnated, if I am permitted the expression, by accidents; and it would be as superficial a judgment to ascribe it necessarily to the former as exclusively to the latter.

The industrial revolution which, during the past thirty years, had turned Paris into the principal manufacturing city of France and attracted within its walls an entire new population of workmen . . . tended more and more to inflame this multitude. Add to this the democratic disease of envy, which was silently permeating it; the economical and political theories which were beginning to make their way and which strove to prove that human misery was the work of laws and not of Providence, and that poverty could be suppressed by changing the conditions of society; the contempt into which the governing class, and especially the men who led it, had fallen, a contempt so general and so profound that it paralyzed the resistance even of those who were most interested in maintaining the power that was being overthrown; the centralization which reduced the whole revolutionary movement to the overmastering of Paris and the seizing of the machinery of government; and lastly, the mobility of all things, institutions, ideas, men and customs, in a fluctuating state of society which had, in less than sixty years, undergone the shock of seven great revolutions, without numbering a multitude of smaller, secondary upheavals. These were the general causes without which the Revolution of February would have been impossible. The principal accidents which led to it were the passions of the dynastic Opposition, which brought about a riot, in proposing a reform; the suppression of this riot, first over-violent, and then abandoned; the sudden disappearance of the old Ministry, unexpectedly snapping the threads of power, which the new ministers, in their confusion, were unable either to seize upon or to reunite; the mistakes and disorder of mind of these ministers, so powerless to re-establish that which they had been strong enough to overthrow; the vacillation of the generals; the absence of the only Princes who possessed either personal energy or popularity; and above all, the senile imbecility of King Louis-Philippe, his weakness, which no one could have foreseen, and which still remains almost incredible, after the event has proved it.

I have sometimes asked myself what could have produced this sudden and unprecedented depression in the King's mind. Louis-Philippe had spent his life in the midst of revolutions, and certainly lacked neither experience, courage, nor readiness of mind, although these qualities all failed him so completely on that day. In my opinion, his weakness was due to his excessive surprise; he was overwhelmed with consternation before he had grasped the meaning of things. The Revolution of February was *unforeseen* by all, but by him more than any other; he had been prepared for it by no warning from the outside, for since many years his mind had withdrawn into that sort of haughty solitude into which in the end the intellect almost always settles down of princes who have long lived happily, and who, mistaking luck for genius, refuse to listen to anything, because they think that there is nothing left for them to learn from anybody. Besides, Louis-Philippe had been deceived . . . imagining that, in order to remain on the throne, all he had to do was to observe the letter of the law while

violating its spirit, and that, providing he himself kept within the bounds of the Charter, the nation would never exceed them. To warp the spirit of the Constitution without changing the letter; to set the vices of the country in opposition to each other; gently to drown revolutionary passion in the love of material enjoyment: such was the idea of his whole life. Little by little, it had become, not his leading, but his sole idea. . . . And when he suddenly saw that it was a false idea, he became like a man who is awakened in the night by an earthquake, and who, feeling his house crumbling in the darkness, and the very ground seeming to yawn beneath his feet, remains distracted amid this unforeseen and universal ruin.

I am arguing very much at my ease today . . . but on the afternoon of that day [February 24] I had many things in my head: I was thinking of the events themselves, and sought less for what had produced them than for what was to follow. . . . I cannot remember ever feeling my soul so full of sadness. It was the second revolution I had seen accomplish itself, before my eyes, within seventeen years! . . .

I had spent the best days of my youth amid a society which seemed to increase in greatness and prosperity as it increased in liberty; I had conceived the idea of a balanced, regulated liberty, held in check by religion, custom, and law; the attractions of this liberty had touched me; it had become the passion of my life; I felt that I could never be consoled for its loss, and that I must renounce all hope of its recovery. . . .

I could not yet know what would issue from this last revolution, but I was already convinced that it could give birth to nothing that would satisfy me; and I foresaw that . . . our own fate was to drag on our lives miserably amid alternate reactions of licence and oppression. . . .

The Constitutional Monarchy had succeeded the Ancien Régime; the Republic, the Monarchy; the Empire, the Republic; the Restoration, the Empire; and then came the Monarchy of July. After each of these successive changes it was said that the French Revolution, having accomplished what was presumptuously called its work, was finished; this had been said and it had been believed. Alas! I myself had hoped it . . . and here is the French Revolution beginning over again, for it is still the same one. As we go on, its end seems farther off and shrouded in greater darkness. Shall we ever . . . attain a more complete and more far-reaching social transformation than our fathers foresaw and desired, and than we ourselves are able to foresee; or are we destined simply to end in a condition of intermittent anarchy, the well-known chronic and incurable complaint of old races? As for me, I am unable to say: I do not know when this long voyage will be ended; I am weary of seeing the shore in each successive mirage, and I often ask myself whether the *terra firma* we are seeking does really exist, and whether we are not doomed to rove upon the seas for ever.

LOUIS BLANC'S ACCOUNT OF THE FAILURE OF THE WORKSHOPS

When Louis Philippe was overthrown, a provisional government served until the Second French Republic could be proclaimed, which was done two days later, on February 26. Workingmen and their leaders played a prominent role in the February Revolution, and they demanded and received much attention by the provisional government, even to the extent of being represented in that government. But despite pledges to guarantee labor to all citizens and a plethora of decrees concerning labor, the majority of the members of the provisional government opposed labor reforms. They appointed two labor representatives, Louis Blanc and Albert (Alexandre Martin) to meet as a "government commission for the workingmen" to occupy itself "with their condition," but they would appropriate no money to establish the workshops for employment of the idle, as Blanc demanded. Instead, a mockery of the national workshops was set up, not under the direction of Blanc or his socialist sympathizers, but under others who neither understood nor followed Blanc's plan. That the idea of a national workshop was not given a fair trial in 1848 is amply attested by Blanc's own justifiably indignant account of those workshops set up.

From BLANC, *1848. Historical Revelations* [1]

The situation of Paris immediately after the great shock of February is well known. The immediate consequences of so violent and unforeseen a crisis were, of course, a disturbance of industrial operations, a panic among capitalists, and a considerable multitude of workingmen thrown upon the streets, starving for want of work, and armed. Such a state of things could not but cause uneasiness to the government. Consequently, on the twenty-seventh of February, 1848, in the first days of the Revolution . . . the Provisional Government decreed the establishment of National Workshops, [and] the Minister of Public Works [M. Marie] was charged with the execution of the decree.

But what were these National Workshops to be? A mere ruinous expedient, or a noble and vigorous experiment in the organisation of labour? A temporary resource to meet the serious problem of the

[1] Louis Blanc, *1848. Historical Revelations Inscribed to Lord Normanby*, London, 1858, 194-98, 205-06.

unemployed, or a starting point for social regeneration? . . . M. Marie knew my opinions better than any one; for only a few days before the Revolution of February, in a rather numerous gathering of deputies and journalists in his own house, I had clearly explained them; and I may add, they had encountered no more decided opponent than M. Marie himself. And yet it was to him, who totally misunderstood and dreaded Socialism, who had sworn in his heart to resist it, *à l'outrance,* that the organisation of the national workshops was to be committed. . . . The actual direction of the workshops, moreover, was intrusted to M. Emile Thomas, whom I did not even know by sight; and one of the claims which recommended that person was his ardent, indefatigable opposition to my doctrines. Later he officially testified, "I have never spoken to M. Louis Blanc in my life; I don't know him." Again, "While I was head of the workshops I saw M. Marie daily, sometimes twice a day; never once M. Ledru-Rollin, nor M. Louis Blanc, nor M. Flocon, nor M. Albert." . . .

Nor let it be objected that though these national workshops were not organised with my concurrence, they were, at all events, in conformity with my principles. The truth is precisely the reverse. . . . In point of fact, it is monstrous to confound the industrial system developed in my *Organization of Labor* with the system, so justly stigmatised, or the national workshops managed by M. Emile Thomas under the sanction of M. Marie.

The *social workshops,* such as I had suggested, were each of them to consist of workmen belonging to the same trade. The *national workshops,* as put in operation by M. Marie, exhibited a collection of workmen got together pell-mell, and yet —prodigious absurdity!—all put to the same kind of work. In the *social workshops* as suggested by me, the workmen were to pursue their business, the State lending them capital, to be repaid according to certain stipulations; they, working exclusively for their own profit, with a view to a joint benefit, that is to say, with all the stimulus of personal interest, combined with the influence generated by the pursuit of a common object, and that point of honour which belongs to *esprit de corps.*

In the *national workshops,* as managed by M. Marie, the State interfered simply as a contractor; the operatives worked only as paid instruments. Now, as the kind of labour in these workshops was utterly unproductive and absurd, besides being such as the greater part of the workers were unaccustomed to . . . the State was simply squandering the public funds; its money was a premium upon idleness; its wages, alms in disguise . . . a rabble of paupers, whom it was enough to feed, from the want of knowing how to employ them, and who had to live together without any other ties than a military organisation, and under chiefs who bore the name, at once so strange and yet so characteristic, of sergeant majors—*brigadiers.* . . .

The national workshops emptied the exchequer with a dead loss; they humiliated the workingman, who was reduced to *accept* the bread which he desired to *earn;* they discredited State interference in industrial matters. In the place of associations of workmen they set up battalions of paid idlers—a strange army, sooner or later to be disbanded at the risk of civil war! The routed logicians of the doctrine of *laissez faire* . . . had, of course, every reason for attempting to fix upon us the responsibility for all this mischief. What a lucky chance for the disciples of the old political economy, could they succeed in playing a trick on public opinion, if they could contrive to pass off as the highest practical form of the organisation of labour those "national workshops," which were nothing more than its ignoble travesties!

THE "JUNE DAYS" (1848)

Repeated and increasingly ugly workers' demonstrations took place in Paris in the spring of 1848. After the elections to the National Assembly (April 23) gave a victory to Lamartine and the moderate Republicans, the workers planned new protests; but the unfriendly National Assembly, terrified by "communism," dissolved the national workshops, a move to which Paris workers replied with insurrection (June 23-26) and the bloodiest street fighting Europe had witnessed. Tocqueville clearly saw it as a class war.

From TOCQUEVILLE, *Recollections* [1]

I come at last to the insurrection of June, the most extensive and the most singular that has occurred in our history, and perhaps in any other: the most extensive, because, during four days, more than a hundred thousand men were engaged in it; the most singular, because the insurgents fought without a war-cry, without leaders, without flags, and yet with a marvellous harmony and an amount of military experience that astonished the oldest officers.

What distinguished it also, among all the events of this kind which have succeeded one another in France for sixty years, is that it did not aim at changing the form of government, but at altering the order of society. It was not, strictly speaking, a political struggle . . . but a combat of class against class, a sort of Servile War. It represented the facts of the Revolution of February in the same manner as the theories of Socialism represented its ideas; or rather it issued naturally from these ideas, as a son does from his mother. We behold in it nothing more than a blind and rude, but powerful, effort on the part of the workmen to escape from the necessities of their condition, which had been depicted to them as one of unlawful oppression, and to open up by main force a road towards that imaginary comfort with which they had been deluded. . . . These poor people had been told that the wealth of the rich was in some way the produce of a theft practised upon themselves. They had been assured that inequality of fortunes was as opposed to morality and the welfare of society as it was to nature. Prompted by their needs and their passions, many had believed this obscure and erroneous notion of right, which, mingled with brute force, imparted an energy, a tenacity and a power which it would never have possessed unaided.

It must also be observed that this formidable insurrection was not the enterprise of a certain number of conspirators, but the revolt of one whole section of the population against another. Women took part in it as well as men. While the latter fought, the former prepared and carried ammunition; and when at last the time had come to surrender, the women were the last to yield. These women went to battle with, as it were, a housewifely ardour: they looked to victory for the comfort of their husbands and the education of their children. . . .

As to the strategic science displayed by this multitude, the warlike nature of the French, their long experience of insurrections, and particularly the military education which the majority of the men of the people in turn receive, suffice to explain it. Half of the Paris workmen had served in our armies, and they are always glad to take up arms again. Generally speaking, old soldiers abound in our riots. . . .

As we know, it was the closing of the national workshops that occasioned the

[1] Tocqueville, *Recollections*, 187.

rising. Dreading to disband this formidable soldiery at one stroke, the Government had tried to disperse it by sending part of the workmen into the country. They refused to leave. On the 22nd of June, they marched through Paris in troops, singing in cadence, in a monotonous chant, "We won't be sent away, we won't be sent away." . . . Their delegates waited upon the members of the Committee of the Executive Power with a series of arrogant demands, and on meeting with a refusal, withdrew with the announcement that next day they would have recourse to arms. Everything, indeed, tended to show that the long-expected crisis had come.

2. The Second Empire (1852-1870)

THE COUP D'ETAT OF LOUIS NAPOLEON (1851-52)

The National Assembly, which had been elected on April 23 by universal suffrage, completed the constitution of the Second Republic on November 4. The constitution provided for a unicameral legislature and a strong President, with separation of powers and direct election by universal suffrage. Presidential elections were held December 10, 1848, and Louis Napoleon, nephew of Napoleon I and pretender to the Napoleonic succession, was elected by a heavy majority. A new Legislative Assembly, however, elected in 1849 and controlled by conservatives in mortal terror of radicalism, soon created new confusions which Louis Napoleon used to his own benefit. The conservatives passed an education bill (the Falloux Law) designed to strengthen Catholic influence in education; then, on May 31, 1850, they passed an electoral law limiting the franchise by disenfranchising about three million laborers, thereby repudiating the principle of universal franchise set forth in the constitution of the Second Republic—a curious spectacle wherein an Assembly elected under universal suffrage disenfranchised the electors whom they were supposed to represent. But it enabled Louis, elected by universal suffrage, to pose as the champion of the constitution against its conservative opponents. To ensure himself continued power, he sought legal means at first, by revising the constitution to enable him to be re-elected for the succeeding term of four years as President. But the attempt failed and he decided to resort to force. On December 2, 1851, the Assembly was dissolved, repressive measures led to the arrest or deportation of opponents, a popular uprising was put down by French troops, and Louis Napoleon, re-establishing universal suffrage, called for a plebiscite either to "give me means to assure your prosperity, or choose another in my place." The circumstances in which the plebiscite was conducted, on December 20, are well described in the following account.

From DICKINSON, *Revolution and Reaction* (1892) [1]

On December 20 the President appealed to the country; he asked for a confirmation of his act of violence and of the authority he had already assumed; the nation was to answer "yes" or "no," that is to say, was either to accept the only Government that remained standing, or was to fling itself deliberately back into the anarchy of parties and passions. "To vote for Louis Napoleon," said Montalembert in a public manifesto, "is not to approve all he has

[1] Dickinson, *Revolution and Reaction in Modern France*, 216-18.

THE SECOND EMPIRE (1852-1870)

done; it is only to choose between him and the total ruin of France; it does not mean that his Government is the one we prefer above all others; it means simply that we prefer a prince who has given proof of resolution and ability, to those who are at this moment giving their proofs of murder and pillage." This opposition of the President who posed as the champion of order to the Socialists who were attempting a democratic revolution in the provinces, was put still more clearly in the proclamation of one of the prefects:—"Yes, is life; no, death by suicide: there is the alternative; choose." By the mere force of the situation, such a vote could hardly be free: but, further, the terror of the *coup d'état* was still weighing on the country; thirty-two departments were under martial law; it was impossible for opposition to be organized by meetings or through the press; the army voted first and gave the cue to the country, and how freely the army voted may be conjectured from an address delivered by a colonel to a corporal who had the audacity to propose to say "no"; the words, though they rest upon hearsay, have a sufficient appearance of authenticity to deserve quotation: "What! You who are reported for promotion and will be nominated to the first vacancy, you formally disobey your colonel, and that in presence of your company! . . . Are you aware, sir, that by this vote of yours you are invoking the destruction of the army, the conflagration of your father's house, the utter annihilation of society? What! You whom I intended to promote! Are these the intentions you avow to my very face!"

Such being the circumstances the result of the *plebiscite* could hardly be doubtful; the President was confirmed in his power by a vote of 7½ million votes [as against 640,000 who dared vote No!] and an even greater number were cast to approve his assumption of the title of Emperor, in November [21] of 1852: the prophecy of Thiers was fulfilled; *"l'empire était fait"* ["the empire was established"].

NAPOLEON LAYS DOWN HIS BASIC POLICIES

On January 14, 1852, Louis Napoleon's new constitution was promulgated, whereby the chief of state, though "responsible to the nation," held "free and unfettered authority" and governed "by means of the ministers, the Council of State, the Senate, and the Legislative Assembly." In the fall of 1852, Napoleon made a tour of French provinces during which he made a number of speeches to describe the policies he had in mind to follow.

From LOUIS NAPOLEON, Address at Bordeaux (October 9, 1852) [1]

Gentlemen,

The invitation of the Chamber and of the tribunal of commerce of Bordeaux which I cheerfully accepted furnishes me an opportunity to thank your grand city for its reception so cordial and its hospitality so replete with magnificence, and I am very glad also, towards the end of my tour, to share with you the impressions which it has left upon me.

The purpose of this tour, as you know, was that I might come to know for myself our beautiful provinces of the south, and that I might appreciate their needs. It has, however, given rise to a much more important result.

Indeed, I say it with a candor as far removed from arrogance as from a false modesty, never has a people testified in a manner more direct, spontaneous, and unanimous the desire to be freed from

[1] Anderson, ed., *The Constitutions and Other Select Documents Illustrative of the History of France*, 558-60. By permission of Frank Maloy Anderson.

anxieties as to the future by consolidation in the same hands an authority which is in sympathy with them. It is because they know at this hour both the false hopes with which they deluded themselves and the dangers with which they are threatened. They knew that in 1852 society would hasten to its destruction, because each party was consoling itself in advance of the general shipwreck with the hope of planting its banner upon the ruins which might float to the surface. They are thankful to me for having saved the ship, merely by raising the banner of France.

Disabused of absurd theories, the people have acquired the conviction that the pretended reformers were only dreamers. . . . Today, France encompasses me with her sympathies, because I am not of the family of ideologists. In order to secure the welfare of the country, it is not necessary to apply new systems; but, before everything else, to inspire confidence in the present and security for the future. That is why France seems to wish to return to the Empire.

There is, nevertheless, a fear which I must refute. In a spirit of distrust, certain persons declare: The Empire means war. But I say: The Empire means peace.

It means peace, because France desires it, and, when France is satisfied, the world is tranquil. Glory, indeed, is bequeathed by hereditary title, but not war. . . .

I admit, however, that I, like the Emperor [Napoleon I], have indeed conquests to make. I wish, like him, to conquer for conciliation the hostile parties and to bring them into the current of the great popular stream from the hostile factions which are now ruining themselves without profit to anybody.

I wish to conquer for religion, morality, and comfortable living that part of the population still so numerous, which, in the midst of a country of faith and belief, scarcely knows of the precepts of Christ:

which, in the midst of the most fertile land in the world, can scarcely enjoy products of the first necessity.

We have enormous uncultivated territories to clear, routes to open, harbors to deepen, rivers to make navigable, canals to finish, and our network of railroads to complete. We have opposite Marseilles an enormous kingdom to assimilate to France [Algeria]. We have to connect our great western ports with the American Continent by those rapid communications which we still lack. In fine, we have everywhere ruins to raise again, false gods to cast down, and truths to make triumphant.

That is how I shall understand the Empire, if the Empire is to be reëstablished. Such are the conquests which I meditate, and all of you who surround me, who wish, like myself, the welfare of our fatherland, you are my soldiers.

CONTEMPORARY OPINION OF NAPOLEON III

A wealth of information about Napoleon III is to be found in the *Conversations* of Nassau Senior (1790-1864), an English barrister and economist who, in various visits to France, talked with leading statesmen and intellectuals. In the following conversation, recorded under the date of February 14, 1854, Dumon, former Minister of Finance in the Guizot Ministry, gives his impression of Napoleon's policies.

From SENIOR, *Conversations* (1854; 1859) [1]

Louis Napoleon was elected on two conditions, prosperity and peace. He gave to us the first; any tolerably fixed Government would have done so. If he had left us to ourselves, if he had merely kept

[1] *Conversations with M. Thiers, M. Guizot, and other Distinguished Persons . . . by the Late Nassau William Senior,* ed. by M. C. M. Simpson, 2 vols., London, 1878, I, 241-43.

down the anarchists, and so given free play to the industry that was anxious to be employed, and to the capital that had been kept idle only by fears, we should have made for ourselves a great and steady, though perhaps less dazzling, prosperity. But he . . . is a political economist after the school of Louis XIV or his uncle. He thinks that he knows what is good for us better than we do; that we require to be directed and encouraged and stimulated. So he set on foot or promoted the wildest speculations: railways that will not pay; banks of issue that will fail; and trust companies that are to borrow and lend milliards. Then he cherishes the common royal doctrine that expenditure is a good in itself, and that the poor profit by the extravagance of the rich.

So he is forcing the municipality of Paris to pull down a fourth of the town. The expense of the mere destruction is ruinous; that of rebuilding it no one ventures to estimate. . . . It will ruin our local finances, which are devoted to public purposes of great importance. All our hospitals and all our works of common utility depend on them. . . . As to his personal expenditure, the millions which he has wasted on his fêtes are little as compared with what he has made other people waste on them. . . . He has led his Court, and his Court has led the rest of the world, to a personal extravagance that was never known before. . . . The prosperity which was the first of his promises is passing away. The other promise, that of peace, may be said to have been broken already. He says that he has been forced into a war [the Crimean War]. Until the publication of the last correspondence we believed him. We thought that he was a victim or the dupe of the ambition of Russia, or of your [English] desire to destroy Cronstadt and Sebastopol, and support Circassia. Now we find that *he* has been the great promoter of war . . . that every decisive

move has been prompted by him. It throws on him the responsibility of the war, and that responsibility will crush him.

[In May, 1859, Senior talked with Prosper Mérimée, the well-known writer, on the motives which led Napoleon III to aid the Kingdom of Piedmont-Sardinia in the war of 1859 against Austria.[1]]

Senior. What do you suppose to have been his real motive for the war, if it were not the fear of the *Carbonari?*

Mérimée. The motives were three. First and foremost was his hatred of Austria and of the Roman Government. He hates them both with the intensity of a conspirator. Such feelings must be his earliest recollections. When, after the insurrection in which his brother died, he was carried a prisoner to the Roman frontier, and then pardoned and driven out, he said that he would pay another visit to the Cardinals.

Senior. I can understand his hating the Cardinals; but what quarrel has he with Austria?

Mérimée. Every Italian, and he is an Italian by education, hates Austria. Then he has to revenge her conduct during the Crimean war.

Senior. So have we, and yet you see that we bear no malice.

Mérimée. A nation may forget her rancunes; an individual, at least the individual of whom we are speaking, does not.

Senior. Has he any real sympathy with the Italian people?

Mérimée. Sympathy with them as the enemies of Austria. . . . His second motive is the desire of military glory, first for himself, next for us. He hopes to add a brilliant page to French history, with his name at the beginning. His third motive is that he believes that his military success will establish his dynasty.

[1] *Ibid.*, II, 244-45.

Senior. In none of these motives is France interested; she does not hate Austria; she has more military glory than she wants, and she would be as happy under an Orleans dynasty as under a Bonaparte one.

Mérimée. Thence the Emperor's anxiety to make our Austria to be the aggressor, in which, by his own dexterity, by the mismanagement of Austria, and by your [England's] assistance, he has in a great degree succeeded.

A PRESENT-DAY ESTIMATE OF NAPOLEON III

Recent students of Napoleon III are disposed to deal more kindly with him than his contemporaries generally were. It becomes increasingly evident that, while Napoleon III appealed constantly to the record of his warlike, despotic uncle, Napoleon I, his policies were leavened by a sincere desire for the public welfare, for international peace, and for the amelioration of poverty and its attendant evils. Albert Guérard has recently (1943) written a brilliant and sympathetic biography of Napoleon III from which the following estimates are derived.

From GUÉRARD, *Napoleon III* (1943) [1]

As the visible head of a great nation he was adequate and at times even impressive. He was no histrion, but he could play his part. The insignificant figure we have seen shuffling and slouching into the Assembly on September 26, 1848, had by 1852 achieved color and a style. A general's uniform gave him distinction. If his legs were short, his torso was long, so he

[1] Reprinted by permission of the publishers from Albert Guérard, *Napoleon III*, in *Makers of Modern Europe*, ed. by Donald C. McKay and Dumas Malone, Harvard University Press, 1943, 144-46, 176-78, 193, 198-201, 203-09.

looked taller on horseback, and, in contrast to Napoleon I, he could ride admirably. The long waxed moustache, the imperial goatee, set a fashion which is still unforgotten. The remote lacklustre gaze of his grey eyes, now that it was fraught with destiny, could be declared sphinx-like or prophetic. In private conversation he had no small talk, few flashes of wit. But his gravity, his courtesy, his gentleness impressed all who approached him. He could win children, princes, scholars— and women, alas!—all too easily. . . . Yet even in the most intimate circles the invisible barrier could not be removed. There were too many aspects to the man, and they could not be brought to the same focus. . . . It seemed that Napoleon III, like the great stoic poet Alfred de Vigny, who sincerely admired him, "never was on familiar terms with any one, not even himself." . . .

This loneliness of the sovereign was due, first of all, to the paradoxical nature of his regime. As an hereditary monarch, he had to surround himself with a court; and every one in his court stood for some kind of privilege, those very privileges which, as a democratic Caesar, it was his mission to destroy. He is reported to have said: "How could you expect the Empire to work smoothly? The Empress is a Legitimist; Morny is an Orleanist; my cousin Napoleon is a Republican; I am known to be a Socialist; only Persigny is a Bonapartist, and he is crazy." The anecdote is probably too neat to be authentic, yet the perplexing facts are literally true— true of his immediate household, true of the court, true of the imperial personnel as a whole. He had with him a few transfuges of the old nobility, but the bulk of that class kept sulking in the Faubourg St. Germain. He had with him some liberal bourgeois, but the upper bourgeoisie as a class was Orleanist through and through, and, from their stronghold in the

THE SECOND EMPIRE (1852-1870)

French Academy, they carried on a futile and irritating warfare against him. He had the support of the Church, but the Roman problem was a constant thorn. He had the rising power of the industrialists on his side, but they lived in dread of his "Utopias," now socialism, now free trade. He had the army, but he was at heart the reverse of a military man. Sovereign by the will of the people, he was hemmed in by those who did not believe in the people. . . .

In March, 1854, on the eve of the Crimean War, Napoleon III said in an address to the Legislative Body: "I have gone as far as honor permitted me to go. . . . Europe knows that France is seeking no aggrandizement. . . . The era of conquests is over, and cannot return; for it is not by extending her territorial boundaries that a nation in our days can be honored and powerful; it is by placing itself in the lead of generous ideas, by causing everywhere the rule of law and justice to prevail."

These words, which have the same ring as the Atlantic Charter, represented his earnest conviction and his hope. He was not . . . crazed with a spirit of conquest. Yet the record offers a very different picture. In eighteen years, the Empire waged three wars with major European powers, and in addition, sent three important expeditions overseas. The contrast between the principles and the performance is glaring.

But the key to this contradiction is not to be found in mere cynicism. . . . Napoleon III was committed to a democratic dogma, the doctrine of nationalities. To him, it was the very condition of permanent peace; but it was bound to disturb the status quo. This conception was in his mind when he spoke of "taking the lead in generous ideas" and "causing justice to prevail." . . . The oppression of one people by another seemed to him an intol-erable wrong. In this he was in full harmony with the romantic humanitarians of his time, with "Young Germany," with Mazzini's "Young Italy," with Michelet, with Proudhon. On the throne, and to the great scandal of his fellow sovereigns, he remained attached to a faith he had professed when he was a conspirator and a Utopian publicist. It is not for us to sneer: his ideal was essentially the same as Woodrow Wilson's principle of self-determination.

If he had been understood and supported, his aims could have been achieved through peaceful readjustments. . . . He had a definite method in view which would have been a substitute for war. His constant desire was to convene a European Congress which, like that of Vienna, would have reorganized the continent, but with *nationality* instead of *legitimacy* as its guiding thought. In this he was frustrated by the diplomats of the old school, too "realistic" to believe in anything but *sacro egoismo* and the balance of power. The only Congress that Napoleon III was able to hold, at Paris, in 1856, was a tribute to his material prestige but a defeat for his ideals: it achieved very little besides registering the paltry results of a senseless war. Thereafter, every suggestion for a Congress was rejected with ironical deference. Napoleon III was thwarted and rejected, as Alexander of Russia had been, and as Woodrow Wilson was to be.

A Congress was intended merely to raise and define the questions to be solved; but no Congress of Powers had any right to take the decision out of the hands of the ultimate judge, the people. National existence and political regime, according to his doctrine, should have the same foundation—the consent of the governed. The will of the people, in both domains, should be ascertained in the most direct fashion, through a plebiscite. . . . This method was applied when Nice and Savoy were annexed to France [1859]. . . .

Just as the keyword of the First Empire was Glory, that of the Second was Prosperity; for two generations, the "good times" under Napoleon III were remembered. . . .

The essential point about Napoleon III is that he was a Socialist. This ought to be a truism: he said so himself; friends and enemies concurred. . . . The problem is to agree upon what is meant by Socialism. . . . The socialism of Napoleon III is not hard to define. It was not Utopian, and it was not doctrinaire (or if you prefer, it was not *scientific*). . . . Socialism with him was more than a sentiment. . . . It was a *tendency*, that is to say, an incentive to action, a guide. . . .

Napoleon III was committed to . . . the government as an agent of collective progress. In his mind, the first concern of the State was "to improve the moral and material condition of the most numerous and poorest class."

The second step is even more definite, but much harder to appraise. The good of the community demands confidence, security, *order*. Ay, there's the rub: to many, who deem themselves good citizens, the word *order* has a sinister ring. It evokes at once the shadow of traditional Bonapartism: the rule of a Super-Policeman. . . . But does the defense of order inevitably mean the protection of privilege? . . . What Napoleon III would have said—and did say in almost every one of his addresses—was "The immediate duty of the State is to curb violence." Every government, autocratic or liberal, must be a government, or abdicate; and the function of a government is first of all to enforce the law, that is to say, to put down lawlessness. . . . We are not attempting to disprove the existence of Napoleon III the Policeman; what we are seeking to establish is that Napoleon III the Policeman

was not in contradiction with Napoleon III the Socialist. Socialism is first of all an orderly society, and the first step toward Socialism is the restoration of order. . . .

We have been attempting to show that a leader could be at the same time a champion of order and a socialist. We are now venturing a bolder paradox: namely, that a true socialist may also seek to foster prosperity. . . . For although he was ready to leave the freest field to individual initiative, he was resolutely opposed to *laissez-faire*. Government, according to him, was not an "ulcer," but an instrument for the common good. He believed in organization and planning. This conviction he had expressed in his pamphlet, *On the Extinction of Pauperism* (1844). . . .

Briefly, his plan was to take over six out of the nine million hectares of uncultivated land, and settle on them colonies of the unemployed, financed by a loan . . . from the State. The colonists were to be supervised by foremen or *prud'hommes* elected by themselves . . . these would be the non-commissioned officers of the labor army. For an army it would be, living on the rough, cheap, and healthy level of army life. Above the *prud'hommes,* there would be technical directors and a governor. Every year, the governors would meet in Paris, to prepare their plans with the Minister of the Interior.

These settlements would not be purely agricultural. They would produce manufactured goods for their own consumption. It was not expected that the colonists would remain permanently in the "collectives." Normally, they would be reabsorbed by free industry. . . . Napoleon III . . . was attempting to keep a balance between the different elements of national prosperity; he refused to commit himself to a purely agrarian policy. He understood that the modern world was to be essentially industrial. . . . His chief interest was industry. . . . His very hobbies were mechanical. . . . Napoleon III realized quite simply that, by its very nature, modern industry is *collectivistic*. It implies the necessary coöperation of the many to serve the needs of the many. . . . He encouraged and subsidized the coöperative system; but he knew that it could not be imposed on consumers or producers, and the French, as a whole, failed to respond. He was not afraid of State Capitalism, or direct operation by the government: if officials could conduct such vital and intricate "big businesses" as the army, the navy, education, the postal service or public works, was it absurd that they should be able to run a mine or a railroad? But he accepted also as a genuine form of collectivism the corporation, created by the State, supervised by the State in the interest of the community. . . . The profit motive is not denied, but it is held in definite subordination to the common good. . . . In such a spirit, and with such a method, industrial enterprise proceeded with an enthusiasm which was clearly lacking under Louis Philippe, and which waned under the Third Republic.

3. *The Third Republic* (1875-1914)

In the midst of the confusion which followed upon the sudden and unexpected fall of Napoleon III in September, 1870, and the newly proclaimed Republic's bloody contest with the Paris Commune (March-May, 1871), considerable doubt existed as to what form the government of France would ultimately take. The monarchical sympathies of the National Assembly (elected February 8, 1871) were among the chief causes of the Paris Commune's resistance to it. But the monarchists were unable to agree upon a candidate, and finally Louis Adolphe Thiers, whom

the Assembly had invested with the executive power, cast in his lot for a republic. He gave his reasons for this decision in a manuscript found among his literary remains.

ARGUMENTS IN FAVOR OF THE THIRD FRENCH REPUBLIC

From THIERS, "Reasons" (*c.* 1875) [1]

In 1873, when the country saw administrative affairs, the army, and the finances reëstablished, and the foreign enemy departed from our soil, a universal cry arose for the abandonment of the provisional form of government, and for the establishment of a permanent government, that is to say, to give to each party, weary of waiting, the government of its choice. But there were three monarchical parties, and but one throne. The idea of gratifying them all had, therefore, to be abandoned. As for myself, my mind was made up. In the presence of these three competitors, the Monarchy was impossible. The Republic was difficult without a doubt, but possible if prudence and wisdom were exercised. Under the Republic France had just been revived. I would have preferred that the question had not been brought up, but it could no longer be evaded. As a simple deputy, elected President of the Republic by my colleagues, I stated the question without allowing myself to solve it. I could do neither more nor less. The three monarchical parties, united in the common design of resisting the establishment of the Republic, proposed to the Assembly that it separate itself from me, and, as I was not less desirous of separating myself from it, I handed in my resignation. . . .

Now I ask every honest man, to what-

[1] Quoted in François Le Goff, *The Life of Louis Adolphe Thiers,* trans. by T. Stanton. New York, 1879, Appendix D, 340, 343-45.

ever party he may belong, if the Count de Chambord could be placed on the throne, with the opinions that he professes and with the flag that he unfurls, or if it is hoped that he may some day be acceptable after he had modified his views? We respect him too much to believe it. I will say nothing of the Orléans princes, who wish to be mentioned only after the Count de Chambord, according to their hereditary rank; but I ask if the country is ready to receive the Prince Imperial [Napoleon III's son], who, though innocent of the misfortuntes of France, suggests them so keenly that the nation still shudders at the bare mention of this name? . . . .

Must France wait until her future masters are ready; until one candidate is brought over to other ways of thinking, until another has made an advance in his right of succession, and until a third has finished his education? In the meanwhile everything will be in suspense, commerce, industry, finances, State affairs. How can business men be asked to engage in great industrial enterprises, and financiers to negotiate loans, when the future threatens fresh political troubles? And how can foreign cabinets be expected to strengthen their relations and form alliances with us, when French policy is liable to be directed by new chiefs and influenced by new ideas? . . .

We persistently ask if there be any other alternative than the following: either the Monarchy, which is impossible because there are three claimants and but one throne; or the Republic, difficult to establish without doubt, not because of itself but because of the opposition of the monarchical parties but nevertheless possible, for it is supported by an immense majority of the people.

It is the duty, therefore, of the immense majority of the people to consult together, to unite and to vote against those who resist the establishment of the only government possible. The Monarchy today, after the three revolutions that have overthrown it, is immediate civil war, if it be established now; and if put off for two years, or three years, the civil war is only postponed until that epoch. The Republic is an equitable participation of all the children of France in the government of their country, according to their abilities, their importance, and their callings—a possible and practical participation, excluding nobody except those who announce that they will govern only by revolution. A republic is absolutely necessary, for everybody who is not blind or deceitful must admit that it alone is possible.

SOME POLITICAL EVENTS IN THE THIRD REPUBLIC

The Threat of General Boulanger

The Third French Republic was organized as a stopgap, pending time for the monarchists to gather their forces anew. Considered a temporary establishment, it was never honored by a formal constitution, only by a loose series of laws, the Constitutional Laws of 1875, which, with a few unimportant amendments, served as the constitution of the Third Republic until its overthrow in 1940. Within this loose constitutional structure, political parties, groups, and coalitions flitted on and off the scene with bewildering rapidity. A plot, a scandal, or the mere rumor thereof, was sometimes enough to topple a ministry or ruin a party. In some such category fell the ill-fated attempt of General Georges E. J. M. Boulanger (1837-1891), backed by a combination of military, conservative, nationalistic, and even radical groups (he was ready to satisfy his ambition by whatever path opened), to seize power after the manner of Napoleon III. A tool of the Monarchists, Boulanger attained wide popularity in the years 1886-89 by urging preparedness against Germany; but he lost his nerve at the critical moment, failed to make himself dictator, and fled, disgraced, into exile, where he committed suicide on his mistress's grave in Brussels. The Boulangist fiasco, however, was a heavy blow to the prestige of the monarchists and their allies in the church, and the elections of 1889 were a triumph for republican elements. The following account by Henri Rochefort, one of Boulanger's defenders, furnishes a good idea of the crosscurrents and eddies in French politics in the late 1880's.

From ROCHEFORT, "General Boulanger" (1888) [1]

The Boulangist movement has in reality a twofold character: it is at once patriotic and anti-parliamentary. France understands perfectly well the necessity upon her at present of fortifying herself against all attacks from the outside, and also the impossibility of continuing to keep alive a republic founded upon monarchical institutions. It has been said repeatedly—and no insinuation or suggestion, however vile, has been neglected which might press the statement home—that General Boulanger was the representative in France of the desire for an immediate revenge upon Germany, and that he was eager for war at all risks. That is simply a calumny borrowed from the German press, which Prince Bismarck keeps alive out of his "reptile fund." Even when he was Minister of War [1886-87], General Boulanger issued the following declaration, which those who know him know to be his real and characteristic opinion. "If I wished

[1] *Fortnightly Review*, N.S. XLIV (July-Dec., 1888), 11-16, 19-20.

war I should be a fool; if I did not prepare for war I should be a vile traitor." And those who saw him at work as Minister for War are able to testify that he did prepare for war with a well-directed energy. . . .

General Boulanger is popular because he has always worked for the defense of the fatherland, while the Opportunists have all laboured for their own personal advancement. . . .

In 1851, a period which some people affect to compare with this year of 1888 under the pretext that there is something of Bonaparte in Boulanger, we had no lost provinces to win back, and we did not hear night and day, upon our frontiers, the insulting rattle of those three million German rifles, with which Bismarck has threatened us in one of his last speeches. At present there is more than a chance—there is a probability—that the new German Emperor will attack us without warning; and it is with the prospect of this aggression before our eyes . . . that all Frenchmen who desire the safety of their country desire to see at the head of the army the one man who possesses their confidence, and whose qualities of resolute energy and patriotism constitute a guarantee which no other Minister of War within the last ten years has been capable of giving. . . .

Experience has proved beyond question the utter powerlessness of the parliamentary system of government as it exists today in France. The present *régime* is, properly speaking, nothing more nor less than a hunt for portfolios unrestrained by any close season. The guiding principle of all our politicians is the simple one, "Get out of that seat in order that I may sit there!" Owing to the adoption of this principle no ministry is stable. A Cabinet is at the mercy of any hostile coalition, and thus energies are paralyzed. . . .

What General Boulanger himself demands . . . is the revision of the constitution by means of an assembly especially elected for that purpose. And yet the Radicals, Opportunists, and followers of M. Ferry, who make this demand a pretext for attacking General Boulanger, were themselves the first to start the cry for revision. Three years ago . . . the Republican party was then unanimous in declaring that the constitution of 1875, having been formed and elaborated by Monarchists, was the stumbling-block in the way of all possible projects of amelioration and progress. Our senate, based upon restricted suffrage, is invested with powers equal to those of the popular chamber. . . . And the constitution is so constructed that if a conflict between the two chambers took place, there would be no possible solution of the difficulty but by a *coup d'état*. Properly speaking, this constitution of 1875 is nothing more or less than organized anarchy. . . . From 1875 to 1885 the Republican party in the Chamber was unanimous in recognizing the abuses inherent in our constitution. Why, then, do these men accuse General Boulanger of aiming at dictatorship because he sees what they saw and advocates the change which they themselves were the first to propose? The explanation is simple. They know well that General Boulanger is earnest in his demand, whereas in the last ten years they have got a liking for the spoils of office, and are now content with the abuses of an institution which they have learnt to turn to their own personal profit.

Emile Zola's Open Letter, J'accuse, on Behalf of Captain Dreyfus (1898)

Close on the heels of the Boulanger incident was another celebrated case in French affairs which came to be fraught with significant political consequences. This was the Dreyfus case. Captain Alfred Dreyfus (1859-1935) was arrested (October, 1894) on a charge of treason, convicted of having betrayed military secrets to the Germans, and sent to Devil's Island in French Guiana. Actually, the charge was a frame-up against a liberal Jew by anti-Semitic, Catholic, royalist members of the General Staff to prevent the revelation of scandal in high places. Subsequently (1897), Dreyfus' brother discovered that one Major Marie Charles F. W. Esterhazy had written the treasonable documents attributed to Dreyfus, and demanded his trial, but Esterhazy was triumphantly acquitted (January 11, 1898). Two days later, Emile Zola, the novelist, entered the fray on behalf of Dreyfus with the following open letter to the President of France, published in *L'Aurore,* a letter which went far to secure Dreyfus a new trial and, ultimately, his freedom and restoration to rank in the army (1906). Meanwhile, the Dreyfus case had become a matter of party politics, an incident leading to the increased power of radicals who supported Dreyfus and to the great discredit of the militarists, Catholics, monarchists, and jingoes who had so basely accused him. Zola's letter persuaded Jean Léon Jaurès to throw the growing weight of the French socialists behind Dreyfus; it was a forceful summary of the whole sordid affair; and it gave the French public its first view of the case as a whole. It ended with these stirring words.

From ZOLA, "J'accuse" (1898) [1]

It is only now that the Affair is beginning, because only now are men assuming clear positions: on one hand, the guilty, who do not wish justice to be done; on

[1] *The Dreyfus Case by the Man—Alfred Dreyfus—and His Son—Pierre Dreyfus,* ed. and trans. by Donald C. McKay, 1937, 118-19. By permission of the Yale University Press.

the other, the adherents of justice, who will give their lives so that justice may triumph. When you drive truth underground, it grows and gathers so great an explosive force that, when it finally does burst forth, it carries everything before it. Indeed, we shall see whether there has not already been prepared—for a future date —the most shocking of disasters.

But this letter has grown long, Mr. President, and it is time to conclude.

I accuse Lieutenant du Paty de Clam of having been the diabolical author of the judicial wrong—unconsciously, I am ready to believe—and of having then for three years defended his pernicious work by the most absurd and culpable machinations.

I accuse General Mercier of having rendered himself the accomplice, at least by want of firmness, of one of the greatest iniquities of the century.

I accuse General Billot of having had in his hands certain proofs of Dreyfus' innocence and of having hushed them up, of having rendered himself guilty of the crime of *lèse-humanité* and *lèse-justice* with a political object and in order to screen the compromised General Staff.

I accuse General de Boisdeffre and General Gonse of having made themselves accomplices of the same crime—the one, doubtless, through clerical prejudice, the other, perhaps, from the *esprit de corps* which makes the War Office a sacred, unassailable ark.

I accuse General de Pellieux and Major Ravary of having made an infamous inquiry—I mean by that an inquiry of monstrous partiality—of which their report is an imperishable monument of naïve audacity.

I accuse the three experts, *Sieurs* Belhomme, Varinard and Couard, of having made a false and fraudulent report, unless a medical examination should find them to be suffering from defective vision and diseased judgment.

I accuse the War Office of having carried on in the press, particularly in the *Eclair* and the *Echo de Paris,* an abominable campaign, in order to screen their mistake and mislead the public.

Lastly, I accuse the first Court-Martial of having violated the law by condemning an accused man on the basis of a secret document, and I accuse the second Court-Martial of having, in obedience to orders, screened that illegality by committing in its turn the judicial crime of knowingly acquitting a guilty man [Esterhazy].

In preferring these charges, I am aware that I bring myself under Articles 30 and 31 of the Press Law of July 29, 1881, which punishes defamation. And I do so voluntarily.

As to the men I accuse, I do not know them, I have never seen them, I have no resentment or animosity toward them. . . . I have but one passion—that of light. This I crave for the sake of humanity, which has suffered so much, and which is entitled to happiness. My passionate protest is merely the cry of my soul. Let them venture then to bring me before the Court of Assize and let an inquiry be made in broad daylight!

I wait.

The Program of the Socialist Party, 1905

"To the Left, to the Left, but never too far Left" well expresses French political-party tendencies, particularly as they have often adopted Leftist names poorly matched by their Center—and even Right of Center—policies. Before 1914, however, genuinely Leftist parties existed in France. In 1895 at a Trade Union Congress at Limoges the C.G.T. was organized (Confédération Générale du Travail), with a program of direct action; that is, to destroy the capitalist state by general strikes, sabotage, and violence. Within ten years, also, largely under the leadership of Jean Jaurès, a united French Socialist Party was organized out of the various splinter groups which had existed in the Third Republic since 1879. In a declaration of January 13, 1905, delegates of the various groups explained somewhat the conditions under which union was achieved, and described the broad policies of the new party.

From the Declaration of the French Socialist Party (1905) [1]

The delegates of the French socialist organizations, "Revolutionary Socialist Labor Party," "Socialist Party of France," "French Socialist Party," "autonomous federations of the Bouches-du-Rhône, Brittany, Hérault, Somme and Yonne," ordered by their respective parties to bring about unity upon the basis indicated by the International Congress of Amsterdam, declare that the action of the unified party ought to be guided by the principles which the international congresses, especially the most recent, those of Paris in 1900 and of Amsterdam in 1904, have established.

They declare that the divergence of views and the interpretations of different tactics which have existed up to the present are due especially to special circumstances in France and to the absence of a general organization.

They affirm their common desire to establish a party of class struggle, which, even when it utilizes to the advantage of the workingmen, the secondary conflicts of the possessors or finds itself accidentally combining its action with that of a political party for the defence of the results and interests of the proletariat, remains always a party of fundamental and irre-

ducible opposition to the totality of the bourgeois class and to the state which is its instrument.

In consequence, the delegates declare that their organizations are ready to collaborate immediately in this work of the unification of the socialistic forces upon the following basis, fixed and accepted by common accord:

1. The "Socialist Party" is a class party which has for its aim to socialize the means of production and exchange, *i.e.,* to transform the capitalistic society into a collectivist or communist society, and has for its method the economic and political organization of the proletariat. By its aim, by its ideal, by the methods which it employs, the "Socialist Party," although striving for the realization of the immediate reforms claimed by the working class, is not a party of reform, but a party of class struggle and of revolution;

2. The representatives of the party in parliament form a single group, confronting the bourgeois political sections. The socialist group in parliament ought to refuse to the government all the means which assure the domination of the *bourgeoisie* and its maintenance in power—to refuse in consequence military credits for colonial conquest, the secret funds, and the whole budget;

Even in the case of exceptional circumstances, the representatives cannot bind the party without its consent;

In parliament, the socialist group ought to consecrate itself to the defense and the extension of the political liberties and the rights of the workingmen, the pursuit and realization of the reforms which improve the conditions of life and of struggle of the working class;

The deputies, like all representatives, ought to hold themselves at the disposition of the party for its action in the country and its general propaganda for the organ-

[1] Anderson, ed., *op. cit.,* 653-54. By permission of Frank Maloy Anderson.

izing of the proletariat and the final aim of socialism.

The representative is released, individually, as each militant, from the control of his federation;

The totality of the representatives, as a group, are released from the control of the central organization. In every case, the congress judges in a sovereign manner. . . .

4. Liberty of discussion is complete in the press for questions of doctrine and of method, but for action all socialist newspapers ought to conform strictly to the decisions of the congress as interpreted by the central organization of the party.

CHURCH AND STATE IN THE THIRD REPUBLIC

The Ferry Laws on Education (*1882*)

From HANOTAUX, *Contemporary France* (1882) [1]

The three leading principles of school reform—*viz.,* that education should be gratuitous, compulsory and secular—were the subject of two bills carefully discussed in both Chambers towards the close of 1880.

M. Jules Ferry had two collaborators, one parliamentary, M. Paul Bert—the other administrative, M. Ferdinand Beusson, Director in the Ministry for Public Instruction.

On April 10th, 1870, speaking in the Salle Molière, M. Jules Ferry had made a solemn vow to keep the education of the people close at heart. This vow was now to be accomplished.

The necessity of educational reform was enforced by universal suffrage and the development of democracy. The high ideal

of harmony between the priest and the teacher was all too seldom realized. Yet M. Jules Ferry endeavoured in all honesty to avoid religious conflict—as he said himself: "There is no conscience more worthy of respect than that of the child." His sincerity cannot be doubted, but the enterprise was full of dangers. The measures he proposed were inspired by eighteenth century philosophy, optimistic philosophy.

"We believe in the natural uprightness of the human mind," he said to his opponents of the Right, "we believe in the ultimate triumph of good over evil, we believe in reason and the power of the people. It is you who do not do so. . . . The *book* and the power to assimilate its teachings are regarded by you and by us from very different points of view. For us, the book, whatever it may be, is the fundamental and irresistible means of developing the intellect."

He opposes *books* to *one* book, he pleads for the liberation of learning from the yoke of tradition. In his speech of 1870, Jules Ferry recalls that he owes his ideas to Condorcet's "magnificent system of Republican instruction, a system of three stages permeated by one principle, that of making men and citizens from the lowest grades up to the highest." The system is both social and civic in its character. The city has a right over the child. She represents the permanent, whereas the family symbolizes what is transient. Not without a violent effort can the bonds of the civic state be broken; those of the family dissolve themselves. . . .

M. Barodet had drawn up a measure which ultimately became a sort of code on primary instruction in 109 articles, and this was reported on by M. Paul Bert: "By the suppression of religious teaching in the school, liberty of conscience for the child, the parent and the teacher, is assured. . . . By putting the teaching in

[1] Gabriel Hanotaux, *Contemporary France,* IV (1877-82), trans. by E. Sparvel-Bayly, 1909, 561-68. By permission of Constable and Company, Ltd., London.

the hands of laymen, public education is intrusted to those who owe obedience only to the State."

In 1876 . . . there were two million children in sectarian schools against 2,-600,000 in undenominational schools.

Since the object of the new measures was to modify this state of things, and to obtain, as Paul Bert expressed it, "the right to supervise the education of the children of France," it is easy to understand the zeal with which they were opposed by the Roman Catholic Right, who looked upon them as atheistical and tyrannous.

The measure for making instruction gratuitous was adopted November 29th. . . . The measures making school instruction obligatory and undenominational had been brought forward by the Ferry Cabinet, January 20th, 1880. Primary instruction was made compulsory for children of both sexes between the ages of six and thirteen . . . [though it] "may be given at home by the parent himself." . . . The secular character of public instruction was determined by the enumeration of the subjects taught . . . a rather heavy program, its "encyclopedic" aspect recalling the origin of the reform. The law allowed no religious instruction to be given in the school; it deprived the clergy of the right of school inspection. . . . But it authorized and favoured the simultaneity of religious and lay instruction by declaring: "That the primary schools should close on one day every week, besides Sunday, in order to allow parents to give their children, if they so desire, religious instruction without the school buildings." . . .

The Right fought desperately for what it deemed the soul of France. . . . The "rights of the parent" and the "part of God" founded an argument that affected only those convinced of its strength. They spoke of Liberty, of Tolerance—but too late. Tolerance, after the abuses of past ages, was now on the side of the authors of the Bill, could they be moderate. . . .

The measure was passed in the Chamber, December 24th, by 329 votes to 134. During the following June it was discussed by the Senate. . . . Jules Ferry again defined his views: "We are called, as I believe, to defend the rights of the State against a certain Catholicism which is not religious Catholicism, but which I will term political. . . . We have indeed desired the Anti-clerical movement—never, though, for a moment aimed against Religion!". . .

These "Ferry Laws" were later completed by a series of legislative and administrative measures . . . under the Goblet Ministry. Only a statesman of Jules Ferry's stamp could have conceived such a work and carried it to its fulfilment. . . . But what has been the practical result of his laws?

As regards expense—in 1870 the budget for primary instruction was 61 millions of francs. . . . In 1902, it reached 236,-598,000 francs (for Algeria included) without reckoning the cost of constructing new buildings, which rose to a milliard.

Within a period of twenty-five years, 851,000 pupils have been added to the State schools; over 96 per cent of conscripts were able to write their own names, against 85 per cent in 1877. In Brittany, however, and in the center of France, there are still 12 and even 17 per cent of men of twenty years who cannot read and write. Education is still far from being properly enforced; and in mountainous districts . . . school attendance often sinks to 51.1 per cent. The Republic, however, has done its duty in offering systematised instruction to the growing generations.

The Separation of Church and State (1905)

The Ferry Laws struck at Catholic Church policy [see page 527], and the church often struck back at the Third Republic, especially through religious orders which inculcated students with ideas hostile to the Republic. To stamp out this influence, the Republic passed the Law of Associations in 1901, which required all religious orders to submit to state authorization and supervision. Four years later, December 9, 1905, the Law of Separation disestablished the French Church and revoked the Concordat which, since the time of Napoleon I [see page 422], had, with some modifications, regulated relations between Church and State in France. Extracts from this Law follow.

From the Law of Separation,
    December 9, 1905 [1]

TITLE I. PRINCIPLES

1. The Republic assures the liberty of conscience. It guarantees the free exercise of religions, subject only to restrictions hereinafter imposed in the interest of the public order.

2. The Republic neither recognizes nor salaries nor subsidizes any religion. In consequence, from the first of January . . . [next], all expenses relative to the exercise of religions shall be suppressed in the budgets of the state, departments, and communes. . . . [Excepting expenses of chaplains in public establishments.]

The public establishments of religion are suppressed, subject to the provisions set forth in article 3.

TITLE II. ASSIGNMENT OF PROPERTY PENSIONS

3. The establishments whose suppression is enacted by article 2, shall continue in operation provisionally, in conformity with the arrangements which at present regulate them, until the assignment of their property to the associations provided for by title IV. . . .

[1] Anderson, ed., *op. cit.*, 663-69. By permission of Frank Maloy Anderson.

From the promulgation of the present law, the agents of the administration of the public lands shall proceed to make a descriptive inventory and valuation: 1st, of the real and personal property of the said establishments; 2nd, of the property of the state, department, and communes of which the same establishments have the enjoyment. . . .

4. Within the period of one year . . . the real and personal property of the *menses, fabriques,* presbyterial councils, consistories, and other public establishments of religion . . . shall be transferred . . . to the associations which . . . shall be legally formed according to the provisions of article 19. . . .

8. In case of failure of an ecclesiastical establishment to proceed to the assignments prescribed above [within a year] . . . the properties shall, until their assignment, be placed under sequestration. . . .

11. The ministers of religion who . . . shall be more than sixty completed years of age and who shall have, during at least thirty years, filled ecclesiastical positions remunerated by the state, shall receive an annual pension for life equal to three-fourths of their salaries. . . . [Those 45 years of age, with 20 years of service, receive pensions equal to one-half of their salaries. Others salaried by the state shall receive one year's full salary, two-thirds for the second year, one-half for the third, and one-third for a fourth year.]

TITLE III. ECCLESIASTICAL BUILDINGS

12. The buildings which have been put at the disposition of the nation and which [in 1802] . . . serve for the public exercise of religions or the housing of their ministers . . . are and shall remain the properties of the state, departments and communes. . . .

13. The buildings in use for the public exercise of religion . . . shall be left

gratuitously at the disposition of the public establishments of religion, then to the associations called upon to replace them. . . .

18. The associations formed in order to provide for the cost, maintenance, and the public exercise of a religion must be constituted in conformity with . . . the law of July 1, 1901 [The Law of Associations]. . . .

19. These associations must have for their exclusive purpose the exercise of a religion and be composed at least: In Communes of less than 1000 inhabitants, of seven persons . . . of 1,000 to 20,000 . . . of fifteen persons . . . of more than 20,000 . . . of twenty-five adult persons. . . .

The associations may receive . . . donations and collections. . . . They shall not, under any form whatsoever, receive subventions from the state, departments, or communes. . . .

25. Meetings for the celebration of worship . . . are public. They . . . remain placed under the surveillance of the authorities in the interest of public order.

JULES FERRY AND MOTIVATION FOR FRENCH IMPERIALISM

Under the Third Republic France re-embarked on imperialistic policies, and before World War I had acquired a vast new empire. A prime mover in the acquisition of this new empire was Jules F. C. Ferry, twice Prime Minister (1880-81 and 1883-85). The motives which lay behind Ferry's policies and acts have been carefully analyzed recently, as follows.

From POWER, *Jules Ferry* (1944) [1]

French expansion in the 1870's was unobtrusively begun by colonial officials without the knowledge of, or with only grudging approval from, Paris. They were predominantly naval and military men who practiced their art of war on relatively backward kingdoms or tribes for the love of *la patrie* and of adventure. Often they were encouraged and abetted by French colonists like those in Réunion, Algeria, and Tunis. . . . Little encouragement from the motherland was given these lonely imperialists for many years. The leaders of France were for a decade much too busy to devote their energies to the empire. . . .

Jules Ferry as a young man had no interest in colonial expansion. He was deeply concerned with domestic problems, his liberal faith was opposed to imperialism. . . . He had no plans for overseas expansion when he came into office and only after his sweeping educational reforms were nearly completed did he become interested in these questions. He was persuaded to embark on his first colonial venture by career diplomats and colleagues, alarmed at Italian ambitions in Tunisia, who proposed to preserve French prestige and guard Algeria by seizing the Regency. Ferry's predecessors had already secured the consent of England and Germany.

Once he was persuaded to act in Tunisia, Ferry launched into a many-pronged imperialistic drive, renewing French projects in Indo-China, Oceania and West Africa. Pronounced vigor in the colonial sphere characterized the balance of his years as Premier. . . . He never had any long-range plan, but he moved opportunistically whenever a chance presented

[1] Reprinted from Thomas F. Power, *Jules Ferry and the Renaissance of French Imperialism*, pp. 194-99. Copyright 1944 by King's Crown Press.

itself. If he thought he could easily add to the French domain, he moved in as he did in Annam and Madagascar. His formula was to subsidize, seize and suppress abroad and then to explain his actions at home. But he was seldom the initiator. . . . The only colony that was entirely his creation . . . was Equatorial Africa, an outgrowth of Brazza's Congo discoveries. In each other field he was the heir of previous French occupation or ambition. His acquisitions included: Tunisia, the Congo, part of the French Sudan, Annam and Tonkin, several Pacific Island archipelagos, and part of French Somaliland. He came close to securing Madagascar and the base he established there was later successfully enlarged, as indeed were most of his territorial gains. . . .

Very important in persuading him to undertake several of his colonial expeditions were high civil servants, professional diplomats and military men. . . . The explorer Brazza fired Ferry's imagination for African expansion; Mahy, a deputy from Réunion, misled him into the Madagascar expedition. Ambassadors like De Noailles, Waddington and Saint-Vallier also encouraged the Premier. . . .

The aggressive imperial policy which Jules Ferry pursued would perhaps not have been possible and certainly would have been more hazardous had it not been for the support of Bismarck. The German Chancellor deliberately encouraged France to build an empire in order to distract her from her lost provinces. During 1884, Bismarck backed French imperial ambitions to use them as a weapon against England. Ferry was well aware of the reasons for Bismarck's support . . . he refused, however, to be pushed by the German statesman beyond the limits he set for himself. . . .

It has often been assumed that Ferry and his colleagues were primarily interested in acquiring new markets for French industry, new fields for French investors; or in protecting French commerce or finance when it was threatened by unsympathetic natives or the vicissitudes of the Great Depression. Such was not the case. Economic factors alone or predominantly were hardly ever responsible for the initiation of French colonial policy. The total French exports to the colonies which were acquired during Ferry's time constituted but an infinitesimal fraction of the nation's trade; French investments were small except in Egypt. . . . Nor was there an immediate rush of French trade, private construction of utilities or investment in the newly acquired colonies. Conspicuously lacking from Ferry's creed was a demand for raw materials. Only later did imports of tropical and mineral products bulk large in French interest. . . . There is no evidence of pressure or influence exerted on Ferry or his colleagues by organized pressure groups. . . . What economic pressure there was came mostly from French colonists. . . . There was no organized colonial propaganda movement. Only a few publicists and academic writers without a following called for an empire. . . . Popular interest in the French empire was only slowly aroused until imaginations were fired by tales of natural and archeological wonders in mysterious Africa and Asia. National pride was inflated by the prestige of owning such mysterious and reputedly wealthy lands. . . .

The need to secure appropriations from Parliament forced Ferry to formulate a rationale of expansion *ex post facto*. On the forge of parliamentary debate, this took its shape of economic imperialism. His early explanations and justifications were principally devoted to arguments of prestige and national honor. But late in 1883 the economic arguments came to the fore, and in retirement Ferry cultivated them to full flower. Those who have read only his later explanations of policy have been misled to believe that they were characteristic of his whole imperialistic career. . . . Ferry also professed to champion a civilizing mission and duty that compelled France to bring the beauties and truths of French culture and Christianity to the backward peoples and free them from such barbaric practices as slavery. This argument was useful to the prosaic Ferry who believed in the power of education,

but was hardly a mainspring of action. Directly bound with considerations of prestige was the necessity of global strategy for an imperial and maritime power. For that reason Ferry acquired naval bases useful both for the merchant marine and warships.

Whatever the means and motives, the policy of Ferry did endow France with a great empire. . . . This empire, for all its shortcomings, made the Third Republic a major world power.

29

THE RISE OF UNITED ITALY TO 1914

1. Nationalistic Stirrings, 1815-1848

"Italy," Prince Metternich is reputed to have said, "is but a geographical expression." This denial of political, national, and cultural unity to Italy was clearly expressed in the settlement at Vienna, whereby Italy was partitioned into eight states under separate rulers, most of them more or less under the tutelage of foreign powers, with Austrian influence predominating. Yet Italy was not devoid of nationalistic impulses. Drawing from the ancient "greatness that was Rome," such Renaissance "nationalists" as Dante and Machiavelli, the examples of their neighbors, the nationalistic influences of the French Revolution, the broken promises of Napoleon, and the teachings of nineteenth-century Liberalism and Romanticism—a small group of Italians longed for unity and freedom. In the latter days of the Napoleonic

Empire, organized resistance to French rule arose, and, after 1815, was carried over against the new foreign "oppressors." Necessarily secret, to avoid first the Napoleonic police and then the watchdogs of Austria and of the Quadruple Alliance, this resistance was spearheaded by the Carbonari. A description of them follows.

THE CARBONARI

From KING, *History of Italian Unity* (1899) [1]

They were practically an offshoot of Italian Freemasonry, with similar statutes and ritual, but with a more definite political aim. The Freemasons had long been numerous and influential in the south of Italy, and the new society was founded by republican refugees, who fled from Joseph Bonaparte's rule to the Abruzzi

[1] Bolton King, *A History of Italian Unity*, 2 vols., 1899, I, 19-23. By permission of Charles Scribner's Sons, New York.

and Calabria. They were joined by others, whose only point of sympathy was a common hatred to French rule; and thus from the first it was uncertain whether they should be counted as republicans or royalists. But they were obviously useful allies against the French, and as such were encouraged by Ferdinand [I, King of the Two Sicilies] and Bentinck. Murat in the latter years of his reign tried to win them, but in vain, and their opposition hastened his fall. After the Restoration Ferdinand naturally persecuted the men who had helped him to his throne. . . . Whether persecuted or protected, the Carbonari spread apace through southern Italy. Their democratic and communistic doctrines, their Christian phraseology swept in converts of different parties; their dim power satisfied men who were groping for authority . . . their fantastic symbolism appealed to an uneducated people, traditionally susceptible to the esoteric and mysterious. They started with a high moral ideal; their leaders hoped to purify society, and initiate an ill-defined socialism, inspired half by Christianity, half by the philosophy of the eighteenth century. Their enigmatic prophecies were inspired by Christian mysticism; "Christ," they said, "was the first victim of tyrants," and the crucifix hung in every Carbonari lodge. They were even tender to the religious orders and the Pope, and sometimes dreamt of a reformed Catholic church that he would lead. Their rules breathed the austerest morality; severe penalties threatened any immoral or dishonorable conduct from a member, and persons of ill-fame were rigorously excluded from the lodges, till, as large numbers thronged for admission, the officers relaxed the strictness of the scrutiny. It is more difficult to say what was their political creed. It was imparted to the higher grades only, and the rank-and-file were contented with vague formulas of liberty

and resistance to tyrants. . . . Sometimes they aimed at a federal government under the presidency of the Pope, sometimes at an united Italy with Rome for its capital; but the fantastic constitutions, which they loved to build, ran through every varying shade of republicanism and democratic monarchy, though the idea of Italian Independence was always present. A large number were more or less republicans, but the loose organization of a society, whose only links were personal and hierarchic, prevented any real unity of principle. They were practically a vast Liberal association, but with more power to destroy than to create. The threads of their complex organization were held by a supreme lodge, which sat at Naples. . . .

From Naples they spread northwards. . . . The earliest public symptom of the new spirit appeared in Lombardy, where it took a social and literary form. Disaffection had grown apace in the Austrian provinces, as hope in the Emperor's "paternal" government broke down. But the political instincts of the Lombards were too weak to allow of more than passive discontent. . . . But the Austrians soon saw the danger of the movement . . . and, harassed and mutilated, it died after a year's existence (October 1819); and the party plunged into conspiracy, as the schemes of the Carbonari matured for revolution.

These schemes were ripest in the south. After the first wave of the Restoration Ferdinand's rule had been more corrupt than tyrannical. . . . No one trusted the government: Ferdinand's word had been too often broken, and the royalist terror of 1799 could never be forgotten. The peasants groaned under the tyranny of their landlords, the drastic forest laws, the revival of conscription. The national pride was hurt by the presence, till 1817, of an Austrian army of occupation. . . . The government was rotten and blundering . . . justice was abused in the interests of the rich. Wide distress added to the discontent; the cotton and brandy industries had declined . . . the corn and oil trade was crippled . . . terrible famines and epidemics . . . left a trail of woe behind. Such a rule, feeble, undignified, corrupt, made a fair seed-bed of conspiracy. The Carbonari were becoming the real government of the country.

[In such circumstances the Neapolitan Revolution began in 1820. Inspired by the Spanish example [see page 467], Neapolitans demanded a constitution (July, 1820), to which Ferdinand at first consented; but soon, with Austrian help, the constitution was denied and the rebellion suppressed. Similar uprisings in northern Italy (Piedmont) were also quickly put down. Austrian troops again policed Italian states; with their protection, the "legitimate" princes revenged themselves savagely upon the Italian peoples. The Carbonari were weakened, their members imprisoned, executed, exiled, their prestige severely injured. When, in 1830-31, a second attempt failed in Romagna, the Carbonari movement faded away.]

JOSEPH MAZZINI'S "YOUNG ITALY," (1831)

Joseph Mazzini (1805-1872), himself a Carbonaro, appreciated the weaknesses of the movement. Born in Genoa, the son of a liberal-thinking professor of anatomy, Mazzini was educated for the bar, but soon turned to politics. He joined the Carbonari, was arrested in the outbreak of 1830, and, while still in prison, conceived the idea of a new society to replace the Carbonari. He objected to the meaningless ritualism, the secrecy, the want of good leaders, the lack of clear-cut principles, and the senility of the Carbonari. He dreamed of a "Young Italy," which would carry the gospel of nationalism to the common people of Italy, and he devoted the rest of his life to the realization of Italian unity, independence, and republican institutions. A far better theorist and propagandist than practical politician, Mazzini was disappointed in the manner in which, ultimately, Italy became unified and independent. But his own influence, and that of Young Italy, nevertheless contributed heavily toward that achievement. Here follows his own account of the origin and purposes of Young Italy.

From MAZZINI, *Young Italy* (1831) [1]

It was during these months of imprisonment that I conceived the plan of the association of Young Italy. . . . I meditated deeply upon the principles upon which to base the organization of the party, the aim and purpose of its labours —which I intended should be publicly declared—the method of its formation, the individuals to be selected to aid me in its creation, and the possibility of linking its operations with those of the existing revolutionary elements in Europe.

We were few in number, young in years, and of limited means and influence; but I believed the whole problem to consist in appealing to the true instincts and tendencies of the Italian heart, mute at that time, but revealed to us both by history and by our own provisions of the future. Our strength must lie in our right appreciation of what those instincts and tendencies really were. . . .

After deep study both of the history and the intimate social constitution of our country, I was led to prefix Unity and the Republic as the aim of the proposed association. . . . I may, however, state

[1] *Life and Writings of Joseph Mazzini*, 6 vols., London, 1891, I, 34-38, 60, 63, 69, 96-97, 99-112.

that I was not influenced by any mere political conception . . . of elevating the condition of the single people whom I saw thus dismembered, degraded, and oppressed; the parent thought of my every design was a presentiment that regenerated Italy was destined to arise the *initiatrix* of a new life, and a new and powerful Unity to all the nations of Europe. . . . I saw regenerate Italy becoming at one bound the missionary of a religion of progress and fraternity, far grander and vaster than she gave to humanity in the past.

The worship of Rome was a part of my being. The great Unity, the One Life of the world, had twice been elaborated within her walls. Other peoples—their brief mission fulfilled—disappeared for ever. To none save her had it been given twice to guide and direct the world. . . . Why should not a new Rome, the Rome of the Italian people—portents of whose coming I deemed I saw—arise to create a third and still vaster Unity; to . . . utter, not to individuals but to peoples, the great word Association—to make known to free men and equals their mission here below? . . .

[Mazzini was liberated from prison in February, 1831. Immediately he affiliated himself with Italian patriots. From Marseille, in 1831, he addressed a letter to Charles Albert, the new King of Sardinia, urging him to place himself at the head of the movement for Italian liberty, unity, and popular government. "The men of freedom," concluded Mazzini, "await your answer in your deeds. Whatsoever that answer may be, rest assured that posterity will either hail your name as that of the greatest of men, or the last of Italian tyrants. Take your choice." Copies of the letter sent to Italy met with favor from Italian patriots, and Mazzini recorded this "was my first encouragement

to *dare*." Rejecting the Carbonari because of its lack of constructive principles—"It called upon men to overthrow; it did not teach them how to build up a new edifice upon the ruins of the old"—Mazzini was impelled to found the Association of Young Italy, with the following statutes as its basis:]

Young Italy is a brotherhood of Italians who believe in *Progress* and *Duty,* and are convinced that Italy is destined to become one nation. . . . They join this association in the firm intent of consecrating both thought and action to the great aim of re-constituting Italy as one independent sovereign nation of free men and equals.

By Italy we understand—1. Continental and peninsular Italy, bounded on the north by the upper circle of the Alps, and the south by the sea, on the west by the mouths of the Varo, and on the east by Trieste; 2. The Islands proved Italian by the language of the inhabitants. . . . By the Nation we understand the universality of Italians bound together by a common Pact, and governed by the same laws. . . .

The aim of the association is revolution; but its labours will be essentially educational, both before and after the day of revolution; and it therefore declares the principles upon which the national education should be conducted, and from which Italy may hope for safety and regeneration. By preaching exclusively that which it believes to be truth, the association performs a work of duty, not of usurpation. . . .

Young Italy is *Republican* and *Unitarian.*

Republican—because theoretically every nation is destined, by the law of God and humanity, to form a free and equal community of brothers; and the republican is the only form of government that insures this future. Because all true sovereignty resides essentially in the nation. . . . Because our Italian tradition is essentially republican . . . whereas the introduction of monarchy amongst us was coeval with our decay and consummated our ruin. . . .

Young Italy is *Unitarian*—Because, without unity, there is no true nation. Because, without unity, there is no real strength; and Italy, surrounded as she is by powerful, united, and jealous nations, has need of strength before all things. Because federalism, by reducing her to the political impotence of Switzerland, would necessarily place her under the influence of one of the neighbouring nations. Because federalism, by reviving the local rivalries now extinct, would throw Italy back upon the Middle Ages. . . . Because Europe is undergoing a progressive series of transformations which are gradually and irresistibly guiding European society to form itself into vast and united masses. . . .

National unity, as understood by Young Italy, does not imply the despotism of any, but the association and concord of all. . . .

The means by which Young Italy proposes to reach its aim are—education and insurrection, to be adopted simultaneously, and made to harmonize with each other. Education must ever be directed to teach by example, word, and pen, the necessity of insurrection. Insurrection, whenever it can be realized, must be so conducted as to render it a means of national education. Education, though of necessity secret in Italy, will be public out of Italy. The members of Young Italy will aid in collecting and maintaining a fund for the expenses of the printing and diffusion of the works of the association.

The character of the insurrection must be national; the . . . aim being the formation of a nation; the insurrection will act in the name of the nation and rely upon the people, hitherto neglected, for its support. . . .

Convinced that Italy is strong enough to free herself without external help; that, in order to found a nationality . . . the feeling and consciousness of nationality should exist; and that it can never be created by any revolution . . . if achieved by foreign arms; convinced, moreover, that . . . the one thing wanting . . . is not power, but *faith,* Young Italy will endeavour to inspire this faith—first by teachings, and afterwards by an energetic initiative.

Young Italy draws a distinction between the period of insurrection, and that of revolution. The revolution begins as soon as the insurrection is triumphant. . . . Insurrection—by means of guerrilla bands —is the true method of warfare for all nations desirous of emancipating themselves from a foreign yoke. . . .

All members of Young Italy will pay into the treasury of the Society a monthly contribution of 50 centimes [or more if they can afford it]. The colours of Young Italy are *white, red,* and *green.* The banner of Young Italy will display these colours, and bear on the one side the words—*Liberty, Equality, Humanity;* and on the other—*Unity, Independence.*

Each member will, upon initiation . . . pronounce the following form of oath . . . In the name of God and of Italy . . . I, A. B. . . . swear to dedicate myself wholly and forever to the endeavour . . . to constitute Italy *one free, independent, republican nation.*

2. *The Revolutions of 1848 in Italy*

The February Revolution of 1848 in France was quickly transmitted to Italy, where, aroused by such propaganda as that set forth by Mazzini's Young Italy, the people of the Italian states struck for independence and unity. The following is a contemporary story of the various abortive insurrections that took place during 1848 and 1849.

From *The Annual Register, 1848 and 1849* [1]

In order to injure the revenue of Austria, the disaffected inhabitants of Lombardy, and especially of Milan, had resolved to give up the use of tobacco, and, in consequence of this, smoking was discountenanced by them as much as possible. Ludicrous as it may seem, cigars thus assumed a political importance, and became a test of the feelings of the population. At the beginning of the present year [1848], the Austrian authorities resolved to bring the tobacco question to a more decisive issue; and early on the morning of the 3d of January a supply of cigars was furnished to the soldiers in barracks in Milan, in order that they might smoke them in the streets. This gave great offence to the populace and, as might be expected, in the course of the day frequent collisions took place between them and the military. The latter drew their swords, and used them with fatal effect, so that a great number of persons were carried to the hospitals severely wounded, and some of them afterwards died. At Pavia also a quarrel about cigar-smoking resulted in a fatal struggle between the students and the soldiers, and the feeling of exasperation became such that it was evident that opportunity alone was wanting to convert it into a general revolt. . . .

The news of the French Revolution [in February, 1848] acted like an electric shock upon Italy, and the time seemed now to have arrived when the Lombardo-Venetian kingdom would rise and make

a bold attempt to throw off the Austrian yoke. No events, however, of importance took place—and it was not until the state of affairs at Vienna . . . had thrown the Austrian government into difficulty and confusion, that a blow for what was called Italian independence was struck. The struggle commenced at Milan where, notwithstanding the old hereditary connection between that territory and the House of Austria, the feeling of hatred against the latter was most intense.

Before, however, proceeding to hostilities, the Milanese demanded: 1. The suppression of the old police, and the establishment of a new corps under the orders of the Municipality. 2. The abolition of the laws regarding state offences, and the immediate liberation of the political prisoners. 3. A provisional regency of the kingdom. 4. Liberty of the press. 5. The convocation of the district councils for the purpose of electing a National Assembly. 6. . . . A Civic Guard under the orders of the Municipality.

A crowd assembled before the Government House, and, becoming tumultuous, the soldiers on duty fired a blank volley. A boy, only sixteen years old, then drew out a pistol, and shouting *Viva l'Italia,* discharged it at the troops. The mob rushed forward and overpowered the guard; the Vice-Governor O'Donnell was made prisoner, and the tricolour flag was hoisted on the palace of the Government. This happened on the 17th of March.

On the following day . . . signals of modern insurrection were everywhere raised in the streets. . . . By . . . the 23d . . . the Austrian troops retired in two columns on Verona and Mantua. . . . At the same time the Provisional Government at Milan issued an energetic proclamation calling upon all Italians to join in the contest. . . . They said:

"Fellow Citizens: We have conquered. We have compelled the enemy to fly, op-

[1] "History," *The Annual Register . . . 1848,* London, 1849, 318-22, 326, 329, 331-32.

pressed by his own shame as much as by our valour. . . . To arms then, to arms, to secure the fruits of our glorious revolution—to fight the last battle of independence and the Italian Union. . . ."

The King of Sardinia, Charles Albert, had already determined to take part in the struggle, and advance with his troops into Milanese territory. In a proclamation which he issued on the 23d of March he said: "For the purpose of more fully showing by exterior signs the sentiments of Italian unity, we wish that our troops should enter the territory of Lombardy and Venice, bearing the arms of Savoy above the Italian tricoloured flag." The assumption, however, of superiority on the part of the Savoy auxiliaries was unpalatable to the Milanese and . . . there was a want of that cordial co-operation which alone could have given the insurgents the slightest chance of success against the armies of Austria.

Venice was not slow in following the example of revolution set by Milan, and a Provisional Government was immediately formed which, on the 26th of March, thus announced to the Lombards its co-operation:

"We hailed with infinite joy the account of the emancipation of our generous sister of Lombardy. On the very day when you shook off the Austrian yoke, a Provisional Government of the Venetian Republic was proclaimed here under the glorious banner of St. Mark. We are influenced by no local prejudice—we are, above all, Italians. . . . We are united to you, Lombards. . . . When the hallowed soil of the country shall have ceased to be sullied by the feet of the foreign oppressor, we shall join you in discussing the form of government most conducive to our common glory." . . .

It is not our intention to narrate in detail the events of the campaign that followed.

They possess little interest, and we have not space to devote to the obscure conflicts which took place from time to time without any effect upon the ultimate result of the war. . . . [By early August, the Austrian forces, reinforced from the homeland, reconquered Milan, and an armistice was concluded.] On the 10th, the King, Charles Albert, issued a proclamation . . . which gave the following account of the cause of his reverses:

"The enemy increased; my army was almost alone in the struggle. The want of provisions forced us to abandon the positions we had conquered. . . . The throbs of my heart were ever for Italian independence; but Italy has not yet shown to the world that she can conquer alone. People of the kingdom! show yourselves strong in misfortune. . . . The cause of Italian independence is not yet lost." . . .

The Pope was naturally unwilling to engage in hostilities against Austria, one of the most powerful and devoted servants of the Papal See. He, therefore, resisted the demands of the people to send troops to join the army that was fighting in Lombardy for Italian independence. A body of Roman volunteers had, however, left the States of the Church. . . . On the 29th of April the Pope . . . disavowed the act of the Papal troops in crossing the frontier. . . . Next day the mob took possession of the Post Office and . . . tumultuous demonstrations took place; and at last, on the 1st of May, the Pope yielded to the popular will and issued a declaration of war against Austria. . . . [But local disturbances continued. Members of the Papal Government were assassinated, and the Pope seemed unable to satisfy popular demands.] On the 24th of November he disguised himself as a livery servant in attendance upon the Count de Spaur, the Bavarian Minister, and . . . drove rapidly away from Rome, arriving on the following day at Gaeta, a town in the Neapolitan territory.[1]

After the flight of Pope Pius IX a Supreme Junta was established at Rome on the 19th of December, 1848 . . . which . . . intended to assume their functions *pro tempore* . . . until the Constituent Assembly should deliberate upon the form of Government . . . claimed by the unanimous wish of the nation. . . . A bill was accordingly presented to the Roman Chambers on the 26th of December whereby it was enacted that the election to the Assembly should take place on the 25th of January, by universal suffrage and ballot; that the Assembly should consist of 200 members . . . and that the Assembly should meet at Rome on the 5th of February [1849]. . . .

At the sitting of the Roman Constituent Assembly on the 8th of February the decree was passed whereby the temporal sovereignty of the Pope was abolished, and a Republic established. . . . On the 12th of February M. Tornaboni moved, and the Assembly decreed, that Joseph Mazzini be invited to Rome, and that the title of citizen be conferred on him. . . . On the 27th of February M. Mazzini was proclaimed a member of the Roman Constituent Assembly. . . . For the purpose of insuring vigour and unity of action, a Triumvirate was appointed in whose hands the whole executive power was placed, and consisting of the following persons: Mazzini, Armellini, and Saffi. . . .

[Against these developments in Rome the Pope, from his exile at Gaeta, issued threatening proclamations, and the Catholic powers—Austria, Spain, and France—were invited to assist His Holiness. Meanwhile, the Austrians suppressed the revolutionary movements in North Italy and, in late April, French troops marched against Rome. After long hesitation, occasioned by uncertainty of policy in French ranks, the French army forced its way into Rome in early July, dissolved the Roman Republic, and took charge of the city pending the Pope's reassumption of power.]

Certainly his Holiness did not evince much disposition to conciliate his rebellious subjects. He did not return to Rome himself, but sent three commissioners, the Cardinals Della Geuga, Vanicelli, and Altieri, into whose hands General Oudinot [the French Commander], on the 3d of August, committed the entire civil administration of affairs.[2]

Naples and Sicily—For a long time the Sicilians had been in a state of discontent at the obstinate refusal of the King of Naples to grant various reforms which they demanded; and it was generally announced at the beginning of 1848, both in Sicily and Naples, that, unless concessions were made by the Neapolitan Government, an insurrection would almost immediately take place. These threats and warnings were, however, neglected or despised. . . . On the 12th of January, which was the King's birthday, the standard of revolt was unfurled at Palermo. The Royal troops made hardly any show of resistance . . . and retired into the barracks, the forts, and the palace. On the morning of the 13th . . . the firing commenced. . . . Detachments of fifteen or twenty persons, armed with fowling pieces, sabres, and cane swords, headed by well-dressed young men, traversed the streets, crying, "Viva Ferdinand II! Viva the Constitution of 1812!" The insurrection then began to expand rapidly, and became very formi-

[1] The following is from *The Annual Register . . . 1849*, London, 1850, 291, 293-95, 297, 306-07.

[2] The following is from *The Annual Register . . . 1848*, 332-37.

dable. After a series of encounters . . . the authority of the Government ceased to be recognized altogether in the city. . . .

When the news of the insurrection at Palermo first reached Naples, the King seemed disposed to act with utmost rigour and crush the rebellion by force. But the determined conduct of the Sicilians alarmed the Ministry, and the popular feeling in Naples was so strongly in favour of the insurgents, that . . . this led immediately to a change of Ministry; and a new one was formed [which] . . . declared that they could not retain office unless a Constitution were granted; and at last, as the aspect of affairs became every hour more serious, the King yielded, and on the 28th of January he signed a decree by which he promised to concede to his subjects a Constitution. . . .

But Sicily still remained in a state of insurrection, and the inhabitants were not disposed to be satisfied with any concessions. . . . On the 29th of January a revolt broke out at Messina, and . . . an English frigate [sought] . . . to moderate the violence of the struggle. . . . The British Government had sent Lord Minto into Italy . . . and, as he happened to be at Naples, he made use of his influence . . . to effect a reconciliation between Ferdinand and his revolted subjects in Sicily. His efforts were, however, vain. . . . Mutual hostilities continued until the 2nd of May, when an armistice was agreed to between the combatants, which lasted until the middle of August. . . .

[Meanwhile, in Naples, the King and Deputies quarreled over the nature of the proposed constitution. The quarrel became a fight in late May. A French squadron interfered to stop the bloodshed] . . . but the King was already master of the situation. Martial law was proclaimed, the National Guard suppressed, and the Chamber of Deputies dissolved. [This action in Naples redoubled the Sicilian

efforts at revolt. Already determined to cast off the yoke of Naples and to set up a separate Sicilian state, the Sicilian Assembly resolved to create a constitutional monarchy and invited the Duke of Genoa to take possession of the throne by the following articles:]

Art. 1. The Duke of Genoa, second son of the present King of Sardinia [Charles Albert], and his posterity, are called to reign in Sicily, according to the constitutional statutes of the 10th of July, 1848.

Art. 2. He will assume the name and title of Albert Amedée I, King of Sicily, in virtue of the Constitution of the Kingdom. . . .

Against this Act the King of Naples drew up a formal protest, declaring it "illegal, null, and of no effect"; and the Duke of Genoa had the prudence to decline the proferred crown. Ferdinand now equipped an expedition against his revolted subjects, and, on the 29th of August, a body of 14,000 soldiers sailed . . . for Messina. . . . On the 2nd of September a simultaneous attack was made upon it from the fire of the garrison, the Neapolitan fleet in the harbour, and a large force which had landed on the shore. The citizens fought with desperation; but the contest was too unequal, and after a bombardment of four days . . . they were compelled to surrender. [Palermo, however, did not surrender until April 22, 1849, when the insurrection finally ended.]

3. Cavour and Italian Unification

CAVOUR ENLISTS THE SYMPATHY OF
FOREIGN POWERS: THE CONGRESS OF
PARIS (1856)

The failure of the Italian Revolutions in 1848-49 convinced many Italian patriots—Mazzini excepted—that freedom from Austria could not be achieved without foreign aid. Among those of this opinion was Count Camillo Benso di Cavour (1810-1861), an aristocratic but liberal Piedmontese editor, commercial and agricultural promoter, and rising statesman of Sardinia. The Kingdom of Sardinia was the only Italian state to survive the defeat of 1848-49 with anything like a liberal constitution. [Charles Albert, on March 4, 1848, promulgated a constitution which became the model for the later constitution of the Kingdom of Italy; and though Charles Albert abdicated (March 23, 1849) in favor of his son, Victor Emmanuel II, the constitution was retained.] Cavour, becoming Premier in 1852, hoped to use his position to expel Austria and achieve Italian independence under Sardinian leadership. To do so, he sought the moral support of Europe, arguing against the accepted axiom that Austria's policing of Italy benefited Europe, and that, instead, Austrian rule in Italy was destructively brutal. Thus when the Crimean War broke out in 1854, Cavour enlisted Sardinia as an ally of England and France and hoped, at the peace conference, to bring the question of Italy before the attention of all Europe. To the Conference of Paris, in 1856, Cavour went with a firm intention to win a resolution that, "in the opinion of the Conference, the condition of Italy is dangerous and deplorable, and the cause of it is Austria." In his masterly biography of Cavour, William Roscoe Thayer gives a graphic account of Cavour's success.

From THAYER, *Cavour* (1911) [1]

To meddle as little as possible in outside discussions . . . was the Emperor's

[1] William Roscoe Thayer, *The Life and Times of Cavour*, 2 vols., 1911, I, 381-86. Permission of The Houghton Mifflin Company, Boston.

[Napoleon III's] true policy: but Cavour had driven his suggestion in so deep that the Italian problem haunted him, and on March 19 he consented that it should be brought before the Congress. He stipulated, however, that the treaty of peace should be signed first, to prevent disputes over side issues from imperiling that. . . . On Sunday, March 30, the treaty was signed. Not until April 8 was held the session at which Walewski, "with a somewhat solemn air," remarked that although their definite tasks had been achieved, the French government thought it would be well for them to discuss, quite informally, some of the questions which might disturb the peace they had just made. He spoke first of the condition of Greece; then he referred to the occupation of the Papal States by French and Austrian garrisons . . . which he hoped might soon be dispensed with. . . . He wondered whether it were not desirable for certain of the Italian princes to abandon their system of despotic repression. . . .

Lord Clarendon spoke next. After touching briefly on the Greek troubles and deploring the excesses of the Belgian press, he turned to the affairs of Italy. The foreign occupation, he pointed out, was tending to become permanent. . . . It virtually upset the European equilibrium. . . . He recognized that the conditions of the Pope's government were such as to render it unsafe to withdraw foreign support at once. That government, he said emphatically, must be reformed from top to bottom. . . . He drew up a terrible indictment against Pius the Ninth's government, going into details. . . . He . . . not merely approved Walewski's tentative criticism of the King of Naples, but asserted that, in spite of his own reluctance to interfere in the affairs of other countries, he believed it the duty of the Powers to compel King Ferdinand to listen to the voice of justice and humanity. . . .

The word now fell to Cavour. At last, after nine years of tireless energy as publicist and statesman and after a life-time of unquenchable hope, he was to speak in behalf of Italy in a Congress of the European Powers. He had a hundred reasons for allowing passion to prompt his eloquence: the sufferings of his down-trodden countrymen and their needs; the insults, the thwarting, the defeats heaped upon his beloved Piedmont. . . . And there nearly opposite, across the green table, as if to tempt him, sat Buol and Hübner—taunting, defiant, supercilious, implacable—the visible embodiment of that Austria who had cursed Italy for fifty years. . . .

Happily, Cavour listened to none of these promptings. Judging wisely that Lord Clarendon's volcanic explosion required no afterclap, he adopted a moderate tone, in which, while protesting formally against the conditions of Italy, he seemed to speak without rancor. Instead of vituperating the Austrian envoys, he began by acknowledging that they had a perfect right to keep out of this discussion, but he urged that it was most important for the welfare of Europe that the opinions of the Powers on the Italian situation should be publicly recorded. "The occupation of the Roman States," he said, confirming Clarendon's charges, "evidently tends to become permanent. It has lasted for eight years, and there is no indication to lead us to suppose that it will ever end. Indeed, the causes—or the pretexts—which brought it about, subsist with the same force as at the epoch when it was begun. The condition of Romagna, instead of improving, has grown worse: which is proved by the fact that Austria feels obliged to maintain the state of seige at Bologna. . . . Such a state of things, contrary to the treaties, destroys the political balance of Italy, and constitutes a very real danger for Pied-

mont. In fact, Austria . . . contrary to the spirit if not the letter of the treaty of Vienna . . . is the actual mistress of the larger part of Italy. The Powers in Congress ought not by their silence to sanction such a state of affairs. Piedmont, in particular, being especially menaced, must protest. For this reason I demand that the opinion of the plenipotentiaries of France and of Great Britain, as well as my formal protest, be inserted in the protocol." . . .

It took nearly a week of wrangling to draft the protocol. The Austrians fought to have every reference to the Italian Question expunged: the English and Cavour insisted that there should be no omission, and Walewski, instructed by the Emperor, sided with them. Still, as finally made public, the official report of that stormy meeting, from which dates a new era in the affairs of Italy, is colorless and emasculate. But the truth spread through Paris by word of mouth . . . and was soon commented upon in the press.

Cavour, who refrained throughout from overestimating the immediate gains to be won at the Congress, wrote, "Nevertheless, two facts will remain, which are not without some importance. First, the stigma branded on the conduct of the King of Naples by France and England in the face of united Europe; and, second, the condemnation aimed by England at the Clerical government in terms as precise and energetic as the most zealous Italian patriot could have desired." Having realized early in the negotiations that he could secure no material benefit, Cavour . . . rejoiced that Austria's stubborness, made more offensive by Buol's personal truculence, must have irritated Napoleon and convinced him, "as I have had the honor to repeat to him several times, that the Italian Question admits of but one real, efficacious solution—the cannon."

NAPOLEON III INTERCEDES ON BEHALF
OF SARDINIA AGAINST AUSTRIA (1859)

Obviously, Cavour had won the moral
support of France and England at Paris.
In July, 1858, Napoleon III conferred
with Cavour at a secret meeting in
Plombières at which the Emperor agreed
to assist Sardinia in a war against Austria if Sardinia provoked Austria to declare war. The plan further called for
the expulsion of Austria from Italy, the
reconstitution of Italy in a federation of
four states with the Pope as honorary
president, though with his own territory
reduced to Rome, and the reimburse-
ment of Napoleon by the cession of
Savoy and Nice to France. By arming
Sardinia and by meddling in the affairs
of neighboring states under Austrian
protection, Cavour provoked Austria
into war on April 28, 1859. On May 3
following, Napoleon III declared war
upon Austria, justifying his act in the
following proclamation to the French
people.

From NAPOLEON III, Proclamation
(May 3, 1859) [1]

Frenchmen! Austria, in causing her
army to enter the territory of the King of
Sardinia, our ally, declares war against us.
She thus violates treaties and justice and
menaces our frontiers. All the Great Powers have protested against this aggression.
. . . What can be the reason of this sudden invasion? It is that Austria has
brought matters to this extremity, that her
dominion must either extend to the Alps,
or Italy must be free to the Adriatic; for
in this country every corner of territory
which remains independent endangers her
power.

[1] Hertslet, The Map of Europe by Treaty, II,
1368-69.

Hitherto moderation has been the rule
of my conduct; now energy becomes my
first duty. Let France arm, and say resolutely to Europe, "I desire no conquest,
but I desire firmly to maintain my national
and traditional policy. I observe the treaties
on condition that no one shall violate them
against me. I respect the territory and
rights of neutral powers, but I boldly avow
sympathy for a people whose history is
mingled with our own, and who groan
beneath foreign oppression. France . . .
has not, therefore, abdicated her task of
civilisation. . . . When she draws the
sword it is not in order to dominate, but to
liberate.

The object of this war, then, is to restore
Italy to herself, not to make her change
masters, and we shall then have next our
frontiers a friendly people, who will owe
to us their independence. We are not going
into Italy to foment disorder or to shake
the power of the Holy Father, whom we
have replaced upon his throne, but to free
him from this foreign pressure which
weighs upon the whole peninsula, and to
help to establish there order upon legitimate satisfied interests.

THE TREATY OF VILLAFRANCA (1859)

Wars are usually filled with surprises.
Napoleon III found several in 1859.
Though their army was victorious in
the first few weeks, the French people
were not enthusiastic; the war was
costly, there was danger of interfering
too greatly in papal affairs, and there
was danger of Prussian attack and of
the war becoming European-wide. The
Austrians were firmly entrenched in
Venetia—which meant more expense
and a prolonged struggle. And lastly,
instead of creating the Italian federation
planned at Plombières, the Italian states,
helped by Cavour's adroit diplomacy,

were casting off their princelings and were uniting enthusiastically with Sardinia. Curiously, then, as it appeared to the outside world, Napoleon III, the victor, sued for peace, and on July 11, 1859, the preliminaries were drawn at Villafranca.

From The Treaty of Villafranca (1859) [1]

Between his majesty the Emperor of Austria and his majesty the Emperor of the French, it has been agreed as follows:

The two Sovereigns favour the creation of an Italian Confederation . . . under the honorary Presidency of the Holy Father. . . .

The Emperor of Austria cedes to the Emperor of the French his rights over Lombardy, with the exception of the Fortresses of Mantua and Peschiera. . . .

The Emperor of the French shall present the ceded territory to the King of Sardinia. . . .

Venetia shall form part of the Italian Confederation, remaining, however, subject to the Crown of the Emperor of Austria. . . .

The Grand Duke of Tuscany and the Duke of Modena return to their States. . . .

The two Emperors shall request the Holy Father to introduce in his States some indispensable reforms.

THE ITALIAN STATES UNITE WITH
SARDINIA: TUSCANY'S EXAMPLE, 1859

Against the proposed terms of Villafranca Cavour stormed with all his power, even to the extent of resigning his Premiership when Victor Emmanuel II indicated his acceptance of the treaty. But difficulties immediately arose in the application of the treaty. The Pope refused to be lured into the pro-

posed confederacy and to consider any reforms in his government; Great Britain objected to the re-establishment of the Dukes of Modena and of Parma and of the Grand Duke of Tuscany, and suggested that the people of those states be allowed to determine their own fate by an election; and while the diplomats of Europe negotiated about the "Italian Question," the peoples of Tuscany, Modena, Parma, and Romagna (a portion of the Papal States), urged on by Cavour and a number of local patriots, conducted elections and peaceably voted to unite with the Kingdom of Sardinia and to accept the sovereignty of Victor Emmanuel II. The war had initiated a movement towards Italian unity which could not be stopped. The following proclamation, issued by the provisional government of Tuscany on September 29, 1859, illustrates this movement.

From A Proclamation of the Provisional
Government of Tuscany (1859) [2]

Tuscans! The Assembly of your legitimate Representatives has declared it to be the firm desire of Tuscany to make part of a strong Constitutional Kingdom under the sceptre of King Victor Emmanuel of the House of Savoy. The Assemblies of Modena, Parma, and the Romagna have unanimously expressed similar declarations. These solemn votes have been accepted. The King Elect has accepted the free act of subjection of the people of Tuscany, Modena, Parma, and the Romagna; and has declared that the first act of his sovereignty shall be to give validity to the rights which had been conferred on him by those peoples.

These acts of the electing peoples and

[1] Ibid., II, 1374-75.

[2] British and Foreign State Papers 1858-1859, London, 1867, XLIX, 236-37.

of the King Elect have constituted the strongest and most legitimate bond that can unite the Ruler and the subject . . . for it is not by force that thrones are established, but by the just national will. . . .

The war undertaken by Napoleon and Victor Emmanuel was a solemn recognition of that right, since it was undertaken to liberate Italy from Austrian dominion, and to constitute Italian nationality. All Italians were called on to profit by the great occasion, and the people of Central Italy flew to arms. . . . This coöperation in a war, not of conquest but of national emancipation, authorized the formation of a new Kingdom of Italy, which the other European States may recognize, but to which they cannot give legitimacy. The latter is the result of the spontaneous consent of the peoples electing and of the King Elect. For them the compact is complete and irrevocable; as regards them, the strong kingdom is a thing established; the King Elect is their King. . . .

Tuscans! your Government proclaims that it will for the future exercise its power in the name of His Majesty Victor Emmanuel of Savoy, the King Elect.

GARIBALDI'S EFFORTS TOWARD A UNITED ITALY

No one dared to interfere in the course of events which, before the end of 1859, had united all northern Italy save Venetia under the crown of Sardinia. But the fate of the Kingdom of Naples was still undecided. The people, vastly discontented under their Bourbon King Francis II, still rose up in sporadic insurrections. Taking advantage of this discontent, and covertly with the connivance of Sardinia, Giuseppe Garibaldi (1807-1882), an Italian patriot and soldier of fortune with an international reputation in guerrilla warfare,

collected about a thousand volunteers (the "Red Shirts") and, with the cry of "Italy and Victor Emmanuel!" descended upon Sicily (May, 1860) and thence to the mainland, intent upon adding the Kingdom of Naples to the new Italian kingdom. Upon his departure for Sicily, Garibaldi set forth the following resounding proclamation as a call to arms.

From GARIBALDI, Proclamation (1860) [1]

Italians! The Sicilians are fighting against the enemies of Italy and for Italy. To help them with money, arms, and especially men, is the duty of every Italian.

Let the Marches, Umbria, Sabine, the Roman Compagna, and the Neapolitan territory rise, so as to divide the enemy's forces.

If the cities do not offer a sufficient basis for insurrection, let the more resolute throw themselves into the open country. A brave man can always find a weapon. In the name of Heaven, hearken not to the voice of those who cram themselves at well-served tables. Let us arm. Let us fight for our brothers; tomorrow we can fight for ourselves.

A handful of brave men, who have followed me in battles for our country, are advancing with me to the rescue. Italy knows them; they always appear at the hour of danger. Brave and generous companions, they have devoted their lives to their country; they will shed their last drop of blood for it, seeking no other reward than that of a pure conscience.

"Italy and Victor Emmanuel!"—that was our battle-cry when we crossed the Ticino; it will resound into the very depths of Aetna. As this prophetic battle-cry

1 "History," *The Annual Register . . . 1860,* London, 1861, 221.

re-echoes from the hills of Italy to the Tarpeian Mount, the tottering thrones of tyranny will fall to pieces, and the whole country will rise like one man.

KING VICTOR EMMANUEL'S ADDRESS TO THE FIRST PARLIAMENT OF UNITED ITALY (FEBRUARY 18, 1861) AND THE POPE'S ATTITUDE

On October 21-22, 1859, Naples and Sicily, by a plebiscite similar to those earlier held in the northern states, voted to unite with Sardinia. Within a year, Italy had been united. Only Venetia and the Patrimony of St. Peter remained outside the newly united state. Elections were held for the first parliament of united Italy in January, 1861. On the eighteenth of February, the parliament met at Turin in a great hall temporarily constructed of wood. King Victor Emmanuel opened the proceedings with the following address.

From *The Annual Register, 1861* [1]

"Gentlemen Senators, Gentlemen Deputies!

"Free, and nearly entirely united, by the wonderful aid of Divine Providence, the concordant will of the peoples, and the splendid valour of the armies, Italy confides in your virtue and wisdom. To you it pertains to give her common institutions and a firm foundation. In endowing with greater administrative freedom peoples that had various usages and institutions, you will take care that political unity, the aspiration of so many centuries, may never be diminished. The opinion of civilized nations is favourable to us; the just and liberal principles, now prevailing in the councils of Europe, are favourable to us. Italy herself, too, will become a guarantee

[1] *The Annual Register . . . 1861,* London, 1862, 186-88, 190-91.

of order and peace, and will once more be an efficacious instrument of universal civilization.

"The Emperor of the French, firmly upholding the maxim of non-intervention —a maxim eminently beneficial to us— nevertheless deemed it proper to recall his envoy. If this fact was a cause of grief to us, it did not change the sentiments of our gratitude nor our confidence in his affection to the Italian cause. . . . The Government and people of England, the ancient country of freedom, loudly took part for our right to be the arbiters of our own destinies. . . . A loyal and illustrious Prince having ascended the throne of Prussia [William I], I sent him an ambassador in token of respect for him personally, and of sympathy with the noble German nation, which I hope will become more and more convinced that Italy, being constituted in her natural unity, cannot offend the rights or interests of other nations. . . .

"Valiant youths, led on by a captain who has filled with his name the most distant countries [Garibaldi], have made it evident that neither servitude nor long misfortunes have been able to weaken the fibre of the Italian peoples. These facts have inspired the nation with great confidence in its own destinies. I take pleasure in manifesting to the first Parliament of Italy the joy I feel in my heart as King and soldier."

The first measure proposed was a Bill declaring Victor Emmanuel King of Italy, which passed almost unanimously, only two votes being given in the negative. Against this Act, the Papal Government protested . . . [as follows:]

"A Catholic King, forgetful of every religious principle, despising every right, trampling upon every law, after having, little by little, despoiled the august Head of the Catholic Church of the greatest and most flourishing part of his legitimate possessions, has now entitled himself King of Italy; with which title he has desired to seal the sacrilegious usurpations already consummated, and which his Government has already manifested its intention of completing to the detriment of the patrimony of the Apostolic See. . . . It would here be superfluous to recall the holiness of the possession of the patrimony of the Church and the right that the Supreme Pontiff has to it—an incontestable right, recognized at all times by all Governments. Therefore it is that the Holy Father will never be able to recognize the title of 'King of Italy,' arrogated to himself by the King of Sardinia, because it is injurious to the sacred property of the Church. On the contrary, he makes the most ample and formal protest against such an usurpation."

[Despite the papal protest, Baron Ricesoli, who succeeded as Premier upon the sudden death of Count Cavour, June 6, 1861, set forth the following policy for the new Kingdom of Italy in an address before the Italian Chamber:]

"What the King's Government sees is a territory to defend, a territory to recover. It sees Rome; it sees Venice! To the Eternal City and the Queen of the Adriatic it turns the thoughts, the hopes, and energies of the nation. The Government feels the heavy task that lies before it; with God's help it will fulfil it. Opportunity, matured by time, will open our way to Venice. In the meantime, we think of Rome. Yes, we will go to Rome. Shall Rome, politically severed from the rest of Italy, continue to be the center of intrigue and conspiracy—a permanent threat to the public order? To go to Rome is for the Italians not merely a right, it is an inexorable necessity."

4. United Italy, 1870-1914: General Trends

CHURCH AND STATE: THE PAPAL LAW OF GUARANTEES (1871)

Venetia and Rome were united to Italy within the next decade, Venetia as a reward for Italy's aid to Prussia in the war between Austria and Prussia in 1866 (the "Seven Weeks' War"), and Rome in 1870, after Napoleon's withdrawal of the French troops from Rome upon the outbreak of the Franco-Prussian War. But Rome was not taken without a battle, and the Italian troops which captured it (September 20, 1870) encountered stiff, though brief, resistance from the papal defenders. After a plebiscite, Rome was annexed to Italy and proclaimed the capital of the now completed Kingdom. Relations with the Papacy, however, remained strained. In March, 1871, the Italian Government sought to define its relations to the Papacy in a Law of Guarantees (March 21), but the Pope refused to recognize or accept it, and proclaimed himself a "prisoner of the Vatican." Relations between the Italian Government and the Papacy were not formally regularized until the Lateran Treaty was successfully negotiated between Mussolini and the Pope in 1929. An English diplomat's report on the proposed Law of Guarantees and its reception by the Vatican follows.

From PAGET, Letter to Earl Granville (1870) [1]

According to the "Bill of Guarantee," &c., for the Pope, the person of the Sovereign Pontiff is declared sacred and inviolable; sovereign honours hitherto

[1] Sir A. Paget to Earl Granville, Florence, December 12, 1870, in British and Foreign State Papers, 1871-1872, London 1877, LXII, 488-89.

awarded to His Holiness are maintained, as well as his right to have his own guard for his palace. A yearly sum (3,225,000 lire) equal to that hitherto inscribed on the Papal budget is to be inscribed on the *grand livre* for His Holiness's own use, and to be paid exempt from all tax; the Pontiff to have the free enjoyment of the Vatican, of Santa Maria Maggiore, of Castel Gondolfo, the above palaces to be exempt from the jurisdiction of the State, as well as the places where conclaves and councils may be held, which the Government binds itself to protect with armed force, if necessary; consequently, no Government official may penetrate into the above-mentioned localities except at the requisition of the Sovereign Pontiff, or of the President of the . . . council. . . . The Pontiff will be free to fulfil all the functions of his Ministry, to affix to the doors of the basilicas at Rome, or to otherwise publish, the acts of his Ministry and those of the sacred congregations, without any impediment on the part of the Government. The Cardinals and other ecclesiastics shall likewise be irresponsible for any ecclesiastical acts performed in Rome having reference to the functions of the Holy See. It shall be allowed to the Pope to correspond with the episcopacy, and to have his own post-office, telegraphs, and couriers for this purpose. Legates and other Representatives of the Pope, as well as Foreign Representatives accredited to His Holiness, are to have the same prerogatives as those accorded to Diplomatic Agents.

The exercise of authority or spiritual jurisdiction by the Pontiff is free from the interference of the Civil Power. . . . The employment of secular compulsion is excluded in ecclesiastical measures. Councils, chapters, and other ecclesiastical reunions can be held without permission from the Government. The nomination to all ecclesiastical appointments in Italy will take place without the interference of the Government, but the nominees, except the "suburbican" Bishops of Rome, must be Italian subjects. . . . The seminaries, academies, colleges, and other Catholic institutions founded at Rome for the education . . . of ecclesiastics will still be dependent upon the Holy See without any interference. . . .

The enactments as a whole . . . must, it appears to me, be considered as offering every necessary security to the Pontiff for the exercise of his spiritual power; but an ecclesiastic of some position and well acquainted with the Vatican whom I saw today declared them utterly unacceptable, and as not offering any sort of guarantee for the Papacy.

POLITICAL TRENDS

From TREVELYAN, *The Italian People* (1920) [1]

For thirty years after the taking of Rome the Italian people labored in the trough of the wave that had carried them to victory. They looked in vain for the prosperity which the patriots had promised them, and an age of industrial revolution brought to the proletariat new suffering which their earlier simplicity had spared them. The South remained a cruel drag upon the more progressive North; taxation was heavy and its incidence unjust; year after year—save for a brief interval from 1875 to 1881—a gaping deficit in every budget swelled the national debt. Capital expenditure of every kind—in railways, in roads, in public buildings—was forced upon the young Kingdom, in order to knit together her diverse populations and to put an end to the medievalism of the South and Center. . . . Not so easily was the terrible heritage of 350 years of oppres-

[1] From Janet Penrose Trevelyan, *A Short History of the Italian People*, 541-43. Copyright 1920, by Janet Penrose Trevelyan, courtesy of G. P. Putnam's Sons.

sion and misrule to be lived down, and if the laborer in Lombardy and the South still remained in a chronic state of semi-starvation; if political corruption fastened on the machine of government and hampered every effort to develop the national resources, the cause must be sought in the hard fate which had given Italy to be exploited for so long by alien and selfish races. . . . It is small wonder that when Cavour's generation had all passed away a race of politicians arose whose only care was to surmount the difficulties of each day, and who were not too fastidious in the means they employed for the purpose. Agostino Depretis, the first Premier produced by the Left or so-called Progressive parties, held office with but two brief interruptions from 1876 to 1887, but although he extended the parliamentary franchise he also invented the system known as *Transformism,* which consisted in buying the votes of this or that parliamentary group by luring its leaders into the Government. The result was that the normal lines of party division disappeared and the Chamber became the home of an unscrupulous opportunism. Francesco Crispi, who followed Depretis, carried the art of applying Government pressure at the elections to a height never before attempted, and . . . ruled the country with a cynical disregard for its hard-won liberties. The neglect of the politicians to the Left to further the interests of the working classes . . . produced an unhappy cleavage between Government and people, and a militant Socialist Party arose on the ruins of the Mazzinian idealists, pledged to fight solely for the material welfare of the workers.

Yet it was to the growth of this Socialist Party that Italy owed her emergence from the state of perpetual disturbances and rioting, culminating in the Milanese massacres of May, 1898. . . . Much infected in its earlier stages with . . . anarchism

. . . Italian Socialism became definitely Marxist and less revolutionary in the early eighties, under the leadership of Andrea Costa and Filippo Turati. As the only living creed that offered hope to the suffering people, it drew to itself the best of the young intellectuals as well as the artisans, and gradually extended its influence over the peasants by accepting the coöperative movement which had already done much to raise the condition of the rural population (1896). Crispi's savage and indiscriminate persecution of Socialists, Republicans and Radicals . . . (1893-96) drew his victims together in a working alliance of the Extreme Left, and it is to the social program advocated by this party, in season and out of season, that Italy owes the saner domestic policy that has followed the opening of the new century.

POLITICAL METHODS

Writing just before 1900, the German scholar Wilhelm Deecke, widely traveled in Italy and personally familiar with Italian affairs, made the following observations upon Italian political methods.

From DEECKE, *Italy* (1899) [1]

The successful working of a liberal constitution and self government presupposes a conscientiousness and disinterestedness among the officials. There is little of these qualities to be seen in Italy. The honorary posts are looked upon as a kind of milk cow, which must be milked with all one's force when one is at the helm. In addition to this, there is a want of scruple as regards public money, which, according to a very general view, exists in

[1] Wilhelm Deecke, *Italy: A Popular Account of the Country, Its People, and Its Institutions,* trans. by H. A. Nesbitt, 1904, 253-54. By permission of The Macmillan Company, New York.

order to be appropriated on any plausible pretext or to be secured for one's family or friends. This is the very cause of the existence of cliques and of party organization, a cause most sharply blamed and detected as much as possible by the opposition of the time, but once in possession of power, the opposition does no better. If on any occasion the scandal becomes too great, or if the levity with which money is spent or the municipality is governed becomes too notorious, the junta and the syndic or certain leaders receive their dismissal. They frequently retire to wait for better times, and no one thinks of bringing them to account for their blunders or their direct breach of law, for the feeling of responsibility towards the community as a whole is absent from the minds of those worthless leaders as well as of their opponents, who, be it said, are afraid of creating a precedent against themselves by any prosecution of the kind.

The country and the poorer population often suffer in an extraordinary manner under these circumstances. For, in spite of the freedom of election, only the more highly rated can vote, and the power in the communes almost always lies in the hands of a kind of aristocracy . . . who . . . determine the amount of the [tax] rates . . . which they foist on the needy people. If the burdens on the ordinary necessities of life (rent, bread, wine, oil, etc.) become too heavy, the people rise, rush together, storm the town hall, set it on fire or burn the toll houses . . . and thus compel either a temporary alleviation of taxation or the fall of the ruling party. This explains the continual disturbances in the Romagna, Southern Italy, Sicily and Sardinia, which can only be permanently quieted by purification of the communal governments and a radical reform of the system of taxation. . . . The country needs a stronger government, and an in-

dependent and better paid body of officials would be a real blessing.

NATIONALISM, IRREDENTISM, AND FUTURISM

From WALLACE, *Greater Italy* (1917) [1]

The unification of Italy had been brought about by putting into practice a long-cherished theory that all men of the same language, customs, and traditions have the right to form a separate political entity. The Italians were the first to bring to a successful conclusion, on a large scale, this great experiment in statecraft, which was to become so impelling a force in nation-building during the ensuing years. . . . As France, a century before, had lit the torch of individual liberty, so Italy first championed successfully the belief that national liberty . . . is the most valuable asset of mankind. . . .

With so firm a faith in the creed of nationality, the Italians could not rest content as long as all the provinces bearing the imprint of Italian culture were not united to the mother country. For, under the stress of necessity, the boundary delimitations of the new Kingdom had been drawn in a manner which left outside the realm more than a million Italians. Thus arose the problem of *"Italia irredenta,"* or "unredeemed Italy," as the districts inhabited by these Italians came to be called. . . . Trentino . . . an enclave between Lombardy and Venetia . . . was arbitrarily annexed to Austria on the fall of Napoleon. . . . The Trentino remains an Italian province, and its people [375,000 Italians] have striven valiantly and patiently to knit ever more closely the ties which bind them to Italy. . . . The other great settlement of Italians who live be-

[1] William Kay Wallace, *Greater Italy*, 1917, 20-27, 30, 32, 34, 36-38. Permission of Charles Scribner's Sons, New York.

yond the pale, and are eager to be joined with their mother country, live in "Venezia Giulia," with the great seaport of Trieste as its chief center. As the name implies, this region, with the exception of Trieste, was formerly under the dominion of Venice, whose colonial domain in the Eastern Adriatic included also Istria and Dalmatia. The irredentist problem in these regions is far more difficult of solution, for, though the coast towns of the Adriatic have retained their Italian character to a large extent, the districts inland, even up to the doors of the cities, are predominantly Slav; Slovene in the northern Adriatic, Serbo-Croat farther south.

To formulate a plan for the redemption of the Italians living outside the realm has preoccupied all Italy from the first day of national independence. Extremists went so far as to include the islands of Malta, Corsica, and even Corfu, besides the Eastern Adriatic mainland as far south as Avlons, in their scheme of *Italia irredenta,* while the more conservative lay claim only to such districts as, like the Trentino and Trieste, are patently Italian. . . . At the most unexpected moments the passions of the Italian people, demanding the liberation of the *irredenta* provinces, burst forth. Every important occasion . . . was seized upon to make a demonstration in favor of the coveted provinces. These in turn sent deputations to Italy and messages of loyalty to the Italian cause. . . . The death of King Victor Emmanuel II, the liberator of Italy, in 1878, gave an opportunity for wide-spread agitation. Garibaldi, whose spiritual authority among the people of Italy was supreme, issued a manifesto in which he exclaimed: "The call of the patriots of Trieste and Trent must find an echo in the hearts of all Italians, and the yoke of Austria, no better than that of the Turk, must once for all be broken off the necks of our brethren." . . . However, Italy was too

weak to fight Austria single-handed; there remained only the alliance [the Triple Alliance]. Events in Germany seemed to pave the way for this understanding. The menacing attitude of France in the Tunisian crisis further contributed to drive Italy into the arms of Germany and Austria, and thus only a year after the most violent "irredentist" campaign, Italy entered into a closely united alliance with her hated enemy, Austria . . . and many of those who had played a leading part in the irredentist movement became convinced that the Triple Alliance was of greater benefit to Italy than the acquisition of the unredeemed provinces would be. It seems reasonable to suppose that had Austria adopted a liberal and enlightened policy towards her Italian subjects . . . the irredentist movement would have finally died out. . . . But Austria, instead of adopting this course . . . incited the Slav populations of the Adriatic, and the Germans of Tyrol, to . . . crush out the Italianism of these districts. . . . The irredentist movement now took on a new aspect. It became a struggle for Italian cultural survival. . . . The Italians . . . formed societies for the maintenance of the Italian culture of the *irredente* provinces. . . . The irredentist movement thus became a literary, patriotic creed rather than a political design. It passed deep into the hearts of the Italian people. It was not "land greed" . . . so much as a spirit like that of the Christian "crusader," who set out to redeem the shrines of the Holy Land, which inspired the Italian people to look forward to the liberation of their nationals still under the Austrian yoke. . . .

If nationalism, as conceived by the Italians, brought forth "irredentism," "irredentism" in turn, by a circuitous path, brought into being what has been termed "futurism." . . . The Italians were sick unto death of hearing of the glories of the Renaissance discussed and commented upon by foreign observers. . . . How could Italy subsist and grow with a world of men, both within and without her boundaries, engrossed only with the period of efflorescence of a golden age of genius already covered with the dust of four elapsed centuries? . . . The futurists, as their name implies, believed that Italy's destiny lay in the future; that looking backward is a sign of senility; that looking to the future is the privilege of youth. . . . Thus arose the demand for independence, liberty of action and self reliance. . . . But futurism has to it another side, which distinguishes it as a phenomenon singularly suggestive. While futurism preaches a cult of progress, it is a progress based on the strength to maintain itself, if need be,

by the force of arms. Arbitration, pacifism, internationalism, the Utopian dreams of a world freed from racial conflicts and wars . . . find no place in Italian futurism. For it is essentially a belligerent doctrine. "War is the only hygiene of the world," was a main tenet enunciated by Italian futurists over a decade ago [c. 1905]. . . . "War is the culminating synthesis of progress, the school of ambition and heroism," was to be the cry of the futurists during the painful days of Italian neutrality [1914-15]. . . . Modern Italians must know how to handle a rifle as well as a paintbrush; a lathe and the motor as well as the sculptor's chisel. Nationalism, irredentism, futurism, were to be the leaven of modern Italy.

30 GERMANIC ALTERATIONS: THE DUAL MONARCHY AND THE RISE OF THE GERMAN EMPIRE

1. The Trend towards Economic Unity: The Zollverein

The militant nationalism engendered in the Germanies during the latter days of Napoleon I [see page 440] and the movement toward greater unity as expressed in the Burschenschaft's objectives [see page 471] continued, especially in Prussian circles, during the first half of the nineteenth century. But the Carlsbad Decrees (1819) and other aspects of the "Metternich System"— plus the conservative policies of most of the German princes themselves, espe-

cially the Prussian Hohenzollerns— were effective in stamping out, or at least in driving underground until 1848, most of the German liberal impulses; and that nationalism which remained was illiberal, rendered almost dynastic by Prussia's competition with Austria for leadership among the German states. Still, while political, constitutional, and social reforms were resisted until, in 1848, the demand for them engulfed all the Germanies in bloody revolt, there was slowly developing, primarily under Prussian leadership, an economic unity among many of the German states.

PRECURSORS OF THE ZOLLVEREIN

One of the principal bases for this economic unity was the Zollverein, or customs union. Instrumental in the agitation for the Zollverein—or something akin to it—was Friedrich List (1789-1846), a Württemberger who became a political economist and pro-Prussian nationalist with considerable influence. List was a severe critic of Adam Smith's individualistic economics. He held that the economic system should be national, not individualistic, and should show how a given nation, in its particular situation, can best direct, regulate, and restrict the economy of individuals in the interest of the greatest possible national power and prosperity. Thus List became an active promoter of a *national* German system—in railway development, manufacturing, and tax regulation. In 1819, List helped to create a union of German businessmen (Handelsverein) to memorialize the Diet in behalf of freer trade within the Bund. Their first petition read in part as follows.

From A Petition of German Merchants to the German Diet (April, 1819) [1]

The humble petition of the German merchants and manufacturers, met together at Frankfurt-on-Main for the Easter Fair of 1819, for the removal of all custom-duties and tolls in the interior of Germany, and the establishment of a universal German system founded on the principle of retaliation against foreign states. Presented by Professor List of Tübingen as agent for the petitioners.

Worshipful Federal Assembly: We, the undersigned German merchants and

[1] This and the next selection are from Margaret E. Hirst, *Life of Friedrich List and Selections from His Writings,* 1909. By permission of John Murray, London. This is 137-40.

manufacturers . . . approach with deep respect this the highest representative assembly of the German nation in order to set forth the causes of our suffering and to beg for help. In a country where it is common knowledge that the majority of manufacturers are either entirely ruined or drag on a precarious and burdensome existence, where the fairs and markets are filled with foreign wares . . . thirty-eight customs boundaries cripple inland trade, and produce much the same effect as ligatures which prevent the free circulation of the blood. The merchant trading between Hamburg and Austria, or Berlin and Switzerland, must traverse ten states, must learn ten customs-tariffs, must pay ten successive transit dues. Any one who is so unfortunate as to live on the boundary-line between three or four states spends his days among hostile tax-gatherers and custom-house officials; he is a man without a country.

This is a miserable condition of things for men of business and merchants. They cast envious glances across the Rhine where, from the Channel to the Mediterranean, from the Rhine to the Pyrenees, from the Dutch to the Italian borders, a great nation [France] carries on its trade over free rivers and free roads without ever meeting a custom-house official. Customs and tolls, like war, can only be justified as a means of defence. But the smaller the country which imposes a duty, the greater is the loss, the more harmful the effect on national enterprise, the heavier the cost of collection; for small countries are all boundary. Hence our thirty-eight customs boundaries are incomparably more injurious than a line of custom-houses on the external boundary of Germany, even if in the latter case the imposts were three times as heavy. And so the power of the very nation which in the time of the Hansards carried on the world's trade under the protection of its own fleet, is now ruined by the thirty-eight lines of customs.

We think that we have brought forward sufficient reasons to prove to your august assembly that only the remission of the internal customs, and the erection of a general tariff for the whole Federation, can restore national trade and industry or help the working classes.

FORMATION OF THE ZOLLVEREIN (1834)

Such petitions as that above bore no fruits directly. Austria was unwilling to join with the other states, and the Diet accomplished nothing. But such petitions awakened other states to the possibilities of economic co-operation. In 1819 Prussia absorbed by treaty into the Prussian customs system the little state of Schwarzburg-Sondershausen and thus took the first step towards the creation of the Zollverein completed nearly fifteen years later. A brief account of these events follows.

From HIRST, *Life of Friedrich List* (1909) [1]

Between the years 1820 and 1825 negotiations were carried on between the Governments of several South and Middle German states, the most important being a conference at Stuttgart in 1825, in which Bavaria, Württemberg, Baden, Hesse-Darmstadt, and Nassau took part. Ultimately, in the year 1828, two "Zollvereins" were formed, the one between Württemberg and Bavaria, the other between Prussia and Hesse. The formation of the Mid-German "Handelsverein" in the same year was due chiefly to the jealousy felt by the smaller states towards Prussia; but this combination had little vitality and soon went to pieces. The three Unions, however, by their very deficiencies prepared the way for transition to a wider system. In 1829 the Bavaria-Württemberg Union made a commercial treaty with Prussia and Hesse, which established practical free trade between the four states. List's friend and publisher, the Freiherr von Cotta, was an active worker in the cause of unification. Saxony was the chief obstacle to any further advance; and for some time longer, on political grounds, it refused to enter into any treaty with Prussia. At last, on January 1, 1834, a German Zollverein was formed between Prussia, Nassau, Württemberg, Bavaria, Saxony, and the Thuringian states; these were joined in the course of the next two years by Baden, Nassau, and the city of Frankfurt. "The elder generation," said a later writer, "can still remember how joyfully the opening hour of the year 1834 was welcomed by the trading world. Long trains of waggons stood on the high-roads, which till then had been cut up by tax barriers. At the stroke of midnight every turnpike was thrown open, and amid cheers the waggons hastened over the boundaries which they could from thenceforward cross in perfect freedom. Every one felt that a great object had been attained."

EFFECTS OF THE ZOLLVEREIN

At the outset the Zollverein embraced eighteen states with a population of more than twenty-three millions. In the course of time, however, other German states joined until, by 1868, all the states, except the Austrian dominions, Hamburg, and Bremen, were members of the Zollverein. Meanwhile, the union entered into commercial negotiations with foreign countries and became so popular that poets praised its effects, singing:

[1] *Ibid.*, 19-21.

You have made the German Nation
Stand united, hand in hand.
More than the Confederation
Ever did for Fatherland.

An English scholar has recently evaluated the influence of the Zollverein as follows.

From HENDERSON, *The Zollverein* (1939) [1]

It is sometimes assumed that the establishment of the German Empire was due almost entirely to political forces and that the rapid rise of her industry and commerce may be dated from the events of 1870-71. Actually the recognition of the advantages of economic unity, which had already been secured, was a factor favourable to the achievement of political unity, and Germany's industrial successes after 1871 were based upon the firm foundations of earlier progress. Between 1815 and 1850 the first steps towards industrial expansion were taken by the founding and extending of the Zollverein and by the improvement of communications. The years 1850 to 1870 saw the rise of German industries—particularly coal, iron, steel and textiles—and the development of a capitalist organization. capable of great expansion in the future.

The development of the Zollverein had thus both an economic and a political significance. It contributed to that expansion of manufactures and commerce in the 'fifties and 'sixties which prepared the way for Germany's rapid rise after 1871 to the position of the chief industrial State on the Continent. It is impossible to estimate the extent to which the Zollverein was responsible. . . . The construction of railways, the enterprise of capitalists, the activity of the great industrialists were

[1] W. O. Henderson, *The Zollverein*, ed. by J. H. Clapham, 1939 (*Cambridge Studies in Economic History*), 337-40. By permission of the Cambridge University Press, Cambridge, England.

probably as important as the customs union in promoting economic welfare. . . . On the other hand, it is clear that if there had been no Zollverein Germany's economic progress would have been hindered, however strong might have been the other economic forces working in favour of expansion. . . .

The Zollverein contributed to the attainment of German unity. The figure of Bismarck dominates Germany in the 'sixties, and students . . . are tempted to confine their attention to his diplomacy and to the wars by which unity was attained. But, so far as her economic life was concerned, Germany had achieved a considerable measure of unification under Prussian leadership some time before Bismarck became Minister President in 1862. Only German states were members of the Zollverein. With the single exception of Luxemburg, every state that joined the Zollverein became a member of the Empire. . . . Above all, the efforts of the Hapsburg dominions to enter the Zollverein were firmly and successfully opposed and here again it was political rather than economic factors that weighed decisively with Prussia. . . .

Over thirty years of economic unity—even though that unity were not absolutely complete—were bound to have a profound influence upon the German peoples. This influence may easily be underestimated because it is so intangible. . . . It is also easy . . . to exaggerate the influence of the customs union upon German affairs and even to regard the establishment of the Empire in 1871 as merely the formal completion of a unity already achieved in the economic sphere.

It is more difficult to steer a middle course between these two extremes—to claim, on the one hand, that the Zollverein had a not unimportant share in fostering both economic expansion and political unity; to admit, on the other hand, that the economic bonds of the Zollverein were not in themselves strong enough to bring the German peoples together permanently and that the Zollverein alone could not have brought about the economic progress that Germany achieved between 1834 and 1871. In any general survey of German history in these years the significance of the Zollverein should receive proper attention—but not at the expense of other factors of equal importance.

2. The German Revolutions of 1848

THE BEGINNINGS IN SOUTHWEST GERMANY

Pent-up demands for reform burst out in open rebellion in the Germanic Confederation almost simultaneously with the February Revolution in France. A contemporary annalist began his relation for 1848 in the following manner.

From *The Annual Register, 1848* [1]

In order to give a clear and distinct narrative of the complicated events which have taken place during the present year in Germany, we have had to consider carefully the question of arrangement; for, independently of the revolutionary movements in the separate kingdoms, there has been a long-sustained attempt to construct a new German nationality on the basis of a Confederation of all the states, with one great Parliament or Diet, and a Central Executive at Frankfurt. . . .

It was in the South-Western States of Germany that the effects of the French Revolution began first to manifest themselves. On the 29th of February the Grand

[1] "History," *The Annual Register . . . 1848,* 356-58.

Duke of Baden received a deputation from his subjects who demanded liberty of the press, the establishment of a national guard, and trial by jury. They succeeded in their object, and M. Welcker, who had distinguished himself as a Liberal leader, was appointed one of the ministers.

On the 3d of March, the Rhenish provinces, headed by Cologne, followed the same example. On the 4th similar demonstrations took place at Wiesbaden and Frankfurt, and on the 5th at Düsseldorf. At Cologne, on the 3d of March, the populace assembled in crowds before the Stadthaus, or town hall, where the town council were sitting, and demanded the concession of certain rights, which were inscribed on slips of paper and handed about amongst the mob. They were as follows: 1. Universal suffrage; all legislation and government to proceed from the people. 2. Liberty of the press and freedom of speech. 3. Abolition of the standing army and the armament of the people, who are to elect their own officers. 4. Full rights of public meeting. 5. Protection to labour, and a guarantee for the supply of all necessaries. 6. State education for all children.

The military were, however, called out, and the streets were cleared without much difficulty.

At Wiesbaden, in Nassau, a large concourse of people met opposite the Palace, on the 4th, and demanded a general arming of the people under their own elective leaders; entire liberty of the press; a German Parliament; right of public meeting; public and oral trial by jury; the control of the Duchy domain; convocation of the Second Chamber to frame a new electoral law on the basis of population; and to remove all restrictions on religious liberty. The Duke was absent at Berlin, but the Duchess, from the balcony of the Palace, assured the people that their demands would be fully conceded by the Duke, her step-son. Subsequently appeared a proclamation in which the Duchess *guaranteed* the concession of these demands; and on the same day, in the afternoon, the Duke returned and, immediately addressing the people, he ratified all the concessions made by the Duchess and his Ministers.

[Similar uprisings followed: in Hesse-Cassel, in Bavaria (where the lecherous old King Louis abdicated in favor of his son, Maximilian II, and fled with his Lola Montez), in Saxony, in Hanover, and so on. Everywhere the demands were similar to those enumerated above, adding, in some instances, requests for the abolition of feudal privileges still retained. As in the instances cited above, in some states the popular demands were conceded—at least temporarily—while in others the military dispersed the people, who were forced to accept the status quo.]

THE ABORTIVE REVOLUTION IN PRUSSIA

The revolutionary wave of 1848 reached Berlin on March 13. The Prussian King, Frederick William IV (1840-61), was a curious mixture of divine-right convictions, dynastic paternalism, and romantic ambition. Already, in 1847, he had convened a United Landtag, combining the provincial diets, only to alienate its members by lecturing to them on the evils of "liberal constitutions." Then, later in 1847, he had sought to recover his prestige by proposing a reorganization of the Germanic Confederation, a sort of revival of the Holy Roman Empire headed by the Hapsburgs and with the King of Prussia as its "Generalissimo." Thus, when Berliners gathered on March 13 to petition for reform, the King dusted off his earlier proposals, added a few

things, such as a promise of liberty of the press and convocation of the United Diet on April 2, and gave the appearance of leading the revolutionary van, even to the extent of promising a constitution! On March 18, however, occurred the first of a series of events which gave the King pause. The crowd, milling about the palace, met with accidental shots from the troops. A clash followed with losses of life on both sides, and the King, greatly agitated, penned the following appeal.

From FREDERICK WILLIAM IV, Appeal "To My Beloved Berliners" (March, 1848) [1]

The shout of joy which greeted me from unnumbered faithful hearts still resounded in my ears when a crowd of peace-breakers mingled with the loyal throng, making seditious and bold demands, and augmenting in numbers as the well-disposed withdrew. As their impetuous intrusion extended to the very portals of the Palace . . . the courtyard was cleared by the cavalry, at *walking pace and with their weapons sheathed;* and two guns of the infantry went off of themselves, without, thanks be to God! causing any injury. A band of wicked men, chiefly consisting of foreigners, who, although searched for, have succeeded in concealing themselves for more than a week, have converted this circumstance into a palpable untruth, and have filled the excited minds of my faithful and beloved Berliners with thoughts of vengeance for supposed bloodshed; and thus have they become the fearful authors of bloodshed themselves. My troops, your brothers and fellow-countrymen, did not make use of their weapons till forced to do so by several shots fired at them from the Königs Strasse. The victorious advance

[1] *Ibid.,* 378-79.

of the troops was the necessary consequence.

It is now yours, inhabitants of my beloved native city, to avert a fearful evil. . . . Return to peace; remove the barricades which are still standing . . . and I pledge you my royal truth that all the streets and squares shall be instantaneously cleared of the troops, and the military garrisons shall be confined solely to the most important buildings. . . . Listen to the paternal voice of your King, ye inhabitants of my true and beautiful Berlin; and forget the past, as I shall forget it, for the sake of that great future which, under the peace-giving blessing of God, is dawning upon Prussia and through Prussia upon all Germany. . . . Written during the night of the 18th and 19th of March, 1848.

[Frederick William suffered much humiliation as a result of his recall of the troops. With the palace unprotected, the rash "beloved Berliners" conducted the funeral services for their fallen comrades in the palace courtyard and the King saluted the corpses of the insurgents as the mob carried them by. Two days later (March 21), the King was paraded through the streets wearing the German tricolor—black, red, and gold—and spoke to the students of the university, concluding: "Mark me, gentlemen, I ask it of you—take it down in writing, that I will not usurp anything!—that I claim nothing except German liberty and unity. Tell it to the students of other universities. I am heartily sorry that they are not here in one body!" When the United Diet assembled on April 2, the King called for a new electoral law whereby a Prussian Constituent Assembly might be chosen to frame a constitution for Prussia. On the 22nd of May the Constituent Assembly

was opened by the King, who spoke to them as follows.]

From FREDERICK WILLIAM IV, Speech to the Prussian Constituent Assembly (May 22, 1848) [1]

With joyful earnestness do I welcome an Assembly proceeding from a general election of the people, whose mission it is with me to unite in the formation of a constitution which is to mark a new era in the history of Prussia and of Germany. I am sure that in beginning this work you will propose to yourselves a twofold task: you will try to secure to the people a large share in the government of the State, and more closely to knit those bonds which for above four centuries indissolubly connected my house with the history of this country. The draft of the constitution will be laid before you by my Ministry. . . .

[The Prussian Constituent Assembly met throughout the summer of 1848, its debates becoming more and more radical, its proceedings less and less to the King's taste. Meanwhile, too, the King's attitude stiffened. Aroused by the "disease" affecting the Assembly, encouraged by the Hapsburg's success in mastering the revolt in Vienna, and prodded by his own generals, Frederick William prorogued the Assembly (October 23), then reconvened it outside Berlin because it had struck from the royal title the words "by the grace of God," and finally, amid much tumult, dispersed the Constituent Assembly by military force as an "illegal meeting" (December 5, 1848). From reliance on "my beloved Berliners" the King had, in the end, fallen back on military power. Simultaneously, the King promulgated a constitution, based in part upon the work

[1] *Ibid.,* 387.

of the Assembly but maintaining the ultimate power of the King. With Berlin in the iron grip of the King's troops, Frederick William presented this constitution to a newly elected United Landtag saying: "I have reserved to you a revision of the Constitution. It is now for you to come to an agreement upon it among yourselves and with my Government." But trouble arose when the Chambers declared illegal the state of siege in Berlin, and on April 26 the King dissolved the Chambers. A new electoral law (May 31) further elaborated the constitution set forth by the King, and this instrument, which remained in force from 1850 to 1918, provided for an upper house (*Herrenhaus*) of the privileged orders and a lower house (Landtag) chosen by universal manhood suffrage under a three-class voting system based on tax-paying ability, and so set up that the wealthy upper fifth of the population controlled two-thirds of the seats in the Landtag. Moreover, though the Landtag could vote new laws and taxes, there was no ministerial responsibility, and royal ordinances issued when the Chambers were not in session had the full force of law. To this constitution, proclaimed on his own authority, Frederick William solemnly swore observance before the Prussian parliament in February, 1850, in the following words.]

From FREDERICK WILLIAM IV, Speech on the New Constitution (February, 1850) [1]

Gentlemen: I request your attention. The words I am about to speak are entirely my own, for I appear before you today as I never have done before, and never shall do again. I am here, not to exercise the innate and hereditary sacred duties of the royal office (which are ex-

[1] *British and Foreign State Papers 1849-1850* (2), London, 1863, XXXIX, 1040-41.

alted high above the opinions and wishes of parties); above all, not sheltered by the responsibility of my highest counsellors, but as myself alone, as a man of honour, who is about to give that which is dearest to him—his word, his yea! energetically and deliberately. Therefore a few words by way of introduction.

The work which I am this day about to sanction began during a year which the loyalty of the coming generation will wish with sorrow, but in vain, to wrest from our history. In the form in which it was submitted to you it was indeed the work of the devoted loyalty of men who have saved this throne; towards whom my gratitude will only be extinguished with my life; but it was in days during which, in the literal sense of the word, the existence of the fatherland was menaced. It was the work of the moment, and bore the broad stamp of its origin.

It is a legitimate question, How can I, with this in mind, give my sanction to this work? Yet I will do it because I can; and it is thanks to you alone, gentlemen, that I can. You have laid an improving hand upon it. You have removed objectionable points from it, and have inserted good in it; by your admirable labours, and by the adoption of my last proposals, you have given me a pledge that you will not, after the sanction, abandon the perfecting work already begun, so that our united, honest endeavours may succeed in rendering it, in the constitutional manner, ever more conformable to the vital requirements of Prussia. I may sanction this work because I can do it with hope. I acknowledge, with the warmest thanks to you, gentlemen—and I say it with joyful emotion—that you have deserved the thanks of the fatherland. And so I declare, God is my witness, that my vow to the constitution is true, sincere, and without reserve. But the existence and success of the constitution, as you and all noble hearts in the country feel, depend upon the fulfilment of necessary conditions.

You, gentlemen, must help me, as well as the diets after you; and the loyalty of my people must help me against those who would use the freedom royally given as a cloak for malice and turn it against its originators, against the authority appointed by God; against those who would wish to regard this document even as a substitute for God's blessed providence, for our history, and for the ancient sacred loyalty. All the good energies of the country must unite in loyal respect for the monarchy and for this throne, which rests upon the victories of our armies, on the observance of the laws, on a faithful fulfilment of the oath of allegiance, as well as of the new oath of loyalty and obedience to the king, and on the conscientious observance of the constitution; in a word, the condition of the constitution's continued existence is that the government may be rendered possible to me with this fundamental law; for in Prussia the King must govern; and I govern, not because it is my pleasure, God knows it, but because it is God's ordinance; on this account, therefore, I am determined to govern. A free people under a free king; that has been my watchword for ten years, so it is still today, and will so remain as long as I breathe.

Before I proceed to the ceremony of the day I will renew before you two former pledges in view of the ten years of my government which have elapsed.

1st, I renew, repeat, and confirm, solemnly and expressly, the vows which I took before God and man at Königsberg and here. Yes, yes, that I will, so help me God.

2ndly, I renew, repeat, and confirm, solemnly and expressly, the sacred vow which I pronounced [at the opening of the United Landtag] on the 11th of April, 1847, "With my House to serve the Lord." Yes, Yes! that I will, so help me God! That vow stands above all others; it must be contained in every one, and must run through all other vows like the pure water of life, if they are to be of any value.

Now, however, whilst in virtue of my royal sovereignty I hereby sanction the Constitution; I vow solemnly, truly, and expressly, before God and man, to maintain the Constitution of my country and realm firmly and inviolably, and to govern in conformity with it and the laws. Yes, yes, that I will, so help me God!

And now I commit the law thus sanctioned into the hands of God Almighty, whose agency in the history of Prussia can plainly be recognised, in order that, out of this work of man, He may make an instrument for the salvation of our dear fatherland, namely, for giving effect to His holy will, rights, and ordinances. Therefore, so be it.

THE FRANKFURT ASSEMBLY: FREDERICK WILLIAM REJECTS THE IMPERIAL CROWN

While revolutions raged in the various German states, a movement was under way to reorganize the entire Confederation along liberal, constitutional lines. On March 5, 1848, a self-constituted committee of fifty-odd prominent liberals met at Heidelberg and, as a result of their plans, a National Assembly elected by direct manhood suffrage in all the Germanies met at Frankfurt-am-Main on May 22 to undertake the reorganization of the Confederation under a new constitution. This body, consisting of over 800 representatives, was a singularly distinguished group, mostly middle-class, including some 200 lawyers, 100 professors, 140 businessmen, and a number of physicians and officials. It suspended the Diet of the Germanic Confederation, appointed Archduke John of Austria (the Emperor's uncle) as Regent and head of an ad interim power to administer "for the whole of the German nation" until a constitution could be drawn and put into operation. This provisional government, however, though temporarily recognized by most of the states—when revolutionary fears ran high—had no military force, and never acquired a firm hold on authority. Meanwhile, too, the Frankfurt Assembly ran into disputes over the extent of German territory to include in the new state, lost time and prestige in a vain attempt to include Schleswig-Holstein in the proposed new Germany, divided sharply over the relative positions of Prussia and the Hapsburg dominions, and did not complete the proposed constitution until March 27, 1849, by which time most of the revolutionary attempts at reform had been quieted both in Prussia and in Austria, and Austria had already indicated her unwillingness to accept the Frankfurt Assembly's proposals. In these circumstances, the Frankfurt Assembly offered "the hereditary imperial dignity, as provided in the said Constitution," to Frederick William IV of Prussia (March 28). On April 3, the King informed a deputation from Frankfurt that he could accept only after the German princes and free cities had accepted the constitution; but after many of the small states had accepted, Frederick William destroyed the plan by declaring that the Hohenzollern King of Prussia, a king by *divine right,* could never accept a crown from a popularly elected assembly. In private letters he made his views emphatically clear.

From FREDERICK WILLIAM IV, Letter to Baron Christian von Bunsen, Potsdam, December 13, 1848 [1]

You say . . . "You want the consent of the ruling princes; very well, that you shall have." But, my dearest friend, you are whipping a dead monkey. I want neither the consent of princes to the election nor the crown itself. Do you understand the words underlined?

I shall enlighten you on the subject as briefly and clearly as possible. First, then, the crown is no crown. The crown which a Hohenzollern could accept, if circumstances rendered such a thing possible at all, is not one created by an Assembly born of revolutionary seed, even if offered with princely approval (*dans le genre de la couronne des pavés de Louis Philippe*). No, it must be a crown set with the seal of the Almighty, one which makes him who assumes it, after the sacred anointment, Sovereign "by the Grace of God," and that because (and as) it has made more than thirty-four princes Kings of the Germans by the grace of God, and gives the latest wearer his place in the ancient line. That crown which was borne by the Ottos, the Hohenstaufens, and the Hapsburgs a Hohenzollern can of course fitly wear, for it honours him inexpressibly with its thousand years of glory. But the crown you unfortunately mean dishonours one inexpressibly, stinking as it does of the Revolution of 1848, the silliest, most stupid and the wickedest, if not, thank God, the most disastrous of the century. Such a fictitious coronet baked out of mire and clay is to be accepted by one who is a legitimate king by the Grace of God, and that, too, by a King of Prussia who has the happiness of wearing, if not the most ancient, at all events

[1] J. G. Legge, *Rhyme and Revolution in Germany,* 1918, 516-17. By permission of Constable and Company, Ltd., London.

the noblest crown, and one that was not stolen from anybody! . . . I tell you roundly: if ever that thousand year old crown of the German nation, which has rested unworn for forty-two years, should again be conferred on any one, then it is I and my peers who are going to confer it, and woe to any one who arrogates a right which is not his due!

From FREDERICK WILLIAM IV, Letter to Baron von Bunsen, May, 1849 [1]

If the majority in the *Paulskirche* [the Frankfurt Assembly] had been really in earnest in the matter, common sense as well as a jot of respect for law and a little faith in the honesty of my official utterances would have told those patriots to obtain first of all the assent of the lawful authorities. I ask why not? . . . To me (and, thank God, to all sound minds) the answer is not doubtful. Because these patriots (!) wished thereby irrevocably to confirm the Revolution; to establish the sovereignty of the German nation they would buckle a dog's collar on the fool, the King of Prussia, which would fetter him indissolubly to the sovereignty of the people, and make him a bondsman of the Revolution of 1848! That, dearest friend, is the gist of the matter, the only excuse for this contemptible business. . . . I and my Ministry did not need any expenditure of mental effort . . . to discover their meaning. Therefore I base my decision on the incompetency of the *Paulskirche* deputation. The meaning of the decision is: "I can answer you neither yes nor no. One only accepts or refuses something which can be offered—and you there, you have nothing to offer: I shall settle the business with my equals, or else good-bye to truth; against democracy only soldiers can avail. Adieu!"

[1] *Ibid.*, 520-21.

[The efforts to reorganize the Germanies broke down after the King of Prussia's refusal to accept the crown, and, in the course of 1850, the Germanic Confederation was re-established in the form set up at Vienna in 1815.]

3. The Revolutions of 1848 in the Hapsburg Dominions

TROUBLES IN HUNGARY

The complex Hapsburg empire was confronted with a complex pattern of revolution in 1848. Besides the attempts of the Frankfurt Assembly to reorganize the German states, the Austrian power was faced with revolts in Italy [see page 574], and with similar attempts in Hungary, Bohemia, and in Vienna itself. In Hungary, Louis (Lajos) Kossuth delivered a daring speech before the Diet at Pressburg which led to serious troubles.

From KOSSUTH, Speech to the Hungarian Diet (March 3, 1848) [2]

The future of our Fatherland is not assured as long as the system of government in the other provinces is in gross contradiction to all constitutional principles, so long as the State Council which has charge of the common affairs of the Monarchy continues . . . to render homage to absolutism. The immobility of the Government condemns the Diet to regular tread-mill work, and makes all the endeavours of the people's friends fruitless. From the charnel house of the Vienna System a pestilential air blows towards us, which paralyses our nerves and lays its ban upon our enthusiasm. The source of all the evil lies in the preposterous policy

[2] *Ibid.*, 261-62.

of the Austrian ministers, for whom it may possibly be painful to see one piece after another of the house fall in which has been built up during a long life, but who compromise the future of the dynasty by their obstinate adherence to their system. Where the foundation is faulty, a downfall is fated and inevitable. It is for us to save the dynasty, to attach its future to the fraternisation of the different races in Austria, and for the evil binding force of bayonets and bureaucratic oppression to substitute the firm cement of a free constitution. . . . In the most intimate fusion of the different provinces of the Monarchy are to be found the guarantees of peace, the support of the dynasty, the safeguard for our freedom. We therefore seek to surround the imperial throne with constitutional organisations, and to obtain the grant of a constitution to all the countries within the Austrian Empire.

THE REVOLUTIONARY SCENE IN VIENNA, MARCH, 1848

Stimulated by the Hungarian's boldness, the Viennese began demonstrations. A diary kept by Count C. F. V. von Eckstädt, Secretary of the Saxon Legation, gives a vivid account of these events.

From ECKSTÄDT, *Diary* (1848) [1]

Vienna, 5th March, 1848. A troubled, sinister mood prevails here in all circles. The Paris revolution has illuminated the obscurity of our position like a thunderbolt. The suburbs are said to be in a very irritated state. The lower middle class is in manifest fermentation. The most pernicious rumours are being circulated. . . . Discontent is general, and I only fear it is not recognised by the au-

[1] *Ibid.*, 267-70.

thorities as it ought to be. . . . It is to be foreseen with certainty that we shall wade through streams of blood.

Sunday, 12th March. In Metternich's salon. Quiet and security. Little anxiety. . . . Count Sedlnitzky (Minister of the Police) engages one thousand men for the secret police and thereby reassures himself.

Monday, 13th March, 8 o'clock. Great procession of students to the Estates house. Masses of well-dressed people surge about in the streets. . . .

11 o'clock. The wishes of the people: . (1) Freedom of the Press. (2) Freedom of teaching. (3) Right of association. (4) General representation, responsible ministers. (5) Open court, oral procedure, trial by jury.

12 o'clock. Great procession. Montecuccoli at the head of the students marches into the palace with the deputation from the Estates. At the same moment a deputation of citizens obtains entry to the palace. Meanwhile the streets assume a threatening aspect. Popular orators are surrounded by groups of people. . . . Four battalions stand at the gates of the palace. Artillery is brought up and loaded. The chancellery is surrounded by troops. The cry "Down with Metternich!" is heard on all sides and becomes the watchword. . . .

2 o'clock. The guard in the Herrengasse is reinforced. Archduke Albrecht seeks to pacify the people. In vain. He is received with stones. After repeated warnings a sharp volley is fired. Four killed, two wounded. A body is carried to Archduke Albrecht.

3 o'clock. . . . Indecision at the palace and the chancellery. . . . The excitement affects everybody. Bayonet attacks. Several deaths. There is talk of fifty deaths.

4 o'clock. . . . The street fighting gets hotter. . . . The people are repulsed. . . .

5 o'clock. The Civic Guard . . . takes

up arms. A deputation . . . (of the Civic Guard) goes to the palace. A kind of truce is arrived at. The officers of the Civic Guard demand (1) the immediate removal of the military from the city; (2) arms for the students; (3) resignation of Prince Metternich, and, with regard to points 2 and 3 are not conceded by 9 P.M. the civic guard will place itself at the head of the rising. . . . Sedlnitzky, Minister of Police, completely paralysed. . . .

8 o'clock. . . . Great butchery. Continued vacillation at the palace. Unwillingness to make any concessions.

8:30 o'clock. Archduke John calls attention to the fact that only half an hour remains. The resignation of Prince Metternich decided upon. . . . Prince Metternich resigns.

9 o'clock. The news runs through the streets. . . .

10 p.m. to 2 a.m. From now onwards separate groups march through the streets rejoicing and shouting "Hurrah!" Some popular orators advise the people not to be content with the two concessions, the resignation of Prince Metternich and the arming of the students.

Tuesday, 14th March . . . 8 o'clock. Dense masses of people march through the city. The students are armed.

9 o'clock. Cockades and ribbons appear. The cry for freedom of the Press becomes general. . . .

1 to 3 o'clock. The whole city has the appearance of one left entirely to itself. The most fabulous rumours contradict one another. The Estates hasten through the streets in uniform, giving assurances that the wishes of the people are conceded. In the palace, where citizens are present, there is much discussion about the term "National Guard"; the thing itself may be granted, but not the name.

3 o'clock. At last the concession of a National Guard is announced. People

crowd to register themselves. The arsenal supplies weapons. . . .

6 o'clock. . . . Prince Metternich, with his family, leaves the city. . . .[1]

Friday, 17th March. All is quiet here. The people show a moderation which is remarkable. . . . The old order of things in Austria has set. Sic transit gloria mundi!

RUSSIA INTERVENES TO ASSIST AUSTRIA

The fall of Metternich and the mob control of Vienna ushered in a critical period in Hapsburg affairs. On all sides the subject peoples rose in rebellion—Hungarians, Czechs, Croats, and others. On May 17, the Emperor fled to Innsbruck, leaving Vienna in revolutionary hands. By June, however, the Imperial Army began to recover the ground lost. Prince Alfred C. F. zu Windisch-Grätz crushed the Czech revolutionary movement (June 17), Baron Josip Jellačič began military operations against Hungary but, being driven back, joined with Windisch-Grätz to pound Vienna into submission (October 31). Soon afterwards, Prince Felix von Schwarzenberg, political and spiritual successor to Metternich, induced the Emperor Ferdinand to abdicate (December 2), and Francis Joseph (1848-1916) succeeded to the throne unfettered by promises to the Hungarians and others still in revolt. On the following March 4 (1849), the new Emperor, ignoring the Reichstag's constitution-making, promulgated a constitution of his own, "not to give liberty to the people, but unity to the empire." So great was the dissatisfaction with the imperial constitution that the

[1] Metternich's flight, attended with considerable danger, ended when he reached London on April 21.

Hungarians, holding that "the house of Lorraine-Hapsburg, as perjured in the sight of God and man, has forfeited its right to the Hungarian throne," issued a declaration of independence (April 14), proclaimed a republic, and chose Kossuth as "governor-president." This new challenge to Austrian control taxed her military powers heavily, and the Czar of Russia, fearing the spread of the revolution to his own territories, responded to Austria's appeal for aid and issued the following manifesto.

From CZAR NICHOLAS, Manifesto
(April 27, 1849) [1]

The insurrection in Hungary has of late made so much progress that Russia cannot possibly remain inactive. A temporary insufficiency of the Austrian forces, divided as they are on many points, has favoured the progress of the insurrection. . . . Their revolutionary plans have swollen in magnitude in proportion to the success of their arms. The Magyar movement has been adulterated by the presence of Polish emigrants . . . who make plans of attack and defence, and it has come to be a general insurrection, especially of Poland . . . Galicia and Cracow . . . the Moldavians and Wallachians. . . . Such a state of things endangers our dearest interests, and prudence compels us to anticipate the difficulties it prepares for us. The Austrian Government being for the moment unable to oppose a sufficient power to the insurgents, it has formally requested His Majesty the Tsar to assist in the repression of a rebellion which endangers the tranquillity of the two empires. It was but natural that the two Cabinets should understand one another on this point of common interest,

and our troops have, consequently, advanced into Galicia to coöperate with Austria against the Hungarian rebellion. We trust the Governments that are equally interested . . . will not misunderstand our motives of action. The Tsar is sorry to quit the passive and expectant position which he has hitherto maintained, but still remains faithful to the spirit of his former declarations, for, in granting to every State the right to arrange its own political constitution . . . His Majesty reserved to himself his full liberty of action in case the reaction of revolutions near him should tend to endanger his own safety. . . . Raised on the basis of anarchy, and imbued with that hostile spirit which the Hungarian chiefs have against Russia, there is . . . a great danger for us in the movement, at the extension of which we dare not to contemplate. In protecting his Polish and Danubian provinces . . . the Emperor flatters himself that he acts in his own interest, and also in the interest of European peace and tranquillity.

AUSTRIA AFTER THE REVOLUTIONS OF 1848-49

The combined armies of Austria and Russia bloodily suppressed the Hungarian revolt by mid-August, 1849. Not one of Austria's enemies who had risen against the Hapsburgs in 1848 remained standing. Externally, Austria appeared powerful and imposing still, but internally she was scarred and riven. The internal weaknesses became manifest when in 1854, despite her obligation to Russia, she failed to come to Russia's aid in the Crimean War. An informed French statesman, commenting on these things in 1855, made the following discerning and prophetic observations with regard to Austria.

[1] "History," *The Annual Register . . . 1849*, 333-34.

From SENIOR, *Conversations* (1855) [1]

She is no longer a great power. Her peculiar strength, her obstinate vitality, is gone. She owed it to her federal origin. The different nations that had coalesced under her sceptre were proud of their respective nationalities, and attached to her as their common protector. They provided her with new armies and new treasures as fast as she wasted what she had. She was constantly defeated, constantly bankrupt, but never without men or without money. These very nationalities which saved her she has attempted to destroy. She has attempted to fuse them into one Austrian empire. She has failed. Instead of fusion she has produced repulsion. We may regret the present development of exclusively national feelings. We may be sorry to see a tendency to constitute Governments rather on moral and ethnological, than on territorial principles, to see a language or a dialect form a frontier, instead of a river or a mountain. The passive resignation with which dissimilar and even hostile races consented to be grouped together, and kindred ones to be separated, was convenient. It gave facilities to the system of exchanges . . . by which the balance of power was maintained. But our regrets are useless. The peoples are taking these matters out of the hands of the diplomatists. And Austria, which was the *"Mauvais idéal"* of that system which was constructed without regard to nationalities, and kept together only by favouring and respecting them, falls to pieces as soon as her rash, ignorant, young Emperor attempts to trample on them. Her German, Polish, Slavonic, Magyar, and Roman elements are separating from one another; they are crystallizing according to their peculiar chemical affinities into

[1] Senior, *Conversations with M. Thiers, M. Guizot, and Other Distinguished Persons*, II, 56-58.

hostile nations. Her cohesion rests on her army, which a single campaign may destroy. Nor is that army to be blindly relied on. Some portions of it are Italians, with all the Italian hate of the German. Others consist of the Hungarian Honveds, or National Guards, whom, after the subjugation of Hungary, she forced as a punishment to serve in the line. . . . I do not believe that even the German part of the population wishes to remain Austrian. It naturally leans to the centre of German intelligence, literature, constitutional freedom, and industry, Prussia. As soon as that throne is occupied by a man of sense and spirit, the German provinces will look towards him as their natural sovereign.

4. The Dual Monarchy of the Hapsburgs: Count von Beust on the Compromise of 1867

The internal weaknesses of the Hapsburg empire were revealed in the war with France and Sardinia in 1859, and Austria was prostrate after the Seven Weeks' War in 1866. Meanwhile, in the years since 1848 the Hapsburg government had set forth a number of sham constitutional plans in an effort to placate the aroused subject nationalities—the insincerity of the programs being accurately revealed by the remark of a critic who pointed out that "absolutism in bankruptcy put on a false constitutional nose in order to extract a few pennies from the public." Of all the subject peoples, the Hungarians held the strongest position. After the defeat in 1866, it was imperative that the Hapsburgs must come to terms with the Magyar leaders. The result of negotiations was the Ausgleich (Compromise) of 1867, leading to the organization of the Dual Monarchy, Austria-Hungary, in which the Magyars enjoyed constitutional dominance in Hungary while the Germans held constitutional control over the peoples of Austria, the two states being joined through personal union in the monarch and through joint ministries to administer common affairs. Count Friedrich Ferdinand von Beust (1809-86), a Saxon who, after 1866, entered the Austrian Ministry and became Prime Minister in 1867, explained in the following words the conditions and motives which impelled him to construct the dual system or, more accurately, to accept the plans of Ferencz Deák, the Hungarian statesman who was principal author of the plan.

From BEUST, *Memoirs* (c. 1867) [1]

The dangers which Austria has to face are of a twofold nature. The first is presented by the tendency of her liberal-minded German population to gravitate towards that larger portion of the German-speaking people now represented by Prussia, Saxony, what was Hanover, Würemberg, and Bavaria; the second is the diversity of language and race in the empire. Of Austria's large Slav population, the Poles have a natural craving for independence after having enjoyed and heroically fought for it for centuries; while the other nationalities are likely at a moment of dangerous crisis to develop pro-Russian tendencies. Everyone who has studied the German problem—which assumed an acute form in 1866, when I was Minister in Saxony—must feel that, setting aside the question of rivalry with France, which sooner or later will be decided at the point of the sword, it re-

solves itself into the question of political supremacy. . . . Bismarck's object is, so far as I know it, to consolidate Germany under one head, probably that of King William as Emperor . . . which means Germany for the Germans. . . .

And now to the second danger I have above mentioned, which presents a far more difficult problem. So long as Austria was a purely despotic State, and the Emperor ruled over it as an absolute monarch —Emperor in Vienna, King in Hungary and Bohemia, Ducal Prince in the other provinces of his vast empire—the local councils had a merely nominal existence, and the governors were there but to register the sovereign's Imperial will and to enforce it by arms if the necessity should arise. The revolutionary wave of 1848 swept over his territories as it did over those of other potentates; laws and decrees which the ignorance and apathy of his people had tolerated, if not approved, in the days of Maria Theresa and the monarchs who succeeded her, raised for the first time among the masses of the population objections and antipathies which generated the firm resolve in their minds to sweep the whole system away. The German element, then as now, took the initiative; but the feeble constitutional measures which were the outcome of popular strife and much bloodshed dwindled down year by year until but a semblance of constitutionalism remained. The comfortable and good-natured Austrian soon forgot what had happened, and occupied himself more with his creature comforts and his dramatic performances than with the development of his constitutional liberties. And—which will show the difficulty of the position—the various nationalities of the empire preferred their servile condition to a state of things which on the very principle of Constitutional government would place all the component parts of the monarchy

[1] *Memoirs of Friedrich Ferdinand Count von Beust,* ed. by Baron Henry de Worms, 2 vols., London, 1887, I, Introduction, xx-xxvi.

on an equality, and cause their representatives to meet in a common parliament on an equal footing. Now my object is to carry out a bloodless revolution—to show the various elements of this great empire that it is to the benefit of each of them to act in harmony with its neighbour, and that no Constitution can permanently exist unless every portion of the State is represented by it. But to this I have made one exception. Hungary is an ancient monarchy, more ancient as such than Austria proper. The kingdom of St. Stephen has a pedigree of centuries; and its constitutional principle was asserted in the earliest times. Its race and language are entirely different from those of the other peoples which constitute the monarchy; its territorial area is larger than theirs; its population, though less by six millions than that of the remainder of the empire, is much larger than that of any of the nationalities composing it. Its people are powerful, brave, united—and, notwithstanding 1848, loyal; for we must not forget that the terrible events of that year in Hungary were to a great extent caused by a system of military despotism . . . which aroused the just indignation of men of such widely different views and position as Batthyany and Kossuth and united them in an effort perhaps less directed against the Hapsburg dynasty than against the generals who, under a boy Emperor, were usurping and abusing the functions of Government. In the scheme which I have developed I have endeavoured to give Hungary not a new position with regard to the Austrian empire, but to secure her in the one which she has occupied. The Emperor of Austria is King of Hungary; my idea was that he should revive in his person the Constitution of which he and his ancestors have been the heads. The leading principles of my plan are, not the creation of a new kingdom and a new Constitution, but the resuscitation of an old monarchy and an old Constitution; not the separation of one part of the empire from the other, but the drawing together of the two component parts by the recognition of their joint positions, the maintenance of their mutual obligations, their community in questions affecting the entire empire, and their proportional pecuniary responsibility for the liabilities of the whole State. It is no plan of separation that I have carried out; on the contrary, it is one of closer union, not by the creation of a new power, but by the recognition of an old one. . . .

I may be asked why I do not apply the same system to Bohemia. The conditions are absolutely different. The rank of King of Bohemia held by the Emperor of Austria has always been rather a titular than a real one; other sovereigns have held it, and it was more an ornament than a power to the Austrian crown. Besides, if I were to advocate a separate kingdom for Bohemia, I could only do so by limiting it to the portion of the country which is inhabited by the Slavs, namely, about one-half of the population. But would it be possible to create a Slav monarchy which should rule over an equal population of Germans, the latter representing in a far higher degree the intelligence and manufacturing industry of the whole of Bohemia? There is no parallel between the two cases.

5. Formation of the German Empire: Highlights of Bismarck's Policies

OTTO VON BISMARCK BECOMES PRUSSIAN MINISTER (SEPTEMBER, 1862)

Frederick William IV was adjudged insane in 1858 and died in 1861. He was succeeded by his brother, William I—first as Regent (1858-61) and then as King (1861-88)—a man of no brilliance but of great industry and common sense. Aroused by the uncertain state of international affairs in 1859, William sought to reform and enlarge the Prussian army. Liberals in the Landtag, opposing militarism, claimed the legal right to control the purse, whereas the King, as head of the army, claimed the right to institute military reforms and to require the necessary funds. A deadlock arose for which the Prussian constitution made no provision. The King considered abdication, but finally fell back upon Otto von Bismarck to break the deadlock. Bismarck (1815-1898) already had a reputation as a Conservative, an antiparliamentarian, a Prussian nationalist, and a man of bold intelligence. While yet a university student he had branded the Burschenschaft movement as "an association between Utopian theories and defective breeding," and had bet an American friend that German unity would be effected within twenty years. A stanch supporter of the King in the Revolution of 1848, he had served as Prussian representative in the Frankfurt Diet (1851-59), as Ambassador to Russia (1859-62), and to France (1862), in which capacities he had acquired a thorough knowledge of the internal affairs of the Germanies as well as of the European diplomatic scene. Bismarck gave the following account of his early ministry.

From BISMARCK, *Reminiscences* (1898) [1]

I arrived at Berlin in the morning of September 20. . . . I was received at Babelsberg on September 22, and the situation only became clear to me when his Majesty defined it in some such words as these: "I will not reign if I cannot do it in such a fashion as I can be answerable for to God, my conscience, and my subjects. But I cannot do that if I am to rule according to the will of the present majority in parliament, and I can no longer find any ministers prepared to conduct my government without subjecting themselves and me to the parliamentary majority. I have therefore resolved to lay down my crown, and have already sketched out the proclamation of my abdication." . . . The King showed me the document in his own handwriting lying on the table, whether already signed or not I do not know. His Majesty concluded by repeating that he could not govern without suitable ministers.

I replied that his Majesty had been acquainted ever since May with my readiness to enter the ministry. . . . After a good deal of consideration and discussion, the King asked me whether I was prepared as minister to advocate the reorganization of the army, and when I assented he asked me further whether I would do so in opposition to the majority in parliament and its resolutions. When I asserted my willingness, he finally declared, "Then it is my duty, with your help, to attempt to continue the battle, and I shall not abdicate." . . .

I succeeded in convincing him that, so far as he was concerned, it was not a question of Liberal or Conservative of this or that shade, but rather of monarchical rule or parliamentary government, and that the latter must be avoided at all costs, if even by a period of dictatorship. I said: "In this situation, I shall, even if your Majesty command me to do things which I do not consider right, tell you my opinion quite openly; but if you finally persist in yours, I will rather perish with the King than forsake your Majesty in the contest with parliamentary

[1] This and the next two selections are from *Bismarck, the Man and the Statesman; Being the Reflections and Reminiscences of Otto, Prince von Bismarck,* trans. under the supervision of A. J. Butler, 2 vols., 1898. Permission of Harper and Brothers, New York. This is I, 294-97, 312-16.

government." This view was at that time strong and absolute in me, because I regarded the negations and phrases of the Opposition of that day as politically disastrous in face of the national task of Prussia, and because I cherished such strong feelings of devotion and affection for William I. . . . It required all the King's honest and noble fidelity for his first servant, to keep him from wavering in his confidence towards me.

In the beginning of October I went as far as Jüterbogk to meet the King, who had been at Baden-Baden for September 30, his wife's birthday. . . . My object in taking this opportunity for an interview was to set his Majesty at rest about a speech made by me in the Budget Commission on September 30, which had aroused some excitement and which, though not taken down in shorthand, had still been reproduced with tolerable accuracy in the newspapers. . . .

I had indicated plainly enough the direction in which I was going. Prussia—such was the point of my speech—as a glance at the map will show, could no longer wear unaided on its long narrow figure the panoply which Germany required for its security; that must be equally distributed over all German peoples. We should get no nearer the goal by speeches, associations, decisions of majorities; we should be unable to avoid a serious contest, a contest which could only be settled by blood and iron. In order to secure our success in this, the deputies must place the greatest possible weight of blood and iron in the hands of the King of Prussia, in order that according to his judgment he might throw it into one scale or the other. I had already given expression to the same idea in the House of Deputies in 1849. . . . [The crucial part of the speech read: ". . . not by speeches and majority votes are the great questions of the day decided—that was the great mistake of 1848 and 1849—but by blood and iron."]

For my part, I was torn between the desire of winning over members to an energetic national policy, and the danger of inspiring the King, whose own disposition was cautious, and shrank from violent measures, with mistrust in me and my intentions. My object in going to meet him at Jüterbogk was to counteract betimes the probable effect of press criticism. . . . When I begged for permission to narrate the events which had occurred during his absence, he interrupted me with the words: "I can perfectly well see where all this will end. Over there, in front of the Opera House, under my windows, they will cut off your head, and mine a little while afterwards." . . .

I answered with the short remark, "Et après, Sire." "Après, indeed; we shall be dead," answered the King. "Yes," I continued, "then we shall be dead; but we must all die sooner or later, and can we perish more honorably? I, fighting for my King's cause, and your Majesty sealing with your own blood your rights as King by the grace of God. . . . Your Majesty is bound to fight, you cannot capitulate; you must, even at the risk of bodily danger, go forth to meet any attempt at coercion." As I continued to speak in this sense, the King grew more and more animated, and began to assume the part of an officer fighting for kingdom and fatherland. . . . He felt as though he had been touched in his military honor, and was in the position of an officer who has orders to hold a certain position to the death. . . . This set him on a course of thought which was quite familiar to him; and in a few minutes he was restored to the confidence which he had lost at Baden, and even recovered his cheerfulness.

[Having thus stiffened the King, Bismarck, in the face of a vote of 274 to 45 in the House of Deputies "that ministers were responsible with their persons and fortunes for unconstitutional expenditures," continued his defiance of the Landtag and, considering himself responsible only to William I, put through the army reforms and served throughout the reign of William I as the "man of blood and iron."]

BISMARCK'S SAGACITY AT THE CONCLUSION OF THE SEVEN WEEKS' WAR (1866)

The tenacity of purpose and the far-sighted wisdom of Bismarck were seldom better demonstrated than near the end of the Seven Weeks' War (1866). Having taken advantage of the Schleswig-Holstein question to maneuver Austria into revealing a test of military power—meanwhile being assured of the assistance of Italy (in return for Venetia) and the probable neutrality of Austria's potential allies—Bismarck saw the expediency of accepting peace as soon as his own political objectives had been won; namely, the humiliation of Austria, the dissolution of the Germanic Confederation, and the recognition of Prussian leadership in North Germany. But the Prussian King and military chiefs, excited by the military conquests possible after the battle of Königgrätz (Sadowa), were bent on following up their victory and continuing the war. Bismarck gave the following relation of his success in persuading the Prussian chiefs to grant Austria a "soft" peace in the interests of future Prussian aggrandizement.

From BISMARCK, *Reminiscences* [1]

After the battle of Königgrätz the situation was such that a favorable response on our part to the first advances of Austria with a view to peace negotiations, was not only possible, but seemed demanded by the interference of France. The latter dates from the telegram, addressed to his Majesty [July 4] . . . in which Louis Napoleon informed the King that the Emperor Francis Joseph had ceded Venetia to him, and had invited his intervention. The brilliant success of the King's arms compelled Napoleon to quit the reserve he had hitherto maintained . . . up to this time Napoleon had calculated on our being defeated and in need of assistance. . . . Subsequently, at Nikolsburg, I asked General von Moltke what he would do if France actively intervened. His reply was: "I should adopt a defensive attitude towards Austria, confining myself to the line of the Elbe, and in the meantime prosecuting the war actively against France."

This opinion confirmed me still more in my resolution to advise his Majesty to make peace on the basis of the territorial integrity of Austria. . . . I believed that the war against France . . . would not be easy. . . . Then, perhaps, we should not be able victoriously to maintain our defensive against Austria on the Elbe if we had to carry on a war of invasion in France, with Austria and South Germany as hostile elements in our rear. I was moved by this prospect to still livelier exertions in the cause of peace. . . .

On July 23, under the presidency of the King, a council of war was held, in which the question to be decided was whether we should make peace under the conditions offered or continue the war. . . . I declared it to be my conviction that

---

[1] *Ibid.*, II, 36-38, 48-54.

peace must be concluded on the Austrian terms, but remained alone in my opinion; the King supported the military majority. . . . I thereupon set to work to commit to paper the reasons which in my opinion spoke for the conclusion of peace. . . .

We had to avoid wounding Austria too severely; we had to avoid leaving behind in her any unnecessary bitterness of feeling or desire for revenge; we ought rather to reserve the possibility of becoming friends again with our adversary of the moment, and in any case to regard the Austrian state as a piece on the European chessboard and the renewal of friendly relations with her as a move open to us. If Austria were severely injured, she would become the ally of France and of every other opponent of ours; she would even sacrifice her anti-Russian interests for sake of revenge on Prussia.

On the other hand, I could see no future acceptable to us for the countries constituting the Austrian monarchy, in case the latter were split up by risings of the Hungarians and Slavs or made permanently dependent on those peoples. . . . Fresh formations on this surface could only be of a permanently revolutionary nature. German Austria we could neither wholly nor partly make use of. The acquisition of provinces like Austrian Silesia and portions of Bohemia could not strengthen the Prussian state; it would not lead to an amalgamation of German Austria with Prussia, and Vienna could not be governed from Berlin as a mere dependency. . . . We must finish off rapidly; before France won time to bring further diplomatic action to bear upon Austria.

To all this the King raised no objection, but declared the actual terms as inadequate. . . . He said that the chief culprit could not be allowed to escape unpunished . . . and he insisted on the cessions of territory from Austria. . . . I replied that we were not there to sit in judgment, but to pursue the German policy. Austria's conflict in rivalry with us was no more culpable than ours with her: *our task was the establishment or initiation of a German national unity under the leadership of the King of Prussia.* . . . I wished to avoid, in the German federation of the future, the sight of mutilated territories, whose princes and peoples might very easily (such is human weakness) retain a lively wish to recover their former possessions by means of foreign help; such allies would be very unreliable. . . .

What seemed to me to be paramount with his Majesty was the aversion of the military party to interrupt the victorious course of the army. The resistance which I was obliged, in accordance with my convictions, to offer to the King's views with regard to following up the military successes, and to his inclination to continue the victorious advance, excited him to such a degree that a prolongation of the discussion became impossible; and, under the impression that my opinion was rejected, I left the room. . . . On returning to my room I was in the mood that the thought occurred to me whether it would not be better to fall out of the open window, which was four stories high; and I did not look round when I heard the door open, although I suspected that the person entering was the Crown Prince. . . . I felt his hand on my shoulder, while he said: "You know that I was against this war. You considered it necessary, and the responsibility for it lies on you. If you are now persuaded that our end is attained, and peace must now be concluded, I am ready to support you and defend your opinion with my father." He then repaired to the King, and came back after a short half-hour, in the same calm, friendly mood, but with the words: "It has been a very difficult business, but my father has consented." This consent found expression in a note written with lead pencil on the margin of one of my last memoranda, something to this effect: "Inasmuch as my Minister-President has left me in the lurch in the face of the enemy, and here I am not in a position to supply his place, I have discussed the question with my son; and as he has associated himself with the Minister-President's opinion, I find myself reluctantly compelled, after such brilliant victories on the part of the army, to bite this sour apple and accept so disgraceful a peace." . . . I gladly accepted the royal assent to what I regarded as politically necessary without taking offence at its ungracious form.

The only residium that the above note of the King's . . . left in my mind was the recollection of the violent agitation into which I had been obliged to put my old master, in order to obtain what I considered essential to the interests of the country if I were to remain responsible. To this day these and similar occurrences have left no other impression upon me than the painful recollection that I had been obliged to vex a master whom personally I loved as I did him.

BISMARCK'S "EMS DESPATCH" ENCOURAGES A FRENCH DECLARATION OF WAR (1870)

Responsibility for the outbreak of the Franco-Prussian War in 1870 is difficult to assess. On the one hand, French officialdom, with the possible exception of Louis Napoleon himself, had been seeking to block Prussia's growing power in Germany since the Seven Weeks' War; and with the clumsy diplomatic treatment accorded the Hohenzollern candidacy for the Spanish throne, a noisy and influential section of French opinion adopted an attitude of reckless bellicosity and did their utmost to render war inevitable—their vain confidence in the outcome well illustrated in the War Minister's boast, "So ready are we that if the war lasts two years, not a gaiter button would be found wanting." On the other hand, Bismarck had considered war with France inevitable since 1866; in a sense, he welcomed it as a means of welding the South German states to the North, thus completing his grand object of German unity. Both sides, then, criminally played with fire. But it is hard to deny that in the final stages of the crisis, in July, 1870, Bismarck's "editing" of the Ems telegram was a deliberate attempt to provoke war. Bismarck himself said so. Here follows Bismarck's story of the Ems despatch.

From BISMARCK, Reminiscences [1]

On July 2, 1870, the Spanish ministry decided in favor of the accession to that throne of Leopold, Hereditary Prince of Hohenzollern. This gave the first stimulus in the field of international law to the subsequent military question, but still only in the form of a specifically Spanish matter. It was hard to find in the law of nations a pretext for France to interfere with the freedom of Spain to choose a King; after people in Paris had made up their minds to war with Prussia, this was sought for artificially in the name Hohenzollern, which in itself had nothing more menacing to France than any other German name. . . . The intervention of France at its beginning concerned Spanish and not Prussian affairs; the garbling of the matter in the Napoleonic policy, by virtue of which the question was to become a Prussian one, was internationally unjustifiable and exasperating, and proved to me that the moment had arrived when

[1] Ibid., II, 87, 90-91, 98-102.

France sought a quarrel against us and was ready to seize any pretext that seemed available. . . .

In view of the attitude of France, our national sense of honor compelled us, in my opinion, to go to war; and if we did not act according to the demands of this feeling, we should lose, when on the way to its completion, the entire impetus towards our national development won in 1866, when the German national feeling south of the Main, aroused by our military successes in 1866, and shown by the readiness of the southern states to enter the alliances, would have to grow cold again. . . . It was confidence in the Germanic power developed by means of Prussia, and the attraction which is inherent in a brave and resolute policy if it is successful, and then proceeds within reasonable and honorable limits. This nimbus had been won by Prussia; it would have been lost irrevocably, or at all events for a long time, if in a question of national honor the opinion gained ground among the people that the French insult, *La Prusse cane,* had a foundation in fact. . . .

All these considerations, conscious and unconscious, strengthened my opinion that war could be avoided only at the cost of the honor of Prussia and the national confidence in it. Under this conviction I made use of the royal authorization communicated to me through Abeken, to publish the contents of the telegram; and in the presence of my two guests I reduced the telegram by striking out words, but without adding or altering, to the following form: "After the news of the renunciation of the hereditary Prince of Hohenzollern had been officially communicated to the imperial government of France by the royal government of Spain, the French ambassador at Ems further demanded of his Majesty the King that he would authorize him to telegraph to Paris that his Majesty the King bound himself for all future time never again to give his consent if the Hohenzollerns should renew their candidature. His Majesty the King thereupon decided not to receive the French ambassador again and sent to tell him through the aide-de-camp on duty that his Majesty had nothing further to communicate to the ambassador." The difference in the effect of the abbreviated text of the Ems telegram as compared with that produced by the original was not the result of stronger words but of the form, which made this announcement appear decisive, while Abeken's version would have only been regarded as a fragment of a negotiation still pending, and to be continued at Berlin.

After I had read out the concentrated edition to my two guests, Moltke remarked: "Now it has a different ring; it sounded before like a parley; now it is like a flourish in answer to a challenge." I went on to explain: "If in the execution of his Majesty's order I at once communicate this text, which contains no alteration in or addition to the telegram, not only to the newspapers, but also by telegraph to all our embassies, it will be known in Paris before midnight, and not only on account of its contents, but also on account of the manner of its distribution, will have the effect of a red rag upon the Gallic bull. Fight we must if we do not want to act the part of the vanquished without a battle. Success, however, essentially depends upon the impression which the origination of the war makes upon us and others; it is important that we should be the party attacked, and this Gallic overweening and touchiness will make us if we announce in the face of Europe, so far as we can without the speaking-tube of the Reichstag, that we fearlessly meet the public threats of France."

This explanation brought about in the

two generals a revulsion to a more joyous mood, the liveliness of which surprised me. They had suddenly recovered their pleasure in eating and drinking and spoke in a more cheerful vein. Roon said: "Our God of old lives still and will not let us perish in disgrace." Moltke so far relinquished his passive equanimity that, glancing up joyously towards the ceiling and abandoning his usual punctiliousness of speech, he smote his hand upon his breast and said: "If I may but live to lead our armies in such a war, then the devil may come directly afterwards and fetch away the 'old carcass.'"

6. Some Aspects of the German Empire, 1871-1914

BISMARCK'S "CONSERVATIVE SOCIALISM": THE WORKERS' INSURANCE LAWS

As Bismarck's repressive measures against Socialism seemed merely to strengthen the Socialist vote, the Chancellor turned to social insurance as a means to allay discontent among workingmen and to draw the teeth of Socialists by embracing some of their demands. Thus the German Workers' Insurance Laws of the 1880's were, in the first instance, introduced as a matter of political opportunism. However, the laws were none the less significant as major contributions to social reform, and they inaugurated a policy widely imitated elsewhere in Europe within a few years. The spirit in which the legislation was undertaken, and a significant comparison of the German and the English attitudes toward labor reform, are well set forth in the following selection.

From DAWSON, *The German Empire* (1919) [1]

Was Bismarck ever a social reformer by study and reasoned conviction? It is doing him no injustice to answer this question negatively. Upon this, as upon most questions, he was guided by intuition and instinct. He saw that things were wrong, and without troubling about scientific theories and sanctions, he tried, by heroic measures and straight cuts, to make them right. Yet his solicitude for the working classes was an acquired solicitude, and he arrived at it under the pressure of political difficulties. The whole bent of his mind was against any interference with the "natural" relations of capital and labour. When, as late as 1877, the Prussian Minister of Commerce prepared a bill which was intended to afford to the working classes greater protection in matters affecting their physical and moral welfare, Bismarck criticized it so severely that it had to be dropped. He regarded the labour question still as essentially one of more or less wages, of longer or shorter hours of employment, and he was far more concerned that employers should not be unduly crippled in their power to meet labour's just demands than that the work should be done under ideal conditions. For traces of any genuine comprehension of social problems, or even of intimate knowledge of the working classes, Bismarck's speeches will be searched in vain. They abound in vivid intuitions of economic truth, in true and sagacious reflections upon social relations, and invaluable dicta of common sense and worldly wisdom, which even the best trained sociologist may still read with profit, but they reflect a mind influenced rather by expediency than deep conviction and impelling

[1] William H. Dawson, *The German Empire, 1867-1914, and Unity Movement*, 2 vols., 1919, II, 38-42. By permission of The Macmillan Company, New York.

enthusiasm. He passed social laws because they were necessary; social reform was never to him a passion, but always a policy.

When, however, Bismarck had once decided to enter this untried path, progress was far easier for him than it was for the early reformers in England, where the prejudices and preconceptions to be overcome were so many and so deeply rooted. Individualism seemed to have conquered in Germany, but the truth was that the victory had merely been that of a handful of men who had for the time controlled fiscal and economic policy in the Ministries, and it lasted only so long as they lasted. Never did individualism obtain a firm hold upon national thought. The theory that the State had an unquestionable right to interfere in any direction in which the common good was endangered, and that it was the special duty of the Crown to hold the balance between conflicting interests, had for generations been a ruling tradition of Prussian statecraft. Now, in the conditions incidental to a time of transition, this tradition proved of immense value. It was not necessary to create precedents for State action; precedents existed in abundance, and all that was needed was to go back to the forsaken ways.

The student who compares the different lines followed by social movements, particularly as reflected in labour law reforms, in England and Germany will find an invaluable clue in the fact that these movements have relied for their chief impetus in one country upon self-help and in the other upon State initiative and furtherance. In England the tendency was to set labour free from fetters and then leave it to fight its own battles. Hence freedom to organize in trade unions was given to the English working classes as early as 1825. In Germany the tendency was the other way. There labour has never yet been free, and such liberty of action as it enjoys today [1919] was gained in England half a century ago. To Governments still steeped in the traditions of absolutism it seemed safer to admit a tacit obligation to do for labour what it was not able or allowed to do for itself. That labour has so seldom given proof of gratitude for the boons conferred upon it is chiefly due to the fact that the State has never seriously tried to view labour questions from the labour standpoint, and that reforms for its benefit have too often been carried out only under pressure. "While we laud and magnify the great deeds of the Imperial Government in social politics," writes a German historian of social movements, Dr. F. Naumann, "it must never be forgotten that many of these great deeds were only necessary because of the gigantic blunders of the same Government, and that all the laws for the protection of skilled workmen are a poor substitute for the free activity of the trade unions."

Inheriting these traditions, Bismarck decided before the Empire was ten years old to embark upon the largest and most original experiment in constructive social reform ever attempted, an experiment which threw into the shade the best that had been done by the heavy-handed but well-meaning patriarchalism of the past. Brushing on one side all questions of wages and hours of labour, as questions which the working classes should be left to settle with their employers, and ignoring all demands for the right of free organization and combination, as opening up a vista of dangerous possibilities at a time when Socialistic doctrines were making ominous headway, he proposed a great scheme of social insurance by which the workers were to be afforded care and provision in all the vicissitudes of industrial life—medical treatment and maintenance in sickness, generous compensation in the event of accident, support during periods of unemployment, and finally pensions in the time of old age and permanent disablement.

"DROPPING THE PILOT": KAISER WILLIAM II'S DIFFERENCES WITH BISMARCK

"It was a matter," said William II, after Bismarck's "enforced" resignation in 1890, "of whether the Hohenzollern or the Bismarck dynasty should rule." This statement, although it expresses an important aspect of the case of Bismarck's dismissal, hardly tells the vital differences in policy between the new Kaiser and the old Chancellor. In his *Memoirs,* the Emperor William II gives the following explanation.

From WILLIAM II, *Memoirs* (1922) [1]

Prince Bismarck's greatness as a statesman and his imperishable services to Prussia and Germany are historical facts of such tremendous significance that there is doubtless no man in existence, whatever his party affiliations, who would dare to place them in question. For this very reason alone it is stupid to accuse me of not having recognized the greatness of Prince Bismarck. The opposite is the truth. I revered and idolized him. Nor could it be otherwise. It should be borne in mind with what generation I grew up —the generation of the devotees of Bismarck. He was the creator of the German Empire, the paladin of my grandfather, and all of us considered him the greatest statesman of his day and were proud that he was a German. Bismarck was the idol in my temple, whom I worshiped. . . .

But my reverence for the great statesman was not such as to make me take

upon my own shoulders, when I became Emperor, political plans or actions of the Prince which I considered mistakes. Even the Congress of Berlin in 1878 was, to my way of thinking, a mistake, likewise the "Kulturkampf." Moreover, the constitution of the Empire was drawn up so as to fit in with Bismarck's extraordinary preponderance as a statesman; the big cuirassier boots did not fit every man.

Then came the labor-protective legislation. I most deeply deplored the dispute which grew out of this, but, at the time, it was necessary for me *to take the road to compromise, which has generally been my road both on domestic and foreign politics.* For this reason I could not wage the open warfare against the Social Democrats which the Prince desired. . . . The tragic element for me, in the Bismarck case, lay in the fact that I became the successor of my grandfather—in other words, that I skipped one generation, to a certain extent. And that is a serious thing. In such a case one is forced to deal constantly with old deserving men, who live more in the past than in the present, and cannot grow into the future. . . . And when Ballin had the Prince cast a glance over the new harbor of Hamburg, Bismarck himself felt a new era had begun which he 'no longer thoroughly understood. . . . This point of view also showed itself on the occasion of the visit of Admiral von Tirpitz . . . at the time when he wished to win the old Imperial Chancellor over to favoring the first Navy bill.

The Foreign Office was conducted with the strictest discipline. . . . The gentlemen there simply flew when they were summoned or dismissed . . . so much so that a joking saying arose at the time that "their coat tails stood straight out behind them." The foreign policy was conducted and dictated by Prince Bismarck alone. . . . Hence *the Foreign Office was noth-*

[1] *The Kaiser's Memoirs: Wilhelm II, Emperor of Germany 1888-1918,* trans. by Thomas R. Ybarra, 1922, 1-4, 6-9. Copyright, 1922, by Harper and Brothers and reprinted with their permission.

ing but an office of the great Chancellor, where work was done according to his directions. Able men, with independent ideas, were not schooled and trained there. . . . The Prince loomed up like a huge block of granite in a meadow; were he to be dragged away, what would be found beneath would be mostly worms and dead roots.

I won the confidence of the Prince, who consulted me about many things. For instance, when the Prince brought about the first German colonial acquisitions (Gross and Klein Popo, Togo, etc.), I informed him, at his wish, concerning the state of mind created in the public and the navy by this move, and described to him the enthusiasm with which the German people had hailed the new road. The Prince remarked that the matter hardly deserved this. Later on I spoke often with the Prince about the colonial question and always found in him the intention to utilize the colonies as commercial objects, or objects for swapping purposes, other than to make them useful to the fatherland or utilize them as sources of raw materials. As was my duty, I called the Prince's attention to the fact that merchants and capitalists were beginning energetically to develop the colonies and that, therefore—as I had learned from Hanseatic circles—they counted upon protection from a navy. For this reason, I pointed out that steps must be taken for *getting a fleet constructed* in time, in order that German assets in foreign lands should not be without protection; that, since the Prince had unfurled the German flag in foreign parts, and the people stood behind it, there must also be a navy behind it.

But the Prince turned a deaf ear to my statements and made use of his pet motto: "If the English should land on our soil I should have them arrested." His idea was that the colonies would be defended by us at home. The Prince attached no importance to the fact that the very assumption that the English could land without opposition in Germany—since Heligoland was English—was unbearable for Germany, and that we, in order to make a landing impossible from the start, needed a sufficiently strong navy, and, likewise, Heligoland. The political interest of the Prince was, in fact, concentrated essentially upon continental Europe; England lay somewhere to one side among the cares that burdened him daily. . . . Prince Bismarck did not realize that, through the acquisition of colonies for Germany, he would be obliged to look beyond Europe and be automatically forced to act, politically, on a large scale—with England especially. . . . For this reason it was that the Foreign Office likewise was involved entirely in the continental interplay of politics, had not the requisite interest in colonies, navy, or England, and possessed no experience in world politics.

GRAND ADMIRAL TIRPITZ AND THE NEW GERMAN NAVAL POLICY

In March, 1898, in response to the Emperor's new foreign and colonial policies, the first Navy Bill passed the German parliament. It was principally the work of Admiral Alfred von Tirpitz, who in 1897 had been Minister of the Marine. Passage of the bill marked the beginning of German naval expansion and a gradual rise of friction with Great Britain on this score, in addition to commercial contests and colonial rivalry. Admiral Tirpitz wrote the following account of the considerations which led to the naval program and the principles which guided the direction it took.

From TIRPITZ, *Memoirs* (1919) [1]

I still maintain today [1919] that the attempt to work our way to real world-political freedom by the construction of a fleet could not be left untried. . . . If people had *not* wanted to build a fleet, but to go on the way of renunciation from the 'nineties onward, then we should have been compelled to slacken trade and industry of our own accord; we should have been compelled to re-start emigration, and to have allowed our foreign interests abroad to go to rack and ruin. Then, as Lichnowsky says, we should have had to leave the field to the "Anglo-Saxons and the sons of Jehovah," and to have contented ourselves with our old reputation of being the salt of the earth, the fertilizer of mankind. It was, and is, an illusion, however, to think that the English would have treated us any better, and have allowed our economic growth to have proceeded unchecked if we had had no fleet. They would have certainly told us to stop much sooner. Anybody who knows the English could have no doubt of this. The threatening outcry in English journalism of the 'nineties is not by any means the only sign that the irksome but impotent German competitor would be struck down at the first safe opportunity. The German considered it his *bona fide* right to spread himself peaceably over the world and outflank English influence everywhere, and in general he did not sufficiently appreciate the feelings of the man in possession who looked upon him as an intruder. Moreover, people in Germany had a wholly inadequate conception of the peculiar composition of English power and of its ability to encircle Germanism with mental and material forces, until the World-War [I] revealed the truth.

[1] From *My Memoirs* by Grand Admiral von Tirpitz, 2 vols., copyright, 1919, by Dodd, Mead & Company, Inc., I, 86-89, 118-21.

The plan of a German battle fleet was evolved without any idea of war with England. It would have seemed perfectly crazy both politically and strategically to have waived the possibility of a later attack upon England. Before 1896—that is, under Caprivi—the popular idea was, as I said, to regard England as the naval complement of the Triple Alliance against France and Russia. There was also no reason at that time to draw up defensive measures against England. The plan of operations which I drew up in 1895 has the "two-front" war in view, and reckons in all its details upon a neutral England. I started on the assumption that we were to open the war against France not as a cruiser war, but with an engagement at sea. This is the origin of our construction of a battle fleet, but the unexpected demonstrations on the part of the British navy at the beginning of 1896, as well as the trade jealousy which was breaking out more and more undisguisedly, were naturally bound soon to add an English front to the French one. After the Krüger telegram the English put a flying squadron in commission against us. This brought a new point of view into our shipbuilding deliberations, and caused Stosch to draw up the plan of operations for defence against England which he had discussed privately with me. The first official plan of operations against England was not drawn up by the Naval Staff until the beginning of the twentieth century. . . .

When I arrived in Potsdam in June, 1897, the Emperor told me that everything was ready for the navy campaign; I only needed to give my consent. . . . The Emperor had had a draft-bill drawn up by a committee, but in my opinion this was of no use. . . . I asked for a few days to think it over.

The fundamental idea of this draft centred round a *foreign-service* fleet. Now there were only a few States left in the world at that time, such as Haiti, etc., in which any infringement of our rights could be corrected by foreign-service cruisers without giving rise to a serious conflict. States like the Argentine already had modern warships at their disposal, so so that every foreign-service cruiser would have to be supported by a naval force in home waters, if it was to fulfil its purpose as an outpost. Moreover we had not a single foreign base. Throughout my whole career I have always had to oppose two ideas, especially beloved of the lay mind—the idea of a special coastal defence, and that of a cruiser fleet. The world-war has proved that the best *coastal defence* is a *battle fleet*. As to the cruiser war, I replied to the Emperor at the time somewhat on the following lines: As a thoroughgoing cruiser war and a war on the high seas against England and other great States is altogether excluded by our lack of foreign bases and by Germany's geographical situation—the foreign admiralties know this quite well—what we need is a battle fleet which can be stationed between Heligoland and the Thames. . . .

We had to increase in general power all round, *i.e.* to qualify ourselves for an alliance with the Great Powers. But alliance-value could only be achieved by a battle fleet. One single ally at sea would have sufficed in the Great War to have enabled us to fight with the most favourable prospects for the freedom of the seas. The first thing therefore was to create for ourselves a fleet which would give us alliance-value; and the second was a corresponding policy of alliance, and the avoidance of all political friction before this end was achieved. These were the two objects for which we had to strive amid the aggravated conditions of the times.

31 | GREAT BRITAIN AND THE NEW BRITISH EMPIRE

1. English Parliamentary Reform in the Nineteenth Century

Further democratization of English political institutions had been a demand of reformers since the English Civil Wars in the seventeenth century [see pages 219, 222, 227]. The shifts in population and the rise of new industrial cities effected by the Industrial Revolution [see page 482] intensified the demands in the late eighteenth century. But the American and French revolutions, by arousing fear of democratic excesses, retarded English reform sentiment, and the Tory governments in England during the era from 1760 to 1820 not only effectively resisted reform proposals but also laid a heavy and sometimes bloody hand upon reformers and reform demonstrations. Consequently, little reform legislation passed Parliament until after 1820. In the course of the rest of the nineteenth century, however, England revolutionized her political and social institutions by parliamentary acts. The first major rift in the conservative Tory front against reform occurred in 1828, when Daniel O'Connell, leader of the Catholic Emancipation movement, was elected to Parliament from County Clare in Ireland. Under the Test Act (1673; see page 232), no Catholic or Protestant Nonconformist could hold public office, but there was real danger of civil war in Ireland unless Catholic disabilities were removed. Accordingly, though it went against the grain, the Duke of Wellington (Prime Minister, 1828-30) forced through Parliament: 1. A repeal of the Test and Corporation Acts, May 9, 1828, removing disabilities from Protestant Nonconformists—mostly a dead letter for a century anyway—and permitting them to hold public office providing they would subscribe to a declaration not to "exercise any power, authority, or influence . . . to injure or weaken the Protestant [Established] Church . . . in England." 2. The Catholic Emancipation Act (April 13, 1829) which granted the franchise to English Catholics and opened to them privileges of officeholding similar to those already extended to Protestant Nonconformists, excepting only that priests were still ineligible for the House of Commons and that no Catholic could become Lord Chancellor of England or Lord Lieutenant of Ireland. But the Iron Duke still resisted parliamentary reform, and only the accession of a new king, William IV (1830-37), which forced a new election whereby a Whig majority was returned to Parliament, enabled the proponents of parliamentary reform to win. John George Lambton, later Lord Durham, and Lord John Russell were the chief authors of the first great Reform Bill, which, after some alterations and a bitter parliamentary struggle, passed in 1832 (March 23). In his speech introducing the bill on March 1, 1831, Russell explained the evils in the English electoral system which the bill sought to combat and outlined the methods employed for their eradication.

THE FIRST STEP IN PARLIAMENTARY REFORM

From RUSSELL, Speech to Introduce the Great Reform Bill (March 1, 1831) [1]

Mr. Speaker: I rise, sir, with feelings of deep anxiety and interest, to bring forward a question which, unparalleled as it is in importance, is likewise unparalleled in difficulty. . . . If, on other occasions, I have called the attention of the House of Commons to this subject, it has been upon my own responsibility, unaided by any one. . . . But, sir, the measure that I have now to bring forward is a measure, not of mine, but of the government in whose name I appear—the deliberate measure of a whole Cabinet, unanimous upon this subject, and resolved to place their measure before this House in redemption of their pledge to their sovereign, to Parliament, and to their country. . . .

Looking at the question, then, as a question of right, the ancient Statutes of Edward 1st contain the germ and vital principal of our political constitution. . . . The 34th Edward 1st, commonly called the Statute de Tallagio Non Concedendo, provides, "that no tallage or aid shall be taken or levied, by us or by our heirs, in our realm, without the good will and assent of archbishops, bishops, earls, barons, knights, burgesses, and other freemen of the land." Although some historical doubts have been thrown upon the authenticity of this statute, its validity in point of law is asserted in the Petition of Rights, was allowed by the Judges in the case of

[1] Hansard's *Parliamentary Debates,* 3d ser., London, 1831, II, 1061, 1063, 1068-72.

Hampden, and is, in fact, the foundation of the Constitution as it has existed since the days of the Stuarts. . . .

Let us now look at the question as one of reason. Allow me to imagine, for a moment, a stranger from some distant country, who should arrive in England to examine our institutions. All the information he had collected would have told him that this country was singular for the degree which it had attained in wealth, in science, and in civilization. He would have learned that in no country have the arts of life been carried further, nowhere the inventions of mechanical skill been rendered more conducive to the comfort and prosperity of mankind. He would have made himself acquainted with its fame in history, and above all, he would have been told that the proudest boast of this celebrated country was its political freedom. If, in addition to this, he had heard that once in six years this country, so wise, so renowned, so free, chose its Representatives to sit in the great Council, where all the ministerial affairs were discussed and determined; he would not be a little curious to see the process by which so important and solemn an operation was effected. What then would be his surprise, if he were taken by his guide, whom he had asked to conduct him to one of the places of election, to see a green mound and told that this green mound sent two Members to Parliament—or, to be taken to a stone wall with three niches in it, and told that these three niches sent two Members to Parliament—or, if he were shown a green park, with many signs of flourishing vegetable life but none of human habitation, and told that this green park sent two Members to Parliament? But his surprise would increase to astonishment if he were carried into the North of England, where he would see large flourishing towns, full of trade and activity, containing vast magazines of wealth and manufactures, and were told that these places had no Representatives in the Assembly which was said to represent the people. Suppose him, after all, for I will not disguise any part of the case, suppose him to ask for a specimen of popular election and to be carried, for that purpose, to Liverpool; his surprise would be turned into disgust at the gross venality and corruption which he would find to pervade the electors. After seeing all this, would he not wonder that a nation which had made such progress in every kind of knowledge and which valued itself for its freedom, should permit so absurd and defective a system of representation any longer to prevail? . . .

We propose that every borough which in that year [1821] had less than 2,000 inhabitants shall altogether lose the right of sending Members to Parliament. The effect will be utterly to disfranchise sixty boroughs. But we do not stop here. . . . We find that there are forty-seven boroughs of only 4,000 inhabitants, and these we shall deprive of the right of sending more than one Member to Parliament. We likewise intend that Weymouth, which at present sends four Members, shall, in future, only elect two. The abolition of sixty boroughs will occasion 119 vacancies, to which are to be added forty-seven for the boroughs allowed to send only one Member, and two of which Weymouth will be deprived, making in the whole 168 vacancies. . . . We do not mean to allow that the remaining boroughs should be in the hands of select corporations—that is to say, in the possession of a small number of persons to the exclusion of the great body of the inhabitants, who have property and interest in the place represented. . . . The right of voting shall be given to the householders paying rates for, or occupying a house of, the yearly value of £10 and upwards. Whether he be the proprietor, or whether he only rent the house, the person rated will have the franchise. . . . I shall now proceed to the manner in which we propose to extend the franchise in counties. The Bill I wish to introduce will give all copyholders to the value of £10 a year . . . a right to vote. . . . The right will depend upon a lease for twenty-one years, where the annual rent is not less than fifty pounds. . . . We propose . . . to fill up a certain number of the vacancies. . . . We intend that seven large towns shall send two Members each, and that twenty other towns shall send one Member each. Some of the towns which are to send two Members each are . . . Manchester and Salford, Birmingham and Aston, Leeds, Greenwich, Deptford. . . . Next we propose an addition to the Members for the larger counties. . . . Those counties contain a variety of interests, and form an admirable constituency; in some, as in Staffordshire, there is a large manufacturing population, better represented in this way than perhaps in any other; and as County Members have unquestionably the most excellent class of constituents, they form of themselves a most valuable class of Representatives. The Bill I shall beg leave to introduce will give two additional Members to each of twenty-seven counties where the inhabitants exceed 150,000.

RESULTS OF THE GREAT REFORM BILL

From MARRIOTT, *England since Waterloo* (1927) [1]

First, as regards disfranchisement: 56 boroughs with less than 2,000 inhabitants were totally disfranchised. Of these 55 had two members each; one, Higham Ferrers,

[1] From *England since Waterloo* by Sir J. A. R. Marriott, 8th ed., 1927, 98-99. Courtesy of G. P. Putnam's Sons, New York.

had one; Weymouth and Melcombe Regis lost two of their four members; and 30 boroughs with less than 4,000 inhabitants lost one of their two members. Thus 143 seats were surrendered. These were redistributed as follows: 65 to English and Welsh counties; 44 to twenty-two English boroughs (two each); 21 to single member boroughs; 8 to Scotland and 5 to Ireland. The total members therefore remained unchanged at 658. In the boroughs a uniform £10 household franchise was established, with the reservation of the rights of resident freemen in corporate towns. In the counties the old 40s. freeholders were reinforced by copyholders and long leaseholders, and by tenants-at-will paying a rent of £50 a year. . . . The final and total result was the addition of some 455,000 electors to the roll—an addition which more than tripled the electorate. In the town political power was vested mainly in the merchants, manufacturers, and shopkeepers; in the counties in the landowners and the farmers.

DEBATES ON THE SECOND REFORM ACT, 1867

The Reform Bill of 1832 left propertyless persons without the franchise. Wage-earners soon clamored for the right to vote [see Chartism, page 502], and English Liberals lent some support to the demand. But the Continental excesses in the Revolutions of 1848 again retarded English action. By the 1860's only one man in six could vote. Finally, in 1866, William Ewart Gladstone, making a bid for Liberal-party leadership, introduced a second reform bill to extend the franchise to workers, small farmers, and tenants, and to redistribute parliamentary seats further in the interest of growing industrial areas. The proposal aroused spirited debate in Commons, as many members feared extension of voting privileges to the working class. The following account of the debates well illustrates the sentiments of all parties at the time.

From *The Annual Register, 1866*[1]

Mr. Hughes [a Radical] supported the bill as an honest attempt to extend the franchise—the most important part of reform—and because . . . it would admit a large body of the best of the working classes. He defended trades unions and their leaders from imputations which had been made against them, described the great results which had been achieved by co-operative societies, and argued that if the working classes had been more directly represented in the House, it would have been able to deal more effectually with such questions as the relations between workmen and employers. . . . He derided the notion that the working classes were not as much divided on political matters as any other class, and urged the national importance of riveting their adherence to the constitution by this concession. . . .

Mr. Lowe [a Conservative] delivered a speech of great argumentative power against the Bill. . . . He pointed out the danger arising from the power of the working classes to combine for the accomplishment of their objects, and the ease with which trades unions might be converted into political organizations. Trades unions were far more unions against the best, most skilful, industrious men themselves, than against the masters. They made war upon all superiority and skilled industry, and made themselves the slaves of clumsiness, idleness, and ignorance. And see what a tremendous machinery they would have if they only

[1] *The Annual Register . . . 1866*, London, 1867, Pt. I, 123-25, 127-28, 130-31, 133, 135.

allowed them to possess the one thing they wanted—the parliamentary vote. Adopt this bill, and there was no saying where they would stop in the downward direction of democracy. . . . Democratize the House of Commons and it would not rest until it had swept away the institutions which now stood between it and the throne and supplied their places by other institutions deriving their origin directly from the people, and not having the quasi-independence which those corporations and privileged classes now enjoyed. When that was done, they would have face to face, with nothing to break the shock between them, the monarch for the time being and a great democracy; and history has taught us little if we thought those two powers would go on harmoniously. . . .

[Mr. Disraeli, the Conservative leader, said:] The franchise would again be extended; all command over the executive would cease; and when that was the state of things they would have a hall of selfish and obscure mediocrities, incapable of anything but mischief, and that mischief devised and regulated by the raging demagogue of the hour. The question before the House was, not whether the working men should be introduced to the franchise, but whether the working of the English constitution could be improved. . . . He did not say that the working classes had their full share of the franchise, but before proceeding to invest them with it, the House ought to obtain accurate information, and, above all, they should legislate in the spirit of the English constitution, so that this House should remain a House of Commons, and not the house of the people or of an indiscriminate multitude. In voting for this bill they would act not in the spirit of the British constitution but in the spirit of the constitution of America. . . .

[Mr. Gladstone, the Liberal leader, "in

one of the most powerful speeches in which his eloquence was ever exhibited," said:] My right honourable friend says we know nothing about the labouring classes. Is not a single word a sufficient reply, and that word is "Lancashire," associated with the sufferings of the last four years, so painful and bitter, but so nobly and gloriously borne? [Gladstone refers to the cotton famine occasioned by the American Civil War.] The qualities then exhibited were the qualities, not of select men here and there among a depraved multitude, but of the masses. . . . I cannot see what argument could be found for some wise and temperate experiment of the extension of civil rights among such people if the experience of the past few years does not afford it. Let us consider the enormous and silent changes which have been going forward among the labouring population. . . . Let us try and raise our views above the fears, suspicions, jealousies, attacks, and recriminations of this place. Let us look onward to the time of our children and our children's children. Let us think what preparation should be made for that time. Is there or is there not a steady movement of the labouring classes, and is or is not that movement onwards and upwards? I do not say you can see it; for, like all great processes, it is unobservable in detail but solid and unassailable in character. . . . You cannot fight against the future. Time is on our side. The great social forces which move on in their might and majesty, and which the tumult of our debates does not for a moment impede or disturb —those great social forces are against you; they are marshalled on our side; and the banner which we now carry, though, perhaps, at some moment it may droop over our sinking heads, yet it soon again will float in the eye of heaven, and it will be borne by the firm hands of the united people of the three kingdoms, perhaps not to an easy, but to a certain and to a not distant victory.

[Gladstone's fervid oratory was to no avail. The bill of 1866 failed to pass—the fifth ministry that had failed to secure passage of legislation of this kind. Disraeli and the Conservatives who followed found the problem on their doorstep, and so great was the public demand that, despite his earlier opposition, Disraeli determined to make a "leap in the dark." He introduced a bill substantially like Gladstone's and saw it successfully passed in 1867—a great personal triumph, though his critics bellowed "that nothing was so elastic as the conscience of a Cabinet Minister," and Mr. Lowe predicted dire disaster when "the bag which holds the winds will be untied, and we shall be surrounded by a perpetual whirl of change, alteration, innovation and revolution."]

THE FRANCHISE BILL OF 1884

The Reform Act of 1867 extended suffrage in towns to all householders paying the poor rates and lodgers paying an annual rent of £10; in rural areas it reduced the property qualification to owners of land of £5 annual value and to tenants paying £12 annual rental. The classes left without voting rights were the owners and tenants of very small agricultural plots, the agricultural laborers, and domestic servants. In 1884, Gladstone's Franchise Bill extended franchise to these rural classes, virtually establishing manhood suffrage in England, the only exceptions being domestic servants, bachelors living with their families, and persons with no fixed abode. Introducing this bill, Gladstone said:

From GLADSTONE, Speech Introducing the
Franchise Bill of 1884 [1]

I am not prepared to discuss admission to the franchise as it was discussed 50 years ago, when Lord John Russell had to state, with almost bated breath, that he expected to add in the Three Kingdoms 500,000 to the constituencies. It is not now a question of nicely calculated less or more. I take my stand on the broad principle that the enfranchisement of capable citizens, be they few or be they many—and if they be many so much the better—gives an addition of strength to the State. The strength of the modern state lies in the Representative System. I rejoice to think that in this happy country and under this happy constitution we have other sources of strength in the respect paid to various orders of the State, and in the authority they enjoy, and in the unbroken course which has been allowed to most of our national traditions; but still, in the main, it is the Representative System which is the strength of the modern State in general, and of the State in this country in particular. . . .

Sir, the only question that remains in the general argument is, who are capable citizens? And, fortunately, that is a question which, on the present occasion, need not be argued at length, for it has been already settled—in the first place by a solemn legislative judgment acquiesced in by both Parties in the State; and, in the second place, by the experience of the last more than fifteen years. Who, Sir, are the capable citizens of the State, whom it is proposed to enfranchise? It is proposed, in the main, to enfranchise the county population on the footing and according to the measure that has already been administered to the population of

the towns. What are the main constituents of the county population? First of all, they are the minor tradesmen of the country and the skilled labourers and artisans in all the common arts of life, and especially in connection with our great mining industry. Is there any doubt that these are capable citizens? You honourable gentlemen opposite [the Conservatives] have yourselves asserted it by enfranchising them in the towns; and we can only say that we heartily subscribe to the assertion. But besides the artisans and the minor tradesmen scattered throughout our rural towns, we have also to deal with the peasantry of the country. Is there any doubt that the peasantry of the country are capable citizens, qualified for enfranchisement, qualified to make good use of their power as voters? This is a question which has been solved for us by the first and second Reform Bills; because many of the places which, under the name of towns, are now represented in this House are really rural communities, based upon a peasant constituency. For my part, I should be quite ready to fight the battle of a peasant upon general and argumentative grounds. I believe the peasant generally to be, not in the highest sense, but in a very real sense, a skilled labourer. He is not a man tied down to one mechanical exercise of his physical powers. He is a man who must do many things, and many things which require in him the exercise of active intelligence. . . .

I say this is not a perfect bill with regard to the franchise. . . . No, Sir; ideal perfection is not the true basis of English legislation. We look at the attainable; we look at the practicable; and we have too much of English sense to be drawn away by those sanguine delineations of what might possibly be attained in Utopia, from a path which promises to enable us to effect great good for the people of England. . . .

[1] Hansard's *Parliamentary Debates,* 3d ser., London, 1884, CCLXXXV, 107-09, 122-23, 131-34.

What does it do, and what does it do in comparison with what has been done before? In 1832 there was passed what was considered a Magna Carta of British liberties; but that Magna Carta of British liberties added, according to the previous estimate of Lord John Russell, 500,000, while according to the results considerably less than 500,000 were added to the entire constituency of the three countries. After 1832 we come to 1866. At that time the total constituency of the United Kingdom reached 1,364,000. By the bills which were passed between 1867 and 1868 that number was raised to 2,448,000. And now, Sir, under the action of the present law the constituency has reached in round numbers what I would call 3,000,000. I will not enter into details; but what is the increase we are going to make? There is a basis of computation, but it is a basis which affords, I admit, ground for conjecture and opinion. That basis of computation is the present ratio in towns, between inhabited houses and the number of town electors. Of course we have availed ourselves of that basis for the purpose of computation. I have gone into the matter as carefully as I can, and the best results I can attain are these. The bill, if it passes as presented, will add to the English constituency over 1,300,000 persons. It will add to the Scotch constituency, Scotland being at present rather better provided for in this respect than either of the other countries, over 200,000, and to the Irish constituency over 400,-000; or, in the main, to the present aggregate constituency of the United Kingdom, taken at 3,000,000, it will add 2,000,000 more, nearly twice as much as was added since 1867, and more than four times as much as was added in 1832. Surely, I say, that is worth doing, that is worth not endangering. Surely that is worth some sacrifice. . . .

"Read your history in a nation's eyes," for you will have deserved it by the benefits you will have conferred. You will have made this strong nation stronger still; stronger by its closer union without; stronger against its foes, if and when it has any foes without; stronger within by union between class and class, and by arraying all classes and all portions of the community in one solid compacted mass round the ancient Throne which it has loved so well, and round a constitution now to be more than ever powerful and more than ever free.

2. Social and Economic Reforms

THE CRIMINAL CODE: BEGINNINGS OF REFORM

In 1800, more than two hundred offenses were legally punishable by the death penalty in England. The severity of the criminal law often defeated its own object, as juries refused to convict for petty offenses when conviction might cost an offender his life. Similarly, judges and courts ignored the law. Thus, of 655 persons indicted for shoplifting between 1805 and 1807, 113 were sentenced to death, but in no case was the penalty enforced. On the other hand, between 1811 and 1818 over 100 persons were hanged for forgery. To reduce such unevenness, undue severity, and irrationalities in the criminal law became the principal object of Sir Samuel Romilly (1757-1818) during the last decade of his life. As lawyer, orator, and parliamentarian, Sir Samuel planted the seeds of reform and himself removed pocket-picking and some few other petty offenses from the list of capital offenses. Sir James Mackintosh lent able assistance to the movement, and Sir Robert Peel reaped the legislative harvest when, in the years 1822-27, he won the repeal of at least 278 harsh and irrational acts, and re-enacted such of their provisions as were still valuable in eight new statutes. The conditions which these acts sought to correct were well described in Romilly's speeches. Excerpts from some of them follow.

From ROMILLY, *Speeches* (c. 1815) [1]

I have always considered it a very great defect in the Criminal Code of this Country that Capital Punishment should be so frequent; that they have been appointed, I cannot say inflicted, for so many crimes. For no principle seems to me more clear than this, that it is the certainty, much more than the severity of punishments, which renders them efficacious. This has been acknowledged, I believe, ever since the publication of the works of the Marquis Beccaria [*Treatise on Crime and Punishment,* first published in Italian in 1764]. The impression, however, which was made in this Country by his writings, has hitherto proved unavailing; for it has not produced a single alteration in our Criminal Law; although in many other states of Europe various amendments have taken place. Indeed, if we were to take the very reverse of the principle to which I have alluded, it would be a faithful description of the English law, in its enactments and administration. It is notorious how few of those who are condemned actually suffer punishment. From the returns which are to be found in the Secretary of State's office, it appears that in the year 1805 there were 350 persons who received sentence of death, of whom only 68 were executed, not quite a fifth part of the number. In the year 1806, 325 re-

ceived sentence of death, of whom 57 were executed; and in 1807, the number was 343, of whom there were executed 63. If we deduct from this number all those who received sentence of death for crimes which are never, or very rarely pardoned, it will, perhaps, be found that out of 20 persons condemned to die, not more than one suffers death.

The question, therefore, is, Whether the execution of the Law is to be the rule or the exception to be observed in the administration of justice; whether a code shall continue to exist in *theory* which has been lately described (in language which one would rather have expected to hear from the lips of a Satirist, than from a seat of Judgment) "as almost abrogated in *practice* by the astuteness of Judges, the humanity of Juries, and the mercy of the Crown." I am far from being disposed either to censure or regret this relaxation of the Law; I am only inquiring whether Statutes so dispensed with can be deemed any longer essential to the well-being of the State.

Such is the general view which I have taken of the subject. But my more immediate purpose is to call the attention of the House to one class only of these severe Statutes, which have, from a change of circumstances, acquired a rigour not originally intended by their framers; Statutes in which the capital part of the charge depends, not on the mode or season in which the offence has been committed, but on the value of the property stolen; such as the Act of Elizabeth, which punishes with death the stealing privately from one person of another to the value of twelve pence; that of William and Mary, which makes privately stealing in a shop to the amount of five shillings, a capital Felony; and other Statues of the same nature. So great an alteration has taken place in the value of money since those Statutes passed that it is astonishing that

---

[1] *The Speeches of Sir Samuel Romilly in the House of Commons,* 2 vols., London, 1820, I, 38-42, 122-25.

the letter of the Law should have been suffered to remain unaltered to the present day, the offences, in the meantime, having become altogether so different. . . .

There are many mischievous consequences resulting from such a state of things. . . . Such Laws cannot be executed. Juries are placed in the painful situation of violating one of two duties; they are reduced to the alternative of violating their oaths, or what they are sometimes mistakenly induced to think more binding on them—the dictates of humanity. Often, against the plainest evidence, Juries have reduced the property stolen to less than half its lowest value in order to dispense with the capital part of the punishment. . . . The law ought not to remain so—it causes offenders to be acquitted against the clearest evidence; and thus, by a necessary consequence, defeats its own ends, and becomes the abettor of its own violation. . . .

The same benevolence and humanity, understood in a more confined or a more enlarged sense, will determine one Judge to pardon and another to punish. . . . Not a great many years ago, upon the Norfolk Circuit, a larceny was committed by two men in a poultry-yard, but only one of them was apprehended; the other having escaped into a distant part of the country had eluded all pursuit. At the next Assizes· the apprehended thief was tried and convicted; but Lord Loughborough, before whom he was tried, thinking the offence a very slight one, sentenced him only to a few months' imprisonment. The news of this sentence having reached the accomplice in his retreat, he immediately returned and surrendered himself to take his trial at the next Assizes. The next Assizes came; but, unfortunately for the prisoner, it was a different Judge who presided . . . Mr.

Justice Gould, who . . . had observed, or thought he had observed, that men who set out with stealing fowls, generally ended by committing the most atrocious crimes; and building a sort of system upon this observation . . . he accordingly, to the astonishment of this unhappy man, sentenced him to be transported. While one was taking his departure for Botany Bay, the term of the other's imprisonment had expired; and what must have been the notions which that little Public, who witnessed and compared these two examples, formed of our system of Criminal Jurisprudence?

THE REPEAL OF THE CORN LAWS

The Corn Laws placed heavy import duties on wheat to protect English landowners. But they also increased the price of food, and this fact, together with prevailing theories of free trade, induced a group of Liberals, many of them manufacturers who desired to reduce food costs in order to hold wages at low levels, to advocate repeal of the Corn Laws. Propaganda was directed by the Anti-Corn Law League, in which Richard Cobden and John Bright were active promoters. Charles Pelham Villiers hammered for repeal in Parliament, but it was Sir Robert Peel who brought it to pass. Peel opposed repeal until preliminary fiscal experiments proved the desirability, for England at least, of lowered tariffs, and the potato famine in Ireland emphasized the need for cheap food supplies. The repeal cost Peel his ministry, but it also placed England at the head of free-trade policies and practices for the remainder of the nineteenth century. In his plea for repeal, Sir Robert gave the following speech in the House of Commons.

From PEEL, Speech on Repeal of the Corn
Laws (February 16, 1846) [1]

This night is to decide between the
policy of continued relaxation of restriction, or the return to restraint and prohibition. This night you will select the
motto which is to indicate the commercial policy of England. Shall it be "advance" or "recede"? Which is the fitter
motto for this great Empire? Survey our
position, consider the advantage which
God and nature have given us, and the
destiny for which we are intended. We
stand on the confines of Western Europe,
the chief connecting link between the old
world and the new. The discoveries of
science, the improvement of navigation,
have brought us within ten days of St.
Petersburgh, and will soon bring us to
within ten days of New York. We have
an extent of coast greater in proportion
to our population and the area of our
land than any other great nation, securing
to us maritime strength and superiority.
Iron and coal, the sinews of manufacture,
give us advantages over every rival in
the great competition of industry. Our
capital far exceeds that which they can
command. In ingenuity, in skill, in
energy, we are inferior to none. Our national character, the free institutions under which we live, the liberty of thought
and action, an unshackled press, spreading the knowledge of every discovery and
of every advance in science—combine
with our natural and physical advantages
to place us at the head of those nations
which profit by the free interchange of
their products. And is this the country to
shrink from competition? Is this the country to adopt a retrograde policy? Is this
the country which can only flourish in
the sickly artificial atmosphere of prohibition? Is this the country to stand

[1] Hansard's *Parliamentary Debates,* 3d ser.,
1846, LXXXIII, 1041-43.

shivering on the brink of exposure to the
healthful breezes of competition?

Choose your motto. "Advance" or "Recede." Many countries are watching with
anxiety the selection you may make. Determine for "Advance," and it will be
the watchword which will animate and
encourage in every state the friends of
liberal commercial policy. Sardinia has
taken the lead. Naples is relaxing her protective duties and favouring British produce. Prussia is shaken in her adherence
to restriction. The Government of France
will be strengthened. . . . Can you doubt
that the United States will soon relax her
hostile Tariff, and that the friends of a
freer commercial intercourse—the friends
of peace between the two countries—will
hail with satisfaction the example of England?

This night, then—if on this night the
debate shall close—you will have to decide what are the principles by which
your commercial policy is to be regulated.
Most earnestly, from a deep conviction,
founded not upon the limited experience
of three years alone, but upon the experience of the results of every relaxation
of restriction and prohibition, I counsel
you to set an example of liberality to other
countries. Act thus, and it will be in
perfect consistency with the course you
have hitherto taken. Act thus, and you
will provide an additional guarantee for
the continued contentment, and happiness, and well-being of the great body of
the people. Act thus, and you will have
done whatever human sagacity can do
for the promotion of commercial prosperity.

You may fail. Your precautions may
be unavailing. They may give no certain
assurance that mercantile and manufacturing prosperity will continue without
interruption. It seems to be incident to
great prosperity that there shall be a
reverse—that the time of depression shall

follow the season of excitement and success. . . . Gloomy winters, like those of 1841 and 1842, may again set in. Are those winters effaced from your memory? From mine they never can be. . . .

When you are again exhorting a suffering people to fortitude under their privations, when you are telling them, "These are the chastenings of an all-wise and merciful Providence, sent for some inscrutable but just and beneficent purpose," . . . when you are encouraging them to bear without repining the dispensations of Providence, may God grant that by your decision of this night you have laid in store for yourselves the consolation of reflecting that such calamities are, in truth, the dispensations of Providence—that they have not been caused, they have not been aggravated by laws of man restricting, in the hour of scarcity, the supply of food!

THE EDUCATION ACT OF 1870

Until 1833 education of the children of the poor in England rested solely in the churches or in private hands. In that year the Treasury began annual grants-in-aid to the church schools. But the dole was too meager and, although, as elsewhere, the churches bitterly opposed state control of education, the want of instruction for the poor became a matter of increasing national concern. Only about one-half of the four million English children of school age were provided with schools of any kind, and those schools which did exist provided educational facilities far inferior to those established in Prussia, Switzerland, and the United States. To correct these conditions, William Edward Forster (1818-1886) introduced the Education Act of 1870, an Act which laid the foundation for a national system of elementary education in England. For-

ster sought to avoid trouble with the churches. "Our object," he said, "is to complete the present voluntary system, to fill up gaps"; and so "if in any one of the districts we find the elementary education to be sufficient, efficient, and suitable . . . we let it alone so long as it continues in that state." All schools, however, were to be open to government inspection. The principal clauses of Forster's Education Act follow.

From The Education Act of 1870 [1]

There shall be provided for every school district a sufficient amount of accommodation in public elementary schools (as hereinafter defined) available for all the children resident in such district for whose elementary education efficient and suitable provision is not otherwise made, and where there is an insufficient amount of such accommodation, in this act referred to as "public school accommodation," the deficiency shall be supplied in manner provided by this act.

Where the education department, in the manner provided by this act, are satisfied and have given public notice that there is an insufficient amount of such accommodation for any school district, and the deficiency is not supplied as hereinafter provided, a school board shall be formed for such district and shall supply such deficiency, and in case of default by the school board the education department shall cause the duty of such board to be performed in manner provided by this act. . . .

Every school provided by a school board shall be conducted under the control and management of such board in accordance with the following regulations: (1) The school shall be a public

[1] G. B. Adams and H. M. Stephens, eds., *Select Documents of English Constitutional History,* 1929, 538-40. By permission of The Macmillan Company, New York.

elementary school within the meaning of this act; (2) No religious catechism or religious formulary which is distinctive of any particular denomination shall be taught in the school. . . .

Every child attending a school provided by any school board shall pay such weekly fee as may be prescribed by the school board, with the consent of the education department, but the school board may from time to time, for a renewable period not exceeding six months, remit the whole or any part of such fee in the case of any child when they are of opinion that the parent of such child is unable from poverty to pay the same, but such remission shall not be deemed to be parochial relief given to such parent. . . .

The school board shall be elected in manner provided by this act—in a borough by the persons whose names are on the burgess roll of such borough for the time being in force, and in a parish not situate in the metropolis by the ratepayers. . . . The school board shall be a body corporate, by the name of the school board of the district to which they belong, having a perpetual succession and a common seal, with power to acquire and hold land for the purposes of this act.

[The Act left local authorities to determine whether attendance was compulsory; in 1880, an additional Act made attendance compulsory. Again, in 1891, the fees paid by the parents were abolished. Thus elementary education became free and compulsory in England.]

THE LEGALIZATION OF TRADE-UNIONS: THE ACTS OF 1871 AND 1906

In spite of the nonlegal status accorded trade-unions by the Combination Laws of 1825, they multiplied rapidly. Industrial disturbances fomented by them in 1866 led to the creation of a Royal Commission, on the strength of whose report the Trade-Union Act of 1871 was enacted.

From The Trade-Union Act of 1871 [1]

The purposes of any trade-union shall not, by reason merely that they are in restraint of trade, be deemed to be unlawful so as to render any member of such trade-union liable to criminal prosecution for conspiracy or otherwise. . . .

The purposes of any trade-union shall not, by reason merely that they are in restraint of trade, be unlawful so as to render void or voidable any agreement or trust. . . .

Any seven or more members of a trade-union may by subscribing their names to the rules of the union, and otherwise complying with the provisions of this Act with respect to registry, register such trade-union under this Act, provided that if any one of the purposes of such trade-union be unlawful such registration shall be void. . . .

The trustees of any trade-union registered under this Act, or any other officer of such trade-union who may be authorised so to do by the rules thereof, are hereby empowered to bring or defend, or cause to be brought or defended, any action, suit, prosecution, or complaint in any court of law or equity, touching or concerning the property, right, or claim to property of the trade-union: and shall and may, in all cases concerning the real or personal property of such trade-union, sue or be sued, plead and be impleaded, in any court of law or equity, in their proper names, without other description than the title of their office; and no such

[1] *Statutes of the Realm:* 34 and 35 Victoria ch. 31, pars. 2, 3, 6, 9, 11.

action, suit, prosecution or complaint shall be discontinued or shall abate by the death or removal from office of such persons or any of them, but the same shall and may be proceeded in by their successor or successors as if such death, resignation, or removal had not taken place. . . .

Every treasurer or other officer of a trade-union registered under this act, at such times as by the rules of such trade-union he should render such account . . . shall render to the trustees of the trade-union, at a meeting of the trade-union, a just and true account of all moneys received and paid by him since he last rendered the like account, and of the balance remaining. . . .

A general statement of the receipts, funds, effects, and expenditure of every trade-union registered under this act shall be transmitted to the registrar before the first day of June in every year . . . and shall show separately the expenditure in respect of the several objects of the trade-union.

[Subsequent legislation in 1875 rendered labor contracts—like other contracts—civil engagements, the two parties being equal before the law, and also legalized picketing. In 1901, however, in the Taff Vale Case, in which the Taff Vale Railway Company sued a trade-union for damages suffered in a strike, the position of trade-unions was again jeopardized. Until then it was understood that a union, not being a corporation, could not be sued. The decision in favor of the railway was upheld by the House of Lords. It hastened the organization of the Labor party, which, by 1905, wielded influence in the new Liberal government then formed. As a consequence, the Trade Disputes Act of 1906 gave the unions additional protection.]

From The Trade Disputes Act of 1906 [1]

An act done in pursuance of an agreement or combination by two or more persons shall, if done in contemplation or furtherance of a trade dispute, not be actionable unless the act, if done without any such agreement or combination, would be actionable. . . .

It shall be lawful for one or more persons, acting on their own behalf or on behalf of a trade-union or of an individual employer or firm in contemplation or furtherance of a trade dispute, to attend at or near a house or place where a person resides or works or carries on business or happens to be, if they so attend merely for the purpose of peacefully obtaining or communicating information, or of peacefully persuading any person to work or abstain from working [that is, peaceful picketing]. . . .

An act done by a person in contemplation or furtherance of a trade dispute shall not be actionable on the ground only that it induces some person to break a contract of employment or that it is an interference with the trade, business, or employment of some other person, or with the right of some other person to dispose of his capital or his labour as he wills. . . .

An action against a trade-union . . . or against any member or official thereof on behalf of themselves and all other members of the trade-union in respect of any tortious act alleged to have been committed by or on behalf of the trade-union, shall not be entertained by any court. Nothing in this section shall affect the liability of the trustees of a trade-union to be sued in the events provided for by the Trade-Union Act, 1871 . . . except in respect of any tortious act committed by or on behalf of the union in contem-

[1] *Statutes of the Realm:* 6 Edward VII, ch. 47, paragraphs 1-5.

plation or in furtherance of a trade dispute. . . .

In this Act . . . the expression "trade dispute" means any dispute between employers and workmen, or between workmen and workmen, which is connected with the employment or non-employment, or the terms of the employment, or with the conditions of labour, of any person, and the expression "workmen" means all persons employed in trade or industry, whether or not in the employment of the employer with whom a trade dispute arises.

3. Aspects of the Irish Question

THE NATIONAL LAND LEAGUE

Among the various issues that constituted the "Irish Question," the agrarian problem was prominent. Fundamental to the agrarian problem was the fact that, in a country primarily agricultural, most of the land was owned by nonresident aliens, who had acquired the soil by conquest and who extended no fixity of tenure, no compensation for improvements made by tenants, nor other "tenant rights" to the native tillers of the soil. In 1850 a Tenant-Right League was founded to obtain the "Three F's"—"fair rents, fixity of tenure, and free sale." In 1879, under the leadership of Michael Davitt and Charles Stewart Parnell, was organized the National Land League. Beginning in August in County Mayo as a local group, it quickly became a nation-wide organization in September, with the same objects and principles outlined in the original constitution as given below. Gladstone's Irish Land Bills (in 1870 and 1881) were designed to ameliorate Irish land conditions, and they prepared the way for ultimate solution of the problem by state-aided purchase by the tenant.

From The Constitution of the National Land League of Mayo (1879) [1]

OBJECTS

The objects for which this body is organized are—

1. To watch over the interests of the people it represents; and to protect the same . . . from an unjust or capricious exercise of power or privilege on the part of landlords or any other class in the community.

2. To resort to every means compatible with justice, morality, and right reason which shall not clash defiantly with the constitution upheld by the power of the British empire in this country, for the abolition of the present land laws of Ireland, and the substitution in their place of such a system as shall be in accord with the social rights and necessities of our people, the traditions and moral sentiments of our race, and which the contentment and prosperity of our country imperatively demand.

3. Pending a final and satisfactory settlement of the land question, the duty of this body will be to expose the injustice, wrong, or injury which may be inflicted upon any farmer in Mayo, either by rackrenting, eviction, or other arbitrary exercise of power which the existing laws enable the landlords to exercise over their tenantry, by giving all such arbitrary acts the widest possible publicity. . . .

4. To undertake the defence of such of its members, or those of local clubs affiliated with it, who may be required to resist

[1] Edmund Curtis and R. B. McDowell, eds., *Irish Historical Documents 1172-1922*, 1943, 255-58. By permission of Methuen and Co., Ltd., London.

by law the actions of landlords or their agents. . . .

5. To render assistance . . . to such farmer-members as may be evicted or otherwise wronged. . . .

6. To undertake the organizing of local clubs or defence associations . . . the holding of public meetings and demonstrations on the land question, and the printing of pamphlets on that and other subjects for the information of the farming classes.

7. And finally to act as a vigilance committee in Mayo, note the conduct of its grand jury, poor law guardians, town commissioners, and members of parliament and pronounce on the manner in which their respective functions are performed. . . .

DECLARATION OF PRINCIPLES

The land of Ireland belongs to the people of Ireland, to be held and cultivated for the sustenance of . . . the inhabitants thereof. Land being created to supply the necessities of existence, those who cultivate it to that end have a higher claim to its absolute possession than those who make it an article of barter. . . . The end for which the land of a country is created requires an equitable distribution of the same among the people. . . . Any restriction, therefore, upon such a distribution by a feudal land system embodying the laws of primogeniture and entail, the amassing of large estates, the claiming of proprietorship under penal obligations from occupiers, and preventing the same from developing the full resources of the land, must necessarily be opposed to the Divine purpose for which it was created, and to the social rights, security, and happiness of the people.

"Before the conquest the Irish people knew nothing of absolute property in land. The land virtually belonged to the entire sept, the Chief was little more than the managing member of the association. The feudal idea, which views all rights as emanating from a head landlord, came in with the conquest, was associated with foreign dominion, and has never to this day been recognized by the moral sentiments of the people. . . . In the moral feelings of the Irish people, the right to hold the land goes, as it did in the beginning, with the right to till it." These were the words of John Stuart Mill, the English political economist.

The landlord system which an alien government has imposed upon our country in the place of that which recognized no intermediate ownership between the cultivator of the soil and the state has reduced Ireland to a degree of poverty and social misery incompatible with the natural productiveness of its land and the progressive prosperity of other civilized nations. The area of Ireland . . . is capable of supporting from twelve to twenty millions of inhabitants. . . . Yet a population of 8,000,000 previous to the year 1847 was reduced by death, starvation, and exile . . . to little over 5,000,000 at the present day. . . . Over 6,000,000 acres of Irish land is owned by less than 300 individuals, twelve of whom are in possession of 1,297,888 acres between them, while 5,000,000 of the Irish people own not a solitary acre. . . . If the land in the possession of 744 landlords in this country were divided into 20-acre farms it would support in ease and comparative independence over two millions and a half of our people.

AGITATION FOR HOME RULE FOR IRELAND

"My first object," said Daniel O'Connell in 1843, "is to get Ireland for the Irish." This was the nub of the Irish question. In the 1880's, Parnell became the dominant leader for Home Rule.

He sought to unite the Irish behind it and to force the English Parliament to grant it by means of obstruction (filibustering)—"Whenever you see a Bill, block it; whenever you see a Raw, rub it." Gladstone's ill-fated Home Rule Bills (1886 and 1893) were vain efforts to respond to the Irish demand. But realization of Home Rule was postponed until after World War I.

From PARNELL, Speech at Wicklow
(October 5, 1885) [1]

When I last spoke in public in Ireland I expressed my conviction that in the new parliament we should be able to form our platform of a single plank, and that plank the plank of legislative independence (cheers), and that we should carry that plank to a successful issue in the same way as during the last parliament we have carried other subordinate planks, such as the extension of the franchise and so forth (cheers). My declaration has been received by the English press and by some, although not all, the English leaders with a storm of disapproval, and they have told us that the yielding of an independent parliament to Ireland is a matter of impossibility. But nothing . . . has in the slightest degree diminished my confidence. . . . On the contrary, very much that has been said by our enemies . . . has very much increased my confidence (cheers). They practically admit that things cannot be allowed to go on as they are. . . . They admit that there must be some change; but the two conditions that they put forward in regard to this change, and as a condition of this change, are—firstly, that the separation of Ireland from England shall not be a consequence of the grant of legislative independence

to Ireland; and, in the second place, they claim that we shall not be allowed to protect our manufactures at the cost of those of England. . . . To take the last point first . . . I have claimed for Ireland a parliament that shall have power to protect these Irish manufactures (cheers), if it be the will of the parliament and of the Irish people that they should be protected (cheers). But it is not for me to say beforehand what the action of such a freely elected Irish assembly would be. . . . I am of the opinion . . . that it would be wise to protect certain Irish industries, at all events for a time. . . . I think also that Ireland could never be a manufacturing nation of such importance as to compete to any great extent with England. . . . I will proceed a little further, and I will deal with the claim that has been put forward, that some guarantee should be given that the granting of legislative powers to Ireland should not lead to the separation of Ireland from England. This claim is one which at first sight may seem a fair one. . . . It is not possible for human intelligence to forecast the future in these matters; but we can point to this—we can point to the fact that under 85 years of parliamentary connection with England, Ireland has become intensely disloyal and intensely disaffected (applause); that notwithstanding the Whig policy of so-called conciliation, alternative conciliation and coercion . . . that disaffection has broadened, deepened and intensified from day to day (cheers). Am I not, then, entitled to assume that one of the roots of this disaffection and feeling of disloyalty is the assumption by England of the management of our affairs? (Cheers.) It is admitted that the present system can't go on, and what are you going to put in its place? (Cries of "Home Rule!") My advice to English statesmen considering this question would

[1] Curtis and McDowell, eds., *Irish Historical Documents 1172-1922*, 284-87. Reprinted by permission of Methuen and Co., Ltd.

be this—trust the Irish people altogether or trust them not at all (cheers). . . . Whatever chance the English rulers may have of drawing to themselves the affection of the Irish people lies in destroying the abominable system of legislative union between the two countries by conceding fully and freely to Ireland the right to manage her own affairs. It is impossible for us to give guarantees, but we can point to the past; we can show that the record of English rule is a constant series of steps from bad to worse (cheers), that the condition of English power is more insecure and more unstable at the present moment than it has ever been (applause). We can point to the example of other countries; of Austria and of Hungary—to the fact that Hungary having been conceded self-government became one of the strongest factors in the Austrian empire. We can show the powers that have been freely conceded to the colonies. . . . We can show that disaffection has disappeared in all the greater English colonies, that while the Irishman who goes to the United States of America carries with him a burning hatred of English rule (cheers) . . . the Irishman . . . who goes to one of the colonies of Canada or one of the colonies of Australia, and finds there another and a different system of English rule to that which he has been accustomed at home, becomes to a great extent a loyal citizen and a strength and a prop to the community amongst whom his lot has been cast; that he forgets the little memories of his experience of England at home, and that he no longer continues to look upon the name of England as a symbol of oppression, and the badge of the misfortunes of his country (cheers). . . . I am confident that the English statesman who is great enough . . . to carry out these teachings . . . to give Ireland full legislative liberty, full power to manage her own domestic concerns, will be regarded in the future by his countrymen as one who has removed the greatest peril to the English empire (hear, hear)—a peril, I firmly believe, which if not removed will find some day . . . an opportunity of revenging itself (loud cheers) to the destruction of the British empire for the misfortunes, the oppressions, and the misgovernment of our country (loud cheers).

4. Shifting Imperial Attitudes, 1815-1840

ANTI-IMPERIAL SENTIMENT

Great Britain's imperial spirit sagged for nearly a generation after 1815. Having lost the thirteen American colonies, she had little pride in the remains of her polyglot empire—French in Canada, Dutch in Cape Colony, Negro in the West Indies, and so on. Not only was the empire stock largely non-British, but also colonies appeared troublesome and costly. Even the economic advantages of colonies were widely questioned. Sir Henry Brooke Parnell (1776-1842), an Anglo-Irish politician and financial writer, gave expression to widely held anti-imperial sentiment in the following words.

From SIR HENRY PARNELL, *On Financial Reform* (1830) [1]

There are only three ways that the colonies can be of any advantage, 1. In furnishing a military force; 2. In supplying the parent state with a revenue; 3. In affording commercial advantages.

1. Instead of furnishing a military force, the colonies are always a drain upon the

[1] Sir Henry Brooke Parnell, *On Financial Reform*, London, 1830, 250-57.

military resources of the country, particularly in war, when they occupy a large portion of the army and fleet in their defence. In the last war, while our own shores were threatened with invasion from Boulogne and Brest, our means of defence were greatly crippled by the number of troops and ships we were obliged to keep in the colonies.

2. With respect to revenue, we have declared by the Act of the 18 Geo. III, that we will not levy any taxes or duties in the colonies except for their use.

3. As to commercial advantages, if the colonial trade were quite free, our commercial relations with the colonies would resemble the intercourse between ourselves and independent countries; and therefore whatever advantages we shall derive from them will be embraced in two questions: 1st. Whether our commerce with them will be more beneficial than with independent countries? 2nd. Whether the capital employed in them will be more beneficially employed than it would be, if employed in the United Kingdom?

With respect to the first question, it is one easily solved, because, where the employment of capital is free, the net profit that may be obtained by the employment of it in commerce with independent countries will always be as great as if it were employed in the colonial trade. The trade we carry on with the United States proves this.

With respect to the second question, it is necessary to trace the operations of capital when employed in colonies, and when employed at home. In the West India islands it goes to feed and clothe slaves; to pay British agents, clerks, and managers; to employ ships and sailors; and although the gross profit upon it seems very high when all the charges and risks are considered, and also the effects of competition, the net profit cannot be greater than it is on capital employed at home.

When capital is employed in the United Kingdom—for instance, on manufactures —it pays wages to English workmen instead of buying clothes and food for slaves; it employs agents, clerks, and managers; it employs ships and sailors to import raw materials and to export the finished goods, and the rate of net profit on it is full as high as that on capital employed in the colonies. The incomes derived by West India proprietors from their profits are spent like incomes derived from rent, and add nothing to the national wealth; but the profits made on capital employed at home are added to capital, and thus promote the constant accumulation of it. It is clear, therefore, that, on the whole, the public derives no commercial advantage from the colonies, which it might not have without them.

They do not even afford any advantage, as some persons suppose, by enlarging the field for the employment of capital; for there are still means enough for employing capital with profit at home; and if new means were wanting, they would be more effectually obtained by removing restrictions on trade and revising the taxes, than by increased trade in colonies.

This general reasoning, which the principles of trade suggest, in refutation of the imaginary advantages of colonies, is completely borne out by the experience of facts. The history of the colonies for many years is that of a series of loss, and of the destruction of capital; and if to the many millions of private capital, which have been thus wasted, were added some hundred millions that have been raised by British taxes and spent on account of the colonies, the total loss to the British public of wealth, which the colonies have occasioned, would appear to be quite enormous.

The only conditions on which it can be wise and politic for us to continue to keep colonial possessions are, that the number of them should be greatly reduced; and that those which we retain should contribute the whole expense incurred in their defence. Even with such conditions, no advantage would be gained . . . unless the planters should prosper and accumulate wealth, and thus add to the general stock of public wealth. . . .

In settling the conditions of the last treaty of peace [1815], it was most unwise to retain so many of the conquered colonies. Trinidad, Demerara, Essequibo, and Tobago were but little advanced in cultivation; a large transfer of capital was necessary for their cultivation, and there was little or no local revenue belonging to them.

At the close of the war the East India Company was anxious to be allowed the Island of Ceylon, and it is not too late to give it up to them; but as large sums of public money have been expended since the war in adding to its value, the Company should repay a large part of them as the condition of becoming masters of this island. As the Cape of Good Hope and Mauritius are of no use except for the defence of the East India Company's possessions, the Company ought to be called on to defray all the expenses of their military protection. . . .

The settlement of Sierra Leone and the military posts on the west coast of Africa should be given up. The public derives no benefit from these possessions, either in a commercial or military point of view. . . .

With respect to Canada (including our other possessions on the Continent of North America), no case can be made out to show that we should not have every commercial advantage we are supposed now to have, if it were made an independent state. Neither our manufac-

tures, foreign commerce, nor shipping would be injured by such a measure. On the other hand, what has the nation lost by Canada? Fifty or sixty millions have already been expended; the annual charge on the British treasury is full £600,000 a year; and we learn from the Second Report of the Committee of Finance, that a plan of fortifying Canada has been for two or three years in progress, which is to cost £3,000,000.

REVIVAL OF THE IMPERIAL INTEREST

By 1840 there were clear signs of a revival of imperial interest in Great Britain, principally upholding colonization as a means of ameliorating domestic conditions of poverty and unemployment occasioned by a rapid growth in population and by recurrent depressions in industry and commerce. An expression of this revival was given by Charles Buller (1806-1848), a Colonial-born member of Parliament and stalwart reformer of the 1830's and 1840's, in a speech in the House of Commons.

From BULLER, "Systematic Colonization" (1843) [1]

I think, Sir, that we cannot contemplate the condition of this country without coming to the conclusion that there is a permanent cause of suffering in the constant accumulation of capital and the constant increase of population within the same restricted field of employment. Every year adds its profits to the amount of capital previously accumulated; and certainly leaves the population considerably larger at its close than at its commencement. This fresh amount both of capital and population have to be employed; and if no further space for their employment

[1] Quoted in Edward Gibbon Wakefield, *A View of the Art of Colonization*, London, 1849, Appendix, 462-63, 471-72, 475-76.

be provided, they must compete for a share of the previous amount of profits and wages. The tendency of this cause to reduce both profits and wages is undoubtedly counteracted by what has fortunately been the still greater tendency of increased demand from foreign countries, of discoveries of fresh products of nature, and of improvements in various processes of art, especially in agriculture, to enlarge the field of employment. . . . But it is as indisputable that this enlargement of the field of employment, though in the long run greater, is not so steady as the growth of capital and population; and that during the intervals that lapse ere fresh employment is found, competition, in a restricted field, oftentimes reduces both wages and profits, and occasions periods of distress. . . . We are now in one of those periods of stagnation. . . .

I propose that you should investigate the efficacy of colonization as a remedy against the distress of the country. I say as a remedy, because I do not bring it forward as a panacea . . . but as one among many remedies which would be valuable. . . . I propose colonization as subsidiary to free trade; as an additional mode of carrying out the same principles and attaining the same object. You advocates of free trade wish to bring food to the people. I suggest to you at the same time to take your people to the food. You wish to get fresh markets by removing the barriers which now keep you from those that exist throughout the world. I call upon you, in addition, to get fresh markets by calling them into existence in parts of the world which might be made to teem with valuable customers. You represent free trade as no merely temporary relief for the distresses of our actual population, but as furnishing outlets of continually extending commerce to the labour of our population, whatever its

increase may be. In these anticipations I fully concur; and I would carry out the same principle, and attempt to make yet more use of these blessed results, by also planting population and capital in the vast untenanted regions of our colonies; and calling into existence markets, which, like those now in being, would go on continually extending the means of employing an increasing population at home. . . .

But the whole, nay the main advantage of colonization, is not secured by that mere removal of the labourer from the crowded mother country. . . . His absence is only the first relief which he affords you. You take him hence to place him on a fertile soil, from which a very small amount of labour will suffice to raise the food which he wants. He soon finds that by applying his spare time and energies to raising additional food, or some article of trade or material of manufacture, he can obtain that which he can exchange for luxuries of which he never dreamed at home. He raises some article of export and appears in your market as a customer. He who a few years ago added nothing to the wealth of the country, but received all from charity . . . comes, after providing his own food, to purchase from you a better quality and a larger quantity of the clothing and other manufactures which he used to take as a dole, and to give employment and offer food to those on whose energies he was a burden before. . . .

It seems a paradox to assert that removing a portion of your population enables a country to support more inhabitants than it could before; and that the place of every man who quits his country because he cannot get a subsistence may speedily be filled up by another whom that very removal will enable to subsist there in comfort. But the assertion is as true as it is strange.

5. Extending the Empire as a Means of Imperial Defense: India

While statesmen in England theorized about the advantages and disadvantages of colonies, the colonial governor often met with practical problems which led to the extension of imperial boundaries. In the late 1830's this became the state of things in India, where there arose reason to fear the advance of Russia, especially through Persia to Afghanistan, which controlled the mountain gateways into northwestern India. At the same time it was feared that disorders and unrest prevalent in border states under native control might encourage the advance of foreign interests unless the English intervened. Consequently, British interests in India were extended widely on the ground of defensive operations. In 1838, when Persian forces, encouraged by Russia, were waging war against Afghanistan, George Eden, Lord Auckland, the Governor-General of India for the East India Company, sent the following dispatches to the Company's Directors.

LORD AUCKLAND'S FEAR OF RUSSIA

From LORD AUCKLAND, Dispatches to the East India Company (1838) [1]

It may be convenient that I should recapitulate briefly my views as to the course proper to be taken by the Government of India in the several contingencies to which we have to look for the course of events in the Afghan countries. If the Persian expedition . . . should fail, fuller opportunity will be afforded for the development of that policy of friendly inter-

[1] Quoted from Muir, The Making of British India, 1756-1858, 317-19. By permission of Longmans, Green & Co., Inc.

course, and exhibition of a desire to recognise and respect all existing interests, by which I had hoped to reconcile in a considerable degree the existing dissensions among the Afghan chiefs. . . . If, contrary to my hope and expectation, the expedition should succeed . . . I do not contemplate any immediate direct interference by arms or money to arrest the enterprise . . . [because] I see so little ground for belief that a weak state like Persia can establish herself with any prospect of permanence in a country and amidst a population such as that of Afghanistan. . . . Should she succeed, against all reasonable anticipations, in acquiring a state authority in Afghanistan, and manifest a disposition to interfere with the territories along the course of the Indus, I should then not hesitate to use all the influence and power of the Government to repel her aggressions. . . . From their local position and our growing influence in the Punjab and in Sind, those states must always, it appears to me, be much dependent on us, and may be expected to place more trust in our friendship than in any aid which may be promised by Persia, even with the support of Russian encouragement. . . . It will remain with the Government of England to aid, as they may judge most proper and advisable, the measures of the Indian administrations, by noticing the part taken by Russia and her agents in these transactions. The letter of the Emperor of Russia [Nicholas I] to Dost Mahomed Khan, of Kabul, in acknowledgment only of the deputation of an agent from that chief, and expressive of a willingness to protect traders proceeding from Kabul to the Russian dominions, appears prima facie liable to no objections. . . . But the entire silence of his Excellency Count Simonitch, the Russian Envoy at Teheran, to Mr. M'Neill, respecting this mission, coupled with the fact . . . of Count Simonitch having opened an unsolicited communication with the chiefs of Kandahar, and having nearly identified himself with the Persian mission to that chiefship . . . affords, as it seems to me, a most reasonable ground for suspicion and inquiry, and may be made, perhaps, the means of exposing these intrigues so detrimental to the perfect tranquillity and good feeling of the countries on our frontier, and of arresting their further progress.

[At the end of the following April, 1838, Lord Auckland wrote further:]

In my former Despatch, I stated that I could not look to any stability of Persian domination in the Afghan countries. But there is a course open to the agents of Russia, in the attempts made by them to extend the power and influence of their country, which they seem ready to pursue, and to prefer to the support of the direct dominion of Persia over Afghanistan. It may be collected from their language and proceedings that they would, on one side, appear to be aiding Persia in the establishment of a general supremacy over the Afghan chiefships, and on the other as protecting those chiefships from any serious aggression and injury. Professions and promises to this effect may at least assist the immediate views of Persia, but they may also have the ultimate effect, in the actual distracted condition of Afghanistan, of giving to Russia an arbitration over the fortunes of all who exercise authority in that region. I need not say that we should seem to have the clearest rights and interest to remonstrate against such proceedings; for Russia can have no legitimate ground for extending her political connections to Afghanistan, while we are necessarily interested in the peace and independence of that country by proximity and position.

QUEEN VICTORIA PROCLAIMS CROWN RULE OF INDIA

While anxiety over Russia's advance led England into the Crimean War, the British continued to enlarge their territories in India. Under the vigorous leadership of James Andrew Broun, Lord Dalhousie (1848-56), the Punjab, Burma, and a number of lesser states were added to the East India Company's territory. At the same time the Europeanization of India was so rapidly advanced that grave discontents arose, which broke out into the savage Sepoy Mutiny in 1857. As soon as this revolt was suppressed a great change occurred whereby the East India Company ceased to exist and India was brought directly under the control of the British Crown, thus culminating a gradual diminution of the company's rights and ending the era of divided authority in India. Queen Victoria's proclamation which accompanied the new legislation follows.

From QUEEN VICTORIA, Proclamation for Crown Rule in India (1858) [1]

We hereby announce to the native princes of India that all treaties and engagements made with them by or under the authority of the Hon. East India Company are by us accepted, and will be scrupulously maintained; and we look for the like observance on their part.

We desire no extension of our present territorial possessions; and while we will permit no aggression upon our dominions or our rights to be attempted with impunity, we shall sanction no encroachment on those of others. We shall respect the rights, dignity, and honour of native princes as our own; and we desire that

[1] "History," *The Annual Register . . . 1858*, London, 1859, 258-59.

they, as well as our own subjects, should enjoy that prosperity and that social advancement which can only be secured by internal peace and good government.

We hold ourselves bound to the natives of our Indian territories by the same obligations of duty which bind us to all our other subjects; and those obligations, by the blessing of Almighty God, we shall faithfully and conscientiously fulfil.

Firmly relying ourselves on the truth of Christianity, and acknowledging with gratitude the solace of religion, we disclaim alike the right and the desire to impose our convictions on any of our subjects. We declare it to be our Royal will and pleasure that none be in anywise favoured, none molested or disquieted by reason of their religious faith or observances, but that all shall alike enjoy the equal and impartial protection of the law; and we do strictly charge and enjoin all those who may be in authority under us that they abstain from all interference with the religious belief or worship of any of our subjects on pain of our highest displeasure.

And it is our further will that, so far as may be, our subjects of whatever race or creed, be freely and impartially admitted to offices in our service, the duties of which they may be qualified, by their education, ability, and integrity duly to discharge.

We know and respect the feelings of attachment with which the natives of India regard the lands inherited by them from their ancestors, and we desire to protect them in all rights connected therewith, subject to the equitable demands of the State; and we will that generally . . . due regard be paid to the ancient rights, usages, and customs of India.

We deeply lament the evils and misery which have been brought upon India by the acts of ambitious men, who have deceived their countrymen by false reports

and led them into open rebellion. Our power having been shown by the suppression of that rebellion in the field, we desire to show our mercy by pardoning the offences of those who have been thus misled. . . . Our clemency will be extended to all offenders, save and except those who have been or shall be convicted of having directly taken part in the murder of British subjects. . . .

When, by the blessing of Providence, internal tranquillity shall be restored, it is our earnest desire to stimulate the peaceful industry of India, to promote works of public utility and improvement, and to administer its government for the benefit of all our subjects resident therein. In their prosperity will be our strength, in their contentment our security, and in their gratitude our best reward. And may the God of all power grant to us . . . strength to carry out these our wishes for the good of our people.

THE EARLY INDIAN ATTITUDE TOWARD BRITISH RULE

Indian opposition to British rule did not become widespread and bitter until early in the present century. At one of the early Indian National Congresses, in 1886, one of the most influential Indian leaders, Dadabhai Naoroji, spoke in his Presidential Speech of the "blessings" of British rule.

From NAOROJI, Speech on British Rule in India (1886) [1]

I ask whether in the most glorious days of Hindu rule, in the days of Rajahs like the great Vikram, you could imagine the possibility of a meeting of this kind, whether even Hindus of all different

[1] Quoted from Sir Valentine Chirol, *India,* in *The Modern World,* ed. by H. A. L. Fisher, 1926, 89-91. Reprinted by permission of Charles Scribner's Sons, New York.

provinces of the Kingdom could have col-lected and spoken as one nation. Coming down to the later Empire of our friends the Mohammedans, who probably ruled over a larger territory at one time than any Hindu monarch, would it have been —even in the days of Akbar himself— possible for a meeting like this to as-semble composed of all classes and com-munities, all speaking one language and all having uniform and high aspirations of their own? . . . It is under the civiliz-ing rule of the Queen and the people of England that we meet here together, hindered by none, and are freely allowed to speak our minds without the least fear and without the least hesitation. Such a thing is possible under British rule and under British rule only. Then I put the question plainly: Is this Congress a nursery for sedition and rebellion against the British government; or is it another stone in the foundation of the stability of that government? There could be but one answer, and that you have already given, because we are thoroughly sensible of the numberless blessings conferred upon us, of which the very existence of this Con-gress is a proof in a nutshell. Were it not for these blessings of British rule I could not have come here today, as I have done, without the least hesitation and without the least fear that my children might be robbed and killed in my absence; nor could you have come from every corner of the land, having performed, within a few days, journeys which in former days would have occupied months. These simple facts bring home to all of us at once some of the great and numberless blessings which British rule has conferred upon us. But there remain even greater blessings for which we have to be grate-ful. It is to British rule that we owe the education we possess; the people of Eng-land were sincere in the declaration made more than half a century ago that India

was a sacred charge entrusted to their care by Providence, and that they were bound to administer it for the good of India, to the glory of their own name, and the satisfaction of God.

6. Rampant Imperialism: Contest in Africa

In the years after 1860, Great Britain —in common with other European countries—indulged in an unprece-dented outburst of imperialist activity. A series of events combined to occasion the new attitude, especially the rise of rival colonial empires, notably those of France and Belgium, and the quick in-terest in colonies shown by the newly united states of Italy and Germany. Much of the competition centered in Africa, where missionary activity in the era after 1800 had been followed by a gradual extension of trading interests. The extraordinary explorations and re-searches of the missionary-explorer David Livingstone between 1840 and 1873, together with the discovery of diamonds in 1867 and of new gold deposits a few years later, led to a mad international scramble in Africa during the latter part of the nineteenth cen-tury. Representatives of rival powers— sometimes self-appointed—vied with one another to obtain trading conces-sions and territory from African tribal "kings"—Henry Morton Stanley for the Belgian King Leopold, Count Pierre P. F. C. de Brazza for France, Carl Peters for Germany, and scores of lesser figures. Great Britain entered the con-test with many advantages. In addition to her industrial, commercial, financial, and maritime growth, Britain had held Cape Colony from the Napoleonic Wars and, in the course of the early

1800's, had gradually extended her control in South Africa and elsewhere. Indeed, Great Britain's advance in Africa took many forms and approached the vast Dark Continent from many different directions simultaneously. A sample of one of the "treaties" with native "kings" by which Great Britain extended her African control follows. The number of such treaties is legion, and agents of a variety of imperialistic European powers negotiated similar agreements in the mad scramble for African colonies. Obviously, the native chieftains often comprehended little of the documents to which they affixed their marks. But Britain's humane efforts to eradicate the slave trade, human sacrifices, piracy, and plundering—as well as her willingness to admit the traders of other nations—gave some weight to the claims to altruism embraced in the widely bruited "white man's burden."

AN EXAMPLE OF NATIVE CONCESSIONS

From An Engagement Between Queen Victoria and the King of Mellella, River Congo, March 19, 1877 [1]

Leicester Chantrey Keppel, Esquire, Commander of Her Britannic Majesty's ship *Avon,* and Senior Officer of the River Congo, on the part of Her Majesty the Queen of Great Britain and Ireland, Empress of India, &c., and the King of Mellella, whose name is hereunto subscribed, on the part of himself, his heirs, and successors, have agreed upon the following Articles:

1. The export of slaves to foreign countries is forever abolished in my territory. . . .

2. No European or other person what-

[1] *British and Foreign State Papers, 1876-1877,* LXVIII, 670-72.

ever shall be permitted to reside in my territories or those of my heirs or successors for the purpose of carrying on in any way the traffic in slaves; and no houses, stores, or buildings of any kind whatsoever shall be erected for the purpose of the slave trade. . . .

3. If at any time it shall appear that the slave trade is being carried on through or from any part of my territories, the slave trade may be put down by force . . . and any British officers may seize my boats . . . found anywhere carrying on the slave trade. . . .

4. The subjects of her Britannic Majesty and all white foreigners may always trade freely with my people . . . in any article they may wish to buy or to sell, at any place whatsoever within my territory; and I, for myself, my heirs or successors, pledge myself to show no favour and to give no privilege to the ships and traders of other countries which I do not show to those of Great Britain.

5. In the event of any British or other foreign vessels running aground in any part of the River Congo near to my territory, I faithfully promise . . . that I will in no way allow them to be interfered with under any pretence whatever. . . .

6. Should any British or other foreign vessel, being aground in the river, apply to me for assistance, I . . . promise to render her all help in my power, provided I am fairly paid for my trouble.

7. Should the ships . . . be attacked by pirates or plunderers, I . . . promise assistance by sending my people with arms, and doing all in my power to punish the robbers.

8. If at any time a naval officer of Great Britain shall require guides or armed people from myself . . . to accompany the said officer against pirates or other enemies of the Queen of Great

Britain, I faithfully promise . . . to provide them.

9. I . . . declare that no human being shall be sacrificed on account of religious or other ceremonies, and that I will prevent the barbarous practice of murdering prisoners of war.

10. Missionaries or other ministers of the Gospel are to be allowed to reside in my territory . . . for the purpose of instructing the people in all useful occupations.

11. And, in consideration of these engagements, all past offences of King Mellella against the Queen of Great Britain, &c., are hereby forgiven.

Concluded on board Her Majesty's ship *Avon*, at Mellella, this 19th day of March, 1877.

Leicester C. Keppel,
Commander H.M.S. Avon.
Mellella, King
of Mellella, River Congo.
His X mark.

Witnesses to signatures of Contracting Parties:

Andrew W. Rogers, *Senior Lieutenant H.M.S.* Avon.

Henry J. Ollard, *Assistant Paymaster H.M.S.* Avon.

Capeta of Mellella   X ⎤
The Sister of   ⎬ Their marks.
Queen Annazoza   X ⎦

EARLY TROUBLES WITH THE BOERS

Great Britain's possession of Cape Colony after 1815 led to repeated troubles with the Dutch settlers, the Boers. At first, the troubles arose chiefly because the Boers objected to the abolition of slavery and to Britain's sympathetic native policies, and they trekked northward to get out from under British authority. Beyond the Vaal River they set up a new Boer state, the Trans-

vaal Republic, which Britain solemnly recognized as an independent state in 1852. British expansion, however, soon overtook the disgruntled Boers, and in 1877, in flagrant violation of the Convention of 1852 and against the vigorous protest of the Boers, Great Britain annexed the South African Republic, as the Transvaal state had been called since 1858. The Proclamation of Annexation, in part, follows.

From the Proclamation Annexing the Transvaal Republic (April 12, 1877. Retroceded in 1881) [1]

Whereas at a meeting held on the 16th day of January . . . 1852, at the Sand River, between Her Majesty's Assistant Commissioners . . . and a deputation from the emigrant farmers then residing north of the Vaal River . . . the said Her Majesty's Assistant Commissioners did "guarantee in the fullest manner . . . to the emigrant farmers north of the Vaal River the right to manage their own affairs, and to govern themselves according to their own laws, without any interference on the part of the British Government";

And whereas the evident objects and inciting motives of the Assistant Commissioners in granting such guarantee or permission to persons who were Her Majesty's subjects were "to promote peace, free trade, and friendly intercourse" . . . in the hope and belief that the territory which a few years later . . . became known by the style and title of "The South African Republic," would become a flourishing and self-sustaining state, a source of strength and security to neighbouring European communities, and a point from which Christianity and civilization might rapidly spread towards Central Africa;

[1] *Ibid.*, 140-45.

And whereas the hopes and expectations upon which this mutual compact was reasonably and honourably founded have been disappointed, and the circumstances . . . show that increasing weakness in the State itself on the one side, and more than corresponding growth of real strength and confidence among the native tribes on the other . . . and this was succeeded by the extinction of all effective rule over extensive tracts of country . . . [so that] some few farmers . . . now occupy their farms on condition of periodical payments to those [native] chiefs. . . . That this decay of power and ebb of authority in the north is being followed by similar processes in the south. . . . That all confidence in its [the Boer Government's] stability . . . has been withdrawn. That Commerce is well nigh destroyed. That the country is in a state of bankruptcy. That the white inhabitants, discontented with their condition, are divided into factions. . . . That the condition above described affords strong temptation to neighbouring native powers . . . to make attacks and inroads upon the State, which from its weakness it cannot repel, and from which it has hitherto been saved by . . . the British Government. . . .

Seeing that the circumstances of the case have, from the inherent weakness of the country already touched upon, become so grave that neither this country nor the British Colonies in South Africa can be saved from the most calamitous circumstances except by the extension over this State of Her Majesty's authority and protection . . . I do, in virtue of the power and authority conferred upon me by Her Majesty's Royal Commission . . . proclaim and make known, that from and after the publication hereof the territory heretofore known as the South African Republic, as now meared and bounded

. . . shall be and shall be taken to be British territory. . . .

And I further proclaim and make known that the Transvaal will remain a separate Government, with its own laws and legislature, and that it is the wish of Her Most Gracious Majesty that it shall enjoy the fullest legislative privileges compatible with the circumstances of the country and the intelligence of its people. That . . . the Dutch language will practically be as much the official language as the English. . . . Equal justice is guaranteed to the persons and property of both white and colored; but the adoption of this principle does not and should not involve the granting of equal civil rights, such as the exercise of the right of voting by savages, or their becoming members of a legislative body, or their being entitled to other civil privileges which are incompatible with their uncivilized condition. The native tribes . . . must be taught due obedience to the paramount authority, and be made to contribute their fair share towards the support of the State that protects them. God save the Queen.

Given under my hand and seal at Pretoria, in the South African Republic, this 12th day of April, in the year of Our Lord, 1877.

T. Shepstone,
Her Majesty's
Special Commissioner
By command of his Excellency,
M. Osborn, Secretary

[By 1880, the Boers of the Transvaal were in revolt against the British. Led by Paul Kruger ("Oom Paul"), the Boers proclaimed a republic; warring with British forces sent to subdue them, the Boers won the early battles and the British Government, under Gladstone's Liberal ministry, was unwilling longer to contest the Boer's desire for freedom. Thus, on April 5, 1881, at the Treaty of Pretoria, the

South African Republic was granted independence, but under the suzerainty of Great Britain—a settlement which left both sides dissatisfied and prepared the way for the Boer War.]

7. Cecil Rhodes: Imperialist Extraordinary

RHODES'S IMPERIALISTIC SENTIMENTS

Perhaps no Englishman better represented the extreme imperialism of the late nineteenth century, both in theory and in practice, than Cecil John Rhodes (1853-1902). Son of a clergyman, Rhodes went to Natal for his health in 1870. Soon he moved to the Orange Free State, where he presently acquired a fortune in the Kimberley diamond fields. His rampant imperialism was early displayed in the first draft of his "Last Will and Testament," drawn up in 1877, before he possessed either the fortune or the political power to give reality to his dreams.

The will proposed to establish a trust fund "To and for the establishment, promotion and development of a Secret Society, the true aim and object whereof shall be the extension of British rule throughout the world, the perfecting of a system of emigration from the United Kingdom, and of colonization by British subjects of all lands where the means of livelihood are attainable by energy, labour and enterprise, and especially the occupation by British settlers of the entire Continent of Africa, the Holy Land, the Valley of the Euphrates, the Islands of Cyprus and Candia, the whole of South America, the Islands of the Pacific not heretofore possessed by Great Britain, the whole of the Malay Archipelago, the seaboard of China and Japan, the ultimate recovery of the United States of America as an integral part of the British Empire, the inauguration of a system of Colonial representation in the Imperial Parliament which may tend to weld together the disjointed members of the Empire and, finally, the foundation of so great a Power as to hereafter render wars impossible and promote the best interests of humanity." [1]

Rhodes's youthful dreams were never realized, but, in a more restricted—though still enormous—area, he nonetheless exerted a tremendous imperial influence. Nor were his early dreams altered in nature. "He used to talk over all his plans and schemes with me," wrote a friend in 1897, after knowing him for twenty years, "and, looking back at them now, it surprises me to note what little change there is in his policy. He had, for instance, even at that early date [1878], formed the idea of doing a great work for the overcrowded British public, by opening up fresh markets for their manufactures. He was deeply impressed with a belief in the ultimate destiny of the Anglo-Saxon race. He dwelt repeatedly on the fact that their great want was new territory, fit for the overflow population to settle permanently." Becoming wealthy, he turned manipulator, and acquired first a virtual monopoly in African diamonds and then an enormous fortune, and interest in gold mines as well. Backed by his wealth, and equipped with a ruthless ability to use it to win his ends, he entered politics in the Cape Colony. "Having read the history of other countries," he said, "I saw that expansion was every-

[1] Quoted in Sir Lewis Michell, *The Life and Times of . . . Cecil John Rhodes*, 2 vols., Kennerley, 1910, I, 72-73.

thing, and that, the world's surface being limited, the great object should be to take as much of it as we could." This object he pursued with undeviating singleness of purpose in British imperial politics. In Africa, especially, he had three aims constantly in view: (1) expansion northward; (2) a federation of African states under the British flag with free trade; and (3) a railroad under British control from the Cape to Cairo—an "inland Suez Canal" extending the full length of Africa. In 1888, as a means of expansion, and as a check upon the ambitions of the stubborn Boers in the Transvaal, Rhodes sent three agents to the extraordinary native, Lobengula, "king" of Matabeleland, Mashonaland, and near-by territories both north and south of the Zambezi River, who negotiated the following grant.

From the Concession of Lobengula
(October 30, 1888) [1]

Know all men by these presents, that whereas Charles Dunell Rudd, of Kimberley; Rochfort Maguire, of London; and Francis Robert Thompson, of Kimberley, hereinafter called the grantees, have covenanted and agreed . . . to pay me . . . the sum of one hundred pounds sterling, British currency, on the first day of every lunar month; and further, to deliver at my royal kraal one thousand Martini-Henry breech-loading rifles, together with one hundred thousand rounds of suitable ball cartridges . . . and further to deliver on the Zambesi River a steamboat with guns suitable for defensive purposes, or in lieu of the said steamboat, should I elect, to pay to me the sum of five hundred pounds sterling, British currency. On the execution of these presents, I, Lo Bengula, King of Matabeleland, Mashonaland, and

other adjoining territories . . . do hereby grant and assign unto the said grantees . . . the complete and exclusive charge over all metals and minerals situated and contained in my kingdoms . . . together with full power to do all things that they may deem necessary to win and procure the same, and to hold, collect, and enjoy the profits and revenues, if any, derivable from the said metals and minerals, subject to the aforesaid payment; and whereas I have been much molested of late by divers persons seeking and desiring to obtain grants and concessions of land and mining rights in my territories, I do hereby authorize the said grantees . . . to take all necessary and lawful steps to exclude from my kingdom . . . all persons seeking land, metals, minerals, or mining rights therein, and I do hereby undertake to render them all such needful assistance as they may from time to time require for the exclusion of such persons, and to grant no concessions of land or mining rights from and after this date without their consent and concurrence. . . . This given under my hand this thirtieth day of October, in the year of our Lord 1888, at my royal kraal.

Lo Bengula X his mark.
C. D. Rudd,
Rochfort Maguire,
F. R. Thompson.

RHODES'S POLICIES AS PRIME MINISTER OF CAPE COLONY (1890-96) AND THE BOER WAR

Armed with the above concession, Rhodes went to London in 1889, where he organized and obtained a charter for the British South Africa Company, capitalized at £1,000,000, to develop and govern Bechuanaland, Matabeleland, and Mashonaland, to extend railways and telegraphs to the region, and to encourage British colonization and

[1] *Ibid.,* I, 255-57.

trade, as well as to exploit the mineral rights acquired. In other words, Rhodes set out to acquire administrative rights in the territories where, from the native chieftain, he had already obtained exclusive mineral concessions. This charter established British administrative control, through the South African Company, over the region later (1895) named Rhodesia. A glance at the map will show that, by this means, Rhodes had gone far to the northward in the expansion of British control in Africa, had pushed the right of way for the Capetown-to-Cairo railroad a long way, and had not only checked the expansion of the Boers in this area but also had placed British-controlled colonies on both sides of the Boer states. Shortly after his return to South Africa, Rhodes became Prime Minister of Cape Colony (July, 1890), a post he held until implication in the Jameson Raid forced his resignation in January, 1896. In a speech in 1890 Rhodes described his objectives.

From RHODES, Speech at Kimberley (September, 1890) [1]

The Government's policy will be a South African policy. What we mean is that we will do all in our power, whilst looking after the interests of the Cape Colony, to draw closer and closer ties between us and the neighbouring States. In pursuance of this we have arranged to meet in December next in Bloemfontein, and hope to extend the railway from Bloemfontein to the Vaal River. We feel it is time to arrive at a settlement of the various questions which divide the States of South Africa. It may not come in our time, but I believe that ultimately the different States will be united. The Government hope that the result of the Swaziland Convention [whereby Cape Colony

recognized the Transvaal's interests in Swaziland in return for which President Kruger of the Transvaal agreed not to interfere in Lobengula's dominions] will prove satisfactory to the Transvaal. *We feel that if fair privileges were granted to every citizen of the Transvaal, the Transvaal would not be dissatisfied at the terms England will deal out to it.* I feel sure that if the Transvaal joins with us and the other States in a Customs' Union, the sister Colony of Natal will also join, and that would be one great step towards a union of South Africa. The projected extension of the railway will likewise prove that we are getting nearer to a United South Africa.

It is customary to speak of a United South Africa as possible within the near future. If we mean a complete Union with the same flag, I see very serious difficulties. I know myself that I am not prepared at any time to forfeit my flag. . . . If you take away my flag, you take away everything. Holding these views, I can feel some respect for the neighbouring States where men have been born under Republican institutions and with Republican feelings. When I speak of South African Union, I mean that we may attain to perfect free trade as to our own commodities, perfect and complete internal railway communication, and a general Customs' Union, stretching from Delagao Bay to Walfisch Bay; and if our statesmen should attain to that, I say they will have done a good work. It has been my good fortune to meet people belonging to both sides of the House, and to hear their approval with regard to the development of the Northern territory. I am glad that the Cape Colony will also share in the development of the Country to the North. I feel assured that within my lifetime the limits of the Cape Colony will stretch as far as the Zambesi. Many of you are interested in the operations of the [British South

[1] *Ibid.*, I, 293-95.

Africa] Chartered Company northwards; and it is a pleasure to me to announce that all risks of collision are over, and that I believe there will be a peaceable occupation of Mashonaland. I have had the pleasure today to receive a telegram announcing the cession of the Barotse country, which I may tell you is over 200,000 square miles in extent. I think we are carrying out a practical object; we have at least sent five hundred of our citizens to occupy a new country. . . . I have often thought that if the people who originally took the Cape Colony had been told that the Colony would today extend to the Orange River, they would have laughed at the idea. I believe that people who live a hundred years hence will think that the present annexation is far too short.

[The italicized portion of Rhodes's speech suggests the final issue between Cape Colony and the Boers which led to the Boer War (1899-1902). Having hedged in the Boer states territorially and vainly brought various pressures to bear upon both the Transvaal and the Orange Free State to win them to a customs union, Rhodes undertook to organize a revolution in the Transvaal against Kruger's government. He pinned his hopes upon the Uitlanders (the Boer name for the foreign element—mostly British—in the Boer states). As Kruger's government repeatedly refused to enfranchise the Uitlanders or to grant them other advantages, Rhodes championed their cause as a means of striking at the Boers' independence. To set off the revolution was the object of the Jameson Raid (December, 1895-January, 1896), the failure of which forced Rhodes's retirement from office. In the next year (1897), Sir Alfred Milner became high commissioner for South Africa; Kruger's re-election as President of the Transvaal (February, 1898) spelled defeat for Uitlanders, who addressed a petition to Queen Victoria recounting their grievances (March, 1899). When a conference between Kruger and Milner failed to patch up the differences, the Orange Free State joined with the Transvaal, and war between the Boer allies and the British broke out in October, 1899. After bitter and bloody fighting, the Boers were defeated, and signed the Treaty of Vereenigig (May 31, 1902) by which they accepted British sovereignty with a promise of representative institutions and an indemnity of £3,000,000 to help rebuild their farms. Rhodes died of heart disease about two months before the treaty was signed.]

8. Imperialistic Apologia: Sir John Robert Seeley

By 1900, the imperial idea was in the ascendancy in Britain. While men like Rhodes labored in far corners of the earth to extend the empire, a generation of imperial apologists rose up at home. One of the greatest of the latter was Robert John Seeley (1834-95), who was Professor of Modern History at Cambridge from 1869 till his death. Seeley felt that history supported the idea of progress, that the English goals were liberty, democracy, and the extension of the English name into other parts of the globe, and that the "Little England" idea was synonymous with national degradation and ruin. He was a popular lecturer, attracted great numbers of students, and awakened the enthusiasm of a generation of English university men for world empire. Moreover, he lectured widely outside Cambridge, and published in 1883 a series of lectures on *The Expansion of England,* a book which went through many editions and reprints to the present day.

The following selection is taken from Professor Seeley's final lecture.

From SEELEY, *Expansion of England* (1883) [1]

I endeavoured to judge the Empire by its own intrinsic merits and to see it as it is, not concealing the inconveniencies which may attend such a vast expansion or the dangers to which it may expose us, nor finding any compensation for these in the notion that there is something intrinsically glorious in an Empire "upon which the sun never sets." . . . But though there is little that is glorious in most of the great Empires mentioned in history, since they have usually been created by force and have remained at a low level of political life, we observed that Greater Britain is not in the ordinary sense an Empire at all. Looking at the colonial part of it alone, we see a natural growth, a mere normal extension of the English race into other lands, which for the most part were so thinly peopled that our settlers took possession of them without conquest. If there is nothing highly glorious in such an expansion, there is at the same time nothing forced or unnatural about it. It creates not properly an Empire, but only a very large state. So far as the expansion itself is concerned, no one does or can regard it but with pleasure. For a nation to have an outlet for its superfluous population is one of the greatest blessings. . . . But should there be an expansion of the State as well as of the nation? "No," say the pessimists, "or only till the colony is grown-up and ready for independence." When a metaphor comes to be regarded as an argument, what an irresistible argument it always seems! I have suggested that in the modern world distance has very much lost its effect, and that there

[1] J. R. Seeley, *The Expansion of England*, 1902, 295-308. By permission of The Macmillan Company, New York.

are signs of a time when states will be vaster than they have hitherto been. . . . In the eighteenth century Burke thought a federation quite impossible across the Atlantic Ocean. In such times the metaphor of the grown-up son might well harden into a convincing demonstration. But since Burke's time the Atlantic Ocean has shrunk till it seems scarcely broader than the sea between Greece and Sicily. Why then do we not drop the metaphor? I have urged that we are unconsciously influenced by a historic parallel which when examined turns out to be inapplicable. . . . These views are founded on the American Revolution, and yet the American Revolution arose out of circumstances and out of a condition of the world which has long since passed away. . . . Even then the separation was not effected without a great wrench. It is true that both countries have prospered since, nevertheless they have had a second war and may have a third, and it is wholly an illusion to suppose that their prosperity has been caused or promoted by their separation. At any rate all the conditions of the world are altered now. The great causes of division, oceans and religious disabilities, have ceased to operate. Vast uniting forces have begun to work, trade and emigration. Meanwhile the natural ties which unite Englishmen resume their influence . . . I mean the ties of nationality, language and religion. The mother-country having once for all ceased to be a step-mother, and to make unjust claims and impose annoying restrictions, and since she wants her colonies as an outlet both for population and trade, and since on the other hand the colonies must feel that there is risk, not to say intellectual impoverishment, in independence, since finally intercourse is ever increasing and no alienating force is at work to counteract it . . . it seems possible that our colonial Empire so-called may more and more deserve to be called Greater Britain, and that the tie may become stronger and stronger. . . .

Perhaps we are hardly alive to the vast results which are flowing in politics from modern mechanism. Throughout the greater part of human history the process of state-building has been governed by strict conditions of space. For a long time no high organization was possible except in very small states. . . . But through the invention of the representative system these states have risen to a higher level. We now see states with vivid political consciousness on territories of two hundred thousand square miles and in population of thirty millions. A further advance is now being made. The federal system has been added to the representative system, and at the same time steam and electricity have been introduced. From these improvements has resulted the possibility of highly organized states on yet a larger scale. Thus Russia in Europe has already a population of near eighty millions on a territory of more than two millions of square miles, and the United States will have by the end of the century a population as large upon a territory of four millions of square miles. . . . At that time which many here present may live to see, Russia and the United States will surpass in power the states now called great as much as the great country-states of the sixteenth century surpassed Florence. Is not this a serious consideration, and is it not especially so for a state like England, which has at the present moment the choice in its hands of two courses of action, the one of which may set it in that future age on a level with the greatest of these great states of the future, while the other will reduce it to the level of a purely European Power looking back, as Spain does now, to the great days when she pretended to be a world-state?

But what I have been saying does not apply to India. If England and her colonies taken together make, properly speaking, not an Empire but only a very large state, this is because the population is English throughout and the institutions are of the same kind. In India the population is wholly foreign and the institutions wholly unlike our own. India is really an Empire and an Oriental Empire. . . . But ostensibly the policy [in acquiring India] was justified by arguments of a philanthropic kind, and they were arguments of such strength that it was difficult to resist them. It was not to be denied that a most deplorable anarchy reigned in India. . . . Aggrandisement might present itself in the light of a simple duty, when it seemed that by extending our Empire the reign of robbery and murder might be brought to an end. . . . And thus we founded our Empire, partly it may be out of an empty ambition of conquest and partly out of a philanthropic desire to put an end to enormous evils. But, whatever our motives might be, we incurred vast responsibilities, which were compensated by no advantages. We have acquired a great Indian trade, but even this we purchase at the expense of a perpetual dread of Russia and of all movements in the Mussulman world and of all changes in Egypt. . . . Another thing almost all observers see, and that is that the experiment must go forward, and that we cannot leave it unfinished if we would. For here too the great uniting forces of the age are at work, England and India are drawn every year for good or for evil more closely together. . . .

My chief aim in these lectures has been to show in what light the more recent history of England ought to be regarded by the student. . . . What great changes has she undergone in this period? Considerable political changes no doubt, but none that have been so memorable as those she underwent in the seventeenth century. Then she made one of the greatest discoveries, and taught all the world how liberty might be adapted to the conditions of a nation-state. On the other hand the modern political movement, that of Reform or Liberalism, began not in England but on the Continent, from whence we borrowed it. The peculiarly English movement, I have urged, in this period has been an unparalleled expansion. Grasp this fact, and you have the clue both to the eighteenth and the nineteenth centuries. The wars with France from Louis XIV to Napoleon fall into an intelligible series. The American Revolution and the conquest of India cease to seem mere digressions, and take their proper places in the main line of English history. The growth of wealth, commerce and manufacture, the fall of the old colonial system and the gradual growth of a new one, are all easily included under the same formula. Lastly, this formula binds together the past of England and her future, and leaves us, when we close the history of our country, not with minds fatigued and bewildered . . . but enlightened and more deeply interested than ever, because partly prepared for what is to come next.

32 CZARIST RUSSIA

1. The Reign of Nicholas I (1825-55)

Alexander I (1801-25), the "Enigmatic Czar," was warmly liberal in the early years of his reign and coldly reactionary in the last decade. His reign illustrates, in miniature, the whole of Russian history in the nineteenth century. While the forces of reaction generally prevailed, there were occasional oscillations of the Russian pendulum toward reform policies, especially after national disasters, such as the defeat in the Crimean War (1856) and that in the Russo-Japanese War (1905). Thus the Russian reform movement slowly gathered strength in the course of the century, became progressively more extremist, and after the Russian disasters in World War I, burst forth in mighty revolution (1917). In 1817, secret societies modeled after those of Germany began in Russia, and in December, 1825, when uncertainty about the successor of Alexander I temporarily arose, the Northern Society at St. Petersburg staged a military revolt. It was half-hearted and wholly unsuccessful. Nicholas I, the new Czar, suppressed it in one day. But the reasonableness of the demands of the "Decembrists"—as these rebels were thereafter called—was emphasized by the cruel treatment accorded their leaders and by the extremes of reactionary policy to which Nicholas I adhered throughout his reign. The Decembrists demanded abolition of serfdom, redistribution of land, and the establishment of constitutional, representative government in Russia—all to be effected, they had hoped, by peaceful methods of reform. Their failure was only a failure of the moment. Subsequent reformers and revolutionists paid homage to their example: Aleksandr Ivanovich Herzen, the mid-century champion of Socialism and editor of the noteworthy émigré paper *The Bell,* acknowledged that he was first aroused by the Decembrists; and Nikolai Lenin wrote that "the Decembrists awakened Herzen and Herzen started the revolutionary agitation" —which culminated in the Russian Revolutions of 1917. Aleksandr Bestuzhev, one of the Decembrists, wrote to Nicholas I the following explanation of the motives which impelled him and his fellows. Bestuzhev was exiled to Siberia for his pains.

THE DEMANDS OF THE DECEMBRISTS

From BESTUZHEV, Letter to Nicholas I (c. 1825) [1]

Your Imperial Highness!

Convinced that You, Sovereign, love the truth, I dare to lay before You the historical development of free thinking in Russia and in general of many ideas which constitute the moral and political basis of the events of December 14. I shall speak in full frankness, without concealing evil, without softening expressions, for the duty of a loyal subject is to tell his Monarch the truth without any embellishment. I commence.

The beginning of the reign of Emperor Alexander was marked with bright hopes for Russia's prosperity. The gentry had recuperated, the merchant class did not object to giving credit, the army

[1] Quoted in Anatole G. Mazour, *The First Russian Revolution,* 1937, Appendix, 277-79. By permission of the University of California Press, Berkeley.

served without making trouble, scholars studied what they wished, all spoke what they thought, and everyone expected better days. Unfortunately, circumstances prevented the realization of these hopes, which aged without their fulfillment. The unsuccessful, expensive war of 1807 and others disorganized our finances, though we had not yet realized it when preparing for the national war of 1812. Finally, Napoleon invaded Russia and then only, for the first time, did the Russian people become aware of their power; only then awakened in all our hearts a feeling of independence, at first political and finally national. That is the beginning of free thinking in Russia. The government itself spoke such words as "Liberty, Emancipation!" It had itself sown the idea of abuses resulting from the unlimited power of Napoleon, and the appeal of the Russian Monarch resounded on the banks of the Rhine and the Seine. The war was still on when the soldiers, on their return home, for the first time disseminated grumbling among the masses. "We shed blood," they would say, "and then we are again forced to sweat under feudal obligations. We freed the Fatherland from the tyrant, and now we ourselves are tyrannized over by the ruling class." The army, from generals to privates, upon its return, did nothing but discuss how good it is in foreign lands. A comparison with their own country naturally brought up the question, Why should it not be so in our own land?

At first, as long as they talked without being hindered it was lost in the air, for thinking is like gunpowder, only dangerous when pressed. Many cherished the hope that the Emperor would grant a constitution, as he himself had stated at the opening of the Legislative Assembly in Warsaw, and the attempt of some generals to free their serfs encouraged that sentiment. But after 1817 everything changed. Those who saw evil or who wished improvement, thanks to the mass of spies were forced to whisper about it, and this was the beginning of the secret societies. Oppression by the government of deserving officers irritated men's minds. Then the military men began to talk: "Did we free Europe in order to be ourselves placed in chains? Did we grant a constitution to France in order that we dare not talk about it, and did we buy at the price of blood priority among nations in order that we might be humiliated at home?" The destructive policy toward schools and the persecution of education forced us in utter despair to begin considering some important measures. And since the grumbling of the people, caused by exhaustion and the abuses of national and civil administrations, threatened bloody revolution, the Societies intended to prevent a greater evil by a lesser one and began their activities at the first opportunity. . . .

You, Sovereign, probably already know how we, inspired by such a situation in Russia and seeing the elements ready for change, decided to bring about a *coup d'état.* . . . Here are the plans we had for the future. We thought of creating a Senate of the oldest and wisest Russian men of the present administration, for we thought that power and ambition would always have their attraction. Then we thought of having a Chamber of Deputies composed of national representatives. . . . For enlightenment of the lower classes we wished everywhere to establish Lancasterian schools. And in order to bring about moral improvement we thought of raising the standard of the clergy by granting to them a means of livelihood. Elimination of nearly all duties, freedom from distillation and road improvement for the state, encouragement of agriculture and general protection of industry would result in satisfying the peasants. Assurance and stability would attract to Russia many resourceful foreigners. Factories would increase with the demand for commodities, while competition would stimulate improvement, which rises along with the prosperity of the people, for the need of commodities for life and luxury is constant.

REACTION UNDER NICHOLAS I: "ORTHODOXY, AUTOCRACY, AND PATRIOTISM"

Thomas Garrigue Masaryk (1850–1937), the famous Czech historian, philosopher, and statesman, wrote the following description picturing the extremes of reaction and brutality to which Nicholas I went as Czar.

From MASARYK, *The Spirit of Russia* (1913) [1]

Tsar Nicholas had a very different education from his two elder brothers. Born in 1796, he was nearly twenty years younger than Alexander, and he was not yet five years old when the latter began to reign. There seemed no probability that he would ever be tsar. Not until it became clear that Alexander would have no legitimate offspring was Constantine induced to renounce the succession. Nicholas' tutor was General Lamsdorf, a rough man who made use of corporal punishment as one of the principal means of education. The prince's only keen interest was in the army. Strict subordination, unquestioning obedience, was Nicholas' system. In his psychology men were mere machines, or at most, animated slaves. "I regard the whole of human life as service," he said on one occasion. The anti-revolutionary mission of Russia therefore began with the reign of this

[1] Thomas Garrigue Masaryk, *The Spirit of Russia,* trans. by Eden and Cedar Paul, 2 vols., 1919, I, 105-12. By permission of The Macmillan Company, New York.

"supreme lord of the narrow world," as Frederick IV termed him. . . .

In European policy, Nicholas, like Alexander, was, therefore, protector of legitimism. He was the declared opponent of Louis Philippe, condemning as unlawful the French monarch's election and investiture by the bourgeoisie. It was in this spirit that in the year 1849 he sent troops to assist in suppressing the revolution in Hungary [see page 602]. In 1853 he ordered Serbia to dismiss the premier Garašanin (senior) because that statesman had been a pupil of Kossuth and Mazzini. Metternich's policy in Austria and Germany was a delight to Nicholas. . . . Metternich, in turn, sought and found in Nicholas a protector against the revolution, of which he had himself been regarded as the chief opponent, and the Austrian chancellor came to terms with Russia in order to keep Germany and Italy dependent. In Europe Nicholas was admired by all conservatives and reactionaries, and by some actually worshipped, as for example his brother-in-law Frederick William IV, who said: "I thank God upon my knees for having vouchsafed to me the profound grief I experience at the death of Tsar Nicholas, for having vouchsafed to me to be the tsar's faithful friend in the best sense of the word." Nicholas, for his part, was devoted to the kings of Prussia, highly esteeming Prussian accuracy and orderliness. He preferred Germans in the army and in the administration.

With Nicholas began the "plague zone which extended from 1825 to 1855." (Herzen) Reaction became a carefully considered police system, the tsar in person assuming the office of chief superintendent of police, for this was the literal signification of the foundation in 1826 of the famous "third section of the departments under his majesty's immediate supervision," which down to the year 1880 was devoted to the attempt to gag Russia intellectually. The notorious Benckendorff, who had secured the tsar's favor through his zeal in the suppression of Decembrism, was appointed chief of this institution. Later he also became chief of the gendarmerie, consecrating all his energies to the work of repression.

In this sketch it would be difficult to give an adequate idea of the abominable stupidity and provocative brutality that characterised reaction under Nicholas. For the utterance of liberal ideas conflicting with the official program, leading men were simply declared insane. This happened to Caadaev and to a number of officers inclined towards revolutionary notions. . . . Not only was the tsar chief officer of police, but in his own exalted person he revised the sentences of the courts. In the year 1837 two Jews were condemned to death in Odessa because, from fear of the plague, they had attempted to escape across the frontier. Nicholas commuted the death penalty as follows: "The convicts are to run the gauntlet—a thousand men—twelve times. God be thanked, with us the death penalty has been abolished, and I will not reintroduce it." This was but one among numerous instances of the theocratic sovereign's power of self-deception and of his cruelty—for who had proposed that the Decembrists should be quartered, and who had commuted their punishment to hanging? In the year 1838 a student named Sočinskii gave the director of the surgical academy a box on the ear. He was sentenced to run the gauntlet—five hundred men—three times. Nicholas revised the sentence thus: "To be carried out in the presence of all the students of the academy. Subsequently the offender, instead of being sent to Siberia, is to spend ten years, wearing fetters, in the disciplinary battalion at Kronstadt." It is hardly necessary to add that though there was no capital punishment, the men thus sentenced died under the blows of the soldiers. . . .

Naturally, the reaction under Nicholas was based upon the state church, just as happened in Austria and Prussia, and quite in accordance with the teachings of de Maistre, de Bonald, Görres, Gentz, and the various other theorists of the anti-revolutionary restoration and reaction.

All independent thought was to be inexorably suppressed; higher education was to be reduced to the minimum of essential knowledge; philosophy and literature, attempts at general culture and at the attainment of a philosophic outlook upon the universe, were to be stifled at the germ. Count Uvarov, minister for education from 1833 to 1849, addressing the governing committees of the schools, announced his advent to office in the following terms: "It is our joint task to secure that the culture of the nation shall be carried on in the unified spirit of Orthodoxy, autocracy and patriotism." Yet more thoroughly did Uvarov, in the course of the same year, formulate this trinitarian doctrine as "the main principle of the social system of education," writing as follows: "Amid the rapid decay of religious and civil institutions of Europe, amid the widespread diffusion of revolutionary ideas, it becomes our duty to establish the foundations of the fatherland so firmly that they cannot be shaken. We must . . . discover energies which will develop the distinctive characteristics of Russia, and will ultimately enable our country to assemble the sacred heritage of nationality into a compact whole, to which we must anchor our salvation. . . . A Russian devoted to his fatherland is as little willing to permit the subtraction of a single dogma from our Orthodox faith as he would be to allow the theft of a pearl from the crown of Monomachus. Autocracy is the main condition of Russia's political existence.

In conformity with these two national bases is the third basis, equally important and equally strong—patriotism."

The official program of reaction—Orthodoxy, autocracy, and patriotism—had thus been formulated. To the present day this program constitutes the alpha and omega of official political wisdom; it is the program of the Russian theocracy, which declares the tsar's will a divine revelation, and deduces bureaucratic politics and administration from God's will thus revealed. In the first section of the fundamental law of 1832 (it became section 4 when the law was reëdited in 1906), autocracy is defined in the following terms: "The tsar of all the Russias is an autocratic and absolute monarch. God himself commands us to obey the tsar's supreme authority, not from fear alone, but as a point of conscience." The theocratic relationship of the tsar to the church is thus defined: "The Russian tsar, as a Christian sovereign, is supreme protector and defender of the dogmas of the Greco-Russian faith and supervisor of Orthodoxy and of good order in general throughout holy church. In this sense he is spoken of as the head of the church." (Fundamental Law of 1906, Section 64) . . .

Nicolas desired in good earnest to realise Uvarov's formula. Russia had the advantage over Europe of possessing the only true faith and uniformity of religious belief was to prevail. The outcome of this ecclesiastical policy was the adoption of harsh police measures against the . . . sectaries . . . and it was the same policy which induced the enforcement of religious uniformity.

Hardly had Nicholas become tsar when he abolished the chair of philosophy at Moscow university. Driving past the university on one occasion, looking very serious, he pointed to the building and said, "There is the wolf's den." The less developed universities were dealt with in accordance with this estimate. . . . In 1835 Uvarov reorganised the universities in conformity with his general program, making the study of theology and ecclesiastical history obligatory in all faculties. In 1850, owing to the alarm inspired by the revolution of 1848, certain disciplines, and notably the study of European constitutional law, were banished from the university. . . . The object of the university was announced to be, "the education of loyal sons for the Orthodox church, of loyal subjects for the tsar, and of good and useful citizens for the fatherland."

ADMINISTRATIVE CORRUPTION IN CZARIST RUSSIA

Aleksander Herzen (1812-70), before his final exile in Europe (1847), was sent away to Eastern Russia, where he had firsthand experiences with Russian officialdom. The following account from his *Memoirs* illustrates the almost universal corruption that prevailed.

From HERZEN, *My Past* (1852-55) [1]

Somewhere in grimy offices, from which we make haste to get away, shabby men write and write on grey paper, and copy on to stamped paper—and persons, families, whole villages are outraged, terrified, ruined. A father is sent into exile, a mother to prison, a son for a soldier, and all this breaks like a thunderclap upon them, unexpected, for the most part undeserved. And for the sake of what? For the sake of money. A tribute must be paid . . . or an inquiry will be held concerning some dead drunkard, burnt up by spirits and frozen to death. And the head-man collects and the village elder collects, the peasants bring their last

[1] Aleksander Ivanovich Herzen, *My Past and Thoughts,* trans. by Constance Garnett, 6 vols., 1924-28, I, 295-96, 304-09. By permission of the publishers, Alfred A. Knopf, Inc., New York.

kopek. The police-inspector must live; the police-captain must live and keep his wife too; the councillor must live and educate his children, the councillor is an exemplary father. . . .

Among my acquaintances was a venerable old man, a police-captain dismissed from his position by a Committee of Inquiry instituted by the Senators' revision. He spent his time drawing up petitions and getting up cases, which was just what he was forbidden to do. This man, who had been in the service immemorial ages, had stolen, doctored official documents, and collected false evidence in three provinces, twice been tried, and so on. This veteran of the rural police liked to tell amazing anecdotes about himself and his colleagues, not concealing his contempt for the degenerate officials of the younger generation.

"They're giddy-pates," he said; "of course they take what they can get, there is no living without it, but it is no use looking for cleverness or knowledge of the law in them. I'll tell you, for instance, about one friend of mine. He was a judge for twenty years and only died last year. He was a man of brains! And the peasants don't remember evil against him, though he has left his family a bit of bread. He had quite a special way of his own. If a peasant came along with a petition, the judge would admit him at once and be as friendly and pleasant as you please.

" 'What is your name, uncle, and what was your father's?'

"The peasant would bow and say, 'Yermolay, sir, and my father was called Grigory.'

" 'Well, good health to you, Yermolay Grigoryevitch, from what parts is the Lord bringing you here?'

" 'We are from Dubilovo.'

" 'I know. I know. You have a mill, I fancy, on the right from the track.'

" 'Yes, sir, the mill of our commune.'

" 'A well-to-do village; the land is good, black soil.' . . .

[And by such wheedling, the judge elicited from the ignorant peasant that the latter had a large family, with grandchildren, that he possessed three horses, cattle, sheep—in short, that he was likely to be good for a touch. This accomplished, the judge continues:]

" 'Ah, I've been too long talking with you. It's the Tsar's service, Yermolay Grigoryevitch, it is time I was in the Court. Had you come about some little business or what?'

" 'Yes, your honour.'

" 'Well, what is it? some quarrel? Make haste and tell me, old man! it is time I was going.'

" 'Well, kind sir, trouble has come upon me in my old age. Just at Assumption, we were in the tavern and came to high words with a peasant of a neighbouring village, such a mischievous man, he is always stealing our wood. We had hardly said a word before he swung his fist and gave me a punch in the chest. "Keep your blows for your own village," I said to him, and just to make an example, I would have given him a push, but, being drunk perhaps, or else it was the devil in it, hit him in the eye—and, well, I spoilt his eye, and he is gone with the church elder straight to the inspector —wants to have me up to be tried in the court.'

"While he tells this story, the judge— our Petersburg actors are nothing to him —grows graver and graver, makes his eyes look dreadful, and does not say a word. The peasant sees and turns pale. . . .

" 'So I have come here to you, kind sir,' says the peasant in a changed tone. . . .

" 'It's a pity! a great pity! to think that a household must be ruined! Why, what will become of the family without you, all young people and little grandchildren, and I'm sorry for your old woman, too.'

"The peasant's legs begin to tremble. 'Well, kind sir, what have I brought on myself?'

" 'Look here, Yermolay Grigoryevitch, read for yourself . . . or perhaps you are no great reader? Well here is the article on maiming and mutilation . . . to be punished by flogging and exile to Siberia.'

" 'Don't let a man be ruined! Don't destroy a Christian! Cannot something be done?' . . .

" 'What a fellow! Can we go against the law? Of course, it is in human hands. Well, instead of thirty strokes we might give five.'

" 'But about Siberia? . . .'

" 'That's not in our power to decide, my good man.'

"The peasant pulls out of his bosom a little bag, takes out . . . two and then three gold pieces, and with a low bow lays them on the table.

" 'What's this, Yermolay Grigoryevitch?'

" 'Save me, kind sir.'

" 'Nonsense, nonsense, what do you mean? Sinful man that I am, I do sometimes accept a token of gratitude. My salary is small, so one is forced to, but if one accepts it, it must be for something! How can I help you? . . . Take your money back.'

"The peasant is crushed.

" 'I'll tell you what I'll do; shall I talk to my colleagues? . . . I have friends, they can do anything, only they are a different sort of people, you won't get off for three gold pieces there. . . . It is no use your offering them less than two grey notes.'

" 'But, kind sir, as God is above, I don't know where I am to turn to get such a mint of money—four hundred roubles— these are hard times.'

" 'Yes, I expect it is difficult. . . . Of course, if you were to sell a couple of horses and one of the cows, and the sheep, you might make it up. . . . On the other hand, if you do keep the horses, you'll have to go off yourself to the ends of the earth. Think it over, Grigoryevitch; there is no hurry . . . but it is time I was going,' adds the judge, and puts the gold pieces he had refused into his pocket, saying, 'This is quite unnecessary. I only take it not to offend you.'

"Next morning you may be sure the old screw brings three hundred and fifty roubles in all sorts of old-fashioned coins to the judge. The judge promises to look after his interests: the peasant is tried and tried and properly scared and then let off with some light punishment, or with a warning to be careful in the future . . . and he remembers the judge in his prayers for the rest of his life.

"That's how they used to do in the old days," the discharged police-inspector told me; "they did things properly."

RUSSIAN SOCIETY IN THE TIME OF NICHOLAS I

A vivid description of Russian society in the latter days of Nicholas I appears in the *Memoirs of a Revolutionist* by Prince Pëtr Alexseevich Kropotkin (1842-1921). Kropotkin himself was a geographer of note, a revolutionist, and a social philosopher; but he spent his boyhood in aristocratic Russian circles, for his father was a wealthy landowner, a nobleman, and "a typical officer of the time of Nicholas I." The following excerpt pictures Russian society about 1850.

From KROPOTKIN, *Memoirs* (1885) [1]

Wealth was measured in those times by the number of "souls" that a landed proprietor owned. So many "souls" meant so many male serfs: women did not count. My father, who owned nearly twelve hundred souls, in three different provinces, and who had, in addition to his peasants' holdings, large tracts of land which were cultivated by these peasants, was accounted a rich man. He lived up to his reputation, which meant that his house was open to any number of visitors, and that he kept a very large household. We were a family of eight, occasionally ten or twelve; but fifty servants at Moscow, and half as many more in the country, were considered not one too many. Four coachmen to attend a dozen horses, three cooks for the masters and two more for the servants, a dozen men to wait upon us at dinner-time (one man, plate in hand, standing behind each person seated at the table), and girls innumerable in the maid-servants' room—how could any one do with less than this?

Besides, the ambition of every landed proprietor was that everything required for his household should be made at home, by his own men. "How nicely your piano is always tuned! I suppose Herr Schimmel must be your tuner?" perhaps a visitor would remark. To be able to answer, "I have my own piano-tuner," was in those times the correct thing. . . .

To have embroideries, harness, furniture—in fact, everything—made by one's own men was the ideal of the rich and respected landed proprietor. As soon as the children of servants attained the age of ten, they were sent as apprentices to the fashionable shops, where they were

[1] Pëtr Alexseevich Kropotkin, *Memoirs of a Revolutionist*, Boston, 1899, 28-30, 36-42, 44-45, 49-51. By permission of Houghton Mifflin Company, Boston.

obliged to spend five to seven years chiefly in sweeping; in receiving an incredible number of thrashings, and in running about town on errands of all sorts. I must own that few of them became masters of their respective arts. The tailors and shoemakers were found only skilful enough to make clothes or shoes for the servants, and when a really good pastry was required for a dinner-party it was ordered at Tremble's. . . .

Nearly every night we had visitors. The green tables were opened in the hall for the card-players, while the ladies and the young people stayed in the reception-room or around Hélène's piano. When the ladies had gone, card-playing continued sometimes till the small hours of the morning, and considerable sums of money changed hands among the players. Father invariably lost. . . . Dancing-parties were not infrequent, to say nothing of a couple of obligatory balls every winter. Father's way, in such cases, was to have everything done in good style, whatever the expense. But at the same time such niggardliness was practised in our house in daily life that if I were to recount it, I should be accused of exaggeration. It is said of a family of pretenders to the throne of France, renowned for their truly regal hunting-parties, that in their every-day life even the tallow candles were minutely counted. The same sort of miserly economy ruled in our house with regard to everything; so much so that when we, the children of the house, grew up, we detested all saving and counting. However, in the Old Equerries' Quarter, such a mode of life only raised my father in public esteem. "The old prince," it was said, "seems to be sharp over money at home; but he knows how a nobleman ought to live." . . .

To maintain such numbers of servants as were kept in our house would have been simply ruinous, if all provisions had to be bought at Moscow; but in those times of serfdom things were managed very simply. When winter came, father sat at his table and wrote the following:

"To the manager of my estate, Nikólskoye, situated in the government of Kalúga, district of Meschóvsk, on the river Siréna, from the Prince Alexéi Petróvich Kropótkin, Colonel and Commander of various orders. On receipt of this, and as soon as winter communication is established, thou art ordered to send to my house, situated in the city of Moscow, twenty-five peasant-sledges, drawn by two horses each, one horse from each house and one sledge and one man from each second house, and to load them with (so many) quarters of oats, (so many) of wheat, and (so many) of rye, as also with all the poultry and geese and ducks, well frozen, which have to be killed this winter, well packed and accompanied by a complete list, under the supervision of a well-chosen man"; and so it went on for a couple of pages, till the next full stop was reached. After this followed an enumeration of the penalties which would be inflicted in case the provisions should not reach the house . . . in due time and in good condition.

Some time before Christmas the twenty-five peasant-sledges really entered our gates, and covered the surface of the wide yard. "Frol!" shouted my father, as soon as the report of this great event reached him. "Kiryúshka! Yegórka! Where are they? Everything will be stolen! Frol, go and receive the oats! Uliána, go and receive the poultry! Kiryúshka, call the princess!" And the household was in commotion, the servants running wildly in every direction, from the hall to the yard, from the yard to the hall, but chiefly to the maid-servants' room, to communicate there the Nikólskoye news: "Pásha is going to marry after Christmas. Aunt Anna has surrendered her soul to God," and so on. . . .

When the sledges had been unloaded, the hall filled with peasants. They had put on their best coats over their sheepskins, and waited till father should call them into his room to have a talk about the snow and the prospects of the next crops. They hardly dared to walk in their heavy boots on the polished floor. A few ventured to sit down on the edge of an oak bench; they emphatically refused to make use of chairs. So they waited for hours, looking with alarm upon every one who entered father's room or issued from it. . . .

Our best time, of course, was in the country. As soon as Easter and Whitsuntide had passed, all our thoughts were directed toward Nikólskoye. However, time went on . . . and father had still thousands of affairs to keep him in town. At last, five or six peasant-carts entered our yard: they came to take all sorts of things which had to be sent to the country-house. The great old coach and the other coaches in which we were going to make the journey were taken out and inspected once more. The boxes began to be packed. . . . Everything was ready: the peasant-carts stood heavily loaded with furniture for the country-house, and almost countless empty glass jars which were to be brought back in the autumn filled with all kinds of preserves. . . . Next afternoon, Frol, the major-domo, and Mikhael Aléeff, the first violin, were called into father's room. A sack containing the "food-money"—that is, a few coppers a day—for each of the forty or fifty souls who were to accompany the household to Nikólskoye, was handed to Frol, with a list. All were enumerated in that list: the band in full; then the cooks and the under-cooks, the laundresses . . . and the rest of them. The first violin received an "order of march." . . .

Next day, at ten instead of six—punctuality is not a Russian virtue ("Thank God, we are not Germans," true Russians used to say)—the carts left the house. The servants had to make the journey on foot; only the children were accommodated with a seat in a bath-tub or basket on top of a loaded cart, and some of the women might find an occasional resting-place on the rim of a cart. The others had to walk all the hundred and sixty miles. As long as they were marching in Moscow, discipline was maintained. . . . But when they were on the road . . . the men and women . . . certainly looked more like a wandering band of gypsies than the household of a wealthy landowner. . . .

The journey was an inexhaustible source of enjoyment for us children. The stages were short and we stopped twice a day to feed the horses. As the ladies screamed at the slightest declivity in the road, it was found more convenient to alight each time the road went up or down hill, which it did continually, and we took advantage of this to have a peep into the woods by the roadside, or run along some crystal brook. . . .

Beyond the forest, and past the ferry which took us over the Ugrá, we left the highroad and entered the narrow country lanes, where green ears of rye bent toward the coach, and the horses managed to bite large mouthfuls of grass on either side of the way. . . . At last we caught sight of the willows which marked the approach to our village, and all of a sudden we saw the elegant pale yellow bell tower of the Nikólskoye church.

For the quiet life of the landlords of those times Nikólskoye was admirably suited. There was nothing in it of the luxury which is seen in the richer estates; but an artistic hand was visible in the planning. . . . Besides the main house, which father had recently built, there were, round a spacious and well-kept yard, several smaller houses. . . . An immense "upper garden" was devoted to fruit trees, and through it the church was reached; the southern slope of the land, which led to the river, was entirely given up to a pleasure garden, where flower-beds were intermingled with alleys of lime trees, lilacs, and acacias. . . . Father was invariably absent from home in the summer, which he spent in military inspections, and our stepmother did not pay much attention to us, especially after her own child, Pauline, was born. We were thus always with M. Poulain [their tutor], who thoroughly enjoyed the stay in the country, and let us enjoy it. The woods; the walks along the river; the climbing over the hills . . . there was no end of new and delightful impressions. . . .

Serfdom was then in the last years of its existence. It is recent history—it seems to be only of yesterday; and yet, even in Russia, few realize what serfdom was in reality. There is a dim conception that the conditions which it created were very bad; but those conditions, as they affected human beings bodily and mentally, are not generally understood. It is amazing, indeed, to see how quickly an institution and its social consequences are forgotten when the institution has ceased to exist, and with what rapidity men and things change. I will try to recall the conditions of serfdom by telling, not what I heard but what I saw.

Uliána, the housekeeper, stands in the passage leading to father's room, and crosses herself; she dares neither to advance nor to retreat. At last, after having recited a prayer, she enters the room, and reports, in a hardly audible voice, that the store of tea is nearly at an end, that there are only twenty pounds of sugar left, and that the other provisions will soon be exhausted.

"Thieves, robbers!" shouts my father. "And you, you are in league with them!"

His voice thunders throughout the house. Our stepmother leaves Uliána to face the storm. But father cries, "Frol, call the princess! Where is she?" And when she enters, he receives her with the same reproaches.

"You also are in league with this progeny of Ham; you are standing up for them"; and so on, for half an hour or more.

Then he commences to verify the accounts. At the same time, he thinks about the hay. Frol is sent to weigh what is left of that, and our stepmother is sent to be present during the weighing, while father calculates how much of it ought to be in the barn. A considerable quantity of hay appears to be missing, and Uliána cannot account for several pounds of such and such provisions. Father's voice becomes more and more menacing; Uliána is trembling; but it is the coachman who now enters the room, and is stormed at by his master. Father springs at him, strikes him, but he keeps repeating, "Your highness must have made a mistake."

Father repeats his calculations, and this time it appears that there is more hay in the barn than there ought to be. . . . But father will not be appeased. He calls in Makár, the piano-tuner and sub-butler, and reminds him of all his recent sins. He was drunk last week, and must have been drunk yesterday, for he broke half a dozen plates. In fact, the breaking of these plates was the real cause of all the disturbance: our stepmother had reported the fact to father in the morning, and that was why Uliána was received with more scolding than was usually the case, why the verification of the hay was undertaken, and why father now continues to shout that "this progeny of Ham" deserve all the punishments on earth.

Of a sudden there is a lull in the storm. My father takes his seat at the table and writes a note. "Take Makár with this note to the police station, and let a hundred lashes with the birch rod be given to him." Terror and absolute muteness reign in the house.

The clock strikes four, and we all go down to dinner; but no one has any appetite, and the soup remains in the plates untouched. We are ten at table, and behind each of us a violinist or a trombone-player stands, with a clean plate in his left hand; but Makár is not among them.

"Where is Makár?" our stepmother asks. "Call him in."

Makár does not appear, and the order is repeated. He enters at last, pale, with a distorted face, ashamed, his eyes cast down. Father looks into his plate, while our stepmother, seeing that no one has touched the soup, tries to encourage us. "Don't you find, children," she says, "that the soup is delicious?"

Tears suffocate me, and immediately after dinner is over I run out, catch Makár in a dark passage, and try to kiss his hand; but he tears it away, and says, either as a reproach or as a question, "Let me alone; you, too, when you are grown up, will you not be just the same?" "No, no, never!"

Yet father was not among the worst of the landowners. On the contrary, the servants and the peasants considered him one of the best. What we saw in our house was going on everywhere, often in much more cruel forms. The flogging of the serfs was a regular part of the duties of the police and of the fire brigade.

2. Reform, Discontent, and Terrorism, 1855-1894

THE ABOLITION OF SERFDOM

Even before the Decembrists, thoughtful Russians had desired to abolish serfdom, although the nobility resisted all suggestions to accomplish this end.

The disasters of the Crimean War opened Russians' eyes to the backwardness and weakness of their social, economic, and governmental structure, and the new Czar, Alexander II (1855-81), undertook a reform program. By Czarist command, a committee worked out plans for emancipation of the serfs. The nobility still resisted, but they were outmaneuvered by the Czar, and the Decree of Emancipation granted the serfs civil freedom—although it did nothing to rid them of economic bondage. Here follows the Czar's decree.

From ALEXANDER II, Decree of Emancipation (March 3, 1861) [1]

By the grace of God, we, Alexander II, Emperor and Autocrat of all the Russias, King of Poland, Grand Duke of Finland, &c., to all our faithful subjects make known . . .

In considering the various classes and conditions of which the State is composed we came to the conviction that the legislation of the empire having wisely provided for the organization of the upper and middle classes and having defined with precision their obligations, their rights, and their privileges, has not attained the same degree of efficiency as regards the peasants attached to the soil, thus designated because either from ancient laws or from custom they have been hereditarily subjected to the authority of the proprietors, on whom it was incumbent at the same time to provide for their welfare. . . . In the most favourable cases this state of things has established patriarchal relations founded upon a solicitude sincerely equitable and benevolent on the part of the proprietors, and on an affectionate submission on the part of the peasants; but in proportion as the simplicity of morals diminished . . . those

1 "History," *The Annual Register . . . 1861,* 207-11.

bonds of mutual good-will slackened, and a wide opening was made for an arbitrary sway, which weighed upon the peasants, and was unfavourable to their welfare. . . .

We thus came to the conviction that the work of a serious improvement of the condition of the peasants was a sacred . . . mission which, in the course of events, Divine Providence called upon us to fulfil. . . .

It is to the nobles themselves, conformable to their own wishes, that we have reserved the task of drawing up the propositions for the new organization of the peasants—propositions which make it incumbent upon them to limit their rights over the peasants, and to accept the onus of a reform which could not be accomplished without some material losses. . . . We have seen the nobles assembled in committees in the districts, through the medium of their confidential agents. . . . These committees, after having collected the necessary data, have formulated their propositions concerning the new organization of the peasants. . . . These propositions having been found very diverse, as was to be expected from the nature of the question, they have been compared, collated, and reduced to a regular system . . . and these new dispositions thus formulated relative to the peasants and the domestics of the proprietors have been examined by the Council of the Empire.

Having invoked the Divine assistance, we have resolved to carry this work into execution.

In virtue of the new dispositions abovementioned, the peasants attached to the soil will be invested within a term fixed by the law with all the rights of free cultivators.

The proprietors retaining their rights of property on all the land belonging to them, grant to the peasants for a fixed regulated rental the full enjoyment of their close [enclosure]; and, moreover, to assure their livelihood and to guarantee the fulfilment of their obligations towards the Government, the quantity of arable land is fixed by the said dispositions, as well as other rural appurtenances. But, in the enjoyment of these territorial allotments, the peasants are obliged, in return, to acquit the rentals fixed by the same dispositions to the profit of the proprietors. In this state, which must be a transitory one, the peasants shall be designated as "temporarily bound."

At the same time, they are granted the right of purchasing their close, and, with the consent of the proprietors, they may acquire in full property the arable lands and other appurtenances which are allotted to them as a permanent holding. By the acquisition in full property of the quantity of land fixed, the peasants are free from their obligations towards the proprietors for land thus purchased, and they enter definitively into the condition of free peasants—landholders.

By a special disposition concerning the domestics, a transitory state is fixed for them. . . . On the expiration of a term of two years . . . they shall receive their full enfranchisement and some temporary immunities. . . .

Although these dispositions . . . have been . . . adapted to economical necessities and local customs, nevertheless, to preserve the existing state where it presents reciprocal advantages, we leave it to the proprietors to come to amicable terms with the peasants, and to conclude transactions relative to the extent of the territorial allotment and to the amount of rental to be fixed in consequence, observing, at the same time, the established rules to guarantee the inviolability of such agreements. . . . [Grants "two years or thereabouts" to complete the changes.]

For which end, we have deemed it advisable to ordain—

1. To establish in each district a special Court for the question of the peasants . . . to investigate the affairs of the rural communes established on the land of the lords of the soil.

2. To appoint in each district justices of the peace to investigate on the spot all misunderstandings and disputes which may arise . . . and to form district assemblies with these justices of the peace.

3. To organize in the seigneurial properties communal administrations, and to this end to leave the rural communes in their actual composition, and to open in the large villages district administrations (provincial boards) by uniting the small communes under one of these district administrations.

4. To formulate, verify, and confirm in each rural district or estate a charter of rules in which shall be enumerated . . . the amount of land reserved to the peasants in permanent enjoyment, and the extent of the charges which may be exacted from them for the benefit of the proprietor as well as for other advantages granted by him.

5. To put these charters of rules into execution . . . within the term of two years. . . .

6. Up to the expiration of this term, the peasants and domestics are to remain in the same obedience towards their proprietors and to fulfil their former obligations without scruple.

7. The proprietors will continue to watch over the maintenance of order on their estates, with the right of jurisdiction and of police until the organization of the districts and of the district tribunals has been effected. . . .

Russia will not forget that the nobility, acting solely upon its respect for the dignity of man and its love for its neighbour, has spontaneously renounced rights given to it by serfdom actually abolished, and laid the foundation of a new future, which is thrown open to the peasants. . . .

To render the transactions between the proprietors and the peasants more easy, in virtue of which the latter may acquire in full property their close (homestead) and the land they occupy, the Government will advance assistance, according to a special regulation, by means of loans or a transfer of debts encumbering an estate. [The Government advanced loans to peasants, bearing interest at a high rate and amortized in forty-nine annual payments, for which each communal board (mir) was held responsible.]

NIHILISM, POPULISM, AND TERRORISM

Alexander II's reforming zeal was short-lived and his reforms were incomplete. As a consequence, opposition to his regime arose rapidly, especially among the intelligentsia. At first the opposition took the relatively inactive, negative form of Nihilism, a philosophical movement; then, from about 1871, it assumed the more active form of Populism, and the cry was "Among the People" as hundreds of enthusiastic propagandists set out to enlighten the peasantry and the workingmen. But the propagandists were arrested, imprisoned, maltreated, and exiled, and the survivors of Populism, embittered and desperate, turned to Terrorism as their weapon against Czarist tyranny. Sergei Mikhailovich Stepnyak (pen-name of Sergei Mikhailovich Kravchinski) was himself one who passed through these stages to Terrorism. In 1882 he wrote the following analysis and description of the growth of revolutionary parties in the reign of Alexander II.

From STEPNYAK, *Underground Russia*
   (1882) [1]

Turgeneff, the novelist, who will certainly live in his writings for many generations, has rendered himself immortal by a single word. It was he who invented "Nihilism." At first the word was used in a contemptuous sense, but afterwards was accepted from party pride by those against whom it was employed, as so frequently has occurred in history. . . .

The genuine Nihilism was a philosophical and literary movement which flourished in the first decade after the Emancipation of the Serfs, that is to say, between 1860 and 1870. It is now [1882] absolutely extinct. . . . Nihilism was a struggle for the emancipation of intelligence from every kind of dependence, and it advanced side by side with that for the emancipation of the labouring classes from serfdom. The fundamental principle of Nihilism, properly so-called, was absolute individualism. It was the negation, in the name of individual liberty, of all the obligations imposed upon the individual by society, by family life, and by religion. Nihilism was a passionate and powerful reaction, not against political despotism, but against the moral despotism that weighs upon the private and inner life of the individual.

But it must be confessed that our predecessors, at least in the earlier days, introduced into this highly pacific struggle the same spirit of rebellion and almost the same fanaticism that characterises the present movement. I will here indicate the general character of this struggle, because it is really a prelude to the great drama, the last act of which is being enacted in the Empire of the night.

The first battle was fought in the domain of religion. But this was neither long nor obstinate. It was gained, so to speak, in a single assault; for there is no country in the world where, among the cultivated classes, religion has such little roots as in Russia. . . . When once this band of young writers, armed with the natural sciences and positive philosophy, full of talent, of fire, and of the ardour of proselytism, was impelled to the assault, Christianity fell like an old, decaying hovel, which remains standing because no one touches it. . . . Atheism excited people like a new religion. . . . Among people in Russia with any education at all, a man now who is not a materialist, a thorough materialist, would really be a curiosity.

The victory was of the highest importance. Absolute atheism is the sole inheritance that has been preserved intact by the new generation, and I need scarcely point out how much advantage the modern revolutionary movement has derived from it. But Nihilism proclaimed war not only against religion but against everything that was not based upon pure and positive reason. . . .

One question in which Nihilism rendered great service to its country . . . was the important question of women. Nihilism recognised her as having equal rights with man . . . and secured for her an almost complete victory. . . . No father now threatens to cut off the hair of his daughter if she wishes to go to St. Petersburg to study medicine, or follow the higher courses there of the other sciences. . . . Nihilism had conquered all along the line. The Nihilist had now only to rest upon his laurels. The first two persons of the trinity of his ideal . . . independence of mind and intelligent female company, were within his reach. The third, an occupation in accordance with his tastes, is lacking, but as he is intelligent, and Russia is wanting in educated people, he will find it easily. . . .

[1] Sergei Mikhailovich Stepnyak (S. M. Kravchinski), *Underground Russia*, 2nd ed., London, 1883, 2-5, 7-20, 24-29, 32-33, 41.

We are now at the year 1871. Through those marvellous inventions by means of which the man of modern days may be called omnipresent, the picture is placed before him of an immense city [Paris in the days of the Commune] which has arisen for a grand idea, that of claiming the rights of the people. . . . But for what are they dying? For what are they weeping? For the emancipation of the working-man. . . .

And at the same time falls upon his ear the plaintive song of the Russian peasant; all wailing and lamentation. . . . His squalid misery, his whole life stands forth full of sorrow, of suffering, of outrage. Look at him; exhausted by hunger, broken down by toil, the eternal slave of the privileged classes, working without pause, without hope of redemption; for the Government purposely keeps him ignorant, and everyone robs him, everyone tramples on him, and no one stretches out a hand to assist him. No one? not so. The young man [the erstwhile Nihilist] knows now "what to do." He will stretch forth his hand. He will tell the peasant how to free himself and become happy. His heart throbs for this poor sufferer, who can only weep. The flush of enthusiasm mounts to his brow, and with burning glances he takes in his heart a solemn oath to consecrate all his life, all his strength, all his thoughts, to the liberation of this population. . . . He will go forth "among the people" in some remote district, and there . . . he will do the hard work of the peasant, enduring every privation in order to carry to him the words of redemption, the Gospel of our age—Socialism. What matters to him if the cutthroats of the Government lay hands upon him? What to him are exile, Siberia, death?

It is thus that the Revolutionary Socialist of 1872-74 arose. . . .

Here then are the two types that represent the Russian intellectual movement. The first, that of the decade 1860-70; the second that from 1871 onwards.

What a contrast! The Nihilist seeks his own happiness at whatever cost. His ideal is a "reasonable" and "realistic" life. The Revolutionist seeks the happiness of others at whatever cost, sacrificing for it his own. His life is a life full of suffering, and a martyr's death. . . .

The Russian revolutionary movement . . . was the result of the examples and ideas developed in Western Europe . . . [communicated, in spite of severe censorship, by] an entire band of very able writers . . . the most intellectual men of whom Russia can boast. . . . There were many causes which determined the youth of Russia to accept so eagerly the principles of the revolutionary Socialism. . . . The ill-fated Crimean War having ruthlessly demonstrated the rottenness of the whole Russian social edifice, it was essential to provide a remedy as expeditiously as possible. . . . The wretched condition . . . of the peasants, that is to say, of nine-tenths of the entire population, could not fail to cause serious reflection to those who had at heart the future of the country. . . . The insurrection in Poland [1863-64], stifled with a ferocity known to all, was the signal for a reaction. . . . As the reaction grew more furious, the revolutionary excitement became more manifest, and secret societies swarmed in all the principal cities. . . . But a most powerful current which came from abroad very soon united with this native current. It was that of the "Internationale" [the First International, founded by Karl Marx in 1864 to organize workers everywhere]. . . . Two writers—the great Michael Bakunin [1814-76], the genius of destruction, the principal founder of the anarchical or federalistic "Internationale," and Peter Lavroff, the distinguished philosopher and writer, rendered great service. . . . The former . . . the ardent tribune and daring thinker, developed his ideas upon the necessity of an immediate popular revolution; the latter as editor of a review, the "Vperiod" ("Onward"). . . . However divergent on certain points— Bakunin being an ardent defender of the extreme party of the "Internationale," and Lavroff being rather inclined towards the more moderate party—the two writers recognised the popular revolution as the sole means of effectively changing the insufferable condition of the Russian people. . . .

All these numerous and powerful influences, acting upon the impressionable minds, so prone to enthusiasm, of Russian youth, produced that vast movement of 1873-74 which inaugurated the new Russian revolutionary era. . . . But a revolution always requires a powerful organisation, which can only be formed by a propaganda, either Socialist or purely revolutionary. As this could not be openly carried on, it was necessary to have recourse to a secret propaganda; and that was absolutely impossible in our villages. Everyone who settles there, whether as artisan, or as communal teacher, or clerk, is immediately under the eyes of all. He is observed, and his every movement is watched, as though he were a bird in a glass cage. Then, too, the peasant is absolutely incapable of keeping secret the propaganda in his midst. . . . Thus, whenever a propagandist visits any of his friends, the news immediately spreads throughout the village, and half an hour afterwards the hovel is full of bearded peasants, who hasten to listen to the newcomer without warning either him or his host. . . .

It is quite evident that, with these customs, the Government would have no difficulty in hearing of the agitation which was being carried on among the peasants. Arrest followed arrest, thick and fast. Thirty-seven provinces were "infected" by the Socialist contagion, as a Government circular declares. The total number of the arrests was never known. . . .

The trials of the agitators which took place in the years 1877 and 1878 indicated the end of this first period of revolutionary activity in Russia, and at the same time were its apotheosis. . . . An entire generation was mown down by Despotism in a fit of delirious fear. The prisons were crammed with propagandists. New prisons were built. . . .

What could the few working-men and peasants do who were inflamed by Socialist ideas? . . . The propagandist movement was a sublime test of the power of Words. By a natural reaction the opposite course was now to be tried, that of Acts.

"We did not succeed because we were mere talkers, incapable of real work." Such was the bitter reproach of the survivors . . . and the cry of "Let us act" became as general as that of "among the people" had been a few years before.

But what kind of action was to be taken. . . .

Against such a Government [as that which so cruelly sentenced a man to fifteen years of hard labor "for two or three speeches made in private to a handful of working-men, or for a single book read or lent"] everything is permitted. It is no longer a guardian of the will of the people, or of the majority of the people. It is organised injustice. A citizen is no more bound to respect it than to respect a band of highwaymen. . . .

But how shake off this *camarilla* entrenched behind a forest of bayonets? How free the country from it? It being absolutely impossible to overcome this obstacle by force, as in other countries more fortunate than ours, a flank movement was necessary, so as to fall upon this *camarilla* before it could avail itself of its forces. . . .

Thus arose the Terrorism.

THE REVOLUTIONARY SOCIALISTS'
PROGRAM (1881)

In March, 1881, after five previous attempts upon the Czar's life since 1866, a terrorist bomb killed Alexander II. Ten days after this event, the Executive Committee of the Revolutionary Socialists addressed the following letter to the new Czar, Alexander III, setting forth conditions for their own dissolution. The Czar of course made no attempt to meet them; but the moderation of the committee's demands is noteworthy as compared with twentieth-century revolutionary pretensions.

From the Letter of the Executive Committee of the Revolutionary Socialists to Alexander III (1881) [1]

Your Majesty: The Executive Committee thoroughly understands the mental prostration you must now be experiencing. It does not, however, consider that it should from a feeling of delicacy, defer the following declaration. There is something higher even than legitimate human feeling; it is the duty towards our country. . . . The sanguinary tragedy on the Catherine Canal [Alexander's assassination] was no mere chance occurrence, and could have surprised no one. After what has happened during the past ten years, it appeared inevitable; and therein lies its profound significance, which should be thoroughly understood by him whom destiny has placed at the head of a State. . . .

Your Majesty will admit that the Government of the late Emperor cannot be accused of "want of energy." The innocent and the guilty were hanged alike; the prisons, like the remotest provinces, were filled with the condemned. The so-called "leaders" were taken and hanged by the dozen. They died tranquilly and

with the calmness of martyrs; but this did not stop the movement; on the contrary, the movement increased. . . . The Government may continue to arrest and hang as long as it likes. . . . But this will not change the state of things. Revolutionists will be created by events; by the general discontent of the whole people; by the tendency of Russia towards new social forms.

An entire nation cannot be suppressed; and still less can the discontent of a nation be suppressed by rigorous measures. These, instead, will increase its bitterness, its energy, its forces. The latter, naturally, will be better organised, profiting by the experience of those who have preceded them. . . . The rigours of the Government after 1878 and 1879 gave birth to the Terrorists. . . . From this imperfect organization more strongly constituted bodies were substituted by a species of "natural selection." At last the Executive Committee appeared, against which the Government still struggles in vain. . . .

But why the sad necessity for this sanguinary struggle?

For this reason, your Majesty; that a just Government, in the true sense of the word, does not exist among us. A Government should . . . be the expression of the aspirations of the people, should carry out only the will of the people. With us, however—pardon us for saying so—the Government is a perfect *camarilla,* and deserves the name of a "band of usurpers" much more than the Executive Committee deserves it. . . . That is why the Government in Russia has no moral influence over the people; this is why Russia produces so many Revolutionists; this is why even an event like the killing of the Tsar excites sympathy among a great part of this very people. Pay no heed to flatterers, your Majesty. Regicide in Russia is very popular.

There are two outlets from such a

<hr/>

[1] *Ibid.,* 287-94.

situation; either a Revolution . . . or the spontaneous surrender of supreme authority to the people to assist in the work of government. In the interests of the country, and to avoid a useless waste of talent and energy, and those terrible disasters by which the Revolution is always accompanied, the Executive Committee addresses itself to your Majesty and counsels you to select the latter course. . . .

The conditions which are necessary in order that the Revolutionary movement should give place to a pacific development have not been created by us, but by events. . . . These conditions, according to our view, should be based upon two principal stipulations. First, a general amnesty for all political offenders, since they have committed no crime, but have simply done their duty as citizens. Second, the convocation of the representatives of the whole of the people, for the examination of the best forms of social and political life, according to the wants and desires of the people.

We, nevertheless, consider it necessary to point out that the legalisation of power by the representation of the people can only be arrived at when the elections are perfectly free. The elections should, therefore, take place under the following conditions: First, the deputies shall be chosen by all classes without distinction, in proportion to the number of inhabitants. Second, there shall be no restriction of any kind upon electors or deputies. Third, the elections and the electoral agitation shall be perfectly free. The Government will, therefore, grant as provisional regulations, until the convocation of the popular assemblies: (a) Complete freedom of the press. (b) Complete freedom of speech. (c) Complete freedom of public meeting. (d) Complete freedom of electoral addresses. These are the only means by which Russia can enter upon the path of peaceful and regular development. We

solemnly declare, before the country, and before the whole world, that our party will submit unconditionally to the National Assembly which meets upon the basis of the above conditions, and will offer no opposition to the Government which the National Assembly may sanction.

And now, your Majesty, decide.

SIBERIAN EXILE: THE SYSTEM OF ADMINISTRATIVE ARREST

Siberian exile as punishment for criminals dates from the seventeenth century in Russia. In the nineteenth century, however, it was used for political offenders, the number of exiles averaging nearly twenty thousand yearly in the last half of the century. During the reign of Alexander III (1881-94), George Kennan, an American writer, visited prisons and exile groups in Siberia and published an informative book on his observations. Here follows his description of the summary Czarist proceedings employed against political offenders, real and imaginary.

From KENNAN, *Siberia and the Exile System* (1891) [1]

Exile by administrative process means the banishment of an obnoxious person from one part of the empire to another without the observance of any of the legal formalities that, in most civilized countries, precede the deprivation of rights and the restriction of personal liberty. The obnoxious person may not be guilty of any crime, and may not have rendered himself amenable in any way to the laws of the state, but if, in the opinion of the local authorities, his presence in a particular place is "prejudicial to public

[1] George Kennan, *Siberia and the Exile System*, 2 vols., London, 1891, I, 242-43, 247-48.

order," or "incompatible with public tranquillity," he may be arrested without a warrant, may be held from two weeks to two years in prison, and may then be removed by force to any other place within the limits of the empire and there be put under police surveillance for a period of from one year to ten years. He may or may not be informed of the reasons for this summary proceeding, but in either case he is perfectly helpless. He cannot examine the witnesses upon whose testimony his presence is declared to be "prejudicial to public order." He cannot summon friends to prove his loyalty and good character, without great risk of bringing upon them the same calamity that has befallen him. He has no right to demand a trial, or even a hearing. He cannot sue out a writ of habeas corpus. He cannot appeal to his fellow-citizens through the press. His communications with the world are so suddenly severed that sometimes even his own relatives do not know what has happened to him. He is literally and absolutely without any means whatever of self-defense. To show the nature of the evidence upon which certain classes of Russians are banished to Siberia, and to illustrate the working of the system generally, I will give a few cases of administrative exile from the large number recorded in my notebooks. . . .

A gentleman named Achkin, in Moscow, was exiled to Siberia by administrative process in 1885 merely because, to adopt the language of the order that was issued for his arrest, he was "suspected of an intention to put himself into an illegal situation." The high crime which Mr. Achkin was "suspected of an intention" to commit was the taking of a fictitious name in the place of his own. Upon what ground he was "suspected of an intention" to do this terrible thing he never knew.

Another exile of my acquaintance, Mr.

Y——, was banished merely because he was a friend of Mr. Z——, who was awaiting trial on the charge of political conspiracy. When Mr. Z——'s case came to a judicial investigation he was found to be innocent and was acquitted; but in the meantime Mr. Y——, merely for being a friend of this innocent man, had gone to Siberia by administrative process.

In another case a young student, called Vladímir Sidórski (I use a fictitious name), was arrested by mistake instead of another and a different Sidórski named Victor, whose presence in Moscow was regarded by somebody as "prejudicial to public order." Vladímir protested that he was not Victor, that he did not know Victor, and that his arrest in the place of Victor was the result of a stupid blunder; but his protestations were of no avail. The police were too much occupied in unearthing what they called "conspiracies" and looking after "untrustworthy" people to devote any time to a troublesome verification of an insignificant student's identity. There must have been something wrong about him, they argued, or he would not have been arrested, and the safest thing to do with him was to send him to Siberia, whoever he might be—and to Siberia he was sent. When the convoy officer called the roll of the outgoing exile party, Vladímir Sidórski failed to answer to Victor Sidórski's name, and the officer, with a curse, cried, "Victor Sidórski! Why don't you answer to your name?"

"It is not my name," replied Vladímir, "and I won't answer to it. It's another Sidórski who ought to be going to Siberia."

"What is your name, then?"

Vladímir told him. The officer cooly erased the name "Victor" in the roll of the party, inserted the name "Vladímir," and remarked cynically, "It doesn't make a —————— bit of difference!" . . .

In the light of such facts terrorism ceases to be an unnatural or an inexplicable phenomenon. Wrong a man in that way, deny him all redress, exile him again if he complains, gag him if he cries out, strike him in the face if he struggles, and at last he will stab and throw bombs. It is useless to say that the Russian Government does not exasperate men and women in this way.

3. Russian Industrial Development

A variety of circumstances combined to stimulate Russian industrial development in the period after 1860—emancipation of the serfs produced a large, mobile labor supply; the extension of railroads facilitated internal commerce; protective tariffs, sounder finance, and foreign loans encouraged greater enterprise. Count Sergei Yulievich Witte (1849-1915), who was Minister of Transportation under Alexander III and Minister of Finance under Nicholas II, pushed forward Russian industrialization against the opposition of Wenzel von Plehve and other ultra-reactionaries who feared the creation of an urban proletariat.

COUNT WITTE ON HIS MINISTERIAL ACCOMPLISHMENTS

From COUNT WITTE, Memoirs (c. 1910) [1]

Among my purely financial reforms the first place belongs, no doubt, to the introduction of the gold standard of currency [1897]. This measure definitely established Russia's credit and put her financially on an equal footing with the European

[1] From: The Memoirs of Count Witte. Copyright 1920, 1921 by Doubleday & Company, Inc., 58-60, 74-76.

Powers. It was owing to this reform that we weathered the wretched Japanese War and the subsequent domestic upheaval. Without it, an economic and financial collapse would have occurred at the very beginning of the war, and all the economic achievements of the recent decades would have been annihilated.

In a slight measure my immediate predecessors, Bunge and Vyshnegradski, prepared our finances for the introduction of the gold standard, but it was left to me to elaborate a detailed and final plan for the currency reform. I worked against great odds, and if I succeeded in carrying the plan into effect it is because His Majesty, Emperor Nicholas, had full confidence in me and because he offered me his support without stint.

In the beginning, nearly the whole of thinking Russia was opposed to the reform. Very few of our financial and economic experts had any theoretical or practical knowledge of the matter in its entirety. The subject was not taught in our institutions of higher learning, and there were no good books in Russian on currency problems. As we had lived under the regime of paper currency since the Crimean War, the very notion of metallic currency had become obscured in the press and in the minds of educated people generally. We had grown accustomed to paper currency as one gets used to chronic disease, in spite of the fact that gradually it ruins the organism.

I was strenuously opposed by those elements of the population which were interested in the export of commodities, especially the farmers. They imagined that paper currency was advantageous for them, because with the depreciation of our money they obtained more for their products exported abroad, i.e., in terms of our depreciated money. Of course, this opinion was erroneous, for the exporter had to pay higher prices for whatever he purchased. Not being an economist, he failed to grasp the correlation of phenomena. . . .

Owing to the confidence of foreign capital in Russia's credit, which I built up, our country obtained several billion rubles of foreign capital. There are people, and their number is not small, who hold this against me. Oh, folly and ignorance! No country has ever developed without foreign capital. Throughout my administration I have defended the idea of the usefulness of foreign capital. In this respect, I had to contend with such statesmen as I. N. Durnovo, Plehve, and other members of the Committee of Ministers. Nicholas, as usual, favoured now one, now the other viewpoint. He went as far as calling a special session to discuss the advisability of importing foreign capital. At this session I declared that I was not afraid of foreign capital, that on the contrary I considered it beneficial for Russia. What I feared, I said, was that our regime is so peculiar that but few foreigners would care to have anything to do with us. Of course, foreign capital would have entered the country more abundantly if so many obstacles had not been created against it during my administration.

A great many people, including the Emperor, opposed the importation of foreign capital to Russia for purely nationalistic considerations. They argued that Russian natural resources should be exploited by "true" Russians and with the aid of Russian money. They overlooked the fact that the amount of available capital in Russia was very small. As a result, industrial concessions were usually granted to "true" Russians, who subsequently sold them to foreigners and pocketed a round sum of totally unearned money. Thus, for instance, I recall that a certain retired Colonel, by the name of Vonlyarlyarski, obtained a concession for mining gold on the Kamchatka Peninsula.

Several months later he sold it to a foreign corporation.

The development of our national labour was another great problem. The productivity of Russian labour is exceedingly low, this being due to the climate, among other reasons. For the latter reason, tens of millions are idle several months during the year. The scarcity of ways of communication is another factor lowering the productivity of labour. After the Turkish War of the '70's railroad construction was suspended, and it fell to my lot to resume the building of railways. In this respect, I have succeeded in achieving a good deal, for during my administration I doubled the railroad mileage. It is noteworthy that the Ministry of War was constantly thwarting my efforts. This Ministry supported me only when I proposed to build railroads of a strategic importance. Often strategic railroads were built counter to my recommendation. . . .

After dealing with the railroads for forty years, I can say that in most cases the strategic considerations of our War Ministry regarding the direction of the road are pure fantasy. The country will be best off if, in building railroads, it is guided by purely economic considerations. On the whole, such railroads would also meet the strategic needs. It is my opinion that this should become a basic principle of railroad construction. For thirty years we were building railroads with a view to a war in the West, and we have wasted no end of energy in that section. In the end the war broke out in the Far East.

To create new sources for the application of labour, it was more than desirable to develop our industry. Alexander the Third, with his characteristic firmness and wisdom, was the first to recognize and carry out this policy. In this respect I was his faithful assistant. It was imperative to develop our industries not only in the interest of the people, but also of the

State. A modern body politic cannot be great without a well-developed national industry. As Minister of Finances, I was also in charge of our commerce and industry. As such, I increased our industry threefold. This again is held against me. Fools! It is said that I took artificial measures to develop our industry. What a silly phrase! How else can one develop an industry? Whatever men do is to a certain extent artificial. The measures taken by me were much less artificial and drastic than those practised by many foreign countries. The only thing I did was to support the protectionist tariff introduced by Vyshnegradski under Alexander III. This I did in the face of a strenuous opposition on the part of the large landowners. All my efforts to facilitate the formation of joint-stock companies were systematically thwarted by the Ministry of the Interior and Plehve particularly. I have also been blamed for having issued industrial loans from the Imperial Bank. In reality, these loans amounted only to some 50,000,000 rubles. Besides, a considerable portion of this sum was lent, without my approval, to members of the court camarilla or their friends. I must say that but few people in Russia grasped the full significance of my work of building up the nation's industries.

RUSSIAN SOCIETY IN 1900: AN EYEWITNESS'S OBSERVATIONS

From NORMAN, "Russia of Today" (1900) [1]

Unless you realize that in Russia the Tsar is everything, literally everything; that not only is his will law but that it is also heaven-inspired right, that his land and his subjects are his to dispose of wholly as he will—I am speaking, of course, of the masses of the people—you

[1] *Scribner's Magazine*, XXVIII, October, 1900, 403-06. By permission of Charles Scribner's Sons.

will not grasp the fundamental condition of Russia today. . . . Indeed this is the most striking aspect of Russian society: at the top, the imperial family, surrounded by the nobility; at the bottom, the "common people." The development of industrialism, with its rapidly made fortunes, is changing this condition so far as the large towns are concerned, but it still remains true of the country as a whole.

What impressions of the Russian people does one gather from several months' travel through the whole empire—a journey of fifteen thousand miles? The first thing that attracts your attention in the two capitals themselves is a curious detail. All the shops which offer wares to the people do so, not in words, as with us, but with pictures. The provision-merchant's shop is a veritable picture-gallery of sausages and cheeses and bread and butter and hams and everything eatable. The ironmonger hangs out illustrations of knives and forks and scissors and chisels and foot-rules and the like. The tailor shows paintings of coats and trousers. Why is this? Simply because a majority of potential customers cannot read! . . . The Russian people, then, is illiterate, in the strict sense of the word. And millions upon millions of people who read no books and no newspapers, write and receive no letters, must inevitably be the helpless victims of superstition and prejudice. This is, of course, the fact. Russia is the home of more religious manias and crazy notions than could be enumerated. Not a month passes without some almost incredible instance of religious fanaticism. . . .

Poverty and illiteracy naturally go hand in hand. In no other great country of the world is poverty—universal, monotonous, hopeless poverty—the national characteristic of the people. The only parallels I know are in some of the Balkan States. At almost any point in rural Russia you might think yourself in the interior of Servia or Bulgaria, except that even in these countries the poor peasant is not quite so poor, and his bearing is more independent. Long train journeys in Russia are depressing experiences. Once past the limits of the towns, every village is the same—a wide street or two—not really streets, of course, but deep dust or mud, according to the season, and from a score to a couple of hundred gray, one-story wooden houses, usually dilapidated, and a church. Russia is still first and foremost an agricultural country; she produces (including Poland) two thousand million bushels of grain, and grain products form more than half her total exports to Europe; therefore at the right season there are great stretches of waving fields, and later the huge mounds of straw, whence the grain has been threshed. But it is in her most fertile districts that the worst famines occur, for famine—a little one every year, a big one every seven years—has now become a regular occurrence. And the country as one flies across it, leaves the general impression of indigence. In sharp and painful contrast with western Europe, there are virtually no fat stock-yards, no cozy farm-house, no château of the local landowner, no squire's hall—pitiful assemblages of men and women just on the hither side of the starvation line. . . .

To this general characterization of the Russian populace I must add one important qualification. The extraordinary—the almost incredible—growth of industrialism in Russia is bringing about a great and vital change in the masses of the people. The peasant who works with hundreds or thousands of his fellows in a mill or factory soon becomes a different being from the peasant toiling on his bit of village land and migrating hither and thither, in seasons of agricultural work, for employment. This, to my thinking, is

by far the most significant and important aspect of Russia of today, and I shall have much to say about it hereafter. In this place I have only endeavored to show the two great characteristics of the Russian social fabric, without an appreciation of which no Russian question or prospect can be intelligently judged—autocracy, the semi-divine, unquestioned, unbounded authority at the top; its counterpart, illiterate, superstitious, brute-like dependence, automatonism, at the bottom.

4. Nicholas II and the Revolution of 1905

COUNT WITTE'S CHARACTERIZATION OF NICHOLAS II

Early in his reign, Nicholas II (1894-1917), the last of the Romanovs, stated: "Let it be known by all that I shall devote my whole power to the best service of the people, but that the principle of autocracy will be maintained by me as firmly and unswervingly as by my lamented father." Nicholas was a weak, ignorant, indecisive, petty, and sentimental man. Count Witte, who had long experience of the Czar's weaknesses, wrote of him as follows.

From COUNT WITTE, *Memoirs* [1]

There is an optimistic strain in His Majesty's character, and he is afflicted with a strange near-sightedness, as far as time and space are concerned. He experiences fear only when the storm is actually upon him, but as soon as the immediate danger is over his fear vanishes. Thus, even after the granting of the constitution, Nicholas considered himself an autocratic sovereign

[1] From: *The Memoirs of Count Witte*, 182-83. 191-92.

in a sense which might be formulated as follows: "I do what I wish, and what I wish is good; if people do not see it, it is because they are plain mortals, while I am God's anointed."

He is incapable of playing fair and he always seeks underhanded means and underground ways. He has a veritable passion for secret notes and methods. Even at the most critical moments, such as the period which immediately preceded the granting of the Constitution, His Majesty did not relinquish his "Byzantine" habits. But inasmuch as he does not possess the talents of either Metternich or Talleyrand, he usually lands in a mud puddle or in a pool of blood. . . .

When, in the course of my official conferences with His Majesty, I referred to public opinion, His Majesty oftentimes snapped angrily: "What have I got to do with public opinion?" He considered, and justly, that public opinion was the opinion of the "intellectuals." As for the Emperor's view of the intellectuals, I recall a story related to me by the Prince Mirski. When Nicholas was visiting the Western provinces, the Prince, in his capacity of local Governor-General, accompanied His Majesty and dined with him. Once at table someone referred to the *intelligentsia* (intellectuals). The Emperor caught the word and exclaimed: "How I detest that word! I wish I could order the Academy to strike it off the Russian dictionary."

The Emperor was made to believe that the people as a whole, exclusive of the intellectuals, stood firmly with him. That was also Her Majesty's conviction. On one occasion, discussing the political situation with the Empress, Prince Mirski remarked that in Russia everybody was against the existing regime. To this the Empress sharply replied that only the intellectuals were against the Czar and his govern-

ment, but that the people always had been and always would be for the Czar. "Yes," retorted the Prince, "that is true enough, but it is the intellectual class that makes history everywhere while the masses are merely an elemental power; today they massacre the revolutionary intellectuals, tomorrow they may loot the Czar's palaces."

The Emperor was surrounded by avowed Jew-haters, such as Trepov, Plehve, and the leaders of the Black Hundreds. As for his personal attitude toward the Jews I recall that whenever I drew his attention to the fact that the anti-Jewish riots could not be tolerated, he either was silent or remarked: "But it is they themselves, *i.e.,* the Jews (His Majesty always used the approbrious *zhidy,* instead of *yevrei*), that are to blame." The anti-Jewish current flowed not from below upward, but in the opposite direction.

BLOODY SUNDAY, JANUARY 22, 1905

Russia's reverses in the war with Japan in 1904-05 led to widespread discontent and industrial strikes. Revolution threatened repeatedly in the course of 1905. On January 22 (January 9 by the Russian calendar), Father Georgi Apollonovich Gapon, a priest whose activities are still something of a mystery, headed an unarmed procession of workers that marched toward the Winter Palace in St. Petersburg with a petition to Nicholas II demanding freedom of speech, press, assembly, and religion; representative, constitutional government; legalization of labor unions; free, public education; and other similar requests. The Czar did not receive them, but the Czar's troops met the workers with gunfire. Men, women, and children were murdered in the snowy streets. Count Witte's final sentence in the following selection adequately summarized the result.

From COUNT WITTE, *Memoirs* [1]

I shall begin my narrative of the revolutionary upheaval of 1905-1906 with my reminiscences relating to the events of January 9, 1905, a day which in the annals of the Russian revolution is known as Bloody Sunday.

A certain Sergey Zubatov, a notorious agent-provocateur, is responsible for the idea of combatting the revolution by applying the principle of "knock out one wedge with another." He inaugurated a system which aimed at fighting the revolution with its own weapons and tactics, and which might be described as police socialism. The revolutionists are winning over the workmen to their side by preaching the doctrine of the socialistic millennium to them, he argued—let us, therefore, imitate the methods and the language of the socialistic agitators, and we shall have the masses with us. And Zubatov proceeded to organize a veritable "labor movement," with trade-unions, workers' meetings, lecture clubs, etc., all under the auspices of the Secret Service. The city of Moscow, with its large industrial population, was Zubatov's headquarters, and his activities had the co-operation and unqualified approval of both Grand Duke Sergey Alexandrovich, Governor-General, and General Trepov, Governor of Moscow. Both the department of factory inspection and myself, in my official capacity, were strenuously opposed to Zubatov's scheme, but we could do nothing against the all-powerful Grand Duke. Sipyagin, Minister of the Interior, merely succeeded in restricting Zubatov's efforts to Moscow. When Sipyagin was assassinated (in 1902), his successor Plehve extended the

[1] *Ibid.*, 250-53.

experiment with police socialism to St. Petersburg. He began to organize there workmen's societies of a counter-revolutionary nature, on the model of the Moscow organizations, in order to keep the labouring masses under the influence of the department of police. The task of organization was entrusted to Father Gapon, who soon succeeded in gaining the entire confidence of the Governor of St. Petersburg. Then, of course, the inevitable happened. The preaching of the socialists and anarchists gradually demoralized the workmen, and they began instinctively to strive to carry into effect the extreme program of socialism. Not only was Gapon unable to stem this movement, but gradually he, too, became infected with the revolutionary spirit. A storm was brewing, while neither Prince Mirski nor I, in my capacity of President of the Committee of Ministers, nor the Government knew anything about the matter.

On January 8th, I was told by the Minister of Justice that in the evening there would be a conference at Prince Mirski's for the purpose of deciding what to do with the workmen who intended the next day to march to the Palace Square and present a petition to His Majesty. The Minister assured me that I would be invited to the conference because of my familiarity with the labour problem, but, as a matter of fact, owing to the opposition of the Minister of Finances, I was not invited to the conference. In the evening a deputation of public-spirited citizens came to see me. I received the committee and recognized among the delegates the academician Shakhmatov, the author Arsenyev, and also Maxim Gorki. The spokesman of the delegation begged me to see to it that the Emperor should appear before the workmen and receive their petition. Otherwise, they said, a great disaster was inevitable. I refused to do anything, for the reason that I had no knowledge whatever of the matter and that it was not within my province. The men left, indignant at the fact that at such a critical time I stood on formalities. As soon as they were gone I informed Prince Mirski over the telephone about the delegation. The next morning, from my balcony, I could see a large crowd moving along the Kamennoostrovski Prospect. There were among it many intellectuals, women, and children. Before ten minutes were over shots resounded in the direction of Troitzky Bridge. One bullet whizzed past me, another one killed the porter of the Alexander Lyceum. The next thing I saw was a number of wounded being carried away from the scene in cabs, and then a crowd running in disorder with crying women here and there. I learned afterwards that it was decided at the above mentioned conference not to allow the marchers to reach the Square, but apparently instructions were not issued in time to the military authorities. There was no one present to speak to the workmen and make an attempt to bring them to reason. I do not know whether the same thing happened everywhere, but on the Troitzky Bridge the troops fired rashly and without rhyme or reason. There were hundreds of casualties in killed and wounded, among them many innocent people. Gapon fled and the revolutionists triumphed: the workmen were completely alienated from the Czar and his Government.

THE OCTOBER MANIFESTO (1905)

After Bloody Sunday, the menace of Revolution became so great that the Russian Government was compelled to issue manifestoes with promises of reform. In March, and again in August, the Czar promised to set up an Imperial Duma "similar to Western parliaments," but defined as "an exclusively consultive institution." As this type of representative body satisfied no one, the famous October Manifesto followed.

From "The October Manifesto" (1905) [1]

The rioting and agitation in the capitals and in many localities of OUR Empire fills OUR heart with great and deep grief. The welfare of the Russian Emperor is bound up with the welfare of the people, and its sorrows are HIS sorrows. The turbulence which has broken out may confound the people and threaten the integrity and unity of OUR Empire.

The great vow of service by the Tsar obligates US to endeavor, with all OUR strength, wisdom, and power, to put an end as quickly as possible to the disturbance so dangerous to the Empire. In commanding the responsible authorities to take measures to stop disorders, lawlessness, and violence, and to protect peaceful citizens in the quiet performance of their duties, WE have found it necessary to unite the activities of the Supreme Government, so as to insure the successful carrying out of the general measures laid down by US for the peaceful life of the state.

We lay upon the Government the execution of OUR unchangeable will:

1. To grant to the population the inviolable right of free citizenship, based on the principles of the freedom of person, conscience, speech, assembly, and union.

2. Without postponing the intended elections for the State Duma and in so far as possible, in view of the short time that

[1] Frank Alfred Golder, ed., *Documents of Russian History, 1914-1917,* trans. by Emanuel Aronsberg, 1927, *The Century Historical Series,* Appendix, 627-28. By permission of D. Appleton-Century Co., Inc., New York.

remains before the assembling of that body, to include in the participation of the work of the Duma those classes of the population that have been until now entirely deprived of the right to vote, and to extend in the future, by the newly created legislative way, the principles of the general right of election.

3. To establish as an unbreakable rule that no law shall go into force without its confirmation by the State Duma and that the persons elected by the people shall have the opportunity for actual participation in supervising the legality of the acts of authorities appointed by us.

We call on all the true sons of Russia to remember their duties toward their country, to assist in combating these unheard-of disturbances, and to join us with all their might in reëstablishing quiet and peace in the country.

Given in Peterhof, on the seventeenth [thirtieth] day of October in the year of our Lord 1905, and the eleventh year of our reign.

Nicholas

[The promises contained in the above document were poorly fulfilled by the Czar. Severe repressive measures continued; a constitution issued (May 6, 1906) retained the autocracy of the Czar; and an electoral law issued arbitrarily by the government (June 16, 1907) restricted suffrage to the propertied classes. Thus the political situation rested until World War I, and the October Manifesto came to appear as another illustration of the Czar's bad faith.]

33 | THE BALKAN PROBLEM IN THE NINETEENTH CENTURY

1. Early Aspects of the Problem

The decadence of Turkish power and institutions, the rebellious discontent of the Christian subject peoples of the Turkish Empire, and the constant interference by rival European powers in Ottoman affairs were the principal ingredients of the Balkan problem in the nineteenth century. Administrative corruption contributed greatly to the decay of Turkish power and prestige. With regard to this evil an English observer wrote in the late eighteenth century as follows.

AN EYEWITNESS'S OBSERVATIONS ON TURKISH CORRUPTION

From PORTER, *The Turks* (1768) [1]

The monarch's despotism is not the greatest evil in Turkey: his subjects would perhaps bear that without much murmuring, or great distress. The radical destruction of all security lies in the iniquitous administration of their laws, which are an impending sword in the hand of cor-

[1] Sir James Porter, *Observations on the Religion, Law, Government, and Manners of the Turks*, 2 vols., London, 1768, II, 1-9.

ruption, ever ready to cut off their lives and properties. . . .

They tell us of some rare examples in Turkey of uncorrupt judges; I have heard of one, but I have known none.

There are in Constantinople several courts where causes are determined, and the plaintiff may choose in which to prefer his suit. The inferior are, the *Moulah* of Galata, and the *Stambole Effendi,* or judge of Constantinople; the higher, the two *Cadi-lesquiers,* or judges of Europe and Asia; and lastly, the Vizir's divan, which is the supreme court of judicature.

Mahomet has exempted his descendants from the authority of these jurisdictions; they are numerous throughout the empire, and are always judged by the heads of their tribe. . . .

The plaintiff has not only a considerable, but almost a certain advantage over the defendant; for as he chooses his judge, his first care is to secure him [that is, to bribe him].

All the judges have a *Naib,* or deputy, who is the real acting man, and generally guides and determines the master: to this man the first application is made, and the bribe is offered: if he finds the sum worth while, and accepts, you are for the most part secure of gaining your suit.

Sometimes, by bribing higher, the defendant may nonsuit his adversary; or he may at least, by quirk and quibble, be enabled to postpone the cause; perhaps to remove it to another court; and thus protracting it, if he is the richer, tire him out, until, at length, the plaintiff is obliged to drop his pretensions, just or unjust, and content himself with a trifling composition.

The means of spinning out a suit, and eluding a decision, are various; a defect in forms of procedure, absence or death of witnesses, denying the validity of seals, the hand-writing of others, or even their own; or, as all proof is determined by witnesses, and that these are found in abundance who will swear any thing for pay, when a cause is desperate, an immediate resource is at hand; for such witnesses may be brought to any point as will puzzle the clearest cause, and justify the law's delay. . . .

The judges have their deputies, who manage their retainers, and other dependents; fellows who constantly attend the courts to bring them custom: their business is to foment litigation, or to raise false suits, called *Avanias,* and attack those on any pretence who are rich and can pay. No man is secure from day to day, especially if he be a Christian or Jew. . . .

Many instances daily happen of demands on property, or complaints of injuries committed, which never had, and never could have, the least grounds of existence.

In general, let the cause be right or wrong, Christians or Jews have no chance against Turks but by dint of money; happy, if that can save them.

Neither Christians nor Jews are admitted as evidence against a Turk; but Christians or Jews can witness for or against each other.

THE ROLE OF EUROPEAN POWERS

European powers, fearful that one might obtain strategic, economic, or territorial advantage over another, were critically vigilant regarding every foreign interference in Turkey. At the opening of the nineteenth century, England and France, though at war with each other, both harbored grave suspicions of Russian motives in Turkey. Provisions of the Treaty of Kuchuk Kainarji, at the end of the Russo-Turkish War in 1774, furnish grounds for these suspicions. The treaty provided guarantees that the Sultan would "protect the Christian Religion in all its Churches," that "Ministers of the Imperial Court of Russia may make representations in favor of the Church to be erected at Constantinople," that Russians might visit the Christian holy places at Jerusalem and elsewhere in Turkish dominions, that Russia might erect a church at Galata to be "under the protection of the Russian Minister" —in short, the treaty gave Russia a splendid opportunity to pose as protector of Christian subjects in Turkey and to interfere in Turkish affairs on their behalf. Thus England (as later other Western powers), while lamenting the evils of Turkish rule, was disposed to support the tottering Moslem empire against Russian extension in the Near East. Sir Robert Murray Keith, veteran British diplomat at Vienna, made clear the British attitude near the opening of the century in one of his charming letters to his sisters. Sir Robert commented as follows.

From KEITH, *Correspondence* (1791) [1]

This country, I pronounce, is not worth living in, because, I will venture to affirm, that there is not one ounce of *genuine love* to be found in the whole extent of Bulgaria. Now, my dear friend, you know that from my cradle upwards, I am Theodosius the Second, "All for love, or the world well lost." I have looked every Turkish man whom I have met deep into the eye (their ladies I have taken in a different point of view), and I have not discovered a single ray of that sensibility which melts men's hearts (without impairing in the least their manly courage) into that species of tender gullibility which marries the minds as well as the bodies of the two sexes; and by the happy transfer

[1] Sir Robert Murray Keith, *Memoirs and Correspondence,* ed. by Mrs. Gillespie Smyth, 2 vols., London, 1849, II, 407-9.

of authority from the strong to the weak, renders every handsome wife, in our henpecked (and consequently blessed) Christendom, the despotic sovereign of her domestic domain. These Mussulmen are made of iron—cold, and rusty iron—they will not bend to happiness; and woman, sweet woman (that dear, queer, irresistible, and unriddle-able divinity), in their estimation, of little more value or animation than a leg of mutton! I have proved to you on former occasions, my dear Anne, that the Ottoman empire cannot stand long. You are *now* convinced that with such men and women in it, it does not signify a button if it should tumble to shivers tomorrow. I am quite of your mind, in a moral and physical (though not in a *political*) light, and my third observation shall prove why the rulers of cabinets must keep it *on its legs* as long as they can.

If Turkey could tumble *into the sea,* good and well. But, alas! the case is quite otherwise. Every bit that crumbles from its consistency falls into the clutches of a certain northern dame [Catherine II of Russia], who has lately fallen into an ugly habit of slaughtering the human race by twenty and thirty thousand at a time, and only for the pleasure of filling a page in a newspaper. I am bold to say, that if we allowed that lady to proceed westward, with the same humane propensities, and an unconquerable thirst of acquisition, she might at length become a troublesome neighbour to some of our Christian princes, who are weak enough to think extirpation but a poor amusement. *Ergo* —Selim the Third is to be supported on his sublime sofa; and it has been very properly determined that the said carnivorous lady shall be prevailed upon to make a few retrograde steps into her quondam boundaries. The Ottomans are to be left to *dwindle down* in their own dull way, whilst her ladyship will be at full liberty to cut and carve her native subjects in the manner best suited to her stout appetite.

2. Rising of the Subject Peoples

GREEK INDEPENDENCE

Under their impressive peasant leader, George Petrović, better known as Karageorge (Black George), the Serbs were the first of the Balkan peoples to stage a nationalist revolt against Turkish rule. The revolt, which began in 1804, seemed doomed to failure in 1813, when Karageorge was forced to flee. But it was revived in 1815 under a new leader, Miloš Obrenović, who speedily won undisputed control of Serbia and proclaimed himself "supreme prince" (1817), although the Sultan refused to recognize the title until 1830. Foreign interference plus internal dissension postponed international recognition of Serb independence until 1878. Meanwhile, the Greeks, having organized (1814) the "Hetairia Philike," a nationalist society resembling the Italian Carbonari, revolted in 1821 and, in 1822, declared their independence.

From the Greek Declaration of Independence (1822) [1]

THE NATIONAL ASSEMBLY TO THE GREEKS

The Greek nation, wearied by the dreadful weight of Ottoman oppression, and resolved to break its yoke, though at the price of the greatest sacrifices, proclaims today, before God and men, by the organ of its lawful representatives, met in a national assembly, its independence.

[1] Quoted in John L. Comstock, *History of the Greek Revolution Compiled from Official Documents,* New York, 1829, Appendix IV, 499-500.

. Descendants of a generous and enlightened nation, witnesses of the happiness which the sacred aegis of law secures to the civilized nations of Europe! Ye all know, that the measure of our sufferings was full. It was impossible for us any longer to bear, without being charged with cowardice and stupidity, the cruel scourge of Ottoman rule. Has not the Turk, during four çenturies, trampling under foot reason and justice, disposed of us as his caprice prompted? We flew to arms then, in order to avenge the injuries which an insolent tyrant had heaped on our country; injuries utterly unexampled, and which left far behind it all the various shapes of oppression which have ever desolated and dyed the earth with carnage.

Our warfare against the Turks, far from being the effect of a seditious and jacobinical movement, or the pretext of an ambitious faction, is a national war, undertaken for the sole purpose of reconquering our rights, and securing our existence and honour. . . . Strong in these principles, and wishing to advance as the equals of the Christians of Europe, in the paths of civilization, we combined into one great war all the partial and secret conflicts which we had long waged against the Ottoman empire. We swore to conquer, and to behold our country governed by just laws, or to disappear from the face of the earth. During ten months God has blessed our steps in this glorious but rugged road. . . .

As soon as circumstances allowed us to think of a plan of government, we saw the Greek continent of the east and west, the Peloponnesus, and the islands, successively proceed in their organization, and prepare the way for that general constitutional system which was necessary to direct the progress of our revolution. For this purpose, the deputies of the provinces and of the islands, being duly authorized, and having met in a national assembly, and after deliberately considering the state of the country, have decreed the basis and the provisional form of the government which is to preside over the future destinies of your country. This government, founded on justice, instituted by universal consent, is now the only legitimate and national government. The nations of Greece will therefore hasten to recognize it.

Two august bodies, the executive power and the senate, will be at the head of the administration, supported by the judicial power, which will discharge its duties quite independently of the former.

The assembly declares to the nation that, having completed its task, it this day dissolves itself. It is the duty of the nation to submit to the laws and the authorities which emanate from it. Grecians! but a little while since, ye said, "no more slavery!" and the power of the tyrant has vanished. But it is concord alone which can consolidate your liberty and independence. The assembly offers up its prayers, that the mighty arm of the Most High may raise the nation towards the sanctuary of his eternal wisdom. Thus discerning their true interests, the magistrates, by vigilant foresight, the people, by a sincere devotion, will succeed in founding the long-desired prosperity of our common country.

Epidaurus, the 15th of January, 1822, and the First Year of Independence.

FOREIGN INTERVENTION

Though the Greeks fought a long war, their independence was won only through the aid of foreign powers. At the outset, the reactionary policies of Metternich and Czar Alexander I led them to frown upon the Greek revolt. But Great Britain and France sought to intercede on the Greeks' behalf and in 1827, after Alexander's death, repre-

sentatives of Great Britain, France, and Russia signed a treaty at London to which the Greeks acceded immediately and to which, after foreign pressure for two years and a Russian declaration of war on Turkey in 1828, the Turks finally agreed in 1829. The next year, the powers agreed in conference to the independence of an abbreviated Greek state. The nature and purpose of the foreign intervention are asserted by the following treaty.

From The Treaty of London (1827) [1]

His Majesty the King of the United Kingdom of Great Britain and Ireland, His Majesty the King of France and Navarre, and His Majesty the Emperor of all the Russias, penetrated with the necessity of putting an end to the sanguinary struggle which, while it abandons the Greek Provinces and the Islands of the Archipelago to all the disorders of anarchy, daily causes fresh impediments to the commerce of the States of Europe, and gives opportunity for acts of Piracy which not only expose the subjects of the High Contracting Parties to grievous losses, but also render necessary measures which are burdensome for their observation and suppression;

His Majesty the King of the United Kingdom of Great Britain and Ireland, and His Majesty the King of France and Navarre, having, moreover, received from the Greeks an earnest invitation to interpose their mediation with the Ottoman Porte; and together with His Majesty the Emperor of all the Russias, being animated with the desire of putting a stop to the effusion of blood, and of preventing the evils of every kind which the continuance of such a state of things may produce;

[1] Quoted in Thomas Erskine Holland, ed., *The European Concert in the Eastern Question*, Oxford, 1885, 7-10.

They have resolved to combine their efforts, and to regulate the operation thereof by a formal Treaty, for the object of re-establishing peace between the contending parties, by means of an arrangement called for, no less by sentiments of humanity, than by interests for the tranquillity of Europe.

For these purposes they . . . have agreed upon the following articles.

Art. 1. The contracting Powers shall offer their mediation to the Ottoman Porte, with the view of effecting a reconciliation between it and the Greeks. . . .

Art. 2. The arrangement to be proposed to the Ottoman Porte shall rest upon the following bases:

The Greeks shall hold under the Sultan as under a Lord paramount; and, in consequence thereof, they shall pay to the Ottoman Empire an annual tribute, the amount of which shall be fixed, once for all, by common agreement. They shall be governed by authorities whom they shall choose and appoint themselves, but in the nomination of whom the Porte shall have a defined right. . . . [In 1830, this article was altered, with Turkish consent, to provide for full independence of Greece with a governing prince selected by the powers. The prince finally chosen, in 1832, was Otho, second son of the King of Bavaria, who became Otto I, King of Greece (1832-62). His successors were likewise named by foreign powers.]

Art. 5. The contracting Powers will not seek in these arrangements, any augmentation of territory, any exclusive influence, or any commercial advantage for their subjects, which those of every other nation may not equally obtain. . . .

ADDITIONAL ARTICLE

In case the Ottoman Porte should not, within the space of one month, accept the mediation which is to be proposed to it,

the High contracting parties agree upon the following measures:

1. It shall be declared to the Porte . . . the necessity of taking immediate measures for forming a connection with the Greeks. It is understood that this shall be effected by establishing commercial relations with the Greeks, and by sending to and receiving from them, for this purpose, consular agents, provided there shall exist in Greece authorities capable of supporting such relations.

2. If, within the said term of one month, the Porte does not accept the armistice proposed in the first article of the Patent Treaty, or if the Greeks refuse to carry it into execution, the High contracting Powers shall declare to either of the contending parties which may be disposed to continue hostilities, or to both of them, that the said High Powers intend to exert all the means which circumstances may suggest to their prudence, for the purpose of obtaining the immediate effects of the armistice . . . without, however, taking any part in the hostilities between the two contending parties.

3. Turkey and the Concert of Powers (1830-1878)

The Greek struggle for independence demonstrated the European powers' sympathy for the subject peoples of the Ottoman Empire and their determination to deal collectively with the Balkan problem. The Turkish Empire was placed, in effect, under the tutelage of Europe, and the powers denied the claim of any single state to settle the destinies of that empire without the concurrence of all. Against the latter policy Russia repeatedly took exception, although in 1844, when Czar Nicholas I visited England, he discussed the "Sick

Man of Europe" (as the Czar had called Turkey) with Sir Robert Peel, then Prime Minister of England, and with George Hamilton Gordon, Earl of Aberdeen, British Foreign Secretary, in terms of Russo-British co-operation. A report of the Czar's conversation ran as follows.

THE SICK MAN OF EUROPE AND THE CZAR

From BARON STOCKMAR, *Memoirs* (1844) [1]

The subject which appears to be occupying most of the Emperor's thoughts is the East, and this, very probably, is the main reason of his visit. Perhaps he wished himself to see, and to sound, and to compare what he may see and hear, with the reports of his diplomatic agents.

He said to Aberdeen: "Turkey is a dying man. We may endeavour to keep him alive, but we shall not succeed. He will, he must die. That will be a critical moment. I foresee that I shall have to put my armies in movement, and Austria must do the same. I fear nobody in the matter, but France. What will she require: I fear much: in Africa, in the Mediterranean, in the East itself. Do you remember the expedition to Ancona? Why should she not undertake similar ones to Candia or Smyrna? In such a case, must not England be on the spot with the whole of her maritime forces? Thus a Russian army, an Austrian army, a great English fleet, all congregated together in those parts. So many powder barrels close to the fire, how shall one prevent the sparks from catching? . . ."

On the occasion of the Emperor's conversation with Sir Robert Peel the windows were open. The Emperor spoke so

[1] *Memoirs of Baron Stockmar,* ed. by Baron E. von Stockmar, trans. by G. A. M., 2 vols., London, 1873, II, 106-09.

loud that the persons outside could hear all that he said, and the Premier was obliged to ask His Majesty to withdraw to the end of the room. . . .

[In a subsequent conversation, Czar Nicholas was again concerned with the Balkan question. He spoke as follows:]

"Turkey," he said, "must fall to pieces. Nesselrode denies this, but *I* for my part am fully convinced of it. The Sultan is no genius, but he is at least a man. Let some misfortune happen to him, what then? A child with a Regency. I don't claim one inch of Turkish soil, but neither will I allow that any other shall have an inch of it."

The Premier replied, that England, in regard to the East, was in a similar position, except that, on one point, the policy of England was slightly modified, namely in regard to Egypt. Too powerful a Government there—a Government that might close the commercial road across Egypt against England, or refuse the transit of the English overland mails—could not be agreeable to England.

The Emperor went on: "We cannot now stipulate as to what shall be done with Turkey when she is dead. Such stipulations would only hasten her death. I shall therefore do all in my power to maintain the *status quo*. But nevertheless, we should keep the possible and eventual case of her collapse honestly and reasonably before our eyes. We ought to deliberate reasonably, and endeavour to come to a straightforward and honest understanding on the subject."

TURKEY'S ADMISSION INTO THE CONCERT OF EUROPE

In 1851, a dispute arose between France and Turkey over the privileges of Roman Catholic monks in the Holy

Places in Palestine. These places had fallen under the control of Greek Orthodox churchmen, supported by Russia. When the Sultan yielded to French demands, Czar Nicholas I, who despised the upstart French Emperor Napoleon III, at first approached England with a view toward Russo-English partition of Turkey, but soon altered his course to demand of Turkey a Russian protectorate over Orthodox churches in the Ottoman Empire. In rejecting the Russian demands, the Sultan was supported by Britain and France. Russian troops occupied the Danubian principalities of Turkey, and by the fall of 1853 the Crimean War was on, with Turkey, France, England, and later Sardinia [see page 579] allied against Russia. In about two years the Allies won and dictated peace at the Paris Conference of 1856. Turkey was admitted to the European Concert of Powers with the understanding that the Sultan would institute reforms in the Turkish administration. The principal articles of the Treaty of Paris ran as follows.

From The Treaty of Paris (1856) [1]

[Articles I and II re-established "Peace and Friendship" between the Allies and Russia and provided for reciprocal evacuation of "the Territories conquered or occupied by their armies."]

Art. VII. Her Majesty the Queen of the United Kingdom of Great Britain and Ireland, His Majesty the Emperor of Austria, His Majesty the Emperor of the French, His Majesty the King of Prussia, His Majesty the Emperor of All the Russias, and His Majesty the King of Sardinia, declare the Sublime Porte admitted to participate in the advantages of the Public Law and System (Concert) of Europe. Their Majesties engage, each on his part, to respect the Independence and the Territorial Integrity of the Ottoman Empire; Guarantee in common the strict observance of that engagement; and will, in consequence, consider any act tending to its violation as a question of general interest.

Art. VIII. If there should arise between the Sublime Porte and one or more of the other Signing Powers, any misunderstanding which might endanger the maintenance of their relations, the Sublime Porte, and each of such Powers, before having recourse to the use of force, shall afford the other Contracting Parties the opportunity of preventing such an extremity by means of their Mediation.

Art. IX. His Imperial Majesty the Sultan having, in his constant solicitude for the welfare of his subjects, issued a Firman, which, while ameliorating their condition without distinction of Religion or of Race, records his generous intentions towards the Christian population of His Empire, and wishing to give a further proof of his sentiments in that respect, has resolved to communicate to the Contracting Parties the said Firman, emanating spontaneously from his Sovereign will. . . .

Art. X. The Convention of 13th of July, 1841, which maintains the ancient rule of the Ottoman Empire relative to the Closing of the Straits of the Bosphorus and of Dardanelles, has been revised by common consent. . . .

Art. XI. The Black Sea is Neutralised; its Waters and its Ports, thrown open to the Mercantile Marine of every Nation, are formally and in perpetuity interdicted to the Flag of War, either of the Powers possessing its Coasts, or of any other Power. . . .

Art. XIII. The Black Sea being Neutralised according to the terms of Article

[1] Hertslet, ed., The Map of Europe by Treaty, II, 1253-68.

XI, the maintenance or establishment upon its Coast of Military-Maritime Arsenals becomes alike unnecessary and purposeless; in consequence, His Majesty the Emperor of All the Russias, and His Imperial Majesty the Sultan, engage not to establish or to maintain upon that Coast any Military-Maritime Arsenal. . . .

[Arts. XV and XVI similarly provide for the free navigation of the Danube River under the supervision of an international commission.]

Art. XXII. The Principalities of Wallachia and Moldavia shall continue to enjoy under the Suzerainty of the Porte, and under the Guarantee of the Contracting Powers, the Privileges and Immunities of which they are in possession. No exclusive Protection shall be exercised over them by any of the guaranteeing Powers. . . .

Art. XXVII. The Principality of Serbia shall continue to hold of the Sublime Porte, in conformity with the Imperial Hats [Charters] which fix and determine its rights and Immunities, placed henceforward under the Collective Guarantee of the Contracting Powers. In consequence, the said Principality shall preserve its Independence and National Administration, as well as full Liberty of Worship.

THE NULLITY OF TURKISH REFORMS

Few treaties have been so poorly kept on all sides as the Treaty of Paris of 1856. The Turkish reform edict (firman) mentioned in the treaty was essentially a dead letter, and subsequent gestures at reform proved equally empty, especially after the accession to power of Abdul Hamid in 1876. The fate of the Turkish constitution of 1876 was described by the British barrister-journalist Sir Edwin Pears.

From PEARS, *Forty Years in Constantinople* (1915) [1]

Abdul Hamid ascended the throne August 31, 1876. During the next nine months he was feeling his way to actual power. A project of a Constitution which was drawn up mainly by Midhat Pasha was submitted for his approval, and whether he liked it or not he had to consent to its promulgation. Probably that which influenced him to give it sanction was the serious political difficulty in which he found himself. His mind was always tricky. There had assembled, December, 1876, in Constantinople, the Conference of the Representatives of the Powers, already mentioned, and the Sultan well knew that a project of reforms was to be submitted which would lessen the Imperial Prerogative and diminish his reputation in the eyes of his subjects. The problem before him was how to defeat the plans of the European Delegates. Rumours of what he proposed to do were widespread at the time. Midhat, who was then Grand Vizier, probably saw a chance of obtaining the grant of a Constitution by playing up to the Sultan's desire to checkmate the Powers. Accordingly a theatrical *coup* was played.

The Conference met in the Admiralty Buildings on the Golden Horn. A few days after they had disclosed their plans, their sittings were interrupted by the booming of a hundred guns, fired from the Turkish ships in the Golden Horn and the Bosporus. Thereupon Sir Henry Elliot, the British Ambassador, proposed to the Delegates that they should discontinue their sittings because those guns

[1] Sir Edwin Pears, *Forty Years in Constantinople*, 1916, 56-58. By permission of D. Appleton-Century Co., Inc., New York.

meant that the Sultan had issued a Constitution, which granted more privileges to the whole of the Empire than those which they had proposed to grant only to Serbia, Bulgaria, and Montenegro, the disaffected provinces. Thereupon, after a little hesitation, General Ignatiev expressed his opinion that he and his colleagues were there, charged with a specific mission by their respective Governments, and had nothing to do with any proclamation of the Sultan. Lord Salisbury supported the same view, and the sittings of the Conference continued.

The most important article in Midhat's Constitution provided for a Chamber of Representatives from all parts of the empire. It was an honest, bold, and praiseworthy attempt to substitute a constitutional form of Government for absolutism. Its proclamation failed in its endeavour to put an end to the Conference, but it was welcomed by the more thoughtful of the subjects of the Sultan of all races. The Chamber met, and its deliberations filled friends of Turkey with hope that the new form of government would put an end to the great abuses in Turkey and give her a new chance of life. Many of the deputies were really able men desirous and hopeful of national progress. Of course there were no traditions of parliamentary government, and many of the speeches made provoked merriment, but the general tone was serious and businesslike. They attacked abuses and the Pashas who were or ought to have been responsible for them. Their earnestness and the keen sense of what the country needed were very striking.

The existence of abuse was largely a revelation to the deputies themselves. The member for Jerusalem or for Salonica, or other distant places, spoke as if he believed that the district from whence he came was exceptional in the rankness of corruption. The discussions showed us outsiders, as well as the members themselves, that the

Government from one end of the country to the other required the most radical reforms. The members became so serious that the Pashas became alarmed, and I remember writing to the *Daily News* that the Chamber would shortly get rid of the offending Pashas or the Pashas of the Chamber. Its President was a certain Ahmed Vefyk, who was a neighbour of mine, and whom I knew well. He had been Ambassador in France, a favourite of Napoleon III, and considered himself, as he was, very much superior in education and intelligence to the mass of the deputies. But as Speaker he was amusingly despotic. From the presidential chair he constantly stopped members, telling them that they knew nothing at all of what they were talking about. Dr. Washburn was present when a Saracli, a white-turbaned Mollah who was prosing along in somewhat dismal fashion, was suddenly brought up by a stentorian shout from the Speaker of, "Shut up, you donkey!" (*Sus eshek!*)

Nevertheless, in spite of many shortcomings and of ignorance of parliamentary usage, the attempt at legislation was an honest one. It was brought abruptly to an end by Abdul Hamid, who gave us, perhaps for the first time, a sample of how he wished to govern. A debate had taken place one day, in which certain charges were made against two Ministers whom the Chamber asked to be brought before it to give explanations. Next morning we learnt that all the deputies had been packed off during the night to the places they represented. No more was heard of attempts to govern Turkey constitutionally until 1908.

OUTBREAK OF THE RUSSO-TURKISH WAR, 1877-78

In July, 1875, an insurrection against Turkish rule began in Bosnia and Herzegovina. The Serbs lent immediate support and Russia evinced great sympathy for the insurgents. In the following May (1876), a similar insurrection broke out in Bulgaria, where Turkish irregular troops suppressed the rebels with such severity and slaughter that the Christian world was horrified at the Turkish atrocities and misrule. In Russia, indignation ran so high that, regardless of the efforts of other powers to maintain peace, the Czar finally ordered his troops to cross the Turkish frontier by the following manifesto.

From ALEXANDER II, Manifesto (April 24, 1877) [1]

We, Alexander II, by the Grace of God Emperor and Autocrat of all the Russians, &c., declare as follows: Our faithful and loving subjects know the lively interest which we have ever manifested towards the destinies of the Christian peoples oppressed in Turkey. Our desire to ameliorate and to guarantee their condition has been shared by the entire Russian nation, which is ever ready to undertake new sacrifices to alleviate the condition of Christians in near-by Balkan states.

The blood and the property of our faithful subjects have always been dear to us. Our entire reign attests our constant solicitude to preserve for Russia the benefits of peace. This solicitude has not prevented our interest in the sad events which have taken place in Herzegovina, Bosnia, and Bulgaria. We have striven to ameliorate the conditions of Christians in the Near East by peaceful negotiations and in concert with the Great European Powers, our allies and our friends. For two years we have made constant efforts to persuade the Porte to institute reforms to preserve the Christians of Bosnia, Herzegovina, and Bulgaria against the arbitrary acts of local authorities. The institution of these reforms was guaranteed, in absolute fashion, by solemn engagements between the Porte and all of Europe. Our efforts, backed by the diplomatic efforts of other powers in common, have sought only to accomplish this desired end. The Porte has remained immovable in its categorical refusal to grant all effective guaranties for the security of its Christian subjects, and in its rejection of the conclusions of the Conference of Constantinople. Desiring to attempt all possible means of reconciliation, in order to persuade the Porte, we have proposed that other states draw up a special protocol embracing the most essential conditions of the Conference of Constantinople, and invite the Turkish Government to join in an international agreement which will fix the extreme limits of our peaceful demands. But our expectation has not been realized. The Porte has not honored the unanimous view of Christian Europe, and has not bowed to the settlement of the Protocol.

Having exhausted our pacific efforts, we are obliged, by the obstinate pride of the Porte, to proceed to more decisive means. . . . By his refusal the Turk places us under the necessity of resorting to the force of arms. Profoundly convinced of the justice of our cause, and humbly depending upon the grace and assistance of the Almighty, we declare to our faithful subjects that the moment foreseen by us . . . has actually come. We have expressed the intention of proceeding independently towards that which we deem necessary and which the honor of Russia requires. Today, appealing for the blessings of God upon our valiant armies, we have given the order for them to cross the frontier of Turkey.

Given at Kischeneff, the 12/24 day of April, in the year of grace 1877, and of our reign the 23^d.

Alexander

[1] *British and Foreign State Papers 1876-1877*, LXVIII, 845-46 (translation).

4. The Congress of Berlin (1878)

In the war against Turkey, Russian troops won speedy and decisive success, forced their way to the outskirts of Constantinople, and dictated the "preliminary" Treaty of San Stefano (March 3, 1878). Among other provisions, such as the recognition of Serbian and Romanian independence and the payment of heavy indemnities by Turkey, this treaty provided for a large, independent Bulgarian state under Russian protection. But the European powers, particularly Great Britain, protested against the Russian action. The Marquis of Salisbury described the British objections as follows.

BRITISH OBJECTIONS TO THE TREATY OF SAN STEFANO

From a British *Foreign Office Circular* (April 1, 1878) [1]

I have received the Queen's commands . . . to explain . . . the course which Her Majesty's Government have thought it their duty to pursue in reference to the Preliminaries of Peace concluded between the Ottoman and Russian Governments, and to the European Congress which it has been proposed to hold for the examination of that Treaty.

On the 14th January, in view of the reports which had reached Her Majesty's Government as to the negotiations for peace which were about to be opened between the Russian Government and the Porte, and in order to avoid any possible misconception, Her Majesty's Government instructed Lord A. Loftus to state to Prince Gortchakow that, in the opinion of Her Majesty's Government, any Treaty concluded between the Government of Russia and the Porte affecting

[1] Hertslet, ed., *The Map of Europe by Treaty,* IV, 2698-2705.

the Treaties of 1856 and 1871 must be a European Treaty, and would not be valid without the assent of the Powers who were parties to those Treaties. . . .

On the 30th January Lord A. Loftus communicated this declaration to Prince Gortchakow, and his Highness replied that to effect an armistice certain Bases of Peace were necessary, but they were only to be considered as Preliminaries and not definitive as regarded Europe; and stated categorically that questions bearing on European interests would be concerted with European Powers, and that he had given Her Majesty's Government clear and positive assurances to this effect.

On the 4th February the Austrian Ambassador communicated a telegram inviting Her Majesty's Government to a Conference at Vienna, and Her Majesty's Government at once accepted the proposal. [The meeting place was changed to Berlin in early March.] . . .

How far the stipulations of the Treaty of San Stefano would commend themselves as expedient to the judgment of the European Powers, it is not at present possible to decide. But even if a considerable portion of them were such as were likely to be approved, the reservation of a right, at discretion, to refuse to accept a discussion of them in a Congress of the Powers would not on that account be the less open to the most serious objection. An inspection of the Treaty will sufficiently show that Her Majesty's Government could not, in a European Congress, accept any partial or fragmentary examination of its provisions. Every material stipulation which it contains involves a departure from the Treaty of 1856. . . .

The most important consequences to which the Treaty practically leads are those which result from its action as a whole upon the nations of South-Eastern Europe. By the Articles erecting the New Bulgaria, a strong Slav State will be created under the auspices and control of Russia, possessing important harbours upon the shores of the Black Sea and the Archipelago, and conferring upon that Power a preponderating influence over both political and commercial relations in those seas. It will be so constituted as to merge in the dominant Slav majority a considerable mass of population which is Greek in race and sympathy, and which views with alarm the prospect of absorption into a community alien to it not only in nationality but in political tendency and in religious allegiance. The provisions by which this new State is to be subjected to a ruler whom Russia will practically choose, its Administration framed by a Russian Commissary, and the first working of its institutions commenced under the control of a Russian army, sufficiently indicate the political system of which in future it is to form a part. . . .

By the other portions of the Treaty analogous results are arrived at upon other frontiers of the Ottoman Empire. The compulsory alienation of Bessarabia from Roumania, the extension of Bulgaria to the shores of the Black Sea, which are principally inhabited by Mussulmans and Greeks, and the acquisition of the important harbour of Batoum, will make the will of the Russian Government dominant over all the vicinity of the Black Sea. The acquisition of the strongholds of Armenia will place the population of that Province under the immediate influence of the Power which holds them; while the extensive European trade which now passes from Trebizond to Persia will, in consequence of the cessions in Kurdistan, be liable to be arrested at the pleasure of the Russian Government by the prohibitory barriers of their commercial system. . . .

Objections may be urged individually against these various stipulations . . . but their separate and individual operation, whether defensible or not, is not that which should engage the most earnest attention of the Signatory Powers. Their combined effect . . . is to depress, almost to the point of entire subjection, the political independence of the Government of Constantinople. The formal jurisdiction of that Government extends over geographical positions which must, under all circumstances, be of the deepest interest to Great Britain. It is in the power of the Ottoman Government to close or to open the Straits which form the natural highway of nations between the Aegean Sea and the Euxine. Its dominion is recognized at the head of the Persian Gulf, on the shores of the Levant, and in the immediate neighbourhood of the Suez Canal. It cannot be otherwise than a matter of extreme solicitude to this country that the Government to which this jurisdiction belongs should be so closely pressed by the political outposts of a greatly superior Power that its independent action, and even existence, is almost impossible.

THE TREATY OF BERLIN (JULY 13, 1878)

At the Congress of Berlin, over which Bismarck presided, Russia was obliged to concede much that she had won at San Stefano, including the independence and large size of her proposed "Big Bulgaria." But while Russian aims were frustrated, Turkey, too, lost several groups of her Balkan subjects, whose status as independent states was recognized, and the powers took pains to urge reforms upon the Sultan's government once more. The chief provisions of the Treaty of Berlin follow.

From The Treaty of Berlin (1878) [1]

Art. I. Bulgaria is constituted an autonomous and tributary Principality under

[1] *Ibid.*, IV, 2766-97.

the suzerainty of His Imperial Majesty the Sultan; it will have a Christian Government and a national militia. . . . [Its boundaries are defined in Art. II.]

Art. III. The Prince of Bulgaria shall be freely elected by the population and confirmed by the Sublime Porte, with the assent of the Powers. No member of the Reigning Dynasties of the Great European Powers may be elected Prince of Bulgaria. . . .

Art. IV. An Assembly of Notables of Bulgaria, convoked at Tirnovo, shall, before the election of the Prince, draw up the Organic Law of the Principality. In the districts where Bulgarians are intermixed with Turkish, Roumanian, Greek, or other populations, the rights and interests of these populations shall be taken into consideration as regards the elections and the drawing up of the Organic Law. . . . [Subsequent articles provide for freedom of religious worship, commercial equality of foreign powers, etc.]

Art. XIII. A province is formed south of the Balkans which will take the name of "Eastern Roumelia," and will remain under the direct political and military authority of His Imperial Majesty the Sultan, under conditions of administrative autonomy. It shall have a Christian Governor-General. . . . [Subsequent articles define boundaries, details of government, religious liberty, and the general oversight of the powers.]

Art. XXV. The Provinces of Bosnia and Herzegovina shall be occupied and administered by Austria-Hungary. The Government of Austria-Hungary, not desiring to undertake the administration of the Sandjak of Novi-Bazar, which extends between Serbia and Montenegro in a south-easterly direction to the other side of Mitrviotza, the Ottoman Administration will continue to exercise its functions there. Nevertheless, in order to assure the maintenance of the new political state of affairs, as well as freedom and security of communications, Austria-Hungary reserves the right of keeping garrisons and having military and commercial roads in the whole of this part of the ancient Vilayet of Bosnia. . . .

Art. XXVI. The independence of Montenegro is recognized by the Sublime Porte and by all those of the High Contracting Parties who had not hitherto admitted it. . . . [Boundaries, religious freedom, and so on, are stipulated in subsequent articles.]

Art. XXXIV. The High Contracting Parties recognize the independence of the Principality of Serbia, subject to the conditions set forth in the following Article [which sets up religious freedom, civil equality, boundaries, and the like]. . . .

Art. XLIII. The High Contracting Parties recognize the independence of Roumania, subject to the conditions set forth in the two following Articles [which establish conditions similar to those for Serbia]. . . .

Art. LII. In order to increase the guarantees which assure the freedom of navigation on the Danube which is recognized as of European interest, the High Contracting Parties determine that all the fortresses and fortifications existing on the course of the river from the Iron Gates to its mouths shall be razed, and no new ones erected. No vessel of war shall navigate the Danube below the Iron Gates with the exception of vessels of light tonnage in the service of the river police and Customs. . . .

Art. LIII. The European Commission of the Danube on which Roumania shall be represented is maintained in its functions, and shall exercise them henceforth as far as Galatz in complete independence of the territorial authorities. . . .

Art. LXI. The Sublime Porte undertakes to carry out, without further delay, the improvements and reforms demanded by local requirements in the provinces inhabited by the Armenians, and to guarantee their security against the Circassians and Kurds.

It will periodically make known the steps taken to this effect to the Powers, who will superintend their application.

Art. LXII. The Sublime Porte having expressed the intention to maintain the principle of religious liberty, and give it the widest scope, the Contracting Parties take note of this spontaneous declaration.

In no part of the Ottoman Empire shall difference of religion be alleged against any person as a ground for exclusion or incapacity as regards the discharge of civil and political rights, admission to the public employments, functions and honours, or the exercise of the various professions and industries.

5. The Turks and Reform

The repeated attempts of the European powers to force governmental reforms upon Turkey met with ill-disguised and constant resistance. The reason is made clear by Sir Charles Eliot, an Englishman who spent many years in the Near East and who came to know the Turks intimately.

THE TURKS' DISTRUST OF CHRISTIAN REFORM EFFORTS

From ELIOT, Turkey in Europe (1900) [1]

It may be that this [the Turks'] horror of reforms springs from a correct instinct that any change in the present order of things would endanger the rule of Moslims over Christians. If we assume that it is desirable to continue the Ottoman Gov-

[1] Sir Charles Eliot, Turkey in Europe, new ed., 1908, 153-54. By permission of Longmans, Green & Co., Inc., London.

ernment—an assumption which no one but a Turk need make—we must admit that this implies the superiority of Turks to Christians. It does not mean the equality of Turks and Christians; that is a thing which is talked of but never realised, for the very good reason that it is impossible. As long as force rules, the Turks are superior to the Christians. They are stronger, braver, and more united. But when force does not rule, when progress, commerce, finance, and law give the mixed population of the Empire a chance of redistributing themselves according to their wits, the Turk and the Christian are not equal; the Christian is superior. He acquires the money and land of the Turk, and proves in a law-court that he is right in so doing. One may criticise the Turkish character, but given their idiosyncrasies, one must admit that they derive little profit from such blessings of civilisation as are introduced into the country. Foreign syndicates profit most, and after them native Christians, but not the Osmanli, except in so far as he can make them disgorge their gains. Those who have associated with Turks will have discovered a fact which it is difficult for the rest of the world to believe, namely, that they are afraid of Christians. The periodical outbreaks formerly called "atrocities," but now described as "events" (a beautiful euphemism which the Sublime Porte has imposed on the diplomatic language of Europe), appear to us as a cowardly slaughter of unarmed men and helpless women and children. But no doubt the average Turk regards these same events as necessary measures of self-defence. He is always ready to believe that the Armenians and Bulgarians are importing arms or planning to burn down Constantinople, and says with sincere alarm that no Moslim's life is safe. I have met many liberal Turks who talked freely of liberty and equality, but never one who did not approve of the Armenian massacres of 1895-6 and attempt to justify them. The converse of this is, that the Christians in Turkey do not feel any more sympathy for liberal or "Young Turks" than they do for old and bigoted ones; for young or old, radical or conservative, their complaints and hopes are confined to their own race and religion, and take no account of the majority of the population in their dominions.

The Turkish reformer and the Christian have nothing in common, and the mass of Turks mistrust the reformer. Even in such a matter as military reform, where there can be no doubt that improvements are in the interest of the Moslim, and the Moslim only, the Turk will not take the view which his friends think he obviously ought to take. Foreign military instructors have again and again presented recommendations, and again and again they have been rejected, sometimes openly, sometimes with a pretence of acceptance, but always quite firmly. The Turk has a dim perception that even in military matters he cannot understand and practise European methods. If he tries to do so, the control will pass out of his hands into those of people who are cleverer than himself. But though he may think them clever, he does not on that account feel any respect for them. He regards them as conjurors who can perform a variety of tricks, which may be, according to circumstances, useful, amusing, or dangerous; but for all Christendom he has a brutal, unreasoning contempt—the contempt of the sword for everything that can be cut, and today the stupid contempt of a blunt sword.

THE "YOUNG TURK" REVOLUTION 1908-1909

Although the Turks generally resisted reform movements imposed by foreign states, there gradually arose, beginning about 1890, a "Young Turk" reform movement. The impulse for this also originated outside Turkey, chiefly with refugees disaffected to Abdul Hamid's rule. They organized committees with headquarters at Paris and soon found it possible to coalesce with reform elements within Turkey, principally in the army. Sir Edwin Pears, who was a sympathetic and informed eye-witness to the events, wrote the following description of the Revolution of 1908.

From PEARS, *Forty Years in Constantinople* [1]

There was gradually growing up in the country, side by side with a disaffected population, a real Turkish party, which had arrived at the conclusion that nothing could be done for the country without a radical change of system. Such Turks saw the childishness of the so-called statesmanship of Abdul Hamid in playing off one race against another, and Abdul Hamid failed to recognise the growing importance of a revolutionary committee in Europe. This committee had already begun the organisation of revolution. One of its most daring emissaries was Dr. Nazim Bey. . . . He is a Moslem, and had obtained a French education as a medical man, and when he offered his services to the Committee in Paris they were readily accepted. If he could be induced to write his life it would be full of wonderful escapes and of daring episodes.

Disguised as a pedlar Dr. Nazim went to Smyrna, entered into communication with officers in the army, and fomented the already existing dissatisfaction with the Sultan. . . . The disaffected Turks already mentioned had formed a commit-

[1] Pears, *op. cit.*, 203-04, 218, 221-23, 228-29 233, 235-36. By permission of D. Appleton Century Co., Inc.

tee in Salonica [about 1905], and in order to get into communication with them Dr. Nazim disguised himself in the Greek brigand's fustanella, joined a band, landed at the Piraeus, crossed the frontier into Turkey and descended into Salonica. . . . He was welcomed by the Committee, many of whom had become members of an Italian lodge of freemasonry, and was once more sent on a confidential mission into Asia Minor. This was the commencement of the famous Committee of Union and Progress which was to revolutionise Turkey. . . .

I have already mentioned that the misgovernment in Turkey had led to the formation of committees, both in and out of Turkey, with the object of bringing about a change of government. Every foreign power interested in the good government of Turkey, but especially England, France, and Italy, was anxious in its own interest to effect reforms throughout the empire generally. The massacres in Armenia had disgusted not merely the whole of the Christian population of the empire, but thoughtful men amongst the Turks. . . .

There were two grievances in particular that made the Moslems, as distinct from the Christians, opposed to the Government. The first was palace espionage, the second the terrible restriction of travel applied both to Moslems and Christians. The average Moslem has the virtues of a dominant race. He is usually one who tells the truth and has the courage of his opinions. But it was commonly said that neither in the streets nor in their private houses were they free from the espionage of the Sultan's agents. . . .

In the country districts the misgovernment was most markedly seen in the want of protection to life and property. A mine-owner would not venture to work the mine without taking the *zaptiehs,* or police, of the neighbourhood into his pay. Many mines were in consequence shut down. Natives and foreigners alike who had acquired tracts of land let them go to rack and ruin rather than pay the sums which the police and local government tried to exact from them.

The condition of the army and navy aroused the indignation of the best men among the Moslems. Young officers who had passed through the military schools were sent off to regiments in the provinces and not allowed to return to the Bosporus. I remember a conversation with a captain amongst them whom I knew well. He declared that there was no *camaraderie* in the army, and that he himself did not know who were the other officers in his regiment. The navy, as I have already mentioned, had been allowed to become nearly worthless. Promotion in it was due to palace favouritism. . . .

It was from such causes that when we reached the year 1908 the disaffection towards the Sultan had become general. The chief committees in Paris and Salonica, after a long search for reforms, had arrived at the conclusion that the most practical remedy was the establishment of constitutional government. A fairly well-drawn Constitution, drafted by Midhat Pasha, had been accepted by Abdul Hamid in December, 1876, and promulgated, as already stated, as a counterstroke to the proposals of reforms made by Lord Salisbury, General Ignatief, and the other members of the European Conference. . . . During these long years of misgovernment the really workable instrument of Midhat had never been forgotten. To have openly advocated its re-establishment would, however, have meant the suppression of any newspaper in the Empire.

The Sultan's spies no doubt sent hundreds of reports on the situation to Yildiz. The Sultan became alarmed, and, ever eager to crush disaffection, sent a Commission to Salonica with instructions to stamp out the movement everywhere, but especially in the army. . . . The Commission was composed of some of the ablest adherents of the Sultan. The general belief existed that it would be followed by many executions. Its immediate effect, however, was very different from what Abdul Hamid anticipated. Two officers in the army took to the Resna Mountains and boldly declared themselves in opposition to Abdul Hamid; these two men . . . were Niazi Bey and Enver Bey, now [1915] Enver Pasha, the Minister of War. Niazi was the first man to raise the flag of revolt. This was on July 5, 1908. . . .

[The revolt spread rapidly among the troops, and the Sultan realized too late that the bulk of the Turkish army was associated with the insurrection.]

Then came a telegram to Yildiz which sounded the knell to Abdul's rule. It was sent either on July 21 or 22, 1908, and demanded the reëstablishment of the Constitution, or abdication, mentioning at the same time that the revolted troops had sworn not to lay down their arms until the Constitution was established. . . .

The Sultan recognised that he must bow to the storm. He sent for the two men whom public opinion generally recognised as the men of the highest reputation in the ministerial class. One was Kutchuk Saïd and the other Kiamil Pasha. . . . They were summoned to the palace because they had the reputation of being favourable to Constitutional Government. . . . On the evening of the 22nd the Sultan published an irade declaring that Parliament would be convoked.

All ranks and classes in Constantinople went delirious with joy. The proprietors of the Turkish newspapers met together and agreed to a resolution which they immediately carried into effect to turn out the censors from each of their offices. The decree only spoke of a Representative Chamber. The Turkish papers chose to interpret it as granting all the rights under Midhat's Constitution, a document which during thirty years had been idolised by Turkish reformers as a symbol of liberty. The popular cries became, *"Vive la Constitution!"* and *"Vive le Sultan!"* A new cry taken up at once followed, "Down with the spies!" a cry so dangerous that Abdul Hamid and the creatures around him who were opposed to the popular movement dared not interfere. . . . The Revolution was an unmistakably popular movement.

[The first flush of popular enthusiasm for the Revolution was short-lived, especially among Christian peoples. The Young Turks soon embarked upon a policy of "Turkey for the Turks," and the system of bribes (baksheesh) was largely retained, though diverted into new channels. An informed English scholar commented as follows on the ultimate outcome of the Young Turk Revolution.]

From SETON-WATSON, *The Balkans* (1917) [1]

The revolution of July, 1908, was followed nine months later by the counter-revolution of April, 1909. The army of Macedonia marched upon the capital. Abdul Hamid was deposed in favour of that amiable nonentity Mohammed V, and deported to a villa on the outskirts of Salonica. The Young Turks assumed complete control of affairs, and their nominee, Hilmi Pasha, became Grand Vizier. The reign of liberty and fraternisation had soon ended. It was followed by a real orgy of jingoism. Turkification was proclaimed as a definite policy. The abstract principle of equality before the law and the refusal

[1] Robert William Seton-Watson, *The Rise of Nationality in the Balkans,* 1917, 137, 139-40. By permission of Constable and Company, Ltd., London.

to recognise any distinctions of race or religion were soon interpreted in a reactionary sense. Henceforth no race save the Ottoman was to be recognised, and, of course, it was unpatriotic to distinguish between Ottoman and Turk, or to claim official recognition for any language save Turkish. Clause 68 of the Constitution makes ineligible for Parliament "those who claim to belong to a foreign nation." Applied as the Young Turks began to apply it, this clause would soon have enabled the authorities to prevent any Macedonian who dared to call himself a Bulgarian or a Greek from standing for Parliament. . . .

The internal policy of the Young Turks, then, was based upon Turkification and terrorism; and one of its many pillars was the "removal" of political opponents. The art of assassination was first practised upon Shemshi Bey, then upon various "Liberal" journalists and minor politicians in Constantinople, and finally upon such prominent personages as Nazim Pasha and Mahmud Shevket Pasha. The machinery of state was clogged more and more by personal jealousies and hates and by the old corrupt and incompetent régime, revived in a different and often cruder form. As time passed, it became more and more obvious that the sole hope of salvation lay in the army.

6. The Balkan Wars (1912-1913)

No doubt the advantage taken by Balkan and other foreign states of Turkey's internal troubles intensified the Young Turks' extreme nationalism. Close on the heels of the Turkish Revolution in 1908, Bulgaria proclaimed independence from Turkey (October 5, 1908), Austria annexed Bosnia and Herzegovina (October 6), and Crete proclaimed her union with Greece (October 7), whereby Eleutherios Venizelos entered Greek politics, becoming Premier in 1910. Not long after these challenges to Turkish power, in 1911, Italy and Turkey went to war as a consequence of the former's seizure of Tripoli. At this point, Bulgaria, Serbia, and Greece were induced by Venizelos, the new Greek leader, to form a Balkan League and declare war on Turkey. Two Balkan Wars followed in quick succession, the first between the Balkan allies and Turkey, and the second between the Balkan allies (Bulgaria vs. Serbia and Greece) over the spoils of the first war—an event which enabled Turkey and Romania to enter the war (vs. Bulgaria) to advantage. Sir Edwin Pears was in Turkey throughout the wars and discussed them as follows.

From PEARS, Forty Years in Constantinople [1]

Serbia and Bulgaria had suffered largely from the disorders in Macedonia, Bulgaria even worse than Serbia. Serbia desired an outlet to the Adriatic, and accordingly an agreement was signed between these two states by which they bound themselves to each other to divide Macedonia and to support each other against Turkey. The Treaty was dated on . . . March 13 [1912]. It provided that the northern part of Macedonia should be taken by Serbia, and the southern portion, including Ochrida and Monastir, by Bulgaria, the boundary line running in a northeasterly direction from Ochrida to Golem. Between Serbian and Bulgarian territory there was a district which is conveniently spoken of as the "contested zone." A secret annexe to the Treaty provided that if the contracting parties could not agree as to the division of the contested zone, the

[1] Pears, op. cit., 326-28, 333-34. By permission of D. Appleton-Century Co., Inc.

decision should be submitted to the arbitration of the Czar of Russia, who consented to act in that capacity. Shortly afterwards Greece claimed to join Bulgaria and Serbia, and her claim was admitted.

Without attempting to trace the war in detail, the important facts are the following: Montenegro declared war on Turkey on October 8, 1912; the armies of Serbia and Bulgaria were already being mobilised. Thereupon, on October 15, Italy and Turkey concluded peace. Three days later Serbia declared war "to secure the liberty and welfare of Macedonia." On October 22 her troops captured Prishtina from the Turks. Six days later, October 28, the Turks were defeated at Kumanova by the Serbians. After forty-eight hours of hard fighting, Uskub [Skoplje], the ancient capital of Serbia, fell to them, and another detachment reached the Adriatic at Durazzo and Alessio.

Meantime the Bulgarians met with even greater success in Thrace. The famous struggles at Kirk Kilissé and the neighbourhood on October 22 and 23 were a surprise to Europe. The Bulgarians completely routed and drove the Turks before them until they reached the Lines of Chatalja, a series of fortifications about twenty-five miles from Constantinople and extending from the Marmara to the Black Sea. There the Turks made a brave stand. It is now known that the Turkish officer commanding sent to Constantinople to state that he could not hold out against another tremendous attack such as the Bulgars had made. Meantime Russia had intervened and had informed Bulgaria that she did not wish the Bulgarians to press on to Constantinople. It is difficult to conjecture what was Russia's idea in making this communication to Bulgaria.

It is easy to be wise after the event, but one can recognise now that if, at the great check which Turkey received at Chatalja,

Bulgarian statesmen had insisted upon terms of peace being there and then signed, the Balkan war might have terminated. The intervention of Russia probably prevented such an event. We in Constantinople watched the progress of the struggle from day to day. We saw thousands of wounded being brought into San Stefano, an absolute breakdown in Turkish military and sanitary organisation, and the general belief was that the Bulgarians would soon enter the city triumphantly.

Unhappily grave dissensions had arisen among the Balkan States. When Austria let it be known that she was opposed to permitting Serbia to have access to the Adriatic she turned for compensation towards obtaining a larger share of Macedonia. It is asserted that a secret arrangement was made between the representatives of Greece and those of Serbia by which Bulgaria was to be excluded altogether from the portion of that province which had been assigned to her by the Treaty of March 13, 1912, while even the disputed section which was to have been left to the decision of the Czar was secretly divided between Serbia and Greece. I am writing without access to the full notes which I made on the subject, and therefore cannot be certain about my dates, but if such a treaty were made it was a gross act of treachery on the part of Serbia and Greece towards their ally.

One of the first incidents which gave rise to the conviction that difficulties had arisen between the Allies was a race between the Greeks and Bulgarians for the occupation of Salonica. The Greeks arrived a few hours before the Bulgarians, and it looked as if there were a possibility there and then of an armed conflict between the two armies for the possession of that city. The Turkish army had made what everyone regarded as a mere show of resistance; in other words had allowed the Greeks to take possession of the city, the suggestion even being made that this was done by arrangement with the Turkish Governor. This took place on November 8, 1912. The Greeks at once installed a Greek Government, but on the arrival of the Bulgarian army a joint occupation was arranged between them and the Greeks, the administration, however, being allowed to remain in Greek hands.

On November 4 Turkey appealed to the Powers for their mediation. The last attack on Chatalja was, I think, on November 17. On December 3 all the belligerents except Greece agreed upon an armistice, and a Conference met in London on December 16. . . . [By May 30, 1913, the Great Powers forced the allies to accept peace terms as set forth in the Treaty of London.]

On June 30 the second Balkanic war commenced. I can only give impressions with regard to it, because all the necessary facts for arriving at a decision are not yet known to me. The Premier of Bulgaria at the time was my friend, M. Gueschoff, whom I have known for thirty years as a man of good judgment, clear insight, and incapable of dishonourable action. He had met Mr. Passitch, the Premier of Serbia, in order to discuss and arrange terms of peace. The discussion progressed and appeared on the point of conclusion, when the military delegate suddenly introduced new conditions which Gueschoff immediately recognised as certain to lead to war between Bulgaria and Serbia. Gueschoff would have nothing to say to them and shortly afterwards resigned. The military representative persisted in his demands, with the result which Gueschoff had foreseen. Serbia and Greece had apparently prepared themselves for war against Bulgaria. To the dismay of all well-wishers to the Balkan States, it broke out with exceptional fury. Bulgaria was badly beaten, withdrew her troops from Adrianople, which after a long siege she had captured, and then Rumania struck in. Bulgaria was quite unable to resist the States thus allied against her, and signed the Treaty of Bucharest in August, 1913, the Rumanian army being then only about fifteen miles from Sofia.

The story is one of the most miserable in modern history. The future historian will be able to say who were mainly to blame for it. Popular opinion rightly or wrongly points to King Ferdinand as the instigator of the second war, but Bulgarians affirm that Serbia and Greece had come to the secret arrangement already mentioned which violated the original treaty, and made a conflict inevitable. The contested zone was not left to the division of the Czar but was divided between Serbia and Greece to the entire exclusion of Bulgaria. This of itself was an act of gross injustice. The defence of Serbia against a charge of acting unfairly would probably be the following: Part of the original understanding was that Serbia should obtain a road to the Adriatic, but at an early stage in the war Austria stepped in and declared that she would not permit this. The desire to have such a road was a natural and legitimate one on the part of Serbia. Austria blocked it as part of her policy of keeping her road clear down to Salonica. When, however, Serbia's desire to get to the Adriatic was thus blocked, she claimed that circumstances had so changed that she was not under any obligation to respect the stipulations in the Treaty of March 13, 1912.

The result of the war was that Bulgaria lost a strip of territory taken possession of by Rumania, which contains the important town of Silistria and a population of about a quarter of a million of Bulgarians; that she lost further the port of Cavalla on the

Aegean and received only the miserable open roadstead of Dédéagatch; that the southern portion of Macedonia, which it had been definitely agreed should belong to Bulgaria, was taken possession of by Greece, and the contested area was not left to the decision of the Czar, but was divided between the enemies of Bulgaria. It is easy to point out blunders and follies committed by the Bulgarians, but they are no justification for the injustice committed by Serbia and Greece.

Part Four

THE TWENTIETH CENTURY:
WARS AND RUMORS OF WARS, 1914-1945

The Twentieth Century: Wars and Rumors of Wars, 1914-1945

34 INTRODUCTION TO THE CURRENT AGE

THE HISTORIAN approaches the treatment of his own age with cautious hesitation. This is not an exhibition of coy modesty, but an honest recognition of a change in his function and of altered conditions in which he exercises it. The past is his province—a past in which the fires of militant opinion are cooled, in which insignificant detail has been vaporized in the crucible of Time, and in which the historical remains lie, like a spent meteor, available for quiet study and calm analysis. To reconstruct the salient features of the past and to wring from it meaningful interpretations for his own generation are his principal functions. The historian can explore the past with a minimum of interference from personal prejudice and passion, separate fact from opinion with little outside interference on the part of pressure groups and partisanship, find a perspective impossible to the living present, and operate without fetters, his only limitations being those inherent in the nature of the evidence from the past and the finite qualities of the human understanding.

But the events of his own age present a different set of problems and circumstances in the midst of which the historian finds himself shackled by the fetters of a living age. As a party to the opinions, pressures, and passions of the time, with his data like a mass of hot lava in a state of constant flux, neither cooled nor dispersed by Time, the historian finds himself hampered by the lack both of an adequate perspective and of a suitable objectivity. Even his task itself is altered. No longer does he interpret the past to the present; rather, he becomes a mere commentator on the events of his own generation. As his data is often uncertain and incomplete, his reconstruction is imperfect; as his objectivity is impaired, his analysis is highly opinionated; and these features, taken together, render his interpretation mere prophecy. All the dangers encountered by the historian in his treatment of the past are magnified a thousandfold as he enters upon the events of his own day.

It is in the spirit engendered by these beliefs that the following analysis of the current age is set forth as a tentative statement for the reader's consideration. In the final reckoning, perhaps, the reader can best judge for himself what are the threads upon which hang the events of the current age. In the writer's opinion, the principal events of European history since 1914—irretrievably and increasingly interrelated to world history as time passes—have been responses to one or another of the following impulses and circumstances: 1. The search for international security. 2. The fear (and the fact) of Communism. 3. The conditions born of world-wide economic depression. 4. The rise of totalitarian states. 5. The struggle between nationalistic aspirations and the reality of "One World." There follows immediately a brief elucidation of each of these five factors, and the selections and sources of Part Four of this book appear, in the main, to illustrate and to clarify them further.

The Search for International Security

Security, viewed nationally and unilaterally, is not identical with peace. But when it is viewed internationally and multilaterally it necessarily demands world peace on a permanent basis. In this latter aspect it coincides with a centuries-old ideal to which all nations have repeatedly given lip service. In a world organized on a national basis, however, with nationalist fervor becoming more and more militant, security tends to be viewed principally from the nationalist standpoint, and the ensuing conflict between national realities ("security for *us*," which can mean war) and international ideals ("security for *all*," which can mean only permanent peace) has, to date, proved little able to resolve itself or to result in the establishment of *effective* methods and machinery for the realization and maintenance of permanent peace on a world basis.

Many efforts have been made and found wanting. In early modern times, a loosely organized "European States System" founded upon the catch-as-catch-can "balance of power" method provided a measure of security, occasional long periods of uneasy peace, and the gradual accumulation of an uncodified body of international "law," that is to say, a body of rules governing international relations which, thanks to international agreements, court decisions, legislative acts, and customary practices came to possess the force of law, though wholly unsupported by any permanently established and effective world "police" or other body with sanctions, and wholly lacking any international judiciary for its interpretation. Unhappily, too, this body of international law included "laws of war," thereby giving legal recognition to war as an instrument of international policy as well as weakening the rules set up for the peaceable resolution of international disputes. The nineteenth century supplied, through the "Concert of Europe" set up during the Napoleonic Wars and regularized at the Congress of Vienna, a more highly organized system which, with all its defects, succeeded in *localizing* European wars for a century and in avoiding a *world* war from 1815 to 1914. The first World War (1914-1918) re-emphasized the need for improved methods of settling international problems without recourse to war, and the current age has been replete with suggestion and experiment in a frantic effort to realize international security and permanent world peace. "This is the central object of our meeting," said President Wilson at the Paris Peace Conference in 1919." Settlements may be temporary, but the actions of the nations in the interests of peace and justice must be permanent. We can set up permanent processes. We may not be able to set up permanent decisions." And the "permanent process" launched was the League of Nations designed, as Wilson had hoped, to establish a "reign of law, based upon the consent of the governed and sustained by the organized opinion of mankind." Accorded uneven and sometimes half-hearted support, and accompanied by a variety of "regional agreements" created to bolster up international security by means of the alliance system, this noble experiment in collective security floundered when, in the early 1930's, it was called upon to take action in the settlement of disputes involving determined major powers. First in the Sino-Japanese dispute over Manchurian (1931) and then in the Italo-Ethiopian affair (1935), the League showed its ineffectiveness. In proportion as its incapacities became clear, the nations hastened to secure themselves by alliances and agreements. The balance of power principle, never wholly supplanted by collective security, came back into play. The Rome-Berlin-Tokyo Axis was soon matched by alliances among the "democratic" powers, and the European World was again organized in a menacing system of alliances which soon plunged into World War II. Before the second World War of the century was over, the major powers resumed the search for international security. The result to date has been the organization of the United Nations, a new experiment in collective security "to save succeeding generations from the scourge of war," as its Charter affirms, and "to unite our strength to maintain international peace and security, and to ensure, by the acceptance of principles and the institution of methods, that armed force shall not be used, save in the common interest." Upon the success of this latest experiment international security and world peace depend. The peace efforts of the current age are on anxious trial in the United Nations.

The Fear of Communism

The latter nineteenth century witnessed a constant struggle on an ever-widening front between the forces of liberalism and the proponents of socialism. The early twentieth century saw the emergence of a new, highly militant group of "professional revolutionists" determined to destroy bourgeois capitalism root and branch by every means available. Though professing Marxian principles, Nicholas Lenin and his fellow conspirators went far beyond the earlier Marxists in their advocacy of violence (see below, p. 761). They sought to capitalize upon every dent in the armor of capitalism—to take advantage of the discontents arising out of mal-distribution, poverty, depression, war, and the like—to destroy capitalistic society and to create in its stead a "dictatorship of the proletariat" for the ultimate realization of a "classless society." Their *aims* differed little from the Marxian socialists; their *methods* outraged the world.

Prior to the Russian Revolutions in 1917, the "Bolsheviks," as Lenin and his fellow conspirators were called (during the Russian Revolutions they began to call themselves "Communists"), attracted little more attention than any other underground group. By their sudden accession to power in Russia in the fall of 1917 they shocked, embittered, and angered the European world. Their acceptance of the hard Peace of Brest-Litovsk early in 1918 shocked the Allies, not only because of Russian defection in war but also because of the actual aid seemingly granted to the erstwhile German foe. The violence of the Russian Revolution, the stubborn hard-headedness and determination of the revolutionary leaders, the barrage of propaganda—implemented by the secret activities of the Third International—aimed at the capitalist, "bourgeois" world, and the calls upon the workingmen of every nation to unite for the overthrow of their "exploiting capitalist overlords" combined further to alienate and to arouse the fears of the non-Russian world. The subsequent actions of the Russian revolutionary government in the early 1920's did nothing to allay the hatred and the fear, especially as the violently anti-clerical and pro-atheistical policies threw the religious world into violent opposition. As the paralysis of economic depression seized the capitalist countries in the late 1920's and early 1930's, a distrust of capitalist institutions arose which not only played into the hands of Communism but also threw the proponents of capitalism into greater torments of fear. "Two Worlds" seemed to be emerging, separated by a mutual lack of exact information regarding each other and by the mutual hatreds, fears, distrust, hypocrisy and lies born of ignorance. To be "bourgeois-minded" in Russia was to court ostracism, exile, the concentration camp, and sudden death; to be a Communist or "fellow-traveler" in the capitalist world was to court ostracism, exile, and imprisonment. The Russian "purges" were in some measure matched by the Communist "witch-hunts" of the capitalist states. During the interwar years the European world, both in its international relations and in its internal national politics, was constantly plagued by the fear of Communist activity, mistrust of Soviet policy, and the insecurity born of these conditions. World War II appears to have offered only a temporary surcease to this state of affairs.

Economic Depression

Periodic "panics" and eras of economic depression have repeatedly taken place in the modern world. After World War I the entire European scene seemed to have its economic nose out of joint. The losses of wealth and manpower occasioned by the war, the financial crises brought on by crushing war debts and the redistribution of bullion and of purchasing power, the hardships arising from indemnities and reparation demands, the recession of demand in some industries and the problems of industrial conversion to peacetime requirements in others—all these factors, after a short period of postwar prosperity, produced convulsions on a wide economic front. Agriculture went into a state of depression in the early twenties. Currency and financial problems assailed most European states, especially France, Italy, Germany, and Austria, throughout the twenties. After the New York stock market "crash" in 1929 and the failure of the Viennese Credit-Anstalt in 1931, depression fastened itself upon the entire world accompanied by business stagnation, unemployment, and all the suffering and social evils attendant upon poverty.

The conditions and circumstances produced by world-wide depression vitally affected national policies and politics. To some extent, the rise of Fascism and Nazism can be initially accounted for as a desperate attempt to deal with the problems of unemployment, trade recession, and depression conditions generally. The internal political control of many states changed hands, in some cases with bewildering rapidity, in similar attempts to solve depression-born problems. Policies, too, were altered. Great Britain reverted to a protectionist economy after about eighty years of free trade; political and economic "New Deals" were rampant; and in their frantic efforts to regain economic prosperity the nations embarked upon unprecedented policies of economic nationalism and socialistic experimentation. It seems doubtful whether any acceptable, permanent solutions were found. With lowering war clouds on every side in the late 1930's, most nations felt impelled to embark upon a war economy. By virtue of extraordinary controls and the artificial stimulation of preparations for war, together with the enormous economic demands of World War II, unemployment and the other economic evils of the Great Depression vanished, at least "for the duration." In the interwar years, however, the search for economic stability and a measure of prosperity equalled, if indeed it did not surpass, the search for international security.

The Rise of Totalitarian States

The "Totalitarian State" was a new creation of the twentieth century. At base, it differed from earlier and non-totalitarian states in the position accorded the individual in the state. In theory and, except in time of war, in fact, in the non-totalitarian, "democratic" state *the state existed for the individual,* and the individual was guaranteed individual rights, a wide measure of social freedom, economic freedom, political freedom, personal security, and private dignity. In theory and in fact, whether in peace or in war, in the totalitarian state *the individual existed for the state,* and the state prescribed individual duties and obligations but granted no individual rights, no social, economic, or political freedom, no personal security, no private dignity; and the state further regimented its citizens in a lock-stepped economy, political machine, and social system, all directed by a one-party oligarchy headed by a dictator who mystically revealed the "national aspirations" in terms of totalitarian policy. The totalitarian state was anti-democratic, anti-parliamentarian, anti-pacifistic, anti-liberal, and professedly capitalist and anti-socialistic, though in practice they often indulged in much "state socialism," that is, in the dictatorial ownership, operation, and regulation of business enterprise. It was jingoistically nationalistic, intolerant of all internationalism whether of a clerical or of a secular origin, and it sought to regiment the minds as well as the bodies and activities of its citizens.

Benito Mussolini and the Italian Fascisti were the earliest totalitarians to win control of a state, although much of the *methods* (though not of the professed ends) of totalitarianism were evident in Russian Communism and in the absolutist regimes of the nineteenth century, notably in the empire of Napoleon I and in the governments of the czars.

Until the late twenties, totalitarianism provoked little criticism. On the contrary, Mussolini's Italian regime brought forth the praises of democratic statesmen and citizens. Fascism, they thought, produced order, industrial peace, prosperity, and such bulwarks against socialism and Communism as to excite the interest of the capitalist world. But when Hitler's Nazi Germany came into being (1933), and the bellicose policies of the totalitarian states endangered both the Paris Peace Settlement and the peace of the world, the democratic peoples and their statesmen, after an initial period of confusion and vain appeasement, went into bitter opposition. The anti-democratic, anti-parliamentarian, and anti-pacifistic policies of the totalitarian nations—together with their absurd racial pretensions—were quickly recognized as a threat to the peace, security, and dignity of mankind. World War II, the post-war activities of the allied occupying forces in the defeated totalitarian countries, and the allied designs for peace were —and are—dedicated to the task of eradicating totalitarianism in the world.

One World

Technological advances, especially in the realms of transportation and communication, the re-grouping of world political and social forces, and the complicated interrelation of world problems have, within the present generation, produced a world unity which transcends the institutional and mental limitations imposed by purely nationalistic organization. Since the outbreak of World War I, the airplane has not only flown the Atlantic but also it has circumnavigated the earth in a time span of ever diminishing proportions. In the same era, the radio has internationalized almost instantaneous world communications. More and more the political and social forces of the world appear to become internationalized: the "Communist front" is international; the capitalist has become conscious of his stake in the preservation of capitalist institutions whether they be institutions of his own or of a foreign state; the "peace front" as represented by the United Nations is an organization of world-wide proportions. Moreover, the major problems of a single state have come to possess, to a degree hitherto unknown, world significance. The internal economic policies of the United States have become a matter of world concern; the internecine quarrels of China have become world problems; the future of India, the politics of France, the constitution of post-war Italy, the post-war economic plans of Russia, a miners' strike in the United States, the individual achievements of thousands of technologists in their private laboratories, the health of Premier Stalin—all have become matters anxiously weighed and considered by the responsible people of the entire world. To be sure, this has always been the case. But in previous generations the concern of responsible persons for such affairs has been cushioned by a time lag of weeks' and even months' duration. This time lag no longer exists. The impact of isolated events upon world opinion has become one of almost immediate reality. Gone are the cushion of the time lag and the perspective and the safety which it often supplied. World problems, East and West,

Old and New, have merged into such a complicated pattern of interrelated features and responses as to clothe every major social, economic, and political issue with *immediate* world significance. In short, the reality of "one world" is upon us, whether or not our institutions and thought processes are capable of coping with it.

35 | THE FIRST WORLD WAR (1914-1918)

1. Diplomatic Prelude: International Relations, 1871-1914

THE UNDERLYING CAUSES OF WORLD WAR I

Probably no survey of the tangled circumstances and international cross-purposes which led to World War I is more thorough and impartial than Professor Sidney Bradshaw Fay's *The Origins of the World War*. A mature scholar before the war began, and a close observer of it, Professor Fay waited until passions had cooled and until the archival records of the opposing powers were largely available before he ventured the following analysis of the underlying causes.

From FAY, *Origins of the World War* (1928) [1]

Obviously, no single volume can hope to deal thoroughly with all these complex and interrelated factors which constitute the underlying causes of the World War. They may be conveniently grouped under five heads: (a) the system of secret alli-

[1] Sidney Bradshaw Fay, *The Origins of the World War*, 2 vols., 1929, I, 33-34, 38-41, 43-48. By permission of The Macmillan Company, New York.

ances; (b) militarism; (c) nationalism; (d) economic imperialism; and (e) the newspaper press.

(a) *The System of Secret Alliances.* The greatest single underlying cause of the War was the system of secret alliances which developed after the Franco-Prussian War. It gradually divided Europe into two hostile groups of Powers who were increasingly suspicious of one another and who steadily built up greater and greater armies and navies. Though this system of alliances in one sense tended to preserve peace, inasmuch as the members within one group often held their friends or allies in restraint for fear of becoming involved in war themselves, the system also made it inevitable that if war did come, it would involve all the Great Powers of Europe. The members of each group felt bound to support each other, even in matters where they had no direct interest, because failure to give support would have weakened the solidarity of the group. Thus, Germany often felt bound to back up Austria-Hungary in her Balkan policies, because otherwise Germany feared to lose her only thoroughly dependable ally. Similarly, France had no direct political (only financial) interests in the Balkans, but felt bound to back up Russia, because otherwise the existence of the Dual Alliance would have been threatened, the balance of power destroyed, and the best guarantee of French safety from a German attack would have been lost. Likewise, the officials of the British Foreign Office became increasingly convinced that England must support France and Russia in order to preserve the solidarity of the Triple Entente [France, Great Britain, Russia] as a check to the Triple Alliance [Germany, Austria-Hungary, Italy]. . . .

(b) *Militarism.* A second underlying cause of the War, closely connected with the system of secret alliances, was militarism. The word is often used vaguely. But usually it includes at least two definite conceptions. First, the dangerous and burdensome mechanism of great standing armies and large navies, with the attendant evils of espionage, suspicion, fear, and hatred. Second, the existence of a powerful class of military and naval officers, headed by the General Staff, who tend to dominate, especially at a time of political crisis, over the civilian authorities. . . .

From the Franco-Prussian War onwards the military and naval armaments of all the Great Powers tended to grow larger and larger, and the financial burden became heavier and heavier. Armaments were alleged to be for defense and in the interests of peace, according to the fallacious maxim, *si vis pacem, para bellum* [if you want peace, prepare for war]. They were intended to produce a sense of security. That was the argument used in getting from legislatures the necessary grants of money. What they really did produce was universal suspicion, fear, and hatred between nations. If one country increased its army, built strategic railways, and constructed new battleships, its fearful neighbors were straightway frightened into doing likewise. So the mad competition in armaments went on in a vicious circle. . . .

Militarism implied also the existence of an influential body of military and naval officers, whose whole psychological outlook was naturally colored by the possibility, if not the "inevitability," of an early war. . . . In a political crisis, therefore, the military leaders were always quick to conclude that war was "inevitable," and exerted all their influence to persuade the ruling civilian authorities to consent to an order for general mobilization at the earliest possible moment, in order to gain the advantage of the offensive. But a general mobilization, according to prevailing military opinion, actually did make war inevitable. It was a process virtually impossible to halt when once begun. This was one of the greatest evils of militarism. It is always at a crisis, precisely when it is most difficult for diplomats to keep their heads clear and their hands free, that militarist leaders exert their influence to hasten decisions for war, or get the upper hand altogether. . . .

Generally speaking, it may be said that this aspect of militarism—the influence of the military upon the civilian authorities—was a serious matter in the three eastern monarchies of Germany, Austria, and Russia. It was much less in France, and virtually non-existent in England, where civilian ministers were ordinarily in charge of the army and navy. . . .

(c) *Nationalism.* Nationalism . . . must be accounted one of the major underlying causes of the War. In its chronic form of Pan-Germanism, Pan-Slavism and *revanche,* it nourished hatred between Germany and her two neighbors on the East and West. It worked in curious and devious ways. It had contributed happily to the unification of Germany and Italy. On the other hand, it had disrupted the Ottoman Empire and threatened to disrupt the Hapsburg Monarchy. In its virulent form, it had contributed for a century to a series of wars for national liberation and unity in the Balkans. . . .

(d) *Economic Imperialism.* Economic imperialism embraces a series of international rivalries which resulted in large part from the Industrial Revolution in England and its subsequent introduction into the other great countries of the world. It led to quantity production of goods which in turn involved the struggle for new markets and new sources of raw materials. It resulted in a great increase of population, part of which sought to emigrate to the still unoccupied regions of the world, thereby sharpening the colonial rivalry of the Great Powers. It brought about the accumulation of capital which sought investment abroad, thus leading to economic exploitation and political competition. In consequence of these and other factors, the Great Powers began to partition Africa among themselves, to secure' territory or exclusive spheres of influence in China, and to build railroads in Turkey and elsewhere. This struggle for markets, raw materials, and colonies became more acute during the last quarter of the nineteenth and the beginning of the twentieth century, owing to the fact that Germany and Italy entered the competition. . . .

Generally speaking, however, this economic imperialism is usually exaggerated as one of the underlying causes of the War. It is often said, for instance, that the industrial development of Germany, and the jealousy with which it was regarded by England, made a war between these two countries "inevitable" sooner or later. This, however, is an unsound view. It arises from the fact that economic rivalry tends to become exaggerated in the mind of the public, because it is a subject which touches the pockets of wide classes, and is more generally discussed and perhaps understood than other questions like secret treaties, militarism, or nationalism.

. . . But if one reads the diplomatic correspondence of the years before the War, one is struck by the relatively slight importance which is given to these economic rivalries which haunt so largely the mind of the average business man and newspaper editor. It is not so much questions of economic rivalry as those of prestige, boundaries, armies and navies, the Balance of Power, and possible shiftings in the system of alliances, which provoke reams of diplomatic correspondence and raise the temperature in Foreign Offices to the danger point.

(e) *The Newspaper Press.* Another underlying cause of the War was the poisoning of public opinion by the newspaper press in all of the great countries. This is a subject which is only beginning to receive the careful investigation which it deserves. Too often newspapers in all lands were inclined to inflame nationalistic feelings, misrepresent the situation in foreign countries, and suppress factors in favor of peace.

EXAMPLES OF SECRET DIPLOMACY: THE TRIPLE ALLIANCE

It is important to recall that the terms of the following treaties of alliance were imperfectly known before 1914 and that the incomplete information which leaked out tended to heighten fears and increase suspicions rather than to allay them. Indeed, the closely veiled secrecy maintained by the diplomats fostered fantastic rumors and ready credence about the treaty stipulations.

The Three Emperors' League (1872)

The Dreikaiserbund, or League of the Three Emperors, was Bismarck's first effort, after the Franco-Prussian War of 1870-71, to forestall France's desire for revenge. Bismarck sought to prevent the creation of a French alliance against Germany and to escape a war which he feared might become a contest between radicalism, as exemplified by the Third French Republic and the forces of international Socialism, and monarchical society as upheld by Germany, Austria, and Russia. Informal at first, the Three Emperors' League was strengthened in 1873 by a written agreement among the three Emperors that they would consult together on matters wherein their interests diverged, and by a secret defensive military agreement between Russia and Germany. Bismarck described its formation as follows.

From BISMARCK, *Reminiscences* (1898) [1]

The triple alliance which I originally sought to conclude after the peace of Frankfurt, and about which I had already sounded Vienna and St. Petersburg, from Meaux, in September 1870, was an alliance of the three Emperors with the further idea of bringing into it monarchical Italy. It was designed for the struggle which, as I feared, was before us; between the two European tendencies which Napoleon called Republican and Cossack, and which I, according to our present ideas, should designate on the one side as the system of order on a monarchical basis, and on the other as the social republic to the level of which the antimonarchical development is wont to sink, either slowly or by leaps and bounds, until the conditions thus created become intolerable, and the disappointed populace are ready for a violent return to monarchical institutions in a Caesarean form. I consider that the task of escaping from this *circulus vitiosus,* or if possible, of

sparing the present generation and their children an entrance into it, ought to be more closely incumbent on the strong existing monarchies, those monarchies which still have a vigorous life, than any rivalry over the fragments of nations which people the Balkan peninsula. If the monarchical governments have no understanding of the necessity for holding together in the interests of political and social order, but make themselves subservient to the chauvinistic impulses of their subjects, I fear that the international revolutionary and social struggles which will have to be fought out will be all the more dangerous, and take such a form that the victory on the part of monarchical order will be more difficult. Since 1871 I have sought for the most certain assurance against those struggles in the alliance of the three Emperors, and also in the effort to impart to the monarchical principle in Italy a firm support in that alliance. I was not without hope of a lasting success when the meeting of the three Emperors took place at Berlin in September 1872, and this was followed by the visits of my Emperor to St. Petersburg in May, of the King of Italy to Berlin in September, and of the German Emperor to Vienna in the October of the next year. The first clouding over of that hope was caused in 1875 by the provocations of Prince Gortchakoff, who spread the lie that we intended to fall upon France before she had recovered from her wounds.

The Austro-German Defensive Alliance

Russia's indignation after the Congress of Berlin in 1878 [see pages 690-693], and her resentment against Bismarck for his part in the proceedings, practically dissolved for the time being the Three Emperors' League. So Bismarck turned to Austria, with whom he concluded a defensive alliance on October 7, 1879—an alliance which,

[1] Quoted in *Bismarck, The Man and the Statesman,* II, 251-52. By permission of Harper & Brothers.

according to Professor Fay, "consolidated the Central Empires and became henceforth, until their collapse in November, 1918, the very foundation rock of German policy." The principal articles of the treaty follow.

From The Austro-German Treaty
(Oct. 7, 1879) [1]

Their Majesties the Emperor of Austria, King of Hungary, and the Emperor of Germany, while solemnly promising each other never to allow their purely defensive Agreement to develop an aggressive tendency in any direction, have determined to conclude an Alliance of peace and mutual defence. . . .

Article I. Should, contrary to their hope, and against the loyal desire of the two High Contracting Parties, one of the two Empires be attacked by Russia, the High Contracting Parties are bound to come to the assistance one of the other with the whole war strength of their Empires, and accordingly only to conclude peace together and upon mutual agreement.

Article II. Should one of the High Contracting Parties be attacked by another Power, the other . . . binds itself hereby, not only not to support the aggressor against its high Ally, but to observe at least a benevolent neutral attitude towards its fellow Contracting Party.

Should, however, the attacking Party in such a case be supported by Russia, either by active co-operation or by military measures which constitute a menace to the Party attacked, then the obligation stipulated in Article I of this Treaty, for reciprocal assistance with the whole fighting force, becomes equally operative. . . .

[1] This and the next selection are reprinted by permission of the publishers from A. F. Pribram, *The Secret Treaties of Austria-Hungary, 1879-1914;* English ed. by A. C. Coolidge, with trans. by D. P. Myers and J. G. D'Arcy Paul, 2 vols., 1920. Permission of Harvard University Press, Cambridge. This is I, 27, 29.

Article IV. This Treaty shall, in conformity with its peaceful character, and to avoid any misinterpretation, be left secret by the two High Contracting Parties, and only communicated to a third Power upon a joint understanding between the two Parties.

The Triple Alliance and the Italian Ministerial Declaration

Italy sought and obtained an alliance with Austria and Germany in 1882 (May 20). Thus originated the famous Triple Alliance. Drawn for five years, it was renewed at intervals—the last renewal was in 1912—and lasted until the outbreak of World War I. Though defensive in character at first, the suspicions engendered by its very existence lent it an aggressive effect. The principal articles of the original treaty in 1882 and the noteworthy Italian declaration at the time ran as follows.

From The Triple Alliance (1882) [2]

Article I. The High Contracting Parties mutually promise peace and friendship, and will enter into no alliance or engagement directed against any one of their States.

They engage to proceed to an exchange of ideas on political and economic questions of a general nature which may arise, and they further promise one another mutual support within the limits of their own interests.

Article II. In case Italy, without direct provocation on her part, should be attacked by France for any reason whatsoever, the two other Contracting Parties shall be bound to lend help and assistance with all their forces to the Party attacked.

This same obligation shall devolve upon Italy in case of any aggression without

[2] *Ibid.,* I, 65, 67, 69.

direct provocation by France against Germany.

Article III. If one, or two, of the High Contracting Parties, without direct provocation on their part, should chance to be attacked and to be engaged in a war with two or more Great Powers nonsignatory to the present Treaty, the *casus foederis* will arise simultaneously for all the High Contracting Parties.

Article IV. In case a Great Power nonsignatory to the present Treaty should threaten the security of the states of one of the High Contracting Parties, and the threatened Party should find itself forced on that account to make war against it, the two others bind themselves to observe towards their Ally a benevolent neutrality. Each of them reserves to itself, in this case, the right to take part in the war, if it should see fit, to make common cause with its Ally.

Article V. If the peace of any of the High Contracting Parties should chance to be threatened under the circumstances foreseen by the preceding Articles, the High Contracting Parties shall take counsel together in ample time as to the military measures to be taken with a view to eventual coöperation.

They engage henceforward, in all cases of common participation in a war, to conclude neither armistice, nor peace, nor treaty, except by common agreement among themselves.

Article VI. The High Contracting Parties mutually promise secrecy as to the contents and existence of the present Treaty.

Ministerial Declaration. The Royal Italian Government declares that the provisions of the secret Treaty concluded May 20, 1882, between Italy, Austria-Hungary, and Germany, cannot, as has been previously agreed, in any case be regarded as being directed against England.

[Besides the above reservation, Italy's adherence to the Triple Alliance became even more unreliable as a result of negotiations with France in the years 1900-02. In a diplomatic exchange during these years, the two governments mutually delimited their respective spheres in North Africa, agreed to maintain neutrality in case of attack by a third power upon either of the contracting parties, and declared that no divergence existed "as to their respective interests in the Mediterranean." Thus Italy violated the spirit, if not the letter, of the Triple Alliance. Poincaré summed up Italy's position accurately in 1912 when he wrote: "Neither the Triple Entente nor the Triple Alliance can count on the loyalty of Italy; the Italian Government will employ all its efforts to preserve the peace; and in case of war, it will begin by adopting a waiting attitude, and will finally join the camp toward which victory will incline."]

EXAMPLES OF SECRET DIPLOMACY: THE TRIPLE ENTENTE

The Franco-Russian Alliance (1890-92)

Despite fundamental differences—notably Russia's absolutism and France's republicanism—common fears and suspicions of Germany and the Triple Alliance led France and Russia to draw together in the 1890's. A number of ties cemented the agreement. Witte, as Finance Minister [see page 672], floated loans in Paris and thus gave Frenchmen a financial interest in Russia; France supplied Russia with armaments; diplomats exchanged views until, by 1891, the two governments agreed to "take counsel together upon every question" likely "to jeopardize the general peace," and to reach a mutual "understanding" in case either party was threatened by aggression. A military convention, rather than a formal alliance, was drawn up, and read as follows.

From the Franco-Russian Military Convention (August 18, 1892) [1]

France and Russia, animated by a common desire to preserve peace and having no other object than to meet the necessities of a defensive war, provoked by an attack of the forces of the Triple Alliance against either of them, have agreed upon the following provisions:

1. If France is attacked by Germany, or by Italy supported by Germany, Russia shall employ all her available forces to fight Germany. If Russia is attacked by Germany, or by Austria supported by Germany, France shall employ all her available forces to fight Germany.

2. In case the forces of the Triple Alliance, or of one of the Powers belonging to it, should be mobilized, France and Russia, at the first news of this event, and without any previous agreement, shall mobilize immediately and simultaneously their entire forces, and shall move them as close as possible to their frontiers.

3. The available forces to be employed against Germany shall be 1,300,000 men on the part of France, and 700,000 or 800,000 on the part of Russia. These forces shall be engaged so completely and so speedily that Germany will be forced to fight simultaneously in the East and in the West.

4. The General Staffs of the armies of the two countries shall at all times consult together to prepare for and to facilitate the execution of the above-mentioned measures. They shall communicate to each other, in time of peace, all information in their possession, or which shall come into their possession, as to the armies of the Triple Alliance. Ways and means of corresponding in time of war shall be studied and prepared in advance.

5. France and Russia shall not conclude peace separately.

6. The present convention shall have the same duration as the Triple Alliance.

7. All the clauses above enumerated shall be kept completely secret.

The Entente Cordiale Between England and France (1904)

Germany's aggressive growth led England and France, despite centuries of traditional hostility, to draw together early in the 1900's. Rapprochement was effected on the part of France by Théophile Delcassé, who became Minister of Foreign Affairs in 1898, and on the part of England by King Edward VII and the Marquis of Lansdowne, British Secretary of State for Foreign Affairs. Edward VII, having spent much of his prolonged youth in France, prepared the ground in 1903 when, upon his first visit to Paris as King of England, he publicly expressed his desire for friendship between the two countries. Diplomats immediately began to explore the possibilities of agreement. On April 8, 1904, was signed the following "Declaration between the United Kingdom and France Respecting Egypt and Morocco, Together with the Secret Articles Signed at the Same Time."

From the Franco-British "Declaration" (1904) [2]

Article 1. His Britannic Majesty's Government declare that they have no intention of altering the political status of Egypt.

[1] France, Ministère des affaires étrangères, *Documents diplomatiques· "L'Alliance Franco-Russe,"* Paris, Imprimerie Nationale, 1918, No. 71, 92 (translation).

[2] Great Britain, *Parliamentary Papers,* CIII, London, 1911, Cd. 5969 (Treaty Series, 1911, No. 24), 162-68.

The Government of the French Republic, for their part, declare that they will not obstruct the action of Great Britain in that country. . . .

It is agreed that the post of Director-General of Antiquities in Egypt shall continue, as in the past, to be entrusted to a French *savant*.

The French schools in Egypt shall continue to enjoy the same liberty as in the past.

Article 2. The Government of the French Republic declare that they have no intention of altering the political status of Morocco.

His Britannic Majesty's Government, for their part, recognise that it appertains to France, more particularly as a Power whose dominions are conterminous for a great distance with those of Morocco, to preserve order in that country, and to provide assistance for the purpose of all administrative, economic, financial, and military reforms which it may require.

They declare that they will not obstruct the action taken by France for this purpose, provided that such action shall leave intact the rights which Great Britain, in virtue of treaties, conventions, and usage, enjoys in Morocco, including the right of coasting trade between the ports of Morocco, enjoyed by British vessels since 1901.

Article 3. His Britannic Majesty's Government, for their part, will respect the rights which France, in virtue of treaties, conventions, and usage, enjoys in Egypt, including the right of coasting trade between Egyptian ports accorded to French vessels.

Article 4. The two Governments, being equally attached to the principle of commercial liberty both in Egypt and Morocco, declare that they will not, in those countries, countenance any inequality either in the imposition of customs duties or other taxes, or of railway transport charges.

The trade of both nations with Morocco and with Egypt shall enjoy the same treatment in transit through the French and British possessions in Africa. An agreement between the two Governments shall settle the conditions of such transit and shall determine the points of entry. . . .

Article 5. His Britannic Majesty's Government declare that they will use their influence in order that the French officials now in the Egyptian service may not be placed under conditions less advantageous than those applying to the British officials in the service.

The Government of the French Republic, for their part, would make no objection to the application of analogous conditions to British officials now in the Moorish service.

Article 6. [Guarantees free passage of the Suez Canal.] . . .

Article 7. In order to secure the free passage of the Straits of Gibraltar, the two Governments agree not to permit the erection of any fortifications or strategic works on that portion of the coast of Morocco comprised between, but not including, Melilla and the heights which command the right bank of the River Sebou.

This condition does not, however, apply to the places at present in the occupation of Spain on the Moorish coast of the Mediterranean.

Article 8. The two Governments, inspired by their feeling of sincere friendship for Spain, take into special consideration the interests which that country derives from her geographical position and from her territorial possessions on the Moorish coast of the Mediterranean. In regard to these interests the French Government will come to an understanding with the Spanish Government.

The agreement which may be come to on the subject between France and Spain shall be communicated to His Britannic Majesty's Government.

Article 9. The two Governments agree to afford to one another their diplomatic support, in order to obtain the execution of the clauses of the present Declaration regarding Egypt and Morocco. . . .

SECRET ARTICLES

Article 1. In the event of either Government finding themselves constrained, by the force of circumstances, to modify their policy in respect to Egypt or Morocco, the engagements which they have undertaken towards each other by articles 4, 6, and 7 of the Declaration of today's date would remain intact.

Article 2. His Britannic Majesty's Government have no present intention of proposing to the Powers any changes in the system of the Capitulations, or in the judicial organisation of Egypt.

In the event of their considering it desirable to introduce in Egypt reforms tending to assimilate the Egyptian legislative system to that in force in other civilised Countries, the Government of the French Republic will not refuse to entertain any such proposals, on the understanding that His Britannic Majesty's Government will agree to entertain the suggestions that the Government of the French Republic may have to make to them with a view of introducing similar reforms in Morocco.

Article 3. The two Governments agree that a certain extent of Moorish territory adjacent to Melilla, Ceuta, and other *présides* should, whenever the Sultan ceases to exercise authority over it, come within the sphere of influence of Spain. . . .

Nevertheless, Spain would previously have to give her formal assent to the provisions of articles 4 and 7 of the Declaration of today's date, and undertake to carry them out.

She would also have to undertake not to alienate the whole, or a part, of the territories placed under her authority or in her sphere of influence.

Article 4. If Spain, when invited to assent to the provisions of the preceding article, should think proper to decline, the arrangement between France and Great Britain, as embodied in the Declaration of today's date, would be none the less at once applicable.

The Anglo-Russian Agreement of 1907

The Anglo-Russian Entente of 1907 marked the completion of the Triple Entente. Since the early nineteenth century, England had been fearful of Russian designs in India [see page 639] and the Near East [see page 680]. From about 1904 on France labored to reconcile her two allies. The efforts were crowned with success when, in 1907, Britain and Russia agreed upon spheres of influence in Persia, as the following relation of the agreement describes.

From *The Annual Register, 1907* [1]

This Convention, which aimed at an amicable settlement of all questions likely to disturb the friendly relations of the two countries in Asia generally, and in Persia, Afghanistan and Tibet in particular, was signed on August 31 and officially communicated to the Powers in St. Petersburg on September 24. After reciting the desire of both Governments to maintain the integrity of Persia, and to allow all nations equal facilities for trade in that country, the Convention states that in certain parts, owing to their geographical proximity to their own terri-

[1] *The Annual Register . . . 1907,* 1908, 375-76. By permission of Longmans, Green & Co., Inc., London.

tories, Great Britain and Russia have special interests. Accordingly (Art. I.); To the north of a line drawn from Kasr-i-Shirin, Ispahan, Yezd and Khakh to the junction of the Persian, Russian and Afghanistan frontiers, Great Britain agrees not to seek for itself or its own subjects or those of any other country any political or commercial concessions, such as railway, banking, telegraph, roads, transport or insurance, or to oppose the acquisition of such concessions by the Russian Government or its subjects.

II. Russia gives a similar undertaking concerning the region to the south of a line extending from the Afghan frontier to Gazik, Birjand, Kerman and Bander Abbas.

III. Russia and Great Britain agree not to oppose, without previous agreement, the granting of concessions to subjects of either country in the regions situated between the lines above mentioned. All existing concessions in the regions above designated are maintained.

IV. The arrangements by which certain Persian revenues were pledged for the payment of the loans contracted by the Shah's Government with the Persian Banque d'Escompte and de Prêts and the Imperial Bank of Persia before the signing of the Convention are maintained.

V. In the event of any irregularities in the redemption or service of these loans Russia may institute a control over the revenues situated within the zone defined by Article I and Great Britain may do the same in the zone defined by Article II. But before instituting such a control the two Governments agree to a friendly exchange of ideas with a view to determining its nature, and avoiding any action in contravention of the principles of the Convention.

With the Convention a letter was published from Sir E. Grey to the British Ambassador at St. Petersburg, announcing that the Persian Gulf lay outside its scope, but that the Russian Government had stated during the negotiations that it did not deny the special interests of Great Britain in the Gulf; and it was intimated that Great Britain reasserted them.

Obviously this Convention is more favourable to Russia than to England in that the northern zone is of far greater commercial value than the southern one. But Russia's influence and commercial position in Northern Persia could hardly have been shaken or checked unless at the risk of war. On the other hand, although the southern zone is of much less commercial value its strategic importance is great, especially as it includes the port of Bander Abbas.

2. Immediate Causes of World War I

The system of alliances which developed after the Franco-Prussian War divided Europe into two hostile groups of powers. Their hostility was intensified by nationalist ambitions, economic rivalry, armament races, and jingoist propaganda. But these dangerous tendencies, taken altogether, did not lead to war. Indeed, the alliances successfully preserved peace for a time, in spite of a series of international crises—notably the Moroccan crisis (1905), the crisis precipitated by Austria's annexation of Bosnia and Herzegovina (1908), the Agadir affair (1911) and the disturbing Balkan Wars (1912-13). It was the assassination of the Archduke Ferdinand in Sarajevo, on June 28, 1914, which consolidated the elements of hostility and set in motion the complicated succession of events which culminated in the outbreak of World War I. This terrorist act, by which the heir to the Austrian throne was struck down, was the work of Bosnian agents of a Serbian nationalist society, "Union or Death" (the Black Hand), a society to which many Serb officials belonged and of whose plot the Serbian Government was cognizant some weeks before its execution. The Black Hand Society had been founded in 1911, one of several Serbian organizations created to bring about the union of all Serbs under a new "Greater Serbia." To the realization of this end the polyglot Hapsburg empire was a major stumbling block. How the Black Hand Society proposed to deal with such barriers is amply illustrated by the following extracts from the society's statutes.

THE PAN-SERBIAN BLACK HAND SOCIETY

From Statutes of Black Hand Society (1911) [1]

Article 1. This organisation has been created with the object of realising the national ideal: The union of all the Serbs. All Serbs . . . and all who are sincerely devoted to this cause, may become members.

Article 2. This organisation prefers terrorist action to intellectual propaganda and for this reason must be kept absolutely secret from persons who do not belong to it.

Article 3. This organisation bears the name "Union or Death."

Article 4. To accomplish its task, the organisation:

1. Brings influence to bear on Government circles, on the various social classes

and on the whole social life of the Kingdom of Serbia. . . .

2. Organises revolutionary action in all territories inhabited by Serbs.

3. Outside the frontiers of Serbia uses every means available to fight the adversaries of this idea.

4. Maintains amicable relations with all . . . who entertain feelings of friendship towards Serbia. . . .

5. Lends help and support in every way possible to all peoples and all organisations struggling for their national liberation and for their union.

Article 5. A Central Committee having its headquarters at Belgrade is at the head of this organisation and exercises executive authority. . . .

Article 25. Members of the organisation are not known to each other personally. It is only the members of the Central Committee who are known to one another.

Article 26. In the organisation itself the members are known by numbers. Only the Central Committee at Belgrade is to know their names. . . .

Article 31. Anyone who once enters the organisation may never withdraw from it. . . .

Article 33. When the Central Committee at Belgrade has . pronounced penalty of death [on one of the members] the only matter of importance is that the execution take place without fail.

THE AUSTRIAN ULTIMATUM TO SERBIA

As the Pan-Serb movement—encouraged by Russia—had been a threat to Austria for several years, the assassination of the Austrian heir furnished the signal for retribution. In a "personal" letter to the German Emperor (written actually by Count Leopold von Berch-

[1] W. Henry Cooke and Edith P. Stickney, eds., *Readings in European International Relations since 1879*, 309. Copyright, 1931, by Harper & Brothers and reprinted with their permission.

told, the Austrian Foreign Minister), Francis Joseph said:[1]

"The perpetration of the assassination of my poor nephew is the direct result of the agitations carried on by the Russian and Serbian Panslavists, the sole object of which is the weakening of the Triple Alliance and the destruction of my realm. According to all the evidence so far brought to light, the Serajevo affair was not merely the bloody deed of a single individual, but the result of a well-organized conspiracy, the threads of which can be traced to Belgrade; and even though it will probably prove impossible to get evidence of the complicity of the Serbian Government, there can be no doubt that its policy, directed toward the unification of all the southern-Slav countries under the Serbian flag, is responsible for such crimes, and that the continuation of such a state of affairs constitutes an enduring peril for my house and my possessions. . . . The efforts of my government must in the future be directed toward the isolation and diminution of Serbia. . . . You, too, must be convinced, after the frightful occurrence in Bosnia, that a reconciliation of the antagonism that now divides Serbia and ourselves is no more to be thought of."

To this letter, the German Emperor and his Chancellor, Theobald von Bethmann-Hollweg, thinking that the Austro-Serb quarrel was a local matter which Austria could handle adequately, replied (July 5) that "The Emperor Franz Joseph may . . . rest assured that His Majesty will faithfully stand by Austria-Hungary, as is required by

the obligations of his alliance and of his ancient friendship." After this assurance, which Berchtold interpreted as a "blank check" despite the danger of Russian intervention on Serbia's behalf—an intervention which threatened to bring into play the Triple Entente and plunge all Europe into war—Austria determined to send an ultimatum to Serbia. Berchtold proposed that *specific* demands should be leveled at Serbia, that the demands should be such that it "would be *wholly impossible for the Serbs to accept,*" that the time allowed for a reply should be "as brief as possible, say forty-eight hours," and that, by these means, Austria would avoid the odium of an attack on Serbia and Serbia "would be put in the wrong." The ultimatum, carefully timed to await the departure from Russia of the French President Poincaré, who had been conferring in St. Petersburg, was sent at 6 P.M. on July 23.

From the Austrian Ultimatum to Serbia (July 23, 1914).[2]

On the 31st of March, 1909, the Royal Serbian Minister at the Court of Vienna made, in the name of his Government, the following declaration to the Imperial and Royal Government:

"Serbia recognizes that her rights were not affected by the state of affairs created in Bosnia, and states that she will accordingly accommodate herself to the decisions to be reached by the Powers in connection with Article 25 of the Treaty of Berlin. Serbia, in accepting the advice of the Great Powers, binds herself to desist from the attitude of protest and opposition which she has assumed with regard to the annexation since October last, and she furthermore binds herself to alter the tendency of her present policy toward

---

[1] This and the next selection are from Max Montgelas and Walter Schücking, eds., *Outbreak of the World War: German Documents Collected by Karl Kautsky*, 1924. By permission of the Carnegie Endowment for International Peace, New York. This is 68-69.

[2] *Ibid.*, Supplement I, 603-06.

Austria-Hungary, and to live on the footing of friendly and neighborly relations with the latter in the future."

Now the history of the past few years, and particularly the painful events of the 28th of June, have proved the existence of a subversive movement in Serbia, whose object it is to separate certain portions of its territory from the Austro-Hungarian Monarchy. This movement, which came into being under the very eyes of the Serbian Government, subsequently found expression outside of the territory of the Kingdom in acts of terrorism, in a number of attempts at assassination, and in murders.

Far from fulfilling the formal obligations contained in its declaration of the 31st of March, 1909, the Royal Serbian Government has done nothing to suppress this movement. . . .

It is clear from the statements and confessions of the criminal authors of the assassination of the twenty-eighth of June, that the murder at Serajevo was conceived at Belgrade, that the murderers received the weapons and the bombs with which they were equipped from Serbian officers and officials who belonged to the *Narodna Odbrana,* and finally, that the dispatch of the criminals and of their weapons to Bosnia was arranged and effected under the conduct of Serbian frontier authorities.

The results brought out by the inquiry no·longer permit the Imperial and Royal Government to maintain the attitude of patient tolerance which it has observed for years toward those agitations which center at Belgrade and are spread thence into the territories of the Monarchy. . . . In order to attain this end, the Imperial and Royal Government finds itself compelled to demand that the Serbian Government give official assurance that it will condemn the propaganda directed against Austria-Hungary. . . . In order to give these assurances a character of solemnity, the Royal Serbian Government will publish on the first page of its official organ of July 26/13, the following declaration:

"The Royal Serbian Government condemns the propaganda directed against Austria-Hungary, that is to say, the whole body of the efforts whose ultimate object it is to separate from the Austro-Hungarian Monarchy territories that belong to it, and it most sincerely regrets the dreadful consequences of these criminal transactions.

"The Royal Serbian Government regrets that Serbian officers and officials should have taken part in the above-mentioned propaganda and thus have endangered the friendly and neighborly relations, to the cultivation of which the Royal Government had most solemnly pledged itself by its declaration of March 31, 1909.

"The Royal Government, which disapproves and repels every idea and every attempt to interfere in the destinies of the population of whatever portion of Austria-Hungary, regards it as its duty most expressly to call the attention of the officers, officials and the whole population of the Kingdom to the fact that for the future it will proceed with the utmost rigor against any persons who shall become guilty of any such activities, activities to prevent and to suppress which, the Government will bend every effort."

This declaration shall be brought to the attention of the Royal army simultaneously by an order of the day from His Majesty the King, and by publication in the official organ of the army.

The Royal Serbian Government will furthermore pledge itself:

1. to suppress every publication which shall incite to hatred and contempt of the Monarchy. . . .

2. to proceed at once to the dissolution of the *Narodna Odbrana,* to confiscate all

of its means of propaganda, and in the same manner to proceed against the other unions and associations in Serbia which occupy themselves with propaganda against Austria-Hungary. . . .

3. to eliminate without delay from public instruction in Serbia, everything . . . that serves or may serve to nourish the propaganda against Austria-Hungary;

4. to remove from the military and administrative service in general all officers and officials who have been guilty of carrying on the propaganda against Austria-Hungary, whose names the Imperial and Royal Government reserves the right to make known. . . .

5. to agree to the cooperation in Serbia of the organs of the Imperial and Royal Government in the suppression of the subversive movement directed against the integrity of the Monarchy;

6. to institute a judicial inquiry against every participant in the conspiracy of the twenty-eighth of June who may be found in Serbian territory. . . .

7. to undertake with all haste the arrest of Major Voislav Tankositch and of one Milan Ciganovitch, a Serbian official. . . .

8. by efficient measures to prevent the participation of Serbian authorities in the smuggling of weapons and explosives across the frontier; to dismiss from the service and to punish severely those members of the Frontier Service . . . who assisted the authors of the crime of Serajevo to cross the frontier;

9. to make explanations to the Imperial and Royal Government concerning the unjustifiable utterances of high Serbian functionaries . . . who . . . have not hesitated to express themselves in a manner hostile toward Austria-Hungary since the assassination of the twenty-eighth of June;

10. to inform the Imperial and Royal Government without delay of the execu-tion of the measures comprised in the foregoing points.

The Imperial and Royal Government awaits the reply of the Royal Government by Saturday, the twenty-fifth instant, at 6 P.M., at the latest.

THE IMMEDIATE CAUSES ASSESSED

To the Austrian ultimatum the Serbian Government, while protesting the facts alleged by Austria, acceded so completely that the German Kaiser wrote: "I propose that we say to Austria: Serbia has been forced to retreat in a very humiliating manner, and we offer our congratulations; naturally, as a result, *no more cause for war* exists; but a *guarantee* that the promises *will be carried out* is probably necessary; that could probably be secured by a temporary military occupation of a portion of Serbia. . . . *On this basis* I am ready to *mediate for peace* with Austria." But the Kaiser's restraining hand was to no avail. Austria declared war on Serbia on July 28, 1914. Germany, fearful of Russia's mobilization activities, declared war on Russia on August 1, on France on August 3, and on Belgium on August 4. On the latter day, also, England declared war on Germany and the major alliances had come to grips in a war which ultimately engulfed every continent. Professor Fay, in his *Origins of the World War* quoted above [page 709], reviewed the immediate causes as follows.

From FAY, *Origins of the World War*[1]

None of the Powers wanted a European War, Their governing rulers and ministers, with very few exceptions, all foresaw

[1] Fay, *The Origins of the World War*, II, 547-48, 550-57. By permission of The Macmillan Company.

that it must be a frightful struggle, in which the political results were not absolutely certain, but in which the loss of life, suffering, and economic consequences were bound to be terrible. . . .

Nevertheless, a European War broke out. Why? Because in each country political and military leaders did certain things, which led to mobilizations and declarations of war, or failed to do certain things which might have prevented them. In this sense, all the European countries, in a greater or less degree, were responsible. . . .

One may, however, sum up very briefly the most salient facts in regard to each country.

Serbia felt a natural and justifiable impulse to do what so many other countries had done in the nineteenth century—to bring under one national Government all the discontented Serb people. She had liberated those under Turkish rule; the next step was to liberate those under Hapsburg rule. She looked to Russia for assistance, and had been encouraged to expect that she would receive it. After the assassination, Mr. Pashitch took no steps to discover and bring to justice Serbians in Belgrade who had been implicated in the plot. One of them, Ciganovitch, was even assisted to disappear. Mr. Pashitch waited to see what evidence the Austrian authorities could find. When Austria demanded co-operation of Austrian officials in discovering, though not in trying, implicated Serbians, the Serbian Government made a very conciliatory but negative reply. They expected that the reply would not be regarded as satisfactory, and, even before it was given, ordered the mobilization of the Serbian army. Serbia did not want war, but believed it would be forced upon her. That Mr. Pashitch was aware of the plot three weeks before it was executed, failed to take effective steps to prevent the assas-sins from crossing over from Serbia to Bosnia, and then failed to give Austria any warning or information which might have averted the fatal crime, were facts unknown to Austria in July, 1915; they cannot therefore be regarded as in any way justifying Austria's conduct; but they are part of Serbia's responsibility, and a very serious part.

Austria was more responsible for the immediate origin of the war than any other Power. Yet from her own point of view she was acting in self-defence—not against an immediate military attack, but against the corroding Greater Serbia and Jugoslav agitation which her leaders believed threatened her very existence. No State can be expected to sit with folded arms and await dismemberment at the hands of its neighbors. Russia was believed to be intriguing with Serbia and Rumania against the Dual Monarchy. The assassination of the heir to the throne, as a result of a plot prepared in Belgrade, demanded severe retribution; otherwise Austria would be regarded as incapable of action, "worm-eaten" as the Serbian Press expressed it, would sink in prestige, and hasten her own downfall. To avert this Berchtold determined to crush Serbia with war. He deliberately framed the ultimatum with the expectation and hope that it would be rejected. He hurriedly declared war against Serbia in order to forestall all efforts at mediation. He refused even to answer his own ally's urgent requests to come to an understanding with Russia, on the basis of a military occupation of Belgrade as a pledge that Serbia would carry out the promises in her reply to the ultimatum. Berchtold gambled on a "local" war with Serbia only, believing that he could rattle the German sword; but rather than abandon his war with Serbia, he was ready to drag the rest of Europe into war. . . .

Germany did not plot a European War, did not want one, and made genuine, though too belated, efforts to avert one. She was the victim of her alliance with Austria and of her own folly. Austria was her only dependable ally, Italy and Rumania having become nothing but allies in name. She could not throw her over, as otherwise she would stand isolated between Russia . . . and France. . . . Therefore, Bethmann felt bound to accede to Berchtold's request for support and gave him a free hand to deal with Serbia; he also hoped and expected to "localize" the Austro-Serbian conflict. Germany then gave grounds to the Entente for suspecting the sincerity of her peaceful intentions by her denial of any foreknowledge of the ultimatum, by her support and justification of it when it was published, and by her refusal of Sir Edward Grey's Conference proposal. However, Germany by no means had Austria so completely under her thumb as the Entente Powers and many writers have assumed. It is true that Berchtold would hardly have embarked on his gambler's policy unless he had been assured that Germany would fulfil the obligations of the alliance, and to this extent Germany must share the great responsibility of Austria. But when Bethmann realized that Russia was likely to intervene, that England might not remain neutral, and that there was danger of a world war of which Germany and Austria would appear to be the instigators, he tried to call a halt on Austria, but it was too late. He pressed mediation proposals on Vienna, but Berchtold was insensible to the pressure, and the Entente Powers did not believe in the sincerity of his pressure, especially as they produced no results. . . .

General mobilization of the continental armies took place in the following order: Serbia, Russia, Austria, France and Germany. General mobilization by a Great Power was commonly interpreted by military men in every country, though perhaps not by Sir Edward Grey, the Tsar, and some civilian officials, as meaning that the country was on the point of making war—that the military machine had begun to move and would not be stopped. Hence, when Germany learned of the Russian general mobilization, she sent ultimatums to St. Petersburg and Paris, warning that German mobilization would follow unless Russia suspended hers within twelve hours, and asking what would be the attitude of France. The answers being unsatisfactory, Germany then mobilized and declared war. It was the hasty Russian general mobilization, assented to on July 29 and ordered on July 30, while Germany was still trying to bring Austria to accept mediation proposals, which finally rendered the European War inevitable. . . .

The part of France is less clear than that of the other Great Powers, because she has not yet made a full publication of her documents. To be sure, M. Poincaré, in the fourth volume of his memoirs, has made a skilful and elaborate plea, to prove *"La France innocente."* But he is not convincing. It is quite clear that on his visit to Russia he assured the Tsar's Government that France would support her as an ally in preventing Austria from humiliating or crushing Serbia. Paléologue renewed these assurances in a way to encourage Russia to take a strong hand. He did not attempt to restrain Russia from military measures which he knew would call forth German counter-measures and cause war. . . .

Sir Edward Grey made many sincere proposals for preserving peace; they all failed owing partly, but not exclusively, to Germany's attitude. Sir Edward could probably have prevented war if he had done either of two things. If, early in the crisis, he had acceded to the urging of France and Russia and given a strong warning to Germany that, in a European War, England would take the side of the Franco-Russian Alliance, this would probably have led Bethmann to exert an earlier and more effective pressure on Austria; and it would perhaps thereby have prevented the Austrian declaration of war on Serbia, and brought to a successful issue the "direct conversations" between Vienna and St. Petersburg. Or, if Sir Edward Grey had listened to German urging, and warned France and Russia early in the crisis, that if they became involved in war, England would remain neutral, probably Russia would have hesitated with her mobilizations, and France would probably have exerted a restraining influence at St. Petersburg. But Sir Edward Grey could not say that England would take the side of France and Russia, because he had a Cabinet nearly evenly divided, and he was not sure, early in the crisis, that public opinion in England would back him up in war against Germany. . . . Therefore, in spite of the pleadings of the French, he refused to give them definite assurances until the probable German determination to go through Belgium made it clear that the Cabinet, and Parliament, and British public opinion would follow his lead in war on Germany. On the other hand, he was unwilling to heed the German pleadings that he exercise restraint at Paris and St. Petersburg, because he did not wish to endanger the Anglo-Russian Entente and the solidarity of the Triple Entente . . . and because he suspected that Germany was backing Austria up in an unjustifiable course and that Prussian militarists had taken the direction of affairs at Berlin out of the hands of Herr von Bethmann-Hollweg and the civilian authorities.

3. The War and Its Extension to Include Italy (1915) and the United States (1917)

GERMANY'S MASTER STRATEGY: THE SCHLIEFFEN PLAN

Space limitations forbid any extended treatment of the military, naval, and air operations of World War I. Air warfare was in its infancy and limited to scouting, artillery spotting, strafing, and small-scale, indiscriminate bombing. Naval operations were of vast importance on both sides—the Allied naval blockade of the Central Powers went far to strangle the latter, and German submarine operations succeeded perilously near to isolating Britain. But it was on the land that the war was won, and among the many theaters of military operations none was so decisive as the Western Front. Here the central factor was the famous German Schlieffen Plan. The Schlieffen Plan carried the threat of a quick German victory; its initial miscarriage set the pattern of fighting on the Western Front; and its ultimate failure cost Germany the war. The plan itself and its initial failure have been recently described as follows.

From CHAMBERS, *This Age of Conflict* (1943) [1]

Ever since the conclusion of the Franco-Russian Alliance in 1893 Germany had been haunted by the fear of simultaneous warfare on two fronts, and Count von Schlieffen, Chief of the German General Staff from 1891 to 1907, devised a plan which would take advantage of the slow

[1] Frank P. Chambers, Christina Phelps Grant, and Charles C. Bayley, *This Age of Conflict*, 1943, 9-12. By permission of Harcourt, Brace and Company, New York.

Russian mobilization to defeat France and Russia in two short successive campaigns. Schlieffen directed that the main force of the German Army should first attack France, and should attack her not by way of the great fortified wall between Verdun and Belfort, but by way of the comparatively open northeastern frontier. The operation would consequently involve the invasion of Belgium and Luxembourg, of whose neutrality Germany was herself a guarantor. It' would take the form of a huge wheeling movement, hinging on Verdun, up the Belgian Meuse and across Champagne, and would end in a decisive battle against the reversed French lines in the western foothills of the Vosges. It was calculated to take about thirty days. Once France had been eliminated, Schlieffen then directed that the victorious German Army should turn at its leisure against the now gathering Russian hordes on the East Prussian frontier. Schlieffen, it is said, bequeathed his plan to his successors with the words "The fight must come. Only make the right wing strong!" On August 2 and 4, 1914, the plan went into operation; German forces crossed the frontiers of Belgium and Luxembourg, and began the investment of the great Belgium fortress of Liége.

The Belgian defense never seriously delayed the German timetable, but the stubbornness of the Belgian garrisons must have been very disconcerting to the "paper strategists" in the German High Command. Some of the forts at Liége held out till August 15. The Belgian field army retired in good order behind the fortified system at Antwerp, where it constituted a standing threat to the advancing German flank. General Joffre, the French commander, in accordance with his own plan, the famous Plan XVII, had attempted the invasion and reconquest of the lost provinces of Alsace-Lorraine. But the French attack was repulsed with serious losses at Morhange, and the French Armies to the left of the French line were soon making contact with the Germans on their sweeping progress through Belgium. The British Expeditionary Force fought its first action at Mons on August 23. Thereafter the Germans followed their appointed schedule until the very pace and magnitude of their maneuver brought them gradually to the point of disorder and breakdown.

Moltke, the German commander, made the serious error of detaching eleven divisions from his right wing for the investment of Antwerp and other remaining centers of resistance in Belgium. He therefore weakened the German deployment at the very point which Schlieffen, in his dying words, had warned his heirs to load most heavily, and as if the plan had not been misread enough, Moltke afterward transferred four of the eleven divisions to East Prussia in answer to an urgent summons for reinforcements from that front.

In the first week of September the German advance had already reached the Marne, and then the French and British armies struck back. They struck at the depleted German right wing, and they struck at an enemy who had lost much of his original cohesion and momentum. Joffre is believed to have been opposed to the attack at first, and its exact timing and direction have been attributed to General Gallieni, the Military Governor of Paris. At all events, the First Battle of the Marne, as the Franco-British counterstroke came to be called, occupied five days, from September 6 to 10, 1914. On September 8 Moltke sent his special emissary, Colonel Hentsch, to visit in turn the five German Armies west of Verdun, and gave him instructions to co-ordinate a general retirement "should it have already been initiated." The Colonel motored from the headquarters of one Army to the next through confused, congested country, meeting everywhere an unaccountable sense of depression. The Franco-British Allies had already won the "psychological" victory. The half-million Germans who for four weeks had tumbled irresistibly through Belgium and northern France halted and drew back, hardly understanding what had beaten them or whether indeed they had been beaten.

The success of Gallieni's attack persuaded Joffre to repeat it, and the opposing armies now entered upon a competition in flanking and counterflanking ever more westward and ever more northward, a competition which developed into what has since been called the "Race to the Sea." Joffre sent General Foch to coordinate the heterogeneous group of French, British and Belgian divisions which now assembled in the North. By mid-October the combatants stretched from the coast of Flanders to the frontier of Switzerland, locked in that curious tactical immobility in which for the next four years they were fated to remain.

ITALY ENTERS THE WAR

Italy held that the circumstances with which the war started in 1914 justified neutrality on her part. However, during the early months of the war, Italy bargained with both groups of belligerents to see which side would pay the more for her participation. The following treaty, signed on April 26, 1915, was the price paid by the Entente for Italian entrance in the war. Its terms proved very embarrassing at the Peace Conference in 1919.

From The Treaty of London (1915) [1]

Article 1. A military convention shall be immediately concluded between the

[1] Great Britain, *Parliamentary Papers,* London, 1920, LI, Cmd. 671; Miscellaneous, No. 7, 2-7.

General Staffs of France, Great Britain, Italy and Russia. This convention shall settle the minimum number of military forces to be employed by Russia against Austria-Hungary in order to prevent that Power from concentrating all its strength against Italy, in the event of Russia deciding to direct her principal effort against Germany. . . .

Article 2. On her part, Italy undertakes to use her entire resources for the purpose of waging war jointly with France, Great Britain and Russia against all their enemies.

Article 3. The French and British fleets shall render active and permanent assistance to Italy. . . .

Article 4. Under the Treaty of Peace, Italy shall obtain the Trentino, Cisalpine Tyrol with its geographical and natural frontier [the Brenner frontier], as well as Trieste, the counties of Gorizia and Gradisca, all Istria as far as the Quarnero and including Volosca and the Istrian islands of Cherso and Lussin, as well as the small islands of Plavnik, Unie, Canidole, Palazzuoli, San Pietro di Nembi, Asinello, Gruica, and the neighbouring islets. . . . [The frontiers are described in detail.]

Article 5. Italy shall also be given the province of Dalmatia within its present administrative boundaries. . . . [The frontiers are described in detail.]

Article 6. Italy shall receive full sovereignty over Valona, the island of Saseno and surrounding territory of sufficient extent to assure defence of these points. . . .

Article 7. Should Italy obtain the Trentino and Istria in accordance with the provisions of Article 4, together with Dalmatia and the Adriatic islands within the limits specified in Article 5, and the Bay of Valona (Article 6), and if the central portion of Albania is reserved for the establishment of a small autonomous neutralised State, Italy shall not oppose the division of Northern and Southern Albania between Montenegro, Serbia and Greece, should France, Great Britain and Russia so desire. . . .

Article 8. Italy shall receive entire sovereignty over the Dodecanese Islands which she is at present occupying.

Article 9. Generally speaking, France, Great Britain and Russia recognise that Italy is interested in the maintenance of the balance of power in the Mediterranean and that, in the event of the total or partial partition of Turkey in Asia, she ought to obtain a just share of the Mediterranean region adjacent to the province of Adalia. . . .

Article 10. All rights and privileges in Libya at present belonging to the Sultan by virtue of the Treaty of Lausanne are transferred to Italy.

Article 11. Italy shall receive a share of any eventual war indemnity corresponding to her efforts and her sacrifices.

Article 12. Italy declares that she associates herself in the declaration made by France, Great Britain and Russia to the effect that Arabia and the Moslem Holy Places in Arabia shall be left under the authority of an independent Moslem Power.

Article 13. In the event of France and Great Britain increasing their colonial territories in Africa at the expense of Germany, those two Powers agree in principle that Italy may claim some equitable compensation, particularly as regards the settlement in her favour of the questions relative to the frontiers of the Italian colonies of Eritrea, Somaliland and Libya and the neighbouring colonies belonging to France and Great Britain.

Article 14. Great Britain undertakes to facilitate the immediate conclusion, under equitable conditions, of a loan of at least £50,000,000, to be issued on the London market. . . .

Article 16. The present arrangement shall be held secret.

THE UNITED STATES ENTERS THE WAR (APRIL 6, 1917)

At the outset of the war in Europe, President Woodrow Wilson, on behalf of the United States, proclaimed (August 4, 1914) "a strict and impartial neutrality" and urged Americans to be "neutral in fact as well as in name." However, on February 3, 1917, the President severed diplomatic relations with Germany; on April 2, he advised a special session of Congress to declare war on Germany; and on April 6, 1917, Congress declared "That the state of war between the United States and the Imperial German Government which has been thrust upon the United States is hereby formally declared." The reasons for this reversal of sentiment and policy—for American entry into World War I—have become subject to heated debate, especially when the approach of World War II prompted reappraisal of American efforts at neutrality. In an article in the *Saturday Review of Literature* for November, 1939, Professor S. B. Fay, already referred to as a leading authority on the causes of World War I [see pages 709 and 722], presented the following analysis of the circumstances which provoked the United States to war in 1917.

From FAY, "Recipes for Neutrality" (1939) [1]

The reasons for American participation in 1917 are very complex. Each one of a hundred million people was actuated by somewhat different motives, and each varied somewhat in his own feeling as

[1] "Recipes for Neutrality," *Saturday Review of Literature*, XXI (Nov. 4, 1939), 3-4, 16. By permission of the Saturday Review Associates, Inc.

new situations continually arose. People did not always find it easy to analyze precisely their own motives. A man's motives are known only to himself and his Maker, and, as modern psychology teaches, not always to himself. How can anyone confidently say that it was Allied propaganda, or the economic motive, or any other one thing that mainly got us into war in 1917? Furthermore, to determine precisely why we went to war it would be necessary to distinguish carefully the motives of, and the influence exercised by, President Wilson, his advisers, senators and congressmen, and the whole people collectively and individually. Our entrance into the war was the resultant of a vast complex of forces. Nevertheless, if one may be so rash as to venture a rough general estimate in the briefest space, the main factors which led us into war might be grouped under six somewhat overlapping heads. Arranging them from the most decisive first, to the least decisive last, they would be something like this:

1. The disregard of American rights involved in the German submarine policy. German disregard of our rights was felt by American sentiment to be more serious than Allied disregard, because the former killed American men, women, and children who could never be brought to life, while the latter merely interfered with American property rights for which compensation could be made.

2. The German methods in beginning and conducting the war: German militarism; support of Austria in July, 1914; invasion of neutral Belgium; severities or "atrocities" which were caused by the panicky feeling of German officers in Belgium and Northern France but which were often deplored by German soldiers, as we know from their captured diaries; deportation of Belgians to forced labor in Germany; introduction of poison gas; blowing up of American bridges and munition plants; and finally the Zimmerman note with its *spurlos versenkt* [being disposed of without a trace] and proposed incitement of Mexico.

3. Anglo-Saxon tradition and sentiment, and native American idealism. The more influential Americans, including of course the President and his advisers, as well as great majority of the newspapers, were pro-English by inheritance and tradition. Through Shakespeare, Wordsworth, Dickens, and a thousand others we had become accustomed to think in much the same terms as our English forefathers. Except for some Irish elements and some naval circles, we had forgotten 1776 and 1812 by 1914, and were more receptive to the cultural and democratic ideals of England than of Imperial Germany. Our native optimism and idealism, probably in part a product of our advancing frontier life and of our great natural resources and fortunate geographical isolation, made us genuinely believe in our mission to make the world safe for democracy—before later events made the very phrase a cause for cynical laughter. But those whose memories are good know that this idealism, as expressed in the President's speeches, was a very real thing to the men who went overseas and to those who stayed at home. As Alice M. Morrissey well says in her excellent study, "American neutrality was never more than a legal status cloaking factual partiality for the Allies."

This American sentiment and idealism perhaps should be put at the head of the list, because it partly explains why we were more angered by German than by British disregard of our rights, why we were so shocked by German methods of war, and why our soil proved so much more fertile for Allied than for German propaganda.

4. Allied propaganda, highly successful because abundant and skillful, and still

more because it fell on ears already conditioned to receptivity. German propaganda, on the other hand, clumsy and ineffective abroad then as today, was more of a boomerang than a success.

5. Economic influences—bankers, munition-makers, profit-seekers—which have been discussed above. [Professor Fay holds earlier that "the influence on President Wilson and Congress of the big bankers, the munition-makers, the profits from Wall Street war babies and war loans, and the economic tie-up resulting from all sorts of Allied purchases in this country" have been much exaggerated; that "no doubt people who bought Allied bonds did not want to lose their investment through the possibility of Allied defeat. No doubt the cotton-farmers, wheat-growers, copper-miners, and munition-makers were interested in the victory of the side that they were supplying so profitably to themselves. But it is a mistake to exaggerate these economic motives and leave out of sight other and more potent factors. . . . Part of the popular success which this economic school has enjoyed is owing to the fact that it can point with more truth to the unwholesome economic after-effects of the war boom. To people suffering from the depression which began to engulf us after 1929, it is pleasant to find a scapegoat and see the blame pinned on the bankers and munition-makers. The condemnation of Wilsonian neutrality which failed to keep us out of war is further applauded because of his failure to win the peace, and because of the disastrous course of European history since Versailles."]

6. Fear for our own ultimate safety if the Kaiser should triumph in Europe—a fear that was emotionally increased by the appearance of German submarines in our waters and that was naturally stronger along the Atlantic seaboard than inland west of the Alleghenies.

4. The Armistice (November 11, 1918)

THE PROPOSED BASIS FOR PEACE

The entry of the United States injected into World War I an idealism which was scarcely comprehensible to the European powers at war. For this idealism President Wilson was in large part responsible. Weeks before the United States entered the war, he addressed the Senate of the United States (January 22, 1917) calling upon the warring parties to conclude "a peace without victory"—a peace between equals, with democracy and freedom for all peoples. Almost a year later (January 8, 1918), after an Interallied Conference had failed to agree upon a statement of war aims and while Russia was seeking a separate peace with Germany, the President laid down fourteen points as the "only possible" program for world peace.

From WILSON, "The Fourteen Points"
(January 8, 1918) [1]

The program of the world's peace . . . is our program; and that program, the only possible program, as we see it, is this:

I. Open covenants of peace, openly arrived at . . . diplomacy shall proceed always frankly and in the public view.

II. Absolute freedom of navigation upon the seas, outside territorial waters, alike in peace and in war, except as the seas may be closed in whole or in part by international action for the enforcement of international covenants.

III. The removal, so far as possible, of all economic barriers and the establishment of an equality of trade conditions

[1] *Congressional Record*, LVI, 1918, Pt. I. 680-81.

among all the nations consenting to the peace and associating themselves for its maintenance.

IV. Adequate guarantees given and taken that national armaments will be reduced to the lowest point consistent with domestic safety.

V. A free, open-minded, and absolutely impartial adjustment of all colonial claims, based upon a strict observance of the principle that in determining all such questions of sovereignty the interests of the populations concerned must have equal weight with the equitable claims of the government whose title is to be determined.

VI. The evacuation of all Russian territory and such a settlement of all questions affecting Russia as will secure the best and freest co-operation of the other nations of the world in obtaining for her an unhampered and unembarrassed opportunity for the independent determination of her own political development and national policy and assure her of a sincere welcome into the society of free nations under institutions of her own choosing. . . .

VII. Belgium, the whole world will agree, must be evacuated and restored, without any attempt to limit the sovereignty which she enjoys in common with all other free nations. . . .

VIII. All French territory should be freed and the invaded portions restored, and the wrong done to France by Prussia in 1871 in the matter of Alsace-Lorraine, which has unsettled the peace of the world for nearly fifty years should be righted. . . .

IX. A readjustment of the frontiers of Italy should be effected along clearly recognizable lines of nationality.

X. The peoples of Austria-Hungary . . . should be accorded the freest opportunity of autonomous development.

XI. Roumania, Serbia, and Montenegro should be evacuated; occupied territories restored; Serbia accorded free and secure access to the sea; and the relations of the several Balkan States to one another determined by friendly counsel along historically established lines of allegiance and nationality. . . .

XII. The Turkish portions of the present Ottoman Empire should be assured a secure sovereignty, but the other nationalities which are now under Turkish rule should be assured an undoubted security of life and an absolutely unmolested opportunity of autonomous development, and the Dardanelles should be permanently opened as a free passage to the ships and commerce of all nations under international guarantees.

XIII. An independent Polish State should be erected which should include the territories inhabited by indisputably Polish populations, which should be assured a free and secure access to the sea, and whose political and economic independence and territorial integrity should be guaranteed by international covenant.

XIV. A general association of nations must be formed under specific covenants for the purpose of affording mutual guarantees of political independence and territorial integrity to great and small States alike.

THE TERMS OF THE ARMISTICE

In two subsequent addresses (July 4 and September 27, 1918), President Wilson enlarged upon and further explained the Fourteen Points. "These great objects," he said on July 4, "can be put in a single sentence. What we seek is the reign of law, based upon the consent of the governed and sustained by the organized opinion of mankind." Meanwhile, Germany suffered decisive military defeat in the summer of 1918 and, on October 6, requested President Wilson "to take steps for the restoration of peace," indicating German willingness to accept peace terms based on the Fourteen Points. President Wilson, replying for the Allies and the United States, agreed to an armistice on these terms but with reservations in regard to Point 2 and in regard to German compensation for damage done to the property and lives of civilians in the Allied Countries. Germany agreed, the following Armistice was signed, and hostilities ceased at 11 A.M., November 11, 1918.

The full text of the Armistice is too extensive for inclusion here, but the following excerpts will illustrate its principal aspects.

From The Armistice with Germany (November 11, 1918) [1]

(A) ON THE WESTERN FRONT

1. Cessation of hostilities on land and in the air six hours after the signature of the Armistice.

2. Immediate evacuation of the invaded countries. . . .

4. Surrender in good condition by the German armies of the following war material:—

5,000 guns (2,500 heavy, 2,500 field).
25,000 machine-guns.
3,000 trench mortars.
1,700 fighting and bombing aeroplanes —in the first place, all D 7's and all night-bombing aeroplanes. . . .

5. Evacuation by the German armies of the territories on the left bank of the Rhine. These territories on the left bank

[1] James Brown Scott, ed., *Official Statements of War Aims and Peace Proposals,* Carnegie Endowment for International Peace, Pamphlet Series, Division of International Law, No. 31, Washington, 1921, 477-81. By permission of the Carnegie Endowment for International Peace.

of the Rhine shall be administered by the local authorities under the control of the Allied and United States armies of occupation. . . .

6. In all the territories evacuated by the enemy there shall be no evacuation of inhabitants; no damage or detriment shall be done to the persons or property of the inhabitants. . . . Military establishments of all kinds shall be handed over intact, as well as military stores, food, munitions and equipment not removed during the periods fixed for evacuation. Stores of food of all kinds for the civil population, cattle, &c., shall be left *in situ*. . . .

7. Roads and means of communication of every kind, railroads, waterways, main roads, bridges, telegraphs and telephones shall be in no way damaged. All civil and military personnel at present employed on them shall be maintained. 5,000 locomotives and 150,000 wagons in good running order, and provided with all necessary spare parts and fittings, shall be delivered to the Associated Powers within the period fixed by Annexe No. 2, which shall not exceed thirty-one days. 5,000 motor lorries in good running order shall also be handed over within thirty-six days. . . .

8. The German Command shall be bound to disclose, within 48 hours after the signature of the Armistice, all mines or delay action apparatus disposed on the territory evacuated by the German troops, and shall assist in their discovery and destruction. . . .

10. Immediate repatriation, without reciprocity, of all Allied and United States prisoners of war. . . .

(B) CLAUSES RELATING TO THE EASTERN FRONTIERS OF GERMANY

12. All German troops at present in any territory which before the war belonged to Austria-Hungary, Roumania, or Turkey, must at once withdraw within the

frontiers of Germany as these existed on August 1, 1914. . . .

15. Annulment of the Treaties of Bucharest and Brest-Litovsk and of supplementary treaties. . . .

(c) IN EAST AFRICA

17. Evacuation of all German forces operating in East Africa within a period fixed by the Allies.

(D) GENERAL CLAUSES . . .

19. *Financial Clauses.*—With the reservation that any future claims and demands of the Allies and United States shall remain unaffected, the following financial conditions are required:—

Reparation for damage done. . . .

(E) NAVAL CONDITIONS

20. Immediate cessation of all hostilities at sea, and definite information to be given as to the location and movements of all German ships. . . .

22. Surrender to the Allies and the United States of all existing submarines (including all submarine cruisers and mine-layers) with armament and equipment complete. . . .

23. The following German surface warships, which shall be designated by the Allies and the United States, shall forthwith be disarmed and . . . placed under the supervision of the Allies and the United States, only guards being left on board, namely:—

　6 battle cruisers.
　10 battleships.
　8 light cruisers, including two mine-layers.
　50 destroyers of the most modern types.

All other surface warships (including river craft) shall be concentrated in German naval bases to be designated by the Allies and the United States, completely disarmed, and there placed under the supervision of the Allies and the United States.

36　THE PEACEMAKERS AND THE PEACE OF PARIS, 1919

1. The Conflicting Interests of the Peacemakers

The Peace Conference opened formally at Paris on January 18, 1919, with seventy delegates and vast corps of "experts" representing twenty-seven of the victorious powers. Representatives of Germany and the other Central Powers were excluded until the peace terms were ready for submission; and, as Russia was in the throes of civil war, the Russians were not represented, although their affairs were of vital import. Moreover, while the German request for peace on the basis of the Fourteen Points had been granted by the Allies with two reservations, the Wilsonian principles lent themselves to differing, even contradictory, interpretations when applied to concrete situations, and among the Allies themselves there arose, between the signing of the Armistice and the conclusion of the peace settlement, such a conflict of views and interests that the Fourteen Points receded far into the background. As a consequence, the peace settlement represented a far from perfect application of the promised basic principles. In a careful study made after World War II had begun—though before American participation in it—and based upon the extensive evidence now available from the diaries, memoirs, and other records of the participants, Professor Paul Birdsall has produced an admirable analysis of the nature and intensity of the diplomatic crosscurrents at work in the Paris Conference. The following excerpts are from Professor Birdsall's book, with topical headings added.

From BIRDSALL, *Versailles Twenty Years After* (1941) [1]

THE FORCES OF REACTIONARY NATIONALISM IN THE UNITED STATES

Unfortunately, purely negative accomplishments, the prevention of positive harm, rarely attract public attention. Yet the record of what Wilson prevented is just as important as his one great positive achievement, the League of Nations, which, however dead at this moment, is certain to be revived in some form in the event of another Allied victory over Germany. The story of Wilson's struggle to restrain nationalist demands is equally important for an understanding of the problems of the next Peace Conference. . . .

The difficulties began before Wilson sailed for Paris, reactionary nationalism being equally at home on both sides of the

[1] *Versailles Twenty Years After,* by Paul Birdsall, 1941, 9-11; 29-32, 207-08; 36-40, 46-47, 51-53; 83-90, 101; 266-69. Reprinted by permission of Reynal and Hitchcock, Inc., New York.

Atlantic. To Wilson it seemed particularly strong in the ranks of the Republican Party. Naturally, though unwisely, he invited the American electorate to return only faithful Democrats to Congress, on the assumption that they alone could be counted upon to support his program. This purge, like a more recent one in American history, failed to come off. Republicans captured control of both branches of the legislature in the elections of November, 1918, and the most conspicuous and bitter opponent of Wilson's program—Henry Cabot Lodge—became chairman of the Senate Committee on Foreign Relations. Lodge's lifelong friend, Theodore Roosevelt, interpreted the election for the benefit of the nationalists of Europe:

"Our allies and our enemies and Mr. Wilson himself should all understand that Mr. Wilson has no authority whatever to speak for the American people at this time. His leadership has just been emphatically repudiated by them. The newly elected Congress comes far nearer than Mr. Wilson to having a right to speak the purposes of the American people at this moment. Mr. Wilson and his Fourteen Points and , . . all his utterances every which way, have ceased to have any shadow of right to be accepted as expressive of the will of the American people. . . ."

Acceptance of the Wilsonian principles referred to had become a contract between the Allied and Associated Powers on the one hand and Germany on the other, as a condition for the granting of an armistice and the convening of a Peace Conference. In effect, Roosevelt was inviting the Allied governments to repudiate their pledges to both President Wilson and the German Government. Though noisy, Theodore Roosevelt was only a private citizen. It was one thing for him to announce that the American people had themselves rejected the whole contractual basis for peace. It was quite another for his friend Henry Cabot Lodge, as Chairman of the Senate Committee on Foreign Affairs, to indulge in similar pronouncements. On December 21, 1918, less than a week after Wilson's arrival in Paris, the *Congressional Record* published the substance of Lodge's speech to the Senate, in which he advised Europe that what it did to Germany was no concern of the United States. Let the Allies administer a severe peace to leave Germany disabled and helpless, and exact heavy indemnities. No attention need be paid to Wilson's principles with regard to new boundaries in Europe, for that was none of his business. Above all, postpone all plans for the construction of a League of Nations until Germany had been summarily disposed of.

The alliance of reactionary nationalisms in Europe and America undermined Wilson's position from the start. The alliance was tacit but real. Colonel House records that "the elections of last November have been a deterrent to free action by our delegates," and Lloyd George is smugness itself in describing the contrast between his own and Wilson's position. Lloyd George enjoyed an overwhelming popular mandate, and knowing the weakness of Wilson's position, could be nonchalant about Wilson's threats to appeal to public opinion. "His occasional threats to appeal to American opinion, when he did not get his way at the Conference, conveyed no real menace. There was no assurance that his country would support him in a break with the Allies on any issue." . . .

THE FRENCH DEMANDS

The real objection of the French to Wilson's program appears in their own concrete proposals, which assigned primary importance to the "federalization" of Germany. The significance of that proposal becomes clear from a remark of Clemenceau (March 7, 1919), "that the more separate and independent republics were established in Germany, the better he would be pleased." . . .

Marshal Foch prepared a memorandum on November 27, 1918. It began where the armistice terms left off, providing the transition from a provisional to a permanent arrangement for French control in the whole Rhineland area. It implements fully the general principles of the Franco-Russian exchange of notes in February 1917, and in some particulars goes far beyond even those principles. It found its justification in the undoubted fact of two German invasions of France within fifty years and in the permanent inferiority of French man-power *vis-à-vis* Germany. . . .

The details of that program add up to the most thinly disguised military imperialism.

1. Extinguish German sovereignty in the purely German territory west of the Rhine.

2. Organize one or more autonomous republics in this former German territory.

3. Conscript the male population of this area into military units to fight Germany in case of war.

4. "Equally treaties or arrangements should assure the conduct of these new states, with a view to specifying their political attitude, and to determining their military burden. . . . That is to say that the different States on the left bank . . . should have a common policy, controlled by some of them in proportion to the risks to be encountered in war [France, Belgium, Great Britain]." . . .

5. "Equally treaties should assure, by maintenance of allied contingents at strongholds of the left bank, the defense of the new frontier for at least a certain period of time."

6. Finally, in order to secure guarantees for German execution in full of all treaty terms, especially reparation payments, it is "indispensable to maintain intact the

occupation of the bridgeheads of the right bank." . . .

Frenchmen might sincerely describe such a program as "not a policy of annexation, but of protection," but they could scarcely object if Lloyd George and Wilson failed to appreciate the distinction. The former would certainly object to the creation of new Alsace-Lorraines in Europe; the latter would as certainly resist such a patent violation of his cardinal principle of self-determination, and would most particularly resent the affront to the League of Nations, which in his view was to provide adequately and permanently for French security within the framework of a new world order. . . .

Lloyd George had suggested to [Colonel E. M.] House, on March 12, a way of meeting the French demand for physical guarantees of French security without permitting the dangerous plan of dismembering Germany. He proposed to offer France a British treaty of alliance against aggression. He conferred with Wilson when the latter arrived in Paris on March 14, before their joint interview with Clemenceau, and they evidently decided on an Anglo-American military guarantee of French security as the only way out of the critical impasse. When the Big Three met in the afternoon, Clemenceau encountered united opposition from the other two, but he fought for the full measure of the Rhenish program, asserting that he would not sign any treaty "which fails to give France the guarantees to which she has a right," the removal of Germany from the French frontier, and the permanent establishment of "military surveillance the length of the Rhine." To this, Wilson said:

"There will be neither the establishment of an independent state on the left bank, nor occupation of the line of the Rhine, but America and England will sign with France a treaty by which they will engage themselves to support France with all

their forces if Germany makes an unprovoked attack on France."

Lloyd George agreed on behalf of Great Britain, the British guarantee to become operative after American ratification of the treaty, and Clemenceau, apparently taken off guard for once, said he would like time "to reflect and consult."

There followed a highly characteristic series of conferences of the French diplomatic general staff, appropriately held at the Ministry of War. In the course of three meetings on March 15 and 16, Clemenceau, Pichon, Loucheur, and Tardieu reconsidered their strategy in the light of the altered situation. They emerged in agreement that it was impossible to refuse the offer of an Anglo-American treaty of guarantee, and that some price must be paid for it by the reduction of French demands in the Rhineland. But they were equally agreed that the proffered treaty was not in itself a satisfactory substitute for the whole of the French program. They might give up the political demand for a separate Rhenish republic; they must still insist on military occupation. . . .

THE ATTITUDE OF GREAT BRITAIN AND HER DOMINIONS

Lloyd George was so little bothered by his commitment to the Pre-Armistice Agreement that he was quite ready to make pledges to the British electorate which defied one of its cardinal principles. His concern for a practical determination of enemy capacity had nothing whatsoever to do with a scrupulous regard for principle or for his pledged word; it was dictated solely by his conception of British economic interest as an exporting nation. Throughout his own account of the Reparation question the constant theme is not his superior virtue, but his superior wisdom. He assumed the complete justification of the British demand for full war costs, provided the enemy practically could pay that much, and provided also that the payment would not injure British trade. Thus at a meeting of the Imperial War Cabinet November 26, 1918, when the Australian premier, Mr. Hughes, "strongly urged the exaction of a full war indemnity," Lloyd George reported:

". . . I asked if it was Mr. Hughes' intention that Australia should be paid in gold, or by Germany selling goods, and to this question Mr. Hughes replied 'by credit.' I then pointed out that, in order to pay the debt in this manner, it would be necessary for Germany to sell goods, and asked who was going to buy them. The total liability of Germany would probably amount to some £20,000,000,000, and it would be very easy for the Allied Powers to say to Germany that she had got to pay this amount, but I suggested that it would mean that for two generations we would make German workmen our slaves. I further pointed out that someone must buy the goods manufactured in Germany, and for the moment, I did not see which nation would provide the dumping ground for such goods. Further, we would have to allow Germany to import raw material for the manufacture of the goods. I thought the only way in which Germany could pay a large indemnity would be by manufacturing cheaper than other nations and by selling to them."

Lloyd George was particularly anxious "that members of the Government should not be responsible during the election for arousing or encouraging any false hopes in the minds of the electorate." Unfortunately on the very eve of the elections Lloyd George's hand-picked committee proposed fantastic figures. He had counted on practical city bankers, officials of the Bank of England, economists, to cure Hughes of his optimism, but Gibbs, Cunliffe, Hewins, Foster, and Long caught the contagion. Both Bonar Law and Lloyd George regarded their report "as a wild and fantastic chimera." It began—reasonably enough in the latter's opinion—with the principle that "the total cost of the War to the Allies is the measure of the indemnity which the Enemy Powers should in justice pay." But it concluded that there was no reason why the Enemy Powers should not pay annually £1,200,000,000 as interest on a capital debt of £24,000,000,000, which was their estimate of the total cost of the war. They saw no reason to fear "economic ill-effects to Allied countries from the repayment of the cost of the War." Worst of all, this report represented the opinions of the Associated Chambers of Commerce and the Federation of British Industries.

"So much," lamented Lloyd George, "for the infallibility of business men in business matters which go beyond their day-to-day transactions." One can grant so much without necessarily endorsing his corollary concerning the superior wisdom of the politician. Once admit the principle of full war indemnity and fantastic figures are sure to follow. It was Lloyd George himself who had opened the floodgates. He was in a hopeless dilemma and he refused to take the one possible and the only honorable way out by retreating to the firm ground of the Pre-Armistice Agreement. . . .

On December 11, 1918, Lloyd George gaily rode both horns of his dilemma into the electoral arena at Bristol to the tune of "Who is to foot the bill?" (A voice— "Germany!" and "The loser pays.") Lloyd George made an ambiguous speech, and, in conclusion, said:

"Let me summarize. First, as far as justice is concerned, *we have an absolute right to demand the whole cost of the war from Germany.* The second point is that *we propose to demand the whole cost of the war.* (Cheers). The third point is that when you come to the exacting of it you must exact it in such a way that it does not do more harm to the country that receives it than to the country which is paying it. The fourth point is that *the Committee appointed by the British Cabinet believe it can be done*. . . . You may depend upon it that the first consideration in the minds of the Allies will be the interests of the people upon whom Germany has made war, and not in the interests of the German people who have been guilty of this crime against humanity." [1]

An enthusiastic electorate may be excused for remembering the positive promise of war costs and for forgetting the reservations, particularly since many of Lloyd George's colleagues were less scrupulous than he in admitting that any practical difficulties of collection existed. The most famous phrase that has ever since echoed out of that hurly-burly is Eric Geddes' triumphant shout in the Cambridge Guildhall, "We shall squeeze the orange until the pips squeak." There was certainly a popular impression that the British Government had promised to collect from Germany every penny that the war had cost them. It may well be, as Harold Nicolson has said, that it was merely unfortunate that "a British Liberal should have placed himself at the mercy of a jingo Commons and a jingo Press," but Lloyd George himself bears the initial responsibility for a cynical departure from President Wilson's principles and from his own pledged word to abide by them. His own betrayal placed the British Liberal on the same level with jingo Press and jingo Commons. . . .

Lloyd George held further meetings of the Imperial War Cabinet to canvass some of the larger questions that he and Wilson were to discuss prior to the Peace Conference. Among these questions the German Colonies bulked large. The Cabinet accepted Wilson's mandatory principle in respect to former enemy possessions—except Southwest Africa and the Pacific islands, New Guinea and Samoa.

Premier Hughes said he had already made it perfectly clear to Wilson ". . . that the demand for the Pacific Islands was being put forward in the interests of Australian security and not in the interests of the British Empire." General Smuts, who had just elaborated the first comprehensive constitution to embody the mandates principle, confined its application chiefly to former Russian, Austro-Hungarian, and Turkish territories. In any case it was not to apply to Southwest Africa, which the Union of South Africa claimed in outright sovereignty.

Premier Borden of Canada made it clear that Canada had not gone to war in order to add territory to the British Empire, but as to the territories conquered by South Africa, Australia, and New Zealand, he would support their retention on the one condition that they were essential to the future security of the Empire. For the rest of the conquered territory, he favored ". . . entrusting their control and dominion to whichever state was appointed as mandatory for that purpose by the League of Nations, on the lines suggested in General Smuts' paper." Lord Milner agreed that Southwest Africa and the Pacific Islands should be excepted from the treatment accorded other occupied colonies, and regarded as the property of the Dominions which had conquered them. . . .

The real storm broke at the Imperial War Cabinet meeting convened to hear Lloyd George's report of his Buckingham Palace conversations with President Wilson; and, characteristically, it was Premier Hughes of Australia who led the attack. . . .

[1] David Lloyd George, *Memoirs of the Peace Conference*, New Haven, 1939. Permission of the Yale University Press. Italics by Professor Birdsall.

Hughes had played a prominent part in the formulation of British demands for war costs and he was the leading exponent of annexationist aims among the Dominion premiers. A man "of frail physique, defective hearing, and eccentric gesticulations," he had a gift for mordant phrase, and a hide like a rhinoceros. He was the living embodiment of everything that was anti-Wilsonian; he gloried in savage attacks on the President's plans for a new world order; he was as hard-boiled a nationalist as any at the Paris Peace Conference. Lloyd George, though he found him difficult, admired him greatly; and Clemenceau fairly doted on him. . . .

Lloyd George's report of Wilson's program provoked Hughes to fury. He took about one-third of the time in a savage attack on the President's "intolerable" claim "to dictate to us how the world should be governed." The British Empire must not permit itself to be dragged "behind the wheels of President Wilson's chariot," for he "had no claim to speak even for his own country," whereas both Clemenceau and Lloyd George enjoyed an overwhelming popular mandate. They "could settle the peace of the world as they liked." As to a League of Nations, that was to Wilson as a toy to a child— "he would not be happy till he got it."

Wilson's one idea seemed to be to establish the League so that he could go home with the proud boast that he had achieved it, leaving all practical matters to the determination of the League. Hughes did not believe that the peace of the world could be settled on any such terms. He wanted to know what Australia, what the British Empire, was to get out of it for all the sacrifices they had made. Once there were adequate guarantees for "reparations and indemnities," once there were safeguards of security in the possession of New Guinea—only eighty miles from Australia—he would have no objection to

handing over other matters to a League of Nations. He insisted that "in any case we should not commit ourselves to the League of Nations until the Conference had completed its labors." . . . He asked, "above all things, that the Prime Minister who now stood clothed with all power by the recent vote of the people, should resolutely insist upon such terms of peace as were necessary for the safety of the Empire." . . .

THE THREE DEMANDS OF THE JAPANESE

"Baron Makino and Viscount Chinda were there for Japan: silent, unemotional, but watchful; rising with power only when their own interests were affected." Such was Colonel House's description of Japan's delegates in the League of Nations Commission. It may well serve to characterize Japan's rôle throughout the Peace Conference.

Their interests were directly affected in only three questions, two of them imperialist claims to territorial and economic rights, the third a claim to explicit equality of treatment in the League of Nations, clearly a matter of prestige. Makino and Chinda concentrated unceasingly on the attainment of these material and moral rights.

They, too, asked for direct and immediate cession of former German islands in the Pacific which they had conquered and now occupied. Possession was nine points of the law, and British treaty obligation was the tenth. The same treaty which bound Japan to support Dominion claims to South Pacific islands bound Great Britain equally to support Japanese claims to North Pacific islands. Lloyd George could hardly press Dominion claims for annexation without making an equivalent case for Japanese annexation. Japan could expect no better treatment than the Dominions, and need fear no worse. Hence her delegates could afford to play a passive rôle during the controversy over the Mandates principle.

Japan did not secure outright annexation, but neither did the British Dominions. Both the Dominions and Japan were assured of Class "C" Mandates for the former German territory they coveted, and if they did not secure an immediate grant of mandatory authority, again Japan was no worse off than the Dominions in this respect. Meantime they had saved their diplomatic shot and shell while Lloyd George had depleted his artillery reserves.

Secondly, Japan wanted extensive rights in the Shantung peninsula on the mainland of China. These rights formerly were exercised by Germany, but had been seized by Japan early in 1915, and Great Britain was also treaty-bound to support this claim. China was equally bound. Moreover, the Japanese Government had promised, under certain conditions, to restore Chinese sovereignty in the Shantung province. What objection could Wilson offer to the Japanese demand for "unconditional cession" of former German rights in Shantung? . . .

Japanese troops conquered Kiao-Chow and overran the entire Shantung province, 250 miles inland to the terminus of the Tsingtao-Tsinan Railway. They established civil government bureaus to replace Chinese authorities. In the spring of 1915 the Japanese Government imposed upon China the notorious Twenty-One Demands, composed of five groups of articles. One of these groups gave Japan free rights of disposal of German privileges in Shantung. Three others gave her extensive economic rights in other parts of China. The fifth established a virtual Japanese protectorate over the whole of China. Not again until 1937 has Japan's policy of a Monroe Doctrine for Asia been so explicit. . . .

Wilson's method was to confront Japanese claims with Chinese counterclaims.

Since Shantung was a province of China, he insisted that China's delegates be heard. At the end of the morning session of the Council of Ten on January 27 Makino asked for a hearing on the Japanese case that afternoon. Wilson agreed, but proposed that it be heard in the presence of the Chinese delegates. Makino squirmed. The suggestion offended his delicate sense of the proprieties. He "did not wish to discuss in the presence of Chinese delegates *Japan's relations with Germany,*" as if there were something indecent about them. Wilson was sure that Makino did not mean "to contend that the disposition of Kiao-Chow did not affect China," and the Council supported his view by inviting Chinese delegates to participate in the discussion of Shantung. . . .

Makino reminded the Chinese delegates that China herself had assented to the fullest discretion for Japan in Shantung. [Wellington] Koo needed no reminder of the Twenty-One Demands and their sequel. He bluntly demanded that they be wiped from the slate by maintaining that China's declaration of war against Germany in 1917 had released her from any treaty commitments to Japan. If Japan were really sincere in her promise to restore the leased territory, the simplest way of fulfilling the promise was direct cession to China. . . .

The Japanese realized that Wilson had frustrated their strategy by confronting them with the Chinese delegates. Secretary of State Lansing, who heard them, said that Koo "simply overwhelmed the Japanese with his argument." The next day, January 29, one of the Japanese delegates called on Lansing "to offset the overwhelming effect of the Koo presentation" by an "indirect threat" of what might happen to the friendly relations between Japan and the United States because of the intensity of feeling in Japan on the subject of Shantung.

Partially satisfied by the Mandates settlement, but completely stalled in Shantung, the Japanese turned their full energy to the attainment of a clause in the League of Nations Covenant to guarantee explicit recognition of the equality of races. This was their third and final objective at the Peace Conference, and it was almost entirely a matter of prestige. It seemed to bear no relation to their aims in Shantung, but the strategic genius of Baron Makino and the shock tactics of Viscount Chinda could combine to give the racial issue a nuisance value far beyond its intrinsic importance. Important in itself to the Japanese as a matter of "face," it might be traded for something more tangible in Shantung. . . .

It was simply a deal in diplomacy. Japan's claims in Shantung had not been met until the very eve of the plenary session of April 28, and the Japanese delegates were restive. Baron Makino made numerous visits to the British Foreign Secretary, Lord Balfour, and the latter's account of one of these visits is so revealing that it deserves to be presented in full: ". . . Makino came to see him again Sunday evening. With great delicacy but perfect clearness he had indicated that Japan wanted a decision on Japanese claims *as a whole.* He had pointed out that Japan was asked to agree to the League of Nations although she could not obtain recognition of her claims for equality of treatment. He had said that public opinion in Japan was much concerned on this question, that if Japan was to receive one check as regards Shantung, and another check as regards the League of Nations, the position would be very serious. . . . *He understood that if Japan received what she wanted in regard to Shantung, her representatives at the Plenary Meeting would content themselves with a survey of the inequality of races and move some abstract resolution which would probably be rejected. Japan then would merely make a protest. If, however, she regarded herself as ill-treated over Shantung, he was unable to say what line the Jap Delegates might take. . . .*"

ITALY'S EXPANSION OF THE TREATY OF LONDON

The Italian demands were extensive enough. They comprised all that had been promised in the Treaty of London of 1915, and more, too. There was already fundamental conflict between Italian claims under the Treaty of London and Wilson's clearly enunciated principle, "A readjustment of the frontiers of Italy should be effected along clearly recognizable lines of nationality." The Treaty of London was a purely strategic line, incorporating within Italy about 200,000 Austrian Germans of the Trentino up to the Brenner Pass in the Alps, and some 500,000 South Slavs of the Dalmatian shore of the eastern Adriatic. Not content with the degree of strategic control which that line gave them in the entire Adriatic area, Italian delegates now proposed extension of the line to include the town and harbor of Fiume which the Treaty of London had specifically awarded to the Austrian province of Croatia, now part of the new Yugoslav kingdom.

The claim on grounds of nationality which the Italians adduced was spurious, since to identify the town of Fiume as Italian was to separate the town from its adjoining Slavic suburb of Susâk and to isolate it entirely from its surrounding Slavic sea. The harbor was, moreover, the only possible economic outlet in the Adriatic area for the new Yugoslav kingdom of the Serbs, Croats, and Slovenes. The real argument underlying the Italian claim was the strategic one that Italy, and Italy alone, must be in a position to dominate the Adriatic. Barzilai, who formulated Italian claims, said frankly, "It will be very difficult for us to keep up the commerce of Trieste unless we control Fiume and are able to divert its trade to Trieste," and Sonnino, the Italian Foreign Minister, wrote Colonel House that the unforeseen collapse of Austria-Hungary created new problems of security for Italy in the Adriatic which made possession of Fiume essential. Orlando, the Italian Premier, frankly regarded the new Yugoslav state as an enemy:

"If in consequence of the breakup of the Austro-Hungarian Empire, new states had been formed, some of which desired to join Serbia, that meant that the Conference no longer had to deal with the Kingdom of Serbia, but with a new state consisting partly of the old kingdom of Serbia and partly of other territories which belonged to an enemy state. . . . Certainly the recognition of the new state would not constitute an amiable act toward Italy. . . . Furthermore he regarded the Croats and Slovenes, that is to say, the people whose frontiers were in question, as his enemies."

Such an attitude removed the Italian case entirely from the category of British, French, and even Japanese imperialist policy. The British Government had accepted the Mandates principle, while asking exceptions only in the case of their own self-governing Dominions, which were themselves brought to recognize a degree of mandatory responsibility. The French program for dismembering Germany had at least the excuse that France had been twice invaded and overrun by German armies within fifty years, and the 1940 débâcle will convince many that their program was justified. They abandoned the major part of their program in the face of Anglo-American objections.

The Japanese, while just as cynical in their demands as the Italians, at least did not ask for more than the letter of their bond, and even glossed that over by arrangements with China which they could represent as generous and renunciatory.

The Italians, who had not been menaced by the war, had chosen to enter it for a price which they now declared to be inadequate, on the extraordinary plea that they had not foreseen the completeness of their enemy's collapse, which had produced a new danger in the Adriatic!

Moreover, they pretended not to rest their claims on the Treaty of London at all, since fulfillment of the letter of that treaty would have assigned Fiume to Yugoslavia. They simply claimed all that the treaty assigned them, *plus* Fiume, using a variety of arguments ranging from strategic necessity, economic requirements, and historical title to appeals to Wilsonian principles of nationality. If the Italians would have renounced Fiume and frankly resorted to the Treaty of London as the basis of their claim, they could have been assured of French and British diplomatic support and Wilson would have had to yield. While denying any commitments to support the Treaty of London where it ran counter to his Fourteen Points, Wilson admitted that Italy had not been clearly committed to the Fourteen Points in making peace with Austria. Yet, by demanding Fiume over and above the Treaty of London, the Italians impaired the validity of all their demands under that treaty which violated the Fourteen Points, and they challenged the American Delegation to battle in the open field without benefit of fortifications.

2. The Treaty of Versailles and the Covenant of the League of Nations

Resurgent nationalism, greed, and diplomatic bungling effected great damage upon the Wilsonian principles of peace settlement. The Paris Conference itself, by its dictatorial and secret methods, violated the first of the Fourteen Points ("Open covenants of peace openly arrived at"). The treaties were prepared by committees, controversial points were settled by the Supreme Council (in point of fact, by the "Big Three"), and final approval by the Plenary Conference was perfunctory. But against all efforts to tamper with Point Fourteen (formation of "a general association of nations") Wilson stood firm as a rock. In an "association of nations" he saw an opportunity to repair the mistakes and inequities of the treaties as well as to ensure future world peace. "This is the central object of our meeting," he told the delegates. "Settlements may be temporary, but the actions of the nations in the interests of peace and justice must be permanent. We can set up permanent processes. We may not be able to set up permanent decisions." On April 28 the Peace Conference formally adopted a covenant or constitution of a League of Nations, largely the handiwork of Lord Robert Cecil of England and General Jan Christiaan Smuts of South Africa. This Covenant, at Wilson's insistence, became an integral part of the treaties which followed —Versailles, St. Germain, Trianon, Neuilly, and Sèvres. The principal treaty, that of Versailles between the Allies and Germany, was signed in the Hall of Mirrors on June 28, 1919, the place a bitter reminder of the peace at the conclusion of the Franco-Prussian War in 1871, and the time the fifth anniversary of ·the Sarajevo assassination. Ratifications were exchanged January 10, 1920, with the exception of the United States, which refused to ratify and remained technically at war with Germany until July 2, 1921. The treaty, comprised of fifteen parts in 440 articles and nearly a score of annexes, is too long to be included here in full.

Part I, the Covenant of the League of Nations, and excerpts from other parts of the Treaty of Versailles follow.

From the Text of the Treaty of Versailles, June 28, 1919

Part I. The Covenant of the League of Nations [1]

The High Contracting Parties,

In order to promote international co-operation and to achieve international peace and security:

by the acceptance of obligations not to resort to war,

by the prescription of open, just and honourable relations between nations,

by the firm establishment of the understandings of international law as the actual rule of conduct among Governments, and

by the maintenance of justice and a scrupulous respect for all treaty obligations in the dealings of organised peoples with one another,

Agree to this Covenant of the League of Nations.

Article 1. 1. The original Members of the League of Nations shall be those of the Signatories which are named in the Annex to this Covenant and also such of those other States named in the Annex as shall accede without reservation to this Covenant. Such accession shall be effected by a Declaration deposited with the Secretariat within two months of the coming into force of the Covenant. Notice thereof shall be sent to all other Members of the League.

2. Any fully self-governing State, Dominion or Colony not named in the Annex may become a Member of the League if its admission is agreed to by two-thirds of the Assembly, provided that it shall give

[1] League of Nations, *Ten Years of World Co-operation*, Secretariat of the League of Nations, Geneva, 1930, 417-30. Amendments to the original draft are shown in italics.

effective guarantees of its sincere intention to observe its international obligations, and shall accept such regulations as may be prescribed by the League in regard to its military, naval and air forces and armaments.

3. Any Member of the League may, after two years' notice of its intention so to do, withdraw from the League, provided that all its international obligations and all its obligations under this Covenant shall have been fulfilled at the time of its withdrawal.

Article 2. The action of the League under this Covenant shall be effected through the instrumentality of an Assembly and of a Council, with a permanent Secretariat.

Article 3. 1. The Assembly shall consist of Representatives of the Members of the League.

2. The Assembly shall meet at stated intervals and from time to time as occasion may require at the Seat of the League, or at such other place as may be decided upon.

3. The Assembly may deal at its meetings with any matter within the sphere of action of the League or affecting the peace of the world.

4. At meetings of the Assembly, each Member of the League shall have one vote, and may have not more than three Representatives.

Article 4. 1. The Council shall consist of Representatives of the Principal Allied and Associated Powers, together with Representatives of four other Members of the League. These four Members of the League shall be selected by the Assembly from time to time in its discretion. Until the appointment of the Representatives of the four Members of the League first selected by the Assembly, Representatives of Belgium, Brazil, Spain and Greece shall be Members of the Council.

2. With the approval of the majority of the Assembly, the Council may name additional Members of the League, whose Representatives shall always be Members of the Council; the Council with like approval may increase the number of Members of the League to be selected by the Assembly for representation on the Council.

2 bis. The Assembly shall fix by a two-thirds majority the rules dealing with the election of the non-permanent Members of the Council, and particularly such regulations as relate to their term of office and the conditions of re-eligibility.

3. The Council shall meet from time to time as occasion may require, and at least once a year, at the Seat of the League, or at such other place as may be decided upon.

4. The Council may deal at its meetings with any matter within the sphere of action of the League or affecting the peace of the world.

5. Any Member of the League not represented on the Council shall be invited to send a Representative to sit as a member at any meeting of the Council during the consideration of matters specially affecting the interests of that Member of the League.

6. At meetings of the Council, each Member of the League represented on the Council shall have one vote, and may have not more than one Representative.

Article 5. 1. Except where otherwise expressly provided in this Covenant or by the terms of the present Treaty, decisions at any meeting of the Assembly or of the Council shall require the agreement of all the Members of the League represented at the meeting. . . .

Article 6. 1. The permanent Secretariat shall be established at the Seat of the League. The Secretariat shall comprise a Secretary-General and such secretaries and staff as may be required.

2. The first Secretary-General shall be the person named in the Annex; there-

after the Secretary-General shall be appointed by the Council with the approval of the majority of the Assembly.

3. The secretaries and staff of the Secretariat shall be appointed by the Secretary-General with the approval of the Council.

4. The Secretary-General shall act in that capacity at all meetings of the Assembly and of the Council.

5. *The expenses of the League shall be borne by the Members of the League in the proportion decided by the Assembly.*

Article 7. 1. The Seat of the League is established at Geneva. . . .

4. Representatives of the Members of the League and officials of the League when engaged on the business of the League shall enjoy diplomatic privileges and immunities.

5. The buildings and other property occupied by the League or its officials or by Representatives attending its meetings shall be inviolable.

Article 8. 1. The Members of the League recognise that the maintenance of peace requires the reduction of national armaments to the lowest point consistent with national safety and the enforcement by common action of international obligations.

2. The Council, taking account of the geographical situation and circumstances of each State, shall formulate plans for such reduction for the consideration and action of the several Governments.

3. Such plans shall be subject to reconsideration and revision at least every ten years.

4. After these plans shall have been adopted by the several Governments, the limits of armaments therein fixed shall not be exceeded without the concurrence of the Council.

5. The Members of the League agree that the manufacture by private enterprise of munitions and implements of war is open to grave objections. The Council

shall advise how the evil effects attendant upon such manufacture can be prevented, due regard being had to the necessities of those Members of the League which are not able to manufacture the munitions and implements of war necessary for their safety.

6. The Members of the League undertake to interchange full and frank information as to the scale of their armaments, their military, naval and air programmes, and the condition of such of their industries as are adaptable to warlike purposes.

Article 9. A permanent Commission shall be constituted to advise the Council on the execution of the provisions of Articles 1 and 8 and on military, naval and air questions generally.

Article 10. The Members of the League undertake to respect and preserve as against external aggression the territorial integrity and existing political independence of all Members of the League. In case of any such aggression or in case of any threat or danger of such aggression the Council shall advise upon the means by which this obligation shall be fulfilled.

Article 11. 1. Any war or threat of war, whether immediately affecting any of the Members of the League or not, is hereby declared a matter of concern to the whole League, and the League shall take any action that may be deemed wise and effectual to safeguard the peace of nations. In case any such emergency should arise the Secretary-General shall on the request of any Member of the League forthwith summon a meeting of the Council. . . .

Article 12. 1. The Members of the League agree that if there should arise between them any dispute likely to lead to a rupture they will submit the matter either to arbitration *or judicial settlement* or to enquiry by the Council and they agree in no case to resort to war until three months after the award by the arbitrators *or the judicial decision* or the report by the Council.

2. In any case under this Article, the award of the arbitrators *or the judicial decision* shall be made within a reasonable time, and the report of the Council shall be made within six months after the submission of the dispute.

Article 13. 1. The Members of the League agree that whenever any dispute shall arise between them which they recognise to be suitable for submission to arbitration *or judicial settlement,* and which cannot be satisfactorily settled by diplomacy, they will submit the whole subject-matter to arbitration *or judicial settlement.*

2. Disputes as to the interpretation of a treaty, as to any question of international law, as to the existence of any fact which, if established, would constitute a breach of any international obligation, or as to the extent and nature of the reparation to be made for any such breach, are declared to be among those which are generally suitable for submission to arbitration *or judicial settlement.*

3. *For the consideration of any such dispute, the court to which the case is referred shall be the Permanent Court of International Justice, established in accordance with Article 14, or any tribunal agreed on by the parties to the dispute or stipulated in any convention existing between them.*

4. The Members of the League agree that they will carry out in full good faith any award *or decision* that may be rendered, and that they will not resort to war against a Member of the League which complies therewith. In the event of any failure to carry out such an award *or decision,* the Council shall propose what steps should be taken to give effect thereto.

Article 14. The Council shall formulate and submit to the Members of the League for adoption plans for the estab-

lishment of a Permanent Court of International Justice. The Court shall be competent to hear and determine any dispute of an international character which the parties thereto submit to it. The Court may also give an advisory opinion upon any dispute or question referred to it by the Council or by the Assembly.

Article 15. 1. If there should arise between Members of the League any dispute likely to lead to a rupture, which is not submitted to arbitration *or judicial settlement* in accordance with Article 13, the Members of the League agree that they will submit the matter to the Council. Any party to the dispute may effect such submission by giving notice of the existence of the dispute to the Secretary-General, who will make all necessary arrangements for a full investigation and consideration thereof.

2. For this purpose the parties to the dispute will communicate to the Secretary-General, as promptly as possible, statements of their case with all the relevant facts and papers, and the Council may forthwith direct the publication thereof.

3. The Council shall endeavour to effect a settlement of the dispute and, if such efforts are successful, a statement shall be made public giving such facts and explanations regarding the dispute and the terms of settlement thereof as the Council may deem appropriate.

4. If the dispute is not thus settled, the Council either unanimously or by a majority vote shall make and publish a report containing a statement of the facts of the dispute and the recommendations which are deemed just and proper in regard thereto.

5. Any Member of the League represented on the Council may make public a statement of the facts of the dispute and of its conclusions regarding the same.

6. If a report by the Council is unanimously agreed to by the Members thereof

other than the Representatives of one or more of the parties to the dispute, the Members of the League agree that they will not go to war with any party to the dispute which complies with the recommendations of the report.

7. If the Council fails to reach a report which is unanimously agreed to by the members thereof, other than the Representatives of one or more of the parties to the dispute, the Members of the League reserve to themselves the right to take such action as they shall consider necessary for the maintenance of right and justice.

8. If the dispute between the parties is claimed by one of them, and is found by the Council, to arise out of a matter which by international law is solely within the domestic jurisdiction of that party, the Council shall so report, and shall make no recommendation as to its settlement.

9. The Council may in any case under this Article refer the dispute to the Assembly. The dispute shall be so referred at the request of either party to the dispute provided that such request be made within fourteen days after the submission of the dispute to the Council.

10. In any case referred to the Assembly, all the provisions of this Article and of Article 12 relating to the action and powers of the Council shall apply to the action and powers of the Assembly, provided that a report made by the Assembly, if concurred in by the Representatives of those Members of the League represented on the Council and of a majority of the other Members of the League, exclusive in each case of the Representatives of the parties to the dispute, shall have the same force as a report by the Council concurred in by all the members thereof other than the Representatives of one or more of the parties to the dispute.

Article 16. 1. Should any Member of the League resort to war in disregard of its covenants under Articles 12, 13 or 15, it shall *ipso facto* be deemed to have committed an act of war against all other Members of the League, which hereby undertake immediately to subject it to the severance of all trade or financial relations, the prohibition of all intercourse between their nationals and the nationals of the covenant-breaking State, and the prevention of all financial, commercial or personal intercourse between the nationals of the covenant-breaking State and the nationals of any other State, whether a Member of the League or not.

2. It shall be the duty of the Council in such case to recommend to the several Governments concerned what effective military, naval or air force the Members of the League shall severally contribute to the armed forces to be used to protect the covenants of the League.

3. The Members of the League agree, further, that they will mutually support one another in the financial and economic measures which are taken under this Article, in order to minimize the loss and inconvenience resulting from the above measures, and that they will mutually support one another in resisting any special measures aimed at one of their number by the covenant-breaking State, and that they will take the necessary steps to afford passage through their territory to the forces of any of the Members of the League which are cooperating to protect the covenants of the League.

4. Any Member of the League which has violated any covenant of the League may be declared to be no longer a Member of the League by a vote of the Council concurred in by the Representatives of all the other Members of the League represented thereon.

Article 17. 1. In the event of a dispute between a Member of the League and a State which is not a Member of the League, or between States not Members of the League, the State or States not Members of the League shall be invited to accept the obligations of membership in the League for the purposes of such dispute, upon such conditions as the Council may deem just. If such invitation is accepted, the provisions of Articles 12 to 16 inclusive shall be applied with such modifications as may be deemed necessary by the Council.

2. Upon such invitation being given the Council shall immediately institute an enquiry into the circumstances of the dispute and recommend such action as may seem best and most effectual in the circumstances.

3. If a State so invited shall refuse to accept the obligations of membership in the League for the purposes of such dispute, and shall resort to war against a Member of the League, the provisions of Article 16 shall be applicable as against the State taking such action.

4. If both parties to the dispute when so invited refuse to accept the obligations of membership in the League for the purposes of such dispute, the Council may take such measures and make such recommendations as will prevent hostilities and will result in the settlement of the dispute.

Article 18. Every treaty or international engagement entered into hereafter by any Member of the League shall be forthwith registered with the Secretariat and shall as soon as possible be published by it. No such treaty or international engagement shall be binding until so registered.

Article 19. The Assembly may from time to time advise the reconsideration by Members of the League of treaties which have become inapplicable, and the consideration of international conditions whose continuance might endanger the peace of the world.

Article 20. 1. The Members of the League severally agree that this Covenant is accepted as abrogating all obligations or understandings *inter se* which are inconsistent with the terms thereof, and solemnly undertake that they will not hereafter enter into any engagements inconsistent with the terms thereof. . . .

Article 21. Nothing in this Covenant shall be deemed to affect the validity of international engagements, such as treaties of arbitration or regional understandings like the Monroe Doctrine, for securing the maintenance of peace.

Article 22. 1. To those colonies and territories which as a consequence of the late war have ceased to be under the sovereignty of the States which formerly governed them and which are inhabited by peoples not yet able to stand by themselves under the strenuous conditions of the modern world, there should be applied the principle that the well-being and development of such peoples form a sacred trust of civilization and that securities for the performance of this trust should be embodied in this Covenant.

2. The best method of giving practical effect to this principle is that the tutelage of such peoples should be entrusted to advanced nations who, by reason of their resources, their experience or their geographical position, can best undertake this responsibility, and who are willing to accept it, and that this tutelage should be exercised by them as Mandatories on behalf of the League.

3. The character of the mandate must differ according to the stage of the development of the people, the geographical situation of the territory, its economic conditions and other similar circumstances.

4. Certain communities formerly belonging to the Turkish Empire have reached a stage of development where their existence as independent nations can be provisionally recognized subject to the

rendering of administrative advice and assistance by a Mandatory until such time as they are able to stand alone. The wishes of these communities must be a principal consideration in the selection of the Mandatory.

5. Other peoples, especially those of Central Africa, are at such a stage that the Mandatory must be responsible for the administration of the territory under conditions which will guarantee freedom of conscience and religion, subject only to the maintenance of public order and morals, the prohibition of abuses such as the slave trade, the arms traffic and the liquor traffic, and the prevention of the establishment of fortifications or military and naval bases and of military training of the natives for other than police purposes and the defence of territory, and will also secure equal opportunities for the trade and commerce of other Members of the League.

6. There are territories, such as Southwest Africa and certain of the South Pacific islands, which, owing to the sparseness of their population, or their small size, or their remoteness from the centres of civilization, or their geographical contiguity to the territory of the Mandatory, and other circumstances, can be best administered under the laws of the Mandatory as integral portions of its territory, subject to the safeguards above mentioned in the interests of the indigenous population.

7. In every case of mandate, the Mandatory shall render to the Council an annual report in reference to the territory committed to its charge.

8. The degree of authority, control or administration to be exercised by the Mandatory shall, if not previously agreed upon by the Members of the League, be explicitly defined in each case by the Council.

9. A permanent Commission shall be constituted to receive and examine the annual reports of the Mandatories, and to advise the Council on all matters relating to the observance of the mandates.

Article 23. Subject to and in accordance with the provisions of international conventions existing or hereafter to be agreed upon, the Members of the League:

(a) will endeavour to secure and maintain fair and humane conditions of labour for men, women, and children, both in their own countries and in all countries to which their commercial and industrial relations extend, and for that purpose will establish and maintain the necessary international organizations;

(b) undertake to secure just treatment of the native inhabitants of territories under their control;

(c) will entrust the League with the general supervision over the execution of agreements with regard to the traffic in women and children and the traffic in opium and other dangerous drugs;

(d) will entrust the League with the general supervision of the trade in arms and ammunition with the countries in which the control of this traffic is necessary in the common interest;

(e) will make provision to secure and maintain freedom of communications and of transit and equitable treatment for the commerce of all Members of the League. In this connection, the special necessities of the regions devastated during the war of 1914-1918 shall be borne in mind;

(f) will endeavour to take steps in matters of international concern for the prevention and control of disease.

Article 24. 1. There shall be placed under the direction of the League all international bureaus already established by general treaties if the parties to such treaties consent. . . .

3. The Council may include as part of the expenses of the Secretariat the expenses of any bureau or commission which

is placed under the direction of the League.

Article 25. The Members of the League agree to encourage and promote the establishment and cooperation of duly authorized voluntary national Red Cross organizations. . . .

Article 26. 1. Amendments to this Covenant will take effect when ratified by the Members of the League whose Representatives compose the Council and by a majority of the Members of the League whose Representatives compose the Assembly.

2. No such amendment shall bind any Member of the League which signifies its dissent therefrom, but in that case it shall cease to be a Member of the League.

Annex

I. *Original Members of the League of Nations* [names omitted]

II. *First Secretary-General of the League of Nations*
The Honourable Sir James Eric Drummond, K.C.M.G., C.B.

Part II. Boundaries of Germany [omitted] [1]

Part III. Political Clauses for Europe . . .

Article 42. Germany is forbidden to maintain or construct any fortifications either on the left bank of the Rhine or on the right bank to the west of a line drawn 50 kilometres to the East of the Rhine. . . .

Article 45. As compensation for the destruction of the coal-mines in the north of France and as part payment towards the total reparation due from Germany for the damage resulting from the war,

[1] The Treaty of Versailles, exclusive of the Covenant of the League of Nations, is taken from the *Treaty of Peace with Germany,* U. S., 66th Congress, 1st Sess., Senate Doc. No. 49, 1919.

Germany cedes to France in full and absolute possession, with exclusive rights of exploitation, unencumbered and free from all debts and charges of any kind, the coal-mines situated in the Saar Basin as defined in Article 48. [Article 48 defines the boundaries.] . . .

Article 49. Germany renounces in favour of the League of Nations, in the capacity of trustee, the government of the territory defined above.

At the end of fifteen years from the coming into force of the present Treaty the inhabitants of the said territory shall be called upon to indicate [by a plebiscite] the sovereignty under which they desire to be placed. [A subsequent article provided for an ad interim government for the Saar Basin by a Commission representing the League of Nations and chosen by the League Council, to include one French citizen, one non-French native of the Saar, and three members "belonging to three countries other than France or Germany."] . . .

The High Contracting Parties, recognising the moral obligation to redress the wrong done by Germany in 1871 both to the rights of France and to the wishes of the population of Alsace and Lorraine, which were separated from their country in spite of the solemn protest of their representatives at the Assembly of Bordeaux,

Agree upon the following Articles:

Article 51. The territories which were ceded to Germany in accordance with the Preliminaries of Peace signed at Versailles on February 26, 1871, and the Treaty of Frankfurt of May 10, 1871, are restored to French sovereignty as from the date of the Armistice of November 11, 1918.

The provisions of the Treaties establishing the delimitation of the frontiers before 1871 shall be restored. . . .

Article 80. Germany acknowledges and will respect strictly the independence of Austria, within the frontiers which may be fixed in a Treaty between that State and the Principal Allied and Associated Powers; she agrees that this independence shall be inalienable, except with the consent of the Council of the League of Nations.

Article 81. Germany, in conformity with the action already taken by the Allied and Associated Powers, recognises the complete independence of the Czecho-Slovak State which will include the autonomous territory of the Ruthenians to the south of the Carpathians. Germany hereby recognises the frontiers of this State as determined by the Principal Allied and Associated Powers and the other interested States. . . .

Article 84. German nationals habitually resident in . . . the Czecho-Slovak State will obtain Czecho-Slovak nationality *ipso facto* and lose their German nationality. . . .

Article 87. Germany, in conformity with the action already taken by the Allied and Associated Powers, recognises the complete independence of Poland. . . .

Article 89. Poland undertakes to accord freedom of transit to persons, goods, vessels, carriages, wagons and mails in transit between East Prussia and the rest of Germany over Polish territory, including territorial waters, and to treat them at least as favourably as the persons, goods, vessels, carriages, wagons and mails respectively of Polish or of any other more favoured nationality, origin, importation, starting-point, or ownership as regards facilities, restrictions and all other matters. . . .

Article 102. The Principal Allied and Associated Powers undertake to establish the town of Danzig, together with the rest of the territory described in Article 100, as a Free City. It will be placed under the protection of the League of Nations. . . .

Article 116. Germany acknowledges and agrees to respect as permanent and inalienable the independence of all the territories which were part of the former Russian Empire on August 1, 1914.

In accordance with the provisions of Article 259 of Part IX (Financial Clauses) and Article 292 of Part X (Economic Clauses) Germany accepts definitely the abrogation of the Brest-Litovsk Treaties and of all other treaties, conventions and agreements entered into by her with the Maximalist Government in Russia.

The Allied and Associated Powers formally reserve the rights of Russia to obtain from Germany restitution and reparation based on the principles of the present Treaty. . . .

Part IV. German Rights and Interests outside Germany

Article 119. Germany renounces in favour of the Principal Allied and Associated Powers all her rights and titles over her oversea possessions. [This renunciation includes Germany's concessions in China.] . . .

Part V. Military, Naval, and Air Claims

Article 159. The German military forces shall be demobilised and reduced as prescribed hereinafter.

Article 160. (1) By a date which must not be later than March 31, 1920, the German Army must not comprise more than seven divisions of infantry and three divisions of cavalry.

After that date the total number of effectives in the Army of the States constituting Germany must not exceed one hundred thousand men, including officers and establishments of depots. The Army shall be devoted exclusively to the maintenance of order within the territory and to the control of the frontiers.

The total effective strength of officers, including the personnel of staffs, whatever their composition, must not exceed four thousand. . . .

(3) The German General Staff and all similar organisations shall be dissolved and may not be reconstituted in any form. . . .

Article 180. All fortified works, fortresses and field works situated in German territory to the west of a line drawn fifty kilometres to the east of the Rhine shall be disarmed and dismantled. . . .

Article 181. After the expiration of a period of two months from the coming into force of the present Treaty the German naval forces in commission must not exceed:

6 battleships of the *Deutschland* or *Lothringen* type,
6 light cruisers,
12 destroyers,
12 torpedo boats,

or an equal number of ships constructed to replace them as provided in Article 190.

No submarines are to be included.

All other warships, except where there is provision to the contrary in the present Treaty, must be placed in reserve or devoted to commercial purposes. . . .

Article 198. The armed forces of Germany must not include any military or naval air forces. . . .

Part VIII. Reparation

Article 231. The Allied and Associated Governments affirm and Germany accepts the responsibility of Germany and her allies for causing all the loss and damage to which the Allied and Associated Governments and their nationals have been subjected as a consequence of the war imposed upon them by the aggression of Germany and her allies.

Article 232. The Allied and Associated Governments recognise that the resources of Germany are not adequate, after taking into account permanent diminutions of such resources which will result from other provisions of the present Treaty, to make complete reparation for all such loss and damage.

The Allied and Associated Governments, however, require, and Germany undertakes, that she will make compensation for all damage done to the civilian population of the Allied and Associated Powers and to their property during the period of the belligerency of each as an Allied or Associated Power against Germany by such aggression by land, by sea and from the air, and in general all damage as defined in Annex I hereto. . . .

Article 233. The amount of the above damage for which compensation is to be made by Germany shall be determined by an Inter-Allied Commission, to be called the *Reparation Commission* and constituted in the form and with the powers set forth hereunder and in Annexes II to VII inclusive hereto.

This Commission shall consider the claims and give to the German Government a just opportunity to be heard.

The findings of the Commission as to the amount of damage defined as above shall be concluded and notified to the German Government on or before May 1, 1921, as representing the extent of that Government's obligations. . . .

Article 234. The Reparation Commission shall after May 1, 1921, from time to time, consider the resources and capacity of Germany, and, after giving her representatives a just opportunity to be heard, shall have discretion to extend the date, and to modify the form of payments, such as are to be provided for in accordance with Article 233; but not to cancel any part, except with the specific authority of the several Governments represented upon the Commission. . . .

Part XIII. Labour

SECTION I. ORGANISATION OF LABOUR

Whereas the League of Nations has for its object the establishment of universal peace, and such a peace can be established only if it is based upon social justice;

And whereas conditions of labour exist involving such injustice, hardship and privation to large numbers of people as to produce unrest so great that the peace and harmony of the world are imperilled; and an improvement of those conditions is urgently required: as, for example, by the regulation of the hours of work, including the establishment of a maximum working day and week, the regulation of the labour supply, the prevention of unemployment, the provision of an adequate living wage, the protection of the worker against sickness, disease and injury arising out of his employment, the protection of children, young persons and women, provision for old age and injury, protection of the interests of workers when employed in countries other than their own, recognition of the principle of freedom of association, the organization of vocational and technical education and other measures;

Whereas also the failure of any nation to adopt humane conditions of labour is an obstacle in the way of other nations which desire to improve the conditions in their own countries;

The High Contracting Parties, moved by sentiments of justice and humanity, as well as by the desire to secure the permanent peace of the world, agree to the following:

CHAPTER I. ORGANISATION

Article 387. A permanent organisation is hereby established for the promotion of the objects set forth in the Preamble.

The original Members of the League of Nations shall be the original Members of this organisation, and hereafter membership of the League of Nations shall carry with it membership and of the said organisation.

Article 388. The permanent organisation shall consist of:

(1) a General Conference of Representatives of the Members, and

(2) an International Labour Office controlled by the Governing Body described in Article 393. . . .

SECTION II. GENERAL PRINCIPLES

Article 427. The High Contracting Parties, recognising that the well-being, physical, moral and intellectual, of industrial wage-earners is of supreme international importance, have framed, in order to further this great end, the permanent machinery provided for in Section I and associated with that of the League of Nations.

They recognise that differences of climate, habits and customs, of economic opportunity and industrial tradition, make strict uniformity in the conditions of labour difficult of immediate attainment. But, holding as they do, that labour should not be regarded merely as an article of commerce, they think that there are methods and principles for regulating labour conditions which all industrial communities should endeavour to apply, so far as their special circumstances will permit.

Among these methods and principles, the following seem to the High Contracting Parties to be of special and urgent importance:

First. The guiding principle above enunciated that labour should not be regarded merely as a commodity or article of commerce.

Second. The right of association for all lawful purposes by the employed as well as by the employers.

Third. The payment to the employed of a wage adequate to maintain a reasonable standard of life as this is understood in their time and country.

Fourth. The adoption of an eight hours' day or a forty-eight hours' week as the standard to be aimed at where it has not already been attained.

Fifth. The adoption of a weekly rest of at least twenty-four hours, which should include Sunday wherever practicable.

Sixth. The abolition of child labour and the imposition of such limitations on the labour of young persons as shall permit the continuation of their education and assure their proper physical development.

Seventh. The principle that men and women should receive equal remuneration for work of equal value.

Eighth. The standard set by law in each country with respect to the conditions of labour should have due regard to the equitable economic treatment of all workers lawfully resident therein.

Ninth. Each State should make provision for a system of inspection in which women should take part, in order to ensure the enforcement of the laws and regulations for the protection of the employed.

Without claiming that these methods and principles are either complete or final, the High Contracting Parties are of opinion that they are well fitted to guide the policy of the League of Nations; and that, if adopted by the industrial communities who are members of the League, and safeguarded in practice by an adequate system of such inspection, they will confer lasting benefits upon the wage-earners of the world.

Part XIV. Guarantees

SECTION I. WESTERN EUROPE

Article 428. As a guarantee for the execution of the present Treaty by Germany, the German territory situated to the west of the Rhine, together with the bridgeheads, will be occupied by Allied and Associated troops for a period of fifteen years from the coming into force of the present Treaty. . . .

Article 431. If before the expiration of the period of fifteen years Germany complies with all the undertakings resulting from the present Treaty, the occupying forces will be withdrawn immediately.

37 THE NEW RUSSIA: UNION OF SOVIET SOCIALIST REPUBLICS

1. The Immediate Background of the Russian Revolution

Revolution, which had been brewing for so long in Czarist Russia [see pages 663, 675], broke out with new intensity when the inefficiency, corruption, and treachery of the Czarist regime became wholly unmasked during World War I. These conditions were clearly set forth by Mikhail Rodzianko (1859-1924), Deputy in and president of the third and fourth Dumas (1911-16). Rodzianko's *Memoirs* cover Russia's war years, and from them the following extracts are taken.

From RODZIANKO, *Memoirs* (c. 1917) [1]

Soon after the first battles, shocking reports came from the front of the incompetency of the sanitary department, of its inability to handle the wounded at the front. There was great confusion. Freight trains came to Moscow filled with wounded, lying on the bare floor, without even straw, in many cases without clothing, poorly bandaged, and unfed. . . . [At Warsaw, in 1914,] I saw a frightful scene. On the floor, without even a bedding of straw, in mud and slush, lay innumerable wounded, whose pitiful groans and cries filled the air. "For God's sake, get them to attend to us. No one has looked after our wounds for five days." . . .

[In spite of these conditions, the Minister in charge of the sanitary division, Evdokimov, blocked efforts of volunteer organizations because the latter "were of a higher order than his"; and all attempts to remove Evdokimov were futile "because he had the protection of Vladimir Aleksandrovich Sukhomlinov (Minister of War) and the Empress Alexandra Fedorovna. It was said that the young Empress persuaded the Emperor to leave Evdokimov in his place in order to spite the old Empress."] . . .

While at Warsaw, I asked permission of Grand Duke Nicholas Nicholaevich [the supreme military commander] to go to Headquarters. I wished to tell him

[1] Frank Alfred Golder, ed., *Documents of Russian History 1914-1917*, trans. by Emanuel Aronsberg, 1927 (*The Century Historical Series*), 82-85, 93, 116, 118-21. By permission of D. Appleton-Century Co., Inc., New York.

[that] . . . General [N. V.] Ruzski had complained to me of lack of ammunition and the poor equipment of the men. There was a great shortage of boots. In the Carpathians, the soldiers fought barefooted. . . . The Grand Duke stated that he was obliged to stop fighting, temporarily, for lack of ammunition and boots. . . .

[Still, when Rodzianko, with the Grand Duke's approval, sought to call a congress of mayors and provincial heads to organize and expedite the manufacture of war materials, the Minister of the Interior, N. A. Maklakov, objected because, according to reports from the secret police, the proposed congress had "for its real object to discuss political questions and demand a constitution." Later he effectively sabotaged the plan and denounced Rodzianko to the Czar as a dangerous revolutionary!]

Rumors began to circulate that the Tsar desired to remove Grand Duke Nicholas Nicholaevitch and assume the supreme command. It was said that this was the wish of the Empress, who hated the Grand Duke and desired to relieve the Tsar from internal affairs, and in this way while he was at the front she could govern the rear. In the Duma and in public circles the removal of the Grand Duke was looked upon as a serious blunder. . . .

[Rodzianko and others pleaded with the Czar not to take this step, but on September 5, 1915, the Czar took supreme command in place of the popular Grand Duke. With the Czar in the field, the Czarina managed affairs, guided constantly by the counsel of the grasping, despicable "monk," Gregori Efimovich Rasputin. Soon afterward, the Duma was adjourned. The Czar, the Czarina, their

Ministers and advisers, became solely responsible for the chaos that followed—a critical shortage of arms and ammunition on the battle fronts, a growing shortage of food, particularly meat, on the home front (though great quantities of meat spoiled because of poor co-ordination of the different ministries), and disquieting rumors of German influence over the Czarina. When the Duma was reassembled (February, 1916), it became more and more estranged from the Czar, the Czarina, and their Ministers. Even the assassination of Rasputin, December 30, 1916, came too late to save the Romanovs from the consequences of their folly. By January, 1917, the army had become disaffected:]

In January, 1917, General Krymov came . . . and asked to be allowed to tell the members of the Duma unofficially of the tragic situation at the front. . . . He said that, until the political horizon cleared, until the Government changed its course or a new Government came in, which the army trusted, there could be no victory. The rear interfered with the war and temporary victories were of no account. He ended with the following words:

"The feeling in the army is such that all will greet with joy the news of a coup d'état. It has to come; it is felt at the front. Should you decide to do this, we will support you. Seemingly, there is no other way out. You, as well as others, have tried everything, but the evil influence of the wife is mightier than the honest words spoken to the Tsar. We cannot afford to lose time."

After Krymov finished, we sat there deeply depressed. The first to speak was Shingarev.

"The General is right—a coup d'état is necessary. But who will dare to undertake it?"

Shidlovski exclaimed in anger, "We cannot waste pity on him [the Czar], if he ruins Russia."

Many of the members of the Duma agreed with Shingarev and Shidlovski. They became noisy in their differences of opinion. Someone quoted Brusilov: "If it comes to a choice between the Tsar and Russia, I will take Russia.". . .

On January 20, I had an audience with the Tsar.

"From my second report, Your Majesty may have seen that I regard the situation as worse than ever. The frame of mind of the country is such that very serious outbreaks may be expected. Political divisions no longer exist, but Russia, as one, demands a change in Government, and the appointment of a responsible Prime Minister who has the confidence of the country. It is necessary to work in agreement with the legislative bodies and public organizations in order to organize the rear and conquer the enemy. To our great shame in these war times, everything is in disorder. There is no government, no system, and no coöperation between front and rear. Wherever one looks he sees only disorder and betrayal. . . . The idea spreads that everything is done that harms Russia and benefits the enemy. Strange rumors circulate about traitors and spies in the rear of the army. There is not one honest man in your entourage; all decent people have either been sent away or have left. . . . It is no secret that the Empress issues State orders without consulting you; that Ministers go to her with their reports; and that at her will those she disapproves of are removed and are replaced by others who are totally unfit. . . . She is regarded as a partisan of Germany, which she protects. Even the common people speak of it.". . .

I then turned the conversation to the front and recalled how I had pleaded with him not to take the supreme command

and that now, after the failure on the Rumanian front, all blame fell upon him.

"Do not bring about a situation, Your Majesty, which will force your subjects to choose between you and the good of the country. Until now, Tsar and country have been one, but lately a distinction has been made."

The Tsar pressed his head with his hands and said, "Is it possible that for twenty-two years I have tried to do some good, and that for twenty-two years I have failed?"

It was a trying moment.

"Yes, Your Majesty, for twenty-two years you have followed the wrong trail."

Notwithstanding this open expression of opinion which could not be agreeable to the Emperor, he bade me good-bye in a friendly way. . . .

On February 23, I had an audience with the Tsar. . . . I was received very coldly. . . . I began to read my report. The Emperor listened not only with indifference, but with a kind of ill-will . . . and he finally interrupted me with the request that I hurry a bit, as Grand Duke Michael Alexandrovich was waiting for him to have a cup of tea. . . .

When I raised the question of the transfer of machine guns, he remarked: "Strange, I know nothing about this." . . . When I spoke of Protopopov, he became irritated. . . . When I called his attention to the threatening situation in the country and the possibility of a revolution, he broke in again by saying: "The information I have is quite contrary to yours, and as to the Duma, I should like to say that if it permits itself such harsh speeches as last time, it will be dissolved."

"Your Majesty, I regard it as my duty to tell you that I have a foreboding, and a conviction that this is my last report to you."

"Why?"

"Because the Duma will be dismissed,

and the course which the Government pursues will lead to no good results. . . . There is still time and opportunity to turn back and form a Government responsible to the [legislative] chambers. But this, seemingly, is not to be. You, Your Majesty, do not agree with me, and things are as they have been. The result will be a revolution and such anarchy as no one will be able to control."

The Emperor made no reply, and bade me good-bye rather formally.

2. The March Revolution (1917)

THE PROVISIONAL GOVERNMENT

Rodzianko's prediction proved right. Early in March (February by the old Russian calendar) strikes and riots broke out in St. Petersburg (now renamed Petrograd; in 1917, Leningrad). On March 10 the troops mutinied in the capital. And on the same day Nicholas II issued the following decree: [1]

"By virtue of Article 99 of the Fundamental Laws of the state, we command:

The work of the State Duma and State Council shall cease March 11 of this year, and the term of its renewal shall be not later than April, 1917, depending upon extraordinary circumstances."

To this command the Duma, after soul-searching debate, refused to accede. Leaders of the political groups (collectively known as the Senior Council) maneuvered the following resolution on March 12 as a reply to the Czar:

"The Senior Council, having met in

[1] This and the next three selections are from Golder, ed., *Documents of Russian History 1914-1917.* By permission of D. Appleton-Century Co., Inc. This is 277-78.

special session and acquainted itself with the decree of prorogation, has resolved:

The State Duma shall not disperse. All Deputies shall remain in their places."

On the same day (March 12), "at half-past two in the afternoon," the Duma named a "Provisional Committee for maintaining order in Petrograd and establishing contact with various institutions and individuals." This committee, early in the morning of March 13, issued appeals to the people of Petrograd and to the army to protect property, maintain order, and assist "in the difficult task of forming a new Government in accordance with the desire of the population and worthy of its confidence." Two days later, on March 15, Czar Nicholas II abdicated the throne in favor of the Grand Duke Michael Alexandrovich, who, in turn, abdicated "in favor of the people," beseeching them (March 16) "to subject themselves to the Provisional Government . . . until the summoning, at the earliest possible moment, of a Constituent Assembly, selected by universal, direct, equal, and secret ballot, which shall establish a government in accordance with the will of the people." On this same day (March 16), the Provisional Executive Committee and the Duma set forth the Provisional Government of Prince Georgi Evgenievich Lvov and announced its program in the following document.

From the Proclamation of the Provisional Government (March 16, 1917) [1]

Citizens, the Provisional Executive Committee of the members of the Duma, with the aid and support of the garrison of the capital and its inhabitants, has tri-

umphed over the dark forces of the Old Régime to such an extent as to enable it to organize a more stable executive power. With this idea in mind, the Provisional Committee has appointed as ministers of the first Cabinet representing the public, men whose past political and public life assures them the confidence of the country.

Prince George E. Lvov, *Prime Minister and Minister of the Interior*
P. N. Miliukov,
Minister of Foreign Affairs
A. I. Gughkov,
Minister of War and Marine
M. I. Tereschenko,
Minister of Finance
A. A. Manuilov,
Minister of Education
A. I. Shingarev,
Minister of Agriculture
N. V. Nekrasov,
Minister of Transportation
A. I. Konovalov,
Minister of Commerce and Industry
A. F. Kerenski, *Minister of Justice*
Vl. Lvov, *Holy Synod*

The Cabinet will be guided in its actions by the following principles:

1. An immediate general amnesty for all political and religious offenses, including terrorist acts, military revolts, agrarian offenses, etc.

2. Freedom of speech and press; freedom to form labor unions and to strike. These political liberties should be extended to the army in so far as war conditions permit.

3. The abolition of all social, religious and national restrictions.

4. Immediate preparation for the calling of a Constituent Assembly, elected by universal and secret vote, which shall determine the form of government and draw up the Constitution for the country.

5. In place of the police, to organize a

---

[1] *Ibid.*, 308-09.

national militia with elective officers, and subject to the local self-governing body.

6. Elections to be carried out on the basis of universal, direct, equal, and secret suffrage.

7. The troops that have taken part in the revolutionary movement shall not be disarmed or removed from Petrograd.

8. On duty and in war service, strict military discipline should be maintained, but when off duty, soldiers should have the same public rights as are enjoyed by other citizens.

The Provisional Government wishes to add that it has no intention of taking advantage of the existence of war conditions to delay the realization of the above-mentioned measures of reform.

President of the Duma,
   M. Rodzianko
President of the Council of Ministers,
   Prince Lvov
Ministers
   Miliukov, Nekrasov, Manuilov, Konovalov, Tereschenko, Vl. Lvov, Shingarev, Kerenski

OPPOSITION FROM THE PETROGRAD SOVIET

Except Aleksandr Feodorovich Kerenski, who was a Socialist Revolutionary, the Provisional Government consisted of members of the Kadets, or Constitutional. Democrat party, predominantly bourgeois, dedicated to the task of continuing the war with Germany, of honoring Russian commitments with the Allies, of instituting civil equality and civil liberties, and of creating by democratic means a liberal constitutional regime which would carry out further social and economic reforms. From the first, however, the Provisional Government was harassed and weakened by the Petrograd Soviet

("Council") of Workers' and Soldiers' Deputies. First organized in 1905, the Soviets had never ceased as an instrument of the Socialist groups. At the outset of the March Revolution, the Petrograd Soviet reorganized (March 12) and issued a proclamation (March 13) urging soldiers to observe order and shoot reactionaries ("Aim seldom, but hit the mark!"), urging workers to organize local committees in every ward, to take over "the management of local affairs," and to arm themselves for "a militia of workmen," and calling upon the "Proletariat of the World" to unite and put a stop to the World War. The presence of Kerenski in the Provisional Government constituted a liaison between that body and the Soviet, but the latter looked with suspicion upon the Provisional Government and supported it only so long as it carried out the Soviet's wishes. In the eyes of the Soviet the revolution was a *bourgeois* revolution only, a preliminary and temporary step towards the *proletarian* revolution to follow. In their eyes, too, the Provisional Government was *responsible* to the Soviet, and to make sure that the government carried out the Soviet program, the Soviet appointed a "Contact Commission . . . to keep the Soviet informed regarding the intentions and acts of the Government; to keep the latter, in turn, informed regarding the demands of the revolutionary people; to exert influence upon the Government for the purpose of satisfying these demands; and to exercise constant control over its actions." [1] The Soviet took pains to have armed forces, both military and civilian, at its disposal, and in an Order No. 1 (March 14) to the garrison of the Petrograd district stated that "the

[1] *Ibid.,* 304.

orders of the military commission of the State Duma are to be fulfilled only in cases which do not contradict the orders and decisions of the Soviet of Workers' and Soldiers' Deputies." Thus the Provisional Government, unsure of its grip anyway, was in a humiliating and intolerable position, awed by the active and vigilant Soviet with which it had inevitable conflicts, ill will, and finally an open break. Editorials in *Izvestia,* the Soviet's journal, on April 7 and 11, 1917, defined relations between the Provisional Government and the Soviet.

From *Izvestia,* April 7 and 11, 1917 [1]

The Provisional Government has two tasks: (1) To prepare for the Constituent Assembly; (2) to govern the country until the Assembly meets. The first task requires no discussion, but the second needs some explanation. The point is that the Government has in its hands a tremendous financial and administrative power and it can, if it so desires, exert great influence on the elections for the Constituent Assembly. It can do even more. It can bring about a state of affairs which the Constituent Assembly, when it meets, must face as accomplished facts, such, for example, as the conclusion of peace, declaration of war, cancellation of commercial agreements, etc. This tremendous power in the hands of the Provisional Government raises the questions (1) whence comes so much power, and (2) how to prevent its use for evil purposes.

First of all, it is important to state most emphatically (and it is for the Provisional Government to say it) that it was not the abdication of Nicholas, and after him Michael Romanov, that called to power the Council of Ministers with Prince Lvov at its head. The Provisional Government was called to power by the will of His Majesty, the Revolutionary People, and no one else. Its power and composition were agreed to by the Committee of the State Duma and the Soviet of Workers' and Soldiers' Deputies. The last named, the real incarnation of the revolution, did not, for weighty reasons, take upon itself the executive power, but handed it to the Council of Ministers, with the understanding that it would carry out immediately certain named reforms.

In addition to these reforms, the Soviet reserved to itself the right of active control over the carrying out of the said reforms.

Does the Provisional Government have executive power over the country? Yes, it has. Does it have full and unlimited power? No, it has not. We have not overthrown one autocrat in order to have twelve. What then limits the power of the Provisional Government?

In the first place, the vigilant and ever wakeful control of the whole nation, organized and meeting freely. It can always stop, instantly, those measures of the Provisional Government which threaten popular liberty. In the second place, the actual control by the organs of the Petrograd Soviet of Workers' and Soldiers' Deputies. . . .

The bourgeois public accuses us of standing in the way of national unity, of bringing about the destructive "Dual Government," of inciting the soldiers against the officers, and thereby interfering with the successful course of the war. At the same time, the bourgeois press does not cease to tell us of the great dangers that threaten Russia from Germany, and lays the blame for military failures on our internal situation.

All these charges and complaints have two specific objects. One is to persuade the soldiers that it is necessary to go on with the war, and the other to sow discord between the soldiers and the workers.

[1] *Ibid.,* 315-18.

As long as the workers and soldiers march hand in hand, the interests of the working population are safe from all attacks of the ruling classes. But if the attempt to divide them should succeed, the cause of the people would be lost, and the bourgeoisie would rejoice in their victory.

Comrades, do not listen to these sowers of discord among you. Remember that in unity there is strength.

LENIN'S "BOLSHEVIK" DEMANDS

The confusion resulting from the "Dual Government" was multiplied in the spring months by the return to Russia of exiles and their political splinter groups. By far the most important of the exiles returning was Vladimir Ilich Ulyanov, better known by his pseudonym, Nikolai Lenin (1870-1924). A professional revolutionary of the extreme Left, Lenin stands forth as the ablest organizer and political analyst of the entire group of conspirators engendered by Czarist methods. He accepted the teachings of Marx and Engels and sought to give reality to the proletarian battle cry of the *Communist Manifesto* [see page 506]. In the opening years of the present century he set forth his plans in the *Iskra* (The Spark), his radical journal. He viewed with contempt the Social-Democratic activities of his fellows. In a lengthy account written in 1901-02 he set forth ideas from which he did not deviate in the years to follow.

From LENIN, "What Is to Be Done?" (1901-02) [1]

The history of all countries shows that the working class, exclusively by its own

effort, is able to develop only trade-union consciousness, *i.e.,* it may itself realize the necessity for combining in unions to fight against the employers and to strive to compel the government to pass necessary labor legislation, etc. . . . The workers can acquire class political consciousness *only from without,* that is, only outside of the sphere of relations between workers and employers . . . [in] the sphere of the inter-relations between *all* classes. . . .

Take the type of Social-Democratic circle that has been most widespread during the past few years, and examine its work. It "has contact with the workers," it issues leaflets—in which abuses in the factories, the government's partiality towards the capitalists, and the tyranny of the police are strongly condemned—and rests content with this. At meetings of workers there are either no discussions or they do not extend beyond such subjects. Lectures and discussions on the history of the revolutionary movement, on questions of the home and foreign policy . . . of the economic evolution of Russia and of Europe, and the position of the various classes in modern society, etc., are extremely rare. Of systematically acquiring and extending contact with other classes of society, no one ever dreams. The ideal leader . . . is something more in the nature of a trade-union secretary than a Socialist political leader. . . . It cannot be too strongly insisted that *this is not* enough to constitute Social-Democracy. The Social-Democrat's ideal should not be a trade-union secretary, but a *tribune of the people,* able to react to every manifestation of tyranny and oppression, no matter where it takes place, no matter what stratum or class of the people it affects; he must be able to group all these manifestations into a single picture of police violence and capitalist exploitation; he must be able to take advantage of every petty event in order to explain his Socialistic convictions and his Social-

[1] *The Collected Works of V. I. Lenin* (36 vols. when completed), IV, *The Iskra Period, 1900-1902,* 1929, Bk. II, 114-15, 158-60, 187-88, 198-99, 204, 206. By permission of International Publishers, New York.

Democratic demands *to all,* in order to explain to *all* and every one the world significance of the struggle for the emancipation of the proletariat. . . .

The political struggle carried on by the Social-Democrats is far more extensive and complex than the economic struggle the workers carry on against the employers and the government. Similarly (and indeed for that reason), the organization of revolutionary Social-Democrats must inevitably *differ* from the organizations of the workers. . . . The workers' organizations must in the first place be trade organizations; secondly, they must be as wide as possible; and thirdly, they must be as public as conditions will allow (here, of course, I have only autocratic Russia in mind). On the other hand, the organizations of revolutionists must be comprised first and foremost of people whose profession is that of revolutionists. . . . As this is the common feature of the members of such an organization, *all distinctions, as between workers and intellectuals,* and certainly distinctions of trade and profession, must be dropped. Such an organization must of necessity be not too extensive and as secret as possible. . . .

"A dozen wise men can be more easily caught than a hundred fools!" This wonderful truth (which the hundred fools will applaud) appears obvious only because in the very midst of the argument you have skipped from one question to another. . . . The fact is, of course, that our movement cannot be caught precisely because it has hundreds and hundreds of thousands of roots deep down among the masses, but that is not the point we are discussing. . . . If you agree to discuss the question of catching the *organizations,* and to stick to that question, then I assert that it is far more difficult to catch ten wise men than it is to catch a hundred fools. . . . As I have already said, by "wise men," in connec-

tion with organization, I mean *professional revolutionists,* irrespective of whether they are students or workingmen. I assert: 1. That no movement can be durable without a stable organization of leaders to maintain continuity; 2. that the more widely the masses are drawn into the struggle and form the basis of the movement, the more necessary it is to have such an organization and the more stable must it be (for it is much easier then for demagogues to side-track the more backward sections of the masses); 3. that the organization must consist chiefly of persons engaged in revolution as a profession; 4. that in a country with a despotic government, the more we *restrict* the membership of this organization to persons who are engaged in revolution as a profession and who have been professionally trained in the art of combating the political police, the more difficult will it be to catch the organization; and 5. the *wider* will be the circle of men and women of the working class or of other classes of society able to join the movement and perform active work in it. . . . We can never give a mass organization that degree of secrecy which is essential for the persistent and continuous struggle against the government. But to concentrate all secret functions in the hands of as small a number of professional revolutionists as possible, does not mean that the latter will "do the thinking for all" and that the crowd will not take an active part in the movement. On the contrary, the crowd will advance from its ranks increasing numbers of professional revolutionists, for it will know that it is not enough for a few students and workingmen waging economic war to gather together and form a "committee," but that professional revolutionists must be trained for years; the crowd will "think" not of primitive ways but of training professional revolutionists. The centralization of the secret functions of the *organization* does not mean the concentration of all the functions of the *movement*. The active participation of the greatest masses in the dissemination of illegal literature will not diminish because a dozen professional revolutionists concentrate in their hands the secret part of the work; on the contrary, it will *increase tenfold*. . . .

Attention must be devoted *principally* to the task of *raising* the workers to the level of revolutionists, but without, in doing so, necessarily *degrading* ourselves to the level of the "labor masses." . . . A workingman who is at all talented and "promising" *must not be left* to work eleven hours a day in a factory. We must arrange that he be maintained by the party, that he may in due time go underground, that he change the place of his activity, otherwise he will not enlarge his experience. . . . When we shall have detachments of specially trained working-class revolutionists who have gone through long years of preparation . . . no political police in the world will be able to contend against them.

LENIN'S CHALLENGE TO THE MARCH REVOLUTION

At a convention of the Russian Social-Democratic Labor party in London, in 1903, Lenin precipitated a split in the party by insisting upon his views. Against the minority (Menshevik) opinion that party membership should be accorded to any person who accepted the party program and lent material support, regardless of whether he took a direct part in revolutionary activity and obeyed every injunction of party discipline, Lenin insisted upon a membership restricted to militant revolutionaries who entered actively into the illegal work of the party. At the convention, Lenin controlled a majority (the Bolsheviks), although *within*

Russia the Mensheviks of the Convention commanded the majority of Socialist support until 1917. Meanwhile, with amazing energy, singleness of purpose, and iron will, Lenin perfected a small, highly disciplined party of Bolsheviks able and willing to take full advantage of every weakness of the Provisional Government in a ruthless bid for political power and a dictatorship in the name of the proletariat. When the German Government, in a move to weaken further the Provisional Government, shipped Lenin to Russia from his Swiss place of exile (mid-April, 1917), Lenin was prepared to throw into action the machinery which he had been perfecting since 1900. His objective was clear from the start: to set up, in Bolshevik hands, a dictatorship in the name of the proletariat. His methods were no less clear: with the cry "All Power to the Soviets" he sought both to overthrow the Provisional Government and to seize control of the Soviets, whose Menshevik and Social-Revolutionary leaders, Lenin alleged, had yielded to bourgeois flattery and betrayed the Soviets into capitalist hands. When the Executive Commission of a Soviet condemned Lenin's propaganda as "no less harmful than any other counter-revolutionary propaganda proceeding from the Right," Lenin was ready to discredit the Mensheviks and Social-Revolutionaries of the Executive Commission as follows.

From LENIN, Editorial in *Pravda* (May 1, 1917) [1]

Let us see now wherein lie the main points of difference between (1) the counterrevolutionary propaganda proceeding from the Right, (2) the propaganda in

[1] *Pravda*, May 1, 1917, in *Collected Works of V. I. Lenin*, XX, *The Revolution of 1917*, 1929, Bk. I, 223-25. By permission of International Publishers.

support of the Provisional Government, and (3) our own propaganda.

The Right desires to overthrow the Provisional Government and the return to a monarchy.

The Provisional Government has *promised* to act in agreement with the Petrograd Soviet of Workers' and Soldiers' Deputies.

Our propaganda consists in demanding that the whole power of the state be turned over to the Soviets . . . and none other, because the Soviets are definitely known to represent an overwhelming majority of the people. . . .

Now, then, the Rights are for a monarchical power. The capitalists are for the power of the capitalists (the Provisional Government is a government of the capitalists); they only promise to act in agreement with the Soviet. . . .

We, on the other hand, wish to convince the majority of the people that power must reside solely in the Soviets of Workers', Soldiers', Peasants' and other Deputies. . . .

Those who advocate an understanding with the Provisional Government . . . are at present themselves relying on the majority of the people! How then can they maintain that our propaganda which urges the majority to seize power is "no less harmful than any counterrevolutionary propaganda proceeding from the Right"?

This is a glaring inconsistency.

The Soviet of Soldiers' Deputies can hardly support this view of its Executive Commission for long.

Let us go a step further. Wherein do we really differ? Chiefly on three points:

1. On the question of land. We demand that the peasants, by the decision of the majority of the peasants themselves in each locality, take over the *entire* land immediately, thus increasing the output of bread and meat for the soldiers.

The Provisional Government favors an "agreement" between the peasants and the landowners, *i.e.,* "an agreement" of three hundred peasants with one landowner.

The future will show whether the majority of the people agrees with us or with the Provisional Government on this question.

2. We favor that type of a republic where, from top to bottom, there is no police, no standing army (instead . . . we believe there should be a general army of the people), no officialdom enjoying in fact the privileges of irremovability and high bourgeois salaries. We want all public offices to be elective, all officials to be subject to recall at any time, and their pay to be that of proletarians.

The Provisional Government stands for the return of the police of the usual type; it favors a standing army and the usual kind of officialdom.

3. The Provisional Government wants to continue the war started by Nicholas the Bloody . . . stands for the confirmation of the secret, predatory treaties *without consulting the will of the people* and even without making them public.

We are against such a war, against the confirmation of the treaties, against their nonpublication.

3. The November Revolution (1917)

THE BOLSHEVIK COUP

Throughout the summer and autumn of 1917 the Provisional Government clung to its precarious existence. Pressed by the Bolsheviks, it was reorganized in May, when Aleksandr Ivanovich Guchkov and Pavel Nikolaevich Milyukov were forced to resign. In July the Bolsheviks attempted prematurely to seize power, but the movement was suppressed, several leaders were arrested, and Lenin himself went into hiding in Finland. On July 20 Prince Lvov resigned and Kerenski became head of the Provisional Government—only to be slowly crushed between the monarchistic Right and the Bolshevik Left. On September 9-14, General Lavr Georgievich Kornilov, dismissed by Kerenski as commander in chief, refused to obey and led a Rightist attack upon the government to free it from Socialist control and to destroy the Soviet. Kornilov was defeated, but Kerenski suppressed the uprising only by appealing to the Bolsheviks for aid and releasing their leaders from prison. And within a few weeks Kerenski found himself under the domination of his Bolshevik allies. In October the Bolsheviks won a majority in the Petrograd Soviet and Leon Trotsky became its chairman. At this point Lenin determined to overthrow the Provisional Government. On November 6 (October by the old Russian calendar), the Bolsheviks, led by their Military Revolutionary Committee, captured most of the governmental offices, took the Winter Palace, and arrested members of the Provisional Government. Kerenski escaped, tried vainly to organize resistance, went into hiding and subsequently into exile abroad. On the morning of November 7, the Military Revolutionary Committee posted such proclamations as the following.

From A Proclamation "To the Citizens of Russia!" (November 7, 1917) [1]

The Provisional Government is deposed. The State Power has passed into the hands of the organ of the Petrograd Soviet of

[1] This and the next two selections are from John Reed, *Ten Days That Shook the World,* 1919. By permission of International Publishers. New York. This is 95.

Workers' and Soldiers' Deputies, the Military Revolutionary Committee, which stands at the head of the Petrograd proletariat and garrison.

The cause for which the people were fighting: immediate proposal of a democratic peace, abolition of landlord property-rights over the land, labor control over production, creation of a Soviet Government—that cause is securely achieved.

LONG LIVE THE REVOLUTION OF WORKMEN, SOLDIERS AND PEASANTS!

THE REVOLUTIONARY ACTS OF THE ALL-RUSSIAN CONGRESS OF SOVIETS (1917)

While the Bolshevik Revolution spread to Moscow and elsewhere in Russia, an All-Russian Congress of Soviets of Workers', Soldiers', and Peasants' Deputies convened in Petrograd on November 8, 1917. John Reed, an American newspaper correspondent who sympathized with the Bolshevik program, was present and wrote the following account of what took place.

From REED, *Ten Days That Shook the World* (1919) [2]

It was just 8:40 when a thundering wave of cheers announced the entrance of the presidium, with Lenin—great Lenin—among them. A short, stocky figure, with a big head set down in his shoulders, bald and bulging. Little eyes, a snubbish nose, wide, generous mouth, and heavy chin; clean-shaven now, but already beginning to bristle with the well-known beard of his past and future. . . . A strange popular leader—a leader purely by virtue of intellect; colorless, humorless, uncompromising and detached, without picturesque idiosyncrasies—but with the power of explaining profound ideas in simple terms. . . . Lenin, gripping the edge of the read-

[2] *Ibid.,* 125-27, 130, 132-34, 137-39, 144-45

ing stand, letting his little winking eyes travel over the crowd as he stood there waiting, apparently oblivious to the long-rolling ovation, which lasted several minutes. When it finished, he said simply, "We shall now proceed to construct the Socialist order!" Again that overwhelming human roar.

"The first thing is the adoption of practical measures to realize peace. . . . We shall offer peace to the peoples of all the belligerent countries upon the basis of Soviet terms—no annexations, no indemnities, and the right of self-determination of peoples. At the same time, according to our promise, we shall publish and repudiate the secret treaties. . . . The question of War and Peace is so clear that I think that I may, without preamble, read the project of a Proclamation to the Peoples of All the Belligerent Countries. . . .

" 'The Workers' and Peasants' Government, created by the revolution of November 6th and 7th and based on the Soviets of Workers', Soldiers' and Peasants' Deputies, proposes to all the belligerent peoples and to their Governments to begin immediately negotiations for a just and democratic peace . . . without annexations (that is to say, without conquest of foreign territory, without forcible annexation of other nationalities), and without indemnities.' " . . .

When the grave thunder of applause died away, Lenin spoke again: "We propose to the Congress to ratify this declaration. . . . This proposal of peace will meet with resistance on the part of the imperialist governments—we don't fool ourselves on that score. But we hope that revolution will soon break out in all the belligerent countries; that is why we address ourselves especially to the workers of France, England and Germany. . . . The revolution of November 6th and 7th," he ended, "has opened the era of the Social Revolution." . . .

It was exactly 10:35 when Kameniev asked all in favor of the proclamation to hold up their cards. . . . Unanimous.

Suddenly, by common impulse, we found ourselves on our feet, mumbling together into the smooth lifting unison of the *Internationale*. . . . "The war is ended! The war is ended!" said a young workman near me, his face shining. . . .

Lenin was reading the Decree on Land: ["We shall secure the confidence of the peasants by one decree which will wipe out the private property of the landowners," he had said.]

"(1.) All private ownership of land is abolished immediately without compensation.

"(2.) All land-owners' estates, and all lands belonging to the Crown, to monasteries, church lands with all their live stock and inventoried property, buildings and appurtenances, are transferred to the disposition of the township Land Committees and the district Soviets of Peasants' Deputies until the Constituent Assembly meets.

"(3.) Any damage whatever done to the confiscated property which from now on belongs to the whole People, is regarded as a serious crime. . . . The district Soviets of Peasants' Deputies shall take all necessary measures for . . . the taking over of the land-owners' estates. . . .

"The lands of peasants and of Cossacks serving in the Army shall not be confiscated." . . .

At two o'clock the Land Decree was put to vote, with only one against and the peasant delegates wild with joy. . . . So plunged the Bolsheviki ahead, irresistible, over-riding hesitation and opposition—the only people in Russia who had a definite program of action while the others talked for eight long months. . . .

At 2:30 A.M. fell a tense hush. Kameniev

was reading the decree of the Constitution of Power:

"Until the meeting of the Constituent Assembly, a provisional Workers' and Peasants' Government is formed, which shall be named the Council of People's Commissars.

"The administration of the different branches of state activity shall be intrusted to commissions. . . . The governmental power is vested in a *collegium* made up of the chairmen of these commissions, that is to say, the Council of People's Commissars.

"Control over the activities of the People's Commissars, and the right to replace them, shall belong to the All-Russian Congress of Soviets of Workers', Peasants' and Soldiers' Deputies, and its Central Executive Committee."

Still silence; as he read the list of Commissars, bursts of applause after each name, Lenin's and Trotzky's especially.

President of the Council: Vladimir Ulianov (*Lenin*)
Interior: A. E. Rykov
Agriculture: V. P. Miliutin
Labor: A. G. Shliapnikov
Military and Naval Affairs—a committee composed of V. A. Avseenko (*Antonov*), N. V. Krylenko, and F. M. Dybenko.
Commerce and Industry: V. P. Nogin
Popular Education: A. V. Lunatcharsky
Finance: E. E. Skvortsov (*Stepanov*)
Foreign Affairs: L. D. Bronstein (*Trotzky*)
Justice: G. E. Oppokov (*Lomov*)
Supplies: E. A. Teodorovitch
Post and Telegraph: N. P. Avilov (*Gliebov*)
Chairman for Nationalities: I. V. Djougashvili (*Stalin*)
Railroads: To be filled later. . . .

Then came the vote on the Constitution of Power, which carried the Council of

People's Commissars into office by an enormous majority. . . .

The election of the new *Tsay-ee-kah* [All-Russian Central Executive Committee of the Soviets of Workers' and Soldiers' Deputies, so-called from its initials], the new parliament of the Russian Replic, took barely fifteen minutes. Trotzky announced its composition: 100 members, of which 70 Bolsheviki. . . . And thereupon the Second All-Russian Congress of Soviets was dissolved, so that the members might hurry to their homes in the four corners of Russia and tell of the great happenings.

DECLARATION OF THE RIGHTS OF THE PEOPLES OF RUSSIA

Among the many decrees of the new government was the following, emanating from Joseph Stalin, as People's Commissar for Nationalities. A glance at the provisions will immediately make evident the new government's reversal of the old Czarist policy of "Russification," and the opportunity granted for decentralization. As a matter of fact, "independent" governments were declared in the Ukraine, Siberia, the Caucasus, and elsewhere, and Russia became a federation of "autonomous republics."

From STALIN, Decree of November 15, 1917 [1]

The first Congress of Soviets, in June of this year, proclaimed the right of the peoples of Russia to self-determination.

The second Congress of Soviets, in November . . . confirmed this inalienable right of the peoples of Russia more decisively and definitely.

Executing the will of these Congresses, the Council of People's Commissars has resolved to establish as a basis for its activ-

[1] *Ibid.*, 260.

ity in the question of Nationalities, the following principles:

(1) The equality and sovereignty of the peoples of Russia.

(2) The right of the peoples of Russia to free self-determination, even to the point of separation and the formation of an independent state.

(3) The abolition of any and all national and national-religious privileges and disabilities.

(4) The free development of national minorities and ethnographic groups inhabiting the territory of Russia.

Decrees will be prepared immediately upon the formation of a Commission on Nationalities.

In the name of the Russian Republic,

People's Commissar for Nationalities,
  Yussov Djugashvili-Stalin
President of the Council of People's Commissars, V. Ulianov (Lenin)

TOWARD CONSOLIDATION OF THE
COMMUNIST REGIME

Years passed before it was clear that the Bolshevik regime which seized power in November, 1917, could stabilize its position and hang on. Furious opposition arose in Russia, and the anticipated support of the "proletariat of the world," which was expected to rise up in revolution against "bourgeois" governments everywhere, never materialized (except temporarily and to a limited degree, as in Hungary). Meanwhile, the Bolsheviks—who began to call themselves "Communists" in the course of the November Revolution— used every means to extend and make permanent their power. Now that "the conditions were changed," Lenin did not hesitate to employ the very instruments which, before his party was in power, he had bitterly condemned in the hands of his enemies. All opposition

was now tarred with the same brush; Kadets, Mensheviks, Socialist-Revolutionists—all were labeled "bourgeois," "capitalist," "counterrevolutionist"; and no opportunity was overlooked to eradicate the opposition parties in order to make the Communist party the master of a single-party state.

Suppression of the Hostile Press (1917)

"The closing of the bourgeois press," ran a Communist Party resolution, "was necessitated . . . as a means of bringing about a new regime . . . that will prevent the capitalists, owners of printing presses and paper, from becoming autocratic makers of public opinion." And while the decree of November 9, 1917, was called "temporary," the policy it instituted has not been altered to the present day (1946). Lenin signed the decree of the Soviet of the People's Commissars, the essence of which ran:[1]

1. Those organs of the press will be closed which (*a*) call for open opposition or disobedience to the Workers' and Peasants' Government; (*b*) sow sedition by a frankly slanderous perversion of facts; (*c*) encourage deeds of a manifestly criminal character.

The Cheka Established (1917)

On November 14, the Communist party set forth "conditions of Agreement with the other Socialists," but the "conditions" imposed complete surrender of opposition parties to the communist policy and power. The arrest of Kadet leaders was already under way and, as opposition persisted, on December 20, a communist political police, like

[1] This and the next two selections are from James Bunyan and H. H. Fisher, eds., *The Bolshevik Revolution 1917-1918,* 1934 (*Hoover War Library Publications*), No. 3. Reprinted by permission of the Stanford University Press, Stanford University. This is 220.

THE NOVEMBER REVOLUTION (1917)

the Czarist "Third Section" in reverse, was established by the following decree: [1]

The Commission is to be named the All-Russian Extraordinary Commission [Russian abbreviation, "Cheka"] and is to be attached to the Soviet of People's Commissars. . . . The duties of the Commission will be:

1. To persecute and break up all acts of counter-revolution and sabotage all over Russia, no matter what their origin.

2. To bring before the Revolutionary Tribunal all counter-revolutionists and saboteurs and to work out a plan for fighting them.

3. To make preliminary investigation only. . . . The Commission is to be divided into sections: (*a*) the information [section], (*b*) the organization section (in charge of organizing the fight against counter-revolution all over Russia) with branches, and (*c*) the fighting section. . . .

The Commission is to watch the press, saboteurs, strikers, and the Socialist-Revolutionists of the Right. Measures . . . [to be taken against these counter-revolutionists are] confiscation, confinement, deprivation of [food] cards, publication of the names of the enemies of the people, etc.

[In 1922 the Cheka was abolished and its functions transferred, first to a "State Political Administration" (GPU) and then to a "Unified State Political Administration" (OGPU). The OGPU was abolished in 1934, but its activities were continued in a newly created Commissariat for Internal Affairs, the NKVD.]

The Communist Dissolution of the Constituent Assembly (1918)

Before the November Revolution, the Bolsheviks had loudly assailed the Provisional Government for its delay

in calling a Constituent Assembly. But after the November Revolution Lenin and his fellows procrastinated also, obviously because the Communist Party could not command a majority in a freely elected Constituent Assembly. So just as the Bolshevik cry had been "All Power to the Soviets" before November, the cry of the Socialist-Revolutionists and other opponents of the Communists became "All Power to the Constituent Assembly" after November. With reluctance, the Communists called for an election on November 25, but managed to postpone the meeting of the newly elected body until January 18, 1918. (Of some 700 members of the Constituent Assembly, only 175 or so were Communists, about 370 Socialist-Revolutionists, and the rest scattered among more than a dozen lesser parties.) To meet the threat of the Assembly, the Communists called the Third All-Russian Congress of Soviets of Workers' and Soldiers' Deputies to meet January 21. Thus prepared to counter Assembly with Congress of Soviets, the Communist Central Executive Committee declared (January 16) that "all power in the Russian Republic is vested with the Soviets and Soviet institutions," that "every attempt on the part of any person or institution to usurp governmental authority will be considered as a counter-revolutionary act . . . and will be suppressed." When the Constituent Assembly gathered on January 18, demonstrators carrying a banner with the words "All Power to the Constituent Assembly" were fired upon by soldiers and the Red Guards and many were killed. Within the Assembly anti-Communist speakers were hissed down and great confusion followed. On the next day (January 19) the Constituent Assembly was dissolved

[1] *Ibid.,* 298-99.

by the following decree (armed forces prevented additional meetings) :[1]

From the very beginning of the Russian Revolution the Soviets . . . came to the front as a mass organization. . . . They learned by experience the futility of compromising with the bourgeoisie, the deception of the bourgeois-democratic-parliamentarism, and came to the conclusion that it is not possible to free the downtrodden classes without completely breaking with these forms and compromises. The November Revolution and the taking over of all power by the Soviets constituted such a break.

The Constituent Assembly which was elected on the [voters'] lists made out before the November Revolution represents the old order when the compromisers and Kadets were in power. . . . To deny full power to the Soviets . . . in favor of a bourgeois parliamentarism or the Constituent Assembly would be a step backward and the deathblow of the November workers'-peasants' revolution.

The Constituent Assembly which opened on January 18 has . . . a majority of Socialist-Revolutionists of the Right, the party of Kerensky. . . . It is natural that this party should refuse to consider the . . . recommendation of the sovereign organ of the Soviet Government and should refuse to recognize the "Declaration of the Rights of the Toiling and Exploited People," the November Revolution, and the Government of the Soviet. By these very acts the Constituent Assembly has cut every tie that bound it to the Soviet of the Russian Republic. Under the circumstances the Bolsheviks and Socialist-Revolutionists of the Left . . . had no choice but to withdraw from the Constituent Assembly.

The majority parties of the Constituent Assembly . . . are carrying on an open war against the Soviet, calling . . . for its overthrow. . . . It is clear that this part of the Constituent Assembly can be of help only to the bourgeois counter-revolution. . . .

In view of the above the Central Executive Committee hereby decrees: The Constituent Assembly is dissolved.

DECLARATION OF THE RIGHTS OF THE TOILING AND EXPLOITED PEOPLE (1918)

After the dissolution of the Constituent Assembly, the Third Congress of Soviets met and, among other things, adopted on January 23, 1918, the following "Declaration" which, with "Constituent Assembly" written in place of the "Third All-Russian Congress of Soviets," had been rejected by the Constituent Assembly. In a revised form, the present Declaration became the first chapter of the Constitution of the Russian Socialist Federated Soviet Republic adopted in July following.

From the "Declaration of Rights"
    (January 23, 1918) [2]

Chapter I. 1. Russia is declared a Republic of Soviets of Workers', Soldiers' and Peasants' Deputies. All authority, central and local, is vested in these Soviets.

2. The Russian Soviet Republic is established on the basis of a free union of free nations, as a federation of Soviet national republics.

Chapter II. 3. Setting as its fundamental aim the abolition of all exploitation of man by man, the complete elimination of the division of society into classes, the ruthless suppression of exploiters, the establishment of a socialistic organization of

[1] *Ibid.*, 385-86.

[2] Samuel N. Harper, "Documents on the Government of the Soviet Union," in *Source Book on European Governments,* ed. by W. E. Rappard and others, 1937, Sec. V, 63-66. By permission of D. Van Nostrand Company, Inc., New York.

society and of the victory of socialism, the Third All-Russian Congress of Soviets of Workers', Soldiers' and Peasants' Deputies further decrees:

(*a*) In realization of the socialization of the land, private property in land is abolished and the entire fund of land is declared public property and it is handed over to toilers without any payment, on the basis of equalized utilization.

(*b*) All forests, mineral deposits and waters of public importance and likewise all live-stock and appurtenances, model private estates and agricultural enterprise are declared national property.

(*c*) As the first step toward the complete transfer of factories, mills, mines, railways and other means of production and of transport to the ownership of the Soviet Republic of Workers and Peasants, there is confirmation of the Soviet legislation on workers' control and on the Supreme Soviet of National Economy, for the purpose of insuring the authority of the toilers over the exploiters.

(*d*) The Third All-Russian Congress of Soviets considers the Soviet law on the repudiation (abolition) of loans contracted by the government of the Tsar, landlords and bourgeoisie. . . .

(*e*) There is ratification of the transfer of all banks to the ownership of the Workman-Peasant State. . . .

(*f*) For the purpose of abolishing the parasitic strata of society and of organizing economic life, universal labor service is introduced.

(*g*) In the interest of insuring complete and full authority to the toiling masses, and of removing all possibility of the reëstablishment of the authority of exploiters, there is decreed the arming of the toilers, the formation of a socialist Red Army of workmen and peasants and the complete disarming of the propertied classes.

Chapter III. 4. Expressing the firm determination to deliver humanity from the claws of financial capital and imperialism, which have drenched the earth with blood in the present most criminal of all wars, the Third All-Russian Congress of Soviets associates itself fully with the policy adopted by the Soviet authority, of repudiating the secret treaties, of organizing the broadest possible fraternization of the workmen and peasants in the armies now engaged in conflict and of attaining at any cost by revolutionary measures a democratic peace of toilers, without annexations and indemnities, on the basis of the free self-determination of nations. . . .

Chapter IV. 7. The Third All-Russian Congress of Soviets of Workers', Soldiers' and Peasants' Deputies considers that now, at the moment of the decisive struggle of the proletariat against its exploiters, these exploiters can have no place in any of the organs of authority. Power must belong wholly and exclusively to the toiling masses, and to their plenipotentiary representatives—to the Soviets of Workers', Soldiers' and Peasants' Deputies.

8. At the same time, while striving to establish a really free and voluntary, and therefore more complete and lasting union of the toiling classes of all the nations of Russia, the Third All-Russian Congress of Soviets confines itself to setting up the basic principles of a federation of Soviet Republics of Russia, leaving to the workers and peasants of each nation to make an independent decision at their own plenipotentiary Soviet Congress, whether they wish, and on what basis, to participate in the federated government and in other federated Soviet institutions.

THE TREATY OF BREST LITOVSK (1918)

"Peace, Bread, and Land" had been the slogan of the March Revolution— and the shout for peace rang out above the cry for bread and the call for land. The Provisional Government's decision to continue World War I had supplied the Bolsheviks with one of their strongest appeals, and their prompt proclamation for peace (November 8) was genuinely popular. But the path to peace was far from smooth. Russia's allies protested warmly against a separate peace, refused to accept a proposal for a general armistice, and resented the Communist exposure of the Allies' secret treaties. The Germans, despite the pressing needs of the Western Front and the necessitous condition of Austria, were the victors over Russia, and they demonstrated to the full their rapacious annexationism in Poland and the Baltic provinces ("I need them for the maneuvring of my left wing in the next war," said Hindenburg during the negotiations), in the Ukraine, where foodstuffs and man power were attractive, and in the Balkans, where Romanian oil was their principal interest. As a consequence, the Communist regime, embarrassed by the threat of civil war in Russia, by the threatening military position of the Germans, by the ignominious failure of the proletariat to raise a revolution in Germany and elsewhere, and, as Lenin put it, by the need of "a breathing space" for the revolution to fasten itself more firmly upon Greater Russia, accepted the Treaty of Brest Litovsk on March 3, 1918. The treaty was subsequently renounced by Germany after her defeat and, except for the immediate effects upon Russia and as an example of the kind of peace Germany would dictate when opportunity offered, the treaty has become, as one author has called it, "The Forgotten Peace." Momentarily, however, it cost Russia "34 per cent of her population, 32 per cent of her agricultural land, 85 per cent

of her beet-sugar land, 54 per cent of her industrial undertakings, and 89 per cent of her coal mines." [1] Some of the territory, such as the Ukraine, was subsequently recovered, but in the end the Soviets signed away Finland, Courland, Livonia, Estonia, Lithuania, Poland, and some lesser areas of southeastern Russia, including Batum. Only the long-awaited world revolution could repair the damage to Russia and justify Lenin's refusal to continue the war with "bourgeois-capitalist" allies. Such were Lenin's arguments for ratification of the treaty.

From LENIN, Speech Supporting Ratification of the Treaty of Brest Litovsk (1918) [2]

Comrades! The question that confronts us is the most crucial in the development of the Russian Revolution and the world revolution. To understand fully the reasons why the Soviet Government signed this humiliating peace and why it now offers it for your ratification, it is necessary to realize the meaning of the November Revolution, the main phases in its development and the causes of the present defeat. . . .

Until now our revolution enjoyed a period of comparative independence. It was a period of great triumphs. We conquered the bourgeoisie, the landlords, and established the dictatorship of the proletariat. This we were able to accomplish because we were left unmolested by the beasts of international imperialism. But now we are entering upon a new period of defeats and trials. We have to give way to forces stronger than ourselves, to forces of international capitalism which are attacking us. The proletariat of the world has not given its assistance in time. We

[1] John Wheeler-Bennett, The Forgotten Peace, Morrow, 1939, 269.
[2] Bunyan and Fisher, eds., op. cit., 530-31. By permission of the Stanford University Press.

had to face the enemy single-handed and we suffered defeat. The thing for us to do now is to retreat and hold at least part of our position while waiting for a more favorable international situation and allowing the proletariat of the world to gather more strength in order to defeat the enemy. . . .

This is where the Socialist-Revolutionists of the Left go wrong. Instead of analyzing the international situation and the conditions of the class struggle, they point to the humiliating character of the treaty and use revolutionary phrases to appeal to our emotions and feelings of indignation. But revolutionary phrases will not do. We have no army; we could not keep the army at the front. We need peace to gain a breathing spell to give the masses a chance to create new forms of life. In all probability that breathing spell will be of short duration. The period of imperialistic wars is over, and we are entering a new period of revolutionary wars on an international scale. We must prepare for the struggle. Victory is certain. The proletariat of the world understands that Russia is fighting its cause. It is our true ally. After we have rested, then, together with the international proletariat, we shall start a new November revolution, but this time on a world scale.

4. War Communism and the NEP

WAR COMMUNISM

From CHAMBERLAIN, *The Russian Revolution* (1935) [1]

The economic system which prevailed in Soviet Russia from 1918 until 1921 has

[1] This and the next selection are from William Henry Chamberlain, *The Russian Revolution 1917-1921*, 2 vols., 1935. By permission of The Macmillan Company. This is II, 96-100, 102.

gone into history under the name: war communism. And the name accurately reflects the double nature of the system, which was a compound of war emergency and socialist dogmatism.

As convinced disciples of Karl Marx the Bolshevik leaders were convinced that state ownership must replace private ownership of the means of production. One of their first decrees was the nationalization of the land; and quite early in their regime they nationalized the banks and the country's shipping and declared foreign trade a state monopoly. But Lenin himself recognized quite clearly that the Soviets were technically unprepared to take over the management of the entire economic life of the country; and during the short breathing-space between the signing of the Peace of Brest-Litovsk and the beginning of hostilities with the Czechs he laid stress not on rapid expropriation of the capitalists, but on inculcating among the workers a spirit of conscious labor discipline and a will to work. During this period he seems to have played with the idea of establishing some kind of *modus vivendi* with those factory-owners who were willing to carry on operations, of setting up a system under which the state, while it retained control over industrial life, would utilize the managerial and technical experience of the factory-owners.

Whether Lenin would have been able or would have desired, in the long run, to resist the impulse of the more aggressive Soviets and local labor organizations to drive away the employers and take over the management of the plants is a hypothetical question. For the outbreak of civil war on a large scale, combined with the acute food crisis, tended to sharpen class antagonism to such a degree that any idea of peaceful coöperation with the capitalists was discarded. . . .

War communism as a system was characterized by six main principles, which were more and more rigorously and intensively applied as the system early in 1921 approached its final crisis, which led to the substitution of the entirely different New Economic Policy. The first of these was that the state through its central or local organs took over all means of production and reduced the sphere of private ownership to the narrowest possible limits. Not only factories, railroads and banks, but private houses of any size, large libraries, privately owned objects of value, such as gold and jewels, were confiscated and taken from their owners.

The second principle of war communism was state control over the labor of every citizen. . . . A decree of February 5, 1920, established in more concrete and definite form the obligation, already written into the Soviet Constitution, of every Soviet citizen to work. Typical of the numerous labor mobilizations of 1920 was an order to all women between the ages of eighteen and forty-five to sew underwear for the Red Army.

A third feature of the system was the effort of the state to produce everything in its own undertakings. With the nationalization even of the smaller workshops and the legal prohibition of private trade (which, incidentally, was continually disregarded and evaded) all production in the towns, on paper at least, was brought under state control. . . .

A fourth characteristic of the system was extreme centralization. There was an effort, quite unprecedented in history, to place the entire regulation of the economic life of a vast country, with a population of well over a hundred millions, in the hands of a few hastily improvised state bureaucratic organizations. Prominent among these was the Supreme Economic Council, created by a decree of December 15, 1917,

which . . . in actual functioning, however . . . became a specialized department for the management of industry. . . . As the Supreme Economic Council became more and more the sole authority in the field of industrial production, the Food Commissariat became the exclusive authorized provider of food and manufactured goods. The Commissariat for Transportation managed the railways and water transport along semi-military lines. . . . The Commissariat for Agriculture endeavored to direct and regulate the production of the peasants; but here the attempts at state regulation were far less effective than in the industrial sphere. It was possible, at the point of the bayonet, to extort from the peasants year after year a growing quantity of grain and of other food products. But it was not possible to make them work efficiently or to arrest the natural tendency of the peasant to plant less as he saw that his surplus grain would be taken away from him without compensation; and this was the most important of several rocks on which the whole experiment in war communism finally foundered.

The fifth principle of war communism was that the state attempted to assume the functions not only of the sole producer, but of the sole distributor. The all-powerful Food Commissariat took from industry whatever it produced for distribution among the population and took from agriculture, mainly on the basis of forced levies, whatever could be extracted from the peasants and distributed it among the town population, which was placed on ration cards. . . .

The sixth outstanding feature of war communism was the attempt to abolish money altogether as a means of exchange, to go over to a system of natural economy, in which all transactions were carried out in kind.

THE NEW ECONOMIC POLICY (1921)

Destructive civil war, the unfriendliness of foreign nations and their armed intervention in Russia, together with internal opposition to war communism, threatened an economic collapse in Russia by the end of 1920. At this point Lenin reverted to his original design of 1918—to compromise with capitalism for the time being, to make a strategic retreat "in order to prepare for a longer step forward." The compromise, known as the New Economic Policy, was hastened by the mutiny (March, 1921) of the sailors at Kronstadt—an early stronghold of Bolshevism. The principal features of the NEP are described in the selection which follows.

From CHAMBERLAIN, *The Russian Revolution* [1]

The cornerstone of this New Economic Policy was the abandonment of the policy of requisitioning all the peasants' surplus produce and the substitution of a fixed tax in kind. Once this tax was paid the peasant was permitted to do what he liked with the remainder of his produce: to consume it himself, to sell it to the state, if the state could offer him any goods in exchange, or to sell it on the private market, which was definitely legalized. This basic change brought in its train a series of other changes, until the economic features of war communism became quite unrecognizable. To trace in detail the rise and subsequent fall of the Nep lies outside the province of this work. One may briefly summarize its more important characteristics as follows: abolition of labor armies and compulsory labor; restoration of a regular currency and taxation system (the tax in kind on the peasantry eventually became a money tax); a rapid spread of private retail trade and a much more

limited toleration of private initiative in other fields, such as small industry and housing construction. . . .

Lenin was quite willing to face the fact that legalization of private trade would mean, to some extent, a return to capitalism. But he considered that the conciliation of the peasantry was such a vital necessity that he was willing to take this risk. He was also willing to permit capitalist relations of a different type by granting concessions to foreign firms. Here he repeated the argument which he had used against the "Left Communists" in 1918: that State capitalism would really be a step forward for a country like Russia, where a great part of the population was living under very primitive economic relations and where the devastation and destruction of seven years of foreign and domestic warfare had been so great.

As a revolutionary strategist Lenin knew that it was sometimes necessary to retreat. The signing of the Brest-Litovsk Peace was one such occasion; the declaration of the New Economic Policy was another. But, like every good general, Lenin was determined that retreat should not turn into disorderly rout. As he said somewhat later:

"Of course freedom of trade means the growth of capitalism. If there are small enterprises, if there is freedom of exchange —capitalism will appear. But is this capitalism dangerous to us, if we keep in our hands the factories, the transportation system and foreign trade? I believe that this capitalism is not dangerous to us. . . . (After characterizing as state capitalism the policy of granting concessions to foreign capital he continued.) . . . Is state capitalism dangerous to us? No, because we will decide in what measure we shall grant concessions."

So there were to be economic guaranties against a full-blooded restoration of capitalism: the retention in the hands of the

[1] *Ibid.*, II, 445, 447.

state of the big industries, the transportation system, the monopoly of foreign trade. There was also to be a political guaranty: the maintenance of the absolute concentration of power in the hands of the Communist Party. Lenin rejected any idea of granting freedom of speech, press and political activity to non-Communist parties.

5. The First Five-Year Plan

Every effort has been made to chart the progress of the Soviet Union in every phase of its economic, social, and political development. State bureaus gather data constantly, and it was with the aid of their findings that a State Planning Commission (Gosplan) drew up a complete economic forecast for Russia for the five-year period 1928-33. Under Joseph Stalin's vigilant eye—and with a constant care for political effect —the first Five-Year Plan was launched on October 1, 1928. The accomplishments were uneven, but the over-all results were satisfactory enough to declare the plan fulfilled on December 31, 1932, only four and a quarter years after its inception. A week later (January 7, 1933) Stalin reported on the objectives and accomplishments.

From STALIN, Leninism (1940) [1]

What is the Five-Year Plan?

What was the fundamental task of the Five-Year Plan?

The fundamental task of the Five-Year Plan was to transfer our country, with its backward, and in part mediaeval, technique, to the lines of new, modern technique.

[1] This and the next selection are from Joseph Stalin, Leninism, 1940. By permission of Lawrence & Wishart, Ltd., London. This is 409-11, 413-15, 421-23.

The fundamental task of the Five-Year Plan was to convert the U.S.S.R from an agrarian and weak country, dependent upon the caprices of the capitalist countries, into an industrial and powerful country, fully self-reliant and independent of the caprices of world capitalism.

The fundamental task of the Five-Year Plan was, in converting the U.S.S.R into an industrial country, fully to eliminate the capitalist elements, to widen the front of Socialist forms of economy, and to create the economic base for the abolition of classes in the U.S.S.R., for the construction of Socialist society.

The fundamental task of the Five-Year Plan was to create such an industry in our country as would be able to re-equip and reorganize, not only the whole of industry, but also transport and agriculture—on the basis of Socialism.

The fundamental task of the Five-Year Plan was to transfer small and scattered agriculture to the lines of large-scale collective farming, so as to ensure the economic base for Socialism in the rural districts and thus eliminate the possibility of the restoration of capitalism in the U.S.S.R.

Finally, the task of the Five-Year Plan was to create in the country all the necessary technical and economic prerequisites for increasing to the utmost the defensive capacity of the country, to enable it to organize determined resistance to any and every attempt at military intervention from outside, to any and every attempt at military attack from without.

What dictated this fundamental task of the Five-Year Plan; what were the grounds for it?

The necessity of putting an end to the technical and economic backwardness of the Soviet Union, which doomed it to an unenviable existence; the necessity of creating in the country such prerequisites as would enable it not only to overtake but in time to outstrip, economically and technically, the advanced capitalist countries.

Consideration of the fact that the Soviet power could not maintain itself for long on the basis of a backward industry; that a modern large-scale industry alone, one that is not only equal to but would in time excel the industries of capitalist countries, can serve as a real and reliable foundation for the Soviet power.

Consideration of the fact that the Soviet government could not for long rest upon two opposite foundations: on large-scale Socialist industry, which *destroys* the capitalist elements, and on small, individual peasant farming, which *engenders* capitalist elements.

Consideration of the fact that until agriculture was placed on the basis of large-scale production, until the small peasant farms were united into large collective farms, the danger of the restoration of capitalism in the U.S.S.R. would be the most real of all possible dangers. . . .

What was the main link in the Five-Year Plan?

The main link in the Five-Year Plan was heavy industry, with machine building as its core. For only heavy industry is capable of reconstructing industry as a whole, as well as the transport system and agriculture, and of putting them on their feet. It was necessary to start the realization of the Five-Year Plan from heavy industry. Hence, the restoration of heavy industry had to be made the basis of the fulfilment of the Five-Year Plan. . . .

What are the results of the Five-Year Plan in four years in the sphere of *industry*?

Have we achieved victory in this sphere?

Yes, we have. And not only that, but we have accomplished more than we expected, more than the hottest heads in our Party could have expected. Even our enemies do not deny this now; and certainly our friends cannot deny it.

We did not have an iron and steel industry, the foundation for the industrialization of the country. Now we have this industry.

We did not have a tractor industry. Now we have one.

We did not have an automobile industry. Now we have one.

We did not have a machine-tool industry. Now we have one.

We did not have a big and up-to-date chemical industry. Now we have one.

We did not have a real and big industry for the production of modern agricultural machinery. Now we have one.

We did not have an aircraft industry. Now we have one.

In output of electric power we were last on the list. Now we rank among the first.

In output of oil products and coal we were last on the list. Now we rank among the first.

We had only one coal and metallurgical base—in the Ukraine—which we barely managed to keep going. We have not only succeeded in improving this base, but have created a new coal and metallurgical base —in the East—which is the pride of our country.

We had only one centre of the textile industry—in the North of our country. As a result of our efforts we will have in the very near future two new centres of the textile industry—in Central Asia and Western Siberia.

And we have not only created these new great industries, but have created them on a scale and in dimensions that eclipse the scale and dimensions of European industry.

And as a result of all this the capitalist elements have been completely and irrevocably eliminated from industry, and Socialist industry has become the sole form of industry in the U.S.S.R.

And as a result of all this our country has been converted from an agrarian into an industrial country; for the proportion of industrial output, as compared with agricultural output, has risen from 48 per cent of the total in the beginning of the Five-Year Plan period (1928) to 70 per cent at the end of the fourth year of the Five-Year Plan period (1932).

And as a result of all this we have succeeded by the end of the fourth year of the Five-Year Plan period in fulfilling the program of general industrial output, which was drawn up for five years, to the extent of 93.7 per cent, and in increasing the volume of industrial output more than *threefold* as compared with the pre-war output, and more than *twofold* as compared with that of 1928. As for the Five-Year Plan program of output for heavy industry, we have fulfilled that to the extent of 108 per cent. It is true that we are 6 per cent short of fulfilling the general program of the Five-Year Plan. But this is due to the fact that in order to improve the defences of the country, in view of the refusal of neighbouring countries to sign pacts of non-aggression with us, and in view of the complications that arose in the Far East, we were obliged hastily to switch a number of factories to the production of modern weapons of defence. And since this involved the necessity of going through a certain period of preparation, these factories had to suspend production for four months, which could not but affect the fulfilment of the general program of output provided for in the Five-Year Plan during 1932. As a result of this operation we have completely closed the breach in the defences of the country. But it could not but affect the fulfilment of the program of output provided for in the Five-Year Plan. It is beyond any doubt that, but for this circumstance, we would not only have fulfilled, but overfulfilled, the figures of the Five-Year Plan.

Finally, as a result of all this the Soviet Union has been converted from a weak country, unprepared for defence, into a country mighty in defence, a country prepared for every contingency, a country capable of producing on a mass scale all modern weapons of defence and of equipping its army with them in the event of an attack from without. . . . .

And what is the position in regard to growth of industrial output in the *capitalist* countries, which are now passing through a severe crisis?

Here are the generally known official figures.

While by the end of 1932 the volume of industrial output in the U.S.S.R. *rose* to 334 per cent of the pre-war output, the volume of industrial output in the U.S.A. *dropped* in this same period to 84 per cent, that of England to 75 per cent, that of Germany to 62 per cent. . . .

Let us pass on to the question of the results of the Five-Year Plan in four years in the sphere of agriculture.

The Five-Year Plan in the sphere of agriculture was a Five-Year Plan of collectivization. What did the Party proceed from in carrying out collectivization?

The Party proceeded from the fact that in order to consolidate the dictatorship of the proletariat and to build up Socialist society it was necessary, in addition to industrialization, to pass from small, individual peasant farming to large-scale collective agriculture equipped with tractors and modern agricultural machinery, as the only firm basis for the Soviet power in the rural districts. . . .

In this connection, the object of the Five-Year Plan in the sphere of agriculture was to unite the scattered and small individual peasant farms, which lacked the opportunity of utilizing tractors and modern agricultural machinery, into large collective farms, equipped with all the modern implements of highly developed agriculture, and to cover unoccupied land with model state farms.

The object of the Five-Year Plan in the sphere of agriculture was to convert the U.S.S.R. from a small-peasant and backward country into a land of large-scale agriculture organized on the basis of collective labour and providing the maximum output for the market.

What has the Party achieved in carrying out the program of the Five-Year Plan in four years in the sphere of agriculture? Has it fulfilled this program, or has it failed?

The Party has succeeded, in a matter of three years, in organizing more than 200,000 collective farms and about 5,000 state farms specializing mainly in grain growing and livestock raising, and at the same time it has succeeded, in the course of four years, in enlarging the crop area by 21,000,000 hectares.

The Party has succeeded in getting more than 60 per cent of the peasant farms, which account for more than 70 per cent of the land cultivated by peasants, to unite into collective farms, which means that we have *fulfilled* the Five-Year Plan *threefold*.

The Party has succeeded in creating the possibility of obtaining, not 500,000,000 to 600,000,000 poods of marketable grain, which was the amount purchased in the period when individual peasant farming predominated, but 1,200,000,000 to 1,400,-000,000 poods of grain annually.

The Party has succeeded in routing the kulaks as a class, although they have not yet been dealt the final blow: the labouring peasants have been emancipated from kulak bondage and exploitation, and a firm economic basis for the Soviet government, the basis of collective farming, has been established in the countryside.

The Party has succeeded in converting the U.S.S.R. from a land of small peasant farming into a land where agriculture is run on the largest scale in the world.

Such, in general terms, are the results of the Five-Year Plan in four years in the sphere of agriculture.

6. The Soviet Constitution of 1936

A new constitution of the Union of Soviet Socialist Republics was adopted December 5, 1936, by the All-Union Congress of Soviets. Widely heralded as a "democratic" instrument, it does indeed include some remarkably democratic features, such as "The Fundamental Rights and Obligations of Citizens" proclaimed in Chapter X, especially Article 123, which is probably the noblest statement of racial equality to be found in constitutional annals. In liberal, "bourgeois" eyes, however, the retention of a one-party political system, with the Communists the only legal political party, together with the continuance of secret, political police, and the "freedom" of the press limited to the *proletarian* press—all these cause the Russian system to fall short of democracy as understood in Western Europe and America. Indeed, the gulf between the *words* of the new constitution and the *institutions* and *practices* in the Soviet Union suggests that the constitution of 1936 is a declaration of Soviet intent for the future, with useful political values for the present, rather than a living framework of Russian society. The recognition of ownership and inheritance of small private properties (Articles 7 and 10) are noteworthy. The statement in Article 12 that "there is being realized the principle of socialism: 'From each according to his ability, to each—according to his toil,'" requires brief explanation.

The earlier statement of the maxim had been according to the principle of *Communism* and had read, "From each according to his ability, to each according to his *needs*." Stalin described the difference between the two in these words: [1]

"The principle of Socialism is that in a Socialist society each works according to his ability and receives articles of consumption, not according to his needs, but according to the work he performs for society. This means that the cultural and technical level of the working class is as yet not a high one, that the distinction between mental and manual labour still exists, that the productivity of labour is still not high enough to insure an abundance of articles of consumption, and, as a result, society is obliged to distribute articles of consumption not in accordance with the needs of its members, but in accordance with the work they perform for society.

"Communism represents a higher stage of development. The principle of Communism is that in a Communist society each works according to his abilities and receives articles of consumption, not according to the work he performs, but according to his needs as a culturally developed individual. This means that the cultural and technical level of the working class has become high enough to undermine the basis of the distinction between mental labour and manual labour, that the distinction . . . has already disappeared, and that productivity of labour has reached such a high level that it can provide an absolute abundance of articles of consumption, and as a result society is able to distribute these articles in accordance with the needs of its members."

[1] *Ibid.*, 548.

Obviously, then, the socialistic phase proclaimed by the following Constitution is a temporary and transitional stage which, in due time, will be replaced by a communist society. The constitution contains thirteen chapters and 146 articles, of which only excerpts can be included.

From *The Constitution of the U.S.S.R.* (1936) [2]

CHAPTER I. THE ORGANIZATION OF SOCIETY

Article 1. The Union of Soviet Socialist Republics is a socialist State of workers and peasants.

Article 2. The political basis of the U.S.S.R. is formed by the councils [Soviets] of toilers' deputies, which have developed and become strong as a result of the overthrow of the power of the landlords and capitalists and the winning of the dictatorship of the proletariat.

Article 3. All power in the U.S.S.R. belongs to the toilers of city and village as represented by the councils of toilers' deputies.

Article 4. The economic basis of the U.S.S.R. is formed by the socialist system of economy and the socialist ownership of implements and means of production, which have been firmly established as a result of the liquidation of the capitalistic system of economy, the abolition of private ownership of implements and means of production, and the destruction of the exploitation of man by man. . . .

[Article 5 declares socialist ownership to be either state or co-operative in form, and Article 6 declares all natural resources, mills, factories, and all manner of trans-

[2] *Text of the New Constitution of the U.S.S.R.,* ed. by Sir Bernard Pares, in *International Conciliation,* February, 1937, 143-63. By permission of the Carnegie Endowment for International Peace.

portation and communication to be state property.]

Article 7. Public undertakings in the collective farms (kolkhozy) and co-operative organizations with their livestock and implements, production effected by the collective farms and co-operative organizations, as well as their public structure are the public, socialist property of the collective farms and co-operative organizations.

Each collective farm household, aside from its basic income from the public collective farm economy, has for its own use a small piece of land attached to the homestead and as individual property the auxiliary economy on this attached piece, a dwelling house, productive livestock, poultry and minor agricultural implements—in accordance with the regulation of the agricultural artel.

Article 8. The land occupied by collective farms is secured to them for use without payment and without time limit, that is, forever.

Article 9. Along with the socialist system of economy, which is the prevailing form of economy in the U.S.S.R., there is permitted by law small private economy of individual peasants and handicraftsmen, based on their personal labor and excluding the exploitation of the labor of another person.

Article 10. The right of personal property of citizens in the income from their toil and in their savings, in their dwelling house and auxiliary domestic economy, in articles of their domestic economy and use, in articles of personal use and comfort, as well as the right of inheritance of personal property of citizens—are protected by law.

Article 11. The economic life of the U.S.S.R. is defined and directed by the State plan of national economy in the interests of the increase of the public wealth, the constant raising of the material and cultural level of the toilers, the strengthening of its defensive ability.

Article 12. Toil in the U.S.S.R. is an obligation and a matter of honor of each citizen who is fit for toil, according to the principle: "He who does not work, does not eat."

In the U.S.S.R. there is being realized the principle of socialism: "From each according to his ability, to each—according to his toil."

CHAPTER II. THE ORGANIZATION OF THE STATE

Article 13. The Union of Soviet Socialist Republics is a union State on the basis of the voluntary association of the [eleven] Soviet Socialist Republics with equal rights. . . .

Article 14. Within the jurisdiction of the Union of Soviet Socialist Republics as represented by its highest organs of power and of organs of State administration belong:

a) the representation of the Union in international relations, the conclusion and ratification of treaties with other States;

b) questions of war and peace;

c) the acceptance of new republics into the organization of the U.S.S.R.;

d) control over the observance of the Constitution of the U.S.S.R. and the ensurance of conformity of the Constitutions of the Union republics with the Constitution of the U.S.S.R.; [organization and direction of the defence of the U.S.S.R., control of the state budget, administration of socialized industries, and so on]. . . .

Article 16. Each Union republic has its own Constitution which takes into account the special features of the republic and is drawn up in full conformity with the Constitution of the U.S.S.R.

Article 17. To each Union republic is preserved the right of free withdrawal from the U.S.S.R. . . .

Article 20. In case of a conflict of the law of a Union republic with the All-Union law, the All-Union law prevails.

Article 21. For citizens of the U.S.S.R. there is one Union citizenship. Every citizen of a Union republic is a citizen of the U.S.S.R. . . .

CHAPTER III. THE HIGHEST ORGANS OF STATE POWER OF THE U.S.S.R.

Article 30. The highest organ of State power of the U.S.S.R. is the Supreme Council [Soviet] of the U.S.S.R.

Article 31. The Supreme Council of the U.S.S.R. exercises all rights granted to the Union of Soviet Socialist Republics, in accordance with Article 14 of the Constitution, in so far as they do not come, by virtue of the Constitution, within the competence of organs of the U.S.S.R. which are accountable to the Supreme Council of the U.S.S.R.: the Presidium of the Supreme Council of the U.S.S.R., the Council of People's Commissars of the U.S.S.R. and the People's Commissariats of the U.S.S.R.

Article 32. The legislative power of the U.S.S.R. is exercised exclusively by the Supreme Council of the U.S.S.R.

Article 33. The Supreme Council of the U.S.S.R. consists of two chambers: the Council of the Union and the Council of Nationalities.

Article 34. The Council of the Union is elected by the citizens of the U.S.S.R. by electoral districts on the basis of one deputy for every 300,000 of population.

Article 35. The Council of Nationalities is elected by the citizens of the U.S.S.R. by Union and Autonomous republics, autonomous regions, and national districts on the basis of: 25 deputies from each Union republic, 5 deputies from each autonomous district and one deputy from each national district.

Article 36. The Supreme Council of the U.S.S.R. is chosen for a term of four years. . . .

Article 38. The Council of the Union and the Council of Nationalities possess in the same measure legislative initiative.

Article 39. A law is considered approved, if it is accepted by both chambers of the Supreme Council of the U.S.S.R. by a simple majority of each. . . .

Article 48. The Supreme Council of the U.S.S.R. chooses at a joint meeting of both chambers the Presidium of the Supreme Council of the U.S.S.R., which consists of: the chairman of the Presidium of the Supreme Council of the U.S.S.R., eleven vice-chairmen, the secretary of the Presidium, and 24 members of the Presidium.

The Presidium of the Supreme Council of the U.S.S.R. is accountable to the Supreme Council of the U.S.S.R. in all its activities.

Article 49. The Presidium of the Supreme Council of the U.S.S.R.

a) convenes sessions of the Supreme Council of the U.S.S.R.;

b) gives interpretations of the laws of the U.S.S.R. in force, issues decrees;

c) dissolves the Supreme Council of the U.S.S.R. . . . and appoints new elections;

d) carries out an interrogation of the whole people (referendum) on its own initiative or on the demand of one of the Union republics;

e) annuls decisions and orders of the Council of People's Commissars of the U.S.S.R. and the Council of People's Commissars of the Union republics in case they do not conform to the law;

f) in the period between sessions of the Supreme Council of the U.S.S.R., relieves of their positions and appoints individual People's Commissars of the U.S.S.R. at the instance of the chairman of the Council of People's Commissars of the U.S.S.R. with the subsequent submission for confirmation by the Supreme Council of the U.S.S.R.

g) awards decorations and bestows titles of honor of the U.S.S.R.;

h) exercises the right of pardon;

i) appoints and removes the high command of the armed forces of the U.S.S.R.;

j) in the period between sessions of the Supreme Council of the U.S.S.R., proclaims a state of war in case of armed attack upon the U.S.S.R. or in case of the necessity of carrying out international treaty obligations for mutual defense against aggression;

k) proclaims general or partial mobilization;

l) ratifies international treaties;

m) appoints and recalls plenipotentiary representatives of the U.S.S.R. in foreign States;

n) receives letters of credence and recall of diplomatic representatives of foreign States accredited to it. . . .

CHAPTER IV. THE HIGHEST ORGANS OF STATE POWER OF THE UNION REPUBLICS

Article 57. The highest organ of State power of the Union republic is the Supreme Council of the Union republic.

Article 58. The Supreme Council of the Union republic is elected by the citizens of the republic for a term of four years.

The ratios of representation are determined by the constitutions of the Union republics. . . .

CHAPTER V. THE ORGANS OF STATE ADMINISTRATION OF THE U.S.S.R.

Article 64. The highest executive and administrative organ of the State power of the Union of Soviet Socialist Republics is the Council of People's Commissars of the U.S.S.R. . . .

Article 68. The Council of People's Commissars:

a) co-ordinates and directs the work of the All-Union and Union-republic People's Commissariats of the U.S.S.R. and other economic and cultural institutions under its jurisdiction;

b) adopts measures to carry out the plan of national economy, the State budget, and the strengthening of the credit-monetary system;

c) adopts measures to maintain public order, defend the interests of the State and guard the rights of citizens;

d) exercises general direction in the sphere of relations with foreign States;

e) determines the yearly quotas of citizens, subject to call for active military service, directs the general organization of the armed forces of the country. . . .

Article 70. The Council of People's Commissars of the U.S.S.R. is formed by the Supreme Council of the U.S.S.R. and consists of:

the Chairman of the Council of People's Commissars of the U.S.S.R.;

the Vice-Chairmen of the Council of People's Commissars of the U.S.S.R.;

the Chairman of the State Planning Commission of the U.S.S.R.;

the Chairman of the Commission of Soviet Control;

the People's Commissars of the U.S.S.R.;

the Chairman of the Committee of Reserves [warehouses];

the Chairman of the Committee on the arts;

the Chairman of the Committee on higher education. . . .

Article 74. The People's Commissariats of the U.S.S.R. are either All-Union or Union-republic. . . .

Article 77. To the All-Union People's Commissariats belong the People's Commissariats of:

Defense;	Communications;
Foreign affairs;	Water transport;
Foreign trade;	Heavy industry;
Railways;	Defense industry;

Article 78. To the Union-republic People's Commissariats belong the People's Commissariats of:

Food industry;   Finances;
Light industry;   Internal trade;
Timber industry;   Internal affairs;
Agriculture;   Justice;
Grain and livestock;   Public health. . . .
        State farms (sovkhoz);

[Chapters VI, VII, and VIII establish organs of local government for the federated republics, based upon Councils of People's Commissars.]

CHAPTER IX. THE COURT AND THE STATE ATTORNEYS

Article 102. Justice in the U.S.S.R. is represented by the Supreme Court of the U.S.S.R., the Supreme Courts of the Union republics, provincial and regional courts, courts of autonomous republics and autonomous regions, district courts, special courts of the U.S.S.R., formed by the decision of the Supreme Council of the U.S.S.R., and People's Courts. . . .

Article 104. The Supreme Court of the U.S.S.R. is the highest judicial organ. To the Supreme Court of the U.S.S.R. is assigned supervision of the judicial activity of all judicial organs of the U.S.S.R. and Union republics. . . .

CHAPTER X. THE FUNDAMENTAL RIGHTS AND OBLIGATIONS OF CITIZENS

Article 118. Citizens of the U.S.S.R. have the right to toil, that is, the right to receive guaranteed work with payment for their toil in accordance with its quantity and quality.

The right to toil is ensured by the socialist organization of national economy, by the unceasing growth of the productive forces of soviet society, the elimination of the possibility of economic crises, and the liquidation of unemployment.

Article 119. Citizens of the U.S.S.R. have the right to rest.

The right to rest is ensured by the shortening of the working day for the overwhelming majority of workers to seven hours, the establishment of yearly leaves to workers and those in service with the maintenance of their labor pay, by reserving for the use of the toilers a wide network of sanatoria, houses of rest, and clubs.

Article 120. Citizens of the U.S.S.R. have the right to material security in old age—and also in case of illness and loss of capacity to toil.

This right is ensured by the wide development of social insurance of workers and those in service at the expense of the State, free medical help for toilers, the reserving for the use of the toilers of a wide network of health resorts.

Article 121. Citizens of the U.S.S.R. have the right to education.

This right is ensured by universal, compulsory elementary education, by the fact that no pay is demanded for education, including higher education. . . .

Article 122. To woman in the U.S.S.R. is offered equal rights with man in all fields of economic, State, cultural, and public-political life.

The possibility of exercising these rights of women is ensured by the granting to woman equal right with man to toil, payment for toil, rest, social insurance, and education, by State protection of the interests of mother and child, the granting to woman during pregnancy of leave with the continuation of maintenance, a wide network of maternity homes, nurseries, and kindergartens.

Article 123. The equal right of citizens of the U.S.S.R., independent of their nationality and race, in all fields of economic, State, cultural, and public-political life is an unalterable law.

Any direct or indirect limitation of rights, or conversely, any establishment of direct or indirect preferences of citizens dependent upon their racial and national membership, as well as all preaching of racial or national exclusiveness, or of hate and contempt, is punishable by law.

Article 124. In the object of ensuring to the citizens freedom of conscience, the church in the U.S.S.R. is separated from the State and the School from the church. Freedom of service of religious cults and freedom of anti-religious propaganda is acknowledged for all citizens.

Article 125. In accordance with the interest of the toilers and in the object of strengthening the socialist system, the citizens of the U.S.S.R. are guaranteed by law:

a) freedom of speech,

b) freedom of press,

c) freedom of assemblies and meetings,

d) freedom of street processions and demonstrations.

These rights of citizens are secured by placing at the disposal of toilers and their organizations printing presses, supplies of papers, public buildings, streets, means of communications, and other material conditions necessary for their exercise.

Article 126. In accordance with the interests of the toilers and with the object of the development of the organized self-expression and political activity of the popular masses, there is ensured to the citizens of the U.S.S.R. the right of union into public organizations, professional unions, co-operative organizations, organizations of youth, sport and defense organizations, cultural, technical and scientific societies, and the most active and conscious citizens from the ranks of the working class and other strata of toilers are united in the All-Union Communist Party [Bolsheviks] which is the vanguard of the toilers in their struggle for the strengthening and development of the socialist order and represents the directing kernel of all organizations of toilers, both public and State.

Article 127. To the citizens of the U.S.S.R. is secured inviolability of person. No one can be subjected to arrest otherwise than on the decision of the court or with the sanction of the State attorney.

Article 128. The inviolability of residence of citizens and the secrecy of correspondence are protected by law. . . .

Article 132. Universal military obligation is a law.

Military service in the Workers' and Peasants' Red Army is an honorable obligation of citizens of the U.S.S.R. . . .

CHAPTER XI. THE ELECTORAL SYSTEM

Article 134. Elections of deputies to all the Councils [national and local] . . . are made by the electors on the basis of universal, equal and direct electoral right with secret ballot.

Article 135. Elections of deputies are universal: all citizens of the U.S.S.R., who have reached the age of eighteen, independent of racial and national affiliations, confession of faith, educational rank, domicile, social origin, property status and past activity, have the right to take part in the election of deputies and to be elected, with the exception of the insane and persons condemned by a court to be deprived of electoral rights. . . .

CHAPTER XIII. THE METHOD OF CHANGING THE CONSTITUTION

Article 146. Change of the Constitution of the U.S.S.R. is made only on the decision of the Supreme Council of the U.S.S.R., accepted by a majority of not less than two-thirds of the votes in each of the chambers.

7. Some Aspects of Soviet Russia in the Early 1940's

THE SECOND AND THIRD FIVE-YEAR PLANS

A second Five-Year Plan, with greater emphasis upon consumer goods, was inaugurated in 1933, and a third in 1938 —the last being sharply diverted to national defense as World War II drew near. Maurice Hindus, a Russian-born American observer, has described the accomplishments of these plans.

From HINDUS, *Mother Russia* (1942) [1]

They paid for the Plans with Russian resources. This is another distinguishing feature of Russian industrialization. Foreign capital, as already indicated, could not be obtained—not in very large sums— nor was it especially wanted; the Soviets would not accept the terms on which they could have it. They chose to pay for everything out of their own pockets, at the expense of their daily bread and shelter. As a consequence, no foreigner holds a mortgage on a single Russian steel shop, power plant, railroad, or any other enterprise. No one received a single dollar in interest on investment in Russian industry. Until the coming of the war, Russia had no external debt, except the prerevolutionary debt which the Soviets have officially repudiated. . . .

In prerevolutionary days about three fourths of Russia's heavy industry was centered in the south, chiefly in the Ukraine. As much as 90 per cent of the coal came from the Donets Basin, which is also in the Ukraine. No less than two thirds of all industry was crowded into the central and southern parts of European

[1] *Mother Russia*, by Maurice Hindus, 166-72. Copyright 1942, reprinted by permission of Doubleday & Company, Inc.

Russia. Siberia was frowned upon as a possible place of industrial development. Central Asia was treated as a backward colony. The Caucasus was regarded as a gay, exciting summer resort. Even the region of the Urals, one of the richest strips of land in the world, literally glutted with raw materials, where there once had been an old and primitive industry, was left largely to itself and to its harsh primitiveness. Until the coming of the Plans there was not a single *modern* blast furnace east of the Volga.

One reason why the Russian Army met with such disaster in the first World War was that so much of Russia's industry was centered in territory which the Germans overran. Had the Soviets centered their industrial development in the old industrial regions, all European Russia, perhaps even the Urals, would by this time [1942] have been under complete German rule. It is because of the wide, far-flung distribution of Russian industry that, no matter how deep into the rear the Red armies retreated, they always had an industry to grind out for them armaments and ammunition. Deliberately and with farsightedness the Russian leaders prepared construction crews that could travel from place to place in the Urals, the Caucasus, Armenia, Siberia, Central Asia, and build new or rehabilitate and enlarge old factories. Without the concentrated training of the three Plans these crews would of course have been impossible.

Russian industry now stretches east all the way to the Pacific Ocean; north to the Arctic Circle and beyond; south to the border of Afghanistan and India. The Red Army can always have an industrial base on which to lean in moments of catastrophe; it can always command weapons with which to fight even if it should be driven beyond the European borders. . . .

The Plans have eliminated all foreign

economic holdings. The Lena gold fields in Siberia, last of the foreign concessions, British in this instance, were taken over by the Soviets before the inauguration of the First Plan. A few small plants (an Austrian sweater factory, a foreign cosmetic works) lingered for some time but in the end were absorbed by Soviet industry. The Plans have made Russia as free from foreign investment as the Soviets have made her free of foreign political influence and intrigue. Though fathered by Bolsheviks who have their roots in international socialism, the Plans have converted Russia in her economic ownership into the most nationalistic country in the world.

The emphasis of the Plans was on heavy industry—steel and machine building. With plenty of steel and abundant machine-building capacity at their command the Soviets felt that they could easily develop in time all the light industries. They could then build factories anywhere without the need of foreign importation. The war [World War II] interrupted the process. Yet the magnitude of the achievement of the Plans can be judged by a few simple figures. In 1913, which marked the peak of Russia's pre-Soviet economic development, industry accounted for 42.1 per cent of the national income, agriculture for the remaining 57.9 per cent. At the beginning of the Third Plan, industry had leaped so far ahead of agriculture that it yielded three and a half times as much income. . . .

In no other country, not even in the United States, was machine building accorded such a crucial place. In 1940 it constituted one fourth of all manufacturing. That is why during the Third Plan Russia was manufacturing excellent trucks and tanks, tractors and combines, planes and locomotives, but inferior, often execrable, shoes, clothes, razors, razor blades, furniture, and plumbing fixtures. Consumption

goods in quality and quantity could wait —such was the theory. If a foreign enemy pounced on the country he would be fought not with razor blades and plumbing fixtures, not with silk stockings and silk underwear, but with guns and shells, with planes and tanks and other modern armaments.

From year to year Russia was building more and more heavy industry. In 1913 the daily output of steel was 11,000 tons. In 1940 it mounted from 58,000 to 59,000 tons. In Europe only Germany surpassed Russia in the production of pig iron and steel. In 1913 the daily output of coal was 85,000 tons, of oil and gas 25,000. In 1940 the first rose to 417,000 tons, the second from 97,000 to 98,000 tons. In 1939 the chemical industry yielded fifteen times as much production as in 1913. Kuzbas, the coal basin in faraway Siberia, accounted in 1913 for only 0.8 millions tons of coal. In 1937 the figure leaped to 17.8 million tons. At the beginning of the Third Plan at least three fourths of all industry and output in Russia came from factories that were new or had been reconstructed and modernized. . . .

But the most distinguishing feature of the Plans and of all Soviet industrialization is their political basis and the implications they presuppose. Bolsheviks speak of their economic system as socialism. Socialists who are not Bolsheviks deny this claim. They contend that Russia has no civil liberties and certain other forms of freedom which are as much a part of a socialist society as collective ownership of property. This is not the place to discuss whether or not the Bolsheviks or their socialist opponents are right. Yet in any account of the Plans and of Russian industrialization it is impossible to overemphasize the fact that private capital and individual enterprise have had no part in it. On the contrary, the Plans, especially the first one, squeezed and throttled to extinction all but a most insignificant number of private enterprises.

Russia is now the only land in the world in which private ownership of income-yielding property is as much at an end as czarism or landlordism. Not a new factory in Russia but was built by the state. . . .

Many of the innovations and interpretations of the Revolution have been found inadequate or dangerous and have been modified or discarded. Theory after theory in education, from the project method of study and lax class discipline to the substitution of the class-struggle saga for history, has been tried, denounced, and finally scrapped. Prerevolutionary values in social life, in esthetics, in music, in the other arts, in daily life, which in the first flush of rebellion against the old world had been mocked and cast away, have been welcomed back with appreciation and fervor. As already stressed in preceding pages, Russia has been zealously rediscovering her own purely Russian past, as well as the past of the human race, and has eagerly and passionately been re-appropriating and reincorporating into daily life usages, customs, and relationships which old Russia had honored and other peoples had for ages made their own.

There has been a significant process of sifting and clarification in social adaptation, individual orientation, in cultural appreciation. There has been a visible return to old and long-tried values. This has led to frequent and loud proclamations—not in Russia but outside—that Sovietism is undergoing a transformation which is pushing Russia closer and closer to the civilization, the economic usage, the human motivation prevailing in England, America, and other advanced modern nations. This is only partially true and, like all partial truths, lends itself to easy distortion of all truth and therefore to rank falsification.

Let it be noted that on the main issue of Sovietism—the ban on capitalism or income-yielding private property in whatever form—there has been neither change nor deviation. The Plans not only envisaged but ruthlessly enforced this ban. The war has not lightened its application. . . .

After a quarter of a century of violent, ceaseless propaganda on the sinfulness and wickedness of private business, Russia is so alienated from the institution that young people under thirty, and even more of them under twenty, in conversation with foreigners find it hard to imagine the system of private enterprise as it exists in the outside world.

IS RUSSIA ABANDONING COMMUNISTIC PRINCIPLES?

A number of observers, impressed by the fact that a highly graduated wage scale was introduced in Russia in March, 1934, that compensation on a piecework basis is employed wherever applicable, that the constitution of 1936 recognized certain private-property rights, and that other incentives similar to those employed in capitalist states have been approved, have maintained that classes are developing in Russian "classless" society and that Russia, perhaps unwittingly, is slipping her communistic moorings. Joseph Davies, the United States Ambassador to Russia in the late 1930's, was one of the earliest advocates of this opinion. He expressed this view in a letter to the Secretary of State in 1937.

From DAVIES, *Mission to Moscow* (1941) [1]

It appears quite clear that the governing powers have, through necessity and for

[1] Reprinted from *Mission to Moscow*, 122-24, by permission of Simon and Schuster, Inc. Copyright, 1941, by Joseph E. Davies.

self-preservation, been compelled to abandon, at least temporarily, many of their communistic principles. The idea of a "classless" society has been and is being destroyed in practice. The government itself is a bureaucracy with all the indicia of class, to wit: special privileges, higher standards of living, and the like. An illustration is found in the fact that the only caviar which can be obtained here is served by the high government officials or possibly obtained as a matter of favor through the Kremlin restaurant, which is provided for the high governmental officials living therein. From the top down, there are to be found indications of class.

Writers, artists, even leaders of jazz bands, receive high compensation and have the class privileges which money provides in luxuries and the like.

Membership in the party constitutes a distinctly privileged class.

In industry, classes have been established and are being rapidly intensified and developed through the system of offering greater pay for greater work. This in turn had induced higher standards of living among certain of the workers, and class consciousness is evidenced in differences in housing and living conditions and indications of style consciousness on the part of women and wives of the workers. This condition is admitted by the officialdom here in confidence; but they seek to justify it on the Marxian theory that there is no class distinction except that which exists between the workers and a capitalistic property-owning class which exploits them, and, inasmuch as this is a socialistic enterprise for the benefit of the state and, therefore, has no capitalistic property-owning class, that therefore, in the proper sense of the word, there are no "classes" because of these differentiations. Of course, the fallacy of this is obvious. "Class," after all, is only a word to define an idea; the basis of which is that there

are different groups of men which are differentiated, as among themselves. Obviously the principal visible distinctions are found in the various standards of living and special privileges that are enjoyed. There can be no doubt that this is essentially a "class" society, and contains the seed of self-interest which the condition breeds.

The significant thing to my mind about this situation is the fact that these theoretical Communists, when clothed with responsibility and faced with the necessity of maintaining themselves in power, were compelled to resort to the elementals of human nature, to wit: self-interest and profit for labor, in order to make their plan function and justify their bureaucracy. A "selfless" industry system, they found, would stagnate. To succeed they were obliged to resort to the fundamental incentive of profit and individualistic self-interest. It is alleged by the leaders here that this is simply a stage in their effort to attain ultimate communism. There is every indication here, however, that again it will be a case of "the monster that makes the meat upon which it grows great"; and that it will be a long time before this capitalistic-socialistic state, with its rulers enjoying the "fleshpots" of luxury and power, will develop into a communistic state and "selfless" society. Again, in the army, the old idea of comrade officers and simplicity has been displaced by titles, gold braid, epaulets, decorations, and smart uniforms, distinguishing the one class from the other.

Another striking indication of departure from the communistic idea is to be found in the attitude of the government toward the home, divorce, parenthood, the fatherland, and nationalistic patriotism. The idea of the world proletariat and revolution has been set aside and replaced with the idea of a nationalistic Russia.

38

FASCISM AND NAZISM

1. Mussolini's Italian Fascist State

MUSSOLINI AND FASCISM

"I want to make a mark on history with my will, like a lion with his claws." So spoke Benito Mussolini (1883-1945) to one of his "official" biographers. And seldom in history has the arrogant will of one man dominated a state more completely than Mussolini's in Fascist Italy, although World War II showed him up as a fair-weather sailor, a victim of fear and indecision when the going was rough, and wholly unlike the incisive "Il Duce" of his peacetime pose. Born in a miserably poor family of Romagna—his father a blacksmith by trade and a Marxian Socialist, anti-Catholic writer by avocation, his mother a pious Catholic schoolteacher—Mussolini was a headstrong, restless youth. Graduated from normal school, he made a brief try at schoolteaching and then migrated to Switzerland (1902) in search of a job. He took unkindly to manual labor and soon became a labor "organizer" and a militant socialist writer. For activities in these latter capacities he was expelled from Switzerland—and later from Austria—and acquired a lengthy police record in Italy as a revolutionary Socialist, antimilitarist, antinationalist, blaspheming atheist, and a defamer of monarchy and the Italian King. In 1912 he became editor in chief of the socialist paper *Avanti!*

and leader of the Italian Socialist party. But he broke with the party over the question of Italian intervention in World War I, resigned as editor of the *Avanti!*, was expelled from the Socialist party, and founded (November, 1914) a daily paper at Milan, *Il Popolo d'Italia,* to advocate intervention on the Allied side in the war and to build up a party of his own (the Fascisti). "I needed a daily paper," he wrote in *My Autobiography,* "it was an instrument for the making of me." From this point on Mussolini was a nationalist and a militarist, and he gradually sloughed off the other attributes of his socialist career. After a brief military career in 1916-17, during which he was severely wounded when a shell exploded prematurely in trench-mortar practice, he resumed his editorship of *Il Popolo d'Italia* (autumn, 1917)—"a life of intense polemics; every day was a battle." The postwar scene in Italy gave Mussolini his opportunity. Undistinguished by her military showing in the war, Italy had nevertheless suffered grievous losses, she was heavily in debt, and her people were angered by the diplomatic failure to realize at Paris the advantages promised by the "secret" Treaty of London of 1915 [see page 727]. Industrial and agrarian unrest, strikes, the growth of Socialism, the red herring of Communism, and an unstable political situation marked by shifting ministries and a lack of firm policies completed the drab picture.

Into this confusion Mussolini cast himself with all his genius of self-dramatization. Through the columns of *Il Popolo d'Italia* he summoned a mass meeting in Milan (March 23, 1919), having for "its object the foundation of a new movement, and the establishment of a program and of methods of action for the success of the battle I was intending to fight against the forces dissolving victory and Nation." Here was organized the first Fasci Italiani di combattimento ("the Italian Bundles of Fight"), the nucleus of the Italian Fascist party, bearing from the outset the personal stamp of Mussolini's ambitious will. Cautious at first, proclaiming themselves nationalists, pacifists, republican, and opposed to dictatorship, the Fascists reversed their policies in time, grew bolder as opportunity offered, and emerged in the early twenties as armed groups (Squadrista) of strikebreakers and terrorists bent upon the conquest of power. As Mussolini frankly said, the movement was not originally a response to a theory. The Fascists seized power first and worked out theoretical justification afterward. But a theory of Fascism did arise, and Mussolini himself explained it flamboyantly and somewhat verbosely in an article for the *Enciclopedia Italiana* in 1932, a translation of which follows.

From MUSSOLINI, *Doctrine of Fascism* (1932) [1]

Fascism was not the nursling of a doctrine worked out beforehand with detailed elaboration; it was born of the need for action and was itself from the beginning practical rather than theoretical; it was not merely another political party but, even in the first two years, in opposition

[1] Benito Mussolini, *The Political and Social Doctrine of Fascism,* trans. by Jane Soames, 1933, 8-14, 16-26. By permission of The Hogarth Press, London.

to all political parties as such, and itself a living movement. The name which I then (1919) gave to the organization fixed its character. And yet, if one were to re-read, in the now dusty columns of that date, the report of the meeting in which the *Fasci Italiani di combattimento* were constituted, one would there find no ordered expression of doctrine, but a series of aphorisms, anticipations and aspirations which, when refined by time from the original ore, were destined after some years to develop into an ordered series of doctrinal concepts, forming the Fascist political doctrine—different from all others either of the past or the present day. . . .

The years which preceded the march to Rome were years of great difficulty, during which the necessity for action did not permit of research or any complete elaboration of doctrine. The battle had to be fought in the towns and villages. There was much discussion, but—what was more important and more sacred—men died. They knew how to die. Doctrine, beautifully defined and carefully elucidated . . . might be lacking; but there was to take its place something more decisive—Faith. Even so, anyone . . . will find that the fundamentals of doctrine were cast during the years of conflict. It was precisely in those years that Fascist thought armed itself, was refined, and began the great task of organization. The problem of the relation between the individual citizen and the State; the allied problems of authority and liberty; political and social problems as well as those specifically national—a solution was being sought for all these while at the same time the struggle against Liberalism, Democracy, Socialism and the Masonic bodies was being carried on. . . . A doctrine of its own . . . was growing . . . first, as happens to all ideas in their beginnings, in the aspect of a violent and dogmatic negation, and then in the aspect of positive construction which has found its realization in the laws and institutions of the regime as enacted successively in the years 1926, 1927, and 1928. . . .

And above all, Fascism . . . believes neither in the possibility nor the utility of perpetual peace.[1] It thus repudiates the doctrine of Pacifism—born of a renunciation of the struggle and an act of cowardice in the face of sacrifice. War alone brings up to its highest tension all human energy and puts the stamp of nobility upon the peoples who have the courage to meet it. All other trials are substitutes, which never really put men into the position where they have to make the great decision—the alternative of life or death. Thus a doctrine which is founded upon this harmful postulate of peace is hostile to Fascism. And thus hostile to the spirit of Fascism, though accepted for what use they can be in dealing with particular political situations, are all the international leagues and societies which, as history will show, can be scattered to the winds when once strong national feeling is aroused by any motive —sentimental, ideal, or practical. This anti-Pacifist spirit is carried by Fascism even into the life of the individual; the proud motto of the *Squadrista, "Me ne frego"* ["We don't give a damn"] . . . is an act of philosophy not only stoic, the summary of a doctrine not only political— it is the education to combat, the acceptation of the risks which combat implies, and a new way of life for Italy. Thus the Fascist accepts life and loves it, knowing nothing of and despising suicide: he rather conceives of life as a duty and struggle and conquest, life which should be high and full, lived for oneself, but above all for others. . . .

Such a conception of life makes Fascism the complete opposition of that doctrine, the base of so-called scientific and Marxian

Socialism, the materialist conception of history; according to which the history of human civilization can be explained simply through the conflict of interests among the various social groups and by the change and development in the means and instruments of production. . . . Fascism, now and always, believes in holiness and in heroism; that is to say, in actions influenced by no economic motive, direct or indirect. . . . It follows that the existence of an unchangeable and unchanging class-war is also denied—the natural progeny of the economic conception of history. And above all Fascism denies that class-war can be the preponderant force in the transformation of society. These two fundamental concepts of Socialism being thus refuted, nothing is left of it but the sentimental aspiration . . . towards a social convention in which the sorrows and sufferings of the humblest shall be alleviated. . . . Fascism denies the validity of the equation, well-being—happiness, which would reduce men to the level of animals, caring for one thing only—to be fat and well-fed—and would thus degrade humanity to a purely physical existence.

After Socialism, Fascism combats the whole complex system of democratic ideology, and repudiates it, whether in its theoretical premises or in its practical application. Fascism denies that the majority, by the simple fact that it is a majority, can direct human society; it denies that numbers alone can govern by means of a periodical consultation, and it affirms the immutable, beneficial and fruitful inequality of mankind, which can never be permanently leveled through the mere operation of a mechanical process such as universal suffrage. The democratic regime may be defined as from time to time giving the people the illusion of sovereignty, while the real effective sovereignty lies in the hands of other concealed and irresponsible forces. . . .

---

[1] For a discussion of some possible romantic forerunners of Fascist thought, see page 539.

Fascism has taken up an attitude of complete opposition to the doctrines of Liberalism, both in the political field and the field of economics. . . . Liberalism only flourished for half a century. . . . And it is symptomatic that such a highly civilized people as the Germans were completely ignorant of the religion of liberty during the whole of the nineteenth century. . . . Germany attained her national unity quite outside the doctrines of Liberalism—a doctrine which seems entirely foreign to the German mind, a mind essentially monarchic—while Liberalism is the logical and, indeed, historical forerunner of anarchy. . . . As for Italian unity, its debt to Liberalism is completely inferior in contrast to that which it owes to the work of Mazzini and Garibaldi, who were not Liberals. Had it not been for the intervention of the anti-Liberal Napoleon, we should not have gained Lombardy; and without the help of the again anti-Liberal Bismarck at Sadowa and Sedan it is very probable that we should never have gained the province of Venice in '66, or been able to enter Rome in '70. From 1870 to 1914 a period began during which even the high priests of the religion themselves had to recognize the gathering twilight of their faith. . . . In addition to this, let it be pointed out that all the political hopes of the present day are anti-Liberal. . . .

But the Fascist negation of Socialism, Democracy and Liberalism must not be taken to mean that Fascism desires to lead the world back to the state of affairs before 1789 . . . we do not desire to turn back. . . . Absolute monarchy has been and can never return, any more than blind acceptance of ecclesiastical authority.

So, too, the privileges of the feudal system "have been" . . . the Fascist conception of authority has nothing to do with such a polity. A party which entirely governs a nation is a fact entirely new in history, there are no possible references or parallels. Fascism uses in its construction whatever elements in the Liberal, Social or Democratic doctrines still have a living value . . . but it rejects all the rest. . . .

The foundation of Fascism is the conception of the State, its character, its duty, and its aim. Fascism conceives of the State as an absolute, in comparison with which all individuals or groups are relative, only to be conceived of in their relation to the State. The conception of the Liberal State is not that of a directing force, guiding the play and development, both material and spiritual, of a collective body, but merely a force limited to the function of recording results: on the other hand, the Fascist State is itself conscious, and has itself a will and a personality—thus it may be called the "ethic" State. In 1929 . . . I said:

"For us Fascists, the State is not merely a guardian . . . nor is it an organization with purely material aims. . . . Nor is it a purely political creation. . . . The State, as conceived of and as created by Fascism, is a spiritual and moral fact in itself, since its political, juridical and economic organization of the nation is a concrete thing; and such an organization must be in its origins and development a manifestation of the spirit. The State is the guarantor of security both internal and external, but it is also the custodian and transmitter of the spirit of the people, as it has grown up through the centuries in language, in customs and in faith. And the State is not only a living reality of the present, it is also linked with the past and above all with the future, and thus transcending the brief limits of individual life, it represents the immanent spirit of the nation. . . . It is the State which educates its citizens in civic virtue, gives them a consciousness of their mission, and welds them into unity; harmonizing their various interests through justice, and transmitting to, future generations the mental conquests of science, of art, of law and the solidarity of humanity." . . .

From 1929 until today [1932], evolution, both political and economic, has everywhere gone to prove the validity of these doctrinal premises. Of such gigantic importance is the State. It is the force which alone can provide a solution to the dramatic contradictions of capitalism, and that state of affairs which we call the crisis can only be dealt with by the State, as between other States. . . . Yet the Fascist State is unique, and an original creation. It is not reactionary, but revolutionary, in that it anticipates the solution of the universal political problems which elsewhere have to be settled in the political field by the rivalry of parties, the excessive power of the Parliamentary regime and the irresponsibility of political assemblies; while it meets the problems of the economic field by a system of syndicalism which is continually increasing in importance, as much in the sphere of labour as of industry: and in the moral field enforces order, discipline, and obedience to that which is the determined moral code of the country. Fascism desires the State to be a strong and organic body, at the same time reposing upon broad and popular support. The Fascist State has drawn into itself even the economic activities of the nation, and, through the corporative social and educational institutions created by it, its influence reaches every aspect of the national life and includes, framed in their respective organizations, all the political, economic and spiritual forces of the nation. A State which reposes upon the support of millions of individuals who recognize its authority, are continually conscious of its power and are ready at once to serve it, is not the old tyrannical State. . . . The individual in the Fascist State is not annulled but rather multiplied, just in the same way that a soldier in a regiment is not diminished but rather increased by the number of his comrades. The Fascist State organizes the nation, but leaves a sufficient margin of liberty to the individual; the latter is deprived of all useless and possibly harmful freedom, but retains what is essential; the deciding power in this question cannot be the individual, but the State alone. . . .

The Fascist State is an embodied will to power and government: the Roman tradition is here an ideal of force in action. According to Fascism, government is not so much a thing to be expressed in territorial or military terms as in terms of morality and the spirit. It must be thought of as an Empire—that is to say, a nation which directly or indirectly rules other nations, without the need for conquering a single square yard of territory. For Fascism, the growth of Empire, that is to say the expansion of the nation, is an essential manifestation of vitality, and its opposite a sign of decadence. Peoples which are rising, or rising again after a period of decadence, are always imperialist; any renunciation is a sign of decay and death. Fascism is the doctrine best adapted to represent the tendencies and the aspirations of a people, like the people of Italy, who are rising again after many centuries of abasement and foreign servitude. But Empire demands discipline, the co-ordination of all forces and a deeply-felt sense of duty and sacrifice: this fact explains . . . the necessarily severe measures which must be taken against those who would oppose this spontaneous and inevitable movement of Italy in the twentieth century.

ASPECTS OF THE ITALIAN CORPORATE STATE

"There is talk of a similarity between Fascism and Bolshevism," said *My Autobiography,* attributed to Mussolini.

"The difference is that Bolshevism believes in the dictatorship of one class, Fascism in the dictatorship of the State over many classes co-operating. While Communism destroyed other classes, Fascism forced them to co-operate and co-ordinate their diverging activities." The corporate state was the Fascist instrument of compulsion, and a basic factor of the corporate state was Italian syndicalism, which advocated the abolition of political government in favor of government by economic groups. Edmondo Rossoni led the Italian syndicalist movement during World War I and immediately afterward. A firm believer in private property rights, capitalism, "class collaboration," and nationalism, Rossoni joined forces with the Fascists, organized syndicates to counterbalance the socialist trade-union movement, and hoped to reform the Italian governmental system so that representation would rest upon organized economic interests rather than upon geographico-political units. Rossoni's syndicates grew rapidly and by 1926 had a membership of nearly two and a half million. At this point, Mussolini embraced the system as a means of controlling the "productive forces" of Italy. Thirteen confederated Fascist syndicates, six of employers, six of employees, and one of intellectuals, were granted legal status by the law.

From *The Legal Discipline of Collective Labor Relations* (April 3, 1926) [1]

PART I. ON THE LEGAL RECOGNITION OF SYNDI-CATES AND ON COLLECTIVE LABOR CONTRACTS

Article 1. Associations of employers and of laborers, intellectual or manual, may be

[1] This and the next selection are from Herbert W. Schneider, ed., "Documents on the Fascist Government of Italy," in *Source Book on European Governments*. By permission of D. Van Nostrand Company, Inc. This is Part III, 32-43.

legally recognized if they can prove that they meet the following requirements:

(1) In the case of associations of employers, that the employers voluntarily registered as members employ at least ten per cent of the workers in the trade and district which the association represents [the same requirement holds for employees]. . . . (2) That, besides protecting the economic and moral interests of its members, the association effectively carries out plans for the insurance, instruction and moral and patriotic education of its members. (3) That the director of the association gives proof of his ability, morality, and unswerving loyalty to the nation.

Article 2. When the conditions prescribed in the foregoing Article are met, legal recognition can be given to associations of persons independently engaged in an art, trade, or profession. . . .

Article 3. The associations referred to in the foregoing Articles shall consist either of employers only or of employees only. Associations of employers and those of employees may be united by means of central co-ordinating bodies with a common hierarchy of higher officers, always maintaining, however, the separate representation of employers and employees. . . .

Article 4. The associations referred to . . . shall be recognized by Royal Decree on proposal of the Minister concerned, acting jointly with the Minister of the Interior, after consultation with the Council of State [later (1930) changed to "after consultation with the National Council of Corporations"]. The constitution of an association shall be approved . . . [and] must be explicit as to the purposes of the association, the mode of . . . appointment of its executive officers, and the conditions prescribed for the admission of members, one of which must be sound political conduct as regards loyalty to the nation. . . .

Article 5. Legally recognized associations

have legal personality and legally represent all the employers, laborers, employees, artists, or professional men of the particular class for which they are formed within the territorial limits of the association, whether they are registered members or not. Legally recognized associations have the right to levy annual dues ["not to exceed one day's wage"] on all employers, laborers, employees, artists, or professional men whom they represent, whether they are registered members or not. . . . At least ten per cent of the sums thus collected must be set aside annually . . . to guarantee the liabilities incurred by the associations with reference to the collective contracts which they have stipulated. . . .

Article 6. Associations may be communal, district, provincial, regional, inter-regional, or national. Federations, or unions of several associations, and confederations of several federations may also be legally recognized. . . . Only one association [federation or confederation] may be legally recognized for any one class of employers, employees, artists, or professional men . . . within the district assigned to each. Whenever a national confederation shall have been recognized for all the classes of employers or employees in agriculture, industry, or commerce, or for all the classes of artists or professional men, the recognition of . . . associations which do not form part of these confederations shall be prohibited.

Article 7. Each association shall have a president or secretary who directs and represents it and is responsible for its work. . . . [These officers are chosen as the constitution of the association provides, subject to approval by Royal Decree—an approval which "may be revoked at any time."]

Article 8. The president or secretary of an association is to be assisted by a Council of Directors elected by the members of the association. . . . [Local associations are subject to supervision of the Prefect, and regional, inter-regional, and national associations are under supervision of the appropriate Minister.]

Article 10. Collective labor contracts made by the legally recognized associations . . . are obligatory on all employers, employees, artists, or professional men in the classes referred to in the contracts or represented in the associations in accordance with . . . Article 5 of the Law. Collective labor contracts are void unless written . . . [and] null and void if they fail to state the period for which they hold good. . . .

[Central co-ordinating bodies, as provided for in Article 3, may establish "general norms and conditions for labor"; all collective contracts must be filed with the appropriate governmental agency and published.]

Article 11. [Provisions of this law do not apply to governmental employees, state or local.] . . .

PART II. OF LABOR COURTS

Article 13. All controversies arising as to the regulation of collective labor relations, whether they concern the application of collective contracts and other existing regulations, or whether they concern demands for new labor conditions, are subject to the jurisdiction of the [sixteen] Courts of Appeal acting as Labor Courts. . . .

Article 14. . . . Such modifications in the judiciary and in the staff of the chancelleries of the Courts as are necessary to carry out the above provisions will be made by Royal Decree. . . .

Article 15. . . . [Each Court of Appeal shall be assisted by a panel of experts "in the problems of production and labor," divided into groups corresponding to the types of business activities under review and revised biennially.] . . .

Article 17. Only legally recognized associations have the right to take action in disputes arising out of collective labor contracts. . . .

PART III. OF LOCK-OUTS AND STRIKES

Article 18. Lock-outs and strikes are prohibited.

[The improvements anticipated in the conditions of labor after legalization of the national syndicates did not measure up to expectations. Accordingly, Rossoni advocated a "Charter of Labor" intended to serve as a codification of concrete rules to be applied to collective contracts. But the original draft was modified until it became a statement of general principles, valuable both as a guide to policy and as an indication of Fascist ideology.]

From "The Charter of Labor"
(April 21, 1927) [1]

1. The Italian nation is an organism having ends, life, and means of action superior to those of the separate individuals or groups of individuals that compose it. It is a moral, political, and economic unity integrated in the Fascist State.

2. Labor in all its forms, organizing, executive, intellectual, technical, and manual, is a social duty. As such and only as such it is safeguarded by the State. From the national point of view the whole of production is a single process; it has a single aim which may be summed up in the welfare of individuals and the growth of the national power. . . .

7. The Corporative State regards private initiative in the field of production as the most effective and useful instrument of the national interest. Since the private organization of production is a function

[1] *Ibid.*, Pt. III, 44-46.

of national interest, the organizer of an enterprise is responsible to the State for its management. From the cooperation of the productive forces [employer and employee] it follows that they have mutual rights and duties. . . .

11. Occupational associations are obliged to regulate by collective contracts the labor relations between the groups of employers and laborers whom they represent.

[The remainder of the Charter of Labor dealt with guarantees to workers, such as additional pay for overtime work, a weekly rest on Sunday, annual paid vacations, social insurance, etc.]

THE CORPORATIVE STATE, 1928-39

The corporative state—"Mussolini's conception of Democracy" and, in his opinion, Fascism's greatest contribution to political science—was incomplete until the syndicalist system was combined with the political system of Italy. This process was effected as described below.

From LANGSAM, *The World since 1914* (1943) [2]

The Corporative State, 1928-39

In 1928 a law was passed which made Italy the first Western state to have a national legislature representing economic divisions. The membership of the Chamber of Deputies was reduced from 560 to 400. These 400 deputies were to be elected by the entire kingdom, acting as a single electoral constituency. Candidates to the number of 800 were to be nominated by the executive councils of the 13 confederated syndicates, sitting at Rome. Each syndicate was given the right to nominate

[2] From Walter Consuelo Langsam, *The World since 1914*, 5th ed., 1943, 346-48. By permission of The Macmillan Company, New York.

a definite number of candidates and in each field of production the employers and employees were to select the same number of nominees. . . . Two hundred additional candidates were similarly to be nominated by a group of cultural and charitable institutions. From the list of 1000 candidates the Fascist Grand Council was to select 400.

The council might, if it chose, add names of its own or even reject the entire list and substitute a new one. When the council had decided upon a satisfactory "four hundred," the approved list was to be made public. On election day the voters would receive a ballot containing the single question: "Do you approve of the list of deputies designated by the Fascist Grand Council?" The answer had to be either "yes" or "no" for the entire list. . . .

Universal suffrage was abolished by this electoral law. The franchise was restricted to those who paid a syndicate rate, or paid a certain minimum of direct taxes, or received pensions or salaries from the state or public institutions, or belonged to the clergy of a recognized cult. Women were excluded from the national franchise, while men, to vote, had to be twenty-one, or eighteen if they were married and had children. The male electorate thus was reduced by approximately three million. The employers, though less numerous than the workers, received equal representation. The entire electoral procedure was undemocratic, but the Fascists were proud of this very fact. . . .

Early in 1929 the executive councils of the syndicates and other institutions met to nominate their candidates under the new law. Mussolini's name came first on nearly every list. The Fascist Grand Council then . . . selected four hundred men of suitable qualifications and "reliable Fascist faith." The list was published and the voters were permitted to accept or reject the entire list. . . . The Fascists carried on an energetic campaign. No opposition speeches were permitted. . . . The official list was endorsed by a proportion of more than 62 to 1 [8,663,412 to 135,761]. The second election under the law was held in 1934 [the result was this time 10,041,998 to 15,265 in favor of the Fascist list]. . . .

In 1934 the Italian Government created twenty-two new corporations, each of which represented the state, capital, and labor. Falling into the three main divisions of agriculture, industry, and services, the corporations stood for the following branches of production: cereals, horticulture and fruit, wine, oils, sugar, stock raising and fishing, wood, textiles, metallurgy and machinery, chemicals, [and so on]. . . . Each corporation included all the interests concerned with its particular branch of national economy. . . . Three functions were assigned to the corporations: to advise the government, settle labor disputes, and regulate production, distribution, and prices. Under this system, said Mussolini, production remained in the hands of self-governing groups of employers and employees, while private initiative was transferred from the individual to the corporate sphere.

After several years of further study, the Fascist Grand Council in 1938 decreed the organization of a new legislative body to take the place of the Chamber of Deputies. Called "the Chamber of Fasces and Corporations," this house was to be composed of about seven hundred "national councillors" representing the state, the Fascist Party, and the twenty-two corporations; all members were to be appointed by the "Head of the Government" (Mussolini). . . . The first meeting of the Chamber of Fasces and Corporations was opened by the king in March 1939. Thus were national elections abolished in Italy.

2. Germany: The Weimar Republic

THE REVOLUTION OF 1918

The conclusion of the Armistice on November 11, 1918, was preceded by scenes of wild confusion in Germany. After Germany's allies began to desert (Bulgaria signed an armistice on September 30), the German High Command, witnessing the continued advance of the Western Powers, became frantic. On October 3, General Field-Marshal Paul von Hindenburg wrote to Prince Max, the new German Chanceller, that "there no longer exists any prospect, according to human calculation, of forcing peace upon our enemies," and he called for "the immediate despatch of the peace offer." While negotiations for the Armistice went on, the German home front degenerated into violence and revolution complicated by a fragmentation of the party structure which had been developing during the war. In 1915, the Independent Socialists, led by Karl Johann Kautsky, Hugo Haase, and Eduard Bernstein, had seceded from the Social-Democratic Party (hereafter referred to as the Majority Socialists), and in 1917 they organized a separate party. In 1917, too, the Spartacists, led by Karl Liebknecht and Rosa Luxemburg, had joined with the Russian Bolsheviks and sought to stir up the German proletariat in preparation for the "world revolution." These extremist groups took prominent parts in the mutiny which broke out in the German Navy (November 3, 1918), in the revolution in Munich (November 7), and similar uprisings elsewhere. Meanwhile, widespread demands arose for the abdication of the Kaiser. On November 9 the Kaiser bolted and, finding that he could

not depend upon the army's loyalty, he fled to Holland the next day. On November 9, too, his abdication was proclaimed in Berlin (although no formal abdication was forthcoming from the Kaiser until November 28), and Philipp Scheidemann, for the Majority Socialists, beat the extremists to the draw and proclaimed the German Republic. A Provisional Government of six People's Representatives, led by Scheidemann and Friedrich Ebert and backed by a coalition of Majority Socialists and Independent Socialists (the latter recoiling from the Spartacists), took control in Berlin, signed the Armistice with the Allies, and subsequently arranged for the election of a National Constituent Assembly. On November 12, against the opposition of the Spartacists and conservatives alike, the Provisional Government issued the following proclamation.

From the Proclamation of the Six Peoples Representatives (November 12, 1918) [1]

To the German People!

The Government created by the Revolution, the policy of which is purely Socialistic, is setting itself the task of carrying out the Socialistic program. With the full force of the law it now promulgates the following:

1. The "state of siege" is suspended.
2. The right of assembly and association is unrestricted. . . .
3. The censorship does not exist. . . .
4. Freedom of speech and of the press is re-established.
5. Religious freedom is guaranteed. . . .

Furthermore, ordinances, social and political, will be published shortly. . . .

[1] *The Making of New Germany: The Memoirs of Philipp Scheidemann,* trans. by J. E. Michell, 2 vols., 1929, II, 274-75. By permission of D. Appleton-Century Co., Inc., New York.

The Government will do its utmost to provide work. . . . All elections to public bodies are henceforward to be conducted according to equal, secret, direct and universal suffrage, based on proportional representation, for all males and females from twenty years old. This electoral law applies to elections for the Constituent Assembly, concerning which further instructions will follow.

THE SPARTACISTS

"The People's Representatives practically did their work as prisoners," said Scheidemann. "Machine-guns rattled day and night in Wilhelmstrasse," and "Noisy processions of many thousands, mostly armed to the teeth, were continuously organized by Liebknecht in front of the Chancellery." The Spartacists were, immediately, the greatest threat. When elections to the Constituent Assembly were announced for January 19, 1919, the Spartacists, aware that they could not win in a free election, determined to "stop the election by force." The result was "Spartacus Week," January 5-15, 1919, a period of civil war prefaced by the Spartacist Manifesto, which ran as follows.

From the "Spartacist Manifesto"
(January 6, 1919)[1]

Comrades! Workers!

The Ebert-Scheidemann Government has rendered itself impossible. It is hereby declared deposed by the undersigned Revolutionary Committee, the representative of the revolutionary socialist workers and soldiers (Independent Social Democratic Party and Communist Party). The undersigned Revolutionary Committee has

[1] Walter Consuelo Langsam, ed., *Documents and Readings in the History of Europe since 1918,* 1939, 649. Reprinted by permission of J. B. Lippincott Company, Chicago.

provisionally assumed the conduct of the business of government.

Comrades! Workers! Support the measures of the Revolutionary Committee.

The Revolutionary Committee
[George] Ledebour
[Karl] Liebknecht
[Paul] Scholze
Berlin, January 6, 1919.

THE WEIMAR CONSTITUTION (1919)

The Spartacist Revolt—and with it the immediate threat of Communism—was put down by force, but not without ugliness and dangerous concessions to the Right. The murders of Liebknecht and Rosa Luxemburg after their arrest marred the reputation of the Provisional Government, and Ebert's appeal to the generals of the demobilized army, secretly permitting them to raise volunteers to crush the Spartacists, gave rise to "free corps," the rallying point of future opponents to the new order and the nucleus of Hitler's Storm Troops. However, the election for the Constituent Assembly went off quietly on January 19. More than thirty million men and women, voting in a dozen or so parties, elected 421 representatives, the Majority Socialists leading with 163 seats, the Centrists second (88 seats), and the Democrats third (75 seats). A coalition of these three groups—the "Weimar Coalition"—controlled the Assembly. It was, broadly speaking, a coalition of moderates. Convening at Weimar to avoid possible mob violence in larger centers, the Assembly met February 6, took over the government from the six People's Representatives, elected Ebert first President of the German Republic, set up a coalition ministry under Scheidemann's leadership, and settled down to the triple task of restoring order, governing, and constitution-making. A crisis occurred in

June, when the Scheidemann ministry resigned rather than sign the Versailles Treaty. A new ministry was created under Gustav Bauer, who took the treaty question directly to the Assembly, which voted (237 to 138) to accept the treaty conditionally, without the "war guilt" articles 227-31 [see page 752]. But the Peace Conference required unconditional acceptance. After an all-night session (June 22-23), the German party leaders, with mutual reaffirmations of faith in the patriotism of all concerned and assurances of military support in case acceptance of the treaty led to popular uprisings, agreed to sign the treaty unconditionally to save the German people from worse suffering than even the peace would impose. This crisis passed, the Assembly completed its work of constitution-making. On July 31 it adopted the Weimar constitution, which went into effect on August 11, 1919, as the fundamental law of the German Republic. It was a noteworthy document on several counts: by its "dormant" socialism (it merely made possible the extension of socialism), it was a counterrevolutionary document directed against the revolutionists who had brought about the collapse of the old regime; its Bill of Rights was singular; and its Article 48 empowered the President to exercise dictatorial powers in an emergency—a provision seized upon by Hitler for the "bloodless" Nazi revolution in 1933. Extracts from the Constitution follow.

From "The Constitution of the German Commonwealth" (1919) [1]

Preamble: The German People, united in all their branches, and inspired by the

[1] William Bennett Munro and Arthur Norman Holcombe, eds. and transls., "The Constitution of the German Commonwealth," in *League of Nations, World Peace Foundation Publications*, II, No. 6, 1919, 354-400. Reprinted by permission of the World Peace Foundation, Boston.

determination to renew and strengthen their Commonwealth in liberty and justice, to preserve peace . . . and to foster social progress, have adopted the following Constitution.

CHAPTER I. STRUCTURE AND FUNCTIONS OF THE COMMONWEALTH

Section I. Commonwealth and States

Art. 1. The German Commonwealth is a republic. Political authority is derived from the People. . . .

Art. 5. Political authority is exercised in national affairs by the National Government in accordance with the Constitution of the Commonwealth, and in State affairs by the State Governments in accordance with the State constitutions. . . .

Art. 12. So long and in so far as the Commonwealth does not exercise its jurisdiction, such jurisdiction remains with the States . . . [except] in cases where the Commonwealth possesses exclusive jurisdiction. . . .

Art. 13. The laws of the Commonwealth are supreme over the laws of the States which conflict with them. . . .

Art. 17. Every State must have a republican constitution. The representatives of the People must be elected by universal, equal, direct and secret suffrage of all German citizens, both men and women, according to principles of proportional representation. . . .

Section II. The National Assembly [Reichstag]

Art. 20. The National Assembly is composed of the delegates of the German people.

Art. 21. The delegates are representatives of the whole People. They are subject only to their own consciences and are not bound by any instructions.

Art. 22. The delegates are elected [for four years] by universal, equal, direct and secret suffrage by all men and women over twenty years of age, in accordance with the principles of proportional representation. . . .

Art. 32. The National Assembly acts by majority vote unless otherwise provided in the Constitution. . . .

Section III. The National President and the National Cabinet

Art. 41. The National President is chosen by the whole German People. Every German who has completed his thirty-fifth year is eligible for election. . . .

Art. 43. The term of the National President is seven years. He is eligible for re-election. . . .

Art. 44. The National President may not at the same time be a member of the National Assembly.

Art. 45. The National President represents the Commonwealth in matters of international law. He concludes in the name of the Commonwealth alliances and treaties with foreign powers. . . . War is declared and peace concluded by national law. Alliances and treaties . . . require the consent of the National Assembly. . . .

Art. 47. The National President has supreme command over all the armed forces. . . .

Art. 48. If any State does not perform the duties imposed upon it by the Constitution or by national laws, the National President may hold it to the performance thereof by force of arms.

If public safety and order in the German Commonwealth is materially disturbed or endangered, the National President may take the necessary measures to restore public safety and order, and, if necessary, to intervene by force of arms. To this end he may temporarily suspend, in whole or in part, the fundamental rights established in Articles 114, 115, 117, 118, 123, 124, and 153. [Subject to revo-

cation "at the demand of the National Assembly."] . . .

Art. 50. All orders and directions of the National President . . . require for their validity the counter-signature of the National Chancellor or of the appropriate National Minister. By the counter-signature responsibility is assumed. . . .

Art. 52. The National Cabinet consists of the National Chancellor and the National Ministers.

Art. 53. The National Chancellor and, on his proposal, the National Ministers are appointed and dismissed by the National President.

Art. 54. The National Chancellor and the National Ministers require . . . the confidence of the National Assembly. Each of them must resign if the National Assembly by formal resolution withdraws its confidence. . . .

Art. 56. The National Chancellor determines the general course of policy and assumes responsibility therefor to the National Assembly. In accordance with this general policy each National Minister conducts independently the particular affairs intrusted to him and is held individually responsible to the National Assembly. . . .

Section IV. The National Council [Reichsrat]

Art. 60. A National Council will be organized to represent the German States in national legislation and administration.

Art. 61. In the National Council each State has at least one vote. In the case of the larger States one vote is accorded for every million inhabitants. . . . [No State shall have more than two-fifths of all votes.]

Art. 63. The States will be represented in the National Council by members of their Cabinets. . . .

Section V. National Legislation

Art. 68. Bills are introduced by the National Cabinet [with the concurrence of the National Council] or by members of the National Assembly. National laws are enacted by the National Assembly. . . .

Art. 74. The National Council has the right to object to laws passed by the National Assembly. . . . In case of objection, the law is returned to the National Assembly [which may override the objection by a two-thirds majority, or, if not, the President may call for a referendum]. . . .

Art. 76. The Constitution may be amended by process of legislation [subject to two-thirds majority]. . . .

Section VI. The National Administration . . .

[Articles 78-101 defined the jurisdiction of the National Administration, including such items as foreign affairs, national defense, colonial policy, customs and the national budget, postal and telegraph services, railroads (which were nationally owned and operated "as a single system of transportation"), and waterways.]

Section VII. The Administration of Justice . . .

[Articles 102-08 provided that a hierarchy of national and state courts should be set up by law, with judges appointed for life by the President.]

CHAPTER II. FUNDAMENTAL RIGHTS AND DUTIES OF GERMANS

Section I. The Individual

Art. 109. All Germans are equal before the law. Men and women have fundamentally the same civil rights and duties. . . .

Art. 114. Personal liberty is inviolable. Any interference . . . is permissible only by authority of law. . . .

Art. 115. The house of every German is . . . inviolable. Exceptions are permissible only by authority of law. . . .

Art. 117. The secrecy of postal, telegraphic, and telephonic communications is inviolable. Exceptions may be permitted only by national law.

Art. 118. Every German has a right within the limits of the general laws to express his opinion freely by word, in writing, in print, by picture, or in any other way. . . . There is no censorship. . . .

Section II. Community Life . . .

[Articles 119-22 set up special protections for marriage and the family and declared the State's responsibility for health, education, the protection of youth against exploitation.]

Art. 123. All Germans have the right of meeting peaceably and unarmed. . . .

Art. 124. All Germans have the right to form associations or societies for purposes not contrary to the criminal law. . . .

Art. 126. Every German has the right to petition. . . .

Section III. Religion and Religious Societies

Art. 135. All inhabitants . . . enjoy complete liberty of belief and conscience. The free exercise of religion is assured by the Constitution and is under public protection. . . .

Art. 137. There is no state church. . . .

Section IV. Education and Schools

Art. 142. Art, science and the teaching thereof are free. . . .

Art. 143. The education of the young shall be provided for through public institutions. . . .

Art. 144. The entire school system is under the supervision of the state. . . .

Art. 145. Attendance at schools is obligatory. . . . Instruction and school supplies . . . are free. . . .

Section V. Economic Life

Art. 151. . . . The freedom of trade and industry is guaranteed in accordance with the national laws.

Art. 152. Freedom of contract prevails . . . in accordance with the laws. . . .

Art. 153. The right of private property is guaranteed by the Constitution. . . . Expropriation may be proceeded with . . . by due process of law. . . .

Art. 159. The right of combination . . . of labor . . . is guaranteed to everybody and to all professions.

THE WEAKNESS OF THE WEIMAR REPUBLIC

"The weakest spot—and it still exists —is that the people have not yet made it a thing of life." So wrote, about 1926, the venerable Philipp Scheidemann of the Weimar constitution. Unhappily, from the outset the Weimar constitution was bitterly assailed both from the Left and from the Right by factions which sought to destroy the Republic. Against these assaults the coalition of moderate parties ultimately could not prevail. An eminent French scholar has analyzed the weaknesses of the Weimar Republic as follows.

From LICHTENBERGER, *The Third Reich* (1935) [1]

The support of the republic was derived in the first place from the Majority Socialists who had united with the petty bourgeoisie to wipe out the extremists. In addition there was the left proper,

[1] Henri Lichtenberger, *The Third Reich,* trans. by Koppel S. Pinson, 1937, 10-14. By permission of Koppel S. Pinson, New York.

which was divided into two rival groups, the Democrats and the People's Party. Finally there was the Catholic Centre Party which, as under the old regime, did not hesitate to assume a preponderant influence in the government, and which furnished to the republic the greater number of its leaders. . . .

The first and most serious weakness was the unsound character of the Social Democratic Party, the party which had from the beginning constituted the major element of the coalition and which, although not forming an absolute majority of the National Assembly, commanded 163 deputies elected by eleven and one-half million votes. The Social Democratic Party had a program, an ideal, and a solid organization. But in action it manifested an almost complete impotence. It is easy to plead extenuating circumstances for it. It was embarrassed by the revolutionary attitude of the extremists and by the necessity for clearly distinguishing itself from the Marxist communism which had triumphed in Russia but which Germany did not want at any price. It had been paralyzed by the necessity of compromising with the bourgeois parties which remained strong enough to check all radical reforms that might frighten the middle classes. It might, therefore, be unjust to be too severe with the Social Democrats. It remains true, nevertheless, that they were taken unawares by the events and that when power was offered them they recoiled before responsibility and practiced a policy of prudent opportunism, confining themselves to defending the interests of the working class and the "conquests of the revolution." The leaders whom the Social Democrats elevated to power lacked "stature." They were men of good intentions, good tacticians, at times intelligent intellectuals, but in general, more often shrewd trade union secretaries rather than veritable leaders. The

Social Democrats may deserve recognition for having been resolutely opposed to every hazardous experiment with bolshevism and this was probably good for Germany. But this is only a negative merit. They did not know how to play the leading role which had devolved upon them.

The bourgeois parties did not meet the test of power with any more good fortune than the Socialists. After a vain effort to constitute a large republican party of the left, they split up into Democrats and German People's Party and they were weakened by internal dissensions and personal quarrels. Personalities of the first order were rare among them. Max Weber died too soon; [Walther] Rathenau was assassinated before he was able to show his measure. [Gustav] Stresemann alone remained.

Stresemann had the very great merit of sensing the need for Germany to pursue a policy of conciliation in foreign affairs and of "sacred union" in domestic affairs. A National Liberal and an imperialist in his origins, he felt as a good realist, however, that nothing could be accomplished in Germany without the participation of the Socialists on one side, and the right on the other. He was equipped with uncommon courage for this well-nigh impossible task. Treated with contempt by the Socialists, he wore himself out in vain efforts to win over the Nationalists. The latter abandoned him on all decisive occasions and the extremists would even have assassinated him if the occasion had presented itself. He died trying to prevent his own party from slipping toward the right. His policy of *rapprochement* earned for him the passionate hatred of his adversaries of the right and at the same time he was always looked upon with a certain mistrust abroad, especially in France. He was accused of "finesse" and duplicity and it is indeed true that Stresemann was

as "national" and as "German" as the fanatics who fought him to the grave. But he differed from them. Of those who knew him intimately, more than one feels that this defeated man who worked himself to death merited more than the injuries, anathemas and disdain which were heaped upon him in his own country and abroad. But he was a defeated man and nothing of his work has survived. With his end, the bourgeoisie, of which he was the most notable exponent, was completely bankrupt.

The Weimar republic above all succumbed under the crushing tasks which circumstances imposed upon it. It had to liquidate the war and the consequences which proceeded from the war; i.e., the armistice, the Versailles Peace, reparations, the Ruhr invasion, the fall of the mark, the ruination of the middle classes and the unprecedented economic crisis that shook the world. The Weimar republic was not responsible for these calamities. It was the men of the old regime and their mistakes that had brought about the ruination of Germany. It was the army chiefs and [Erich] Ludendorf [sic] in particular who had imperiously called for an armistice. But neither one nor the other was called upon to find the means of warding off the disaster. This is understandable. Ludendorf could not be sent to negotiate the armistice with Foch nor could William II be charged with signing the peace treaty. It was the "civil officers" who, during the war, had been stripped of all power yet, in the hour of distress, remained bravely to take the reins of government into their hands. But it was inevitable that the men who accepted this unenviable mission should be ruined in public opinion when they found themselves forced to advocate the acceptance and execution by their fellow citizens of the very severe conditions which were imposed upon Germany. The innocent ones continued to pay for the faults of the guilty.

The impossibility of the task of the new men was rendered complete by the fact that while they bore the responsibility for the sacrifices imposed by the victors, they never thereby gained the confidence of the Allies themselves. Democrats have often alleged that the Entente should have dealt kindly with the Weimar republic and its policy of fulfilment. By the severity of the conditions imposed and by the persistent mistrust which they showed to their German partners, the Allies are in part responsible for the collapse of the very republic whose advent they favored.

This thesis obviously has substantial basis in fact. It runs counter, however, to a persistent doubt found especially in France. Some wondered, and they still wonder, whether there really was much of a change between the pre-war Germany and the new republican Germany; in other words whether the German "revolution" had really been a "crisis of conscience" and the index of a change in the very mentality of the German. They wondered whether Germany had driven out her old leaders because she sincerely repudiated her imperialist past or simply because they had been wrong in not being successful. A suspicion persisted that the revolution of 1918 was nothing but an instinctive defensive attitude assumed by the Germans. Feeling themselves lost they hastily cringed low in order to avoid collapse; but they remained invincibly faithful to their realistic temperament and to their policy of force. Their democracy from that time on was considered to be a function of their weakness. It was felt that in the measure in which they would regain their forces they would return to their true nature, to their imperialist mentality and to their ambitions of world expansion. This deep-seated doubt increased

in proportion to and in measure with the increase of the second wave of the counter-revolution, that of nationalism, which ended by submerging the entire country in the triumph of Hitler.

THE ATTACK FROM THE RIGHT: THE PROGRAM OF THE NATIONAL SOCIALIST GERMAN WORKERS' PARTY (NAZIS)

A number of postwar German nationalist parties pursued a purely negative policy of pitiless criticism against Communists, Socialists, and Social-Democrats alike, placing on the doorstep of the Weimar Republic's creators all the ills of postwar Germany. In nationalists' eyes, pacifistic socialists and democrats, by counsels of timidity, had snatched victory from German arms during the war; by strikes, defeatist propaganda, and the revolution of November 9, they had undermined the morale of the troops and delivered a "dagger thrust in the back" of the German army; by pinning faith in President Wilson, they had been lured into the Armistice and deluded into accepting the humiliating Treaty of Versailles; by attempts to fulfill the terms of the Versailles Treaty and the reparations settlements they had subjected German economy to Allied control and jeopardized the very existence of the Fatherland; by creation of the Republic they had broken with Germany's glorious, monarchical past and set up a detestable, corrupt, divided parliamentary regime, powerless to protect private property or national prosperity against the "socialist fraud," or to maintain the national prestige in the face of vengeful foes. In short, the nationalists refused to admit that Germany had lost the war or to accept the consequences of defeat. They believed only in the final victory of might, and they saw no future for Germany save by a revival of the nationalistic impulses and institutions (like the regenerating movements of Napoleonic times), by a restoration of monarchy or some other strong central authority, and by a Bismarckian regrouping of world forces which would permit the destruction of the order established by the Peace of Paris and the League of Nations. Their tactics always consisted in drawing comparisons between the glorious past and the distressing present, and they lost no opportunity, by means fair or foul, to discredit the Weimar Republic or its leaders. Indeed, in a number of "putsches" during the early 1920's, they attempted to overturn the Republic and to seize power in their own hands.

That nationalist group destined for the highest position—though more troublesome than dangerous until the late 1920's—was the German Workers' party, which in August, 1920, changed its name to the National Socialist German Workers' party (*Nationalsozialistische Deutsche Arbeiter-partei—NSDAP*, or Nazi party). Organized in January, 1919, and still an obscure local group, the party set forth at Munich an ambitious Twenty-five-Point Program on February 24, 1920. The program was the work of four men, Anton Drexler, the founder of the party, Gottfried Feder, an engineer turned economist, Dietrich Eckart, a journalist and editor of the *Völkischer Beobachter* ("People's Observer"), and Adolf Hitler, a soldier who, sickened by the revolution of November 9 and all that followed, "resolved now to become a politician" and had become (September 19, 1919) the seventh member of the German Workers' party. It was Hitler who, at a mass meeting in Munich on February 24, 1920, presented and expounded the Twenty-five-

Points. "A fire had been lighted," he later wrote. ". . . I sensed that there walked the goddess of inexorable revenge for the perjured act of the 9 of November, 1918."

From the "Twenty-five Points" of the National Socialist Party (1920) [1]

The Program of the German Workers' Party is limited as to period. The leaders have no intention, once the aims announced in it have been achieved, of setting up fresh ones, merely in order to increase the discontent of the masses artificially, and so ensure the continued existence of the Party.

1. We demand the union of all Germans to form a Great Germany on the basis of the right of the self-determination enjoyed by nations.

2. We demand equality of rights for the German People in its dealings with other nations, and abolition of the Peace Treaties of Versailles and St. Germain.

3. We demand land and territory (colonies) for the nourishment of our people and for settling our superfluous population.

4. None but members of the nation may be citizens of the State. None but those of German blood, whatever their creed, may be members of the nation. No Jew, therefore, may be a member of the nation.

5. Anyone who is not a citizen of the State may live in Germany only as a guest and must be regarded as being subject to foreign laws.

6. The right of voting on the State's government and legislation is to be enjoyed by the citizen of the State alone. We demand therefore that all official appointments, of whatever kind, whether in the Reich, in the country, or in the

[1] Raymond E. Murphy and others, eds., *National Socialism*, U. S. Department of State, Publication 1864, 1943, 222-25.

smaller localities, shall be granted to citizens of the State alone. We oppose the corrupting custom of Parliament of filling posts merely with a view to party considerations, and without reference to character or capability.

7. We demand that the State shall make it its first duty to promote the industry and livelihood of citizens of the State. If it is not possible to nourish the entire population of the State, foreign nationals (non-citizens of the State) must be excluded from the Reich.

8. All non-German immigration must be prevented. . . .

9. All citizens of the State shall be equal as regards rights and duties.

10. It must be the first duty of each citizen of the State to work with his mind or with his body. The activities of the individual may not clash with the interests of the whole, but must proceed within the frame of the community and be for the general good.

We demand therefore:

11. Abolition of incomes unearned by work.

ABOLITION OF THE THRALDOM OF INTEREST

12. In view of the enormous sacrifice of life and property demanded of a nation by every war, personal enrichment due to a war must be regarded as a crime against the nation. We demand therefore ruthless confiscation of all war gains.

13. We demand nationalisation of all businesses (trusts). . . .

14. We demand that the profits from wholesale trade shall be shared out.

15. We demand extensive development of provision for old age.

16. We demand creation and maintenance of a healthy middle class, immediate communalisation of wholesale business premises, and their lease at a cheap rate to small traders, and that extreme consideration shall be shown to all small purveyors to the State, district authorities and smaller localities.

17. We demand land-reform suitable to our national requirements. . . .

18. We demand ruthless prosecution of those whose activities are injurious to the common interest. Sordid criminals against the nation, usurers, profiteers, etc. must be punished with death, whatever their creed or race.

19. We demand that the Roman Law, which serves the materialistic world order, shall be replaced by a legal system for all Germany.

20. With the aim of opening to every capable and industrious German the possibility of higher education and of thus obtaining advancement, the State must consider a thorough re-construction of our national system of education. The curriculum of all educational establishments must be brought into line with the requirements of practical life. Comprehension of the State idea (State sociology) must be the school objective, beginning with the first dawn of intelligence in the pupil. We demand development of the gifted children of poor parents, whatever their class or occupation, at the expense of the State.

21. The State must see to raising the standard of health in the nation by protecting mothers and infants, prohibiting child labour, increasing bodily efficiency by obligatory gymnastics and sports laid down by law, and by extensive support of clubs engaged in the bodily development of the young.

22. We demand abolition of a paid army and formation of a national army.

23. We demand legal warfare against conscious political lying and its dissemination in the Press. In order to facilitate creation of a German national Press we demand:

(a) that all editors of newspapers and

their assistants, employing the German language, must be members of the nation;

(b) that special permission from the State shall be necessary before non-German newspapers may appear. These are not necessarily printed in the German language;

(c) that non-Germans shall be prohibited by law from participation financially in or influencing German newspapers. . . .

It must be forbidden to publish papers which do not conduce to the national welfare. We demand legal prosecution of all tendencies in art and literature of a kind likely to disintegrate our life as a nation, and the suppression of institutions which militate against the requirements above-mentioned.

24. We demand liberty for all religious denominations in the State, so far as they are not a danger to it and do not militate against the moral feelings of the German race.

The Party, as such, stands for positive Christianity, but does not bind itself in the matter of creed to any particular confession. It combats the Jewish-materialist spirit within us and without us, and is convinced that our nation can only achieve permanent health from within on the principle:

THE COMMON INTEREST BEFORE SELF

25. That all the fore-going may be realised we demand the creation of a strong central power of the State. Unquestioned authority of the politically centralized Parliament over the entire Reich and its organisations; and formation of Chambers for classes and occupations for the purpose of carrying out the general laws promulgated by the Reich in the various States of the Confederation.

The leaders of the Party swear to go straight forward—if necessary to sacrifice their lives—in securing fulfilment of the fore-going Points.

3. Features of Nazism

ADOLF HITLER AS REVEALED IN "MEIN KAMPF" (1925-26)

Adolf Hitler (1889-1945?), the paranoiac Führer of National Socialism, began *Mein Kampf* while imprisoned after the abortive Nazi putsch at Munich in 1923.[1] Originally entitled *Four and a Half Years' Fight against Lying, Stupidity, and Cowardice,* the truculent title was shortened, and the book, which came to be known as the "Nazi Bible," was published in two volumes in 1925-26. Gustav Stresemann, with a prophetic capacity which no one could fully appreciate at the time, characterized the "struggle" aptly when, in a speech shortly after the Munich putsch, he quoted the following lines:

Ihr habt bei Nacht und Nebel gekriegt,
Und euer Feind er lagt besiegt;
Doch als Ihr die Leiche bei Licht erkannt,
War es das eigene Vaterland.

["You fought in the night and the mist, and your enemy lay vanquished; but when in the dawn you recognized the corpse, it was your own Fatherland."]

Hitler's writings and speeches were rambling, repetitive, and often difficult to translate because of unorthodox expressions and mythical meanings. He seems always to have written as he spoke, in white-hot hatred. In the autobiographical sections of *Mein Kampf,* Hitler relates that he was born in Braunau, on the River Inn, "providentially" located on the border between Germany and Austria, two German states

[1] The German terms, in wide usage during the Nazi era, mean: Führer, "leader"; *Mein Kampf,* "My Struggle"; putsch, "revolutionary outbreak," or coup d'état.

whose reunion Hitler claimed as a boy-hood objective. Hitler's father, Alois, was an Austrian civil servant and a stern, unimaginative parent; his mother, Klara Pölzl, was, within the family's limited means, overindulgent. While Adolf was a small boy his father moved, first to Passau in Germany, then to Linz in Austria, where he was pen-sioned off, and then to a farm near Lambach in Upper Austria. Here it was, as Hitler said, that his first ideals were formed; here his "oratorical tal-ent" began to appear in rows with his playfellows; here he became "a little ringleader," difficult to handle. Here he began to read a little—he never read much—falling upon an old history of the Franco-Prussian War, which fanned the latent boyhood fires of nationalism and militarism and led him to become an ardent admirer of Bismarck's Reich. He and his father became mutually embittered over many issues, chief of which was that Adolf, desirous of be-coming a painter, rebelled against his father's demand that he, like his par-ent, become an Austrian customs offi-cial; and Adolf, angry and frustrated, "sabotaged" all that displeased him at home and in school, stubbornly deter-mined to defy his father and to have his own way. Let him continue the narrative at this point.

From HITLER, *Mein Kampf* (1925-26) [1]

If now, after so many years, I examine the results of this period, I regard two outstanding facts as particularly signifi-cant:

First: *I became a [German] nationalist.*
Second: *I learned to understand and grasp the meaning of history.*

[1] Adolf Hitler, *Mein Kampf*, trans. by Ralph Manheim, 1943, 10-13, 21-22, 52, 56-58, 64-65, 204, 206. By permission of The Houghton Mifflin Company.

Old Austria was a *"state of nationali-ties."* . . .
What they [the German Austrians] failed to appreciate was that, unless the German in Austria had really been of the best blood, he would never have had the power to set his stamp on a nation of fifty-two million souls to such a degree that . . . the erroneous opinion could arise that Austria was a German state. . . . A glowing testimonial to the ten million Germans in the *Ostmark* [Aus-tria]. Only a handful of Germans . . . had the slightest conception of the eternal and merciless struggle for the German language, German schools, and a German way of life. . . . It is a struggle for the soul of the child, and to the child its first appeal is addressed:
"German boy, do not forget you are a German," and, "Little girl, remember that you are to become a German mother." . . .
I, too, while still comparatively young, had an opportunity to take part in the struggle of nationalities in old Austria. . . . In a short time I had become a fanatical 'German Nationalist.' . . .

[Meanwhile, in 1903, Hitler's father died. Shortly afterward, Hitler persuaded his doting mother to allow him to leave school (1905). He traveled some, loafed a lot, and studied art in Munich for a time. In 1907 he went to Vienna and, supported by his mother and other rela-tives, he studied in the Academy of Fine Arts. But twice failing in the entrance examinations, he was rejected by the Academy's School of Painting and failed to qualify in architecture. When his mother died (1908), he severed all home connections and remained in Vienna, friendless, bitter, and alone, eking out a precarious living by painting post cards, advertisements, furniture, and, occasion-ally, when his brushes failed utterly, by beggary. He appears to have been allergic to manual labor. Of these difficult, un-happy years he wrote:]

I owe it to that period that I grew hard and am still capable of being hard. . . . Hunger was then my faithful bodyguard; he never left me for a moment. . . . And yet during this time I studied as never before . . . [and] forged in a few years' time the foundations of a knowledge from which I still draw nourishment today. . . .

[Hitler also acquired two of his life-long prejudices in Vienna: a hatred of Jews and of Social-Democracy—both ac-quired, in part, at least, by contact with Dr. Karl Lueger (1844-1910), founder of the anti-Semitic, anti-Socialist Christian-Social Party in Austria. Hitler continued:]

There were few Jews in Linz. In the course of the centuries their outward ap-pearance had become Europeanized and had taken on a human look; in fact, I even took them for Germans. . . . Then I came to Vienna. . . .

Once, as I was strolling through the Inner City, I suddenly encountered an apparition in a black caftan and black hair locks. Is this a Jew? was my first thought. . . . They had not looked like that in Linz. I observed the man furtively and cautiously, but the longer I stared . . . the more my first question assumed a new form: Is this a German?

As always in such cases, I now began to try to relieve my doubts by books. . . . I bought the first anti-Semitic pamphlets of my life. . . .

The cleanliness of this people, moral and otherwise, I must say, is a point in itself. By their very exterior you could tell that these were no lovers of water, and, to your distress, you often knew it with your eyes closed. . . .

All this could scarcely be called very attractive; but it became positively repul-sive when, in addition to their physical uncleanliness, you discovered the moral stains on this "chosen people." . . .

What had to be reckoned heavily against the Jews in my eyes was when I became acquainted with their activity in the press, art, literature, and the the-ater. . . . The fact that nine tenths of all literary filth, artistic trash, and theatrical idiocy can be set to the account of a people, constituting hardly one hundredth of all the country's inhabitants, could sim-ply not be talked away: it was the plain truth. . . .

[Soon Hitler thought he saw the evil hand of Jewry everywhere: the press was controlled by Jews, and the journalistic style suddenly became intolerable, the con-tent shallow and consciously directed against Germans and Germanism; prosti-tution and the white-slave traffic appeared to be peculiarly Jewish enterprises.]

But then a flame flared up within me. I no longer avoided . . . the Jewish ques-tion; no, now I sought it. And when I learned to look for the Jew in all branches of cultural and artistic life and its various manifestations, I suddenly encountered him in a place where I would least have expected to find him. . . . I recognized the Jew as the leader of the Social De-mocracy. . . . A long soul struggle had reached its conclusion. . . .

I had ceased to be a weak-kneed cosmo-politan and become an anti-Semite. . . .

The Jewish doctrine of Marxism rejects the aristocratic principle of nature and replaces the eternal privilege of power and strength by the mass of numbers and their dead weight. Thus it denies the value of personality in man, contests the signifi-cance of nationality and race, and thereby withdraws from humanity the premise of its existence and its culture. . . . If, with the help of his Marxist creed, the Jew is victorious over the other peoples of the world, his crown will be the funeral wreath of humanity. . . . Hence today I believe that I am acting in accordance with the will of the Almighty Creator: *by defending myself against the Jew, I am fighting for the work of the Lord.* . . .

[Hitler left Vienna and went to Munich in 1913. When World War I began the next year, he volunteered for the Bavarian army. Here, for the first time, Hitler appears to have been happy. He was a good soldier, especially as a dispatch-carrier, won the Iron Cross for bravery, and became a sergeant. In October, 1918, he was gassed, went blind for a time, and was sent to a hospital at Pasewalk, near Berlin. Here he was when the German Revolution broke out in November—"the greatest villainy," he said, "of the century." He heard of the sailors' mutiny, led by "a few Jew boys." On November 10, a chaplain informed the hospitalized men of the revolution. Hitler gave the following account of his own reaction:]

When the old gentleman tried to go on, and began to tell us that we must now end the long War, yes, that now it was lost and we were throwing ourselves upon the mercy of the victors, our fatherland would for the future be exposed to dire oppression, that the armistice should be accepted with confidence in the magnanimity of our previous enemies—I could stand it no longer. . . . I tottered and groped my way back to the dormitory, threw myself on my bunk, and dug my burning head into my blanket and pillow. . . .

There followed terrible days and even worse nights—I knew that all was lost. Only fools, liars, and criminals could hope in the mercy of the enemy. In these nights hatred grew in me, hatred for those responsible for this deed.

In the days that followed, my own fate became known to me. . . . At last it became clear to me that what had happened was what I had so often feared. . . . Kaiser William II was the first German Emperor to hold out a conciliatory hand to the leaders of Marxism, without suspecting that scoundrels have no honor. While they still held the imperial hand in theirs, their other hand was reaching for the dagger.

There is no making pacts with Jews; there can only be the hard: either—or.

I, for my part, decided to go into politics.

THE CORE OF NAZI THEORY: THE "VOLK," THE "PARTEI," AND THE "FÜHRER."

The Nazi state was said by its apologists to rest on three basic concepts, the *Volk,* the *Partei,* and the *Führer,* to each of which was ascribed a somewhat mystical meaning.

The Nazi Volk (Gemeinschaftsvolk— "Community People")

The Nazi party, said Hitler, fought for "an idea—a *Weltanschauung* [world outlook]; and in the forefront stands a fundamental principle: Men do not exist for the State, the State exists for men. First and far above all else stands the idea of the people: the State is a form of organization of this people . . . to assure the life of the people." [1] The state itself was considered as a "living organism" in which the individual was totally submerged as a "cell," incapable of a separate existence outside the organism of which he was an integral part. [For some antecedents of this idea, see page 542.] In

[1] Speech at Munich, Sept. 16, 1930, as quoted in Adolf Hitler, *My New Order,* ed. by Raoul de Roussy de Sales, 1941, 89. By permission of Reynal and Hitchcock, Inc., New York.

opposition to the democratic notion of a state consisting of the sum of individuals within its borders or under its jurisdiction, each individual possessing an inherent, independent part in the life of the state (*Gesellschaftsvolk*, or "society people"), Nazism subscribed to the idea of a "community people" (*Gemeinschaftsvolk*) functioning as a totality, as a uniform whole. Friedrick Alfred Beck expressed this Nazi view in 1936 as follows:[1]

"This idea of totality must be radically distinguished from the liberalistic conception of the mass. According to the liberalistic interpretation the whole consists of a summation of its parts. According to the National Socialist organic conception the whole comes before the parts; it does not arise from the parts but it is already contained in the parts themselves; all parts are microcosmic forms of the whole. This organic conception of the whole is the deepest natural justification of the basic political character of all organic life."

Democratic states developed their concept of the people from the wrong approach: they started with the concept of the state and its functions and considered the people as being made up of all the elements which fall within the jurisdiction of the state. National Socialism, on the other hand, started with the concept of the people, which forms a political unity, and built the state upon this foundation. The elements which constitute a people are, in the Nazi view, beyond human comprehension, but the most important of them is a uniformity of blood (race) which results in a "similarity of nature" which, in turn, manifests itself in a common language, a community of

feeling, a common destiny, and a consciousness of "a common mission." Land and history further mold these features. Ernst Rudolf Huber, in a book on constitutional law in the Nazi state, developed the Nazi view of "community people" as follows.

From HUBER, Constitutional Law (1939) [2]

There is no people without an objective unity, but there is also none without a common consciousness of unity. A people is determined by a number of different factors: by racial derivation and by the character of its land, by language and other forms of life, by religion and history, but also by the common consciousness of its solidarity and by its common will to unity. For the concrete concept of a people, as represented by the various peoples of the earth, it is of decisive significance which of these various factors they regard as determinants for the nature of the people. The new German Reich proceeds from the concept of the political people, determined by the natural characteristics and by the historical idea of a closed community. The political people is formed through the uniformity of its natural characteristics. Race is the natural basis of the people. . . . As a political people the natural community becomes conscious of its solidarity and strives to form itself, to develop itself, to defend itself, to realize itself. "Nationalism" is essentially this striving of a people which has become conscious of itself toward self-direction and self-realization, toward a deepening and renewing of its natural qualities.

This consciousness of self, springing from the consciousness of a historical idea, awakens in a people its, will to historical formation: the will to action. The political

[1] *Die Erziehung im dritten Reich,* Dortmund and Breslau, 1936, 57, as trans. in Raymond E. Murphy and others, *National Socialism,* 30.

[2] *Verfassungsrecht des grossdeutschen Reiches,* Hamburg, 1939, 156-57, as trans. in *ibid.,* 158-59.

people is no passive, sluggish mass, no mere object for the efforts of the state at government or protective welfare work. . . . The great misconception of the democracies is that they can see the active participation of the people only in the form of plebiscites according to the principle of majority. In a democracy the people does not act as a unit but as a complex of unrelated individuals who form themselves into parties. . . . The new Reich is based on the principle that real action of a self-determining people is only possible according to the principle of leadership and following.

The Partei (Party)

"In the State," said Hitler, ". . . there is only one bearer of the political will, and that is the National Socialist party." And in a speech at Nuremberg he described the nature and role of the party.

From HITLER, Speech at Nuremberg, September 10, 1934 [1]

When the National Socialist party appealed for the first time to the German people it resolutely refused to pledge itself to champion the cause of any separate group which was committed to the support either of religious or economic interests within the nation: its appeal was from the first directed to the heroic instincts of the people. . . .

Thus a new Party was formed, that is true; its membership was limited, but its leaders and its fighters were not to be measured by any economic standards: they possessed the essential quality of leadership. . . .

And because we were racially the most valuable section of the German nation, because we proudly valued ourselves as

[1] Hitler, *My New Order*, 290-93. By permission of Reynal and Hitchcock.

such, because we courageously, boldly demanded that to us should be entrusted the leadership of the Reich and of the people, the people in ever growing numbers joined us and acknowledged our leadership. Its innermost consciousness rightly told it that its better self had found in the National Socialist party its point of concentration and its expression. Thus it was that our movement as an "historic minority" could grasp supremacy in Germany in understanding with and with the will of the overwhelming majority of the German nation. . . .

The basis which formed the foundation for our rise and growth in the past is valid also for the future. The following principle must be recognized: always only a part of the people will be composed of really active fighters. They have been in Germany the supporters of the National Socialist struggle: they were the fighters in the National Socialist revolution and it is they who uphold the National Socialist State. From them more is demanded than from the millions of their fellow-countrymen. For them the mere profession "I believe" is not enough: their vow must be "I fight."

The Party will for all time form the picked body of the leaders of the German people. It will develop a State of political apostles and combatants who then as obedient officers, true to their duty, will serve the Movement. It will be that great school which attracts to itself the millions of our people, educates them and then sends them out into the world. In it there will develop a tradition in the art of leading a people which will not permit that men of alien spirit should ever again confuse the brain and the heart of the Germans.

It will be in its teaching unalterable, in its organization hard as steel, in its tactics supple and adaptable, but in its whole appearance it will resemble an Order.

It is for all time the mustard-seed of the

National Socialist idea, the teacher of the art of National Socialist organization, the school of National Socialist propaganda.

The aim must be that all decent Germans shall be National Socialists: only the best National Socialists shall be members of the Party.

The Führer

The Führer was the *Volk* in miniature; but whereas the keynotes of the Führer were *authority* and *responsibility,* those of the *Volk* were *discipline* and *obedience.* Huber, in his book on Nazi constitutional law already quoted, described the Führer principle as follows.

From HUBER, *Constitutional Law* [1]

The Führer Reich of the [German] people is founded on the recognition that the true will of the people cannot be disclosed through parliamentary votes and plebiscites but that the will of the people in its pure and uncorrupted form can only be expressed through the Führer. Thus a distinction must be drawn between the supposed will of the people in a parliamentary democracy, which merely reflects the conflict of the various social interests, and the true will of the people in the Führer-state, in which the collective will of the real political unit is manifested. . . .

The Führer is the bearer of the people's will; he is independent of all groups, associations, and interests, but he is bound by laws which are inherent in the nature of his people. In this twofold condition: independence of all factional interests but unconditional dependence on the people, is reflected the true nature of the Führer principle. Thus the Führer has nothing in common with the functionary, the agent,

[1] Murphy and others, *National Socialism,* 160-62.

or the exponent who exercises a mandate delegated to him and who is bound to the will of those who appoint him. The Führer is no "representative" of a particular group whose wishes he must carry out. He is no "organ" of the state in the sense of the mere executive agent. He is rather the bearer of the collective will of the people. In his will the will of the people is realized. He transforms the mere feelings of the people into a conscious will. . . . Thus it is possible for him, in the name of the true will of the people which he serves, to go against the subjective opinions and convictions of single individuals within the people if these are not in accord with the objective destiny of the people. . . . He shapes the collective will of the people within himself and he embodies the political unity and entirety of the people in opposition to individual interests. . . .

But the Führer, even as the bearer of the people's will, is not arbitrary and free of all responsibility. His will is not the subjective, individual will of a single man, but the collective national will is embodied within him in all its objective, historical greatness. . . . Such a collective will is not a fiction, as is the collective will of the democracies, but it is a political reality which finds its expression in the Führer. The people's collective will has its foundation in the political idea which is given to a people. It is present in the people, but the Führer raises it to consciousness and discloses it. . . .

In the Führer are manifested also the natural laws inherent in the people: It is he who makes them into a code governing all national activity. In disclosing these natural laws he sets up the great ends which are to be attained and draws up the plans for the utilization of all national powers in the achievement of the common goals. Through his planning and directing he gives the national life its true purpose and value. . . .

The Führer principle rests upon unlimited authority but not upon mere outward force. . . . It can only be maintained by mutual loyalty which must find its expression in a free relation. The Führer-order depends upon the responsibility of the following, just as it counts on the responsibility and loyalty of the Führer to his mission and to his following. . . . There is no greater responsibility than that upon which the Führer principle is grounded. . . .

That the will of the people is embodied in the Führer does not exclude the possibility that the Führer can summon all members of the people to a plebiscite on a certain question. In this "asking of the people" the Führer does not, of course, surrender his decisive power to the voters. The purpose of the plebiscite is not to let the people act in the Führer's place or to replace the Führer's decision with the result of the plebiscite. Its purpose is rather to give the whole people an opportunity to demonstrate and proclaim its support of an aim announced by the Führer. It is intended to solidify the unity and agreement between the objective people's will embodied in the Führer and the living, subjective conviction of the people as it exists in the individual members. . . . This approval of the Führer's decision is even more clear and effective if the plebiscite is concerned with an aim which has already been realized rather than with a mere intention.

4. The Creation of the Nazi State

The Weimar constitution was never formally abrogated by the Nazis. Rather, it was rendered ineffectual by a series of basic laws promulgated shortly after

Hitler's rise to power in 1933. The first of these, set forth less than a month after Hitler became Chancellor, suspended "until further notice" the basic rights of the individual guaranteed in the Weimar Constitution, as follows:

THE LIQUIDATION OF THE WEIMAR CONSTITUTION

From the "Decree of the Reich's President for the Protection of the People and State" (February 28, 1933) [1]

In virtue of paragraph 2, Article 48, of the German Constitution, the following is decreed as a defensive measure against Communist acts of violence, endangering the state:

Art. 1. Sections 114, 115, 117, 118, 123, 124, and 153 of the Constitution of the German Reich are suspended until further notice. Thus, restrictions on personal liberty, on the right of free expression of opinion, including freedom of the press, on the right of assembly and the right of association, and violations of the privacy of postal, telegraphic communications, and warrants for house-searches, orders for confiscations as well as restrictions on property, are also permissible beyond the legal limits otherwise prescribed.

[The second basic law, known as the "Enabling Act," swept away parliamentary government by the following provisions.]

From the "Law to Remove the Distress of People and State" (March 24, 1933) [2]

The Reichstag has resolved the following law, which is, with the approval of the National Council, herewith promulgated, after it has been established that the re-

[1] *Reichsgesetzblatt*, 1933, trans. in *National Socialism*, Appendix, 215.
[2] *Ibid.*, 217-18.

quirements have been satisfied for legislation altering the Constitution.

Art. 1. National laws can be enacted by the National Cabinet. . . .

Art. 2. The national laws enacted by the National Cabinet may deviate from the Constitution so far as they do not affect the position of the Reichstag and the National Council. The powers of the President remain undisturbed. [This article was amended by the law of January 30, 1934. See page 818.]

Art. 3. The national laws enacted by the National Cabinet are prepared by the Chancellor. . . .

Art. 4. Treaties of the Reich with foreign states which concern matters of national legislation do not require the consent of the bodies participating in legislation. The National Cabinet is empowered to issue the necessary provisions for the execution of these treaties.

[A third law soon dissolved all opposing political parties.]

From the "Law Creating a One-Party State" (July 14, 1933) [1]

The German Cabinet has resolved the following law. . . .

Art. 1. The National Socialist German Workers' Party constitutes the only political party in Germany.

Art. 2. Whoever undertakes to maintain . . . another political party or to form a new political party will be punished with penal servitude up to three years or with imprisonment of from six months to three years, if the deed is not subject to a greater penalty according to other regulations.

[A fourth law identified the Nazi party and the state.]

[1] *Ibid.*, 220.

From the "Law to Safeguard the Unity of Party and State" (December 1, 1933) [2]

The German Cabinet has resolved the following law. . . .

Art. 1 (1) After the victory of the National Socialist revolution, the National Socialist German Workers' Party is the bearer of the German state-idea and indissolubly joined to the state.

(2) It is a corporation in public law. The Führer determines its statutes.

Art. 2. In order to guarantee the closest cooperation of the party and the SA [Sturm Abteilung—Storm Section] with the public officials, the Führer's Deputy and the Chief of Staff of the SA are made members of the Cabinet.

Art. 3 (1) The members of the NSDAP or the SA, including its subordinate formations, as the leading and animating forces of the National Socialist state, have increased obligations toward the Führer, people, and state.

(2) For violation of these obligations they are subject to a special party and SA jurisdiction.

(3) The Führer can extend these regulations to the members of other organizations.

THE NAZI CORPORATE STATE

Industrial Organization

Nazism denied the notion of the class struggle. It considered industrial enterprise as an indissoluble whole in which both employer and employee should loyally co-operate. Private property and individual initiative were held as fundamentals of Nazism. Labor unions were abolished in 1933 when—

"At ten o'clock in the morning on May 2, Dr. Robert Ley, at the head of a 'committee of action for the protection of German labor' occupied by force the

[2] *Ibid.*, 221.

offices of all the trade unions and imprisoned several of their most important leaders. He met with no resistance.
In the course of several days all the
socialist as well as Christian associations, together with 169 trade union
organizations, were placed under the
control of the Nazis. On May 10 the
Nazis held the first meeting of the
organization which was designed to
replace the trade unions, namely the
German Labor Front (*Deutsche Ar-
beitsfront*)." [1]

Employers' associations were similarly
absorbed in the Labor Front, the functions of which have been described as
follows.

From LANGSAM, *The World since 1914*
    (1943) [2]

Completely controlled by Dr. Robert
Ley, this body was intended to coördinate
all German intellectual and manual employers and workers [it embraced about
30 million members by 1939]. Its prime
function was to be the indoctrination of
Nazi principles, but it was given some
power to arbitrate in labor disputes. Associated with this Labor Front was an
elaborate recreational organization called
"Strength through Joy." The latter arranged cheap vacation trips for workers
and their families.

Relations between capital and labor
were regulated by laws that took effect in
May 1933 and May 1934. This legislation,
rejecting the idea of an inevitable capital-
labor conflict, upheld the principles of
leadership and "the common welfare before individual welfare." Strikes and
lockouts were prohibited. Employers in
enterprises with more than twenty workers
were designated as "leaders," while their

employees officially became "followers."
Each such business was required to choose
a "council of confidence" to advise on the
running of the business, working conditions, and possible ways of increasing the
general efficiency. The council members
were to be nominated by the leader and
elected by the followers. In case of dispute,
the workers might appeal to the appropriate "trustee of labor."

Provision was made for thirteen such
labor trustees to supervise thirteen geographical areas. Charged with the maintenance of industrial peace, these appointees
of the Reich Government were empowered
to supervise the councils of confidence, fix
wage scales, check any wholesale dismissal
of employees, act as referees in cases of
dispute between leaders and councils, and
even oust exceptionally inefficient or inconsiderate employers from their own
businesses. Violators of the new social
ethics were to be haled for punishment
before Economic Courts of Honor. . . .

In respect of foreign trade and commerce the Nazis put into practice all the
principles of economic nationalism. Every
means was employed to create a self-
sufficient "balanced" economy, that is, to
make Germany an autarchic state (*Au-
tarkie*). Pressure was exerted to decrease
imports and increase exports. Raw materials were rationed. Tariffs were raised
and citizens were urged to "buy home
products." No one could engage in a new
business without governmental permission. . . . The development of synthetics
or *Ersatzmittel* was feverishly pushed. The
government controlled all currency movements. Coördination, unity, and economic
independence were the keywords of all
striving.

Agriculture

The corporate organization of German agriculture consisted, in broad
analysis, of three interrelated acts—all

[1] Lichtenberger, *The Third Reich*, 234. By permission of Koppel S. Pinson.
[2] Langsam, *The World since 1914*, 448-49. By
permission of The Macmillan Company.

aimed, among other things, at autarchy, or agricultural self-sufficiency. The first act was the centralization of all agricultural groups into one vast organization under the Minister of Agriculture, R. Walther Darré; the second consisted of measures to fix prices on agricultural products; the third, in line with the party program [page 807], was an effort to create an "Aryan farmer aristocracy" from which to draw future German leaders. It was set forth in a statute which began as follows.

From "The Hereditary Farms Law"
    (September 29, 1933) [1]

The Cabinet, by safeguarding old German customs of inheritance of property, wishes to preserve the peasantry as the blood source of the German people.

The property of peasants shall be protected from overburdening and splitting up so that it will remain permanently as the property of the family in the hands of free peasants. A fair distribution of agricultural properties shall be worked out since a great number of productive smaller and medium sized peasant properties, distributed as evenly as possible all over the country, gives the best guarantee for the health of the people and state.

The Cabinet has decided upon the following law. The basic ideas of the law are:

Agricultural and forest properties of the size of at least one soil subsistence (ackernahrung) and of not more than 125 hectares [i.e., about 2 to 300 acres] are hereditary properties if they belong to a person who qualifies as a peasant.

The owner of an hereditary property is

called a peasant. Only one who is a German citizen of German or kindred blood and who is honorable can be a peasant. [Jews and colored persons are unqualified.]

The hereditary property passes on undivided to the next principal heir. The rights of the co-heirs are limited to the remaining fortune of the peasant. Heirs who are not principal heirs receive a professional training and portion corresponding to the value of the property; in case of financial difficulties for which they are not guilty, they shall be given home shelter.

The right of inheritance cannot be excluded or limited through disposal on account of death.

The hereditary property is basically unsaleable and not subject to mortgage.

[The male line has preference in inheritance; doubtful cases were determined by a special Inheritance Court.]

THE NUREMBERG LAWS ON CITIZENSHIP AND RACE (1935)

Nazi race prejudice, especially anti-Semitism, found expression in a series of laws promulgated in the autumn of 1935 by a special session of the Reichstag held at Nuremberg. The first, known as the Law for Protection of German Blood and German Honor, dated September 15, 1935, ran as follows.

From the "Nuremberg Laws" (1935) [2]

Clearly realizing that the purity of the German blood is the prerequisite for perpetuating the German people, and inspired by an inflexible determination to secure the existence of the German nation for all

[1] This and the next selection are from James K. Pollock, ed., "Documents on the Nazi Government of Germany" in Source Book on European Governments, 1937. By permission of D. Van Nostrand Company, Inc. This is Pt. IV, 94-95.

[2] Ibid., Pt. IV, 80-81, 77-79.

time to come, the Reichstag has unanimously passed the following law. . . .

1. (1) Marriages between Jews and citizens of German or kindred stock are prohibited. . . .

(2) Only the public prosecutor shall bring suit for annulment.

2. Non-marital sexual intercourse between Jews and citizens of German or kindred stock shall be prohibited.

3. Jews shall not employ in their household female citizens of German or kindred stock under 45 years of age.

4. (1) Jews shall not hoist the Reich or national flag nor display the Reich colors.

(2) They are, however, permitted to display the Jewish colors.

[The second of the Nuremberg Laws, passed the same day, was the Reich Citizenship Law and Decree:]

The Reichstag has unanimously enacted the following law. . . .

1. (1) A citizen is one who belongs to the protective union of the German Reich and who is under special obligations to it.

(2) Citizenship shall be acquired in conformity with . . . the national and state citizenship law.

2. (1) Only such persons as are of German or kindred stock and who have proved by their conduct that they are willing and fit loyally to serve the German people and Reich are citizens of the Reich.

(2) The right to Reich citizenship is acquired by the grant of a certificate of Reich citizenship.

(3) Reich citizens shall be the sole possessors of complete political rights.

[A third law, the Decree for Reich Citizenship, followed on November 14, 1935. It declared: "A Jew cannot be a Reich citizen. He is not allowed to vote in political affairs; he cannot hold a public office." It announced that all Jewish officials would be dismissed at the end of 1935 and provided a retirement allowance for those who were veterans of World War I. It defined a Jew as follows:]

5. (1) A Jew is one who is descended of at least three generations of Jewish grandparents [i.e., persons "who have belonged to the Jewish religious faith"]. . . .

(2) One is also considered a Jew if he is descended of two grandparents of Jewish mixture who are nationals of the state, (a) Who upon promulgation of the law belonged to a Jewish religious organization or is taken in afterward; (b) Who upon promulgation of the law was married to a Jew or is married to one afterward; (c) Who is descended out of matrimony from a Jew in the sense of section 1 . . . after the law for the protection of German blood and honor. . . . (d) Who was born as a result of illegitimate intercourse with a Jew in the sense of section 1, and who is born illegitimately after July 31, 1936.

39

HIGHLIGHTS IN EUROPEAN INTERNAL
DEVELOPMENTS, 1920-1939

1. England and the British Empire

PROS AND CONS OF BRITAIN'S RETURN
TO A PROTECTIONIST ECONOMY IN 1932

World War I produced the earliest departure from Great Britain's free-trade policy since repeal of the Corn Laws in 1846 [see page 627]. In 1915 the McKenna duties placed tariffs on luxuries as a means to reduce their war-time consumption and as a revenue measure—and paved the way for a postwar return to protectionist policies. After the war, a variety of circumstances conspired to weaken Britain's position as an export nation: high costs of production because of heavy taxation and inefficient methods; changes in world demand because of the widespread substitution of oil for coal, silk and artificial silk for cotton, and the like; new industrial competition, especially from the United States and Japan; and the raising of tariff walls and other forms of economic nationalism. Britain sought to meet these challenges to English trade supremacy by industrial reorganization in the interest of greater efficiency and, as imports increased, by a return to tariff protection. The McKenna duties were retained (they were re-enacted in 1925), and in 1921 the Safeguarding of Industries Act enlarged the area of protective duties. The Labor Government of Ramsay MacDonald in 1929-30 tried to stem the tide of protec-

tionism, but the world-wide depression after 1929 hampered the attempt, and the financial crisis of 1931 led England to abandon the gold standard. In the same year, MacDonald's defection from the Labor party and the formation under him of the National Coalition Government (predominantly Conservative) practically guaranteed an outright return to protectionist principles. In January, 1932, the Import Duties Bill was introduced in Parliament and became law on March 1. Mr. Neville Chamberlain, Chancellor of the Exchequer in the National Coalition Government, introduced the bill in Commons and, as indicated in his speech quoted below, hoped to integrate the new tariff policy with one of "reciprocal preference" on the part of British Dominions. At the subsequent Ottawa Imperial Economic Conference (July-August, 1932) the Dominions reluctantly assented to a carefully limited amount of imperial preference, thereby creating a restricted policy of "Imperial Preference and Tariff Reform" similar to that which Joseph Chamberlain (Neville's father) and other imperialists and conservatives had advocated since 1903. The following speeches are from the Commons' debates on the Import Duties Bill. The first, by Neville Chamberlain, sketches the objectives and provisions of the bill as envisaged by a majority of the Cabinet; the second, by Mr. Clement Attlee, sets forth objections on behalf of the Labor party and suggests policies clearly presaging those of the Labor Government under Prime Minister Attlee after World War II [see page 831].

From The Commons Debates, 1932 [1]

Feb. 4, 1932, Mr. Neville Chamberlain, Chancellor of Exchequer, introducing Import Duties Bill:

A great exporting country like ours is forced to look overseas for a great part of its trade. The catastrophic fall in the gold prices of commodities which has been taking place, and which as yet shows no signs of having reached bottom, has brought world trade into a truly deplorable condition. One of the first signs of this distress in world trade is the extraordinary growth of trade restrictions. There is hardly any device, ranging from surtaxes to quotas, which has not been applied by one country or another; and . . . which have raised almost impassable barriers to normal trading relations. Then there is that great problem which keeps Europe, or a great part of Europe, in a constant state of doubt and anxiety, the problem of Reparations and War Debts, still unsettled. Recent events in the Far East have raised a new source of anxiety. . . . The figures of unemployment still remain of colossal dimensions. . . . The main industries of the country are very slow to move. Iron and steel remain in a stagnant condition; shipping and agriculture are still in the depths of depression. The effect of depreciation of the pound . . . is being gradually whittled away as one country after another has departed from the Gold Standard. . . .

In 1929 the value . . . of the surplus of imports over exports was £382,000,000.

The value of the invisible exports was £482,000,000, leaving a favourable surplus of £100,000,000. In 1931 the surplus of imports over exports was £409,000,000, but the invisible exports were only £296,000,000, leaving an adverse balance in the neighbourhood of £113,000,000. In two years, therefore, the balance of payments had gone against us to the extent of over £200,000,000. . . . I submit . . . that those figures establish the vital necessity for any action which it is in the power of the Government to take which may restore the balance of payments once more to the right side. . . . We had to put to ourselves the problem, How are we at one and the same time to diminish our imports and to increase our exports? . . .

The basis of our proposals is what we call a general *ad valorem* duty of 10 per cent upon all imports into this country, with certain exceptions to which I shall allude a little later [wheat, meat, other foodstuffs, and critical raw materials, such as raw cotton and raw wool]. The purposes of that general duty are two-fold. We desire to raise by it a substantial contribution to the Revenue, and we desire also to put a general brake upon the total of the imports coming in here. . . . I now pass to the superstructure which it is proposed to build upon the general *ad valorem* duties. That superstructure takes the form of additional duties which may be imposed upon non-essential articles. . . . I mean either articles of luxury which are not essential to the individual, or articles which are not essential to the nation, in the sense that they either can be now or could be very shortly produced at home. . . . We do not propose to specify these additional duties in the Bill; we propose that these duties may be imposed by Order of the Treasury after consultation with the appropriate Department . . . the Board of Trade or the Ministry of Agriculture, or other Department concerned. [The initia-

[1] Great Britain, *Parliamentary Debates: Official Report*, 5th ser., Vol. 261, 1932, Cols. 282-85, 288-93, 298-99, 301-05.

tive to be in the hands of a special advisory committee, and "all Orders made by the Treasury imposing duties will be subject to confirmation by a Resolution of this House."] . . .

I now come to the position of the Empire in connection with this change in our fiscal system. . . . Next July the Imperial Conference is to be held at Ottawa, when the economic relations of the members of the British Commonwealth will be discussed. His Majesty's Government attach the utmost importance to that Conference, and they intend to approach it with a full determination of promoting arrangements which will lead to a great increase of inter-Imperial trade. I have no doubt that the Dominions would no more question our right to impose duties in our own interests . . . than we have questioned theirs to do the same, but considerations of that kind have to be weighed against the advantages to be obtained from preferential entry into Dominion markets, even though they should involve some surrender of revenue or lessening of the reduction of imports . . . and since we desire . . . to approach this Conference in the true spirit of Imperial unity and harmony, we have decided that, so far as the Dominions are concerned . . . neither the general nor the additional duties shall become operative before the Ottawa Conference has been concluded. After the Conference, its results can be embodied in whatever modifications of these duties may have been agreed upon. . . .

I should like to touch for a moment on the provisions in connection with foreign countries. They are of two kinds. The first deals with the case where the treatment . . . amounts to discrimination against the United Kingdom. The Board of Trade will be authorised . . . to impose a duty which may amount to as much as 100 per cent, in addition to the existing duties, upon any goods coming from the offend-

ing country. . . . The second provision is designed to facilitate the lowering of tariff barriers in foreign countries by offering to reduce our own in return for an advantage of that kind. . . . We attach a good deal of importance to this provision as a bargaining factor, but . . . we do not intend to conclude any arrangements of this kind with any foreign country until we have made our agreements with the Conference at Ottawa. . . .

[Mr. Attlee rose "to state the views of the Labour Party" in opposition to the proposals, as follows:]

We have heard from the right honourable Gentleman the considerations which have led the Government to put forward these Measures. The first one—and I think the chief one—was an endeavour to balance our trade. . . . Almost every country is trying in some way or another to balance its trade. . . . All the creditor nations—and we are still a creditor nation —are endeavouring to keep a favourable balance of trade, while at the same time insisting that debts should be paid. The only real argument . . . is, that when in Rome do as Rome does, and that when in a lunatic asylum you must behave like a lunatic. The struggle for a balance of trade, and the idea that by some miraculous way you can restore trade by keeping out the goods of others, and at the same time make them receive yours are, unfortunately, very widespread. It is a complete confusion of thought. . . . In our opinion, all attempts to seek a favourable balance of trade are futile so long as you do not deal with inter-Allied Debts and Reparations. . . .

We are suffering not from an attack upon our trade by some particular nation, but the fact that the whole world is suffering from a slump and that there is a decrease of purchasing power all over the world, owing very largely to currency and exchange problems. . . . What the right honourable Gentleman really envisaged is a tariff wall. That is what these tariff bargains lead to. . . . Can he give us any instance where a tariff war has led to a reduction of tariffs? I do not believe that it is a good way of cementing our friendship with Dominions. . . . The unfortunate thing is that the goods we want to sell to the Dominions are precisely the goods which they wish to manufacture for themselves. . . .

We object to the whole system because we believe it to be thoroughly unscientific and thoroughly bad. . . . There is a strong case for saying that we want to have so much of our labour and our capital devoted to agriculture. There may be a case for iron and steel and for this or that industry, but to say, haphazard, that we are going to put on a tariff and that we are going to stimulate this, that or the other will not lead to the rationalisation or the stabilisation of our economic life, but will lead to the creation of a large number of vested interests and will make it more and more difficult for us to reconstruct. . . . There is no protection for the consumer or for the worker, and there is nothing to ensure efficiency. What the scheme amounts to is a very large dole to separate industries. . . .

My complaint is not against the boldness but against the timidity of the Government's scheme. They have not the courage to say that the economic life of the country must be controlled by the Government. In effect, they say: "We surrender to pressure from below the Gangway." . . . I believe that it will lead on to industrial warfare . . . to an attempt to set up an economic bloc of the British Empire and probably some allies. That will mean economic competition with some other bloc, and that economic warfare will lead to political warfare. It is surprising that we should get economic nationalism by a national Government at a time when all the world is crying out for internationalism. We oppose the proposal not because of any of the old views or arguments in regard to Free Trade or Protection but on the ground that it is not calculated to deal with the evils from which the country and the world are suffering, but is calculated to corrupt political life, to raise up a host of vested interests, and, so far from helping the recovery of the world, will lead to economic warfare in the future.

THE EMERGENCE OF THE IRISH FREE STATE (1921)

In about twenty-five years English Liberals introduced in Parliament three Home Rule bills for Ireland [see pages 633-635]. The first (1886) was rejected by the Commons, the second (1893) by the Lords. The third (1912) passed both houses and received royal assent in September, 1914, but by the Suspensory Act its operation was postponed until the end of World War I. Meanwhile, nationalist organizations expanded Irish sentiment for independence. Douglas Hyde (1860-), a Celtic enthusiast and professor of the Irish language, founded (1893) the Gaelic League "to keep the Irish language spoken in Ireland," and he hammered incessantly "on the necessity for de-anglicizing Ireland." Arthur Griffith (1872-1922) founded *The United Irishman* (1899-1906) to advocate a separate parliament for Ireland, passive resistance to British rule, and Irish economic development through industrialization and agricultural reform. Griffith was also prominent in the organization (in 1902) of the nationalist movement known as Sinn Fein ("We Ourselves"), and in 1906 adopted the name for his journal, although he opposed the appeal to force which certain Sinn Fein factions fostered. It was these latter groups which, relying upon German aid, led the Easter Rebellion in 1916 (April 24-29), set up a Provisional Government, proclaimed the Irish Republic as "a sovereign, independent state," and protested that "Until our arms have brought the opportune moment for the establishment of a permanent national government . . . the Provisional Government, hereby constituted, will administer the civil and military affairs of the republic in trust for the people." The rebellion was bloodily suppressed by British arms, but in Ireland's first postwar election (December, 1918) the Sinn Fein members, led by Eamon de Valera, refused to attend the British Parliament, met in Dublin, declared themselves the parliament of Ireland (the Dail Eireann), and issued the Irish Declaration of Independence (January 21, 1919). Again British arms interposed, De Valera fled to the United States, and Ireland was convulsed by ferocious conflict for more than a year. On December 23, 1920, the British Parliament passed the Government of Ireland Act, providing Home Rule with separate parliaments for Northern and Southern Ireland and a Council for Ireland, representing both parts, to work for common action and ultimate Irish consolidation. Northern Ireland accepted the Act, but when elections were held for the parliament in Southern Ireland (May, 1921) the Sinn Fein won 124 out of 128 seats, declared themselves the Dail Eireann, and rejected the British Act. There followed conferences between Irish and British leaders. In the first (July 14-21, 1921), De Valera rejected British offers of Dominion status for Ireland; in the second (October 11-December 6), De Valera did not attend and Arthur

Griffith and Michael Collins, negotiating on behalf of the less extravagant Sinn Fein factions, came to a settlement with Lloyd George and other English representatives known in Ireland as a "treaty" and in England as "articles of agreement." This settlement, though later modified in some vital respects, granted Southern Ireland (the twenty-six largely Catholic counties of West and South Ireland) Dominion status as the Irish Free State (the six northeastern, mostly Protestant, "Ulster" counties retained the arrangement set up in the Government of Ireland Act and became officially known as Northern Ireland).

From the Anglo-Irish Treaty, December 6, 1921 [1]

1. Ireland shall have the same constitutional status in the community of nations known as the British Empire as the Dominion of Canada . . . with a parliament having powers to make laws for the peace and good government of Ireland and an executive responsible to that parliament, and shall be styled and known as the Irish Free State. . . .

4. The oath to be taken by members of the parliament of the Irish Free State shall be in the following form: I —— do solemnly swear true faith and allegiance to the constitution of the Irish Free State as by law established and that I will be faithful to H. M. King George V, his heirs and successors by law in virtue of the common citizenship of Ireland with Great Britain and her adherence to and membership of the group of nations forming the British Commonwealth of Nations. . . .

11. Until the expiration of one month from the passing of the act of parliament for the ratification of this instrument, the powers of the parliament and the govern-

[1] Great Britain, *Parliamentary Papers, 1921,* Sess. 2, Cmd. 1560, I, 3-5.

ment of the Irish Free State shall not be exercisable as respects Northern Ireland, and the provisions of the *Government of Ireland Act,* 1920, shall, so far as they relate to Northern Ireland, remain of full force and effect. . . .

12. If before the expiration of the said month, an address is presented to his majesty by both houses of the parliament of Northern Ireland to that effect,[1] the powers of . . . the Irish Free State shall no longer extend to Northern Ireland, and the provisions of the *Government of Ireland Act,* 1920 (including those relating to the council of Ireland), shall so far as they relate to Northern Ireland, continue to be of full force and effect. . . . Provided that if such an address is so presented a commission consisting of three persons, one . . . of the Irish Free State, one . . . of Northern Ireland, and one who shall be chairman to be appointed by the British government shall determine in accordance with the wishes of the inhabitants, so far as may be compatible with economic and geographic conditions the boundaries between Northern Ireland and the rest of Ireland.

[Although the Dail Eireann accepted the above treaty, Eamon de Valera rejected it, principally because of the oath required of Irish parliament members (Article 4), because it fell short of recognition of Irish nationhood, and because it kept Irish economy tied to the British imperial system. While his erstwhile colleagues put through a constitution for the Irish Free State (October 25, 1922), De Valera organized opposition (the new Republican Society) and resorted to insurrection. Not until 1927 did he and his Republican colleagues agree to take the oath and assume seats in the Dail. By 1932 the Republicans, supported by La-

[1] Such an address was presented on December 7, 1922.

bor Deputies, controlled the Dail, and in March, 1932, De Valera was elected President on a program of abolishing the oath to the British king, of the suspension of land annuity payments to Britain, and of high protective tariffs for Ireland. Within a year, the Dail abolished the oath of loyalty (May 3, 1933), but the remainder of De Valera's program led to a tariff war with Great Britain, a conflict for which Ireland was ill prepared and from which she suffered tremendously. The situation was slightly bettered by a coal and cattle agreement with Britain in 1935, and the tariff war ended when, on February 17, 1936, an Anglo-Irish Trade Pact was concluded, the Irish agreeing to resume payment of land annuities. In 1937, De Valera put through a new Irish constitution which entirely ignored Ireland's relationship to Great Britain. The next year a series of agreements with Great Britain (April 25, 1938) provided for mutual destruction of the tariff barriers, a satisfactory settlement of the annuity problem and other British claims, and the return to Ireland of the Irish coastal defenses. Until well into World War II Anglo-Irish relations remained on a close friendly basis.]

IMPERIAL REORGANIZATION

The tendency, long operative in the British Empire, for the Dominions to assert independent nationhood was accelerated by World War I. Creation (in 1917) of the Imperial War Cabinet (the British War Cabinet plus representatives of the Dominions) gave the Dominions a part in the formulation of imperial policy; and the independent role of Dominions at the Paris Conference and in the League of Nations virtually completed recognition of their sovereign status in "the British Commonwealth of Nations," as General

Smuts termed it. At the Imperial Conference of 1926, Arthur James Balfour, as head of a committee to define interimperial relations, reported that "They [the United Kingdom, the Dominion of Canada, the Commonwealth of Australia, the Dominion of New Zealand, the Union of South Africa, the Irish Free State, and Newfoundland] are autonomous communities within the British Empire, equal in status, in no way subordinate one to another in any aspect of their domestic or external affairs, though united by a common allegiance to the Crown, and freely associated as members of the British Commonwealth of Nations." As if this were insufficient, the Balfour Report also declared that "every self-governing member of the Empire is now the master of its destiny. In fact, if not always in form, it is subject to no compulsion whatever"; and it held further that Governors-General should stand in the same relation to Dominion governments as that of the King to the Government of the United Kingdom—a "regalization" of Governors-General. The Balfour Report went far to clarify imperial relationships, but it was clear that "constitutional surgery" in the form of statutory action was needed to give it the full weight of constitutionality. This "surgery" was effected by the Statute of Westminster, passed by Parliament December 11, 1931.

From the Statute of Westminster (1931)[1]

Whereas the delegates of His Majesty's Governments . . . at Imperial Conferences holden at Westminster in the years of our Lord nineteen hundred and twenty-six and nineteen hundred and thirty did concur in making the declarations and

[1] Great Britain, *Statutes of the Realm*, 22 Geo. 5, *c.* 4.

resolutions set forth in the Reports of the said Conferences:

And whereas it is meet and proper to set out by way of preamble to this Act that, inasmuch as the Crown is the symbol of the free association of the members of the British Commonwealth of Nations, and as they are united by a common allegiance to the Crown, it would be in accord with the established constitutional position of all the members of the Commonwealth in relation to one another that any alteration in the law touching the Succession to the Throne or the Royal Style and Titles shall hereafter require the assent as well of the Parliaments of all the Dominions as of the Parliament of the United Kingdom:

And whereas it is in accord with the established constitutional position that no law hereafter made by the Parliament of the United Kingdom shall extend to any of the said Dominions as part of the law of that Dominion otherwise than at the request and with the consent of that Dominion:

And whereas it is necessary for the ratifying, confirming and establishing of certain of the said declarations and resolutions of the said Conferences that a law be made and enacted in due form by authority of the Parliament of the United Kingdom:

And whereas the Dominion of Canada, the Commonwealth of Australia, the Dominion of New Zealand, the Union of South Africa, the Irish Free State and Newfoundland have severally requested and consented to the submission of a measure to the Parliament of the United Kingdom for making such provision with regard to the matters aforesaid as is hereafter in this Act contained:

Now, therefore, be it enacted by the King's most Excellent Majesty by and with the advice and consent of the Lords Spiritual and Temporal, and Commons, in this present Parliament assembled, and by the authority of the same, as follows:

1. In this Act the expression "Dominion" means any of the following Dominions, that is to say, the Dominion of Canada, the Commonwealth of Australia, the Dominion of New Zealand, the Union of South Africa, the Irish Free State and Newfoundland.

2. (1) The Colonial Laws Validity Act, 1865, shall not apply to any law made after the commencement of this Act by the Parliament of a Dominion.

(2) No law and no provision of any law made after the commencement of this Act by the Parliament of a Dominion [or by a state or provincial legislature of a Dominion] shall be void or inoperative on the ground that it is repugnant to the law of England, or to the provisions of any existing or future Act of Parliament of the United Kingdom, or to any order, rule or regulation made under any such Act, and the powers of the Parliament of a Dominion shall include the power to repeal or amend any such Act, order, rule or regulation in so far as the same is part of the law of the Dominion.

3. It is hereby declared and enacted that the Parliament of a Dominion has full power to make laws having extraterritorial operation.

4. No Act of Parliament of the United Kingdom passed after the commencement of this Act shall extend, or be deemed to extend, to a Dominion as part of the law of that Dominion, unless it is expressly declared in that Act that that Dominion has requested, and consented to, the enactment thereof. . . .

7. (1) Nothing in this Act shall be deemed to apply to the repeal, amendment or alteration of the British North America Acts, 1867 to 1930, or any order, rule or regulation made thereunder. . . .

8. Nothing in this Act shall be deemed to confer any power to repeal or alter the Constitution or the Constitution Act of the Commonwealth of Australia or the Constitution Act of the Dominion of New Zealand otherwise than in accordance with the law existing before the commencement of this Act. . . .

11. Notwithstanding anything in the Interpretation Act, 1889, the expression "Colony" shall not, in any Act of the Parliament of the United Kingdom passed after the commencement of this Act, include a Dominion or any Province or State forming part of a Dominion.

INDIA BECOMES AN IMPERIAL PROBLEM: GANDHI ON PASSIVE RESISTANCE

Until the Anglo-Russian Agreement of 1907 [see page 717], Britain's administration of Indian affairs was conducted with an ever watchful eye on Russia [see page 639]. Meanwhile, the Indian attitude toward British overlordship [see page 641] underwent a great change. Indian leaders became familiar with European political ideas —with national self-consciousness, democratic self-government, socialism, and communism—and they grew increasingly impatient of British rule. The Indian National Congress, organized in 1885, began about 1905 to demand reforms in British administration and to talk of Dominion status for India, with democratic self-government. Other organizations, such as the Moslem League (1906) and a variety of radical groups, made more extreme demands, some of them resorting to bomb-throwing tactics. World War I intensified Indian unrest, and a British policy inaugurated in 1918-19 looking toward a gradual evolution to Dominion status did little to allay it, as the National Congress declared that the British plan was wholly unacceptable. Most prominent among the postwar Indian leaders was

Mohandas Karamchand Gandhi, christened "Mahatma" ("Great Soul") by the common people of India. Born in 1869, Gandhi was trained in law, migrated (1893) to South Africa, where his mistreatment by whites for his defense of Asiatic immigrants led him to develop and to institute widely a policy of passive resistance. His reputation as a religious man and a political leader preceded him to India, to which he returned in 1914. He gave loyal support to the British during World War I, but when a threatening face on Indian affairs led the British to institute the Rowlatt Acts (1919) making it possible to intern agitators without trial and to try their cases without juries, Gandhi went into quick opposition. In 1920, the National Congress, led by Gandhi, launched a campaign of passive resistance, or Satyagraha (Truth-force or Soul-force), and a boycott of British goods, British government, and British civilization (Hartal). Campaigns of nonviolent resistance of this nature were repeatedly instituted by Gandhi and his disciples during the next quarter-century. The Mahatma, himself a Hindu, advocated co-operation and mutual tolerance of Indian religious sects, social reforms (including abolition of child marriage and modification of the caste system), and a rigorous self-discipline in accordance with Oriental asceticism. He rejected the whole of European civilization as materialistic and immoral, and urged India to return to the simple village life of old, substituting self-government (Swaraji) for British rule, Hindu for English, homespun for factory-made clothing, economic self-sufficiency based upon village industries for reliance upon foreign factory-made goods, and a life devoted to soul perfection for materialistic go-getting. Gandhi's peculiar compound of Oriental philosophy, Hindu mysticism, and political philosophy render his writings difficult for Western comprehension, but his central object—Swaraji (self-government) by Ahimsa (nonviolence), Swadeshi (use of native products), and Satyagraha (truth- or soul-force)—is unmistakable. Representative selections from his writings follow.

From GANDHI, *Speeches and Writings* [1]

On Soul-Force and Indian Politics. The English expression "Passive Resistance" hardly denotes the force about which I propose to write. But Satyagraha, *i.e.,* Truth-force, correctly conveys the meaning. Truth-force is soul-force, and is the opposite of the force of arms. The former is a purely religious instrument; its conscious use is, therefore, possible only in men religiously inclined. . . . A "Passive Resister" has no spirit of envy in him. It is not anger that bids him court death. But it is by reason of his ability to suffer that he refuses to surrender. . . . Thus a "Passive Resister" has need to have courage, forgiveness, and love. . . . "Passive Resistance" is the religion of *Ahimsa.* . . . It is limited only by the insufficiency of the Passive Resister's strength to suffer. . . .

Both Soul-Force and force of arms are from times immemorial. Both have received their due . . . praise. . . . They respectively represent Forces of Good and Evil. The Indian belief is that there was in this land a time when the forces of Good were predominant. That state still remains our ideal. Europe furnishes a forcible illustration of predominance of the Forces of Evil.

Either of these is preferable to rank cowardice. Neither *Swaraji* [self-government] nor an Awakening among us is

---

[1] *Speeches and Writings of M. K. Gandhi,* ed. by C. F. Andrews, Madras, n.d., 157-59, 235-37.

possible without resort to one or the other. "Swaraji" is no Swaraji which is gained without Action. . . . No Awakening is possible without the people at large realizing their power. In spite of protestations by leaders and effort by the Government, if they and we do not give "Passive Resistance" due predominance, methods of violence will automatically gain strength. . . . For a cultivation of "Passive Resistance," endeavour and courage form the necessary manure; and as weeds, if they are not rooted out, overwhelm a crop, even so will violence grow like weeds, if the ground is not kept clean by self-sacrifice for the growth of "Passive Resistance." . . .

Meaning of Swadeshi [Belonging to, or made in, one's own country]. In my humble opinion fearlessness is the first thing indispensable before we could achieve anything permanent and real. This quality is unattainable without religious consciousness. Let us fear God and we shall cease to fear man. . . . And when we have sufficiently cultivated this spirit of fearlessness, we shall see that there is no salvation for us without true Swadeshi. . . . I would like us to apply it to our religious, political, and economic life. It is not therefore merely confined to wearing on occasions a Swadeshi cloth. . . . It is a duty we owe to our dear country. We commit a breach of the Swadeshi spirit certainly if we wear foreign-made cloth, but we do so also if we adopt the foreign cut. Surely the style of our dress has some correspondence with our environment. In elegance and tastefulness it is immeasurably superior to the trousers and the jacket. . . . Swadeshi in religion teaches one to measure the glorious past and to re-enact it in the present generation. . . . Modern civilization represents forces of evil and darkness whereas the ancient, *i.e.,* Indian, civilization represents in its essence the divine force. Modern civilization is chiefly materialistic

as ours is chiefly spiritual. Modern civilization occupies itself in the investigation of the laws of matter and employs the human ingenuity in inventing or discovering means of production and weapons of destruction; ours is chiefly occupied in exploring spiritual laws. . . . Our civilization tells us with daring certainty that a proper and perfect cultivation of the quality of *Ahimsa* [nonviolence], which in its active form means purest love and pity, brings the whole world to our feet. . . . Examine its result in the political life. There is no gift so valued . . . as the gift of life. Consider what our relations would be with our rulers if we gave absolute security of life to them. If they could but feel that no matter what we might feel about their acts, we would hold their bodies as sacred as our own, there would immediately spring up an atmosphere of mutual trust . . . [so] as to pave the way for an honourable and just solution of many problems that worry us today. It should be remembered that in practising *Ahimsa* there need not be any reciprocation, though as a matter of fact in its final stages it commands reciprocation.

An Early Example of the Use of Passive Resistance. [In a year of poor crops, when the government refused to suspend collection of revenue for that year, more than two hundred men in one Indian village signed the following declaration drawn up under Gandhi's leadership: [1]]

We, the undersigned, hereby solemnly declare that we shall not pay the full or remaining revenue, but we will let the Government take such legal steps as they may think fit to collect the same and we shall gladly suffer all the consequences of our refusal to pay. We shall allow our lands to be confiscated, but we shall not of our own accord pay anything and thereby lose our self-respect and prove

[1] *Ibid.,* 167.

ourselves wrong. . . . The reason why those of us who have the money to pay and still do not, is that if they do the poorer might in panic sell their things or borrow to pay and thereby suffer.

Under the circumstances we believe it is the duty of those who are able to pay to protect the poor.

THE PROGRAM OF THE BRITISH LABOR PARTY

The rise of the British Labor party was the result of ceaseless "education, agitation, and organization" since the enfranchisement of the British laborer in 1884. The party itself is, broadly speaking, a federation of three groups, differences among which have often seriously impaired party solidarity. These groups are: (1) Radical (Marxian but *not* Communist) Socialists, who seek to effect socialist ends by revolutionary means; (2) Moderate Socialists, such as the Fabian Society, founded in 1883, and the Independent Labor party (I.L.P.), founded in 1893, who seek to effect socialist ends by evolutionary (parliamentary) means; and (3) trade-unions, especially the Trade-Union Congress (T.U.C.), which seek all means to improve the workers' estate. Membership in the party is, then, both individual and affiliate, the latter consisting of various trade-unions, socialistic societies, professional organizations, and the like. From the outset, the party was frankly socialistic; its program generally keynoted by the I.L.P.'s policy "to secure the collective ownership of all means of production, distribution, and exchange." For years the party suffered from grave internal dissensions and from the tendency of other parties, especially the Liberals, to siphon off potential Labor support by enacting portions of the Labor program. Only once

before World War I did the Labor party poll more than half a million votes and return as many as forty-two members to Parliament. After the war, however, the Labor vote rose quickly,[1] and in 1924, and again in 1929-31, the party, though still a minority group, organized Labor governments in the United Kingdom. Such, in brief, was the background when, on July 27, 1945, returns from Great Britain's first parliamentary election since the beginning of World War II showed that the Labor party had become the majority party, with 11,962,678 votes and 393 seats in Parliament (out of a total of 640). Labor's triumph marked not only the political overthrow of Britain's colorful war leader, the Conservative Mr. Winston Churchill, by the steady Mr. Clement R. Attlee, but also a peaceful revolution in national policy. Previous Labor governments, too weak to effect socialization, had confined their efforts to reform legislation; but after the election of 1945 the Labor government, for the first time supported by a majority party, could embark upon its proposed socialist program. This program was set forth by the party's Executive Committee in April, 1945, in a declaration of policy entitled "Let Us Face The Future." It read, in part, as follows.

From "Let Us Face the Future" (1945) [2]

The nation wants food, work and homes. It wants more than that—it wants good food in plenty, useful work for all,

[1] The Labor vote in 1918 was 2,244,945; in 1924, 5,487,620; and in 1929, 8,364,883. In 1935, the vote was over eight millions, but it was so scattered that only 154 M.P.'s were returned by the party.

[2] Harry W. Laidler, *British Labor's Rise to Power*, 1945, League for Industrial Democracy Pamphlet Series, 20-25. By permission of the League for Industrial Democracy, Inc., New York.

and comfortable, labor-saving homes that take full advantage of the resources of modern science and productive industry. It wants a high and rising standard of living, security for all against a rainy day, an educational system that will give every boy and girl a chance to develop the best that is in them.

These are the aims. In themselves they are no more than words. All parties may declare that in principle they agree with them. But the test of a political program is whether it is sufficiently in earnest about the objectives to adopt the means to realize them. It is very easy to set out a list of aims. What matters is whether it is backed by a genuine workmanlike plan conceived without regard to sectional vested interests and carried through in a spirit of resolute concentration. . . .

The Labor party's program is a practical expression of that spirit applied to the tasks of peace. It calls for hard work, energy and sound sense.

We must prevent another war, and that means we must have such international organization as will give all nations real security against future aggression. But Britain can only play her full part in such an international plan if our spirit as shown in our handling of home affairs is firm, wise and determined. This statement of policy, therefore, begins at home.

And in stating it we give clear notice that we will not tolerate obstruction of the people's will by the House of Lords.

The Labor party stands for freedom— for freedom of worship, freedom of speech, freedom of the press. The Labor party will see to it that we keep and enlarge these freedoms, and that we enjoy again the personal civil liberties we have, of our own free will, sacrificed to win the war. The freedom of the trade unions, denied by the Trade Disputes and Trade Unions Act, 1927, must also be restored. But there are certain so-called freedoms that Labor will not tolerate: freedom to exploit other people; freedom to pay poor wages and to push up prices for selfish profit; freedom to deprive the people of the means of living full, happy, healthy lives.

The nation needs a tremendous overhaul, a great program of modernization and re-equipment of its homes, its factories and machinery, its schools, its social services.

All parties say so—the Labor party means it. For the Labor party is prepared to achieve it by drastic policies of replanning and by keeping a firm constructive hand on our whole productive machinery; the Labor party will put the community first and the sectional interests of private business after. Labor will plan from the ground up—giving an appropriate place to constructive enterprise and private endeavour in the national plan, but dealing decisively with those interests which would use high-sounding talk about economic freedom to cloak their determination to put themselves and their wishes above those of the whole nation. . . .

What will the Labor party do?

First, the whole of the national resources, in land, material and labour must be fully employed. Production must be raised to the highest level and related to purchasing power. Over-production is not the cause of depression and unemployment; it is under-consumption that is responsible. It is doubtful whether we have ever, except in war, used the whole of our productive capacity. This must be corrected because, upon our ability to produce and organize a fair and generous distribution of the product, the standard of living of our people depends.

Secondly, a high and constant purchasing power can be maintained through good wages, social services and insurance, and taxation which bears less heavily on the lower-income groups. But everybody knows that money and savings lose their value if prices rise, so rents and the prices of the necessities of life will be controlled.

Thirdly, planned investment in essential industries and on houses, schools, hospitals and civic centers will occupy a large field of capital expenditure. A National Investment Board will determine social priorities and promote better timing in private investment. In suitable cases we would transfer the use of efficient government factories from war production to meet the needs of peace. The location of new factories will be suitably controlled, and where necessary the government will itself build factories. There must be no depressed areas in the New Britain.

Fourthly, the Bank of England with its financial powers must be brought under public ownership, and the operations of the other banks harmonized with industrial needs.

By these and other means full employment can be achieved. But a policy of Jobs for All must be associated with a policy of general economic expansion and efficiency as set out in the next section of this Declaration. Indeed, it is not enough to ensure that there are jobs for all. If the standard of life is to be high—as it should be—the standard of production must be high. This means that industry must be thoroughly efficient if the needs of the nation are to be met. . . .

By the test of war some industries have shown themselves capable of rising to new heights of efficiency and expansion. Others, including some of our older industries fundamental to our economic structure, have wholly or partly failed.

Today we live alongside economic giants—countries where science and technology take leaping strides year by year. Britain must match those strides—and we must take no chances about it. Britain needs an industry organized to enable it to yield the best that human knowledge and skill can provide. Only so can our

people reap the full benefits of this age of discovery and Britain keep her place as a Great Power.

The Labor party intends to link the skill of British craftsmen and designers to the skill of British scientists in the service of our fellowmen. The genius of British scientists and technicians who have produced radio-location, jet-propulsion, penicillin, and the Mulbery Harbors in wartime, must be given full rein in peacetime too.

Each industry must have applied to it the test of national service. If it serves the nation, well and good; if it is inefficient and falls down on the job, the nation must see that things are put right.

These propositions seem indisputable, but for years before the war anti-Labor government set them aside, so that British industry over a large field fell into a state of depression, muddle and decay. Millions of working and middle-class people went through the horrors of unemployment and insecurity. It is not enough to sympathize with these victims: we must develop an acute feeling of national shame—and act.

The Labor party is a socialist party, and proud of it. Its ultimate purpose at home is the establishment of the socialist commonwealth of Great Britain—free, democratic, efficient, progressive, public-spirited, its material resources organized in the service of the British people.

But socialism cannot come overnight, as the product of a week-end revolution. The members of the Labor party, like the British people, are practical-minded men and women.

There are basic industries ripe and overripe for public ownership and management in the direct service of the nation. There are many smaller businesses rendering good service which can be left to go on with their useful work.

There are big industries not yet ripe for public ownership which must nevertheless be required by constructive supervision to further the nation's needs and not to prejudice national interests by restrictive antisocial monopoly or cartel agreements. . . .

In the light of these considerations, the Labor party submits to the nation the following industrial program:

1. *Public Ownership of the Fuel and Power Industries*—[Coal, gas and electricity] . . . will bring great economies in operation and make it possible to modernize production methods and to raise safety standards. . . .

2. *Public Ownership of Inland Transport.* Co-ordination of [rail, road, air and canal] transport services . . . [by] unification under [public] ownership.

3. *Public Ownership of Iron and Steel* . . . [in the interest of efficiency].

These socialized industries, taken over on a basis of fair compensation, to be conducted efficiently in the interests of consumers, coupled with proper status and conditions for the workers. . . .

4. *Public Supervision of Monopolies and Cartels* with the aim of advancing industrial efficiency in the service of the nation. . . .

5. *A First and Clear-cut Program for the Export Trade.* We would give State help in any necessary form to get our export trade on its feet and enable it to pay for the food and raw materials without which Britain must decay and die. But State help on conditions—conditions that industry is efficient and go-ahead. . . .

6. *The Shaping of Suitable Economic and Price Controls* to secure that first things shall come first in the transition from war to peace and that every citizen . . . shall get fair play. . . .

7. *The Better Organization of Government Departments* and the Civil Service for work in relation to these ends. The economic purpose of government must be to spur industry forward and not to choke it with red tape.

2. France Between the World Wars

The bewildering French political scene, with its multiplicity of parties and its frequent ministerial shifts (there were 110 ministries during the seventy years' existence of the Third Republic), presented a somewhat exaggerated appearance of instability. Doubtless, a variety of factors—such as the French individualistic temperament, French electoral practices, French traditions, and French circumstances of geography, economics, and diplomacy—accounted for the political peculiarities of the Third Republic. The following selections are helpful explanations.

THE SPIRIT OF MODERN FRANCE:
"THE TWO FRANCES"

From MILLER, *France* (1944) [1]

The French Revolution split in two the internal politics of France; from that time to our own there have been twin Frances, mortal enemies. The left-over bitterness of the American Civil War is still a political factor, yet in the United States the geographic unity of the opposing sides has been a softening influence. The French Revolution was a civil war in which, over large areas, the lines were drawn not on a geographic but on a social basis. When it was over, the ex-combatants had to live side by side in persisting bitterness. As the completeness of the democratic victory, with the passage of time and the coming of reaction, became less complete, two Frances confronted each other: authoritarian France, founded on the institutional trinity of monarchy, army and church, with industry as an ally after World War I; and democratic

[1] Helen Hill Miller, *France: Crossroads of a Continent,* 1944 (*Headline Series* No. 49), 33-40. By permission of the publisher, Foreign Policy Association, Inc., New York.

France, founded on the ideological trinity of liberty, equality and fraternity among individual citizens.

From the Revolution of 1789 to the founding of the Third Republic in 1870, changes in the form of government—empire, restoration, constitutional monarchy, empire again—occurred about once a generation, punctuated by revolutionary interludes. And while the Third Republic lasted some seventy years before it was interred by Marshal Pétain and the collaborationists in 1940, its stability was more than once in doubt. It was threatened in the 1880's by a man-on-horseback, Boulanger, and again at the turn of the century at the time of the Dreyfus case. . . .

That time, the Republic was vindicated. But in the 1930's, another notorious case put the shoe on the other foot. Restlessness with the regime had been growing during the interwar years, based on an uneasy certainty that too many of its officials were little men, at best blandly unaware of the deepening crisis; at worst, venal and corrupt. That was why the Stavisky swindle [see pages 841-842] . . . took on the proportions of a national scandal.

Distrust of a government which seemed to be party to such corruption was widespread even among citizens who did not belong to the authoritarian camp. This affords some explanation of the acceptance by a defeated France in 1940 of the slogan, "work, family, fatherland," as a substitute for "liberty, equality, fraternity." . . .

In order to understand the social struggles of France in our time, struggles which will provide unfinished business for postwar leadership, it is important to know the geography of the country—not only its physical geography . . . but the political, economic and religious geography. . . . The centralization of life in Paris is too apt to blind the foreigner to the diversity of provincial France, no less real and no

less important than the diversity among American regions. . . .

Take the map of France as a study in political geography. Straight across the country, south of the Loire, lay the France of nineteenth century democracy. The effects of the French Revolution were most sweeping in the south. It is not surprising that Toulouse, the early capital of radicalism, was among the first cities to rise in the summer of 1944. The Breton peninsula of the west, where the Revolution was unsuccessful, also changed but little after those bloody days; in this country of Celtic extremes, in recent years, the black conservatism of church and château lowered over the red radicalism of the fishing fleet. In the northeast is Alsace-Lorraine, the vulnerable frontier with Germany, scene of recurrent war, fortification, anxiety, desire for strong government. In the north-center is Paris, with the function of exerting on these very diverse elements the unifying influence of a political capital.

Take a map of France as a study in economic geography. With the Revolution, the south and east became the home of the French peasant proprietor, of most of the four and a half million Frenchmen who between wars had holdings of less than fifteen acres, of the million more holdings of less than seventy-five. In the west, where the large landed estates were not broken up, tenure changed little through a century. Eighty-five per cent of the industrial wealth of France lay in the north-north-east and the Paris region; the major part of the iron, steel and mining industries were within gunshot of the frontier. In the cities—Paris, Lyons, Marseilles—were entrenched the class-conscious workers.

Take a map of France as a study in religious geography. In the 1930's thirty-six of the forty million French were adherents of the Roman Catholic Church, but in studying the political aspect of their religion it was important to distinguish between those who were Catholics by conviction and those who were Catholics by convention. There were some twelve million Catholics by conviction, the intensity of whose religious life caused them to be classified as *catholiques pratiquants* (practicing Catholics). There were twice as many others whose conventional Catholicism was directly comparable to conventional Protestantism in the United States. They called the priest for weddings and funerals; they thronged the churches for the principal services of Christmas and Easter. The Frenchman who said *"Je suis athée, mais naturellement, je suis catholique* ("I am an atheist but, naturally, I am Catholic") summarized the nature of their conformity. . . .

The religious map also shows certain exceptional groups. The Bretons of the west are Catholics, but because they are also Celts their mystic approach to religion has more in common with the Catholicism of Ireland than with that of the rest of France. The Catholics of Alsace-Lorraine are also of another tradition. Scattered over the country, but concentrated to some extent in the cities, were 1,000,000 Protestants and 165,000 Jews: both groups were prominent in the public life of the interwar years beyond their proportionate popular strength.

These three maps, superimposed on one another, give a rough picture of the sectional politics as regularly reflected every four years by prewar elections to the Chamber of Deputies. Viewed against this background, the election returns belie the prevailing opinion that French politics were erratic. Cabinet changes were frequent exactly because the election results, year after year, showed so nearly equal a division between the France of authority and the France of democracy that the cabinet of the day always balanced on a

knife edge. The bloc system in parliament resulted in the formation of unstable majorities which could be upset by a very small shift, and so bring down the ministry of the day. The French Cabinet, moreover, unlike the British, could not discipline parliament by a threat of calling an election and going to the country on the issue which brought it down; the premier of the day merely resigned and bestowed on his successor the dubious task of finding a new and if possible a less precarious majority.

French national and local politics were closely linked, as in the United States, and there was a corresponding tendency to vote for persons and parties rather than on issues. The parties, moreover, had been so long established that their issues were traditional rather than immediate, and they were unable to present to French voters certain contemporary questions on which action could not safely be postponed.

As long as the framework of the Third Republic endured, all but the extremist political fringe had to pay at last lipservice to the democratic ideal. On the far left, in the 1930's, the Communists extolled another system, and an offshoot of the Socialist party urged something very like national socialism. At the same time, on the far right, a small but vociferous group proposed restoration of the pre-Revolutionary monarchy, and certain reactionary industrial leaders campaigned for centralization of governmental power in the President.

But between these extremes, the chief parties bore names which showed how the winds of politics blew to the left. The furthest right group called itself the Republican Federation; the right-center, the Democratic Alliance. In the middle-of-the-road, wielding the balance-of-power, were the Radical Socialists; left-of-center stood the Socialists. These party alignments offered relatively satisfactory divisions for votes on issues that concerned politics or religion. But they were brittle with age. The developments of the twentieth century required action on social and economic issues which the existing parties were ill-equipped to undertake.

PROBLEMS AND POLICIES OF POSTWAR FRANCE

Into the hands of the ill-adapted political setup described above, the end of World War I dumped some of the most critical problems ever to challenge French leadership—problems of postwar reconstruction, finance, and security. Ten per cent of the active male population had been killed in the war, and 11 per cent more had been permanently maimed—losses felt the more keenly in view of France's loss of demographic superiority during the previous century: for between 1800 and 1930, the French population, though rising absolutely from 27,000,000 to 41,000,000, had dropped relatively from 14.6 per cent to 8.5 per cent of the total population of Europe, and Russia, Germany, Great Britain, and even Italy surpassed her in manpower by 1930. Moreover, the war had caused tremendous financial outlays and had annihilated French resources: ten departments lay devastated—the richest in population and industrial resources, formerly producing 70 per cent of French coal, over 60 per cent of French steel, and nearly 80 per cent of French sugar. To reconstruct these areas, the man-power situation being as it was, France had imported nearly two million foreign laborers by 1931—mostly Italians, Czechs, Poles, Spaniards and Germans, including, by 1939, an effi-

cient number of "fifth-columnists." Such, in brief retrospect, were some of the major conditions which plagued French statecraft, multiplying party divisions and raising political temperatures during the interwar era. André Tardieu, an old Clemenceau supporter, described the scene as it appeared to French leaders in 1922.

From TARDIEU, "The Policy of France" (1922) [1]

What France was yesterday, such she is today. But in three years of peace she has been bitterly disillusioned.

France counted on the co-operation of her recent comrades in arms in carrying out the long-term clauses of the just peace which they signed in common. She counted on it in vain.

In March, 1920, the United States refused to ratify the Treaty of Versailles and the Tripartite Military Guarantee [see page 736]. In 1921 it concluded with Germany a separate peace by which it definitely rejected the mutual engagements implied in the treaty of 1919. From that moment Germany knew that America would not insist on the execution of a peace treaty in which she had no further interest.

In the same way Great Britain has turned her back on her 1919 policy. It was Great Britain who had called for the most draconian clauses—for the punishment of war criminals, for example, and for repayment of war pensions. Less than six months after the ratification of the treaty she repudiated these stipulations. . . . In his successive conferences Mr. Lloyd George has followed a definite policy of mutilating the peace terms, thus time and

[1] André P. A. A. Tardieu, "The Policy of France," Foreign Affairs, I (September, 1922), 11-13, 21-22. By permission of Foreign Affairs, New York.

again imposing sacrifices on France without granting her any corresponding compensation. So it happens that during the past few months my country has come to feel herself isolated, without feeling that she was responsible for this isolation. . . .

If France insists upon the execution of the treaty it is not solely because it is a contract; it is because its non-execution would very shortly place her in an impasse.

The war bled us terribly. Out of our population of less than 38,000,000 there were mobilized 8,500,000; 5,300,000 of them were killed or wounded (1,500,000 killed, 800,000 *mutilés,* 3,000,000 wounded), not counting 500,000 men who have come back to us from German prisons in a very bad physical condition.

Almost 4,000,000 hectares [about 10,000,000 acres] of land were devastated, together with some 4,000 towns and villages; 600,000 buildings were destroyed, among them 20,000 factories and workshops, besides 5,000 kilometers [over 3,000 miles] of railroads and 53,000 kilometers [about 33,000 miles] of roads. About 1,400,000 head of cattle were carried off. Altogether a quarter of our productive capital was annihilated.

The financial consequences . . . bear down on us heavily today. The war cost us 150 billions of francs. The damage to property and persons comes to 200 billions. Our ordinary budget has increased from 4½ billions to 25 billions; our debt from 36 billions to 330 billions. Since the armistice we have spent on reconstruction and on pensions a total of 90 billions, and we have received from Germany in one form or another less than two billions of gold marks (about six billions of francs), or about six per cent of what we have had to spend on restoring our provinces—a task as yet but half completed. . . . In the last two years France has spent on reconstruction and pensions 7½ billions of dollars, or $5,700 a minute, while in the same period Germany has only spent 500 millions of dollars, or $381 a minute. In other words, we have accumulated a deficit of $5,319 every minute; and it is we who have paid it, in place of Germany who was responsible for creating the damage.

We think that this cannot go on. You would think the same in our place. The interest and amortization on the sums borrowed by us since the armistice to make up for Germany's default have cost us 4½ billions of francs a year. The interest on our debt absorbs 55 per cent of our taxes. We ask that all this be ended. Who can say it is not a legitimate demand? . . .

Having said all of this I feel in a better position to reply to the question that has been put to me: "What does France want? What is her policy?" My reply lies in a single phrase: "France wants to live."

France wants to live. By that I mean she wants not to succumb beneath the burden of her victory—that she wants to rebuild her ruins instead of being crushed beneath them. . . .

France wants to live, and her acts have proved it. The work of reconstruction accomplished since the armistice is the admiration of all who have come to study it. Without any outside assistance we have restored all our railroads and highways, have put back into condition 80 per cent of our devastated fields, have brought home 90 per cent of the people driven away by the war, have rebuilt half of our factories and have put up temporary houses which . . . will serve until permanent structures can be erected. . . . We showed no less energy in reorganizing our finances. . . . France is full of action, but she wants to have fulfilled the two conditions which will permit her efforts to bear fruit: one, lasting security; two, effective reparations. The pursuit of these two conditions determines her policy.

STABILIZING THE DEPRECIATED FRANC, 1919-1928

French difficulties at home and abroad caused the franc to decline in international exchange value until, by 1926, it was quoted at 2 cents, or about one-tenth of its prewar value. Meanwhile, owing to Germany's defaults in reparations payments and France's failure to float sizable foreign loans, the situation became so critical that party lines were temporarily laid aside and Raymond Poincaré formed a National Union ministry which, with only minor changes, guided French destinies from July, 1926, to July, 1929. In these years the franc was stabilized and revalued at about 4 cents, a process which, while it amounted to a repudiation of four-fifths of the internal debt, was nevertheless upheld at the polls, and Poincaré came to be hailed as the "Savior of France." In a careful study of the depreciation and stabilization of the franc, Miss Eleanor Lansing Dulles has described French financial stabilization as follows.

From DULLES, *The French Franc* (1929) [1]

The French franc lost eighty per cent of its value as a result of the World War. It fell from an exchange value of 19.29 cents in 1914 to 3.90 cents in 1928, and its internal purchasing power fell to the same extent. Such depreciation . . . has caused notable changes in France. In the first place, the temporary loss in financial prestige and power has been considerable. In the second place, production has come to be dominated more and more by large manufacturing units and corporate forms of enterprise. The results of this change are likely to persist. In the third place, the

[1] Eleanor Lansing Dulles, *The French Franc, 1914-1928*, 1929, 1-6, 8-12, 412-14, 416-18, 437-38. By permission of The Macmillan Company.

shift of power from the middle classes to the industrial leaders and to those with more flexible incomes appears to have changed the character of French life and ideals to a notable extent. . . .

The special fact in the French case was the size and urgency of her reconstruction problem [estimated to have cost 100 billion francs by 1924]. This led to her policy of reparations, the growth of the internal debt, and most of the important events in her foreign and domestic history after the war. . . . It is obvious that the fact that France wished to collect reparation payment from Germany to meet an immediate need, and that she was the main creditor nation [she was awarded 52 per cent of the reparation payments under the Spa agreement in 1920], placed her in a peculiar position. It was to her interest more than to that of any other country to see that Germany paid. It is possible that the complete default of Germany would have forced France to repudiate . . . her internal debt, and probably also her external debt. The result was an immediate and inevitable conflict of interest between France and England. France needed money or goods to replace the destruction of her northern departments, England needed money but, even more . . . she desired the reëstablishment of foreign markets and the recovery of international trade. . . . Moreover, her claim on Germany was less than half that of France [22 per cent], and her interest in collecting it was comparatively slight. Even though her exchequer would suffer through the failure of reparations, her commerce was apt to benefit. France, however, had little to gain in the way of expanding her foreign commerce, and she had much to lose through national bankruptcy. The result was tension, misunderstanding, and divided interests. . . . The situation of France, then, as regards reparations, was exceptional. . . . A study of the factors influencing the franc makes it apparent that if this problem could have been solved to the satisfaction of the French, the franc might conceivably have returned to par. . . .

At the close of the war, the most immediate influence working against the franc was the unfavorable balance of trade. The second in direct relation was the internal debt, which bore with it the threat of inflation or repudiation, and, therefore, of depreciation on both the commodity and the foreign exchange markets. . . . Of course, the increase in the internal debt of France was a serious matter; it had risen from 32½ billion francs to 140 billion francs at the end of 1918. . . . Thus it was the two-fold strain of interest and capital expenditures which made necessary the inflation of later years. The internal debt practically doubled during the eight years following the armistice.

France, in 1919, anticipated a far different development of economic affairs from that which took place. In the first place, the French expected, or at any rate they hoped, that the United States would advance money to finance reconstruction. . . . In the second place, the French confidently expected that every cent that went to pay for rebuilding the North would come eventually from Germany. . . . [As neither of these anticipations materialized,] France went on spending money on reconstruction with a growing debt and a diminishing prospect of financial recovery, and the turn of speculation against France was the direct result.

It was natural that, as the size of budget expenditures and loans for reconstruction purposes increased, there were heated political struggles over questions which should have been settled mainly by impartial technical experts. The party or group in power, the *Bloc national,* bidding for popular favor, promised that the cost would be met by Germany . . . and various unsound financial measures were used to postpone the bitter disillusionment of the French electors. The complications thus introduced . . . were . . . the most important result of the reconstruction tangle, and a prime cause of the depreciation of the franc. . . .

The French problem of stabilization was . . . different from that of any other nation. This was true, first, because of her economic situation, and second, because of her political conditions. The instability of political life . . . was aggravated in matters of finance by the strong influence of the *rentier* class. It was natural that the large number of government bond holders formed a serious obstacle to early stabilization. Since they had pocketed a very serious loss in the value of their securities, they felt that their interests should be given some weight in the choice of the new value of the franc. It was, therefore, not possible to come quickly to the final decision because of strong public sentiment favoring a higher gold value. . . .

A second reason for the delay in stabilization was the condition of the internal debt, which was peculiar to the French situation. The large mass of short-time credits . . . made the situation difficult to handle from a technical point of view. . . .

Then, in the third place, the external debts of France were troublesome. They interfered, not so much because there was urgent need of payment, as because they prevented securing foreign credits which were considered necessary for stabilization. . . .

These three factors are the inevitable outgrowth of the war and reconstruction expenditures. It was the budget deficits which led to depreciation, and therefore to the heavy losses sustained by the *rentier*. It was the cost of reconstruction which increased the internal debt, and made it impossible to discharge external debts. If the severe crises attributable to government embarrassment in handling the debt and the budget in 1924 and 1926 could have been avoided, if the budget could have been passed with reasonable speed in 1925, there is no reason to suppose that France would have found stabilization impossible in 1925 or 1926. It is important, then, to realize that the French difficulties were a combination of the exceptionally heavy postwar burdens and a political system unadapted to handling such difficult problems. . . .

The last plunge of the franc in 1926 led almost inevitably to the recovery which followed so quickly. . . . Poincaré took office on July 24. He arranged for the immediate transfer of the Morgan funds to the treasury. He secured a vote of confidence on July 27. . . . It was sufficient to divert attention from the underlying difficulties until more constructive measures could be passed. . . .

The final act of stabilization of June 25, 1928 . . . increased confidence and economic activity. Thus the franc which had been worth about 20 cents before the war came to have a fairly steady value of 3.93 cents after the war. This change of ratio . . . really brought no change at the time it was recognized by law. The adjustment had been so complete . . . that the new government measures simply confirmed what had been already widely accepted. . . . There was, indeed, little to concern the average business man, except the fact that he need not worry any longer about sudden changes of export and import prices nor make abnormal efforts to build up bank balances abroad.

To the student of monetary theory . . . there are . . . points of interest in the provisions for stabilization. . . . France passed almost imperceptibly to a full gold standard in place of the limping standard which had existed before the war. . . . In contrast to the procedure in other countries, France secured no large foreign loans to facilitate stabilization. And, finally . . . the legal act of stabilization brought no adverse economic reaction, but rather hastened the recovery of industry which was, already, fairly general.

THE STAVISKY SCANDAL AND THE PARIS RIOTS OF FEBRUARY, 1934

The National Union ministries, French prosperity, and the prospects for French security ended in quick succession in the years 1929 to 1933. Poincaré resigned (July 27, 1929) because of ill-health; world-wide economic depression, highlighted by the New York Stock Market crash in October, 1929, and the failure of the Austrian Creditanstalt in May, 1931, brought a swift conclusion to French economic well-being; and the outbreak of Sino-Japanese troubles in 1931, together with the rise of Hitler to power in Germany (January, 1933), threatened world peace in general and French security in particular. With the return of economic disaster and international danger, chaotic divisions, indecision, and corruption became the most marked features of French political leadership. Ministries appeared and disappeared with extraordinary rapidity (there were five ministries in thirteen months in 1932-33), and, with French tempers on edge, a scandal came to light which justifiably directed grave suspicion toward incumbent ministers, undermined people's confidence in their government, fanned political passions into white heat, brought into the open a series of leagues, societies, and "fronts" of a dangerously dubious nature, and provoked riots and revolutionary unrest until "there was ever present the danger that the streets might try to take from the chamber the right to govern French affairs." The incident which set off this

unhappy train of events was the Stavisky scandal. A description by a contemporary annalist follows.

From *The Annual Register* (1934) [1]

In the closing days of December, 1933,
there had been discovered a financial
fraud involving the Municipal Loan
Office of Bayonne, which, at the suggestion of an adventurer named [Serge
Alexandre] Stavisky, had placed in circulation 200 milliards [billions] worth of
forged bonds. Stavisky, who was known
as an old offender [Paris papers had referred to him since 1926 as "the king of
crooks"], was already in flight. Soon after
came the news of his violent death, on
January 9, in a villa at Chamonix, to
which he had been tracked down by the
police.

M. Dalimier, now Minister for the
Colonies, had, when Minister of Commerce, induced the insurance companies
to invest their funds in bonds of municipal loan offices. For this, he found himself
obliged to resign on January 9. The Prime
Minister, M. [Camille] Chautemps . . .
retained the support of Parliament, [but]
the behaviour of the street crowds already
showed the agitation prevailing in Paris
and the feeling aroused by the scandals.
The Keeper of the Seals, M. Raynaldy,
and other high officials were openly
charged with complicity; the name of M.
Pressard, the brother-in-law of M. Chautemps, was also dragged in; and on January 28 M. Chautemps and his colleagues
resigned. . . . On January 30 M. Daladier
formed a Ministry . . . and declared his
intention of striking "hard and quickly"
at all the guilty. . . .

On February 6 the Cabinet met in an
atmosphere of gloom. A number of groups,

[1] "Foreign History," *The Annual Register . . .
for the Year 1934*, London, 1935, 167-70. By
permission of Longmans, Green & Co., Ltd.

among them a very strong contingent of
ex-soldiers [mostly Royalists and pseudo-
fascists], had resolved to demonstrate in
the evening in the vicinity of the Palais
Bourbon. The danger of incidents arising
became acute. . . . While a dramatic sitting was going on within, the ex-soldiers
tried to approach the Chamber. Atrocious
scenes took place in the Place de la Con-
corde, fifteen persons being killed and
hundreds wounded. On the next day M.
Daladier . . . felt himself obliged by the
excitement in the streets to resign. Fresh
disorders took place on February 7 and 9
in Paris, the former provoked by mischief-
makers, the latter by the Communists.

The President . . . now appealed to
M. Gaston Doumergue, an ex-President
of the Republic. . . . M. Doumergue arrived in Paris on February 8, and on the
next day formed a Cabinet in which all
parties were represented except the unified
Socialists and the Communists [in reality
a Rightist ministry]. . . . It came before
the Chamber on February 15 as a Government of truce, appeasement and justice,
and secured a big majority. . . .

The task awaiting the Cabinet of
National Union was even more difficult
than that which had devolved on the
Poincaré Cabinet in 1926. To financial
and budgetary difficulties there were added
grave external problems, while the crisis
arising from the scandals still persisted.
It was bad enough that the swindler had
used official recommendations to unload
on the public his fraudulent bonds. But
behind the affair lurked the danger of a
bitter conflict between those who desired
an ever increasing State control of industry (that is to say, the Socialists, not to
mention the Communists, and a part of
the Radicals), and the upholders of the
existing régime of bourgeoisie and economic liberty.

FRENCH FASCISM

From WOLFE, *France* (1940) [1]

In France, as in the rest of Europe, the depression saw the growth of a crop of fascist and authoritarian movements with glittering programs to attract the masses. The people, apparently unwilling to find their own way out of trouble, often naïvely believed that a messianic leader will open all doors for them. Fortunately for the liberal, democratic Republic, there were no Hitlers or Mussolinis at the heads of the French fascist movements. The several budding fascist organizations were not to have an immediate opportunity to regulate French life, but in 1934 there were several groups anxious to assume the role. The most formidable was [Colonel François de] La Rocque's Croix de Feu. With several hundred thousand followers, mostly war veterans, La Rocque struck heroic attitudes, and vaguely muttered imprecations upon the heads of French politicians.[2] If given a chance, he would "restore France to the French" by creating some sort of totalitarian regime. Closely allied with the Croix de Feu were the royalist Action Française and the blue-shirted Solidarité Française. There is some reason to suppose that these movements were not ignored by the fascist states on France's frontiers, but there is no avail-

able evidence of the sort of assistance that they received. L'Action Française had a subsidiary organization, Les Camelots du Roi, which, apparently, was composed of tennis-playing, rather wealthy, young hoodlums, and students with a taste for "authority" and disorder. This group noisily proclaimed the necessity for a monarchical restoration, and acted as the shock troops of the extreme right against socialists and communists. There were other—less important, perhaps—fascist or semifascist organizations here and there in depression-ridden France; now they appear to have been weak and harmless, but at the time it was impossible to say whether or not one of them might carry within its destiny the destruction of the liberal democratic regime. This was especially true since several of these groups began to accumulate stores of arms for a possible test of strength with the government.

THE RISE OF THE POPULAR FRONT

From WERTH, *The Twilight of France* (1942) [3]

The beginning of the "anti-Fascist rally" in France dates back to the days immediately following the riot of February 6, 1934. In the course of 1934 the Socialists and Communists drew closer together, and on August 27 . . . they signed the United Action Pact, which marks the formal beginning of what came to be known as the Front Commun.

Its purpose was, among other things, to "mobilize the entire working population against the Fascist organizations," and to "defend democratic liberties." Actually, the rank and file, much more than the

[1] John B. Wolfe, *France 1815 to the Present*, ed. by Carl Wittke, 1940 (Prentice-Hall Books on History), 525-26. By permission of Prentice-Hall, Inc., New York.

[2] He spoke of a "plan of action," embodying "the mystic consciousness of France," to rehabilitate the nation, to eliminate "irresponsible, underhand and self-seeking interests," and to establish an "interrelated framework of a national discipline, rejuvenated and authoritarian." He was especially bitter against "votism"—"the far too widespread misconception that the people's verdict, whether the vote be limited or universal, subserve some higher end." All of which smacked suspiciously of the Nazi antidemocratic "Führer principle."

[3] Alexander Werth, *The Twilight of France, 1933-1940*, 1942, 50-54. By permission of Hamish Hamilton, London.

leaders, wanted this "united action." The Communist leaders at first rejected the overtures made by the Socialists, and when, shortly afterwards, in February, 1934, they suddenly went all out for co-operation, this *volte-face* aroused the Socialists' suspicion. M. [Léon] Blum thought the directives from Moscow a little too nationalist. . . .

It so happened that June 1935 was marked by a sudden reappearance on the French political scene of the Croix de Feu. . . . The Croix de Feu leaders suddenly realized that there now sat at the head of the Government not a hostile [Pierre Etienne] Flandin, but [Pierre] Laval who, they had reason to believe, was not un-sympathetic to the movement, and with whom friendly co-operation . . . might be possible. As time went on, and as the hostility between Laval and the Socialists and Communists grew, the relations be-tween him and the Croix de Feu became more cordial. An intimate friend of his repeated to me . . . the following reflec-tion that Laval made to him in a moment of candor: "Yes, I am on good terms with the Croix de Feu. *Ce sont des vrais Français* [They are the true French]." . . . As was to be expected, the Left became greatly alarmed by the sudden revival in the energies of the Croix de Feu. . . .

June 28 . . . was an important land-mark in the history of the Front Populaire. A meeting took place that night at the Mutualité. . . . The three speakers at the meeting were MM. Daladier, Blum, and [Maurice] Thorez.

M. Daladier received a tremendous ova-tion from the audience—for it was his presence at the meeting that symbolized the extension of the Front Commun to the proportions of a Front Populaire. He proceeded to show that the greatest evil in France was the financial oligarchy. The Fascists merely represented this oligarchy. The Premier of the 6th of February was clearly rehabilitating himself in his new role.

M. Blum said he hoped the Front Populaire victory . . . would "extend to the whole of France."

M. Thorez, the young Communist leader, declared that the Communists also wished to join the Front Populaire, to defend the liberties of the working class. All three speakers agreed that their ad-herence to the Front Populaire did not imply any loss of independence.

The meeting created a sensation in France as the beginning of something very big. . . . [Both the nascent Popular Front and the Croix de Feu planned mighty demonstrations for Bastille Day (July 14), 1935.]

At last the great day came. Some of the London papers were full of panic stories of how a civil war might break out in Paris that day. They were to be disap-pointed. All the police did was to separate East from West, and to see that neither procession transgressed the limit fixed for them. And everything went off perfectly smoothly. The . . . procession of the Left was the most impressive thing of its kind ever seen in Paris. Some 300,000 to 400,000 people took part in it. . . . Later, at the opposite end of the town, the Croix de Feu . . . some 30,000 of them . . . [marched] in the procession. . . . Numerically it was insignificant, compared with the vast Bas-tille procession; but the military discipline of La Rocque's men was impressive. The 14th of July 1935 marked not only the beginning of the Front Populaire; it was also the apotheosis of the Croix de Feu. At no moment had La Rocque's prestige stood higher. The Left knew it; and were determined not to allow his prestige to grow any bigger.

THE POPULAR FRONT IN POWER

"The Front Populaire," said Léon Blum in a widely quoted speech made soon after the victory of the Popular Front in May, 1936,[1] "is a new thing. It represents not merely a combination of parties but a powerful mass movement. It will be new by its methods and by the character of its action. Our mission as a party is to build up a new society, but I shall tell you frankly that the task of the Front Populaire Government is different. Neither the Socialists alone nor the Socialists together with the other proletarian parties have a majority. Our duty is simply to carry out the Front Populaire program. We are going to act within the framework of the present régime, whose very vices we have denounced. The question is whether there is a possibility of at least securing within the present régime relief for those who suffer, and of creating a peaceful transition from this Society to the Society which remains our aim? Are a small ration of justice and well-being and a large ration of hope possible in the present society?"

Thus Blum indicated both that the Popular Front was a coalition, not a union, of parties, and that despite the fact that the program fell short of socialist-revolutionary aspirations, his government intended to stick to it. During the next year (June 5, 1936-June 19, 1937), Blum labored valiantly against great odds, not the least of which was the weakness of the Popular Front itself—for both the Communists and the C.G.T., while promising support in the Chamber, refused to accept Cabinet appointments. At best, the Blum Government headed off a possible revolution in France; but its day

was short, and its accomplishments of temporary duration, as the following account of it shows.

From JACKSON, *The Postwar World* (1943) [2]

Blum came to power at the worst possible moment. Italy had just completed the conquest of Abyssinia, Hitler had just defied Locarno by marching into the Rhineland, civil war was about to break out beyond the Pyrenees. In France itself, impatient laborers were taking the law into their own hands by a wave of strikes of the "stay-in" variety in the automobile and other factories. Blum could hope for little success in the international diplomatic field, but he took advantage of the internal unrest to launch a program of sweeping social reform. He promised the French workers the forty-hour week, the right to make collective contracts, and annual holidays with pay.

These promises were sufficient to put an end to the strike wave. But when they were put into practice, somewhat tentatively, the effect was to force up industrial costs. Prices rose, the volume of production declined, unemployment increased. Capitalists, foreseeing a devaluation of the franc, hastened to send their gold out of the country.

To meet these setbacks Blum set in motion three further reforms. The first was to authorize the Bank of France to stop exports of gold, a step which was accompanied by a devaluation of the franc and a Three-Power Declaration with Britain and the United States in favor of monetary cooperation and the maintenance of world prices. The second was to reorganize the Bank of France itself so as to bring that all-powerful financial institution under a measure of Government

[1] Quoted in *Ibid.*, 97.

[2] J. Hampden Jackson, *The Postwar World 1918-1939*, 1943, 64-66. By permission of Little, Brown and Company, Boston.

control. Hitherto the directors of the bank had been nominated by the two hundred biggest shareholders—members of the hated *deux cent familles* who among them held a great part of the directorships in the most important industrial concerns and had not hesitated to use their position in the bank to turn official financial policy to their own account. Blum's Act arranged for twenty Bank directors; nine of these were to be nominated by the Government departments, six by the Finance Minister from lists sent in by Cooperative Societies, Trade Unions and Chambers of Commerce, and only two of the remainder by the Bank's shareholders—and these were to be elected by the total 40,000 shareholders, each having one vote, instead of by the two hundred families. The third reform was the nationalization of the arms industries. The great Creusot combine and the aeroplane factories were brought under Government supervision. . . . As Alexander Werth remarked in *The Destiny of France:* "The Popular Front will go down in history as the Government which went a long way towards the total abolition of the private arms business."

In spite of these triumphs Blum's Government lasted hardly more than a year. Behind the breakdown were two causes, one general and one particular. In general, the social reforms led to a rise in the cost of living and a fall in industrial output, which the financial reforms might alleviate but could not altogether check. In particular, Blum's foreign policy antagonized the extremist sections and disappointed all sections of the Popular Front. His policy, put simply, was a *rapprochement* with Britain. In itself this would have antagonized nobody: there was general approval when Blum's ministry followed Britain's lead in stopping sanctions against Italy. But when, in August, 1936, Blum actually took the lead in imposing an embargo on arms and war materials destined for Spain, the Left Wing raised the cry that the independence of Spain was being betrayed. . . . Blum could not foresee, in August, that the Fascist countries would defy the Nonintervention Committee and take part on the grand scale in Franco's rebellion. On the other hand, he was bound to agree with the British view that interference in Spain would precipitate a European war. But the result was that by the beginning of 1937 Italy was in control of the Balearic Isles, and Germany had air bases in northern Spain and Morocco. Blum was blamed for this, and . . . resigned.

For the next two years the Popular Front remained in power under successive ministries, but each ministry moved a little further to the Right. The social legislation remained on the statute book, but no further progress was made. And every attempt to extend Government control over financial agencies was sabotaged by French capitalists. The ruling passion in France in those years was fear of Hitler. When Hitler threatened Czechoslovakia in September 1938 the French, now led by Daladier and Georges Bonnet, abandoned their ally and fell back on a gigantic rearmament scheme to be financed by economies and cuts in the social services. The forty-hour week was set aside and employers were empowered to work their men up to fifty hours. . . . The Popular Front was dead. Security was once again the slogan of France.

3. The Papacy on Current Problems

Pope Pius XI (1922-39), whose pontificate very nearly coincided with the era between World Wars, set forth a series of remarkable encyclical letters in an effort to remind the world that

Christian ethics and morality, as interpreted by the Roman Catholic Church, offered solutions to many of the current social problems. Strongly reminiscent of the conservative stand adopted by the Church in the last century [see pages 525-531], the encyclicals were powerful assertions of the Roman Catholic viewpoint and served as clarion calls to the faithful throughout the world. Excerpts from a few of these documents follow.

THE PAPAL POLICY ON EDUCATION

On the control of education, a thorny issue between Church and State in many parts of the world throughout the last century and still a source of heated controversy, Pius XI set forth the following policy.

From PIUS XI, Encyclical: *Christian Education of Youth* (1929) [1]

Indeed never has there been so much discussion about education as nowadays. . . .

The reason is that men, created by God . . . realize today more than ever amid the most exuberant material progress, the insufficiency of earthly goods to produce true happiness. . . . And hence they feel more keenly in themselves the impulse towards a perfection that is higher. . . . This perfection they seek to acquire by means of education. But many of them . . . pretend to draw education out of human nature itself and evolve it by its own unaided powers. Such easily fall into error, because instead of fixing their gaze on God, first principle and last end of the whole universe, they fall back upon themselves, becoming attached exclusively to passing things of earth. . . .

[1] This and the next two selections are from *Five Great Encyclicals*. By permission of The Paulist Press. This is 38-40, 49-52, 56-57, 60.

In fact, since education consists essentially in preparing man for what he must be and for what he must do here below, in order to attain the sublime end for which he was created, it is clear that there can be no true education which is not wholly directed to Man's last end . . . there can be no ideally perfect education which is not Christian education. . . .

And first of all education belongs preeminently to the Church, by reason of a double title in the supernatural order, conferred exclusively upon her by God Himself: absolutely superior therefore to any other title in the natural order. . . .

It pertains to the State, in view of the common good, to promote in various ways the education and instruction of youth. It should begin by encouraging and assisting, of its own accord, the initiative and activity of the Church and the family. . . . It should moreover supplement their work whenever this falls short of what is necessary, even by means of its own schools and institutions. . . . The State can exact, and take measures to secure that all its citizens have the necessary knowledge of their civic and political duties, and a certain degree of physical, intellectual and moral culture, which . . . is really necessary for the common good. . . .

All that We have said so far regarding the activity of the State in educational matters rests on . . . the Catholic doctrine of the Christian Constitution of States set forth in such masterly fashion by Our Predecessor Leo XII [1823-29] . . . "God has divided the government of the human race between two authorities, ecclesiastical and civil, establishing one over things divine, the other over things human. Both are supreme, each in its own domain; each has its own fixed boundaries which limit its activities." . . .

Now the education of youth is precisely one of those matters that belong both to the Church and to the State, "though in different ways." . . . "Therefore," continues Leo XIII [1878-1903], "between the two powers there must reign a well-ordered harmony." . . .

Whoever refuses to admit these principles, and hence to apply them to education, must necessarily deny that Christ has founded His Church, for the eternal salvation of mankind, and maintain instead that civil society and the State are not subject to God and to His law. . . . Such a doctrine is manifestly impious, contrary to right reason, and, especially in this matter of education, extremely harmful to the proper training of youth and disastrous . . . for the well-being of all mankind. . . . [For citizens who live up to the teachings of Christ are "the greatest safeguard of the State."]

Another grave danger is that naturalism which nowadays invades the field of education in that most delicate matter of purity of morals. Far too common is the error of those who with dangerous assurance and under the ugly term propagate a so-called sex-education, falsely imagining they can forearm youth against the dangers of sensuality by means purely natural. . . . [This, if necessary at all, should be left to the family and to the Church; ". . . every precaution must be taken."]

False also and harmful to Christian education is the so-called method of "co-education." This, too . . . is founded upon naturalism and the denial of original sin. . . . The Creator has ordained and disposed perfect union of the sexes only in matrimony, and, with varying degrees of contact, in the family and in society. Besides there is not in nature itself, which fashions the two quite different in organisms, in temperament, in abilities, anything to suggest that there can or ought to be promiscuity, and much less equality, in the training of the two sexes. . . .

We renew and confirm . . . declarations . . . in which the frequenting of non-Catholic schools, whether neutral or mixed, those namely which are open to Catholics and non-Catholics alike, is forbidden for Catholic children, and can at most be tolerated, on the approval of the Ordinary alone, under determined circumstances of place and time, and with special precautions. Neither can Catholics admit that other type of mixed school . . . in which the students are provided with separate religious instruction, but receive other lessons in common with non-Catholic pupils from non-Catholic teachers. . . .

And let no one say that in a nation where there are different religious beliefs, it is impossible to provide for public instruction otherwise than by neutral or mixed schools. In such a case it becomes the duty of the State . . . to leave free scope to the initiative of the Church and family . . . [for] "Catholic education in Catholic schools for all the Catholic youth." . . . If such education is not aided from public funds, as distributive justice requires, certainly it may not be opposed by any civil authority. . . .

Whatever Catholics do in promoting and defending the Catholic school for their children, is a genuinely religious work and therefore an important task of "Catholic Action." For this reason the associations which in various countries are so zealously engaged in this work of prime necessity are especially dear to Our paternal heart and are deserving of every commendation.

ECONOMIC AND SOCIAL POLICY OF THE PAPACY

Exactly forty years after Leo XIII's encyclical, *Rerum Novarum, "On the Condition of Labor"* [see page 528], Pope Pius XI issued the encyclical

Quadragesimo Anno, "On Reconstructing the Social Order," in which he reasserted his illustrious predecessor's principles, offered corrective interpretations in view of altered conditions, and made significant additions. Pius XI praised Leo XIII's bold stand against Liberalism and Communism, vindicated his defense of the right of private property, and enumerated under three heads the benefits alleged to have emanated from Pope Leo's encyclical. To do these justice, said Pius XI, "it would be necessary to recall almost the whole social history of the past forty years," but they might be summarized thus: 1. "Under the teaching and guidance of the Church," learned clergy and laymen elaborated and put into practical application by organizations of workingmen "a truly Christian social science" by "adapting to modern needs the unchanging and unchangeable doctrine of the Church." 2. As "Leo XIII boldly passed beyond the restrictions imposed by Liberalism, and fearlessly proclaimed the doctrine that the civil power is more than the mere guardian of law and order" and "completely overthrew those tottering tenets of Liberalism which had long hampered interference by the government," his encyclical "prevailed upon the people themselves to develop their social policy more intensely." As a consequence, "there has arisen a new branch of jurisprudence unknown to earlier times, whose aim is the energetic defense of those sacred rights of the workingmen" concerning "the soul, the health, the strength, the housing, workshops, wages, dangerous employments, in a word, all that concerns the wage-earners." 3. Despite the hostility of Liberals, and even "of Catholics who viewed with suspicion the efforts of the laboring classes to form . . . unions, as if

they reflected the spirit of Socialistic or revolutionary agitators," Leo XIII had encouraged the organization of workingmen and employers, either jointly or separately, to draw the two classes more closely together. Thus, a wide variety of Christian workingmen's associations arose which, "though unfortunately still inferior in number to the organizations of Socialists and Communists . . . maintain successfully . . . the rights and legitimate demands of Catholic laborers." In sum, wrote Pius XI, "Leo's Encyclical has proved itself the Magna Charta on which all Christian activities in social matters are ultimately based." After this lengthy encomium, Pius XI reiterated the principle "that it is Our right and Our duty to deal authoritatively with social and economic problems . . . in so far as they refer to moral issues," and, after a vigorous denial of the charge that the Church, by upholding private property rights, upheld "the wealthier classes against the proletariat," continued on "The Reconstruction of the Social Order" as follows.

From PIUS XI, Encyclical: *Quadragesimo Anno: On Reconstruction of the Social Order* (1931) [1]

When We speak of the reform of the social order it is principally the State We have in mind. Not indeed that all salvation is to be hoped for from its intervention, but because on account of the evil of Individualism, as We called it, things have come to such a pass that the highly developed social life which once flourished in a variety of prosperous institutions organically linked with each other, has been damaged and all but ruined, leav-

[1] *Ibid.*, 147-53, 155-57, 166. Reprinted by permission of The Paulist Press.

ing thus virtually only individuals and the State. . . .

Now this is the primary duty of the State and of all good citizens; to abolish conflict between classes with divergent interests, and thus foster and promote harmony between the various ranks of society. . . .

Still another aim must be kept in view. Just as the unity of human society cannot be built upon class warfare, so the proper ordering of economic affairs cannot be left to free competition alone. From this source have proceeded in the past all the errors of the "Individualistic" school [which] . . . teaches that the State should refrain in theory and practice from interfering therein, because these possess in free competition and open markets a principle of self-direction better able to control them than any created intellect. . . . More lofty and noble principles must . . . be sought in order to control this supremacy sternly and uncompromisingly: to wit, social justice and social charity. To that end all the institutions of public and social life must be imbued with the spirit of justice, and this justice must above all be truly operative. . . .

Within recent times, as all are aware, a special syndical and corporative organization has been inaugurated which in view of the subject of the present Encyclical, demands of Us some mention and opportune comment.

The State here grants legal recognition to the syndicate or union, and thereby confers on it some of the features of a monopoly, for in virtue of this recognition, it alone can represent respectively workingmen and employers, and it alone can conclude labor contracts and labor agreements [see pages 794-797]. . . . The corporations are composed of representatives of the unions of workingmen and employers of the same trade or profession, and as true and genuine organs and

institutions of the State they direct and coördinate the activities of the unions in all matters of common interest. Strikes and Lock-outs are forbidden. If the contending parties cannot come to an agreement, public authority intervenes.

Little reflection is required to perceive the advantage of the institution thus summarily described; peaceful collaboration of the classes, repression of Socialist organizations and efforts, the moderating influence of a special ministry. . . . We feel bound to add that to Our knowledge there are some who fear that the State is substituting itself in place of private initiative . . . that the new syndical and corporative institution possesses an excessively bureaucratic and political character, and that notwithstanding the general advantages referred to above, it risks serving particular political aims rather than contributing to the initiation of a better social order.

We believe that to attain this last named lofty purpose . . . there is need before and above all the blessing of God, and in the second place of the coöperation of all men of good will. We believe, moreover . . . that the end intended will be the more certainly attained . . . by men of technical, commercial and social competence, and more still by Catholic principles and their application. . . .

It remains for Us to turn Our attention to the actual condition of the economic order and to its adversary and accuser: We mean Socialism. . . .

Since the time of Leo XIII important changes have taken place both in economic conditions and in regard to Socialism. . . . Not alone is wealth accumulated, but immense power and despotic economic domination is concentrated in the hands of a few . . . frequently not the owners, but only the trustees and directors of invested funds, who administer them at their good pleasure. . . . This concentration of power has led to a three-fold struggle for domination. First, there is the struggle for dictatorship in the economic sphere itself; then, the fierce battle to acquire control of the State, so that its resources and authority may be abused in the economic struggles. Finally, the clash between States themselves. . . .

Socialism, too . . . has undergone profound changes. . . . One section of Socialism has undergone approximately the same change . . . as . . . the capitalistic economic regime has passed: it has degenerated into Communism. Communism teaches and pursues a twofold aim: Merciless class warfare and complete abolition of private ownership. . . . To obtain these ends, Communists shrink from nothing and fear nothing. . . . We do not think it necessary to warn upright and faithful children of the Church against the impious and nefarious character of Communism. . . .

The other section, which has retained the name of Socialism, is much less radical in its views. Not only does it condemn recourse to physical force; it even mitigates and moderates to some extent class warfare and the abolition of private property. It does not reject them entirely. It would seem as if Socialism were afraid of its own principles and of the conclusion drawn therefrom by the Communists, and in consequence were drifting towards the truth . . . for it cannot be denied that its programs often strikingly approach the just demands of Christian social reformers. . . . We pronounce as follows: Whether Socialism be considered as a doctrine, or as a historical fact, or as a movement, if it really remain Socialism, it cannot be brought into harmony with the dogmas of the Catholic Church, even after it has yielded to truth and justice in the points We have mentioned: the reason being that it conceives human society

in a way utterly alien to Christian truth. . . .

Present circumstances, therefore, Venerable Brethren and Beloved Children, indicate clearly the course to be followed. . . . We are confronted with a world which in large measure has almost fallen back into paganism. In order to bring back to Christ these whole classes of men who have denied Him, we must gather and train from amongst their very ranks auxiliary soldiers of the Church, men . . . who with kindly fraternal charity will be able to win their hearts.

THE PAPACY AND COMMUNISM

In 1937, Pope Pius XI, again deploring the materialism of "Bolshevistic and Atheistic Communism" and noting with alarm its spread from Russia into Mexico and other parts of the world, issued a Papal Encyclical to review the Church's opposition to Communism and to call upon all the forces of the Church to combat it.

From PIUS XI, Encyclical: *On Atheistic Communism* (March 19, 1937) [1]

Ever since the days when groups of "intellectuals" were formed in an arrogant attempt to free civilization from the bonds of morality and religion, Our Predecessors overtly and explicitly drew the attention of the world to the consequences of the de-Christianization of human society. With reference to Communism, Our Venerable Predecessor, Pius IX, of holy memory, as early as 1846 pronounced a solemn condemnation, which he confirmed in the words of the *Syllabus* directed against "that infamous doctrine of so-called Communism which is absolutely contrary to the natural law itself, and if

[1] *Ibid.*, 178, 183, 200-01. By permission of The Paulist Press.

once adopted would utterly destroy the rights, property and possessions of all men, and even society itself." Later on, another of Our Predecessors, the immortal Leo XIII . . . defined Communism as "the fatal plague which insinuates itself into the very marrow of human society only to bring about its ruin." With clear intuition he pointed out that the atheistic movements existing among the masses of the Machine Age had their origin in that school of philosophy which for centuries had sought to divorce science from the life of the Faith and of the Church. . . . We, too, have frequently . . . denounced the current trend to atheism which is alarmingly on the increase. . . .

If we would explain the blind acceptance of Communism by so many thousands of workmen, we must remember that the way had been already prepared for it by the religious and moral destitution in which wage-earners had been left by liberal economics. . . .

To priests in a special way We recommend anew the oft-repeated counsel of Our Predecessor, Leo XIII, to go to the workingman. We make this advice Our own, and faithful to the teaching of Jesus Christ and His Church, We thus complete it: "Go to the workingman, especially where he is poor; and in general, go to the poor." The poor are obviously more exposed than others to the wiles of agitators who, taking advantage of their extreme need, kindle their hearts to envy the rich and urge them to seize by force what fortune seems to have denied them unjustly. If the priest will not go to the workingman and to the poor, to warn them or to disabuse them of prejudice and false theory, they will become an easy prey for the apostles of Communism. . . .

After this appeal to the clergy, We extend Our paternal invitation to Our beloved sons among the laity who are doing battle in the ranks of Catholic Action. On another occasion we have called this movement so dear to Our heart "a particularly providential assistance" in the work of the Church during these troublous times. Catholic Action is in effect a *social* apostolate also, inasmuch as its object is to spread the Kingdom of Jesus Christ. . . . The militant leaders of Catholic Action, thus properly prepared and armed, will be the first and immediate apostles of their fellow workmen . . . an invaluable aid to the priest.

4. The Conflicting Forces in the Spanish Civil War

Spain, strikingly industrialized during World War I, exhibited a sorry spectacle of particularism, class cleavage, and political corruption during the years before World War II. Torn between the extremes of conservatism, supported by large landowners, the church, and the army, and extreme proletarianism, backed by a variety of socialists, anarcho-syndicalists, and communists of the new industrial society, and with a vastly underdeveloped middle class of genuinely liberal sympathies, Spanish society exhibited many of the evils of the French pre-Revolutionary Old Regime and of the Russian pre-Revolutionary proletarian extravagancies. In this community of contrasts civil war broke out on July 18, 1936, and continued until March 28, 1939, ending in a victory for the Rightist factions led by General Francisco Franco, whose ultimate success was probably made possible because of material military aid from Fascist Italy and Nazi Germany, a timid neutrality on the part of France and England, and an incapacity on the part of Russia born of geography and unpreparedness. It was promptly followed (April 7) by Spanish adhesion to the German-Italian-Japanese Anti-Comintern Pact and the gradual organization of a fascist regime in Spain. Mr. Lawrence A. Fernsworth, a correspondent for the London *Times* and the *New York Times*, wrote from Barcelona the following analysis of the conflicting forces soon after the Civil War had begun.

From FERNSWORTH, "Back of the Spanish Rebellion" (1936) [1]

Red revolutionists—Anarcho-Syndicalists, Socialists and various brands of Marxists—have made common cause with the government to save Spain from fascism. It is recognized, both within and without the country, that fascism versus popular rule has become the sharply defined issue. But when the revolutionary minded proletariat shall have done with the fascists, they will still have to come to an understanding with the constitutional government. Can Republican constitutional government prosper in Spain or has a proletarian social system, long incubating, settled upon it for an indefinite stay? That is a question which to a foreign observer like myself looms fully as large as the one of fascism versus popular rule. . . . The constitutional government meanwhile is bravely fighting with its back to the wall, hoping to save the Republic as against both fascism and communistic proletarian rule. But the odds against it are heavy. The decision may be long postponed. . . .

First, how did the actual rebellion begin? On Sunday, July 12 [1936], a lieutenant of the shock police, José del Castillo, was assassinated in the streets of Madrid. It was the culmination of a long series of fascist provocations and murders,

openly admitted by fascist spokesmen. They had of course been answered in kind. Similar acts of violence and retaliation had been going on ever since the elections of February 16 last restored a Left government to power. The Left victory was by an overwhelming popular majority. . . . The assassination of Lieutenant del Castillo was answered that same night by the assassination of the monarchist leader and finance minister of the Primo de Rivera dictatorship, Calvo Sotelo. The shock police invaded his home in force . . . and took him away. That was the last seen of him until his body with a mortal bullet wound in the head was delivered to the porter of a Madrid cemetery. Was Sotelo the secret leader of the fascists? . . . The shock police, an organization set up by the Republic in its first year to defend it in an emergency, was certainly convinced that he was.

The killing of Sotelo was followed by a most violent uproar on the part of the fascists, the monarchists and their allies. At his graveside monarchist leaders took solemn oath that his death should be avenged. At a meeting of the permanent commission of the Cortes two days later, there were unbridled speeches, one of the most violent being made by the Catholic Party's leader, Gil Robles, who warned the Government that "responsibility" would overtake "the highest" therein, "and will fall upon the parties which support you in the Popular Front coalition, and will strike the whole parliamentary system and spatter the very regime with mud, with misery and with blood." . . . Four days after this speech was pronounced the garrisons in Spanish Morocco under General Francisco Franco rebelled. The next day saw the uprising on the mainland. . . .

The present uprising is the climax of a revolutionary process which has been under way ever since the proclamation of

[1] Lawrence A. Fernsworth, "Back of the Spanish Rebellion," *Foreign Affairs*, XV (1936), 87-101. By permission of *Foreign Affairs*, New York.

the Spanish Republic on April 14, 1931. Three distinct periods may be noted:

(1) The "first biennium"—the period of pure republicanism; of the adoption of the constitution; of the granting of autonomy to Catalonia . . . of the curbing of the excessive powers and pretensions of the·army; of the separation of church and state; of a series of revolutionary attempts against the Government by the Anarcho-Syndicalists; of trials and errors and tardy rectifications. The first biennium ended in the elections of November 1933, which turned out the Azaña regime and gave power to the Right, acting in combination with the Radical Party bloc.

(2) The "black biennium," the re-actionary period which followed and which lasted until the elections of February 1936. This was the period of waste, of marking time, of corruption, of the undermining of the constitution, of the wrecking of Catalan autonomy, of the glorification of the army, of the suspension or disregard of the religious laws and the replacing of the clergy on the payroll. Finally, it was the period of the Catalan and the Asturias revolutions and of the wholesale and cruel repressions that followed.

(3) The brief period after the recent elections which brought back to power the "pure" Republicans led by [President] Don Manuel Azaña, in agreement with the Socialists and Communists, though not with their participation in the cabinet. These groups together constituted the Popular Front, with a minimum social program accepted by all. This period saw the rehabilitation of the constitution; the abrogation of illegal laws and decrees, the restoration of Catalan autonomy; the liberation of political and social prisoners; the enactment of laws and decrees giving employment to workers and increasing their pay; and the settling of the peasants upon the land in large numbers. It also

saw the development of a fatal circle of violence and retaliations, and finally the loosing of civil war.

The rebellion against the Republic is the work of three main forces united in a well-understood pact, sealed by the fact of mutual and interrelated interests. The forces in question are the privileged and propertied classes, the army and the church.

The privileged and propertied classes have kept the people in misery. That is a fact. The tale of its how and why has been told so frequently that to tell it again now would be mere wearisome repetition. The position of the army, and in even greater degree the position of the church, are not so well known. Indeed, with respect to the church many persons inquire in amazement how it can be that in a Catholic country a Catholic people can turn against the church with as much vehement fury as was ever recorded of Protestants in the old days of church persecutions. The army and the church, therefore, deserve more extensive examination, particularly as regards the positions they took up vis-à-vis the Republic.

But first it may be well to view somewhat more *in extenso* certain aspects of the second of the three revolutionary periods mentioned, the period in which Gil Robles was the moving figure, not only because it is closely linked with the present attitude of the army and the church, but because the maneuvers of that time paved the way for what has now come. The rebellion is the great cry of frustration of all those reactionary elements which had hoped to profit by what was in preparation during the "black biennium." . . .

José María Gil Robles [Quiñones], a professor of law at Salamanca and also a journalist of the staff of the Madrid Catholic paper, *El Debate,* came into prominence a year or two after the advent of the Republic by his organization of a

Catholic party, "Acción Popular," to defend the interests of the church. This party became the principal unit of the CEDA (Spanish Confederation of Autonomous Right Parties). Gil Robles was a monarchist who later, for reasons soon to be seen, finally declared himself to be a republican and became minister of war . . . in 1935. The following extract . . . may serve to throw light on his peculiar mentality:

"For us [he said] Democracy is a transitory means of influencing the politics of the country. . . . When we find ourselves confronted by a reality we seek to procure two things: to derive the greatest benefit from it, and to transform it to our ideology. The present Spanish political system . . . is . . . a supporting base on whatever offers itself to me in order to transform it, and, if necessary, to destroy it. I do not refer to . . . the form of government, but to the problem of the fundamental change of the country." . . .

In 1933 the Pope issued the Encyclical *Dilectissima Nobis,* which . . . stated: "All know that the Catholic Church . . . finds no difficulty in accommodating itself to various civil institutions, be they monarchic or be they republican." Taking this as its cue, the Catholic organ *El Debate,* on December 15, 1933, published an editorial which was meant to be a message to devout Catholics . . . sponsored "political action of the Right," which it defined as "political action of Catholics and as Catholics" . . . henceforth to be the dominant note of "Acción Popular" and its allies. Indeed, Gil Robles . . . was building up his party on fascist lines, with himself as the "supreme chief" whom all should unquestioningly obey. . . .

Gil Robles, in addition to his alliance with the church, entered into an alliance with the army. He glorified it repeatedly in his public speeches . . . a direct bid for the army's favor and support, the more so as while he was at the war ministry . . . [he] curried the good will of the army by reinstating generals and other high officers whom the Republic had dismissed as disloyal, and by procuring for it huge budgetary appropriations. . . .

The Spanish army is a vestige of feudal times, a strangely incongruous institution in this twentieth century. In the Middle Ages there existed various castes, each having its *fueros* or rights and privileges, the *fueros* of the military caste running nip and tuck with those of the church. The officer was a direct representative of the king. . . . An offense against the army was therefore an offense against the king. Officers could not be criticized, much less disobeyed. They were virtually immune from the law as it applied to most citizens.

This sacred character of the Spanish army was maintained under the monarchy; and though somewhat modified under the Republic, the tradition survived. . . . Ex-King Alfonso preferred the company of military men to all others, and their influence over him, and consequently over the government, was great. In his day there was passed the law of jurisdictions which gave to the army authority, not only over offenses committed against its personnel, but over any criticism or comment or action which might be construed as hostile to the king, the state or the regime. Thus republican agitation was a *military* offense. The army became obsessed with the idea that its special mission was to be the "Savior of Spain." It controlled its own internal regime, disciplined refractory members, and intervened in political affairs by means of secret committees called Juntas. These Juntas frequently fomented conspiracies against the government itself. . . .

With the advent of the Republic the power of the army was considerably curbed. The press, radio speakers and public speakers in general were freed from the jurisdiction of military courts. Courts of honor were abolished. The law was laid down that the army must be amenable to civil authority. Officers out of harmony with the new regime were given the opportunity of withdrawing on retirement pay. Many accepted, but the most intransigent monarchists remained to continue their plotting. . . .

The plain fact is that the attempts of the Republic to curb the power of the army . . . constituted a blow to its pride which it could never forgive. And when the Republic's enemies flattered the army with fair words, whispered to it that it was still the anointed "Savior of Spain," it seized the opportunity of salvaging its private interests under the guise of saving the state. . . .

Unpleasant as is the tale of the church's alliance with the Republic's enemies, the facts must be faced; the tale must be told. To do otherwise would be insincere and cowardly. . . .

Popular uprisings against the church in Spain are not new. In 1835 there was a widespread burning of churches and monasteries, one of the principal grievances in that day being the church's excessive holdings of land and wealth in contrast to the misery of the people. But the church "came back," again grew great in power and wealth. Everywhere it again had churches and monasteries enormously rich.

Up to the advent of the Republic there existed a kind of union of church and state which meant that the clergy and the hierarchy were paid from the public treasury; the Bishops were the nominees of the King . . . certain Bishops were members of the Senate; the church had intervention in the national schools for the purpose of teaching religion. In other words, the church was the ally of the state; but the state was regarded by the people as their oppressor. At least, illiterate and hungering masses saw it that way. Moreover, the church constituted a heavy drain upon the economic resources of the country. It was top-heavy with clergy. . . . Let *El Socialista* (April 11, 1936) complete the record of the opposition's complaint against the church:

"The monarchy did nothing but deliver itself over to the intrigues of Rome, whose tendency to exercise temporal power and privilege in the affairs of state is irrepressible. Bishops and parish priests shared political control with governors and mayors. The Papal Nuncio was accustomed to have greater influence than the Prime Minister. There existed the anachronistic situation of two systems of law incompatible with the sovereignty of a lay and indivisible state: the canonical law and the civil law. Religious indifference was deemed an offense against the fatherland. . . . The consequences of this . . . were that the people reacted in equal degree against the church and the monarchy which appeared in umbilical union. Upon the fall of the monarchy there was severed this morbid juncture. The state proclaimed its absolute power in matters of law and laicism. . . . The church, however, has not resigned itself, and its latest offense is that which is represented by the CEDA. . . . We men of earth, respectful of the ecstacies of others, merely ask that the priestly caste do not stir up the rancor of its sheep against our political institutions." . . .

I do not mean to suggest that within the Spanish church organization there were not sincere and self-sacrificing men and women . . . priests, monks and nuns dedicated to the service of humanity. . . . All these sincere and innocent people were the unwitting victims of "the system," of the Spanish church's imprudent procedure, of its absolutism. . . .

Let us now examine briefly the "antichurch" measures to which the Republic had recourse. The hierarchy and the clergy were cut off from the public payroll. They were permitted to exercise their sacerdotal functions as they pleased but were forbidden to earn their livelihood as teachers. Cemeteries were laicized. . . . A special law dissolved the Jesuit order and confiscated its property. Another special law . . . suppressed religious schools, and limited the activities of the religious orders. . . . The third of the trilogy of religious laws provided for the nationalization of church property [that is, "to be the property of the nation"] . . . The nationalization of church property did not mean its confiscation. All such property was left in the possession of the church [but it could not be disposed of as private property; it became the state's trust]. . . . Finally, diplomatic relations with the Holy See were not severed. The Papal Nuncio remained at Madrid. . . .

Nevertheless, the church threw all the weight of its clergy, its press and its amenable followers into the political struggle. There was formed, simultaneously with "Acción Popular," a great organization of laymen, women and children, and even clergy, known as "Acción Católica" . . . an adjunct to "Acción Popular";

and when the elections of 1936 were preparing it boldly flung itself . . . against the Popular Front. . . . Voters were deluged with literature (of which I retain some specimens) informing them that "their consciences did not permit" them to vote for a Left candidate. . . .[1]

Having taken account of the forces engaged in the struggle against the Spanish Republic, one is impelled to draw up the following indictment:

In a moment when a duly elected and constitutional government was fighting, its back to the wall, to save Spanish democracy both from the onslaughts of its enemies of the right and from the excessive demands of revolutionaries of the kind commonly called red, the privileged classes, the army and the church, to salvage their own material interests, deliberately made common cause in an attack upon the government, deliberately unloosed a reign of terror in which both sides have since had an equal share of guilt, deliberately opened the gates to the revolution of untutored and infuriated masses bent upon wiping out democratic government and establishing the supreme domination of the proletariat.

---

40 SOUTHEASTERN EUROPE AND THE NEAR EAST, 1918-1939

1. Dissolution of the Austro-Hungarian Empire

The Dual Monarchy of the Hapsburgs, which had been straining against forces of dissolution since the Revolutions of 1848 [see pages 600-604], broke asunder under the strain of World War I. The Paris Conference, as Charles Seymour shows in the following selection, was not primarily responsible for

[1] A Catholic catechism circulated in Spain at this time included the following—with much more of a similar nature:
"Q. What sin is committed by those who vote Liberal?
"A. Usually, mortal sin."

the breakup; it merely gave the stamp of approval to an accomplished fact. The boundaries drawn for the Hapsburg heirs have been subject, however, to violent criticism and became a contributing factor, especially in the case of Austria and the Sudetenland, in the disturbances leading to World War II. Mr. Seymour, a professor of history at, and after 1937 president of, Yale University, was Chief of the Austro-Hungarian Division of the American Commission to negotiate peace at Paris. His account, which follows, bears the stamp, then, of an eyewitness's testimony.

From SEYMOUR, "The End of an Empire" (1921) [1]

"If Austria did not exist, it would be necessary to create her." This diplomatic aphorism, coined by a member of one of the very nationalities oppressed by the Hapsburgs, had rung in the ears of European statesmen for many decades. It had become almost axiomatic that the union of Danubian territories was essential to the economic welfare and political tranquillity of southeastern Europe. There were few who did not recognize the service performed for Europe by the Hapsburgs in holding together regions naturally interdependent, and in obstructing the advance up the Danube of that internecine strife which has characterized the political habits of the Balkans. The disruption of the Hapsburg empire would threaten economic dislocation at the same time that it would inflame the nationalistic jealousy and ambition of the peoples that had been crushed under the Hapsburg yoke. The

prospect was regarded with a doubt that bordered upon dismay even by the nations that were fighting Austria in the Great War.

But the statesmen of the Peace Conference were confronted by a condition and not a theory. However clearly they recognized the dangers coincident with the disintegration of Austria-Hungary, it was not for them to decide. The question had already been settled by the nationalities of the dying empire, which in the last weeks of the war had set up their own governments, contemptuously brushing away the traditions of centuries. Austria-Hungary as a political entity had crumbled like the one-hoss shay, and the most solemn peace conference imaginable could not put her together again. . . .

The development of revolutionary organization during the war was slow. It came first and most effectively among the Czechs, who organized wholesale desertion of Czech battalions from the Hapsburg armies and the betrayal to the Allies of Austrian military secrets. The Jugo-Slavs were more cautious. Especially after the entrance of Italy into the war they showed themselves suspicious of Allied propaganda, for they feared lest emancipation from the Hapsburg yoke might become simply the first step toward enslavement by Italy. Nor were the Allies anxious, at first, to foster revolution, since the disruption of Austria did not enter completely into their diplomatic plans. But the growing conviction that Austria had become the catspaw of Germany, combined with the disgust of the subject nationalities, resulted in the encouragement and the success of the revolution. In 1918 Czecho-Slovakia was recognized as an independent Allied state. The newly formulated aims of the Jugo-Slavs for independence and union with Serbia were generally approved, and a cordial, though

[1] Charles Seymour, "The End of an Empire: Remnants of Austria-Hungary," in Charles Seymour and E. M. House, eds., *What Really Happened at Paris*, 1921, 87-91, 93-95. By permission of Charles Scribner's Sons, New York.

informal and temporary, understanding with Italy was established.

With the surrender of Bulgaria, the rolling back of the German tide in France, and the defeat of Austrian armies on the Piave the revolution was inaugurated. Irresistibly and with extraordinary quiet it gathered headway. Hapsburg officials and organs of government were not assailed, but simply passed over, and in their place arose the provisional councils representing the nationalities. Within the space of a month the artificial cement that held the empire together had crumbled, loyalty to the emperor had evaporated, and the over-lordship of Germans and Magyars had been cast aside. The Tyrol and Trieste were occupied by Italians; at Prague the new Czecho-Slovak Government was solidified; in Croatia the Jugo-Slavs seized the reins of power and prepared for union with Serbia, while on the coast they took over the Austrian fleet; in Galicia the Poles negotiated with the new national government of Warsaw; in Transylvania the Rumanians were greeted as liberators.

When the peace conference opened, therefore, the empire of Austria-Hungary was a thing of the past. . . . The United States and Great Britain would have been glad to create a federation of the Danubian nationalities which, without the vices that had led to the fall of the Hapsburgs, might have accomplished the economic integration and preserved the political order so essential to the tranquillity and prosperity of southeastern Europe. The suggestion would have been no more effective than a tenor solo in a boiler-shop. The nationalities would have none of it. They had freed themselves, they were instinct with the sense of their own capacity, bursting with nationalistic ambitions, suspicious of any federation as likely to revive the tyranny under which they had so long suffered. The Conference lacked the right, as well as the power, to impose union upon them. By virtue of the principle of self-determination it was for the nationalities to determine their own destiny, and if they preferred disunion no one could deny them. The independent sovereignty of the Czechs had been recognized; the union of the Poles of Galicia with the mass of the nationality in Russia and Germany was generally admitted; the right of Rumania to Transylvania had been acknowledged; and there were few inclined to dispute the union of the Serbs, Croats, and Slovenes of southern Hungary, Austria, and Bosnia, with their kinsmen in Serbia and Montenegro, although the prospect was not hailed with enthusiasm by Italy. . . .

The Peace Conference was, accordingly, placed in the position of executor of the Hapsburg estate. The heirs were generally recognized—Czecho-Slovakia, Poland, Rumania, Jugo-Slavia, the new lesser Austria, lesser Hungary, and Italy. The duty of the Conference was to determine the character of the division. . . .

The hearings took place in Secretary [of Foreign Affairs Stéphen J. M.] Pichon's study in the Quai d'Orsay, with its old pearly gray carpet marked with red roses, its rich Gobelin tapestries, and high French windows opening on to the perfect lawns of the foreign office gardens. In the centre, behind the empire desk, sat Clemenceau, squat, stolid, gray of face, his hands clasped quietly, covered by the eternal gray gloves, on his countenance an expression of bored tolerance. In his cynical wisdom he had never believed that the end of the war would bring the millennium; these nationalistic quarrels seemed to him entirely natural, even though inconvenient. His arid humor, his biting sarcasm displayed in an infrequent question, contrasted with the patient earnestness of President Wilson, who sat upon his right, and to whom, it is not uninteresting to note, the claimants appealed by their manner, if not in form, as the man of justice upon whom their hopes rested. Next to the Americans sat Lloyd George and Balfour, perfect contrast. The British prime minister, consumed with an electric energy, always on the edge of his chair, questioning and interrupting; Balfour, with his long legs outstretched, his head on the back of his chair, eyes not infrequently closed, philosophic in his attitude, completely proof against those sudden gusts of enthusiasm which sometimes assailed his chief. Next, on the right were the Japanese, with features immobile as the Sphinx, enigmatic as the Mona Lisa. Facing Clemenceau sat the Italians: Orlando, florid in manner, eloquent in speech; Sonnino, with eagle features, powerful nose, and jaw set like a vise. In the corners were the secretaries. Behind the principals sat the attachés and experts, with their maps and tables of statistics, whispering corrections of the *ex parte* statements which the delegates of the nationalities presented.

The latter stood or sat before Clemenceau's desk, presenting the particular claims of their newly founded or expanding states. There was the black-bearded [Ion] Bratiano [Bratianu] of Rumania, rather moody, fighting for the treaty of 1916, resentful of opposition. Or, contrasting type, the young and smiling foreign minister of the Czecho-Slovak Republic, Edward Beneš, magnetic in manner, frank in negotiation. He had done much to organize the revolution that swept aside the Hapsburgs and to build up the Czecho-Slovak army in Siberia; his diplomatic skill had combined with the solid honesty of President Masaryk to win the recognition of the Allies for the infant state. Then again the claimant would be the Pole, [Roman] Dmowski, with furrowed visage, clear logic, and power of satire that wounded as effectively, though less ostentatiously, as the scalding invective of Bratiano. [Ignace] Paderewski came to Paris only late in the history of the Conference. There also were the Serbs, the patriarchal Pachitch [Nikola Pašić], with white flowing beard, veteran of many a diplomatic battle in the Balkans, and the smooth-spoken Vesnitch [Milenko Vesnich], both representing the Serbia of old, together with Trumbitch [Ante Trumbich] and Zholger, representatives of the newly freed Austrian Jugo-Slavs.

2. Steps toward Balkan Unity

THE BALKAN CONFERENCES

Before World War I, most of the efforts to give a measure of political unity and economic solidarity to the Balkan peoples originated in the imperialistic designs of non-Balkan states —in the pan-Slavism of Russia, in the political ambitions of the Hapsburg empire, in the economic ambitions of William II's Germany, and so on. After the war, however, a number of promising movements arose in the Balkan states themselves looking toward Balkan economic co-operation, greater social solidarity, and political federation. First in point of time was the organization, in 1920, of the Green International by Aleksandr Stamboliski. This was an attempt to co-ordinate various Peasant parties, especially Stamboliski's Bulgarian Federation of Soil-Tillers, the Croat Peasant party (founded by the Radić brothers, Stefan and Ante), and the Romanian Peasant party (led by Iuliu Maniu), into a vast agrarian co-operative movement leading to a Southern-Slav Federation. The ill success of the Peasant parties in their respective national political arenas, together with the assassination of the principal leaders (Stamboliski in 1923 and Stefan Radić in 1928), limited the achievements of the Green International to educational objectives, chiefly in agricultural improvement. Subsequent movements toward Balkan unity, however, profited from the Green International's beginning. The second movement originated at Athens in 1929, during a session of the Universal Congress of Peace. Alexander Papanastasiou, a former Greek Premier, presided at the Congress and brought to its attention a Greek memorandum which proposed the creation of a permanent institute of Balkan Entente. Pleading union among Balkan peoples, including the new, reformed Turkey [see page 863], Papanastasiou urged the organization of a series of Balkan Conferences to explore the possibilities. The proposal found favor in all Balkan states—though not without hesitation, especially in Albania and Bulgaria, both of which were "dissatisfied" states with respect to territorial boundaries and the disposition of national minorities. The First Balkan Conference opened at Athens, October 5, 1930, with unofficial representatives from Greece, Yugoslavia, Albania, Romania, Bulgaria, and Turkey. Subsequent conferences—four in all—met in Istanbul (1931), in Bucharest (1932), and in Salonika (1933). Though private in character, because governments did not officially participate and were not bound by the decisions, the conferences accomplished much in the way of economic, cultural, and political rapprochement. Despite the explosive problems of national minorities and territorial changes urged by Bulgaria and Albania, the conferences succeeded in setting up permanent machinery for Balkan cooperation, furnished an opportunity for discussion of Balkan questions, and established a number of regional institutions, such as the Press Association, the Medical Union, the Chamber of Commerce and Industry. Unhappily, though further conferences were intended, the creeping paralysis of economic depression, together with communist intrigue (a new kind of Russian pan-Slavism), the diplomatic opposition of Fascist Italy, and the advent of Hitlerism in Germany, led the Balkan states to take a hand directly by introducing a third form of Balkan unity; namely, the Balkan Pact of 1934, a "Little Entente" of four of the Balkan states in the interest of mutual defense and maintenance of the territorial status quo. The following selections are illustrative, first, of the work of the Balkan Conferences, and second, of the Balkan Pact. Immediately following is the "constitution" of the Balkan Conferences drawn up by the six states at the First Conference held at Athens in October, 1930.

From the Statutes of the Balkan Conference (October 12, 1930) [1]

The first Balkan Conference held at Athens, from October 5th to 12th, 1930, decided to establish a permanent organization under the title of "Balkan Conference." It shall be governed by the present Statutes.

Aims of the Conference. Article 1. The aim of the Balkan Conference is to contribute to the *rapprochement* and collaboration of the Balkan peoples in their economic, social, cultural, and political relations, so as to direct this collaboration toward the ultimate establishment of the Union of Balkan States (Albania, Bulgaria, Greece, Rumania, Turkey, and Yugoslavia).

Seat of the Conference. Article 2. The Balkan Conference shall meet in turn in each country.

[1] Reprinted from Theodore I. Geshkoff, *Balkan Union*, pp. 240-45. Copyright 1940 by Columbia University Press.

Organs of the Conference. Article 3. The organs of the Conference shall be: (a) the General Assembly; (b) the Council; (c) the Bureau [of the Assembly] and the Secretariat; (d) the National Groups.

The National Groups of the Conference. Article 4. 1. The delegates at the First Balkan Conference, as well as those who take part in the successive Conferences, shall constitute the National Groups of the Balkan Conference in their own countries. These groups shall endeavor to [advance within their respective states the objects and purposes of the Balkan Conference]. . . .

The General Assembly. Article 5. 1. The General Assembly of the Conference shall meet regularly each year in October on a date fixed by the Council.

2. Three months before that date each National Group shall act in concert with the government of its own country in order to constitute . . . its delegation to the Assembly.

3. Each delegation shall include only thirty delegates, aside from experts and secretaries. . . . [Diplomatic representatives of the Balkan states and observers from the League of Nations and the International Labor Office were invited to attend.]

Article 8. The following six committees shall function within the framework of the Conference: (a) Organization; (b) Political Relations; (c) Intellectual Co-operation; (d) Economics; (e) Communications; (f) Hygiene and Social Policy. . . .

Article 9. The discussions in the Assembly and in the Committees shall be in French. . . .

Article 11. Each delegate shall be entitled to one vote . . . [but] no delegation shall have a total of more than thirty votes. . . .

The Council of the Conference. Article 15. 1. The Council . . . shall consist of the head and two other members of each delegation. . . .

Article 16. The Council shall be the supreme executive organ of the Assembly [that is, of the Conference]. It shall represent the Conference . . . between sessions of the Assembly. . . . It shall fix the precise date and the agenda of the next Assembly. . . .

Secretariat. Article 21. The Secretariat shall consist of the secretary-general and five other secretaries, one appointed by each delegation. It shall be responsible for the correspondence, the publication of the proceedings of the Assembly, the archives. . . . It shall as soon as possible publish a periodical bulletin in French, and all the National Groups shall be invited to contribute to it. . . .

The Finances of the Conference. Article 23. 1. The annual dues of the National Groups shall be fixed by the Assembly. . . .

Final Provisions. . . . Article 25. It shall be the duty of each delegation to do everything possible within its own country for the execution of the resolutions and the accomplishment of the ideals of the Conference.

THE BALKAN ENTENTE (1934)

The Third Balkan Conference, held at Bucharest in 1932, operating without Bulgarian co-operation, drew up a Draft Balkan Pact as a preliminary step to Balkan union. The draft proposed to establish mutual guarantees of non-aggression and to create means for the pacific settlement of disputes that might arise. Nothing materialized directly—although the Draft Balkan Pact was recommended to the various Balkan governments. But in 1934, fearing outside interference in Balkan affairs, and disturbed by Bulgaria's aggressive attitude and Albania's unrest (aggravated by Italian machinations), four Balkan states concluded the following pact, leaving the door open for the future inclusion of the other Balkan states.

From the "Pact of Balkan Entente" (February 9, 1934) [1]

The President of the Hellenic Republic, His Majesty the King of Rumania, the President of the Turkish Republic, and His Majesty the King of Yugoslavia, being desirous of contributing to the consolidation of peace in the Balkans; animated by the spirit of understanding and conciliation which inspired the drawing up of the Briand-Kellogg Pact and the decisions of the Assembly of the League of Nations in relation thereto; firmly resolved to ensure the observance of the contractual obligations already in existence and the maintenance of the territorial situation in the Balkans as at present established; have resolved to conclude a "Pact of Balkan Entente and . . . have agreed upon the following provisions:

Article 1. Greece. Rumania, Turkey, and Yugoslavia mutually guarantee the security of each and all their Balkan frontiers.

Article 2. The High Contracting Parties undertake to concert together in regard to the measures to be taken in contingencies liable to affect their interests as defined by the present Agreement. They undertake not to embark upon any political action in relation to any other Balkan country not a signatory of the present Agreement without previous mutual consultation, nor to incur any political obligation to any other Balkan country without the consent of the other Contracting Parties.

Article 3. The present agreement shall come into force on the date of its signature

[1] League of Nations *Treaty Series*, CLIII, No. 3514, Geneva, 1934, 155-59.

by all the Contracting Parties, and shall be ratified as rapidly as possible. It shall be open to any Balkan country whose accession thereto is favourably regarded by the Contracting Parties, and such accession shall take effect as soon as the other signatory countries have notified their agreement. . . .

[A "Protocol-Annex" to the above Agreement declared that "The Pact of Balkan Entente is not directed against any other Power. Its object is to guarantee the security of the several Balkan frontiers against any aggression on the part of any Balkan State. . . . The Pact of Balkan Entente is a defensive instrument. . . . The maintenance of the territorial situation in the Balkans as at present established is binding definitely on the High Contracting Parties." The pact was to endure for at least seven years.]

3. The New Turkey

MUSTAPHA KEMAL DESCRIBES TURKISH CONDITIONS IN 1919

In October, 1918, the Turkish armies collapsed, the government of Sultan Mohammed VI [1918-22] signed the Armistice of Mudros (October 30), and the Western Allies, in keeping with secret agreements made in 1916, prepared to partition the Ottoman Empire. Allied military commanders took over the administration of Constantinople, and early in 1919 Italian, Greek, and other Allied forces landed in Asiatic Turkey preparatory to division of the spoils of victory. On May 19, Mustapha Kemal (1881-1938) landed at Samsun. Ostensibly an inspector of Turkish armies in Anatolia, he began at once to organize resistance against further dismemberment of Turkey. In the course of a few months he rallied the bulk of the Turkish army and Turkish public opinion, defied the Sultan, organized a series of national congresses, and prepared the way for a new Turkish national state. In a remarkable speech before a Congress of the Republican People's party at Ankara (the speech took six days to deliver, October 15-20, 1927), Mustapha Kemal described the conditions which impelled him to undertake his nationalistic crusade.

From MUSTAPHA KEMAL,
        Speech of October 15-20, 1927 [1]

Morally and materially, the enemy Powers were openly attacking the Ottoman Empire and the country itself. They were determined to disintegrate and annihilate both. The Padishah-Caliph had one sole anxiety—namely, to save his own life and to secure the tranquillity of himself and the Government. Without being aware of it, the nation had no longer any one to lead it, but lived in darkness and uncertainty, waiting to see what would happen. Those who began to understand clearly the terrors and the extent of the catastrophe were seeking some means to save the country, each guided by the circumstances that surrounded him and the sentiments that inspired him. The Army existed merely in name. The commanders and other officers were still suffering from the exhaustion resulting from the war. . . .

Here I must add and explain a very important point. The Nation and the Army had no suspicion at all of the Padishah-Caliph's treachery. On the contrary, on account of the close connection between religion and tradition handed down for centuries, they remained loyal to the throne and its occupant. Seeking

[1] *A Speech Delivered by Ghazi Mustapha Kemal . . . October 1927*, Leipzig, 1929, 15-17.

for means of salvation under the inflence of this tradition, the security of the Caliphate and the Sultanate concerned them far more than their own safety. That the country could possibly be saved without a Caliph and without a Padishah was an idea too impossible for them to comprehend. And woe to those who ventured to think otherwise! . . .

I must mention another point here. In seeking how to save the situation it was considered especially important to avoid irritating the Great Powers—England, France and Italy. The idea that it was impossible to fight even one of these Powers had taken root in the mind of nearly everybody. . . .

Not only the mass of the people thought in this strain, but those also who must be regarded as their chosen leaders shared the same opinion. Therefore, in seeking a way out of the difficulty, two questions had to be eliminated from discussion. First of all, no hostility was to be shown towards the Entente Powers; secondly, the most important thing of all was to remain, heart and soul, loyal to the Padishah-Caliph.

Now, Gentlemen, I will ask you what decision I ought to have arrived at in such circumstances to save the Empire?

As I have already explained, there were three propositions that had been put forward:

1. To demand protection from England;
2. To accept the United States of America as a mandatory Power.

The originators of these two proposals had as their aim the preservation of the Ottoman Empire in its complete integrity and preferred to place it as a whole under the protection of a single Power, rather than to allow it to be divided among several States.

3. The third proposal was to deliver the country by allowing each district to

act in its own way and according to its own capability. Thus, for instance, certain districts, in opposition to the theory of separation, would have to see that they remained an integral part of the Empire. Others holding a different opinion already appeared to regard the dismemberment of the Empire as an accomplished fact and sought only their own safety. . . .

None of these three proposals could be accepted as the correct one, because the arguments and considerations on which they were based were groundless. In reality, the foundations of the Ottoman Empire were themselves shattered at that time. Its existence was threatened with extermination. All the Ottoman districts were practically dismembered. . . . Such expressions as: the Ottoman Empire, Independence, Padishah-Caliph, Government —all of them were mere meaningless words. Therefore, whose existence was it essential to save? and with whose help? and how? . . .

In these circumstances, one resolution alone was possible, namely, to create a New Turkish State, the sovereignty and independence of which would be unreservedly recognized by the whole world.

This was the resolution we adopted before we left Constantinople and which we began to put into execution immediately we set foot on Anatolian soil at Samsun.

TREATY RECOGNITION OF THE NEW TURKEY

For a time Turkey had two competing governments. While the Sultan negotiated from Constantinople with the Allies, and ultimately accepted the abortive Treaty of Sèvres (August 10, 1920), the Nationalists set up a provisional government at Ankara (April 23, 1920) and adopted the Fundamental Law (January 20, 1921), which declared that "The sovereignty belongs to the nation," and that Turkish government resides in the Grand National Assembly elected by manhood suffrage; it also set up a responsible ministry and elected Mustapha Kemal President with wide powers. After a bitter war, Turkish Nationalist forces expelled the Greeks (who had been encouraged by the Allies) and Mustapha Kemal proclaimed the abolition of the Sultanate (November 1, 1922). In the meantime, the Allied position was crumbling. Kemalist Turkey succeeded in negotiating treaties with a number of states, including Italy and France, and between November 20, 1922, and July 24, 1923, the Lausanne Conference concluded peace between the Allies and Nationalist Turkey. The Treaty of Lausanne was a remarkable document, partly because it was the first *negotiated* treaty after World War I between the Allies and a former enemy power, but even more importantly because by its provisions the long contest between the European Powers and Turkey was concluded. The European Powers not only recognized the new Turkey, but also gave up their principal means of interfering in Turkish affairs (see below, Article 28); and Turkey not only agreed to the dissolution of the Ottoman Empire and confined herself largely within her national borders (Article 16), but also gave ironclad guarantees (Articles 37-44) to reform her own institutions and to grant freedom and protection to her non-Moslem minorities such as European powers had repeatedly demanded in the nineteenth century [see pages 686-688, 693-694]. A few of the provisions of this lengthy document read as follows.

From The Treaty of Lausanne
    (July 24, 1923) [1]

Art. 16. Turkey hereby renounces all rights and title whatsoever over or respecting the territories situated outside the frontiers laid down in the present Treaty. . . .

Art. 23. The High Contracting Parties are agreed to recognise and declare the principle of freedom of transit and navigation, by sea and air, in time of peace as in time of war, in the strait of the Dardanelles, the Sea of Marmora and the Bosphorus, as prescribed in the separate Convention signed this day, regarding the régime of the Straits. . . .

Art. 25. Turkey undertakes to recognise the full force of the Treaties of Peace and additional Conventions concluded by the other Contracting Powers with the Powers who fought on the side of Turkey, and to recognise whatever dispositions have been or may be made concerning the territories of the former German Empire, of Austria, of Hungary and of Bulgaria, and to recognise the new States within their frontiers as there laid down. . . .

Art. 28. Each of the High Contracting Parties accepts, in so far as it is concerned, the complete abolition of the Capitulations in Turkey in every respect. . . .

Art. 37. Turkey undertakes that the stipulations contained in Articles 38 and 44 shall be recognised as fundamental laws, and that no law, no regulation, nor official action shall conflict or interfere with these stipulations. . . .

Art. 38. The Turkish Government undertakes to assure full and complete protection of life and liberty to all inhabitants of Turkey without distinction of birth, nationality, language, race or religion.

All inhabitants of Turkey shall be entitled to free exercise . . . of any creed, religion or belief, the observance of which

[1] Great Britain, *Parliamentary Papers,* 1923, XXV, Cmd. 1929, 21, 23, 25, 29-33.

shall not be incompatible with public order and good morals.

Non-Moslem minorities will enjoy full freedom of movement and of emigation, subject to the measures applied . . . to all Turkish nationals . . . for national defence, or for the maintenance of public order.

Art. 39. Turkish nationals belonging to non-Moslem minorities will enjoy the same civil and political rights as Moslems.

All the inhabitants of Turkey, without distinction of religion, shall be equal before the law.

Differences of religion, creed or confession shall not prejudice any Turkish national in matters relating to the enjoyment of civil or political rights, as, for instance, admission to public employments. . . .

Art. 40. Turkish nationals belonging to non-Moslem minorities shall enjoy the same treatment and security in law and in fact as other Turkish nationals. In particular, they shall have an equal right to establish, manage, and control at their own expense, any charitable, religious and social institutions, any schools and other establishments for instruction and education, with the right to use their own language and to exercise their own religion freely therein.

Art. 41. As regards public instruction, the Turkish government will grant in those towns and districts where a considerable proportion of non-Moslem nationals are resident, adequate facilities for ensuring that in the primary schools the instruction shall be given to children of such Turkish nationals through the medium of their own language. This provision will not prevent the Turkish Government from making the teaching of the Turkish language obligatory in the said schools. . . .

Art. 44. Turkey agrees that, in so far as the preceding Articles of this Section affect non-Moslem nationals of Turkey, these provisions constitute obligations of international concern and shall be placed under the guarantee of the League of Nations. They shall not be modified without the assent of the majority of the Council of the League of Nations. . . .

Turkey agrees that any Member of the Council of the League of Nations shall have the right to bring to the attention of the Council any infraction . . . of any of these obligations, and that the Council may thereupon take such action . . . as it may deem proper and effective.

THE GOVERNMENT OF THE NEW TURKEY

About three months after the Treaty of Lausanne, the Grand National Assembly of Turkey at Ankara formally proclaimed the Turkish Republic and unanimously elected Mustapha Kemal its first President. On March 3 following (1924) the Grand National Assembly abolished the Islamic Law (which had been the basis of all law under the Ottoman Empire), declared that "the laying down and execution of law in cases concerning civil transactions in the Republic of Turkey falls within the province of the Great National Assembly of Turkey and the Government which it has constituted." With this act of secularization, the Assembly also passed laws on the same day which stated: "The Caliph is deposed. The office of the Caliph is abolished. . . . The deposed Caliph and all male and female members of the Imperial Family of the now extinguished Ottoman Sultanate . . . are deprived in perpetuity of the right to reside within the boundaries of . . . the Republic of Turkey." Additional Acts deprived members of the imperial family "of the status and rights of Turkish nationality" and transferred their real

properties in Turkey to the nation. On April 20 following, a constitution of the Republic of Turkey was adopted, an elaboration of the Fundamental Law of 1921, prepared largely by Mustapha Kemal himself. With some later amendments, as indicated, it ran as follows.

From the Constitution of the Republic of Turkey (1924) [1]

BASIC PROVISIONS

Art. 1. The Turkish State is a Republic.

Art. 2. The religion of the Turkish State is Islam; the official language is Turkish; the seat of government is Angora. [Amended February 5, 1937, to read: "The Turkish State is republican, nationalist, populist, étatist, laïque, and revolutionist. The official language of the State is Turkish, its capital is the city of Ankara."]

Art. 3. Sovereignty belongs unconditionally to the nation.

Art. 4. The Grand National Assembly of Turkey is the sole lawful representative of the nation, and exercises sovereignty in the name of the nation.

Art. 5. The legislative function and executive power are . . . concentrated in the Grand National Assembly.

Art. 6. The Assembly exercises its legislative function directly.

Art. 7. The Assembly exercises the executive power through the . . . President of the Republic, whom it elects, and through a Cabinet chosen by him. The Assembly controls the acts of the government and may at any time withdraw power from it.

Art. 8. The judicial power is exercised

[1] This and the next selection are from Donald Everett Webster, *The Turkey of Atatürk,* 1939 (Monographs of The American Academy of Political and Social Science, No. 3). By permission of The American Academy of Political and Social Sciences, Philadelphia. This is Appendix D, 297-306.

in the name of the Assembly by independent tribunals constituted in accordance with the law.

SECOND SECTION: THE LEGISLATIVE FUNCTION

Art. 9. The Grand National Assembly
is composed of members elected by the
nation in conformity with the electoral
law. [Legislative elections are held every
four years.]

Art. 10. Every male Turk who has
completed his eighteenth year has the
right to vote in elections to the Parliament.
[Amended December 5, 1934, to include
women and to change the minimum voting age to twenty-one.]

Art. 11. Every male Turk at least thirty
years of age is eligible for election as a
Deputy. [Subsequent articles exclude
traitors, criminals, and illiterates; and Article 11 was amended December 5, 1934,
to include women and to reduce the age
to twenty-two.] . . .

Art. 15. Initiation of legislation rests
with the members of the Assembly and
the Cabinet. . . .

THIRD SECTION: THE EXECUTIVE FUNCTION

Art. 31. The President of the Turkish
Republic is elected by the Grand National
Assembly in plenary session from among
its own membership to hold office during
its own term. He continues to exercise his
function until a new President is elected.
He is eligible for reëlection.

Art. 32. The President of the Republic
is the head of the State . . . he . . . may
not take part in the discussions or in the
deliberations of the Assembly and may
not vote. . . .

Art. 35. The President . . . shall promulgate within ten days of its enactment
any law by the Assembly. The President
. . . must return within ten days any law
which he does not consider worthy of
promulgation, together with a statement
of his reasons, for consideration by the

Assembly; amendments to the Constitution and legislation concerning the Budget
are not subject to the President's suspen-
sive veto. The President is obliged to promulgate any law which is enacted by
majority vote of the Assembly after reconsideration. . . .

Art. 44. The Prime Minister is chosen
by the President of the Republic from
among the Deputies. The other Cabinet
members are chosen from among the
Deputies by the Premier, who, with the
approval of the President . . . submits the
Cabinet list to the Assembly. . . .

Art. 45. The Ministers, under the presidency of the Prime Minister, constitute the
Cabinet.

Art. 46. The members of the Cabinet
are collectively responsible for the general
policies of the government. . . .

Art. 51. There shall be established a
Council of State which shall be called
upon to decide administrative controversies and to give its advice on contracts,
concessions and proposed laws. . . . The
Council of State shall be composed of
persons chosen by the Grand National
Assembly, from among those who have
held important posts, who possess great
experience, who are specialists, or who are
otherwise qualified. . . .

FOURTH SECTION: THE JUDICIAL FUNCTION

Art. 53. The organization, the jurisdiction, and the functions of the courts shall
be determined by law.

Art. 54. Judges are independent in the
conduct of trials and in the rendering of
their judgments. They shall be protected
from any sort of intervention and are
subject only to the law. . . .

FIFTH SECTION: THE COMMON LAW OF THE
TURKS

Art. 68. Every Turk is born free and
free he lives. Liberty consists in the right
to live and enjoy life without offense or

injury to others. The only limitations on liberty—which is one of the natural rights of all—are those imposed in the interest of the rights and liberties of others. Such limitations on personal liberty shall be defined only in strict accordance with the law.

Art. 69. All Turks are equal before the law. . . .

Art. 70. Inviolability of person; freedom of conscience, of thought, of speech, of press; freedom of travel and of contract; freedom of labor; freedom of private property, of assembly, of association; freedom of incorporation, are among the natural rights of Turks.

Art. 71. The life, the property, the honor, and the home of each and all are inviolable.

Art. 72. No one shall be arrested or deprived of his goods and chattels except by due process of law. . . .

[Article 86 provides for the temporary suspension of many of these "natural rights of Turks" by the Cabinet in case of war or conspiracy against the Republic.]

Art. 87. Primary education is obligatory for all Turks and shall be gratuitous in the government schools.

Art. 88. The word "Turk," as a political term, shall be understood to include all citizens of the Turkish Republic, without distinction of, or reference to, race or religion. . . .

SIXTH SECTION: MISCELLANEOUS PROVISIONS

Art. 89. Turkey is divided into vilâyets [provinces], based upon geographic situation and economic relationship. . . .

Art. 90. The affairs of the vilâyets are administered and governed by law, in accordance with the principles of local autonomy and the separation of functions. . . .

Art. 102. Amendments to this Constitution may be made only upon the following conditions: The proposal to amend must be signed by at least one-third of the total number of Deputies. The proposed amendment must be thereafter discussed by the Assembly and adopted by vote of two-thirds of the total number of Deputies.

No proposal to alter or amend Article 1 of this Constitution, specifying that the form of government is a Republic, shall be entertained.

THE PRINCIPLES OF KEMALISM

By the time of his death in 1938, Mustapha Kemal had become not only Turkey's "Strong Man," but also her "Ghazi" ("savior"), the founder of Kemalism ("Perfectionism"), and Atatürk ("father of the Turks"). Of obscure parentage, he had run away from school to attend military college, was given the name of Kemal ("perfection") for excellence in mathematics, was associated with (though was too radical for) the Young Turk movement of 1908 [see page 694], acquired a splendid military record, organized the Nationalist Movement in 1919, and became the founder of the People's party in 1923. With this party behind him— no other was permitted in the Republic, though Atatürk evidently hoped to allow opposition parties after Turkish Republican politics had matured— Mustapha Kemal inaugurated a widespread program of reform to "Westernize" and modernize Turkish society. With freedom from outside molestation and freedom within the new state to develop along scientific, nationalist lines as his two overall objectives, he undertook the dual role of dictator and teacher, abolished wearing of the fez (1925), introduced European clothes, abolished polygamy, emancipated Turkish women, substituted Latin script for

Arabic, and introduced (1926) new law codes based upon European models. His policies, and those of the People's party, came to be summarized under six heads, symbolized by six arrows on the party banner; they were incorporated in the constitution in 1937 and known as Kemalism. These were republicanism (that is, representative government), nationalism, populism (that is, the principle of popular government), étatism (state socialism), laicism (secularism), and revolution (as opposed to evolutionary methods). At the Fourth Grand Congress of the People's party in May, 1935, a program was adopted from which the following extracts constitute an illuminating explanation of the six principles of Kemalism.

From Program of the People's Party (1935) [1]

Introduction. The fundamental ideas that constitute the basis of the Program of the Republican Party of the People are evident in the acts and realizations which have taken place from the beginning of our Revolution until today.

On the other hand, the main ideas have been formulated in the general principles of the Statutes of the Party, adopted also by the Grand Congress of the Party in 1927, as well as the Declaration published on the occasion of the elections to the Grand National Assembly in 1931.

The main lines of our intentions, not only for a few years, but for the future as well, are here put together in a compact form. All these principles which are the fundamentals of the Party constitute Kemalism. . . .

Part II. The Essential Characteristics of the Republican Party of the People. . . . The Republican Party of the People is: (a) Republican (b) Nationalist (c) Popu-

list (d) *Etatist* (e) Secular (f) Revolutionary. a. The Party is convinced that the Republic is the form of government which represents and realizes most safely the ideal of national sovereignty. . . . The Party defends, with all its means, the Republic against all danger.

b. The Party considers it essential to preserve the special character and entirely independent identity of the Turkish social community. . . .

c. The source of Will and Sovereignty is the Nation. The Party considers it an important principle that this Will and Sovereignty be used to regulate the proper fulfillment of the mutual duties of the citizen to the State and of the State to the citizen. . . . It is one of our main principles to consider the people of the Turkish Republic . . . as a community. . . . The aims of our Party . . . are to secure social order and solidarity instead of class conflict, and to establish harmony of interests. . . .

d. Although considering private work and activity a basic idea, it is one of our main principles to interest the State actively in matters where the general and vital interests of the nation are in question, especially in the economic field, in order to lead the nation and the country to prosperity in as short a time as possible. The interest of the State in economic matters is to be an actual builder, as well as to encourage private enterprises, and also to regulate and control the work that is being done. The determination of the economic matters to be undertaken by the State depends upon the requirements of the greatest public interest of the nation. If the enterprise, which the State itself decides to undertake actively as a result of this necessity, is in the hands of private entrepreneurs, its appropriation shall, each time, depend upon the enactment of a law, which will indicate the way in which the State shall indemnify the loss sustained

[1] *Ibid.,* Appendix E, 307-18.

by private enterprise as a result of this appropriation. . . .[1]

e. The Party considers it a principle to have the laws, regulations, and methods . . . of the State prepared and applied in conformity with . . . the fundamentals . . . provided . . . by Science and Technique. . . . The Party considers it to be one of the chief factors of the success of our nation . . . to separate ideas of religion from politics, and from the affairs of the world and of the State.

f. The Party does not consider itself bound by progressive and evolutionary principles in finding measures in the State administration. The Party holds it essential to remain faithful to the principles born of revolutions which our nation has made with great sacrifices.

4. Nationalism and Imperialism in the Near East: The Arabs and Palestine

THE ALLIES SUPPORT ARAB NATIONALISM

Arab nationalism and demand for an Arab state, independent of the Ottoman Empire, became increasingly evident

[1] In a later article, the Party declared further: "Every economic enterprise shall harmonize with united national work as well as with the general interest. This harmony is also the principle in the union of work between the employer and worker. With the Labor Law the mutual relations of workers and employers shall be regulated. Labor conflicts shall be dealt with by means of conciliation, and where this is impossible, through the arbitration of Reconciliation Agencies to be set up by the State. Strikes and lockouts shall be prohibited. We are interested in the life and rights of the nationalist Turkish workers within the framework of these principles. . . .

"The industries which the State or individuals shall establish . . . shall conform to a general program . . . as to render the country an industrial unit. . . . The State shall organize price control."

after 1875. When World War I began and Turkey joined the Central Powers, the Allies were quick to employ Arab discontent for their own strategic advantage. In the main, Arab aid was successfully solicited by the British by means of subsidies and by a series of agreements and understandings marked with suspicious secrecy and strange inconsistencies. Among these understandings one of the most notable was the arrangement with Hussein ibn-Ali, Grand Sherif of Mecca, made by Sir Arthur Henry McMahon, the British High Commissioner in Egypt. In a series of letters in 1915 and 1916—though not made fully public until 1939—the British promised support for an Arab confederacy in the event of the successful prosecution of the war. The gist of this correspondence follows.

From the McMahon-Hussein Correspondence (1915-16) [2]

SHERIF HUSSEIN TO SIR HENRY MC MAHON, JULY 14, 1915

Whereas the whole of the Arab nation without any exception have decided in these last years to live, and to accomplish their freedom, and grasp the reins of their administration both in theory and practice; and whereas they have found and felt that it is to the interest of the Government of Great Britain to support them and aid them to the attainment of their firm and lawful intentions . . . and whereas it is to their (the Arabs') interest also to prefer the assistance of . . . Great Britain in consideration of their geographical position and economic interests, and also of the attitude of the above-mentioned Government . . .

For these reasons the Arab nation see

[2] Great Britain, Parliamentary Papers, 1938-39, XXVII; Miscellaneous No. 3, 1939, Cmd. 5957, 3-14.

fit to limit themselves, as time is short, to asking the Government of Great Britain, if it should think fit, for the approval . . . of the following fundamental propositions. . . .

Firstly. England to acknowledge the independence of the Arab countries, bounded on the north by Mersina and Adana up to the 37° of latitude . . . up to the border of Persia; on the east by the borders of Persia up to the Gulf of Basra; on the south by the Indian Ocean, with the exception . . . of Aden to remain as it is; on the west by the Red Sea, the Mediterranean Sea up to Mersina. England to approve of the proclamation of an Arab Caliphate of Islam. [This area included the whole of the Arabian Peninsula except Aden, together with present-day Iraq, Syria, Transjordan, and Palestine.]

Secondly. The Arab Government . . . to acknowledge that England shall have the preference in all economic enterprises in the Arab countries. . . .

Thirdly. . . . Both high contracting parties to offer mutual assistance . . . to face any foreign Power which may attack either party. Peace not to be decided without agreement of both parties. . . .

Fifthly. England to acknowledge the abolition of foreign privileges in the Arab countries, and to assist . . . in an International Convention for confirming such abolition.

[To this letter Sir Henry McMahon replied on August 30, 1915, to thank the Sherif "for your frank expression . . . of your feeling towards England," to reassert "our desire for the independence of Arabia," and to approve the proposed Arab Caliphate. But as to the boundaries of the new Arab state, Sir Henry felt it "to be premature . . . in discussing such details in the heat of war, and while, in many portions . . . the Turk is up to

now in effective occupation." Sherif Hussein took exception, in his next letter (September 9) to Sir Henry's view regarding boundaries, regretting Sir Henry's "ambiguity" and "coldness" on this point, and insisting that upon these limits the Arabs were united and determined. Sir Henry's next letter ran as follows:]

SIR HENRY MC MAHON TO SHERIF HUSSEIN, OCTOBER 24, 1915

I regret that you should have received . . . the impression that I regarded the question of the limits and boundaries with coldness and hesitation; such was not the case, but it appeared to me that the time had not yet come when that question could be discussed in a conclusive manner.

I have realized, however . . . that you regard this question as one of vital and urgent importance. I have, therefore, lost no time in informing the Government of Great Britain . . . and . . . I communicate to you on their behalf the following statement. . . .

The two districts of Mersina and Alexandretta and portions of Syria lying to the west of the districts of Damascus, Homs, Hama, and Aleppo cannot be said to be purely Arab, and should be excluded from the limits demanded. With the above modification, and without prejudice to our existing treaties with Arab chiefs, we accept these limits.

As for those regions lying within those frontiers wherein Great Britain is free to act without detriment to the interests of her ally, France, I am empowered . . . to give the following assurances and make the following reply to your letter:

(1) Subject to the above modifications, Great Britain is prepared to recognise and support the independence of the Arabs in all the regions within the limits demanded by the Sherif of Mecca.

(2) Great Britain will guarantee the Holy Places against all external aggression and will recognise their inviolability.

(3) When the situation admits, Great Britain will give to the Arabs her advice and will assist them to establish . . . the most suitable forms of government in those various territories [such assistance to be given *only* by British advisers]. . . .

I am convinced that this declaration will assure you beyond all possible doubt of the sympathy of Great Britain towards the aspirations of her friends the Arabs and will result in a firm and lasting alliance, the immediate results of which will be the expulsion of the Turks from the Arab countries and the freeing of the Arab peoples from the Turkish yoke.

[Sherif Hussein, writing November 5, agreed to renounce the vilayets of Mersina and Adena, but insisted that the vilayets "of Aleppo and Beirut . . . are purely Arab." To this statement Sir Henry replied (December 14, 1915) that, as to the vilayets of Aleppo and Beirut, the British took note of the Arab position "but, as the interests of our ally, France, are involved in them both, the question will require careful consideration and a further communication on the subject." The next two letters in the series treated further of the subject. Sherif Hussein wrote (January 1, 1916) that the citizens of Beirut would admit no dismemberment from the proposed Arab state, and that the Arabs did not "care to negotiate with any other Power" but England. However, they were anxious to win the war, and did not wish to "injure the alliance of Great Britain and France." At this point the issue was dropped, so far as this correspondence went, and the remaining letters treat of details of joint prosecution of the war against Turkey and the Central Powers.]

THE BALFOUR DECLARATION (NOVEMBER 2, 1917)

Unhappily, the clarity of the Mc-Mahon-Hussein correspondence was marred by a series of additional more or less secret treaties and agreements. These can best be summarized as follows:

1. Arab leadership was not clearly established. Besides Sherif Hussein, another Arab leader, Abd-al-Aziz ibn-Saud, dominant in Nejd and traditional enemy of Hussein, was courted by the British in order to ensure access to the Anglo-Persian oil fields. Hence arose the peculiar situation in which the British sent arms and ammunition to contending Arab leaders who occasionally used the means afforded to fight each other. In the end, by 1926, Ibn-Saud conquered the Hejaz, forced the abdication of Hussein and his son Ali, proclaimed himself King of the Hejaz and Nejd and, in 1932, changed the name of his kingdom to Saudi Arabia. Meanwhile, however, both Sherif Hussein, principally through his sons, Ali and Faisal—the latter King, first of Syria [1920] and then of Iraq [1921-33], and Ibn-Saud gave material support to the British forces in the Near East campaigns of World War I.

2. By a series of secret treaties and agreements, the Allies (Britain, France, Russia, and later Italy) prepared to partition Ottoman territories in the event of victory over the Turks. To these plans, the national ambitions of the Arabs were decidedly inconvenient, and the clash of interests between France and the Arabs—and therefore between France and Britain—sometimes became acute, the conflict being nurtured by suspicion on all sides created by the secrecy of the negotiations. Thus, for example, the McMahon-Hussein ar-

rangements were not made known to the French, and an agreement made between the British and the French in 1916 was not made known to the Arabs. This was the Sykes-Picot Agreement of May 9, 1916, named after the British negotiator, Sir Mark Sykes, and the French [François Marie Denis] Georges Picot. The agreement provided for the division of the land between the Mediterranean and the Persian Gulf in five zones, part under British control (Haifa and Iraq), part under French (Syria, Cilicia, southern Armenia), part to be internationalized (Palestine), and part (Aleppo, Damascus, and other interior provinces) to be "Independent Arab," under distinct, separate British and French political oversight. No amount of diplomacy could harmonize the Allies' secret agreements with each other and with the Arabs—a fact which led to endless difficulties at the Paris Peace Conference, to repeated revolts in the Near and Middle East against the mandates set up under the League of Nations, to an atmosphere of uncertainty and intrigue, and to occasional outbursts of violence which plagued the entire interwar era and has survived World War II.

3. Parallel to the rise of Arab nationalism in the Near East was the development of Jewish nationalism, especially as pushed forward by the Zionist Organization created in 1897. Inspired by Biblical prophecy, by the Jewish historical claim to Palestine, by opposition to Moslem control over the Promised Land, and by the need created by anti-Semitism for a haven of refuge for oppressed Jews, Zionists set out "to create for the Jewish people a home in Palestine secured by public law." Some Zionists were content to preserve and develop Jewish cultural institutions and to assist their oppressed brethren to colonize in Palestine under the protection of existing political conditions; others, often called "political Zionists," demanded the creation in Palestine of an independent Jewish national state. The object of the latter, however, ran counter to Arab aspirations in geographic, economic, strategic, and political senses—not to include religious and social differences between Jew and Arab. It seems clear, though, that Arab nationalists were both aware of the Jewish ambition and, prior to the McMahon-Hussein correspondence, ready (however reluctantly) to make adjustments as necessary to satisfy the Zionist demands. Unfortunately, the McMahon-Hussein correspondence made no specific provision for Zionist demands in Palestine, and Arab leaders, anxious to follow up every advantage, profess to believe that the British pledged to support the creation of an independent Arab state including Palestine within its territorial limits. But British leaders already were sympathetic to Zionism, and this fact, together with the Christian concern for the Holy Places in Palestine, had led Sykes and Picot, in their secret agreement in 1916, to provide: "With a view to securing the religious interests of the Entente Powers, Palestine, with the Holy Places, is separated from Turkish territory and subjected to a special regime to be determined by agreement between Russia, France, and Great Britain." Czarist Russia, however, in keeping with its anti-Semitic policy, had disapproved of Zionism, and it was not until after revolution had caused Russia to withdraw from the war that Britain and France gave open approval to Zionist aspirations. This approval took the form of the famous Balfour Declaration of November 2, 1917. As early as 1906, Dr. Chaim Weizmann, a prominent chem-

ist and Zionist leader, had interested Arthur James Balfour in Zionism. Now, in 1917, when Balfour was British Foreign Secretary, he and Dr. Weizmann interceded in British governmental circles on behalf of Zionism. With the full previous approval of the United States Government and subsequent approval from the French and Italian governments, the policy was made public in a letter from Mr. Balfour to Baron Edmond de Rothschild, leader of the Zionists in Britain, as follows:[1]

Foreign Office,
November 2nd, 1917

Dear Lord Rothschild,

I have much pleasure in conveying to you, on behalf of His Majesty's Government, the following declaration of sympathy with Jewish Zionist aspirations which has been submitted to, and approved by, the Cabinet: "His Majesty's Government view with favour the establishment in Palestine of a National Home for the Jewish people, and will use their best endeavours to facilitate the achievement of this object, it being clearly understood that nothing shall be done which may prejudice the civil and religious rights of existing non-Jewish communities in Palestine, or the rights and political status enjoyed by Jews in any other country." I should be grateful if you would bring this declaration to the knowledge of the Zionist Federation.

Yours sincerely,
(Signed) Arthur James Balfour

THE MANDATE FOR PALESTINE (1922)

After long delays, inevitable in the tangled situation, Palestine was set up as a Mandate under the League of Nations with Great Britain as Mandatory. The allocation was made by the Supreme Council of the League in April, 1920, but specific terms of the Mandate were not drawn until July 24, 1922, and the Mandate did not go into full operation until September 29, 1923, as the League Council delayed until the French Mandate for Syria could be simultaneously promulgated. Terms of the British Mandate for Palestine ran, in part, as follows.

From the British Mandate for Palestine (1922)[2]

The Council of the League of Nations:

Whereas the Principal Allied Powers have agreed . . . to entrust to a Mandatory . . . the administration of the territory of Palestine . . . and

Whereas the Principal Allied Powers have also agreed that the Mandatory should be responsible for putting into effect the declaration originally made on November 2, 1917, by the Government of His Britannic Majesty, and adopted by the said Powers, in favor of the establishment in Palestine of a National Home for the Jewish people [here follow the provisions of the Balfour Declaration] . . . and

Whereas the Principal Allied Powers have selected His Britannic Majesty as the Mandatory . . . and . . . His Britannic Majesty has accepted the Mandate . . . and . . . it is provided [in the Covenant of the League of Nations, Article 22] that the degree of authority . . . shall be explicitly defined by the Council of the League of Nations . . . [it] defines its terms as follows:

Art. 1. The Mandatory shall have full powers of legislation and of administration, save as they may be limited by the terms of this Mandate.

Art. 2. The Mandatory shall be responsible for placing the country under

[1] *The Times,* London, Nov. 9, 1917, 7.

[2] Great Britain, *Parliamentary Papers,* 1923, XXV, Cmd. 1785, 2-5.

such political, administrative, and economic conditions as will secure the establishment of the Jewish National Home . . . and the development of self-governing institutions, and also for safeguarding the civil and religious rights of all the inhabitants of Palestine, irrespective of race and religion. . . .

Art. 4. An appropriate Jewish Agency shall be recognised as a public body for the purpose of advising and co-operating with the Administration . . . in such . . . matters as may affect the establishment of the Jewish National Home. . . . The Zionist organization, so long as its organization and constitution are in the opinion of the Mandatory appropriate, shall be recognised as such agency. . . .

Art. 6. The Administration . . . while insuring that the rights and position of other sections of the population are not prejudiced, shall facilitate Jewish immigration under suitable conditions and shall encourage, in co-operation with the Jewish agency referred to in Article 4, close settlement by Jews on the land. . . .

Art. 9. The Mandatory shall be responsible for seeing that the judicial system established in Palestine shall assure to foreigners, as well as to natives, a complete guarantee of their rights. . . .

Art. 11. The Administration . . . shall take all necessary measures to safeguard the interests of the community in connection with the development of the country, and . . . shall have full power to provide for public ownership or control of any of the natural resources . . . or of the public works, services, and utilities. . . . It shall introduce a land system appropriate to the needs of the country . . . [and] may arrange with the Jewish Agency [Zionist Organization] . . . to construct or operate . . . any public works, services and utilities, and to develop any of the natural resources. . . .

Art. 13. All responsibility in connection with the Holy Places . . . is assumed by the Mandatory, who shall be responsible solely to the League of Nations in all matters concerned herewith.

THE PALESTINE QUESTION AND BRITISH POLICY (1939)

As Mandatory over Palestine, Great Britain's position was not enviable. Arab leaders, citing the McMahon-Hussein correspondence, demanded all of Palestine as a means of consolidating the Arab states.[1] Political Zionists, on the other hand, bitterly denied the Arab contention and, appealing to the Balfour Declaration, asserted that its words, "a National Home for the Jewish people," clearly presaged the establishment of Palestine as a Jewish National State, "as Jewish as England is English." In an atmosphere charged with such bitterness and disillusionment, and amid a mixed population of Arab and Jew, the actual administration and development of Palestine under the terms of the Mandate posed problems both dif-

[1] As late as 1938, Arab delegates in London argued, "There is no room for doubt that Palestine was in fact and in intention included by both parties in the McMahon-Hussein Correspondence in the area of Arab independence." British spokesmen admitted that "the language in which its exclusion was expressed was not so specific and unmistakable as it was thought to be at the time," but insisted "that the effect of the Correspondence when read in the light of all the surrounding circumstances . . . was to exclude what is now called Palestine from the area in which Great Britain was to recognize and support the independence of the Arabs." Sir Henry McMahon himself stated (1937), "I feel it my duty to state, and I do so definitely and emphatically, that it was not intended by me in giving the pledge to King Hussein to include Palestine in the area in which Arab independence was promised."— "Report of a Committee Set up to Consider Certain Correspondence between Sir Henry McMahon . . . and The Sherif of Mecca in 1915 and 1916," Great Britain, *Parliamentary Papers, 1938-39,* XIV, Cmd. 5974, 5, 7-8, 10.

ficult and delicate. Again and again Britain has sought to placate the opposing parties; Royal Commissions, parliamentary committees, and private investigators have surveyed the situation and made recommendations in vain. In 1937, a Royal Commission headed by William Robert Wellesley, Lord Peel, suggested the partition of Palestine between Jew and Arab, but the British Government, after a year's study of the proposal, rejected it as "impracticable." The next year, in May, 1939, Great Britain issued a new "Statement of Policy" with reference to Palestine. This "Statement of Policy" became the source of much criticism, especially in Jewish quarters, during and immediately after World War II, when the need for a haven of refuge for displaced Jews in Europe was especially severe. In its major provisions, the British "Statement" ran as follows.

From the British "Statement of Policy" (1939) [1]

His Majesty's Government are convinced that in the interests of the peace and well-being of the whole people of Palestine a clear definition of policy and objectives is essential. The proposal of partition recommended by the Royal Commission would have afforded such clarity, but the establishment of self-supporting independent Arab and Jewish States within Palestine has been found to be impracticable. It has therefore been necessary for His Majesty's Government to devise an alternative policy which will, consistently with their obligations to Arabs and Jews, meet the needs of the situation in Palestine. Their views and proposals are set forth below under three heads, (I) The Constitution, (II) Immigration, and (III) Land.

[1] Ibid., 1939, Cmd. 6019, 3-6, 8-12.

I. THE CONSTITUTION. It has been urged that the expression "a national home for the Jewish people" offered a prospect that Palestine might in due course become a Jewish State or Commonwealth. His Majesty's Government do not wish to contest the view, which was expressed by the Royal Commission, that the Zionist leaders at the time of the issue of the Balfour Declaration recognised that an ultimate Jewish State was not precluded by the terms of the Declaration. But, with the Royal Commission, His Majesty's Government believe that the framers of the Mandate in which the Balfour Declaration was embodied could not have intended that Palestine should be converted into a Jewish State against the will of the Arab population of the country. That Palestine was not to be converted into a Jewish State might be held to be implied in the passage from the Command Paper of 1922 which reads as follows: [1]

". . . His Majesty's Government regard any such expectation as impracticable and have no such aim in view. Nor have they at any time contemplated . . . the disappearance or the subordination of the Arabic population, language or culture in Palestine. They would draw attention to the fact that the terms of the (Balfour) Declaration . . . do not contemplate that Palestine as a whole should be converted into a Jewish National Home, but that such a Home should be founded in Palestine."

But this statement has not removed doubts, and His Majesty's Government now declare unequivocally that it is not part of their policy that Palestine should become a Jewish State. It would indeed

[1] This Command Paper (Cmd. 1700) was a formal interpretation of the Balfour Declaration set forth by Winston Churchill, then (1922) Colonial Secretary, both as a guide to British policy and as a reply to the demands of political Zionists. It is often referred to as the Churchill Memorandum.

regard it as contrary to their obligations to the Arabs under the Mandate, as well as to the assurances that have been given to the Arab people in the past, that the Arab population of Palestine should be made the subjects of a Jewish State against their will. . . .

The nature of the Jewish National Home in Palestine was further described in the Command Paper of 1922 as follows:

". . . When it is asked what is meant by the development of the Jewish National Home in Palestine, it may be answered that it is not the imposition of a Jewish nationality upon the inhabitants of Palestine as a whole, but the further development of the existing Jewish community with the assistance of Jews in other parts of the world, in order that it may become a centre in which the Jewish people as a whole may take, on grounds of religion and race, an interest and a pride." . . .

In the recent discussions the Arab delegations have repeated the contention that Palestine was included within the area in which Sir Henry McMahon . . . undertook to recognise and support Arab independence. . . . His Majesty's Government regret the misunderstandings which have arisen. . . . For their part they can only adhere . . . to the view that the whole of Palestine west of Jordan was excluded from Sir Henry McMahon's pledge, and they therefore cannot agree that the McMahon correspondence forms a just basis for the claim that Palestine should be converted into an Arab State. . . .

His Majesty's Government are charged as the Mandatory authority "to secure the development of self-governing institutions" in Palestine. . . . His Majesty's Government are unable at present to foresee the exact constitutional forms which government in Palestine will eventually take, but their objective is self-government, and they desire to see established ultimately an independent Palestine State. It should be a State in which the two peoples in Palestine, Arabs and Jews, share authority in government in such a way that the essential interests of each are secured. . . . An independent State . . . would require such relations between the Arabs and the Jews as would make good government possible. Moreover, the growth of self-governing institutions in Palestine, as in other countries, must be an evolutionary process. A transitional period will be required before independence is achieved, throughout which the ultimate responsibility for the Government of the country will be retained by His Majesty's Government as the Mandatory authority. . . . The objective . . . is the establishment within ten years of an independent Palestine State. . . .

II. IMMIGRATION. . . . Under Article 6 of the Mandate, the Administration of Palestine "while ensuring that the rights and position of other sections of the population are not prejudiced," is required to "facilitate Jewish immigration under suitable conditions." Beyond this, the extent to which Jewish immigration . . . is to be permitted is nowhere defined in the Mandate. But in the Command Paper of 1922 it was laid down that for the fulfilment of the policy of establishing a Jewish National Home

"it is necessary that the Jewish community in Palestine should be able to increase . . . by immigration. This immigration cannot be so great in volume as to exceed whatever may be the economic capacity of the country at the time to absorb new arrivals." . . .

In practice, from that date onwards until recent times, the economic absorptive capacity of the country has been treated as the sole limiting factor. . . .

This interpretation has been supported by resolutions of the Permanent Mandates Commission. But His Majesty's Government do not read . . . that the Mandate requires them, for all time and in all circumstances, to facilitate the immigration of Jews . . . subject only to . . . the country's economic absorptive capacity. . . . If immigration has an adverse effect on the economic position in the country, it should clearly be restricted; and equally, if it has a seriously damaging effect on the political position in the country, that is a factor that should not be ignored. . . . The fear of the Arabs that this influx will continue indefinitely until the Jewish population is in a position to dominate them has produced consequences which are extremely grave for Jews and Arabs alike and for the peace and prosperity of Palestine. . . . His Majesty's Government cannot take the view that . . . they should ignore these circumstances in framing immigration policy. . . .

It has been the hope . . . ever since the Balfour Declaration was issued that in time the Arab population . . . would become reconciled to the further growth of the Jewish National Home. This hope has not been fulfilled. The alternatives . . . are either (i) to seek to expand the Jewish National Home indefinitely by immigration, against the strongly expressed will of the Arab people of the country; or (ii) to permit further expansion . . . only if the Arabs are prepared to acquiesce in it. The former policy means rule by force . . . contrary to the whole spirit of . . . the League of Nations, as well as to the . . . Mandate. Therefore His Majesty's Government . . . have decided that the time has come to adopt in principle the second of the alternatives referred to above. . . .

His Majesty's Government . . . conscious of the present unhappy plight of large numbers of Jews who seek a refuge from certain European countries . . . believe that they will be acting consistently with their Mandatory obligations to both Arabs and Jews . . . by adopting the following proposals regarding immigration:

"(1) Jewish immigration during the next five years will be at a rate which, if economic absorptive capacity permits, will bring the Jewish population up to approximately one-third of the total population of the country. . . . This would allow of the admission . . . of some 75,-000 immigrants over the next five years. These immigrants would, subject to the criterion of economic absorptive capacity, be admitted as follows:

"(a) For each of the next five years a quota of 10,000 Jewish immigrants will be allowed. . . .

"(b) In addition, as a contribution towards the solution of the Jewish refugee problem, 25,000 refugees will be admitted as soon as the High Commission is satisfied that adequate provision . . . is ensured. . . .

"(3) After a period of five years no further Jewish immigration will be permitted unless the Arabs of Palestine are prepared to acquiesce in it." . . .

His Majesty's Government are satisfied that, when the immigration over five years which is now contemplated has taken place, they will not be justified in facilitating, nor will they be under any obligation to facilitate, the further development of the Jewish National Home by immigration regardless of the wishes of the Arab population.

III. LAND. . . . Owing to the natural growth of the Arab population and the steady sale in recent years of Arab land to Jews, there is now in certain areas no room for further transfers of Arab land. . . . In these circumstances, the High

Commissioner will be given general powers to prohibit and regulate transfers of land. . . .

In framing these proposals His Majesty's Government have sincerely endeavoured to act in strict accordance with their obligations under the Mandate to both the Arabs and the Jews. . . . His Majesty's Government cannot hope to satisfy the partisans of one party or the other in such controversy as the Mandate has aroused. Their purpose is to be just as between the two peoples in Palestine whose destinies . . . have been affected by the great events of recent years, and who, since they live side by side, must learn to practice mutual tolerance, good will, and co-operation.

41   THE WESTERN POWERS AND THE FAR EASTERN QUESTION

A full treatment of the "Far Eastern question" lies beyond the scope of this chapter, as it would require an excursion into more than a century of inter-hemispheric relations between East and West and the resultant developments in the Oriental countries. In the present century, however, the Far Eastern question has become a part of the European-world scene, and after World War I it cannot be wholly ignored in treating of European affairs. In consequence, the present chapter is concerned with twentieth-century aspects of the Far Eastern question, prefaced by a short statement of the nature of the problem.

In broad analysis, the Far Eastern question, prior to World War II, was a compound of the imperialistic interests of Western Powers in the Orient, the powers' competition with one another, and the effects of their presence upon the Oriental peoples. Chief among these effects were the Westernizing influences of the imperialistic powers; the emulation of Western imperialism on the part of an awakened, highly nationalistic Japan; and the rise of nationalism in China and among other Asiatic peoples.

Great Britain took the lead in the extension of imperialistic interests in the Far East, followed by the United Netherlands, Russia, France, the United States, Germany, and Italy. Stung by the Chinese Emperor's proud, and seemingly stupid, refusal to treat with the "English barbarians" except as an inferior, tributary people, by the harsh treatment accorded British subjects in China, and by Chinese restrictions upon and corruption in the conduct of trade, the British, during the Anglo-Chinese War (the "Opium War") of 1839-42 and the treaty arrangements which followed, set the pattern for Western penetration in China. Other nations demanded "equal rights," and concessions were subsequently wrung from China in the form of treaty ports, extraterritoriality, customs control, and "spheres of influence," until Chinese sovereignty was weakened, a series of foreign "colonies" practically created states within the Chinese state, and by 1900 China was in serious danger of being partitioned among foreign powers. To obviate this danger, the United States, in 1899-1900, formulated the Open Door policy, which, in the words of Secretary John Hay, was to "preserve Chinese territorial and administrative entity, protect all rights guaranteed to friendly powers by treaty and international law, and safeguard for the world the principle of equal and impartial trade with all parts of the Chinese Empire." To this policy European powers and Japan reluctantly assented. But already, besides the foreign concessions in China proper, imperialistic powers held all the surrounding territory—India, Burma, Indo-China, Malaya, and the East Indies—and Japan held Formosa and was contesting with Russia the control of Korea and Manchurian interests.

Japan, released in 1853 by Commodore Matthew Calbraith Perry and the United States Navy from more than two centuries of self-imposed seclusion, underwent a series of rapid internal changes and, in a remarkably short time, emerged as a new world power. "It was perceived," said the Japanese Minister of Foreign Affairs in 1897, "that in order to attain an equal footing with the Powers it was necessary to change the national institutions, learning, and education." Accordingly, in order to centralize and strengthen the government, the Emperor was restored to power in 1867, and, in an atmosphere of ill-digested liberalism, a constitution was promulgated in 1889. Although the new document nominally changed Japan into a constitutional monarchy, actually it did little more than envelop traditional Japanese political principles in a cloak of deceptive representative institutions; for according to the constitution the Emperor (Mikado) remained hereditary sovereign, combining the offices of high priest, civil ruler, and supreme commander of the army and navy. He was declared "sacred and inviolable," and believed to be "Heaven-descended, divine, and sacred. . . . He has indeed to pay due respect to the law, but the law has no power to hold Him accountable to it."[1] In this theocratic climate, the Imperial Diet, whose consent was constitutionally required for every law, exerted comparatively little real power; and the Mikado, with his hand-picked advisers, reigned, governing through the Ministers of State. Meanwhile, Japan was rapidly industrialized, and, with an army and navy equipped with up-to-date weapons, astonished the world by her speedy defeats of China (1895) and Russia (1905), emerging as a Great Power in the Far East, with Formosa (acquired from China in 1895), a free hand in "independent" Korea (which she annexed outright in 1910), expanding interests in Manchuria, and an ambition to seize exclusive domination in the Far East.

Meanwhile, China, borne down by poverty, internal disunity, and bad government, squirmed in the clutches of foreign powers. Before 1900, however, evidences of regeneration appeared as Chinese nationalism arose. Taking the form of organized clubs, nationalists in China were separated, roughly, into two groups, one determined to expel the "foreign barbarians" from China's shores, the other anxious to reform and modernize China along Western lines. The first group, led by the order of "Righteous Harmonious Fists" (Boxer Clubs), precipitated the unsuccessful

[1] See Marquis Hirobumi Ito, *Commentaries on the Constitution of the Empire,* trans. by Baron Miyoji Ito, 2nd ed., Tokyo, 1906, 6-7 *passim.*

Boxer Rebellion in 1900-01; the second group, led by Dr. Sun Yat-sen, sought to prepare China for constitutional government, to eject the Manchu dynasty, and to set up a republic. This group, though never free from dangerous internal divisions, carried through a successful revolution in 1911, expelled the boy Emperor, Hsüan Tung (he retired in 1912, becoming in private life Henry Pu-yi), and proclaimed the Republic of China.

1. Dr. Sun Yat-sen and the Kuomintang

The leading spirit of the Chinese Republic, and its most revered founder, was Dr. Sun Yat-sen (1866-1925). Born of peasant stock in Kwantung Province in South China, Dr. Sun spent five years of his youth in Honolulu, was later trained in medicine in Hong Kong, but turned to political activity early in his career. His life was marked by a progressive trend toward revolutionary thinking. From 1884 to 1905, he emerged first as an ardent nationalist and advocate of peaceful reform, then (in 1894) as a revolutionist who, by means of revolutionary societies, such as the Revive China party (Hsin Chung Hui) organized in 1894, determined to overthrow the Manchu dynasty and to establish a democratic republic in China with positive social and economic reforms. Between 1905 and 1919, Dr. Sun won world-wide recognition as a leading Chinese revolutionary. He founded the Brotherhood party (Tung Meng Hui) in 1905, carried on propaganda and financial campaigns throughout the Far East, in Europe, and in America, fostered revolutionary attempts to overthrow the Emperor, and finally, when

the revolution was successful in 1911, was elected first President of the Chinese Republic. In an effort mistakenly supposed to contribute to Chinese unity, Dr. Sun resigned his post early in 1912 in favor of an ambitious war lord, Yüan Shih-ḳai—a move which led to serious internal divisions throughout the era of World War I—and later in the same year transformed the Brotherhood party into the Kuomintang, or Chinese People's party, which survived Yüan (who died in 1916) and the confusion of World War II to become the governing party of China. Already, in 1907, Dr. Sun had set forth the "Three Principles of the People" (*San Min* doctrine) of "Nationalism, Democracy, and Livelihood" as the platform of his party. Now, in 1919, he began a nation-wide campaign of propaganda and education in these principles and set out to reorganize the Kuomintang as an instrument for social and economic, as well as political, reform. Like his contemporary in Turkey, Mustapha Kemal, Dr. Sun set himself up as schoolmaster to the nation, culminating forty years' of activity in a whirlwind of lectures and speeches which not only elevated the *San Min* doctrine into the realm of a major social philosophy but also led the Kuomintang to canonize it as the focus of the new Chinese nationalism. In his "Political Testament," written less than three weeks before his death on March 12, 1925, Dr. Sun wrote: "For forty years I have devoted myself to the cause of the people's revolution with but one end in view: the elevation of China to a position of freedom and equality among the nations." [1] More than a year before, the reorgan-

[1] The entire document appears in *An Outline of the Organization of the Kuomintang and the Chinese Government,* The China Information Committee, Chungking, 1940, 14.

ized Kuomintang, at its First National Convention (January, 1924), incorpo rated in its "Declaration" the *San Min* Doctrine, which remains to this day the basic platform of the Chinese Nationalist movement. The "Declaration," prepared by Dr. Sun, consisted of three parts: A. On the Present Situation in China. B. The Principles of Kuomintang. C. The Kuomintang Platform. The first, as it repeats much of the information summarized above, is omitted in the following extract.

From the Kuomintang Declaration (1924) [1]

The principles of the Kuomintang are really the *San Min* Doctrine or the Three Principles of the People as outlined by Dr. Sun. As the faithful execution of these principles is the only way to national salvation, the political platform of the Party is based upon these principles and the entire program of the people's revolution has been determined in accordance with them. . . . We give here . . . a brief summary of the Doctrine to serve as an introduction to our political program for remedying the present Chinese situation.

THE DOCTRINE OF NATIONALISM. The Kuomintang's Doctrine of Nationalism has two implications: the first is the emancipation of the Chinese people, and the second is the equality of all the races within China.

First of all, the purpose of the Kuomintang's Doctrine of Nationalism is to restore liberty and independence to the Chinese people. Before 1911, the Chinese people were governed by the Manchus who, in turn, were not free, but were under the dominant influence of the imperialistic Powers. At that time, the function of the Nationalist movement was,

on the one hand, to free the Chinese people from the Manchu rule, and on the other hand, to prevent the partition of China by the Powers. The first object, namely, the overthrowing of the Manchu rule, was accomplised by the revolution of 1911. But the imperialistic Powers have still kept a dominant influence in China.

Although the danger of political partition seems to be averted, the danger of international control is imminent. In other words, the Powers have substituted for their policy of military conquest a policy of economic exploitation; and the result of imperialistic economic exploitation is the same as the result of military conquest, namely, the loss of independence and liberty on the part of the Chinese people. Not only are the militarists in the country allying themselves with the imperialists, but the capitalist class is also trying to get as much as possible from the common people. Thus, the Chinese people are prevented from making progress in economic activities as well as in political activities.

Seeing the present status of affairs, the members of the Kuomintang feel in duty bound to work for the liberation of the Chinese people from economic and political exploitation. In this struggle, we must have the supprt of the mass of the people including support from the intellectual class, from the farmers, from the workers, as well as from the merchants.

Since Nationalism aims to stop the imperialistic invasion of China, it is a doctrine by which all classes will be equally benefited. Without the realization of the Doctrine of Nationalism, the manufacturers will be forever hindered from achieving economic prosperity and development by the foreign domination of business in China. At the same time, the workers will have to depend for their living upon either foreign capitalists or

[1] Leonard Shihlien Hsü, ed., *Sun Yat-Sen: His Political and Social Ideals*, 1933, 126-41. By permission of the University of Southern California Press, Los Angeles.

Chinese militarists, and so will have to keep on living in a status of slavery.

The motto in the present struggle for national liberation is "Anti-imperialism," because the downfall of imperialism in China will enable the mass of people to organize, to consolidate, and to continue the nationalist struggle. We pray, therefore, for close co-operation between the Kuomintang and the mass of the people in order to enable the Chinese people to regain their real liberty and their independence.

The second aspect of the Doctrine of Nationalism is racial equality. . . . Unfortunately, the present government of China is controlled by the surviving elements of old officialdom who know nothing of racial equality and freedom; and consequently the other races in China are discontented with the present status of affairs. These discontented people have even questioned the sincerity of the Kuomintang's policy of racial equality and racial co-operation. The Kuomintang must convince these people as to the sincerity of its efforts and the honesty of its motive if the party is to carry out the Doctrine of Nationalism. We have over and over insisted upon the common interest of all peoples within China and the necessity of their consolidation in the people's revolution and in solving all interracial problems. We hereby repeat solemnly that we recognize the right of self-determination for all peoples in China, and that a free united Republic of China based upon the principles of free alliance of the different peoples will be established after the downfall of imperialism and militarism.

THE DOCTRINE OF DEMOCRACY. The Kuomintang's Doctrine of Democracy includes direct democracy and indirect democracy. This means that the people will not only have the right of suffrage, but also the rights of initiative, referendum, and recall. Through what channels, and in what ways these rights of the people are to be exercised, will be stated in the constitution. . . .

It has been found that so-called representative governments often have not been truly representative of the people, and that they have been only tools used by capitalists to exploit the common people. According to the Kuomintang's Doctrine of Democracy, the people's rights should be enjoyed by all the people, not by a few privileged individuals only.

It should also be pointed out that the Kuomintang's Doctrine of Democracy is different entirely from the doctrine of natural rights. Our doctrine is based upon the actual needs of the present revolutionary cause in China; for the safety of the nation can be maintained only when all the political power is enjoyed by all the people of the Republic, not by those individuals who are opposed to the Republic and who may use the power to work indirectly against the interest of the nation. In other words, all individuals or organizations sincerely opposed to militarism may enjoy all the direct rights of the people, and all the individuals or organizations who are betraying the nation's interest by working in the interest of the imperialists or militarists will forfeit their rights.

THE DOCTRINE OF LIVELIHOOD. The Kuomintang's Doctrine of Livelihood includes two essential points: first, the equalization of land ownership; and second, the regulation of capital. The greatest cause of economic inequality in society is the private ownership of land. It is necessary, therefore, for the state to enact laws to regulate the ownership of land and the collection of land tax. Land owned by private individuals should be assessed and reported to the government, which will levy the tax according to the value of the land; and, if necessary, buy it from private owners at the assessed rate. This is the essence of the principle of equalization of land ownership.

As to the regulation of capital: big industries such as banks, railways, and steamship lines which can be favorably operated by a monopoly or are of such dimensions as to exceed the power of individual investment, should be managed by the state. In this way, the private capitalists can have no power to interfere with the normal economic life of the people.

We believe that if these two principles are successfully carried out, a sound foundation will have been laid for the solution of the problem of the people's livelihood. We should like to say this to the farmers: China has been and still is an agricultural nation, and of all the classes of people, the agricultural class has suffered the most from economic exploitation.

According to our Doctrine of Livelihood, the state will provide land for cultivation to those farmers who have been deprived of their land or to those who have suffered from their landlords. Irrigation systems will be provided, and colonization schemes will be devised to help those farmers who are without land of their own. Farmers' banks will be established to facilitate rural credits. It is the earnest hope of the Party that everything be done to restore normal happiness to the farmers.

To the workers, the Kuomintang has also a special message. For centuries, the Chinese government has not done anything to ensure the livelihood of the working class. According to our principles, the state should help the unemployed and pass laws to improve the conditions of the laborers. Systems for the relief of the aged, for the care of children, for providing pensions for the disabled, and for providing education for the mass of the people will also be attended to by the Party in order to better the conditions of the less fortunate classes. . . .

Both the farmers and the workers are asked to join the Kuomintang and to give their continuous devotion and efforts to promoting the People's Revolution. Inasmuch as the Kuomintang is opposed to the imperialists and the militarists who are the most dangerous enemies of the workers and farmers, participation in the struggle of the Party is to struggle also for their own interests. . . .

THE KUOMINTANG PLATFORM. In order to secure unified action among the members of the Party and in order to define clearly our objectives in the important task of national salvation and political reconstruction, we present the following platform. As China is facing a crisis in which she is in danger of national extinction, we wish patriotic citizens who put the national interest above personal or factional interest to give their utmost co-operation in carrying out the following provisions:

GENERAL INTRODUCTION. 1. The People's Government will reconstruct the Republic of China in accordance with the *San Min* Doctrine and the Five-Power Constitution.

2. The first step in reconstruction is to promote the economic well-being of the people by providing for their four greatest necessities of life: namely, food, clothing, shelter, and transportation. . . .

3. Next is the promotion of democracy. The Government will educate the people and give them the necessary political training for the exercise of their rights of suffrage, initiative, referendum, and recall.

4. The third step is the development of nationalism. The Government will give assistance to the weaker classes of people and make them capable of self-government and self-determination. At the same time, the Government will resist foreign aggression and revise our treaties with foreign powers so as to re-establish our national independence and international equality.

FOREIGN POLICIES. 1. All unequal treaties, such as those prevailing for the extra-territorial rights of foreign nations, the foreign control of the Maritime Customs, and those that imply an infringement of China's sovereignty by allowing foreign nationals political rights on Chinese territory, should be abolished, and in their place treaties should be concluded which are based on equality and a mutual respect for sovereign rights. . . .

INTERNAL POLICIES. 1. The powers of the Central Government and those of the provincial governments are to be equally distributed. . . .

2. The people of each province may draw up their own constitutions and elect their own governors. The provincial constitutions must not conflict with the national constitution. The provincial governors will be at the head of provincial self-government, while at the same time receiving orders from the central government regarding the execution of national governmental affairs.

3. The hsien, or district, is to be the unit of the people's self-government. The people of every self-governing hsien will have the right of electing and recalling their own officials, and the rights of initiative and referendum in making the laws. . . .

METHODS OF CARRYING OUT THE PROGRAM. 1. The reconstruction program will be divided into three periods: (1) the period of military dictatorship; (2) the period of political tutelage; and (3) the period of constitutional government.

2. During the period of military dictatorship, all political machinery will be placed under the direct control of the military government. . . .

3. When a province has been completely brought within military control, the period of political tutelage begins and the period of military dictatorship ends. During the period of political tutelage, the Govern-ment will send to different hsien qualified experts who have passed satisfactorily the required civil service examinations to assist the people of the different hsien in organizing local self-government. . . .

4. When all the hsien in a province have evolved a working self-government, then the provinces are to pass into the period of constitutional government. . . .

5. At the outset of constitutional government, the Central Government will establish five separate departments to administer the five political functions: namely, the Executive Department, the Legislative Department, the Judicial Department, the Examining Department, and the Board of Control. . . .

6. When the majority of the provinces in the country have reached the period of constitutional government, that is, when these provinces have secured effective local self-government, a People's Conference will be held to consider, promulgate, and adopt the constitution. After the Constitution has been promulgated, the highest political power of the Central Government will be vested in the People's Conference. . . .

7. The promulgation of the national Constitution will end the third period, that is, the period of constitutional government. A national general election will be held in accordance with the provisions of the Constitution. This will be the successful completion of the program of national reconstruction.

2. Japan's Twenty-One Demands on China (1915)

At the outbreak of World War I in Europe in 1914, Japan moved swiftly to take advantage of the powers' occupation with European disputes. As a subsidiary of the Triple Entente, by virtue of the Anglo-Japanese Agreement of 1902,[1] Japan demanded (August 15, 1914) that the German fleet withdraw from Far Eastern waters and that Germany surrender her concessions at Kiaochow. When Germany failed to comply, Japan declared war (August 23), laid siege to Kiaochow, and captured it in early November. Thus possessed of this additional mainland area, Japan immediately sought to enlarge it —to capitalize upon China's internal weakness by demanding the whole of Shantung Province, together with other economic, political, and military concessions. On January 18, 1915, Japan submitted to China the following Twenty-One Demands, obviously intended to subordinate China and to establish Japanese preponderance in the Far East.

From Japan's "Twenty-One Demands" (1915)[2]

Group I [Relating to Japanese succession to German rights in Shantung].

The Japanese Government and the Chi-

nese Government, being desirous to maintain the general peace in the Far East and to strengthen the relations of amity and good neighborhood existing between the two countries, agree to the following articles:

Art. I. The Chinese Government engage to give full assent to all matters that the Japanese Government may hereafter agree with the German Government respecting the disposition of all rights, interests and concessions, which, in virtue of treaties or otherwise, Germany possesses *vis-à-vis* China in relation to the Province of Shantung.

Art. II. The Chinese Government engage that, within the Province of Shantung or along its coast, no territory or island will be ceded or leased to any other Power. . . .

Art. III. The Chinese Government agree to Japan's building a railroad connecting Chefoo or Lungkow with the Kiaochou-Tsinanfu Railway.

Art. IV. The Chinese Government engage to open of their own accord, as soon as possible, certain important cities and towns in the Province of Shantung for the residence and commerce of foreigners. The places to be so opened shall be decided upon in a separate agreement.

Group II [Relating to Japanese concessions in South Manchuria and Inner Mongolia].

The Japanese Government and the Chinese Government, in view of the fact that the Chinese Government has always recognized the predominant position of Japan in South Manchuria and Eastern Inner Mongolia, agree to the following articles:

Art. I. The two Contracting Parties mutually agree that the term of the lease of Port Arthur and Dairen and the term respecting the South Manchuria Railway and the Antung-Mukden Railway shall be extended to a further period of 99 years respectively.

---

[1] This agreement was made prior to the Anglo-French Entente of 1904 [see page 715] when both Japan and Great Britain were eying Russian advances in Asia with suspicion and fear. It provided for mutual recognition of each nation's interests in China and Korea, declared mutual guarantees for the independence and territorial integrity of China and Korea, promised neutrality in case either power became involved in war with a third power "in defense of their respective interests," and mutual assistance in case any fourth power joined "in hostilities against the Ally." The agreement became a source of considerable embarrassment to Great Britain after the Anglo-Russian Entente of 1907 [see page 717] but it was renewed in 1911 in spite of Japan's seizure of Korea in 1910.

[2] James Brown Scott, ed., *The Sino-Japanese Negotiations of 1915,* Carnegie Endowment for International Peace, Division of International Law, Pamphlet No. 45, 1921, 2-8. The Japanese version of the English text is given, as being sufficiently aggressive in tone. By permission of the Carnegie Endowment for International Peace, Washington.

Art. II. The Japanese subjects shall be permitted in South Manchuria and Eastern Inner Mongolia to lease or own land required either for erecting buildings for various commercial and industrial uses or for farming.

Art. III. The Japanese subjects shall have liberty to enter, reside and travel in South Manchuria and Eastern Inner Mongolia, and to carry on business of various kinds—commercial, industrial and otherwise.

Art. IV. The Chinese Government grant to the Japanese subjects the right of mining in South Manchuria and Eastern Inner Mongolia. As regards the mines to be worked, they shall be decided upon in a separate agreement.

Art. V. The Chinese Government agree that the consent of the Japanese Government shall be obtained in advance, (1) whenever it is proposed to grant to other nationals the right of constructing a railway or to obtain from other nationals the supply of funds for constructing a railway in South Manchuria and Eastern Inner Mongolia, and (2) whenever a loan is to be made with any other Power, under security of the taxes of South Manchuria and Eastern Inner Mongolia.

Art. VI. The Chinese Government engage that whenever the Chinese Government need the services of political, financial or military advisers or instructors in South Manchuria or in Eastern Inner Mongolia, Japan shall first be consulted.

Art. VII. The Chinese Government agree that the control and management of the Kirin-Changchun Railway shall be handed over to Japan for a term of 99 years. . . .

Group III [Relating to Japanese interests in Chinese collieries and iron mines].

The Japanese Government and the Chinese Government, having regard to the close relations existing between Japanese capitalists and the Han-Yeh-Ping

Company and desiring to promote the common interests of the two nations, agree to the following articles:

Art. I. The two Contracting Parties mutually agree that when the opportune moment arrives the Han-Yeh-Ping Company shall be made a joint concern of the two nations, and that, without the consent of the Japanese Government, the Chinese Government shall not dispose or permit the Company to dispose of any right or property of the Company.

Art. II. The Chinese Government engage that, as a necessary measure for protection of the invested interests of Japanese capitalists, no mines in the neighborhood of those owned by the Han-Yeh-Ping Company shall be permitted without the consent of the said Company, to be worked by anyone other than the said Company; and further that whenever it is proposed to take any other measure which may likely affect the interests of the said Company . . . the consent of the said Company shall first be obtained.

Group IV [Relating to Chinese territorial integrity].

The Japanese Government and the Chinese Government, with the object of effectively preserving the territorial integrity of China, agree to the following article:

The Chinese Government engage not to cede or lease to any other Power any harbor or bay on or any island along the coast of China.

Group V [Relating to Chinese acceptance of Japanese political, financial, and military advisers].

1. The Chinese Central Government to engage influential Japanese as political, financial and military advisers;

2. The Chinese Government to grant the Japanese hospitals, temples and schools in the interior of China the right to own land;

3. In the face of many police disputes

which have hitherto arisen between Japan and China . . . the police in localities (in China), where such arrangements are necessary, to be placed under joint Japanese and Chinese administration, or Japanese to be employed in police offices in such localities, so as to help at the same time the improvement of the Chinese Police Service;

4. China to obtain from Japan supply of a certain quantity of arms, or to establish an arsenal in China under joint Japanese and Chinese management and to be supplied with experts and materials from Japan;

5. In order to help the development of the Nanchang-Kiukiang Railway, with which Japanese capitalists are so closely identified . . . China to agree to give to Japan the right of constructing a railway to connect Wuchang with the Kiukiang-Nanchang line, and also the railways between Nanchang and Hangchou and between Nanchang and Chaochou;

6. In view of the relations between the Province of Fukien and Formosa and of the agreement respecting the non-alienation of that province, Japan to be consulted first whenever foreign capital is needed in connection with the railways, mines and harbor works (including dockyards) in the Province of Fukien;

7. China to grant to Japanese subjects the right of preaching [Buddhism] in China.

[China was unable to deny all of the Japanese demands. In negotiations extending through 1915, China signed a series of treaties acceding to Group I and most of Groups II and III. However, with reference to Group III, Article 2, China found it impossible to comply, inasmuch as the Han-Yeh-Ping Company was a private corporation. Further, China rejected Group IV as an intolerable restriction upon her sovereignty, although she made a volun-

tary statement "that she would not alienate any portion of her coast line." And lastly, China refused most of Group V on the grounds that these demands conflicted "with the sovereign rights of China, the treaty rights of other Powers, and the principle of equal opportunity." In all, however, China acceded to fifteen of Japan's Twenty-One Demands.]

3. The Washington Conference and the Nine-Power Treaty (1922)

Japan's aggressive policies in China aroused grave apprehension, especially in the United States, which guarded jealously the Open Door policy. In 1917, a Japanese envoy, Viscount Kikujiro Ishii, arrived in the United States to quiet American fears and, if possible, to obtain a modification of the Open Door. The resulting compromise, known as the Lansing-Ishii Agreement (November 2, 1917), satisfied nobody. While Japan agreed to adhere "always" to "the principle of the so-called 'Open-door,'" and renewed her guarantees regarding the "territorial sovereignty in China," the United States also recognized "that territorial propinquity creates special relations" and that "consequently the Government of the United States recognizes that Japan has special interests in China."[1] Subsequent efforts at the Paris Peace Conference failed to loosen Japan's grip on the Asiatic mainland. Indeed, it was not until Far Eastern questions came up for review at the Washington Conference in 1921-22 that the Japanese position was redefined to the greater satisfaction of China and the Western Powers. At this Conference

[1] The Lansing-Ishii Agreement was canceled in April, 1923, after the Nine-Power Treaty rendered it obsolete.

were set forth—besides the Naval Arms Limitation Treaty [see page 906]—a number of highly important resolutions and treaties respecting the Far East. These included:

1. A series of resolutions by Belgium, France, Great Britain, Italy, Japan, The Netherlands, Portugal, and the United States to the effect that: (a) The powers would establish a Joint Commission to inquire into the state of Chinese law and judicial practices and to assist in their further reform with a view to the surrender of extraterritorial rights in China. (b) The powers would limit the use of radio stations set up in China. (c) The powers would withdraw their armed forces from China "whenever China shall assure the protection of the lives and property of foreigners in China."

2. A Sino-Japanese Treaty (February 4, 1922) whereby Japan agreed: (a) To "restore to China the former German leased territory of Kiaochow." (b). To evacuate Japanese troops from Shantung. (c) To transfer to China the Tsingtao-Tsinanfu railway in return for its assessed value plus Japanese improvements. (d) To relinquish exclusive Japanese control over mining rights formerly conceded to Germany in return for joint operation of them by a company chartered by the Chinese Republic, "in which the amount of Japanese capital shall not exceed that of Chinese capital."

3. A "Treaty regarding principles and policies to be followed in matters concerning China," signed February 6, 1922. This settlement, often referred to as the Nine-Power Treaty, was hailed in the United States Senate as "a Magna Carta for China," which provided multilateral guarantees of the territorial and administrative integrity of China and of the Open Door policy. The treaty was ratified by all nine signatories by August 5, 1925.

From the Nine-Power Treaty (1922) [1]

The United States of America, Belgium, the British Empire, China, France, Italy, Japan, the Netherlands and Portugal:

Desiring to adopt a policy designed to stabilize conditions in the Far East, to safeguard the rights and interests of China, and to promote intercourse between China and the other Powers upon the basis of equality of opportunity . . . have agreed as follows:

Article I. The Contracting Powers, other than China, agree:

(1) To respect the sovereignty, the independence, and the territorial and administrative integrity of China;

(2) To provide the fullest and most unembarrassed opportunity to China to develop and maintain for herself an effective and stable government;

(3) To use their influence for the purpose of effectually establishing and maintaining the principle of equal opportunity for the commerce and industry of all nations throughout the territory of China;

(4) To refrain from taking advantage of conditions in China in order to seek special rights or privileges which would abridge the rights of subjects or citizens of friendly States, and from countenancing action inimical to the security of such States.

Article II. The Contracting Powers agree not to enter into any treaty, agreement, arrangement, or understanding, either with one another, or, individually or collectively, with any Power or Powers, which would infringe or impair the principles stated in Article I.

Article III. With a view to applying more effectually the principles of the

[1] The League of Nations, *Treaty Series* XXXVIII, No. 982, 1925, 278-83.

Open Door or equality of opportunity in China for the trade and industry of all nations, the Contracting Powers, other than China, agree that they will not seek. nor support their respective nationals in seeking—

(a) any arrangement which might purport to establish in favour of their interests any general superiority of rights with respect to commercial or economic development in any designated region of China;

(b) any such monopoly or preference as would deprive the nationals of any other Power of the right of undertaking any legitimate trade or industry in China, or of participating with the Chinese Government, or with any local authority, in any category of public enterprise, or which by reason of its scope, duration or geographical extent is calculated to frustrate the practical application of the principle of equal opportunity.

It is understood that the foregoing stipulations of this Article are not to be so construed as to prohibit the acquisition of such properties or rights as may be necessary to the conduct of a particular commercial, industrial, or financial undertaking or to the encouragement of invention and research.

China undertakes to be guided by the principles stated in the foregoing stipulations of this Article in dealing with applications for economic rights and privileges from Governments and nationals of all foreign countries, whether parties to the present Treaty or not.

Article IV. The Contracting Powers agree not to support any agreements by their respective nationals with each other designed to create Spheres of Influence or to provide for the enjoyment of mutually exclusive opportunities in designated parts of Chinese territory.

Article V. China agrees that, throughout the whole of the railways in China,

she will not exercise or permit unfair discrimination of any kind. . . .

The Contracting Powers, other than China, assume a corresponding obligation in respect of any of the aforesaid railways over which they or their nationals are in a position to exercise any control in virtue of any concession, special agreement or otherwise.

Article VI. The Contracting Powers, other than China, agree fully to respect China's rights as a neutral in time of war to which China is not a party; and China declares that when she is a neutral she will observe the obligations of neutrality.

Article VII. The Contracting Powers agree that, whenever a situation arises which in the opinion of any one of them involves the application of the stipulations of the present Treaty, and renders desirable discussion of such application, there shall be full and frank communication between the Contracting Powers concerned.

Article VIII. Powers not signatory to the present Treaty . . . shall be invited to adhere to the present Treaty.

4. The Tanaka Memorial
(July 25, 1927)

Japanese history teems with ambitious schemes of world hegemony. In 1858 Premier Hotta was reported to have advised the Emperor that "in establishing relations with foreign countries the object should always be kept in view of laying the foundation for securing the hegemony over all nations." In 1927 Premier Baron Gi-ichi Tanaka was supposed to have placed before the Emperor a blueprint for conquest whereby, through a policy of "blood and iron," Japanese power might be extended over Manchuria, Mongolia, China, and the United States as a solid beginning for world dominion. First released through Chinese sources, the Tanaka Memorial was disclaimed by the Japanese as a forgery; but subsequent Japanese policy gave a tone of verisimilitude to the document, and, whether forged or not, the Tanaka Memorial exerted a tremendous influence over Far Eastern affairs as the powers came to accept it as a reality. The gist of it is presented through the following extracts.

From *The Tanaka Memorial* (1927) [1]

Since the European War, Japan's political as well as economic interests have been in an unsettled condition. This is due to the fact that we have failed to take advantage of our special privileges in Manchuria and Mongolia and fully to realize our acquired rights. But upon my appointment as premier, I was instructed to guard our interests in this region and watch for opportunities for further expansion. . . . So in order that we may lay plans for the colonization of the Far East and the development of our new continental empire, a special conference was held from June 27th to July 7th. . . . It was attended by all the civil and military officers connected with Manchuria and Mongolia, whose discussions result in the following resolutions. These we respectfully submit to Your Majesty for consideration. . . .

The term Manchuria and Mongolia includes the provinces Fengtien, Kirin, Heilungkiang and Outer and Inner Mongolia. It extends over an area of 74,000 square miles, having a population of 28,000,000 people. The territory is more than three times as large as our own empire not counting Korea and Formosa, but it is inhabited by only one-third as many

[1] Carl Crow, ed., *Japan's Dream of World Empire: The Tanaka Memorial,* 2nd ed., 1942, 22-29, 32-33. Copyright, 1942, by Carl Crow, and reprinted by permission of Harper & Brothers, New York.

people. The attractiveness of the land does not arise from the scarcity of population alone; its wealth of forestry, minerals and agricultural products is also unrivaled elsewhere in the world. In order to exploit these resources for the perpetuation of our national glory, we created especially the South Manchurian Railway Company.

The total investment involved in our undertakings in railway, shipping, mining, forestry, steel manufacture, agriculture, and in cattle raising, as schemes pretending to be mutually beneficial to China and Japan, amount to no less than Yen 440,-000,000,000. It is veritably the largest single investment and the strongest organization of our country. Although nominally . . . under the joint ownership of the government and the people, in reality the government has complete power and authority. In so far as the South Manchurian Railway is empowered to undertake diplomatic, police, and ordinary administrative functions so that it may carry out our imperialistic policies, the Company forms a peculiar organization which has exactly the same powers as the Governor-General of Korea. . . .

Unfortunately, since the European War there have been constant changes in diplomatic as well as domestic affairs. The authorities of the Three Eastern Provinces are also awakened. . . . It has affected the spread of our influence in a most serious way, and has put us to so many disadvantages that the dealings with Manchuria and Mongolia of successive governments have resulted in failure. Furthermore, the restrictions of the Nine Power Treaty signed at the Washington Conference have reduced our special rights and privileges . . . to such an extent that there is no freedom left for us. The very existence of our country is endangered.

Unless these obstacles are removed, our national existence will be insecure and our national strength will not develop. . . .

The result is that while our people cannot migrate into Manchuria as they please, the Chinese are flowing in as a flood. . . . They have jeopardized our acquired rights in Manchuria and Mongolia to such an extent that our annual surplus population of eight hundred thousand have no place to seek refuge. In view of this we have to admit our failure in trying to effect a balance between our population and our food supply. If we do not devise plans to check the influx of Chinese immigrants immediately, in five years' time the number of Chinese will exceed 6,000,000. Then we shall be confronted with greater difficulties in Manchuria and Mongolia.

It will be recalled that when the Nine Power Treaty was signed which restricted our movements in Manchuria and Mongolia, public opinion was greatly aroused. . . . I was sent to Europe and America to ascertain secretly the attitude of the important statesmen toward it. They were all agreed that the Nine Power Treaty was initiated by the United States. The other Powers which signed it were willing to see our influence increase in Manchuria and Mongolia in order that we may protect the interests of international trade and investments. This attitude I found out personally from the political leaders of England, France and Italy. . . .

Unfortunately just as we were ready to carry out our policy and declare void the Nine Power Treaty with the approval of those whom I met on my trip, the . . . Cabinet suddenly fell and our policy failed of fruition. It was indeed a great pity. . . .

For the sake of self-protection as well as the protection of others, Japan cannot remove the difficulties in Eastern Asia unless she adopts a policy of "Blood and Iron." But in carrying out this policy we have to face the United States which has been turned against us by China's policy of fighting poison with poison. In the future if we want to control China, we must first crush the United States just as in the past we had to fight in the Russo-Japanese War. But in order to conquer China we must first conquer Manchuria and Mongolia. In order to conquer the world, we must first conquer China. If we succeed in conquering China the rest of the Asiatic countries and the South Sea countries will fear us and surrender to us. Then the world will realize that Eastern Asia is ours and will not dare to violate our rights. This is the plan left to us by our Emperor Meiji, the success of which is essential to our national existence. . . .

After studying the present conditions and possibilities of our country, our best policy lies in the direction of taking positive steps to secure rights and privileges in Manchuria and Mongolia. These will enable us to develop our trade. This will not only forestall China's own industrial development, but also prevent the penetration of European Powers. This is the best policy possible!

The way to gain actual rights in Manchuria and Mongolia is to use this region as a base and under the pretense of trade and commerce penetrate the rest of China. Armed by the rights already secured, we shall seize the resources all over the country. Having China's entire resources at our disposal, we shall proceed to conquer India, the Archipelago, Asia Minor, Central Asia, and even Europe. But to get control of Manchuria and Mongolia is the first step if the Yamato race wishes to distinguish themselves on Continental Asia.

5. The "Mukden Incident" (1931) and the Lytton Commission Report (1932)

Internal peace and order in China were by no means realized by the reorganized Kuomintang after 1924. The Chinese Communist party, which had been organized in 1921 and which, until 1927, co-operated with the Kuomintang for the realization of Dr. Sun's *San Min* doctrine, made such demands upon the Kuomintang that the latter, in July, 1927, excluded the Communists. The latter immediately rose up in revolt against the Kuomintang-controlled Nationalist government, and General Chiang Kai-shek, as Generalissimo of the Nationalist forces and heir apparent to Dr. Sun's position as leader of the Kuomintang, set out to exterminate the Communists by force. Thus internal strife arose anew in China, to continue, in a complicated ebb and flow, until after World War II.

Nor did the Nine-Power Treaty and the machinery previously set up at the Paris Peace Conference succeed in defending China from further imperialistic aggression and in maintaining peace in the Far East. Taking advantage of China's internal weakness and disorder, Japan, seeking to sidestep the legal restraints imposed by the Covenant of the League of Nations, the Nine-Power Treaty, and the Kellogg-Briand Pact, struck out at Chinese forces in Manchuria in the night of September 18-19, 1931, and quickly extended her control over the whole of Manchuria. China appealed immediately (September 21) to the League of Nations "to take immediate steps to prevent the further development of a situation endangering the peace of nations." After many assurances from both parties of their peaceful intentions (Japan denied any territorial designs upon Manchuria), the League Council won promises of co-operation with a League Commission of Enquiry. This Commission, appointed January 14, 1932, and commonly known as the Lytton Commission, was composed of Lord Lytton (Britain, Chairman), Count Luigi Aldrovandi (Italy), Henri Claudel (France), Major-General Frank Ross McCoy (United States), and Dr. Heinrich Schnee (Germany). The commission was empowered to examine the issues and causes of the dispute and to make recommendations to the League Council for a solution which would reconcile the interests of both China and Japan. Its report, dated September 4, 1932, after the Commissioners had devoted six months to active inquiry in the Far East, is both a splendid résumé of the Sino-Japanese difficulties and an example of the work of the League of Nations in the face of a major threat to world peace. "We have insisted," said the Commissioners, "less on the responsibility for past actions than on the necessity of finding means to avoid their repetition in the future." Nevertheless, the Commissioners could not ignore the complex background of the trouble, as their report demonstrates.

From the Lytton Commission Report (1932) [1]

The events of September 18th, 1931, which first brought the present conflict to the notice of the League of Nations, were but the outcome of a long chain of minor occasions of friction, indicating a growing tension in the relations between China and Japan. . . . The national aspirations of the Republic of China, the expansionist policy of the Japanese Empire, and of the former Russian Empire, the present dissemination of Communism from the U.S.S.R., the economic and strategic needs of these three countries: such matters as these, for example, are factors of funda-

[1] League of Nations, *Report of the Commission of Enquiry*, 1932, Series of League of Nations Publications VII; Official No., C. 663, M. 320, 1932, VII, 13, 38, 67-71, 111, 127, 132-33.

mental importance in any study of the Manchurian problem. . . .

The long list of Japan's rights in Manchuria [leased territory, railway concessions, extraterritorial rights, financial control, and so on] shows clearly the exceptional character of the political, economic and legal relations created between that country and China in Manchuria. There is probably nowhere in the world an exact parallel to this situation, no example of a country enjoying in the territory of a neighbouring State such extensive economic and administrative privileges. A situation of this kind could possibly be maintained without leading to incessant complications and disputes if it were freely desired or accepted on both sides, and if it were the sign and embodiment of a well-considered policy of close collaboration in the economic and in the political sphere. But, in the absence of those conditions, it could only lead to friction and conflict. . . .

On the morning of Saturday, September 19th, the population of Mukden woke to find their city in the hands of Japanese troops. . . . Appreciating the great importance of this occurrence, which, as will be shown, was the first step . . . in the military occupation of practically the whole of Manchuria, the Commission conducted an extensive enquiry into the events of that night. . . .

According to the Japanese versions, Lieutenant Kawamoto, with six men under his command, was on patrol duty on the night of September 18th, practising defence exercises along the track of the South Manchuria Railway to the north of Mukden. They were proceeding southwards in the direction of Mukden. The night was dark but clear and the field of vision was not wide. When they reached a point at which a small road crosses the line, they heard the noise of a loud explosion a little way behind them. . . . The explosion took place at the point of junction of two rails; the end of each rail had been cleanly severed, creating a gap in the line of 31 inches. On arrival at the site of the explosion, the patrol was fired upon from the fields on the east side of the line. . . . [Finding the force large, the Japanese officer telephoned for reinforcements from Battalion Headquarters at Mukden.]

At this moment the south-bound train from Changchun was heard approaching. Fearing that the train might be wrecked . . . the Japanese patrol . . . placed detonators on the line in the hope of warning the train in time. The train, however, proceeded at full speed. When it reached the site of the explosion it was seen to sway and heel over to one side, but it recovered and passed on without stopping. . . . Due at Mukden at 10:30 P.M. . . . it arrived punctually.

Fighting was then resumed. . . . Meanwhile, Lieutenant-Colonel Shimamoto, the Battalion Commander, on receipt of a telephone message, at once ordered [reinforcements to] . . . Lieutenant Kawamoto's patrol. . . . Although his force was then only 500, and he believed the Chinese army in the North Barracks numbered 10,000, Lieutenant-Colonel Shimamoto at once ordered an attack on the Barracks, believing, as he told us, that "offence is the best defence." . . . When the Japanese reached the North Barracks, which were described as glittering with electric light, an attack was made . . . vigorously contested by the Chinese troops within, and there was fierce fighting for some hours. . . . By six o'clock A.M. the entire barracks were captured [and burned] at the cost of two Japanese privates killed and twenty-two wounded. . . . The Japanese stated that they buried 320 Chinese, but only found about 20 wounded.

In the meantime . . . Colonel Hirata

. . . decided to attack the walled city. . . . No resistance was offered, only occasional fighting on the streets, mostly with the Chinese police, of whom 75 were killed. . . . By 3:40 A.M. he had captured it. . . . The arsenal and aerodrome were captured at 7:30. The East Barracks . . . were occupied without fighting. . . . The [Japanese] Chief of Staff received a telegraphic report at 11:46 A.M. . . . giving details of the attack, and orders were immediately sent to the troops at Liaoyang, Yingkow and Fenghuangsheng to proceed to Mukden. The fleet was ordered to leave Port Arthur and proceed to Yingkow and the Commander-in-Chief of the Japanese Garrison Army in Korea was asked to send reinforcements. . . .

According to the Chinese version, the Japanese attack on the Barracks . . . was entirely unprovoked and came as a complete surprise. On the night of September 18th, all the soldiers of the 7th Brigade, numbering about 10,000, were in the North Barracks. As instructions had been received [September 6th] . . . that special care was to be taken to avoid any clash with the Japanese troops in the tense state of feeling existing at the time, the sentries at the walls of the Barracks were only armed with dummy rifles. For the same reason, the west gate . . . which gave access to the railway had been closed. The Japanese had been carrying out night manoeuvres around the barracks. . . . At 7 P.M. on the evening of the 18th, they were manoeuvring at a village called Wenkuantum. At 9 P.M., Officer Liu reported that a train composed of three or four coaches, but without the usual type of locomotive, had stopped there. At 10 P.M. the sound of a loud explosion was heard, immediately followed by rifle fire. This was reported over the telephone by the Chief of Staff to the Commanding Officer, General Wang I-Cheh, who was at his private house situated near the railway, about six or seven miles from the barracks, to the south. While the Chief of Staff was still at the telephone, news was brought to him that the Japanese were attacking the barracks. . . . The Chief of Staff gave orders for the lights to be extinguished, and again reported to General Wang I-Cheh by telephone. The latter replied that no resistance was to be offered. Distant artillery fire was heard at 10:30 o'clock. . . . At midnight, live shells began to fall inside the barracks. . . . The only resistance was offered by the 620th regiment . . . [which] found themselves cut off, and had no option but to fight their way through. . . . This was the only actual fighting that took place in the barracks and was responsible for most of the casualties. . . .

As soon as they were all assembled, the Chinese troops . . . made their way to a village near Kirin. . . . The Japanese residents at Kirin were so alarmed at the approach of the Chinese soldiers that . . . the Chinese turned back towards Mukden. They left their trains 13 miles outside Mukden, separated into nine groups, and marched around Mukden by night. To escape detection by the Japanese, General Wang I-Cheh himself rode through the town disguised as a peasant. In the morning, the Japanese obtained news of their presence and sent aeroplanes to bomb them. They were obliged to lie hidden by day, but continued their march at night. Eventually they reached a station on the Peiping-Mukden railway, and here they were able to order seven trains, which brought them to Shanhaikwan by October 4th.

Such are the two stories of the so-called incident of September 18th as they were told to the Commission. . . . Clearly, and not unnaturally in the circumstances, they are different and contradictory.

Appreciating the tense situation . . . the Commission . . . interviewed as many as possible of the representative foreigners who had been in Mukden at the time. . . . After a thorough consideration of such opinions, as well as of the accounts of the interested parties, and after a mature study of the considerable quantity of written material and a careful weighing of the great mass of evidence . . . the Commission has come to the following conclusions:

Tense feeling undoubtedly existed between the Japanese and Chinese military forces. The Japanese . . . had a carefully prepared plan to meet the case of possible hostilities. . . . On the night of September 18th-19th, this plan was put into operation with swiftness and precision. The Chinese . . . had no plan of attacking the Japanese troops, or of endangering the lives or property of Japanese nationals at this particular time or place. They made no concerted or authorized attack on the Japanese forces and were surprised by the Japanese attack and subsequent operations. An explosion undoubtedly occurred on or near the railroad between 10 and 10:30 P.M. on September 18th, but the damage, if any, to the railroad did not in fact prevent the punctual arrival of the southbound train from Changchun, and was not in itself sufficient to justify military action. The military operations of the Japanese troops during this night . . . cannot be regarded as measures of legitimate self-defence. In saying the above, the Commission does not exclude the hypothesis that the officers on the spot may have thought they were acting in self-defence.

[The Japanese followed up the "Mukden Incident" with a swift military occupation of the whole of Manchuria. Some military operations took place in Inner Mongolia (Jehol), the Japanese insisting that disorders there would endanger the "peace and order" of Manchuria—a circumstance which led the Lytton Commissioners to observe that "an extension of

the area of conflict . . . must be reckoned with." Before the end of 1931 the Chinese forces had retired south of the Great Wall, and Japan was busily organizing "self-government" in Manchuria. The three provinces were combined into one "separate and independent state" which, under the new name of "Manchukuo" set forth a Declaration of Independence on February 18, 1932, and, on March 9th inaugurated Henry Pu-yi, the former Chinese Emperor, as head of the new "state." Meanwhile, the United States had notified (January 7) all signatories of the Nine-Power Treaty that the United States would recognize no Japanese gains won by armed force. Also, the Lytton Commission, convinced that Manchukuo "cannot be considered to have been called into existence by a genuine and spontaneous independence movement," determined to investigate the matter. In the face of considerable danger, the Commissioners toured Manchuria and, despite every obstacle placed in their way by the Japanese (who sought by terroristic methods to prevent the Chinese inhabitants from testifying before the League Commission), gathered evidence [1] which they felt justified the following conclusion:]

After careful study of the evidence presented to us in public and private interviews, in letters and written statements, we have come to the conclusion that there is no general Chinese support for the "Manchukuo Government," which is regarded by the local Chinese as an instrument of the Japanese.

[Further on the Commission noted the following peculiar aspects of the dispute

[1] For example, of 1,550 letters received by the Commission from people in all walks of life in Manchuria, all except two were found to be "bitterly hostile to the new 'Manchukuo Government' and to the Japanese."

and ended its report with suggestions for its solution:]

The dispute has arisen between two States, both Members of the League, concerning a territory the size of France and Germany combined, in which both claim to have rights and interests, only some of which are clearly defined by international law; a territory which, although legally an integral part of China, had a sufficiently autonomous character to carry on direct negotiations with Japan on the matters which lay at the root of this conflict.

Japan controls a railway and a strip of territory running from the sea right up into the heart of Manchuria, and she maintains for the protection of that property a force of about 10,000 soldiers, which she claims the right by treaty to increase, if necessary, up to 15,000. She also exercises the rights of jurisdiction over all her subjects in Manchuria and maintains consular police throughout the country. . . .

It is a fact that, without declaration of war, a large area of what was indisputably the Chinese territory has been forcibly seized and occupied by the armed forces of Japan and has . . . been separated from and declared independent of the rest of China. The steps by which this was accomplished are claimed by Japan to have been consistent with the obligations of the Covenant of the League of Nations, the Kellogg Pact and the Nine-Power Treaty of Washington, all of which were designed to prevent action of this kind. . . . The justification . . . has been that all the military operations have been legitimate acts of self-defence, the right of which is implicit in all the . . . above. . . . Furthermore, the administration [of Manchukuo] . . . is justified in that its establishment was the act of the local population, who, by a spontaneous assertion of their independence, have severed all connection with China. . . . Such a genuine independence movement, it is claimed, is not prohibited by any international treaty or by . . . the League of Nations. . . . It is this plea of justification which makes this particular conflict at once so complicated and so serious. It is not the function of our Commission to argue the issue, but we have tried to provide sufficient material to enable the League of Nations to settle the dispute consistently with the honour, dignity and national interest of both the contending parties. . . .

We suggest, in the first place, that the Council of the League should invite the Governments of China and Japan to discuss a solution of their dispute. . . . If the invitation is accepted, the next step would be the summoning as soon as possible of an Advisory Conference, to discuss and to recommend detailed proposals for the constitution of a special régime for the administration of the Three Eastern Provinces [Manchuria].

Such a conference . . . might be composed of representatives of the Chinese and Japanese Governments and of two delegations representing the local population, one . . . by the Chinese . . . and one . . . by the Japanese Government. If agreed by the parties, the assistance of neutral observers might be secured. . . .

Finally, we suggest that the results of these discussions and negotiations should be embodied in four separate instruments:

1. A Declaration by the Government of China constituting a special administration of the Three Eastern Provinces, in the terms recommended by the Advisory Conference;

2. A Sino-Japanese Treaty dealing with Japanese interests;

3. A Sino-Japanese Treaty of Conciliation and Arbitration, Non-Aggression and Mutual Assistance.

4. A Sino-Japanese Commercial Treaty. . . .

When once these broad principles have

been agreed upon beforehand the fullest possible discretion as regards the details would be left to the . . . Advisory Conference. . . . Further reference to the Council of the League of Nations would only take place in the event of failure to agree.

[The League Assembly approved the Lytton Report on February 24, 1933, and adopted the United States formula of non-recognition of the Japanese conquests in China.[1] But Japan, protesting that she was never conscious of "having transgressed the due limits of the right of self-defense" and that "the movement for the proclamation of the independence of Manchuria was a genuine, spontaneous, popular and natural one," refused to accept the League's invitation and announced (May 27, 1933) her resignation from the League of Nations, to take effect two years later. In this manner, the League's efforts failed, the world acquiesced in the Japanese fait accompli in "Manchukuo," and the first major failure in the system of collective security established at Paris to maintain world peace became a fact— and a grim precedent for warmongering dictators arising in Europe.]

6. The Clash at Marco Polo Bridge and the Beginning of the "Chinese Incident" (1937)

THE CLASH AT MARCO POLO BRIDGE (JULY 7, 1937)

Although the conflict precipitated by the Mukden Incident largely died down in the summer of 1933, Sino-Japanese relations remained strained, character-

ized by constant intrigue and occasional outbursts of violence. In July, 1937, hostilities were renewed on a major, ever widening scale until, after the Japanese attack on Pearl Harbor on December 7, 1941, the Chinese "Incident" merged with World War II. The initial clash of this new conflict took place at Lukouchiao, usually referred to in English as Marco Polo Bridge, less than ten miles from Peiping. A Committee of the League of Nations sifted the evidence and prepared the following account of it.

From "First Report of the Sub-Committee of the Far-East Advisory Committee," October 5-6, 1937[2]

This initial incident occurred at Lukouchiao [Marco Polo Bridge], thirteen kilometres to the southwest of Peiping, between the Chinese garrison and the Japanese troops carrying out night manoeuvres in that district. The Chinese and Japanese versions of the incident differ.

According to the Japanese version, it was the Chinese soldiers . . . who opened fire; a temporary cessation of hostilities was arranged on the morning of July 8 . . . to permit of the immediate opening of negotiations . . . with a view to the settlement of the incident; the Chinese soldiers did not abide by this agreement, nor by the agreement concluded next day for the mutual withdrawal of . . . troops; this aggressive attitude on the part of the Chinese troops rendered vain the . . . [pacific] settlement of the incident. . . .

According to the Chinese version, on the pretext that one of their men was missing, the Japanese troops which were carrying out manoeuvres in the night of July 7th asked permission to enter Wan-

---

[1] Japan had already created additional problems by giving formal recognition to "Manchukuo" on September 15, 1932.

[2] League of Nations, *Official Journal,* Special Supplement No. 177, Geneva, 1937, 38.

ping (Lukuochiao) in order to make investigations; this having been refused, Wanping . . . was attacked by the Japanese infantry and artillery; the Chinese garrison resisted; the situation was aggravated, not by the action of the Chinese troops, which even before the Japanese troops had begun their withdrawal, complied with the agreement for the withdrawal of troops, but by the action of the Japanese troops, which, having received large reinforcements, resumed the offensive . . . extending their operations to the immediate vicinity of Peiping . . . moreover . . . the Japanese army extended its operations in Northern China.

Leaving on one side the obvious discrepancies between these Chinese and Japanese versions of the events, it may be observed that . . . extensive movements of troops were making the situation worse. As a result of the arrival at Tientsin and in the suburbs of Peiping of reinforcements, hastily sent from Manchuria, the Japanese effectives on July 12th, according to Chinese reports, exceeded 20,000 men, and the Japanese Air Force consisted of 100 aeroplanes. It was also announced that troops of the Central Chinese Government were moving north. . . .

At the end of July hostilities began in North China. . . . The Japanese occupied Peiping and Tientsin and seized the railway lines running south which connect these two cities with Central China. A new Government which favoured the Japanese influence was set up in Hopei. The Japanese army then progressed towards the west along the railway which connects Peiping and Sui-yuen through Kalgan and Ta-tung. It also progressed along the frontier between Hopei and Chahar Province; the taking of the Nankow Pass, some 80 kilometres northwest of Peiping, facilitated the penetration of the Japanese Manchurian divisions into Inner Mongolia.

GENERALISSIMO CHIANG KAI-SHEK ON CHINA'S STRATEGIC AIMS (1937)

Japan prosecuted the war in China with vigor, advancing steadily and committing shocking atrocities among the civilian population. Throughout the long contest, however, Generalissimo Chiang Kai-shek, the Chinese Nationalist leader, professed a firm faith in China's ability to survive and in her ultimate realization of Dr. Sun's *San Min* doctrine, for which national survival was an initial step. There follow excerpts from some of his addresses to the Chinese people early in the war. They proclaim not only the Generalissimo's faith in the face of great odds, but also the Chinese over-all plan of defense against the invader.

From CHIANG KAI-SHEK, Address to the Chinese People (1937) [1]

Since the beginning of this war, our total casualties in dead and wounded at the front have been more than three hundred thousand.[2] The loss of civilian lives and property is beyond computation. Such heavy sacrifice is unprecedented in China's history of opposition to foreign aggressors. . . .

In the face of the great crisis confronting us at this moment, there is no use in looking back with vain regrets. If we look ahead . . . we may say that the present situation is definitely favorable to China. The basis of our confidence in China's ultimate success in prolonged resistance is not to be found in Nanking, nor in the big cities or municipalities, but

[1] Chiang Kai-shek, *Resistance and Reconstruction: Messages during China's Six Years of War 1937-1943*, trans. by Albert French Lutley and others, 26-29, 42, 49-50. Copyright, 1943, by Chinese News Service, and reprinted by permission of Harper & Brothers, New York.

[2] This address was delivered December 16, 1937, five months after hostilities had begun.

in the villages, and in the widespread and unshaken determination of the people. Let our fellow-countrymen realize that there is no possible way of avoiding Japan's wanton aggression; let fathers inform their children, and elder brothers encourage the younger ones; then, animated by general hatred of the enemy, our people will erect defenses everywhere. . . . In the present situation you must not be swayed by temporary victories or reverses. Rather you should seek to understand the true meaning of prolonged resistance, and hold firmly to your belief in the ultimate triumph of our cause.

Let me mention briefly a few points for your encouragement. First, the present armed resistance against Japan is an inevitable stage in the progress of China's national revolution. Externally China desires independence, internally she seeks to maintain her existence as a nation; China therefore strives to loose the bonds that bind her people, and to complete the establishment of a new state. This war with all its bitter suffering was bound to come sooner or later. Our war is a war of the Three Principles of the People against the brutal forces of imperialism. It is a war against aggression waged by a people whose land has been invaded, a war for survival and independence. . . .

The present Japanese invasion of China has for its chief objectives not merely the occupation of our territory, the massacre of our people, and the destruction of our culture and civilization, but also the eradication of our Three Principles, and the suppression of our revolutionary spirit. So long as this revolutionary spirit exists, our nation cannot be destroyed. . . .

Fellow-countrymen, you must realize that no nation can free itself from oppression, and bring its revolution to a successful completion, without paying a high price. . . . Suffering cannot be avoided

and it must not be refused. This is what prolonged resistance really means.

In the second place, if we realize that China . . . must fight this war to the very end, then no matter how the present situation may change, we will only press forward, and not on any account stop halfway or surrender. . . . If we submit, there is no hope of our rising again as a nation. . . . We shall perish forever. . . .

The enemy's original plan and hope was to subdue us without having to fight. But from first to last our answer has been to fight back; we have refused to submit. As long as we can hold out, the enemy will never be able to reach his goal. The deeper the Japanese penetrate into the interior, the more they will be forced on the defensive. If they want to occupy the whole four million square miles of Chinese territory, and destroy our four hundred million people, what an enormous army they will have to place in the field! If all our people resolve neither to submit nor to be dismayed; if as one falls, another takes his place . . . Japan's military strength will be completely exhausted, and China will be completely victorious.

[In later addresses, Generalissimo Chiang enlarged somewhat upon the Chinese strategy:]

The Japanese planned originally to fight "a short war with a swift conclusion," while we, a prolonged one in order to exhaust the enemy's strength and thus to win the final victory. . . . The farther they penetrate into China, the stronger is our resistance and the greater their losses. In other words, as the war-fronts extend, the strength of our resistance will increase, whereas our enemy's exhaustion will be aggravated. . . . From the beginning, our plan has been to establish the bases of our resistance . . . in the vast interior. In accordance with the military strategy and policy consistently pursued by our government, our western provinces are the real base of our resistance. [In

November, 1937, the National Government transferred its capital to Chungking, in the western province of Szechwan.]

42   INTERNATIONAL RELATIONS BETWEEN WORLD WARS, 1920-1939

1. The Diplomatic Search for Security, 1920-1930

A demand for peace and security was universal in the war-weary world of 1920. But unfortunately national views as to what constituted *security* differed so sharply as to jeopardize *peace*. For example, France's idea of security required a weak, disunited, friendless Germany, whose future was mortgaged with heavy reparation payments; Britain's view of security demanded a revival of trade, for which a measure of German prosperity and purchasing power was anticipated; and Germany's concept of security cried out for modification of the Versailles Treaty, ostensibly to make it conformable to the Fourteen Points upon which it was to have been founded, but actually to remove the economic, political, territorial, and military restrictions imposed by the treaty in order that Germany might pursue her national aims on a parity with other powers. Around the fear and hatred between France and Germany centered much of the diplomacy of the interwar years. Over and beyond this focal point, however, a world-wide fear and detestation of Communism overlay the diplomatic scene—a fear which, outside Russia, was

slow to mitigate in the face of economic difficulties and depression conditions that fostered the Third International's efforts to organize a Communist party in every country. Throughout the interwar years the diplomatic search for security was colored at nearly every point either by the conflicting ambitions of France and Germany or by the fear of Communism.

The methods by which European nations sought to ensure peace and security likewise varied. Collective security, that is, the settlement of international disputes by an appeal to law through a "World Court," and the maintenance of world peace by collective action, was the ideal of the League of Nations. But the structure was weakened at the outset by the failure to include the erstwhile enemy powers, by the exclusion of Soviet Russia, and by the failure of the United States to adhere to the Versailles settlement. Moreover, France, and some other states, had co-operated with misgivings in the creation of the League, and they had little faith in the effectiveness of League machinery for the guarantee of their own national security. Accordingly, with the failure of the Anglo-American treaty proposed at Paris to guarantee assistance to France in case of an unprovoked German attack [see page 736], France turned at once to the age-old method of seeking security by alliances. Indeed, as early as September, 1920, France had entered into a "military understanding" with Belgium. Like most of the French agreements to follow, this "understanding" asserted that its object was "to reinforce the guarantees of peace and security resulting from the Covenant of the League of Nations." The following letter, sent by Belgian officials to Alexandre Millerand, the French Foreign Minister, tells of the Franco-Belgian entente; Millerand's reply, dated five days later, was in practically the same words.

THE FRANCO-BELGIAN ENTENTE (1920)

From the Belgian Letter Confirming the Understanding [1]

Brussels, Sept. 10, 1920

His Excellency M. Millerand,
    President of the Council,
Minister of Foreign Affairs, Paris.

Excellency: We have the honour to inform your Excellency that the Belgian Government gives its approval to the Military Understanding, the text of which was signed September 7, 1920, by Marshal Foch, General Maglinse, Chief of Staff of the Belgian Army, and General Buat, Chief of Staff of the French Army, designated for this purpose by their respective Governments.

The object of this understanding is to reinforce the guarantees of peace and security resulting from the Covenant of the League of Nations.

It is recognized as a matter of course that the two States retain undiminished their rights of sovereignty in respect of the imposition of military burdens upon their respective countries and in regard to determining in each case whether the eventuality contemplated by the present understanding has in fact arisen. . . .

(Signed) Paul Emile Janson, *Minister of National Defense*
(Signed) Delacroix, *Prime Minister*

THE FRANCO-POLISH AGREEMENT (1921)

A second step in France's new security-by-alliance policy was her Political Agreement with the new Polish state signed at Paris on February 19, 1921. A defensive agreement "in accordance with the Covenant of the League of Nations," the accord held great strategic value for both signatories. It read as follows.

From the Franco-Polish Political Agreement (1921) [2]

The Polish Government and the French Government, both desirous of safeguarding, by the maintenance of the Treaties which both have signed or which may in future be recognized by both Parties, the peace of Europe, the security of their territories and their common political and economic interests, have agreed as follows:

1. In order to co-ordinate their endeavours towards peace, the two Governments undertake to consult each other on all questions of foreign policy which concern both States, so far as those questions affect the settlement of international relations in the spirit of the Treaties and in accordance with the Covenant of the League of Nations.

2. . . . The two Governments . . . will endeavour to develop their economic relations, and for this purpose will conclude

---

[1] League of Nations, *Treaty Series*, 1920, II, 2, 128-29.

[2] *Ibid.*, 1923, XVIII (No. 449), 13.

special agreements and a Commercial Treaty.

3. If, notwithstanding the sincerely peaceful views and intentions of the two Contracting States, either or both of them should be attacked without giving provocation, the two Governments shall take concerted measures for the defence of their territory and the protection of their legitimate interests, within the limits specified in the preamble.

4. The two Governments undertake to consult each other before concluding new agreements which will affect their policy in Central and Eastern Europe.

THE LITTLE ENTENTE TREATIES, 1920 AND BEYOND

While the Paris Conference was in session, leaders of the "succession states" of the erstwhile Hapsburg empire—especially Masaryk and Beneš of Czechoslovakia, Take Ionescu of Romania, and Ninčić of Yugoslavia—made plans for their future co-operation and mutual defense. Activated by the desire to preserve their security against hostile powers (especially, in the early 1920's, against Hungary, Bulgaria, and Soviet Russia), to prevent the restoration of the Hapsburgs, to promote political and economic co-operation for their mutual welfare, to establish and maintain internal order, and to consolidate the gains of their common revolution against the old regime, they negotiated a web of interlocking treaties which bound Czechoslovakia, Romania, and Yugoslavia (then known as the Kingdom of the Serbs, Croats and Slovenes) in a regional alliance commonly known as the Little Entente. In a short time the Little Entente expanded, and a cluster of affiliates developed, including Poland, France, Greece, and other states.

The first three agreements by which the Little Entente was inaugurated were practically identical in terminology. They were Conventions of Defensive Alliance between: 1. The Kingdom of the Serbs, Croats, and Slovenes and Czechoslovakia, August 14, 1920; (2) The Kingdom of Romania and Czechoslovakia, April 23, 1921; and (3) The Kingdom of Romania and the Kingdom of the Serbs, Croats, and Slovenes, June 7, 1921. Each of them was to be valid for two years, although—as will be noted—they were extended and enlarged before their expiration. The first of the series, with the addition of Article 4 from the next two, will serve to illustrate them all.

From "The Convention of Defensive Alliance between the Kingdom of the Serbs, Croats and Slovenes and the Czecho-slovak Republic," Belgrade, August 14, 1920 [1]

Firmly resolved to maintain the Peace obtained by so many sacrifices, and provided for by the Covenant of the League of Nations, as well as the situation created by the Treaty concluded at Trianon on June 4, 1920, between the Allied and Associated Powers . . . and Hungary, the President of the Czechoslovak Republic and His Majesty, the King of the Serbs, Croats and Slovenes have agreed to conclude a defensive Convention. . . .

Art. 1. In case of an unprovoked attack on the part of Hungary against one of the High Contracting Parties, the other Party agrees to assist in the defence of the Party attacked, in the manner laid down . . . in Article 2 of the present Convention:

Art. 2. The competent Technical Au-

[1] *Ibid.*, 1921, VI (No. 154), 211-13.

thorities . . . [of both parties] shall decide, by mutual agreement, upon the provisions necessary for the execution of the present Convention.

Art. 3. Neither of the High Contracting Parties shall conclude an Alliance with a third Power without preliminary notice to the other.

[Romania was an unofficial partner to this agreement from August 19, 1920. A formal convention between Romania and Czechoslovakia, signed at Bucharest, April 23, 1921, added the provision (Article 4) that:]

For the purpose of co-ordinating their efforts to maintain peace, the two Governments undertake to consult together on questions of foreign policy concerning their relations with Hungary.[1] [". . . and Bulgaria" was added to the same article in the Convention between Romania and Yugoslavia signed at Belgrade on June 7, 1921.]

[In the course of 1922 and 1923, each of the above-mentioned conventions was renewed and extended as a "Treaty of Alliance," establishing the basis for a remarkable economic co-operation among the members of the Little Entente and enabling them to present a solid political and economic front to the rest of the world. At the same time, as agreements had already been negotiated with states outside the Little Entente, recognition of these "political and military treaties" was formally given. In 1929, at a Little Entente Conference at Belgrade, the Little Entente treaties were prolonged for five years, subject to automatic renewal at the end of each five-year term; and at Geneva, in 1933, by the "Statute of the Little

Entente" (February 16), A "Permanent Council" of the Little Entente Ministers of Foreign Affairs was set up to handle problems affecting the three powers and to regularize and pass upon agreements with outside powers, and the original Little Entente treaties were renewed "for an indefinite period." Thus the Little Entente continued until the annihilation of Czechoslovakia in 1939 and the outbreak of World War II destroyed it as a factor in international relations. In the meantime, by a series of interlocking agreements, a number of European states had become affiliated with the Little Entente —Austria, Greece, France, Poland, and others. The gist of one of these "outside" agreements is shown in the following excerpt from a "Convention for a Defensive Alliance between the Polish Republic and the Kingdom of Rumania, Bucharest, March 3, 1921," as follows:[2]]

Art. 1. Poland and Rumania undertake to assist each other in the event of their being the object of an unprovoked attack on their present eastern frontiers. Accordingly, if either State is the object of an unprovoked attack, the other shall consider itself in a state of war and shall render armed assistance.

FRANCE AND THE LITTLE ENTENTE

France became affiliated with the Little Entente both indirectly and directly. By her agreement with Poland (and Poland's with Romania), France set up an indirect connection in 1921; and in 1924 France forged a direct link with the Little Entente by a treaty with Czechoslovakia—a link strengthened by a Franco-Romanian treaty in 1926. Terms of the treaty uniting France and Czechoslovakia ran as follows.

[1] *Ibid.*, 1921, VI (No. 155), 218.

[2] *Ibid.*, 1922, VII (No. 175), 79.

From "Treaty of Alliance and Friendship
  between France and Czechoslovakia".
  (January 25, 1924) [1]

The President of the French Republic
and the President of the Czechoslovak
Republic, being earnestly desirous of upholding the principle of international
agreements which was solemnly confirmed
by the Covenant of the League of Nations,
  being further desirous of guarding
against any infraction of the peace, the
maintenance of which is necessary for the
political stability and economic restoration of Europe,
  being resolved for this purpose to ensure respect for the international juridical
and political situation created by the
Treaties of which they were both signatories,
  and having regard to the fact that, in
order to attain this object, certain mutual
guarantees are indispensable for security
against possible aggression and for the
protection of their common interests,
  have . . . agreed to the following provisions:
  Art. 1. The Governments of the French
Republic and of the Czechoslovak Republic undertake to concert their action
in all matters of foreign policy which may
threaten their security or which may tend
to subvert the situation created by the
Treaties of Peace of which both parties
are signatories.
  Art. 2. The High Contracting Parties
shall agree together as to the measures to
be adopted to safeguard their common
interests in case the latter are threatened.
  Art. 3. The High Contracting Parties,
being fully in agreement as to the importance, for the maintenance of the
world's peace, of the political principles
laid down in Article 88 of the Treaty of
Peace of St. Germain-en-Laye of September 10, 1919, and in the Protocols of

[1] *Ibid.*, 1924, XXIII (No. 588), 165-67.

Geneva dated October 4, 1922, undertake
to consult each other as to the measures
to be taken in case there should be any
danger of an infraction of these principles. . . .
  Art. 5. The High Contracting Parties
solemnly declare that they are in complete
agreement as to the necessity, for the
maintenance of peace, of taking common
action in the event [of] any attempt to
restore the Hohenzollern dynasty in Germany. . . .
  Art. 7. The High Contracting Parties
undertake to communicate to each other
all Agreements affecting their policy in
Central Europe which they may have
previously concluded, and to consult one
another before concluding any further
Agreements. They declare that, in this
matter, nothing in the present Treaty is
contrary to the above Agreements, and
in particular to the Treaty of Alliance
between France and Poland, or to the
Conventions and Agreements concluded
between Czechoslovakia with . . . Austria, Rumania, the King of the Serbs,
Croats and Slovenes . . . [and so on]

DISARMAMENT: THE WASHINGTON
NAVAL TREATY (1922), WITH NOTES
ON ITS EMASCULATION TO 1938

While European states built new alliances to guarantee the Paris Peace
Settlement and to strengthen the League
Covenant (and, incidentally, to encircle
Germany and construct bulwarks
against Russia!), the United States
sired the Washington Conference of
1921-22, already referred to [page 889].
Anxious to demonstrate pacific intentions after self-exclusion from the
League of Nations, the United States
called the Washington Conference into
existence for a variety of purposes: to
reaffirm the Open Door and Chinese
rights, to re-establish a balance of power

in the Pacific area, to bury the Anglo-Japanese Alliance (which since World War I had lost its raison d'être), and to avoid a naval-armaments race with Great Britain and Japan. Among the treaties negotiated at this historic gathering was "A Treaty between the United States of America, the British Empire, France, Italy and Japan, Limiting Naval Armament," February 6, 1922. By this treaty a ten-year naval holiday was proclaimed during which no capital ships (that is, ships over 10,000 tons bearing larger than 8-inch guns) were to be built, and a ratio of capital ships of 5-5-3-1.67-1.67 was established. The first chapter of this treaty, containing "General Provisions Relating to the Limitation of Naval Armament," read, in essence, as follows.

From "A Treaty Limiting Naval Armament" (1922) [1]

The United States of America, the British Empire, France, Italy and Japan: Desiring to contribute to the maintenance of the general peace and to reduce the burdens of competition in armament; Have resolved, with a view to accomplishing these purposes, to conclude a Treaty to limit their respective naval armament. . . .

Art. 1. The Contracting Powers agree to limit their respective naval armament as provided in the present Treaty.

Art. 2. The Contracting Powers may retain respectively the capital ships which are specified in Chapter II, Part I [a detailed list]. On the coming into force of the present Treaty, but subject to the following provisions of this Article, all other capital ships, built or building . . . shall be disposed of as prescribed in Chapter II, Part 2.

In addition to the capital ships specified in Chapter II, Part I, the United States may complete and retain two ships of the *West Virginia* class now under construction. On the completion of these two ships the *North Dakota* and *Delaware* shall be disposed of. as prescribed in Chapter II, Part 2.

The British Empire may . . . construct two new capital ships not exceeding 35,000 tons (35,560 metric tons) standard displacement each . . . [providing, when these two are completed,] the *Thunderer, King George V, Ajax,* and *Centurion* shall be disposed of. . . .

Art. 3. Subject to the provisions of Article 2, the Contracting Powers shall abandon their respective capital-ship building. programs. . . .

Art. 4. The total capital ship replacement tonnage of each of the Contracting Powers shall not exceed in standard displacement, for the United States 525,000 tons (533,400 metric tons); for the British Empire 525,000 tons (533,400 metric tons); for France 175,000 tons (177,800 metric tons); for Italy 175,000 tons (177,800 metric tons); for Japan 315,000 tons (320,040 metric tons).

Art. 5. No capital ship exceeding 35,000 tons (35,560 metric tons) . . . shall be acquired by, or constructed by, for, or within the jurisdiction of, any of the Contracting Powers.

Art. 6. No capital ship of any of the Contracting Powers shall carry a gun with a calibre in excess of 16 inches (406 millimetres).

Art. 7. The total tonnage for aircraft carriers of each of the Contracting Powers shall not exceed . . . for the United States 135,000 tons (137,160 metric tons); for the British Empire 135,000 tons (137,160 metric tons); for France 60,000 tons (60,960 metric tons); for Italy 60,000 tons (60,960 metric tons); for Japan 81,000 tons (82,296 metric tons). . . .

Art. 9. No aircraft carrier exceeding 27,000 tons (27,432 metric tons) . . .

[1] *Ibid.,* XXV (No. 609), 202-09.

shall be acquired by . . . any of the Contracting Powers. However, any of the Contracting Powers may, provided that its total tonnage allowance of aircraft carriers is not thereby exceeded, build not more than two aircraft carriers, each of a tonnage of not more than 33,000 tons (33,528 metric tons) . . . and in order to effect economy any of the Contracting Powers may use . . . any two of their ships . . . which would otherwise be scrapped under . . . Article 2. . . .

Art. 10. No aircraft carrier of any of the Contracting Powers shall carry a gun with a calibre in excess of 8 inches (203 millimetres). . . . If the armament carried includes guns exceeding 6 inches (152 millimetres) in calibre the total number of guns carried, except anti-aircraft guns and guns not exceeding 5 inches (127 millimetres), shall not exceed ten. [No limit was established if the guns did not exceed 6 inches.] . . .

Art. 11. No vessel of war exceeding 10,000 tons (10,160 metric tons) . . . other than a capital ship or aircraft carrier, shall be acquired by . . . any of the Contracting Powers. . . .

No vessel of war of any of the Contracting Powers, hereafter laid down, other than a capital ship, shall carry a gun with a calibre in excess of 8 inches (203 millimetres). . . .

Art. 14. No preparations shall be made in merchant ships in time of peace for the installation of warlike armaments for . . . converting . . . into vessels of war, other than the necessary stiffening of decks for the mounting of guns not exceeding 6-inch (152 millimetres) calibre.

Art. 15. No vessel of war constructed within the jurisdiction of any of the Contracting Powers for a non-Contracting Power shall exceed the limitations . . . prescribed by the present Treaty for vessels of a similar type . . . of the Contracting Powers. . . .

Art. 18. Each of the Contracting Powers undertakes not to dispose by gift, sale or any mode of transfer any vessel of war . . . [to] the Navy of any foreign Power.

Art. 19. The United States, the British Empire and Japan agree that the *status quo* at the time of the signing of the present Treaty, with regard to fortifications and naval bases, shall be maintained in their respective territories and possessions specified hereunder: (1) The insular possessions which the United States now holds or may hereafter acquire in the Pacific Ocean, except (a) those adjacent to the coast of the United States, Alaska and the Panama Canal Zone, not including the Aleutian Islands, and (b) the Hawaiian Islands;

(2) Hongkong and the insular possessions which the British Empire now holds or may hereafter acquire in the Pacific Ocean, east of the meridian 110 east longitude, except (a) those adjacent to the coast of Canada, (b) the Commonwealth of Australia and its Territories, and (c) New Zealand;

(3) The following insular territories and possessions of Japan . . . to wit: the Kurile Islands, the Bonin Islands, Amami-Oskima, the Loochoo Islands, Formosa and the Pescadores, and any insular territories or possessions in the Pacific Ocean which Japan may hereafter acquire.

[By progressive steps, the Washington Treaty was scrapped. The beginning was made in 1930, at the London Naval Conference. By this time France and Italy were engaged in rivalry for naval control of the western Mediterranean and refused to sign parts of the London Naval Treaty agreed to by Great Britain, the United States, and Japan (April 22, 1930), whereby tonnage limits were extended over other categories of war vessels, including cruisers, destroyers, and submarines. Moreover, by the "escalator clause"

(Art. 21) of the London Treaty, Great Britain, the United States, and Japan opened the door for competition by permitting an increase over specified tonnages in lighter war craft (excluding capital ships and aircraft carriers): "if . . . the requirements of the national security of any High Contracting Party . . . are, in the opinion of that Party, materially affected by new construction of any other Power . . . that High Contracting Party will notify the other Parties . . . as to the increase required to be made . . . specifying particularly the proposed increases and the reasons therefor, and shall be entitled to make such increase. Thereupon the other Parties . . . of this Treaty shall be entitled to make a proportionate increase in the category or categories specified; and the said other Parties shall promptly advise with each other through diplomatic channels as to the situation thus presented." [1] Meanwhile, Japan had grown restive because of the powers' refusal to grant her naval parity with Great Britain and the United States, and on December 29, 1934, Japan gave notice of her intent to terminate the Washington Treaty on December 31, 1936. Moreover, on June 18, 1935, England concluded an agreement with Germany whereby the latter power was granted the right to construct naval vessels up to 35 per cent of the British tonnage—an agreement which defied the Versailles Treaty and which greatly troubled France. Accordingly, when the powers, by previous agreement, assembled in London late in 1935 to replace the London Treaty of 1930, Japan quickly withdrew, and the British Empire, the United States, and France signed a new tripartite London Naval Treaty (March 25, 1936)—to which Italy, Germany, and the Soviet Union subsequently adhered, the latter with reserva-

tions regarding her Asiatic fleet. The Treaty of 1936 placed no limit to the overall tonnage of each naval power, but it set up limits with regard to individual ships in each category. Thus capital ships were limited to 35,000 tons and their guns could not exceed a caliber of 16 inches, and aircraft carriers were restricted to 23,000 tons with guns not to exceed 6.1 inches (155 millimeters). The London Treaty of 1936 also repeated the "escalator clause" with reference to light craft and provided further that, in case of war, any signatory power might suspend "any or all of the obligations of the present Treaty" providing that it notify the other signatories of the action—whereupon the other signatories might likewise suspend the treaty. About two years later, the United States, Great Britain, and France set forth a new Protocol signed at London, June 30, 1938, whereby, "Following the refusal of Japan to furnish information with regard to its naval construction, or its plans for future construction," the three powers announced "their intention to escalate." The limit on the size of capital ships was advanced from 35,000 to 45,000 tons, with their guns' caliber (16 inches or 406 millimeters) unaltered. Thus, by 1938, the Washington Naval Treaty of 1922 had become meaningless.]

THE LOCARNO TREATIES (1925)

On February 9, 1925, the German Government, acting principally on the motion of Gustav Stresemann, Minister for Foreign Affairs, sent a note to France suggesting that

"Germany might . . . announce her readiness to conclude a Pact by which all the Powers interested in the Rhine, and especially England, France, Italy, and Germany, should solemnly pledge themselves for a considerable time . . . not to make war upon each other. . . .

[1] *Ibid.*, 1931, CXII (No. 2608), 87-88.

It might be combined with a far-reaching arbitration treaty between Germany and France." [1]

The suggestion was timely. The Dawes Plan of 1924 had "brought the first signs of cessation of the policy of sanctions and force against Germany"; the Allies, in accordance with the Versailles Treaty, were beginning to evacuate troops from the Cologne zone of occupied Germany; France coveted every possible guarantee for the security of her postwar frontier with Germany; and England, having recently rejected the Geneva Protocol (1924) for the pacific settlement of international disputes, was anxious to show a sign of international goodwill. Accordingly, the German note led to a fruitful exchange of views which resulted in the Locarno Conference, October 5-16, 1925, a series of treaties which inaugurated the "Locarno Spirit" of security, and Germany's admission (at French insistence) to the League of Nations (September 8, 1926). The principal flaw in the new European outlook was Germany's refusal to extend any guarantees as regards her eastern and southern frontiers. "This obligation," said Stresemann, "we undertook in the West, but we refused it in the East." In consequence, a new series of alliances among the states to the east and south of Germany—with France a party to some of them—followed close on the heels of the Locarno Conference. For Western Europe, however, the Locarno Treaties had a positive, though short-lived, effect in creating a new feeling of security and goodwill. The "Final Protocol of the

Locarno Conference" will serve to introduce the Locarno Treaties.

From the "Final Protocol of the Locarno Conference" (1925) [1]

. The representatives of the German, Belgian, British, French, Italian, Polish and Czechoslovak Governments, who have met at Locarno from October 5 to 16, 1925, in order to seek by common agreement means for preserving their respective nations from the scourge of war and for providing for the peaceful settlement of disputes of every nature which might eventually arise between them, have given their approval to the draft Treaties and Conventions which respectively affect them and which, framed in the course of the present Conference, are mutually independent:

Treaty between Germany, Belgium, France, Great Britain and Italy (Annex A) [given below].

Arbitration Convention between Germany and Belgium (Annex B).

Arbitration Convention between Germany and France (Annex C).

Arbitration Treaty between Germany and Poland (Annex D).

Arbitration Treaty between Germany and Czechoslovakia (Annex E).

These instruments . . . will bear today's date, the representatives of the interested Parties agreeing to meet in London on December 1 next, to proceed . . . to the formality of the signature of the instruments which affect them.

The Minister for Foreign Affairs of France states that as a result of the draft arbitration treaties mentioned above, France, Poland and Czechoslovakia have also concluded . . . draft agreements in order reciprocally to assure to themselves the benefit of the said treaties. . . .

---

[1] *Gustav Stresemann, His Diaries, Letters, and Papers,* ed. and trans. by Eric Sutton, 3 vols., 1937, II, 59. By permission of The Macmillan Company, New York.

[1] League of Nations, *Treaty Series,* 1926, LIV (No. 1292), 297-99.

The representatives of the Governments . . . declare their firm conviction that the entry into force of these treaties and conventions will contribute greatly in bringing about a moral relaxation of the tension between nations, that it will help powerfully towards the solution of many political or economic problems . . . and that, in strengthening the peace and security of Europe, it will hasten on effectively the disarmament provided for in Article 8 of the Covenant of the League of Nations.

Done at Locarno, October 16, 1925

    (Signed) Dr. Luther.
           Stresemann.
           Emile Vandervelde.
           Aristide Briand.
           Austen Chamberlain.
           Benito Mussolini.
           Al. Skrzynski.
           Eduard Benes.

ANNEX A: TREATY OF MUTUAL GUARANTEE BE-
TWEEN GERMANY, BELGIUM, FRANCE, GREAT
BRITAIN, AND ITALY

The President of the German Reich, His Majesty the King of the Belgians, the President of the French Republic, His Majesty the King of the United Kingdom of Great Britain and Ireland and of the British Dominions beyond the Seas, Emperor of India, and His Majesty the King of Italy;

Anxious to satisfy the desire for security and protection which animates the peoples upon whom fell the scourge of the war of 1914-18; taking note of the abrogation of the treaties for the neutralisation of Belgium, and conscious of the necessity for ensuring peace in the area which has so frequently been the scene of European conflicts; animated also with the sincere desire of giving to all the signatory Powers concerned supplementary guarantees within the framework of the Covenant of the League of Nations and the treaties in force between them; have determined to conclude a treaty with these objects . . . and have agreed as follows:

Art. 1. The High Contracting Parties collectively and severally guarantee, in the manner provided in the following Articles, the maintenance of the territorial *status quo* resulting from the frontiers between Germany and Belgium and between Germany and France and the inviolability of the said frontiers as fixed by or in purance of the Treaty of Peace signed at Versailles on June 28, 1919, and also the observance of the stipulations of Articles 42 and 43 of the said Treaty concerning the demilitarized zone.

Art. 2. Germany and Belgium, and also Germany and France, mutually undertake that they will in no case attack or invade each other or resort to war against each other. This stipulation shall not, however, apply in case of:

1. The exercise of the right of legitimate defence. . . .

2. Action in pursuance of Article 16 of the Covenant of the League of Nations.

3. Action as the result of a decision taken by the Assembly or by the Council of the League of Nations or in pursuance of Article 15, paragraph 7, of the Covenant of the League of Nations, provided that in this last event the action is directed against a State which was the first to attack.

Art. 3. In view of the undertakings entered into in Article 2 of the present treaty, Germany and Belgium and Germany and France undertake to settle by peaceful means and in the manner laid down herein all questions of every kind which may arise between them and which it may not be possible to settle by the normal methods of diplomacy:

Any question . . . as to their respective rights shall be submitted to judicial decision, and the Parties undertake to comply with such decision.

All other questions shall be submitted

to a conciliation commission. If the proposals of this commission are not accepted by the two Parties, the question will be brought before the Council of the League of Nations, which will deal with it in accordance with Article 15 of the Covenant of the League.

The detailed arrangements for effecting such peaceful settlement are the subject of special arrangements signed this day.[1]

Art. 4. (1) If one of the High Contracting Parties alleges that a violation of Article 2 [above] . . . or a breach of Articles 42 or 43 of the Treaty of Versailles has been or is being committed, it shall bring the question at once before the Council of the League of Nations.

(2) As soon as the Council of the League . . . is satisfied that such violation . . . has been committed, it will notify . . . the Powers signatory of the present Treaty, who severally agree that in such case they will each of them come immediately to the assistance of the Power against whom the act complained of is directed.

(3) In case of a flagrant violation of Article 2 [above] . . . or of a flagrant breach of Articles 42 or 43 of the Treaty of Versailles by one of the contracting parties, each of the other Contracting Parties hereby undertakes immediately to come to the help of the Party . . . [without waiting for a League decision, which, however, will be given in due course and in accord-

ance with which the parties will accommodate their action].

Art. 5. . . . If one of the Powers referred to in Article 3 refuses to submit a dispute to peaceful settlement or to comply with . . . [a] decision . . . the provisions of Article 4 shall apply. . . .

Art. 6. The provisions of the present treaty do not affect the rights and obligations of the High Contracting Parties under the Treaty of Versailles or under arrangements supplementary thereto. . . .

Art. 7. The present Treaty . . . shall not be interpreted as restricting the duty of the League to take whatever action may be deemed wise . . . to safeguard the peace of the world.

Art. 8. The present Treaty shall be registered at the League of Nations. . . .

Art. 9. The present Treaty shall impose no obligation upon any of the British dominions, or upon India, unless the Government of such dominion, or of India, signifies its acceptance thereof.

THE KELLOGG-BRIAND OR PARIS PACT (1928)

On April 6, 1927, Aristide Briand, the French Foreign Minister, proposed to the United States a bilateral treaty "outlawing war." The American Secretary of State, Frank Billings Kellogg, countered with the suggestion that the treaty be widened into a multilateral antiwar pact open to all nations. After months of correspondence, the French acceded to the American proposal and on August 27, 1928, fifteen states signed the Treaty for the Renunciation of War as an Instrument of National Policy. Additional adherents speedily gave the pact almost world-wide acceptance, as the pact involved a mere renunciation of aggressive war with no provision for sanctions save the force of world opinion. The latter, however, was forceful

---

[1] This refers to the Arbitration Conventions of the Final Protocol. An example from the Arbitration Convention between Germany and France reads: "The undersigned . . . charged by their respective Governments to determine the methods by which . . . a peaceful solution shall be attained of all questions which cannot be settled amicably between Germany and France, Have agreed as follows:

Part. I. Article I. All disputes of every kind between Germany and France . . . which it may not be possible to settle amicably by the normal methods of diplomacy, shall be submitted either to an arbitral tribunal or to the Permanent Court of International Justice." Cf. League of Nations, *Treaty Series*, 1926, LIV (No. 1294), 317.

enough to give rise to that new phenomenon in international affairs known as the "undeclared war." The pact read as follows.

From *The Pact for the Renunciation of War* (1928) [1]

The President of the German Reich, the President of the United States of America, His Majesty the King of the Belgians, the President of the French Republic, His Majesty the King of Great Britain, Ireland and the British Dominions beyond the Seas, Emperor of India, His Majesty the King of Italy, His Majesty the Emperor of Japan, the President of the Republic of Poland, the President of the Czechoslovak Republic,

Deeply sensible of their solemn duty to promote the welfare of mankind;

Persuaded that the time has come when a frank renunciation of war as an instrument of national policy should be made to the end that the peaceful and friendly relations now existing between their peoples may be perpetuated;

Convinced that all changes in their relations with one another should be sought only by pacific means and be the result of a peaceful and orderly process, and that any signatory Power which shall hereafter seek to promote its national interests by resort to war should be denied the benefits furnished by this Treaty;

Hopeful that, encouraged by their example, all the other nations of the world will join in this humane endeavor and by adhering to the present Treaty as soon as it comes into force bring their peoples within the scope of its beneficent provisions, thus uniting the civilized nations of the world in a common renunciation of war as an instrument of their national policy;

[1] U.S. Department of State, *The General Pact for the Renunciation of War, Text of the Pact Signed, Notes and Other Papers*, 1928, 1-3.

Have decided to conclude a Treaty and . . . have agreed upon the following articles:

Art. 1. The High Contracting Parties solemnly declare in the names of their respective peoples that they condemn recourse to war for the solution of international controversies, and renounce it as an instrument of national policy in their relations with one another.

Art. 2. The High Contracting Parties agree that the settlement or solution of all disputes or conflicts of whatever nature or of whatever origin they may be, which may arise among them, shall never be sought except by pacific means.

Art. 3. The present Treaty shall be ratified by the High Contracting Parties . . . in accordance with their respective constitutional requirements. . . .

This Treaty shall . . . remain open as long as may be necessary for adherence by all the other Powers of the world. Every instrument evidencing the adherence of a Power shall be deposited at Washington. . . .

It shall be the duty of the . . . United States to furnish each Government named in the Preamble and every Government subsequently adhering to this Treaty with a certified copy of the Treaty and of every instrument of ratification or adherence.

2. The Return to International Anarchy, 1930-1936

In 1930 the peace of the world was safeguarded by the Paris peace settlement, the League of Nations, and a chain of fortifying alliances to guarantee protection against aggression. By 1937, however, this structure had been destroyed, and the entire world stood poised dangerously between peace and war. Japan, Germany, Italy, and some lesser states had launched a series of aggressive acts which scrapped the Paris treaties, revealed the League's impotence to maintain peace, and divided the world into two competing parts, the Anti-Comintern powers (which later became the Rome-Berlin-Tokyo Axis), and the "democratic" or "peace" front. Japan had taken the first move [at Mukden, in 1931, see page 893]; Germany, after the accession of Adolf Hitler to the Chancellorship (January 30, 1933), took the second. Years before, Hitler had denounced the Versailles Treaty: "It was no Treaty of Peace which was signed," he said in 1923, "but a betrayal of Peace. . . . So long as this Treaty stands there can be no resurrection of the German people. . . . At its foundation our [Nazi] Movement formulated three demands: 1. Setting aside of the Peace Treaty. 2. Unification of all Germans. 3. Land and soil to feed our nation." [1] Within a few months after his rise to power, Hitler began a series of acts designed to implement this threefold policy.

GERMANY REASSERTS HER "NATIONAL EQUALITY"

German Withdrawal from the League of Nations (1933)

On February 2, 1932, sixty nations met at Geneva under the auspices of the League of Nations to institute general disarmament in accordance with the League Covenant. The Conference continued until May 30, 1934, before it broke up without any general agreement. Meanwhile, on October 14, 1933,

[1] This and the next two selections are from *The Speeches of Adolf Hitler*, ed. by Norman H. Baynes, 2 vols., Royal Institute of International Affairs, London, 1942. By permission of the Oxford University Press. This is I, 56-57.

Germany suddenly withdrew from the Disarmament Conference and announced her resignation from the League of Nations (Japan had resigned the previous March; the resignations went into effect after two years). Hitler's Proclamation of these acts read as follows.

From HITLER, Proclamation and Speech of October 14, 1933 [2]

Filled with the sincere desire to carry through the work of the peaceful internal reconstruction of our people and of its political and economic life, former German Governments, trusting that a just equality of rights would be granted them, declared their willingness to enter the League of Nations and to take part in the Disarmament Conference.

But in so doing Germany suffered a bitter disillusionment.

In spite of our willingness at any time, if necessary, to continue to its utmost limits the German disarmament which had already been effected, other Governments could not make up their minds to fulfill the promises made . . . in the [Versailles] Peace Treaty. . . .

After the German Government, on the basis of the express recognition of German equality of rights laid down on 11 December 1932, had recently declared itself willing to resume its participation in . . . the Disarmament Conference, it was later communicated to the Foreign Minister of the Reich and to our delegates . . . that this equality of rights could no longer be granted. . . .

Since the German Government regards this action as a discrimination against the German people which is as unjust as it is degrading, under such conditions, as a

[2] *Ibid.*, II, 1088-89, 1092-94, 1100, 1102.

second-class nation, deprived of its rights, it feels itself no longer able to take any further part in deliberations which could only lead to further "Diktats."

Therefore while the German Government asserts afresh its unalterable will for peace, in the face of these humiliating and dishonouring suggestions, to its profound regret it declares that it is forced to leave the Disarmament Conference. And in consequence it must also give notice of its retirement from the League of Nations.

[At the same time, Hitler called for a national plebiscite on the question: "Does the German people approve the policy of its Government as here set forth, and is it willing to declare this policy to be the expression of its own views and of its own will and solemnly to pledge itself thereto?" The plebiscite was held November 12, in characteristic Nazi fashion, and 95 per cent voted *"Ja!"* But Hitler took care to limit German bellicosity to a mere assertion of equality of rights. In a radio address to the German people (October 14), he spoke further:]

When in November 1918 in trustful reliance upon the assurances defined in President Wilson's Fourteen Points the German people laid down its arms, a disastrous struggle reached its close. . . . If in those months after the War the world had loyally given its hand to the prostrate foe, mankind would have been spared much suffering and many a disillusionment. The profoundest disillusionment of all was suffered by the German people. . . . The German people destroyed its armaments "in fanatical loyalty": a small professional army quite inadequately armed took the place of an army millions strong. . . . The German people might thus reasonably expect that the rest of the

world would similarly keep its promises. . . . For a decade and a half the German people has hoped and waited. . . . The German people and the German Government have not demanded arms at all; what they have demanded is equality of rights. . . . If the world permits to every people certain types of arms, we are not prepared, as though we were a people with less rights than others, to allow ourselves on principle to be excluded from their possession. . . . But this demand of Germany cannot . . . constitute a threat to the other Powers. . . . Germany does not demand any offensive arms but only those defensive arms which . . . are permitted to all nations.

Germany Reintroduces Universal Military Service (1935)

On March 16, 1935, in one of his early "Saturday coups," Hitler issued a proclamation to reintroduce universal military conscription in Germany. The act defied the Versailles Treaty, led other nations quickly to scrap whatever disarmament plans they may have had, and hastened the formation of European alliances aimed at protection against Germany. But Hitler pleaded that it was an act of self-defense, to render Germany "able to safeguard peace for the Reich and thereby for the whole of Europe." He insisted that Germany had "offered to all neighbouring States the conclusion of pacts of non-aggression," had signed (January 26, 1934) a ten-year nonaggression pact with Poland (although she refused an "Eastern Locarno Pact" on September 10), and had "given to France the solemn assurance that Germany, now that the question of the Saar has been settled, will not make or raise any further territorial claims on France." Hitler continued:

From HITLER, Proclamation of
March 16, 1935 [1]

The German Government must, how-
ever, to its regret, observe that for months
past there has been taking place a continuous increase in armaments on the part
of the rest of the world. It sees in the
creation of a Soviet-Russian army of 101
divisions, i.e., an admitted peace-strength
of 960,000 men, an element that could not
have been contemplated at the . . . Treaty
of Versailles.

It sees the speeding-up of similar measures in other States further proofs of the
rejection of the idea of disarmament. . . .

The German Government feels that in
these circumstances it is impossible any
longer to delay the measures which are
necessary for the security of the Reich or
indeed to fail to disclose those measures
to others. . . . At this hour the German
Government renews before the German
people and before the entire world the
affirmation of its resolve never to go beyond that which the protection of German
honour and the freedom of the Reich demand and especially affirms that it wishes
in the national German armament to create no instrument of military aggression,
but on the contrary to create exclusively
an instrument of defence and therefore
an instrument for the maintenance of
peace. . . .

It is with this end in view that the
Government of the German Reich has
today decided on the following law: [2]

A Law for the Recreation of the National
Defense Forces. . . .

1. Service in the defensive forces is
predicated on universal military service.

2. The German peace army, including
police units . . . shall comprise twelve

army corps commands and thirty-six divisions [324,000 men, exclusive of naval
forces and the air corps, which, in contradiction of the Versailles Treaty, had been
reinstituted on March 1 previously].

3. Supplementary laws for regulating
universal military service will be drafted
and submitted to the Reich Cabinet by the
Reich Minister for Defense.

Berlin, March 16, 1935

[On the same day the Nazi party issued
the following jubilant piece of propaganda
for German internal consumption.]

From the Nazi Party "Statement on Military
Policy" (March 16, 1935) [3]

The proclamation of the Fuehrer is for
the German people a historic event of the
greatest importance. Since the day when
Germany collapsed through treason, since
the days in which the Diktat of Versailles
was imposed upon her, this is the German
people's greatest moment. Through this
proclamation, which is a document of
peace but also of determination, the German people have been freed from the
oppressive shame which has burdened
them for sixteen years.

With the present day the honor of the
German nation has been restored. We
stand erect as a free people among nations.
. . . We again possess the German army
in order to defend our German fatherland
by force of arms. The liberty and life of
our people are sacred treasures which in
arms-bristling Europe can be safeguarded
only through the rebirth of the German
army. . . .

No miracles have happened. This equality of rights . . . this liberty has not fallen
into our laps; we have won it for ourselves. The Fuehrer's struggle has won it
for us. It is his accomplishment. . . .

---

[1] *Ibid.*, II, 1209-11.

[2] Frederick T. Birchall in the *New York Times,*
March 17, 1935, 1. This and the next selection
by permission of the *New York Times.*

[3] *Ibid.,* 31.

Within two years after seizing power he has conquered for his people political equality.

The Franco-Russian Treaty (1935)

One of the most immediate results of the German Conscription Law was the signing of a Franco-Russian Treaty of Mutual Assistance on May 2, 1935, and, two weeks later, of a similar security pact between Czechoslovakia and Russia—the latter states guaranteeing aid to one another in case of unprovoked aggression on condition that the victim of aggression also received aid from France. France and Russia had already concluded a Nonaggression Pact (November 29, 1932); their new treaty, which was to remain in force for five years, subject to renewal indefinitely, ran as follows.

From the Franco-Russian Treaty of Mutual Assistance (May 2, 1935) [1]

The Central Executive Committee of the Union of Soviet Socialist Republics and the President of the French Republic, being desirous of strengthening the peace of Europe and of guaranteeing its benefits to their respective countries by securing a fuller and stricter application of those provisions of the Covenant of the League of Nations which are designed to maintain national security, territorial integrity and political independence of States; determined to devote their efforts to the preparation and conclusion of a European agreement for that purpose, and in the meantime to promote as far as lies in their power, the effective application of the provisions of the Covenant of the League of Nations, have resolved to conclude a

[1] League of Nations, *Treaty Series,* 1936, CLXVII (No. 3881), 404-05.

Treaty to this end and . . . have agreed upon the following provisions:

Art. 1. In the event of France or the Union of Soviet Socialist Republics being threatened with or in danger of aggression on the part of any European State, the U.S.S.R. and reciprocally France undertake mutually to proceed to an immediate consultation as regards the measures to be taken for the observance of the provisions of Article 10 of the Covenant of the League of Nations.

Art. 2. Should, in the circumstances specified in Article 15, paragraph 7, of the Covenant of the League of Nations, France or the U.S.S.R. be the object, notwithstanding the sincerely peaceful intentions of both countries, of an unprovoked aggression on the part of a European State, the U.S.S.R. and reciprocally France shall immediately come to each other's aid and assistance.

Art. 3. In consideration of the fact that under Article 16 of the Covenant of the League of Nations any Member of the League which resorts to war in disregard of its covenants under Articles 12, 13 or 15 of the Covenant is *ipso facto* deemed to have committed an act of war against all other Members of the League, France and . . . the U.S.S.R. undertake, in the event of one of them being the object . . . of an unprovoked aggression on the part of a European State, immediately to come to each other's aid and assistance in application of Article 16 of the Covenant.

German Denunciation of the Locarno Treaties and Remilitarization of the Rhineland (1936)

On March 7, 1936, the German Ambassador to London handed the British Foreign Minister "a memorandum which fell into two parts. The first part stated that in the opinion of the German Government, the now imminent conclusion by France of a pact with

Soviet Russia had created an entirely new situation and destroyed the political system of the Locarno Treaty, which Germany consequently regarded as no longer binding on her. Taking advantage of this fact, the German Government had restored the full and unrestricted sovereignty of Germany over the demilitarized zone of the Rhineland; in token of which German troops had already marched in large numbers into that district." [1] On the same day, Hitler gave a long speech to the Reichstag ending with another appeal by plebiscite "that the German people may give their verdict as to my leadership" (95 per cent again voiced approval in the elections held March 29). In earlier portions of his speech Hitler explained the German action as follows.

From HITLER, Speech to the Reichstag (March 7, 1936) [2]

Unfortunately the treaties of alliance that had already been made by France were the first obstacles laid in the practical path of this Pact, namely the Rhine Pact of Locarno. To this Pact Germany made a contribution which represented the greatest sacrifice; because while France fortified her frontier with steel and concrete [the Maginot Line] . . . a condition of complete defencelessness was imposed upon us on our Western frontier. Nevertheless, we abided by that obligation . . . that we might serve the cause of European peace. . . .

The agreement concluded between France and Russia last year, and already signed and accepted by the French Cham-

ber, is in open contradiction to this Pact. This new Franco-Soviet Agreement introduces the threatening military power of a mighty Empire into the centre of Europe by the roundabout way of Czechoslovakia, the latter country having also signed an agreement with Russia. . . . France has not concluded this Treaty with a European Power of no special significance. Even before the Rhine Pact came into existence France already had treaties of assistance with Czechoslovakia and with Poland. Germany made no objection to this. . . . But Soviet Russia is the exponent of a revolutionary political and philosophical system. . . . Its political creed is the confession of faith in the world revolution. It cannot be foreseen whether this philosophy will not be victorious . . . in France as well. But should this happen . . . then it is certain that this new Bolshevic State would be a section of the Bolshevic International . . . [and that] headquarters would not be in Paris but in Moscow. . . . This gigantic mobilization of the East against Central Europe is opposed not only to the letter but above all to the spirit of the Locarno Pact. . . . After a hard inner struggle with myself I therefore decided . . . to hand the following Memorandum to the French Government today and to the other signatories of the Locarno Pact . . .

1. It is an undisputed fact that the Franco-Soviet Pact is exclusively directed against Germany.

2. It is an undisputed fact that in the Pact France undertakes . . . obligations . . . far beyond her duty as laid down in the Covenant of the League of Nations, and which compel her to take military action against Germany even when she cannot appeal . . . to . . . the Council of the League.

3. It is an undisputed fact that France . . . claims for herself the right to decide . . . who is the aggressor.

[1] "English History," The Annual Register . . . for the Year 1936, 1937, 20. By permission of Longmans, Green and Co., Ltd.

[2] The Speeches of Adolf Hitler, ed. Baynes, II, 1287-89, 1291, 1293-95, 1297. By permission of the Oxford University Press.

4. It is thereby established that France has undertaken . . . to act as if neither the Covenant of the League of Nations, nor the Rhine Pact, which refers to the Covenant, were valid. . . .

In this manner . . . the Locarno Rhine Pact has lost its inner meaning and ceased in practice to exist. Consequently, Germany regards herself for her part as no longer bound by this dissolved treaty. The German Government are now constrained to face the new situation created by this [Franco-Russian] alliance. . . . In accordance with the fundamental right of a nation to secure its frontiers and ensure its possibilities for defence, the German Government have today restored the full and unrestricted sovereignty of Germany in the demilitarized zone of the Rhineland.

[Hitler went on to offer seven proposals for creation of "a system of peaceful security for Europe," including demilitarized zones on *both sides* of the boundaries between Germany and France and Belgium, nonaggression pacts with both eastern and western German neighbors, and, "now that Germany's equality of rights . . . have finally been attained," a German offer to re-enter the League of Nations.]

BREAKDOWN OF PEACE MACHINERY: THE ITALO-ETHIOPIAN WAR (1934-1936)

A major disappointment of the 1930's was the inability of the peace machinery to maintain peace. The League of Nations, which had accomplished much in the twenties, broke down as soon as its members were called upon to apply its machinery against a Great Power; the regional pacts either dissolved or turned into systems of competing alliances; and the Kellogg-Briand Pact, possessing no effective sanctions, was ignored. Most

disappointing was the League. China found it ineffective in halting Japanese aggression in Manchuria [see page 899]; against Germany's unilateral rejection of the Versailles and Locarno Treaties the League did little more than register formal protests; and in the years 1934-37, the final disillusionment occurred when, in the face of League condemnation and a halfhearted application of economic sanctions, Italy succeeded in the conquest of Ethiopia. Highlights of the Italo-Ethiopian troubles and of the League's action therewith follow.

The Walwal Incident (1934-35)

From League of Nations, Council Report on Dispute between Ethiopia and Italy (1935) [1]

It appeared that, from November 23rd, 1934, onwards, incidents had occurred in the Walwal area after the arrival in that area, which contained wells, of the Anglo-Ethiopian Joint Commission for the delimitation of the frontier between Ethiopia and British Somaliland. This Commission, which had instructions to make a survey of the grazing-grounds in the Ethiopian province of Ogaden, and which, from Ado onwards, was accompanied by a strong Ethiopian escort, had found Walwal occupied by an Italian native force. Following various incidents, the Commission had withdrawn on November 25th, without its escort. After its departure, an engagement took place on December 5th between the Italian and Ethiopian troops. Other incidents followed. Each of the two Governments protested to the other, holding it responsible.

Whereas Ethiopia requested the appli-

1 "Dispute between Ethiopia and Italy . . . Report of the Council," *League of Nations Publications.* VII. Political 1935. VII. 16 (C. 411 (1). M. 207 (1). 1935. VII.), 1-2, 6.

cation of the arbitration procedure . . . the Italian . . . Government could not see what question there was to submit to arbitration. The Ethiopian Government replied that arbitration was possible on the two following main questions: (1) There was an Italian aggression first at Walwal and . . . in the interior of Ogaden. . . . (2) Walwal is Ethiopian territory illegally occupied by Italian troops. . . . The Italian Government maintained, on the other hand, that Walwal belonged to the Italian colony of Somaliland and had been occupied by Italian troops for several years past. . . . The controversy was inflamed by mutual accusations regarding the policy of the two countries prior to the Walwal incident.

[Ethiopia appealed to the League of Nations on December 14, 1934. When, in January, 1935, the League Council was on the point of taking up the problem, Italy, showing reluctance to have the matter aired before the League, agreed to arbitrate with Ethiopia under a Treaty of Amity signed between the two countries in 1928. Amid a storm of continuing accusations from both sides, arbitration proceedings took place and finally, on September 3, 1935, a singularly inconclusive award was given, as follows:]

1. That neither the Italian Government nor its agents on the spot can be held responsible in any way for the actual Walwal incident; the allegations brought against them by the Ethiopian Government are disproved. . . .

2. That, although the Ethiopian Government . . . had no reasonable interest in provoking that engagement, its local authorities . . . may have given the impression that they had aggressive intentions . . . but that nevertheless it had not been shown that they can be held

responsible for the actual incident of December 5th.

Italian Aggression and Economic Sanctions

Prior to the arbitration award of September 3, Ethiopia had repeatedly accused Italy of further troop concentrations in East Africa. Great Britain and France—both with colonies bordering on Ethiopia—attempted tripartite negotiations with Italy in Paris, but Italy rejected their overtures in August (Ethiopia rejected a later attempt in December). And on September 4, the day after the arbitration award, Italy presented a detailed memorandum to the League Council stating that "Italy's dignity as a civilized nation would be deeply wounded were she to continue a discussion in the League on a footing of equality with Ethiopia." Although this was contrary to a fundamental principle of the League Covenant conferring equality upon League members, Italy held that Ethiopia failed to measure up because it had no stable government, no effective administration, and no well-defined frontiers, and because it permitted slavery and traffic in arms which no "civilized" nation could condone. Less than a month later (October 3), Ethiopia notified the League Council that Italian military planes had, that day, bombarded Adowa and Adigrat, that ground troops were also engaged in battle, and that these facts "involved a violation of Ethiopian frontiers and a breach of the Covenant by Italian aggression." Obviously, League action was demanded, and on October 11, fifty members voted in the League Assembly that Italy has "resorted to war in disregard of its Covenants under Article 12 of the Covenant of the League of Nations." On the same day, the Assembly set up committees to expedite League action under the Covenant. On the same day the events recounted below also took place.

From "Report on the Work of the League 1935/36"[1]

The Committee of Eighteen submitted to the Co-ordination Committee, which adopted it, a first proposal dealing with arms, ammunition and implements of war, in which it was proposed (a) that Governments which were at that time enforcing an arms embargo on Ethiopia should immediately lift such embargo, and (b) chat Governments should at once impose an embargo on the exportation, re-exportation or transit of arms, ammunition and implements of war to Italy and the Italian Colonies.

[Subsequent proposals, accepted to go into effect by November 18, extended the embargo on "all loans and credits to the Italian Government" and provided that governments should prohibit the importation of Italian goods and the export or re-export to Italy of certain raw materials. More than fifty member States accepted and applied—each in its own way—these proposals, in accordance with the resolution of the Co-ordination Committee of October 16 concerning the "obligations which flow from Article 16 of the Covenant":]

The Committee of Co-ordination, considering that it is important to ensure rapid and effective application of the measures which have been and may subsequently be proposed . . .
Considering that it rests with each country to apply these measures in accordance with its public law and, in particular, the powers of its Government in regard to execution of treaties:

Calls attention to the fact that Members of the League, being bound by the obligations which flow from Article 16 of the Covenant, are under a duty to take the necessary steps to enable them to carry out these obligations with all requisite rapidity.

[Unhappily, the economic sanctions were not sufficiently effective to stop Italian aggression. A League survey early in 1936 showed that Italian exports and imports had been severely reduced, but a number of difficulties arose to impair the efficacy of economic sanctions, notably the following: 1. The system was economically incomplete, as petroleum, petroleum products, iron, and steel were not included. 2. The system was not universally applied, although states outside the League, especially the United States, generally co-operated loyally. 3. As each member applied the measures "in accordance with its own public law," the sanctions were unevenly administered. 4. Existing treaties of amity and commerce, and economic contracts in process of execution, conflicted with members' Covenant obligations. 5. Application of sanctions entailed economic losses to states applying them, thereby cooling their ardor for the system. 6. In conflict with an undeveloped country like Ethiopia, Italian stock piles sufficed for a quick conquest and, as it turned out, economic sanctions were in operation too short a time to have had their full, cumulative effect. While League Committees deplored (April 18, 1936) that no opportunity existed "of facilitating and hastening the settlement of the dispute through an agreement between the parties within the framework of the Covenant,"[2] Italy hastened her conquest.

[1] "Report on the Work of the League 1935/36," Pt. I, *League of Nations Publications,* General 1936. 5 (A. 6. 1936), 48-49.

[2] "Report on the Work of the League 1935/36," Pt. I, *League of Nations Publications,* General 1936. 5 (A. 6. 1936), 34.

On May 9, 1936, the King of Italy signed a decree saying that:] [1]

The territories and peoples which belonged to the Empire of Ethiopia are placed under the full and entire sovereignty of the Kingdom of Italy. The title of Emperor of Ethiopia is assumed by the King of Italy for himself and his successors.

[Thereafter, Italy refused further to discuss the dispute, holding that Ethiopia no longer existed, as its erstwhile Emperor had fled, "menaced by the revolt of the people," that "Italy was therefore compelled to accept such responsibilities as were entailed by the situation," and that:[2]]

Italy views the work she has undertaken in Ethiopia as a sacred mission of civilization, and proposes to carry it out according to the principles of the Covenant of the League of Nations and of other international deeds which set forth the duties and tasks of the civilizing Powers. . . . Slavery and forced labour, which were a blot of infamy on the old régime, are now abolished. . . .
Italy will consider it an honour to inform the League of Nations of the progress achieved in her work of civilizing Ethiopia, of which she has assumed the heavy responsibility.
While expecting the League . . . to appraise the situation now existing in Ethiopia in a spirit of fair understanding, the Italian Government declares itself ready to give once more its willing and practical co-operation to the League of Nations in order to achieve a settlement of the grave problems upon which rests the future of Europe and of the world. . . . The Italian Government cannot but recall

the abnormal situation in which Italy has been placed and the necessity for the immediate removal of such obstacles as have been and are in the way of the international co-operation which Italy sincerely seeks, and to which she is prepared to give a tangible contribution for the sake of, and the maintenance of, peace.

[Thus faced with a fait accompli, League members gave little heed to the warning given by Ethiopia on May 12:[3]]

The Ethiopian delegation asks that all the provisions of Article 16 of the Covenant should at last be enforced, so that all States, weak or powerful . . . may be reassured. The moment is a tragic one for Ethiopia. It is no less grave for the League of Nations. On the resolution that the Council takes to-day depends the future and the very existence of the League of Nations.

[On June 30, the exiled Ethiopian Emperor, Haile Selassie I, addressed a moving appeal to the League Assembly:[4]]

On behalf of the Ethiopian people, a Member of the League of Nations, I ask the Assembly to take all measures proper to secure respect for the Covenant. I renew my protest against the violations of treaties of which the Ethiopian people has been the victim. I declare before the whole world that the Emperor, the Government and the people of Ethiopia will not bow before force, that they uphold their claims. . . .
I ask that fifty-two nations who have given the Ethiopian people a promise to help them in their resistance to the aggressor: What are they willing to do for Ethiopia?
I ask the great Powers, who have prom-

[1] *Ibid.*, 43.
[2] *Ibid.*, Pt. II (A. 6(a). 1936), 11-12.

[3] *Ibid.*, Pt. I, 44-45.
[4] *Ibid.*, Pt. II, 13.

ised . . . collective security to small states . . . What measures do they intend to take?

Representatives of the world, I have come to Geneva to discharge in your midst the most painful of the duties of the head of a State. What answer am I to take back to my people?

[As a reply to the Emperor's appeal, League members began to discuss the proposition put forth by Chile that: [1]]

Since the war is finished, sanctions should be raised. Sanctions no longer have any object, and they affect not only the country against which they have been enforced, but also the countries applying them.

[On July 6, the League voted to lift sanctions against Italy as of July 15, 1936. And, as if repentant for its poor showing in the Italo-Ethiopian War, the League began to consider a question which occupied much of its attention for the next two years;[2] namely, how to strengthen "the real effectiveness of the guarantees of security which the League affords to its Members"!]

ITALO-GERMAN RAPPROCHEMENT

The Rome-Berlin Axis was slow to mature. Indeed, until after the Italian conquest of Ethiopia, Italy and Germany pursued conflicting foreign objectives. Their conflict centered around Austria. In 1931—before Hitler—when Germany sought to effect tariff unity with Austria, Italy joined in the opposi-

tion. And in 1934, by the Rome Protocol (March 17), Italy joined Austria and Hungary in an agreement designed "to develop economic relations" and to preserve Austrian independence. The Rome Protocol was renewed in 1936, but, with his position weakened by the Ethiopian venture, Mussolini soon found himself unable further to oppose German designs on Austria. Already Hitler had spoken honeyed words to the Italian dictator. In 1922, he had declared that "Italy and Germany have the same enemies and their mission is to work together for the cause of civilization." Again, on the eve of the Ethiopian conquest Hitler made a point of extending cordiality to Italy. Now, in the autumn of 1936, was formed the Rome-Berlin Axis, marking the division of Europe into contending alliances. A contemporary annalist described it as follows.

From a Contemporary Account of the Formation of the Rome-Berlin Axis (1936) [3]

Count Ciano had conversations at Berlin, and then at Berchtesgaden, with the German Foreign Minister and with Chancellor Hitler from October 20 to 23. The Reich officially recognised the Empire of Ethiopia. On November 1, at Milan, Signor Mussolini proclaimed the creation of the "Rome-Berlin axis." From November 9 to 12 Count Ciano was present at the Italo-Austrian-Hungarian conference at Vienna. He then went to Hungary, where he stayed till the 17th. On November 24 the Hungarian Regent, Admiral Horthy, arrived in Rome on an official visit, and stayed till the 25th. . . . In regard to Spain [whose civil war had begun on July 18], Italy very early manifested her sympathy with the rebellion of

---

[1] *Ibid.*, Pt. I, 45.

[2] *Ibid.*, Pt. II, 15. For further interesting and valuable materials on this question, see "Report of the Special Committee set up to Study the Application of the Principles of the Covenant," *League of Nations Publications* VII. Political 1938. VII. 1. (A. 7. VII.)

[3] *The Annual Register . . . for the Year 1936,* 1937, Pt. I, 183. By permission of Longmans, Green and Co., Ltd.

General Franco. . . . After Count Ciano's visit to Germany, Italy declared herself opposed to the establishment of Bolshevism whether in the whole of Spain or in one part of it.

GERMAN-JAPANESE RAPPROCHEMENT (1936)

The Italian declaration against Communism sounded the keynote which served, a month later, as the diplomatic excuse for an agreement between bellicose Germany and aggressive Japan. The Anti-Comintern Pact, signed between the latter powers on November 25, 1936, later included Italy (November 6, 1937), Hungary and "Manchukuo" (February 24, 1939), and Spain (March 27, 1939). Thus it marked the union of totalitarian states in the East and the West and heralded the extension of the Rome-Berlin Axis to include Tokyo in 1939. The original German-Japanese Pact ran as follows.

From the German-Japanese Anti-Comintern Pact (November 25, 1936) [1]

The German Government and the Japanese Government, recognizing that the aim of the Communist Internationale known as the Comintern is directed at disrupting and violating existing States with all means at its command and convinced that to tolerate the Communist Internationale's interference with the internal affairs of nations not only endangers their internal peace and social well-being but threatens world peace at large, animated by a desire to work in common against Communist disruptive influences, have arrived at the following agreement:

I. The high contracting parties agree to mutually inform each other concerning the activities of the Communist Inter-

[1] New York Times, Nov. 26, 1936, 27. By permission of the New York Times.

nationale, to consult with each other concerning measures to combat this activity, and to execute these measures in close coöperation with each other.

II. The two high contracting parties will jointly invite third parties whose domestic peace is endangered by the disruptive activities of the Communist Internationale to embark upon measures for warding these off with the spirit of this agreement or to join in it.

III. . . . This agreement . . . becomes effective the day of signing and is in force for a period of five years. . . .

SUPPLEMENTARY PROTOCOL. A. The competent authorities of both . . . parties will coöperate most closely . . . concerning the activities of the Communist Internationale, as well as in connection with publicity and defense measures against the Communist Internationale.

B. The competent authorities of both . . . parties will, within the framework of existing laws, take strict measures against those who, at home or abroad, directly or indirectly are active in the service of the Communist Internationale. . . . With a view to facilitating the coöperation of the competent authorities of both . . . parties, specified in (A), a permanent commission will be created. . . .

Berlin, November 25, 1936; that is, the November 25 of the eleventh year of the Showa Period.

[Signed] Ribbentrop
Mushakoji

3. The Immediate Background of World War II: Aggression vs. Appeasement

The years immediately preceding World War II were marked, until six months before war actually began, by two ill-assorted policies, aggression and appeasement. The former—aggression

—was merely a continuation of the Axis powers' previous activities, extended, in the course of 1937-39, to include Italo-German aid to ensure a fascist victory in Spain (whose civil war ended in a victory for General Franco, March 28, 1939); the outbreak of fresh hostilities in the Far East [see page 899]; the German incorporation (Anschluss) of Austria (March, 1938); the partition of Czechoslovakia at Munich (September, 1938); the German annihilation of Czechoslovakia (March, 1939); the German annexation of Memel (March, 1939); the Italian conquest of Albania (April, 1939); and the Danzig-Polish crisis (August, 1939), which led directly to war. Appeasement, on the other hand, was the policy of the "democratic," or "peace," front, sturdily maintained until the German annihilation of Czechoslovakia in March, 1939, after which the democratic powers stiffened in the face of Axis aggression. It was founded upon a genuine thirst for peace, a lack of preparation for war, a refusal to believe either in the Axis powers' capacity for war or in their base willingness to plunge Europe into war, and a seldom-voiced hope that, if war came, it would be a death struggle between the Axis and Soviet Russia, fatal to both of Europe's terrors, Nazism and Communism. The chief spokesman of appeasement was Neville Chamberlain, who in May, 1937, became Prime Minister of Great Britain. A "Go-Getter for Peace," Chamberlain held that, in order to secure peace, it must be positively worked for. Accordingly, he sought to reach agreements with the Axis powers, even at the expense of considerable concessions. In November, 1937, he dispatched Lord Halifax to Germany to explore possibilities in that direction, and early in 1938 he sought an agreement with Italy without waiting for a settlement of the Spanish problem. As a consequence of Chamberlain's latter move, Anthony Eden, who had championed collective security, resigned as Foreign Secretary (February 20, 1938). Eden's resignation precipitated a debate on foreign policy in the House of Commons, during which Prime Minister Chamberlain gave the following account of his policy.

THE POLICY OF APPEASEMENT

From CHAMBERLAIN, Speech of
  February 21, 1938 [1]

In order that the House may have before it as complete a picture as possible of the events which have led up to the present situation, I must ask their indulgence while I endeavour to state once again my own views upon certain aspects of foreign policy. . . . On a former occasion I described that policy as being based upon three principles—first, on the protection of British interests and the lives of British nationals; secondly, on the maintenance of peace, and, as far as we can influence it, the settlement of differences by peaceful means and not by force; and, thirdly, the promotion of friendly relations with other nations who are willing to reciprocate our friendly feelings and who will keep those rules of international conduct without which there can be neither security nor stability. [2]

[1] Great Britain, *Parliamentary Debates, House of Commons*, 5th ser., London, 1938, 332: 53-54, 64.

[2] Opponents of the appeasement policy charged that the Prime Minister merely played into the hands of the dictators. "The Prime Minister," said Mr. Attlee, "laid down three principles which he observed in foreign affairs, and then proceeded to show that in practice he disregarded them all. . . . The Foreign Secretary [Eden] has been thrown to the wolves. . . . He was willing, as we all are, to enter into conversations with other countries, but he was quite definite that there must be a public law in Europe. . . . The Prime Minister disregards that entirely."—*Ibid.*, 332: 65-66.

It is not enough to lay down general principles. If we truly desire peace, it is . . . necessary to make a sustained effort to ascertain, and if possible remove, the causes which threaten peace. . . . There is another fact which points in the same direction. We are . . . now engaged upon a gigantic scheme of rearmament. . . . Other countries are doing the same. Indeed, we were the last of the nations to rearm, but this process of general rearmament has been forced upon us all, because every country is afraid to disarm lest it should fall a victim of some armed neighbour. I recognise the force of that hard fact, but I have never ceased publicly to deplore what seems to me a senseless waste of money. . . . I cannot believe that, with a little good will and determination, it is not possible to remove genuine grievances and to clear away suspicions which may be entirely unfounded.

For these reasons, then, my colleagues and I have been anxious to find some opportunity of entering upon conversations with the two European countries with which we have been at variance, namely, Germany and Italy, in order that we might find out whether there was any common ground on which we might build up a general scheme of appeasement in Europe. . . .

The peace of Europe must depend upon the attitude of the four major Powers—Germany, Italy, France and ourselves. For ourselves, we are linked to France by common ideals of democracy, of liberty and Parliamentary government. France need not fear that the resignation of my right hon. Friend [Eden] upon this issue signifies any departure from the policy of the closest friendship with France. . . . On the other side we find Italy and Germany linked by affinities of outlook and in the forms of their government. The question that we have to think of is this: Are we to allow these two pairs of nations to go on glowering at one another across the frontier, allowing the feeling between the two sides to become more and more embittered, until at last the barriers are broken down and the conflict begins which many think would mark the end of civilisation? Or can we bring them to an understanding of one another's aims and objects, and to such discussion as may lead to a final settlement? If we can do that, if we can bring these four nations into friendly discussion, into a settling of their differences, we shall have saved the peace of Europe for a generation.

APPEASEMENT IN ACTION, 1937-1938

Anglo-Italian relations had deteriorated rapidly during the Italo-Ethiopian War. After the outbreak of the Spanish Civil War (July, 1936), Italian interference—especially Italian naval interference in the western Mediterranean—caused grave concern in Great Britain. In consequence of diplomatic conversations, the Italian Foreign Minister gave verbal assurances (September 12, 1936) that "the Italian Government had not, either before or since the revolution in Spain, engaged in any negotiations with General Franco whereby the *status quo* in the western Mediterranean would be altered, nor would they engage in any negotiations in the future." This verbal promise was confirmed in the following "Gentlemen's Agreement."

Appeasement with Italy

From "The Anglo-Italian Mediterranean Declaration" (January 2, 1937) [1]

His Majesty's Government in the United Kingdom and the Italian Government:

Animated by the desire to contribute

[1] *Ibid.*, 1936-37, XXIX; State Papers, Italy, No. 1 (1937), Cmd. 5348, 2.

increasingly, in the interests of the general cause of peace and security, to the betterment of relations between them and between all the Mediterranean Powers, and resolved to respect the rights and interests of those Powers;

Recognise that the freedom of entry into, exit from, and transit through, the Mediterranean is a vital interest both to the different parts of the British Empire and to Italy, and that these interests are in no way inconsistent with each other;

Disclaim any desire to modify or, so far as they are concerned, to see modified the *status quo* as regards national sovereignty of territories in the Mediterranean area;

Undertake to respect each other's rights and interests in the said area;

Agree to use their best endeavours to discourage any activities liable to impair the good relations which it is the object of the present declaration to consolidate.

This declaration is designed to further the end of peace and is not directed against any other Power.

Appeasement with Spain

From the outset, the Spanish Civil War sharpened the division of Europe into fascist and nonfascist groups. Germany and Italy gave active support to the Spanish insurgents, and Russia, though hampered by geography, assisted the Loyalists. Lest Spain become a cockpit in which all Europe fell to fighting, Great Britain and France arranged an international nonintervention agreement—which was generally ignored by the powers interested in the Spanish war. In fact, Italy gave little heed to her "Gentlemen's Agreement" with Great Britain, and in June, 1937, the Axis powers withdrew from the neutrality naval patrol off Spanish coasts because of "unprovoked" attacks by Spanish Loyalists. Immediately afterward, numerous acts of "piracy"

occurred in the Mediterranean, mostly consisting of submarine attacks on neutral vessels carrying cargoes to "Loyalist" Spain. To deal with this situation, Britain and France called a conference of powers to meet at Nyon, near Geneva, on September 9. Italy and Germany refused to be represented (because Russia was), but on September 14 nine powers signed the following Nyon Agreement—Great Britain, France, Russia, Greece, Romania, Turkey, Bulgaria, Yugoslavia, and Egypt.

From the Nyon Agreement
(September 14, 1937) [1]

Whereas arising out of the Spanish conflict attacks have been repeatedly committed in the Mediterranean by submarines against merchant ships not belonging to either of the conflicting Spanish parties; and

Whereas these attacks are violations of the rules of international law . . . ; and

Whereas without . . . admitting the right of either party to the conflict in Spain to exercise belligerent rights or to interfere with merchant ships on the high seas . . . and without prejudice to the right of any Participating Power to take such action as may be proper to protect its merchant shipping . . . it is necessary . . . to agree upon certain special collective measures against piratical acts by submarines:

In view whereof the undersigned . . . have met in conference at Nyon between the 9th and the 14th September 1937, and have agreed upon the following provisions which shall enter immediately into force:

I. The Participating Powers will instruct their naval forces to take the action indicated in paragraphs II and III below with a view to the protection of all mer-

[1] League of Nations, *Treaty Series 1937-1938*, CLXXXI (No. 4184), 137-39.

chant ships not belonging to either of the conflicting Spanish parties.

II. Any submarine which attacks such a ship contrary to the rules of international law . . . shall be counter-attacked and, if possible, destroyed.

III. The instruction mentioned in the preceding paragraph shall extend to any submarine encountered in the vicinity of . . . a ship not belonging to either of the conflicting Spanish parties [which] has been recently attacked in violation of the rules referred to . . . in circumstances which give valid grounds for the belief that the submarine was guilty of the attack.

IV. In order to facilitate . . . the above arrangements in a practical manner, the Participating Powers have agreed upon the following arrangements. . . . [These involve patrol-zone delimitations, with British and French fleets carrying the major assignments. A supplementary agreement, signed September 17, extended the Nyon Agreement to include protection against aircraft and surface craft.]

Further Appeasement with Italy

Prior to the Munich settlement [see immediately below], the high-water mark of Britain's appeasement policy was reached by the Anglo-Italian Pact of April 16, 1938. Eager to be free of Italian hostility in the Mediterranean and the Near East, Britain undertook negotiations with Italy, while Mussolini evidently welcomed a counterpoise to the oppressive friendship of Hitler. As a result, a Protocol was signed at Rome on April 16, 1938, followed by eight annexes and an exchange of notes. According to the Protocol, each of the Agreements and Declarations in the annexes "shall be regarded as a separate and self-contained instrument." They were:

From the Anglo-Italian Pact (April 16, 1938) [1]

(1) Reaffirmation of the Declaration of the 2nd January, 1937, regarding the Mediterranean . . . [see page 926].

(2) Agreement regarding the Exchange of Military Information [providing annual exchange of information].

(3) Agreement regarding certain Areas in the Middle East [Article 2 provided: "Neither Party will obtain or seek to obtain a privileged position of a political character in . . . Saudi Arabia or the Yemen"].

(4) Declaration regarding Propaganda [providing that each party would abstain from "methods of publicity or propaganda . . . in order to injure the interests of the other"].

(5) Declaration regarding Lake Tsana.

(6) Declaration regarding the Military Duties of Natives of Italian East Africa [which were confined to "local policing and territorial defence"].

(7) Declaration regarding the free Exercise of Religion and the Treatment of British religious Bodies in Italian East Africa [guaranteeing religious freedom].

(8) Declaration regarding the Suez Canal ["which guarantees at all times and for all Powers the free use of the Suez Canal"].

[In the exchange of notes which followed, Italy: 1. Agreed to reduce her military forces in Libya to "peace strength." 2. Gave assurances as regards her interference in Spain. 3. Acceded to the London Naval Treaty of 1936 [see page 909]. Britain: 1. Recognized Italian sovereignty over Ethiopia. 2. Agreed to use her influence to induce other states to do likewise. Two of the notes follow:]

[1] Great Britain, *Parliamentary Papers 1937-1938*, XXXI; Treaty Series, No. 31; 1938, Cmd. 5726, 4, 28-29, and *passim*.

Your Excellency: Your Excellency will remember that, in the course of our recent conversations, I gave Your Excellency certain assurances regarding the policy of the Italian Government in . . . Spain. I now wish to reaffirm those assurances and to place them on record.

First, the Italian Government have the honour to confirm their full adherence to the United Kingdom formula for the proportional evacuation of the foreign volunteers from Spain, and pledge themselves to give practical and real application to such an evacuation at the moment and on the conditions which shall be determined by the Non-Intervention Committee on the basis of the above-mentioned formula.

I desire secondly to reaffirm that if this evacuation has not been completed at the moment of the termination of the Spanish civil war, all remaining Italian volunteers will forthwith leave Spanish territory and all Italian war material will simultaneously be withdrawn.

I wish thirdly to repeat my previous assurance that the Italian Government have no territorial or political aims, and seek no privileged economic position, in or with regard to either Metropolitan Spain, the Balearic Islands, any of the Spanish possessions overseas, or the Spanish zone of Morocco, and that they have no intention whatever of keeping any armed forces in any of the said territories.

[To the above note, Lord Perth, the British Ambassador to Italy, wrote an acknowledgment of the same date which read, in part:]

I hardly need to remind Your Excellency [Count Ciano] that His Majesty's Government regard a settlement of the Spanish question as a prerequisite of the entry into force of the Agreement between our two Governments.

I have further the honour to inform Your Excellency that His Majesty's Government, being desirous that such obstacles as may at present be held to impede the freedom of member States as regards recognition of Italian sovereignty over Ethiopia should be removed, intend to take steps at the forthcoming meeting of the Council of the League of Nations for the purpose of clarifying the situation of member States in this regard.

Appeasement with Germany

Czechoslovakia, as constituted in 1918-19, embraced a polyglot population of nearly 14,000,000, including about 7,000,000 Czechs, over 2,000,000 Slovaks, 750,000 Magyars, 450,000 Ruthenes, over 3,000,000 Germans, and a variety of others. Though Czechoslovak minorities legislation was liberal and gently administered, discriminations existed, especially as Czechs tended to monopolize administrative posts. And, while great favor was shown to the German population, especially to the Sudetenland Germans, friction arose between the German minority and their Czech rulers. With the rise of Hitlerism in Germany, the Germans in Czechoslovakia became Nazified and, under the leadership of Konrad Henlein, began to howl about Czech repression and ill-treatment. By 1938, Hitler began openly to espouse the cause of German minorities outside the Reich, lamenting (February 20) that because of "the violence done to the map of Europe in the mad act of Versailles, over ten million Germans live in two of the States adjoining our frontiers" (Czechoslovakia and Poland). After German annexation of Austria in March, 1938, Czechoslovakia was in a poor strategic position, with the rising

German Empire on three sides of it. Almost immediately "incidents" between Czechs and the German minority began to multiply. On April 24, Henlein set forth an 8-point program (the Karlsbad Program), demanding full equality of status for Germans and Czechs, delimitation of German areas with full autonomy, reparations for all damages suffered by Germans since 1918, full liberty for the German language, culture, and ideology, a revision of Czech foreign policy, and other extravagant claims. When Henlein's program was rejected by the Czech Government, a new outburst of disorders followed throughout the summer of 1938, leading to mobilization of troops by both Czechoslovakia and Germany. By early August, all Europe looked on anxiously, and even Britain and France began to make military and naval preparations. On August 3, Prime Minister Chamberlain dispatched Lord Runciman to Prague to investigate. Before Lord Runciman had completed his mission, Hitler gave a passionate speech at Nuremberg, referring to Czechoslovakia as follows:[1]

"The conditions in this State . . . are intolerable. Here in political life over seven and a half millions in the name of the right of self-determination of a certain Mr. Wilson are deprived of their right of self-determination. . . . This misery of the Sudeten Germans is indescribable. It is sought to annihilate them. . . . When three and a half million members of a people which numbers nearly eighty millions may not sing a song they like simply because it does not please the Czechs, or when they are beaten until the blood flows solely because they wear stockings . . . which offend the Czechs, or when they

are terrorized and ill-treated because they use a form of greeting which the Czechs dislike . . . this may perhaps cause the . . . democracies no concern . . . but . . . this *does* concern us. . . . The depriving of these people of their rights must come to an end."

Hitler ended with a promise of German aid if the Sudeten Germans could not obtain their "rights" in any other way. The next day, in the face of even more serious incidents, the Czech Government established martial law, and the Sudeten leaders, breaking off all negotiations with the Czech Government, declared their unalterable intent to return to the Reich. By this time, Lord Runciman had concluded that cession to Germany of the predominantly German areas of Czechoslovakia was the only solution left.[2]

"Responsibility for the final break [he wrote to Prime Minister Chamberlain in his formal report of September 21] must, in my opinion, rest upon Herr Henlein and Herr Frank and upon those of their supporters inside and outside the country who were urging them to extreme and unconstitutional action. I have much sympathy, however, with the Sudeten case. It is a hard thing to be ruled by an alien race; and I have been left with the impression that Czechoslovak rule in the Sudeten areas . . . though not actively oppressive and certainly not "terroristic," has been marked by tactlessness, lack of understanding, petty intolerance and discrimination, to a point where . . . the German population was inevitably moving in the direction of revolt."

It was at this stage of events that Prime Minister Chamberlain, with French agreement, appealed to Hitler

---

[1] *The Speeches of Adolf Hitler*, II, 1489-90. By permission of the Oxford University Press.

[2] Great Britain, *Parliamentary Papers 1937-38*, XXX; Miscellaneous No. 7, 1938, Cmd. 5847, 4-5.

for a personal conference "to find a peaceful solution." Three conferences followed within a fortnight. In the first, at Berchtesgaden, September 15, Hitler demanded annexation of the German areas of Czechoslovakia and indicated a readiness to go to war for them. In consequence, Britain and France drew up proposals to the Czech Government (September 19), holding that "both Governments have been compelled to the conclusion that the maintenance of peace and the safety of Czechoslovakia's vital interests cannot effectively be assured unless these areas are now transferred to the Reich." And further, assuming Czech acquiescence, Britain and France proposed "to join in an international guarantee of the new boundaries of the Czechoslovak State." To these proposals Czechoslovakia reluctantly assented, but when Chamberlain took up the matter in a second conference with Hitler at Godesberg (September 22-23), the German Chancellor enlarged his demands, joined to them Hungarian and Polish claims, and insisted upon *immediate* transfer of all *predominantly* German areas with all military, industrial, and agrarian assets intact, together with a plebiscite in other German areas by November 25. Chamberlain refused the Führer's demands as an unwarranted extension of the original request, and Jan Masaryk, the Czech Minister, declared that "Herr Hitler's demands in their present form are absolutely and unconditionally unacceptable. . . . Against these new and cruel demands my Government feel bound to make their utmost resistance, and we shall do so, God helping. The nation of St. Wenceslas, John Hus and Thomas Masaryk will not be a nation of slaves."

An acute international crisis followed, broken only after President Franklin D. Roosevelt appealed (September 27) for another conference in an effort to avoid an appeal to force. The next day Hitler invited Chamberlain, Mussolini, and Daladier to a conference in Munich. There, on September 29-30, Hitler, Ribbentrop, Mussolini, Ciano, Chamberlain, and Daladier conferred and, without consulting Czech officials or other interested powers (such as the other members of the Little Entente and Russia), signed the following agreement acceding to practically all of Hitler's demands.

From "The Munich Agreement" (1938) [1]

Germany, the United Kingdom, France and Italy, taking into consideration the agreement, which has been already reached in principle for the cession to Germany of the Sudeten German territory, have agreed on the following terms and conditions governing the said cession . . . and by this agreement they each hold themselves responsible for the steps necessary to secure its fulfilment:

1. The evacuation will begin on the 1st October.

2. The United Kingdom, France and Italy agree that the evacuation of the territory shall be completed by 10th October, without any existing installations having been destroyed, and that the Czechoslovak Government will be held responsible for carrying out the evacuation without damage to the said installations.

3. The conditions governing the evacuation will be laid down in detail by an international Commission composed of representatives of Germany, the United Kingdom, France, Italy and Czechoslovakia.

4. The occupation by stages of the pre-

[1] *Ibid.*, XXX; Miscellaneous No. 8, 1938, Cmd 5848, 3-5.

dominantly German territory by German troops will begin on the 1st October. [The order of German occupation was described on an attached map.] . . .

5. The international Commission referred to in paragraph 3 will determine the territories in which a plebiscite is to be held. . . .

6. The final determination of the frontiers will be carried out by the international Commission. . . .

7. There will be a right of option into and out of the transferred territories . . . to be exercised within six months. . . .

8. The Czechoslovak Government will within a period of four weeks . . . release from their military and police forces any Sudeten Germans who may wish to be released . . . and Sudeten German prisoners who are serving terms of imprisonment for political offences. . . .

Annex to the Agreement: His Majesty's Government in the United Kingdom and the French Government have entered into the above agreement on the basis that they stand by the offer . . . relating to an international guarantee of the new boundaries of the Czechoslovak State against unprovoked aggression.

When the question of the Polish and Hungarian minorities in Czechoslovakia has been settled,[1] Germany and Italy for their part will give a guarantee to Czechoslovakia. . . .

Declaration. The Heads of the Governments of the four Powers declare that the problems of the Polish and Hungarian minorities in Czechoslovakia, if not settled within three months by agreement between the respective Governments, shall

form the subject of another meeting of the Heads of the Governments of the four Powers here present.
Munich, September 29, 1938

> [Signed] Adolf Hitler
> Neville Chamberlain
> Edouard Daladier
> Benito Mussolini

[Chamberlain returned to London by air September 30, proclaiming to crowds in Downing Street that night: "My good friends, this is the second time in our history that there has come back from Germany to Downing Street peace with honour. I believe it is peace for our time."]

Further Appeasement with Germany

Last among the major results of appeasement was the following self-evident Declaration.

From the Franco-German Declaration (December 6, 1938) [2]

Herr Joachim von Ribbentrop, German Minister for Foreign Affairs, and M. Georges Bonnet, French Minister for Foreign Affairs, acting in the name and by order of their Governments, have at their meeting in Paris, on December 6, 1938, agreed as follows:

1. The German . . . and the French Government fully share the conviction that peaceful and neighborly relations between Germany and France constitute one of the most essential elements for the consolidation of the situation in Europe and the maintenance of general peace. The two Governments will in consequence use all their efforts to ensure the development in this direction of the relations between their countries.

2. The two Governments recognize that between the two countries there is no

---

[1] Poland demanded (September 29) and won (October 2) the Teschen region, about 400 square miles and 240,000 people (less than 100,000 of whom were Poles); Hungary, after serious clashes, gained (November 2) a strip of southern Slovakia and Ruthenia, about 4,200 square miles with 1,060,000 inhabitants. In all, Czechoslovakia lost about 16,000 square miles and 5,000,000 persons.

[2] *Documents on the Events Preceding the Outbreak of the War,* German Library of Information, New York, 1940, No. 329, 353.

territorial question outstanding, and they solemnly recognize as final the frontiers between their countries as they now exist.

3. The two Governments are resolved . . . to remain in contact with regard to all questions concerning their two countries, and mutually to consult, should the later evolution of those questions lead to international difficulties.

In token whereof the representatives of the two Governments have signed the present Declaration, which comes into immediate effect.

4. The Outbreak of World War II (September 1, 1939)

GERMAN ABSORPTION OF THE CZECHO-SLOVAK STATE, MARCH 14-15, 1939

The problem of German minorities in Czechoslovakia, said Hitler on the eve of the Munich settlement, is "the last problem that must be solved and will be solved. It is the last territorial claim which I have to make in Europe." Nevertheless, by mid-March, 1939, Hitler employed alleged new anti-German activities as an excuse to annihilate the rump Czechoslovak state. Summoning the new Czech President, Emil Hácha, and his Foreign Minister, Frantisek Chvalkovsky, to Berlin, Hitler and his supporters browbeat them into signing over their state. M. Coulondre, the French Ambassador in Berlin, described the scene vividly.

From COULONDRE, *Report* to Bonnet (March 17, 1939) [1]

Immediately on arrival, M. Hacha and his Minister, who were received with

[1] M. Coulondre to M. Bonnet, Berlin, March 17, 1939, in *The French Yellow Book*, 1940, No. 77, 96-97. Reprinted by permission of Reynal & Hitchcock, New York.

military honors, were taken to the Chancellery where Herr Hitler, Field-Marshal Goering, Herr von Ribbentrop, and Herr Kepler were waiting for them.

The document to be signed lay waiting on the table, in its final form, as well as a memorandum relating to the future Statute for the administration of Bohemia and Moravia.

The Fuehrer stated very briefly that the time was not one for negotiation but that the Czech Ministers had been summoned to be informed of Germany's decisions, that these decisions were irrevocable, that Prague would be occupied on the following day at 9 o'clock, Bohemia and Moravia incorporated within the Reich and constituted a Protectorate, and whoever tried to resist would be "trodden underfoot." With that, the Fuehrer wrote his signature and went out. It was about 12:30 A.M. A tragic scene then took place between the Czech Ministers and the three Germans.

For hours on end Dr. Hacha and M. Chvalkovsky protested against the outrage done to them. . . . The German ministers were pitiless. They literally hunted Dr. Hacha and M. Chvalkovsky round the table on which the documents were lying, thrusting them continually before them, pushing pens into their hands, incessantly repeating if they continued in their refusal, half Prague would lie in ruins from aerial bombardment within two hours. . . . Hundreds of bombers were awaiting only the order to take off, and they would receive that order at six in the morning if the signatures were not forthcoming by then.

President Hacha was in such a state of exhaustion that he more than once needed medical attention from the doctors, who, by the way, had been there ready . . . since the beginning. . . . At 4:30 in the morning, Dr. Hacha, in a state of total collapse, and kept going only by means of injections, resigned himself with death in his soul to give his signature. As he left the Chancellery, M. Chvalkovsky declared: "Our people will curse us, and yet we have saved their existence. We have preserved them from a horrible massacre."

BRITISH REACTIONS TO THE DESTRUCTION OF CZECHOSLOVAKIA

From CHAMBERLAIN, Speech at Birmingham, March 17, 1939 [1]

One thing is certain. Public opinion in the world has received a sharper shock than has ever yet been administered to it, even by the present régime in Germany. . . .

How can these events this week be reconciled with those assurances which I have read out to you? Surely, as a joint signatory of the Munich Agreement, I was entitled, if Herr Hitler thought it ought to be undone, to that consultation which is provided for in the Munich declaration. Instead of that he has taken the law into his own hands. Before even the Czech President was received, and confronted with demands which he had no power to resist, the German troops were on the move, and within a few hours they were in the Czech capital. . . .

What has become of this declaration of "No further territorial ambition"? What has become of the assurance, "We don't want Czechs in the Reich"? What regard had been paid here to that principle of self-determination on which Herr Hitler argued so vehemently with me at Berchtesgaden when he was asking for the severance of Sudetenland . . . and its inclusion in the German Reich? . . .

Does not the question inevitably arise in our minds, if it is so easy to discover good reasons for ignoring assurances so solemnly and so repeatedly given, what reliance can be placed upon any other assurances that come from the same source? . . .

Germany, under her present régime, has sprung a series of unpleasant surprises upon the world. The Rhineland, the Austrian *Anschluss,* the severance of Sudetenland—all these things shocked and affronted public opinion throughout the world. Yet, however much we might take exception to the methods which were adopted . . . there was something to be said, whether on account of racial affinity or of just claims too long resisted—there was something to be said for the necessity of a change in the existing situation.

But the events which have taken place this week in complete disregard of the principles laid down by the German Government itself seem to fall into a different category, and they must cause us all to be asking ourselves: "Is this the end of an old adventure, or is it the beginning of a new? Is this the last attack upon a small State, or is it to be followed by others? Is this, in fact, a step in the direction of an attempt to dominate the world by force?" . . .

We ourselves will naturally turn first to our partners in the British Commonwealth of Nations and to France, to whom we are so closely bound. . . . I feel bound to repeat that . . . no greater mistake could be made than to suppose that, because it believes war to be a senseless and cruel thing, this nation has so lost its fibre that it will not take part to the utmost of its power in resisting such a challenge [as an attempt to dominate the world by force] if it ever were made.

[1] Great Britain, *Parliamentary Papers 1938-39,* XXVII; Miscellaneous No. 9, 1939, Cmd. 6106, No. 9, 5, 8-10.

FRENCH REACTIONS TO THE DESTRUCTION OF CZECHOSLOVAKIA

From COULONDRE, *Report* to Bonnet
(March 19, 1939) [1]

A direct challenge to world opinion by the treachery, the cynicism, and the brutality it shows, the "coup" by which Germany has just wiped Czechoslovakia off the map cannot simply be dismissed as a break in the general political line taken by Germany since last autumn. . . . On the very morrow of the Munich Agreement, it was clear that beyond the Rhine this Agreement was taken to imply a free hand for Germany in Central and Eastern Europe. . . . For months this version found daily expression in the great German newspapers, officially inspired. . . . I myself have more than once noted the same state of mind in Herr von Ribbentrop. . . . As the Fuehrer said in his speech of January 30, "Central Europe was a region where the Western Powers had no concern." . . .

Though we have no reason whatever to be surprised at this new advance of German influence in the East, on the other hand we have every right to condemn the unspeakable methods used by the Reich to achieve it. It is these methods which, properly speaking, constitute the break in the policy of appeasement. . . . France and Britain were entitled to expect that in the event of fresh Central European difficulties they would be consulted by the Reich. . . . France and Great Britain also had the right to assume that Germany would not reject the racial principle which at Munich had guided the settlement . . . nor that, having invoked the rights of nationalities, Germany would violate them so wantonly.

[1] M. Coulondre to M. Bonnet, Berlin, March 19, 1939, in *The French Yellow Book,* No. 80, 100-02. By permission of Reynal & Hitchcock.

THE END OF APPEASEMENT

On March 23, 1939, Germany annexed Memel and followed with demands upon Poland regarding the Free City of Danzig and the Province of Pormorze (the "Polish Corridor"). Immediately, Anglo-French policy stiffened, and on March 31, Prime Minister Chamberlain announced an agreement with Poland which, by August, hardened into a mutual assistance pact.

From CHAMBERLAIN, Speech on the Anglo-Polish Agreement (March 31, 1939) [2]

I am glad to take this opportunity of stating again the general policy of His Majesty's Government. They have constantly advocated the adjustment, by way of free negotiation between the parties concerned, of any differences that may arise. . . . As the House is aware, certain consultations are now proceeding with other Governments. In order to make perfectly clear the position of His Majesty's Government in the meantime before those consultations are concluded, I have now to inform the House that during that period, in the event of any action which clearly threatened Polish independence, and which the Polish Government accordingly considered it vital to resist with their national forces, His Majesty's Government would feel themselves bound at once to lend the Polish Government all support in their power. They have given the Polish Government an assurance to this effect.

I may add that the French Government have authorised me to make it plain that they stand in the same position in this matter as do His Majesty's Government.

[2] Great Britain, *Parliamentary Papers 1938-39,* XXVII; Miscellaneous No. 9, 1939, Cmd. 6106, No. 17, 36.

GERMAN DEMANDS ON POLAND

The Anglo-French Agreement with Poland incensed Hitler, who began screaming against Britain's "policy of encirclement." Late in April, Germany presented a memorandum to England, stating that "By means of this encirclement policy the British Government has unilaterally deprived the Naval Agreement of the 18th June, 1935, of its basis," and that, therefore, the German Government regarded the treaty "as having lapsed." The next day (April 28), Germany denounced the ten-year German-Polish Nonaggression Pact of 1934, holding that the "new arrangement between Poland and Great Britain, whatever its final form may be, is intended by both partners as a regular treaty of alliance . . . directed solely against Germany." On the same day, Hitler gave another long speech to the Reichstag, heaping ridicule upon President Roosevelt, who had written an open letter (April 14) to Hitler and Mussolini [1] asking them to give a ten-year pledge of nonaggression against thirty small states; and he announced demands on Poland painfully like those made upon Czechoslovakia a year earlier.

From HITLER, Speech of April 28, 1939 [2]

There is little to be said as regards German-Polish relations. Here, too, the Treaty of Versailles—of course intentionally—inflicted a most severe wound on Germany. The strange way in which the Corridor, giving Poland access to the sea, was marked out was meant above all to prevent for all time the establishment of an understanding between Poland and Germany. . . . Nevertheless, I have never ceased to uphold the view that the necessity of free access to the sea for the Polish State cannot be ignored. . . . The late Marshal Pilsudski . . . was prepared to go into the question of taking the sting out of German-Polish relations, and finally to conclude an Agreement whereby Germany and Poland expressed their intention of renouncing war altogether as a means of settling the questions which concerned them both [the Nonaggression Pact of 1934]. . . .

Nevertheless there remained one unsettled question . . . which naturally had to be solved sooner or later—the question of the German city of Danzig. Danzig is a German city and wishes to belong to Germany. On the other hand, this city has treaties with Poland, which, however, were forced upon her by the dictators of Versailles. But since the League of Nations, formerly the greatest fomenter of trouble, is now represented by a High Commissioner of extraordinary tact, the problem of Danzig must in any case come up for discussion, to be solved at the latest when this calamitous institution finally comes to an end. I regard the peaceful settlement of this problem as a further contribution to a final relaxation of European tension. . . . Since the problem of Danzig has been repeatedly discussed some months ago, I have now made a concrete offer to the Polish Government. I will reveal this offer to you, members of the Reichstag, and you yourselves shall judge whether it does not represent the greatest concession conceivable in the interests of European peace. . . . I am no democratic statesman, but a National-Socialist and a realist. I do, however, consider it necessary to make it clear to the Government in Warsaw that just as they desire access to the sea, so Germany needs access to her province of East Prussia. . . .

[1] On April 13, Italy formally annexed Albania, having invaded it on April 7.
[2] Documents on the Events Preceding the Outbreak of the War, German Library of Information, No. 214, 226-29.

I have now had the following proposal submitted to the Polish Government:

1. Danzig returns as a Free State into the framework of the German Reich.

2. Germany receives a route through the Corridor and a railway line at her own disposal, and having the same extraterritorial status for Germany as the Corridor itself has for Poland. In return Germany is prepared: 1. To recognize all Polish economic rights in Danzig. 2. To ensure for Poland a free harbor in Danzig. . . . 3. . . . To accept the frontiers between Germany and Poland . . . as final. 4. To conclude a 25-year non-aggression pact with Poland. . . .

The Polish Government have rejected my offer and have only declared that they are prepared

1. To negotiate concerning the question of a substitute for the League Commissioner, and

2. To consider facilities for through traffic across the Corridor.

I sincerely regretted this incomprehensible attitude on the part of the Polish Government. But that alone is not the decisive factor. Far worse is the fact that Poland, like Czechoslovakia a year ago, now believes, under the pressure of lying international agitation, that she must call up troops, although Germany on her part has not called up a single man and has not thought of taking any kind of action against Poland. . . . Some day posterity will decide whether it was really right to refuse this proposition, which I make once and only once. . . .

Germany's alleged aggressive intentions, a mere figment of the international press, led, as you know, to . . . Poland's incurring an obligation for mutual assistance, which would compel her under certain circumstances to take military action against Germany. . . . This obligation is contrary to the Agreement which I made with Marshal Pilsudski some years ago.

. . . I therefore look upon the Agreement . . . as having been unilaterally infringed by Poland and thereby no longer in existence.

NEW ALLIANCES: THE RUSSO-GERMAN NONAGGRESSION PACT (1939)

Throughout the summer of 1939, reports of "atrocities" perpetrated by Poles against the German minority in Poland, together with expressions of indignation against Britain, poured from the Nazi press. Likewise, new international alignments took place. Britain and France negotiated mutual assistance pacts with Turkey (May-June), gave guarantees to Romania and Greece, and formalized their commitment with Poland (August 25); Germany and Italy enlarged the Rome-Berlin Axis into a full political and military alliance (May 22), and Germany entered into nonaggression agreements with Denmark, Estonia, and Latvia (May-June). But most surprising and disquieting of all was the Russo-German Nonaggression Pact announced August 23. Since March, France and Great Britain had sought to bring Russia into the orbit of the democratic front, but Russia found excuses and delayed. Nevertheless, considering Nazi-Communist bitterness, Russia's agreement with Germany struck the democracies like a bombshell, as the height of Bolshevik perfidy—and it placed signatories of the Anti-Comintern Pact in a strange position. Terms of the treaty ran as follows.

From the Russo-German Nonaggression Pact (August 23, 1939) [1]

Guided by the desire to strengthen the cause of peace between Germany and the Union of Socialist Soviet Republics, and

[1] *Ibid.*, No. 348, 370-71.

basing themselves upon the fundamental stipulations of the Neutrality Agreement concluded . . . in April, 1926, the German Government and the Government of the Union of Socialist Soviet Republics have come to the following agreement:

Art. 1. The two contracting parties undertake to refrain from any act of force, any aggressive act and any attacks against each other . . . either singly or in conjunction with any other Powers.

Art. 2. If one of the . . . parties should become the object of war-like action on the part of a third Power, the other . . . party will in no way support the third Power.

Art. 3. The Governments of the two . . . parties will . . . remain in consultation in order to inform each other about questions which touch their common interests.

Art. 4. Neither of the two . . . parties will join any group of Powers which is directed . . . against the other party.

Art. 5. In case disputes . . . should arise between the two . . . parties, the two partners will solve these disputes . . . exclusively by friendly exchange of views or . . . by arbitration. . . .

Art. 6. The present agreement is concluded for . . . ten years. . . .

Art. 7. The present agreement . . . comes into force immediately it has been signed. . . .

Moscow, August 23, 1939. . . .

[Signed] Ribbentrop. Molotov.

WAR DISPLACES DIPLOMATIC EFFORTS, AUGUST 22-SEPTEMBER 1, 1939

About 9 P.M. on August 22, Sir Nevile Meyrick Henderson, the British Ambassador at Berlin, received instructions to convey a personal letter from Prime Minister Chamberlain to Hitler. As Hitler was at Berchtesgaden, Henderson flew there the next day. The Prime Minister's letter contained three main points: 1. To insist upon Britain's determination to stand by Poland. 2. To reassert Britain's readiness to continue negotiations for settlement of issues between Germany and England. 3. To urge Germany to enter into direct discussion with Poland in regard to Polish-German difficulties. Henderson found Hitler in a violent, excitable mood (it was the day Ribbentrop signed the Russian pact in Moscow), and he returned to Berlin without satisfaction from the Führer. However, two days later, after Hitler had returned to Berlin, the Chancellor softened somewhat, summoned Henderson to the Chancellery (August 25), and urged him personally to lay proposals—his "last offer" —before the Prime Minister. Hitler's proposals—"a large comprehensive offer"—involved, first, the necessity of an immediate settlement of the dispute between Germany and Poland, and, second, an offer of friendship and alliance with Britain after the Polish troubles had been peaceably settled. Sir Nevile flew to London on August 26, spent two days in conference with the British ministers, and returned to Berlin in the afternoon of August 28 with the British reply.

Henderson's Account of the British Communication, August 28, 1939

From HENDERSON, "Final Report" (September 20, 1939) [1]

Therein, while the obligations of His Majesty's Government to Poland were re-

[1] "Final Report by . . . Sir Nevile Henderson, September 20, 1939," in *Parliamentary Papers 1938-39*, XXVII (Germany No. 1, 1939), Cmd. 6115, 12. Daladier, President Roosevelt, and others made similar appeals to Hitler about the same time. Cf. *The French Yellow Book*, No. 261; *Parliamentary Papers 1938-39*, XXVII; Miscellaneous No. 9, 1939, Cmd. 6106, 181 ff.

affirmed, it was stated that the Polish Government were ready to enter into negotiations with the German Government for a reasonable solution of the matter in dispute on the basis of the safeguarding of Poland's essential interests and of an international guarantee for the settlement eventually arrived at. His Majesty's Government accordingly proposed that the next step should be the initiation of direct discussions between the Polish and German Governments on that basis and the adoption of immediate steps to relieve the tension in the matter of the treatment of minorities. Furthermore, His Majesty's Government undertook to use all their influence with a view to contributing toward a solution which might be satisfactory to both parties and which would, they hoped, prepare the way for the negotiation of that wider and more complete understanding between Great Britain and Germany which both countries desired.

The German Reply to the British Communication, August 29, 1939

After noting with satisfaction the British proposals of August 28, Germany pointed out that "since the autumn of 1938, and for the last time in March, 1939," she had sought vainly to settle peaceably her disputes with Poland. But Poland had rejected all offers, had mobilized her troops, and, with regard to the German minority, had subjected them "to atrocious and barbarous ill-treatment' and . . . persecution"—"a state of affairs which can no longer be remedied in a matter of days or even weeks but for which perhaps only a few hours remain." However, "despite their sceptical judgment of the prospects of such direct negotiations, the German Government are nevertheless prepared to accept the English proposal, and to enter into direct discussions." The German reply closed with

the following preposterous proposal—preposterous especially because it was handed to the British Ambassador at 7:15 P.M. on August 29.

From HITLER, "Reply to the British Proposal" (August 29, 1939) [1]

The German Government therefore agree to accept the proposed intermediation of the British Government to send to Berlin a Polish representative invested with plenipotentiary powers. They expect his arrival on Wednesday, August 30, 1939.

The German Government will immediately draft the proposals for a solution acceptable to them, and, if possible, will make such proposals available for the British Government also before the Polish negotiator arrives.

The Breakdown of Diplomacy (1939)

In the course of August 30, British diplomats made three important observations with regard to the German reply of August 29: 1. The time allotted for the appearance in Berlin of a fully empowered Polish emissary was unreasonably short—so short, in fact, that Sir Nevile Henderson told Hitler and Ribbentrop that it sounded like an ultimatum, which incensed the Germans. 2. The entire setting was so similar to that prepared for President Hácha in the previous March [see page 933] that Britain hesitated to ask Poland to accede to it, urging, instead, that the German proposals be transmitted through the Polish Ambassador to Warsaw, with a view to arrangements being made for the conduct of further negotiations. 3. That both Germany and Poland must avoid frontier incidents and refrain from military action which

[1] *Documents on the Events Preceding the Outbreak of the War,* German Library of Information, No. 464, 480-82.

might jeopardize negotiations. Exactly at midnight, on August 30, Sir Nevile Henderson waited on Ribbentrop, the German Foreign Minister, choosing his time carefully, because, while no Polish emissary had arrived, neither had Germany tendered her propositions as a basis for settlement, and, as Sir Nevile said, "it was utterly unreasonable to expect a Polish plenipotentiary to present himself at Berlin without even knowing in advance the basis of the proposals about which he was expected to negotiate." [1] Sir Nevile's telegraphic report of the interview follows.

From HENDERSON, Report on Interview with Ribbentrop (August 30-31, 1939) [2]

I told Herr von Ribbentrop . . . that His Majesty's Government found it difficult to advise Polish Government to accept procedure adumbrated in German reply, and suggested that he should adopt normal contact, *i.e.,* that when German proposals were ready to invite Polish Ambassador to call and to hand him proposals for transmission to his Government with a view to immediate opening of negotiations. . . .

Herr von Ribbentrop's reply was to produce a lengthy document which he read out in German aloud at top speed. Imagining that he would eventually hand it to me I did not attempt to follow too closely the sixteen or more articles which it contained. . . .

When I asked Herr von Ribbentrop for text of these proposals in accordance with undertaking in the German reply of yesterday, he asserted that it was too late as Polish representative had not arrived in Berlin by midnight.

I observed that to treat the matter in this way meant that request for Polish representative to arrive . . . on 30th August constituted, in fact, an ultimatum in spite of what he and Herr Hitler had assured me yesterday. This he denied, saying that idea of an ultimatum was figment of my imagination. Why then I asked could he not adopt normal procedure and give a copy of proposals and ask Polish Ambassador to call on him . . . ? In the most violent terms Herr von Ribbentrop said that he would never ask the Ambassador to visit him. . . . We parted on that note.

[Late the next day a representative of the German Foreign Office presented Henderson with a copy of the sixteen proposals with a statement, published in the German version of the interview, which read as follows.]

From German Memorandum of Conversation with the British Ambassador (Midnight, August 30, 1939) [3]

Henderson asked whether the German proposals were ready, and whether these proposals could be handed over to him.

The German Foreign Minister replied, first, that British intervention had so far led to only one tangible result, namely, general mobilization on the part of Poland [Germany had mobilized too, establishing food rationing and blackout on August 27]; and second, that Germany had been counting on the arrival of a Polish representative that day. This had not constituted an ultimatum, as the British Ambassador erroneously assumed, but, as the Fuehrer had already explained . . . a practical proposal dictated by prevailing conditions. By midnight Germany had

[1] "Final Report by . . . Sir Nevile Henderson, September 20, 1939," *loc. cit.,* 16.
[2] Great Britain, *Parliamentary Papers 1938-39,* XXVII; Miscellaneous No. 9, 1939, Cmd. 6106, No. 92, 145-46.

[3] *Documents on the Events Preceding the Outbreak of the War,* German Library of Information, No. 466, 483.

received no answer from Poland. The question of a possible proposal therefore no longer existed. In order to show, however, what proposals Germany had intended to make if Polish representative had come, the Foreign Minister read aloud the German proposals contained in the Appendix and explained them in detail.

[But Sir Nevile Henderson denied that the proposals had been presented in this manner. Later he wrote of this interview, and of its fateful sequel, as follows.]

From HENDERSON, *Failure of a Mission* (1940) [1]

In themselves and taken at their face value they [the German proposals] were not unreasonable and might well have served as a basis for negotiation. That is why one can only assume that Ribbentrop did not wish them to be discussed, and his attitude that night was not only one of ill manners, but also of ill faith. He endeavoured to conceal this later by a deliberate distortion of the truth. In the note which was handed to me . . . the next evening and which contained at last the text of those proposals . . . it was stated that Herr von Ribbentrop had given the British Ambassador [at the midnight interview] . . . precise information as to the text of the German proposals. . . . The German White Paper on the origins of the war repeats this complete perversion of the actual facts. None of the points at issue in the memorandum were discussed at all. . . . Did Ribbentrop have such a high opinion of my memorizing faculty as to think. that, after listening to his jabber of words, I could . . . give either His Majesty's or the Polish Government an authoritative account of the exact sense

[1] From *Failure of a Mission*, 286-88. Copyright 1940 by Sir Nevile Henderson. Courtesy of G. P. Putnam's Sons.

of a long and complicated text? Yet that apparently was what Ribbentrop was pleased to call "precise information" about a document of vital importance, upon which peace or war depended. . . .

There was, in fact, for Herr Hitler only one conceivable alternative to brute force, and that was that a Polish plenipotentiary should humbly come to him, after the manner of Dr. Schuschnigg or President Hacha, and sign on the dotted line to the greater glory of Adolf Hitler. . . .

There was, however, a further delay. . . . [August 31] The Polish Government had . . . authorized their Ambassador to establish contact with Ribbentrop; and Hitler waited to learn what message M. Lipski would bring . . . whether his qualifications would be those of a plenipotentiary . . . to conduct and conclude negotiations. . . . The meeting . . . proved, however, quite futile. [It was held about 6 P.M. on August 31.] M. Lipski stated that he was acting solely in his capacity as an ambassador without plenary powers . . . and handed to the Minister for Foreign Affairs a brief communication to the effect that the Polish Government were weighing favourably the [British] proposal . . . for direct discussion. . . . He did not ask for the German proposals, and Ribbentrop did not offer to give them to him. Their meeting lasted but a few minutes. When, after his interview, the Polish Ambassador attempted once more to telephone to his Government, he found that it was no longer possible for him to do so. Hitler had, in fact, chosen his moment to precipitate the conflict. He did not want direct negotiations with the Poles. It was zero hour. . . .

In point of fact the advance into Poland had been ordered immediately after Lipski's meeting with Ribbentrop, and in the early hours of September 1st without any declaration of war the German Army crossed the frontier, and the German Air

Force proceeded to bomb the Polish airdromes and lines of communications.

THE LEADERS' SPEECHES IN JUSTIFICATION OF WAR

The German Apologia

From HITLER, Speech to the Reichstag, September 1, 1939 [1]

[Hitler began with the familiar review of his "peace efforts," including his acceptance of the British offer of mediation between Poland and Germany:]

For these discussions I had drawn up the fundamentals which are known to you. And then I and my Government sat expectantly for two whole days in order to find out whether the Polish Government saw fit finally to dispatch an authorized representative or not. Up to last night the Polish Government did not dispatch an authorized representative, but informed us by their Ambassador that at present they were considering the question whether and to what extent they might be able to accept the British proposals. . . .

My love of peace and my endless patience must not be mistaken for weakness, much less for cowardice. Last night I informed the British Government that . . . I have found it impossible to detect any inclination on the part of the Polish Government to enter into a really serious discussion with us.

These proposals of mediation are thus wrecked, for in the meantime the answer to these offers of mediation had been, first, the order for Polish general mobilization, and, secondly, serious additional outrages. Repetitions of the latter incidents occurred last night. Only recently during one single night 21 frontier incidents occurred, last night there were 14, three of them of a most serious character. For that reason, I have now decided to address Poland in exactly the same language as Poland has been using toward us for months. . . .

In the night Polish soldiers of the Regular Army fired the first shots in our own territory. Since 5:45 A.M. we have been returning their fire. And from now onwards every bomb will be answered by another bomb. . . . I will carry on this fight, no matter against whom, until such time as the safety of the Reich and its rights are secured! . . .

Therefore, I have once again put on that uniform which was always so sacred and dear to me. I shall not lay it aside until after the victory—or I shall not live to see the end.

Should anything happen to me in this war, my first successor shall be Party Member [Field Marshal Hermann] Göring. Should anything happen to Party Member Göring, his successor shall be Party Member [Rudolf] Hess. To these men as your leaders you would then owe the same absolute loyalty and obedience that you owe me. In the event that something fatal should happen to Party Member Hess, I am about to make legal provisions for the convocation of a Senate appointed by me, who shall then elect the worthiest, that is to say the most valiant among themselves.

As a National Socialist and a German soldier I enter upon this fight with a stout heart! . . . One word I have never known: Capitulation. . . .

As for the rest of the world, I can only assure them that November, 1918, shall never occur again in German history.

I ask of every German what I myself am prepared to do at any moment: to be ready to lay down his life for his people and for his country. . . .

Germany—*Sieg Heil!*

[1] *Documents on the Events Preceding the Outbreak of the War,* The German Library of Information, No. 471, 500, 502-4.

The British Explanation

Great Britain and France mobilized for war as soon as the German attack on Poland was known, but they notified Germany of their willingness still to negotiate if German forces were withdrawn from Poland. Italy declared an intention to remain neutral and (September 2) proposed a five-power conference. But England refused to negotiate while German forces were on Polish soil. Early in the morning of September 3, England demanded German withdrawal and "satisfactory assurances" by 11 A.M. or "we shall inform the German representative that a state of war exists as from that hour." About noon, the German rejection of the ultimatum arrived. France, making a similar demand and meeting with a similar response, declared war at 5 P.M. on the same day. Thus, exactly twenty-five years from the beginning of World War I, World War II of the twentieth century began. The next day, September 4, Prime Minister Chamberlain addressed the German people by radio as follows.

From CHAMBERLAIN, Radio Address to the German People, September 4, 1939 [1]

GERMAN PEOPLE—Your country and mine are at war. . . . God knows this country has done everything possible to prevent this calamity. But now that the invasion of Poland by Germany has taken place, it has become inevitable.

You were told by your Government that you are fighting because Poland rejected your Leader's offer and resorted to force. What are the facts? The so-called "offer" was made to the Polish Ambassador on Thursday evening, two hours before the announcement by your Government that it had been "rejected." So far

[1] Great Britain, *Parliamentary Papers 1938-39,* XXVII; Miscellaneous No. 9, 1939, Cmd. 6106, No. 144, 194-95.

from having been rejected, there had been no time even to consider it.

Your Government had previously demanded that a Polish representative should be sent to Berlin within twenty-four hours to conclude an agreement . . . to sign an agreement which he had not even seen. This is not negotiation. This is a dictate. To such methods no self-respecting and powerful State could assent. Negotiations on a free and equal basis might well have settled the matter in dispute.

You may ask why Great Britain is concerned. We are concerned because we gave our word of honour to defend Poland against aggression. Why did we feel it necessary to pledge ourselves to defend this Eastern Power when our interests lie in the West? The answer is—and I regret to have to say it—that nobody in this country any longer places any trust in your Leader's word.

He gave his word that he would respect the Locarno Treaty; he broke it. He gave his word that he neither wished nor intended to annex Austria; he broke it. He declared that he would not incorporate the Czechs in the Reich; he did so. He gave his word after Munich that he had no further territorial demands in Europe; he broke it. He has sworn for years that he was the mortal enemy of Bolshevism; he is now its ally.

Can you wonder his word is, for us, not worth the paper it is written on?

The German-Soviet Pact was a cynical *volte-face,* designed to shatter the Peace Front against aggression. This gamble failed. The Peace Front stands firm. . . .

In this war we are not fighting against you, the German people, for whom we have no bitter feeling, but against a tyrannous and forsworn régime which has betrayed not only its own people but the whole of Western civilisation and all that you and we hold dear.

May God defend the right!

43

THE SECOND WORLD WAR (1939-1945)

Materials for the history of World War II lie on every side of us. For, whether or not it was the "best-reported war" in history, it was certainly the most-reported one. The mass of this material remains inchoate, as yet winnowed neither by time nor by critical minds, and molded into no well-defined pattern by balanced, reasonably objective treatments. Moreover, readers of this book, within the next decade at least, are almost certain to have personal and poignant memories of these hard and bitter war years. In such circumstances, the materials of this chapter cannot be fortified by reference to historical syntheses already made, and it can accomplish little more than to remind the reader of a few of the peaks—and, unhappily, some of the valleys—of this vast contemporary scene.

1. The Years of Axis Offensive (1939-1942)

On September 17, 1939, little more than two weeks after Germany took up arms, Russian troops entered East Poland in an effort, only later apparent, to build a buffer between Russia and her newest "ally." Poland's allies could give—immediately—only token aid, and Poland, caught between two Great Powers, collapsed in less than a month. On October 29, Germany and Russia

subjected the devastated Polish state to its fifth partition. Meanwhile, on October 6 Hitler reviewed the events of the first month of the war before the Reichstag, and offered peace to Great Britain and France—an offer which was coldly rejected. Parts of Hitler's speech follow.

THE "LAST PEACE OFFER"

From HITLER, Speech of October 6, 1939 [1]

After one week of fighting there could no longer be any doubt as to the outcome. Whenever Polish troops met German units, they were driven back or dispersed. . . . Death-defying in attack, advancing at an unconquerable rate of progress, infantry, armored detachments, air force and units of the navy were soon dictating the course of events. . . .

That the last remnants of the Polish Army were able to hold out in Warsaw, Modlin, and on Hela Peninsula until October 1 was not due to their prowess in arms, but only to our cool thinking and our sense of responsibility. I forbade the sacrifice of more human lives than was absolutely necessary[!]. . . .

The attempt to convince the responsible Polish command—in so far as it existed—that it was futile and in fact insane to attempt resistance, especially in a city of more than a million inhabitants, proved

[1] This and the next selection are from Hitler, *My New Order*. By permission of Reynal & Hitchcock. This is 722-25, 727-28, 737-42, 749-51, 755-56.

entirely fruitless. A "generalissimo," who himself took to inglorious flight, forced upon the capital of his country a resistance which could never lead to anything but its destruction. . . . The entire city [Warsaw] was converted into a fortress and barricaded in every direction. . . . Sheer sympathy for women and children caused me to . . . offer . . . to let civilian inhabitants leave the city. I declared a temporary armistice and safeguards necessary for evacuation. . . . The proud Polish commander . . . did not even . . . reply. . . . Twice I attempted to evacuate at least the international colony from the city. In this I finally succeeded . . . in the case of the Russian colony actually at the last moment. I then ordered a general attack on the city for September 25. . . . Warsaw capitulated on the 27th. . . .

The outcome of the war was the annihilation of all Polish armies, followed by the dissolution of the Polish State. . . .

Versailles was the cradle of a Polish State. . . . Poland, who for centuries past had proved herself incapable of existence, was in 1916 artificially begotten and in 1919 no less artificially born by a German government just as incapable of existence. . . . [Here Hitler launched into a description of the political, economic, and social weaknesses of the Polish state in an obvious attempt to persuade the Allies that Poland was not worth fighting for, and that "One of the most senseless deeds perpetrated at Versailles is thus a thing of the past." He went on to proclaim unity of purpose as between Germany and Russia in relieving "one of the most acute danger spots in Europe of its threatening character."]

Germany and the Soviet Union have therefore clearly defined the boundaries of their own spheres of interest with the intention of being singly responsible for law and order and preventing everything which might cause injury to the other partner.

·The aims and tasks which emerge from the collapse of the Polish State are, insofar as the German sphere of interest is concerned, roughly as follows:

1. Demarcation of the boundary for the Reich, which will do justice to historical, ethnographical and economic facts.

2. Pacification of the whole territory. . . .

3. Absolute guarantees of security . . . for the entire sphere of interest.

4. Re-establishment and reorganization of economic life . . . involving development of culture. . . .

5. As the most important task, however, to establish a new order of ethnographic conditions, that is to say, resettlement of nationalities . . . *so as to remove at least part of the material for European conflict.* Germany and the Union of Soviet Republics have come to an agreement to support each other in this matter. . . .

As Germany and Soviet Russia undertake this work of re-establishment, the two States are entitled to point out that the attempt to solve this problem by the methods of Versailles has proved an utter failure. . . .

And I personally take exception at seeing foreign statesmen stand up and call me guilty of having broken my word because I have now put these revisions through. On the contrary I pledged my sacred word to the German people to do away with the Treaty of Versailles and to restore to them their natural and vital rights as a great nation. . . . [Here Hitler gave the familiar account of his "peaceful" attempts to revise the Versailles settlement.]

It was fortunate for humanity and no misfortune at all that I succeeded in removing the craziest, most impossible clauses of the Versailles Treaty by peaceful methods. . . . The last revision of this treaty could have been brought about in exactly the same peaceful way. . . . That is chiefly the fault of those who not only took no pleasure in the former peaceful revision, but on the contrary complained of the fact that by peaceful methods a new Central Europe was being built up; that is to say, a Central Europe that was able once more to give its inhabitants work and bread.

As I have already mentioned, it was one of the aims of the . . . Reich to clear up the relation between ourselves and our neighbors. . . .

[Hitler went on to review his attempts to establish peaceful relations with his neighbors—nonaggression pacts, efforts to come to terms with France and Great Britain, and so forth. His speech concluded on the following note:]

Why should this war in the West be fought? For restoration of Poland? Poland of the Versailles Treaty will never rise again. This is guaranteed by two of the largest States in the world. . . . What other reason exists? Has Germany made any demands of England which might threaten the British Empire or endanger its existence? On the contrary, Germany has made no such demands on either France or England. But if this war is really to be waged only in order to give Germany a new regime, that is to say, in order to destroy the present Reich once more and thus to create a new Treaty of Versailles, then millions of human lives will be sacrificed in vain, for neither will the German Reich go to pieces nor will a second Treaty of Versailles be made. And even should this come to pass after three, four, or even eight years of war, then this second Versailles would once more become the source of fresh conflict in the future. . . .

Mr. Churchill and his companions may interpret these opinions of mine as weakness or cowardice if they like. I need not occupy myself with what they think. . . . *If, however, the opinions of Messrs. Churchill and followers should prevail, this statement will have been my last. Then we shall fight. . . .*

Destiny will decide who is right.

One thing only is certain. In the course of world history, there have never been two victors, but very often only losers. This seems to me to have been the case in the last war. *May those people and their leaders who are of the same mind now make their reply. And let those who consider war to be the better solution reject my outstretched hand.*

THE WAR IN THE WEST, 1940

The German Conquest of France

Prime Minister Chamberlain rejected Hitler's "last peace offer" on October 12, 1939. So quiet, however, were the military fronts during the following winter that commentators began to speak of the conflict as a "phony war." The only important engagement was that which took place off the coasts of Brazil and Uruguay in mid-December, when three British cruisers outmaneuvered the more heavily gunned German "pocket battleship" *Admiral Graf von Spee,* so that the German commander scuttled his ship. Meanwhile, too, a seemingly unconnected war began between Russia and Finland. Russia, engaged in rounding out her western defenses, made demands upon Finland for territory on which to construct Russian military installations. When Finland refused, Russia invaded her (November 30, 1939). Because Russia had become a treaty partner with Germany, allied circles generally sympathized with Finland. But on March 12,

1940, when the Finns surrendered, Russia added territory which after the German attack in 1941 went far to save Leningrad from German hands. The "phony war" in the West ended suddenly when, on April 9, 1940, Germany invaded Denmark (which quickly capitulated) and Norway, and followed up these conquests a month later (May 10) with a blitzkrieg attack upon France via the Netherlands, Belgium, and Luxembourg. British and French troops rushed into the Low Countries, but the Dutch capitulated on May 15 and the Belgians on May 28. Meanwhile, Hitler, by a reversal of the Schlieffen Plan [see page 725], bottled up the Allied forces at Dunkirk (May 30-June 4). Italy, hoping to ride to victorious conquest on Germany's coattails, declared war on June 10. And France, deprived of British aid and caught between the Germans and the Italians, shocked the world by her capitulation on June 21, 1940. In less than three months Hitler had become master of the mainland of western Europe, and the way appeared clear for a successful blow against England. In characteristic fashion, Hitler blamed the necessity for these conquests upon the machinations of Great Britain and France.

From HITLER, Speech to the Reichstag, July 19, 1940 [1]

During March . . . we received information about Anglo-French intentions of intervening in the Russo-Finnish conflict, presumably not so much for the sake of helping the Finns, as in order to damage Russia which was regarded as a power working with Germany. These intentions developed into the decision to take an active part . . . in the Finnish war in order to obtain a base for carrying the war

[1] *Ibid.*, 817-18, 820-22.

into the Baltic. At the same time, however, the proposals of the Allied Supreme War Council became more and more insistent, either to set the Balkans and Asia Minor on fire in order to cut off Germany's supply of oil from Russia and Rumania, or to obtain possession of the Swedish iron ore. With this object in view, a landing was to have been made in Norway with the main object of occupying the iron ore railway leading from Narvik across Sweden to the port of Lulea.

The conclusion of peace between Russia and Finland caused the contemplated action in the Northern States to be withheld at the last moment; but a few days later intentions again became more definite and a final decision was reached. Britain and France had agreed to carry out an immediate occupation of a number of the most important points in Norway under the pretext of preventing Germany from benefiting from further war supplies of Swedish ore. . . .

That this danger was imminent we learned through the uncontrollable verbosity of no less a person than the First Lord of the Admiralty . . . [and] through a hint given by the French Premier, Mr. Reynaud, to a foreign diplomat. Until a short time ago, however, we were unaware that . . . this action . . . was to have taken place on the 8th [of April]. In fact, this was not definitely confirmed until the finding of the records of the Allied Supreme War Council [allegedly found in a French railway car on June 19]. As soon as the danger of the Northern States being dragged into the war became apparent, I gave the necessary orders to the German forces. [The Germans attacked Norway via Denmark on April 9.] . . .

Before the campaign in Norway had come to an end [May 3], the news from the West became more and more threatening . . . the necessity became evident, in the course of the first months of the war, of envisaging some action against Belgium or Holland if need be . . . noticeable concentration of French forces was taking place along the Franco-Belgian frontier. The massing of practically all the tank divisions and mechanized divisions in this sector in particular, indicated the intention—in any case, however, the possibility—of their being thrown forward in a lightning dash through Belgium to the German frontier. . . .

I therefore acquainted the German forces with the possibility of such a development and gave them the necessary detailed instructions. . . . The careful observations which had been made everywhere gradually compelled us to realize that an Anglo-French thrust was to be expected at any moment after the beginning of May. Between May 6 and 7 fears that the advance of the Allies into Holland and Belgium could be expected any moment were multiplied. . . . The following day, on the 8th, I therefore gave orders for immediate attack at 5:35 in the morning, on May 10.

The basic idea for these operations was, disregarding small unimportant successes, so to dispose the entire forces, principally the Army and the Air Force, that the total destruction of the Anglo-French Armies would be the inevitable consequence. . . .

In contradiction to the Schlieffen Plan of 1914, I arranged for the operations to bear mainly on the left wing of the front, where the break-through was to be made, though ostensibly retaining the principles of the opposite plan. This strategy succeeded. The establishment of the entire plan of operations was made easier for me, of course, by the measures adopted by the enemy himself. For the concentration of the entire Anglo-French mechanized forces along the Belgian frontier [relying on the Maginot Line to the east], made it appear that the High Command of the

Allied Armies had resolved to proceed into this area as rapidly as possible . . . a blow directed at the right flank of the Anglo-French Motorized Army Corps must, in these circumstances, lead to the complete destruction and breaking up, in fact, probably to the surrounding, of the enemy forces. As a second operation, I had planned to aim for the Seine and Le Havre and . . . Somme and the Aisne, from which a third attack could be made . . . to advance . . . to the Swiss frontier. . . . At the conclusion of the operations, it was intended to reach the coast south of Bordeaux. The operations were carried out in accordance with this plan and in this order.

Post-Mortem on the Fall of France

"What has *happened* to this country?" is the question which, since her humiliating surrender on June 21, 1940, has haunted the minds of responsible Frenchmen and of all who have known and loved France. While Hitler pirouetted ecstatically before movie cameras, patriotic Frenchmen and their friends wrung their hands in agony. Englishmen were especially concerned, mostly because England now stood alone against Hitler, but partly because the memory was still fresh of the Anglo-French Declaration, signed March 28, by which Great Britain and the French Republic declared "that during the present war they will neither negotiate nor conclude an armistice or treaty of peace except by mutual agreement." Now, in July, 1940, the Third Republic lay dead, its territory divided between German-occupied portions (which embraced the entire Atlantic coastline and the northern industrial areas) and an unoccupied zone, which the Assembly had turned over, with dubious legality, to Marshal Henri Philippe Pétain with "all power" to promulgate a new constitution. A third France existed also, mostly outside the homeland, led by General Charles A. J. M. de Gaulle, who, refusing to accept surrender, fled to London, organized the French National Committee (the "Free French"), and proclaimed that "France has lost a battle; she has not lost the war."

But the question still persisted—and still persists: What has happened to France? Mystery? Tragedy? Failure? Betrayal? Suicide? Dry rot? "Too few children, too few arms, too few allies," said Pétain—although his diagnosis represents a peculiarly neofascist attitude of mind. The fact is, no one knows —perhaps it will never be fully known —what happened to France. Below is an account by a disillusioned French soldier, written in a London hospital after his escape from France, "to clear his mind and heart, to understand if he could the causes of Compiègne and Vichy." "I am not writing history," he said. "The historian must study and write with detachment. He has a corpse to dissect. I am bowed above an open wound, and cries wrung from me by the anguish of it are what I have to express." He continues:

From "JACQUES," *A French Soldier Speaks* (1941) [1]

Have we been betrayed? I do not know. I have no way of coming at the facts without which considered judgment is impossible. I shall only say this: the men in charge should have known our own strength. They should have informed themselves as to the forces of the enemy. If we were the weaker, we should not have run headlong upon suicide. If we

were the stronger, where did our strength go?

But our defeat has causes more remote than these. Here there is no need of documentation or evidence in writing: my own memory will suffice. And the memories that crowd upon me bring me to this conclusion. France died because her soul was sick. She was snapped from the tree of life, and fell into Hitler's hands, like a rosy apple, rotten at the heart. This country, once masculine and proud, torchbearer of civilization in the vanguard of the nations, was become (despite certain appearances) a woman, with a woman's qualities and a woman's defects: and the French themselves no better than insufferable children, quarrelsome and ill-bred.

It is with régimes as with individuals: they have their youth, their flowering, their decadence and their death. The decadence of democracy is demagogy, its death dictatorship. With the assistance of the foreigner, France finds herself a dictatorship, but she only reached that pass because a crazy demagogy had brought her down by the stern to suicide.

A people is a democracy when it governs itself by means of representatives whose business it is to reconcile the general interest with the liberty of the individual, in the equality of all. A people is a demagogy when its representatives neglect the general interest, and think only of their own. For long years France has been a demagogy.

I grant you that she kept up the democratic forms. She even posed as champion of the democracies. . . . The French . . . ended by becoming stripped of the political sense. Her leaders, finding the régime profitable, took good care not to enlighten them. They were degenerates themselves . . .

Of the Parliamentary Office that should have been a duty, the members made a career: how many briefless barristers, how

[1] "Jacques," pseud., *A French Soldier Speaks,* trans. by Helen Waddell, 1941, 30-35. By permission of Constable and Company, Ltd., London, and The Macmillan Company.

many doctors without practice, sat in the Chamber, with hardly a sincere conviction amongst them? When the fancy took them to stand for election, they sniffed the air to see which way the wind blew; chose the slogan most likely to secure the maximum of votes, prepared to abandon it the moment they were elected, if the wind had changed and there was a chance of office. Certain of them, starting off from socialism, wound up on the extreme Right. Is not that so, M. Laval? Others, after marching in the ranks of the *Jeunesse Catholique,* became leaders of the Popular Front. Is not that so, M. Pierre Cot? In short, every member felt it his duty to become a Minister; every Minister would have felt himself disgraced if he had not been at least once in his career Premier.

The descent was imperceptible: yet in the end all executive power was dependent on the legislative; hence the temptation to provoke, by one pretext or another, the fall of the Ministry in office, with the secret hope of a seat in its successor. The Third Republic lived for seventy years and had known about a hundred and ten Ministries. These gentlemen had, moreover, a universal competence: they could pass with nonchalance from Finance to Justice, from National Education to the Colonies. Every candidate after his election, every deputy after reaching Cabinet rank, had to satisfy his Camarilla, place his friends. For the smaller appetites a tobacconist's licence or a job as postman; for the larger, the promise of a Bill, an amendment to a Bill, a demand for an amnesty, an important contract to come one's way. Too many of our leaders were themselves led by the nose, puppets whose strings were in the hands of high finance. The *Affaire Stavisky* that made such a stir exposed some of those strings. . . .

The basis of the régime, election, was itself completely counterfeit. . . . Contested elections are normal in a democracy. The régime cannot exist without several political parties. This is essential. Admit but one party and the Country finds itself automatically a dictatorship. But excess in anything is a defect. France suffered from a plethora of so-called parties which were nothing but groups. . . . Since none of these groups was strong enough to stand alone, the Minister who took office must make alliances with his neighbours, water down his Cabinet, renounce his personal program in whole or in part to secure support: A fine prospect for constructive policy. . . . Unluckily, in this struggle between particular interests, the general interest of the nation was ground to powder.

Britain's Finest: Winston Churchill's "Blood, Toil, Tears, and Sweat"

Great Britain's failure to stem the Nazi tide in Norway cost Prime Minister Chamberlain his office. Severely criticized in Commons (May 7-8) by speakers from all parties, Chamberlain resigned on May 10, 1940, and Winston Churchill headed a coalition Cabinet as Prime Minister. In his first speech to the House of Commons (May 13), the new Prime Minister sounded a call which galvanized democratic opinion 'round the world.

From CHURCHILL, Speech of May 13, 1940 [1]

To form an Administration of this scale and complexity is a serious undertaking in itself, but it must be remembered that we are in the preliminary stage of one of the greatest battles in history, that we are in action in many points in Norway and Holland, that we have to be prepared in the Mediterranean, that the air battle is

[1] This and the next two selections are from *Blood, Sweat, and Tears,* Copyright, 1941 by Winston S. Churchill. Courtesy of G. P. Putnam's Sons. This is 276.

continuous, and that many preparations have to be made here at home. In this crisis I hope I may be pardoned if I do not address the House at any length to-day. I hope that any of my friends and colleagues, or former colleagues, who are affected by the political reconstruction, will make all allowance for any lack of ceremony with which it has been necessary to act. I would say to this House, as I said to those who have joined this Government: "I have nothing to offer but blood, toil, tears, and sweat."

We have before us an ordeal of the most grievous kind. We have before us many, many long months of struggle and of suffering. You ask, What is our policy? I will say: "It is to wage war, by sea, land and air, with all our might and with all the strength that God can give us: to wage war against a monstrous tyranny, never surpassed in the dark, lamentable catalogue of human crime. That is our policy." You ask, What is our aim? I can answer in one word: Victory—victory at all costs, victory in spite of all terror, victory however long and hard the road may be; for without victory there is no survival. Let that be realized; no survival for the British Empire; no survival for all that the British Empire has stood for; no survival for the urge and impulse of the ages, that mankind will move forward towards its goal. But I take up my task with buoyancy and hope. . . . At this time I feel entitled to claim the aid of all, and I say, "Come, then, let us go forward together with our united strength."

[Before the end of May, 1940, the swift German envelopment of the Allied armies had knocked Holland and Belgium out of the war and pinned the British Expeditionary Forces, together with more than a hundred thousand French and Belgian troops, against the sea at Dunkirk.

A total of about 400,000 allied soldiers appeared doomed. Then came "Operation Dynamo" or, as John Masefield called it, the Nine Days' Wonder. While the Germans pressed Dunkirk on all sides, their air forces bombing and strafing from above, every available ship was gathered in England, including small motorboats and fishing craft—in all 665 civilian craft and 222 naval units. While the Royal Air Force lent telling aid, the evacuation from Dunkirk began. Between May 26 and June 4, over 335,000 men, French, British, and Belgian, were carried "out of the jaws of death and shame." British casualties totaled over 50,000, and the losses in matériel were tremendous—most of the heavy guns, armored vehicles, and motor transports of the BEF were left on the sands of Dunkirk. Moreover, the fall of France was clearly near at hand, and the danger of a German invasion of England was imminent. Commenting upon these things in Commons on June 4, after the "Miracle of Dunkirk" was over, Prime Minister Churchill concluded his address with these defiant and determined words.]

From CHURCHILL, Speech of June 4, 1940 [1]

Even though large tracts of Europe and many old and famous States have fallen or may fall into the grip of the Gestapo and all the odious apparatus of Nazi rule, we shall not flag or fail. We shall go on to the end, we shall fight in France, we shall fight on the seas and oceans, we shall fight with growing confidence and growing strength in the air, we shall defend our Island, whatever the cost may be, we shall fight on the beaches, we shall fight on the landing grounds, we shall fight in the fields and in the streets, we shall fight in the hills; we shall never surrender, and even if, which I do not for a moment believe, this Island or a

[1] *Ibid.*, 297.

large part of it were subjugated and starving, then our Empire beyond the seas, armed and guarded by the British Fleet, would carry on the struggle, until, in God's good time, the New World, with all its power and might, steps forth to the rescue and the liberation of the old.

THE BATTLE OF BRITAIN: UNITED STATES LEND-LEASE

Prime Minister Churchill's reference to the New World's possible "rescue" of the Old acquired new meaning in the fall and winter of 1940. In August, 1940, the "Battle of Britain" began, with fierce German attacks upon British shipping and indiscriminate bombing, strafing, and burning of British cities. Germany hoped to terrorize the British into surrender or, failing that, to weaken Britain's defenses so as to make possible a German invasion with ground forces. The German failure to achieve either of these objectives marked, as events turned out, the first important one of the Axis setbacks leading to the ultimate defeat of the Axis powers. In spite of heavy British losses in life and property, the British fought on, and the Royal Air Force exacted such heavy losses from the German attackers that the German Bomber Arm never fully recovered. "Never in the field of human conflict," said Churchill of the RAF, "was so much owed by so many to so few."

In the meantime, the dark days of Dunkirk, the fall of France, and the blitz over England aroused the anxious concern of the United States of America. Despite the national hatred of war —expressed in a series of Neutrality Acts reaching back to 1935—American sentiment was overwhelmingly anti-Axis, and in the course of 1940 there arose a growing realization that Brit-

ain's fight was America's fight—that a British defeat would leave America isolated in a hostile world. President Roosevelt was outspoken in his anti-Axis attitude. He had condemned Mussolini's declaration of war on France as "a stab in the back" and promised (June 10, 1940) "to extend to opponents of force the material resources of this nation." On September 3, 1940, the United States made its first important contribution to the war—the transfer to Britain of fifty over-age destroyers in return for 99-year leases on a series of defense bases extending from Newfoundland to British Guiana. President Roosevelt was re-elected in the autumn of 1940 on a platform demanding all aid to Britain "short of war." Wendell Willkie, his opponent, had firmly supported the President's foreign policy and in the winter of 1940-41, when Willkie went to Britain, he carried a personal message from the President to Prime Minister Churchill. The Prime Minister referred to it in a radio address on February 9, 1941.

Churchill's Plea: "Give Us the Tools"

From CHURCHILL, Address of
    February 9, 1941 [1]

The other day, President Roosevelt gave his opponent in the late Presidential Election a letter of introduction to me, and in it he wrote out a verse, in his own handwriting, from Longfellow, which, he said, "applies to you people as it does to us." Here is the verse:

. . . Sail on, O Ship of State!
Sail on, O Union, strong and great!
Humanity with all its fears,
With all the hopes of future years,
Is hanging breathless on thy fate!

[1] *Ibid.*, 462.

What is the answer that I shall give, in your name, to this great man, the thrice-chosen head of a nation of a hundred and thirty millions? Here is the answer which I will give to President Roosevelt: Put your confidence in us. Give us your faith and your blessing, and, under Providence, all will be well.

We shall not fail or falter; we shall not weaken or tire. Neither the sudden shock of battle, nor the long-drawn trials of vigilance and exertion will wear us down. Give us the tools, and we will finish the job.

Lend-Lease and the Four Freedoms

America's reply to Churchill's plea was already in the making. On December 29, 1940, President Roosevelt had called upon the United States to become "the great arsenal of democracy." When the new Congress convened in January, 1941, he called upon it for authority and funds to push forward American defense preparations, went on to request means of supplying Britain with "the tools," and ended with a statement of the "Four Freedoms," which heralded the wartime ideological drive of the democratic front. The President began as follows.

From ROOSEVELT, Message to Congress (January 6, 1941) [1]

At no previous time has American security been so seriously threatened from without as it is today. . . . The safety of our country and of our democracy are overwhelmingly involved in events far beyond our borders. . . . Obviously, as long as the British Navy retains its power, no . . . danger [of immediate, direct invasion] exists. . . . The immediate need is a swift and driving increase in our armament production. . . .

[1] *Congressional Record*, 1941, Vol. 87, Pt. 1, 44-47.

I . . . ask this Congress for authority and for funds sufficient to manufacture additional munitions and war supplies of many kinds, to be turned over to those nations which are now in actual war with aggressor nations. Our most useful and immediate role is to act as an arsenal for them as well as for ourselves. They do not need manpower. They do need billions of dollars' worth of weapons of defense.

The time is near when they will not be able to pay for them in ready cash. We cannot, and will not, tell them they must surrender merely because of present inability to pay for the weapons which we know they must have.

I do not recommend that we make them a loan of dollars. . . . I recommend that we make it possible for those nations to continue to obtain war materials in the United States, fitting their orders into our own program. Nearly all of their materiel would, if the time ever came, be useful for our own defense.

Taking counsel of expert military and naval authorities . . . we are free to decide how much should be kept here and how much should be sent abroad to our friends who, by their determined and heroic resistance, are giving us time in which to make ready our own defense.

For what we send abroad we shall be repaid, within a reasonable time following the close of hostilities, in similar materials, or at our option, in other goods of many kinds which they can produce and which we need. Let us say to the democracies, "We Americans are vitally concerned in your defense of freedom. We are putting forth our energies, our resources, and our organizing powers to give you the strength to regain and maintain a free world. We shall send you, in ever-increasing numbers, ships, planes, tanks, guns. This is our purpose and our pledge.". . .

In the future days, which we seek to

make secure, we look forward to a world founded upon four essential human freedoms.

The first is freedom of speech and expression everywhere in the world.

The second is freedom of every person to worship God in his own way everywhere in the world.

The third is freedom from want, which, translated into world terms, means economic understandings which will secure to every nation a healthy peacetime life for its inhabitants everywhere in the world.

The fourth is freedom from fear—which, translated into world terms, means a world-wide reduction of armaments to such a point and in such a thorough fashion that no nation will be in a position to commit an act of physical aggression against any neighbor—anywhere in the world.

That is no vision of a distant millenium. It is a definite basis for a kind of world attainable in our own time and generation. That kind of world is the very antithesis of the so-called new order of tyranny which the dictators seek to create with the crash of a bomb.

[In pursuance of the President's recommendation, the United States Congress passed the Lend-Lease Act, which the President signed March 11, 1941. By terms of this Act, the President was empowered, "when he deems it in the interest of national defense," to authorize manufacture of "defense articles," and "to sell, transfer title to, exchange, lease, lend, or otherwise dispose of . . . any defense article" to the "government of any country whose defense the President deems vital to the defense of the United States." Under the Lend-Lease Act the President entered into Lend-Lease Agreements by which Britain and later Russia and other states were supplied with "the tools . . . [to] finish the job."]

THE WAR IN EASTERN EUROPE

Another major point in Allied victory, as experts see it now, was Hitler's brash decision to launch an attack upon Russia on June 22, 1941. Already, in the fall and winter of 1940-41, the Axis powers had extended the war into the Balkans and into North Africa. Italy, in characteristic hope of easy conquests, had invaded British Somaliland (August, 1940), and after Germany had occupied Romania "to protect the oil fields," Italy invaded Greece (October 28, 1940). Before winter was well advanced, Italian forces were in difficulty both in Africa (where British troops were successfully occupying Libya) and in Greece (where Greek forces were repelling the Italians). Accordingly, Germany felt compelled to rescue her Axis partner. German troops reinforced the Italians in Africa, and, in March-April, 1941, German forces overran Bulgaria, Yugoslavia, and Greece. This conquest of the Balkan states was followed closely by a sudden German attack upon Russia, without warning and in perfidious betrayal of the Nonaggression Pact of August 23, 1939. As usual, Hitler sought to justify his action by "pious frauds," holding that Russia had violated the Nonaggression Pact by mobilizing troops on her western frontiers and by aiding Germany's enemies.

Germany's Attack on Russia

From HITLER, Proclamation of June 22, 1941 [1]

German people! National Socialists! Weighted down with heavy cares, condemned to months-long silence, the hour has now come *when at last I can speak frankly.* . . .

[1] Hitler, *My New Order,* ed. De Sales, 977, 979-82, 986-87. By permission of Reynal & Hitchcock.

It was . . . only with extreme difficulty that I brought myself in August, 1939, to send my foreign minister to Moscow in an endeavor there to oppose the British encirclement policy against Germany. . . . during our advance in Poland, Soviet rulers suddenly, contrary to the treaty, also claimed Lithuania. . . . As Russia undertook to subjugate . . . not only Finland but also the Baltic States, she suddenly motivated this action by the assertion, as ridiculous as it was false, that she must protect these countries from an outside menace or forestall it. *This could only be meant to apply to Germany. . . .* While our soldiers from May 5, 1940, on had been breaking Franco-British power in the west, Russian military deployment on our eastern frontier was being continued. . . . Russia's advance into Rumania and Greece's tie-up with England threatened to turn these regions, too . . . into a . . . theater of war. . . .

Thus Moscow not only broke but miserably betrayed the stipulations of our friendly agreement. All this was done while the rulers in the Kremlin . . . pretended peace and friendship. . . .

The moment has now come when to continue as a mere observer would not only be a sin of omission but a crime against the German people—yes, even against the whole of Europe.

Today something like 160 Russian divisions are standing at our frontiers. For weeks constant violations of this frontier have taken place. . . . This has brought us to the hour when it is necessary for us to take steps against this plot devised by the Jewish-Anglo-Saxon warmongers and equally Jewish rulers of the Bolshevist center in Moscow.

German people! *At this moment a march is taking place that, as regards extent, compares with the greatest the world hitherto has seen.* United with their Finnish comrades, the fighters of the victory of Narvik are standing in the . . . Arctic.

German divisions . . . in co-operation with the heroes of Finnish freedom . . . are protecting Finnish soil. Formations of the German eastern front extend from East Prussia to the Carpathians. . . . *The task of this front, therefore, no longer is the protection of single countries, but the safeguarding of Europe and thereby the salvation of all.*

I therefore decided today again to lay the fate and future of the German Reich and our people in the hands of our soldiers.

May God help us especially in this fight!

Anglo-Russian Rapprochement

From CHURCHILL, Broadcast on the New War (June 22, 1941) [1]

I have taken occasion to speak to you tonight because we have reached one of the climacterics of the war. In the first of these intense turning points, a year ago, France fell . . . and we had to face the storm alone.

The second was when the Royal Air Force beat the Hun raiders out of the daylight air and thus warded off the Nazi invasion of our islands. . . .

The third turning point was when the President and Congress of the United States passed the lease and lend enactment, devoting nearly 2,000,000,000 sterling of the wealth of the New World to help us defend our liberties and their own.

Those were the three climacterics. The fourth is now upon us.

At 4 o'clock this morning Hitler attacked and invaded Russia. . . .

All this was no surprise to me. In fact I gave clear and precise warnings to Stalin of what was coming. I gave him warnings. . . . I can only hope that these warnings did not fall unheeded. All we know at present is that the Russian people are defending their native soil and that their

[1] *The British Library of Information*, New York. Pamphlet.

leaders have called upon them to resist to the utmost. . . .

The past, with its crimes, its follies and its tragedies, flashes away. I see the Russian soldiers standing on the threshold of their native land, guarding the fields which their fathers have tilled from time immemorial. . . . And then my mind goes back across the years to the days when the Russian armies were our Allies against the same deadly foe. . . . But now I have to declare the decision of His Majesty's Government and I feel sure it is a decision in which the great Dominions will, in due course, concur. . . . I have to make the declaration, but can you doubt what our policy will be?

We have but one aim and one single irrevocable purpose. We are resolved to destroy Hitler and every vestige of the Nazi régime. From this nothing will turn us. Nothing. We will never parley; we will never negotiate with Hitler or any of his gang. . . .

Any man or State who fights against Nazism will have our aid. Any man or State who marches with Hitler is our foe. This applies not only to organized States but to all representatives of that vile race of Quislings who make themselves the tools and agents of the Nazi régime against their fellow-countrymen and against the lands of their births. . . . That is our policy and that is our declaration.

It follows, therefore, that we shall give whatever help we can to Russia and to the Russian people. We shall appeal to all our friends and Allies in every part of the world to take the same course and pursue it as we shall, faithfully and steadfastly to the end.

We have offered to the Government of Soviet Russia any technical or economic assistance which is in our power. . . . We shall bomb Germany by day as well as by night in ever-increasing measure. . . .

Hitler . . . wishes to destroy the Russian power because he hopes that if he succeeds in this he will be able to bring back the main strength of his army and air force from the East and hurl it upon this island, which he knows he must conquer or suffer the penalty of his crimes. . . .

The Russian danger is therefore our danger and the danger of the United States.

THE ATLANTIC CHARTER

"We have found in President Roosevelt's message to Congress in January 1941 the keynote of our own purpose." Thus spoke Mr. Anthony Eden, the British Minister of Foreign Affairs, of President Roosevelt's "Four Freedoms" [see page 953]. In August, 1941, President Roosevelt and Prime Minister Churchill held conferences on Lend-Lease problems aboard warships somewhere in the North Atlantic. One of the products of this meeting was the historic "Atlantic Charter," obviously issued to internationalize and inspire the ideological drive of the democratic front. The document read as follows.

From the "Atlantic Charter"
(August 14, 1941) [1]

The President of the United States of America and the Prime Minister, Mr. Churchill, representing His Majesty's Government in the United Kingdom, being met together, deem it right to make known certain common principles in the national policies of their respective countries on which they base their hopes for a better future for the world.

FIRST, Their countries seek no aggrandizement, territorial or other;

[1] *White House Press Release*, August 21, 1941.

SECOND, They desire to see no territorial changes that do not accord with the freely expressed wishes of the peoples concerned;

THIRD, They respect the right of all peoples to choose the form of government under which they will live; and they wish to see sovereign rights and self-government restored to those who have been forcibly deprived of them;

FOURTH, They will endeavor, with due respect for their existing obligations, to further the enjoyment by all States, great or small, victor or vanquished, of access, on equal terms, to the trade and to the raw materials of the world which are needed for their economic prosperity;

FIFTH, They desire to bring about the fullest collaboration between all nations in the economic field with the object of securing, for all, improved labor standards, economic advancement and social security;

SIXTH, After the final destruction of the Nazi tyranny, they hope to see established a peace which will afford to all nations the means of dwelling in safety within their own boundaries, and which will afford assurance that all the men in all the lands may live out their lives in freedom from fear and want;

SEVENTH, Such a peace should enable all men to traverse the high seas and oceans without hindrance;

EIGHTH, They believe that all of the nations of the world, for realistic as well as spiritual reasons, must come to the abandonment of the use of force. Since no future peace can be maintained if land, sea or air armaments continue to be employed by nations which threaten, or may threaten, aggression outside of their frontiers, they believe, pending the establishment of a wider and permanent system of general security, that the disarmament of such nations is essential. They will likewise aid and encourage all other practicable measures which will lighten for peace-loving peoples the crushing burden of armaments.

August 14, 1941

> (Signed) Franklin D. Roosevelt
> (Signed) Winston S. Churchill

THE WAR BECOMES GLOBAL: THE JAPANESE ATTACK PEARL HARBOR (DECEMBER 7, 1941)

Japan Joins the Rome-Berlin Axis

From The Three-Power Pact
(September 27, 1940) [1]

The Governments of Germany, Italy and Japan consider it the prerequisite of lasting peace that every nation in the world shall receive the space to which it is entitled. They have, therefore, decided to stand by and co-operate with one another in their efforts in Greater East Asia and the regions of Europe respectively. In doing this it is their prime purpose to establish and maintain a new order of things, calculated to promote the mutual prosperity and welfare of the peoples concerned.

It is, furthermore, the desire of the three Governments to extend co-operation to other nations . . . who are inclined to direct their efforts along lines similar to their own for the purpose of realizing their ultimate object, world peace.

Accordingly, the Governments of Germany, Italy and Japan have agreed as follows:

Art. 1. Japan recognizes and respects the leadership of Germany and Italy in the establishment of a new order in Europe.

Art. 2. Germany and Italy recognize and respect the leadership of Japan in the establishment of a new order in Greater East Asia.

Art. 3. Germany, Italy and Japan agree

[1] German Library of Information, *Facts in Review*, New York, 1941, II, 486.

to co-operate in their efforts on the aforesaid lines. They further undertake to assist one another with all political, economic and military means if one of the three Contracting Powers is attacked by a Power at present not involved in the European War or in the Chinese-Japanese conflict [clearly aimed at the United States!].

Art. 4. With a view to implementing the present pact, joint technical commissions . . . will meet without delay. . . .

Art. 6. The present pact shall become valid immediately upon signature and shall remain in force ten years. . . .

Done in triplicate at Berlin, the 27th day of September, 1940, in the eighteenth year of the Fascist era, corresponding to the 27th day of the ninth month of the fifteenth year of Showa.

Treachery Documented: President Roosevelt's Summary of American-Japanese Relations (1941)

On December 15, 1941, eight days after Japan's treacherous attack upon Pearl Harbor, President Roosevelt presented to Congress a "full record of our past relations with Japan." This document reviews the whole sordid story of Axis aggression, with particular attention to Japan and to American-Japanese relations immediately preceding the Pearl Harbor attack. Parts of the Presidential Message follow.

From ROOSEVELT, Message to Congress (December 15, 1941) [1]

Pursuing this policy of conquest, Japan had first worked her way into and finally seized Manchuria. Next she had invaded China; and has sought for the past four and one-half years to subjugate her.

[1] U. S. Department of State, *Bulletin*, V, No. 130, Dec. 20, 1941, 532-35.

Passing through the China Sea close to the Philippine Islands, she then invaded and took possession of Indo-China. Today the Japanese are extending this conquest throughout Thailand—and seeking the occupation of Malaya and Burma. The Philippines, Borneo, Sumatra, Java come next on the Japanese timetable; and it is probable that further down the Japanese page, are the names of Australia, New Zealand, and all the other islands of the Pacific—including Hawaii and the . . . Aleutian Islands.

To the eastward of the Philippines, Japan violated the mandate under which she had received the custody of the Caroline, Marshall, and Mariana Islands after the World War, by fortifying them, and not only closing them to all commerce but her own but forbidding any foreigner even to visit them.

Japanese spokesmen, after their custom, cloaked these conquests with innocent-sounding names. They talked of the "New Order in Eastern Asia"; and then of the "co-prosperity sphere in Greater East Asia." What they really intended was the enslavement of every nation which they could bring within their power. . . . Here too they were following the Nazi pattern. . . .

It became clear that, unless this course of affairs in the Far East was halted, the Pacific area was doomed to experience the same horrors which have devastated Europe.

Therefore, in this year of 1941, in an endeavor to end this process by peaceful means while there seemed still to be a chance, the United States entered into discussions with Japan.

For nine months these conversations were carried on, for the purpose of arriving at some understanding acceptable to both countries.

Throughout all of these conversations,

this Government took into account not only the legitimate interests of the United States but also those of Japan and other countries. When questions relating to the legitimate rights and interests of other countries came up, this Government kept in appropriate contact with the representatives of those countries.

In the course of these negotiations, the United States steadfastly advocated certain basic principles which should govern international relations. These were:

The principle of inviolability of territorial integrity and sovereignty of all nations.

The principle of non-interference in the internal affairs of other countries.

The principle of equality—including equality of commercial opportunity and treatment.

The principle of reliance upon international co-operation and conciliation for the prevention, and pacific settlement, of controversies.

The Japanese Government, it is true, repeatedly offered qualified statements of peaceful intention. But it became clear, as each proposal was explored, that Japan did not intend to modify in any way her greedy designs upon the whole Pacific world. Although she continually maintained that she was promoting only the peace and greater prosperity of East Asia, she continued her brutal assault upon the Chinese people.

Nor did Japan show any inclination to renounce her unholy alliance with Hitlerism.

In July of this year the Japanese Government connived with Hitler to force from the Vichy Government of France permission to place Japanese armed forces in southern Indo-China; and began sending her troops and equipment into that area.

The conversations between this Govern-ment and the Japanese Government were thereupon suspended.

But during the following month, at the urgent and insistent request of the Japanese Government, which again made emphatic profession of peaceful intent, the conversations were resumed. . . .

Finally, on November 20, 1941, the Japanese Government presented a new and narrow proposal which called for supplying by the United States to Japan of as much oil as Japan might require, for suspension of freezing measures, and for discontinuance by the United States of aid to China. It contained however no provision for abandonment by Japan of her warlike operations or aims.

Such a proposal obviously offered no basis for a peaceful settlement or even for a temporary adjustment. The American Government, in order to clarify the issues, presented to the Japanese Government on November 26, a clear-cut plan for a broad but simple settlement. . . .

In the midst of these conversations, we learned that new contingents of Japanese armed forces and new masses of equipment were moving into Indo-China. Toward the end of November these movements were intensified. During the first week of December new movements of Japanese forces made it clear that, under cover of the negotiations, attacks on unspecified objectives were being prepared.

I promptly asked the Japanese Government for a frank statement of the reasons for increasing its forces in Indo-China. I was given an evasive and specious reply. Simultaneously, the Japanese operations went forward with increased tempo.

We did not know then, as we know now, that they had ordered and were even then carrying out their plan for a treacherous attack upon us.

I was determined, however, to exhaust every conceivable effort for peace. With this in mind, on the evening of December sixth last, I addressed a personal message to the Emperor of Japan.

To this Government's proposal of November twenty-sixth the Japanese Government made no reply until December seventh. On that day the Japanese Ambassador here and the Special Representative whom the Japanese Government had sent to the United States to assist in peaceful negotiations, delivered a lengthy document to our Secretary of State,[1] one hour after the Japanese had launched a vicious attack upon American territory and American citizens in the Pacific.

That document was a few minutes after its receipt aptly characterized by the Secretary of State [Mr. Cordell Hull] as follows:

"I must say that in all my conversations with you [the Japanese Ambassador] during the last nine months I have never uttered one word of untruth. This is borne out absolutely by the record. In all my fifty years of public service I have never seen a document that was more crowded with infamous falsehoods and distortions —infamous falsehoods and distortions on a scale so huge that I never imagined until today that any Government on this planet was capable of uttering them."

I concur emphatically in every word of that statement.

[1] This document was a Memorandum, the burden of which was well set forth in the following excerpt: "Obviously it is the intention of the American Government to conspire with Great Britain and other countries to obstruct Japan's efforts toward the establishment of peace through the creation of a new order in East Asia, and especially to preserve Anglo-American rights and interests by keeping Japan and China at war. This intention has been revealed clearly during the course of the present negotiation. . . . The Japanese Government . . . consider that it is impossible to reach an agreement through further negotiations."

2. The Rise of the United Nations, 1942-1943

A few hours after the attack on Pearl Harbor, Japan declared war on the United States and the British Empire. The European Axis partners—already at war with Britain and others—declared war on the United States on December 11, and the Axis puppet states followed suit: Romania on December 12, Hungary and Bulgaria on December 13, and Thailand on January 25, 1942. Meanwhile, on December 11, 1941, Germany, Italy, and Japan reaffirmed their pact of 1940 [see pages 957-958], each power promising not to conclude a separate peace and all agreeing to co-operate "after victory" to establish "a new and just order." One important consequence of these Axis proceedings was that the anti-Axis states drew more closely together in order to effect better co-operation for a global war. The United States' declaration of war on Japan on December 8 —followed by reciprocal declarations against the other Axis powers—brought in its wake a number of like declarations from Central American and South American nations. On January 1, twenty-six nations, representing Europe, Asia, and both Americas, signed at Washington an agreement pledging each signatory to use all its resources to defeat the Axis Powers, not to sign a separate peace, and to accept the provisions of the Atlantic Charter.

FORERUNNER OF THE UNITED NATIONS CHARTER

From the "Declaration by United Nations" (January 1, 1942) [1]

A joint declaration by the United States of America, the United Kingdom of Great

[1] White House Press Release, January 1, 1942.

Britain and Northern Ireland, the Union of Soviet Socialistic Republics, China, Australia, Belgium, Canada, Costa Rica, Cuba, Czechoslovakia, Dominican Republic, El Salvador, Greece, Guatemala, Haiti, Honduras, India, Luxembourg, Netherlands, New Zealand, Nicaragua, Norway, Panama, Poland, South Africa, Yugoslavia.

The governments signatory hereto, having subscribed to a common program of purposes and principles embodied in the Joint Declaration of the President of the United States of America and the Prime Minister of the United Kingdom of Great Britain and Northern Ireland dated August 14, 1941, known as the Atlantic Charter;

Being convinced that complete victory over their enemies is essential to defend life, liberty, independence and religious freedom, and to preserve human rights and justice in their own lands as well as in other lands, and that they are now engaged in a common struggle against the savage and brutal forces seeking to subjugate the world, DECLARE:

1. Each government pledges itself to employ its full resources, military or economic, against those members of the Tripartite Pact and its adherents with which such government is at war.

2. Each government pledges itself to co-operate with the governments signatory hereto and not to make a separate armistice or peace with the enemies.

The foregoing declaration may be adhered to by other nations which are, or which may be, rendering material assistance and contributions in the struggle for victory over Hitlerism.[1]

[Inter-Allied co-operation, as set forth in the above Declaration, was fortified at points by bilateral alliances between members of the United Nations. Of these treaties—so far as made public to date—two are worthy of brief mention, both of them entered into by Russia, the first with England, the second with China. The first was the Anglo-Russian twenty-year Alliance and Mutual Aid Treaty of May 26, 1942. By this treaty, the agreement of July, 1941, for joint action in the war against Germany was replaced by a formal treaty and, in addition, both signatories promised to adhere to the Atlantic Charter; to give mutual assistance during the war as well as after the war, "should either of the . . . parties during the post-war period become involved in hostilities with Germany or any of the [Axis] States"; to make no separate armistice or peace with the Axis states; to "render one another all possible economic assistance after the war"; and to assert "their desire to unite with other like-minded States in adopting proposals for common action to preserve peace and resist aggression in the post-war period."

[The second treaty, signed on August 14, 1945, shortly before the Japanese surrender and the end of World War II, was a Sino-Russian Treaty of Alliance, with Supplementary Agreements. Its terms were almost identical, as between Russia and China and as against Japan, to those of the Anglo-Russian Treaty of 1942 against Germany. Annexed Agreements provided: 1. For joint operation, under Chinese sovereignty, of the Chinese Eastern and South Manchurian railways (thereafter known as the Changchun Railway). 2. For the establishment of Dairen as a demilitarized free port, under Chinese administration, with piers and warehouses under lease to Russia. 3. For military collaboration in the recovery of the three Eastern Provinces from Japan and, upon cessation of hostilities, Russian recognition of Chinese sovereignty over and territorial integrity of these provinces. 4. For Rus-

---

[1] Subsequently, in 1942, Mexico, the Commonwealth of the Philippines, and Ethiopia joined in the "Declaration"; in 1943 were added Bolivia, Brazil, Iran, Iraq, and Colombia; and in 1944, Liberia and France signed also.

sian recognition of the Chinese National Government (Kuomintang-controlled), without any "intention to interfere with China's internal affairs"—that is, without Russian aid and support to Chinese Communists against the National Government. 5. For a joint agreement whereby, if the people of Outer Mongolia desire independence at the end of the war, both parties will recognize it.

[Another group of Russian treaties was less evidently designed to strengthen Allied co-operation, appearing rather as an attempt on the part of Russia to construct a Slavic cordon sanitaire about her European borders. The first of these was with the Czechoslovakian Government-in-Exile, signed December 13, 1943. This treaty confirmed Russo-Czech mutual assistance pacts of 1935 and 1941, and, with two significant differences, was quite similar to the Anglo-Russian Treaty summarized above. The differences were: 1. Reference to the Atlantic Charter and the United Nations Declaration was omitted. 2. The treaty was left open for future adherence of third parties, like the Anglo-Russian Treaty, but the object was specifically directed against any postwar renewal of Germany's policy of Drang nach Osten. On May 8, 1944, when Russian troops stood poised on Czech borders to liberate the state from the Germans, the two parties signed an additional pact which placed Czechoslovak territory entirely under Soviet military authority until liberated, after which a Czech government would assume civilian control. Thus Czechoslovakia linked her security with Russia, a "guarantee," said Dr. Beneš meaningly, "that Munich will never happen again." Before the end of the war, similar Russian treaties were signed with Yugoslavia and Poland, and hints of similar accords with Hungary and Romania were in the air—giving rise to a feeling in non-Slavic circles of the United Nations that Russia sought to build up spheres of influence hardly in harmony with United Nations objectives of general security.]

LEND-LEASE AND RECIPROCAL ("REVERSE LEND-LEASE") AID

The United States of America, by its Lend-Lease aid to the Allies (to say nothing of its tremendous military accomplishments on land and sea and in the air), contributed heavily to allied victory. After the Pearl Harbor attack, provisions were made for reciprocal aid among the Allies (often called "Reverse Lend-Lease"). Mr. Edward R. Stettinius, Jr., the American Administrator of Lend-Lease, published the following account of Lend-Lease mutual benefits to the summer of 1943.

From STETTINIUS, *Lend-Lease* (1944) [1]

This development of the machinery of United Nations collaboration has made full use of Lend-Lease as a two-way street. In fact, the value of reciprocal aid provided to the United States under the Lend-Lease Act was demonstrated only a few days after Pearl Harbor. The smashing blow at Hawaii caught this country without enough barrage balloons for the protection of the West Coast and without enough anti-aircraft guns for our coastal cities. A year before, the British had given us working models and manufacturing specifications for the Bofors 40 mm. anti-aircraft gun, which our Army found superior to the type we had been manufacturing and made standard equipment for United States forces. However, the Bofors guns had not begun to come off the production lines in this country at the time

[1] Edward R. Stettinius, Jr., *Lend-Lease, Weapon for Victory*, 1944, 163-64, 313-15, 319-20, 323-24. By permission of The Macmillan Company, New York.

of Pearl Harbor, and the British sent us anti-aircraft guns to reinforce our Panama Canal defenses and to supplement the air raid defenses of continental United States. They also rushed for use on our West Coast several thousand barrage balloons, some of which had been flying over English cities.

To help us fight the Nazi U-boat campaign off our Atlantic coast, the British, although they were hard-pressed themselves, turned over to us more than a score of corvettes and trawlers.

We christened these first acts of reciprocal aid "Reverse Lend-Lease," and the amount of such aid we have since received from our allies has grown to very large proportions. Reverse Lend-Lease, however, is only one of several benefits received by the United States under the Lend-Lease Act. All these benefits are set forth in the Master Lend-Lease Agreements with our principal allies, the first of which—with the United Kingdom—was signed on February 23rd, 1942, eleven weeks after Pearl Harbor.

For the prosecution of the war the United States agrees, in the Lend-Lease Agreements, to continue to supply Lend-Lease aid as authorized by the President. The other governments agree "to continue to contribute to the defense of the United States" and to supply us with Reverse Lend-Lease aid.

The contribution which Britain, the Soviet Union, China and the others make to the "defense of the United States" by fighting the Axis is, of course, the most important war benefit we receive in return for our Lend-Lease aid. As I reported to the Congress on January 25th, 1943: "This is a benefit which cannot be measured in figures. There is no standard of values by which the loss of a thousand Russian lives, for instance, can be compared with a thousand fighter planes. Those who have died fighting in Britain, in China and in Russia, in Africa and in Asia, died in defense of their own countries. But these peoples have fought, and they fight now against enemies that are ours as well as theirs. Their sacrifices are saving American lives. China's five-year struggle against Japan, the terrible toll taken of the Nazis by the Red Army, the defense of Britain and the destruction of German production centers by England's R.A.F., and the protection of vital sea lanes by the British Navy—all have combined to save the United States from invasion, to preserve to us the means of victory and to speed its coming."

The Lend-Lease Agreements also provide for the return after the war of such equipment, not destroyed or lost, as the President decides will be useful to us. . . .

The exact terms of the final Lend-Lease settlement, however, are left, by the Agreements, to be determined after the "progress of events" has made clearer how they can best be worked out in the mutual interests of this country and our allies. But the Agreements do provide that the final settlement shall be directed toward the "attainment of all the economic objectives" of the Atlantic Charter. . . .

The United States has put into Lend-Lease about twelve cents out of every dollar that we have spent to fight this war. By the middle of 1943—two years and four months after Lend-Lease began —the total cost of our Lend-Lease aid amounted to $12,900,000,000, and that figure has since been going up at the rate of a little more than a billion dollars a month. . . .

What does $12,900,000,000 of Lend-Lease by June 30th, 1943, actually mean in terms of fighting strength?

First of all, it means about thirteen thousand airplanes—a few hundred of our big four-motor bombers, four thousand medium bombers, five thousand fighters, many trainers and some military transport planes. And it means also the spare parts necessary to keep these planes in the air, and many motors for airframes built in the factories of our allies. All this accounts for close to two billion dollars.

Of these thirteen thousand airplanes, more have gone to Russia than to any other battlefront. In the early days, of course, most Lend-Lease planes went to the British forces in Egypt and in the British Isles. But as the sea lanes and the ferry routes to Russia have been expanded, the Soviet's share of our Lend-Lease airplanes has steadily risen. By the middle of 1943, the Russians were receiving over a third of them. The next largest shipments went to the British Isles, and the balance to the Mediterranean, the Pacific and the Far Eastern theaters.

The Lend-Lease planes we are sending from the United States represent about sixteen out of every hundred that our factories are turning out. The other eighty-four are going to our own Army and Navy. The percentage of planes we lend-lease in any one month depends, of course, on the strategic decisions of the Combined Chiefs of Staff as these are carried out by the Munitions Assignment Board. From month to month, the percentage fluctuates. In one recent month, we went twenty-two percent of our plane production under Lend-Lease; in another recent month, it was down to ten percent. . . .

The proportion of our tanks that we are sending to our allies under Lend-Lease has been much higher than the proportion of planes. In this field, probably more than anywhere else, we have been the arsenal of our allies. Over fourteen thousand tanks had gone abroad under Lend-Lease by the middle of 1943, and many more were on the docks or rolling out of the factories. This means today about thirty-eight out of every hundred tanks produced in the United States—a higher percentage for Lend-Lease probably than of any other military item we produce.

Tanks account for over a billion dollars of the total figure of Lend-Lease aid.

Three hundred thousand trucks, jeeps, scout cars and other vehicles account for another half a billion dollars. Out of every seven Lend-Lease motor vehicles, three have gone to Russia, two to the Pacific and the Far East, and the other two to Egypt, Britain, Iran or other theaters of war. American Lend-Lease trucks are fighting the war of supply all over the globe, although we have only sent ten out of every hundred we produce.

The planes, tanks and trucks, together with more than a billion and a half dollars' worth of guns and ammunition, a billion dollars' worth of fighting ships, landing craft and merchant vessels leased to our allies, and thousands of other smaller items total up to a little over six billion dollars. Or, put in another way, about six cents out of every dollar we have spent for the war have gone to buy weapons and ships for the fighting forces of our allies. . . .

From the beginning of Lend-Lease to the middle of 1943, we were able to lend-lease over five million tons of food. In addition to that, about 700,000 tons of other agricultural products were sent. Taken together, these account for another two billion dollars of the $12,900,-000,000 total of Lend-Lease aid.

In the over-all picture, the Lend-Lease slice of American food has been small—six percent in 1942 and about ten percent in 1943. In crucial items the Lend-Lease percentage has been even smaller. Half a pound of beef out of every hundred pounds, three quarts of milk out of every hundred, two cans of canned fruit and less than one can of canned vegetables out of every hundred have been lend-leased. We have sent only one pound of butter out of every hundred pounds, and that has gone to Russia. The drain on our supply of other less critical foods, however, has been greater. We have lend-leased about twelve pounds of pork and five pounds of lamb and mutton out of every hundred pounds, ten eggs out of a hundred, twenty percent of our canned fish, and eighteen percent of our dried fruit. . . .

This is the breakdown, then, of the $12,900,000,000 total of Lend-Lease aid—$6,200,000,000 worth of planes, tanks, guns, ammunition, ships, trucks, and other fighting supplies; $2,800,000,000 of raw materials and industrial equipment; $1,900,000,000 of food and other agricultural products; $2,000,000,000 of shipping, ship repairs, factories and other services. We provide these things under Lend-Lease because they fight for our cause just as our own soldiers do. A Luftwaffe bomber is no less out of the fight because the American gun that shot it down was manned by a Russian. A base in New Guinea is no less captured because some of the American tanks that blasted out the Japanese were manned by Australians.

We Americans are a hard-headed people, however, and the average American will naturally say to himself, "$12,900,-000,000 is a lot of money. Have we got our money's worth?"

I think that we have in more than double measure. The total impact of Lend-Lease on our economy has been relatively small. The dividends it has paid have been enormous. We are, it is true, drawing heavily upon our national resources to fight this war, mostly to arm and equip our own fighting men, but also to aid our allies. If we had not had Lend-Lease, however, if Britain had gone under, Hitler had isolated Russia, Japan had completed the conquest of China, and finally we in the Western Hemisphere had stood alone against an Axis-dominated world, who can measure the expenditure of men and of our material wealth we would have had to make if our liberties were to survive?

DEFINING THE PEACE TERMS AND PLANS FOR POSTWAR SECURITY

The Moscow Conference

As the "Big Three" powers—the United States, Russia, and Great Britain—bore the heaviest burden of the war and enjoyed the greatest international prestige, during the war they took the lead in United Nations deliberations and decisions. Representatives of these powers held many conferences to organize joint military undertakings, integrate their efforts, plan campaigns, and make decisions with regard to the principles upon which future policies should be founded. One of the most important of these was the Tripartite Conference held in Moscow from October 19 to October 30, 1943. In a Joint Communiqué issued November 1, the Big Three reported that they had canvassed the military outlook thoroughly and laid joint plans for future campaigns. "Second only to the importance of hastening the end of the war," continued the communiqué, "was the unanimous recognition . . . that it was essential . . . to continue the present close collaboration and co-operation . . . into the period following the end of hostilities, and that only in this way could peace be maintained and the political, economic and social welfare of their peoples fully promoted." To this end the Big Three, with the Chinese Ambassador in Moscow joining in on behalf of his government, issued the following Four-Power Declaration.

From the Four-Power Declaration on General Security, Moscow (October 30, 1943) [1]

The Governments of the United States of America, the United Kingdom, the Soviet Union and China:

[1] U. S. Department of State, *Bulletin,* IX, No. 228 (Nov. 6, 1943), 308-09.

united in their determination, in accordance with the Declaration by the United Nations of January 1, 1942, and subsequent declarations, to continue hostilities against those Axis powers with which they respectively are at war until such powers have laid down their arms on the basis of unconditional surrender;

conscious of their responsibility to secure the liberation of themselves and the peoples allied with them from the menace of aggression;

recognizing the necessity of ensuring a rapid and orderly transition from war to peace and, of establishing and maintaining international peace and security with the least diversion of the world's human and economic resources for armaments;

jointly declare:

1. That their united action, pledged for the prosecution of the war against their respective enemies, will be continued for the organization and maintenance of peace and security.

2. That those of them at war with a common enemy will act together in all matters relating to the surrender and disarmament of that enemy.

3. That they will take all measures deemed by them to be necessary to provide against any violation of the terms imposed upon the enemy.

4. That they recognize the necessity of establishing at the earliest practicable date a general international organization, based on the principle of the sovereign equality of all peace-loving states, and open to membership by all such states, large and small, for the maintenance of international peace and security.

5. That for the purpose of maintaining international peace and security pending the re-establishment of law and order and the inauguration of a system of general security, they will consult with one another and as occasion requires with other members of the United Nations with a view to joint action on behalf of the community of nations.

6. That after the termination of hostilities they will not employ their military forces within the territories of other states except for the purposes envisaged in this declaration and after joint consultation.

7. That they will confer and co-operate with one another and with other members of the United Nations to bring about a practicable general agreement with respect to the regulation of armaments in the postwar period.

Moscow, *30th October, 1943*

> V. Molotov
> Anthony Eden
> Cordell Hull
> Foo Ping-Sheung

The "Pacific Charter"

The Moscow Declaration demonstrated complete accord among the Big Three to wage war to the end against Fascism and Nazism. A few weeks later (November 22-26, 1943), President Roosevelt, Prime Minister Churchill, and Generalissimo Chiang Kai-shek[1] met at Cairo and on December 1 released a similar statement with regard to Japanese aggression in the Far East.

From the Cairo Statement
(December 1, 1943)[2]

The several military missions have agreed upon future military operations against Japan. The three great Allies expressed their resolve to bring unrelenting pressure against their brutal enemies by sea, land and air. This pressure is already rising. The three great Allies are fighting this war to restrain and punish the aggression of Japan. They covet no gain for themselves and have no thought

[1] As Russia was not then at war with Japan, she did not associate herself with this statement.
[2] U. S. Department of State, *Bulletin,* IX, No. 232 (Dec. 4, 1943), 393.

of territorial expansion. It is their purpose that Japan shall be stripped of all the islands in the Pacific which she has seized or occupied since the beginning of the first World War in 1914, and that all the territories Japan has stolen from the Chinese, such as Manchuria, Formosa and the Pescadores, shall be restored to the Republic of China. Japan will also be expelled from all other territories which she has taken by violence and greed. The aforesaid three great powers, mindful of the enslavement of the people of Korea, are determined that in due course Korea shall become free and independent.

With these objects in view, the three Allies, in harmony with those of the United Nations at war with Japan, will continue to persevere in the serious and prolonged operations necessary to procure the unconditional surrender of Japan.

The Tehran Conference

From Cairo, President Roosevelt and Prime Minister Churchill flew to Tehran, Iran, where they met Marshal Stalin in a four-day conference to complete plans for military operations in Europe. Their joint Declaration, released simultaneously with the Cairo Statement on December 1, 1943, not only reaffirmed the Moscow Declaration as regards postwar security, but also welcomed the co-operation of all democratic nations in "a world family."

From the Three-Power Declaration at Tehran (December 1, 1943) [1]

We—the President of the United States, the Prime Minister of Great Britain, and the Premier of the Soviet Union, have met these four days past, in this, the Capital of our Ally, Iran, and have shaped and confirmed our common policy.

We express our determination that our nations shall work together in war and in the peace that will follow.

As to war—our military staffs have joined in our round table discussions, and we have concerted our plans for the destruction of the German forces. We have reached complete agreement as to the scope and timing of the operations to be undertaken from the east, west and south.

The common understanding which we have here reached guarantees that victory will be ours.

And as to peace—we are sure that our concord will win an enduring Peace. We recognize fully the supreme responsibility resting upon us and all the United Nations to make a peace which will command the goodwill of the overwhelming mass of the peoples of the world and banish the scourge and terror of war for many generations.

With our Diplomatic advisers we have surveyed the problems of the future. We shall seek the co-operation and active participation of all nations, large and small, whose peoples in heart and mind are dedicated, as are our own peoples, to the elimination of tyranny and slavery, oppression and intolerance. We will welcome them, as they may choose to come, into a world family of Democratic Nations.

No power on earth can prevent our destroying the German armies by land, their U Boats by sea, and their war plants from the air. Our attack will be relentless and increasing.

Emerging from these cordial conferences we look with confidence to the day when all peoples of the world may live free lives, untouched by tyranny, and according to their varying desires and their own consciences.

We came here with hope and determination. We leave here, friends in fact, in spirit and in purpose.

Roosevelt, Churchill and Stalin

[1] *Ibid.*, IX, No. 233 (Dec. 11, 1943), 409.

3. Allied Victory, 1944-1945

VICTORY IN EUROPE, 1944-1945

Allied arms liberated most of Axis-dominated Europe in the course of 1944. Finland signed an armistice on September 4, and the Baltic states were generally cleared of German forces by the end of October. Romania, similarly, signed an armistice on September 12, and by the end of 1944 the Balkans had been freed of Axis troops. Meanwhile, on the Western Front, Allied landings in France, beginning June 6, had succeeded in driving the bulk of the German forces out of France. On October 23, the Big Three simultaneously recognized the Provisional Government of General Charles de Gaulle in France.

The End of Mussolini (April 28-29, 1945)

In Italy, however, a less happy situation had developed. Mussolini's popularity had reached the vanishing point in 1943, and on July 25, shortly after the Allied invasion of Sicily (July 10), the Italian dictator was arrested by Marshal Pietro Badoglio, who, with the approval of King Victor Emmanuel III, formed a new government. After Allied forces invaded the Italian mainland on September 3, the new Italian Government declared its unconditional surrender; but Mussolini was rescued from captivity by the Germans and, on September 23, proclaimed a "Republican Fascist" government under German protection in northern Italy. In the meantime, the Allied conquest of Italy had been slowed down by a combination of difficult terrain and firm German resistance. The condition of Italy was one of wild confusion. Not until June 4, 1944, after severe fighting, did the Allies rout the Axis forces from Rome and push northward. At this

point, too, in recognition of Italian anti-monarchical sentiment, the King withdrew—but did not abdicate—in favor of his son, Prince Humbert, who was proclaimed "Lieutenant-General of the Realm" (June 5). Shortly afterward, the Badoglio government fell, and a new ministry under Ivanoe Bonomi, an aged Socialist, was created under Allied sponsorship. On October 23, this government was granted Allied recognition as a cobelligerent (Italy had declared war on Germany a year earlier, October 13, 1943). Throughout the winter of 1944-45 the struggle in northern Italy continued, with Italians fighting on both sides, some supporting Mussolini and the Germans, and others—in increasing proportion—fighting with the Allies. Many of the latter fought as partisans—that is, guerrillas—behind the Axis lines. Into their, the partisans', hands fell Benito Mussolini on April 28, 1945, after a heated dispute with his German partners who, in giving up Milan, were charged by the former Duce with betrayal. Mussolini's end, "as horrible as any ever visited on a tyrant," was currently described by a *New York Times* correspondent.

From BRACKER, Dispatch to the *New York Times*, April 30, 1945 [1]

At 9:30 A.M. today [April 29], Mussolini's body lay on the rim of the mass of corpses, while all around surged a growing mob wild with the desire to have the last look at the man who once was a Socialist editor in this same city [Milan]. The throng pushed and yelled. Partisans strove to keep them back largely in vain. Even . . . shots in the air did not dissuade them.

Mussolini had changed in death, but not enough to be anyone else. His closely

[1] Milton Bracker, *op. cit.,* Apr. 30, 1945, 1.

shaved head and his bull neck were un-mistakable. . . . At least one bullet had passed through his head. . . . There was another small hole nearer his forehead where another bullet seemed to have gone in. As if he were not dead or dishonored enough, at least two young men in the crowd broke through and aimed kicks at his skull. One glanced off. But the other landed full on his right jaw and there was a hideous crunch that wholly disfigured the once-proud face. . . .

Mussolini lay with his head on the breast of his mistress, Clara Petacci, who had sought to rise to movie fame through him. Younger even than his daughter, she had been executed with him in a suburb of Como on the shore of Lake Como. . . . The other bodies . . . included those of Alessandro Pavolini, Mussolini's Secretary of State [and some eighteen or twenty others]. . . .

Some time on Thursday morning [April 28], in a caravan of some thirty cars, Mussolini headed north up the west shore of Lake Como. He was wearing a black coat over his [Squadrist] uniform. Near Dongo . . . a Partisan named Urbano Lazari spotted him. . . . He was made to alight and temporarily sheltered in a cottage. . . . Signorina Petacci was with him but the others in the caravan were held separate. After a brief trial they were executed.

From this point the details came from a Committee of National Liberation leader in this area known only as Eduardo. When word of the arrest reached him, he sent ten men from Milan with an un-named colonel from the Milan area of the Italian Command. The colonel handled the details of the trial and sentence, but for the moment, at least, this phase of the story is unascertainable. Eduardo's men brought back the bodies last night and they gave this version through him.

When Mussolini first saw the Italian officer with the group from Milan, he sought to embrace them, thinking that they were Fascists and his friends. Dis-abused, he was shocked and later, after the trial and the death sentence, he said . . . "Let me save my life and I will give you an empire." But this incredible plea was vain and the execution was carried out at 4:10 P.M. yesterday.

The Fall of Hitler, May 1, 1945

In the absence of final proof of the death of Adolf Hitler, the following documents are presented. There is no doubt that, whether or not Hitler died, he was succeeded on May 1, 1945, by Grand Admiral Karl Doenitz as Presi-dent, who continued German resist-ance for a week afterward. After the fall of Germany, Allied authorities pub-lished (December 30, 1945) a document by Hitler which read, in part, as fol-lows.

From HITLER, "My Political Testament" (April 29, 1945) [1]

More than thirty years have passed since I made my modest contribution as a volunteer in the First World War, which was forced upon the Reich.

In these three decades, love and loyalty to my people alone have guided me in all my thoughts, actions and life. They gave me power to make the most difficult deci-sions which have ever confronted mortal man. I have spent all my time, my powers and my health in these three decades.

It is untrue that I or anybody else in Germany wanted war in 1939. It was wanted and provoked exclusively by those international statesmen who either were of Jewish origin or worked for Jewish interests. . . .

After six years of war, which, in spite of all setbacks, will one day go down in

[1] *Ibid.*, Dec. 31, 1945, 6.

history as the most glorious and heroic manifestation of the struggle for existence of a nation, I cannot forsake the city that is the capital of this state. As our forces are too small to withstand an enemy attack on this place any longer, and our own resistance will gradually be worn down by men who are merely blind automata, I wish to share my fate with that which millions of others have also taken upon themselves by staying in this town. Further, I shall not fall into the hands of the enemy, who requires a new spectacle, presented by the Jews, to divert their hysterical masses.

I have therefore decided to remain in Berlin and there to choose death voluntarily at that moment when I believe that the position of the Fuehrer and the Chancellery itself can no longer be maintained. I die with a joyful heart in my knowledge of the immeasurable deeds and achievements of our soldiers at the front, of our women at home, the achievements of our peasants and workers and of a contribution unique in history, of our youth that bears my name.

That I express to them all the thanks that come from the bottom of my heart is as clear as my wish that they should therefore not give up the struggle under any circumstances but carry it on wherever they may be against the enemies of the Fatherland, true to the principles of the great Clausewitz.

From the sacrifice of our soldiers and from my own comradeship with them to death itself, the seed has been sown that will grow one day in the history of Germany to the glorious rebirth of the National Socialist movement and thereby to the establishment of a truly united nation. . . .

Before my death, I expel the former Reich Marshal Hermann Goering from the party and withdraw from him all the rights that were conferred on him by the decree of 29 June, 1941, and by my Reichstag speech of the first of September, 1939. . . . [Hitler also expelled Heinrich Himmler, Minister of the Interior and former SS leader.]

Apart altogether from their disloyalty to me, Goering and Himmler have brought irreparable shame on the country and the whole nation by secretly negotiating with the enemy without my knowledge and against my will, and also by illegally attempting to seize control of the state.

In order to give the German people a government composed of honorable men who will fulfill the task of continuing the war with all means, as the leader of the nation I appoint the following members of the new Cabinet:

President, Doenitz; Chancellor, Dr. Goebbels; Party Minister, Bormann; Foreign Minister, Seyss-Inquart. . . .

Although a number of these men, such as Martin Bormann, Goebbels, etc., as well as their wives, have come to me of their own free will, wishing under no circumstances to leave the Reich capital, but instead to fall with me here, I must nevertheless ask them to obey my request and, in this case, put the interests of the nation above their own feelings. [Goebbels refused to obey and, with his family, supposedly perished by Hitler's side.] . . .

May they finally be conscious that our task, the establishment of a National Socialist State, represents the work of centuries to come and obliges each individual person always to serve the common interest before his own advantage. I ask all Germans, all National Socialists, men, women and all soldiers of the army, to be loyal and obedient to the new Government and its President until death.

Above all, I enjoin the Government of the nation and the people to uphold the racial laws to the limit and to resist mercilessly the poisoner of all nations, international Jewry.

Berlin, 29 April, 1945, 0400 hours

A. Hitler

Witnesses: Dr. Joseph Goebbels, Wilhelm Burgdorf, Martin Bormann, Hans Krebs.

[In the afternoon of May 1, 1945, the Hamburg radio broadcast the following announcement:]

From the Hamburg Radio Broadcast
   (May 1, 1945) [1]

It is reported from the Fuehrer's headquarters that our Fuehrer, Adolf Hitler, fighting to the last breath against bolshevism, fell for Germany this afternoon in his operational headquarters in the Reich Chancellery.

On April 30 the Fuehrer appointed Grand Admiral Doenitz his successor. The Grand Admiral and successor of the Fuehrer now speaks to the German people.

Doenitz: German men and women, soldiers of the armed forces:

Our Fuehrer, Adolf Hitler, has fallen. In the deepest sorrow and respect the German people bow. . . . The Fuehrer has appointed me to be his successor. Fully conscious of the responsibility, I take over the leadership of the German people at this fateful hour. . . .

[On the same day, Admiral Doenitz issued the following statement:]

From DOENITZ, "Order of the Day,"
   May 1, 1945

German armed forces, my comrades: The Fuehrer has fallen. Faithful to his great ideal to save the nations of Europe from bolshevism, he has given his life and has met a hero's death. In him one of the greatest heroes of German history has

[1] *Ibid.,* May 2, 1945, 4.

departed. With proud respect and grief we lower our standards.

The Fuehrer has designated me to be the head of the state and supreme commander. . . . I take over the supreme command . . . resolved to continue the struggle against the Bolsheviks. . . . Against the British and Americans I am bound to continue to fight as far and as long as they impede me in the . . . struggle against Bolshevism. . . . I demand discipline and obedience. . . . For every single one of you the oath of loyalty to the Fuehrer is transferred straight to my person as the Fuehrer's appointed successor.

German soldiers! Do your duty! The existence of our people is at stake.

[Evidence later pointed to the conclusion that Adolf Hitler had died by his own hand. With his bride of a few days (possibly hours), Eva Braun, who had been his mistress for years before, and allegedly had borne him two children, Adolf Hitler was said to have committed suicide in the bomb shelter of the Reichschancellery, while Allied bombs and Bolshevik artillery fire rained on Berlin and Russian troops were advancing in the city of Berlin.]

The German Surrender (May 8, 1945)

German resistance collapsed almost as soon as Hitler's fall was announced. On May 4, all German forces in Holland, northwest Germany, and Denmark surrendered unconditionally to the British General Sir Bernard Law Montgomery. At the same time, General Friedeburg, of the German High Command, admitted that all Germany was in turmoil, that German soldiers were refusing to fight further, and that the German High Command was ready to surrender. A brief delay followed, as the Allies refused to recognize the government of Admiral Doenitz and required properly accredited representatives of the German High Command. Finally, General Gustav Jodl, German Chief of Staff, representing both the German High Command and Admiral Doenitz, met with Allied officials at Rheims, in France, and signed the following Act of Military Surrender at 2:41 A.M., May 7, 1945, to take effect 11:01 P.M., May 8.

From the Act of Military Surrender
(May 7, 1945) [1]

1. We, the undersigned, acting by authority of the German High Command, hereby surrender unconditionally to the Supreme Commander, Allied Expeditionary Force, and simultaneously to the Soviet High Command, all forces on land, sea, and in the air who are at this date under German control.

2. The German High Command will at once issue orders to all German military, naval and air authorities and to all forces under German control to cease active operations at 2301 hours [11:01 P.M.] Central European Time on 8 May and to remain in the positions occupied at the time. No ship, vessel, or aircraft is to be scuttled, or any damage done to their hull, machinery or equipment.

3. The German High Command will at once issue to the appropriate commanders, and ensure the carrying out of any further orders issued by the Supreme Commander, Allied Expeditionary Force, and by the Soviet High Command.

4. This Act of Military Surrender is without prejudice to, and will be superseded by, any general instrument of surrender imposed by, or on behalf of the United Nations and applicable to Germany and the German Armed Forces as a whole.

[1] U. S. Department of State, *Bulletin*, XIII, No. 317 (July 22, 1945), 106.

5. In the event of the German High Command or any of the forces under their control failing to act in accordance with this Act of Surrender, the Supreme Commander, Allied Expeditionary Force, and the Soviet High Command will take such punitive or other action as they deem appropriate.

Signed at Rheims, France, at 0241 [2:41 A.M.] on the 7th day of May, 1945
On behalf of the German High Command
—Jodl
In the presence of:
On behalf of the Supreme Commander, Allied Expeditionary Force—W. B. Smith
On behalf of the Soviet High Command —[Ivan] Sousloparoff
F. Sevez, Major General, French Army (Witness)

THE TURNING POINTS OF THE WAR

In a masterly analysis, General George C. Marshall, United States Chief of Staff, outlined the course of the entire World War II in his "Biennial Report to the Secretary of War, September 1, 1945." The following excerpts from his report represent the General's views with regard to the turning points in the War in Europe.

From MARSHALL, "Biennial Report"
(September 1, 1945) [2]

This generation . . . can still remember the black days of 1942 when the Japanese conquered all of Malaysia, occupied Burma, and threatened India while the German armies approached the Volga and the Suez. In those hours Germany and Japan came so close to complete domination of the world that we do not realize

[2] From the "Text of the Report of General Marshall," *New York Times*, Oct. 10, 1945. This is used by permission of the *New York Times*.

how thin the thread of Allied survival had been stretched.

In good conscience this Nation can take little credit for its part in staving off disaster in those critical days. It is certain that the refusal of the British and Russian peoples to accept what appeared to be inevitable defeat was the great factor in the salvage of our civilization. Of almost equal importance was the failure of the enemy to make the most of the situation. In order to establish for the historical record where and how Germany and Japan failed I asked General Eisenhower to have his intelligence officers promptly interrogate the ranking members of the German High Command who are now our prisoners of war. The results of these interviews are of remarkable interest. They give a picture of dissension among the enemy nations and lack of long range planning that may well have been decisive factors of the world struggle at its most critical moments. . . .

The available evidence shows that Hitler's original intent was to create, by absorption of Germanic peoples in the areas contiguous to Germany . . . a greater Reich which would dominate Europe. . . . No evidence has been found that the German High Command had any over-all strategic plan. Although the High Command approved Hitler's policies in principle, his impetuous strategy outran Germany military capabilities and ultimately led to Germany's defeat. The history of the German High Command from 1938 on is one of constant conflict of personalities in which military judgment was increasingly subordinated to Hitler's personal dictates. . . . In each case Hitler's views prevailed and the astounding success of each succeeding campaign raised Hitler's military prestige to the point where his opinions were no longer challenged. His military self-confidence became unassailable after the victory in France. . . .

Thus no General Staff objection was expressed when Hitler made the fatal decision to invade Soviet Russia.

When Italy entered the war Mussolini's strategic aims contemplated the expansion of his empire under the cloak of German military success. . . . Italy's declaration of war was contrary to her agreement with Germany. . . . From the very beginning Italy was a burden on the German war potential. . . . Mussolini's unilateral action in attacking Greece and Egypt forced the Germans into the Balkan and African campaigns, resulting in over-extension of the German armies which subsequently became one of the principal factors in Germany's defeat.

Nor is there evidence of close co-ordination between Germany and Japan. . . . It is believed that Japan also acted unilaterally and not in accordance with a unified strategic plan. Here were three criminal nations eager for loot and seeking greedily to advance their own self-interest by war, yet unable to agree on a strategic over-all plan for accomplishing a common objective.

1. *Failure to Invade England*—Hitler's first military set-back occurred when, after the collapse of France, England did not capitulate. . . . It was estimated that with the fall of France, England would not continue the fight. The unexpectedly swift victory over France and Great Britain's continuation of the war found the General Staff unprepared for an invasion of England. Although the armistice with France was concluded on 22 June 1940, no orders to prepare for the invasion of Britain were issued prior to 2 July. Field Marshal Kesselring . . . urged the invasion since it was generally believed in Germany that England was in a critical condition. Field Marshal Keitel, Chief of Staff . . . stated that the risk was thought to be the existence of the British fleet. He said the army was ready but the air force was limited by

weather, the navy very dubious. Meanwhile, in the air blitz over England the German Air Force suffered irreparable losses from which its bombardment arm never recovered.

2. *The Campaign of 1941 in the Soviet Union*—In the autumn of 1941 . . . the Germans stood exhausted but apparently victorious before Moscow. According to Jodl, the General Staff . . . considered that one last energetic push would . . . finish the Soviets. The German High Command had neither envisioned nor planned for a winter campaign. A sudden change in the weather brought disaster. The Red Army defense, a terrific snow storm, and extremely unseasonable cold in the Christmas week of 1941 precipitated the strategic defeat of the German armed forces. Impatient of all restraint, Hitler publicly announced that he had more faith in his own intuition than in the judgment of his military advisers. He relieved the Commander in Chief of the Army, General von Brauchitsch. It was the turning point of the war.

3. *Stalingrad*—Even after the reverse before Moscow in 1941, Germany might have avoided defeat had it not been for the campaign in 1942 which culminated in the disaster at Stalingrad. Disregarding the military lessons of history, Hitler, instead of attacking the Soviet armies massed in the north, personally planned and directed a campaign of which the immediate objectives were to deprive the Soviet Union of her vital industries and raw materials by cutting the Volga at Stalingrad and seizing the Caucasian oil fields. Beyond these concrete objectives was evidently the Napoleonic dream of a conquest of the Middle East and India by a gigantic double envelopment with one pincer descending from the Caucasus through Tiflis and the other from North Africa across Egypt, Palestine, and the Arabian desert. The campaign collapsed before Stalingrad with the magnificent Russian defense of that city. . . .

4. *Invasion of North Africa*—Allied landings in North Africa came as a surprise to the German High Command. . . . Since no advance preparations had been made by the Germans to repel such an Allied invasion of North Africa, all subsequent efforts to counter the Allies suffered from hasty improvisation. Defense continued however, because . . . since evacuation was impossible, the Germans had only the choice of resisting or surrendering.

5. *The Invasion of France*—All German headquarters expected the Allied invasion of France. . . . Both the general direction and the strength of the initial assault in Normandy were correctly estimated; but . . . the Germans were not sure exactly where the Allies would strike and considered Brittany as more probable because of the three major U-boat bases located in that region. Both Keitel and Jodl believed that the invasion could be repulsed or at worst contained, and both named the Allied air arm as the decisive factor in the German failure.

Prior to invasion, important divergencies of opinion developed between Field Marshal von Rundstedt, Commander in Chief West, and Rommel, commander of the threatened Army Group. Rundstedt desired to hold his armored forces in a group around Paris and in eastern France; Rommel to push them forward to positions in readiness close to the coast. The Rommel view prevailed. . . . Soon after the Allied capture of Cherbourg, dissension again broke out in the High Command. Von Kluge [who had relieved von Rundstedt] and Rommel wished to evacuate all southwestern France, blocking or destroying its usable ports [lest their western armies be destroyed]. . . . Hitler refused to accept this recommendation, relieved von Kluge . . . and reappointed von Rundstedt as Commander in Chief West. Under direct instructions, Rundstedt continued the battle of Normandy to its final denouement. . . .

6. *The Ardennes Counter-Attack*—The German offensive in December, 1944, was Hitler's personal conception. . . . It irreparably damaged the comparatively fresh armored divisions of the Sixth Panzer Army, the principal element of Germany's strategic reserve, at a moment when every available reserve was needed to repulse the expected Soviet attack in the East.

7. *The Crossing of the Rhine*—Even after the failure of the German counter-offensive in the Ardennes, the Germans believed that the Rhine line could be held. The loss of the Remagen bridge, however, exploded that hope. The entire Rhine defensive line had to be weakened in the attempt to contain the bridgehead, and the disorderly German retreat in the Saar and Palatinate rendered easy the subsequent drive eastward of the Allied Armies towards Hamburg, Leipzig, and Munich.

Not only were the European partners of the Axis unable to co-ordinate their plans and resources . . . but the eastern partner, Japan, was working in even greater discord. The Axis, as a matter of fact, existed on paper only. . . . Japan was so greedy for her own immediate conquests that she laid her strategy, not to help Germany defeat Russia and Great Britain, but to accumulate her own profit. . . . This principle of expansion was outlined in the "Tanaka Memorial" [see page 891]. . . . Authentic or not, it provided the pattern which Japan has followed, culminating in the great Pacific conflict. . . .

Japan's objective was the conquest, consolidation, and eventual domination of the whole Far East. . . . The best estimate of Japan's plan for the accomplishment of her objectives appears to be the following:

(1) Neutralize or destroy the United States Pacific Fleet by an attack on Pearl Harbor.

(2) Drive rapidly south, overcoming the Philippines and the Southwest and South Pacific Islands in order to cut sea routes of supply or attack from the East and gain the vast natural resources of the East Indies.

(3) Cut China's supply line from the west by an invasion of Burma.

(4) Form a flank by the seizure of . . . Singapore and the islands of Sumatra and Java.

(5) Isolate or possibly invade Australia.

(6) Invade the Hawaiian Islands via Midway.

(7) Invade the Aleutian Islands to form a northern flank. . . .

(8) Bring the American Northwest under aerial bombardment, raid our West Coast aviation industries and then seize critical areas.

(9) Stimulate unrest to eventual revolution in India. . . .

The Japanese strategic plan initially failed when she missed the opportunity of landing troops on Hawaii, capturing Oahu and the important bases there, and denying us a necessary focal point from which to launch operations in the Western Pacific.

There can be no doubt that the greed and mistakes of the war-making nations as well as the heroic stands of the British and Soviet peoples saved the United States a war on her own soil. The crisis had come and passed at Stalingrad and El Alamein before this nation was able to gather sufficient resources to participate in the fight in a determining manner.

ALLIED OCCUPATION OF GERMANY

The Yalta Conference, 1945

In February, 1945, prior to the German collapse, President Roosevelt,

Prime Minister Churchill, and Marshal Stalin, with their staffs, held a Big Three conference in the Crimea to perfect plans for Germany's final overthrow and establish principles for postwar occupation and settlement in Europe. Commonly called the Yalta Conference, this was the last Big Three conference attended by President Roosevelt, as he died suddenly on April 12, too soon to see victory crown his brilliant war efforts. The principles and objectives set forth at this conference were those by which the postwar occupation of Germany and the Allies' policies with regard to Europe in general were governed. At the Potsdam Conference, held soon after Germany's surrender (July-August, 1945), the Big Three arranged details "to carry out the Crimea Declaration on Germany."

From Report of the Crimea Conference (February 11, 1945) [1]

We have agreed on common policies and plans for enforcing the unconditional surrender terms which we shall impose on Nazi Germany. . . . These terms will not be made known until the final defeat of Germany. . . . Under the agreed plan, the forces of the three powers will each occupy a separate zone of Germany. Coordinated administration and control has been provided for . . . through a central control commission consisting of the Supreme Commanders of the three powers with headquarters in Berlin. It has been agreed that France should be invited . . . to take over a zone of occupation, and to participate as a fourth member of the control commission. . . .

It is our inflexible purpose to destroy German militarism and Nazism and to ensure that Germany will never again be

[1] U. S. Department of State, *Bulletin*, XII, No. 295 (Feb. 18, 1945), 214-16.

able to disturb the peace of the world. We are determined to disarm and disband all German armed forces; break up for all time the German General Staff . . . remove or destroy all German military equipment; eliminate or control all German industry that could be used for military production; bring all war criminals to just and swift punishment and exact reparation in kind for the destruction wrought by the Germans; wipe out the Nazi Party, Nazi laws, organizations and institutions, remove all Nazi and militarist influences from public office and from the cultural and economic life of the German people; and take in harmony such other measures in Germany as may be necessary to the future peace and safety of the world. It is not our purpose to destroy the people of Germany, but only when Nazism and militarism have been extirpated will there be hope for a decent life for Germans, and a place for them in the comity of nations.

REPARATIONS BY GERMANY. We have considered the question of the damage caused by Germany . . . and recognized it as just that Germany be obliged to make compensation . . . in kind to the greatest extent possible.[2] A commission for the compensation of damage will be established . . . to consider the . . . extent and methods for compensation . . . to the allied countries. The commission will work in Moscow. . . .

DECLARATION ON LIBERATED EUROPE. The [Allied Chiefs] . . . have consulted with each other in the common interests of the peoples of their countries and those of liberated Europe. They jointly declare

[2] At the Potsdam Conference (July-August, 1945), the Big Three decided that the reparation claims of each power should be met by removals from the zone which it occupied and "from appropriate German external assets." Russia was to receive additional reparations from the western zones. The amounts of equipment to be removed were to be fixed within six months and deliveries completed within two years.

their mutual agreement to concert during the temporary period of instability in liberated Europe the policies of their three governments in assisting the peoples liberated . . . to solve by democratic means their pressing political and economic problems.

The establishment of order in Europe and the rebuilding of national economic life must be achieved by processes which will enable the liberated peoples to destroy the last vestiges of Nazism and Fascism and to create democratic institutions of their own choice. This is a principle of the Atlantic Charter—the right of all peoples to choose the form of government under which they will live. . . .

To foster the conditions in which the liberated peoples may exercise these rights, the three governments will jointly assist the people in any European liberated state or former Axis satellite state in Europe where in their judgment conditions require (A) to establish . . . internal peace; (B) to carry out emergency measures for the relief of distressed peoples; (C) to form interim governmental authorities broadly representative of all democratic elements . . . pledged to the earliest possible establishment through free elections of governments responsive to the will of the people; and (D) to facilitate where necessary the holding of such elections.

The three governments will consult the other United Nations and provisional authorities or other governments in Europe when matters of direct interest to them are under consideration. . . .

By this declaration we reaffirm our faith in the principles of the Atlantic Charter, our pledge in the declaration of the United Nations, and our determination to build in co-operation with other peace-loving nations world order under law, dedicated to peace, security, freedom and general well-being of all mankind.

[The Big Three also created a commission to reorganize the government of liberated Poland on "a broader democratic basis," this government to hold "free and unfettered elections as soon as possible on the basis of universal suffrage and secret ballot." They further considered that the eastern frontier of Poland "should follow the Curzon line with digressions from it in some regions of five to eight kilometers in favor of Poland. They recognize that Poland must receive substantial accessions of territory in the North and West" (that is, compensation for territorial losses at German expense). The Big Three also reviewed Balkan questions, agreeing especially to recommend that a new government be established in Yugoslavia by Marshal Tito and Dr. Subasić.]

The Berlin Conference (June, 1945)

On June 5, 1945, after the German surrender, representatives of the United States, Russia, Great Britain, and France met in Berlin to work out details of German occupation in accordance with the principles laid down at the Crimea Conference. Parts of their statements made on that occasion follow.

From the Four Major Allies' Statements on Control of Occupied Germany (June 5, 1945) [1]

By the declaration made at Berlin on June 5 the Governments [of the four Allies] . . . have assumed supreme authority with respect to Germany. . . .

1. Germany, within her frontiers as they were on Dec. 31, 1937, will, for the purposes of occupation, be divided into four zones, one to be allotted to each power as follows:

An eastern zone to the Union of Soviet Socialist Republics [Mecklenburg, Saxony, Thuringia, and part of Brandenburg];

[1] *New York Times,* June 6, 1945, 4. By permission of the *New York Times.*

a northwestern zone to the United Kingdom [the Ruhr, Hanover, Westphalia, Hamburg, Bremen, Schleswig-Holstein];

a southwestern zone to the United States of America [Bavaria, Württemberg, Hesse, Hesse-Nassau];

a western zone to France [both sides of the Rhine about Coblenz south to near Karlsruhe and on to the Swiss border, to include area about Freiburg].

The occupying forces in each zone will be under a commander in chief designated by the responsible power. . . .

2. The area of "Greater Berlin" will be occupied by forces of each of the four powers. An inter-Allied governing authority consisting of four commandants, appointed by their respective commanders in chief, will be established to direct jointly its administration. . . .

[Each commander in chief held supreme authority in all matters affecting his zone; a Control Council, of the four commanders in chief, regulated matters affecting Germany as a whole. A political adviser, and other specialized officers, were associated with each commander in chief. No other responsible government was recognized as competent in Germany, in keeping with the German unconditional surrender. German military forces were to be completely disarmed, a civil police force equipped with small arms being retained for guard duties. The Allies took possession of all German arms, ammunition, military equipment, stores, naval vessels, aircraft, transportation and communication facilities, military installations (airfields, naval bases, and so on), factories, plants, laboratories, technical data, patents, and the like. The principal Nazi leaders, as specified by the Allies, and all war criminals, were to be surrendered to the Allies. And all German authorities were to "carry out uncondi-

tionally the requirements of the Allied representatives."]

PLANS FOR EUROPEAN PEACE SETTLEMENT: THE COUNCIL OF FOREIGN MINISTERS

The Potsdam Conference

No final peace treaties between the Allies and the conquered powers were drawn up by the end of 1945, although machinery and methods for their ultimate establishment had been determined upon. In July, President Harry S. Truman, Generalissimo Stalin, and Prime Minister Churchill—the last being supplanted on July 28 by Clement Richard Attlee, who had become British Prime Minister after a Labor-party victory in a postwar parliamentary election—met at Potsdam, near Berlin, where, among other things, the following arrangements for ultimate peace settlement were made.

From the Potsdam Agreement
(July 26, 1945) [1]

The conference reached an agreement for the establishment of a Council of Foreign Ministers representing the five principal powers [the United States, Great Britain, Russia, China, and France] to continue the necessary preparatory work for the peace settlements. . . . The Council shall normally meet in London, which shall be the permanent seat of the joint secretariat which the Council will form. . . . The first meeting of the Council shall be held in London not later than September 1, 1945. . . .

As its immediate important task, the Council shall be authorized to draw up, with a view to their submission to the United Nations, treaties of peace with

[1] U. S. Department of State, *Bulletin*, XIII, No. 319 (Aug. 5, 1945), 153-54.

Italy, Rumania, Bulgaria, Hungary, and Finland, and to propose settlements of territorial questions outstanding on the termination of the war in Europe. The Council shall be utilized for the preparation of a peace settlement for Germany to be accepted by the government of Germany when a government adequate for the purpose is established.

[The first Council of Foreign Ministers met in London in September, but, in the words of the American Secretary of State, Mr. James F. Byrnes, it "closed in a stalemate." The principal issues arose over interpretation of the Berlin (Potsdam) Agreement, especially with regard to the competency of France and others of the five powers to take part in treaty arrangements with states with which they had not been at war, and as to whether this council was to draw up final treaty arrangements or merely to do preparatory work. A complete deadlock between Russia and the other powers arose on these questions. At a second meeting, at Moscow, in December, 1945, a happier atmosphere prevailed—possibly because only the Big Three were present. The issues which plagued the London Conference were determined as follows, France and China being "requested" to adhere.]

From the Moscow Communiqué of the
  Council of Foreign Ministers
  (December 26, 1945) [1]

1. In drawing up by the Council of Foreign Ministers of treaties of peace with Italy, Rumania, Bulgaria, Hungary, Finland, only members of the council who are, or under the terms of the agreement establishing the Council of Foreign Ministers adopted at the Berlin Conference are deemed to be, signatory of the surren-

der terms will participate, unless and until the council takes further action under the agreement to invite other members of the council to participate. . . . That is to say:

A. The terms of the peace treaty with Italy will be drafted by the Foreign Ministers of the United Kingdom, the United States, the Soviet Union and France;

B. The terms of the peace treaties with Rumania, Bulgaria and Hungary by the Foreign Ministers of the Soviet Union, the United States and the United Kingdom;

C. The terms of the peace treaty with Finland by the Foreign Ministers of the Soviet Union and the United Kingdom. . . .

2. When the preparation of all these drafts has been completed, the Council of Foreign Ministers will convoke a conference for the purpose of considering the [five] treaties. . . . The conference will consist of . . . the Council of Foreign Ministers together with all members of the United Nations which actively waged war with substantial military force against enemy European states, namely: [The Big Three, plus China, France, the British Dominions, Belgium, the Netherlands, Byelo-Russian Soviet Socialist Republic, Brazil, Czechoslovakia, Ethiopia, Greece, India, Norway, Poland, Yugoslavia, and the Ukrainian Soviet Socialist Republic]. . . . The conference will be held not later than May 1, 1946.

3. After the . . . conference and upon consideration of its recommendations, the states signatory to the terms of armistice with Italy, Rumania, Bulgaria, Hungary and Finland—France being regarded as such . . . with Italy—will draw up the final texts of peace treaties.

4. The final texts of the respective peace treaties as so drawn will be signed by . . . the states represented at the conference which are at war with the enemy states in question. The texts of the respective treaties will then be submitted to the other

United Nations which are at war with the enemy states in question.

5. The peace treaties will come into force immediately after they have been ratified by the Allied states signatory to the respective armistices, France being regarded as such in the case of the peace with Italy. These treaties are subject to ratification by the enemy states in question.

THE SURRENDER OF JAPAN (1945)

Allied Demands upon Japan

The end of the war in Europe led to renewed concentration of Allied efforts in the war against Japan. On July 26, 1945, President Truman, Generalissimo Chiang Kai-shek, and Prime Minister Attlee issued a Declaration from the Berlin Conference, to which Russia later adhered, which amounted to an ultimatum to Japan.

From the Potsdam Declaration
   (July 26, 1945) [1]

The following are our terms; we will not deviate from them; there are no alternatives; we shall brook no delay.

There must be eliminated for all time the authority and influence of those who have deceived and misled the people of Japan into embarking on a world conquest. We insist that a new order of peace, security and justice will be impossible until irresponsible militarism is driven from the world.

Until such a new order is established and until there is convincing proof that Japan's war-making power is destroyed, points in Japanese territory to be designated by the Allies shall be occupied to secure the achievement of the basic objectives we are here setting forth.

The terms of the Cairo Declaration shall

[1] *Ibid.*, July 27, 1945, 5.

be carried out and Japanese sovereignty shall be limited to the islands of Honshu, Hokkaido, Kyushu, Shikoku and such minor islands as we determine.

The Japanese military forces, after being completely disarmed, shall be permitted to return to their homes with the opportunity to lead peaceful and productive lives.

We do not intend that the Japanese shall be enslaved as a race or destroyed as a nation, but stern justice shall be meted out to all war criminals, including those who have visited cruelties upon our prisoners. The Japanese Government shall remove all obstacles to the revival and strengthening of democratic tendencies among the Japanese people. Freedom of speech and religion and of thought, as well as respect for the fundamental human rights, shall be established.

Japan shall be permitted to maintain such industries as will sustain her economy and permit the exaction of just reparations in kind, but not those industries which will enable her to rearm for war. To this end access to, as distinguished from control of, raw materials shall be permitted. Eventual Japanese participation in world trade relations shall be permitted.

The occupying forces of the Allies shall be withdrawn from Japan as these objectives have been accomplished and there has been established, in accordance with the freely expressed will of the Japanese people, a peacefully inclined and responsible Government.

We call upon the Government of Japan to proclaim now the unconditional surrender of all Japanese armed forces, and to provide proper and adequate assurances of their good faith in such action. The alternative for Japan is prompt and utter destruction.

The Atomic Bombs (August 6 and 8, 1945)

Japan chose to "ignore" the Potsdam Declaration, but two almost simultaneous events soon followed to cause her to alter the decision. The first occurred on August 6, when a lone American bomber flew over Hiroshima, a Japanese city of about 350,000, and dropped a single bomb packed with the destructive force of 20,000 tons of TNT. This was the first atomic bomb, heralding, it was said, a new "atomic age," an age for which the most fantastic prophecies have been made but which, at present writing, is known only for a new destructive weapon of breath-taking proportions. The bomb was the result of a race between Nazi and Allied scientists, the former principally Germans, the latter English, Americans, and German and other refugees, to create a weapon which would utilize man's newly discovered ability to split atoms and to harness and direct the enormous energy —the basic power of the universe— loosed from their cores. The first bomb destroyed 60 per cent of Hiroshima and perhaps a hundred thousand inhabitants at one blow. A second (improved) bomb was dropped on Nagasaki on August 8. William L. Laurence, a consultant to the United States War Department and science writer for the *New York Times,* went on the flight which dropped the bomb and gave the following eyewitness account of the scene.

From LAURENCE, Report on the Bombing of Nagasaki (August 8, 1945) [1]

We heard the prearranged signal on our radio, put on our arc-welder's glasses and watched tensely the maneuverings of the

[1] *Ibid.,* Sept. 9, 1945, 35.

strike ship about half a mile in front of us.

"There she goes!" someone said.

Out of the belly of *The Great Artiste* what looked like a black object went downward.

Captain Bock swung around to get out of range; but even though we were turning away in the opposite direction, and despite the fact that it was broad daylight in our cabin, all of us became aware of a giant flash that broke through the dark barrier of our arc-welder's lenses and flooded our cabin with intense light.

We removed our glasses after the first flash, but the light still lingered on, a bluish-green light that illuminated the entire sky all around. A tremendous blast wave struck our ship and made it tremble from nose to tail. This was followed by four more blasts in rapid succession, each resounding like the boom of cannon fire hitting our plane from all directions.

Observers in the tail of our ship saw a giant ball of fire rise as though from the bowels of the earth, belching forth enormous white smoke-rings. Next they saw a giant pillar of purple fire, 10,000 feet high, shooting skyward with enormous speed.

By the time our ship had made another turn in the direction of the atomic explosion, the pillar of purple fire had reached the level of our altitude. Only about forty-five seconds had passed. Awestruck, we watched it shoot upward like a meteor coming from the earth instead of from outer space, becoming ever more alive as it climbed skyward through the white clouds. It was no longer smoke, or dust, or even a cloud of fire. It was a living thing, a new species of being born before our incredulous eyes.

At one stage of its evolution, covering millions of years in terms of seconds, the entity assumed the form of a giant square totem pole, with its base about three miles long, tapering off to about a mile at the top. Its bottom was brown, its center was amber, its top white. But it was a living totem pole, carved with many grotesque masks grimacing at the earth.

Then, just when it appeared as if the thing had settled down into a state of permanence, there came shooting out of the top a giant mushroom that increased the height of the pillar to a total of 45,000 feet. The mushroom top was even more alive than the pillar, seething and boiling in a white fury of creamy foam, sizzling upward and then descending earthward, a thousand Old Faithful geysers rolled into one.

It kept struggling in an elemental fury, like a creature in the act of breaking the bonds that held it down. In a few seconds it had freed itself from its gigantic stem and floated upward with tremendous speed, its momentum carrying into the stratosphere to a height of about 60,000 feet.

But no sooner did this happen than another mushroom, smaller in size than the first one, began emerging out of the pillar. It was as though the decapitated monster were growing a new head.

As the first mushroom floated off into the blue, it changed its shape into a flower-like form, its giant petal curving downward, creamy white outside, rose-colored inside. It still retained that shape when we last gazed at it from a distance of about 200 miles.

The Japanese Surrender (September 2, 1945)

The second event which caused the Japanese to alter their decision with regard to the Potsdam Declaration was Russia's declaration of war on Japan on August 8. Russia's declaration of war culminated many months of Allied efforts to persuade her to take the step, a step which she resolutely refused to take until after the German defeat ob-

viated the necessity for her to fight on two fronts simultaneously—and a step, as it now appears, although perhaps not all the evidence is made public, which was hastened by secret Allied agreements made at the Crimean Conference to grant Russia economic and territorial concessions in the Far East at the expense of China and Japan.

Faced with such odds, shorn of many of her South Pacific conquests by the brilliant exploits of American forces and the rest cut off, left to "wither on the vine," and with American and British forces on her doorstep, roaming at will the Japanese home waters and the air over the Japanese islands, the Japanese offered to surrender on August 10, on condition that acceptance of the Potsdam Declaration would not prejudice "the prerogatives of His Majesty [the Japanese Emperor] as a sovereign ruler." To this offer the Allies replied cautiously, indicating that the future status of the Emperor would depend, ultimately, upon the will of the Japanese people as expressed in a free election. On August 14, by an Imperial Rescript, the Japanese Emperor announced unconditional acceptance of the Potsdam Declaration. While emissaries went out to arrange details with Admiral Chester William Nimitz and General Douglas MacArthur for a bloodless occupation of Japan, a giant Allied fleet assembled and moved into Tokyo Bay. There, on September 2, aboard the American battleship *Missouri*, the surrender was signed.

From the "Instrument of Surrender" (September 2, 1945) [1]

We, acting by command of and in behalf of the Emperor of Japan, the

---

[1] Facsimile in the U. S. Department of State, *Bulletin*, XIII, No. 324 (Sept. 9, 1945), 364-65.

Japanese Government and the Japanese Imperial General Headquarters, hereby accept the provisions set forth in the declaration issued by the heads of the Governments of the United States, China and Great Britain on 26 July, 1945, at Potsdam, and subsequently adhered to by the Union of Soviet Socialist Republics, which four powers are hereafter referred to as the Allied Powers.

We hereby proclaim the unconditional surrender to the Allied Powers of the Japanese Imperial General Headquarters and of all Japanese armed forces and all armed forces under Japanese control wherever situated.

We hereby command all Japanese forces wherever situated and the Japanese people to cease hostilities forthwith, to preserve and save from damage all ships, aircraft, and military and civil property and to comply with all requirements which may be imposed by the Supreme Commander for the Allied Powers or by agencies of the Japanese Government at his direction. . . .

We hereby command all civil, military and naval officials to obey and enforce all proclamations, orders and directives deemed by the Supreme Commander for the Allied Powers to be proper to effectuate this surrender and issued by him or under his authority. . . .

We hereby undertake for the Emperor, the Japanese Government and their successors to carry out the provisions of the Potsdam Declaration in good faith. . . .

We hereby command the Japanese Imperial Government and the Japanese Imperial General Headquarters at once to liberate all allied prisoners of war and civilian internees now under Japanese control and to provide for their protection, care, maintenance and immediate transportation to places as directed.

The authority of the Emperor and the Japanese Government to rule the state shall be subject to the Supreme Commander for the Allied Powers who will take such steps as he deems proper to effectuate these terms of surrender.

> Signed at Tokyo Bay, Japan at 0904 I on the Second day of September, 1945
>
> (Signed) Mamoru Shigemitsu, By Command and in behalf of the Emperor of Japan and the Japanese Government
>
> (Signed) Yoshijiro Umezu, By Command and in behalf of the Japanese Imperial General Headquarters

Accepted at Tokyo Bay, Japan at 0908 I on the Second day of September, 1945, for the United States, Republic of China, United Kingdom and the Union of Soviet Socialist Republics, and in the interests of other United Nations at war with Japan.

> (Signed) Douglas MacArthur, Supreme Commander for the Allied Powers

[The signatures of representatives of the United States, China, Great Britain, Russia, Australia, Canada, France, the Netherlands, and New Zealand follow.]

44

THE NEW STRUCTURE FOR SECURITY

1. The Charter of the United Nations (June 26, 1945)

To implement the objectives set forth by President Roosevelt's "Four Freedoms," to seek to give reality to the Atlantic Charter, to establish and maintain the peace, and to bind up the wounds of war, a series of organizations was created by the United Nations, which from the twenty-six states that signed the United Nations Declaration of January 1, 1942, had grown to fifty-one in number by the end of the war. Chief among these interrelated organizations were:

1. The United Nations Relief and Rehabilitation Administration (UNRRA), created by an Agreement signed at Washington on November 9, 1943, "To plan, co-ordinate, administer or arrange for the administration of measures for the relief of victims of war in any area under the control of any of the United Nations through the provision of food, fuel, clothing, shelter and other basic necessities, medical and other essential services."

2. The creation at the United Nations Monetary and Financial Conference, held at Bretton Woods, New Hampshire, July 10-22, 1944, of: a. An International Monetary Fund of $8,000,000,000 as a "world kitty" administered to "promote international monetary co-operation . . . facilitate the expansion and balanced growth of international trade,

and to contribute thereby to the promotion and maintenance of high levels of employment and real income . . . [and] to promote exchange stability." b. An International Bank for Reconstruction and Development, "To assist in the reconstruction and development of territories of members . . . promote private foreign investments by means of guarantees or participation in loans . . . [and] to promote the long-range balanced growth of international trade."

3. The establishment, under a newly drawn Charter, of the United Nations, a world security organization to prevent the reoccurrence of war, strengthen the will to peace, and promote social progress.

Organization of the United Nations grew out of the successful co-operation of the Allies in the prosecution of the war. Presaged by the results of various conferences held during the war [see page 960], especially by the Four-Power Declaration at Moscow in October, 1943, the Charter of the "new League of Nations" was the direct outgrowth of the Dumbarton Oaks Conference, held between August 21 and October 7, 1944. At this conference, the Big Three—with China consulting with the United States and Great Britain after the Russian delegates' departure— agreed upon a draft proposal for a new international security organization, the draft to be submitted to an assembly of the United Nations at San Francisco.

The United Nations Conference on International Organization met at San Francisco on April 25, 1945, with delegations representing fifty nations. Until June 26, the delegates debated the draft submitted from the Dumbarton Oaks Conference—with many sharp exchanges of opinion, particularly with reference to the question of the allocation of power between great and small states—and agreed to submit the following Charter to member states for approval. By October 24, 1945, the requisite number of nations had ratified it and, under the provisions of the document itself, the United Nations Charter became operative. Fifty-one nations had approved of the Charter before the end of 1945.

To realize the purposes set forth in the Preamble, the United Nations Charter provided six instruments: 1. The Security Council, an agency to assist nations to settle their disputes peaceably and to enforce peace. 2. The General Assembly, an international forum to which any and all kinds of international questions may be taken for discussion and possible action. 3. The Economic and Social Council, an instrument to foster economic and social developments in the interests of international harmony, progress, and peace. 4. The International Court of Justice to adjust justiciable international disputes in accordance with the principles of international law and justice. 5. The Trusteeship Council, an agency to supervise the international trusteeship for dependent states. 6. The Secretariat, the permanent civil service of the United Nations. The success of these interrelated instruments lies, of course, in the lap of the gods. Should they achieve the purposes for which they are instituted, the words of President Truman at the final session of the San Francisco Conference will be gloriously fulfilled: "Oh, what a great day this can be in history!"

From The Charter of the United Nations (1945) [1]

We the peoples of the United Nations, determined to save succeeding generations from the scourge of war, which twice in our lifetime has brought untold sorrow to mankind, and

to reaffirm faith in fundamental human rights, in the dignity and worth of the human person, in the equal rights of men and women and of nations large and small, and

to establish conditions under which justice and respect for the obligations arising from treaties and other sources of international law can be maintained, and

to promote social progress and better standards of life in larger freedom,

and for these ends to practice tolerance and live together in peace with one another as good neighbors, and

to unite our strength to maintain international peace and security, and to ensure, by the acceptance of principles and the institution of methods, that armed force shall not be used, save in the common interest, and

to employ international machinery for the promotion of the economic and social advancement of all peoples,

have resolved to combine our efforts to accomplish these aims.

Accordingly, our respective Governments, through representatives assembled in the city of San Francisco, who have exhibited their full powers found to be in good and due form, have agreed to the present Charter of the United Nations

[1] "Report to the President on the Results of the San Francisco Conference by . . . the Secretary of State," U. S. Department of State *Publication 2349,* Conference Series 71 (June 26, 1945), Appendix A, 176 ff.

and do hereby establish an international organization to be known as the United Nations.

CHAPTER I. PURPOSES AND PRINCIPLES

Art. 1. The Purposes of the United Nations are:

1. To maintain international peace and security, and to that end: to take effective collective measures for the prevention and removal of threats to the peace, and for the suppression of acts of aggression or other breaches of the peace, and to bring about by peaceful means, and in conformity with the principles of justice and international law, adjustment or settlement of international disputes or situations which might lead to a breach of the peace;

2. To develop friendly relations among nations based on respect for the principle of equal rights and self-determination of peoples, and to take other appropriate measures to strengthen universal peace;

3. To achieve international co-operation in solving international problems of an economic, social, cultural, or humanitarian character, and in promoting and encouraging respect for human rights and for fundamental freedoms for all without distinction as to race, sex, language, or religion; and

4. To be a center for harmonizing the actions of nations in the attainment of these common ends.

Art. 2. The Organization and its Members, in pursuit of the Purposes stated in Article 1, shall act in accordance with the following Principles.

1. The Organization is based on the principle of the sovereign equality of all its Members.

2. All Members, in order to ensure to all of them the rights and benefits resulting from membership, shall fulfill in good faith the obligations assumed by them in accordance with the present Charter.

3. All Members shall settle their international disputes by peaceful means in such a manner that international peace and security, and justice, are not endangered.

4. All Members shall refrain in their international relations from the threat or use of force against the territorial integrity or political independence of any state, or in any other manner inconsistent with the Purposes of the United Nations.

5. All Members shall give the United Nations every assistance in any action it takes in accordance with the present Charter, and shall refrain from giving assistance to any state against which the United Nations is taking preventive or enforcement action.

6. The Organization shall ensure that states which are not Members of the United Nations act in accordance with these Principles so far as may be necessary for the maintenance of international peace and security.

7. Nothing contained in the present Charter shall authorize the United Nations to intervene in matters which are essentially within the domestic jurisdiction of any state or shall require the Members to submit such matters to settlement under the present Charter; but this principle shall not prejudice the application of enforcement measures under Chapter VII.

CHAPTER II. MEMBERSHIP

Art. 3. The original Members of the United Nations shall be the states which, having participated in the United Nations Conference on International Organization at San Francisco, or having previously signed the Declaration by United Nations of January 1, 1942, sign the present Charter and ratify it in accordance with Article 110.

Art. 4. 1. Membership in the United Nations is open to all other peace-loving states which accept the obligations contained in the present Charter, and, in the judgment of the Organization, are able and willing to carry out these obligations.

2. The admission of any such state to membership in the United Nations will be effected by a decision of the General Assembly upon the recommendation of the Security Council.

Art. 5. A Member of the United Nations against which preventive or enforcement action has been taken by the Security Council may be suspended from the exercise of the rights and privileges of membership by the General Assembly upon the recommendation of the Security Council. The exercise of these rights and privileges may be restored by the Security Council.

Art. 6. A Member of the United Nations which has persistently violated the Principles contained in the present Charter may be expelled from the Organization by the General Assembly upon the recommendation of the Security Council.

CHAPTER III. ORGANS

Art. 7. 1. There are established as the principal organs of the United Nations: a General Assembly, a Security Council, an Economic and Social Council, a Trusteeship Council, an International Court of Justice, and a Secretariat.

2. Such subsidiary organs as may be found necessary may be established in accordance with the present Charter.

Art. 8. The United Nations shall place no restrictions on the eligibility of men and women to participate in any capacity and under conditions of equality in its principal and subsidiary organs.

CHAPTER IV. THE GENERAL ASSEMBLY: COMPOSITION

Art. 9. 1. The General Assembly shall consist of all the Members of the United Nations.

2. Each Member shall have not more than five representatives in the General Assembly.

Functions and Powers

Art. 10. The General Assembly may discuss any questions or any matters within the scope of the present Charter or relating to the powers and functions of any organs provided for in the present Charter, and, except as provided in Article 12, may make recommendations to the Members of the United Nations or to the Security Council or to both on any such questions or matters.

Art. 11. 1. The General Assembly may consider the general principles of co-operation in the maintenance of international peace and security, including the principles governing disarmament and the regulation of armaments. . . .

2. The General Assembly may discuss any questions relating to the maintenance of international peace and security brought before it by any Member of the United Nations, or by the Security Council, or by a state which is not a Member of the United Nations. . . .

3. The General Assembly may call the attention of the Security Council to situations which are likely to endanger international peace and security. . . .

Art. 12. 1. While the Security Council is exercising in respect of any dispute or situation the functions assigned to it in the present Charter, the General Assembly shall not make any recommendations with regard to that dispute or situation unless the Security Council so requests. . . .

Art. 13. 1. The General Assembly shall initiate studies and make recommendations for the purpose of:

a. promoting international co-operation in the political field and encouraging the progressive development of international law and its codification;

b. promoting international co-operation

in the economic, social, cultural, educational, and health fields, and assisting in the realization of human rights and fundamental freedoms for all without distinction as to race, sex, language, or religion. . . .

Art. 14. Subject to the provisions of Article 12, the General Assembly may recommend measures for the peaceful adjustment of any situation, regardless of origin, which it deems likely to impair the general welfare or friendly relations among nations. . . .

Art. 15. 1. The General Assembly shall receive and consider annual and special reports from the Security Council. . . .

2. The General Assembly shall receive and consider reports from the other organs of the United Nations.

Art. 16. The General Assembly shall perform such functions with respect to the international trusteeship system as are assigned to it under Chapters XII and XIII, including the approval of the trusteeship agreements for areas not designated as strategic.

Art. 17. 1. The General Assembly shall consider and approve the budget of the Organization.

2. The expenses of the Organization shall be borne by the Members as apportioned by the General Assembly. . . .

Voting

Art. 18. 1. Each member of the General Assembly shall have one vote.

2. Decisions of the General Assembly on important questions shall be made by a two-thirds majority of the members present and voting. These questions shall include: recommendations with respect to the maintenance of international peace and security, the election of the non-permanent members of the Security Council, the election of the members of the Economic and Social Council, the election of members of the Trusteeship Council in

accordance with paragraph 1 (c) of Article 86, the admission of new Members to the United Nations, the suspension of the rights and privileges of membership, the expulsion of Members, questions relating to the operation of the trusteeship system, and budgetary questions.

3. Decisions on other questions, including the determination of additional categories of questions to be decided by a two-thirds majority, shall be made by a majority of the members present and voting. . . .

Procedure

Art. 20. The General Assembly shall meet in regular annual sessions and in such special sessions as occasion may require. Special sessions shall be convoked by the Secretary-General at the request of the Security Council or of a majority of the Members of the United Nations.

Art. 21. The General Assembly shall adopt its own rules of procedure. It shall elect its President for each session.

Art. 22. The General Assembly may establish such subsidiary organs as it deems necessary for the performance of its functions.

CHAPTER V. THE SECURITY COUNCIL: COMPOSITION

Art. 23. 1. The Security Council shall consist of eleven Members of the United Nations. The Republic of China, France, the Union of Soviet Socialist Republics, the United Kingdom of Great Britain and Northern Ireland, and the United States of America shall be permanent members of the Security Council. The General Assembly shall elect six other Members of the United Nations to be non-permanent members of the Security Council, due regard being specially paid, in the first instance to the contribution of Members of the United Nations to the maintenance of international peace and security and to the other purposes of the Organization, and also to equitable geographical distribution.

2. The non-permanent members of the Security Council shall be elected for a term of two years. In the first election of the non-permanent members, however, three shall be chosen for a term of one year. A retiring member shall not be eligible for immediate re-election.

3. Each member of the Security Council shall have one representative.

Functions and Powers

Art. 24. 1. In order to ensure prompt and effective action by the United Nations, its Members confer on the Security Council primary responsibility for the maintenance of international peace and security, and agree that in carrying out its duties under this responsibility the Security Council acts on their behalf.

2. In discharging these duties the Security Council shall act in accordance with the Purposes and Principles of the United Nations. . . .

3. The Security Council shall submit annual and, when necessary, special reports to the General Assembly for its consideration.

Art. 25. The Members of the United Nations agree to accept and carry out the decisions of the Security Council in accordance with the present Charter.

Art. 26. In order to promote the establishment and maintenance of international peace and security with the least diversion for armaments of the world's human and economic resources, the Security Council shall be responsible for formulating, with the assistance of the Military Staff Committee referred to in Article 47, plans to be submitted to the Members of the United Nations for the establishment of a system for the regulation of armaments.

Voting

Art. 27. 1. Each member of the Security Council shall have one vote.

2. Decisions of the Security Council on procedural matters shall be made by an affirmative vote of seven members.

3. Decisions of the Security Council on all other matters shall be made by an affirmative vote of seven members, including the concurring votes of the permanent members; provided that, in decisions under Chapter VI, and under paragraph 3 of Article 52, a party to a dispute shall abstain from voting.

Procedure

Art. 28. 1. The Security Council shall be so organized as to be able to function continuously. Each member of the Security Council shall for this purpose be represented at all times at the seat of the Organization.

2. The Security Council shall hold periodic meetings at which each of its members may, if it so desires, be represented by a member of the government or by some other specially designated representative.

3. The Security Council may hold meetings at such places other than the seat of the Organization as in its judgment will best facilitate its work.

Art. 29. The Security Council may establish such subsidiary organs as it deems necessary for the performance of its functions.

Art. 30. The Security Council shall adopt its own rules of procedure, including the method of selecting its President.

Art. 31. Any Member of the United Nations which is not a member of the Security Council may participate, without vote, in the discussion of any question brought before the Security Council whenever the latter considers that the interests of that Member are specially affected.

Art. 32. Any Member of the United Nations which is not a member of the Security Council or any state which is not a Member of the United Nations, if it is a party to a dispute under consideration by the Security Council, shall be invited to participate, without vote, in the discussion relating to the dispute. The Security Council shall lay down such conditions as it deems just for the participation of a state which is not a Member of the United Nations.

CHAPTER VI. PACIFIC SETTLEMENT OF DISPUTES

Art. 33. 1. The parties to any dispute, the continuance of which is likely to endanger the maintenance of international peace and security, shall, first of all, seek a solution by negotiation, enquiry, mediation, conciliation, arbitration, judicial settlement, resort to regional agencies or arrangements, or other peaceful means of their own choice.

2. The Security Council shall, when it deems necessary, call upon the parties to settle their dispute by such means.

Art. 34. The Security Council may investigate any dispute, or any situation which might lead to international friction or give rise to a dispute, in order to determine whether the continuance of the dispute or situation is likely to endanger the maintenance of international peace and security.

Art. 35. 1. Any Member of the United Nations may bring any dispute, or any situation of the nature referred to in Article 34, to the attention of the Security Council or of the General Assembly.

2. A state which is not a Member of the United Nations may bring to the attention of the Security Council or of the General Assembly any dispute to which it is a party if it accepts in advance, for the purposes of the dispute, the obligations of pacific settlement provided in the present Charter. . . .

Art. 36. 1. The Security Council may, at any stage of a dispute of the nature referred to in Article 33 or of a situation of like nature, recommend appropriate procedures or methods of adjustment. . . .

3. In making recommendations under this Article the Security Council should also take into consideration that legal disputes should as a general rule be referred by the parties to the International Court of Justice in accordance with the provisions of the Statute of the Court.

Art. 37. 1. Should the parties to a dispute of the nature referred to in Article 33 fail to settle it by the means indicated in that Article, they shall refer it to the Security Council.

2. If the Security Council deems that the continuance of the dispute is in fact likely to endanger the maintenance of international peace and security, it shall decide whether to take action under Article 36 or to recommend such terms of settlement as it may consider appropriate. . . .

CHAPTER VII. ACTION WITH RESPECT TO THREATS TO THE PEACE, BREACHES OF THE PEACE AND ACTS OF AGGRESSION

Art. 39. The Security Council shall determine the existence of any threat to the peace, breach of the peace, or act of aggression and shall make recommendations, or decide what measures shall be taken in accordance with Articles 41 and 42, to maintain or restore international peace and security.

Art. 40. In order to prevent an aggravation of the situation, the Security Council may, before making the recommendations or deciding upon the measures provided for in Article 39, call upon the parties concerned to comply with such provisional measures as it deems necessary or desirable. Such provisional measures shall be without prejudice to the rights, claims, or position of the parties concerned. The Security Council shall duly take account of failure to comply with such provisional measures.

Art. 41. The Security Council may decide what measures not involving the use of armed force are to be employed to give effect to its decisions, and it may call upon the Members of the United Nations to apply such measures. These may include complete or partial interruption of economic relations and of rail, sea, air, postal, telegraphic, radio, and other means of communication, and the severance of diplomatic relations.

Art. 42. Should the Security Council consider that measures provided for in Article 41 would be inadequate or have proved to be inadequate, it may take such action by air, sea, or land forces as may be necessary to maintain or restore international peace and security. Such action may include demonstrations, blockade, and other operations by air, sea, or land forces of Members of the United Nations.

Art. 43. 1. All Members of the United Nations, in order to contribute to the maintenance of international peace and security, undertake to make available to the Security Council, on its call and in accordance with a special agreement or agreements, armed forces, assistance, and facilities, including rights of passage, necessary for the purpose of maintaining international peace and security.

2. Such agreement or agreements shall govern the numbers and types of forces, their degree of readiness and general location, and the nature of the facilities and assistance to be provided.

3. The agreement or agreements shall be negotiated as soon as possible on the initiative of the Security Council. They shall be concluded between the Security Council and Members or between the Security Council and groups of Members and shall be subject to ratification by the signatory states in accordance with their respective constitutional processes.

Art. 44. When the Security Council has decided to use force it shall, before calling upon a Member not represented on it to provide armed forces in fulfillment of the obligations assumed under Article 43, invite that Member, if the Member so desires, to participate in the decisions of the Security Council concerning the employment of contingents of that Member's armed forces.

Art. 45. In order to enable the United Nations to take urgent military measures, Members shall hold immediately available national air-force contingents for combined international enforcement action. The strength and degree of readiness of these contingents and plans for their combined action shall be determined, within the limits laid down in the special agreement or agreements referred to in Article 43, by the Security Council with the assistance of the Military Staff Committee.

Art. 46. Plans for the application of armed force shall be made by the Security Council with the assistance of the Military Staff Committee.

Art. 47. 1. There shall be established a Military Staff Committee to advise and assist the Security Council on all questions relating to the Security Council's military requirements for the maintenance of international peace and security, the employment and command of forces placed at its disposal, the regulation of armaments, and possible disarmament.

2. The Military Staff Committee shall consist of the Chiefs of Staff of the permanent members of the Security Council or their representatives. Any Member of the United Nations not permanently represented on the Committee shall be invited by the Committee to be associated with it when the efficient discharge of the Committee's responsibilities requires

the participation of that Member in its work.

3. The Military Staff Committee shall be responsible under the Security Council for the strategic direction of any armed forces placed at the disposal of the Security Council. Questions relating to the command of such forces shall be worked out subsequently.

4. The Military Staff Committee, with the authorization of the Security Council and after consultation with appropriate regional agencies, may establish regional subcommittees. . . .

Art. 50. If preventive or enforcement measures against any state are taken by the Security Council, any other state, whether a Member of the United Nations or not, which finds itself confronted with special economic problems arising from the carrying out of those measures shall have the right to consult the Security Council with regard to a solution of those problems.

Art. 51. Nothing in the present Charter shall impair the inherent right of individual or collective self-defense if an armed attack occurs against a Member of the United Nations, until the Security Council has taken the measures necessary to maintain international peace and security. Measures taken by Members in the exercise of this right of self-defense shall be immediately reported to the Security Council and shall not in any way affect the authority and responsibility of the Security Council under the present Charter to take at any time such action as it deems necessary in order to maintain or restore international peace and security.

CHAPTER VIII. REGIONAL ARRANGEMENTS

Art. 52. 1. Nothing in the present Charter precludes the existence of regional arrangements or agencies for dealing with such matters relating to the maintenance of international peace and security as are appropriate for regional action, provided that such arrangements or agencies and their activities are consistent with the Purposes and Principles of the United Nations. . . .

3. The Security Council shall encourage the development of pacific settlement of local disputes through such regional arrangements or by such regional agencies either on the initiative of the states concerned or by reference from the Security Council. . . .

Art. 53. 1. The Security Council shall, where appropriate, utilize such regional arrangements or agencies for enforcement action under its authority. But no enforcement action shall be taken under regional arrangements or by regional agencies without the authorization of the Security Council, with the exception of measures against any enemy state. . . .

2. The term enemy state as used in paragraph 1 of this Article applies to any state which during the Second World War has been an enemy of any signatory of the present Charter.

Art. 54. The Security Council shall at all times be kept fully informed of activities undertaken or in contemplation under regional arrangements or by regional agencies for the maintenance of international peace and security.

CHAPTER IX. INTERNATIONAL ECONOMIC AND SOCIAL CO-OPERATION

Art. 55. With a view to the creation of conditions of stability and well-being which are necessary for peaceful and friendly relations among nations based on respect for the principle of equal rights and self-determination of peoples, the United Nations shall promote:

a. higher standards of living, full employment, and conditions of economic and social progress and development;

b. solutions of international economic, social, health, and related problems; and international cultural and educational co-operation; and

c. universal respect for, and observance of, human rights and fundamental freedoms for all without distinction as to race, sex, language, or religion.

Art. 56. All Members pledge themselves to take joint and separate action in co-operation with the Organization for the achievement of the purposes set forth in Article 55. . . .

CHAPTER X. THE ECONOMIC AND SOCIAL COUNCIL: COMPOSITION

Art. 61. 1. The Economic and Social Council shall consist of eighteen Members of the United Nations elected by the General Assembly.

2. Subject to the provisions of paragraph 3, six members of the Economic and Social Council shall be elected each year for a term of three years. A retiring member shall be eligible for immediate re-election.

3. At the first election, eighteen members of the Economic and Social Council shall be chosen. The term of office of six members so chosen shall expire at the end of one year, and six other members at the end of two years, in accordance with arrangements made by the General Assembly.

4. Each member of the Economic and Social Council shall have one representative.

Functions and Powers

Art. 62. 1. The Economic and Social Council may make or initiate studies and reports with respect to international economic, social, cultural, educational, health, and related matters and may make recommendations with respect to any such matters to the General Assembly, to the Members of the United Nations, and to the specialized agencies concerned.

2. It may make recommendations for the purpose of promoting respect for, and observance of, human rights and fundamental freedoms for all.

3. It may prepare draft conventions for submission to the General Assembly, with respect to matters falling within its competence.

4. It may call, in accordance with the rules prescribed by the United Nations, international conferences on matters falling within its competence. . . .

Art. 65. The Economic and Social Council may furnish information to the Security Council and shall assist the Security Council upon its request. . . .

Voting

Art. 67. 1. Each member of the Economic and Social Council shall have one vote.

2. Decisions of the Economic and Social Council shall be made by a majority of the members present and voting.

Procedure

Art. 68. The Economic and Social Council shall set up commissions in economic and social fields and for the promotion of human rights, and such other commissions as may be required for the performance of its functions. . . .

Art. 72. 1. The Economic and Social Council shall adopt its own rules of procedure, including the method of selecting its President.

2. The Economic and Social Council shall meet as required in accordance with its rules, which shall include provision for the convening of meetings on the request of a majority of its members.

CHAPTER XI. DECLARATION REGARDING NON-SELF-GOVERNING TERRITORIES

Art. 73. Members of the United Nations which have or assume responsibilities for the administration of territories whose peoples have not yet attained a full measure of self-government recognize the principle that the interests of the inhabitants of these territories are paramount, and accept as a sacred trust the obligation to promote to the utmost, within the system of international peace and security established by the present Charter, the well-being of the inhabitants of these territories, and, to this end:

a. to ensure, with due respect for the culture of the peoples concerned, their political, economic, social, and educational advancement, their just treatment, and their protection against abuses;

b. to develop self-government, to take due account of the political aspirations of the peoples, and to assist them in the progressive development of their free political institutions, according to the particular circumstances of each territory and its peoples and their varying stages of advancement;

c. to further international peace and security;

d. to promote constructive measures of development, to encourage research, and to co-operate with one another and, when and where appropriate, with specialized international bodies with a view to the practical achievement of the social, economic, and scientific purposes set forth in this Article; and

e. to transmit regularly to the Secretary-General for information purposes, subject to such limitation as security and constitutional considerations may require, statistical and other information of a technical nature relating to economic, social, and educational conditions in the territories for which they are respectively responsible other than those territories to which Chapters XII and XIII apply.

Art. 74. Members of the United Nations also agree that their policy in respect of the territories to which this Chapter applies, no less than in respect of their metropolitan areas, must be based on the general principle of good-neighborliness, due account being taken of the interests and well-being of the rest of the world, in social, economic, and commercial matters.

CHAPTER XII. INTERNATIONAL TRUSTEESHIP SYSTEM

Art. 75. The United Nations shall establish under its authority an international trusteeship system for the administration and supervision of such territories as may be placed thereunder by subsequent individual agreements. These territories are hereinafter referred to as trust territories.

Art. 76. The basic objectives of the trusteeship system, in accordance with the Purposes of the United Nations laid down in Article 1 of the present Charter, shall be:

a. to further international peace and security;

b. to promote the political, economic, social and educational advancement of the inhabitants of the trust territories, and their progressive development towards self-government or independence as may be appropriate to the particular circumstances of each territory and its peoples and the freely expressed wishes of the peoples concerned, and as may be provided by the terms of each trusteeship agreement;

c. to encourage respect for human rights and for fundamental freedoms for all without distinction as to race, sex, language, or religion, and to encourage recognition of the interdependence of the peoples of the world; and

d. to ensure equal treatment in social, economic, and commercial matters for all Members of the United Nations and their nationals, and also equal treatment for the latter in the administration of justice, without prejudice to the attainment of the foregoing objectives and subject to the provisions of Article 80.

Art. 77. 1. The trusteeship system shall apply to such territories in the following categories as may be placed thereunder by means of trusteeship agreements:

a. territories now held under mandate;

b. territories which may be detached from enemy states as a result of the Second World War; and

c. territories voluntarily placed under the system by states responsible for their administration.

2. It will be a matter for subsequent agreement as to which territories in the foregoing categories will be brought under the trusteeship system and upon what terms.

Art. 78. The trusteeship system shall not apply to territories which have become Members of the United Nations. . . .

Art. 79. The terms of trusteeship for each territory to be placed under the trusteeship system, including any alteration or amendment, shall be agreed upon by the states directly concerned, including the mandatory power in the case of territories held under mandate by a Member of the United Nations, and shall be approved as provided for in Articles 83 and 85.

Art. 80. 1. Except as may be agreed upon in individual trusteeship agreements, made under Articles 77, 79, and 81, placing each territory under the trusteeship system, and until such agreements have been concluded, nothing in this Chapter shall be construed in or of itself to alter in any manner the rights whatsoever of any states or any peoples or the terms of existing international instruments to which Members of the United Nations may respectively be parties.

2. Paragraph 1 of this Article shall not be interpreted as giving grounds for delay or postponement of the negotiation and conclusion of agreements for placing man-

dated and other territories under the trusteeship system as provided for in Article 77.

Art. 81. The trusteeship agreement shall in each case include the terms under which the trust territory will be administered and designate the authority which will exercise the administration of the trust territory. Such authority, hereinafter called the administering authority, may be one or more states or the Organization itself. . . .

Art. 83. 1. All functions of the United Nations relating to strategic areas, including the approval of the terms of the trusteeship agreements and of their alteration or amendment, shall be exercised by the Security Council.

2. The basic objectives set forth in Article 76 shall be applicable to the people of each strategic area. . . .

Art. 84. It shall be the duty of the administering authority to ensure that the trust territory shall play its part in the maintenance of international peace and security. To this end the administering authority may make use of volunteer forces, facilities, and assistance from the trust territory in carrying out the obligations towards the Security Council undertaken in this regard by the administering authority, as well as for local defense and the maintenance of law and order within the trust territory.

Art. 85. 1. The functions of the United Nations with regard to trusteeship agreements for all areas not designated as strategic, including the approval of the terms of the trusteeship agreements and of their alteration or amendment, shall be exercised by the General Assembly.

2. The Trusteeship Council, operating under the authority of the General Assembly, shall assist the General Assembly in carrying out these functions.

Art. 86. 1. The Trusteeship Council shall consist of the following Members of the United Nations:

a. those Members administering trust territories;

b. such of those Members mentioned by name in Article 23 as are not administering trust territories; and

c. as many other Members elected for three-year terms by the General Assembly as may be necessary to ensure that the total number of members of the Trusteeship Council is equally divided between those Members of the United Nations which administer trust territories and those which do not.

2. Each member of the Trusteeship Council shall designate one specially qualified person to represent it therein.

Functions and Powers

Art. 87. 1. The General Assembly and, under its authority, the Trusteeship Council, in carrying out their functions, may:

a. consider reports submitted by the administering authority;

b. accept petitions and examine them in consultation with the administering authority;

c. provide for periodic visits to the respective trust territories at times agreed upon with the administering authority; and

d. take these and other actions in conformity with the terms of the trusteeship agreements.

Art. 88. The Trusteeship Council shall formulate a questionnaire on the political, economic, social, and educational advancement of the inhabitants of each trust territory, and the administering authority for each trust territory within the competence of the General Assembly shall make an annual report to the General Assembly upon the basis of such questionnaire.

Voting

Art. 89. 1. Each member of the Trusteeship Council shall have one vote.

2. Decisions of the Trusteeship Council shall be made by a majority of the members present and voting.

Procedure

Art. 90. 1. The Trusteeship Council shall adopt its own rules of procedure, including the method of selecting its President.

2. The Trusteeship Council shall meet as required in accordance with its rules, which shall include provision for the convening of meetings on the request of a majority of its members.

Art. 91. The Trusteeship Council shall, when appropriate, avail itself of the assistance of the Economic and Social Council and of the specialized agencies in regard to matters with which they are respectively concerned.

CHAPTER XIV. THE INTERNATIONAL COURT OF
JUSTICE

Art. 92. The International Court of Justice shall be the principal judicial organ of the United Nations. It shall function in accordance with the annexed Statute, which is based upon the Statute of the Permanent Court of International Justice and forms an integral part of the present Charter.

Art. 93. 1. All Members of the United Nations are *ipso facto* parties to the Statute of the International Court of Justice.

2. A state which is not a Member of the United Nations may become a party to the Statute of the International Court of Justice on conditions to be determined in each case by the General Assembly upon the recommendation of the Security Council.

Art. 94. 1. Each Member of the United Nations undertakes to comply with the decision of the International Court of Justice in any case to which it is a party.

2. If any party to a case fails to perform the obligations incumbent upon it under a judgment rendered by the Court, the other party may have recourse to the Security Council, which may, if it deems necessary, make recommendations or decide upon measures to be taken to give effect to the judgment.

Art. 95. Nothing in the present Charter shall prevent Members of the United Nations from entrusting the solution of their differences to other tribunals by virtue of agreements already in existence or which may be concluded in the future.

Art. 96. 1. The General Assembly or the Security Council may request the International Court of Justice to give an advisory opinion on any legal question.

2. Other organs of the United Nations . . . may also request advisory opinions of the Court on legal questions arising within the scope of their activities.

CHAPTER XV. THE SECRETARIAT

Art. 97. The Secretariat shall comprise a Secretary-General and such staff as the Organization may require. The Secretary-General shall be appointed by the General Assembly upon the recommendation of the Security Council. He shall be the chief administrative officer of the Organization.

Art. 98. The Secretary-General shall act in that capacity in all meetings of the General Assembly, of the Security Council, of the Economic and Social Council, and of the Trusteeship Council, and shall perform such other functions as are entrusted to him by these organs. The Secretary-General shall make an annual report to the General Assembly on the work of the Organization.

Art. 99. The Secretary-General may bring to the attention of the Security Council any matter which in his opinion

may threaten the maintenance of international peace and security.

Art. 100. 1. In the performance of their duties the Secretary-General and the staff shall not seek or receive instructions from any government or from any other authority external to the Organization. They shall refrain from any action which might reflect on their position as international officials responsible only to the Organization.

2. Each Member of the United Nations undertakes to respect the exclusively international character of the responsibilities of the Secretary-General and the staff and not to seek to influence them in the discharge of their responsibilities.

Art. 101. 1. The staff shall be appointed by the Secretary-General under regulations established by the General Assembly.

2. Appropriate staffs shall be permanently assigned to the Economic and Social Council, the Trusteeship Council, and, as required, to other organs of the United Nations. These staffs shall form a part of the Secretariat. . . .

CHAPTER XVI. MISCELLANEOUS PROVISIONS

Art. 102. 1. Every treaty and every international agreement entered into by any Member of the United Nations after the present Charter comes into force shall as soon as possible be registered with the Secretariat and published by it.

2. No party to any such treaty or international agreement which has not been registered in accordance with the provisions of paragraph 1 of this Article may invoke that treaty or agreement before any organ of the United Nations.

Art. 103. In the event of a conflict between the obligations of the Members of the United Nations under the present Charter and their obligations under any other international agreement, their obligations under the present Charter shall prevail.

Art. 104. The Organization shall enjoy in the territory of each of its Members such legal capacity as may be necessary for the exercise of its functions and the fulfillment of its purposes.

Art. 105. 1. The Organization shall enjoy in the territory of each of its Members such privileges and immunities as are necessary for the fulfillment of its purposes.

2. Representatives of the Members of the United Nations and officials of the Organization shall similarly enjoy such privileges and immunities as are necessary for the independent exercise of their functions in connection with the Organization. . . .

CHAPTER XVIII. AMENDMENTS

Art. 108. Amendments to the present Charter shall come into force for all Members of the United Nations when they have been adopted by a vote of two thirds of the members of the General Assembly and ratified in accordance with their respective constitutional processes by two thirds of the Members of the United Nations, including all the permanent members of the Security Council.

Art. 109. 1. A General Conference of the Members of the United Nations for the purpose of reviewing the present Charter may be held at a date and place to be fixed by a two-thirds vote of the members of the General Assembly and by a vote of any seven members of the Security Council. Each Member of the United Nations shall have one vote in the conference. . . .

3. If such a conference has not been held before the tenth annual session of the General Assembly following the coming into force of the present Charter, the proposal to call such a conference shall be placed on the agenda of that session of the General Assembly, and the conference shall be held if so decided by a majority

vote of the members of the General Assembly and by a vote of any seven members of the Security Council.

CHAPTER XIX. RATIFICATION AND SIGNATURE

Art. 110. 1. The present Charter shall be ratified by the signatory states in accordance with their respective constitutional processes.

2. The ratifications shall be deposited with the Government of the United States of America, which shall notify all the signatory states of each deposit as well as the Secretary-General of the Organization when he has been appointed.

3. The present Charter shall come into force upon the deposit of ratifications by the Republic of China, France, the Union of Soviet Socialist Republics, the United Kingdom of Great Britain and Northern Ireland, and the United States of America, and by a majority of the other signatory states. A protocol of the ratifications deposited shall thereupon be drawn up by the Government of the United States of America, which shall communicate copies thereof to all the signatory states.

4. The states signatory to the present Charter which ratify it after it has come into force will become original Members of the United Nations on the date of the deposit of their respective ratifications.

2. Notes on the Statute of the International Court of Justice

Organization. The International Court of Justice is established by a separate Statute as the principal judicial organ of the United Nations. It consists of fifteen members elected by the General Assembly and the Security Council. Members are elected for nine years and no two of them may be nationals of the same state. No member of the Court is permitted to hold any other political or administrative office, to engage in any other occupation or profession, or to act as agent, counsel, or advocate in any case. Court members hold diplomatic privileges and immunities while engaged in Court business. The seat of the Court is at The Hague, though it may function elsewhere at will. The Court remains in permanent session, except for vacation periods. A quorum of nine judges suffices to constitute the Court. The Court may form separate Chambers of three or more judges to deal with special cases. Court expenses are borne by the United Nations.

Competence. Only states may be parties in cases before the Court. The Court is open to all Members of the United Nations and to others as determined by the Security Council. Jurisdiction includes all cases which the parties refer to it and all matters provided for in the United Nations Charter and treaties and conventions in force. It includes the interpretation of treaties, questions of international law, questions of breach of international obligation and reparations for the same. The Court decides questions in accordance with international law, which include: international conventions which establish rules recognized by contending states, international custom, general principles of law as recognized by civilized nations, and judicial decisions and teachings of highly qualified national publicists. All Members of the United Nations, party to a dispute before the Court, agree to comply with the Court's decision. Failure to do so will be brought to the notice of the Security Council.

Procedure. The official languages of the Court are French and English. Parties to cases before the Court are represented by agents and counsel. Procedures are in two parts, written memorials and oral testimony. Hearings are public except in special cases. Minutes are made of each hearing. After the evidence is in, the deliberations of the Court are private and secret. Questions are decided by majority vote of the judges present. Decisions must cite reasons upon which they are based. Minority opinions are permissible. The decision of the Court has no binding force except between the parties concerned and to the particular case. Judgments are final, without appeal, subject to review only upon discovery of vital new evidence within ten years.